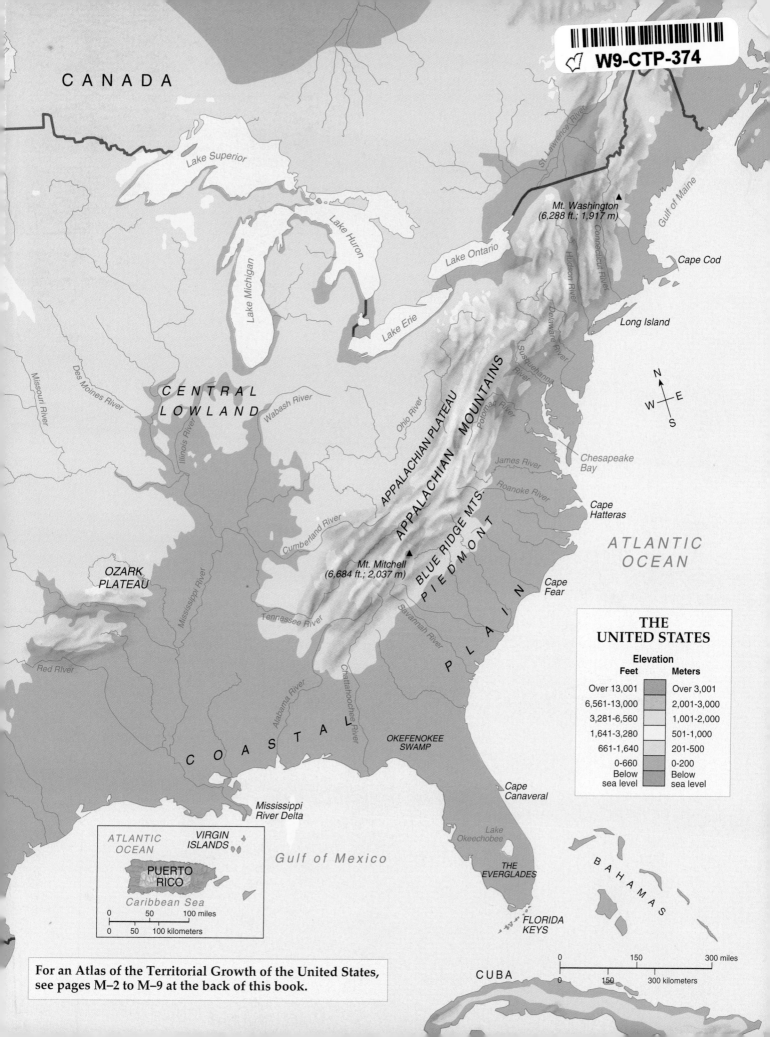

CANADA

W9-CTP-374

Lake Superior

Lake Michigan

Lake Huron

Lake Ontario

Lake Erie

St. Lawrence River

Gulf of Maine

Mt. Washington
(6,288 ft.; 1,917 m)

Cape Cod

Connecticut River

Hudson River

Long Island

Missouri River

Des Moines River

CENTRAL
LOWLAND

Illinois River

Wabash River

Ohio River

APPALACHIAN PLATEAU

APPALACHIAN MOUNTAINS

Delaware River

Susquehanna River

Potomac River

James River

Chesapeake
Bay

Roanoke River

Cape
Hatteras

ATLANTIC
OCEAN

OZARK
PLATEAU

Mississippi River

Cumberland River

Mt. Mitchell
(6,684 ft.; 2,037 m)

BLUE RIDGE MTS.

PIEDMONT

Tennessee River

Cape
Fear

Red River

Alabama River

Chattahoochee River

COASTAL

P L A I N

OKEFENOKEE
SWAMP

Savannah River

Cape
Canaveral

THE
UNITED STATES

Elevation

Feet	Meters
Over 13,001	Over 3,001
6,561-13,000	2,001-3,000
3,281-6,560	1,001-2,000
1,641-3,280	501-1,000
661-1,640	201-500
0-660	0-200
Below sea level	Below sea level

Mississippi
River Delta

Gulf of Mexico

Lake
Okeechobee

THE
EVERGLADES

B A H A M A S

ATLANTIC
OCEAN

VIRGIN
ISLANDS

PUERTO
RICO

Caribbean Sea

FLORIDA
KEYS

0   50   100 miles
0   50   100 kilometers

N
W   E
S

0   150   300 miles
0   150   300 kilometers

CUBA

For an Atlas of the Territorial Growth of the United States,
see pages M–2 to M–9 at the back of this book.

THE CONTEMPORARY WORLD

ARCTIC OCEAN

NORWAY
SWEDEN
FINLAND
ESTONIA
LATVIA
LITHUANIA
DEN.
NETH.
GERMANY
POLAND
BELARUS
BEL.
LUX. CZ. REP.
SLK.
AUS. HUNG. UKRAINE
SLN. ROMANIA MOLDOVA
SWITZ. CR.
ITALY S.M. BULGARIA
B.H. F.Y.R.O.M.
ALB. GREECE
TURKEY
TUNISIA
MALTA
CYPRUS
ISRAEL
LEBANON
SYRIA
Gaza Strip
West Bank
JORDAN
GEORGIA
ARMENIA
AZERBAIJAN
IRAQ
IRAN

RUSSIAN FEDERATION

KAZAKHSTAN
MONGOLIA

UZBEKISTAN
KYRGYZSTAN
TURKMENISTAN
TAJIKISTAN
AFGHANISTAN
PAKISTAN

CHINA

N. KOREA
S. KOREA
JAPAN

PACIFIC OCEAN

ALGERIA
LIBYA
EGYPT

KUWAIT
BAHRAIN
SAUDI ARABIA
QATAR
UNITED ARAB
EMIRATES
OMAN
YEMEN

NEPAL
BHUTAN
BANGLADESH
INDIA
MYANMAR
(BURMA)
LAOS
VIETNAM
THAILAND
CAMBODIA

Taiwan
(China)

Mariana Is.
(U.S.)

Guam
(U.S.)

MARSHALL
IS.

NIGER
CHAD
SUDAN
ERITREA
DJIBOUTI
ETHIOPIA
SOMALIA

MALDIVES

SRI
LANKA

PHILIPPINES

PALAU

FEDERATED STATES
OF MICRONESIA

NAURU

KIRIBATI

NIGERIA
BENIN
TOGO
CENTRAL
AFRICAN REP.
CAMEROON
EQ.
GUINEA
GABON
CONGO
RWANDA
UGANDA
KENYA
DEM. REP. OF
THE CONGO
BURUNDI
TANZANIA
SÃO
TOMÉ
& PRÍNCIPE

COMOROS
SEYCHELLES

BRUNEI

MALAYSIA

SINGAPORE

INDONESIA

PAPUA
NEW
GUINEA

SOLOMON
IS.

TUVALU

INDIAN OCEAN

EAST
TIMOR

ANGOLA
ZAMBIA
MALAWI
NAMIBIA
ZIMBABWE
BOTSWANA
MADAGASCAR
MAURITIUS

VANUATU

FIJI

New Caledonia
(Fr.)

AUSTRALIA

MOZAMBIQUE
SWAZILAND
SOUTH
AFRICA
LESOTHO

NEW
ZEALAND

Tasmania
(Aust.)

ABBREVIATIONS	
ALB.	ALBANIA
AUS.	AUSTRIA
BEL.	BELGIUM
B.H.	BOSNIA AND HERZEGOVINA
CR.	CROATIA
CZ. REP.	CZECH REPUBLIC
DEN.	DENMARK
F.Y.R.O.M.	FORMER YUGOSLAV REPUBLIC OF MACEDONIA
HUNG.	HUNGARY
LUX.	LUXEMBOURG
NETH.	NETHERLANDS
SLK.	SLOVAKIA
SLN.	SLOVENIA
S.M.	SERBIA AND MONTENEGRO
SWITZ.	SWITZERLAND

ANTARCTICA

20 E   40 E   60 E   80 E   100 E   120 E   140 E   160 E

The American Promise

A HISTORY OF THE UNITED STATES

Third Edition

CLASSROOM, c. 1850, IN THE EMERSON SCHOOL FOR GIRLS (BOSTON, MASS.?)
Daguerreotype by Southworth & Hawes. Reproduced by permission of The Granger Collection, New York.

The American Promise

A HISTORY OF THE UNITED STATES

Third Edition
Volume I: To 1877

James L. Roark
Emory University

Michael P. Johnson
Johns Hopkins University

Patricia Cline Cohen
University of California, Santa Barbara

Sarah Stage
Arizona State University West

Alan Lawson
Boston College

Susan M. Hartmann
The Ohio State University

BEDFORD/ST. MARTIN'S
Boston ◆ New York

FOR BEDFORD/ST. MARTIN'S

Executive Editor for History: Mary Dougherty
Director of Development for History: Jane Knetzger
Senior Developmental Editor: Heidi L. Hood
Senior Production Editor: Karen S. Baart
Senior Production Supervisor: Joe Ford
Senior Marketing Manager: Jenna Bookin Barry
Editorial Assistant: Elizabeth Harrison
Production Assistants: Amy Derjue, Anne E. True
Copyeditor: Patricia Herbst
Text Design and Page Layout: Wanda Kossak Design
Photo Research: Pembroke Herbert/Sandi Rygiel, Picture Research Consultants & Archives, Inc.
Indexer: Maro Riofrancos
Cover Design: Donna Lee Dennison
Cartography: Mapping Specialists Ltd.
Composition: TechBooks
Printing and Binding: R.R. Donnelley & Sons Ltd.

President: Joan E. Feinberg
Editorial Director: Denise B. Wydra
Director of Marketing: Karen Melton Soeltz
Director of Editing, Design, and Production: Marcia Cohen
Managing Editor: Elizabeth M. Schaaf

Library of Congress Control Number: 2004102163

Manufactured in the United States of America.

9 8 7 6 5
f e d c b

For information, write: Bedford/St. Martin's, 75 Arlington Street, Boston, MA 02116 (617-399-4000)

ISBN: 0–312–40687–8 (combined edition)   EAN: 978–0–312–40687–5
ISBN: 0–312–40688–6 (Vol. I)   EAN: 978–0–312–40688–2
ISBN: 0–312–40689–4 (Vol. II)   EAN: 978–0–312–40689–9

Cover Art: *Classroom, c. 1850, in the Emerson School for Girls (Boston, Mass.?).* Daguerreotype by Southworth & Hawes. Reproduced by permission of The Granger Collection, New York.

BRIEF CONTENTS

CONTENTS

CHAPTER 1

Ancient America: Before 1492   3

CHAPTER 10

Republicans in Power, 1800–1824 319

CHAPTER 11

The Expanding Republic, 1815–1840 355

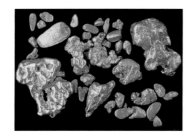

(continued)

MAPS, FIGURES, AND TABLES

Maps

CHAPTER 14

CHAPTER 15

CHAPTER 16

Figures and Tables

AMERICAN PLACES

BEYOND AMERICA'S BORDERS

DOCUMENTING THE AMERICAN PROMISE

HISTORICAL QUESTION

THE PROMISE OF TECHNOLOGY

PREFACE

THIS NEW EDITION OF *The American Promise* is a cause for celebration, for it proudly announces the successful reception of earlier editions. Preparing this edition, however, allowed us the opportunity to revisit our original premises, evaluate our earlier efforts, take stock of what worked, and decide how to build on those successes. The result of our careful reexamination is a major revision of *The American Promise*. While the third edition rests securely on our original goals and draws on our continuing engagement with American history as classroom teachers, we have also benefited from the invaluable suggestions of many of our adopters. As our textbook established its place among introductory surveys of American history, an ever-growing community of book users informed our efforts to make this good text even better. We are grateful for their suggestions and are confident the result is a text that will be even more useful to students and instructors.

From the beginning, *The American Promise* has been shaped by our firsthand knowledge that the survey course is the most difficult to teach and the most difficult to take. Collectively, we have logged more than a century in introductory American history classrooms in institutions that range from small community colleges to large research institutions. Drawing on our practical experience, we set an ambitious goal, one that we continue to focus on in the third edition: to produce the most teachable and readable introductory American history textbook available.

Our experience as teachers informs every aspect of our text, beginning with its framework. Many survey texts emphasize either a social or a political approach to history, and by focusing on one, they inevitably slight the other. In our classrooms, we have found that students need **both** the structure a political narrative provides **and** the insights gained from examining social and cultural experience. To write a comprehensive,

> We set an ambitious goal to produce the most teachable and readable introductory American history textbook available.

balanced account of American history, we focused on the public arena—the place where politics intersects social and cultural developments—to show how Americans confronted the major issues of their day and created far-reaching historical change.

We also thought hard about the concerns most frequently voiced by instructors: that students often find history boring, unfocused, and difficult and their textbooks lifeless and overwhelming. Getting students to open the book is one of the biggest hurdles instructors face. We asked ourselves how our text could address these concerns and engage students in ways that would help them understand and remember the main developments in American history. To make the political, social, economic, and cultural changes vivid and memorable and to portray fully the diversity of the American experience, we stitched into our narrative the voices of hundreds of contemporaries—from presidents to pipefitters, sharecroppers to suffragists—whose ideas and actions shaped their times and whose efforts still affect our lives. By incorporating a rich selection of authentic American voices, we seek to capture history as it happened and to create a compelling narrative that captures students' interests and sparks their historical imagination.

Our title, *The American Promise,* reflects our emphasis on human agency and our conviction that American history is an unfinished story. For millions, the nation has held out the promise of a better life, unfettered worship, representative government, democratic politics, and other freedoms seldom found elsewhere. But none of these promises has come with guarantees. And promises fulfilled for some have meant promises denied to others. As we see it, much of American history is a continuing struggle over the definition and realization of the nation's promise. Abraham Lincoln, in the midst of what he termed the "fiery trial" of the Civil War, pronounced the nation "the last best hope of Earth." Kept alive by countless sacrifices, that hope has been marred by compromises, disappointments, and denials, but it lives still. We believe that *The American Promise*, Third Edition, with its increased attention to making history come alive, will help students become aware of the legacy of hope bequeathed to them by previous generations of Americans stretching back nearly four centuries, a legacy that is theirs to preserve and build on.

Features

From the beginning, readers have proclaimed this textbook a visual feast, richly illustrated in ways that extend and reinforce the narrative. The third edition furthers this benefit by nearly doubling the number of **illustrations** to more than 750. Many in full color and large enough to study in detail, these illustrations are contemporaneous with the period of the chapter in which they appear. In our effort to make history tangible and memorable, we expanded and enriched the art program's acclaimed use of **artifacts** and added **all-new embedded artifacts**—100 small images of material culture—from boots and political buttons to guns and sewing machines—folded into the lines of the narrative. These, combined with full-page **chapter-opening artifacts** and other captioned artifacts throughout, emphasize the importance of material culture in the study of the past and enrich the historical account. Similarly, within our **new illustrated chapter chronologies** we placed thumbnail-size images from the chapter to reinforce the narrative and stimulate students' power of recall. A striking **new design** highlights the illustration program and makes the most of our **comprehensive captions** while enticing students to delve deeper into the text itself.

Our highly regarded **map program** offers more maps than any other U.S. survey text—over 170 maps in all (20 more than in the previous edition). Each chapter offers, on average, four **full-size maps** showing major developments in a wide range of areas, from environmental and technological issues to political, social, cultural, and diplomatic matters. New maps reflect our increased attention to Native American peoples

and to the West in particular, and they cover such varied topics as zones of empire in eighteenth-century North America; Indian war in the West, 1777–1781; western mining, 1848–1890; urban riots, 1965–1968; and the election of 2000. In addition, each chapter includes two to three **spot maps,** small, single-concept maps embedded in the narrative to strengthen students' grasp of crucial issues. Unique to *The American Promise,* new spot maps in the third edition highlight such topics as Spanish missions in California, frontier land opened by Indian removal in the 1830s, the Mexican cession, the Battle of Glorieta Pass, the Samoan Islands, selected Indian relocations from 1950 to 1970, the Cuban missile crisis, contemporary Liberia, contemporary Israel, and the recent conflict in Afghanistan. Another unique feature is our brief **Atlas of the Territorial Growth of the United States,** a series of full-color maps at the end of each volume that reveal the changing cartography of the nation.

Spanish Missions in California

Imaginative and effective pedagogy remains a hallmark of our text. All chapters are constructed to preview, reinforce, and review the narrative in the most memorable and engaging means possible. To prepare students for the reading to come, each chapter begins with a **new chapter outline** to accompany the vivid **opening vignette** that invites students into the narrative with lively accounts of individuals or groups who embody the central themes of the chapter. Each vignette ends with a **narrative overview** of all of the chapter's main topics. New vignettes in this edition include, among others, Roger Williams being banished from Puritan Massachusetts, runaway slave William Gould enlisting in the Union navy, Native American boarding school students celebrating Indian Citizenship Day, Henry Ford putting

America on wheels, Colonel Paul Tibbets dropping the bomb on Hiroshima, Phyllis Schlafly promoting conservatism, and Colin Powell adjusting to the post–cold war world. To further prepare students as they read, major sections within each chapter have **introductory paragraphs** that preview the subsections that follow. Throughout each chapter, **two-tiered running heads** with dates and topical headings remind students where the sections they are reading fall chronologically, and **call-outs** reinforce key points. In addition, **new thematic chronologies** reinforce and extend points in the narrative, and a **new Glossary of Historical Vocabulary** makes history even more accessible. To help students understand the role of geography in American history and to teach them how to read maps and how map content relates to chapter content, we include twice as many of our popular **map exercises** as in the last edition—now two per chapter.

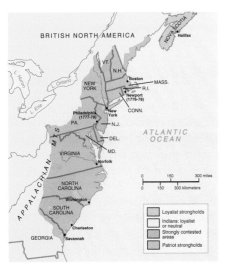

MAP 7.2 Loyalist Strength and Rebel Support
The exact number of loyalists can never be known. No one could have made an accurate count at the time; in addition, political allegiance often shifted with the winds. This map shows the regions of loyalist strength on which the British relied—most significantly the lower Hudson valley and the Carolina Piedmont.

READING THE MAP: Which forces were stronger, those loyal to Britain or those rebelling? (Consider size of areas, centers of population, and vital port locations.) What areas were contested? If the contested areas ultimately sided with the British, how would the balance of power change?

CONNECTIONS: Who was more likely to be a loyalist, and why? How many loyalists left the United States? Where did they go?

FOR MORE HELP ANALYZING THIS MAP, see the map activity for this chapter in the Online Study Guide at bedfordstmartins.com/roark.

At the end of each chapter, an annotated and **illustrated chapter chronology** reviews important events, and a **conclusion** critically reexamines central ideas and provides a bridge to the next chapter.

An enriched array of special features reinforces the narrative and offers teachers more points of departure for assignments and discussion. By providing two entirely new types of features (on 41 topics) in this edition, we supply a widened variety of choices to spark students' interest while helping them understand that history is both a body of knowledge and an ongoing process of investigation. The two new types of boxed features we added are designed to expand and deepen students' understanding

of the American story and make it come alive for them. The **new American Places** feature brings history home to students through a brief essay in each chapter on an American locale related to the discussion at hand—such as Jamestown, the California Mission Trail, Lowell National Historic Park, Antietam National Battlefield, the Lower East Side Tenement Museum, and Alcatraz Island—that students can visit today in person and on the Web. Too often, written history seems to float detached from the landscape in which events occurred, untouched by the powerful influences of place. By discussing the history of specific historical sites and describing what visitors today will find there, we hope to illustrate that history is rooted in both time *and* place and provide students with a tangible, and thus memorable, bridge to the past. This feature concludes with a cross-reference to our **new PlaceLinks** feature on the book's companion Web site (at bedfordstmartins.com/roark) for virtual visits to each described site and to other sites throughout the United States.

AMERICAN PLACES

Antietam National Battlefield, Sharpsburg, Maryland

Bloody Lane.
Antietam National Battlefield.

Fresh from their victory at Second Manassas, General Robert E. Lee's troops reached Sharpsburg, Maryland, on September 15 and took up positions on the low ridge that runs along the western side of Antietam Creek. General George McClellan's army arrived on and firing with demoniacal fury and shouting and laughing hysterically." So intense was the firing, Hooker remembered, that quickly "every stalk of corn in the . . . field was cut as closely as could have been done with a knife." Rival soldiers surged back and forth. Ac-

Because we understand that students need help making connections with historical geographies outside the United States as well, we complement attention to international topics in the narrative with twelve essays in our **new Beyond America's Borders** feature. Essays as varied as "American Tobacco and European Consumers," "Back to Africa: The United States and Liberia," "Transnational Feminisms," and "Jobs in a Globalizing Era" challenge students to consider the effects of transnational connections. These essays seek to widen students' perspectives, to help them see that this country did not develop in isolation. This broader notion of American history will help students understand more fully

BEYOND AMERICA'S BORDERS

Transnational Feminisms

When large numbers of American women began to protest sex discrimination in the 1960s, most were unaware that they belonged to a movement stretching more than one hundred years back in history and across oceans. In 1850, Ernestine Rose, who had been born in Poland and lived in Berlin, Paris, and London, told a women's rights convention in Massachusetts, "We are not contending here for the rights of the women of New England, or of old England,

assumption of superiority or of patronage on the part of Europe or America . . . will alienate . . . the womanhood of Asia and Africa." White, Christian women from the United States and Europe dominated the organization and all too readily assumed that they could speak for all women. But oppression and discrimination placed quite different to women in other parts of the world. For example, in colonized countries such as India and Egypt, feminism arose alongside movements for inde-

jected sex discri pressed hard for including Eleano delegate to the U the commission declaration; Har and women's rig India; and Miner the Dominican R

These and c commitments to went far beyond teed to women b legal system or t nations, thereby and raising expe for example, asse to equal pay in 1 before the U.S. C

the complex development of their nation's history and help prepare them to live in the world.

Fresh topics in our three enduring special features further enrich this edition. Each **Documenting the American Promise** feature juxtaposes three or four primary documents to dramatize the human dimension of major events and show varying perspectives on a topic or issue. Feature introductions and document headnotes contextualize the sources, and Questions for Analysis and Debate promote critical thinking about primary sources. New topics in this edition include "Missionaries Report on California Missions," "Families Divide over the Revolution," "Young Women Homesteaders and the Promise of the West," and "Voices of Protest." Illustrated **Historical Questions** essays pose and interpret specific questions of continuing interest so as to demonstrate the depth and variety of possible answers, thereby countering the belief of many beginning students that historians simply gather facts and string them together into a chronological narrative. New questions in this edition include "How Long Did the Seven Years' War Last in Indian Country?" and "Social Darwinism: Did Wealthy Industrialists Practice What They Preached?" The **Promise of Technology** essays examine the ramifications—positive and negative—of technological developments in American society and culture. New topics in this edition include "Stoves Transform Cooking," "C.S.S. *H. L. Hunley:* The First Successful Submarine," "Artificial Limbs: Filling the 'Empty Sleeve,'" and "Solar Energy."

nings of American history means fresh material throughout the text and a new post–Civil War chapter, "The West in the Gilded Age." We also give more coverage to the environment, Native Americans, Mexicans, Latinos, Chinese workers, and other topics often related to the history of the West. We enriched the discussion of pre-Columbian America in chapter 1 (the prologue in the second edition) with more discussion of Native Americans on the eve of European contact, to complement the chapter's introduction to the process—and limits—of historical investigation.

To strengthen coverage and increase clarity and accessibility, we reorganized certain chapters. In particular, reorganization in the chapters on antebellum America and the Gilded Age provides clearer themes with smoother transitions and better places the West in the national narrative. We also provide stronger post-1945 chapters, reorganized to make themes more compelling and chronology clearer. These post-1945 chapters also include a fresh array of voices, pay greater attention to the West and related topics, and, of course, provide up-to-date coverage of the George W. Bush administration, the Middle East, and the war on terrorism.

Staying abreast of current scholarship is of perennial concern to us, and this edition reflects that keen interest. We incorporated a wealth of new scholarship into the third edition in myriad ways to benefit students. Readers will note that we made good use of the latest works on a number of topics, such as Spanish borderlands, Native Americans in the Seven Years' War, the role of political wives in the early Republic, the social history of the gold rush, the active participation of blacks in their own liberation during the Civil War, mining and commercial farming in the Gilded Age West, race and Americanization, Mexican migration into the American Southwest and how this compares to black migration into the North, the story of the atomic bomb, the black civil rights struggle in global context, and the rise of contemporary conservatism.

Textual Changes

In our ongoing effort to offer a comprehensive text that braids all Americans into the national narrative, we give particular attention to diversity and the influence of class, religion, race, ethnicity, gender, and region. For example, increased coverage of the West and its peoples from the begin-

Supplements

Developed with our guidance and thoroughly revised to reflect the changes in the third edition, the comprehensive collection of print and electronic resources accompanying the textbook provide a host of practical learning and teaching aids. Again, we learned much from the book's community of adopters, and we broadened the scope of the supplements to create a learning package that responds to the real needs of instructors and students. Cross-references in the textbook to the groundbreaking Online Study Guide and to the primary source reader signal the tight integration of the core text with the supplements.

For Students

Reading the American Past: Selected Historical Documents, **Third Edition.** Edited by Michael P. Johnson (Johns Hopkins University), one of the authors of *The American Promise,* and designed to complement the textbook, *Reading the American Past* provides a broad selection of over 150 primary source documents, as well as editorial apparatus to help students understand the sources. Emphasizing the important social, political, and economic themes of U.S. history courses, 31 new documents (one per chapter) were added to provide a multiplicity of perspectives on environmental, western, ethnic, and gender history and to bring a global dimension to the anthology.

Online Study Guide at bedfordstmartins.com/ roark. The popular Online Study Guide for *The American Promise* is a free and uniquely personalized learning tool to help students master themes and information presented in the textbook and improve their historical skills. Assessment quizzes let students evaluate their comprehension and pro-

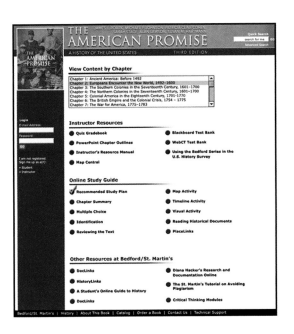

vide them with customized plans for further study through a variety of activities. Instructors can monitor students' progress through the online Quiz Gradebook or receive e-mail updates.

NEW *Maps in Context: A Workbook for American History.* Written by historical cartography expert Gerald A. Danzer (University of Illinois, Chicago), this skill-building workbook helps students comprehend essential connections between geographic literacy and historical understanding. Organized to correspond to the typical U.S. history survey course, *Maps in Context* presents a wealth of map-centered projects and convenient pop quizzes that give students hands-on experience working with maps.

NEW *History Matters: A Student Guide to U.S. History Online.* This new resource, written by Alan Gevinson, Kelly Schrum, and Roy Rosenzweig (all of George Mason University), provides an illustrated and annotated guide to 250 of the most useful Web sites for student research in U.S. history as well as advice on evaluating and using Internet sources. This essential guide is based on the acclaimed "History Matters" Web site developed by the American History Social Project and the Center for History and New Media.

Telecourse Guide for *Shaping America: U.S. History to 1877.* This guide by Kenneth G. Alfers (Dallas County Community College District) is designed for students using *The American Promise* in conjunction with the Dallas TeleLearning telecourse *Shaping America* (see p. xxxvii below). Lesson overviews, assignments, objectives, and focus points provide structure for distance learners, while enrichment ideas, suggested readings, and brief primary sources extend the unit lessons. Practice tests help students evaluate their mastery of the material. *Note:* The telecourse and guide for *Transforming America: U.S. History since 1877* will be available in fall 2005.

Bedford Series in History and Culture. Over 70 titles in this highly praised series combine first-rate scholarship, historical narrative, and important primary documents for undergraduate courses. Each book is brief, inexpensive, and focused on a specific topic or period. Package discounts are available.

Historians at Work Series. Brief enough for a single assignment yet meaty enough to provoke thoughtful discussion, each volume in this series examines a single historical question by combining unabridged selections by distinguished historians, each with a different perspective on the issue, with helpful learning aids. Package discounts are available.

PlaceLinks at bedfordstmartins.com/roark. Extending the goals of the "American Places" textbook feature, PlaceLinks provides access to over 100 Web sites about locations in all fifty states, such as specific monuments, parks, and museums, that connect students to the places where history happened.

DocLinks at bedfordstmartins.com/doclinks. This Web site provides over 750 annotated Web links to online primary documents, including links to speeches, legislation, treaties, social commentary, Supreme Court decisions, essays, travelers' accounts, personal narratives and testimony, newspaper articles, visual artifacts, songs, and poems. Students and teachers alike can search documents by topic, date, or specific chapter of *The American Promise*. Links can be selected and stored for later use or published to a unique Web address.

HistoryLinks at bedfordstmartins.com/history links. Recently updated, HistoryLinks directs instructors and students to over 500 carefully selected and annotated links to history-related Web sites, including those containing image galleries, maps, and audio and video clips for supplementing lectures or assignments. Users can browse these Internet starting points by date, subject, medium, keyword, or specific chapter in *The American Promise*. Instructors can assign these links as the basis for homework assignments or research projects, or students can use them in their own history research. Links can be selected and stored for later use or published to a unique Web address.

A Student's Online Guide to History Reference Sources at bedfordstmartins.com/benjamin. This Web site provides links to history-related databases, indexes, and journals, plus contact information for state, provincial, local, and professional history organizations.

Research and Documentation Online at bedfordstmartins.com/resdoc. This Web site provides clear advice on how to integrate primary and secondary sources into research papers, how to cite sources correctly, and how to format in MLA, APA, *Chicago,* or CBE style.

The St. Martin's Tutorial on Avoiding Plagiarism at bedfordstmartins.com/plagiarismtutorial. This online tutorial reviews the consequences of plagiarism and explains what sources to acknowledge, how to keep good notes, how to organize research, and how to integrate sources appropriately. The tutorial includes exercises to help students practice integrating sources and recognize acceptable summaries.

Critical Thinking Modules at bedfordstmartins .com/historymodules. This Web site offers over two dozen online modules for interpreting maps, audio, visual, and textual sources, centered on events covered in the U.S. history survey. An online guide correlates modules to textbook chapters and to books in the Bedford Series in History and Culture.

For Instructors

Instructor's Resource Manual. This popular manual by Sarah E. Gardner (Mercer University) offers both experienced and first-time instructors tools for presenting textbook material in exciting and engaging ways—annotated chapter outlines, lecture strategies, discussion starters, and film and video recommendations. The new edition includes in-class activities on analyzing visual sources and primary documents from the textbook, as well as a chapter-by-chapter guide to all of the supplements available with *The American Promise*. An extensive guide for first-time teaching assistants and sample syllabi are also included.

Transparencies. This set of over 160 full-color acetate transparencies includes all full-size maps and many other images from the textbook to help instructors present lectures and teach students important map-reading skills.

Book Companion Site at bedfordstmartins.com/ roark. The companion Web site gathers all the electronic resources for *The American Promise*, including the Online Study Guide and related Quiz Gradebook, at a single Web address, providing convenient links to lecture, assignment, and research materials such as PowerPoint chapter outlines, DocLinks, HistoryLinks, and Map Central.

Computerized Test Bank. This test bank by Bradford Wood (Eastern Kentucky University) and Peter Lau (University of Rhode Island) provides easy-to-use software to create tests. Over 80 exercises are provided per chapter, including multiple-choice, fill-in-the-blank, map analysis, short essay, and full-length essay questions. Instructors can customize quizzes, add or edit both questions and answers, as well as export questions and answers to a variety of formats, including WebCT and Blackboard. The disc includes correct answers and essay outlines.

Instructor's Resource CD-ROM. This disc provides instructors with ready-made and customizable PowerPoint multimedia presentations built around chapter outlines, maps, figures, and selected images from the textbook. The disc also includes images in jpeg format, an electronic version of the *Instructor's Resource Manual,* outline maps in pdf format for quizzing or handouts, and quick start guides to the Online Study Guide.

Map Central at bedfordstmartins.com/mapcentral. Map Central is a searchable database of over 750 maps from Bedford/St. Martin's history texts for classroom presentation and over 50 basic political and physical outline maps for quizzing or handouts.

Using the Bedford Series in History and Culture in the U.S. History Survey at bedfordstmartins .com/usingseries. This online guide helps instructors integrate volumes from the highly regarded Bedford Series in History and Culture into their U.S. history survey course. The guide not only correlates themes from each series book with the survey course but also provides ideas for classroom discussions.

Blackboard Course Cartridge and **WebCT e-Pack.** Blackboard and WebCT content are available for this book.

Videos and Multimedia. A wide assortment of videos and multimedia CD-ROMs on various topics in American history is available to qualified adopters. Also available are segments from the telecourse *Shaping America.*

***The American Promise* via Telecourse.** We are pleased to announce that *The American Promise* has been selected as the textbook for the award-winning U.S. history telecourse *Shaping America* and the forthcoming *Transforming America* telecourse by Dallas TeleLearning, the LeCroy Center, Dallas County Community College District. Guides for students and instructors fully integrate the narrative of *The American Promise* into each telecourse. The telecourse package for *Shaping America: U.S. History to 1877,* updated for *The American Promise,* Third Edition, will be available for examination in fall 2004. The telecourse package for *Transforming America: U.S. History since 1877* will premiere in fall 2005. For more information on these distance-learning opportunities, visit the Dallas TeleLearning Web site at http://telelearning.dcccd.edu, e-mail tlearn@dcccd.edu, or call 972-669-6650.

Acknowledgments

We gratefully acknowledge all of the helpful suggestions from those who have read and taught from the previous editions of *The American Promise,* and we hope that our many classroom collaborators will be pleased to see their influence in the third edition. In particular, we wish to thank the talented scholars and teachers who gave generously of their time and knowledge to review this book; their critiques and suggestions contributed greatly to the published work: Eric Arnesen, *University of Illinois, Chicago;* Carl H. Boening, *Shelton State Community College;* Tommy L. Bynum, *Georgia Perimeter College;* Lawrence Cebula, *Missouri Southern State College;* Michael Connolly, *Tidewater Community College;* Gary Darden, *Rutgers University;* David Engerman, *Brandeis University;* Maurine W. Greenwald, *University of Pittsburgh;* David Igler, *University of Utah;* Peter F. Lau, *University of Rhode Island;* Charles H. Martin, *University of Texas, El Paso;* April Masten, *State University of New York, Stony Brook;* Jim R. McClellan, *Northern Virginia Community College;* Constance McGovern, *Frostburg State University;* Karen Merrill, *Williams College;* Peggy Renner, *Glendale Community College;* Steven Reschly, *Truman State University;* Leo Ribuffo, *The George Washington University;* Christine Sears, *University of Delaware;* Michael Sherry, *Northwestern University;* Steven Stoll, *Yale University;* Diana Turk, *New York University;* Elliott West, *University of Arkansas;* Jon A. Whitfield, *Central Texas College, Fort Knox;* Thomas Winn, *Austin Peay State University;* and Thomas Zeiler, *University of Colorado at Boulder.*

A project as complex as this requires the talents of many individuals. First, we would like to acknowledge our families for their support, forbearance, and toleration of our textbook responsibilities. Pembroke Herbert and Sandi Rygiel of Picture Research Consultants, Inc., contributed their unparalleled knowledge, soaring imagination, and diligent research to make possible the extraordinary illustration program. Susan Dawson at the Ohio State University provided helpful research assistance.

We would also like to thank the many people at Bedford/St. Martin's who have been crucial to this project. No one contributed more than senior editor Heidi L. Hood, who managed the entire revision and oversaw the development of each chapter. The results of her dedication to excellence and commitment to creating the best textbook imaginable are evident on every page. We thank as well executive editor Elizabeth Welch, senior editor Louise Townsend, and free-lance editor Ellen Kuhl for their help with the manuscript. Thanks also go to editorial assistant Elizabeth Harrison, who provided unflagging assistance and who coordinated the supplements. We are also grateful to Jane Knetzger, director of development for history, and Mary Dougherty, executive editor, for their support and guidance. For their imaginative and tireless efforts to promote the book, we want to thank Jenna Bookin Barry, marketing manager, and Amanda Byrnes, marketing associate. With great skill and professionalism, Karen Baart, senior production editor, pulled together the many pieces related to copyediting, design, and typesetting, with the able assistance of Amy Derjue and Anne True and the guidance of managing editor Elizabeth Schaaf and assistant managing editor John Amburg. Senior production supervisor Joe Ford oversaw the manufacturing of the book. Designer and page makeup artist Wanda Kossak, copyeditor Patricia Herbst, and proofreaders Janet Cocker and Mary Lou Wilshaw-Watts attended to the myriad details that help make the book shine. Maro Riofrancos provided an outstanding index. Associate new media editor Bryce Sady and new media production coordinator Coleen O'Hanley made sure that *The American Promise* remains at the forefront of technological support for students and instructors. Editorial director Denise Wydra provided helpful advice throughout the course of the project. Finally, Joan E. Feinberg, president, and Charles H. Christensen, former president, took a personal interest in *The American Promise* from the start and guided all editions through every stage of development.

JAMES L. ROARK

Born in Eunice, Louisiana, and raised in the West, James L. Roark received his B.A. from the University of California, Davis, in 1963 and his Ph.D. from Stanford University in 1973. His dissertation won the Allan Nevins Prize. He has taught at the University of Nigeria, Nsukka; the University of Nairobi, Kenya; the University of Missouri, St. Louis; and, since 1983, Emory University, where he is Samuel Candler Dobbs Professor of American History. In 1993, he received the Emory Williams Distinguished Teaching Award, and in 2001–2002 he was Pitt Professor of American Institutions at Cambridge University. He has written *Masters without Slaves: Southern Planters in the Civil War and Reconstruction* (1977). With Michael P. Johnson, he is author of *Black Masters: A Free Family of Color in the Old South* (1984) and editor of *No Chariot Let Down: Charleston's Free People of Color on the Eve of the Civil War* (1984). He has received research assistance from the American Philosophical Society, the National Endowment for the Humanities, and the Gilder Lehrman Institute of American History. Active in the Organization of American Historians and the Southern Historical Association, he is also a fellow of the Society of American Historians.

MICHAEL P. JOHNSON

Born and raised in Ponca City, Oklahoma, Michael P. Johnson studied at Knox College in Galesburg, Illinois, where he received a B.A. in 1963, and at Stanford University in Palo Alto, California, earning a Ph.D. in 1973. He is currently professor of history at Johns Hopkins University in Baltimore, having previously taught at the University of California, Irvine, San Jose State University, and LeMoyne (now LeMoyne-Owen) College in Memphis. His publications include *Toward a Patriarchal Republic: The Secession of Georgia* (1977); with James L. Roark, *Black Masters: A Free Family of Color in the Old South* (1984)

and *No Chariot Let Down: Charleston's Free People of Color on the Eve of the Civil War* (1984); *Abraham Lincoln, Slavery, and the Civil War: Selected Speeches and Writings* (2001); *Reading the American Past: Selected Historical Documents*, the documents reader for *The American Promise*; and articles that have appeared in the *William and Mary Quarterly*, the *Journal of Southern History*, *Labor History*, the *New York Review of Books*, the *New Republic*, the *Nation*, and other journals. Johnson has been awarded research fellowships by the American Council of Learned Societies, the National Endowment for the Humanities, and the Center for Advanced Study in the Behavioral Sciences and Stanford University, and the Times Mirror Foundation Distinguished Research Fellowship at the Huntington Library. He has directed a National Endowment for the Humanities Summer Seminar for College Teachers and has been honored with the University of California, Irvine, Academic Senate Distinguished Teaching Award and the University of California, Irvine, Alumni Association Outstanding Teaching Award. He won the *William and Mary Quarterly* award for best article in 2002 and the Organization of American Historians ABC-CLIO *America: History and Life* Award for best American history article in 2002. He is an active member of the American Historical Association, the Organization of American Historians, and the Southern Historical Association.

PATRICIA CLINE COHEN

Born in Ann Arbor, Michigan, and raised in Palo Alto, California, Patricia Cline Cohen earned a B.A. at the University of Chicago in 1968 and a Ph.D. at the University of California, Berkeley in 1977. In 1976, she joined the history faculty at the University of California, Santa Barbara. Cohen has written *A Calculating People: The Spread of Numeracy in Early America* (1982; reissued 1999) and *The Murder of Helen Jewett: The Life and Death of a Prostitute in Nineteenth-Century New York* (1998). She has also published articles on quantitative literacy, mathematics education, prostitution, and murder in journals including the *Journal of Women's History, Radical History Review*, the *William and Mary Quarterly*, and the *NWSA Journal*. Her scholarly work has received support from the National Endowment for the Humanities, the National Humanities Center, the University of California President's Fellowship in the Humanities, the Mellon Foundation, the American Antiquarian Society, the Schlesinger Library, and the Newberry Library. She is an active associate of the Omohundro Institute of Early American History and Culture, sits on the advisory council of the Society for the History of the Early American Republic, and is president of the Western Association of Women Historians. She has served as chair of the Women's Studies Program and as acting dean of the humanities and fine arts at the University of California at Santa Barbara. In 2001–2002 she was the Distinguished Senior Mellon Fellow at the American Antiquarian Society. Currently she is chair of the history department at Santa Barbara and is working on a book about women's health advocate Mary Gove Nichols.

SARAH STAGE

Sarah Stage was born in Davenport, Iowa, and received a B.A. from the University of Iowa in 1966 and a Ph.D. in American studies from Yale University in 1975. She has taught U.S. history for more than twenty-five years at Williams College and the University of California, Riverside. Currently she is professor of Women's Studies at Arizona State University West, in Phoenix. Her books include *Female Complaints: Lydia Pinkham and the Business of Women's Medicine* (1979) and *Rethinking Home Economics: Women and the History of a Profession* (1997), which has been translated for a Japanese edition. Among the fellowships she has received are the Rockefeller Foundation Humanities Fellowship, the American Association of University Women dissertation fellowship, a fellowship from the Charles Warren Center for the Study of History at Harvard University, and the University of California President's Fellowship in the Humanities. She is at work on a book entitled *Women and the Progressive Impulse in American Politics, 1890–1914.*

ALAN LAWSON

Born in Providence, Rhode Island, Alan Lawson received his B.A. from Brown University in 1955 and his M.A. from the University of Wisconsin in 1956. After Army service and experience as a high school teacher, he earned his Ph.D. from the University of Michigan in 1967. Since winning the Allan Nevins Prize for his dissertation, Lawson has served on the faculties of the University of California, Irvine, Smith College, and, currently, Boston College. He has written *The Failure of Independent Liberalism* (1971) and coedited *From Revolution to Republic* (1976). While completing the forthcoming *Ideas in Crisis: The New Deal and the Mobilization of Progressive Experience*, he has published book chapters and essays on political economy, the cultural legacy of the New Deal, multiculturalism, and the arts in public life. He has served as editor of the *Review of Education* and the *Intellectual History Newsletter* and contributed articles to those journals as well as to the *History of Education Quarterly*. He has been active in the field of American studies as director of the Boston College American studies program and as a contributor to the *American Quarterly*. Under the auspices of the United States Information Agency, Lawson has been coordinator and lecturer for programs to instruct faculty from foreign nations in the state of American historical scholarship and teaching.

SUSAN M. HARTMANN

Professor of history at Ohio State University, Susan M. Hartmann received her B.A. from Washington University and her Ph.D. from the University of Missouri. After specializing in the political economy of the post–World War II period and publishing *Truman and the 80th Congress* (1971), she expanded her interests to the field of women's history, publishing many articles and three books: *The Home Front and Beyond: American Women in the 1940s* (1982); *From Margin to Mainstream: American Women and Politics since 1960* (1989); and *The Other Feminists: Activists in the Liberal Establishment* (1998). Her work has been supported by the Truman Library Institute, the Rockefeller Foundation, the National Endowment for the Humanities, and the American Council of Learned Societies. At Ohio State she has served as director of women's studies, and in 1995 she won the Exemplary Faculty Award in the College of Humanities. Hartmann has taught at the University of Missouri, St. Louis, and Boston University, and she has lectured on American history in Australia, Austria, France, Germany, Greece, Japan, Nepal, and New Zealand. She is a fellow of the Society of American Historians, has served on award committees of the American Historical Association, the Organization of American Historians, the American Studies Association, and the National Women's Studies Association, and currently is on the Board of Directors at the Truman Library Institute. Her current research is on gender and the transformation of politics since 1945.

The American Promise

A HISTORY OF THE UNITED STATES

Third Edition

ANASAZI EFFIGY
Ancient North Americans crafted human likenesses in stone, clay, and wood, as well as depicting human forms on canyon walls, pottery, and elsewhere. An Anasazi Indian in the Southwest carved this artifact from stone sometime around AD 1200. The unmistakably human features of the object tempt us to believe that it might be an ancient American self-portrait. Certainly the carver took care to give the object a recognizably human face, neck, arms, hands, legs, and feet. The brightly colored pigments suggest clothing or body decorations. The Anasazi who painted the object had a clear idea of what should be painted orange, turquoise, and red. Red belonged on wrists, not on lips. This color code that made perfect sense to the Anasazi remains obscure to us, a hint that the carver may have intended to depict a deity or supernatural being who had some human features. For example, the artifact lacks ears and sexual organs. The polished tip of the nose contrasts with the rough surface of the torso and legs, suggesting that Anasazi often rubbed the nose. Experts refer to this artifact and others like it as effigies, that is, objects that presumably had ritualistic or spiritual significance. Instead of showing us what the Anasazi considered a self-portrait, this effigy probably depicts one of their many gods. Yet, since the Anasazi—like other human beings—probably created gods in their own image, the effigy may somewhat resemble Anasazi people.
Jerry Jacka Photography.

Ancient America
Before 1492

G EORGE MCJUNKIN, the manager of the Crowfoot Ranch near Folsom, New Mexico, rode out to mend fences and to look for missing cattle after a violent rainstorm in August 1908. An American of African descent, McJunkin had been born a slave in Texas and had been riding horses since he was a boy. After he became free at the end of the Civil War in 1865, McJunkin worked as a cowboy in Colorado and New Mexico before becoming the Crowfoot manager in 1891. Now, as he rode across the ranch land he knew so well to survey damage caused by the recent storm, McJunkin noticed that floodwater had washed away the bank of a gulch called Wild Horse Arroyo and exposed a deposit of stark white bones. Curious, he dismounted and chipped away at the deposit until he uncovered an entire fossilized bone. The bone was much larger than the parched skeletons of range cattle and buffalo that McJunkin often saw, so he strapped it to his saddle and saved it, hoping someday to identify it.

Four years later, in 1912, McJunkin met Carl Schwachheim, a white man in Raton, New Mexico. Schwachheim, a blacksmith, shared McJunkin's curiosity about fossils, and the two men became friends. McJunkin told Schwachheim about the fossil deposit he had discovered, but Schwachheim could not get out to the ranch to take a look for himself. Ten years later, a few months after McJunkin's death, Schwachheim finally drove out to Wild Horse Arroyo, dug out several bones, and brought them back to Raton. But, like McJunkin, he could not identify an animal that had such big bones.

In 1926, Schwachheim delivered cattle to the stockyards in Denver, and he took some of the old bones to the Denver Museum of Natural History and showed them to J. D. Figgins, a paleontologist who was an expert on fossils of ancient animals. Figgins immediately recognized the significance of the fossils and a few months later began an excavation of the Folsom site that revolutionized knowledge about the first Americans.

When Figgins began his dig at Folsom, archaeologists (individuals who examine **artifacts** left by long-vanished peoples as part of the study of **archaeology**) believed that Native Americans had arrived relatively recently in the Western Hemisphere, probably no more than three or four thousand years earlier when, experts assumed, they had paddled small boats across the icy waters of the Bering Strait from what is now Siberia. At Folsom, Figgins learned that the bones McJunkin had first spotted belonged to twenty-three giant bison, a species known to have been extinct for at least 10,000 years. Far more startling, Figgins found among the bones nineteen flint spear points

George McJunkin

This photo shows McJunkin a few years after he discovered the Folsom site but about fifteen years before anyone understood the significance of his find. He appears here in his work clothes on horseback, as he probably was when he made the discovery. The fossilized bones he discovered belonged to an extinct bison species that was much larger than modern bison; the horns of the ancient animal often spanned six feet, wide enough for McJunkin's horse to have stood sideways between the horns.

Eastern New Mexico University, Blackwater Draw Site, Portales, New Mexico 88130.

(Folsom points, they have since been called), proof that human beings had been alive at the same time as the giant bison. One spear point remained stuck between two ribs of a giant bison, just where a Stone Age hunter had plunged it more than 10,000 years earlier. No longer could anyone doubt that human beings had inhabited North America for at least ten millennia.

The Folsom discovery sparked other major finds of ancient artifacts that continue to this day. Since the 1930s, archaeologists have tried to reconstruct the history of ancient Americans, to understand not only the hunters who killed giant bison with flint-tipped spears, but also their ancestors who first arrived in North America, their descendants who built southwestern pueblos and eastern burial mounds, and *their* descendants who encountered the Europeans who arrived in 1492. Although the story scholars have assembled is incomplete and controversial, they have learned enough to bring into focus the identity of ancient Americans, where they came from, and some basic features of their complex cultures and histories during the thousands of years before that moment in 1492 when a few of them stood on the beach of a small island in the Caribbean and watched Christopher Columbus and his men row ashore.

Archaeology and History

Archaeologists and historians share the desire to learn about people who lived in the past, but they usually employ different methods to obtain information. Both archaeologists and historians study artifacts as clues to the activities and ideas of the humans who created them. They concentrate, however, on different kinds of artifacts. Archaeologists tend to focus on physical objects such as bones, stones, pots, baskets, jewelry, textiles, clothing, graves, and buildings. Historians direct their attention mostly to writings, which encompass personal and private jottings such as diary entries and love letters, official and public pronouncements such as laws and speeches, as well as an enormous variety of other documents such as court decisions, censuses, business ledgers, newspapers, books, and even shopping lists. Although historians are interested in other artifacts and archaeologists do not neglect written sources if they exist, the characteristic concentration of historians on writings and archaeologists on other physical objects denotes a rough cultural and chronological boundary between the human beings studied by the two groups of scholars, a boundary marked by the use of writing.

Writing is defined as a system of symbols that record spoken language. Writing originated among ancient peoples in China, Egypt, and Central America about 8,000 years ago, within the most recent 2 percent of the 400 millennia that modern human beings (*Homo sapiens*) have existed. Writing came into use even later in most other places in the world. The ancient Americans who inhabited North America in 1492, for example, possessed many forms of symbolic representation, but not writing.

The people who lived during the millennia before writing were biologically nearly identical to us. Their DNA was the template for ours. But they differed from us in many other ways. Unlike us, they did not use writing to communicate across space and time. They had a long history, both individual and collective. They moved across the face of the globe; they invented hundreds of spoken languages; they learned to survive and even to thrive in almost every natural environment; they chose and honored leaders; they traded, warred, and worshipped; and, above all, they learned from and taught each other. Much of what we would like to know about their experiences remains unknown because it took place before writing existed. The absence of writing forever muffled their words and thus their history.

Archaeologists specialize in learning about people who did not document their history in writing. They study the millions of artifacts created by these people, trying to decipher what the objects tell us about their lives. By also scrutinizing soil, geological strata, pollen, climate, and other environmental features, they attempt to reconstruct the outlines of the history of ancient peoples. Still, much of their history remains unknowable. No documents chronicle their births and deaths, comings and goings, pleasures and pains, victories and defeats. Despite these silences, archaeologists have learned to make ancient artifacts tell a great deal about the people who made them.

Anasazi Pictograph

This unusual pictograph was painted about AD 1300 on the wall of an Anasazi dwelling in what is now Canyonlands National Park in Utah. The colorful design presumably had a specific meaning for the Anasazi who created it, but that meaning remains indecipherable to experts today.

J. Q. Jacobs.

Since ancient America was the long first phase of the history of the United States, this chapter relies on the work of archaeologists to sketch a brief overview of this important era. Our desire to understand the origins and development of our own society in the last five centuries requires beginning that story when humans first arrived in the Western Hemisphere. These ancient Americans and their descendants did not consider their history a prelude to a future that included us. They resided in North America for thousands of years before Europeans arrived. They created societies and cultures of amazing diversity and complexity. But because they did not use written records, their history cannot be reconstructed with the detail and certainty made possible by writing. Yet their remarkable longevity and creativity make it far preferable to abbreviate and oversimplify their history than to ignore it.

The First Americans

The first human beings to arrive in the Western Hemisphere immigrated from Asia. They brought with them hunting skills, weapon- and tool-making techniques, and a full range of other forms of human knowledge and expertise developed during previous millennia in Africa, Europe, and Asia. These first Americans specialized in hunting mammoths, giant elephant-like creatures they had learned in Europe and Asia to kill, butcher, and process for food, clothing, building materials, and many other purposes. Most likely, these first Americans wandered into the Western Hemisphere more or less accidentally, hungry and in pursuit of their prey.

African and Asian Origins

Human beings lived elsewhere in the world for hundreds of thousands of years before they reached the Western Hemisphere. In effect, humans lacked an effective means of transportation to it because, millions of years before humans evolved anywhere on the globe, North and South America became detached from the gigantic common landmass scientists now call Pangaea. About 240 million years ago, powerful forces deep within the earth began to fracture Pangaea and slowly to push the continents apart to approximately their present positions (Map 1.1). This process of continental drift encircled the

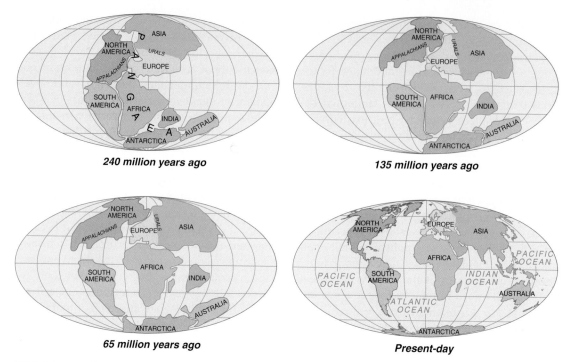

240 million years ago

135 million years ago

65 million years ago

Present-day

MAP 1.1 Continental Drift
Massive geological forces separated North and South America from other continents eons before
human beings evolved in Africa in the last 1.5 million years.

READING THE MAP: Which continents separated from Pangaea earliest? Which ones separated from
each other last? Which are still closely connected to each other?
CONNECTIONS: How does continental drift explain why human life developed elsewhere on the planet
for hundreds of thousands of years before the first person entered the Western Hemisphere during
the last 15,000 years?

FOR MORE HELP ANALYZING THIS MAP, see the map activity for this chapter in the Online Study Guide at
bedfordstmartins.com/roark.

land of the Western Hemisphere with large
oceans that isolated it from the other continents,
long before early human beings (*Homo erectus*)
first appeared in Africa about 2 million years
ago. (Hereafter in this chapter, the abbreviation
BP—archaeologists' notation for "years before
the present"—is used to indicate dates earlier
than 2,000 years ago. Dates more recent than
2,000 years ago are indicated with the common
and familiar notation *AD*—for example, AD
1492.)

More than a million and a half years after
Homo erectus appeared, or about 400,000 BP,
modern humans (*Homo sapiens*) evolved in
Africa. All human beings throughout the world
today are literally descendants of these ancient
Africans. Slowly, over many millennia, *Homo
sapiens* migrated out of Africa and into Europe
and Asia. Unlike North and South America,
Europe and Asia retained land connections to
Africa, making migration possible for *Homo sapi-*

ens, who traveled principally on foot and occasionally in small boats that could navigate rivers
and lakes but could not survive the rigors of
transoceanic travel. The vast oceans encircling
North and South America kept human beings
away for roughly 97 percent of the time *Homo
sapiens* have been on earth.

Two major developments made it possible
for human beings to migrate to the Western
Hemisphere. First, humans successfully adapted
to the frigid environment near the Arctic Circle.
Second, changes in the earth's climate recon-
nected North America to Asia.

By about 25,000 BP, *Homo sapiens* had spread
from Africa throughout Europe and Asia.
People, presumably women, had learned to use
bone needles to sew animal skins into warm
clothing that permitted them to become permanent residents of extremely cold regions like
northeastern Siberia. Ancient Siberians made the
trip to North America on land that now lies sub-

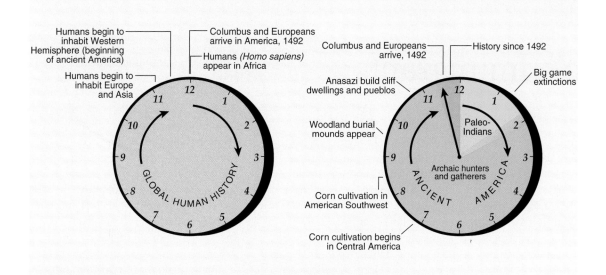

FIGURE 1.1   Human Habitation of the World and the Western Hemisphere
These clock faces illustrate the long global history of modern humans (left) and of human history in the Western Hemisphere since the arrival of the first ancient Americans (right). If the total period of human life on earth is considered, American history since the arrival of Columbus in 1492 comprises less than one minute (or 1/10 of 1 percent) of modern human existence. And if the total period of human life in the New World is converted from millennia to a 12-hour clock, then ancient American history makes up the first 11½ hours and all history since the arrival of the Europeans in 1492 occupies only the last half hour.

merged beneath sixty miles of water that separates easternmost Siberia from westernmost Alaska. But during the last great global cold spell—the Wisconsin glaciation, which endured from about 80,000 BP to about 10,000 BP—snow piled up in glaciers that did not melt, causing the sea level to drop as much as 350 feet below its current level. This natural transformation of seawater into glacial ice exposed the sea floor currently submerged beneath the waters of the Bering Strait and turned it into dry land that formed what experts refer to as a land bridge between Asian Siberia and American Alaska. This land bridge, which scientists call Beringia, opened a pathway about a thousand miles wide between the Eastern and Western Hemispheres.

Siberian hunters presumably roamed into Beringia for centuries in search of game animals. (See "Beyond America's Borders," page 8.) Grasses and small shrubs that covered Beringia supported

Beringia

herds of mammoth, bison, and numerous smaller animals. As the hunters ventured farther and farther east, they had no idea that they walked where humans had never before set foot. They had no awareness that their pursuit of prey made them pioneers of human life in the Western Hemisphere. Their migrations probably had very little influence on their own lives, which continued more or less in the traditional ways they had learned from their Siberian ancestors. Unbeknownst to them, however, their migrations revolutionized the history of the world, both for their descendants in the Western Hemisphere and for the descendants of their ancestors back in Asia, Europe, and Africa.

Archaeologists speculate that these Siberian hunters traveled in small bands of no more than twenty-five people. How many such bands arrived in North

> The transformation of seawater into glacial ice exposed the sea floor beneath the waters of the Bering Strait and turned it into a land bridge between Asian Siberia and American Alaska.

Nature's Immigrants

Like the first human beings who came to the New World, most of the large animals in ancient America were descendants of migrants from elsewhere on the globe. Mammoths, the signature prey of the Clovis hunters of ancient America, illustrate the persistent immigration of animals from Asia to North America. The ancestors of the mammoths that Clovis hunters stalked about 12,000 years ago had immigrated from Asia about 1.7 million years earlier. The first mammoth migrants from Asia followed in the tracks of hundreds of other animal species that had made their way across Beringia to North America for more than 60 million years. These immigrants and their descendants populated the natural environment of America that ancient Americans first encountered. Clearly, America was a land of immigrants long before the first humans arrived.

An extraterrestrial event created the basic precondition for these animal migrations. Scientists have discovered convincing evidence that about 65 million years ago a meteorite about six miles in diameter slammed into the Yucatán peninsula in Mexico. Experts estimate that the meteorite sped toward Yucatán at about 54,000 miles an hour and cratered into the earth with an explosion equivalent to trillions of atomic bombs. Coming in at a low angle to the curvature of the earth from the direction of the Southern Hemisphere, the meteorite incinerated almost all the exposed animals and plants in North America with a blast of heat a thousand times hotter than that reaching the earth from the sun. The plume of dust and smoke propelled into the atmosphere by the impact of the meteorite darkened skies, reduced or eliminated photosynthesis, and showered the earth with sulfuric acid. These catastrophic changes in the global environment caused the extinction of many animals worldwide, including dinosaurs who had ruled the earth for more than 100 million years. But outside the fiery blast zone that extended thousands of miles north from ground zero in Yucatán, many animals survived the mass extinction and became the ancestors of animals that eventually migrated to North America.

Among the animals that survived the great extinction were small ratlike creatures, the ancestors of mammals that began to multiply and remultiply, ultimately filling many of the environmental niches previously occupied by dinosaurs and other extinct species. For example, a tiny hoofed mammal now called *Procerberus* made the trek across Beringia from Asia to North America and within about 4 million years spawned dozens of new species of hoofed mammals in the New World, the largest the size of a small pony. *Procerberus* became the ancient ancestor of both horses and camels, species that evolved first in North America.

In the millions of years that followed ancestor species' initial migration from Asia, distinctive North American descendants evolved, just as horses and camels did. The ancestor of North American cats migrated from Asia about 17 million years ago, but within a few million years, North America had evolved distinctive cat species, including lions roughly twice as large as the largest male African lions today. Similarly, nature's migrants from Asia developed into distinctive North American elephants (including mammoths), rhinoceroses, and pigs, as well as many smaller creatures such as beavers, skunks, and weasels. Although the migration of ancient birds is less well known because of the scarcity of fossil remains, the ancestor of today's common raven made the colossal journey to North America over millions of years by flying through Asia from its starting point in Australia.

Some animals that evolved in North America eventually migrated back to Asia and beyond. Horses and camels illustrate this two-way traffic on the Beringian land bridge. Horses evolved in North America for about 20 million years before they first wandered across the land bridge to Asia. They didn't stop there. Modern-day zebras on the plains of Africa are the descendants of those

Meteor Impact in North America, 65 Million Years Ago

North America

ATLANTIC OCEAN

PACIFIC OCEAN

South America

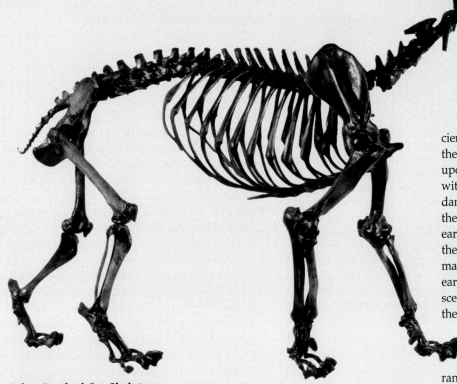

Saber-Toothed Cat Skeleton

Saber-toothed cats ranged throughout North America when the first Americans arrived. This fossilized skeleton came from the La Brea tar pits in present-day Los Angeles, California. For millennia before the arrival of human beings in the New World, these cats and 660 other animal species became bogged down in the tar pits, which ultimately served to preserve their remains. Hundreds of thousands of saber-toothed cat bones have been recovered from the tar pit deposits. The cats probably used their huge incisors to tear open the throats or abdomens of their prey. Unlike the swift-footed big cats of today, saber-toothed cats did not chase down their prey. Since they weighed about twice as much as modern lions, they crouched in ambush and leaped on unsuspecting victims nearby. This mode of attack probably accounts for the many fossils in the tar pits. Cats who attacked prey mired in the sticky tar probably became trapped themselves sometimes. Like many other big mammals that inhabited North America during the Paleo-Indian era, the saber-toothed cat became extinct about 11,000 BP.

George C. Page Museum.

On the eve of the arrival of ancient Americans in the New World, the large mammals they would prey upon—and in some cases compete with for prey—were the descendants of migrants who had preceded the first Americans millions of years earlier. The giant bison who roamed the plains—and whose fossilized remains George McJunkin excavated early in the twentieth century—descended from Asian migrants. So did the giant sloths that measured eighteen feet from nose to tail and weighed three tons. So did the massive short-faced bear that ran down its prey despite weighing the better part of a ton. So did the saber-toothed cat that, fossil deposits prove, feasted on young mammoths. And so did the mammoths themselves. The human beings who first set foot in the New World were pioneers of human migration to North America, but they were only the latest of latecomers among the thousands of nature's migrants from Asia that had been pioneering in North America for more than 60 million years.

BIBLIOGRAPHY

Jordi Agusti and Mauricio Anton, *Mammoths, Sabertooths, and Hominids* (2002).

Miles Barton et al., *Prehistoric America: A Journey through the Ice Age and Beyond* (2002).

Claudine Cohen, *The Fate of the Mammoth: Fossils, Myth, and History* (2002).

Tim Flannery, *The Eternal Frontier: An Ecological History of North America and Its Peoples* (2001).

Richard Fortey, *Life: A Natural History of the First Four Billion Years of Life on Earth* (1997).

Ian Lange, *Ice Age Mammals of North America* (2002).

ancient American migrant horses. Camels were much more recent outmigrants, wending their way from North America to Asia only about 4 million years ago. Dogs, evidently one of the few native North American mammals, also migrated to Asia, along with other distinctive species. But the dominant stream of nature's migrants was in the other direction, from Asia to North America. The greater variety of well-established species in the larger Asian landmass made it difficult for many North American species to get a foothold there. Conversely, migrants from Asia more readily carved out an environmental niche for themselves in the New World.

Mammoth Cave Painting
Like Clovis people in ancient America, human beings elsewhere in the world hunted mammoths. An ancient artist painted this portrait of mammoths on the wall of a cave in southern France about 16,000 BP. The painting conveys the artist's close observation of mammoths. It is easy to understand why the artist and hunters throughout the world paid respectful attention to mammoths. North American mammoths hunted by Clovis Paleo-Indians stood about fourteen feet tall at the shoulder and weighed eight to ten tons. Their tusks stretched to sixteen feet in length. Each of their four teeth was about the size of a shoebox. Although mammoths were vegetarians, they presumably knew how to throw their weight around against puny humans. Hunters armed with stone-tipped wooden spears needed to study such formidable prey to identify their vulnerabilities.
Musée de l'Homme.

America before Beringia once again disappeared beneath the sea will never be known. When they came is hotly debated by experts. The first migrants probably arrived sometime after 15,000 BP. Scattered and inconclusive evidence suggests that they may have arrived a few thousand years earlier. Certainly humans inhabited the Western Hemisphere by 13,000 BP.

Archaeologists refer to these first migrants and their descendants for the next few millennia as Paleo-Indians. While the date of their arrival is somewhat uncertain, they certainly originated in Asia. Some archaeologists have speculated that the Paleo-Indians may have sailed across the South Pacific from Polynesia or across the North Atlantic from Europe, but no evidence conclusively supports such views. Instead, detailed analyses of Native American languages, blood proteins, and DNA patterns, along with extensive archaeological discoveries, provide conclusive evidence of the first Americans' Asian origins.

Paleo-Indian Hunters

When humans first arrived in the Western Hemisphere, massive glaciers covered most of present-day Canada. A narrow corridor not entirely obstructed by ice ran along the eastern side of the Canadian Rockies, and most archaeologists believe that Paleo-Indians migrated through the ice-free passageway in pursuit of game. They may also have traveled along the coast in small boats, hopscotching from one desirable landing spot to another. At the southern edge of the glaciers, Paleo-Indians entered a hunters' paradise. North, Central, and South America teemed with wildlife that had never before confronted wily two-legged predators armed with razor-sharp spears. The abundance of game presumably made hunting relatively easy. Ample food permitted the Paleo-Indian population to grow. Within a thousand years or so, Paleo-Indians had migrated to the southern tip of South America and virtually everywhere else in the Western Hemisphere.

Paleo-Indians used a distinctively shaped spearhead known now as a Clovis point, named for the place in New Mexico where it was first excavated. Archaeologists' discovery of Clovis points throughout North and Central America in sites occupied between 11,500 BP and 11,000 BP is powerful evidence that these nomadic hunters shared a common ancestry and way of life. The Paleo-Indians probably hunted smaller animals, but most of the artifacts that have survived from this era indicate that the first Americans specialized in hunting mammoths. One mammoth kill supplied meat for weeks or, if dried, for months. Mammoth hide and bones provided clothing, shelter, tools, and much more.

About 11,000 BP, Paleo-Indians confronted a major crisis. The mammoths and other big-game

Clovis Spear Straightener
Clovis hunters used this bone spear straightener about 11,000 BP at a campsite in Arizona where archaeologists discovered it lying among the butchered remains of two mammoth carcasses and thirteen ancient bison. Similar objects often appear in ancient sites in Eurasia, but this is the only bone artifact yet discovered in a Clovis-era site in North America. Presumably Clovis hunters stuck their spear shafts through the opening and then grasped the handle of the straightener and moved it back and forth along the length of the shaft to remove imperfections and make the spear a more effective weapon.
Arizona State Museum, University of Arizona.

animals they hunted became extinct. Scientists are not completely certain why the extinction occurred, although the changing environment probably contributed to it. About this time the Wisconsin glacial period came to an end, glaciers melted, and sea levels rose. Some large mammals probably had difficulty adapting to the warmer climate. Many archaeologists also believe, however, that Paleo-Indians contributed to the New World extinctions by killing these animals more rapidly than they could reproduce. Within just a few thousand years of their arrival in the Western Hemisphere, Paleo-Indian hunters helped bring about a radical change in the natural environment—namely the extinction of large mammals that had existed for millions of years and whose presence had initially drawn hunters west across Beringia.

Paleo-Indians adapted to the drastic environmental change of the big-game extinctions by making at least two important changes in their way of life. First, hunters began to prey more intensively on smaller animals. Second, Paleo-Indians devoted more energy to foraging, that is, to collecting wild plant foods such as roots, seeds, nuts, berries, and fruits. When Paleo-Indians made these changes, they replaced the apparent uniformity of the big-game-oriented Clovis culture* with great cultural diversity. This diversity arose because ancient Americans adapted to the many natural environments throughout the hemisphere, ranging from icy tundra to steamy jungles.

Post-Clovis adaptations to local environments resulted in the astounding variety of Native American cultures that existed when Europeans arrived in AD 1492. By then, more than three hundred major tribes and hundreds of lesser groups inhabited North America alone. Hundreds more lived in Central and South America. These peoples spoke different languages, practiced different religions, lived in different dwellings, followed different subsistence

---

* The word *culture* is used here to connote what is commonly called "way of life." It refers not only to how a group of people supplied themselves with food and shelter but also to their family relationships, social groupings, religious ideas, and other features of their lives. For most prehistoric cultures—as for the Clovis people—more is known about food and shelter because of the artifacts that have survived. Ancient American's ideas, assumptions, hopes, dreams, and fantasies were undoubtedly important, but we know very little about them.

strategies, and observed different rules of kinship and inheritance. Hundreds of other ancient American cultures had disappeared or transformed themselves as their people constantly adapted to environmental and other changes. A full account of those changes and the cultural diversity they created is beyond the scope of this textbook. But we cannot ignore the most important changes and adaptations made by ancient Americans during the last eleven millennia.

> About 11,000 BP, Paleo-Indians confronted a major crisis. The mammoths and other big-game animals they hunted became extinct.

Archaic Hunters and Gatherers

Archaeologists use the term **Archaic** to describe both the many different hunting and gathering cultures that descended from Paleo-Indians and the long period of time when those cultures dominated the history of ancient America, roughly from 10,000 BP to somewhere between 3000 BP and 4000 BP. Although the cultural and the chronological boundaries of the Archaic era are not sharply defined, the term usefully describes the important era in the history of ancient America that followed the Paleo-Indian big-game hunters and preceded the development of agriculture. It also denotes a hunter-gatherer way of life that persisted throughout most of North America well into the era of European colonization.

Like their Paleo-Indian ancestors, Archaic Indians hunted with spears; but they also took smaller game with traps, nets, and hooks. Unlike their Paleo-Indian predecessors, most Archaic peoples used a variety of stone tools to prepare food from wild plants. A characteristic Archaic artifact is a grinding stone used to pulverize seeds into edible form. Most Archaic Indians migrated from place to place to harvest plants and hunt animals. They usually did not establish permanent villages, although they often returned to the same river valley or fertile meadow from year to year to take advantage of abundant food resources. In certain regions with especially rich resources—such as present-day California and the Pacific Northwest—they developed permanent settlements. Many groups became highly proficient basket makers in order to collect and

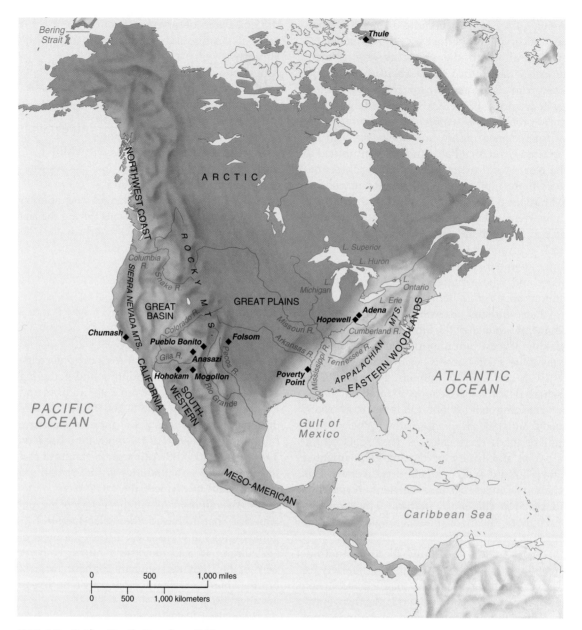

MAP 1.2 Native North American Cultures
Environmental conditions defined the boundaries of the broad zones of cultural similarity among ancient North Americans.

READING THE MAP: What crucial environmental features set the boundaries of each cultural region? (The topography indicated on Map 1.3, "Native North Americans about 1500," may be helpful.)
CONNECTIONS: How did environmental factors and variations affect the development of different groups of Native American cultures? Why do you think historians and archaeologists group cultures together by their regional positions?

FOR MORE HELP ANALYZING THIS MAP, see the map activity for this chapter in the Online Study Guide at
bedfordstmartins.com/roark.

store plant food. Above all, Archaic folk did not depend on agriculture for food. Instead, they gathered wild plants and hunted wild animals. Archaic peoples expressed these general traits in distinctive ways in the major environmental regions of North America (Map 1.2).

Great Plains Bison Hunters

After the extinction of large game such as mammoths, some hunters began to concentrate on huge herds of bison that grazed the grassy, arid plains stretching for hundreds of miles east of the Rocky Mountains. For almost a thousand years after the big-game extinctions, Archaic Indians hunted bison with Folsom points like those found at the site discovered by George McJunkin.

Like their nomadic predecessors, Folsom hunters moved constantly to maintain contact with their prey. Often two or three hunters from a band of several families would single out a few bison from a herd and creep up close enough to spear them. Great Plains hunters also developed trapping techniques that made it easier to kill large numbers of animals. At the original Folsom site, careful study of the bones McJunkin found suggests that early one winter hunters drove

bison into the arroyo and speared twenty-three of them. At many other sites, hunters stampeded large numbers of bison over cliffs, killing some and injuring others, which Indians then readily slaughtered.

Bows and arrows reached Great Plains hunters from the north about AD 500. They largely replaced spears, which had been the hunters' weapon of choice for millennia. Bows permitted hunters to wound an animal from farther away, and arrows made it easy to shoot repeatedly. These new weapons did not otherwise alter the age-old techniques of bison hunting that ancient Americans had practiced since the Folsom era.

Great Basin Cultures

Archaic peoples in the Great Basin between the Rocky Mountains and the Sierra Nevada inhabited a region of great environmental diversity. Some Great Basin Indians lived along the shores of large marshes and lakes that formed during rainy periods. They ate fish of every available size and type, catching them with bone hooks and nets. Other cultures survived in the foothills of mountains between the blistering heat on the desert floor and the cold, treeless mountain heights. Hunters killed deer, antelope, and sometimes bison, as well as smaller game like rabbits, rodents, and snakes. These broadly defined zones of habitation changed constantly, depending largely on the amount of rainfall.

Despite the variety and occasional abundance of animals, Great Basin peoples relied on plants as the most important source of food. Unlike meat and fish, plant food could be collected in large quantities and stored in baskets for long periods to protect against shortages caused by the fickle rainfall. Many Great Basin peoples depended on ample supplies of piñon nuts as a dietary staple. By diversifying their food sources and migrating to favorable locations to collect and store them, Great Basin peoples adapted to the severe environmental challenges of the region and maintained their Archaic hunter-gatherer way of life for centuries after AD 1492.

Pacific Coast Cultures

The richness of the natural environment made present-day California the most densely settled area in all of ancient North America. The abundant resources of both land and ocean offered

Folsom Point at Wild Horse Arroyo

In 1927, paleontologist J. D. Figgins found this spear point (subsequently named a Folsom point) at the site discovered by George McJunkin. Embedded between the fossilized ribs of a bison that had been extinct for 10,000 years, this point proved that ancient Americans had inhabited the hemisphere at least that long. The importance of this find led one paleontologist to hold up several Folsom points and proclaim, "In my hand I hold the answer to the antiquity of man in America." Although he exaggerated (Folsom was only part of the answer), this discovery in Wild Horse Arroyo stimulated archaeologists to rethink the history of ancient Americans and to uncover fresh evidence of their many cultures.

such ample food that California peoples remained hunters and gatherers for hundreds of years after AD 1492. The diversity of California's environment encouraged corresponding diversity among native peoples. The mosaic of Archaic settlements in California included about five hundred separate tribes speaking some ninety languages, each with local dialects. No other region of comparable size in North America exhibited such cultural variety.

The Chumash, one of the many California cultures, emerged in the region surrounding what is now Santa Barbara about 5000 BP. Comparatively plentiful food resources—especially acorns—permitted Chumash people to establish relatively permanent villages. Conflict frequently broke out among the villages, documented by the notable proportion of skeletons in Chumash burial grounds that display signs of violent deaths. Archaeologists believe that these conflicts arose in part from efforts by Chumash villagers to restrict access to their valuable acorn-gathering territory. Although few other California cultures achieved the population density and village settlements of the Chumash, all shared the hunter-gatherer way of life and reliance on acorns as a major food source.

> Fishing freed Northwest peoples to develop sophisticated woodworking skills.

Chumash Necklace

Long before the arrival of Europeans, ancient Chumash people in southern California made this elegant necklace of abalone shell. The carefully formed, polished, and assembled pieces of shell illustrate the artistry of the Chumash and their access to the rich and diverse marine life of the Pacific coast. Since living abalone cling stubbornly to submerged rocks along the coast, Chumash divers presumably pried abalone from their rocky perches to obtain their delicious flesh; then one or more Chumash artisans recycled the inedible shell to make this necklace. Its iridescent splendor demonstrates that Chumash people wore beautiful as well as useful adornments. Natural History Museum of Los Angeles County.

Ancient California

Another rich natural environment lay along the Pacific Northwest coast. Like the Chumash, Northwest peoples built more or less permanent villages. Abundant fish and marine life permitted ancient Americans in this region to devote substantial time and energy to activities other than hunting and gathering. After about 5500 BP, they concentrated on catching large quantities of salmon, halibut, and other fish, which they dried to last throughout the year and to trade with people who lived hundreds of miles from the coast. Fishing freed Northwest peoples to develop sophisticated woodworking skills. They fashioned elaborate wood carvings that denoted wealth and status as well as huge canoes, some big enough to hold fifty people, for fishing,

hunting, and conducting warfare against neighboring tribes. Much of the warfare among Archaic northwesterners grew out of attempts to defend or gain access to prime fishing sites. Northwestern peoples also carved distinctive totem poles to adorn their houses with images of animals, ancestors, and supernatural beings.

Eastern Woodland Cultures

East of the Mississippi River, Archaic peoples adapted to a forest environment that included many local variants, such as the major river valleys of the Mississippi, Ohio, Tennessee, and Cumberland; the Great Lakes region; and the Atlantic coast (see Map 1.2). Throughout these

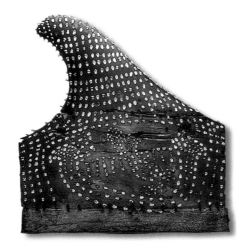

Ozette Whale Effigy
This carving of a whale fin decorated with hundreds of sea otter teeth was discovered along with thousands of other artifacts of daily life at Ozette, an ancient village on the tip of the Olympic Peninsula in present-day Washington that was inundated by a catastrophic mud slide about five hundred years ago. The fin illustrates the importance of whale hunting to the residents of Ozette, who set out in canoes carrying eight men armed with harpoons to catch and kill animals weighing twenty to thirty tons.
Richard Alexander Cooke III.

diverse locales, Archaic peoples followed similar survival strategies.

Woodland hunters stalked deer as their most important prey. Deer supplied Woodland people with food as well as with hides and bones that they crafted into clothing, weapons, needles, and many other tools. Like Archaic peoples elsewhere, Woodland Indians gathered edible plants, seeds, and especially nuts. Most commonly, they gathered hickory nuts, but they also collected pecans, walnuts, acorns, and hazelnuts. About 6000 BP, some Woodland groups established more or less permanent settlements of 25 to 150 people, usually near a river or lake that offered a wide variety of plant and animal resources. The existence of such settlements has permitted archaeologists to locate numerous Archaic burial sites that suggest Woodland people had a life expectancy of about eighteen years.

Around 4000 BP, Woodland cultures added two important new features to their basic hunter-gatherer lifestyles: agriculture and pottery. Gourds and pumpkins that originated thousands of years earlier in Mexico spread to North America through trade and migration, and Woodland peoples began to grow them in parts of Missouri and Kentucky. After the introduction of these Mexican crops, Woodland peoples also began to cultivate local species such as sunflowers. They probably also grew small quantities of tobacco, another import from South America, since stone pipes for smoking appeared by about 3500 BP. Corn, the most important plant food in Mexico, became a significant Woodland food crop more than a thousand years later. These cultivated crops added to the quantity, variety, and predictability of Woodland food sources, but they did not fundamentally alter Woodland peoples' dependence on gathering wild plants, seeds, and nuts.

Techniques for making ceramic pots probably also originated in Mexico. Traders and migrants probably brought them into North America along with Central and South American seeds. Pots were more durable than baskets for cooking and storage of water and food, but they were also much heavier. Nomadic people elsewhere in North America relied on baskets since pots were too heavy to move readily. The permanent settlements of Woodland peoples made the heavy weight of pots much less important than their advantages compared to leaky and fragile baskets.

> Around 4,000 years ago, the Woodland cultures added two important features to their hunter-gatherer lifestyles: agriculture and pottery.

Woodland Hairpins
Ancient Americans in present-day Florida crafted these hairpins from bone between roughly 4500 BP and AD 800. The intricate designs incised on the pins demonstrate the artists' interest and skill in decoration. The differences in design hint at the diversity of cultural styles among the Woodland people who produced them.
Courtesy of Barbara A. Purdy; photo by Roy Craven.

While pottery and agriculture introduced changes in Woodland cultures, ancient Woodland Americans retained the other basic features of their Archaic hunter-gatherer lifestyle, which persisted in most areas to 1492 and beyond.

> All southwestern peoples confronted the challenge of a dry climate and unpredictable fluctuations in rainfall that made the supply of wild plant food very unreliable. These ancient Americans probably adopted agriculture in response to this basic environmental condition.

Agricultural Settlements and Chiefdoms

Among Eastern Woodland peoples and other Archaic cultures, agriculture supplemented rather than replaced hunter-gatherer subsistence strategies. Reliance on wild animals and plants required most Archaic groups to remain small and mobile. But beginning about 4000 BP, distinctive southwestern cultures slowly came to depend on agriculture and to build permanent settlements. Later, around 2500 BP, Woodland peoples in the vast Mississippi valley began to construct burial mounds and other earthworks that suggest the existence of social and political hierarchies that archaeologists term chiefdoms. Although the hunter-gatherer lifestyle never entirely disappeared, the development of agricultural settlements and chiefdoms represented important innovations to the Archaic way of life.

Southwestern Cultures

Ancient Americans in what is now Arizona, New Mexico, and southern portions of Utah and Colorado developed cultures characterized by agriculture and eventually by multiunit dwellings called pueblos. All southwestern peoples confronted the challenge of a dry climate and unpredictable fluctuations in rainfall that made the supply of wild plant food very unreliable. These ancient Americans probably adopted agriculture in response to this basic environmental condition.

Until about 5000 BP, few people lived in the Southwest. As the population slowly grew during the next 1,500 years, southwestern hunters and gatherers began to cultivate their signature food crop, corn, which had been grown in Central and South America since about 7000 BP. During the next 3,000 years, corn became the most important cultivated crop for ancient Americans throughout North America. In the Southwest, the demands of corn cultivation encouraged hunter-gatherers to restrict their migratory habits in order to tend the crop. A vital consideration was access to water. Southwestern Indians became irrigation experts, conserving water from streams, springs, and rainfall and distributing it to thirsty crops.

Ancient Agriculture
Dropping seeds into holes punched in cleared ground by a pointed stick, known as a "dibble," this ancient American farmer sows a new crop while previously planted seeds—including the corn and beans immediately opposite him—bear fruit for harvest. Created by a sixteenth-century European artist, the drawing misrepresents who did the agricultural work in many ancient American cultures—namely women rather than men. However, the three-foot dibble would have been used as shown here.
The Pierpont Morgan Library/Art Resource, NY; Jerry Jacka Photography.

About AD 200, small farming settlements began to appear throughout southern New Mexico, marking the emergence of the Mogollon culture. Typically, a Mogollon settlement included a dozen pit houses, made by digging out a rounded pit about fifteen feet in diameter and a foot or two deep and then erecting poles to support a roof of branches or dirt. Larger villages usually had one or two bigger pit houses that may have been the predecessors of the circular *kivas*, the ceremonial rooms that became a characteristic of nearly all southwestern settlements. About AD 1000, Mogollon culture began to decline, for reasons that remain obscure. Its descendants included the Mimbres peoples in southwestern New Mexico, who produced spectacular pottery often adorned with human and animal designs. By about AD 1250, the Mimbres culture also disappeared.

Around AD 500, while the Mogollon culture prevailed in New Mexico, other ancient people migrated from Mexico to southern Arizona and established the distinctive Hohokam culture. Hohokam settlements used sophisticated grids of irrigation canals to take advantage of the abundant sunshine that permitted them to plant and harvest twice a year. Irrigation produced comparatively high crop yields, permitting the Hohokam population to grow and seek out more land to settle. Hohokam culture reflected the continuing influence of its origins in Mexico. The people built sizable platform mounds and ball courts characteristic of many Mexican cultures to the south. Hohokam culture declined about AD 1400, for reasons that remain a mystery.

North of the Hohokam and Mogollon cultures, in a region that encompassed southern Utah and Colorado and northern Arizona and New Mexico, the Anasazi culture began to flourish about AD 100. The early Anasazi built pit houses on mesa tops and used irrigation much like their neighbors to the south. Beginning around AD 1000 (again, it is not known why), Anasazi began to move to large, multistory cliff dwellings whose spectacular ruins still exist at Mesa Verde, Colorado, and

Southwestern Cultures

Canyon de Chelly, Arizona. Other Anasazi communities—like the one whose impressive ruins can be visited at Chaco Canyon, New Mexico (see "American Places," page 20)—erected huge, stone-walled pueblos with enough rooms to house everyone in the settlement. Pueblo Bonito at Chaco Canyon, for example, contained more than eight hundred rooms. Anasazi pueblos and cliff dwellings typically contained one or more kivas used for secret ceremonies, restricted to men, that sought to communicate with the supernatural world.

Drought began to plague the region about AD 1130, and it lasted for more than half a century, triggering the disappearance of Anasazi culture. By AD 1200, the large Anasazi pueblos had been abandoned. The prolonged drought probably intensified conflict among pueblos and made it impossible to depend on the techniques of irrigated agriculture that worked for centuries. Some Anasazi migrated toward regions with more reliable rainfall and settled in Hopi, Zuñi, and Acoma pueblos that their descendants in Arizona and New Mexico have occupied ever since.

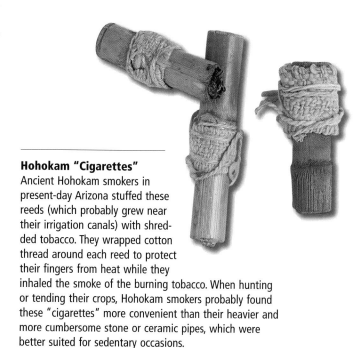

Hohokam "Cigarettes"
Ancient Hohokam smokers in present-day Arizona stuffed these reeds (which probably grew near their irrigation canals) with shredded tobacco. They wrapped cotton thread around each reed to protect their fingers from heat while they inhaled the smoke of the burning tobacco. When hunting or tending their crops, Hohokam smokers probably found these "cigarettes" more convenient than their heavier and more cumbersome stone or ceramic pipes, which were better suited for sedentary occasions.
Jerry Jacka Photography.

Mexican Ball Court Model

Mexican and other ancient Central American cultures commonly built special courts (or playing fields) for their intensely competitive ball games. This rare model of a ball court, made in Mexico sometime between 2200 BP and AD 250, shows a game in progress, complete with players and spectators. Players wore padded belts and used their hips to hit the hard rubber ball through the goal. Spectators watched intently, not only to admire the skills of the players but also because a lot was at stake. Spectators bet on the game, and losing players were often killed. A few ball courts have been excavated in North America, providing compelling evidence of one of the many connections between ancient Mexicans and North Americans.

Yale University Art Gallery. Stephen Carlton Clark, B.A. 1903, Fund.

Woodland Burial Mounds and Chiefdoms

No other ancient Americans created dwellings similar to pueblos, but around 2500 BP, Woodland cultures throughout the vast drainage of the Mississippi River began to build burial mounds. The size of the mounds, the labor and organization required to erect them, and the differences in the artifacts buried with certain individuals suggest the existence of a social and political hierarchy that archaeologists term a chiefdom. Experts do not know the name of a single chief, nor do they know the organizational structure a chief headed. But the only way archaeologists can account for the complex and labor-intensive burial mounds and artifacts found in them is to assume that one person—whom scholars term a chief—had the ability to command the labor and obedience of very large numbers of other people, who comprised the chief's chiefdom.

Between 2500 BP and 2100 BP, Adena people built hundreds of burial mounds radiating from central Ohio. In the mounds, the

Major Mississippian Mounds, AD 800–1500

Adena usually accompanied burials with a wide variety of grave goods, including spear points and stone pipes as well as decorative and ritualistic items such as thin sheets of mica (a glasslike mineral) crafted into shapes of birds, beasts, and human hands. Over the body and grave goods Adena people piled basketful after basketful of dirt until a mound formed. Sometimes burial mounds were constructed all at once, but often they were built up slowly over many years.

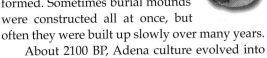

About 2100 BP, Adena culture evolved into the more elaborate Hopewell culture, which lasted about 500 years. While centered in Ohio, Hopewell culture extended throughout the vast drainage of the Ohio and Mississippi rivers. Hopewell people built larger mounds and filled them with more magnificent grave goods than had their Adena predecessors.

Burial was probably reserved for the most important members of Hopewell groups. Most people were cremated. Burial rituals appear to have brought many people together to honor the dead person and to help build the mound. Hopewell mounds were often 100 feet in diameter and 30 feet high. Careful analysis of skeletons in one Hopewell mound suggests the high status of hunters. Elbows of men in the more important graves showed signs of arthritis associated with stress to the elbow joint caused by repetitive spear-throwing. Grave goods at Hopewell sites testify to the high quality of Hopewell crafts and to the existence of a thriving trade network that ranged from Wyoming to Florida. Archaeologists believe that Hopewell chiefs probably played an important role in this sprawling interregional trade.

Ashley Creek Petroglyph
Ancient Americans incised this large petroglyph on a rock wall in present-day Utah. The elaborate shield and regalia (the headdress, breastplate, belt, and skirt) suggest that the larger figure depicts a chief or a warrior (who may also have been a chief). Experts do not know the meaning of these and other petroglyphs, although the care with which they were rendered proves that they were significant to the ancient Southwestern artists who made them. J. Q. Jacobs.

FOR MORE HELP ANALYZING THIS IMAGE, see the visual activity for this chapter in the Online Study Guide at bedfordstmartins.com/roark.

Hopewell culture declined about AD 400 for reasons that are obscure. Archaeologists speculate that bows and arrows, along with increasing reliance on agriculture, made small settlements more self-sufficient and, therefore, less dependent on the central authority of the Hopewell chiefs who were responsible for the burial mounds.

Four hundred years later, another mound-building culture flourished. The Mississippian culture emerged in the floodplains of the major southeastern river systems about AD 800 and lasted until about AD 1500. Major Mississippian sites included huge mounds with platforms on top for ceremonies and for the residences of great chiefs. The largest Mississippian site was Cahokia, located in present-day Illinois near the confluence of the Mississippi and Missouri rivers at St. Louis, Missouri.

At Cahokia, more than one hundred mounds of different sizes and shapes were grouped around large open plazas. Monk's Mound, the largest, covered sixteen acres at its base and was one hundred feet tall. Dwellings at one time covered five square miles and may have housed as many as thirty thousand inhabitants, easily qualifying Cahokia as the largest settlement in ancient North America. At Cahokia and other Mississippian sites, people evidently worshipped a sun god; the mounds probably were supposed to elevate elites nearer to the divine power of the sun. One Cahokia burial mound suggests the authority a great chief exercised. One man—presumably the chief—was buried with the bodies of more than sixty people who had been killed at the time of burial, including fifty young women who had been strangled. Such a mass sacrifice shows the coercive power a Cahokia chief wielded and the obedience he commanded.

Cahokia and other Mississippian cultures had dwindled by AD 1500. When Europeans arrived, most of the descendants of Mississippian cultures, like those of the Hopewell culture, lived in small dispersed villages supported by hunting and gathering supplemented by agriculture.

Woodland Eagle Carving
This eagle effigy topped a post in a charnel house where Woodland Indians deposited the remains of their dead ancestors sometime between 1,500 and 1,000 years ago at a site in present-day Florida. The significance of the eagle is unknown; it may have represented the clan of the deceased in the charnel house. The Detroit Institute of Arts.

Chaco Culture National Historical Park, Nageezi, New Mexico

Visitors to Chaco Culture National Historical Park can literally walk in the footsteps of ancient Americans. You can roam around plazas of Anasazi pueblos where hundreds of people lived; stroll through rooms where they cooked, conversed, and slept; enter kivas where they worshipped and performed secret rituals; climb up stairs they carved in steep cliffs; and hike for miles along straight roadways they built that seemingly lead to nowhere. Located in northwestern New Mexico about 200 miles west of George McJunkin's discovery at Folsom, Chaco is one of the most spectacular ancient sites in North America. About AD 1000, the massive residential and ceremonial buildings you can visit today stood at the center of Chacoan culture that extended over more than 20,000 square miles into the present-day Four Corners region at the intersection of Utah, Colorado, Arizona, and New Mexico.

The Chaco people were expert builders, constructing hundreds of masonry structures of awe-inspiring size and complexity. Like other Southwestern peoples, the Anasazi at Chaco hunted game and used irrigation to grow corn and other crops. But the scale and magnificence of their buildings strongly suggests that they were engaged in far more than simple subsistence. Large quantities of turquoise have been found in Chaco sites, providing evidence that Anasazi brought this valuable stone to Chaco Canyon for gifts, offerings, or trade. The numerous large kivas suggest that many people may have come to Chaco to participate in ceremonies and rituals. Major buildings appear to have been aligned to mark important astronomical events, such as the spring and winter solstices and the phases of the lunar cycle.

These solar and lunar alignments provide striking evidence that Chaco people were keenly attuned to heavenly events. They hint that the ceremonies held at Chaco may have symbolized the site's potent connection between earth and sky, between humans and the omnipotent celestial ruler. Even the carefully constructed roads that radiated for miles from major Chaco buildings seem to have been used for ceremony rather than transportation. Researchers continue to study the multitude of Chacoan artifacts to attempt to unravel the many mysteries of Anasazi history. Few visitors to Chaco will fail to be amazed by the stunning achievements of Anasazi minds and hands. And few will fail to be awed by the silent majesty of this premier ancient American place.

FOR WEB LINKS RELATED TO THIS SITE AND OTHER AMERICAN PLACES, see "PlaceLinks" at bedfordstmartins.com/roark.

Pueblo Bonito, Chaco Canyon, New Mexico
Richard Alexander Cooke III.

Native Americans in the 1490s

About thirteen millennia after Paleo-Indians first migrated to the Western Hemisphere, a new migration—this time from Europe—began in 1492 with the journey of Columbus. In the decades before the arrival of Columbus, Native Americans continued to employ their ancestors' time-tested survival strategies of hunting, gathering, and agriculture. Those strategies succeeded in both populating and shaping the new world Europeans encountered.

By the 1490s, Native Americans lived throughout North America, but their total population is a subject of heated debate among scholars. Some experts claim Native Americans numbered 18 million to 20 million, while others place the population at no more than a million. A prudent estimate is about 4 million. On the eve of European colonization, the small island nation of England had about the same number of people as all of North America. This comparison highlights the low population density in North America. In England, every hundred square miles of land had a population of about 8,000. In North America, the same area had only about sixty people. Compared to England and elsewhere in Europe, Native Americans were spread thin across the land, an outgrowth of their survival strategies of hunting, gathering, and agriculture.

FIGURE 1.2 Native American Population in North America, about 1492 (Estimated)
On the eve of the arrival of Europeans, about a fifth of all native North Americans lived along the Pacific coast—in California and the Northwest—where rich marine resources supported hunter-gatherers in much higher population densities than elsewhere in North America. About a quarter of native North Americans resided in the Southwest, where they depended on agriculture, unlike the Pacific coast peoples. Since sparse rainfall made the southwestern environment less bountiful than that of the Pacific coast, the population density in the Southwest was roughly half that on the West Coast. Woodland peoples east of the Mississippi River—in the Northeast and Southeast—comprised almost a third of native North Americans. Woodland deer and plants supplemented by agriculture supported a lower population density than in the Southwest or the West Coast. The population density on the enormous expanses of the Great Plains, Great Basin, and Arctic regions was very low, although in total about a quarter of all native North Americans resided in these areas. Overall, the population density in North America was less than 1 percent of the population density of England, which helps explain why European colonists tended to view North America as a comparatively empty wilderness.

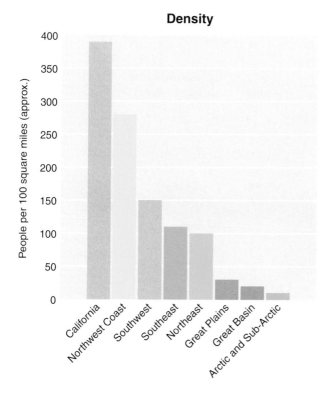

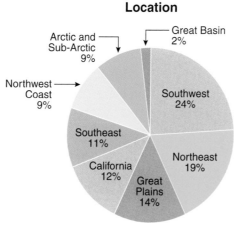

Regions in North America with abundant resources had relatively high population densities. In food-rich California and the Northwest Coast, the population density was, respectively, six times greater and four times greater than the average for the whole continent. In the food-scarce Great Plains and Great Basin, the population density was, respectively, half and one-third as much as the continental average. But even in the most densely inhabited region of North America, California, the population density was still just one-twentieth of England's.

By the 1490s, about a third of Native Americans lived in the Eastern Woodland region, which stretched west from the Atlantic coast nearly to the Mississippi, and from the Great Lakes south to the Gulf of Mexico. Eastern Woodland peoples clustered into three broad linguistic and cultural groups: Algonquian, Iroquoian, and Muskogean.

Algonquian tribes inhabited the Atlantic seaboard, the Great Lakes region, and much of the upper Midwest (Map 1.3). The relatively mild climate along the Atlantic permitted the coastal Algonquians to grow corn and other crops as well as to hunt and fish. Around the Great Lakes and in northern New England, however, cool summers and severe winters made agriculture impractical. Instead, the Abenaki, Penobscot, Chippewa, and other tribes concentrated on hunting and fishing, using canoes both for transportation and for gathering wild rice.

MAP 1.3   Native North Americans about 1500

Distinctive Native American peoples resided throughout the area that, centuries later, would become the United States. This map indicates the approximate location of some of the larger tribes about 1500. In the interest of legibility, many other peoples who inhabited North America at the time are omitted from the map.

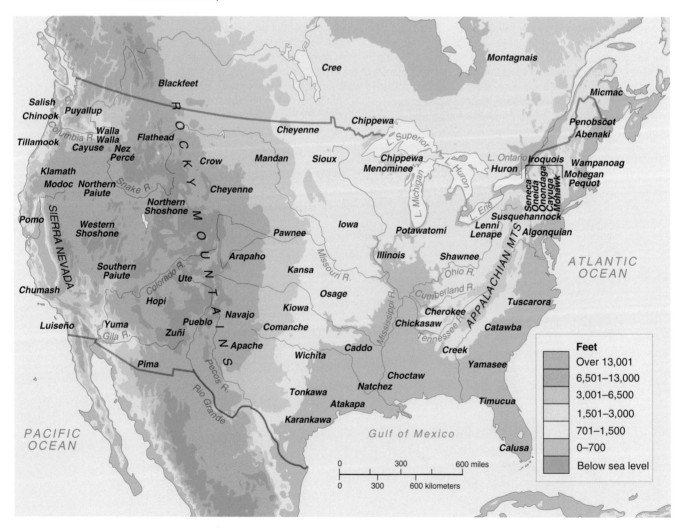

Inland from the Algonquian region, Iroquoian tribes occupied territories centered in Pennsylvania and upstate New York, as well as the hilly upland regions of the Carolinas and Georgia. Several features distinguished Iroquoian tribes from their neighbors. First, their success in cultivating corn and other crops allowed them to build permanent settlements, usually consisting of several bark-covered longhouses up to one hundred feet long and housing five to ten families. Second, Iroquoian societies adhered to matrilineal rules of descent. Property of all sorts, including land, children, and inheritance, belonged to women. Women headed family clans and even selected the chiefs (normally men) who governed tribes. Third, for purposes of war and diplomacy, an Iroquoian confederation—including the Seneca, Onondaga, Mohawk, Oneida, and Cayuga tribes—formed the League of Five Nations, which remained powerful well into the eighteenth century.

Muskogean peoples spread throughout the Southeast, south of the Ohio River and east of the Mississippi. Including Creek, Choctaw, Chickasaw, and Natchez tribes, Muskogeans inhabited a bountiful natural environment that provided abundant food from hunting, gathering, and agriculture. Remnants of the earlier Mississippian culture still existed in the religious rites common among the Muskogean. They practiced a form of sun worship, and the Natchez even built temple mounds modeled after those of their Mississippian ancestors.

Great Plains peoples accounted for about one out of seven Native Americans. Inhabiting the huge region west of the Eastern Woodland people and east of the Rocky Mountains, many tribes had migrated to the Great Plains within the last century or two, forced westward by Iroquoian and Algonquian tribes. Some Great Plains tribes—especially the Mandan and Pawnee—farmed successfully, growing both corn and sunflowers. But the Teton Sioux, Blackfeet, Comanche, Cheyenne, and Crow on the northern plains and the Apache and other nomadic tribes on the southern plains depended on buffalo for subsistence.

Southwestern cultures included about a quarter of all native North Americans. These descendants of the Mogollon, Hohokam, and Anasazi cultures lived in settled agricultural communities, many of them pueblos. They continued to grow corn, beans, and squash with methods they had refined for centuries. However, their communities came under attack by a large number of warlike Athapascan tribes who invaded the Southwest beginning around AD 1300. The Athapascans—principally Apache and Navajo—were skillful warriors who preyed on the sedentary pueblo Indians, reaping the fruits of agriculture without the work of farming.

About a fifth of all native North Americans resided along the Pacific coast. In California, abundant acorns and nutritious marine life supported high population densities but retarded the development of agriculture. Similar dependence on hunting and gathering persisted along the Northwest coast, where fishing reigned supreme. Salmon was so abundant that at the Dalles site on the Columbia River, Northwest peoples caught millions of pounds of salmon every summer and traded it as far away as California and the Great Plains. Although important trading centers existed throughout North America, particularly in the Southwest, it is likely that the Dalles site was the largest Native American trading center on the continent.

While trading was common—especially for such luxury items as highly nutritious dried salmon, or much prized stones, shells, and feathers—all native North Americans in the 1490s still depended on hunting and gathering for a major portion of their food. Most of them also practiced agriculture. Some used agriculture to supplement hunting and gathering; for others, the balance was reversed. People throughout North America used bows, arrows, and other weapons for hunting and warfare. None of them employed writing, expressing themselves instead in many other ways. They made drawings on stones, wood, and animal skins. They wove patterns in baskets and textiles. (See "The Promise of Technology," page 24.) They painted designs on pottery and crafted beadwork, pipes, and other decorative items. They danced, sang, and played music. They performed elaborate burial ceremonies and other religious rites.

These rich and varied cultural resources of Native Americans did not include features of life common in Europe during the 1490s. Native Americans did not use wheels; sailing ships were unknown to them; they had no large domesticated animals such as horses, cows, or

> Iroquoian societies adhered to matrilineal rules of descent. Property of all sorts, including land, children, and inheritance, belonged to women.

Ancient American Weaving

Weaving—like other ancient American activities such as cooking, hunting, and worship—required transmission of knowledge from person to person. The workbasket of a master weaver shown here illustrates the technology of ancient American textile production. Found in the Andes in a woman's grave dating from 1,000 years ago, the workbasket contains tools for every stage of textile production.

Most likely, the ancient American woman who owned this workbasket taught her skills to her daughters and other kinswomen. Novices learned by watching, by copying, and by listening to advice about what they did wrong. Since ancient Americans had no instruction manuals for weaving or anything else, all technological knowledge had to be remembered and passed from one person to another. Over time, details of knowledge accumulated into sophisticated technologies that produced marvels of human artistry such as the weaving shown here.

Mastery of the technology of weaving took many years of training and experience. Imagine that you were handed this workbasket and asked to make the weaving pictured here. First of all, you would need to know how to use the various tools in the workbasket. You would need to take fiber from cotton plants or animal wool (such as llama or alpaca) and spin it into thread. To make colored threads, you would dye the fibers before spinning, using different vegetable and mineral concoctions. The pointed sticks wrapped with thread (left center) are spindles for transforming the colored fibers into thread. You would use the small ceramic cup to hold one end of the spindle while you twisted the fiber through your fingers to create strong, thin thread. The two pieces of chalk (to the right of the ceramic cup) served to make a powder that lubricated your fingers to allow the thread to wind smoothly onto the spindle. Skeins of finished thread removed from their spindles are just to the left of the ceramic cup. This small workbasket contained more than 150 spindles for the many varieties of thread required. The beadlike objects at the center are whorls for placing on spindles to anchor the thread and provide decoration. On the right, above the ceramic cup, are bobbins used to pass the thread through the weaving, a bone pick to press down on the threads to tighten the weave, and a long spine needle with a tiny hole, to use for sewing and embroidery.

This simple example demonstrates that technology involves more than just physical objects—tools. Human beings must learn how to use the tools. The tools themselves embody the results of human learning that took place over many centuries. Presumably, a woman once discovered that it was easier to twist thread by holding the end of the spindle in a small cup. She probably taught the technique to friends. Eventually, this piece of knowledge became common

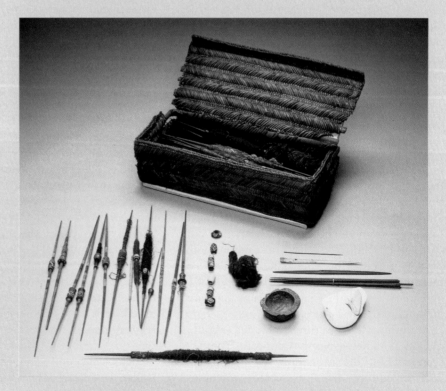

An Ancient American Weaver's Workbasket
Gift of Charles H. White. Courtesy of Museum of Fine Arts, Boston.

knowledge among weaving women, and they acquired a cup like the one in this workbasket.

Chances are, however, even if trained to use the tools in the weaver's workbasket, you could never weave fabrics like the one shown here. Weavers had to learn how to combine color, texture, and shape into a specific design or pattern. Designs were learned and passed from one person to another. Patterns such as those depicted on the weaving shown here required the weaver to learn, express, and transmit knowledge about much more than textile production. To weave an appropriate pattern, the weaver needed to know, for example, how to represent gods, omens, powerful leaders, or sacred places. She had to be familiar with the culture of the people she lived among—their religion, politics, economy, and social organization. Even in the unlikely event that you could *copy* this weaving, you could not possibly design other fabrics like an ancient American weaver without knowing and understanding her culture as she did. While weavers possessed specialized training and skill, their technological knowledge had to be used within the specific cultural contours of the people they lived among. A design for a commoner was not fit for a chief, nor was a woman's outfit suitable for a warrior.

The technologies of weaving, pottery-making, cooking, hunting, agriculture, and much more fit into distinctive cultural patterns among the thousands of diverse ancient American societies. Archaeologists use these cultural patterns to distinguish one group of ancient Americans from another. The enormous diversity of these patterns over the millennia of human occupation of the Western Hemisphere and throughout the vast geography of

Ancient Weaving
This tunic for Peruvian royalty illustrates the artistry a master weaver could achieve. Woven with wool and cotton sometime between AD 250 and AD 550, the tunic incorporates complex images denoting religious and political authority. In order to know what images to use and how to portray them, the weaver had to be as familiar with Peruvian culture as with the techniques of weaving.
Art Institute of Chicago.

North, Central, and South America reflects a basic fact about ancient American technology. Technological developments—such as weaving—occurred when and where they did partly because of subsistence needs and challenges posed by the natural environment. But the technology of weaving, like other technologies, depended above all on human knowledge that passed from one person to another in cycle after cycle of teaching and learning.

Over time, technological knowledge accumulated and achievements—like this weaving—could reach masterful levels of artistry. But the cycle of teaching and learning was fragile. A weaver's knowledge could die with her if it had not been

taught to somebody else. Wars, famines, droughts, epidemics, and other disasters could—and did—extinguish technological knowledge along with its possessors. The fragility of the transmission of human knowledge helps explain the tremendous diversity among ancient American cultures. When the cycle of teaching and learning was broken, technologies and cultures died. Fresh and often distinctive technological knowledge had to be created anew, accumulated, and passed on. The technology of weaving practiced by the owner of this workbasket was developed by the women she learned from and passed on to the women she taught.

oxen; their use of metals was restricted to copper; and metallurgy did not exist in North America. However, the absence of these European conveniences was profoundly irrelevant to native North Americans. Their cultures had developed as adaptations to the natural environment local to each tribe and to the social environment among neighboring peoples. That great similarity—adaptation to natural and social environments—underlay all the cultural diversity among native North Americans.

> The absence of European conveniences was profoundly irrelevant to native North Americans.

It would be a mistake, however, to conclude that native North Americans lived in blissful harmony with nature and each other. Archaeological sites provide ample evidence of violent conflict among Native Americans. Skeletons bear the marks of wounds as well as of ritualistic human sacrifice and even cannibalism. Other forms of conflict—such as religious, economic, and familial—must have existed, but they left few archaeological traces and therefore remain in obscurity. In general, fear and anxiety must have been at least as common among Native Americans as feelings of peace and security.

Native Americans not only adapted to the natural environment; they also changed it in many ways. They built thousands of structures, from small dwellings to massive pueblos and enormous mounds, permanently altering the landscape. Their gathering techniques selected productive and nutritious varieties of plants, thereby shifting the balance of local plants toward useful varieties. The first stages of North American agriculture, for example, probably resulted from Native Americans gathering wild seeds and then sowing them in a meadow for later harvest. It is almost certain that fertile and hardy varieties of corn were developed in just this way, first in Mexico and later in North America.

Native Americans also altered the natural environment by fires. In addition to cooking, Indians used fires to provide food, communicate, and make war. Fires set for hunting probably left the largest imprint on the landscape. Great Plains hunters often set fires to hunt buffalo. Sometimes they circled a herd with a ring of fire that concentrated the animals and made them easy to slaughter. At other times hunters left an outlet in the ring of fire and killed buffalo as they passed through the opening. They also set widely separated parallel lines of fire and drove frightened buffalo between the fires toward a cliff over which they plunged to their destruction.

Eastern Woodland, Southwest, and Pacific coast Indians also used fire to hunt deer and other valuable prey. Frequently, hunters waited downwind from a brushy area while their companions set a fire upwind; the hunters then killed the animals that fled toward them from the burning underbrush. Over thousands of square miles throughout North America, Indians set fires along the edges of woods to burn off shrubby undergrowth and encroaching tree seedlings. These burns encouraged the growth of tender young plants that attracted deer and other game animals, bringing them within convenient range of hunters' weapons. Such burns also encouraged the growth of numerous plants Indians relished, such as blackberries, strawberries, and raspberries.

Because fires usually burned until they ran out of fuel or were extinguished by rain or wind, enormous regions of North America were burned over. In some places, fires were set once or twice a year; in other areas, decades passed between fires. In the long run, fires created and maintained light-dappled meadows for hunting and agriculture, cleared entangling underbrush from forests, and promoted a diverse and productive natural environment. Fires, like other activities of Native Americans, shaped the landscape of North America long before Europeans arrived in 1492.

The Mexica: A Meso-American Culture

The indigenous population of the New World numbered roughly 80 million in the 1490s, about the same as the population of Europe. Almost all these people lived in Central and South America. Like their much less numerous North American counterparts, they too lived in a natural environment of tremendous diversity. They too developed hundreds of cultures, far too numerous to catalog here. But among all the Central and South American cultures, the Mexica stood out. (Europeans often called these people Aztecs, a name the Mexica did not use.) Their empire stretched from coast to coast across central Mexico, encompassing as many as 25 million people. We know more about the Mexica than about any other Native American society of the time, principally because of their massive monuments and their Spanish conquerors' well-documented interest in subduing them. Their significance in the history of the New World after 1492 dictates a brief consideration of their culture and society.

The Mexica began their rise to prominence about 1325 when small bands settled on a marshy island in Lake Texcoco, the site of the future city of Tenochtitlán, the capital of the Mexican empire. Resourceful, courageous, and cold-blooded warriors, the Mexica often hired out as mercenaries for richer, more settled tribes. By 1430, the Mexica succeeded in asserting their dominance over their former allies and leading their own military campaigns in an ever-widening arc of empire building. Despite pockets of resistance, by the 1490s the Mexica ruled an empire that covered more land than Spain and Portugal combined and contained almost three times as many people.

The empire exemplified the central values of Mexican society. The Mexica worshipped the war god Huitzilopochtli. Warriors held the most exalted positions in the Mexican social hierarchy, even above the priests who performed the sacred ceremonies that won Huitzilopochtli's favor. In the almost constant battles necessary to defend and extend the empire, young Mexican men exhibited the courage and daring that would allow them to rise in the carefully graduated ranks of warriors. The Mexica considered capturing prisoners the ultimate act of bravery. Warriors usually turned over the captives to Mexican priests, who sacrificed them to Huitzilopochtli by cutting out their hearts. (See "Historical Question," page 28.)

The empire contributed far more to Mexican society than victims for sacrifice. At the most basic level, the empire functioned as a military and political system that collected tribute from subject peoples. The Mexica forced conquered tribes to pay tribute in goods, not money. Tribute redistributed to the Mexica as much as one-third of the goods produced by conquered tribes. It included everything from candidates for human sacrifice to textiles and basic food products such as corn and beans as well as exotic luxury items such as gold, turquoise, and rare bird feathers.

Tribute reflected the fundamental relations of power and wealth that pervaded the Mexican empire. The relatively small nobility of Mexican warriors, supported by a still smaller priesthood, possessed the military and religious power to command the obedience of thousands of non-noble Mexicans and of millions of other non-Mexicans in subjugated provinces. The Mexican elite exercised their power to obtain tribute and thereby to redistribute wealth from the conquered to the conquerors, from the commoners to the nobility, from the poor to the rich. This redistribution of wealth made possible the achievements of Mexican society that eventually amazed Spaniards: the huge cities, fabulous temples, teeming markets, and luxuriant gardens, not to mention the storehouses stuffed with gold and other treasures.

On the whole, the Mexica did not interfere much with the internal government of conquered regions.

> Despite pockets of resistance, by the 1490s the Mexica ruled an empire that covered more land than Spain and Portugal combined and contained almost three times as many people.

Salado Ritual Figure
About AD 1350—more than a century before Columbus arrived in the Western Hemisphere—this figure was carefully wrapped in a reed mat with other items and stored in a cave in a mountainous region of New Mexico by people of the Salado culture, descendants of the Mimbres, who had flourished three centuries earlier. The face of this figure is as close to a self-portrait of ancient Americans on the eve of their encounter with Europeans as we are ever likely to have. Adorned with vivid pigments, cotton string, bright feathers, and stones, the effigy testifies to the human complexity of all ancient Americans, a complexity visible in artifacts that have survived the millennia before the arrival of Europeans.
© 2000 The Art Institute of Chicago.

Why Did the Mexica Practice Human Sacrifice?

The Mexica practiced human sacrifice on a scale unequaled in human history. That does not mean that they intentionally killed more people than any other society. Plenty of other societies, both before and since, have systematically killed other human beings. Only a partial accounting from the years 1930 to 1945, for example, would include millions of Jews and others murdered by German Nazis and their European sympathizers, millions of Russians killed by the Soviet leader Joseph Stalin, hundreds of thousands of Chinese slaughtered by the Japanese, and hundreds of thousands of Japanese annihilated by atomic bombs the United States dropped on Hiroshima and Nagasaki. Warfare of any kind involves intentional sacrifice of human life. However, the human sacrifice practiced by the Mexica was different. For them, human sacrifice was an act of worship—in fact, the ultimate act of worship.

Looking back from our vantage point five hundred years later, we may find it difficult to understand why the Mexica accepted human sacrifice as a normal and reasonable activity. Yet it is perfectly clear that they did. Although the precise number of victims is unknown, experts estimate that about 20,000 people were sacrificed each year throughout the Mexican empire. Celebration of an important victory or the appointment of a new emperor often involved the sacrifice of hundreds, sometimes thousands.

Most of the victims were prisoners captured in battle or rendered in tribute. However, ordinary Mexican citizens—especially young men, women, and children—were often sacrificed in religious rituals. Every eighteen months, for example, a greatly honored young man was sacrificed to Tezcatlipoca, the god of human fate. From time to time, all Mexica practiced sacrificial bloodletting, piercing themselves with stingray spines or cactus thorns to demonstrate their religious devotion. Both as symbol and in reality, human sacrifice was an integral part of daily life in Mexican communities.

Mexica employed several different techniques of sacrifice, all supervised and carried out by priests. By far the most common sacrifice was performed at an altar on the top of a temple, where a priest cut out the still-beating heart of a victim and offered it to the gods. The victim's

Mexican Human Sacrifice
This graphic portrait of human sacrifice was drawn by a Mexican artist in the sixteenth century, after Spanish conquest. It shows the typical routine of human sacrifice practiced by the Mexica for centuries before Europeans arrived. The victim climbed the temple steps, then was stretched out over a stone pillar (notice the priest's helper holding the victim's legs) to make it easier for the priest to plunge a stone knife into the victim's chest, cut out the still-beating heart, and offer it to the bloodthirsty gods. The body of the previous victim has already been pushed down from the temple heights and is about to be dragged away. The Mexica's blood-caked priests and temples repulsed Spanish conquerors, who considered human sacrifice barbaric. The intent watchfulness among the people portrayed at the base of the temple suggests their keen interest in the gory spectacle as a way of obtaining favors from supernatural powers.
Scala / Art Resource, NY; Biblioteca Nazionale, Florence, Italy.

Mexican Sacrificial Knife

This flint knife—embellished and personalized with eyes and teeth made of shell, turquoise, and obsidian—was a symbol of human sacrifice. The knife, as well as two additional knives, human skulls, and other objects, was excavated from a temple where ancient Mexica placed them as offerings to Huitzilopochtli, the powerful god of war. Since this specific knife was an offering, it probably was not used to cut out the hearts of sacrifice victims. But knives just like it, made of flint and seven or eight inches long, were used by Mexican priests to sacrifice tens of thousands of people.

Photo by Michel Zabe / Banco Mexicano de Imagenes (BMI).

head and limbs were then severed, and the torso was fed to wild animals kept in cages in and near the temple. Heads were displayed on large racks at the base of the temple; limbs were cooked and eaten in sacred rituals. It is likely that participation in this ritualistic cannibalism was restricted to a minority of Mexica, principally warriors, priests, and wealthier merchants. However, every Mexica participated in symbolic cannibalism by eating small cakes made of flour mixed with blood and shaped into human forms.

To us, these rituals may seem ghoulish and disgusting, as they certainly did to sixteenth-century Europeans who eventually witnessed them. Yet the Mexica devoted so much time, energy, and resources to such rituals that it is impossible to doubt their importance to them. But why was human sacrifice so important?

In recent times, some scholars have argued that the Mexica practiced human sacrifice and cannibalism to remedy protein deficiencies in their diet. However, the Mexican diet contained many sources of protein, including turkeys, chickens, fish, turtles, and eggs as well as corn and beans. For most Mexica, dietary protein was adequate or better.

Mexican religious beliefs offer a far more persuasive explanation for human sacrifice. Scholars know a good deal about Mexican religion because, in the years immediately following European conquest, Catholic priests studied Mexican religion in order to convert the people more readily to Christianity. These sources make clear that the Mexica inhabited a world suffused with the power of supernatural beings. A special deity oversaw nearly every important activity. Mexica believed that their gods communicated with human beings through omens, signs that the gods were either happy or displeased. In turn, the people communicated their own reverence for the gods by observing appropriate rituals. Bad omens such as an unexplained fire or a lightning bolt striking a temple meant that a god was angry and needed to be appeased with the proper rituals. Since almost every occurrence could be interpreted as an omen that revealed the will of a god, the routine events of daily life had a profound, supernatural dimension.

The Mexica's most powerful gods were Huitzilopochtli, the war god, and Quetzalcoatl, the god who gave sustenance to human beings. Mexica believed that these two gods had created the world, the sun, the moon, the first human beings, the whole array of lesser deities, and everything else in the universe. Since the moment of creation, the earth had passed through four different epochs, which Mexica called the Four Suns, each of which had ended in catastrophe. It fell to Quetzalcoatl and other potent deities to begin the Fifth Sun by re-creating human beings and all the other features of the universe. After years of work, Quetzalcoatl and the other gods had accomplished everything except the creation of the sun. Finally, two gods agreed to sacrifice themselves by jumping into a fire. Thereby they became the sun and the moon, and other gods quickly followed them into the fire to keep the sun burning. But the sacrifice of the gods was sufficient only to ignite the sun. To maintain the light of the sun and keep it moving across the sky every day required human beings to follow the example of the gods and to feed the sun with human blood. Without the sacrificial blood, the world would go dark and time would stop. Mexica considered the Fifth Sun the final stage of the universe, which would end when cataclysmic earthquakes destroyed the earth and supernatural monsters ravaged human life. By feeding the sun with human sacrifices, Mexica believed they could delay that horrible final reckoning.

For the Mexica, human sacrifice was absolutely necessary for the maintenance of life on earth. Victims of sacrifice fulfilled the most sacred of duties. Through the sacrifice of their lives, they fed the sun and permitted others to live. The living demonstrated their respect and reverence for victims of sacrifice by eating their flesh. As one sixteenth-century Catholic priest explained, "The flesh of all those who died in sacrifice was held truly to be consecrated and blessed. It was eaten with reverence, ritual, and fastidiousness—as if it were something from heaven." From the Mexica's perspective, it was not wrong to engage in human sacrifice; it was wrong not to.

Instead, they usually permitted the traditional ruling elite to stay in power—so long as they paid tribute. For their efforts, the conquered provinces received very little from the Mexica, except immunity from punitive raids by the dreaded Mexican warriors. Subjugated communities felt exploited by the constant payment of tribute to the Mexica. By depending on military conquest and constant collection of tribute, the Mexica failed to create among their subjects a belief that Mexican domination was, at some level, legitimate and equitable. The high level of discontent among subject peoples constituted the soft, vulnerable underbelly of the Mexican empire. Instead of making friends for the Mexica, the empire created many bitter and resentful opponents, a fact Spanish intruders exploited after AD 1492 to conquer the Mexica.

Conclusion: The World of Ancient Americans

Ancient Americans shaped the history of human beings in the New World for more than twelve thousand years. They established continuous human habitation in the Western Hemisphere from the time the first big-game hunters crossed Beringia until 1492 and beyond. Much of their history remains irretrievably lost because they relied on oral rather than written communication. But much can be pieced together from artifacts they left behind, like the Folsom points among the bones discovered by George McJunkin. Ancient Americans achieved

their success through resourceful adaptation to the hemisphere's many and ever-changing natural environments. They also adapted to social and cultural changes caused by human beings— such as marriages, deaths, political struggles, and warfare—but the sparse evidence that has survived renders those adaptations almost entirely unknowable. Their creativity and artistry are unmistakably documented in the artifacts they left behind at kill sites, camps, and burial mounds. Those artifacts sketch the only likenesses of ancient Americans we will ever have— blurred, shadowy images that are indisputably human but forever silent.

In the five centuries after 1492—just 4 percent of the time human beings have inhabited the Western Hemisphere—Europeans and their descendants began to shape and eventually to dominate American history. Native American peoples continued to influence major developments of American history for centuries after 1492. But the new wave of strangers that at first trickled and then flooded into the New World from Europe and Africa forever transformed the peoples and places of ancient America.

FOR ADDITIONAL FIRSTHAND ACCOUNTS OF THIS PERIOD, see Chapter 1 in Michael Johnson, ed., *Reading the American Past*, Third Edition.

TO ASSESS YOUR MASTERY OF THE MATERIAL IN THIS CHAPTER, see the Online Study Guide at bedfordstmartins.com/ roark.

FOR WEB LINKS RELATED TO TOPICS IN THIS CHAPTER, see "HistoryLinks," "DocLinks," and "PlaceLinks" at bedfordstmartins.com/roark.

CHRONOLOGY

("BP" is an abbreviation used by archaeologists for "years before the present.")

c. 80,000–10,000 BP
- Wisconsin glaciation exposes Beringia, land bridge between Siberia and Alaska.

c. 13,000 BP
- First humans arrive in North America.

c. 11,500–11,000 BP
- Paleo-Indians in North and Central Americas use Clovis points to hunt big game.

c. 11,000 BP
- Mammoths and many other big-game prey of Paleo-Indians become extinct.

c. 10,000–3,000 BP
- Archaic hunter-gatherer cultures dominate ancient America.

c. 7000 BP
- Corn cultivation begins in Central and South Americas.

c. 4000 BP
- Some Eastern Woodland peoples grow gourds and pumpkins and begin making pottery.

c. 3500 BP
- Southwestern cultures begin corn cultivation.
- Stone pipes for tobacco smoking appear in Eastern Woodland regions.

c. 2500 BP
- Eastern Woodland cultures start to build burial mounds.

c. 2500–2100 BP
- Adena culture develops in Ohio.

c. 2300 BP
- Some Eastern Woodland peoples begin to cultivate corn.

c. 2100 BP–AD 400
- Hopewell culture emerges in Ohio and Mississippi valleys.

c. AD 200–AD 900
- Mogollon culture emerges in New Mexico.

c. AD 500
- Bows and arrows appear in North America south of Arctic.
- Pacific Northwest cultures denote wealth and status with elaborate wood carvings.

c. AD 500–AD 1400
- Hohokam culture develops in Arizona.

c. AD 800–AD 1500
- Mississippian culture flourishes in Southeast.

c. AD 1000–AD 1100
- Anasazi peoples build cliff dwellings at Mesa Verde, Colorado, and pueblos at Chaco Canyon, New Mexico.

c. AD 1325–AD 1500
- Mexica conquer neighboring peoples and establish Mexican empire.

AD 1492
- Christopher Columbus arrives, beginning European colonization of New World.

BIBLIOGRAPHY

General Works

Robson Bonnichsen and Karen L. Turnmire, *Ice Age Peoples of North America* (1999).

Thomas M. Bonniksen, *America's Ancient Forests: From the Ice Age to Discovery* (2000).

Karen Olsen Bruhns, *Ancient South America* (1994).

Karen Olsen Bruhns and Karen E. Stothert, *Women in Ancient America* (1999).

Michael D. Coe and Rex Koontz, *Mexico: From the Olmecs to the Aztecs* (5th ed., 2002).

Michael Coe, Dean Snow, and Elizabeth Benson, *Atlas of Ancient America* (1986).

Thomas D. Dillehay, *The Settlement of the Americas: A New Prehistory* (2000).

E. James Dixon, *Quest for the Origins of the First Americans* (1993).

Roger Downey, *Riddle of the Bones: Politics, Science, Race, and the Story of Kennewick Man* (2000).

Penelope Ballard Drooker and Laurie D. Webster, *Beyond Cloth and Cordage: Archaeological Textile Research in the Americas* (2000).

Brian M. Fagan, *The Journey from Eden: The Peopling of Our World* (1990).

Brian M. Fagan, *Ancient North America: The Archaeology of a Continent* (1991).

Brian M. Fagan, *Kingdoms of Gold, Kingdoms of Jade: The Americas before Columbus* (1991).

Stuart J. Fiedel, *Prehistory of the Americas* (2nd ed., 1992).

Virginia M. Fields and Victor Zamudio-Taylor, *The Road to Aztlan: Art from a Mythic Homeland* (2002).

Robert L. Hall, *An Archaeology of the Soul: North American Indian Belief and Ritual* (1997).

David Henige, *Numbers from Nowhere: The American Indian Contact Population Debate* (1998).

Francis Jennings, *The Founders of America: How Indians Discovered the Land . . .* (1993).

Jesse D. Jennings, *Prehistory of North America* (1974).

Jesse D. Jennings, ed., *Ancient North Americans* (1983).

Alvin M. Josephy Jr., *America in 1492: The World of the Indian Peoples before the Arrival of Columbus* (1992).

Jake Page, *In the Hands of the Great Spirit: The Twenty-Thousand-Year History of American Indians* (2003).

David Hurst Thomas, *Skull Wars: Kennewick Man, Archaeology, and the Battle for Native American Identity* (2000).

Richard Townsend, ed., *The Ancient Americas: Art from Sacred Landscapes* (1992).

Frederick Hadleigh West, ed., *American Beginnings: The Prehistory and Paleoecology of Beringia* (1996).

North American Cultures

Mary J. Adair, *Prehistoric Agriculture in the Central Plains* (1988).

Kenneth M. Ames and Herbert D. G. Maschner, *Peoples of the Northwest Coast: Their Archaeology and Prehistory* (1999).

David G. Anderson, *The Savannah River Chiefdoms: Political Change in the Late Prehistoric Southeast* (1994).

Alex W. Barker and Timothy R. Pauketat, eds., *Lords of the Southwest: Social Inequality and the Native Elites of Southeastern North America* (1992).

Timothy G. Baugh and Jonathon E. Ericson, eds., *Prehistoric Exchange Systems in North America* (1994).

John Howard Blitz, *Ancient Chiefdoms of the Tombigbee* (1993).

Sally A. Kitt Chappell, *Cahokia: Mirror of the Cosmos* (2002).

Linda S. Cordell, *Prehistory of the Southwest* (1984).

Linda S. Cordell and George R. Gumerman, eds., *Dynamics of Southwest Prehistory* (1989).

Richard J. Dent Jr., *Chesapeake Prehistory: Old Traditions, New Directions* (1995).

E. James Dixon, *Bones, Boats, and Bison: Archeology and the First Colonization of Western North America* (1999).

Don Dumond, *Eskimos and Aleuts* (2nd ed., 1987).

Thomas E. Emerson and R. Barry Lewis, eds., *Cahokia and the Hinterlands: Middle Mississippian Cultures of the Midwest* (1991).

Thomas E. Emerson et al., eds., *Late Woodland Societies: Tradition and Transformation across the Midcontinent* (2000).

Brian M. Fagan, *The Great Journey: The Peopling of Ancient America* (1987).

William Fitzhugh, ed., *Crossroads of Continents: Cultures of Siberia and Alaska* (1988).

William W. Fitzhugh and Valerie Chaussonnet, eds., *Anthropology of the North Pacific Rim* (1994).

Franklin Folsom, *Black Cowboy: The Life and Legend of George McJunkin* (1992).

Nelson Foster and Linda S. Cordell, eds., *Chilies to Chocolate: Food the Americas Gave to the World* (1992).

Julie E. Francis, *Ancient Visions: Petroglyphs and Pictographs From . . . Wyoming and Montana* (2002).

Kendrick Frazier, *People of Chaco: A Canyon and Its Cultures* (1986).

George C. Frison, *Prehistoric Hunters of the High Plains* (2nd ed., 1991).

George Gumerman, *A View from Black Mesa* (1984).

George Gumerman, ed., *Themes in Southwest Prehistory* (1994).

Robert F. Heizer, ed., *Handbook of North American Indians*, vol. 8, *California* (1978).

R. Douglas Hurt, *Indian Agriculture in America: Prehistory to the Present* (1987).

Barry L. Isaac, ed., *Prehistoric Economies of the Pacific Northwest Coast* (1988).

Sissel Johannessen and Christine A. Hastorf, eds., *Corn and Culture in the Prehistoric New World* (1994).

Roger G. Kennedy, *Hidden Cities: The Discovery and Loss of Ancient North American Civilization* (1994).

Sarah A. Kerr, *Beyond Chaco: Great Kiva Communities on the Mogollon Rim Frontier* (2001).

J. C. H. King, *First People, First Contacts: Native Peoples of North America* (1999).

Ruth Kirk, *Hunters of the Whale* (1975).

Theodora Kroeber, *Ishi in Two Worlds* (1965).

Steven A. LeBlanc, *The Mimbres People: Ancient Pueblo Potters of the American Southwest* (1983).

Steven A. LeBlanc, *Prehistoric Warfare in the American Southwest* (1999).

Stephen H. Lekson, *The Chaco Meridian: Centers of Political Power in the Ancient Southwest* (1999).

Edward J. Lenik, *Picture Rocks: American Indian Rock Art in the Northeast Woodlands* (2002).

Mary Ann Levine et al., eds., *The Archaeological Northeast* (1999).

R. G. Matson, *The Origins of Southwestern Agriculture* (1991).

William E. McGoun, *Prehistoric Peoples of South Florida* (1993).

Jonathan Merli, *Shadow House: Interpretations of Northwest Coast Art* (2001).

Jerald T. Milanich, *Archaeology of Precolumbian Florida* (1994).

Claudia G. Mink, *Cahokia: City of the Sun: Prehistoric Urban Center in the American Bottom* (1992).

Michael J. Moratto, *California Archaeology* (1984).

William N. Morgan, *Precolumbian Architecture in Eastern North America* (1999).

Jon Muller, *Archaeology of the Lower Ohio Valley* (1986).

Alfonso Ortiz, ed., *Handbook of North American Indians,* vol. 9, *Southwest* (1979).

Alfonso Ortiz, ed., *Handbook of North American Indians,* vol. 10, *Southwest* (1983).

Timothy R. Pauketat, *The Ascent of Chiefs: Cahokia and Mississippian Politics in Native North America* (1994).

Timothy R. Pauketat and Thomas E. Emerson, eds., *Cahokia: Domination and Ideology in the Mississippian World* (2000).

Jefferson Reid and Stephanie Whittlesley, *The Archaeology of Ancient Arizona* (1997).

Karl H. Schlesier, *Plains Indians, A.D. 500–1500: The Archaeological Past of Historic Groups* (1994).

Lynne Sebastian, *The Chaco Anasazi: Sociopolitical Evolution in the Prehistoric Southwest* (1992).

Lynda Shaffer, *Native Americans before 1492: The Moundbuilding Centers of the Eastern Woodlands* (1992).

Dennis Slifer, *Signs of Life: Rock Art of the Upper Rio Grande* (1998).

Bruce D. Smith, ed., *The Mississippian Emergence* (1990).

Marvin T. Smith, *Coosa: The Rise and Fall of a Southeastern Mississippian Chiefdom* (2000).

Dean Snow, *The Archaeology of New England* (1980).

Katherine A. Spielmann, *Interdependence in the Prehistoric Southwest: An Ecological Analysis of Plain-Pueblo Interaction* (1991).

David E. Stuart, *Anasazi America* (2000).

Kenneth B. Tankersley and Barry L. Isaac, eds., *Early Paleoindian Economies of Eastern North America* (1990).

Bruce G. Trigger, *The Children of Aataentsic: A History of the Huron People to 1660* (1972).

Bruce G. Trigger, *Natives and Newcomers* (1985).

Bruce G. Trigger, ed., *Handbook of North American Indians,* vol. 15, *Northeast* (1978).

J. A. Tuck, *Onondaga Iroquois Prehistory* (1971).

Christy G. Turner II and Jacqueline A. Turner, *Cannibalism and Violence in the Prehistoric American Southwest* (1999).

R. Gwinnn Vivian and Bruce Hilpert, *The Chaco Handbook* (2002).

William Snyder Webb, *The Adena People* (1974).

Randolph J. Widmer, *The Evolution of the Calusa: A Nonagricultural Chiefdom on the Southwest Florida Coast* (1988).

Joseph C. Winter, *Tobacco Use by Native North Americans: Sacred Smoke and Silent Killer* (2000).

Biloine Whiting Young and Melvin L. Fowler, *Cahokia: The Great Native American Metropolis* (1999).

The Mexica

Philip P. Arnold, *Eating Landscape: Aztec and European Occupation of Tlalocan* (1999).

Elizabeth Hill Boone, *Stories in Red and Black: Pictorial Histories of the Aztecs and Mixtecs* (2000).

David Carrasco, *Quetzalcoatl and the Irony of Empire: Myths and Prophecies in the Aztec Tradition* (1992).

David Carrasco, *City of Sacrifice: The Aztec Empire and the Role of Violence in Civilization* (1999).

David Carrasco et al., eds., *Mesoamerica's Classic Heritage: From Teotihuacan to the Aztecs* (2000).

Inga Clendinnen, *Aztecs: An Interpretation* (1991).

Marty W. Eubanks, *Corn in Clay: Maize Paleoethnobotany in Pre-Columbian Art* (1999).

Ross Hassig, *War and Society in Ancient Mesoamerica* (1992).

Ross Hassig, *Time, History, and Belief in Aztec and Colonial Mexico* (2001).

Alan Knight, *Mexico: From the Beginning to the Spanish Conquest* (2002).

Mary Ellen Miller, *The Art of Meso-America: From Olmec to Aztec* (2001).

Eduardo Matos Moctezuma and Felipe Solis Olguin, *Aztecs* (2002).

Felipe Solis and Ted Leyenaar, *Art Treasures of Ancient Mexico* (2002).

Richard F. Townsend, *The Aztecs* (1992).

E. Michael Whittington, *The Sport of Life and Death: The Mesoamerican Ballgame* (2002).

TAINO ZEMI BASKET
This basket is an example
of the effigies Tainos made
to represent *zemis*, their
deities. The effigy illustrates the
artistry of the basket maker, almost
certainly a Taino woman. Crafted sometime between
1492 and about 1520, the effigy demonstrates that Tainos readily incorporated goods obtained through contacts
with Europeans into their own traditional beliefs and practices. The basket maker used African ivory and European
mirrors as well as Native American fibers, dyes, and designs.

Archìvio Fotogràfico del Museo Preistòrico Etnografico L. Pigorini, Roma.

Europeans Encounter the New World

1492–1600

A HALF HOUR BEFORE SUNRISE on August 3, 1492, Christopher Columbus commanded three ships to catch the tide out of a harbor in southern Spain and sail west. Just over two months later, in the predawn moonlight of October 12, 1492, Columbus glimpsed an island on the western horizon. At last, he believed, he had found what he had been looking for—the western end of a route across the Atlantic Ocean to Japan, China, and India. At daybreak, Columbus could see people on the shore who had spotted his ships. He rowed ashore and, as the curious islanders crowded around, he claimed possession of the land for Ferdinand and Isabella, king and queen of Spain, who had sponsored his voyage. He named the island San Salvador, in honor of the Savior, Jesus Christ.

A day or two afterward, Columbus described that first encounter with the inhabitants of San Salvador in an extensive diary he kept during his voyage. He called these people Indians, assuming that their island lay somewhere in the East Indies near Japan or China. The Indians were not dressed in the finery Columbus expected. "All of them go around as naked as their mothers bore them; and the women also," he observed. Their skin color was "neither black nor white." They were not familiar with the Spaniards' weapons. "I showed them swords," Columbus wrote, "and they took them by the edge and through ignorance cut themselves." This first encounter led Columbus to conclude, "They should be good and intelligent servants, for I see that they say very quickly everything that is said to them; and I believe that they would become Christians very easily, for it seemed to me that they had no religion."

The people Columbus called Indians called themselves Tainos, which to them meant "good" or "noble." They inhabited most of the Caribbean islands Columbus visited on his first voyage, as had their ancestors for more than two centuries. The Tainos were an agricultural people who grew cassava, a nutritious root, as well as sweet potatoes, corn, cotton, tobacco, and other crops. To fish and to travel from island to island, they built canoes from hollowed-out logs. The Tainos worshipped gods they called *zemis*, the spirits of ancestors and of natural objects like trees and stones. They made effigies of zemis and performed rituals to honor them. "It seemed to me that they were a people very poor in everything," Columbus wrote. But the Tainos mined gold in small quantities, enough to catch the eye of Columbus and his men.

What the Tainos thought about Spaniards we can only surmise, since they left no written documents. At first, Columbus believed that the Tainos thought he and his men came from heaven. After six weeks of contact, Columbus

Cacique's Canoe
This sixteenth-century drawing of a large canoe carrying a cacique, or chief, and powered by twenty oarsmen probably resembles the canoes used by Tainos and the other Native Americans who paddled out to visit the ships of Columbus and other European explorers. The influence of such European contacts may be reflected in the flags flying from the corners of the leafy awning that shades the enthroned cacique and rowers.
The Pierpont Morgan Library / Art Resource, NY.

concluded that in fact he did not understand Tainos. Late in November 1492, he wrote that "the people of these lands do not understand me nor do I, nor anyone else that I have with me, them. And many times I understand one thing said by these Indians . . . for another, its contrary."

The confused communication between Europeans and Tainos suggests how different, how strange, each group seemed to the other. Columbus's perceptions of Tainos were shaped by European ideas, attitudes, and expectations, just as Tainos's perceptions of Europeans must have been colored by their own culture. Yet the word that Columbus coined for the Tainos— *Indians*, a word that originated in a colossal misunderstanding—hinted at the direction of the future. To Europeans, *Indians* came to mean all native inhabitants of the New World, the name they gave to the lands in the Western Hemisphere. After 1492, the perceptions, the cultures, and even the diseases of Europeans began to exert a transforming influence on the New World and its peoples.

Long before 1492, certain Europeans restlessly expanded the limits of the world known to them. Their efforts made possible Columbus's encounter with the Tainos. In turn, Columbus's landfall in the Caribbean changed the history not only of the Tainos, but also of Europe and

the rest of the world. Beginning in 1492, the promise of the New World lured more and more Europeans to venture their lives and fortunes on the western shores of the Atlantic, a promise realized largely at the expense of New World peoples like Tainos.

Europe in the Age of Exploration

Historically, the East—not the West—attracted Europeans. Around the year 1000, Norsemen ventured west across the North Atlantic and founded a small fishing village as L'Anse aux Meadows on the tip of Newfoundland. After a decade or so, the Norse left and did not return because the world's climate cooled, choking the North Atlantic with ice. Viking sagas memorialized the Norse "discovery," but it had virtually no other impact in the New World or in Europe. Instead, wealthy Europeans developed a taste for luxury goods from Asia and Africa, and merchants competed to satisfy that taste. As Europeans traded with the East and with one another, they acquired new information about the world they inhabited. Some learned that the world they knew was not all there was to know. A few people—sailors, merchants, and aristocrats—took the risks of exploring beyond the limits of the world known to Europeans. Those risks were genuine and could be deadly. But sometimes they paid off in new information, new opportunities, and eventually in the discovery of a world entirely new to Europeans.

Mediterranean Trade and European Expansion

From the twelfth through the fifteenth centuries, spices, silk, carpets, ivory, gold, and other exotic goods traveled overland from Persia, Asia Minor, India, and Africa and then were funneled into continental Europe through Mediterranean trade routes (Map 2.1). Dominated primarily by the Italian cities of Venice, Genoa, and Pisa, this lucrative trade enriched Italian merchants

and bankers, who fiercely defended their near-**monopoly** of access to eastern goods. Instead of trying to displace the Italians, merchants in other European countries chose the safer alternative of trading with them. The vitality of the Mediterranean trade offered few incentives to look for alternatives. New routes to the East and the discovery of new lands were the stuff of fantasy.

Preconditions for turning fantasy into reality developed in fifteenth-century Europe. In the mid-fourteenth century, Europeans suffered a catastrophic epidemic of bubonic plague. The Black Death, as it was called, killed about a third of the European population. This devastating pestilence had

> The risks of exploring were genuine and could be deadly. But sometimes they paid off in new information, new opportunities, and eventually in the discovery of a world entirely new to Europeans.

MAP 2.1   European Trade Routes and Portuguese Exploration in the Fifteenth Century

The strategic geographic position of Italian cities as a conduit for overland trade from Asia was slowly undermined during the fifteenth century by Portuguese explorers who hopscotched along the coast of Africa and eventually found a sea route that opened the rich trade of the East to Portuguese merchants.

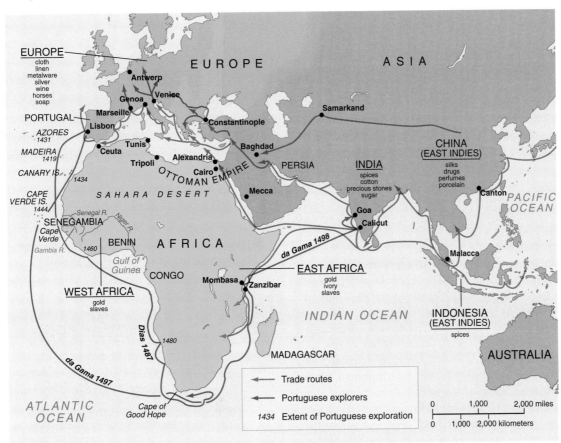

major long-term consequences. It significantly reduced the pressure of Europe's now-reduced population on food resources. Many who survived inherited property from plague victims, giving new chances for advancement. The turmoil caused by the plague also prompted peasants to move away from their homes and seek opportunities elsewhere.

Understandably, most Europeans perceived the world as a place of alarming risks where the delicate balance of health, harvests, and peace could quickly be tipped toward disaster by epidemics, famine, and violence. Most people protected themselves from the constant threat of calamity by worshipping the supernatural, by living amid kinfolk and friends, and by maintaining good relations with the rich and powerful. Curiously, the insecurity and uncertainty of fifteenth-century European life encouraged a few people to take greater chances, such as embarking on a dangerous sea voyage through uncharted waters to points unknown.

Monarchs who hoped to enlarge their realms and enrich their dynasties also had reasons to sponsor journeys of exploration. More territory meant more subjects who could pay more taxes, provide more soldiers, and participate in more commerce, magnifying monarchs' power and prestige. Voyages of exploration also could stabilize monarch's regimes by diverting the military energies of unruly noblemen toward distant lands. Sometimes monarchs sponsored expeditions by young sons of aristocratic families that had fallen on hard times. Other explorers, like Columbus, were not of noble birth and hoped to be elevated to the aristocracy as a reward for their daring achievements. Exploration promised fame and fortune in European societies to those who succeeded, whether they were commoners or kings.

Scientific and technological advances also helped set the stage for exploration. The invention of movable type made printing easier and cheaper, stimulating diffusion of information, including news of discoveries, among literate Europeans. By 1400, crucial navigational aids employed by maritime explorers like Columbus were already available: compasses; hourglasses, which allowed calculation of elapsed time, useful in estimating speed; and the astrolabe and the quadrant, devices for determining latitude. Detailed sailing maps called *portulanos* illustrated shoreline topography and noted compass headings for sailing from one port to another. Many people throughout fifteenth-century

Ivory Saltcellar

This exquisitely carved sixteenth-century ivory saltcellar combines African materials, craftsmanship, and imagery in an artifact for Portuguese tables. Designed to hold table salt in the central globe, the saltcellar portrays a victim about to be beheaded by the armed man who has already beheaded five others. To Portuguese eyes, the saltcellar dramatized African brutality and quietly suggested the superiority of Portuguese virtues and their beneficial influence in Africa.

Archivio Fotogràfico del Museo Preistòrico Etnografico L. Pigorini, Roma.

Europe knew about these and other technological advances. The Portuguese were the first to use them in a campaign to sail beyond the limits of the world known to Europeans.

A Century of Portuguese Exploration

In many ways, Portugal was an unlikely candidate to take the lead in exploration. With less than 2 percent of the population of Christian Europe, the country devoted far more energy and wealth to the geographical exploration of the world between 1415 and 1460 than all the other countries of Europe combined.

Facing the Atlantic on the Iberian Peninsula, the Portuguese lived on the fringes of the thriving Mediterranean trade. As a Christian kingdom, Portugal cooperated with Spain in the Reconquest, the centuries-long drive to expel Muslims from the Iberian Peninsula. The religious zeal that propelled the Reconquest also justified expansion into what the Portuguese considered heathen lands. The key victory came in 1415 when Portuguese forces conquered Ceuta, the Muslim bastion at the mouth of the Strait of Gibraltar that had blocked Portugal's access to the Atlantic coast of Africa.

The most influential advocate of Portuguese exploration was Prince Henry the Navigator, son of the Portuguese king. From 1415 until his death in 1460, Henry collected the latest information about sailing techniques and geography, supported new crusades against the Muslims, encouraged fresh sources of trade to fatten Portuguese pocketbooks, and pushed explorers to go farther still. Both the Portuguese king and the Christian pope supported Henry's efforts to extend the Reconquest down the African coast. African expeditions also promised to wrest wheat fields from their Moroccan owners and to obtain gold, the currency of European trade. Gold was scarce in Europe because the quickening pace of commerce increased the need for currency while purchases in the East drained gold away from European markets.

Neither the Portuguese nor anybody else in Europe knew the immensity of Africa or the length or shape of its coastline, which, in reality, fronted the Atlantic for more than 7,000 miles—about five times the considerable distance from Genoa, Columbus's hometown, to Lisbon, the Portuguese capital. At first, Portuguese mariners cautiously hugged the west coast of Africa, seldom venturing beyond sight of land. By 1434, they had reached the northern edge of the

Sahara Desert, where strong westerly currents swept them out to sea. They soon learned to ride those currents far away from the coast before catching favorable winds that turned them back toward land, a technique that allowed them to reach Cape Verde by 1444 (see Map 2.1). To stow the supplies necessary for long periods at sea and to withstand the battering of waves in the open ocean, the Portuguese developed the caravel, a sturdy ship that became explorers' vessel of choice. In caravels, Portuguese mariners sailed into and around the Gulf of Guinea and as far south as the Congo by 1480.

Fierce African resistance confined Portuguese expeditions to coastal trading posts, where they bartered successfully for gold, slaves, and ivory. Portuguese merchants learned that relatively peaceful trading posts on the coast were far more profitable than attempts at violent conquest and **colonization** of inland regions. In the 1460s, the Portuguese used African slaves to develop sugar plantations on the Cape Verde Islands, inaugurating an association between enslaved Africans and plantation labor that would be transplanted to the New World in the centuries to come.

About 1480, Portuguese explorers began a conscious search for a sea route to Asia. In 1488, Bartolomeu Dias sailed around the Cape of Good Hope at the southern tip of Africa and hurried back to Lisbon with the exciting news that it appeared to be possible to sail on to India and China. In 1498, after ten years of careful preparation, Vasco da Gama commanded the first Portuguese fleet to sail to India. Portugal quickly capitalized on the commercial potential of da Gama's new sea route. By the early sixteenth century, the Portuguese controlled a far-flung commercial empire in India, Indonesia,

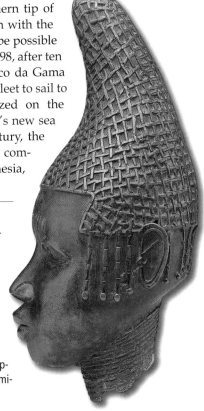

Benin Queen Mother
Early in the sixteenth century, as the Portuguese began their forays along the African coast, the Oba (king) of Benin, in present-day Nigeria, introduced the notion of a queen mother who possessed the ability to communicate with supernatural deities. Brass castings of Benin queen mothers like the one shown here appeared on altars in royal palaces. The distinctive headdress apparently signified the queen mother's semi-divine status.
The National Museums, Liverpool.

and China (collectively referred to as the East Indies). Their new sea route to the East eliminated overland travel and the numerous intermediate merchants and markups of the old Mediterranean trade routes controlled by the Italians. The new route allowed Portuguese merchants to charge much lower prices for the eastern goods they imported, and still make handsome profits.

Portugal's African explorations during the fifteenth century broke the monopoly of the old Mediterranean trade with the East, dramatically expanded the world known to Europeans, established a network of Portuguese outposts in Africa and Asia, and developed methods of sailing the high seas that Columbus employed on his revolutionary voyage west.

A Surprising New World in the Western Atlantic

In retrospect, the Portuguese seemed ideally qualified to venture across the Atlantic. They had pioneered the **frontiers** of seafaring, exploration, and geography for almost a century. However, the knowledge and experience they gained while navigating around Africa made them cautious about the risks of trying to sail west across the Atlantic. Portuguese and most other European experts believed doing so was literally impossible. The European discovery of America required someone bold enough to believe that the experts were wrong and the risks were surmountable. That person was Christopher Columbus. His explorations inaugurated a geographical revolution that forever altered Europeans' understanding of the world and its peoples, including themselves. Columbus's landfall in the Caribbean originated a thriving exchange between the people, ideas, cultures, and institutions of the Old and New Worlds that continues to this day.

The Explorations of Columbus

Born in 1451 into the family of an obscure master weaver in Genoa, Italy, Columbus went to sea when he was about fourteen. Sometime around 1476, he arrived in Lisbon

and within a few years married Felipa Moniz. Felipa's father had been raised in the household of Prince Henry the Navigator, and her family retained close ties to the prince. Through Felipa, Columbus gained access to explorers' maps and papers crammed with information about the tricky currents and winds encountered in sailing the Atlantic. Columbus himself ventured into the Atlantic frequently and at least twice sailed all the way to the central coast of Africa.

Like other educated Europeans, Columbus believed that the earth was a sphere and that theoretically it was possible to reach the East Indies by sailing west. Most Europeans believed, however, that the earth was simply too big for anyone to sail west from Europe to Asia. Sailors would die of thirst and starvation long before they reached Asia.

Columbus rejected this conventional wisdom. With flawed calculations, he estimated that Asia was only about 2,500 miles from the westernmost boundary of the known world, a shorter distance than Portuguese ships routinely sailed between Lisbon and the Congo. In fact, the shortest distance to Japan from Europe's jumping-off point was nearly 11,000 miles. Convinced by his erroneous calculations, Columbus became obsessed with a scheme to prove he was right.

First, Columbus tried to convince the Portuguese king to sponsor an expedition to the west. But Columbus's peculiar notions about geography did not divert the Portuguese monarchy from its lucrative African voyages. After years of unsuccessful lobbying in Spain, England, and France, Columbus finally won financing for his journey from Spain's King Ferdinand and Queen Isabella in 1492. The Spanish monarchs saw Columbus's venture as an inexpensive gamble: The potential loss was small while the potential gain was huge. The Spanish monarchs gave Columbus a letter of introduction to China's Grand Khan of the Mongols, the ruler they hoped he would meet on the other side of the Atlantic.

After scarcely three months of hurried preparation, Columbus and his small fleet—the *Niña* and *Pinta*, both caravels, and the *Santa María*, a larger merchant vessel—headed west. Six weeks after leaving the Canary

Columbus's First Voyage to the New World, 1492–1493

12 Oct. 1492
First landing on
San Salvador I.

Gulf of Mexico

Cuba

ATLANTIC OCEAN

Santiago (Jamaica)

Hispaniola

Santo Domingo

Caribbean Sea

0   200   400 miles

0   400 kilometers

Islands, where he stopped for supplies, Columbus landed on a tiny Caribbean island about three hundred miles north of the eastern tip of Cuba.

Columbus and his men understood that they had made a momentous discovery. Yet they found it frustrating. Although the Tainos proved friendly, they did not have the riches Columbus expected to find in the East. For three months Columbus cruised from island to island, looking for the king of Japan and the Grand Khan of China. In mid-January 1493, he started back to Spain, taking seven Tainos with him. When he reached Isabella and Ferdinand, they were overjoyed by his news. With a voyage that had lasted barely eight months, Columbus appeared to have catapulted Spain from a secondary position in the race for a sea route to Asia into that of a serious challenger to Portugal, whose explorers had not yet sailed to India or China. Columbus and his Taino companions became the toast of the royal court. The Spanish monarchs elevated Columbus to the nobility and awarded him the title "Admiral of the Ocean Sea." The seven Tainos were baptized as Christians, and King Ferdinand became their godfather.

Soon after Columbus arrived in Spain, the Spanish monarchs rushed to obtain the pope's support for their claim to the new lands in the west. When the pope, a Spaniard, complied, the Portuguese feared their own claims to recently discovered territory were in jeopardy. To protect their claims, the Portuguese and Spanish monarchs negotiated the Treaty of Tordesillas in 1494. The treaty drew an imaginary line eleven hundred miles west of the Canary Islands (Map 2.2). Land discovered west of the line belonged to Spain; Portugal claimed land to the east.

Ferdinand and Isabella moved quickly to realize the promise of their new claims. In the fall of 1493 they dispatched Columbus once again, this time with a fleet of seventeen ships and more than a thousand men who planned to locate the Asian mainland, find gold, and get rich. When Columbus returned to the island of Hispaniola, where a shipwreck near the end of his first voyage had forced him to leave behind thirty-nine of his sailors, he received disturbing news. In Columbus's absence, his sailors had terrorized the Tainos, kidnapping their women and confining them to harems. In retaliation, Taino chiefs had killed all the Spaniards. This small episode prefigured much of what was to happen in encounters between Native Americans and Europeans in the years ahead.

Before Columbus died in 1506, he returned to the New World two more times without relinquishing his belief that the East Indies were there, someplace. Other explorers continued to search for a passage to the East or some other source of profit. Before long, however, prospects of beating the Portuguese to Asia began to dim along with the hope of finding vast hoards of gold. Nonetheless, Columbus's discoveries forced sixteenth-century Europeans to think about the world in new ways. He proved that it was possible to sail from Europe to the western rim of the Atlantic and return to Europe. Most important, Columbus made clear that beyond the western shores of the Atlantic lay lands entirely unknown to Europeans.

> Columbus made clear that beyond the western shores of the Atlantic lay lands entirely unknown to Europeans.

The Geographic Revolution and the Columbian Exchange

Within thirty years of Columbus's initial discovery, Europeans' understanding of world geography underwent a revolution. An elite of perhaps twenty thousand people with access to Europe's royal courts and trading centers learned the exciting news about global geography. But it took a generation of additional exploration before they could comprehend the larger contours of Columbus's discoveries.

European monarchs hurried to stake their claims to the newly discovered lands. In 1497, King Henry VII of England, who had spurned Columbus a decade earlier, sent John Cabot to look for a "Northwest Passage" to the Indies across the North Atlantic (see Map 2.2). Cabot reached the tip of Newfoundland, which he believed was part of Asia, and hurried back to England, where he assembled a small fleet and sailed west again in 1498. But he was never heard from again. Three thousand miles to the south, a Spanish expedition landed on the northern coast of South America in 1499 accompanied by Amerigo Vespucci, an Italian businessman. In 1500, Pedro Álvars Cabral commanded a Portuguese fleet bound for the Indian Ocean that accidentally made landfall on the coast of Brazil as it looped westward into the Atlantic.

By 1500, European experts knew that several large chunks of land cluttered the western Atlantic. A few cartographers speculated that these chunks were connected to one another in a landmass that was not Asia. In 1507, Martin Waldseemüller, a German cartographer, published the first map that showed the New World separate from Asia; he named the land America, in honor of Amerigo Vespucci.

Two additional discoveries confirmed Waldseemüller's speculation. In 1513, Vasco Núñez de Balboa crossed the isthmus of Panama and reached the Pacific Ocean. Clearly, more water lay between the New World and Asia.

MAP 2.2   European Exploration in Sixteenth-Century America

This map illustrates the approximate routes of early European explorations of the New World.

READING THE MAP: Which countries were most actively exploring the New World? Which countries were exploring later than others?

CONNECTIONS: What were the motivations behind the explorations? What were the motivations for colonization?

FOR MORE HELP ANALYZING THIS MAP, see the map activity for this chapter in the Online Study Guide at bedfordstmartins.com/roark.

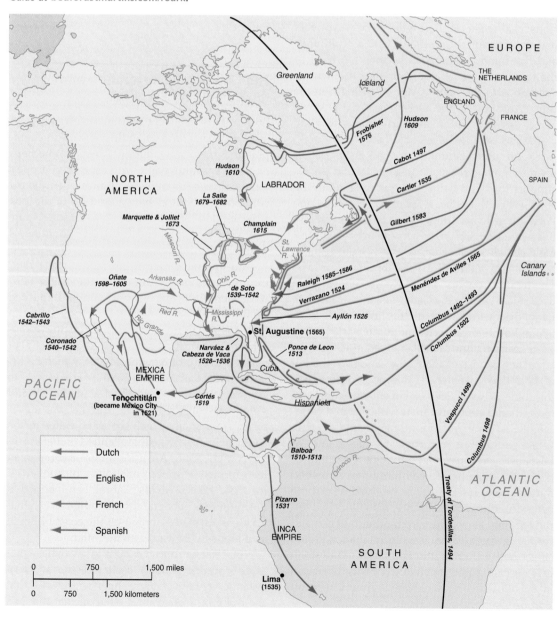

Columbian Exchange

The arrival of Columbus in the New World initiated an ongoing transatlantic exchange of goods, people, and ideas. Spaniards brought domesticated animals from the Old World, including horses, cattle, goats, chickens, cats, and sheep (left). The novelty of such animals is demonstrated by the Nahua words the Mexican people initially used to refer to these strange new beasts: for horses, they used the Nahua word for deer; a cow was "one with horns"; a goat was a "bearded one with horns"; a chicken was a "Spanish turkey hen"; a cat was a "little cougar"; a sheep was referred to with the word for cotton, linking the animal with its fibrous woolen coat. Spaniards brought many other alien items such as cannon, which the Mexica at first termed "fat fire trumpets," and guitars, which the Mexica called "rope drums." Spaniards also carried Old World microorganisms that caused devastating epidemics of smallpox, measles, and other diseases (center). Ancient American people, goods, and ideas made the return trip across the Atlantic. Columbus's sailors quickly learned to use Indian hammocks and became infected with syphilis in sexual encounters with Indian women; then they carried both hammocks and syphilis back to Europe. Smoking tobacco, like the cigar puffed by the ancient Mayan lord (right), became such a fashion in Europe that some came to believe, as a print of two men relaxing with their pipes was captioned, "Life Is Smoke." The strangeness of New World peoples and cultures also reinforced Europeans' notions of their own superiority. Although the Columbian exchange went in both directions, it was not a relationship of equality. Europeans seized and retained the upper hand.

University of California at Berkeley, The Bancroft Library; Arxiu Mas; Collection of Dr. Francis Robicsek.

How much water Ferdinand Magellan discovered when he led an expedition to circumnavigate the globe in 1519. Sponsored by King Charles I of Spain, Magellan's voyage took him first to the New World, around the southern tip of South America, and into the Pacific late in November 1520. Crossing the Pacific took almost four months. By the time he reached the Philippines, his crew had been decimated by extreme hunger and thirst. Magellan himself was killed by Philippine tribesmen. A remnant of his expedition continued on to the Indian Ocean and managed to transport a cargo of spices back to Spain in 1522.

In most ways Magellan's voyage was a disaster. One ship and 18 men crawled back from an expedition that had begun with five ships and more than 250 men. But the geographic information it provided left no doubt that America was a continent separated from Asia by the enormous Pacific Ocean. The voyage made clear that Columbus was dead wrong about the identity of what he had discovered. It was possible to sail west to reach the East Indies, but that was a

After Magellan, most Europeans who sailed west had their sights set on the New World, not on Asia.

terrible way to go. After Magellan, most Europeans who sailed west set their sights on the New World, not on Asia.

Columbus's arrival in the Caribbean anchored the western end of what might be imagined as a sea bridge that spanned the Atlantic, connecting the Western Hemisphere to Europe. That sea bridge ended the age-old separation of the hemispheres and initiated the **Columbian exchange**, a transatlantic exchange of goods, people, and ideas that has continued ever since.

Spaniards brought novelties to the New World that were commonplace in Europe, including Christianity, iron technology, sailing ships, firearms, wheeled vehicles, horses and other domesticated animals, and much else. (See "The Promise of Technology," page 46.) Unknowingly, they also smuggled along many Old World microorganisms that caused epidemics of smallpox, measles, and other diseases that would kill the vast majority of Indian peoples during the sixteenth century and continue to decimate survivors in later centuries. European diseases made the Columbian exchange catastrophic for Native Americans. In the long term, these diseases were decisive in transforming the dominant peoples of the New World from descendants of Asians, who had inhabited the hemisphere for millennia, to descendants of Europeans and Africans, recent arrivals from the Old World by way of the newly formed sea bridge.

Ancient American goods, people, and ideas made the return trip across the Atlantic. Europeans were introduced to New World foods such as corn and potatoes as well as exotic fruits like pineapples, named for their resemblance to pinecones. Columbus's sailors became infected with syphilis in sexual encounters with New World women and then unwittingly carried the deadly parasite back to Europe, where it may already have had a foothold. New World tobacco created a European fashion for smoking that ignited quickly and has yet to be extinguished. But for almost a generation after 1492, this Columbian exchange did not reward Spaniards with the riches they yearned to find.

Hernán Cortés, who became the richest and most famous conquistador, arrived in the New World in 1504, an obscure nineteen-year-old Spaniard seeking adventure and the chance to make a name for himself.

Spanish Exploration and Conquest

During the sixteenth century, the New World helped Spain become the most powerful monarchy in both Europe and the Americas. Initially, Spanish expeditions reconnoitered the Caribbean, scouted stretches of the Atlantic coast, and established settlements on the large islands of Hispaniola, Puerto Rico, Jamaica, and Cuba. Spaniards enslaved Caribbean tribes and put them to work growing crops and mining gold. But the profits from these early ventures barely covered the costs of maintaining the settlers. After almost thirty years of exploration, the promise of Columbus's discovery seemed illusory.

Soon after 1519, however, that promise was fulfilled, spectacularly. The mainland phase of exploration began in 1519 with Hernán Cortés's march into Mexico. By about 1545, Spanish conquests extended from northern Mexico to southern Chile, and New World riches filled Spanish treasure chests. Cortés's expedition served as the model for Spaniards' and other Europeans' expectations that the New World could yield bonanza profits for its conquerors.

The Conquest of Mexico

Hernán Cortés, who became the richest and most famous conquistador (conqueror), arrived in the New World in 1504, an obscure nineteen-year-old Spaniard seeking adventure and the chance to make a name for himself. He fought in the conquest of Cuba and elsewhere in the Caribbean. In 1519, the governor of Cuba authorized Cortés to organize an expedition to investigate rumors of a fabulously wealthy kingdom somewhere in the interior of the mainland. A charming, charismatic leader, Cortés quickly assembled a force of about six hundred men, loaded his ragtag army aboard eleven ships, and set out.

Cortés's confidence that he could talk his way out of most situations and fight his way out of the rest fortified the small band of Spaniards. But Cortés could not speak any Native American language. Landing first on the Yucatán peninsula, he had the good fortune to receive a gift from a chief of the Tobasco people. Among about twenty other women given to Cortés was a fourteen-year-old girl named Malinali who spoke several native languages, including Mayan and Nahuatl, the language of Mexica, the most powerful people in what is now Mexico and Central America (see chapter 1). Malinali had acquired her linguistic fluency painfully. Born into a family of the Mexican nobility, she learned Nahuatl as a young child. After her father died and her mother remarried and had a son, Malinali's stepfather sold her as a slave to Mayan-speaking Indians who subsequently gave the slave girl to the Tobascans. Malinali, whom the Spaniards called Marina, soon learned Spanish and became Cortés's interpreter. She also became one of Cortés's several mistresses and bore him a son. (Several years later, after Cortés's wife arrived in New Spain, Cortés cast Marina aside, and she married one of his soldiers.) Although no word uttered by Marina survives in historical documents, her words were the Spaniards' essential conduit of communication with the Indians. "Without her help," wrote one of the Spaniards who accompanied Cortés, "we would not have understood the language of New Spain and Mexico." With her help, Cortés talked and fought with Indians along the Gulf coast of Mexico, trying to discover the location of the fabled kingdom. By the time Marina died at age twenty-four, the people she had grown up among—the people who had taught her languages, enslaved her, and given her to Cortés—had been conquered by the Spaniards with her help.

In the capital of the Mexican empire, Tenochtitlán, the emperor Montezuma heard rumors about some strange creatures sighted along the coast. (Montezuma and his people are often called Aztecs, but they called themselves Mexica.) He feared that the strangers were led by the god Quetzalcoatl, returning to Tenochtitlán as predicted by Mexican religion. Montezuma sent representatives to meet with the strangers and bring them gifts fit for gods. Marina had told Cortés about Quetzalcoatl, and when Montezuma's messengers arrived, Cortés donned the regalia they had brought, almost certain proof to the Mexica that he was indeed the god they feared. The Spaniards astounded the messengers by blasting their cannon and displaying their swords.

The messengers hurried back to Montezuma with their amazing news. The emperor arranged for large quantities of food to be sent to the coast to welcome the strangers and perhaps to postpone Quetzalcoatl's dreaded arrival in the capital. Before the food was served to the Spaniards, the Mexica sacrificed several hostages and

Cortés Arrives in Tenochtitlán
This portrayal of the arrrival of Cortés and his army in the Mexican capital illustrates the importance of Malinali, who stands at the front of the Spaniards' procession, serving as their translator and intermediary with Montezuma (not pictured), who has come out to greet the invaders. Painted by a Mexican artist after the conquest, the work contrasts Cortés—dressed as a Spanish gentleman, respectfully doffing his hat to Montezuma and accompanied by his horse and African groom—with his soldiers, who are armed and ready for battle. The painting displays the choices confronted by the Mexica: accepting the pacific overtures of Cortés or facing the lances, swords, and battle axes of the Spanish soldiers. Also notable is the importance of Indian porters who carried the Spaniards' food and other supplies. What do you think was the significance of the winged image on the flag?
Bibliothèque Nationale, Paris.

soaked the food in their blood. This fare disgusted the Spaniards and might have been enough to turn them back to Cuba. But along with the food, the Mexica also brought the Spaniards another gift, a "disk in the shape of a sun, as big as a cartwheel and made of very fine gold," as one of the Mexica recalled. Here was conclusive evidence that the rumors of fabulous riches heard by Cortés had some basis in fact.

In August 1519, Cortés marched inland to find Montezuma. Leading about 350 men armed with swords, lances, and muskets and supported by ten cannon, four smaller guns, and sixteen horses, Cortés had to live

Cortés's Invasion of Tenochtitlán, 1519–1521

Gulf of Mexico

Otumba
Zautla
Texcoco
Jalapa
Tenochtitlán
Tlaxcala
Veracruz
Cholula

→ Cortés' original route, 1519
→ Cortés' retreat, 1520
→ Cortés' return route, 1520–1521

Horses: A New Native American Technology

An Indian on horseback: few images better evoke the American West. Yet Native Americans had no knowledge of horses before Columbus and other Spaniards arrived in the New World. Only after Spanish conquest did Native Americans learn to ride horses. Horses illustrate the widespread transfer of European technology to America in the wake of conquest and its transformation in the new context of the American West.

Horses existed throughout the hemisphere (and the world) when the first humans arrived in North America about 13,000 years ago. Like mammoths and other large mammals, however, ancient horses became extinct in America about 11,000 years ago. Paleo-Indians almost certainly contributed to their extinction by killing them for food. They reappeared in the New World less than two years after the arrival of Europeans. In January 1494, Columbus brought 24 stallions and 10 mares from Spain to the island of Hispaniola. Spaniards brought hundreds more horses on later voyages and began to breed and raise horses in New Spain.

The reappearance of horses in the New World epitomized the connections that already interlaced the globe by 1494. Columbus, an Italian mariner born in Genoa, a center of the old Mediterranean trade, had married a woman from Portugal, a monarchy that had pioneered voyages of exploration along the African coast that eventually undermined the Mediterranean trade. Now Columbus, who commanded a Spanish fleet seeking a western route to the East to compete with both the Portuguese trade around Africa and the old Mediterranean trade, brought back to the New World the descendants of horses that had originally evolved there millions of years earlier, after *their* ancestors had migrated to North America from Asia millions of years earlier still.

Horses had survived for millennia outside North America for two basic reasons. First, horses can convert the energy stored in tough, sparse grasses into strong bones and muscles. Horses achieve this energy conversion with a specialized intestine that allows them to digest large quantities of poor-quality grass that cannot sustain cattle.

Second, horses survived because they proved to be very useful to human beings. For hundreds of thousands of years, ancient humans probably saw horses mainly as a source of meat, just as Paleo-Indians did. But about 6,000 years ago in the Ukraine, a young nomad got close enough to a horse to leap on its back and hold on for dear life, initiating a revolution in human transportation. The domestication of horses, probably launched by a wild ride on the Ukrainian plains, spread throughout Eurasia.

From China to England, people learned to harness the great strength and energy of horses to carry burdens and pull loads. Horse users invented numerous technological devices and tinkered with them endlessly: saddles for carrying riders and packs; harnesses for control and to connect with carts or plows; spurs and whips to goad and punish; stirrups for a rider's comfort and to provide leverage for driving a lance through an opponent's chest; and much else, from magnificent armor to lowly horseshoes.

Columbus and other Spaniards made room for horses on their ships partly because the prevailing technology of horses made them useful for hauling loads and tilling fields. But above all, horses were on board Spanish ships because they carried conquistadors. Horses were as much a part of conquistadors' military equipment as swords and cannon. For a glimpse of the superiority of a

off the land, establishing peaceful relations with indigenous tribes when he could and killing them when he thought necessary. On November 8, 1519, Cortés reached Tenochtitlán. Montezuma came out to welcome the Spaniards. After presenting Cortés with gifts, Montezuma welcomed the Spaniards to the royal palace and showered them with lavish hospitality. Quickly, Cortés took Montezuma hostage and held him under house arrest, hoping to make him a puppet through which the Spaniards could rule the Mexican empire. This uneasy peace existed for several months until, after a brutal massacre of many Mexican nobles by one of Cortés's subor-

conquistador on horseback compared to a plebeian on foot, imagine a mounted soldier swinging a long, razor-sharp sword at everyone within reach. The deadly combination of mobility, speed, and height that horses gave conquistadors created an aura of power and authority around any Spaniard on horseback. The military technology of horses helped Spaniards exercise the political authority of conquest.

The Mexica who first saw Cortés's horses thought they were strange supernatural deer. Before long, however, the Mexica and other Native Americans learned that horses were neither deer nor supernatural. Native Americans soon grasped that technology that was good for the conquerors could also be good for the conquered.

Despite Spaniards' best efforts, some of their horses were stolen by Indians or ran away and thrived in the wild by grazing marginal lands, as their ancestors had done for millennia. The horses that ultimately made their way to North America were wild descendants of the domesticated horses brought to the New World in the holds of Spanish ships. By the early seventeenth century, Spanish merchants in the Southwest and elsewhere also traded horses to Native Americans along with guns and many other goods.

Native Americans adapted horses to their own cultures. They collected horses by taming wild animals, breeding, and raiding the herds of Spaniards and nearby tribes. Tasks that had previously been assigned to domesticated dogs, such as pulling loads or carrying packs, were now given to horses that readily hauled four times more weight. With their ability to move heavy loads while they searched for grazing and hunting lands, nomadic Indians accumulated all kinds of goods, including ceremonial items that reinforced tribal political and religious hierarchies. Horses also made age-old methods of buffalo hunting faster and more efficient, freeing young men to undertake other activities, particularly raids and reprisals against their enemies.

Horses probably intensified and certainly modified warfare among Native Americans in the West. Tactics shifted from massed groups of warriors engaged in pitched battles to small numbers of highly mobile horsemen springing surprise attacks. Bows and spears became shorter and shields smaller and lighter. The goals of warriors often included capturing their enemies' horses, which increased the warriors' military might while correspondingly diminishing that of their enemies. In these and many other ways, Indians in the American West adopted and transformed the technology of horses initiated by ancient Ukrainians and imported by fifteenth- and sixteenth-century Spaniards.

Teton Sioux Hide Painting
This hide painting illustrates the significance of horses in Indian warfare on the Great Plains. Painted by a Teton Sioux artist in the late nineteenth century, the images document the prowess of Indian warriors in combining their deadly weapons with the strength and speed of horses. Unhorsed individuals had little chance against their mounted adversaries, the painting shows. Horses are the dominant figures in the painting and are rendered as distinctive individual animals, suggesting the artist's understanding of their importance to the warriors astride them. Horses had become so deeply integrated into Teton Sioux culture that a warrior and a horse were considered a single fighting unit. These assumptions and military tactics developed in the centuries after the arrival of Columbus, when Spaniards reintroduced horses to the New World.
Thaw Collection, Fenimore Art Museum, Cooperstown, NY. John Bigelow Taylor, NYC.

dinates, the population of Tenochtitlán revolted, murdered Montezuma, and mounted a ferocious assault on the Spaniards. On June 30, 1520, Cortés and about a hundred other Spaniards fought their way out of Tenochtitlán and retreated toward the coast about one hundred miles to Tlaxcala, a stronghold of bitter enemies of the Mexica. The friendly Tlaxcalans—who had long resented Mexican power—allowed Cortés to regroup, obtain reinforcements, and plan a strategy to conquer Tenochtitlán.

In the spring of 1521, Cortés mounted a complex campaign against the Mexican capital. The Spaniards and tens of thousands of Indian allies laid siege to the city. With a relentless, scorched-earth strategy, Cortés finally defeated the last Mexican defenders on August 13, 1521. (See "Historical Question," page 46.) The great capital of the Mexican empire "looked as if it had been ploughed up," one of Cortés's soldiers remembered. A few years later, one of the Mexica described the utter despair of the defeated:

> Broken spears lie in the roads;
> we have torn our hair in grief.
> The houses are roofless now, and their walls
> are red with blood. . . .
> We have pounded our hands in despair
> against the adobe walls,
> for our inheritance, our city, is lost and dead.

The Search for Other Mexicos

Lured by their insatiable appetite for gold, conquistadors quickly fanned out from Tenochtitlán in search of other sources of treasure like Mexico. The most spectacular prize fell to Francisco Pizarro, who conquered the Incan empire in Peru. The Incas controlled a vast, complex region that contained more than nine million people and stretched along the western coast of South America for more than two thousand miles. In 1532, Pizarro and his army of fewer than two hundred men captured the Incan emperor Atahualpa and held him hostage. As ransom, the Incas gave Pizarro the largest treasure yet produced by the conquests: gold and silver equiva-

Artifacts of Spanish Conquest

Spaniards reveled in their victories over the Mexica and other native peoples in the New World. About 1522, Cortés sent this Mexican shield as a trophy of conquest to a bishop in Spain. Made by a Mexican featherworker and probably looted from its Mexican owner by Cortés's soldiers, the shield was constructed of reeds, reenforced by sticks and rawhide, and decorated with feathers of exotic Central American birds. The animal outlined in strips of gold on the shield probably depicts the coyote effigy of Mexican warriors. The shield displayed to Spaniards the artistry of the Mexica as well as their weakness: Feathers, reeds, and coyotes were no match for Spaniards' steel, gunpowder, and Christianity. Contrast the vulnerability of the featherwork shield to Spaniards' razor-sharp swords and the comparative invulnerability of the Spanish war helmet to the Mexica's wooden spears and stone points. Like the shield, the helmet was a sign of Spaniards' technological superiority, which made conquest possible and justified it: People of feathers and reeds would—and should—be conquered by people of steel, the trophies suggested to Spaniards. The gold ingot was another trophy of conquest. Shortly after Cortés and his army entered Tenochtitlán, they found the treasure-house of Montezuma filled with golden artifacts. The Spaniards confiscated the treasure and melted the golden artworks into ingots slightly bent to allow them to be strapped in belts around soldiers' waists. In 1521, when the Mexica revolted against the Spaniards and temporarily drove them out of Tenochtitlán, many of Cortés's soldiers were forced to drop their heavy waistbands of gold in order to escape. This gold ingot, excavated in Mexico City in 1982, is probably one dropped by the retreating Spaniards. The ingot hints of the looting and destruction that accompanied conquest.

Museum of Volkerkunde, Vienna; Wallace Collection, London, UK / Bridgeman Art Library; Museo Nacional de Antropologia, CONACULTA-INAH, 10-220012.

lent to half a century's worth of precious-metal production in Europe. With the ransom safely in their hands, the Spaniards executed Atahualpa. The Incan treasure proved that at least one other Mexico did indeed exist, and spurred the search for others.

Juan Ponce de León had sailed along the Florida coast in 1513. Encouraged by Cortés's success, he went back to Florida in 1521 to find riches, only to be killed in battle with Calusa Indians. A few years later, Lucas Vázquez de Ayllón explored the Atlantic coast north of Florida to present-day South Carolina. In 1526 he established a small settlement on the Georgia coast that he named San Miguel de Gualdape, the first Spanish attempt to establish a foothold in what is now the United States. Within a few months, however, Ayllón and most of the other settlers sickened and died, and the few survivors retreated to Spanish settlements in the Caribbean.

Pánfilo de Narváez surveyed the Gulf coast from Florida to Texas in 1528. The Narváez expedition ended disastrously with a shipwreck on the Texas coast near present-day Galveston. Indians enslaved the few survivors of the Narváez expedition. After several years in Indian captivity, four of the survivors managed to escape and were rescued by Spanish slave hunters in northern Mexico.

In 1539, Hernando de Soto, a seasoned conquistador who had taken part in the conquest of Peru, set out with nine ships and more than six hundred men to find another Peru in North America. Landing in Florida, de Soto literally slashed his way through much of southeastern North America for three years, searching for the rich, majestic civilizations he thought were there. After many brutal battles and much hardship, de Soto became sick and died in 1542. His men buried him in the Mississippi River before turning back to Mexico, disappointed.

Tales of the fabulous wealth of the mythical Seven Cities of Cíbola also lured Francisco Vásquez de Coronado to search the Southwest and Great Plains of North America. In 1540, Coronado left northern Mexico with more than three hundred Spaniards, a thousand Indians, fifteen hundred horses, and a priest who claimed to know the way to what he called "the greatest and best of the discoveries." Cíbola turned out to be a small Zuñi pueblo of about a hundred families. When the Zuñi shot arrows at the Spaniards, Coronado attacked the pueblo and routed the defenders after a hard battle. Convinced that the

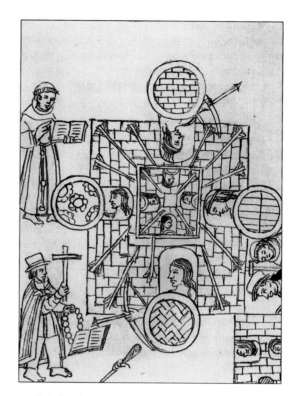

Zuñi Defend Pueblo against Coronado
This sixteenth-century drawing by a Mexican artist shows Zuñi bowmen fighting back against the arrows of Coronado's men and the entreaties of Christian missionaries. Intended to document the support some Mexican Indians gave to Spanish efforts to extend the conquest into North America, the drawing depicts the Zuñi defender at the bottom of the pueblo aiming his arrow at a Mexican missionary armed only with religious weaponry: a crucifix, a rosary, and a book—presumably the Bible.
Hunterian Museum Library, University of Glasgow. Glasgow University Library, Department of Special Collections.

rich cities must lie somewhere over the horizon, Coronado kept moving all the way to central Kansas before deciding in 1542 that the rumors he had pursued were just that, nothing more.

Juan Rodríguez Cabrillo led an expedition in 1542 that sailed along the coast of California. Cabrillo died on Santa Catalina Island, offshore from present-day Los Angeles, but his men sailed on to the border of Oregon, where a ferocious storm forced them to turn back toward Mexico.

These probes into North America by de Soto, Coronado, and Cabrillo persuaded Spaniards that enormous territories stretched northward but their inhabitants had little to loot or exploit. After a generation of vigorous exploration, Spaniards concluded that there was only one Mexico and one Peru.

Why Did Cortés Win?

By conquering Mexico, Hernán Cortés demonstrated that Columbus had in fact discovered a New World of enormous value to the Old. But how did a few hundred Spaniards so far away from home defeat millions of Indians fighting on their home turf?

First, several military factors favored the Spaniards. They possessed superior military technology, which partially offset the Mexica's numerical superiority. They fought with weapons of iron and steel against the Mexica's stone, wood, and copper. They charged on horseback against Mexican warriors on foot. They ignited gunpowder to fire cannon and muskets toward attacking Mexica, whose only source of power was human muscle. But the Mexica's immense numerical superiority could overpower the Spaniards' weaponry.

Spaniards also possessed superior military organization, although they were far from a highly disciplined, professional fighting force. Cortés's army was composed of soldiers of fortune, young men who hoped to fight for God and king and get rich. The unsteady discipline among the Spaniards is suggested by Cortés's decision to beach and dismantle the ships that had brought his small army to the Mexican mainland. After that, his men had no choice but to go forward.

The Spaniards were a well-oiled military machine compared with the Mexica, who tended to attack from ambush or in waves of frontal assaults, showing great courage but little organization or discipline.

The Mexica seldom sustained attacks, even when they had the Spaniards on the run. In the siege of Tenochtitlán, for example, the Mexica often paused to sacrifice Spanish soldiers they had captured, taking time to skin "their faces," one Spaniard recalled, "which they afterward prepared like leather gloves, with their beards on." Spanish tactics, in contrast, concentrated their soldiers to magnify the effect of their firepower and to maintain communication during the thick of battle.

But perhaps the Spaniards' most fundamental military advantage was their concept of war. The Mexican concept was shaped by the nature of the empire. The Mexica fought to impose their tribute system on others and to take captives for sacrifices. They believed that war would make their adversaries realize the high cost of continuing to fight and would give them a big incentive to surrender and pay tribute. To the Spaniards, war meant destroying the enemy's ability to fight. In short, the Spaniards sought total victory; the Mexica sought surrender. All these military factors weakened the Mexica's resistance but were insufficient to explain Cortés's victory.

Disease played a major part in the Mexica's defeat. When the Mexica confronted Cortés, they were not at full strength. An epidemic of smallpox and measles had struck the Caribbean in 1519, arrived in Mexico with Cortés and his men, and lasted through 1522. Thousands of Indians died, and many others became too sick to fight. When the Spaniards were regrouping in Tlaxcala after their disastrous evacuation of Tenochtitlán, a great plague broke out in the Mexican capital. As one Mexica explained to a Spaniard shortly after the conquest, the plague lasted for seventy days, "striking everywhere in the city and killing a vast number of our people. Sores erupted on our faces, our breasts, our bellies. . . . The illness was so dreadful that no one could walk or move. . . . They could not get up to search for food, and everybody else was too sick to care for them, so they starved to death in their beds."

The sickness was not confined to Tenochtitlán. It also killed and weakened people in the areas surrounding the city, spreading back along the network of trade and tribute that fed the city, reducing its food supply and further weakening the survivors. While the Mexica were decimated by their first exposure to smallpox and measles, the Spaniards were for all practical purposes immune, having previously been exposed to the diseases. European viruses probably played at least as large a role in the conquest as weapons and military tactics.

Religion also contributed to the Mexica's defeat. Mexican religious doctrine led Montezuma to be hesitant and uncertain in confronting the Spaniards during the months when they were most vulnerable. While Cortés marched toward Tenochtitlán, the Indians thought that the Spaniards and their horses were immortal deities. Cortés worked hard to maintain the illusion, hiding Spaniards who died. But by the time Cortés retreated from Tenochtitlán, the Mexica knew that the Spaniards could be killed, and their resistance stiffened accordingly.

While the Mexica's religion reduced their initial resistance to the

Mexican Warrior

Warriors held the most exalted status in Mexican society. This sixteenth-century Mexican painting of a warrior in full battle regalia illustrates the Mexica's careful attention to their magnificent, awe-inspiring costumes. The elaborate clothing and decorative adornments (notice the ornamental stone plug in the warrior's lower lip) expressed warriors' high status; they also were intended to intimidate enemies who dared oppose the fearsome Mexica. Spanish soldiers developed healthy respect for the military skills of the Mexica but were not intimidated by the costumes of Mexican warriors. They did not understand the meaning the costumes had for the Mexica—for example, the costumes' evocation of supernatural support. In addition, although Mexican wooden swords lined with sharp stones could inflict deadly wounds, they proved no match for Spanish body armor, steel swords, horses, and guns.

Bibliothèque Nationale, Paris.

Mexican military commanders often turned to their priests for military guidance. Spaniards routinely celebrated mass and prayed before battles, but Cortés and his subordinates—tough, wily, practical men—made the military and diplomatic decisions. When the Spaniards suffered defeats, they did not worry that God had abandoned them. However, when the Mexica lost battles advised by their priests, they confronted the distressing fear that their gods no longer seemed to listen to them. The deadly sickness sweeping through the countryside also seemed to show that their gods had abandoned them. "Cut us loose," one Mexica pleaded, "because the gods have died."

Finally, political factors proved decisive in the Mexica's defeat. Cortés shrewdly exploited the tensions between the Mexica and the people they ruled in their empire. Cortés's small army was reinforced by thousands of Indians who were eager to seek revenge against the Mexica. With skillful diplomacy, Cortés obtained cooperation from thousands of Indian porters and food suppliers. Besides fighting alongside Cortés, the Spaniards' Indian allies provided the invaders with a fairly secure base from which to maneuver against the Mexican stronghold. Hundreds of thousands of Indians helped the Spaniards by not contributing to the Mexica's defense. These passive allies of the Spaniards prevented the Mexica from fully capitalizing on their overwhelming numerical superiority. In the end, although many factors contributed to the conquest, Cortés won because the Mexican empire was the source not only of the Mexica's impressive wealth and power but also of their crippling weakness.

conquistadors, Christianity strengthened the Spaniards. The Spaniards' Christianity was a confident and militant faith that commanded its followers to destroy idolatry, root out heresy, slay infidels, and subjugate nonbelievers. Their religious zeal had been honed for centuries in the battles of the Reconquest. Christianity was as much a part of the conquistadors' armory as swords and gunpowder.

Spaniards created the distinctive colonial society of New Spain that gave other Europeans a striking illustration of how the New World could be made to serve the purposes of the Old.

New Spain in the Sixteenth Century

For all practical purposes, Spain was the dominant European power in the Western Hemisphere during the sixteenth century (Map 2.3). Portugal claimed the giant territory of Brazil under the Tordesillas treaty but was far more concerned with exploiting its hard-won trade with the East Indies than in colonizing the New World. England and France were absorbed by domestic and diplomatic concerns in Europe and largely lost interest in America until late in the century. In the decades after 1519, Spaniards created the distinctive colonial society of New Spain that gave other Europeans a striking illustration of how the New World could be made to serve the purposes of the Old.

The Spanish monarchy claimed ownership of most of the land in the Western Hemisphere and gave the conquistadors permission to explore and plunder. (See "Documenting the American Promise," page 54.) The crown took one-fifth, called the "royal fifth," of any loot confiscated and allowed the conquerors to divide the rest. In the end, most conquistadors received very little after the plunder was divided among Cortés and his favorite officers. After the conquest of Tenochtitlán, Cortés decided to compensate

MAP 2.3 New Spain in the Sixteenth Century
Spanish control spread throughout Central and South America during the sixteenth century, with the important exception of Portuguese Brazil. North America, though claimed by Spain under the Treaty of Tordesillas, remained peripheral to Spain's New World empire.

READING THE MAP: Track Spain's efforts at colonization by date. How did political holdings, the physical layout of the land, and natural resources influence where the Spanish directed their energies?

CONNECTIONS: What was the purpose of the Treaty of Tordesillas? How might the location of silver and gold mines have affected Spain's desire to assert its claims over regions still held by Portugal after 1494, and Spain's interest in California, New Mexico, and Florida?

FOR MORE HELP ANALYZING THIS MAP, see the map activity for this chapter in the Online Study Guide at bedfordstmartins.com/roark.

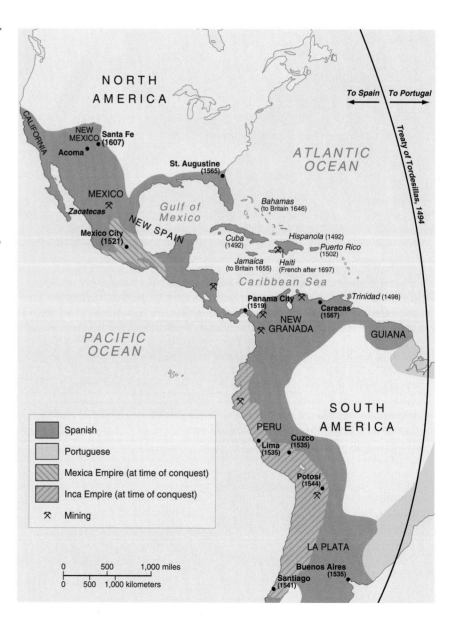

Testerian Catechism
After conquest, Catholic missionaries tried to teach the Mexica the basic doctrines of Christianity by using pictures (pictographs) that resembled the symbols in preconquest Mexican codices (books composed of pictographs). Missionaries hoped to appeal to the Mexica's respect for the authority of the ancient texts. These Testerian catechisms demonstrate the missionaries' awareness that the Mexica often retained their faith in their preconquest gods. The catechism shown here incorporates symbols of both Christian and Mexican belief. Try to puzzle out the identity of the various figures and the meanings Catholic missionaries intended them to convey to the Mexica.

his disappointed, battle-hardened men by giving them towns the Spaniards had subdued.

The distribution of conquered towns institutionalized the system of *encomienda*, which empowered conquistadors to rule the Indians and the lands in and around their towns. The concept of encomienda was familiar to the Spaniards, who had used it to govern regions recaptured from the Muslims during the Reconquest. In New Spain, encomienda transferred to the Spanish *encomendero* (the man who "owned" the town) the tribute that the town had previously paid to the Mexican empire.

In theory, encomienda involved a reciprocal relationship between the encomendero and "his" Indians. In return for the tribute and labor of the Indians, the encomendero was supposed to encourage the Indians to convert to Christianity, to be responsible for their material well-being, and to guarantee order and justice in the town. Catholic missionaries labored earnestly to convert Indians to Christianity. Missionaries fervently believed that God expected them to save Indians' souls by convincing them to abandon their old, sinful beliefs and to embrace the one true Christian faith. After baptizing tens of thousands of Indians, the missionaries learned that many Indians continued to worship their own gods along with the Christian God. Most friars came to believe that the Indians

Justifying Conquest

The immense riches Spain reaped from its New World empire came largely at the expense of Indians. A few individual Spaniards raised their voices against the brutal exploitation of Indians. Their criticisms prompted the Spanish monarchy to formulate an official justification of conquest that, in effect, blamed Indians for resisting Spanish dominion.

DOCUMENT 1
Montecino's 1511 Sermon

In 1511, a Dominican friar named Antón Montecino delivered a blistering sermon that astonished the Spaniards gathered in the church in Santo Domingo, headquarters of the Spanish Caribbean.

Your greed for gold is blind. Your pride, your lust, your anger, your envy, your sloth, all blind. . . . You are in mortal sin. And you are heading for damnation. . . . For you are destroying an innocent people. For they are God's people, these innocents, whom you destroyed. By what right do you make them die? Mining gold for you in your mines or working for you in your fields, by what right do you unleash enslaving wars upon them? They have lived in peace in this land before you came, in peace in their own homes. They did nothing to harm you to cause you to slaughter them wholesale. . . . Are you not under God's command to love them as you love yourselves? Are you out of your souls, out of your minds? Yes. And that will bring you to damnation.

Source: Zvi Dor-Ner, *Columbus and the Age of Discovery* (New York: Morrow, 1991), 220–21.

DOCUMENT 2
The Requerimiento

Montecino returned to Spain to bring the Indians' plight to the king's attention. In 1512 and 1513, King Ferdinand met with philosophers, theologians, and other advisers and concluded that the holy duty to spread the Christian faith justified conquest. To buttress this claim, the king had his advisers prepare the Requerimiento. According to the Requerimiento, Indians who failed to welcome Spanish conquest and all its blessings deserved to die. Conquistadors were commanded to read the Requerimiento to Indians before any act of conquest. Beginning in 1514, they routinely did so, speaking in Spanish while other Spaniards brandishing unsheathed swords stood nearby.

On the part of the King . . . [and] queen of [Spain], subduers of the barbarous nations, we their servants notify and make known to you, as best we can, that the Lord our God, living and eternal, created the heaven and the earth, and one man and one woman, of whom you and we, and all the men of the world, were and are descendants. . . .

God our lord gave charge to one man called St. Peter, that he should be lord and superior to all the men in the world, that all should obey him, and that he should be the head of the whole human race, wherever men should live . . . and he gave him the world for his kingdom and jurisdiction.

And he commanded him to place his seat in Rome, as the spot most fitting to rule the world from. . . . This man was called Pope, as if to say, Admirable Great Father and Governor of men. The men who lived in that time obeyed that St. Peter and took him for lord, king, and superior of the universe. So also they have regarded the others who after him have been elected to the pontificate, and so has it been continued even till now, and will continue till the end of the world.

One of these pontiffs, who succeeded that St. Peter as lord of the world . . . made donation of these islands and mainland to the aforesaid king and queen [of Spain] and to their successors. . . .

were lesser beings inherently incapable of fully understanding the Christian faith.

In practice, encomenderos were far more interested in what the Indians could do for them than in what they or missionaries could do for the Indians. Encomenderos subjected Indians to chronic overwork, mistreatment, and abuse. As one Spaniard remarked, "Everything [the Indians] do is slowly done and by compulsion. They are malicious, lying, [and] thievish." Economically, however, encomienda recognized a fundamental reality of New Spain: The most important treasure the Spaniards could plunder from the New World was not gold but uncompensated Indian labor. To exploit that labor, New Spain's richest natural resource, encomienda

So their highnesses are kings and lords of these islands and mainland by virtue of this donation; and . . . almost all those to whom this has been notified, have received and served their highnesses, as lords and kings, in the way that subjects ought to do, with good will, without any resistance, immediately, without delay, when they were informed of the aforesaid facts. And also they received and obeyed the priests whom their highnesses sent to preach to them and to teach them our holy faith; and all these, of their own free will, without any reward or condition have become Christians, and are so, and the highnesses have joyfully and graciously received them, and they have also commanded them to be treated as their subjects and vassals; and you too are held and obliged to do the same. Wherefore, as best we can, we ask and require that you consider what we have said to you, and that you take the time that shall be necessary to understand and deliberate upon it, and that you acknowledge the Church as the ruler and superior of the whole world, and the high priest called Pope, and in his name the king and queen [of Spain] our lords, in his place, as superiors and lords and kings of these islands and this mainland by virtue of the said donation, and that you consent and permit that these religious fathers declare and preach to you. . . .

If you do so . . . we . . . shall receive you in all love and charity, and shall leave you your wives and your children and your lands free without servitude, that you may do with them and with yourselves freely what you like and think best, and they shall not compel you to turn to Christians unless you yourselves, when informed of the truth, should wish to be converted to our holy Catholic faith. . . . And besides this, their highnesses award you many privileges and exemptions and will grant you many benefits.

But if you do not do this or if you maliciously delay in doing it, I certify to you that with the help of God we shall forcefully enter into your country and shall make war against you in all ways and manners that we can, and shall subject you to the yoke and obedience of the Church and of their highnesses; we shall take you and your wives and your children and shall make slaves of them, and as such shall sell and dispose of them as their highnesses may command; and we shall take away your goods and shall do to you all the harm and damage that we can, as to vassals who do not obey and refuse to receive their lord and resist and contradict him; and we protest that the deaths and losses which shall accrue from this are your fault, and not that of their highnesses, or ours, or of these soldiers who come with us.

Indians who heard the Requerimiento could not understand Spanish, of course.

No native documents survive to record the Indians' thoughts upon hearing the Spaniards' official justification for conquest, even when it was translated in a language they recognized. But one conquistador reported that when the Requerimiento was translated for two chiefs in Colombia, they responded that if the pope gave the king so much territory that belonged to other people, "the Pope must have been drunk."

SOURCE: Adapted from A. Helps and M. Oppenheim, eds., *The Spanish Conquest in America and Its Relation to the History of Slavery and to the Government of the Colonies,* 4 vols. (London and New York, 1900–1904), 1:264–67.

QUESTIONS FOR ANALYSIS AND DEBATE

1. How did the Requerimiento answer the criticisms of Montecino? According to the Requerimiento, why was conquest justified? What was the source of Indians' resistance to conquest?

2. What arguments might a critic like Montecino have used to respond to the Requerimiento's justification of conquest? What arguments might the Mexican leader Montezuma have made against those of the Requerimiento?

3. Was the Requerimiento a faithful expression or a cynical violation of Spaniards' Christian faith?

gave encomenderos the right to force Indians to work when, where, and how the Spaniards pleased.

Encomienda engendered two groups of influential critics. A few of the missionaries were horrified at the brutal mistreatment of the Indians. The cruelty of the encomenderos made it difficult for priests to persuade Indians of the tender mercies of the Spaniards' God. "What will [the Indians] think about the God of the Christians," Fray Bartolomé de Las Casas asked, when they see their friends "with their heads split, their hands amputated, their intestines torn open? . . . Would they want to come to Christ's sheepfold after their homes had been destroyed, their children imprisoned, their wives

Catholic Feather Mosaic

In sixteenth-century Europe, Catholic churches conveyed religious messages in paintings, sculptures, and stained glass. The visual images both dramatized Christian stories and made religious doctrines accessible to the majority of Europeans who could not read. This feather mosaic produced by Mexican craftsmen in 1539 had a similar purpose. It follows European Christians' example of portraying a major event in Christian faith—Christ's resurrection after his death on the cross—in the distinctively Mexican medium of a mosaic of feathers collected from New World birds. Can you detect any other hints that the mosaic was designed to be understood by the Mexica?

The Mass of St. Gregory, 1539, feather mosaic, Auch, Musée des Jacobins, France (Gers).

chy moved to abolish encomienda in an effort to replace swashbuckling old conquistadors with royal bureaucrats as the rulers of New Spain.

One of the most important blows to encomienda was the imposition in 1549 of a reform called the *repartimiento,* which limited the labor an encomendero could command from his Indians to forty-five days per year from each adult male. The repartimiento, however, did not challenge the principle of forced labor, nor did it prevent encomenderos from continuing to cheat, mistreat, and overwork their Indians. Slowly, as the old encomenderos died, repartimiento replaced encomienda as the basic system of exploiting Indian labor.

The practice of coerced labor in New Spain grew directly out of the Spaniards' assumption that they were superior to the Indians. As one missionary put it, the Indians "are incapable of learning. . . . The Indians are more stupid than asses and refuse to improve in anything." Therefore, most Spaniards assumed, Indians' labor should be organized by and for their conquerors. Indians who resisted Spaniards' labor demands did so at great peril. Spaniards seldom hesitated to use violence to punish and intimidate recalcitrant Indians.

From the viewpoint of Spain, the single most important economic activity in New Spain after 1540 was silver mining. Spain imported more New World gold than silver in the early decades of the century, but that changed with the discovery of major silver deposits at Potosí, Bolivia, in 1545 and Zacatecas, Mexico, in 1546. As the mines swung into large-scale production, an ever-growing stream of silver flowed from New Spain to Spain (Figure 2.1). Overall, exports of precious metals from New Spain during the sixteenth century were worth about twenty-five times more than hides, the next most important export. The mines required large capital investments and many miners. Typically, a few Spaniards supervised large groups of Indian miners, who were supplemented by African slaves later in the sixteenth century. The mines and their products were valuable principally for their contribution to the wealth of Spain, not to that of the colony.

For Spaniards, life in New Spain was relatively easy. Only a few thousand Spaniards actually fought during the conquests. Although the riches they won fell far short of their expectations, the benefits of encomienda gave them a comfortable, leisurely life that was the envy of many Spaniards back in Europe. As one colonist

raped, their cities devastated, their maidens deflowered, and their provinces laid waste?" Las Casas and other outspoken missionaries softened few hearts among the encomenderos, but they did win some sympathy for the Indians from the Spanish monarchy and royal bureaucracy. Royal officials interpreted encomenderos' brutal treatment of the Indians as part of the larger general problem of the troublesome autonomy of encomenderos. The Spanish monar-

wrote to his brother in Spain, "Don't hesitate [to come]. . . . This land [New Spain] is as good as ours [in Spain], for God has given us more here than there, and we shall be better off."

During the century after 1492, about 225,000 Spaniards settled in the colonies. Virtually all of them were poor young men of common (non-noble) lineage who came directly from Spain. Laborers and **artisans** made up the largest proportion, but soldiers and sailors were also numerous. Throughout the sixteenth century, men vastly outnumbered women, although the proportion of women grew from about one in twenty before 1519 to nearly one in three by the 1580s. The gender and number of Spanish settlers shaped two fundamental features of the society of New Spain. First, despite the thousands of immigrants, Europeans never made up more than 1 or 2 percent of the total population. Although Spaniards ruled New Spain, the population was almost wholly Indian. Second, the shortage of Spanish women meant that Spanish men frequently married Indian women or used them as concubines.

The tiny number of Spaniards, the masses of Indians, and the frequency of intermarriage created a steep social hierarchy defined by perceptions of national origin and race. Natives of Spain—*peninsulares* (people born on the Iberian Peninsula)—enjoyed highest social status in New Spain. Below them but still within the white elite were creoles, the children born in the New World to Spanish men and women. Together, peninsulares and creoles made up barely 1 or 2 percent of the population. Below them on the social pyramid was a larger group of mestizos, the offspring of Spanish men and Indian women, who comprised 4 or 5 percent of the population. So many of the mestizos were illegitimate that the term *mestizo* (after the Spanish word for "mixed") became almost synonymous with *bastard* in the sixteenth century. Some mestizos worked as artisans and labor overseers and lived well, and a few rose into the ranks of the elite, especially if their Indian ancestry was not obvious from their skin color. Most mestizos, however, were lumped with Indians, the enormous bottom mass of the population.

The society of New Spain established the precedent for what would become a pronounced pattern in the European colonies of the New World: a society stratified sharply by social origin and race. All Europeans of whatever social origin considered themselves superior to Native Americans; in New Spain, they were a dominant minority in both power and status.

> New Spain established the precedent for what would become a pronounced pattern in the European colonies of the New World: a society stratified sharply by social origin and race.

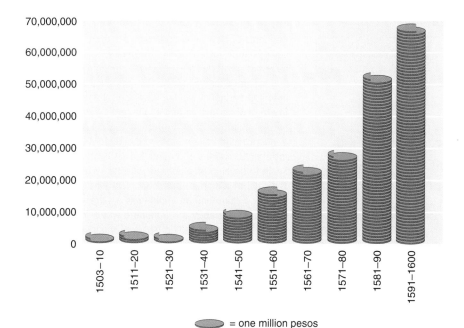

70,000,000
60,000,000
50,000,000
40,000,000
30,000,000
20,000,000
10,000,000
0

1503–10   1511–20   1521–30   1531–40   1541–50   1551–60   1561–70   1571–80   1581–90   1591–1600

= one million pesos

FIGURE 2.1 New World Gold and Silver Imported into Spain during the Sixteenth Century, in Pesos
Spain imported more gold than silver during the first three decades of the sixteenth century, but the total value of this treasure was quickly eclipsed during the 1530s and 1540s when rich silver mines were developed. Silver accounted for most of the enormous growth in Spain's precious-metal imports from the New World.

Español con India, Mestizo.

Mestizo con Española Castizo.

Castizo con Española Español.

Español con Mora Mulato.

5

6

Mulato con Española Morisco.

Morisco con Española Chino.

7

Chino con India Salta atras.

Salta atras con Mulata Lobo.

The Toll of Spanish Conquest and Colonization

By 1560, the major centers of Indian civilization had been conquered, their leaders overthrown, their religion held in contempt, and their people forced to work for the Spaniards. Profound demoralization pervaded Indian society. As a Mexican poet wrote:

> Nothing but flowers and songs of sorrow
> are left in Mexico . . .
> where once we saw warriors and wise men. . . .
> We are crushed to the ground;
> we lie in ruins.
> There is nothing but grief and suffering
> in Mexico.

Adding to the culture shock of conquest and colonization was the deadly toll of European diseases. As conquest spread, Indians succumbed to virulent epidemics of measles, smallpox, and respiratory illnesses. Indians had built up no immunity to these diseases because they had not been exposed to them before the arrival of Europeans. By 1570, only a half-century after Cortés entered Tenochtitlán, the Indian population of New Spain had fallen about 90 percent from what it had been when Columbus arrived. The destruction of the Indian population was a

Mixed Races

Residents of New Spain maintained a lively interest in each person's racial lineage. These eighteenth-century paintings illustrate forms of racial mixture common in the sixteenth century. In the first painting, a Spanish man and an Indian woman have a mestizo son; in the fourth, a Spanish man and a woman of African descent have a mulatto son; in the fifth, a Spanish woman and a mulatto man have a *morisco* daughter. The many racial permutations of parents led residents of New Spain to develop an elaborate vocabulary of ancestry. The child of a morisco and a Spaniard was a *chino*; the child of a chino and an Indian was a *salta abas*; the child of a salta abas and a mulatto was a *lobo*; and so on. Can you detect hints of some of the meanings of racial categories in the clothing depicted in these paintings?
Bob Schalkwijk/INAH.

FOR MORE HELP ANALYZING THIS IMAGE, see the visual activity for this chapter in the Online Study Guide at bedfordstmartins.com/roark.

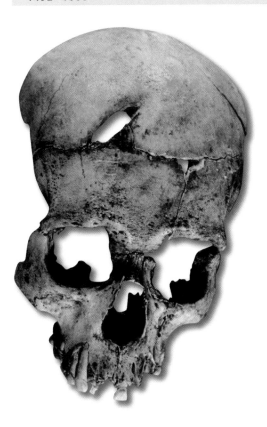

A Sign of Conquest

This skull of an Indian man in his fifties was recently excavated from the site of a Native American village in southwestern Georgia visited by de Soto's expedition in 1540. The skull shows that the man suffered a fatal sword wound above his right eye. Combined with slashed and severed arm and leg bones from the same site, the skull demonstrates the brutality de Soto employed against indigenous peoples on his voyage through the Southeast. No native weapons could have inflicted the wounds indelibly left on this skull and the other bones.

Robert L. Blakely.

African Slaves Mining Gold *(below)*

This sixteenth-century illustration depicts African slaves mining gold in New Spain. Spaniards imported African slaves in substantial numbers after the Native American population had been decimated by conquest and disease. Here, the two slaves on the right dig ore, from which the gold is separated by the slave in the center and then washed in hot water over the fire, before the clean nuggets are given to the Spaniard, who carefully weighs and saves them. How did the artist emphasize the differences between the Spaniard and the slaves? Is it possible to detect the artist's point of view about who was more "civilized"?

The Pierpont Morgan Library, New York. MA 3900, f.100.

catastrophe unequaled in human history. A Mayan Indian recalled that when sickness struck his village, "Great was the stench of the dead. . . . The dogs and vultures devoured the bodies. The mortality was terrible. . . . So it was that we became orphans. . . . We were born to die!" For most Indians, New Spain was a rapidly growing graveyard.

For Spaniards, Indian deaths meant that the most valuable resource of New Spain—Indian labor—dwindled rapidly. By the last quarter of the sixteenth century, Spanish colonists felt the pinch of a labor shortage. To help redress the need for laborers, the colonists began to import African slaves. Some Africans had come to Mexico with the conquistadors; one Mexica recalled that among Cortés's men were "some black-skinned one with kink hair." In the years before 1550 while Indian labor was still adequate, only 15,000 slaves were imported from Africa. Even after Indian labor began to decline, the relatively high cost of African slaves kept imports low, approximately 36,000 from 1550 to the end of the century. During the sixteenth century, New Spain continued to rely primarily on a diminishing number of Indians.

Spanish Outposts in Florida and New Mexico

After the explorations of de Soto, Coronado, and Cabrillo, officials in New Spain lost interest in North America. The monarchy claimed that Spain owned North America and insisted that a few North American settlements be established to give some tangible reality to its claims. Settlements in Florida would have the additional benefit of protecting Spanish ships from pirates and privateers who lurked along the southeastern coast, waiting for the Spanish treasure fleet sailing toward Spain.

In 1565, the Spanish king sent Pedro Menéndez de Avilés to create settlements along the Atlantic coast of North America. In early September, Menéndez founded St. Augustine in Florida, the first permanent European settlement within what became the United States. By 1600, St. Augustine had a population of about five hundred, the remaining Spanish beachhead on the vast Atlantic shoreline of North America (see "American Places," page 61).

More than sixteen hundred miles west of St. Augustine, the Spaniards founded another outpost in 1598. Juan de Oñate led an expedition of about five hundred people to settle northern Mexico, now called New Mexico, and claim the booty rumored to exist there. Oñate had impeccable credentials for both conquest and mining. His father had helped to discover the bonanza silver mines of Zacatecas, and his wife was Isabel Tolosa Cortés Montezuma—the granddaughter of Cortés, the conqueror of Mexico and the great-granddaughter of Montezuma, the emperor of Mexico before conquest.

After a two-month journey from Mexico, Oñate and his companions reached pueblos near present-day Albuquerque and Santa Fe. He solemnly convened the pueblos' leaders and received their oath of loyalty to the Spanish king and to the Christian God. Oñate sent out scouting parties to find the legendary treasures of the region and to locate the ocean, which he believed must be nearby. Meanwhile, many of his soldiers planned to mutiny, and relations with the Indians deteriorated. When Indians in the Acoma pueblo revolted against the Spaniards, Oñate ruthlessly suppressed the uprising, killing 800 men, women, and children. Although Oñate reconfirmed the Spaniards' military superiority, he did not bring peace or stability to the region. Another pueblo revolt occurred in 1599, and many of Oñate's settlers returned to Mexico, dis-

illusioned. New Mexico lingered as small, dusty assertions of Spanish claims to the North American Southwest.

The New World and Sixteenth-Century Europe

The riches of New Spain helped make the sixteenth century the Golden Age of Spain. After the deaths of Queen Isabella and King Ferdinand, their sixteen-year-old grandson became King Charles I of Spain in 1516. Three years later, just as Cortés ventured into Mexico, Charles I used judicious bribes to secure his selection as Holy Roman Emperor Charles V. His empire encompassed more than that of any other European monarch. Charles V used the wealth of New Spain to protect his sprawling empire and promote his interests in the fierce dynastic battles of sixteenth-century Europe. He also sought to defend orthodox Christianity from the insurgent heresy of the **Protestant Reformation**. The power of the Spanish monarchy spread throughout sixteenth-century Europe the clear message that a New World empire could bankroll Old World ambitions.

The Protestant Reformation and the European Order

In 1517, Martin Luther, an obscure Catholic priest in central Germany, initiated the Protestant Reformation by publicizing his criticisms of the Catholic Church. Luther's ideas, though shared by many other Catholics, were considered extremely dangerous by church officials and by Charles V and many other monarchs who believed with total conviction that, just as the church spoke for God, they ruled for God.

Luther preached a doctrine known as *justification by faith*: Individual Christians could obtain salvation and life everlasting only by having faith that God would save them. Giving offerings to the church, following the orders of priests, or participating in church rituals would not put believers one step closer to heaven. Also, the only true source of information about God's will was the Bible, not the church. By reading the Bible, any Christian could learn as much about God's commandments as any priest. Indeed, Luther called for a "priesthood of all believers."

St. Augustine, Florida

St. Augustine, Florida, occupies the site of the oldest continuous settlement of Europeans in the United States. Founded in 1565 by the Spanish explorer Don Pedro Menéndez de Avilés on lands of a Timucuan Indian village, St. Augustine represented a projection of the power of the Spanish monarchy into the unknown lands of North America. Spaniards intended the settlement to defend Spanish ships that cruised along the Florida coast on their return to Spain and to assert Spain's claims against those of European and Native American rivals. A priest arrived with the first settlers and soon began missionary work among the Timucuan Indians.

The Mission of Nombre de Dios stands on the site of the first church and can be visited today.

Shortly after the Spaniards arrived, they mounted an attack on a nearby settlement of French Protestants (called Huguenots). More than 100 of the French settlers were killed when they refused to renounce their faith. At the site of the massacre, the Spaniards erected temporary fortifications and, much later, Fort Matanzas, which can still be visited. Other Spanish fortifications in St. Augustine were replaced in the late seventeenth century by what became Castillo de San Marcos, which is now the oldest fort built by Europeans in the United States.

Spaniards took care to fortify Castillo de San Marcos against attacks from sea and land. The drawbridge shown in the photograph allowed access to the only doorway entering the fort. In case of attack, the drawbridge would be raised; attackers who tried to cross the flooded moat would be vulnerable to weapons fired from the notched openings along the top of the fort. The design and size of Castillo de San Marcos demonstrate the military significance of St. Augustine in Spain's New World empire.

Visitors to St. Augustine today can have a taste of the daily life of settlers in colonial Spanish Florida by exploring Spanish Quarter Village, a vivid reminder of the long history of Spanish influence in North America.

FOR WEB LINKS RELATED TO THIS SITE AND OTHER AMERICAN PLACES, see "PlaceLinks" at bedfordstmartins.com/roark.

Castillo de San Marcos Fortification
Casa de San Marcos; photo by Linda Chandler.

In effect, Luther charged that the Catholic Church was in many respects fraudulent. Despite the church's claims to the contrary, Luther insisted that priests were unnecessary for salvation, and that they encouraged Christians to violate God's will by promoting religious practices not specifically commanded by the Bible. The church, Luther declared, had neglected its true purpose of helping individual Christians understand the spiritual realm revealed in the Bible and had wasted its resources in worldly conflicts of politics and wars. Luther hoped his ideas would reform the Catholic Church, but instead they ruptured forever the unity of Christianity in western Europe.

> Luther hoped his ideas would reform the Catholic Church, but instead they ruptured forever the unity of Christianity in western Europe.

Charles V pledged to exterminate Luther's **Protestant** heresies. The wealth pouring into Spain from the New World fueled his efforts to defend orthodox Catholic faith against Protestants, as well as against Muslims in eastern Europe and against any nation bold or foolhardy enough to contest Spain's supremacy. As the wealthiest and most powerful monarch in Europe, Charles V, followed by his son and successor, Philip II, assumed responsibility for upholding the existing order of sixteenth-century Europe.

New World Treasure and Spanish Ambitions

Both Charles V and Philip II fought wars throughout the world during the sixteenth century. Mexican silver funneled through the royal treasury into the hands of military suppliers, soldiers, and sailors wherever in the world Spain's forces fought. New World treasure was dissipated in military adventures that served the goals of the monarchy but did little to benefit most Spaniards.

In a sense, American wealth made the Spanish monarchy too rich and too powerful among the states of Europe. The ambitions of Charles V and Philip II were so great that the expenses of constant warfare far outstripped the revenues arriving from New Spain. To help meet military expenditures, both kings raised taxes in Spain more than fivefold during the sixteenth century. Since the nobility, by far the wealthiest class, was exempt from taxation, the burdensome new taxes fell mostly on poor peasants. The ambitions of the monarchy impoverished the vast majority of Spain's population and brought the nation to the brink of bankruptcy. When taxes failed to produce enough revenue to fight its wars, the monarchy borrowed heavily from European bankers. By the end of the sixteenth century, interest payments on royal debts swallowed two-thirds of the crown's annual revenues. In retrospect, the riches from New Spain proved a short-term blessing but a long-term curse.

But sixteenth-century Spaniards did not see it that way. As they looked at their accomplishments in the New World, they saw unmistakable signs of progress. They had added enormously to their knowledge and wealth. They had built mines, cities, Catholic churches, and even universities on the other side of the Atlantic. Their military, religious, and economic achievements gave them great pride and confidence.

Europe and the Spanish Example

The lessons of sixteenth-century Spain were not lost on Spain's European rivals. Spain proudly displayed the fruits of its New World conquests. In 1520, for example, Charles V exhibited some of the gifts Montezuma had given to Cortés. The objects astonished the German artist Albrecht Dürer, who wrote in his diary about "the things which were brought to the King from the New Golden Land: a sun entirely of gold, a whole fathom [six feet] broad; likewise a moon, entirely of silver, just as big. . . . I have never seen in all my days what so rejoiced my heart. . . . For I saw among them amazing objects, and I marveled over the subtle ingenuity of the men in these distant lands." Dürer's reaction illustrates the excitement the New World generated among some Europeans. But the most exciting news about "the men in these distant lands" was that they could serve the interests of Europeans as Spain had shown. With a few notable exceptions, Europeans saw the New World as a place for the expansion of European influence, a place where, as one Spaniard wrote, Europeans could "give to those strange lands the form of our own."

France and England tried to follow Spain's example. Both nations warred with Spain in Europe, preyed on Spanish treasure fleets, and ventured to the New World, where they too hoped to find an undiscovered passageway to the East Indies or another Mexico or Peru.

In 1524, France sent Giovanni da Verrazano to scout the Atlantic coast of North America from North Carolina to Canada, looking for a

Algonquian Ceremonial Dance

When the English artist John White visited the coast of present-day North Carolina in 1585 as part of Raleigh's expedition, he painted this watercolor portrait of an Algonquian ceremonial dance. This and White's other portraits are the only surviving likenesses of sixteenth-century North American Indians that were drawn from direct observation in the New World. White's portrait captures the individuality of these Indians' appearances and gestures while depicting a ceremony that must have appeared bizarre and alien to a sixteenth-century Englishman. The significance of this ceremonial dance is still a mystery, although the portrait's obvious signs of order, organization, and collective understanding show that the dancing Indians knew what it meant.

Copyright © The British Museum.

Northwest Passage (see Map 2.2). Eleven years later, France probed farther north with Jacques Cartier's voyage up the St. Lawrence River. Encouraged, Cartier returned to the region with a group of settlers in 1541, but the colony they established—like the search for a Northwest Passage—came to nothing.

English attempts to follow Spain's lead were slower but equally ill fated. Not until 1576, almost eighty years after John Cabot's voyages, did the English try again to find a Northwest Passage. This time Martin Frobisher sailed into the frigid waters of northern Canada. His spon-

sor was the Cathay Company, which hoped to open trade with China (see Map 2.2). Like many other explorers who preceded and followed him, Frobisher was mesmerized by the Spanish example and was sure he had found gold. But the tons of "ore" he hauled back to England proved worthless, the Cathay Company collapsed, and English interests shifted southward.

English explorers' attempts to establish North American settlements were no more fruitful than their search for a northern route to China. Sir Humphrey Gilbert led expeditions in 1578 and 1583 that made feeble efforts to found colonies in Newfoundland until Gilbert vanished at sea. Sir Walter Raleigh organized an expedition in 1585 to settle Roanoke Island off the coast of present-day North Carolina. The first group of explorers left no colonists on the island, but two years later Raleigh sent a contingent of more than one hundred settlers to Roanoke under John White's leadership. White returned to England for supplies, and when he came back to Roanoke in 1590, the colonists had disappeared, leaving only the word *Croatoan* (whose meaning is unknown) carved on a tree. The Roanoke colonists most likely died from a combination of natural causes and unfriendly Indians. By the end of the century, England had failed to secure a New World beachhead.

Roanoke Settlement, 1585–1590

Conclusion: The Promise of the New World for Europeans

The sixteenth century in the New World belonged to the Spaniards, who employed Columbus, and to the Indians, who greeted him as he stepped ashore. Spaniards initiated the Columbian exchange between the New World and the Old that continues to this day. The exchange subjected Native Americans to the ravages of European diseases and Spanish conquest. Spanish explorers, conquistadors, and colonists forced Indians to serve the interests of Spanish settlers and the Spanish monarchy. The exchange illustrated one of the most important lessons of the sixteenth century: After millions of years, the Atlantic no longer was an impermeable barrier separating the Eastern and Western Hemispheres. After the voyages of Columbus, European sailing ships regularly bridged the Atlantic and carried people, products, diseases, and ideas from one shore to the other.

No European monarch could forget the seductive lesson taught by Spain's example: The New World could vastly enrich the Old. Spain remained a New World power for almost four centuries, and its language, religion, culture, and institutions left a permanent imprint. By the end of the sixteenth century, however, other European monarchies had begun to contest Spain's dominion in Europe and to make forays into the northern fringes of Spain's New World preserve. To reap some of the benefits the Spaniards enjoyed from their New World domain, the others had to learn a difficult lesson: how to deviate from Spain's example. That discovery lay ahead.

For additional firsthand accounts of this period, see Chapter 2 in Michael Johnson, ed., *Reading the American Past,* Third Edition.

To assess your mastery of the material in this chapter, see the Online Study Guide at bedfordstmartins.com/roark.

For Web links related to topics in this chapter, see "HistoryLinks," "DocLinks," and "PlaceLinks" at bedfordstmartins.com/roark.

CHRONOLOGY

1415 • Portugal conquers Ceuta at Strait of Gibraltar, gaining access to western coast of Africa.

1444 • Portuguese explorers reach Cape Verde.

1451 • Christopher Columbus born in Genoa, Italy.

1480 • Portuguese ships reach Congo.

1488 • Bartolomeu Dias rounds Cape of Good Hope.

1492 • Columbus lands on Caribbean island that he names San Salvador, initiating contact between Europe and the New World.

1493 • Columbus makes second voyage to the New World. In retaliation for mistreatment, Tainos kill many of Columbus's sailors.

1494 • Portugal and Spain negotiate Treaty of Tordesillas to establish their claims to newly discovered lands.

1497 • John Cabot searches for Northwest Passage.

1498 • Columbus makes third voyage to the New World and lands in Venezuela. Vasco da Gama sails to India.

1500 • Pedro Álvars Cabral makes landfall in Brazil.

1502 • Columbus makes fourth voyage to New World.

1507 • German mapmaker Martin Waldseemüller names the New World "America."

1513 • Vasco Núñez de Balboa crosses isthmus of Panama and learns that the Pacific Ocean separates America from Asia.

1517 • Protestant Reformation begins in Germany, intensifying religious and political turmoil in Europe.

1519 • Hernán Cortés leads expedition to find and conquer Mexico.

• Malinali (Doña Marina) becomes Cortés's translator and mistress.

• Ferdinand Magellan sets out to sail around the world.

• Charles I of Spain becomes Holy Roman Emperor Charles V.

1520 • Mexica in Tenochtitlán revolt against Spaniards.

1521 • Cortés, with the help of his Indian allies, conquers the Mexica at Tenochtitlán.

• Juan Ponce de León lands in Florida.

1526 • Lucas Vázquez de Ayllón establishes San Miguel de Gualdape on Georgia coast.

1528 • Pánfilo de Narváez leads expedition to survey Gulf coast from Florida to Texas.

1532 • Francisco Pizarro begins conquest of Peru.

1535 • Jacques Cartier explores St. Lawrence River.

1539 • Hernando de Soto launches exploration of southeastern North America.

1540 • Francisco Vásquez de Coronado starts to explore the Southwest and Great Plains of North America.

1542 • Juan Rodríguez Cabrillo explores California coast.

1549 • Repartimiento reforms begin to replace encomienda.

1565 • Pedro Menéndez de Avilés establishes St. Augustine, Florida.

1576 • Martin Frobisher sails into northern Canadian waters.

1578 • Sir Humphrey Gilbert attempts to found colonies in Newfoundland.

1587 • English colonists under Sir Walter Raleigh settle Roanoke Island.

1598 • Juan de Oñate leads expedition into New Mexico.

1599 • Pueblos revolt against Oñate.

BIBLIOGRAPHY

General Works

Richard Boyer and Geoffrey Spurling, eds., *Colonial Lives: Documents on Latin American History, 1550–1850* (2000).

Alfred W. Crosby Jr., *The Columbian Exchange: Biological and Cultural Consequences of 1492* (1972).

Barry W. Cunliffe, *Facing the Ocean: The Atlantic and Its Peoples, 8000 BC–AD 1500* (2001).

Zvi Dor-Ner, *Columbus and the Age of Discovery* (1991).

J. H. Elliott, *The Old World and the New, 1462–1650* (1970).

Felipe Fernández-Armesto, *Before Columbus: Exploration and Colonization from the Mediterranean to the Atlantic, 1229–1492* (1987).

Jonathan Locke Hart, *Representing the New World: The English and French Uses of the Example of Spain* (2001).

Jonathan Locke Hart, *Columbus, Shakespeare, and the Interpretation of the New World* (2003).

John L. Kessell, *Spain in the Southwest: A Narrative History of Colonial New Mexico, Arizona, Texas, and California* (2002).

D. W. Meinig, *The Shaping of America* (1986).

William D. Phillips and Carla Rahn Phillips, *The Worlds of Christopher Columbus* (1992).

David B. Quinn, *North America from Earliest Discovery to First Settlements* (1977).

A. J. R. Russell-Wood, *The Portuguese Empire, 1415–1808: A World on the Move* (1998).

Jayme A. Sokolow, *The Great Encounter: Native Peoples and European Settlers in the Americas, 1492–1800* (2003).

Stanley J. Stein and Barbara H. Stein, *Silver, Trade, and War: Spain and America in the Making of Early Modern Europe* (2000).

Hugh Thomas, *Conquest: Montezuma, Cortés, and the Fall of Old Mexico* (1993).

John Thornton, *Africa and Africans in the Making of the Atlantic World, 1400–1680* (1992).

David J. Weber, *The Spanish Frontier in North America* (1992).

Explorers and Empires

Jan De Vries, *The Economy of Europe in an Age of Crisis, 1600–1750* (1976).

William Eccles, *Canadian Frontier, 1534–1760* (1969).

Mary E. Giles, *Women in the Inquisition: Spain and the New World* (1999).

Henry Arthur Francis Kamen, *Spain's Road to Empire: The Making of a World Power, 1492–1763* (2002).

Karen Ordahl Kupperman, *Roanoke: The Abandoned Colony* (1984).

Peggy K. Liss, *Isabel the Queen: Life and Times* (1992).

John Lynch, *Spain, 1516–1598: From Nation State to World Empire* (1992).

Harry A. Miskimin, *The Economy of Later Renaissance Europe, 1460–1600* (1977).

David B. Quinn, *England and the Discovery of America, 1481–1620* (1974).

David B. Quinn, *Set Fair for Roanoke* (1985).

Francesc Relaño, *The Shaping of Africa: Cosmographic Discourse and Cartographic Science in Late Medieval and Early Modern Europe* (2002).

A. C. de C. M. Saunders, *A Social History of Black Slaves and Freedmen in Portugal, 1441–1555* (1982).

Roger C. Smith, *Vanguard of Empire: Ships of Exploration in the Age of Columbus* (1993).

Robert S. Weddle, *The Gulf of Mexico in North American Discovery, 1500–1685* (1985).

Europeans Encounter the New World

James Axtell, *Natives and Newcomers: The Cultural Origins of North America* (2002).

Robert F. Berkhofer Jr., *The White Man's Indian: Images of the American Indian from Columbus to the Present* (1978).

Philip P. Boucher, *Cannibal Encounters: Europeans and Island Caribs, 1492–1763* (1992).

Nicholas Canny and Anthony Pagden, *Colonial Identity in the Atlantic World, 1500–1800* (1987).

Rebecca Catz, *Christopher Columbus and the Portuguese, 1476–1498* (1993).

Alfred W. Crosby, *Ecological Imperialism: The Biological Expansion of Europe, 900–1900* (1986).

James Robert Enterline, *Erikson, Eskimos, and Columbus: Medieval European Knowledge of America* (2002).

William W. Fitzhugh, ed., *Cultures in Contact: The Impact of European Contacts on Native American Cultural Institutions, 1000–1800* (1985).

Valerie J. Flint, *The Imaginative Landscape of Christopher Columbus* (1992).

Anthony Grafton, *New Worlds, Ancient Texts: The Power of Tradition and the Shock of Discovery* (1992).

Peter Hulme, *Colonial Encounters: Europe and the Native Caribbean, 1492–1797* (1986).

William F. Keegan, *The People Who Discovered Columbus: An Introduction to the Prehistory of the Bahamas* (1992).

Anthony Pagden, *The Fall of Natural Man: The American Indian and the Origins of Comparative Ethnology* (1981).

Anthony Pagden, *European Encounters with the New World: From Renaissance to Romanticism* (1993).

Anthony Pagden, *Lords of All the World: Ideologies of Empire in Spain, Britain, and France, 1500–1800* (1995).

Irving Rouse, *The Tainos: Rise and Decline of the People Who Greeted Columbus* (1992).

Samuel M. Wilson, *Hispaniola: Caribbean Chiefdoms in the Age of Columbus* (1990).

Conquest and New Spain

Ida Altman, *Emigrants and Society: Extremadura and Spanish America in the Sixteenth Century* (1989).

Ida Altman, *Transatlantic Ties in the Spanish Empire: Brihuega, Spain, and Puebla, Mexico, 1560–1620* (2000).

Gary Clayton Anderson, *The Indian Southwest, 1580–1830: Ethnogenesis and Reinvention* (1999).

Kenneth J. Andrien, *Andean Worlds: Indigenous History, Culture, and Consciousness under Spanish Rule, 1532–1825* (2001).

Santa Arias, ed., *Mapping Colonial Spanish America: Places and Commonplaces of Identity, Culture, and Experience* (2002).

Elinore M. Barrett, *Conquest and Catastrophe: Changing Rio Grande Settlement Patterns in the Sixteenth and Seventeenth Centuries* (2001).

Herman L. Bennett, *Africans in Colonial Mexico: Absolutism, Christianity, and Afro-Creole Consciousness, 1570–1640* (2003).

Peter J. Blackwell, *Silver Mining and Society in Colonial Mexico: Zacatecas, 1546–1700* (1971).

Peter J. Blackwell, *Miners of the Red Mountain: Indian Labor in Potosí, 1545–1650* (1984).

Virginia Marie Bouvier, *Women and the Conquest of California, 1548–1840* (2001).

Frederick P. Bowser, *The African Slave in Colonial Peru, 1524–1650* (1974).

Gordon Brotherston, *Image of the New World: The American Continent Portrayed in Native Texts* (1979).

Louise M. Burkhart, *The Slippery Earth: Nahua-Christian Moral Dialogue in Sixteenth-Century Mexico* (1989).

Magali Marie Carrera, *Imagining Identity in New Spain: Race, Lineage and the Colonial Body in Portraiture and Casta Paintings* (2003).

Inga Clendinnen, *Aztecs: An Interpretation* (1991).

Noble David Cook, *Born to Die: Disease and New World Conquest, 1492–1650* (1998).

Noble David Cook, ed., *Secret Judgments of God: Old World Disease in Colonial Spanish America* (2001).

Kathleen A. Deegan, ed., *America's Ancient City: Spanish St. Augustine, 1565–1763* (1991).

David Ewing Duncan, *Hernando de Soto: A Savage Quest in the Americas* (1995).

Richard Flint and Shirley Cushing Flint, *The Coronado Expedition* (2003).

Patricia Galloway, *The Hernando de Soto Expedition: History . . . and "Discovery" in the Southeast* (1997).

Charles Gibson, *Spain in America* (1966).

Serge Gruzinski, *The Conquest of Mexico: The Incorporation of Indian Societies into the Western World, Sixteenth–Eighteenth Centuries* (1993).

Ramón A. Gutiérrez, *When Jesus Came, the Corn Mothers Went Away: Marriage, Sexuality, and Power in New Mexico, 1500–1846* (1991).

Robert T. Himmerich, *The Encomenderos of New Spain, 1521–1555* (1991).

Paul E. Hoffman, *A New Andalacía and a Way to the Orient: The American Southeast during the Sixteenth Century* (1990).

Robert H. Jackson, *Race, Caste, and Status: Indians in Colonial Spanish America* (1999).

Robert H. Jackson, ed., *Indians, Franciscans, and Spanish Colonization: The Impact of the Mission System on California Indians* (1995).

Richard L. Kagan, *Urban Images of the Hispanic World, 1493–1793* (2000).

Robert L. Kapitzke, *Religion and Politics in Colonial St. Augustine* (2001).

Kenneth F. Kiple and Stephen V. Beck, eds., *Biological Consequences of European Expansion, 1450–1800* (1997).

Andrew L. Knaut, *The Pueblo Revolt of 1680: Conquest and Resistance in Seventeenth-Century New Mexico* (1995).

James Lang, *Conquest and Commerce: Spain and England in the Americas* (1975).

Clark Spencer Larsen and George R. Milner, eds., *In the Wake of Contact: Biological Responses to Conquest* (1994).

James Lockhart, *The Nahuas after Conquest: A Social and Cultural History of the Indians of Central Mexico, Sixteenth through Eighteenth Centuries* (1992).

James Lockhart, ed., *We People Here: Nahuatl Accounts of the Conquest of Mexico* (1993).

Lyle N. McAlister, *Spain and Portugal in the New World, 1492–1700* (1984).

Sabine McCormack, *Religion in the Andes: Vision and Imagination in Early Colonial Peru* (1991).

Bonnie G. McEwan, *The Spanish Missions of La Florida* (1993).

Jerald T. Milanich, *Florida Indians and the Invasion from Europe* (1995).

Jerald T. Milanich, *Laboring in the Fields of the Lord: Spanish Missions and Southwestern Indians* (1999).

Jerald T. Milanich and Charles Hudson, *Hernando De Soto and the Indians of Florida* (1993).

Shannon Miller, *Invested with Meaning: The Raleigh Circle in the New World* (1998).

Barbara E. Mundy, *The Mapping of New Spain: Indigenous Cartography and the Maps of the Relaciones Geográficas* (2000).

Colin A. Palmer, *Slaves of the White God: Blacks in Mexico, 1570–1650* (1976).

José Rabasa, *Writing Violence on the Northern Frontier: The Historiography of Sixteenth Century New Mexico and Florida and the Legacy of Conquest* (2000).

Carroll L. Riley, *Rio del Norte: People of the Upper Rio Grande from Earliest Times to the Pueblo Revolt* (1995).

Carroll L. Riley, *The Kachina and the Cross: Indians and Spaniards in the Early Southwest* (1999).

Susan Schroeder, *Native Resistance and the Pax Colonial in New Spain* (1998).

Stuart B. Schwartz, ed., *Victors and Vanquished: Spanish and Nahua Views of the Conquest of Mexico* (2000).

Robert Silverberg, *The Pueblo Revolt* (1994).

Steve J. Stern, *Peru's Indian Peoples and the Challenge of Spanish Conquest: Huamanga to 1640* (1982).

David Hurst Thomas, ed., *Ethnology of the Indians of Spanish Florida* (1991).

David Hurst Thomas, ed., *The Missions of Spanish Florida* (1991).

Richard F. Townsend, *The Aztecs* (2000).

Charles A. Truxillo, *By the Sword and the Cross: The Historical Evolution of the Catholic World Monarchy in Spain and the New World, 1492–1825* (2001).

Thomas M. Whitmore and Billie Lee Turner II, *Cultivated Landscapes of Middle America on the Eve of Conquest* (2001).

Stephanie Gail Wood, *Transcending Conquest: Nahua Views of Spanish Colonial Mexico* (2003).

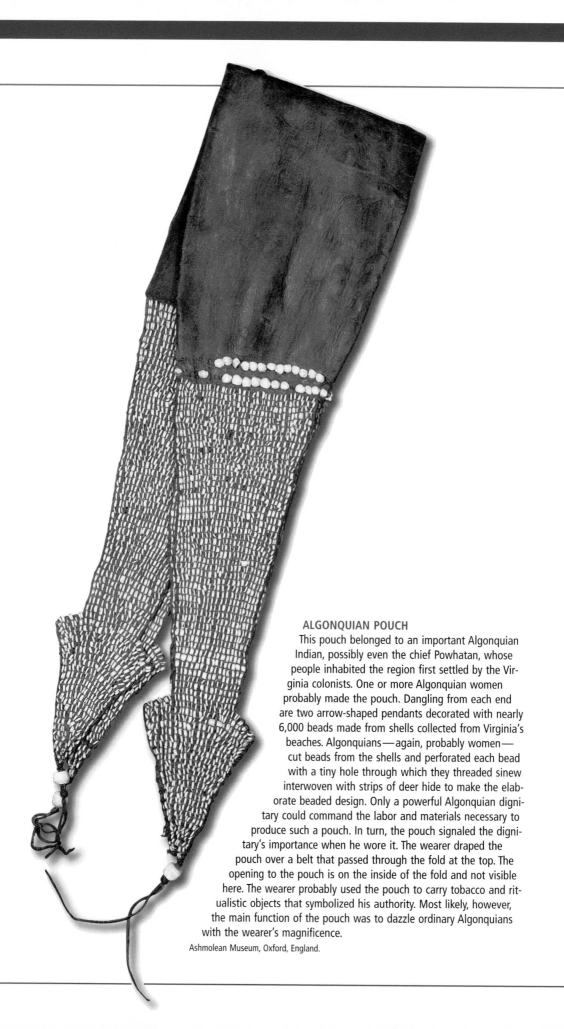

ALGONQUIAN POUCH

This pouch belonged to an important Algonquian Indian, possibly even the chief Powhatan, whose people inhabited the region first settled by the Virginia colonists. One or more Algonquian women probably made the pouch. Dangling from each end are two arrow-shaped pendants decorated with nearly 6,000 beads made from shells collected from Virginia's beaches. Algonquians—again, probably women—cut beads from the shells and perforated each bead with a tiny hole through which they threaded sinew interwoven with strips of deer hide to make the elaborate beaded design. Only a powerful Algonquian dignitary could command the labor and materials necessary to produce such a pouch. In turn, the pouch signaled the dignitary's importance when he wore it. The wearer draped the pouch over a belt that passed through the fold at the top. The opening to the pouch is on the inside of the fold and not visible here. The wearer probably used the pouch to carry tobacco and ritualistic objects that symbolized his authority. Most likely, however, the main function of the pouch was to dazzle ordinary Algonquians with the wearer's magnificence.

Ashmolean Museum, Oxford, England.

The Southern Colonies in the Seventeenth Century

1601–1700

I N DECEMBER 1607, barely six months after arriving at Jamestown with the first English colonists, Captain John Smith was captured by warriors of Powhatan, the supreme chief of about fourteen thousand Algonquian people who inhabited the coastal plain of present-day Virginia, near the Chesapeake Bay. According to Smith, Powhatan "feasted him after their best barbarous manner." Then, after the chief consulted with his men, "two great stones were brought before Powhatan: then as many [Indians] as could layd hands on [Smith], dragged him to [the stones], and thereon laid his head, and being ready with their clubs, to beate out his braines." At that moment, Pocahontas, Powhatan's eleven-year-old daughter, rushed forward and "got [Smith's] head in her armes, and laid her owne upon his to save him from death." Pocahontas, Smith wrote, "hazarded the beating out of her owne braines to save mine, and . . . so prevailed with her father, that I was safely conducted [back] to James towne."

This romantic story of an Indian maiden rescuing a white soldier and saving not only his life but also Jamestown and ultimately English **colonization** of North America has been enshrined in the writing of American history since 1624 when Smith published his *Generall Historie of Virginia* and was even dramatized in a Disney movie. Historians believe that this episode actually happened more or less as Smith described it. But Smith did not understand why Pocahontas acted as she did. Many commentators have claimed that her love for Smith caused her to rebel against her father's authority. Pocahontas herself left no document that explains her motives; most likely, she could not write. Everything known about her comes from the pens of Smith or other Englishmen. When their writings are considered in the context of what is known about the Algonquian society Pocahontas was born into, her actions appear in an entirely different light.

When Pocahontas intervened to save Smith, she almost certainly was a knowing participant in an Algonquian ceremony that expressed Powhatan's supremacy and his ritualistic adoption of a subordinate chief, or *werowance.* Most likely, what Smith interpreted as Pocahontas's saving him from certain death was instead a ceremonial enactment of Powhatan's willingness to incorporate Smith and the white strangers at Jamestown into Powhatan's empire. The ceremony displayed Powhatan's power of life or death over a subordinate chief—Smith—and Powhatan's willingness to give protection to those who acknowledged his supremacy—in this case, the interlopers at Jamestown. By appearing to save Smith, Pocahontas was probably acting out Smith's new status as an adopted member of Powhatan's extended family. Rather than a rebellious, love-struck girl, Pocahontas was almost certainly a dutiful daughter playing the part prescribed for her by her father and her culture.

Smith went back to England about two years after the adoption ritual. In the meantime, Pocahontas frequently visited the English settlement and often brought gifts of food to the colonists from her father. Powhatan routinely at-

Pocahontas in England

Shortly after Pocahontas and her husband John Rolfe arrived in England in 1616, an engraver made this portrait of her dressed in English clothing suitable for a princess. The portrait captures the dual novelty of England for Pocahontas and of Pocahontas for the English. Ornate, courtly clothing probably signified to English observers that Pocahontas was royalty and to Pocahontas that the English were accepting her as befitted the "Emperor" Powhatan's daughter. The mutability of Pocahontas's identity is displayed in the engraving's identification of her as "Matoaka" or "Rebecca."

Library of Congress.

tached his sons and daughters to subordinate tribes as an expression of his protection and his dominance. It appears that Pocahontas's attachment to the English colonists grew out of Powhatan's attempt to treat the tribe of white strangers at Jamestown as he did other tribes in his empire, an attempt that failed.

In 1613, after relations between Powhatan and the English colonists had deteriorated into bloody raids by both parties, the colonists captured Pocahontas and held her hostage at Jamestown. Within a year she converted to Christianity and married one of the colonists, a widower named John Rolfe. After giving birth to a son, Thomas, Pocahontas, her husband, and the new baby sailed for England in the spring of 1616. There, promoters of the Virginia colony dressed her as a proper Englishwoman and arranged for her to meet dignitaries. She even went to a ball attended by the English king and queen.

When John Smith heard that Pocahontas was in London, he went to see her. According to Smith, Pocahontas said, "You did promise Powhatan what was yours should bee his, and he the like to you; you called him father, being in his land a stranger, and by the same reason so must I doe you." It seems likely that Pocahontas understood what was happening to her in England as a counterpart to the adoption ritual Powhatan had staged for John Smith in Virginia back in 1607.

Pocahontas died in England in 1617. Her son, Thomas, ultimately returned to Virginia, and by the time of the American Revolution his descendants numbered in the hundreds. But the world Thomas Rolfe and his descendants inhabited was shaped by a reversal of the power ritualized when his mother "saved" John Smith. By the end of the seventeenth century, Native Americans were far from vanquished, but—unlike Powhatan—they no longer dominated the newcomers who arrived in the Chesapeake with John Smith.

During the seventeenth century, English colonists learned how to deviate from the example of New Spain (see chapter 2) by growing tobacco, a crop Native Americans had cultivated in small quantities for centuries. The new settlers, however, grew enormous quantities of tobacco, far more than they could smoke, chew, or sniff themselves, and they exported most of it to England. Instead of incorporating Powhatan's people into their new society, the settlers encroached on lands surrounding the Chesapeake

Bay that had supported ancient Americans for millennia, and they built new societies on the foundation of tobacco agriculture and transatlantic trade.

To produce large crop surpluses for export required hard labor and people who were willing—or could be forced—to do it. For the most part, Native Americans refused to be conscripted into the colonists' fields. Instead, the settlers depended on the labor of family members, **indentured servants**, and, by the last third of the seventeenth century, African slaves. By the end of the century, the southern colonies had become sharply different both from the world dominated by Powhatan when the Jamestown settlers first arrived and from contemporary English society. In ways unimaginable to Powhatan, Pocahontas, or John Smith, the colonists paid homage to the international market and the English monarch by working mightily to make a good living growing crops for sale to the Old World.

An English Colony on the Chesapeake

When James I became king of England after the death of Queen Elizabeth I in 1603, he eyed North America as a possible location for colonies. Spain claimed all of North America under the 1494 Treaty of Tordesillas (see chapter 2), but Spain's claim meant little if it could not be defended. King James had reason to believe England could encroach on the outskirts of Spain's New World empire. In 1588, England had defeated the Spanish Armada, a large fleet of warships sent to invade England and bring it under Spanish rule. England's success in defending itself from this Spanish attack suggested that England might now succeed in defending new colonies in North America. And English colonies might well become enormously profitable, just as Spain's New World empire had proved for more than a century to be profitable for Spain.

In 1606, a number of "knightes, gentlemen, merchauntes, and other adventurers of our cittie of London" organized the Virginia Company, a joint stock company. English merchants had used joint stock companies for many years to pool capital and share risks in trading voyages to Europe, Asia, and Africa. The Virginia Company

Secotan Village

This engraving, published in 1612, was copied from an original drawing John White made in 1585 when he visited the village of Secotan on the coast of North Carolina. The drawing provides a schematic view of daily life in the village, which may have resembled one of Powhatan's settlements. White noted on the original that the fire burning behind the line of crouching men was "the place of solemne prayer." The large building in the lower left was a tomb where the bodies of important leaders were kept. Dwellings similar to those illustrated on John Smith's map of Virginia lined a central space, where men and women ate. Corn is growing in the fields along the right side of the village. The engraver included hunters shooting deer at the upper left. Hunting was probably never so convenient—no such hunters or deer appear in White's original drawing. This drawing conveys the message that Secotan was orderly, settled, religious, harmonious, and peaceful (notice the absence of fortifications), and very different from English villages.

Princeton University Libraries, Department of Rare Books and Special Collections.

FOR MORE HELP ANALYZING THIS IMAGE, see the visual activity for this chapter in the Online Study Guide at bedfordstmartins.com/roark.

had ambitions larger than trade. The company petitioned King James for permission to establish a colony in North America. The king complied, giving the company over six million acres extending inland from the Atlantic coast. In effect, the king's **land grant** to the Virginia Company was a royal license to poach on both Spanish claims and Powhatan's chiefdom.

The investors in the Virginia Company hoped to found an empire that would strengthen England both overseas and at home. Richard Hakluyt, a strong proponent of colonization, claimed that a colony would provide work for swarms of poor "valiant youths rusting and hurtfull by lack of employment" in England. Jobless Englishmen could find work in the colony, producing goods that England now had to import from other nations. They could also provide a ready colonial market for English manufactured goods. More trade and more jobs would benefit many people in England, but the main reason the Virginia Company investors were willing to risk their capital in Virginia was their fervent hope for quick profits.

Investors did not know exactly how they could make money in Virginia. Enthusiastic reports from the Roanoke voyages twenty years earlier (see chapter 2) declared that in Virginia "the earth bringeth foorth all things in aboundance, as in the first creation, without toile or labour." Even if these reports exaggerated, investors reasoned, maybe some valuable exotic crop could be grown profitably in this Eden. Maybe the apparently limitless forests could be tapped to produce pitch and tar, essentials for watertight ships. Or maybe rich lodes of gold and silver awaited discovery, as they had in New Spain. Gold and silver that did not need to be discovered nestled in the holds of Spanish ships that cruised up the Atlantic coast to catch the trade winds that would take them home. Virginia Company investors dreamed about the quick and easy profits they could reap from an occasional raid on these Spanish treasure ships. One way or another, the new colony promised to reward the company's investors. Or so they thought. They failed to appreciate the difficulties of adapting European desires and expectations to the New World environment, especially the Native Americans who already inhabited the region. Within two decades, the struggling Jamestown settlement managed to survive in unexpected ways, and royal government replaced the private Virginia Company, which never earned a penny for its investors.

The Fragile Jamestown Settlement

In December 1606, the ships *Susan Constant*, *Discovery*, and *Godspeed* carried 144 Englishmen toward Virginia. They arrived at the mouth of the Chesapeake Bay on April 26, 1607. That night while the colonists rested on shore, one of them later recalled, a band of Indians "creeping upon all foure, from the Hills like Beares, with their Bowes in their mouthes," attacked and dangerously wounded two men. The attack gave the colonists an early warning that the North American wilderness was not quite the paradise described by the Virginia Company's publications in England. On May 14, they went ashore on a small peninsula in the midst of Powhatan's chiefdom. With the memory of their first night in America fresh in their minds, they quickly built a fort, the first building in the settlement they named Jamestown. (See "American Places," page 73.)

The Jamestown fort showed the colonists' awareness that they needed to protect themselves from Indians and Spaniards. Spain employed spies to stay informed about the new English colony. Spain planned to wipe out Jamestown when the time was ripe, but that time never came. Powhatan's people defended Virginia as their own. During May and June 1607, the settlers and Powhatan's warriors skirmished repeatedly. English muskets and cannon repelled Indian attacks on Jamestown, but the Indians' superior numbers and knowledge of the Virginia wilderness made it risky for the settlers to venture far beyond the peninsula. Late in June, Powhatan sensed a stalemate and made peace overtures.

The settlers soon confronted dangerous, invisible threats: disease and starvation. During the summer, many of the Englishmen lay "night and day groaning in every corner of the Fort most pittiful to heare," wrote George Percy, one of the settlers. By September, 50 of the colonists had died. "Our men were destroyed with cruel diseases [such] as Swellings, Fluxes, [and] Burning Fevers," Percy recalled. The colonists increased their misery by bickering among themselves, leaving crops unplanted and food supplies shrinking. "For the most part [the settlers] died of meere famine," Percy wrote; "there were never Englishmen left in a forreigne Countrey in such miserie as wee were in this new discovered Virginia."

Powhatan's people came to the rescue of the weakened and demoralized Englishmen. Early

Jamestown, Virginia

The first colonists chose the site for Jamestown in 1607 because it seemed defensible. Located about thirty miles up the James River from the open waters of the Chesapeake Bay, the site offered protection against surprise attack by marauders from Spain. A small island separated from the mainland promised protection against Indian attacks and a convenient escape route down the James River, should escape become necessary. Quickly, the colonists built a triangular fort and mounted artillery at the corners in order, George Percy wrote, to make "our selves sufficiently strong for these Savages." Although colonists ventured outside the fort to explore, trade with Indians, plant crops, and eventually to live, the fort remained a well-entrenched safe haven for Jamestown's early inhabitants.

At first, the Jamestown settlers held religious services under an old ship's sail stretched between several trees. Inside their fort they soon erected a wooden church, "a homely thing like a barn," John Smith observed. When that church burned in 1608, the colonists put up another wooden structure, where Pocahontas and John Rolfe solemnized their marriage. Between 1617 and 1619, Jamestown residents built a larger wooden church on a foundation of big cobblestones still visible in the floor of the church shown here. Twenty years later, prosperous planters funded the replacement of the wooden structure with a new brick church, which included the tower visible at the right end of the church in the photo. In September 1676, during Bacon's Rebellion, the rebels burned down the brick church, but the tower survived. It stood for the next two centuries until it was incorporated into the present-day church. Today, the church tower is the only seventeenth-century building at Jamestown.

Fire and decay eventually eliminated every visible sign of the original fort. Since 1994, careful archaeological excavations have uncovered the outlines of the fort and many other structures. Under the surface of the soil, archaeologists found unmistakable evidence of the wooden posts that made up the walls of the fort. And jumbled together in and around the fort were numerous **artifacts** the early settlers lost or tossed away.

Today, visitors to Jamestown can see the site of the original fort and watch the continuing archaeological investigations. Exhibits display examples of armor and weapons used by the colonists, pipes they smoked, coins they spent, and dishes that held their food. At least as revealing as the many fascinating archaeological finds is the swampy, heavily wooded natural environment that surrounds Jamestown. On a stroll, bicycle ride, or drive through the wilderness around Jamestown, visitors can imagine what this strange new land must have looked like to the early colonists.

For Web links related to this site and other American Places, see "PlaceLinks" at bedfordstmartins.com/roark.

Jamestown Church
The Association for the Preservation of Virginia Antiquities.

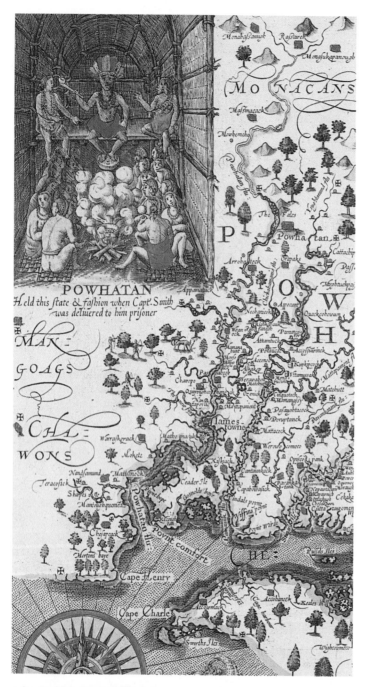

John Smith's Map of Virginia
In 1612, John Smith published a detailed map that showed not only geographic features of early Virginia but also the limits of exploration (indicated by small crosses), the locations of the houses of the Indian "kings" (indicated by dwellings that look like Quonset huts), and "ordinary houses" of indigenous people (indicated by dots). The map shows the early settlers' intense interest in knowing where the Indians were—and were not. Notice the location of Jamestown (upriver from Point Comfort) and of Powhatan's residence at the falls (just to the right of the large *P* outside the hut in the upper left corner). The drawing of Powhatan surrounded by some of his many wives (upper left corner) was almost certainly made by an English artist who had never been to Virginia or seen Powhatan but tried to imagine the scene as described by John Smith.

Princeton University Libraries, Department of Rare Books and Special Collections.

in September 1607, they began to bring corn to the colony for barter. When that was insufficient to keep the colonists fed, the settlers sent Captain John Smith to trade (and plunder) for corn with Indians upriver from Jamestown. His efforts managed to keep 38 of the original settlers alive until a fresh supply of food and 120 more colonists arrived from England in January 1608.

It is difficult to exaggerate the fragility of the early Jamestown settlement. Although the Virginia Company sent hundreds of new settlers to Jamestown each year, few survived. During the "starving time" winter of 1609–10, food became so short that one or two famished settlers resorted to eating their recently deceased neighbors. When a new group of colonists arrived in 1610, they found only about 60 of the 500 previous settlers still alive. When told they might be taken back to England, the survivors responded with "a general acclamation, and shoutte of joy," an observer wrote. The Virginia Company continued to pour people into the colony, promising in a 1609 pamphlet that "the place will make them rich." But most settlers went instead to an early grave.

Cooperation and Conflict between Natives and Newcomers

Powhatan's people stayed in contact with the English settlers but maintained their distance. The Virginia Company boasted that the settlers bought from the Indians "the pearles of earth [corn] and [sold] to them the pearles of heaven [Christianity]." In fact, few Indians converted to Christianity, and the English devoted scant effort to proselytizing. Marriage between Indian women and English men was also rare, despite the acute shortage of English women in Virginia in the early years. Few settlers other than John Smith troubled to learn the Indians' language. His notes on the Indians' vocabulary show that settlers quickly adopted the Virginia Algonquian words *tomahawk* and *moccasin*. It is safe to speculate that few English words entered Powhatan's vocabulary, given the distance the Indians maintained.

Powhatan's people regarded the English with suspicion, for good reasons. While the settlers often made friendly overtures to the Indians, they did not hesitate to use their guns and swords to enforce English notions of proper Indian behavior. More than once the Indians refused to trade their corn to the settlers, evidently hoping to starve them out. Each time the English broke the boycott by attacking the uncooperative Indians, pillaging their villages, and confiscating their corn.

Powhatan's people retaliated against English violence, but for fifteen years they did not organize an all-out assault on the European intruders, probably for several reasons. Although Christianity held few attractions for the Indians, the power of the settlers' God impressed them. One chief told John Smith that "he did believe that our [English] God as much exceeded theirs as our guns did their bows and arrows." Powhatan probably concluded that these powerful strangers would make better allies than enemies. As allies, the English strengthened Powhatan's dominance over the tribes in the region. They also traded with his people, usually exchanging European goods for corn. Native Virginians had some copper weapons and tools before the English arrived, but they quickly recognized the superiority of the intruders' iron and steel knives, axes, and pots and traded eagerly to obtain them.

The trade that supplied Indians with European conveniences provided English settlers with a necessity: food. But why did the settlers prove unable to feed themselves for more than a decade? First, as the staggering death rate suggests, many settlers were too sick to be productive members of the colony. Second, very few farmers came to Virginia in the early years. Instead, most of the newcomers were gentlemen and their servants, men who, in John Smith's words, "never did know what a day's work was." The proportion of gentlemen in Virginia in the early years was six times greater than in England, a reflection of the Virginia Company's urgent need for investors and settlers. In a 1610 pamphlet, the company declared that nobody should think that Virginia "excludeth Gentlemen . . . for though they cannot digge, use the square, nor practise the axe and chizell, yet [they know] . . . how to employ the force of knowledge, the exercise of counsel, the operation and power of their best breeding and qualities." In Virginia breeding and quality proved worthless for growing corn, catching fish, or even hunting deer. John Smith declared repeatedly that in Virginia "there is no country to pillage [as in New Spain] . . . all you can expect from [Virginia] must be by labor." For years, however, colonists clung to English notions that gentlemen should not work with their hands and tradesmen should work only in trades for which they had been trained,

John Smith's Dictionary of Powhatan's Language

In 1612, John Smith published this list of the English equivalents of words used by Powhatan's people, almost the only record of the coastal Algonquian language that exists. Smith probably compiled this list by pointing and listening carefully. Can you find any of Powhatan's words that made their way into common English usage? What do the words in the list suggest about Smith's encounters with Powhatan's people? What interested Smith? What compelled the interest of his informants?

Princeton University Libraries, Department of Rare Books and Special Collections.

Becauſe many doe deſire to know the manner of their Language, I haue inſerted theſe few words.

KA katorawincs yowo. What call you this.
Nemarough, a man.
Crenepo, a woman.
Marowancheſſo, a boy.
Yehawkans, Houſes.
Matchcores, Skins, or garments.
Mockaſins, Shooes.
Tuſſan, Beds. *Pokatawer,* Fire.
Attawp, A bow. *Attonce,* Arrowes.
Monacookes, Swords.
Aumouhhowgh, A Target.
Pawcuſſacks, Gunnes.
Tomahacks, Axes.
Tockahacks, Pickaxes.
Pamcſacks, Kniues.
Accowprets, Sheares.
Pawpecones, Pipes. *Mattaſſin,* Copper
Uſſawaſſin, Iron, Braſſe, Silver, or any white mettall. *Muſſes,* Woods.
Attaſſkuſſ, Leaues, weeds, or graſſe.
Chepſin, Land. *Shacquohocan.* A ſtone.
Wepenter, A cookold.
Suckahanna, Water. *Noughmaſſ,* Fiſh.
Copotone, Sturgeon.
Weghſhaughes, Fleſh.
Sawwehone, Bloud.
Netoppew, Friends.
Marrapough, Enemics.
Maskapow, the worſt of the enemies.
Mawchick chammay, The beſt of friends
Caſacunnakack, peya quagh acquintan vttaſantaſough, In how many daies will there come hither any more Engliſh Ships.
Their Numbers.
Necut, 1. *Ningh,* 2. *Nuſſ,* 3. *Yowgh,* 4.
Paranske, 5. *Comotinch,* 6. *Toppawoſſ,* 7
Nuſſwaſh, 8. *Kekatawgh,* 9. *Kaskeke* 10
They count no more but by tennes as followeth.
Caſe, how many.
Ningh ſapooeksku, 20.
Nuſſapooeksku, 30.

Yowghapooeksku, 40.
Parankeſta ſapoockſku, 50.
Comatinchta ſapoockſku, 60.
Nuſſwaſhta ſſapooekſku, 70.
Kekataughta ſapooekſku, 80.
Necuttoughtyſinough, 100.
Necuttwevnquaough, 1000.
Rawcoſowghs, Dayes.
Keſkowghes, Sunnes:
Toppqunough. Nights.
Nepawweſhowghs, Moones.
Pawpaxſoughes, Yeares.
Pummahumps, Starres.
Oſies, Heavens.
Okees, Gods.
Quiyoughcoſoughs, Pettie Gods, and their affinities.
Righcomoughes, Deaths.
Kekughes, Liues.
Mowchick woyawgh tawgh noeragh kaquere mecher, I am very hungry ? what ſhall I eate ?
Tawnor nehiegh Powhatan, Where dwels Powhatan.
Mache, nehiegh yourowgh, Orapaks. Now he dwelsa great way hence at Orapaks.
Vittapitchewayne anpechitchs nehawper Werowacomoco, You lie, he ſtaid ever at Werowacomoco.
Kator nehiegh mattagh neer vttapitchewayne, Truely he is there I doe not lie.
Spaughtynere keragh werowance mawmarinough kekate wawgh peyaquaugh. Run you then to the King Mawmarynough and bid him come hither.
Vtteke, e peya weyack wighwhip, Get you gone, & come againe quickly.
Kekaten Pokahontas patiaquagh ningh tanks manotyens neer mowchick rawrenock audowgh, Bid Pokahontas bring hither two little Baskets, and I will giue her white Beads to make her a Chaine. *FINIS.*

Trade Goods

These objects excavated from the site of early Jamestown illustrate the trade between the settlers and Powhatan's people. Colonists desperately needed the Indians' corn to survive. To trade for corn, settlers had to have a surplus of something the Algonquians desired. The Indians wanted firearms, but the struggling colonists could ill afford to increase the Indians' military strength. Instead, the colonists tried to appeal to the Indians' interest in items for decoration and display. Jamestown residents often traded cheap glass beads like the one shown here (top left). Made in Venice, Italy, this colorful bead incorporated sophisticated techniques of glassmaking unknown to Indians; they readily used such glass beads as substitutes for the shell beads they had made so laboriously for centuries. Algonquians used copper before the arrival of Europeans, but their supplies were limited and difficult to obtain, as Jamestown settlers quickly learned. Colonists cut their own sheets of copper into shapes desired by the Indians for jewelry, like the triangular copper ornament at bottom left, pierced for easy attachment. As colonists learned more about Indians' fashions, they began to craft items like the bone pendant shown here (bottom, center). To our eyes, it looks as if it were made by Indians, but iron file marks along the edges are strong evidence that English settlers made the pendant, using materials and designs familiar to the Indians. In modern language, the pendant reflects the results of Jamestown settlers' market research about what Algonquians would accept in exchange for corn. The pottery shards are from an Indian clay pot that probably contained corn English settlers received for their trade goods.

The Association for the Preservation of Virginia Antiquities.

ideas about labor that made more sense in labor-rich England than in labor-poor Virginia. In the meantime, the colonists depended on the Indians' corn for food. (See "The Promise of Technology," page 78.)

The persistence of the Virginia colony, precarious as it was, created difficulties for Powhatan's chiefdom. Steady contact between natives and newcomers spread European viruses among the Indians, who suffered deadly epidemics in 1608 and between 1617 and 1619. The settlers' insatiable appetite for corn introduced other tensions within Powhatan's villages. Producing enough corn for both survival and trade with the English made agriculture, which was women's work, more important for Indians. But from the Indians' viewpoint, the most important fact about the Virginia colony was that it was surviving, barely.

Powhatan died in 1618, and his brother Opechancanough replaced him as supreme

Wolf Head Pendant

A Susquehanna man probably wore this pendant suspended from the deer hide necklace (dyed red) extending from the back of the wolf head. The Native American who made the pendant in the mid-seventeenth century took the jawbone and teeth of a wolf and skillfully stitched them into a head shaped from deer hide stuffed with deer hair, taking care to display the wolf's menacing teeth. Inside the wolf's jaws, the maker sewed a realistic tongue (not visible in the picture) made of blue cloth obtained in trade with European colonists. Whether a wolf's tongue crafted from a European textile conveyed Susquehanna interpretation of words spoken by Europeans is unknown.

Courtesy, Skokloster Castle, Uppland, Sweden.

chief. In 1622, Opechancanough organized an all-out assault on the English settlers. Striking on March 22, the Indians killed 347 settlers, nearly a third of the English population. But the attack failed to dislodge the colonists. In the aftermath, the settlers unleashed a murderous campaign of Indian extermination that in a few years pushed Indians beyond the small circumference of white settlement. Before 1622, the settlers knew that the Indians, though dangerous, were necessary to keep the colony alive. After 1622, most colonists considered Indians their perpetual enemies.

From Private Company to Royal Government

The 1622 uprising came close to achieving Opechancanough's goal of pushing the colonists back into the Atlantic—so close that it prompted a royal investigation of affairs in Virginia. The investigators discovered that the appalling mortality among the colonists was caused more by disease and mismanagement than by Indian raids. In 1624, King James revoked the charter of the Virginia Company and made Virginia a royal colony, subject to the direction of the royal government rather than to the company's private investors, an arrangement that lasted until 1776.

The king now appointed the governor of Virginia and his council, but most other features of local government established under the Virginia Company remained intact. In 1619, for example, the company had inaugurated the House of Burgesses, an assembly of representatives (called burgesses) elected by the colony's inhabitants. (Historians do not know exactly which settlers were considered inhabitants and were thus qualified to vote.) Under the new royal government, laws passed by the burgesses had to be approved by the king's bureaucrats in England rather than by the company. Otherwise,

Advertisement for Jamestown Settlers
While Virginia imported thousands of indentured servants to labor in tobacco fields, the colony advertised in 1631 for settlers like those pictured here. The notice features men and women equally, although men heavily outnumbered women among actual newcomers to the Chesapeake. How would the English experiences of the individuals portrayed in the advertisement be useful in Virginia? Why would such individuals want to leave England and go to Virginia? If indentured servants were pictured, how might they differ in appearance from these people?
Harvard Map Collection, Pusey Library, Harvard University.

Corn, the "Life-Giver"

Europeans first learned about corn from Columbus. As soon as he returned to Spain in 1493, he told the royal court about amazing things he had seen on his voyage to the other side of the Atlantic, including a plant he called maize, his version of *mahiz*, the Taino word for corn, which meant "life-giver." Ancient Americans had been growing corn for about seven thousand years. From its origin in central Mexico, corn had spread throughout the Western Hemisphere by the time Columbus arrived. Although the rest of the world had never seen or heard of corn, within a generation after 1493 travelers carried seeds throughout the Old World. By the early sixteenth century, corn seeds had sprouted in Europe, the Middle East, Africa, India, and China.

Accustomed to growing wheat and eating foods derived from it, Europeans at first did not like corn. A few years before the settlers arrived in Jamestown, an English botanist expressed the common European view that "the barbarous Indians which know no better, are constrained to make a vertue of necessitie, and think [corn is] a good food; whereas we may easily judge that it nourisheth but little, and is of hard and evill digestion, a more convenient foode for swine than for man."

Early in the seventeenth century, English settlers in North America discovered that hunger quickly made a virtue of necessity. John Smith wrote that during the spring of 1609 Jamestown residents became so hungry that "they would have sould their soules" for a half-basket of Powhatan's corn. Before settlers could reliably subsist in the Chesapeake region, they had to learn the technology of corn.

From the perspective of the twenty-first century, it may seem odd to speak of the technology of corn. Today, we tend to think that the word *technology* refers only to machinery such as engines, computer chips, or airplanes. But it also refers to a much broader range of human experience involving the use of knowledge for practical purposes. Nowadays, technological knowledge has found countless practical uses for corn as food, sweetener, and oil, as well as in such products as medicines, tires, batteries, and lipstick. The roots of these modern-day uses of corn stretch back to ancient Americans who first developed the technology of growing, processing, and consuming corn, a technology English settlers of North America sought to learn for the practical purpose of eating.

Corn needs help to grow. If you bury an ear of corn in the soil, the seeds that sprout will strangle each other in an overcrowded quest for light. But if you strip the husk from a ripe ear of corn, rub the seeds out of the cob, and plant the separated seeds on a spring day in a spot with sufficient heat, light, and water, then during the summer each seed will be capable of producing a stalk with two or more ears, each bearing hundreds of edible corn seeds. An awestruck English visitor described corn's "marveillous great increase; of a thousand, fifteene hundred and some two thousand fold."

To obtain this impressive yield, early-seventeenth-century European settlers throughout North America watched Native Americans cultivate corn. "In place of ploughs" commonly used in England, one observer reported, "they use an instrument of hard wood, shaped like a spade" to break up the soil and prepare it for planting, work

Ancient Corn Popper
Long before movies and microwaves, ancient Americans munched popcorn. This corn popper comes from the Mochica culture, which thrived on the northern coast of Peru for about 600 years after the birth of Christ. The Mochica presumably nestled the popper on a bed of coals with the opening facing up, placed corn inside, and covered the opening with a lid (not shown) while the kernels popped. The Mochica and other ancient Americans did not pop most of the corn they grew. Instead, they ground it into cornmeal, which they used in a wide variety of dishes, probably including ancient counterparts of modern tortillas.
The Field Museum #A112961c, Chicago. Photographer: Diane Alexander Whites.

usually done by men. Then women used a stick to "make a hole [in the soil] wherein they put out four grains . . . And cover them." Another colonist acknowledged that Native Americans were "our first instructors for the planting of their Indian corne, by teaching us to cull out the finest seede, to observe the fittest season, to keepe distance for holes, and fit measure for hills, to worme it, and weede it; to prune it, and dresse it as occasion shall require." Jamestown's early settlers did not depend on chance observations of this planting technology. John Smith boasted that two hostages the colonists captured from Powhatan "taught us how to order and plant our fields" while they were held as "fettered prisoners."

Along with corn, Indians usually planted beans. "When they [beans] grow up they interlace with the corn. . . . And they keep the ground very free from weeds," one newcomer noticed. Ancient Americans' association of beans with corn had a sound biochemical basis. Beans fixed nitrogen in the soil, a function corn roots cannot perform. Corn plants then absorbed the nitrogen to produce higher yields. Beans also made corn more nutritious. Beans contain niacin, an essential nutrient lacking in corn. Together, corn and beans provided the basic ingredients for a healthy diet.

As every popcorn eater knows, corn kernels are hard enough to crack a tooth. European settlers had no difficulty eating green or sweet corn, the immature form of ripening corn commonly consumed today as corn on the cob. But to obtain the nutritious interior of mature corn

Corn God Figurine
This Mayan figurine signals the importance of corn among ancient Americans who lived in present-day Guatemala. Made sometime between 1400 BP and 1100 BP, the figurine shows the corn god dancing in honor of the source of human sustenance, corn.
Museo Nacional de Arqueologia y Etnologia, Guatemala City. Photograph © Justin Kerr.

kernels without cracking their teeth they had to learn ancient American technology. For millennia Native Americans had soaked or boiled corn kernels with wood ash or other alkaline material. The alkali softened and loosened the tough hull protecting the corn's nutrients. Treated in this way, corn kernels that otherwise were rock-hard could be separated from their hulls and readily mashed into dough for tortillas or mixed with beans or other foods in tasty stews. Early colonists copied this process to make the softened corn

foods they called samp, or hominy, or grits.

Since settlers were accustomed to wheat ground into a fine flour, they preferred cornmeal obtained by the much more laborious process of pulverizing corn kernels with a mortar and pestle or grinding them between stones, both processes familiar to Native Americans. From cornmeal dough cooked on an iron griddle or baked in the coals of a cookfire, Europeans made corn bread, corn pone, hoecake, and johnnycake—English names for ancient American food.

Unlike wheat, many varieties of corn pop open when heated, an astonishing trait Columbus duly reported to his Spanish sponsors. **Archaeologists** speculate that ancient Americans first thought to cultivate corn when a few grains accidentally landed in a campfire and out popped a morsel of readily edible food. For millennia, ancient Americans enjoyed popcorn, not least because it so easily avoided the need to soak, boil, or grind hard corn kernels. They also ground popped corn into a nutritious and portable powder that could be mixed with water and other foods for a satisfying meal. The New England minister Roger Williams wrote that he "made a good dinner and supper" with "a spoonfull of this meale and a spoonfull of water from the brooke." Other colonists, too, learned the ancient technology of popcorn. Today, at the cineplex and on the couch, every American consumes about 50 quarts of popped corn each year, participating—usually unwittingly—in a technology that reaches back in unbroken continuity to a campfire in central Mexico about 7,000 years ago.

the House of Burgesses continued as before, acquiring distinction as the oldest representative legislative assembly in the British colonies. Under the new royal government, all free adult men in Virginia could vote for the House of Burgesses, giving it a far broader and more representative constituency than the English House of Commons.

> All free adult men in Virginia could vote for the House of Burgesses, giving it a far broader and more representative constituency than the English House of Commons.

The demise of the Virginia Company marked the end of the first phase of colonization of the Chesapeake region. From the first 105 adventurers in 1607, the population had grown to about 1,200 by 1624. Despite mortality rates higher than the worst epidemics in London, new settlers still came. Their arrival and King James's willingness to take over the struggling colony reflected a fundamental change in Virginia. After years of fruitless experimentation, it was becoming clear that English settlers could make a fortune in Virginia by growing tobacco.

Tobacco Wrapper
This wrapper labeled a container of "Virginia Planters Best Tobacco." It shows a colonial planter supervising slaves who hold the hoes they use to chop weeds that rob the leafy tobacco plants of nutrients and moisture. The planter enjoys a pipe in the shade of an umbrella held by a slave. After the tobacco was harvested and dried, it was pressed tightly into barrels, like those shown here, for shipment overseas. How does this illustration indicate the differences between the planter and the slaves?
Colonial Williamsburg Foundation.

A Tobacco Society

Tobacco grew wild in the New World, and Native Americans used it for thousands of years before Europeans arrived. *Tobacco* was a Caribbean Indian word that referred to a leaf of the tobacco plant rolled into a cigar-like shape. Indians lit the rolled leaf and inhaled the smoke, a practice Columbus observed in Cuba on his first journey of discovery. Many sixteenth-century European explorers commented on the Indians' odd habit of "drinking smoke." During the sixteenth century, Spanish colonists in the New World sent tobacco to Europe, where it was an expensive luxury used sparingly by a few. During the next century, English colonists in North America sent so much tobacco to European markets that it became an affordable indulgence used often by many people. (See "Beyond America's Borders," page 82.)

Tobacco never featured in the initial plans of the Virginia Company. "As for tobacco," John Smith wrote, "we never then dreamt of it." John Rolfe—Pocahontas's husband-to-be—planted West Indian tobacco seeds in 1612 and learned that they flourished in Virginia. By 1617, the colonists had grown enough tobacco to send the first commercial shipment to England, where it sold for a high price. After that, the same Virginia colonists who had difficulty growing enough corn to feed themselves learned quickly to grow as much tobacco as possible. Virginia pivoted from a colony of rather aimless adventurers into a society of dedicated tobacco **planters**.

Dedicated they were. In 1620, with fewer than a thousand colonists, Virginia shipped 60,000 pounds of tobacco to England. By 1700, nearly 100,000 colonists lived in the Chesapeake region (encompassing Virginia, Maryland, and northern North Carolina), and they exported over 35 million pounds of tobacco. Per capita tobacco exports grew fivefold during the century, demonstrating that Chesapeake colonists had mastered the demands of tobacco agriculture. To a large degree, the "Stinkinge Weede" (a seventeenth-century Marylander's term for tobacco) also mastered the colonists. Settlers lived by the rhythms of tobacco agriculture, and their endless need for labor attracted droves of English indentured servants to work in Chesapeake tobacco fields (Map 3.1).

Tobacco Agriculture

A demanding crop, tobacco required close attention and a great deal of hand labor year-round. Colonists sowed the tiny seeds in the spring, transplanted the sprouts, and hoed around the growing plants all summer while carefully grooming the plants to produce marketable leaves. Early in the fall when the leaves began to yellow, colonists cut down the plants and strung them up in a shed to dry and cure. The next

spring when the dried leaves became pliable in the moist climate, workers stripped the tobacco leaves from the stalks and packed them tightly into hogsheads (large barrels) for shipment to market. By the time last year's crop was being packed, this year's crop already had to be in the ground.

Primitive tools and methods made this intensive cycle of labor taxing. Like the Indians, colonists "cleared" fields by cutting a ring of bark from trees (a procedure known as *girdling*), thereby killing them. Girdling brought sunlight to clearings but left fields studded with tree stumps, making the use of plows impractical. Instead, colonists tilled their tobacco fields with heavy hoes, one hoe-chop at a time. To plant, a visitor observed, colonists "just make holes [with a stick] into which they drop the seeds," much as the Indians did. Because colonists also

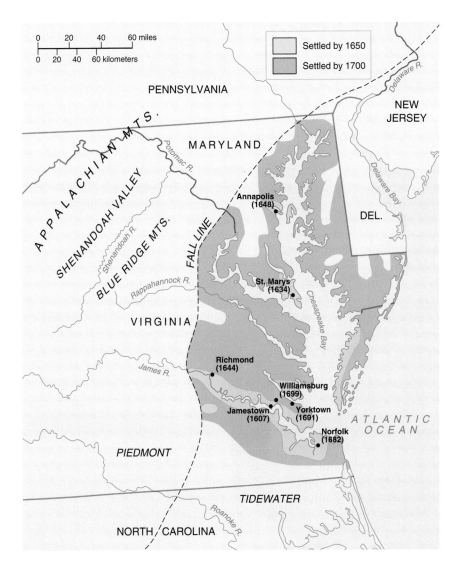

MAP 3.1 The Chesapeake Colonies in the Seventeenth Century

The intimate association between land and water in the settlement of the Chesapeake in the seventeenth century is illustrated by this map. The fall line indicates the limit of navigable water, where rapids and falls prevented further upstream travel. Although Delaware had excellent access to navigable water, it was claimed and defended by the Dutch colony at New Amsterdam (discussed in chapter 4) rather than by the English settlements in Virginia and Maryland shown on this map.

READING THE MAP: Using the notations on the map, create a chronology of the establishment of towns and settlements. What physical features correspond to the earliest habitation by English settlers?

CONNECTIONS: Why was access to navigable water so important? Given the settlers' need for defense against native tribes, what explains the distance between settlements?

FOR MORE HELP ANALYZING THIS MAP, see the map activity for this chapter in the Online Study Guide at bedfordstmartins.com/roark.

American Tobacco and European Consumers

English colonies in the Chesapeake were "wholly built upon smoke," King Charles I remarked. The king's shrewd comment highlighted the fundamental reason why the seventeenth-century Chesapeake colonies prospered by growing ever-increasing crops of tobacco: because people on the eastern side of the Atlantic were willing to buy ever-increasing quantities of tobacco to smoke—and to sniff, chew, and drink, and even to use for enemas. Europeans' desire for tobacco was the only reason it had commercial value. If Europeans had considered tobacco undesirable, the history of both the British North American colonies and the rest of the world would have been very different.

Some Europeans did hate tobacco, England's King James I foremost among them. In *A Counterblaste to Tobacco*, a pamphlet published in 1611, James declared that smoking was "A custome lothsome to the eye, hatefull to the Nose, harmefull to the braine, dangerous to the Lungs, and in the blacke stinking fume thereof, neerest resembling the horrible . . . smoke of the pit that is bottomelesse." James pulled out all the stops in attacking smoking. "What honour or policie can moove us to imitate the barbarous and beastly manners of the wilde, godlesse, and slavish *Indians*, especially in so vile and stinking a custome?" he asked. "Why doe we not as well imitate them in walking naked as they doe? in preferring glasses, feathers, and such toyes, to golde and precious stones, as they do? yea why do we not denie God and adore the Devill, as they doe?" James reviled the "filthy smoke," the "stinking Suffumigation," the "spitting," the "lust," the "shameful imbecilitie," and the "sin" of tobacco. James's fulminations acknowledged that "the

Tobacco Cutter
Tobacconists in Europe used this machine to chop tobacco leaves into small pieces. Then they often flavored the chopped tobacco with oils, herbs, and spices much as coffeehouse baristas today add hazelnut, mocha, or vanilla flavors to lattes and cappucinos. The picture on the side of the cutter refers to the Native American origins of the tobacco processed by the cutter's screws, clamps, and blades.
Niemeyer Nederlands Tabacologisch Museum.

generall use of Tobacco" was "daily practiced . . . by all sorts and complexions of people." He noted, "The publike use [of tobacco], at all times, and in all places, hath now so farre prevailed that a man cannot heartily welcome his friend now, but straight they must bee in hand with *Tobacco*. . . . It is become . . . a point of good fellowship, and he that will refuse to take a pipe of *Tobacco* among his fellows . . . is accounted peevish and no good company." Clearly, James championed a lost cause.

When Spaniards first brought tobacco to Europe during the sixteenth century, physicians praised it as a wonder drug. One proclaimed that "to seek to tell the virtues and greatness of this holy herb, the ailments which can be cured by it, and have been, the evils from which it has saved thousands would be to go on to infinity . . . this precious herb is so general a human need [that it is] not only for the sick but for the healthy." Such strong recommendations from learned men were reinforced by everyday experiences of commoners. Sailors returning from the New World "suck in as much smoke as they can," one Spaniard observed, "[and] in this way they say that their hunger and thirst are allayed, their strength is restored and their spirits are refreshed; [and] . . . their brains are lulled by a joyous intoxication." That joyous intoxication—"a bewitching quality" King James called it—made tobacco irresistible to most Europeans. And, as we know all too well today, the bewitching intoxication of tobacco was highly addictive.

Feeding that habit was expensive at the beginning of the seventeenth century because tobacco was scarce. In 1603, for example, England imported only about 25,000

Smoking Club

In Europe, tobacco smokers congregated in clubs to enjoy the intoxicating weed. This seventeenth-century print satirizes smokers' promiscuous gatherings of fashionable men, women, and children who indulged their taste for tobacco. Emblems of the tobacco trade adorn the wall; pipes, spittoons, and other smoking implements are close at hand; and the dog cleans up after those who cannot hold their smoke.

Koninklijke Bibliotheek, The Hague.

pounds of tobacco, all from New Spain. By 1700, England imported nearly 40 million pounds of tobacco, almost all from the Chesapeake colonies. The huge increase in tobacco supply caused prices to plummet. A quantity of tobacco that sold for a dollar in 1600 cost less than two and a half cents by 1700.

The low prices made possible by bumper crops harvested by planters in the Chesapeake transformed tobacco consumption in England and elsewhere in Europe. Per capita tobacco use in England grew over 200-fold during the seventeenth century, from less than a fifth of an ounce in the 1620s to 2.3 pounds by 1700. American tobacco became the first colonial product of mass consumption by Europeans, blazing a trail followed by New World sugar, coffee, and chocolate.

Tobacco altered European culture. It spawned new industries, new habits, and new forms of social life. Smoking was the most common form of tobacco consumption in the seventeenth century, and smokers needed far more than tobacco to light up. They needed pipes, and hundreds of pipe makers supplied them with millions of ceramic pipes. They needed boxes or tins to hold their tobacco and a container to hold the embers they used to light the tobacco, or a flint and steel to strike sparks; they needed pipe cleaners; they needed spittoons if they were smoking in a respectable place that disapproved of spitting on the floor. European merchants and manufac-

turers supplied all these needs, along with tobacco itself, which had to be graded, chopped, flavored, packaged, stored, advertised, and sold. Men and women smoked in taverns, in smoking clubs, around dinner tables, and in bed. A visitor to London noted that tobacco was not only in "frequent use . . . at every hour of the day but even at night [smokers] keep the pipe and steel at their pillows and gratify their longings."

The somewhat cumbersome paraphernalia of smoking caused many tobacco users to shift to snuff, which became common in the eighteenth century. Snuff use eliminated smoke, fire, and spitting with the more refined arts of taking a pinch of powdered, flavored tobacco from a snuffbox and sniffing it into one or both nostrils, which produced a fashionable sneeze followed by a genteel wipe with a dainty handkerchief. Sneezing induced by snuff was considered not only fashionable but healthful. One snuff taker explained that "by its gently pricking and stimulating the membranes, [snuff] causes Sneezing or Contractions, whereby the Glands like so many squeezed Sponges, dismiss their Seriosities and Filth."

Whether consumed by smoking, by sniffing, or in other ways, tobacco profoundly changed European habits, economies, and societies. It is no exaggeration to conclude that planters, servants, and eventually slaves in the Chesapeake made it possible for Europeans to become hooked on tobacco.

BIBLIOGRAPHY

Jordan Goodman, *Tobacco in History: The Cultures of Dependence* (1993).

Jason Hughes, *Learning to Smoke: Tobacco Use in the West* (2003).

Joseph C. Winter, *Tobacco Use by Native North Americans: Sacred Smoke and Silent Killer* (2000).

had to grow food crops in the midst of the tobacco production cycle, there was little time for idleness. But in spare moments, they enjoyed the fruits of their labor. One traveler reported that "Everyone smokes while working or idling . . . men, women, girls, and boys, from the age of seven years."

English settlers worked hard because their labor promised greater rewards in the Chesapeake region than in England. One colonist proclaimed that "the dirt of this Province affords as great a profit to the general Inhabitant, as the Gold of Peru doth to . . . the Spaniard." Although he exaggerated, it was true that a hired man could expect to earn two or three times more in Virginia tobacco fields than in England. Better still, in Virginia land was so abundant that it was extremely cheap, compared to land in England. By the mid-seventeenth century, common laborers could buy a hundred acres for less than their annual wages—an impossibility in England. New settlers who paid their own transportation to the Chesapeake received a grant of fifty acres of free land (termed a *headright*). The Virginia Company initiated the headright policy to encourage settlement, and the royal government continued it for the same reason.

A Servant Labor System

Headrights, cheap land, and high wages gave poor English folk powerful incentives to immigrate to the New World. Yet many potential immigrants could not scrape together the fare to cross the Atlantic. Their poverty and the colonists' crying need for labor formed the basic context for the creation of a servant labor system.

Today, people think of the colonial South as a slave society. The seventeenth-century Chesapeake region, however, was fundamentally a servant society. Twenty Africans arrived in Virginia in 1619, and they probably were enslaved, although scanty records make it impossible to be certain. For the next fifty years, however, only a small number of slaves labored in Chesapeake tobacco fields. (Large numbers of slaves came in the eighteenth century, as chapter 5 explains.) About 80 percent of the immigrants to the Chesapeake during the seventeenth century were indentured servants. Along with tobacco, servants profoundly influenced nearly every feature of Chesapeake society.

> The seventeenth-century Chesapeake region was fundamentally a servant society.

To buy passage aboard a ship bound for the Chesapeake, an English immigrant had to come up with about £5, roughly a year's wages for an English servant or laborer. Saving a year's wages was no easier then than it is now. The purchasing power of wages was declining because England's population was growing faster than its food supply, causing prices to rise. Earning wages at all was difficult since job opportunities were shrinking. Many country gentlemen needed fewer farmhands because they fenced fields they had formerly planted with crops and began to pasture sheep in the enclosures. Unemployed people drifted into seaports like Bristol, Liverpool, and London, where they learned about the plentiful jobs in North America.

Unable to pay for their trip across the Atlantic, poor immigrants agreed to a contract called an *indenture*. In effect, an indenture functioned as a form of credit. By signing an indenture, an immigrant borrowed the cost of transportation to the Chesapeake from a merchant or ship captain in England. To repay this loan, the indentured person agreed to work as a servant for four to seven years in North America. Once the indentured person arrived in the colonies, the merchant or ship captain sold his right to the immigrant's labor to a local tobacco planter. To obtain the servant's labor, the planter paid about twice the cost of transportation and agreed to provide the servant with food and shelter during the term of the indenture. When the indenture expired, the planter owed the former servant "freedom dues," usually a few barrels of corn and a suit of clothes.

Ideally, indentures allowed poor immigrants to trade their most valuable assets—their freedom and their ability to work—for a trip to the New World and four to seven years of servitude followed by freedom in a land of opportunity. Planters reaped more immediate benefits. Servants meant more hands to grow more tobacco. As one Virginian declared, "our principall wealth . . . consisteth in servants." For every newly purchased servant, planters also received a headright of fifty acres of land from the colonial government. Since a planter expected a servant to grow enough tobacco in one year to cover the price the planter paid for the indenture, the next three to six years of the indenture promised a handsome profit for the planter. But roughly half of all servants became sick and died before serving out their indentures, reducing planters' gains.

About three out of four servants were men, the great majority between the ages of fifteen and twenty-five when they arrived in the Chesapeake. Typically they shared the desperation of sixteen-year-old Francis Haires, who indentured himself for seven years because "his father and mother and All friends [are] dead and he [is] a miserable wandering boy." Like Francis, most servants had no special training or skills, although the majority had some experience with agricultural work. "Hunger and fear of prisons bring to us onely such servants as have been brought up to no Art or Trade," one Virginia planter complained. A skilled craftsman could obtain a shorter indenture, but few risked coming to the colonies since their prospects were better at home.

Women were almost as rare as skilled craftsmen in the Chesapeake and more ardently desired. In the early days of the tobacco boom, the Virginia Company shipped young single women servants to the colony as prospective wives for male settlers willing to pay "120 weight [pounds] of the best leaf tobacco for each of them," in effect getting both a wife and a servant. The company reasoned that, as one official wrote in 1622, "the plantation can never flourish till families be planted, and the respect of wives and children fix the people on the soil." The company's efforts as a marriage broker proved no more successful than its other ventures. Women remained a small minority of the Chesapeake population until late in the seventeenth century. The servant labor system perpetuated the gender imbalance. Although female servants cost about the same as males and generally served for the same length of time, only about one indentured servant in four was a woman. Planters preferred male servants for fieldwork, although many servant women hoed and harvested tobacco fields. Most women servants also did household chores such as cooking, washing, cleaning, gardening, and milking.

Servant life was harsh by the standards of seventeenth-century England and even by the **frontier** standards of the Chesapeake. Unlike servants in England, Chesapeake servants had no control over who purchased their labor—and thus them—for the period of their indenture. Many servants were bought and sold several times before their indenture expired. A Virginia servant protested in 1623 that his master "hath sold me for £150 sterling like a damnd slave." A ship captain reported in 1625 that "servants were sold here [in Virginia] upp and downe like

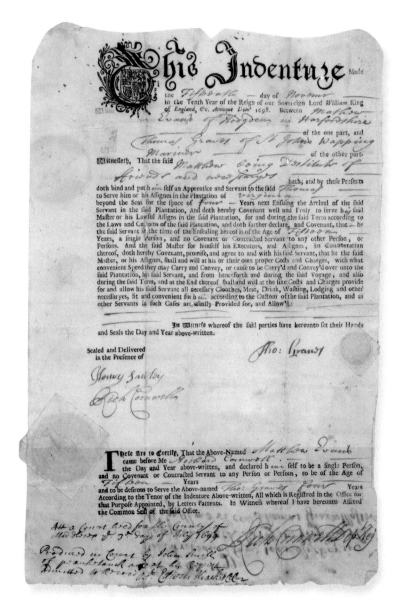

Indenture Contract
Indenture contracts were so common that forms were printed with blank spaces for details to be written in. In mid-November 1698, fifteen-year-old Matthew Evans, a friendless boy from Harfordshire, agreed to serve mariner Thomas Graves, or anybody to whom Graves sold his rights, for four years in Virginia. The contract specifies that Graves will carry Evans to Virginia and provide during the term of the indenture "all necessary Cloathes, Meat, Drink, Washing, Lodging and other necessaryes, fit and convenient for him according to the Custom of the said Plantation, as other Servants in such Cases are usually Provided for. . . ."
The Library of Virginia.

horses." But tobacco planters' need for labor muffled such qualms about treating servants as property.

Some former servants argued that indentured servitude had advantages, despite its rigors. But most found otherwise. James Revel, an

Tobacco Plantation
This print illustrates the processing of tobacco on a seventeenth-century plantation. Workers cut the mature plants and put the leaves in piles to wilt (left foreground and center background). After the leaves dry somewhat, they are suspended from poles in a drying barn (right foreground), where they are seasoned before being packed in casks for shipping. Sometimes, tobacco leaves are left to dry in the fields (center background). The print suggests the labor demands of tobacco by showing twenty-two individuals, all but two of them actively at work with the crop. The one woman, hand in hand with a man in the left foreground, may be on her way to work, on the harvested leaves, but it is more likely that she and the man are overseeing the labor of their servants or employees.
From "About Tobacco," Lehman Brothers.

eighteen-year-old thief who was punished by being indentured to a Virginia tobacco planter, described experiences common to most servants. In verse, Revel chronicled what happened when he arrived at his new master's plantation:

My Europian clothes were took from me,
Which never after I again could see.
A canvas shirt and trowsers then they gave,
With a hop-sack frock in which I was to slave:
No shoes nor stockings had I for to wear,
Nor hat, nor cap, both head and feet were bare.
Thus dress'd into the Field I next must go,
Amongst tobacco plants all day to hoe,
At day break in the morn our work began,
And so held to the setting of the Sun.

Severe laws aimed to keep servants in their place. Punishments for petty crimes stretched servitude far beyond the original terms of indenture. Christopher Adams, for example, had to serve three extra years for running away for six months. Richard Higby received six extra years of servitude for killing three hogs. After midcentury, the Virginia legislature added three or more years to the indentures of most servants by requiring them to serve until they were twenty-four years old.

Women servants were subject to special restrictions and risks. They were prohibited from marrying until their servitude had expired. A servant woman, the law assumed, could not serve two masters at the same time: one who owned her indentured labor and another who was her husband. However, the predominance of men in the Chesapeake population inevitably pressured women to engage in sexual relations. The pressure was strong enough that about a third of immigrant women were pregnant when they got married. Pregnancy and childbirth sapped a woman's strength, and a new child diverted her attention, reducing her usefulness to her master. As a rule, if a woman servant gave birth to a child, she had to serve two extra years and pay a fine. However, for some servant women, premarital pregnancy was a path out of servitude: The father of an unborn child sometimes purchased the indenture of the servant mother-to-be, freed, and married her.

Such punishments reflected four fundamental realities of the servant labor system. First, planters' hunger for labor caused them to demand as much labor as they could get from their servants, including devising legal ways to extend the period of servitude. Second, servants hoped to survive their servitude and use their freedom to obtain land and start a family. Third, servants' hopes frequently conflicted with planters' demands. Since servants saw themselves as free people in a temporary status of servitude, they often made grudging, half-hearted workers. Finally, both servants and planters put up with this contentious arrangement because the alternatives were less desirable.

Planters could not easily hire free men and women because land was readily available and free people preferred to work on their own land, for themselves. Nor could planters depend on much labor from family members. The preponderance of men in the population meant that families were few, were started late, and thus had few children. And, until the 1680s and 1690s, slaves were expensive and hard to come by. Before then, masters who wanted to expand their labor force and grow more tobacco had few alternatives to buying indentured servants.

Cultivating Land and Faith

Villages and small towns dotted the rural landscape of seventeenth-century England, but in the Chesapeake acres of wilderness were interrupted here and there by tobacco farms. Tobacco was such a labor-intensive crop that one field-worker could tend only about two acres of the plants in a year (an acre is slightly smaller than a football field), plus a few more acres for food crops. A successful farmer needed a great deal more land, however, because tobacco quickly exhausted the fertility of the soil. Since each farmer cultivated only 5 or 10 percent of his land at any one time, a "settled" area comprised swatches of cultivated land surrounded by forest. Arrangements for marketing tobacco also contributed to the dispersion of settlements. Tobacco planters sought land that fronted a navigable river in order to minimize the work of transporting the heavy hogsheads of tobacco onto ships. A settled region thus resembled a lacework of farms stitched around waterways.

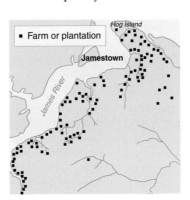

Settlement Patterns along the James River

Most Chesapeake colonists were nominally **Protestants**. Attendance at Sunday services and conformity to the doctrines of the Church of England were required of all English men and women. Few clergymen migrated to the Chesapeake, however, and too few of those who did come were models of righteousness and piety. Certainly some colonists took their religion seriously. Church courts punished fornicators, censured blasphemers, and served notice on parishioners who spent Sundays "goeing a fishing." But on the whole, religion did not awaken the zeal of Chesapeake settlers, certainly not as it did the New England settlers in these same years (see chapter 4). What quickened the pulse of most Chesapeake folk was a close horse race, a bloody cockfight, or—most of all—an exceptionally fine tobacco crop. The religion of the Chesapeake colonists was Anglican, but their faith lay in the turbulent, competitive, high-stakes gamble of survival as tobacco planters.

The situation was similar in the Catholic colony of Maryland. In 1632, England's King Charles I granted his Catholic friend Lord Baltimore about six and a half million acres in the northern Chesapeake region. In return, the king specified that Lord Baltimore pay him the token rent of "two Indian arrowheads" a year. Lord Baltimore intended to create a refuge for Catholics, who suffered severe discrimination in England. He fitted out two ships, the *Ark* and the *Dove*, gathered about 150 settlers, and sent them to the new colony, where they arrived on March 25, 1634. However, Maryland failed to live up to Baltimore's hopes. The colony's population grew very slowly for twenty years, and most settlers were Protestants rather than Catholics. The religious turmoil of the **Puritan** Revolution in England (discussed in chapter 5) spilled across the Atlantic, creating conflict between Maryland's few Catholics—most of them wealthy and prominent—and the Protestant majority, most of them neither wealthy nor prominent. During the 1660s, Maryland began to attract settlers as readily as Virginia, mostly Protestants. Although Catholics and the Catholic faith continued to exert influence in Maryland, the colony's society, economy, politics, and culture became nearly indistinguishable from Virginia's. Both colonies shared a devotion to tobacco, the true faith of the Chesapeake.

> The religion of the Chesapeake colonists was Anglican, but their faith lay in the turbulent, competitive, high-stakes gamble of survival as tobacco planters.

The Evolution of Chesapeake Society

The system of indentured servitude sharpened inequality in Chesapeake society by the mid-seventeenth century, propelling social and political polarization that culminated in 1676 with Bacon's Rebellion. The rebellion prompted reforms that stabilized relations between elite planters and their lesser neighbors and paved the way for a social hierarchy based less overtly on land and wealth than on race. (See "Historical Question," page 90.) Amid this social and political evolution, one thing did not change: the dedication of Chesapeake colonists to growing tobacco.

Social and Economic Polarization

The first half of the seventeenth century in the Chesapeake was the era of the **yeoman**—a farmer who owned a small plot of land sufficient to support a family and tilled largely by servants and a few family members. A small number of elite planters had larger estates and commanded ten or more servants. But for the first several decades, few men lived long enough to accumulate a fortune sufficient to set them much apart from their neighbors. Until midcentury, the principal division in Chesapeake society was less between rich and poor planters than between free farmers and unfree servants. While these two groups contrasted sharply in their legal and economic status, their daily lives had many similarities. Servants looked forward to the time when their indentures would expire and they would become free and eventually own land. On the whole, a rough, frontier equality characterized free families in the Chesapeake until about 1650.

Three major developments splintered that equality during the third quarter of the century. First, as planters grew more and more tobacco, the ample supply depressed tobacco prices in European markets. Cheap tobacco reduced planters' profits and made it more difficult for freed servants to save enough to become landowners. Second, because the mortality rate in the Chesapeake colonies declined, more and more servants survived their indentures, and landless freemen became more numerous and grew more discontented. Third, declining mortality also encouraged the formation of a planter elite. By living longer, the most successful planters compounded their success. The wealthiest planters also began to serve as merchants, marketing crops for their less successful neighbors, importing English goods for sale, and giving credit to hard-pressed customers.

By the 1670s, the society of the Chesapeake had become polarized. Landowners—the planter elite and the more numerous yeoman planters—clustered around one pole. Landless colonists, mainly freed servants, gathered at the other. Each group eyed the other with suspicion and mistrust. For the most part, planters saw land-

less freemen as a dangerous rabble rather than as fellow colonists with legitimate grievances. Governor William Berkeley feared the political threat to the governing elite posed by "six parts in seven [of Virginia colonists who] . . . are poor, indebted, discontented, and armed."

Government Policies and Political Conflict

In general, government and politics amplified the distinctions in Chesapeake society. The most vital distinction separated servants and masters, and the colonial government enforced it with an iron fist. Poor men like William Tyler complained that "nether the Governor nor Counsell could or would doe any poore men right, but that they would shew favor to great men and wronge the poore." Most Chesapeake colonists, like most Europeans, assumed that "great men" should bear the responsibilities of government. Until 1670, all freemen could vote, and they rou-

Governor William Berkeley
This portrait illustrates the distance that separated Governor Berkeley and the other Chesapeake grandees from poor planters, landless freemen, servants, and slaves. Berkeley's clothing suited the genteel interiors of Jamestown, not the rustic dwellings of lesser Virginians. His haughty, satisfied demeanor suggests his lack of sympathy for poor Virginians, who, he was certain, deserved their lot.
Courtesy of Berkeley Castle Charitable Trust, Gloucestershire.

tinely elected prosperous planters to the legislature. No former servant served in either the governor's council or the House of Burgesses after 1640. Yet Tyler and other poor Virginians believed that the "great men" used their government offices to promote their selfish personal interests, rather than governing impartially.

As discontent mounted among the poor during the 1660s and 1670s, colonial officials tried to keep political power in safe hands. Beginning in 1661, for example, Governor Berkeley did not call an election for the House of Burgesses for fifteen years. In 1670, the House of Burgesses outlawed voting by poor men, permitting only men who headed a household and were landowners to vote.

In 1660, the king also began to tighten the royal government's control of trade and to collect substantial revenue from the Chesapeake. The 1660 Navigation Act required all tobacco and other colonial products to be sent only to English ports. The act supplemented laws of 1650 and 1651 that specified that colonial goods had to be transported in English ships with predominantly English crews. A 1663 law stipulated that all goods sent to the colonies must pass through English ports and be carried in English ships by English sailors. Together, these navigation acts were designed to funnel the colonial import trade exclusively into the hands of English merchants and shippers. The navigation acts reflected the English government's **mercantilist** assumptions about the colonies: What was good for England should determine colonial policy.

These mercantilist assumptions also underlay the import duty on tobacco inaugurated by the 1660 Navigation Act. The law assessed an import tax of two pence on every pound of colonial tobacco brought into England, about the price a Chesapeake tobacco farmer received. The tax gave the king a major financial interest in the size of the tobacco crop. During the 1660s, these tobacco import taxes yielded about a quarter of all English customs revenues.

Inside a Poor Planter's House
The houses of seventeenth-century Chesapeake settlers were typically "earthfast": The structural timbers that framed the house were simply placed in holes in the ground, and the floor was packed dirt. No seventeenth-century house was substantial enough to survive until today. This photo shows a carefully documented historical reconstruction of the interior of a poor planter's house at St. Mary's City, Maryland. The wall of this one-room dwelling with a loft features a window with a shutter but no glass; when the shutter was closed, the only source of light was a candle or a fire. Notice the rustic, unfinished bench, table, and walls. These meager furnishings were usually accompanied by a storage chest and some bedding but not a bed. If and when planters became more prosperous, a bed was likely to be their first acquisition, suggesting that the lack of a good night's sleep was one of their major discomforts.
Image courtesy of Historic St. Mary's City.

Bacon's Rebellion

Colonists, like residents of European monarchies, accepted social hierarchy and inequality as long as they believed government officials ruled for the general good. When rulers violated that precept, ordinary people felt justified in rebelling. In 1676, Bacon's Rebellion erupted as a dispute over Virginia's Indian policy. Before it was over, the rebellion convulsed Chesapeake politics and society, leaving in its wake death, destruction, and a legacy of hostility between the great planters and their poorer neighbors.

Opechancanough, the Algonquian chief who had led the Indian uprising of 1622 in Virginia, mounted another surprise attack in 1644

Why Did English Colonists Consider Themselves Superior to Indians and Africans?

Were seeds of the racial prejudice that has been such a powerful force in American history planted in the seventeenth-century Chesapeake? To answer that question, historians have paid close attention to the language colonists used to describe Indians, Africans, and themselves.

In the mid-1500s, the English adopted the words *Indian* and *Negro* from Spanish, where they had come to mean, respectively, an aboriginal inhabitant of the New World and a black person of African ancestry. Both terms were generic, homogenizing an enormous diversity of tribal affiliations, languages, and cultures. Neither term originated with the people to whom it referred. The New England minister Roger Williams, who published a book on Indian languages in 1643, reported, "They have often asked mee, why we call them Indians," a poignant question that reveals the European origins of the term.

After *Indians*, the word the settlers used most frequently to describe Native Americans was *savages*. The Indians were savages in the colonists' eyes because they lacked the traits of English civilization. As one Englishman put it in 1625, the natives of Virginia were "so bad a people, having little of humanitie but shape, ignorant of Civilitie, of Arts, of Religion; more brutish than the beasts they hunt, more wild and unmanly than that unmanned wild countrey, which they range rather than inhabite; captivated also to Satans tyranny in foolish pieties, mad impieties, wicked idlenesse, busie and bloudy wickednesse." Some English colonists counterbalanced this harsh indictment with admiration for certain features of Indian behavior. They praised Indians' calm dignity and poise, their tender love and care for family members, and their simple, independent way of life in apparent harmony with nature.

Color was not a feature of the Indians' savagery. During the seventeenth century, colonists never referred to Indians as "red." Instead, they saw Indians' skin color as tawny or tanned, the "Sun's livery," as one settler wrote. Many settlers held the view that Indians were innately white like the English but in other ways woefully un-English.

Despite their savagery in English eyes, Indians controlled two things colonists desperately wanted: land and peace. Early in the seventeenth century, when English settlements were small and weak, peace with Indians was a higher priority than land. In this period, English comments on Indian savagery noted the obvious differences between settlers and Indians, but the colonists' need for peace kept them attuned to ways to coexist with Indians. By the middle of the seventeenth century, as colonial settlements grew and the desire for land increased, violent conflict with Indians erupted repeatedly. The violence convinced settlers that the only way to achieve both land and peace was to eliminate Indians, either by killing them or pushing them far away from colonial settlements. Colonists' convictions about Indians' savagery became the justification for chronic violence against Indians. English assumptions of their superiority to savage Indians gave a gloss of respectability to colonists' relentless grab of Indian lands.

The colonists identified Africans quite differently. Only a few Africans lived in the Chesapeake early in the seventeenth century. The first recorded arrival of Africans occurred in 1619, when a Dutch man-of-war brought to Virginia "20. and odd Negroes," as John Rolfe wrote. Rolfe's usage illustrates the colonists' most common term for Africans: *Negroes*. But the other word the colonists frequently used to refer to Africans was not *savage* or *heathen* but *black*. What struck English colonists most forcefully about Africans was not their un-English ways but their un-English skin color.

Black was not a neutral color to the colonists. According to the *Oxford English Dictionary* (which catalogs the changing meaning of words), *black* meant to the English people who settled the Chesapeake "deeply stained with dirt; soiled, dirty, foul . . . having dark or deadly purposes, malignant; pertaining to or involving death, deadly; baneful, disastrous, sinister . . . foul, iniqui-

Katarina, "Moorish Woman"
Albrecht Dürer, one of the foremost artists of the Renaissance, drew this portrait of Katarina early in the sixteenth century. It is among the first portraits of Africans made in Renaissance Europe. Katarina was the servant of a Portuguese merchant whom Dürer visited in the Netherlands in the spring of 1521. The portrait was completed before the Atlantic slave trade had begun to boom, but well after Portuguese merchants had brought thousands of African slaves to Europe. Dürer's meticulous portrait betrays no trace of racial prejudice. Katarina wears European clothing and is depicted with the same respect and dignity Dürer accorded Europeans whose likenesses he drew. In what ways might this portrait have been different if it had been executed by an artist in the southern colonies of North America in the late seventeenth century?
Foto Marburg / Art Resource, NY.

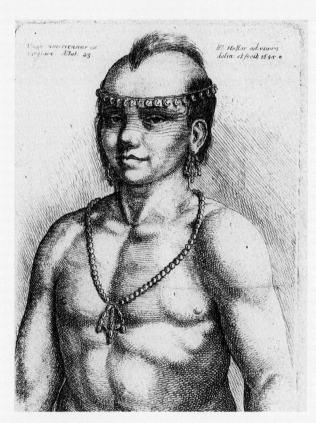

A Young Virginian
In 1645, the Dutch artist Wenceslaus Hollar drew this portrait of a twenty-three-year-old Indian man from Virginia. The young man had evidently been brought to London, where he posed for this likeness. Hollar portrayed the exotic adornment of the man—the animal claw headband, shell earrings and necklace, facial markings, Mohawk haircut, and bare-chested torso. Yet these distinctly non-European features did not cause Hollar to compromise his humane, dignified depiction of this man, whose gaze seems to be fixed steadily and without shame on the observer. If this young Virginian had been back in the Chesapeake rather than in London, he would probably have been engaged in the deadly warfare triggered by Opechancanough's 1644 uprising. How might this portrait have been different if it had been drawn by a Virginia colonist in 1645?
© Copyright The British Museum.

tous, atrocious, horrible, wicked." Black was the opposite of white, which connoted purity, beauty, and goodness—attributes the colonists identified with themselves. By the middle of the seventeenth century, the colonists referred to themselves

not only as English but also as free, implying that people who were not English were not free. After about 1680, colonists often stated that implication in racial terms by referring to themselves as white. By the end of the seventeenth century, blacks were

triply cursed in English eyes: un-English, un-white, and un-free.

A few Englishmen dissented from such views. Thomas Phillips, a slave ship captain, declared in 1694

(continued)

(continued)

that he could not "imagine why they [blacks] should be despis'd for their colour, being what they cannot help, and the effect of the climate it has pleas'd God to appoint them. I can't think there is any intrinsick value in one colour more than another, nor that white is better than black, only we think it so because we are so, and are prone to judge favourably in our own case, as well as the blacks, who in odium of the colour, say, the devil is white, and so paint him." But these observations did not prevent Phillips or other colonists from enslaving Africans for their labor.

Virginians did not legally define slavery as permanent, lifelong, inherited bondage until 1660. The sparse surviving evidence demonstrates, however, that colonists practiced slavery long before that. Although there is no way to be certain, it is likely that the "20. and odd Negroes" who arrived in 1619 were slaves. And the punishments handed out to blacks who broke the law usually took for granted that their servitude could not be extended, presumably because they were already in bondage for life, not—like servants—for a limited number of years.

The debasements of slavery strengthened colonists' prejudice toward blacks, while racial prejudices buttressed slavery. A Virginia law of 1662, for instance, provided that "if any christian shall committ Fornication with a negro man or woman, hee or shee soe offending" had to pay a double fine. The law also demonstrates that, despite racial prejudices, sexual relations between white and black settlers were prevalent enough to attract the attention of the legislature.

For most of the seventeenth century, possession of a black skin did not automatically and necessarily condemn a person to the status of slave in the eyes of whites. Some Africans in the Chesapeake served for limited periods of time like white servants, became free like white servants, and even acquired land, reared families, and participated in local affairs like former white servants. In fact, white colonists' prejudice against blacks echoed wealthy colonists' attitudes toward servants and other poor white people. Masters often considered white servants, like blacks, "the vile and brutish part of mankind."

Colonists' attitudes toward Indians and Africans exaggerated and hardened English notions about social hierarchy, about superiority and inferiority. Colonists' convictions of their own superiority to Indians and Africans justified, they believed, their exploitation of Indians' land and Africans' labor. Those justifications planted the seeds of pernicious racial prejudices that flourished in America for centuries.

and killed about 500 Virginia colonists in two days. During the next two years of bitter fighting, the colonists eventually gained the upper hand, capturing and murdering the old chief. The treaty that concluded the war established policies toward the Indians that the government tried to maintain for the next thirty years. The Indians relinquished all claims to land already settled by the English. Wilderness land beyond the fringe of English settlement was supposed to be reserved exclusively for Indian use. The colonial government hoped to minimize contact between settlers and Indians and thereby maintain the peace.

Had the Chesapeake population remained constant, the policy might have worked. But the number of land-hungry colonists, especially poor, recently freed servants, continued to multiply. In their quest for land, they pushed beyond the treaty limits of English settlement and encroached steadily on Indian land. During the 1660s and 1670s, violence between colonists and Indians repeatedly flared along the advancing frontier. The government, headquartered in the tidewater region near the coast, far from the danger of Indian raids, took steps to calm the disputes and reestablish the peace. Frontier settlers thirsted for revenge against what their leader, Nathaniel Bacon, termed "the protected and Darling Indians." Bacon minced no words about his intention: "Our Design [is] not only to ruine and extirpate all Indians in Generall but all Manner of Trade and Commerce with them." Indians were not the only enemies Bacon and his men singled out. Bacon also urged colonists to "see what spounges have suckt up the Publique Treasure." He charged that "Grandees," or elite planters, operated the government for their private gain, a charge that made sense to many colonists. Bacon crystallized the grievances of the small planters and poor farmers against both the Indians and the colonial rulers in Jamestown.

Hoping to maintain the fragile peace on the frontier in 1676, Governor Berkeley pronounced Bacon a rebel, threatened to punish him for treason, and called for new elections of burgesses who, Berkeley believed, would endorse his get-tough policy. To Berkeley's surprise, the elections backfired. Almost all the old burgesses were voted out of office, their places taken by local leaders, including Bacon. The legislature was now in the hands of minor grandees who, like Bacon, chafed at the rule of the elite planters.

In June 1676, the new legislature passed a series of reform measures known as Bacon's Laws. Among other changes, the laws gave local settlers a voice in setting tax levies, forbade office-holders from demanding bribes or other extra fees for carrying out their duties, placed limits on holding multiple offices, and restored the vote to all freemen. Under pressure, Berkeley pardoned Bacon and authorized his campaign of Indian warfare. But elite planters soon convinced Berkeley that Bacon and his men were a greater threat than Indians.

When Bacon learned that Berkeley had once again branded him a traitor, he declared war against Berkeley and the other grandees. For three months, Bacon's forces fought the Indians, sacked the grandees' plantations, and attacked Jamestown. Berkeley's loyalists retaliated by plundering the homes of Bacon's supporters. The fighting continued until late October, when Bacon unexpectedly died, most likely from dysentery, and several English ships arrived to bolster Berkeley's strength. With the rebellion crushed, Berkeley hanged several of Bacon's allies and destroyed farms that belonged to Bacon's supporters.

The rebellion did not dislodge the grandees from their positions of power. If anything, it strengthened their position. When the king learned of the turmoil in the Chesapeake and its devastating effect on tobacco exports and customs duties, he ordered an investigation. Royal officials replaced Berkeley with a governor more attentive to the king's interests, nullified Bacon's Laws, and instituted an export tax on every hogshead of tobacco as a way of paying the expenses of government without having to obtain the consent of the tightfisted House of Burgesses.

In the aftermath of Bacon's Rebellion, tensions between great planters and small farmers gradually lessened. Bacon's Rebellion showed, a governor of Virginia said, that it was necessary "to steer between . . . either an Indian or a civil war." The ruling elite concluded that it was safer

for colonists to fight Indians rather than each other, and the government made little effort to restrict settlers' encroachment on Indian lands. Tax cuts were another policy welcomed by all freemen. The export duty on tobacco imposed by the king allowed the colonial government to reduce taxes by 75 percent between 1660 and 1700. In the long run, however, the most important contribution to political stability was the declining importance of the servant labor system. During the 1680s and 1690s, fewer servants arrived in the Chesapeake, partly because of improving economic conditions in England. Accordingly, the number of poor, newly freed servants also declined, reducing the size of the lowest stratum of free society. In 1700, as many as one-third of the free colonists still worked as tenants on land owned by others, but the social and political distance between them and the great planters, enormous as it was, did not seem as profound as it had been in 1660. The main reason was that by 1700 the Chesapeake was in the midst of transition to a slave labor system that minimized the differences between poor farmers and rich planters and magnified the differences between whites and blacks.

> Bacon crystallized the grievances of the small planters and poor farmers against both the Indians and the colonial rulers in Jamestown.

Religion and Revolt in the Spanish Borderland

While English colonies in the Chesapeake grew and prospered with the tobacco trade, the northern outposts of the Spanish empire in New Mexico and Florida stagnated. Instead of attracting settlers and growing crops for export, New Mexico and Florida appealed to Spanish missionaries seeking to harvest Indian souls. The missionaries baptized thousands of Indians in Spanish North America during the seventeenth century, but they also planted the seeds of Indian uprisings against Spanish rule.

Few Spaniards came to New Spain's northern borderland during the seventeenth century. Only about 1,500 Spaniards lived in Florida and roughly twice as many inhabited New Mexico. One royal governor complained that "no [Spaniard] comes . . . to plow and sow [crops], but only to eat and loaf." In both colonies, Indians outnumbered Spaniards ten or twenty to one.

Royal officials seriously considered eliminating both colonies because their costs greatly exceeded their benefits. Every three years, oxen pulled a caravan of wagons out of Mexico City crammed with things Spaniards in New Mexico considered necessities, including nails, raisins, oysters, and communion wine. Florida required even larger subsidies because, unlike New Mexico, it housed a garrison of soldiers to menace European interlopers who sought to prey on Spanish ships. The soldiers also protected the missionaries and their faith; Christian crosses even adorned the stirrups on their saddles. Catholic missionaries persuaded the Spanish government that, instead of being losing propositions, the colonies represented golden opportunities to convert heathen Indians to Christianity. Royal officials reasoned that the missionaries' efforts would pacify Indians and be a relatively cheap way to preserve Spanish footholds in North America.

Dozens of missionaries came to Florida and New Mexico, as one announced, to free Indians "from the miserable slavery of the demon and from the obscure darkness of their idolatry." Pueblo Indians in New Mexico and southeastern tribespeople in Florida had to be taught, missionaries believed, that their religious beliefs and rituals were idolatrous devil worship and that their way of life was barbaric. Missionaries followed royal instructions that Indians should be taught "to live in a civilized manner, clothed and wearing shoes . . . [and] given the use of bread and wine and oil and many other essentials of life—bread, linen, horses, cattle, tools, and weapons, and all the rest that Spain has had." In effect, missionaries sought to convert Indians not just into Christians but also into surrogate Spaniards.

Missionaries supervised the building of scores of Catholic churches across Florida and New Mexico. Typically, they conscripted Indian women and men to do the construction labor. Adopting practices common elsewhere in New Spain, missionaries forced Indians both to work and to pay tribute in the form of food, blankets, and other goods. Supported by Indians' coerced labor, missionaries taught Christian doctrines, performed Christian rituals, and celebrated Christian—that is, Spanish—civilization. While missionaries congratulated themselves on the many Indians they converted, their coercive methods subverted their goals. A missionary reported that an Indian in New Mexico asked him, "if we [missionaries] who are Christians caused

so much harm and violence [to Indians], why should they [i.e., Indians] become Christians?"

Indians retaliated repeatedly against Spanish exploitation, but Spaniards suppressed the violent uprisings by taking advantage of the disunity among Indians much as Cortés did in the conquest of Mexico (see chapter 2). In 1680, however, Pueblo Indians organized a unified revolt under the leadership of Popé, who ordered his followers, as one recounted, to "break up and burn the images of the holy Christ, the Virgin Mary, and the other saints, the crosses, and everything pertaining to Christianity." During the Pueblo Revolt, Indians desecrated churches, killed two-thirds of Spanish missionaries, and drove Spaniards out of New Mexico to present-day El Paso, Texas. Spaniards managed to return to New Mexico by the end of the seventeenth century, but only by curtailing missionaries and reducing labor exploitation. Florida Indians never mounted a unified attack on Spanish rule, but they too organized sporadic uprisings and resisted conversion, causing a Spanish official to report by the end of the seventeenth century that "the law of God and the preaching of the Holy Gospel have now ceased."

Toward a Slave Labor System

Spaniards had few qualms about exploiting Indian labor, but European diseases continued to wreak havoc among vulnerable Native Americans. During the sixteenth century, Spaniards and Portuguese supplemented Indian laborers in the New World with enslaved Africans. On this foundation, European colonizers built African slavery into the most important form of coerced labor in the New World. During the seventeenth century, British colonies in the West Indies followed the Spanish and Portuguese examples and developed sugar plantations with slave labor. In the British North American colonies, however, a slave labor system did not emerge until the last quarter of the seventeenth century. During the 1670s, settlers from Barbados brought slavery to the new English mainland colony of Carolina, where the imprint of the West Indies remained strong for decades. In Chesapeake tobacco fields at about the same time, slave labor began to replace servant labor, marking the transition toward a society of freedom for whites and slavery for Africans.

Sugar Mill
This seventeenth-century drawing of a Brazilian sugar mill highlights the heavy equipment needed to extract the juice from sugarcane. A vertical waterwheel turns a large horizontal gear that exerts force on the jaws of the press that squeezes the cane. Workers remove crushed cane from the press and replace it with freshly harvested cane as it is unloaded from an oxcart. Except for the overseer (just to the right of the waterwheel), all of the workers are black, presumably slaves from Africa, as suggested by their clothing. All of the mill workers appear to be men, a hint of the predominance of men among newly imported African slaves.
Musées Royaux des Beaux-Arts de Belgique.

The West Indies: Sugar and Slavery

The most profitable part of the British New World empire in the seventeenth century lay in the Caribbean (Map 3.2). The tiny island of Barbados, colonized in the 1630s, was the jewel of the British West Indies. During the 1640s, Barbadian planters began to grow sugarcane with such success that a colonial official proclaimed Barbados "the most flourishing Island in all those American parts, and I verily beleive in all the world for the production of sugar." Sugar commanded high prices in England, and planters rushed to grow as much as they could. By midcentury, annual sugar exports from the British Caribbean totaled about 150,000 pounds; by 1700, exports reached nearly 50 million pounds.

Sugar transformed Barbados and other West Indian islands. Poor farmers could not afford the expensive machinery that extracted and refined the sugarcane juice. Planters who had the necessary capital to grow sugar got rich. By 1680, the wealthiest Barbadian sugar planters were, on average, four times richer than tobacco grandees in the Chesapeake. The sugar grandees differed from their Chesapeake counterparts in another crucial way: The average sugar baron in Barbados in 1680 owned 115 slaves.

African slaves planted, cultivated, and harvested the sugarcane that made West Indian planters wealthy. Beginning in the 1640s, Barbadian planters purchased thousands of slaves to work their plantations, and the African population on the island mushroomed. During the 1650s, when blacks made up only 3 percent of the Chesapeake population, they had already become the majority on Barbados. By 1700, slaves constituted more than three-fourths of the island's population.

> By 1700, slaves constituted more than three-fourths of the population of Barbados.

For slaves, work on a sugar plantation was a life sentence to brutal, unremitting labor. Slaves had short life expectancies and high death rates. Since slave men outnumbered slave women two to one, few slaves could form families and have children. These grim realities meant that in Barbados and elsewhere in the West Indies, the slave population did not grow by natural reproduction. Instead, planters continually purchased enslaved Africans. Although sugar plantations did not gain a foothold in North America in the seventeenth century, the West Indies nonetheless exerted a powerful influence on the development of slavery in the mainland colonies.

Carolina: A West Indian Frontier

The early settlers of what became South Carolina were immigrants from Barbados. In 1663, a Barbadian planter named John Colleton and a group of seven other men obtained a charter from England's King Charles II to establish a colony south of the Chesapeake and north of the Spanish territories in Florida. The men, known as "proprietors," hoped to siphon settlers from Barbados and other colonies and encourage them to develop a profitable export crop comparable to West Indian sugar and Chesapeake tobacco. Following the Chesapeake example, the proprietors offered headrights of up to 150 acres of land for each settler. In 1670, they established the first permanent English settlement in the colony, on the west bank of the Ashley River just across from the peninsula where the king's namesake city, Charles Towne (later spelled Charleston), was founded (see Map 3.2).

As the proprietors had planned, most of the early settlers were from Barbados. In fact, Carolina was the only seventeenth-century English colony to be settled principally by colonists from other colonies rather than from England. The Barbadian immigrants brought their slaves with them. More than a fourth of the early settlers were slaves, and as the colony continued to attract settlers from Barbados, the black population multiplied. By 1700, slaves made up about

MAP 3.2 The West Indies and Carolina in the Seventeenth Century
Although Carolina was geographically close to the Chesapeake colonies, it was culturally closer to the West Indies in the seventeenth century because its early settlers—both blacks and whites—came from Barbados. South Carolina retained strong ties to the West Indies for more than a century, long after the arrival of many of its subsequent settlers from England, Ireland, France, and elsewhere.

READING THE MAP: Locate English colonies in America and English holdings in the Caribbean. Which European country controlled most of the mainland bordering the Caribbean? Where was the closest mainland English territory?
CONNECTIONS: Why were colonists in Carolina so interested in Barbados? What goods did they export? Describe the relationship between Carolina and Barbados in 1700.

FOR MORE HELP ANALYZING THIS MAP, see the map activity for this chapter in the Online Study Guide at bedfordstmartins.com/roark.

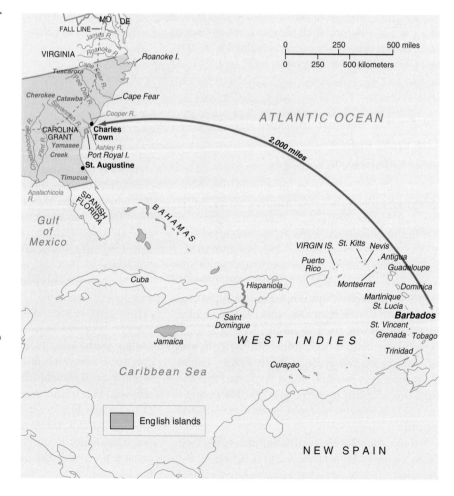

half the population of Carolina. The new colony's close association with Barbados caused English officials to refer routinely to "Carolina in ye West Indies."

The Carolinians experimented unsuccessfully to match their semitropical climate with profitable export crops of tobacco, cotton, indigo, and olives. In the mid-1690s, colonists identified a hardy strain of rice and took advantage of the knowledge of rice cultivation among their many African slaves to build rice plantations. During the first generation of settlement, however, Carolina remained an economic colony of Barbados. Settlers sold livestock and timber to the West Indies. They also exploited another "natural resource": They captured and enslaved several thousand local Indians and sold them to Caribbean planters. Both economically and socially, seventeenth-century Carolina was a frontier outpost of the West Indian sugar economy.

Slave Labor Emerges in the Chesapeake

By 1700, more than eight out of ten people in the southern colonies of British North America lived in the Chesapeake. Until the 1670s, almost all Chesapeake colonists were white people from England. In 1700, however, one out of eight people in the region was a black person from Africa. Although a few blacks had lived in the Chesapeake since the 1620s, the black population increased fivefold between 1670 and 1700 as hundreds of tobacco planters made the transition from servant to slave labor, purchasing slaves rather than servants to work in their tobacco fields. For planters, slaves had several obvious advantages over servants. Although slaves cost three to five times more than servants, slaves never became free. Since the mortality rate had declined by the 1680s, planters could reasonably expect slaves to live longer than a servant's period of indenture. Slaves also promised to be a perpetual labor force, since children of slave mothers inherited the status of slavery.

For planters, slaves had another important advantage over servants: They could be controlled politically. Bacon's Rebellion had demonstrated how disruptive former servants could be when their expectations were not met. A slave labor system promised to avoid the political problems caused by the servant labor system. Slavery kept discontented laborers in permanent servitude, and their color was a badge of their bondage.

Bell of Slave Ship
The English slave ship *Henrietta Marie* sailed from England to the west African coast in 1699, loaded a cargo of slaves, made the **Middle Passage** to the West Indies, where the slaves were sold, then started back to England, but sank with all aboard off the Florida Keys. Centuries later, this bronze bell was recovered from the wreckage.
© 1991 Mel Fisher Maritime Heritage Society, Key West, FL. Photo: Dylan Kibler.

The slave labor system polarized Chesapeake society along lines of race and status: All slaves were black, and nearly all blacks were slaves; almost all free people were white, and all whites were free or only temporarily bound in indentured servitude. Unlike Barbados, however, the Chesapeake retained a vast white majority. Among whites, huge differences of wealth and status still existed. In fact, the emerging slave labor system sharpened the economic differences among whites because only prosperous planters could afford to buy slaves. By 1700, more than three-quarters of white families had neither servants nor slaves. Nonetheless, poor white farmers enjoyed the privileges of free status. They could own property; they could marry, have families, and bequeath their property and their freedom to their descendants; they could move when and where they wanted; they could associate freely with other people; they could serve on juries, vote, and hold political office; and they could work, loaf, and sleep as they chose. Such distinctions between free people and slaves made lesser white folk feel they had a genuine stake in the existence of slavery, even if they did not own a single slave. By emphasizing the privileges of freedom shared by all white people, the slave labor system reduced the tensions between poor folk and grandees that had plagued the Chesapeake region in the 1670s.

In contrast to Barbados, most slaves in the seventeenth-century Chesapeake colonies had frequent and close contact with white people.

> Both economically and socially, seventeenth-century Carolina was a frontier outpost of the West Indian sugar economy.

Slaves and white servants performed the same tasks on tobacco plantations, often working side by side in the fields. For slaves, work on a tobacco plantation was less onerous than on a sugar plantation. But slaves' constant exposure to white surveillance made Chesapeake slavery especially confining. Slaves took advantage of every opportunity to slip away from white supervision and seek out the company of other slaves, "going abroad" to visit slaves on neighboring plantations. Planters often feared that slaves would turn such seemingly innocent social pleasures to political ends, either to run away or to conspire to strike against their masters. Slaves often ran away, but they usually were captured or returned after a brief absence. Despite planters' nightmares, slave insurrections did not occur.

While slavery resolved the political unrest caused by the servant labor system, it created new political problems. By 1700, the bedrock political issue in the Chesapeake was keeping slaves in their place, at the business end of a hoe in a tobacco field. The Chesapeake was developing a slave labor system that stood midway, both geographically and socially, between the sugar plantations and black majority of Barbados to the south and the small farms and homogeneous villages that developed in seventeenth-century New England to the north (see chapter 4).

Conclusion: The Growth of English Colonies Based on Export Crops and Slave Labor

By 1700, the colonies of Virginia, Maryland, and Carolina were firmly established. The staple crops they grew for export provided a livelihood for many, a fortune for a few, and valuable revenues for shippers, merchants, and the English monarchy. Their societies differed markedly from English society in most respects, yet the colonists considered themselves English people who happened to live in North America. They claimed the same rights and privileges as English men and women while they denied those rights and privileges to Native Americans and African slaves.

The English colonies also differed from the example of New Spain. Settlers and servants flocked to English colonies, in contrast to Spaniards who trickled into New Spain. Few English missionaries sought to convert Indians to Protestant Christianity, unlike the numerous Catholic missionaries in New Mexico and Florida. Large quantities of gold and silver never materialized in British North America. English colonists never adopted the system of encomienda (see chapter 2) because Indians were too few and too hostile and their communities too small and decentralized compared with those of the Mexica. Yet forms of coerced labor and racial distinction that developed in New Spain had North American counterparts, as English colonists employed servants and slaves and defined themselves as superior to Indians and Africans.

By 1700, the remnants of Powhatan's people still survived. As English settlement pushed north, west, and south of the Chesapeake Bay, Indians faced the new colonial world that Powhatan and Pocahontas had encountered when John Smith and the first colonists arrived at Jamestown. By 1700, the many descendants of Pocahontas's son, Thomas, as well as other colonists and Native Americans, understood that the English had come to stay.

FOR ADDITIONAL FIRSTHAND ACCOUNTS OF THIS PERIOD, see Chapter 3 in Michael Johnson, ed., *Reading the American Past,* Third Edition.

TO ASSESS YOUR MASTERY OF THE MATERIAL IN THIS CHAPTER, see the Online Study Guide at bedfordstmartins.com/roark.

FOR WEB LINKS RELATED TO THE TOPICS IN THIS CHAPTER, see "HistoryLinks," "DocLinks," and "PlaceLinks" at bedfordstmartins.com/roark.

CHRONOLOGY

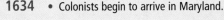

1588 • England defeats Spanish Armada.

1606 • Virginia Company of London receives royal charter to establish colony in North America.

1607 • English colonists found Jamestown settlement; Pocahontas "rescues" John Smith.

1609 • Starvation plagues Jamestown.

1612 • John Rolfe begins to plant tobacco in Virginia.

1617 • First commercial tobacco shipment leaves Virginia for England.
• Pocahontas dies in England.

1618 • Powhatan dies, and Opechancanough becomes supreme chief of the Algonquians.

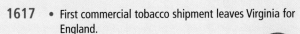

1619 • First Africans arrive in Virginia.
• House of Burgesses begins to meet in Virginia.

1622 • Opechancanough leads Indian uprising against Virginia colonists.

1624 • Virginia becomes royal colony.

1632 • King Charles I grants Lord Baltimore land for colony of Maryland.

1634 • Colonists begin to arrive in Maryland.

1640s • Barbados colonists begin to grow sugarcane with labor of African slaves.

1644 • Opechancanough leads Indian uprising against Virginia colonists.

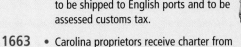

1660 • Navigation Act requires colonial tobacco to be shipped to English ports and to be assessed customs tax.

1663 • Carolina proprietors receive charter from King Charles II for Carolina colony.

1670 • Charles Towne, South Carolina, founded.

1670–1700 • Slave labor system emerges first in Carolina and more gradually in Chesapeake colonies.

1676 • Bacon's Rebellion convulses Virginia, leading eventually to the decline of indentured servitude and the rise of slavery.

1680 • Pueblo Revolt erupts in New Mexico, temporarily pushing Spanish officials out of pueblos.

BIBLIOGRAPHY

Please consult the bibliographies of chapters 2 and 4 for more readings on related topics.

General Works

Kenneth R. Andrews, *Trade, Plunder, and Settlement: Maritime Enterprise and the Genesis of the British Empire* (1984).

David Armitage and Michael Braddick, eds., *The British Atlantic World, 1500–1800* (2002).

James Axtell, *Natives and Newcomers: The Cultural Origins of North America* (2001).

Bernard Bailyn and Philip D. Morgan, eds., *Strangers within the Realm: Cultural Margins of the First British Empire* (1991).

Robert M. Bliss, *Revolution and Empire: English Politics and the American Colonies in the Seventeenth Century* (1990).

Ruth H. Bloch, *Gender and Morality in Anglo-American Culture, 1650–1800* (2003).

Joyce E. Chaplin, *Subject Matter: Technology, the Body, and Science on the Anglo-American Frontier, 1500–1676* (2001).

Linda Colley, *Captives* (2002).

Seymour Drescher and Stanley L. Engerman, eds., *A Historical Guide to World Slavery* (1998).

Betty Fussell, *The Story of Corn* (1992).

Alison Games, *Migration and the Origins of the English Atlantic World* (1999).

Iain Gately, *Tobacco: The Story of How Tobacco Seduced the World* (2001).

Richard Godbeer, *Sexual Revolution in Early America* (2002).

Jack P. Greene and J. R. Pole, eds., *Colonial British America: Essays in the New History of the Early Modern Era* (1984).

Eric Hinderaker and Peter C. Mancall, *At the Edge of Empire: The Backcountry in British North America* (2003).

Winthrop D. Jordan, *White over Black: American Attitudes towards the Negro, 1550–1812* (1968).

Karen Ordahl Kupperman, *Indians and English: Facing Off in Early America* (2000).

John J. McCusker and Russell R. Menard, *The Economy of British America, 1607–1789* (1985).

Edmund S. Morgan, *American Slavery, American Freedom: The Ordeal of Colonial Virginia* (1975).

Mary Beth Norton, *Founding Mothers and Fathers: Gendered Power and the Forming of American Society* (1996).

David Ormrod, *The Rise of Commercial Empires: England and the Netherlands in the Age of Mercantilism, 1650–1770* (2003).

James Walvin, *Fruits of Empire: Exotic Produce and British Trade, 1660–1800* (1997).

Indians

James Axtell, *The Indians' New South: Cultural Change in the Colonial Southeast* (1997).

Philip L. Barbour, *Pocahontas and Her World* (1970).

Kathryn E. Holland Braund, *Deerskins and Duffels: The Creek Indian Trade with Anglo-America, 1685–1815* (1993).

James F. Brooks, *Confounding the Color Line: The Indian-Black Experience in North America* (2002).

Wesley Frank Craven, *White, Red, and Black: The Seventeenth-Century Virginian* (1971).

Robbie Etheridge and Charles Hudson, eds., *The Transformation of the Southeastern Indians, 1540–1760* (2002).

Alan Gallay, *The Indian Slave Trade: The Rise of the English Empire in the American South, 1670–1717* (2002).

Frederic W. Gleach, *Powhatan's World and Colonial Virginia: A Conflict of Cultures* (1997).

Charles Hudson and Carmen Chaves Tesser, eds., *The Forgotten Centuries: Indians and Europeans in the American South, 1521–1704* (1994).

J. A. Leo Lemay, *Did Pocahontas Save Captain John Smith?* (1992).

James H. Merrell, *The Indians' New World: Catawbas and Their Neighbors from European Contact through the Era of Removal* (1989).

Michael Leroy Oberg, *Dominion and Civility: English Imperialism and Native America, 1585–1685* (1999).

Daniel K. Richter, *Facing East from Indian Country: A Native History of Early America* (2001).

Helen C. Rountree, *Pocahontas's People: The Powhatan Indians of Virginia through Four Centuries* (1990).

Helen C. Rountree and E. Randolph Turner III, *Before and after Jamestown: Virginia's Powhatans and Their Predecessors* (2002).

Bernard W. Sheehan, *Savagism and Civility: Indians and Englishmen in Colonial Virginia* (1980).

Timothy Silver, *A New Face on the Countryside: Indians, Colonists, and Slaves in South Atlantic Forests, 1500–1800* (1990).

Jayme A. Sokolow, *The Great Encounter: Native Peoples and European Settlers in the Americas, 1492–1800* (2003).

Peter H. Wood et al., eds., *Powhatan's Mantle: Indians in the Colonial Southeast* (1989).

Chesapeake Society

Stephen Adams, *The Best and Worst Country in the World: Perspectives on the Early Virginia Landscape* (2001).

Edward L. Bond, *Damned Souls in a Tobacco Colony: Religion in Seventeenth-Century Virginia* (2000).

Carl Bridenbaugh, *Jamestown, 1544–1699* (1980).

Kathleen Brown, *Good Wives, Nasty Wenches, and Anxious Patriarchs: Gender, Race, and Power in Colonial Virginia* (1996).

Lois Green Carr et al., *Robert Cole's World: Agriculture and Society in Early Maryland* (1991).

Lois Green Carr et al., eds., *Colonial Chesapeake Society* (1988).

James Deetz, *Flowerdew Hundred: The Archaeology of a Virginia Plantation, 1619–1864* (1993).

James Horn, *Adapting to a New World: English Society in the Seventeenth-Century Chesapeake* (1994).

Ivor Noël Hume, *The Archaeology of Martin's Hundred* (2001).

David W. Jordan, *Foundations of Representative Government in Maryland, 1632–1715* (1987).

Jon Kukla, *Political Institutions in Virginia, 1619–1660* (1989).

Aubrey C. Land et al., eds., *Law, Society, and Politics in Early Maryland* (1977).

Kenneth A. Lockridge, *The Diary, and Life, of William Byrd II of Virginia, 1674–1744* (1987).

Gloria Lund Main, *Tobacco Colony: Life in Early Maryland, 1650–1720* (1982).

Debra Meyers, *Common Whores, Vertuos Women, and Loveing Wives: Free Will Christian Women in Colonial Maryland* (2003).

John Ruston Pagan, *Anne Orthwood's Bastard: Sex and Law in Early Virginia* (2003).

James Perry, *The Formation of a Society on Virginia's Eastern Shore, 1615–1655* (1990).

Jacob M. Price, *Perry of London: A Family and a Firm on the Seaborne Frontier, 1615–1753* (1992).

Darrett B. Rutman and Anita H. Rutman, *A Place in Time: Middlesex County, Virginia, 1650–1750*, 2 vols. (1984).

Terri L. Snyder, *Brabbling Women: Disorderly Speech and the Law in Early Virginia* (2003).

Linda L. Sturtz, *Within Her Power: Propertied Women in Colonial Virginia* (2002).

Thad W. Tate and David L. Ammerman, eds., *The Chesapeake in the Seventeenth Century: Essays on Anglo-American Society* (1979).

Margaret Holmes Williamson, *Powhatan Lords of Life and Death: Command and Consent in Seventeenth-Century Virginia* (2003).

Servants and Slaves

Ira Berlin, *Many Thousands Gone: The First Two Centuries of Slavery in North America* (1998).

Robin Blackburn, *The Making of New World Slavery: From the Baroque to the Modern, 1492–1800* (1997).

David Eltis, *The Rise of African Slavery in the Americas* (2001).

Leland G. Ferguson, *Uncommon Ground: Archaeology and Early African America, 1650–1800* (1992).

David W. Galenson, *White Servitude in Colonial America: An Economic Analysis* (1981).

David W. Galenson, *Traders, Planters, and Slaves: Market Behavior in Early English America* (1986).

Paul E. Lovejoy, ed., *Africans in Bondage: Studies in Slavery and the Slave Trade* (1986).

Russell R. Menard, *Migrants, Servants and Slaves: Unfree Labor in Colonial British America* (2001).

Hugh Thomas, *The Slave Trade* (1997).

Spanish Borderlands

Gary Clayton Anderson, *The Indian Southwest, 1580–1830: Ethnogenesis and Reinvention* (1999).

James F. Brooks, *Captives and Cousins: Slavery, Kinship, and Community in the Southwest Borderlands* (2002).

Ramón A. Gutiérrez, *When Jesus Came, the Corn Mothers Went Away: Marriage, Sexuality, and Power in New Mexico, 1500–1846* (1991).

John L. Kessell, *Spain in the Southwest: A Narrative History of Colonial New Mexico, Arizona, Texas, and California* (2002).

Jane Landers, *Black Society in Spanish Florida* (1999).

Jerald T. Milanich, *Laboring in the Fields of the Lord: Spanish Missions and Southeastern Indians* (1999).

Robert W. Preucel, *Archaeologies of the Pueblo Revolt: Identity, Meaning, and Renewal in the Pueblo World* (2002).

Carroll L. Riley, *The Kachina and the Cross: Indians and Spaniards in the Early Southwest* (1999).

David J. Weber, *The Spanish Frontier in North America* (1992).

Carolina Society

Cara Anzilotti, *In the Affairs of the World: Women, Patriarchy, and Power in Colonial South Carolina* (2002).

Alan Vance Briceland, *Westward from Virginia: The Exploration of the Virginia-Carolina Frontier, 1650–1710* (1987).

Kirsten Fischer, *Suspect Relations: Sex, Race, and Resistance in Colonial North Carolina* (2002).

Lorri Glover, *All Our Relations: Blood Ties and Emotional Bonds among the Early South Carolina Gentry* (2000).

Thomas M. Hatley, *The Dividing Paths: Cherokees and South Carolinians through the Era of the American Revolution* (1993).

Daniel C. Littlefield, *Race and Slaves: Ethnicity and the Slave Trade in Colonial South Carolina* (1981).

Aaron M. Shatzmann, *Servants into Planters: The Origin of an American Image: Land Acquisition and Status Mobility in Seventeenth-Century South Carolina* (1989).

Richard Waterhouse, *A New World Gentry: The Making of a Merchant and Planter Class in South Carolina, 1670–1770* (1989).

Robert M. Weir, *Colonial South Carolina: A History* (1983).

Peter H. Wood, *Black Majority: Negroes in Colonial South Carolina from 1670 through the Stono Rebellion* (1974).

The West Indies

Carl Bridenbaugh and Roberta Bridenbaugh, *No Peace beyond the Line: The English in the Caribbean, 1624–1690* (1972).

Richard S. Dunn, *Sugar and Slaves: The Rise of the Planter Class in the English West Indies, 1624–1713* (1972).

Jerome S. Handler and Frederick W. Lange, *Plantation Slavery in Barbados* (1978).

Kenneth F. Kiple, *The Caribbean Slave: A Biological History* (1984).

Herbert S. Klein, *African Slavery in Latin America and the Caribbean* (1986).

Sidney W. Mintz, *Sweetness and Power: The Place of Sugar in Modern History* (1985).

Richard B. Sheridan, *Sugar and Slavery: An Economic History of the British West Indies, 1623–1775* (1974).

Eric Williams, *From Columbus to Castro: The History of the Caribbean, 1492–1969* (1970).

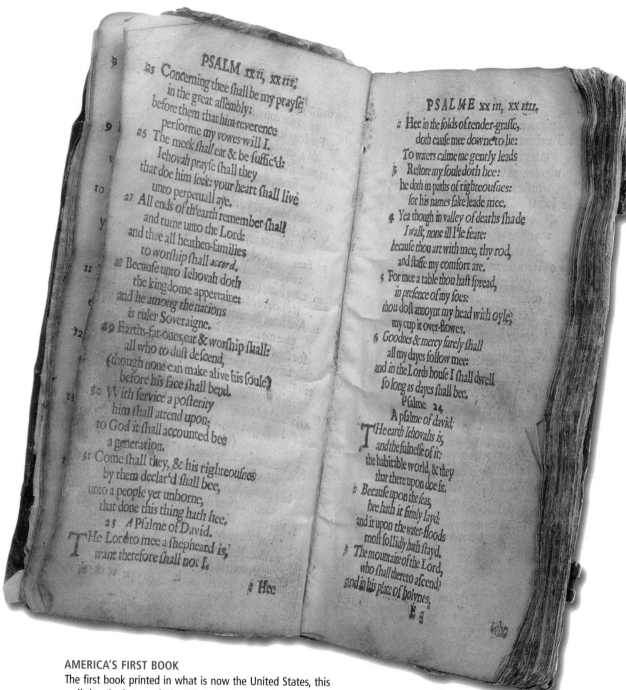

AMERICA'S FIRST BOOK

The first book printed in what is now the United States, this
well-thumbed copy of *The Whole Booke of Psalmes Faithfully Translated into English
Metre* was published in Cambridge, Massachusetts, in 1640. Puritan services banned musical
instruments and other diversions from God's holy word. Worshippers used this book and others to sing psalms, celebrating with a chorus of voices the wonders of God's Truth. The famous Twenty-third Psalm begins near the bottom of the left-hand page and concludes on
the facing page. Read the psalm aloud to re-create the experience of seventeenth-century
New England Puritan congregations.

4

The Northern Colonies in the Seventeenth Century

1601–1700

ROGER WILLIAMS AND HIS WIFE MARY arrived in Massachusetts in February 1631. Fresh from a superb education at Cambridge University and a stint as a private chaplain for a wealthy family, the twenty-eight-year-old Williams was "a godly [Puritan] minister," noted John Winthrop, governor of the new colony. The Boston church honored Williams with an invitation to become its minister. Williams refused because the church had not openly declared its utter rejection of the corrupt Church of England. The leading church of Puritan New England was not pure enough for Williams.

Williams and his wife moved to Plymouth colony for two years; while there, he assisted another minister and spent a great deal of time among the Narragansett Indians. "My soul's desire was to do the natives good," he said. By doing good he meant trying to learn about their language, their religion, and their culture, not trying to covert them to Christianity. Although Williams believed Indians were pagans, he insisted that their religion and other beliefs should be respected since all human beings should live according to their consciences as revealed to them by God. Williams avowed that "Nature knows no difference between Europeans and Americans in blood, birth, [or] bodies . . . God having made of one blood all mankind." His respect for Indians led him to condemn English colonists for their "sin of unjust usurpation" of Indian lands. The colonists' land claims were legally, morally, and spiritually invalid, Williams proclaimed.

Massachusetts officials defended colonists' settlement on Indian land. If land "lies common, and hath never been replenished or subdued, [it] is free to any that possess or improve it," Governor Winthrop explained. Besides, he said, "if we leave [the Indians] sufficient [land] for their use, we may lawfully take the rest, there being more than enough for them and us." Although Winthrop's arguments prevailed, Williams refused to knuckle under. "God Land," he said, "[is] as great a God with us English as God Gold was with the Spaniards." While New Englanders claimed to worship God in heaven, Williams observed, "the truth is the great Gods of this world are God-belly, God-peace, God-wealth, God-honour, [and] God-pleasure."

William Bradford, the governor of Plymouth, praised Williams as "a man godly and zealous, having many precious parts" but also "some strange opinions." Most New England leaders were less generous. One minister censured

Williams for his "self-conceited, and unquiet, and unlamblike frame of . . . Spirit." Rather than submitting lamblike to the colony's rulers, Williams continued to espouse his strange opinions, which ultimately caused him to be banished from the colony.

Williams accepted an invitation to become the minister at Salem, Massachusetts, in 1633. Like other New England Puritans, the members of the Salem church had solemnly agreed to "**Covenant** with the Lord and one with another; and doe bynd our selves in the presence of God, to walke together in all his waies, according as he is pleased to reveale himself unto us in his Blessed word of truth [the Bible]." Most New England Puritans believed that since the Bible clearly defined God's way, churches and governments should enforce both godly belief and behavior. Like other Puritans, Williams believed that the Bible revealed the word of God. But unlike New England's leaders who claimed that "the Word of God is so clear," Williams believed the Bible shrouded the word of God in "mist and fog." Williams pointed out that devout and pious Christians could and did differ about what the Bible said and what God expected. That observation led him to denounce the emerging New England order as impure, ungodly, and tyrannical.

New England's government required everyone to attend church service, whether or not they were church members. Williams argued that forcing people who were not Christians to attend church was wrong in four major ways. First, Williams preached, it was akin to requiring "a dead child to suck the breast, or a dead man [to] feast." The only way for any person to become a true Christian was by God's gift of faith revealed to the person's conscience. Second, churches should be reserved exclusively for those already converted. Churches, Williams declared, must separate "holy from unholy, penitent from impenitent, [and] godly from ungodly." He characterized requiring godly and ungodly to attend church as "False Worshipping" that would create "spiritual drunkenness and whoredom, a soul sleep and a soul sickness." Third, the government—any government—had no business ruling on spiritual matters. Williams termed New England's regulation of religious behavior and belief "spiritual rape" that inevitably would lead governments to use coercion and even violence to enforce the government's misguided way, not God's true way. Finally and most fundamentally, Williams believed that governments should tolerate all religious beliefs, whether Christian or not. He argued that because only God knows the truth, all people of all religions have to struggle to decipher God's inscrutable will; no person and no religion can understand God with absolute certainty. "I commend that man," Williams wrote, "whether Jew, or Turk, or Papist, or whoever, that steers no otherwise than his conscience dares." In Williams's view, toleration of religious belief and liberty of conscience were the only paths to religious purity and political harmony.

New England's leaders denounced Williams's arguments. One minister wrote that Williams sought "liberty to enfranchise all false Religions," which was "the greatest impiety in the World." Genuine **liberty**, he said, was "to contend earnestly for the Truth; to preserve unity of Spirit, Faith, ordinances, to be all like minded, of one accord." Like-minded New Englanders banished Williams for his "extreme and dangerous" opinions. He escaped from an attempt to ship him back to England and in January 1636, "exposed to the mercy of an howling Wilderness in Frost and Snow," spent fourteen weeks walking south to Narragansett Bay. There he founded the colony of Rhode Island, which enshrined "Liberty of Conscience" as a fundamental ideal and became a refuge for other dissenters from Puritan like-mindedness.

Although New England's leaders expelled Williams from their holy commonwealth, his dissenting ideas arose from orthodox Puritan doctrines. By urging believers to search for evidence of God's grace, **Puritanism** encouraged the faithful to listen for God's whisper of truth and faith. Puritanism combined rigid insistence on conformity to God's law and aching uncertainty about how to identify and act upon it. Despite the best efforts of New England's leaders to render God's instructions in no uncertain terms, Puritanism inspired believers like Roger Williams to draw their own conclusions and stick to them.

During the seventeenth century, New England's Puritan zeal—exemplified by Roger Williams and his persecutors—cooled. The goal of founding a holy New England faded. Late in the century, new "middle" colonies—New York, New Jersey, and Pennsylvania—featuring greater religious and ethnic diversity than New England were founded. Religion remained important throughout all the colonies, but it competed with a growing faith that the promise of a better life required less of the Puritans' intense focus on salvation and more attention to the mundane affairs of family, work, and trade.

As settler populations increased throughout the British mainland colonies—northern and southern—settlements encroached on Indian lands, causing violent conflict to flare up repeatedly. Political conflict also arose among colonists, particularly in response to major political upheavals in England. By the end of the seventeenth century, the English monarchy exerted greater control over its far-flung North American empire. The lifeblood of the empire remained, however, the continual flow of products, people, and ideas that pulsed between England and the colonies, energizing both.

Puritan Origins: The English Reformation

The religious roots of the Puritans who founded New England reached back to the Protestant Reformation, which arose in Germany in 1517 (see chapter 3). The **Reformation** spread quickly to other countries, but the English church initially remained within the Catholic fold and continued its allegiance to the pope in Rome. King Henry VIII, who reigned from 1509 to 1547, understood that the Reformation offered him an opportunity to break with Rome and take control of the church in England. In 1534, Henry formally initiated the English Reformation. At his insistence, Parliament passed the Act of Supremacy, which outlawed the Catholic Church and proclaimed the king "the only supreme head on earth of the Church of England." Henry seized the vast properties of the Catholic Church in England as well as the privilege of appointing bishops and other members of the church hierarchy.

In the short run, the English Reformation allowed Henry VIII to achieve his political goal of controlling the church. In the long run, however, the Reformation brought to England the political and religious turmoil that Henry had hoped to avoid. Henry himself sought no more than a halfway Reformation. Protestant doctrines held no attraction for Henry; in almost all matters of religious belief and practice he remained an orthodox Catholic. Many English Catholics wanted to revoke the English Reformation; they

English Monarchy and the Protestant Reformation

1509–1547	Henry VIII	Leads the English Reformation, outlawing the Catholic Church in England and establishing the English monarch as supreme head of the Church of England.
1547–1553	Edward VI	Moves religious reform in a Protestant direction.
1553–1558	Mary I	Outlaws Protestantism and strives to reestablish the Catholic Church in England.
1558–1603	Elizabeth I	Reaffirms the English Reformation and tries to position the Church of England between extremes of Catholicism and Protestantism.
1603–1625	James I	Authorizes a new, Protestant, translation of the Bible, but is unsympathetic to Puritan reformers.
1625–1649	Charles I	Continues James I's move away from the ideas of Puritan reformers. Puritan-dominated Parliament orders his beheading during the Puritan Revolution.
1642		Puritan Revolution (English Civil War) begins.
1644–1660	Oliver Cromwell	Leads Puritan side to victory in the English Civil War. Parliament proclaims England a Puritan republic (1649) and declares Cromwell the nation's "Lord Protector" (1653).
1660–1685	Charles II	Is restored to the monarchy by Parliament and attempts to enforce religious toleration of Catholics and Protestant dissenters from Church of England.
1685–1688	James II	Mounts aggressive campaign to appoint Catholics to government posts, then flees to France when English Protestants in Parliament offer the throne to his Dutch son-in-law, William. The peaceful accession of William and his wife (the daughter of James II) as corulers is called a "Glorious Revolution" (1688).
1689–1694	William III and Mary II	Reassert Protestant influence in England and its empire.

> Many English Catholics wanted to revoke the English Reformation. But many other English people insisted on a genuine, thoroughgoing Reformation; these people came to be called Puritans.

hoped to return the Church of England to the pope and to restore Catholic doctrines and ceremonies. But many other English people insisted on a genuine, thoroughgoing Reformation; these people came to be called Puritans.

During the sixteenth century, Puritanism was less an organized movement than a set of ideas and religious principles that appealed strongly to many dissenting members of the Church of England. They sought to purify the Church of England by eliminating what they considered the offensive features of Catholicism. For example, they demanded that the church hierarchy be abolished and that ordinary Christians be given greater control over religious life. They wanted to do away with the rituals of Catholic worship and instead emphasize an individual's relationship with God developed through Bible study, prayer, and introspection. Although there were many varieties and degrees of Puritanism, all Puritans shared a desire to make the English church thoroughly Protestant.

The fate of **Protestantism** waxed and waned under the monarchs who succeeded Henry VIII. When he died in 1547, the advisers of the new king, Edward VI—the nine-year-old son of Henry and his third wife, Jane Seymour—initiated religious reforms that moved in a Protestant direction. The tide of reform reversed in 1553 when Edward died and was succeeded by Mary I, the daughter of Henry and Catherine of Aragon, his first wife. Mary was a steadfast Catholic, and shortly after becoming queen, she married Philip II of Spain, Europe's most powerful guardian of Catholicism. Mary attempted to restore the pre-Reformation Catholic Church. She outlawed Protestantism in England and persecuted those who refused to conform, sentencing almost three hundred to burn at the stake.

The tide turned again in 1558 when Mary died and was succeeded by Elizabeth I, the daughter of Henry and his second wife, Anne Boleyn. During her long reign, Elizabeth reaffirmed the English Reformation and tried to position the English church between the extremes of Catholicism and Puritanism. Like her father, she asserted her control over the Church of England. Elizabeth was less concerned with theology than with politics. Above all, she desired a church that would strengthen the monarchy and the nation. By the time Elizabeth died in 1603, many people in England looked on Protestantism as a defining feature of national identity.

When her successor, James I, came to the throne, English Puritans petitioned for further reform of the Church of England. The king authorized a new translation of the Bible, known ever since as the King James version. However, neither James I nor his son Charles I, who became king in 1625, was receptive to the ideas of Puritan reformers. James and Charles moved the Church of England away from Puritanism. They enforced conformity to the Church of England and punished dissenters, both ordinary Christians and ministers. In 1629, Charles I dissolved Parliament—where Puritans were well represented—and initiated aggressive anti-Puritan policies. Many Puritans despaired about continuing to defend their faith in England and began to make plans to emigrate. Some left for Europe, others for the West Indies. The largest number set out for America.

Persecution of English Protestants

This sixteenth-century drawing shows Protestant prisoners being marched to London to be tried for heresy during the reign of Queen Mary I, a staunch Catholic. The artist emphasizes the severity of the Catholic persecutors by depicting the use of four well-armed guards, two on horseback, to escort some fifteen prisoners, including at least five women who are roped together but not because they appear menacing or likely to run away. The guards seem to be necessary less to maintain order among the prisoners than to discourage sympathetic citizens from rushing forward and freeing the prisoners. The artist seems to assume that most citizens opposed the queen's persecution of Protestants. The Bible verse from the book of Matthew underscores the Protestants' fealty to Christ rather than to mere "Princes and rulers" like Queen Mary. Folger Shakespeare Library.

Puritans and the Settlement of New England

Puritans who emigrated aspired to escape the turmoil and persecution of England and to build a new, orderly, Puritan version of England. Their faith shaped the colonies they established in almost every way. Although many New England colonists were not Puritans, Puritanism remained a paramount influence in New England's religion, politics, and community life during the seventeenth century.

The Pilgrims and Plymouth Colony

One of the first Protestant groups to emigrate, later known as Pilgrims, espoused a heresy known as separatism: These Separatists sought to withdraw—separate—from the Church of England, which they considered hopelessly corrupt. In 1608, they moved to Holland; by 1620, they realized that they could not live and worship there as they had hoped. William Bradford, a leading member of the group, recalled that "many of their children, by . . . the great licentiousness of youth in [Holland], and the manifold temptations of the place, were drawn away by evil examples." Believing that America was a place where they might protect their children's piety and preserve their community, the Separatists obtained permission to settle in the extensive lands granted to the Virginia Company (see chapter 3). To finance their journey, they formed a joint stock company with London investors. The investors provided the capital; the Separatists, their labor, lives, and a share in all profits for seven years. In August 1620, following months of delay in Holland and England, 102 settlers, mostly families, finally boarded the *Mayflower*. After eleven weeks at sea, all but one of them arrived at the outermost tip of Cape Cod, in present-day Massachusetts.

The Pilgrims realized immediately that they had landed far north of the Virginia grant and had no legal authority from the king to settle in the area. To provide order and security as well as a claim to legitimacy, they drew up the Mayflower Compact on the day they arrived. In signing the document, they agreed to "covenant and combine ourselves together into a civil Body Politick, for our better Ordering and Preservation"; the signers (all men) agreed to enact and obey necessary and just laws.

The Pilgrims settled at Plymouth and elected William Bradford their governor. That first winter "was most sad and lamentable," Bradford wrote later. "In two or three months' time half of [our] company died . . . being the depth of winter, and wanting houses and other comforts [and] being infected with scurvy and other diseases."

In the spring, Indians rescued the floundering Plymouth settlement. First Samoset, then Squanto—both of whom had learned English from previous contacts with sailors and fishermen—befriended the settlers. Samoset arranged for the Pilgrims to meet and establish good relations with Massasoit, the chief of the Wampanoags, whose territory included Plymouth. Squanto, Bradford recalled, "was a special instrument sent of God for their [the Pilgrims'] good. . . . He directed them how to set their corn, where to take fish, and to procure other commodities, and was also their pilot to bring them to unknown places." With Squanto's help and their own hard labor, the Pilgrims managed to store enough food to guarantee their survival through the coming winter, an occasion they celebrated in the fall of 1621 with a feast of thanksgiving attended by Massasoit and many of his warriors.

Still, the colony struggled to survive. Only seven dwellings were erected that first year; half the original colonists died; and a new group of thirty-six threadbare, sickly settlers arrived in November 1621, requiring the colony to adopt stringent food rationing. The colonists quarreled with their London investors, who became frustrated when the colony failed to produce the expected profits.

Although the colony's status remained precarious, the Pilgrims lived quietly and simply, coexisting in relative peace with the Indians. They paid Massasoit when settlers gradually encroached on Wampanoag lands. By 1630, Plymouth had become a permanent settlement, but it failed to attract many other English Puritans. (See "American Places," page 109.)

The Founding of Massachusetts Bay Colony

In 1629, shortly before Charles I dissolved Parliament, a group of Puritan merchants and country gentlemen obtained a royal charter for the Massachusetts Bay Company. The charter provided the usual privileges granted to joint stock companies. It granted land for **colonization** in an area spanning present-day Massachusetts, New Hampshire, Vermont, Maine, and upstate New York. In addition, the charter contained a unique provision: The government of the Massachusetts Bay Company could be located in the colony rather than in England. Thus, with royal permission, Puritans could exchange their position as a harassed minority in England for self-government in Massachusetts.

To lead the emigrants, the stockholders of the Massachusetts Bay Company elected John Winthrop, a prosperous lawyer and landowner, to serve as governor. In March 1630, eleven ships crammed with seven hundred passengers sailed for Massachusetts; six more ships and another five hundred emigrants followed a few months later. Winthrop's fleet arrived in Massachusetts Bay in early June. Unlike the Separatists, Winthrop's Puritans aspired to reform the corrupt Church of England (rather than separate from it) by setting an example of godliness in the New World. Winthrop and a small group chose to settle on the peninsula that became Boston, and other settlers clustered at promising locations nearby (Map 4.1).

In a sermon to his companions aboard the *Arbella* while they were still at sea — probably the most famous sermon in American history — Winthrop explained the cosmic significance of their journey. The Puritans had "entered into a covenant" with God to "work out our salvation under the power and purity of his holy ordinances," Winthrop proclaimed. This sanctified agreement with God meant that "the Lord will [not] bear with such failings at our hands as he doth from those among whom we have lived" in England. The Puritans had to make "extraordinary" efforts to "bring into familiar and constant practice" religious principles that most people in England merely preached. The Puritans had to subordinate their individual interests to the common good. "We must be knit together in this work as one man," Winthrop declared. "We must delight in each other, make others' conditions our own, rejoice together, mourn together, labor and suffer together, always having before our eyes . . . our community as members of the same body." The stakes could not be higher, Winthrop told his listeners: "We must consider that we shall be as a city upon a hill. The eyes of all people are upon us."

That belief shaped seventeenth-century New England as profoundly as tobacco shaped the Chesapeake. Winthrop's vision of a city on a hill fired the Puritans' fierce determination to keep their covenant and live according to God's laws, unlike the backsliders and compromisers who accommodated to the Church of England. Their determination to adhere strictly to God's plan charged nearly every feature of life in seventeenth-century New England with a distinctive, high-voltage piety.

> The vision of a city on a hill fired the Puritans' fierce determination to keep their covenant and live according to God's laws.

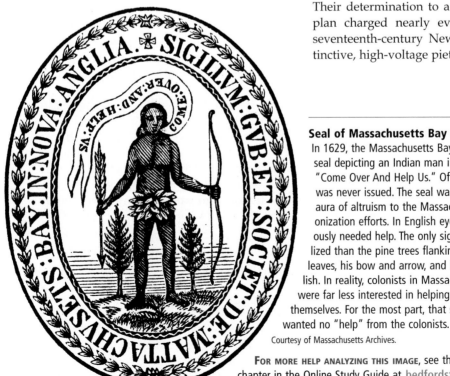

Seal of Massachusetts Bay Colony

In 1629, the Massachusetts Bay Company designed this seal depicting an Indian man inviting English settlers to "Come Over And Help Us." Of course, such an invitation was never issued. The seal was an attempt to lend an aura of altruism to the Massachusetts Bay Company's colonization efforts. In English eyes, the Indian man obviously needed help. The only signs that he was more civilized than the pine trees flanking him were his girdle of leaves, his bow and arrow, and his miraculous use of English. In reality, colonists in Massachusetts and elsewhere were far less interested in helping Indians than in helping themselves. For the most part, that suited the Indians, who wanted no "help" from the colonists.

Courtesy of Massachusetts Archives.

FOR MORE HELP ANALYZING THIS IMAGE, see the visual activity for this chapter in the Online Study Guide at bedfordstmartins.com/roark.

AMERICAN PLACES

Plimoth Plantation, Plymouth, Massachusetts

Plymouth Fort and Meetinghouse
Courtesy of Plimoth Plantation, Inc., Plymouth, MA.

William Bradford, the governor of Plymouth colony, expressed the aspirations of the Plymouth settlers and many other seventeenth-century New Englanders when he wrote, "As one small candle may light a thousand, so the light here kindled hath shone unto many, yea in some sort to our whole nation." A recent authoritative poll by the Pew Forum on Religion in Public Life found evidence that Bradford's small candle, among other sources, succeeded in kindling religious illumination among Americans. The March 2002 poll reported that two-thirds of all Americans believe that the United States is a Christian nation; nearly 60 percent believe that the strength of America

derives from the religious faith of its people; and despite the Islamist terrorist attacks of September 11, 2001, almost half believe that the United States has enjoyed special protection from God for most of its history.

While most Americans today — like Bradford and other colonists at Plymouth and elsewhere in New England — affirm the significance of religious faith, few people today would find the Plymouth colonists' routines of daily life familiar or particularly desirable. When Bradford strolled through the woods shortly after arriving at Plymouth, he noticed a sapling bent over some acorns scattered on the ground. When he went over to look at the bent sapling, "it gave a sudden jerk

up, and he was immediately caught by the leg" in a deer trap, one of his companions wrote. Visitors who walk through Plimoth Plantation today do not risk getting snared by a deer trap, but they can experience the flavor of daily life in Plymouth and elsewhere in seventeenth-century New England.

Reproductions of seventeenth-century buildings, based on scrupulous archaeological excavations and historical research, permit visitors to stroll through a colonial village populated by well-informed interpreters who go about daily chores that would be familiar to Bradford and his fellow colonists. Plimoth Plantation includes a careful reproduction of the *Mayflower*, a Wampanoag house, and many other features of Native American and colonial activity. Visitors can watch interpreters act as if they were seventeenth-century colonists cultivating gardens, harvesting crops, cooking meals, sewing clothes, chopping wood, and going about the colonists' myriad other tasks. The arduous work demonstrates that the colonists had much more than religion on their minds. Visitors are encouraged to question the interpreters, who are trained to answer as if they were voicing the thoughts of the original colonists. In the bustle of all this unfamiliar activity, however, it is easy for a visitor to lose sight of the light of faith kindled by the small candle so important to Bradford and other New Englanders.

FOR WEB LINKS RELATED TO THIS SITE AND OTHER AMERICAN PLACES, see "PlaceLinks" at bedfordstmartins.com/roark.

The new colonists, as Winthrop's son John wrote later, had "all things to do, as in the beginning of the world." Unlike the early Chesapeake settlers, the first Massachusetts Bay colonists encountered few Indians because the local population had been almost entirely exterminated by an epidemic more than a decade earlier. Still, as in the Chesapeake, the colonists fell victim to

MAP 4.1 New England Colonies in the Seventeenth Century

New Englanders spread across the landscape town by town during the seventeenth century. (For the sake of legibility, only a few of the more important towns are shown on the map.)

READING THE MAP: Using the notations on the map, create a chronology of the establishment of towns in New England. What physical features correspond to the earliest habitation by English settlers?

CONNECTIONS: Why were towns so much more a feature of seventeenth-century New England than of the Chesapeake (see also chapter 3)? How did Puritan dissent influence the settlement of New England colonies?

FOR MORE HELP ANALYZING THIS MAP, see the map activity for this chapter in the Online Study Guide at bedfordstmartins.com/roark.

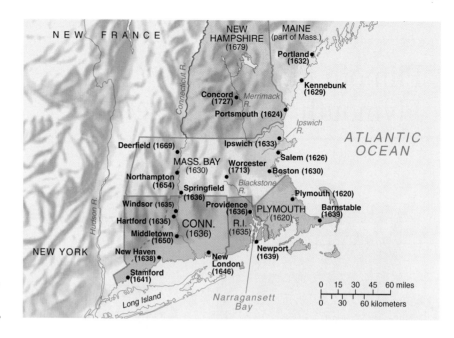

deadly ailments. More than 200 settlers died during the first year, including one of Winthrop's sons and eleven of his servants. About the same number decided by the spring of 1631 that having "all things to do, as in the beginning of the world," was more than they had bargained for, and they returned to England on the first outbound ship. But Winthrop maintained a confidence that proved infectious. "I like so well to be heer," he wrote his wife, "as I do not repent my comminge. . . . I would not have altered my course, though I had forseene all these Afflictions." And each year from 1630 to 1640, ship after ship followed in the wake of Winthrop's fleet. In all, more than 20,000 new settlers came, their eyes fixed on the Puritans' city on a hill.

Often, when the Church of England cracked down on a Puritan minister in England, he and many of his followers uprooted and moved together to New England. By 1640, New England had one of the highest ratios of preachers to population in all of Christendom. But the ratio was still not high enough to provide a trained minister for every band of settlers who hungered for religious instruction; one colonist complained that ordinary "fellowes which keepe hogges all weeke preach on the Saboth." A few ministers sought to carry the message of Christianity to Indians, accompanied by instructions about proper civilized (that is, English) behavior to re-

place what missionary John Eliot termed Indians' "unfixed, confused, and ungoverned . . . life, uncivilized and unsubdued to labor and order." (See "Documenting the American Promise," page 116.) For the most part, however, the colonists focused on saving Indians' souls less than on saving their own.

The occupations of New England immigrants reflected the social origins of English Puritans. On the whole, the immigrants came from the middle ranks of English society. Few representatives of the nobility or the landed gentry came to Massachusetts; Winthrop was an exception. The vast majority of immigrants were either farmers or tradesmen, including carpenters, tailors, and textile workers. Servants, whose numbers dominated the Chesapeake settlers, accounted for only about a fifth of those headed for New England. Most New England immigrants paid their way to Massachusetts, even though the journey often took their life savings. To such people, reports like the one Winthrop sent his son must have been encouraging: "Here is as good land as I have seen there [in England]. . . . Here can be no want of anything to those who bring means to raise out of the earth and sea."

In contrast to the Chesapeake, where immigrant women and children were nearly as rare as atheists in Boston, New England immigrants usually arrived as families. In fact, more Puritans came with family members than did any other group of immigrants in all of American history. A ship that left Weymouth, England, in 1635 carried 106 passengers, 98 of whom belonged to one of the 14 families aboard—typically a husband, wife, and children, sometimes accompanied by a servant or two. In this group, women and children made up a solid majority.

As Winthrop reminded the first settlers in his *Arbella* sermon, each family was a "little commonwealth" that mirrored the hierarchy among all God's creatures. Just as humankind was sub-ordinate to God, so young people were subordinate to their elders, children to their parents, and wives to their husbands. The immigrants' family ties reinforced their religious beliefs with universally understood notions of hierarchy and mutual dependence. While immigrants to the Chesapeake were disciplined mostly by the coercions of servitude and the caprices of the tobacco market, immigrants to New England entered a social order defined by the interlocking institutions of family, church, and community.

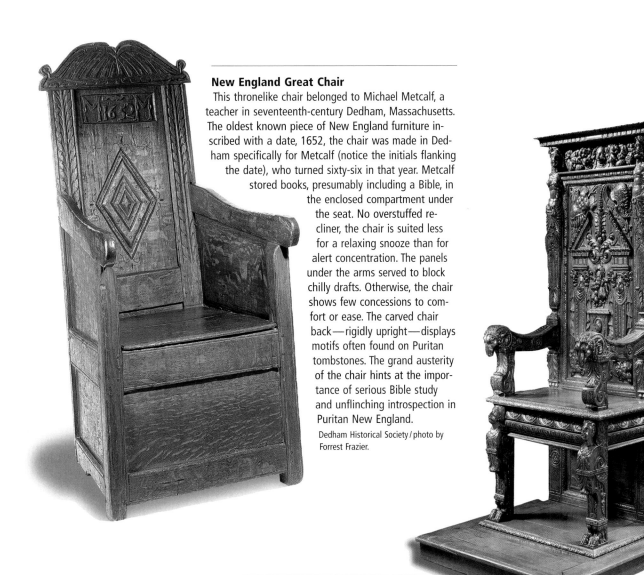

New England Great Chair
This thronelike chair belonged to Michael Metcalf, a teacher in seventeenth-century Dedham, Massachusetts. The oldest known piece of New England furniture inscribed with a date, 1652, the chair was made in Dedham specifically for Metcalf (notice the initials flanking the date), who turned sixty-six in that year. Metcalf stored books, presumably including a Bible, in the enclosed compartment under the seat. No overstuffed recliner, the chair is suited less for a relaxing snooze than for alert concentration. The panels under the arms served to block chilly drafts. Otherwise, the chair shows few concessions to comfort or ease. The carved chair back—rigidly upright—displays motifs often found on Puritan tombstones. The grand austerity of the chair hints at the importance of serious Bible study and unflinching introspection in Puritan New England.
Dedham Historical Society / photo by Forrest Frazier.

European Throne Chair
In contrast to the New England great chair, this late-sixteenth-century European throne chair is embellished on every surface with elaborate carvings proclaiming the worldly magnificence of the chair's owner. This chair illustrates the ostentatious display of luxury and refinement that disgusted Puritans considered signs of the vanity and false pride that distracted people from seeking and following God's Truth.
Courtesy of Huntington Antiques Ltd., Gloucestershire, England.

The Evolution of New England Society

The New England colonists, unlike their counterparts in the Chesapeake, settled in small towns, usually located on the coast or by a river (see Map 4.1). Massachusetts Bay colonists founded 133 towns during the seventeenth century, each with one or more churches. Church members' fervent piety, buttressed by the institutions of local government, enforced remarkable religious and social conformity in the small New England settlements. During the century, tensions within the Puritan faith and changes in New England communities splintered religious orthodoxy and weakened Puritan zeal. By 1700, however, Puritanism still maintained a distinctive influence in New England.

Church, Covenant, and Conformity

Puritans believed that the church consisted of men and women who had entered a solemn covenant with one another and with God. Winthrop and three other men signed the original covenant of the first Boston church in 1630, agreeing to "Promisse, and bind our selves, to walke in all our wayes according to the Rule of the Gospell, and in all sincere Conformity to His holy Ordinaunces, and in mutuall love, and respect to each other, so neere as God shall give us grace." Each new member of the covenant had to persuade existing members that she or he had fully experienced conversion. Fervent Puritans among the early colonists, whose faith had been tempered by persecution in England and by the journey to Massachusetts, had little difficulty meeting the test of covenant membership. By 1635, the Boston church had added more than 250 names to the four original subscribers to the covenant.

Puritan views on religion and church membership derived from **Calvinism**, the doctrines of John Calvin, a sixteenth-century Swiss Protestant theologian who insisted that Christians strictly discipline their behavior to conform to certain religious ideas. As followers of Calvin's ideas, the Puritans believed in **predestination**—the idea that all-powerful God, before the creation of the world, decided which few human souls would receive eternal life, and that nothing a person did in his or her lifetime could alter God's inscrutable choice. According to Calvinist doctrine, only God knows the identity of these fortunate, predestined individuals—the "elect" or "saints." And no person can know for certain whether she or he is predestined for salvation in heaven with the elected few or for damnation in hell with the doomed multitude.

Despite this looming uncertainty, Puritans believed that if a person lived a rigorously godly life—constantly winning the daily battle against sinful temptations—his or her behavior was likely to be a hint, a visible sign, that he or she was one of the elect. Puritans thought that "sainthood" would become visible in individuals' behavior, especially if they were privileged to know God's Word as revealed in the Bible.

The connection between sainthood and saintly behavior, however, was far from certain. Some members of the elect, Puritans believed, had not heard God's word as revealed in the Bible, and therefore their behavior did not necessarily signal their sainthood. One reason Puritans required all town residents to attend church services was to enlighten anyone who was ignorant of God's Truth. The slippery relationship between saintly behavior—observable by anybody—and God's predestined election—invisible and unknowable to anyone—caused Puritans to worry constantly that individuals who acted like saints were fooling themselves and others. Nevertheless, Puritans thought that "visible saints"—persons who passed their demanding tests of conversion and church membership—probably, though not certainly, were among God's elect.

Members of Puritan churches ardently hoped that God had chosen them to receive eternal life and tried to demonstrate saintly behavior. Their covenant bound them to help each other attain salvation and to discipline the entire community by saintly standards. Church members kept an eye on the behavior of everybody in town. Infractions of morality, order, or propriety were reported to Puritan elders, who summoned the wayward to a church inquiry. The watchfulness that set the tone of life in Puritan communities is suggested by one minister's note that "the church was satisfied with Mrs. Carlton as to the weight of her butter." By overseeing every aspect of life, including Mrs. Carlton's butter, the visible saints enforced a remarkable degree of righteous conformity in Puritan communities. Total conformity, however, was never achieved, and Puritan doctrine even spelled out the fiery punishment for failure to conform: A servant in Roxbury declared that "if hell were ten times

THE
World turn'd upfide down:
OR,
A briefe defcription of the ridiculous Fafhions
of thefe diftracted Times.

By T. J. a well-willer to King, Parliament and Kingdom.

London : Printed for *John Smith.* 1647.

The Puritan Challenge to the Status Quo
This title page of "The World Turn'd Upside Down" satirizes the Puritan notion that the contemporary world was deeply flawed. Printed in London in 1647, the pamphlet refers to the "distracted Times" of the Puritan Revolution in England. The drawing ridicules criticisms of English society that were also common among New England Puritans. The drawing shows at least a dozen examples of the conventional world of seventeenth-century England turned upside down. Can you identify them? Puritans, of course, would claim that the artist had it wrong—that the conventional world turned God's order upside down. How might the drawing have been different if a devout Puritan had drawn it?
By permission of The British Library.

hotter, [I] had rather be there than [I] would serve [my] master."

Despite the central importance of religion, churches played no direct role in the civil government of New England communities. Puritans did not want to emulate the Church of England, which they considered a puppet of the king rather than an independent body that served the Lord. They were determined to insulate New England churches from the contaminating influence of the civil state and its merely human laws. Although ministers were the most highly respected figures in New England towns, they were prohibited from holding government office.

Puritans had no qualms, however, about their religious beliefs influencing New England governments. As much as possible, the Puritans tried to bring public life into conformity with their view of God's law. Most Puritans agreed that the Sabbath began at sunset on Saturday evening, and enforcement of proper Sabbath behavior was taken seriously. On the Sabbath, townsfolk could not work, play, or travel. Fines were issued for Sabbath-breaking activities such as playing a flute, smoking a pipe, and visiting neighbors.

Puritans mandated other purifications of what they considered corrupt English practices. They refused to celebrate Christmas or Easter because the Bible did not mention either one. They outlawed religious wedding ceremonies; couples were married by a magistrate in a civil ceremony (the first wedding in Massachusetts to be performed by a minister did not occur until 1686). Puritans prohibited elaborate, colorful clothing, censuring finery such as lace trim and frowning on short sleeves—"whereby the nakedness of the arm may be discovered." Cards, dice, shuffleboard, and other games of chance were banned, as were music and dancing. The distinguished minister Increase Mather insisted that "Mixt or Promiscuous Dancing . . . of Men and Women" could not be tolerated since "the unchaste Touches and Gesticulations used by Dancers have a palpable tendency to that which is evil." On special occasions, Puritans proclaimed days of fasting and humiliation, which, as one preacher boasted, amounted to "so many Sabbaths more."

> As much as possible, the Puritans tried to bring public life into conformity with their view of God's law.

Government by Puritans for Puritanism

It is only a slight exaggeration to say that seventeenth-century New England was governed by Puritans for Puritanism. The charter of the Massachusetts Bay Company empowered the company's stockholders, or freemen, to meet as a body known as the General Court and make the laws needed to govern the company's affairs. The colonists transformed this arrangement for running a joint stock company into a structure for governing the colony. Hoping to ensure that godly men would decide government policies,

Sabbath Breakers

These seventeenth-century prints show some of the punishments to which Sabbath breakers could be subjected by man and God. In the upper illustration, a person who gathered sticks on the Sabbath is stoned to death as Puritans believed the Bible commanded. In the lower print, three women who broke the Sabbath by preparing flax to be spun and woven into linen suffer God's retribution when they are burned to death. New Englanders differed about exactly when the Sabbath began. Some thought it started at sunset on Saturday evening, but John Winthrop believed the Sabbath began about three o'clock Saturday afternoon. Given the extreme punishments inflicted on Sabbath breakers, New Englanders needed to be careful about what they did between Saturday afternoon and Monday morning.

Divine Examples of God's Severe Judgements upon Sabbath-Breakers (London, 1671).

the General Court ruled in 1631 that freemen had to be male church members. Only freemen had the right to vote for governor, deputy governor, and other colonial officials. As new settlers were recognized as freemen, the size of the General Court grew until it became too large to meet conveniently. So in 1634, the freemen in each town agreed to send two deputies to the General Court to act as the colony's legislative assembly. All other men were classified as "inhabitants," and they had the right to vote, hold office, and participate fully in town government.

A "town meeting," composed of a town's inhabitants and freemen, chose the selectmen and other officials who administered local affairs. New England town meetings routinely practiced a level of popular participation in political life that was unprecedented elsewhere during the seventeenth century. Almost every adult man could speak out in town meetings and fortify his voice with a vote. However, all women—even church members—were prohibited from voting, and towns did not permit "contrary-minded" men to become or remain inhabitants. Although town meeting participants wrangled from time to time, widespread political participation tended to reinforce conformity to Puritan ideals.

One of the most important functions of New England government was land distribution. Settlers who desired to establish a new town entered a covenant and petitioned the General Court for a grant of land. The court granted town sites to suitably pious petitioners but did not allow settlement until the Indians who inhabited a grant agreed to relinquish their claim to the land, usually in exchange for manufactured goods. For instance, William Pynchon purchased the site of Springfield, Massachusetts, from the Agawam Indians for "eighteen fathams [arms' lengths] of Wampam, eighteen coates, 18 hatchets, 18 hoes, [and] 18 knives."

Having obtained their grant, town founders apportioned land among themselves and any newcomers they permitted to join them. Normally, each family received a house lot large enough for an adjacent garden as well as one or more strips of agricultural land on the perimeter of the town. Although there was a considerable difference between the largest and smallest family plots, most clustered in the middle range—roughly fifty to one hundred acres—resulting in a more nearly equal distribution of land in New England than in the Chesapeake. Towns reserved some common land, which all inhabitants could use for grazing livestock and cutting wood, and

Joseph Capen House
This substantial house was built in 1683 for Joseph Capen, a Harvard graduate who had recently arrived in Topsfield, Massachusetts, to serve as the local minister. The town granted Capen twelve acres for a homesite, and he probably paid for the house with the dowry of his new wife, Priscilla Appleton, the daughter of a wealthy colonist in nearby Ipswich, Massachusetts. The plain but imposing house suggests the sturdy ties between preachers and their congregations and, more generally, between families, faith, and communities. Capen lived in the house and preached to the Topsfield church for more than forty years until his death in 1725. Now, more than three centuries after Capen built the house, it still stands, a monument to New England colonists' convictions that they were building a society to endure for the ages.
Picture Research Consultants & Archives.

saved the rest for new settlers and the descendants of the founders.

The physical layout of New England towns encouraged settlers to look inward toward their neighbors, multiplying the opportunities for godly vigilance. Most people considered the forest that lay just beyond every settler's house an alien environment that was interrupted here and there by those oases of civilization, the towns. Footpaths connecting one town to another were so rudimentary that even John Winthrop once got lost within half a mile of his house and spent a sleepless night in the forest, circling the light of his small campfire and singing psalms.

The Splintering of Puritanism

Almost from the beginning, John Winthrop and other leaders had difficulty enforcing their views of Puritan orthodoxy. In England, persecution as a dissenting minority had unified Puritan voices in opposition to the Church of England. In New England, the promise of a godly society and the Puritans' emphasis on individual Bible study led New Englanders toward different visions of godliness. Puritan leaders, however, interpreted dissent as an error caused either by a misguided believer or by the malevolent power of Satan. Whatever the cause, errors could not be tolerated. As one Puritan minister proclaimed, "God doth no where in his word tolerate Christian States, to give Tolerations to . . . adversaries of his Truth, if they have power in their hands to suppress them. The Scripture saith . . . there is no Truth but one."

Shortly after banishing Roger Williams, Winthrop confronted another dissenter, this time—as one New Englander observed—a "Woman that Preaches better Gospell then any of your black-coates that have been at the Ninneversity." The woman was Anne Hutchinson, a devout Puritan steeped in Scripture and absorbed by religious questions. Hutchinson had received an excellent education from her father in England. The mother of fourteen children, she served her neighbors as a skilled midwife. After she settled into her new

> Almost from the beginning, John Winthrop and other leaders had difficulty enforcing their views of Puritan orthodoxy.

King Philip Considers Christianity

Beginning in 1646, the Puritan minister John Eliot served as a missionary to New England's Indians, trying to teach the doctrines of Christianity and proper English behavior. During his half-century tenure as leader of the Puritan congregation in Roxbury, Massachusetts, Eliot studied the languages, customs, and beliefs of Native Americans, hoping to help them along the path to Christian piety and to strengthen them against colonists' unscrupulous encroachment on their lands. The efforts of Eliot and other missionaries convinced some Indians to leave their own communities and settle in "praying towns" populated by Native Americans who had agreed to live in conformity with English ways. Most Indians, however, did not move into praying towns or adopt the faith or manners of the colonists.

In Indian Dialogues, *a book published in 1671, Eliot illustrated the challenge he and other missionaries confronted as they tried to convince Native Americans of the errors of their ways. Based on his decades of missionary experience, Eliot created imaginary conversations between converted Indians and those who resisted Christianity. Eliot's invented conversations echoed arguments he and other missionaries had encountered repeatedly. The following selection from an imaginary dialogue between two praying Indians, Anthony and William, and King Philip (or*

Metacomet), the chief (or sachem) of the powerful Wampanoags, documents Eliot's perception of the attractions of Christianity and one Indian leader's doubts about it, doubts that ultimately prevailed when King Philip led the Wampanoags in an all-out attack against the settlers in 1675.

Anthony: Sachem, we salute you in the Lord, and we declare unto you, that we are sent by the church, in the name of our Lord Jesus Christ, to call you, and beseech you to turn from your vain conversation unto God, to pray unto God, and to believe in Jesus Christ for the pardon of your sins, and for the salvation of your soul. . . . So we are come this day unto you, in the name of Jesus Christ, to call you to come unto the Lord, and serve him. . . . We hear that many of your people do desire to pray to God, only they depend on you. We pray you to consider that your love to your people should oblige you to do them all the good you can. . . . You will not only yourself turn from sin unto God . . . , but all your people will turn to God with you, so that you may say unto the Lord, oh Lord Jesus, behold here am I, and all the people which thou hast given me. We all come unto thy service, and promise to pray unto God so long as we live. . . . Oh how happy will all your people be. . . . It

will be a joy to all the English magistrates, and ministers, and churches, and good people of the land, to hear that Philip and all his people are turned to God, and become praying Indians. . . .

Philip: Often have I heard of this great matter of praying unto God, and hitherto I have refused. . . . Mr. Eliot himself did come unto me. He was in this town, and did persuade me. But we were then in our sports, wherein I have much delighted, and in that temptation, I confess, I did neglect and despise the offer, and lost that opportunity. Since that time God hath afflicted and chastised me, and my heart doth begin to break. And I have some serious thoughts of accepting the offer, and turning to God, to become a praying Indian, I myself and all my people. But I have some great objections, which I cannot tell how to get over, which are still like great rocks in my way, over which I cannot climb. And if I should, I fear I shall fall down the precipice on the further side, and be spoiled and undone. By venturing to climb, I shall catch a deadly fall to me and my posterity.

The first objection that I have is this, because you praying Indians do reject your sachems, and refuse to pay them tribute, in so much that if any of my people turn to pray unto God, I do reckon that I have lost him. He will no longer own me for his sachem, nor pay me any tribute. And hence it will come to pass, that if I should pray to God, and all my people with me, I must become as a common man among them, and so

home in Boston in 1634, women gathered there to hear her weekly lectures on recent sermons, a proper female activity since, according to one minister, it "water[ed] the seeds publikely sowen." As the months passed, Hutchinson began

to lecture twice a week, and crowds of sixty to eighty women and men gathered to listen to her.

Hutchinson expounded on the sermons of John Cotton, her favorite minister. Cotton stressed what he termed the "covenant of

lose all my power and authority over them. This is such a temptation as . . . I, nor any of the other great sachems, can tell how to get over. Were this temptation removed, the way would be more easy and open for me to turn praying Indian. I begin to have some good likance of the way, but I am loth to buy it at so dear a rate.

William: . . . I say, if any of the praying Indians should be disobedient (in lawful things) and refuse to pay tribute unto their sachems, it is not their religion and praying to God that teaches them so to do, but their corruptions. . . . I am sure the word of God commandeth all to be subject to the higher powers, and pay them tribute. . . . And therefore, beloved sachem, let not your heart fear that praying to God will alienate your people from you . . . for the more beneficent you are unto them, the more obligation you lay upon them. And what greater beneficence can you do unto them than to further them in religion, whereby they may be converted, pardoned, sanctified, and saved? . . .

Philip: I have another objection stronger than this, and that is, if I pray to God, then all my men that are willing to pray to God will (as you say) stick to me, and be true to me. But all such as love not and care not to pray to God, especially such as hate praying to God, all these will forsake me, yea will go and adjoin themselves unto other sachems that pray not to God. And so it will come to pass, that if I be a praying sachem, I shall be a poor and weak one, and

easily trod upon by others, who are like to be more potent and numerous. And by this means my tribute will be small, and my people few, and I shall be a great loser by praying to God. In the way I am now, I am full and potent, but if I change my way and pray to God, I shall be empty and weak. . . .

William: . . . Suppose all your subjects that hate praying to God should leave you. What shall you lose by it? You are rid of such as by their sins vitiate others, and multiply transgression, and provoke the wrath of God against you and yours. But consider what you shall gain by praying to God. . . . All the praying Indians will rejoice at it, and be your friends, and they are not a few. . . . [And] you shall gain a more intimate love of the Governor, and Magistrates. . . . They will more honor, respect, and love you, than ever they did. . . . The Governor and Magistrates of the Massachusetts will own you, and be fatherly and friendly to you. . . . Yea more, the King of England, and the great peers who . . . yearly send over means to encourage and promote our praying to God, they will take notice of you.

Philip: I perceive that in your praying to God, and in your churches, all are brought to an equality. Sachems and people they are all fellow brethren in your churches. Poor and rich are equally privileged. The vote of the lowest of the people hath as much weight as the vote of the sachem. Now I doubt [worry] that this way will lift up the heart of the poor to

too much boldness, and debase the rulers to[o] low. This bringing all to an equality will bring all to a confusion. . . . [T]here is yet another thing that I am much afraid of, and that is your church admonitions and excommunications. I hear that your sachems are under that yoke. I am a sinful man as well as others, but if I must be admonished by the church, who are my subjects, I know not how I shall like that. I doubt [worry] it will be a bitter pill, too hard for me to get down and swallow. . . . I feel your words sink into my heart and stick there. You speak arrows. . . . I desire to ponder and consider of these things. . . . I am willing they should still lie soaking in my heart and mind.

SOURCE: John Eliot, *Indian Dialogues* (Cambridge, 1671) in Henry W. Bowden and James P. Ronda, eds., *John Eliot's Indian Dialogues: A Study in Cultural Interaction* (Westport, Conn.: Greenwood Press, 1980), 120–31.

QUESTIONS FOR ANALYSIS AND DEBATE

1. To what degree is Eliot's dialogue a reliable guide to Philip's doubts about the wisdom of becoming a praying Indian?

2. According to Eliot, was Philip's religion a stumbling block to his acceptance of Christianity? What made Philip fear that he would "fall down the precipice"?

3. If Philip had written a dialogue proposing that Eliot convert to the Wampanoag way of life, what arguments might he have made?

grace"—the idea that individuals could be saved only by God's grace in choosing them to be members of the elect. Cotton contrasted this familiar Puritan doctrine with the "covenant of works," the erroneous belief that a person's behavior— one's works—could win God's favor and ultimately earn a person salvation. Belief in the covenant of works and in the possibility of salvation for all was known as Arminianism. Cotton's sermons strongly hinted that many Puritans, including ministers, embraced Arminianism, which claimed—falsely, Cotton declared—that human beings could influence God's will. Anne Hutchinson agreed with Cotton. Her lectures emphasized her opinion that many of the colony's leaders affirmed the Arminian covenant of works. Like Cotton, she preached that only God's covenant of grace led to salvation.

The meetings at Hutchinson's house alarmed her nearest neighbor, John Winthrop, who believed that she was subverting the good order of the colony. In 1637, Winthrop had formal charges brought against Hutchinson and confronted her in court as her chief accuser. He denounced Hutchinson's lectures as "not tolerable nor comely in the sight of God nor fitting for your sex." He told her, "You have stept out of your place, you have rather bine a Husband than a Wife and a preacher than a Hearer; and a Magistrate than a Subject."

As Winthrop and Hutchinson confronted each other in court, he proved no match for her learning, wit, and insight. Hutchinson pointed to passages in the Bible that instructed women to meet and teach one another. When Winthrop claimed that those scriptures did not apply to her, she asked him, "Must I shew my name written therein?" Besides, she said, if it was "not lawful for me to teach women . . . why do you call me to teach the court?" Outsmarted and off-balance, Winthrop pressed forward with the investigation, fishing for a heresy he could pin on Hutchinson.

Winthrop and other Puritan elders referred to Hutchinson and her followers as **antinomians**, people who oppose the law. Hutchinson's opponents charged that she believed that Christians could be saved by faith alone and did not need to act in accordance with God's law as set forth in the Bible and as interpreted by Winthrop and the colony's other leaders. Hutchinson nimbly defended herself against the accusation of antinomianism. Yes, she acknowledged, she believed that men and women were saved by faith alone; but no, she did not deny the need to obey God's law. "The Lord hath let me see which was the clear ministry and which the wrong," she said. Finally, her interrogators cornered her. How could she tell which ministry was which? "By an immediate revelation," she replied, "by the voice of [God's] own spirit to my soul." Winthrop spotted in this statement the heresy of prophecy, the view that God revealed his will directly to a believer instead of exclusively through the Bible, as every right-minded Puritan knew.

In 1638, the Boston church formally excommunicated Hutchinson. The minister decreed, "I doe cast you out and . . . deliver you up to Satan that you may learne no more to blaspheme to seduce and to lye. . . . I command you . . . as a Leper to withdraw your selfe out of the Congregation." Banished, Hutchinson and her family moved first to Roger Williams's Rhode Island and then to present-day New York, where she and most of her family were killed by Indians.

The strains within Puritanism exemplified by Anne Hutchinson and Roger Williams caused it to splinter repeatedly during the seventeenth century. Thomas Hooker, a prominent minister, clashed with Winthrop and other leaders over the composition of the church. Hooker argued that men and women who lived godly lives should be admitted to church membership even if they had not experienced conversion. This issue, like most others in New England, had both religious and political dimensions, for only church members could vote in Massachusetts. In 1636, Hooker led an exodus of more than 800 colonists from Massachusetts to the Connecticut River valley, where they founded Hartford and neighboring towns. In 1639, the towns adopted the Fundamental Orders of Connecticut, a quasi-constitution that could be altered by the vote of freemen, who did not have to be church members, though nearly all of them were.

Other Puritan churches divided and subdivided throughout the seventeenth century as acrimony developed over doctrine and church government. Sometimes churches split over the appointment of a controversial minister. Sometimes families who had a long walk to the meetinghouse simply decided to form their own church nearer their houses. These schisms arose from ambiguities and tensions within Puritan belief. As the colonies matured, other tensions developed as well.

Religious Controversies and Economic Changes

A revolutionary transformation in the fortunes of Puritans in England had profound consequences in New England. Disputes between King Charles I and Parliament, dominated by Puritans, escalated in 1642 to civil war in England, a conflict known as the Puritan Revolution. Parliamentary forces led by the staunch Puritan Oliver Cromwell were victorious, executing Charles I in 1649 and proclaiming England a Puritan republic. From 1649 to 1660, England's rulers—principally Oliver Cromwell—were not monarchs who suppressed Puritanism but believers who championed it. In a half century, English Puritans had risen from being a harassed group of religious dissenters to become a dominant power in English government.

When the Puritan Revolution began, the stream of immigrants to New England dwindled to a trickle, creating hard times for the colonists. They could no longer consider themselves a city on a hill setting a godly example for humankind. English society was being reformed by Puritans in England, not New England. Furthermore, when immigrant ships became rare, the colonists faced sky-high prices for scarce English goods and few customers for their own colonial products. As they searched to find new products and markets, they established the enduring patterns of New England's economy.

New England's rocky soil and short growing season ruled out cultivating the southern colonies' crops of tobacco and rice that found a ready market in Atlantic ports. Exports that New Englanders could not get from the soil they took instead from the forest and the sea. During the first decade of settlement, colonists traded with Indians for animal pelts, which were in demand in Europe. By the 1640s, fur-bearing animals had become scarce unless traders ventured far beyond the **frontiers** of English settlement. Trees from the seemingly limitless forests of New England proved a longer-lasting resource. Masts for ships and staves for barrels of Spanish wine and West Indian sugar were crafted from New England timber.

But the most important New England export was fish. During the religious and political turmoil of the 1640s, English ships withdrew from the rich North Atlantic fishing grounds, and New England fishermen quickly took their place. Dried, salted codfish found markets in southern Europe and the West Indies. The fish trade also stimulated colonial shipbuilding and trained generations of fishermen, sailors, and merchants, creating a commercial network that endured for more than a century. But the export economy remained peripheral to most New England colonists. Their lives revolved around their farms, their churches, and their families.

Although immigration came to a standstill in the 1640s, the population continued to boom, doubling every twenty years. In New England, almost everyone married and women often had eight or nine children. Long, cold winters prevented the warm-weather ailments of the south-

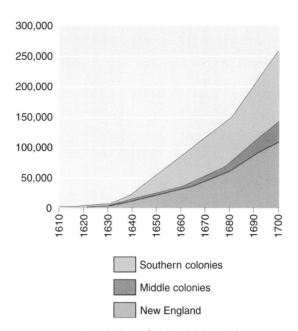

FIGURE 4.1 Population of the British North American Colonies in the Seventeenth Century The colonial population grew at a steadily accelerating rate during the seventeenth century. New England and the southern colonies each comprised about half the total colonial population until after 1680, when growth in Pennsylvania and New York contributed to a surge in the population of the middle colonies.

ern colonies and reduced New England mortality. The descendants of the immigrants of the 1630s multiplied and remultiplied, boosting the New England population to roughly equal that of the southern colonies (Figure 4.1).

During the last half of the seventeenth century, under the pressures of steady population growth and integration into the Atlantic economy, the white-hot piety of the founders cooled. After 1640, the population grew faster than church membership. All residents attended sermons on pain of fines and punishment, but many could not find seats in the meetinghouses. Boston's two churches in 1650 could house only about a third of the city's population. By the 1680s, women were the majority of full church members throughout New England. In some towns, only 15 percent of the adult men were members. A growing fraction of New Englanders, especially men, embraced what one historian has termed "horse-shed Christianity": They attended sermons but loitered outside near the horse shed, gossiping about the weather, fishing, their crops, or the scandalous behavior of neighbors.

David, Joanna, and Abigail Mason

This 1670 painting depicts the children of Joanna and Anthony Mason, a wealthy Boston baker. The artist lavished attention on the children's elaborate clothing. Fashionable slashed sleeves, fancy laces, silver-studded shoes, six-year-old Joanna's and four-year-old Abigail's necklaces, and nine-year-old David's silver-headed cane suggest not only the Masons' wealth but also their desire to display and memorialize their possessions and adornments. The painting hints that the children themselves were adornments, young sprouts of the Mason lineage, which could afford such finery. The portrait is unified not by signs of warm affection, innocent smiles, or familial solidarity but by trappings of wealth and sober self-importance. The painting expresses the growing respect for wealth and its worldly rewards in seventeenth-century New England.

Fine Arts Museums of San Francisco. Gift of Mr. and Mrs. John D. Rockefeller III.

This slackening of piety led Puritan minister Michael Wigglesworth to ask, in verse,

> How is it that I find
>   In stead of holiness Carnality,
> In stead of heavenly frames an Earthly mind,
>   For burning zeal luke-warm Indifferency,
> For flaming love, key-cold Dead-heartedness,
>   For temperance (in meat, and drinke, and cloaths) excess?
> Whence cometh it, that Pride, and Luxurie
>   Debate, Deceit, Contention, and Strife,
> False-dealing, Covetousness, Hypocrisie
>   (With such Crimes) amongst them are so rife,
> That one of them doth over-reach another?
>   And that an honest man can hardly trust his Brother?

Most alarming to Puritan leaders, many of the children of the visible saints of Winthrop's gen-

eration failed to experience conversion and attain full church membership. Puritans tended to assume that sainthood was inherited—that the children of visible saints were probably also among the elect. Acting on this premise, churches permitted saints to baptize their infant sons and daughters, symbolically cleansing them of their contamination with original sin. As these children grew up  during the 1640s and 1650s, however, they seldom experienced the inward transformation that signaled conversion and qualification for church membership. The problem of declining church membership and the watering-down of Puritan orthodoxy became urgent during the 1650s when the children of saints, who had grown to adulthood in New England but had not experienced conversion, began to have children themselves. Their sons and daughters—the grandchildren of the founders of the colony—could not receive the protection that baptism afforded against the terrors of death because their parents had not experienced conversion.

Puritan churches debated what to do. To allow anyone, even the child of a saint, to become a church member without conversion was an unthinkable retreat from fundamental Puritan doctrine. In 1662, a synod of Massachusetts ministers reached a compromise known as the **Halfway Covenant**. Unconverted children of saints would be permitted to become "halfway" church members. Like regular church members, they could baptize their infants. But unlike full church members, they could not participate in communion or have the voting privileges of church membership. The Halfway Covenant generated a controversy that sputtered through Puritan churches for the remainder of the century. With the Halfway Covenant, Puritan churches came to terms with the "luke-warm Indifferency" that had replaced the founders' burning zeal.

Nonetheless, New England communities continued to enforce piety with holy rigor. Beginning in 1656, small bands of Quakers—or members of the Society of Friends, as they called themselves—began to arrive in Massachusetts. Many of their beliefs were at odds with orthodox Puritanism. Quakers believed that God spoke directly to each individual through an "inner light," and that individuals needed neither a preacher nor the Bible in order to discover God's Word. Maintaining that all human beings were equal in God's eyes, Quakers refused to conform to mere temporal powers such as laws and governments unless God requested otherwise. Quakers affronted Puritan doctrines of faith and social order. For example, they refused to observe the Sabbath because they insisted that God had not set aside any special day for worship but instead expected the faithful to worship every day.

New England communities treated Quakers with ruthless severity. Some Quakers were branded on the face "with a red-hot iron with [an] H. for heresie." Several Quaker women were stripped to the waist, tied to the back of a cart, and whipped as they were paraded through towns. When Quakers refused to leave Massachusetts, Boston officials sentenced two men and a woman to be hanged in 1659. The three Quakers walked to the gallows "Hand in Hand, all three of them, as to a Weding-day, with great cheerfulness of Heart," one colonist observed.

New Englanders' only partial success in realizing the promise of a godly society ultimately

undermined the intense appeal of Puritanism. In the pious Puritan communities of New England, leaders tried to eliminate sin. In the process, they diminished the sense of utter human depravity that was the wellspring of Puritanism. By 1700, New Englanders did not doubt that human beings sinned, but they were more concerned with the sins of others than with their own.

Witch trials held in Salem, Massachusetts, were signs of the erosion of religious confidence and assurance. In 1692, the frenzied Salem proceedings accused more than 100 people of witchcraft, a capital crime. (See "Historical Question," page 122.) Most of the accused were middle-aged women who, according to their accusers, were in thrall to Satan, who had tortured and bedeviled the accusers. The Salem court executed 19 accused witches, signaling enduring belief in the supernatural origins of evil and gnawing doubt about the strength of Puritan New Englanders' faith.

The Founding of the Middle Colonies

South of New England and north of the Chesapeake, a group of middle colonies were founded in the last third of the seventeenth century. Before the 1670s, few Europeans settled in the region. For the first two-thirds of the seventeenth century, the most important European outpost in the area was the relatively small Dutch colony of New Netherland. By 1700, however, the English monarchy had seized New Netherland, renamed it New York, and encouraged the creation of a Quaker colony led by William Penn. Unlike the New England colonies, the middle colonies of New York, New Jersey, and Pennsylvania originated as **land grants** by the English monarch to one or more proprietors, who then possessed both the land and the extensive, almost monarchical, powers of government (Map 4.2). These middle colonies attracted settlers of more diverse European origins and religious faiths than were found in New England.

From New Netherland to New York

In 1609, the Dutch East India Company dispatched Henry Hudson to search for a Northwest Passage to the Orient. Hudson sailed

Valuables Chest
This sturdy chest used to hold jewelry and valuable papers commemorated the wedding of Joseph and Bathsheba Pope in 1679. Quakers, the Popes lived in Salem, Massachusetts. Thirteen years after acquiring this chest, the Popes became participants in the 1692 Salem witch trials. They both accused neighbors of being witches. Bathsheba succumbed to fits that she attributed to the witchcraft of Martha Corey. Joseph testified that John Proctor claimed to have powers to exorcise Satan. Both Corey and Proctor were convicted of witchcraft and hanged.
Peabody Essex Museum, Salem, MA.

Why Were Some New Englanders Accused of Being Witches?

Almost everybody in seventeenth-century North America—whether Native Americans, slaves, or colonists—believed that supernatural spirits could cause harm and misfortune. Outside New England, however, few colonists were legally accused of being witches—that is, persons who had become possessed by Satan. More than 95 percent of all legal accusations of witchcraft in the North American colonies occurred in New England, a hint of Puritans' enduring preoccupation with sin and evil. In 1691 and 1692, an epidemic of witchcraft accusations broke out in Salem, Massachusetts, but long before that many New Englanders had whispered privately that particular individuals were witches. To accuse a person of witchcraft was a serious matter. A 1641 Massachusetts law stated, "If any man or woman be a witch . . . they shall be put to death." The other New England colonies had identical laws. During the seventeenth century, courts carried out the letter of the law: Thirty-four accused witches were legally executed, nineteen of them during the Salem outbreak.

To understand the peculiar New England obsession with witchcraft,

historians have gathered a great deal of information about accused witches and the dark deeds their accusers attributed to them. Almost anyone could be accused of being a witch, but 80 percent of the accusations were leveled against women. About two-thirds of the accused women were over forty years old, past the normal age of childbearing. About half of the men who were accused as witches were relatives of accused women. Usually, one family member did not accuse another. Nor did accusers single out a stranger as a witch. Instead, accusers pointed to a neighbor they knew well.

Almost always the accused person denied the charge. Occasionally, the accused confessed to having made a pact with the devil. A confession could sometimes win sympathy and a reduced punishment from officials. During the Salem witch-hunt, those who confessed usually saved their own skins by naming other people as witches. The testimony of a confessed witch was then used to accuse others.

Accusers of all descriptions stepped forward to testify against alleged witches. Witchcraft investigations often stretched over weeks, months, or even years as courts

accumulated evidence against (and sometimes in favor of) the accused. About 90 percent of accusers were adults, about six out of ten of them men. Young women between the ages of sixteen and twenty-five made up almost all of the remaining 10 percent of accusers; typically, they claimed to be tortured by the accused.

At Salem, for example, afflicted young girls shrieked in pain, their limbs twisted into strange, involuntary contortions as they pointed out the witches who tortured them. At the trial of Bridget Bishop in Salem, the court record noted that if Bishop "but cast her eyes on them [the afflicted], they were presently struck down. . . . But upon the touch of her hand upon them, when they lay in their swoons, they would immediately revive." The bewitched girls testified that "the shape of the prisoner did oftentimes very grievously pinch them, choke them, bite them, and afflict them; urging them to write their names in a book"—the devil's book.

Such sensational evidence of torture by a witch was relatively rare in witch-hunts and trials. Usually, accusers attributed some inexplicable misfortune they had suffered to the evil influence of an accused witch. One woman testified against a woman who, she insisted, had bewitched her cow, causing it to give discolored milk. Another woman accused a witch whom she feared would "smite my chickens," and "quickly after [the suspected witch went away] one chicken died." A man was accused as a witch because

along the Atlantic coast and ventured up the large river that now bears his name until it dwindled to a stream that obviously did not lead to China. A decade later, the Dutch government granted the West India Company—a group of

Dutch merchants and shippers—exclusive rights to trade with the Western Hemisphere. In 1626, Peter Minuit, the resident director of the company, purchased Manhattan Island from the Manhate Indians for trade goods worth the

Witches Show Their Love for Satan
Mocking pious Christians' humble obeisance to God, witches willingly debased themselves by standing in line to kneel and kiss Satan's buttocks—or so it was popularly believed. This seventeenth-century print portrays Satan with clawlike hands and feet, the tail of a rodent, the wings of a bat, and the head of a lustful ram attached to the torso of a man. Notice that women predominate among the witches eager to express their devotion to Satan and to do his bidding.
UCSF Library / Center for Knowledge Management.

something bad happened, an unhappy God may have caused it to show his displeasure with the victim, who had perhaps sinned in some way. But maybe the victim was not in fact responsible for the misfortune. Maybe Satan, acting through a witch, had caused it. If misfortunes could be pinned on a witch in thrall to Satan, the accuser was absolved from responsibility. The accuser became a helpless victim rather than a guilty party. Witches were an explanation for the disorder that continually crept into New England communities, an explanation that attributed the disorder not to chance or to the faults of individuals but to the witches' evil deeds, commanded by Satan.

Accusers usually targeted a vulnerable neighbor, such as an older, often poor woman. Historians have noted that accusers often complained that the accused individuals were quarrelsome, grumbled about being mistreated, muttered vague threats about getting even, and seemed to be dissatisfied with their lives. Researchers have pointed out that many New Englanders had such feelings after about 1650, but most people did not express them openly or, if they did, felt guilty about doing so. Accused witches often expressed and acted on feelings that other people shared but considered inappropriate, shameful, or sinful in their zeal to lead the saintly lives prescribed by their Puritan religion. Witches made it somewhat easier for New Englanders to consider themselves saints rather than sinners.

his "spirit bewitched the pudding," which was inexplicably "cut lengthwise . . . as smooth as any knife could cut it." Mary Parsons testified that she suspected her husband, Hugh, of being a witch "because almost all that he sells to anybody does not prosper."

From our present-day perspective, the accusers seem to have been victims not of witchcraft but of simple accidents, of overheated imaginations, or—in the case of the possessed young women—of emotional distress. But why did seventeenth-century New Englanders find the testimony of accusers persuasive?

Seventeenth-century New Englanders believed that almost nothing happened by chance. Supernatural power, whether God's or Satan's, suffused the world and influenced the smallest event, even the color of a cow's milk. When

equivalent of a dozen beaver pelts. New Amsterdam, the small settlement established at the southern tip of Manhattan Island, became the principal trading center in New Netherland and the colony's headquarters.

Unlike the English colonies, New Netherland did not attract many European immigrants. Like New England and the Chesapeake colonies, New Netherland never realized the profits of its sponsors' dreams. The company tried to stimulate immigration by granting patroonships—allotments of eighteen miles of land along the Hudson River—to wealthy stockholders who would bring fifty families to the colony and settle them as serflike tenants on their huge domains. Only one patroonship succeeded; the others failed to attract settlers, and much of the land was sold back to the company.

> Although few in number, the New Netherlanders were remarkably diverse. Religious dissenters and immigrants from Holland, Sweden, France, Germany, and elsewhere made their way to the colony.

Although few in number, the New Netherlanders were remarkably diverse, especially compared with the homogeneous English settlers to the north and south. Religious dissenters and immigrants from Holland, Sweden, France, Germany, and elsewhere made their way to the colony. A minister of the Dutch Reformed Church complained to his superiors in Holland that several groups of Jews had recently arrived, adding to the religious mixture of "Papists, Mennonites and Lutherans among the Dutch [and] many Puritans . . . and many other atheists . . . who conceal themselves under the name of Christians."

The West India Company struggled to govern the motley colonists. Peter Stuyvesant, governor from 1647 to 1664, tried to enforce conformity to the Dutch Reformed Church, but the company declared that "the consciences of men should be free and unshackled," making a virtue of New Netherland necessity. The company never permitted the colony's settlers to form a representative government. Instead, the company appointed government officials who set policies, including taxes, which many colonists deeply resented.

In 1664, New Netherland became New York. Charles II, who became king of England in 1660 when Parliament restored the monarchy, gave his brother James, the Duke of York, an enormous grant of land that included New Netherland. Of course, the Dutch colony did not belong to the king of England. But that legal technicality did not impede the king or his brother. The duke quickly organized a small fleet of warships, which appeared off Manhattan Island in late summer 1664, and demanded that Stuyvesant surrender. With little choice, he did.

As the new proprietor of the colony, the Duke of York exercised almost the same unlimited authority over the colony as had the West India Company. The duke never set foot in New York, but his governors struggled to impose order on the unruly colonists. Like the Dutch, the duke permitted "all persons of what Religion soever, quietly to inhabit . . . provided they give no disturbance to the publique peace, nor doe molest or disquiet others in the free exercise of their religion." This policy of religious toleration was less an affirmation of liberty of conscience and more a recognition of the reality of the most heterogeneous colony in seventeenth-century North America.

New Jersey and Pennsylvania

The creation of New York led indirectly to the founding of two other middle colonies, New Jersey and Pennsylvania (see Map 4.2). In 1664, the Duke of York subdivided his grant and gave the portion between the Hudson and Delaware

New Amsterdam

In the background of this 1673 Dutch portrait of New Amsterdam appears the settlement on Manhattan Island—complete with a windmill. Wharves connect Manhattan residents to the seaborne commerce of the Atlantic world. In the foreground, the Dutch artist placed native inhabitants of the mainland, drawing them in such a way that they resemble Africans rather than Lenni Lenape (Delaware) Indians. Dutch merchants carried tens of thousands of African slaves to New World ports, New Amsterdam among them. Probably, the artist had never seen Indians, had never been to New Amsterdam, and depended on well-known artistic conventions about the appearance of Africans to create his Native Americans. The portrait contrasts orderly, efficient, businesslike New Amsterdam with the exotic natural environment of America, to which the native woman clings as if she is refusing to succumb to the culture represented by those neat rows of rectangular houses across the river.
© Collection of the New-York Historical Society.

MAP 4.2   Middle Colonies in the Seventeenth Century
For the most part, the middle colonies in the seventeenth century were inhabited by settlers who clustered along the Hudson or Delaware rivers. The vast geographic extent of the colonies shown in this map reflects land grants authorized in England. Most of this area was inhabited by Native Americans rather than settled by colonists.

The Quakers' concept of an open, generous God who made his love equally available to all people manifested itself in unusually egalitarian worship services and in social behavior that continually brought Quakers into conflict with the English government. Quaker leaders were ordinary men and women, not specially trained preachers. More than any other seventeenth-century sect, Quakers allowed women to assume positions of religious leadership. "In souls there is no sex," they said. Since all people were equal in the spiritual realm, Quakers considered social hierarchy false and evil. They called everyone "friend" and shook hands instead of curtsying or removing their hats—even when meeting the king. These customs enraged many non-Quakers and provoked innumerable beatings and worse.

William Penn
This portrait was drawn about a decade after the founding of Pennsylvania. At a time when extravagant clothing and fancy wigs proclaimed that their wearer was an important person, Penn is portrayed informally, lacking even a coat, his natural hair neat but undressed—all a reflection of his Quaker faith. Penn's full face and double chin show that his faith did not make him a stranger to the pleasures of the table. No hollow-cheeked ascetic or wild-eyed enthusiast, Penn appears sober and observant, as if sizing up the viewer and reserving judgment. The portrait captures the calm determination—anchored in faith—that inspired Penn's hopes for his new colony.
Historical Society of Pennsylvania.

rivers to two of his friends. The proprietors of this new colony, New Jersey, soon discovered that Puritan and Dutch settlers already in the region stubbornly resisted the new government. The continuing strife persuaded one of the proprietors to sell his share to two Quakers. When the Quaker proprietors began to quarrel, they called in a prominent English Quaker, William Penn, to arbitrate their dispute. Penn eventually worked out a settlement that continued New Jersey's proprietary government but did little to end the conflict with the settlers. In the process, Penn became intensely interested in what he termed a "holy experiment" of establishing a genuinely Quaker colony in America.

Unlike most Quakers, William Penn came from an eminent family. His father had served both Cromwell and Charles II and had been knighted. Born in 1644, the younger Penn trained for a military career, but the ideas of dissenters from the reestablished Church of England appealed to him, and he became a devout Quaker. By 1680, he had published fifty books and pamphlets and spoken at countless public meetings, although he had not won official toleration for Quakers in England.

Penn was jailed four times for such offenses, once for nine months.

Despite his many run-ins with the government, Penn remained on good terms with Charles II, who granted him land to found a Quaker colony in America. Partly to rid England of the troublesome Quakers, in 1681 Charles made Penn the proprietor of 45,000 square miles for his new colony, called Pennsylvania.

Toleration and Diversity in Pennsylvania

When Penn announced the creation of his colony, Quakers flocked to English ports in numbers exceeded only by the great Puritan migration to New England fifty years earlier. Between 1682 and 1685, nearly 8,000 immigrants arrived in Pennsylvania, most of them Quakers from England, Ireland, and Wales. They represented a cross section of the **artisans**, farmers, and laborers who predominated among English Quakers. Quaker missionaries also encouraged immigrants from the European continent, and many came, giving Pennsylvania greater ethnic diversity than any other English colony except New York. Pennsylvania prospered, and the capital city, Philadelphia, soon rivaled New York—though not yet Boston—as a center of commerce. By 1700, the city's 5,000 inhabitants participated in a thriving trade exporting flour and other food products to the West Indies and importing textiles and manufactured goods.

> Despite its toleration and diversity, Pennsylvania was as much a Quaker colony as New England was a stronghold of Puritanism.

Penn was determined to live in peace with the Indians who inhabited the region. His Indian policy expressed his Quaker ideals and contrasted sharply with the hostile policies of the other English colonies. As he explained to the chief of the Lenni Lenape (Delaware) Indians, "God has written his law in our hearts, by which we are taught and commanded to love and help and do good to one another . . . [and] this great God has been pleased to make me concerned in your parts of the world, and the king of the country where I live has given unto me a great province therein, but I desire to enjoy it with your love and consent." Penn instructed his agents to obtain the Indians' consent by purchasing their land, respecting their claims, and dealing with them fairly.

Penn declared that the first principle of government was that every settler would "enjoy the free possession of his or her faith and exercise of worship towards God." Accordingly, Pennsylvania tolerated Protestant sects of all kinds as well as Roman Catholics. All voters and officeholders had to be Christians, but the government did not compel settlers to attend religious services, as in Massachusetts, or to pay taxes to maintain a state-supported church, as in Virginia.

Despite its toleration and diversity, Pennsylvania was as much a Quaker colony as New England was a stronghold of Puritanism. Penn had no hesitation about using civil government to enforce religious morality. One of the colony's first laws provided severe punishment for "all such offenses against God, as swearing, cursing, lying, profane talking, drunkenness, drinking of healths, obscene words . . . all prizes, stage plays, cards, dice, May games, gamesters, masques, revels, bull-baitings, cock-fightings, bear-baitings, and the like, which excite the people to rudeness, cruelty, looseness, and irreligion." The ethnic and religious diversity of Pennsylvania prevented strict enforcement of pious behavior, but Quaker expectations of godly order and sobriety set the tone of Pennsylvania society.

As proprietor, Penn had extensive powers, subject only to review by the king. He appointed a governor who maintained the proprietor's power to veto any laws passed by the colonial council, which was elected by property owners who possessed at least one hundred acres of land or who paid taxes. The council had the power to originate laws and administer all the affairs of government. A popularly elected assembly served as a check on the council; its members had the authority to reject or approve laws framed by the council.

Penn stressed that the exact form of government mattered less than the men who served in it. In Penn's eyes, "good men" staffed Pennsylvania's government because Quakers dominated elective and appointive offices. Quakers, of course, differed among themselves. Members of the assembly struggled to win the right to debate and amend laws, especially tax laws. They finally won the battle in 1701 when a new Charter of Privileges gave the proprietor the power to appoint the council and in turn stripped the council of all its former powers and gave them to the assembly, which became the only unicameral legislature in all the British colonies.

The Colonies and the British Empire

From the king's point of view, proprietary grants of faraway lands to which he had tenuous claims were a cheap way to reward friends. As the colonies grew, however, the grants became more valuable. After 1660, the king took initiatives to channel colonial trade through English hands and to consolidate royal authority over colonial governments. These initiatives defined the basic relationship between the colonies and England that endured until the American Revolution (Map 4.3).

Royal Regulation of Colonial Trade

English economic policies toward the colonies were designed to yield customs revenues for the monarchy and profitable business for English merchants and shippers. In addition, the policies were intended to divert the colonies' trade from England's enemies, especially the Dutch and the French.

The Navigation Acts of 1650, 1651, and 1660 set forth two fundamental regulations governing colonial trade. First, all colonial goods imported into England had to be transported in English ships using primarily English crews. Second, the Navigation Acts listed ("enumerated," in the language of the time) specific colonial products

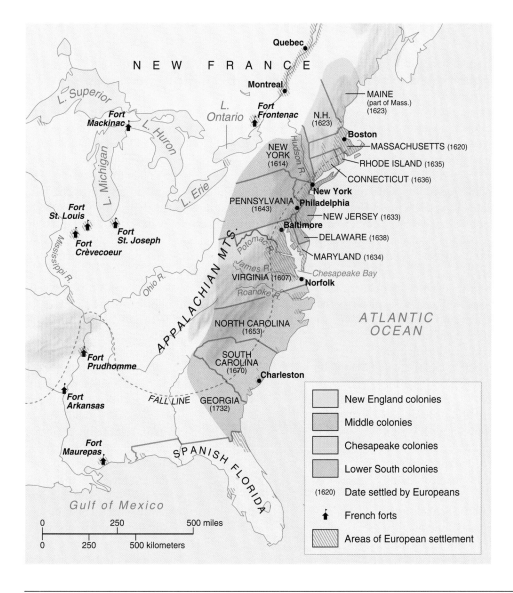

MAP 4.3 American Colonies at the End of the Seventeenth Century
By the end of the seventeenth century, settlers inhabited a narrow band of land that stretched more or less continuously from Boston to Norfolk, with pockets of settlement farther south. The colonies' claims to enormous tracts of land to the west were contested by Native Americans as well as by France and Spain.

READING THE MAP: What geographic feature acted as the western boundary for colonial territorial claims? Which colonies were the most settled and which the least?
CONNECTIONS: The map divides the colonies into four regions. Can you think of an alternative organization? On what criteria would it be based?

FOR MORE HELP ANALYZING THIS MAP, see the map activity for this chapter in the Online Study Guide at bedfordstmartins.com/roark.

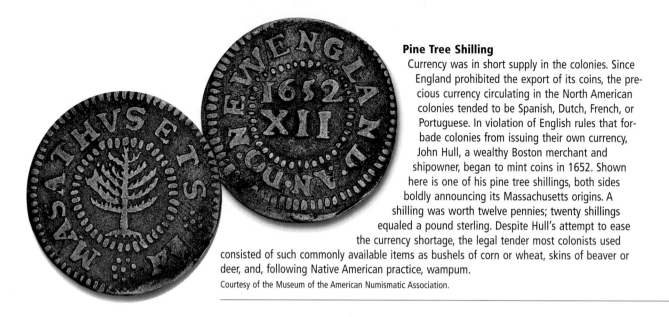

Pine Tree Shilling

Currency was in short supply in the colonies. Since England prohibited the export of its coins, the precious currency circulating in the North American colonies tended to be Spanish, Dutch, French, or Portuguese. In violation of English rules that forbade colonies from issuing their own currency, John Hull, a wealthy Boston merchant and shipowner, began to mint coins in 1652. Shown here is one of his pine tree shillings, both sides boldly announcing its Massachusetts origins. A shilling was worth twelve pennies; twenty shillings equaled a pound sterling. Despite Hull's attempt to ease the currency shortage, the legal tender most colonists used consisted of such commonly available items as bushels of corn or wheat, skins of beaver or deer, and, following Native American practice, wampum.

Courtesy of the Museum of the American Numismatic Association.

that could be shipped only to England or to other English colonies. The Staple Act of 1663 imposed a third regulation on colonial trade. It required all goods imported into the colonies to pass through England (see chapter 3). While these regulations prevented Chesapeake **planters** from shipping their tobacco directly to the European continent, they interfered less with the commerce of New England and the middle colonies, whose principal exports—fish, lumber, and flour—were not enumerated and could legally be sent directly to their most important markets in the West Indies.

By the end of the seventeenth century, colonial commerce was defined by regulations that subjected merchants and shippers to royal supervision and gave them access to markets throughout the British empire. In addition, colonial commerce received protection from the British navy. By 1700, colonial goods (including those from the West Indies) accounted for one-fifth of all British imports and for two-thirds of all goods reexported from England to the European continent. In turn, the colonies absorbed more than one-tenth of British exports. The commercial regulations gave economic value to England's proprietorship of American colonies.

King Philip's War and the Consolidation of Royal Authority

The monarchy also took steps to exercise greater control over colonial governments. Virginia had been a royal colony since 1624; Maryland, South Carolina, and the middle colonies were proprietary colonies with close ties to the crown. The New England colonies possessed royal charters, but they had developed their own distinctively Puritan governments. Charles II, whose father, Charles I, had been executed by Puritans in England, took a particular interest in harnessing the New England colonies more firmly to the British Empire. The occasion was a royal investigation following King Philip's War.

In 1675, warfare between Indians and colonists erupted in the Chesapeake and New England. Although Massachusetts settlers had massacred hundreds of Pequot Indians in 1637, they had established relatively peaceful relations with the more potent Wampanoags. But in the decades that followed, New Englanders steadily encroached on Indian lands, and, in 1675, the Wampanoags struck back with attacks on settlements

King Philip's War, 1675

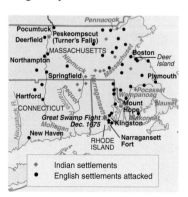

• Indian settlements
• English settlements attacked

King Philip (Metacomet)
No portrait of Metacomet, or King Philip, was made during his lifetime. The artist of this likeness imagines him as a proud warrior wrapped in a shawl and armed with a musket, which indicates both his adoption of this European weapon and his willingness to use it against English colonists.
Library of Congress.

dozen. By the spring of 1676, Indian warriors ranged freely within seventeen miles of Boston. The colonists finally defeated the Indians, principally with a scorched-earth policy of burning their food supplies. King Philip's War left the New England colonists with an enduring hatred of Indians, a large war debt, and a devastated frontier. And in 1676, an agent of the king arrived to investigate whether New England was abiding by English laws.

Not surprisingly, the king's agent found all sorts of deviations from English rules, and the English government decided to govern New England more directly. In 1684, an English court revoked the Massachusetts charter, the foundation of the distinctive Puritan government. Two years later, royal officials incorporated Massachusetts and the other colonies north of Maryland into the Dominion of New England. To govern the dominion, the English sent Sir Edmund Andros to Boston. Some New England merchants cooperated with Andros, but most colonists were offended by his flagrant disregard of such Puritan traditions as keeping the Sabbath. Worst of all, the Dominion of New England invalidated all land titles, confronting every

> King Philip's War left the New England colonists with an enduring hatred of Indians, a large war debt, and a devastated frontier.

King Philip's Sash
This woolen sash belonged to Wampanoag chief Metacomet, or King Philip. Small white glass beads, obtained through trade with Europeans, are stitched into the sash in the shape of a serpent.
Peabody Museum of Archaeology and Ethnology, Harvard University.

in western Massachusetts. Metacomet—whom the colonists called King Philip—was the chief of the Wampanoags and the son of Massasoit, who had befriended William Bradford and his original band of Separatists. Metacomet probably neither planned the attacks nor masterminded a conspiracy with the Nipmucks and the Narragansetts, as the colonists feared. But when militias from Massachusetts and other New England colonies counterattacked all three tribes, a deadly sequence of battles killed over a thousand colonists and thousands more Indians. The Indians utterly destroyed thirteen English settlements and partially burned another half

landowner in New England with the horrifying prospect of losing his or her land.

Events in England, however, permitted Massachusetts colonists to overthrow Andros and retain title to their property. When Charles II died in 1685, he was succeeded by his brother James II, a zealous Catholic. James's aggressive campaign to appoint Catholics to government posts engendered such unrest that in 1688 a group of Protestant noblemen in Parliament invited the Dutch ruler William of Orange, James's son-in-law, to claim the English throne. When William landed in England at the head of a large army, James fled to France and William and his wife Mary (James's daughter) became corulers in a bloodless "Glorious Revolution," which reasserted Protestant influence in England and its empire. Rumors of the revolution raced across the Atlantic and emboldened colonial uprisings against royal authority in Massachusetts, New York, and Maryland.

In Boston, rebels seized Andros and other English officials and tossed them in jail. Then the rebellious colonists destroyed the Dominion of New England and reestablished the former charter government. New Yorkers followed the Massachusetts example. Under the leadership of Jacob Leisler, rebels seized the royal governor and ruled the colony for more than a year. But when King William's governor of New York arrived in 1691, he executed Leisler for treason. In Maryland, the Protestant Association, led by John Coode, overthrew the colony's pro-Catholic government in 1689, fearing it would not recognize the new Protestant king. Coode's men ruled until the new royal governor arrived in 1692 and ended both Coode's rebellion and Lord Baltimore's proprietary government.

Much as they chafed under increasing royal control, the colonists still valued English protection from hostile neighbors. While the northern colonies were distracted by the Glorious Revolution, French forces from the fur-trading regions along the Great Lakes and in Canada attacked villages in New England and New York. Known as King William's War, the conflict with the French was a colonial outgrowth of William's war against France in Europe. The war dragged on until 1697 and ended inconclusively in both Europe and the colonies. But it made clear to many colonists that along with English royal government came a welcome measure of military security.

In Massachusetts, John Winthrop's city on a hill became another royal colony in 1691, when a new charter was issued. The charter said that the governor of the colony would be appointed by the king rather than elected by the colonists' representatives. But perhaps the most unsettling change was the new qualification for voting. Possession of property replaced church membership as a prerequisite for voting in colony-wide elections. Wealth replaced God's grace as the defining characteristic of Massachusetts citizenship.

Conclusion: An English Model of Colonization in North America

By 1700, the diverse English colonies in North America had developed along lines quite different from the example New Spain had set in 1600. In the North American colonies, English immigrants and their descendants created societies of settlers unlike the largely Indian societies in New Spain ruled by a tiny group of Spaniards. Although many settlers came to North America from other parts of Europe and a growing number of Africans arrived in bondage, English laws, habits, ideas, and language dominated all the colonies.

Economically, the English colonies thrived on agriculture and trade instead of mining silver and exploiting Indian labor as in New Spain. Southern colonies grew huge crops of tobacco and rice with the labor of indentured servants and slaves, while farmers in the middle colonies planted wheat and New England fishermen harvested the sea. Although servants and slaves could be found throughout the North American colonies, many settlers depended principally on the labor of family members. Relations between settlers and Native Americans often exploded in bloody warfare, but Indians seldom served as an important source of labor for settlers, as they did in New Spain.

Protestantism prevailed in the North American settlements, relaxed in some colonies and straitlaced in others. The convictions of Puritanism that motivated John Winthrop and others to build a new England in the colonies became muted as the New England colonies matured and dissenters like Roger Williams multiplied. Catholics, Quakers, Anglicans (members of the Church of England), Jews, and others settled in the middle and southern colonies, creating considerable religious toleration, especially in Pennsylvania and New York.

Politics and government differed from colony to colony, although the imprint of English institutions and practices existed everywhere. And everywhere, local settlers who were free adult white men had an extraordinary degree of political influence, far beyond that of colonists in New Spain or ordinary citizens in England. A new world of settlers that Columbus could not have imagined, that Powhatan only glimpsed, had been firmly established in English North America by 1700. During the next half century,

that English colonial world would undergo surprising new developments built on the achievements of the seventeenth century.

FOR ADDITIONAL FIRSTHAND ACCOUNTS OF THIS PERIOD, see Chapter 4 in Michael Johnson, ed., *Reading the American Past*, Third Edition.

TO ASSESS YOUR MASTERY OF THE MATERIAL IN THIS CHAPTER, see the Online Study Guide at bedfordstmartins.com/roark.

FOR WEB LINKS RELATED TO THE TOPICS IN THIS CHAPTER, see "HistoryLinks," "DocLinks," and "PlaceLinks" at bedfordstmartins.com/roark.

CHRONOLOGY

1534 • King Henry VIII breaks with Roman Catholic Church and initiates English Reformation.

1609 • Henry Hudson searches for Northwest Passage for Dutch East India Company.

1620 • English Pilgrims found Plymouth colony and elect William Bradford governor.

1626 • Peter Minuit purchases Manhattan Island for Dutch West India Company and founds New Amsterdam.

1629 • Massachusetts Bay Company receives royal charter for colony.

1630 • John Winthrop leads Puritan settlers to Massachusetts Bay, founding the largest New England colony.

1636 • Roger Williams, banished from Massachusetts, establishes Rhode Island colony as a haven for religious dissenters.
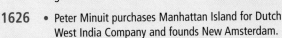
• Thomas Hooker leaves Massachusetts and helps found Connecticut colony.

1638 • Anne Hutchinson, accused of antinomianism, is excommunicated from Boston church.

1642 • Puritan Revolution inflames England, pitting Puritans against royalists in civil war and sharply reducing immigration to New England.

1649 • English Puritans win civil war, execute King Charles I, and declare England a Puritan republic.

1656 • Quakers arrive in Massachusetts and are persecuted there.

1660 • Monarchy restored in England; Charles II becomes king.
• Navigation Act requires colonial goods to be shipped in English ships through English ports.

1662 • Many Puritan congregations adopt Halfway Covenant, relaxing standards for baptism and church membership.
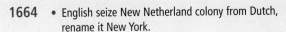

1663 • Staple Act requires all colonial imports to come from England.

1664 • English seize New Netherland colony from Dutch, rename it New York.
• Duke of York subdivides colony, creating colony of New Jersey.

1675 • Indians and colonists clash in King Philip's War, leaving a legacy of hostility toward Indians and prompting English monarchy to attempt to govern New England more directly.

1681 • King Charles II grants William Penn a charter for colony of Pennsylvania, which becomes a haven for Quakers and other religious dissenters.

1686 • Royal officials create Dominion of New England.

1688 • King James II ousted in a "Glorious Revolution"; William III and Mary II become corulers of England.

1691 • Massachusetts becomes royal colony.

1692 • Witch trials flourish at Salem, Massachusetts.

BIBLIOGRAPHY

Please consult the bibliographies of chapters 2 and 3 for more readings on related topics.

General Works

Patricia U. Bonomi, *Under the Cope of Heaven: Religion, Society, and Politics in Colonial America* (1986).

Jon Butler, *Awash in a Sea of Faith: Christianizing the American People* (1990).

Colin G. Calloway, *New Worlds for All: Indians, Europeans, and the Remaking of Early America* (1998).

Patrick Collinson, *The Birthpangs of Protestant England: Religious and Cultural Change in the Sixteenth and Seventeenth Centuries* (1988).

David Hackett Fischer, *Albion's Seed: Four British Folkways in America* (1989).

Stephen Foster, *The Long Argument: English Puritanism and the Shaping of New England Culture, 1570–1700* (1991).

Alison Games, *Migration and the Origins of the English Atlantic World* (1999).

Jack P. Greene, *Pursuits of Happiness: The Social Development of Early Modern British Colonies and the Formation of American Culture* (1988).

David D. Hall, *Worlds of Wonder, Days of Judgment: Popular Religious Belief in Early New England* (1989).

Stephen Innes, *Creating the Commonwealth: The Economic Culture of Puritan New England* (1995).

David Jaffee, *People of the Wachusett: Greater New England in History and Memory, 1630–1860* (1999).

David S. Lovejoy, *Religious Enthusiasm in the New World: Heresy to Revolution* (1985).

Perry Miller, *The New England Mind: From Colony to Province* (1953).

Carla Pestana and Sharon V. Salinger, *Inequality in Early America* (1999).

Robert Blair St. George, *Possible Pasts: Becoming Colonial in Early America* (2000).

Martha Saxton, *Being Good: Women's Moral Values in Early America* (2002).

Alan Taylor, *American Colonies* (2001).

Helena M. Wall, *Fierce Communalism: Family and Community in the American Colonies in the Seventeenth Century* (1990).

Native Americans

Russell Bourne, *Gods of War, Gods of Peace: How the Meeting of Native and Colonial Religions Shaped Early America* (2002).

Colin G. Calloway, *The Western Abenaki of Vermont, 1600–1800: War, Migration, and the Survival of an Indian People* (1990).

Richard W. Cogley, *John Eliot's Mission to the Indians before King Philip's War* (1999).

William Cronon, *Changes in the Land: Indians, Colonists, and the Ecology of New England* (1983).

Matthew Dennis, *Cultivating a Landscape of Peace: Iroquois-European Encounters in Seventeenth-Century America* (1993).

Carol Devens, *Countering Colonization: Native American Women and Great Lakes Missions, 1630–1900* (1992).

James David Drake, *King Philip's War: Civil War in New England, 1675–1676* (2000).

Nicholas Griffiths and Fernando Cervantes, eds., *Spiritual Encounters: Interactions between Christianity and Native Religions in Colonial America* (1999).

Francis Jennings, *The Ambiguous Iroquois Empire: The Covenant Chain Confederation of Indian Tribes with English Colonies from Its Beginnings to the Lancaster Treaty of 1744* (1983).

Yasughide Kawashima, *Puritan Justice and the Indian: White Man's Law in Massachusetts, 1630–1763* (1986).

Jill Lepore, *The Name of War: King Philip's War and the Origins of American Identity* (1998).

James W. Mavor, *Manitou: The Sacred Landscape of New England's Native Civilization* (1989).

Michael Leroy Oberg, *Dominion and Civility: English Imperialism and Native America, 1585–1685* (1999).

Jean M. O'Brien, *Dispossession by Degrees: Indian Land and Identity in Natick, Massachusetts, 1650–1790* (1997).

Ann Marie Plane, *Colonial Intimacies: Indian Marriages in Early New England* (2000).

Daniel K. Richter, *The Ordeal of the Longhouse: The Peoples of the Iroquois League in the Era of European Colonization* (1992).

Daniel K. Richter and James H. Merrell, *Beyond the Covenant Chain: The Iroquois and Their Neighbors in Indian North America, 1600–1800* (1987).

Neal Salisbury, *Manitou and Providence: Indians, Europeans, and the Making of New England, 1500–1643* (1982).

Alden T. Vaughan, ed., *New England Encounters: Indians and Euroamericans, ca. 1600–1850* (2000).

Richard White, *The Middle Ground: Indians, Empires, and Republics in the Great Lakes Region, 1650–1815* (1991).

New England

David Grayson Allen, *In English Ways: The Movement of Societies and the Transferal of English Local Law and Custom to Massachusetts Bay in the Seventeenth Century* (1981).

Douglas Anderson, *William Bradford's Book of Plimmoth Plantation and the Printed Word* (2003).

Virginia Dejohn Anderson, *New England's Generation: The Great Migration and the Formation of Society and Culture in the Seventeenth Century* (1991).

Paul Boyer and Stephen Nissenbaum, *Salem Possessed: The Social Origins of Witchcraft* (1974).

Theodore Dwight Bozeman, *To Live Ancient Lives: The Primitivist Dimension in Puritanism* (1988).

Louise A. Breen, *Transgressing the Bounds: Subversive Enterprises among the Puritan Elite in Massachusetts, 1630–1692* (2001).

Francis J. Bremer, *Shaping New Englands: Puritan Clergymen in Seventeenth-Century England and New England* (1994).

Francis J. Bremer, *John Winthrop: America's Forgotten Founding Father* (2003).

Jonathan M. Chu, *Neighbors, Friends, or Madmen: The Puritan Adjustment to Quakerism in Seventeenth-Century Massachusetts Bay* (1985).

Charles Lloyd Cohen, *God's Caress: The Psychology of Puritan Religious Experience* (1986).

James F. Cooper Jr., *Tenacious of Their Liberties: The Congregationalists in Colonial Massachusetts* (1999).

David Cressy, *Coming Over: Migration and Communication between England and New England in the Seventeenth Century* (1987).

Bruce C. Daniels, *The Connecticut Town: Growth and Development, 1635–1790* (1979).

Bruce Colin Daniels, *Puritans at Play: Leisure and Recreation in Colonial New England* (1995).

Cornelia Hughes Dayton, *Women before the Bar: Gender, Law, and Society in Connecticut, 1639–1789* (1995).

John Demos, *A Little Commonwealth: Family Life in Plymouth Colony* (1970).

John Putnam Demos, *Entertaining Satan: Witchcraft and the Culture of Early New England* (1982).

Stephen Foster, *The Long Argument: English Puritanism and the Shaping of New England Culture, 1570–1700* (1991).

Edwin S. Gaustad, *Liberty of Conscience: Roger Williams in America* (1999).

Richard P. Gildrie, *The Profane, the Civil, and the Godly: The Reformation of Manners in Orthodox New England, 1679–1749* (1994).

Richard Godbeer, *The Devil's Dominion: Magic and Religion in Early New England* (1992).

Lisa M. Gordis, *Opening Scriptures: Bible Reading and Interpretive Authority in Puritan New England* (2003).

Judith S. Graham, *Puritan Family Life: The Diary of Samuel Sewall* (2000).

Philip Gura, *A Glimpse of Sion's Glory: Puritan Radicalism in Seventeenth-Century New England, 1620–1660* (1984).

Michael G. Hall, *The Last American Puritan: The Life of Increase Mather, 1639–1723* (1988).

Stephen Innes, *Labor in a New Land: Economy and Society in Seventeenth-Century Springfield* (1983).

Sydney V. James, *The Colonial Metamorphoses in Rhode Island: A Study of Institutions in Change* (2000).

Jane Kamensky, *Governing the Tongue: The Politics of Speech in Early New England* (1997).

Carol F. Karlsen, *The Devil in the Shape of a Woman: Witchcraft in Colonial New England* (1987).

Karen Ordahl Kupperman, *Providence Island, 1630–1641: The Other Puritan Colony* (1993).

Mary Lou Lustig, *The Imperial Executive in America: Sir Edmund Andros, 1637–1714* (2002).

Gloria L. Main, *Peoples of a Spacious Land: Families and Cultures in Colonial New England* (2001).

Bruce H. Mann, *Neighbors and Strangers: Law and Community in Early Connecticut* (1987).

Carolyn Merchant, *Ecological Revolutions: Nature, Gender, and Science in New England* (1989).

Edmund S. Morgan, *The Puritan Dilemma: The Story of John Winthrop* (1958).

Edmund S. Morgan, *Visible Saints: The History of a Puritan Idea* (1963).

Edmund S. Morgan, *Roger Williams: The Church and the State* (1967).

Margaret Ellen Newell, *From Dependency to Independence: Economic Revolution in Colonial New England* (1999).

Mary Beth Norton, *In the Devil's Snare: The Salem Witchcraft Crisis of 1692* (2002).

Carla Gardina Pestana, *Quakers and Baptists in Colonial Massachusetts* (1991).

Mark A. Peterson, *The Price of Redemption: The Spiritual Economy of Puritan New England* (1998).

Amanda Porterfield, *Female Piety in Puritan New England: The Emergence of Religious Humanism* (1992).

Michael J. Puglisi, *Puritans Besieged: The Legacies of King Philip's War in the Massachusetts Bay Colony* (1991).

Elizabeth Reis, *Damned Women: Sinners and Witches in Puritan New England* (1997).

Phillip H. Round, *By Nature and by Custom Cursed: Transatlantic Civil Discourse and New England Cultural Production, 1620–1660* (1999).

Robert Blair St. George, *Conversing by Signs: Poetics of Implication in Colonial New England Culture* (1998).

Timothy J. Sehr, *Colony and Commonwealth: Massachusetts Bay, 1649–1660* (1989).

Kenneth Silverman, *The Life and Times of Cotton Mather* (1984).

Richard C. Simmons, *Studies in the Massachusetts Franchise, 1631–1691* (1989).

Darren Staloff, *The Making of an American Thinking Class: Intellectuals and Intelligentsia in Puritan Massachusetts* (1997).

Harry S. Stout, *The New England Soul: Preaching and Religious Culture in Colonial New England* (1986).

Rebecca J. Tannenbaum, *The Healer's Calling: Women and Medicine in Early New England* (2002).

Roger Thompson, *Divided We Stand: Watertown, Massachusetts, 1630–1680* (2001).

Lawrence William Towner, *A Good Master Well Served: Masters and Servants in Colonial Massachusetts, 1620–1750* (1998).

Laurel Thatcher Ulrich, *Good Wives: Image and Reality in the Lives of Women in Northern New England, 1650–1750* (1982).

Lisa Wilson, *Ye Heart of a Man: The Domestic Life of Men in Colonial New England* (1999).

Michael P. Winship, *Seers of God: Puritan Providentialism in the Restoration and Early Enlightenment* (1996).

Michael P. Winship, *Making Heretics: Militant Protestantism and Free Grace in Massachusetts, 1636–1641* (2002).

Avihu Zakai, *Exile and Kingdom: History and Apocalypse in the Puritan Migration to America* (1992).

Middle Colonies

Thomas J. Archdeacon, *New York City, 1664–1710: Conquest and Change* (1976).

Patricia U. Bonomi, *A Factious People: Politics and Society in Colonial New York* (1971).

Richard S. Dunn and Mary Maples Dunn, eds., *The World of William Penn* (1986).

Sung Bok Kim, *Landlord and Tenant in Colonial New York: Manorial Society, 1664–1775* (1978).

Cathy Matson, *Merchants and Empire: Trading in Colonial New York* (1998).

Donna Merwick, *Possessing Albany, 1630–1710: The Dutch and English Experiences* (1990).

Donna Merwick, *Death of a Notary: Conquest and Change in Colonial New York* (1999).

David E. Narrett, *Inheritance and Family Life in Colonial New York City* (1992).

Gary B. Nash, *Quakers and Politics: Pennsylvania, 1681–1726* (1968).

John E. Pomfret, *Colonial New Jersey: A History* (1973).

Oliver A. Rink, *Holland on the Hudson: An Economic and Social History of Dutch New York* (1986).

Robert C. Ritchie, *The Duke's Province: A Study of New York Politics and Society, 1664–1691* (1977).

Allen Tully, *Forming American Politics: Ideals, Interests, and Institutions in Colonial New York and Pennsylvania* (1994).

Stephanie Grauman Wolf, *Urban Village: Population, Community, and Family Structure in Germantown, Pennsylvania, 1683–1800* (1976).

Karin A. Wulf, *Not All Wives: Women of Colonial Philadelphia* (2000).

COLONIAL SLAVE DRUM

An African in Virginia made this drum sometime around the beginning of the eighteenth century. The maker of the drum was probably a man who had been enslaved in Africa, transported across the Atlantic in the hold of a slave ship, and sold to a tobacco planter in the Chesapeake. The drum combines deerskin and cedar wood from North America with African skills and designs the maker had mastered before enslavement. The drum signifies the millions of enslaved African men, women, and children who were among the many goods bought and sold in the booming transatlantic trade of the eighteenth century. At a time when Benjamin Franklin and other whites—both native-born and immigrants from Europe—were finding opportunities to better their lives in America, tens of thousands of Africans were arriving in the British North American colonies in hereditary, lifetime bondage. The drum embodies slaves' use of African cultural resources in the alien and oppressive environment of New World slavery. During moments of respite from work, slaves played drums to accompany dances learned in Africa. They also drummed out messages from plantation to plantation. Whites knew slaves used drums for communication, but they could not decipher the meanings of the rhythms and sounds. Fearful that drums signaled rebellious up-risings, whites outlawed drumming but could not eliminate it. Most likely, the messages expressed by the hands that struck this drumhead included lamentations about a life of bondage in America.

5

Colonial America in the Eighteenth Century

1701–1770

EARLY ON A SUNDAY MORNING in October 1723, young Benjamin Franklin stepped from a wharf along the Delaware River onto the streets of Philadelphia. As he recalled in his autobiography, "I was dirty from my Journey; my Pockets were stuff'd out with Shirts and Stockings; I knew no Soul, nor where to look for Lodging. I was fatigu'd with Travelling, Rowing and Want of Rest. I was very hungry."

Born in 1706, Benjamin Franklin grew up in Boston, where his father, Josiah, worked making soap and candles. The father of seventeen children, Josiah apprenticed each of his sons to learn a trade. At the age of twelve, Benjamin signed a contract to serve for nine years as an apprentice to his brother James, a printer. In James's shop, Benjamin learned the printer's trade and had access to the latest books and pamphlets, which he read avidly. In 1721, James inaugurated the *New England Courant*, avowing to "expose the Vice and Follies of Persons of all Ranks and Degrees" with articles written "so that the meanest ploughman . . . may understand them."

Benjamin's responsibilities in the print shop grew quickly, but he chafed under his brother's supervision. "My Brother was passionate and had often beaten me," he remembered. Benjamin resolved to escape from his apprenticeship "to assert my Freedom" and to run away to New York, nearly three hundred miles from anyone he knew. When he could not find work, he wandered to the Delaware River and then talked his way aboard a small boat heading toward Philadelphia. After rowing half the night, Franklin arrived in the city and went straight to a bakery where he purchased "three great Puffy Rolls." Then he set off for the wharf, "with a Roll under each Arm," to wash down the bread with "a Draught of the River Water." After quenching his thirst, Franklin followed "many clean dress'd People . . . to the great Meeting House of the Quakers. . . . I sat down among them, and . . . I fell fast asleep, and continu'd so till the Meeting broke up."

Franklin's account of his life in Boston and his arrival in Philadelphia is probably the most well-known portrait of life in eighteenth-century America. It illustrates everyday experiences that Franklin shared with many other colonists: a large family; long hours of labor subject to the authority of a parent, relative, or employer; and a restless quest for escape from the ties that bound, for freedom. Franklin's account hints at other, less tangible trends: ambition to make something of oneself in this world rather than worry too much about the hereafter; eagerness to subvert orthodox opinion by publishing dissenting views expressed in simple, clear language understandable by

- **A Growing Population and Expanding Economy in British North America**

- **New England: From Puritan Settlers to Yankee Traders**
  Natural Increase and Land Distribution
  Farms, Fish, and Trade

- **The Middle Colonies: Immigrants, Wheat, and Work**
  German and Scots-Irish Immigrants
  Pennsylvania: "The Best Poor [White] Man's Country"

- **The Southern Colonies: Land of Slavery**
  The Atlantic Slave Trade and the Growth of Slavery
  Slave Labor and African American Culture
  Tobacco, Rice, and Prosperity

- **Unifying Experiences**
  Commerce and Consumption
  Religion, Enlightenment, and Revival

- **Bonds of the British Empire**
  Defending the Borderlands of Empire: Indians and French and Spanish Outposts
  Colonial Politics in the British Empire

- **Conclusion: The Dual Identity of British North American Colonists**

Mrs. Charles Willing

This portrait of Mrs. Charles Willing of Philadelphia illustrates the prosperity achieved by numerous women and men in the eighteenth-century colonies. Painted by the Philadelphia artist Robert Feke in 1746, the portrait depicts the close connections between Europe and the North American colonies made possible by thriving transatlantic commerce. Scholars have discovered that Anna Maria Garthwaite, an established textile designer in Spitalfields—a silk-weaving center near London—designed the silk used to make Mrs. Willing's dress in 1743. A Spitalfields weaver, Simeon Julins, then wove the fabric in the months between the fall of 1743 and the spring of 1744 and sold it to a merchant who exported it to Philadelphia in 1744. Mrs. Willing must have spotted the silk in a shop much like the one Benjamin Franklin eventually ran with his wife Deborah after he had become more established in Philadelphia. Mrs. Willing would have purchased enough to have this fashionable gown sewn and fitted for her portrait, only three years after Anna Garthwaite first sketched the design in Spitalfields. The portrait demonstrates that, like other prosperous colonists, Mrs. Willing kept abreast of the latest London fashions available in the shops of colonial merchants.

Courtesy, Winterthur Museum, gift of Mrs. George P. Bissell Jr.

"the meanest ploughman"; confidence that, with a valued skill and a few coins, a young man could make his way in the world, confidence few young women could dare assert; and a slackening of religious fervor displayed, for example, in Franklin's quiet snooze—rather than rapt attention—during the Quaker meeting he wandered into on his first day in Philadelphia.

Franklin's story introduces some of the major changes that affected all the British colonies in eighteenth-century North America. Social and economic changes tended to reinforce the differences among New England, the middle colonies, and the southern colonies, while important cultural and political developments tugged in the opposite direction, creating common experiences, aspirations, and identities. In 1776, when *E Pluribus Unum* (Latin meaning "From Many, One") was adopted as the motto for the Great Seal of the United States, the changes in eighteenth-century America that strengthened *Pluribus* also planted the seeds of *Unum*.

In contrast to the British colonies, which experienced vigorous economic growth and political maturation, the Spanish and French colonies in North America remained thinly populated outposts of European empires interested principally in maintaining a toehold in the vast North American territories they claimed. The social, cultural, and religious developments that tended to unify the British North American colonies were unique to what would soon become the United States of America.

A Growing Population and Expanding Economy in British North America

The most important fact about eighteenth-century British America is its phenomenal population growth: In 1700, colonists numbered about 250,000; by 1770, they tallied well over 2 million. An index of the emerging significance of colonial America is that in 1700 there were 19 people in England for every American colonist, but by 1770 there were only 3. The eightfold growth of the colonial population signaled the maturation of a distinctive colonial society. That society was by no means homogeneous. Colonists of different ethnic groups, races, and religions lived in varied environments under thirteen different colonial governments, all of them part of the British Empire.

In general, the growth and diversity of the eighteenth-century colonial population derived from two sources: immigration and natural increase (growth through reproduction). Natural increase contributed about three-fourths of the population growth, immigration about one-fourth. Immigration shifted the ethnic and racial balance among the colonists, making them by 1770 less English and less white than ever before. Fewer than 10 percent of eighteenth-century immigrants came from England; about 36 percent were Scots-Irish, mostly from northern Ireland; 33 percent arrived from Africa, almost all of them slaves; nearly 15 percent had left the many German-language principalities (the nation of Germany did not exist until 1871); and almost 10 percent came from Scotland. In 1670, more than 9 out of 10 colonists were of English ancestry, and only 1 out of 25 was of African ancestry. By 1770, only about half the colonists were of English descent, while more than 20 percent descended from Africans. By 1770, the people of the colonies had a distinctive colonial—rather than English—profile (Map 5.1).

The booming population of the colonies hints at a second major feature of eighteenth-century colonial society: an expanding economy. Today, societies with rapidly growing populations often have more people than they can adequately feed; or, put another way, they have a high ratio of people to land. In the eighteenth-century colonies, very different conditions prevailed.

In 1700, after almost a century of settlement, nearly all the colonists lived within fifty miles of the Atlantic coast, on the edge of a vast wilderness peopled by native Indians and a few trappers and traders. The almost limitless wilderness gave the colonies an extremely low ratio of people to land. Consequently, land was cheap. Land in the colonies commonly sold for a fraction of its price in the Old World, often for only a shilling an acre, at a time when a carpenter could earn three shillings a day. Along the **frontiers** of settlement, many newcomers who lacked the money to buy land lived as squatters on unoccupied land, hoping it might eventually become theirs.

Without labor, land was almost worthless for agriculture. The abundance of land in the colonies made labor precious, and the colonists

> The most important fact about eighteenth-century colonial America is its phenomenal population growth.

"Dummy Board" of Phyllis, a New England Slave

This life-size portrait of a slave woman named Phyllis, a mulatto who worked as a domestic servant for her owner, Elizabeth Hunt Wendell, was painted sometime before 1753. Known as a "dummy board," it was propped against a wall or placed in a doorway or window to suggest that the residence was occupied and to discourage thieves, a hint of the strangers from throughout the Atlantic world who strolled by prosperous homes in colonial cities. Phyllis is portrayed as a demure, well-groomed woman whose dress and demeanor suggest that she was capable, orderly, and efficient. Unlike Mrs. Willing, Phyllis did not appear in the latest fashions of silk and lace. Instead, she wore the clothing of a servant woman, like thousands of other slave women who labored in the homes of prosperous white families. Phyllis illustrates the integration of the mundane tasks of housekeeping with the shifting currents of transatlantic commerce. Although tens of thousands of slaves were brought from Africa to the British North American colonies during the eighteenth century (like the maker of the drum shown at the beginning of this chapter), Phyllis was probably not one of them. Instead, she was most likely born in the colonies of mixed black and white parentage.

Courtesy of the Society for the Preservation of New England Antiquities / photo by David Bohl.

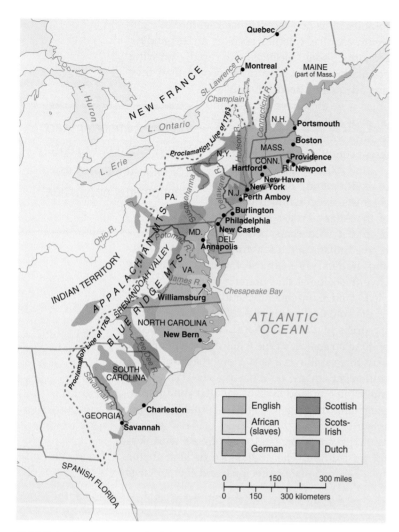

MAP 5.1 Europeans and Africans in the Eighteenth Century
This map illustrates regions where Africans and certain immigrant groups clustered. It is important to avoid misreading the map. Predominantly English and German regions, for example, also contained colonists from other places. Likewise, regions where African slaves resided in large numbers also included many whites, slave masters among them. The map suggests the polyglot diversity of eighteenth-century colonial society.

New England: From Puritan Settlers to Yankee Traders

The New England population grew sixfold during the eighteenth century but lagged behind the growth in the other colonies. Why did New England fail to keep pace? Most immigrants chose other destinations because of New England's relatively densely settled land and because Puritan orthodoxy made these colonies comparatively inhospitable to religious dissenters and those indifferent to religion. As the population grew, many settlers in search of farmland dispersed from towns, and Puritan communities lost much of their cohesion. Nonetheless, networks of economic exchange laced New Englanders to their neighbors, to Boston merchants, and to the broad currents of Atlantic commerce. In many ways, trade became a faith that competed strongly with the traditions of **Puritanism**.

Natural Increase and Land Distribution

The New England population grew mostly by natural increase, much as it had during the seventeenth century. Nearly every adult woman married. Most married women had children—often many children, thanks to the relatively low mortality rate in New England. The perils of childbirth gave wives a shorter life expectancy than husbands, but wives often lived to have six, seven, or eight babies. When a wife died, her husband usually remarried quickly. A wife's labor and companionship were too vital for a family to do without. Benjamin Franklin's father had seven children with his first wife and ten (including Benjamin) with his second.

The burgeoning New England population pressed against a limited amount of land. The interior of New England was smaller than that of colonies farther south (see Map 5.1). Moreover, as the northernmost group of colonies, New England had a contested northern and western frontier. Powerful Indian tribes, especially the Iroquois and Mahicans, jealously guarded their territories. When provoked by colonial or European disputes, the French (and Catholic) colony of Quebec also menaced the English (and **Protestant**) colonies of New England.

During the seventeenth century, New England towns parceled out land to individual families. In most cases, the original settlers prac-

always needed more. The colonists' insatiable demand for labor was the fundamental economic environment that sustained the mushrooming population. Economic historians estimate that the standard of living of free colonists (those who were not **indentured servants** or slaves) improved during the eighteenth century. By 1770, most free colonists had a higher standard of living than the majority of people elsewhere in the Atlantic world. The unique achievement of the eighteenth-century colonial economy was not the wealth of the most successful colonists but the modest economic welfare of the vast bulk of the free population.

ticed partible inheritance (they subdivided land more or less equally among sons). By the eighteenth century, the original land allotments had to be further subdivided to accommodate grandsons and great-grandsons, and many plots of land became too small for subsistence. Sons who could not hope to inherit sufficient land to farm had to move away from the town where they were born.

During the eighteenth century, colonial governments in New England abandoned the seventeenth-century policy of granting land to towns. Needing revenue, the governments of both Connecticut and Massachusetts sold land directly to individuals, including speculators. Now money, rather than membership in a community bound by a church **covenant**, determined whether a person could obtain land. The new land policy eroded the seventeenth-century pattern of settlement. As colonists moved into western Massachusetts and Connecticut and north into present-day New Hampshire and Maine, they tended to settle on individual farms rather than in the towns and villages that characterized the seventeenth century. New Englanders still depended on their relatives and neighbors for help in clearing land, raising a house, worshiping God, and having a good time. But far more than in the seventeenth century, they regulated their behavior in newly settled areas by their own individual dictates.

Farms, Fish, and Trade

A New England farm was a place to get by, not to get rich. New England farmers grew food for their families, but their fields did not produce a huge marketable surplus. Instead of one big crop, farmers grew many small ones. If they had extra, they sold to or traded with neighbors. Poor roads made travel difficult, time-consuming, and expensive, especially with bulky and heavy agricultural goods. The one major agricultural product the New England colonies exported—livestock—walked to market on its own legs. By 1770, New Englanders had only one-fourth as much wealth as free colonists in the southern colonies.

As consumers, New England farmers were the foundation of a diversified commercial economy that linked remote farms to markets throughout the world. Merchants large and small stocked imported goods—English textiles, ceramics, and metal goods; Chinese tea; West Indian sugar; and Chesapeake tobacco. Farmers'

needs for sturdy shoes, a warm coat, a sound cart, and a solid building supported local shoemakers, tailors, wheelwrights, and carpenters. Larger towns and especially Boston, housed skilled tradesmen such as cabinetmakers and silversmiths, along with printers like Benjamin Franklin's brother. Shipbuilders clustered in Boston and other ports, and they tended to do better than other **artisans** because they served the most dynamic sector of the New England economy.

Many New Englanders made their fortunes at sea, as they had since the seventeenth century. Fish accounted for more than a third of New England's eighteenth-century exports; livestock and timber made up another third. The West Indies absorbed two-thirds of all New England's exports. Slaves on Caribbean sugar plantations ate dried, salted codfish caught by New England fishermen, filled barrels crafted from New England timber with molasses and refined sugar, and loaded those barrels aboard ships bound ultimately for Europeans with a sweet tooth (Map 5.2). Almost all the rest of New England's exports went to England and continental Europe. This Atlantic commerce benefited the entire New England economy, providing jobs for laborers and tradesmen as well as for ship captains, clerks, and merchants.

Merchants dominated the commercial economy of New England and stood at the hub of trade between local folk and the international market. The largest and most successful merchants lived in Boston, where they not only bought and sold imported goods but also owned and insured the ships that carried the merchandise. When John Adams, a Massachusetts lawyer who became a leader during the American Revolution and ultimately the second president of the United States, was invited to a wealthy Boston merchant's home, he was stunned by its magnificence. It was a house "for a noble Man, a Prince," he wrote: "The Turkey Carpets, the painted Hangings, the Marble Tables, the rich Beds with crimson Damask Curtains and Counterpins, the beautiful Chimney Clock, the Spacious Garden, are the most magnificent of any Thing I have ever seen." The contrast Adams noted between the luxurious home of this merchant prince and the lives of other New Englanders indicates the polarization

> New Englanders still depended on relatives and neighbors, but far more than in the seventeenth century, they regulated their behavior in newly settled areas by their own individual dictates.

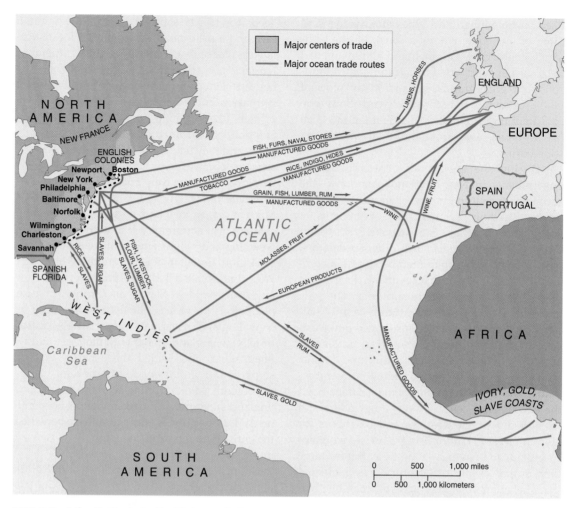

MAP 5.2   Atlantic Trade in the Eighteenth Century
This map illustrates the economic outlook of the colonies in the eighteenth century—east toward the Atlantic world rather than west toward the interior of North America. The long distances involved in the Atlantic trade and the uncertainties of seaborne travel suggest the difficulties Britain experienced governing the colonies and regulating colonial commerce.

READING THE MAP: What were the major markets for trade coming out of Europe? What goods did the English colonies import and export?
CONNECTIONS: In what ways did the flow of raw materials from the colonies affect English industry? How did English colonial trade policies influence the Atlantic trade?

FOR MORE HELP ANALYZING THIS MAP, see the map activity for this chapter in the Online Study Guide at bedfordstmartins.com/roark.

---

of wealth that occurred in Boston and other seaports during the eighteenth century. By 1770, the richest 5 percent of Bostonians owned about half the city's wealth; the poorest two-thirds of the population owned less than one-tenth.

Although the rich got richer and everybody else had a smaller share of the total wealth, the incidence of genuine poverty did not change much. Roughly 5 percent of the New England population qualified for poor relief throughout the eighteenth century. The colonies' growing population increased the sheer numbers of unemployed or sick, but compared with the poor in England, the colonists were better off. A Connecticut traveler wrote from England in 1764, "We in New England know nothing of poverty and want, we have no idea of the thing, how much better do our poor people live than 7/8 of the people on this much famed island."

The contrast with English poverty had meaning because the overwhelming majority of New Englanders traced their ancestry to England; New England was more homogeneous than any other region. People of African ancestry (almost all of them slaves) remained few. New Englanders had no hesitation about acquiring slaves, and many Puritan ministers owned one or two. In the Narragansett region of Rhode Island, numerous slaves were imported by the colony's prominent slave traders to raise livestock. But New England's family farms were unsuited for slave labor. Instead, slaves concentrated in towns, especially Boston, where most of them worked as domestic servants and laborers. Although the black population of New England grew to over 15,000 by 1770, it barely diluted the region's 97 percent white majority.

By 1770, the population, wealth, and commercial activity of New England differed from what they had been in 1700. Ministers still enjoyed high status, but Yankee traders had replaced Puritan saints as the symbolic New Englanders.

The Middle Colonies: Immigrants, Wheat, and Work

In 1700, almost twice as many people lived in New England as in the middle colonies of Pennsylvania, New York, New Jersey, and Delaware. But by 1770, the population of the middle colonies had multiplied tenfold—mainly from an influx of German, Irish, Scottish, and other immigrants—and nearly equaled the population of New England. Immigrants made the middle colonies a uniquely diverse society. By 1800, barely one-third of Pennsylvanians and less than half the total population of the middle colonies traced their ancestry to England.

German and Scots-Irish Immigrants

Germans made up the largest contingent of migrants from the European continent to the middle colonies. By 1770, about 85,000 Germans had arrived in the colonies. Their fellow colonists often referred to them as "Pennsylvania Dutch," an English corruption of *Deutsch,* the word the immigrants used to describe themselves.

Most German immigrants came from what is now southwestern Germany, although some hailed from German-speaking parts of Switzerland, Austria, and the Netherlands. Throughout Europe, peasants suffered from exploitation by landowners and governments and had few opportunities to improve their lives. Many German peasants, one observer noted, were "not as well off as cattle elsewhere." Devastating French invasions of Germany during Queen Anne's War (1702–1713) made ordinarily bad conditions even worse and triggered the first large-scale migration. German immigrants included numerous artisans and a few merchants, but the great majority were farmers and laborers. Economically, they represented "middling" folk, neither the poorest (who could not afford the trip) nor the better off (who did not want to leave).

By the 1720s, Germans who had established themselves in the colonies wrote back to their friends and relatives, as one reported, "of the civil and religious liberties [and] privileges, and

German Hymnal

This manuscript hymnal contains words and music created by Johann Conrad Beissel, the founder of the Seventh-Day Baptists and among the earliest musical composers in the colonies. A German sect that migrated to Pennsylvania in 1732, the Seventh-Day Baptists, like many other German immigrants, continued to worship in their native German long after arriving in the British colonies. Once owned by Benjamin Franklin, this book expresses on its title page the hymns' evocation of the Seventh-Day Baptists' vision of this world and the next: "The Bitter good, or the song of the turtledove, the Christian church here on earth, in the valley of sadness, where it bemoans its 'widowhood'; and at the same time sings of another future reunion [with God]."
Roger Foley/Library of Congress.

of all the goodness I have heard and seen." Such letters prompted still more Germans to pull up stakes and embark for America, to exchange the miserable certainties of their lives in Germany for the uncertain attractions of life in the colonies.

Similar motives propelled the Scots-Irish, who considerably outnumbered German immigrants. The term *Scots-Irish* was another misleading label coined in the colonies. Immigrants labeled "Scots-Irish" actually hailed from the north of Ireland, Scotland, and northern England. Some of the Scots-Irish were Irish natives who had no personal or ancestral connection whatever with Scotland.

Like the Germans, the Scots-Irish were Protestants, but with a difference. Most German immigrants worshipped in Lutheran or German Reformed churches; many others belonged to dissenting sects such as the Mennonites, Moravians, and Amish, whose adherents sought relief from persecution they had suffered in Europe for their refusal to bear arms and to swear oaths, practices they shared with Quakers. In contrast, the Scots-Irish tended to be militant Presbyterians who seldom hesitated to bear arms or swear oaths. Like German settlers, however, Scots-Irish immigrants were clannish, residing when they could among relatives or neighbors from the old country.

In the eighteenth century, wave after wave of Scots-Irish immigrants arrived, beginning in 1717, cresting every twelve or fifteen years thereafter, and culminating in a flood of immigration in the years just before the American Revolution. Deteriorating economic conditions in northern Ireland, Scotland, and England pushed many toward America. Most of the immigrants were farm laborers or tenant farmers fleeing droughts, crop failures, high food prices, or rising rents. By 1773, British officials became so concerned about the drain of people to the colonies that they began to quiz prospective settlers about why they were leaving. The answers Scots-Irish gave echoed the motives of their predecessors: "out of work"; "poverty"; "tyranny of landlords"; and the desire to "do better in America."

Both Scots-Irish and Germans probably heard the common saying that "Pennsylvania is heaven for farmers [and] paradise for artisans," but they almost certainly did not fully understand the risks of their decision to leave their native lands. Gottfried Mittelberger, a musician who traveled from Germany to Philadelphia in 1750, described the grueling passage to America commonly experienced by eighteenth-century emigrants. Mittelberger's trip from his home village in the interior to the port of Rotterdam took seven weeks and cost four times more than the trip from Rotterdam to Philadelphia. Nearly two-thirds of all German emigrants arrived at their port of departure with no money to stock up on extra provisions for the trip or even to buy a ticket. Likewise, they could not afford to go back home. Ship captains, aware of the hunger for labor in the colonies, eagerly signed up the penniless emigrants as "redemptioners," a variant of indentured servants. A captain would agree to provide transportation to Philadelphia, where redemptioners would obtain the money to pay for their passage by borrowing it from a friend or relative who was already in the colonies or, as most did, by selling themselves as servants. Impoverished Scots-Irish emigrants, especially the majority who traveled alone rather than with families, typically paid for their passage by contracting before they sailed to become indentured servants.

Mittelberger enjoyed the amenities reserved for passengers who paid their way to Pennsylvania, but he witnessed the distress among the four hundred other Germans aboard his ship, most of them redemptioners. They were packed "as closely as herring" in bunks two feet by six feet. Seasickness compounded by exhaustion, poverty, poor food, bad water, inadequate sanitation, and tight quarters encouraged the spread of disease. The dismal conditions on Mittelberger's ship were not unusual. One historian has noted that on the sixteen immigrant ships arriving in Philadelphia in 1738, over half of all passengers died en route.

When his ship finally approached land, Mittelberger wrote, "everyone crawls from below to the deck . . . and people cry for joy, pray, and sing praises and thanks to God." Unfortunately, their troubles were far from over. Once the ship docked, passengers who had paid their fare could go ashore. Redemptioners and indentured servants—the majority of the passengers—had to stay on board until somebody came to purchase their labor. Unlike indentured servants, redemptioners negotiated independently with their purchasers about their period of servitude.

> Both Scots-Irish and Germans heard the saying that "Pennsylvania is heaven for farmers [and] paradise for artisans," but they almost certainly did not fully understand the risks of leaving their native lands.

Typically, a healthy adult redemptioner agreed to four years of labor. Indentured servants commonly served five, six, or seven years, as did weaker, younger, and less skilled redemptioners. Children ten years old or younger usually had to become indentured servants until they were twenty-one.

Pennsylvania: "The Best Poor [White] Man's Country"

New settlers, whether free or in servitude, poured into the middle colonies because they perceived unparalleled opportunities, particularly in Pennsylvania, "the best poor Man's Country in the World," as indentured servant William Moraley wrote in 1743. Although Moraley reported that "the Condition of bought Servants is very hard" and masters often failed to live up to their promise to provide decent food and clothing, opportunity abounded because there was more work to be done than workers to do it.

Most servants toiled in Philadelphia, New York City, or one of the smaller towns or villages. Artisans, small manufacturers, and shopkeepers prized the labor of male servants. Female servants

> New settlers, whether free or in servitude, poured into the middle colonies because they perceived unparalleled opportunities.

New York City Street

This painting depicts John Street, a residential neighborhood of New York City, in 1768, as recalled by the artist Joseph B. Smith early in the nineteenth century. The painting highlights the urbane pleasures of casual encounters and friendly conversations on the street. Unlike many urban streets today, John Street was quiet. People could talk casually while a horseman rode past. The street appears safe and secure. Men, women, and children show no sign of caution about theft or assault. People sit on their porches, doors ajar. Modest dwellings adjoin more elaborate homes, suggesting a mix of wealth and taste among John Street residents. Notice that fences separate house yards from the street, rather than houses from one another, hinting of friendly relations among neighbors.

Old John Street United Methodist Church.

Wampum Belt and Game Table
Delaware Indians presented this wampum belt to William Penn in the late seventeenth century to attest to peaceful land transfer and continuing friendship between the Indians and the Pennsylvania colonists. Delawares and other Indians valued wampum as currency, but the land they alienated to Penn and other colonists in the middle colonies became the foundation of prosperous farms that undermined and ultimately eliminated wampum as a form of wealth. By the eighteenth century, the hands joined on this wampum belt might have been reinterpreted by Delawares less as a symbol of friendship than of grasping colonists snatching land from reluctant Indians.

Wealth accumulated by prosperous eighteenth-century colonists supported urban artisans, such as the cabinetmaker in New York who built this elegant Chippendale table for sociable games of backgammon and cards. The table symbolizes the shift from hands joined in amity and friendship (on the wampum belt) to hands in competition with one another in games of chance that rewarded luck, shrewdness, and self-interest.
Belt: Historical Society of Pennsylvania; table: The Metropolitan Museum of Art, Rogers Fund, 1937. (37.122) Photograph by Richard Cheek. Photograph © 1984 The Metropoliton Museum of Art.

made valuable additions to households, where nearly all of them cleaned, washed, cooked, or minded children. From the masters' viewpoint, servants were a bargain. A master could purchase five or six years of a servant's labor for approximately the wages a common laborer would earn in four months. Wage workers could walk away from their jobs when they pleased, and they did so often enough to be troublesome to employers. Servants, however, were legally bound to work for their masters until their terms expired.

A few black slaves worked in shops and homes in Philadelphia and New York City. After Benjamin Franklin became prosperous, he purchased five slaves. Since a slave cost at least three times as much as a servant, only affluent colonists could afford the long-term investment in slave labor. While the population of African ancestry (almost all slaves) in the middle colonies grew to over 30,000 in 1770, it represented only about 7 percent of the total population, and in most of the region much less. The reason more slaves were not brought to the middle colonies was that farmers, the vast majority of the population, had little use for them. Most farms operated with family labor. Wheat, the most widely grown crop, did not require more

labor than farmers could typically muster from relatives, neighbors, and a hired hand or two.

During the eighteenth century, most slaves came to the middle colonies and New England from the West Indies. Enough arrived to prompt colonial assemblies to pass slave codes that punished slaves much more severely than servants for the same transgressions. "For the least trespass," servant Moraley reported, slaves "undergo the severest Punishment." In practice, both servants and slaves were governed more by their masters than by the laws. But in cases of abuse, servants could and did charge masters with violating the terms of their indenture contracts. The terms of a slave's bondage were set forth in a master's commands, not in a written contract.

Small numbers of slaves managed to obtain their freedom, but free African Americans did not escape whites' firm convictions about black inferiority and white supremacy. Whites' racism and blacks' lowly social status made African Americans scapegoats for European Americans' suspicions and anxieties. In 1741, when arson and several unexplained thefts plagued New York City, officials suspected a murderous slave conspiracy. On the basis of little more than evidence of slaves' "insolence" (refusal to conform fully to whites' expectations of servile behavior), city authorities had thirteen slaves burned at the stake and eighteen others hanged. Although slaves were certifiably poor (they usually had no property whatever), they were not included among the poor for whom the middle colonies were reputed to be the best country in the world.

Immigrants swarmed to the middle colonies because of the availability of land. The Penn family encouraged immigration to bring in potential buyers for their enormous tracts of land in Pennsylvania. From the beginning, Pennsylvania followed a policy of negotiating with Indian tribes to purchase additional land. This policy greatly reduced the violent frontier clashes evident elsewhere in the colonies. Yet the Penn family did not shrink from pushing its agreements with Indian tribes to the limit and beyond. In a dispute with tribes on the northern Delaware River in 1737, the Penn family pulled out a document showing that in 1686 local tribes had granted the Penns land that stretched as far as a man could walk in a day and a half. Under the terms of this infamous "Walking Purchase," the Penns sent out three runners, two of whom collapsed before the thirty-six hours expired. The third runner managed to cover sixty miles of wilderness, approximately doubling the size of the Penns' claim.

Few colonists drifted beyond the northern boundaries of Pennsylvania. Owners of the huge estates in New York's Hudson valley preferred to rent rather than sell their land, and thus they attracted fewer immigrants. The Iroquois dominated the lucrative fur trade of the St. Lawrence valley and eastern Great Lakes, and they had the political and military strength to defend their territory from colonial encroachment. Few settlers wanted to risk having their scalps lifted by Iroquois warriors in northern New York when they could choose to settle instead in the comparatively safe environs of Pennsylvania.

The price of farmland depended on soil quality, access to water, distance from a market town, and the extent of improvements. One hundred acres of improved land that had been cleared, plowed, fenced, and ditched, and per-

Patterns of Settlement, 1700–1770

haps had a house and barn built on it, cost three or four times more than the same acreage of uncleared, unimproved land. Since the cheapest land always lay at the margin of settlement, would-be farmers tended to migrate to promising areas just beyond already improved farms. From Philadelphia, settlers moved north along the Delaware River and west along the Schuylkill and Susquehanna rivers. By mid-century, settlement had reached the eastern slopes of the Appalachian Mountains, and newcomers spilled south down the fertile valley of the Shenandoah River into western Virginia and the Carolinas. Thousands of settlers migrated from the middle colonies through this back door to the South.

Farmers made the middle colonies the breadbasket of North America. They planted a wide variety of crops to feed their families, but they grew wheat in abundance. Flour milling was the number-one industry and flour the number-one export, constituting nearly three-fourths of all exports from the middle colonies. Pennsylvania flour fed residents in other colonies, in southern Europe, and, above all, in the West Indies (see Map 5.2). For farmers, the world grain market proved risky but profitable. Grain prices rose steadily after 1720; by 1770, a bushel of wheat was worth twice (in real terms, that is, adjusted for inflation) what it had been fifty years earlier.

The standard of living in rural Pennsylvania was probably higher than in any other agricultural region of the eighteenth-century world. The comparatively widespread prosperity of all the middle colonies permitted residents to indulge in a half-century shopping spree for English imports. The middle colonies' per capita consumption of imported goods from England more than doubled between 1720 and 1770, far outstripping the per capita consumption of English goods in New England and the southern colonies.

At the crossroads of trade in wheat exports and English imports stood Philadelphia. By 1776, Philadelphia had a larger population than any other city in the entire British Empire except London. Merchants occupied the top stratum of Philadelphia society. In a city where only 2 percent of the residents owned enough property to qualify to vote, merchants built grand homes and dominated local government. Many of Philadelphia's wealthiest merchants were Quakers. Quaker traits of industry, thrift, honesty, and sobriety encouraged the accumulation of wealth. A colonist complained that a Quaker "prays for his neighbor on First Days [the Sabbath] and then preys on him the other six."

The ranks of merchants reached downward to aspiring tradesmen like Benjamin Franklin. After he started to publish the *Pennsylvania Gazette* in 1728, Franklin opened a shop, run mostly by his wife, Deborah, that sold a little bit of everything: cheese, codfish, coffee, goose feathers, sealing wax, soap, and now and then a slave. In 1733, Franklin began to publish *Poor*

Bethlehem, Pennsylvania

This view of the small community of Bethlehem, Pennsylvania, in 1757 dramatizes the profound transformation of the natural landscape wrought in the eighteenth century by highly motivated human labor. Founded by Moravian immigrants in 1740, Bethlehem must have appeared at first like the dense woods on the upper left horizon. In fewer than twenty years, precisely laid-out orchards and fields replaced forests and glades. By carefully penning their livestock (lower center right) and fencing their fields (lower left) farmers safe-guarded their livelihoods from the risks and disorders of untamed nature. Individual farmsteads (lower center) and impressive multistory brick town buildings (upper center) integrated the bounty of the land with the delights of community life. Few eighteenth-century communities were as orderly as Bethlehem, but many effected a comparable transformation of the environment.

Print Collection, Miriam and Ira D. Walsh Division of Art, Prints and Photographs, The New York Public Library. Astor, Lenox, and Tilden.

FOR MORE HELP ANALYZING THIS IMAGE, see the visual activity for this chapter in the Online Study Guide at bedfordstmartins.com/roark.

ARCH STREET FERRY, PHILADELPHIA.

Philadelphia Wharf
This early-nineteenth-century drawing of the Arch Street wharf in Philadelphia approximates the world Benjamin Franklin entered when he stepped ashore in 1723. The wharf was a center of industrious activity; almost everyone depicted appears to be working. The pulse of Atlantic commerce propels casks of products from the deck of the small local sailboat (right) toward the hold of large ocean-going ships (center) bound for England and Europe, ships that had unloaded European products in Philadelphia, such as the silk brocade for Mrs. Willing's dress (page 136). The small rowboat carrying four people (just to the right of the large ships) is probably similar to the boat Franklin rowed to the city. Coordinating the complicated comings and goings of people and goods that moved through the wharf required individuals who combined intelligence, energy, and discipline with efficiency, reliability, and trustworthiness—traits Franklin and other eighteenth-century colonists sought to cultivate.
Rare Book Department, The Free Library of Philadelphia.

Richard's Almanack, a calendar of weather predictions, astrological alignments, and pithy epigrams. Poor Richard preached the likelihood of long-term rewards for tireless labor. The *Almanack* sold thousands of copies, quickly becoming Franklin's most profitable product.

The popularity of *Poor Richard's Almanack* suggests that many Pennsylvanians thought less about the pearly gates than about their pocketbooks. Where were the mysteries of divine providence in what might be considered Poor Richard's motto for the middle colonies, "God gives all Things to Industry"? The promise of a worldly payoff made work a secular faith in the middle colonies. Poor Richard advised, "Work as if you were to live 100 years, Pray as if you were to die Tomorrow."

William Penn's Quaker utopia became a center of worldly affluence whose most famous citizen, Franklin, was neither a Quaker nor a utopian. Quakers remained influential, but Franklin spoke for most colonists with his aphorisms of work, discipline, and thrift that echoed Quaker rules for outward behavior. Franklin's maxims did not look to the Quakers' divine inner light for guidance. They depended instead on the spark of ambition and the glow of gain.

The Southern Colonies: Land of Slavery

Between 1700 and 1770, the population of the southern colonies of Virginia, Maryland, North Carolina, South Carolina, and Georgia grew almost ninefold. By 1770, about twice as many people lived in the South as in either the middle colonies or New England. As elsewhere, natural increase and immigration accounted for the rapid population growth. Many Scots-Irish and German immigrants funneled from the middle colonies into the southern backcountry. Other immigrants were indentured servants (mostly English and Scots-Irish) who followed their seventeenth-century predecessors. But slaves made the most striking contribution to the booming southern colonies, transforming the racial composition of the population. Slavery became the defining characteristic of the southern colonies during the eighteenth century, shaping the region's economy, society, and politics.

The Atlantic Slave Trade and the Growth of Slavery

The number of southerners of African ancestry (nearly all of them slaves) rocketed from just over 20,000 in 1700 to well over 400,000 in 1770. The black population increased nearly three times faster than the South's briskly growing white population. Consequently, the proportion of southerners who were black grew from 20 percent in 1700 to 40 percent in 1770.

Southern colonists clustered into two distinct geographic and agricultural zones. The colonies in the upper South, surrounding the Chesapeake Bay, specialized in growing tobacco, as they had since the early seventeenth century. Throughout the eighteenth century, nine out of ten southern whites and eight out of ten southern blacks lived in the Chesapeake region. The upper South retained a white majority during the eighteenth century.

In the lower South, a much smaller cluster of colonists inhabited the coastal region and spe-

cialized in the production of rice and indigo (a plant used to make blue dye). Lower South colonists made up only 5 percent of the total population of the southern colonies in 1700 but inched upward to 15 percent by 1770. South Carolina was the sole British colony along the southern Atlantic coast until 1732, when Georgia was founded. (North Carolina, founded in 1711, was largely an extension of the Chesapeake region.) Blacks in South Carolina, in contrast to every other British mainland colony, outnumbered whites almost two to one; in some low-country districts, the ratio of blacks to whites exceeded ten to one.

The enormous growth in the South's slave population occurred through natural increase

MAP 5.3 The Atlantic Slave Trade

Although the Atlantic slave trade lasted from about 1450 to 1870, its peak occurred during the eighteenth century, when more than six million African slaves were imported to the New World. Only a small fraction of the African slaves imported to the Western Hemisphere were taken to British North America; most went to sugar plantations in Brazil and the Caribbean.

READING THE MAP: From where in Africa did most slaves originate? Approximately how far was the trip from the busiest ports of origin to the two most common New World destinations?
CONNECTIONS: Why were so many more African slaves sent to the West Indies and Brazil than to British North America?

FOR MORE HELP ANALYZING THIS MAP, see the map activity for this chapter in the Online Study Guide at bedfordstmartins.com/roark.

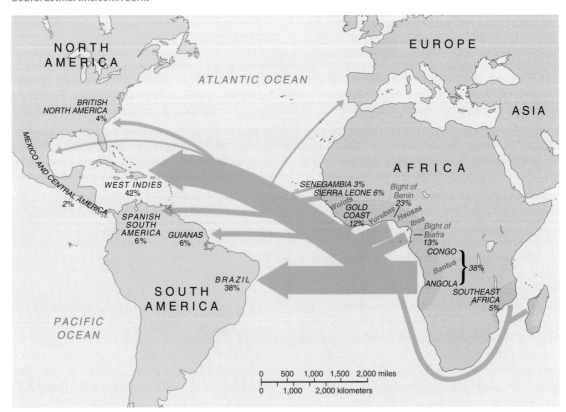

TABLE 5.1	SLAVE IMPORTS, 1451–1870

Estimated Slave Imports to the Western Hemisphere

1451–1600	275,000
1601–1700	1,341,000
1701–1810	6,100,000
1811–1870	1,900,000

and the flourishing Atlantic slave trade (Map 5.3 and Table 5.1). Slave ships brought almost 300,000 Africans to British North America between 1619 and 1780. Of these Africans, 95 percent arrived in the South and 96 percent arrived during the eighteenth century. Unlike indentured servants or redemptioners, these Africans did not choose to come to the colonies. Most of them had been born into free families in villages located within a few hundred miles of the West African coast. Although they shared African origins, they came from many different African cultures, including Akan, Angolan, Asante, Bambara, Gambian, Igbo, Mandinga, and others. They spoke different languages, worshipped different deities, followed different rules of kinship, grew different crops, and recognized different rulers. The most important experience they had in common was enslavement. Captured in war, kidnapped, or sold into slavery by other Africans, they were brought to the coast, sold to African traders who assembled slaves for resale, and sold again to European or colonial slave traders or ship captains, who bought them for shipment to the New World. Packed below decks in the holds of a slave ship, two to three hundred or more slaves were subjected to the infamous **Middle Passage** crossing of the Atlantic and then sold yet again by the ship captain to a colonial slave merchant or to a southern **planter**.

The voices of Africans caught up in the slave trade have been enveloped in a deafening historical silence, with one major exception. In 1789, Olaudah Equiano published *The Interesting Narrative*, an account of his own enslavement that hints at the stories that might have been told by the thousands of silenced Africans. Equiano was born in 1745 in the interior of what is now Nigeria. "I had never heard of white men or Europeans, nor of the sea," he recalled. One day when Equiano was eleven years old, two men and a woman, all Africans, broke into his home, seized him and his sister, and carried them off. The kidnappers soon separated Equiano from his sister, leaving him "in a state of distraction not to be described. I cried and grieved continually, and for several days did not eat anything but what they forced into my mouth."

During the next six or seven months, Equiano was sold to several different African masters, each of whom moved him closer to the coast. When he arrived at the coast, a slave ship waited offshore. Equiano feared that he had "gotten into a world of bad spirits," that he was going to be killed and "eaten by those white men with horrible looks, red faces, and loose hair."

Olaudah Equiano
This portrait was painted by an unknown English artist about 1780, when Equiano was in his mid-thirties, more than a decade after he had bought his freedom. The portrait evokes Equiano's successful acculturation to the customs of eighteenth-century England. His clothing and hairstyle reflect the fashions of respectable young Englishmen. In his *Interesting Narrative*, Equiano explained that he had learned to speak and understand English while he was a slave. He wrote that he "looked upon [the English] . . . as men superior to us [Africans], and therefore I had the stronger desire to resemble them, to imbibe their spirit and imitate their manners; I therefore embraced every occasion of improvement, and every new thing that I observed I treasured up in my memory." Equiano's embrace of English culture did not cause him to forsake his African roots. He honored his dual identity by campaigning against slavery. His *Narrative* was one of the most important and powerful antislavery documents of the time.
Royal Albert Memorial Museum, Exeter, Devon, UK / Bridgeman Art Library.

Once the ship set sail, many slaves died from sickness, crowded together in suffocating heat fouled by filth of all descriptions. "The shrieks of the women and the groans of the dying rendered the whole a scene of horror almost inconceivable," Equiano recalled. Most of the slaves on the ship were sold in Barbados, but Equiano and other leftovers were shipped off to Virginia, where Equiano "saw few or none of our native Africans and not one soul who could talk to me." Equiano felt isolated and "exceedingly miserable" because he "had no person to speak to that I could understand." He finally was sold to a white man, the captain of a tobacco ship bound for England. Equiano remained a slave for ten years, traveling frequently from England to the West Indies and North America until he bought his freedom in 1766.

Only about 15 percent of the slaves brought into the southern colonies came as Equiano did, aboard ships from the West Indies. Merchants in the North American colonies often specialized in this trade; Equiano himself was owned for several years by a Quaker merchant from Philadelphia who traded extensively with the West Indies. All the other slaves brought into the southern colonies came directly from Africa, and almost all the ships that brought them (roughly 90 percent) belonged to British merchants. Most slaves on board were young adults, men usually outnumbering women two to one. Children under the age of fourteen, like Equiano, were typically no more than 10 or 15 percent of a cargo.

Mortality during the Middle Passage varied considerably from ship to ship. On average, about 15 percent of the slaves died, but sometimes half or more perished. The average mortality among the white crew of slave ships was often nearly as bad. In general, the longer the voyage lasted, the larger was the number of deaths. Recent studies suggest that many slaves succumbed not only to virulent epidemic diseases such as smallpox and dysentery but also to acute dehydration caused by fluid loss from heavy perspiration, vomiting, and diarrhea combined with a severe shortage of drinking water.

Normally an individual planter purchased at any one time a relatively small number of newly arrived Africans, or "new Negroes," as they were called. Planters preferred to purchase small groups of slaves to permit the newcomers to be trained by the planters' other slaves. Like Equiano, newly arrived Africans were often profoundly depressed, demoralized, and disoriented. Planters counted on their other slaves—either those born into slavery in the colonies (often called "country-born" or "creole" slaves) or Africans who had arrived earlier—to help new Negroes become accustomed to their strange new surroundings.

Planters' preferences for slaves from specific regions of Africa aided slaves' acculturation (or "seasoning," as it was called) to the routines of bondage in the southern colonies. Chesapeake planters preferred slaves from Senegambia, the Gold Coast, or—like Equiano—the Bight of Biafra, the origin of 40 percent of all Africans imported to the Chesapeake. South Carolina planters favored slaves from the central African Congo and Angola regions, the origin of about 40 percent of the African slaves they imported (see Map 5.3). Although slaves within each of these regions spoke many different languages, enough linguistic and cultural similarities existed that they could usually communicate with other Africans from the same region.

Seasoning acclimated new Africans to the physical as well as the cultural environment of the southern colonies. Slaves who had just endured the Middle Passage were poorly nourished, weak, and sick. In this vulnerable state they encountered the alien diseases of North America without having developed a biological arsenal of acquired immunities. As many as 10 or 15 percent of newly arrived Africans, sometimes more, died during their first year in the southern colonies.

While newly enslaved Africans poured into the southern colonies, slave women made an especially significant contribution to the growth of the black population by giving birth to slave babies, causing the slave population in the South to mushroom. Slave owners encouraged these births. Thomas Jefferson explained, "I consider the labor of a breeding [slave] woman as no object, that a [slave] child raised every 2 years is of more profit than the crop of the best laboring [slave] man." The growing number of slave babies set the southern colonies apart from other New World slave societies, which experienced a natural decrease of the slave population (slave deaths exceeded births). The high rate of natural increase in the southern colonies meant that by the 1740s the majority of southern slaves were country-born. The large numbers of newly enslaved Africans made the influence of African culture in the eighteenth-century South stronger than ever before—or since.

Negro's houses

a fire

Boys playing
under that Rooff

a Woman with
her Child on her back

y door

The African Slave Trade

The African slave trade existed to satisfy the New World's demand for labor and Europe's voracious appetite for such New World products as sugar, tobacco, and rice. African men, women, and children, like those pictured in this early-eighteenth-century engraving of a family residence in Sierra Leone, were kidnapped or captured in wars—typically by other Africans—and enslaved. Uprooted from their homes and kin, they were usually taken to coastal enclaves where African traders and European ship captains negotiated prices, made deals, and often branded the newly enslaved people. The collaboration between Europeans and their African trading partners is evident in the seventeenth-century Benin bronze box in the shape of a royal palace in Nigeria guarded by massive predatory birds and two Portuguese soldiers. Jammed into the holds of slave ships, enslaved Africans made the dreaded Middle Passage to the New World. The model of a slave ship shown here was used in parliamentary debates by antislavery leaders in Britain to demonstrate the inhumanity of shipping people as if they were just so much tightly packed cargo. The model does not show another typical feature of slave ships: weapons. Slaves vastly outnumbered the crews aboard the ships, and crew members justifiably feared slave uprisings.

Staatliche Museen Zu Berlin, Preussischer Kulturbesitz; Courtesy, Earl Gregg Swen Library, College of William and Mary, Williamsburg, Virginia; Wilberforce House, Hull City Museums and Art Galleries, UK / Bridgeman Art Library.

Slave Labor and African American Culture

Southern planters expected slaves to work from sunup to sundown and beyond. George Washington wrote that his slaves should "be at their work as soon as it is light, work til it is dark, and be diligent while they are at it." The conflict between the masters' desire for maximum labor and the slaves' reluctance to do more than necessary made the threat of physical punishment a constant for eighteenth-century slaves. Masters preferred black slaves to white indentured servants, not just because slaves served for life but also because colonial laws did not limit the force masters could use against slaves. As a traveler observed in 1740, "A new negro . . . will require more discipline than a young spaniel. . . . let a hundred men show him how to hoe, or drive a wheelbarrow; he'll still take the one by the bottom and the other by the wheel and . . . often die before [he] can be conquered." Slaves, the traveler noted, were not stupid or simply obstinate; despite the inevitable punishment, they resisted their masters' demands because of their "greatness of soul," their stubborn unwillingness to conform to their masters' definition of them as merely slaves.

Some slaves escalated their acts of resistance to direct physical confrontation with the master, mistress, or an overseer. But a hoe raised in anger, a punch in the face, or a desperate swipe with a knife led to swift and predictable retaliation by whites. Throughout the southern colonies, the balance of physical power rested securely in the hands of whites.

Rebellion occurred, however, at Stono, South Carolina, in 1739. Before dawn on a September Sunday, a group of about twenty slaves attacked a country store, killed the two storekeepers, confiscated the store's guns, ammunition, and powder, and set out toward Spanish Florida after pausing to set the severed heads of their victims on the store's front steps. Enticing other rebel slaves to join the march south, the group plundered and burned more than a half dozen plantations and killed more than twenty white men, women, and children. A mounted force of whites quickly suppressed the rebellion. They placed rebels' heads atop mileposts along the road, grim reminders of the consequences of rebellion. The Stono rebellion illustrated that eighteenth-century slaves had no chance of overturning slavery and very little chance of defending themselves in any

bold strike for freedom. After the rebellion, South Carolina legislators enacted repressive laws designed to guarantee that whites would always have the upper hand. No other similar uprising occurred during the colonial period.

Slaves maneuvered constantly to protect themselves and to gain a measure of autonomy within the boundaries of slavery. In Chesapeake tobacco fields, most slaves were subject to close supervision by whites. In the lower South, the task system gave slaves some control over the pace of their work and some discretion in the use of the rest of their time. A "task" was typically defined as a certain area of ground to be planted, cultivated, and harvested or a specific job to be completed. A slave who completed the assigned task might use the remainder of the day to work in a garden, fish, hunt, spin, weave, sew, or cook. When masters sought to boost productivity by increasing tasks, slaves did what they could to defend customary practices.

Eighteenth-century slaves also planted the roots of African American lineages that branch out to the present. Historians are only beginning to explore the kin networks slaves built; much remains unknown. But it is clear that slaves valued family ties and that, as in West African societies, kinship structured slaves' relations with one another. Slave parents often gave a child the name of a grandparent, aunt, or uncle. In West Africa, kinship not only identified a person's place among living relatives; it also linked the person to ancestors among the dead and to descendants in the future. Newly imported African slaves usually arrived alone, like Equiano, without kin. Often slaves who had traversed the Middle Passage on the same ship adopted one another as "brothers" and "sisters." Likewise, as new Negroes were seasoned and incorporated into existing slave communities, established families often adopted them as "fictive" kin.

When possible, slaves expressed many other features of their West African origins in their lives on New World plantations. They gave their children traditional dolls and African names such as Cudjo or Quash, Minda or Fuladi. They grew food crops familiar to those in Africa, such as yams and okra. They constructed huts with mud walls and thatched roofs similar to African residences. They fashioned banjos, drums, and other musical instruments, held dances, and observed funeral rites that echoed African practices. In these and many

Eliza Lucas Pinckney's Gown
When Eliza Lucas was sixteen years old in 1738, she took over day-to-day management of her father's rice plantations when he was called to duty in the British army. Highly educated, independent, and energetic, Lucas relished her duties and introduced numerous innovations on the plantations, including the cultivation of indigo—which became a major export crop in South Carolina—and silk worms. She married Charles Pinckney, a wealthy rice planter, in 1744 and continued her interest in agricultural innovation while raising four children. The gown shown here was made for Eliza Lucas Pinckney out of silk she grew on her plantation and sent to England to be dyed and woven.
Smithsonian Institution, Washington, D.C.

other ways, slaves drew upon their African heritages to endow their personal lives with relationships and meanings that they controlled, as much as the oppressive circumstances of slavery permitted.

Tobacco, Rice, and Prosperity

Slaves' labor bestowed prosperity on their masters, British merchants, and the monarchy. The southern colonies supplied 90 percent of all North American exports to England. Rice exports from the lower South exploded from less than half a million pounds in 1700 to eighty million pounds in 1770, nearly all of it grown by slaves. Exports of indigo also boomed. Together, rice and indigo made up three-fourths of lower South exports, nearly two-thirds of them going to England and most of the rest to the West Indies, where sugar-growing slaves ate slave-grown rice. Tobacco was by far the most important export from British North America; by 1770, it represented almost one-third of all colonial exports and three-fourths of all Chesapeake exports. And under the provisions of the Navigation Acts (see chapter 4), nearly all of it went to England, where the monarchy collected a lucrative tax on each pound. British merchants then reexported more than 80 percent of the tobacco to the European continent, pocketing a nice markup for their troubles.

These products of slave labor made the southern colonies by far the richest in North America. The per capita wealth of free whites in the South was four times greater than that in New England and three times that in the middle colonies. At the top of the wealth pyramid stood the rice grandees of the lower South and the tobacco gentry of the Chesapeake. These elite families commonly resided on large estates in handsome mansions adorned by luxurious gardens, maintained and supported by slaves. The extravagant lifestyle of one gentry family astonished a young tutor from New Jersey, who noted that during the winter months the family kept twenty-eight large fires roaring, requiring six oxen to haul in a heavy cartload of slave-cut wood four times a day. By contrast, **yeoman** families—who supported themselves on small plots of land without slaves and cut their own wood—normally warmed themselves around one fire.

The vast differences in wealth among white southerners engendered envy and occasional tension between rich and poor, but remarkably

Westover Plantation House
William Byrd II, a leading Virginia planter and large slaveholder, built this house about 1730 and named it Westover, after a relative of a previous Virginia governor. Facing the James River and visible from every ship that sailed past, the house embodies the devotion of Byrd and other prominent Virginians to principles of order, symmetry, and balance commonly found among fine English homes of the era. The house evokes the Virginia gentry's widely shared sense of confidence, stability, and permanence.
Picture Research Consultants & Archives.

little open hostility. In private, the planter elite spoke disparagingly of humble whites but in public acknowledged their lesser neighbors as equals, at least in belonging to the superior—in their minds—white race. Looking upward, white yeomen and tenants (who owned neither land nor slaves) sensed the gentry's condescension and veiled contempt. But they also appreciated the gentry for granting favors, upholding white supremacy, and keeping slaves in their place. While racial slavery made a few whites much richer than others, it also gave those who did not get rich a powerful reason to feel similar (in race) to those who were so different (in wealth).

The slaveholding gentry dominated the politics and economy of the southern colonies. In Virginia, only adult white men who owned at least one hundred acres of unimproved land or twenty-five acres of land with a house could vote. This property-holding requirement prevented about 40 percent of white men in Virginia from voting for representatives to the House of Burgesses. In South Carolina, only fifty acres of land were required to vote, and most adult white men qualified. But in both colonies, voters elected members of the gentry to serve in the colonial legislature. The gentry passed elected political offices from generation to generation, almost as if they were hereditary. Politically, the gentry built a self-perpetuating oligarchy—rule by the elite few—with the votes of their many humble neighbors.

The gentry also set the cultural standard in the southern colonies. They entertained lavishly, gambled regularly, and attended Anglican (Church of England) services more for social than for religious reasons. Above all, they cultivated the leisurely pursuit of happiness. They did not condone idleness, however. Their many pleasures and responsibilities as plantation owners kept them busy. Thomas Jefferson, a phenomenally productive member of the gentry, recalled that his earliest childhood memory was of being carried on a pillow by a family slave—a powerful image of the slave hands supporting the gentry's leisure and achievement.

Unifying Experiences

While the societies of New England, the middle colonies, and the southern colonies became more sharply differentiated during the eighteenth century, colonists throughout British North America shared certain unifying experiences that eluded settlers in Spanish and French colonies. The first was economic. The economies of all three British regions had their roots in agriculture. But the tempo of commerce quickened during the eighteenth century. Colonists sold their distinctive products in markets that, in turn, offered to consumers throughout British North America a more or less uniform array of goods. A second unifying experience was a decline in the importance of religion. Some settlers called for a revival of religious intensity, but for most people religion mattered less, the affairs of the world more, than they had in the seventeenth century. Third, white inhabitants throughout British North America became aware that they shared a distinctive identity as *British* colonists. Thirteen different governments presided over these North American colonies, but all of them answered to the British monarchy. Royal officials who expected loyalty from the colonists often had difficulty obtaining obedience. The British colonists asserted their prerogatives as British subjects to defend their special colonial interests.

Commerce and Consumption

Eighteenth-century commerce whetted the appetite to consume. Colonial products spurred the development of mass markets throughout the Atlantic world (Figure 5.1). Huge increases in the supply of colonial tobacco and sugar brought the price of these small luxuries within reach of most free whites. Colonial goods brought into focus an important lesson of eighteenth-century commerce: Ordinary people, not just the wealthy elite, would buy the things that they desired in addition to what they absolutely needed. Even

news, formerly restricted mostly to a few people through face-to-face conversations or private letters, became an object of public consumption through the innovation of newspapers. (See "The Promise of Technology," page 156.) With the appropriate stimulus, market demand seemed unlimited.

The Atlantic commerce that took colonial goods to markets in England brought objects of consumer desire back to the colonies. English merchants and manufacturers recognized that colonists made excellent customers, and the Navigation Acts (see chapter 4) gave English exporters privileged access to the colonial market. By midcentury, export-oriented industries in England were growing ten times faster than firms attuned to the home market. Most English exports went to the vast European market, where potential customers outnumbered those in the colonies by more than one hundred to one. But as European competition stiffened, colonial markets became increasingly important. English exports to North America multiplied eightfold between 1700 and 1770, outpacing the rate of population growth after midcentury (Figure 5.1). When the colonists' eagerness to consume exceeded their ability to pay, English exporters willingly extended credit, and colonial debts soared.

Imported mirrors, silver plate, spices, bed and table linens, clocks, tea services, wigs, books, and more infiltrated parlors, kitchens, and bedrooms throughout the colonies. Despite the many differences among the colonists, the consumption of English exports built a certain material uniformity across region, religion, class, and status. Consumption of English exports did not simply tie the colonists to the British economy. It also made the colonists look and feel more British even though they lived at the edge of a wilderness an ocean away from England.

The rising tide of colonial consumption had other less visible but no less important consequences. Consumption presented women and men with a novel array of choices. In many respects, the choices might appear trivial: whether to buy knives and forks, teacups, or a clock. But such small choices confronted eighteenth-century consumers with a big question: "What do

> Colonial goods brought into focus an important lesson of eighteenth-century commerce: Ordinary people, not just the wealthy elite, would buy the things that they desired in addition to what they absolutely needed.

The Printing Press: "The Spring of Knowledge"

James Franklin's Printing Press
Newport Historical Society.

In the eighteenth century, colonial printers began to publish newspapers. Since the 1630s, colonial printers had used presses to churn out books, pamphlets, broadsides, government announcements, legal forms, invitations, and even promissory notes. The innovation of compiling newsworthy information and publishing it on a regular schedule began in 1704 with the appearance of the *Boston News-Letter*, which was usually printed on both sides of a single sheet of paper smaller than conventional typing paper. Each week the *News-Letter* contained reprints of articles that had appeared in English newspapers, along with a few tidbits of local news such as deaths, fires, storms, and ship arrivals.

For years, the audience for such information remained small; the editor complained in 1719 that he could not sell three hundred copies of each issue. Nonetheless, a competing newspaper, the *Boston Gazette*, began publication in that year. It was printed by James Franklin on his press, which he had brought from England. Both the *Gazette* and the *News-Letter* submitted their copy to the governor for official approval before the newspapers were printed. Frustrated by this official scrutiny, Franklin started a new paper, the *New England Courant*, which set out to thumb its nose at officialdom, both governmental and religious. The *Courant* pledged "to entertain the Town with the most comical and diverting Incidents of Humane Life" and to "expose the Vice and Follies of Persons of all Ranks and Degrees." Franklin's press—operated faithfully by his apprentice brother, Benjamin—broadcast to the reading public dissenting opinions previously confined to private conversations.

By 1740, more than a dozen newspapers were being published in the colonies, and their numbers continued to increase. Relatively high rates of literacy gave them a large audience. In the northern colonies, readers included well over half of adult men and nearly half of adult women. In the southern colonies, literacy rates among whites were slightly lower but still considerably above those in Europe. Since whites tried to prevent slaves from learning to read, literacy rates remained low among southern blacks.

The information that newspapers printed spread far beyond readers. Newspapers were often read aloud, not just at home but in workshops, taverns, and courthouses. In these public places, people who could not read listened to the controversial ideas, partisan accusations, and salacious rumors that printers relished. An eighteenth-century poem illustrates the many connections between news and audiences cultivated by colonial newspapers:

News'papers are the spring of
knowledge,
The gen'ral source throughout the
nation.
Of ev'ry modern conversation.
What would this mighty people do,
If there, alas! were nothing new?

A News-paper is like a feast,
Some dish there is for ev'ry guest;
Some large, some small, some strong,
some tender,
For ev'ry stomach, stout or slender;
Those who roast beef and ale delight
in,
Are pleas'd with trumpets, drums, and
fighting;
For those who are more puny made,
Are arts and sciences, and trade;
For fanciful and am'rous blood,
We have a soft poetic food;
For witty and satyric folks,
High-season'd, acid, BITTER JOKES;
And when we strive to please the mob,
A jest, a quarrel, or a job.

If any gentleman wants a wife,
(A partner, as 'tis termed, for life)
An advertisement does the thing,
And quickly brings the pretty thing.

If you want health, consult our pages,
You shall be well, and live for ages. . . .

Our services you can't express,
The good we do you hardly guess;
There's not a want of human kind,
But we a remedy can find.

When newspapers employed the technology of printing to publish everything from political news to advertisements for a spouse, all kinds of information and ideas began to diffuse more readily beyond official channels and to help form public opinion. Combining the old technology of printing with the new currents of commerce, dissent, and enlightenment, eighteenth-century newspapers created a novel awareness of the problems and possibilities of public life.

Numb. XIII.

THE

New-York Weekly JOURNAL.

Containing the freſheſt Advices, Foreign, and Domeſtick.

MUNDAY January 28, 1733.

Lege fræuata omnis poteſtas Eſto,
BRACTON.

SIR,

MEN in a Torrent of Proſperity ſeldom think of a Day of Diſtreſs, or Great Men that their greatneſs will ever Ceaſe. This ſeems to be a Sort of a Curſe upon Power, a Vanity and Infatuation blended with the Nature of it: As if it were Poſſible nay eaſy to bind the Fickleneſs of Fortune, and enſure Happyneſs for a Term of Years. Tis from this Aſſureance, often cleaving to very able Men that thoſe in Authority often act with ſuch Boldneſs and Inſolence as if their Reign were never to End, and they were for ever ſecure againſt all After-reckonings, all caſualties and diſgrace. From whence elſe comes it, but from ſuch blindSecurity in the Permanence of their Condition, and in the Impunity of their Actions, that Miniſters have ſometimes concerted SCHEMES OF GENERAL OPPRESSION AND PILLAGE, SCHEMES TO DEPRECIATE OR EVADE THE LAWs, RESTRAINTS UPON LIBERTY AND PROIECTS FOR ARBITRARY WILL? Had they thought that ever they themſelves ſhould ſuffer in the common Oppreſſion would they have adviſed *Methods of Oppreſſing*? Should they have been for *Weakning* or *abrogating the Laws*, had they Dreamed that they ſhould come to want THE PROTECTION OF THE LAW? Would they have aimed at *Aboliſhing Liberty*, had they apprehended that they were at any time to fall from Power; or at eſtabliſhing *deſpotick Rule*, but for the Sake of *having the Direction of it* againſt others, without feeling ITS Weight and Terrors in their own Particulars?

How few Men in Power have ſecured to themſelves a Reſource of Friendſhip and Affection from the Publick, in Caſe of a Storm at Court and the Frowns of a Croun! Nay what ſome of them have done to ſerve the Crown againſt the People, has been a Motive with the Crown (and a politic Motive, tho not always a juſt one, at leaſt not generous) to Sacrifice them to the Pleaſure and Revenge of the People, thus *Cæſar Borgio*, uſed *Romiro D'orco* Governour of *Ramagna*, one firſt employed to commit Cruelties then executed for having committed them. Thus were EMPSON and DUDLEY uſed, and thus the great Turk often uſes his Baſhaws.

The GENERAL SECURITY, is the only certain Security of particulars; and tho'DeſperateMen often find ſafety in publick Deſtruction, yet they cannot inſure the ſame ſafety to their Children, who muſt ſuffer with the reſt in the miſery of all. If Great wicked Men would conſider this, the World would not be plagued with their Ambition, their Poſterity ſcarce ever miſs to reap the bitter Fruits of their Actions, and the Curſe of their iniquities rarely fails to follow them to the third and fourth Generation.

The INSTRUMENTS OF PUBLICK RUIN have generally at once intailed miſery upon their Country and their own Race. Thoſe who were the Inſtruments and Miniſters of *Cæſar* and *Auguſtus*, and put the Common Wealth under their Feet AND THEM ABOVE THE LAWS, did not conſider that they were not only forging Chains for their Country, but whetting Swords againſt their own Families, who were all cut off under ſucceeding Tyrants: Nay, moſt of their Children fell early

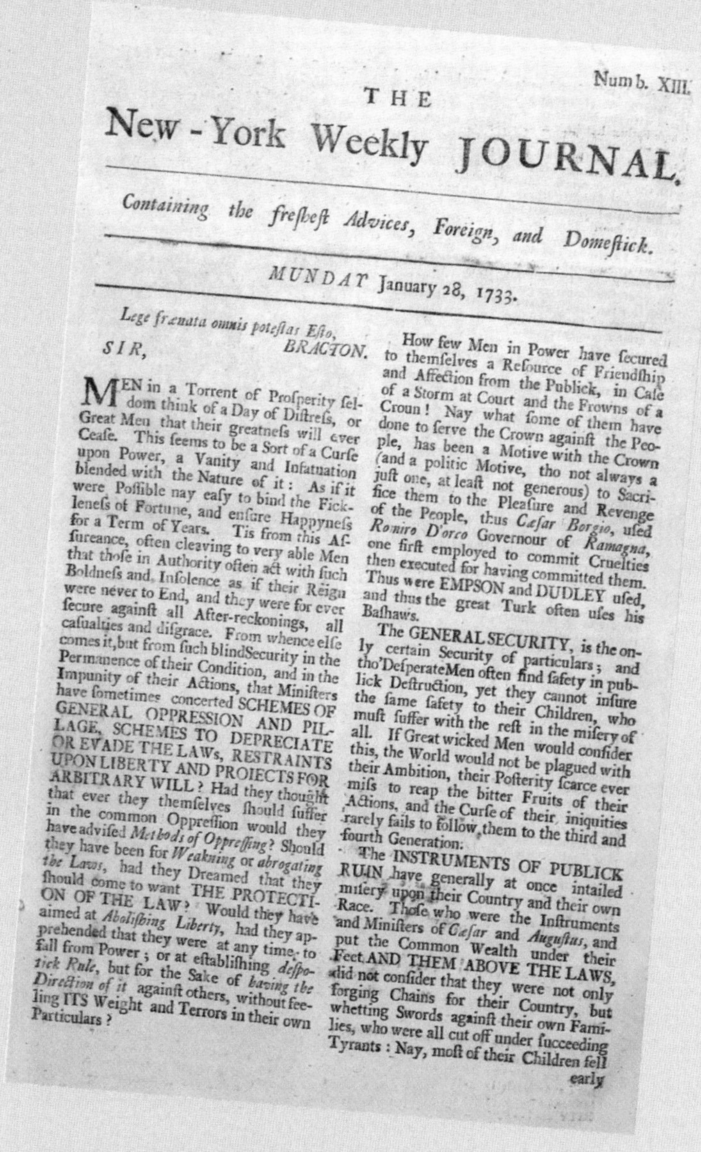

John Peter Zenger's Newspaper
This issue of John Peter Zenger's *New-York Weekly Journal* contained on the third of its four pages an article criticizing New York's governor. For this and other critical articles, the governor had Zenger tried for seditious libel in 1735. The jury sided with Zenger and acquitted him, although the law favored the governor. Like Zenger, printers throughout the colonies continued to be harassed by public officials who tried to censor irreverent and independent publishers. But colonial governments were too weak to suppress dissenting opinions for very long. Vigorous political commentary like that featured on the page shown here found an avid audience among colonial readers.
Courtesy, American Antiquarian Society.

FIGURE 5.1
Colonial Exports, 1768–1772

These pie charts provide an overview of the colonial export economy in the 1760s. The first two show that almost two-thirds of colonial exports came from the South and that the majority of the colonies' exports went to Great Britain. The remaining charts illustrate the distinctive patterns of exports in each colonial region. Fish, livestock, and wood products were New England's most important exports; they were sent primarily to the West Indies, only a small fraction going to Great Britain. From the colonial breadbasket in the middle colonies, grain products made up three-fourths of all exports, most of which went to the West Indies or to southern Europe. The Chesapeake also exported some grain, but tobacco accounted for three-fourths of the region's export trade, nearly all of it bound for Great Britain as mandated by the Navigation Acts. Rice and indigo comprised three-fourths of the exports from the lower South, the bulk of which was sent to Great Britain. Taken together, these charts reveal Britain's economic interest in the exports of the North American colonies.

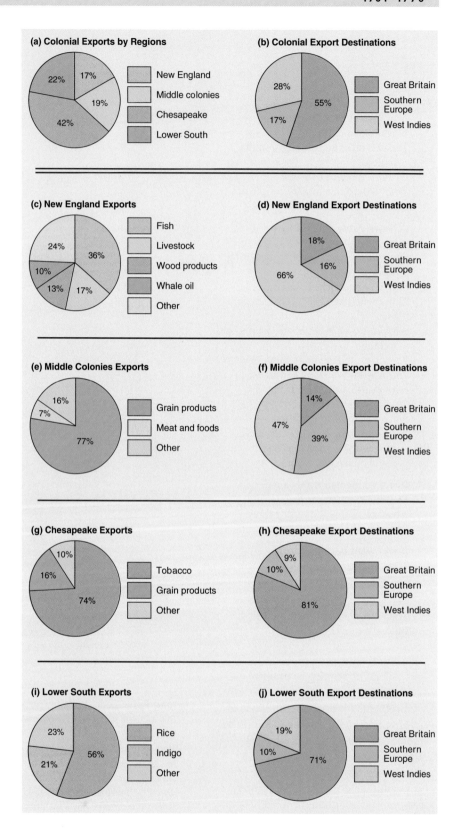

you want?" As colonial consumers defined and expressed their desires with greater frequency during the eighteenth century, they became accustomed to thinking of themselves as individuals who had the power to make decisions that influenced the quality of their lives—attitudes of significance in the hierarchical world of eighteenth-century British North America.

Religion, Enlightenment, and Revival

Eighteenth-century colonists could choose from almost as many religions as consumer goods. Virtually all of the bewildering variety of religious denominations represented some form of Christianity, almost all of them Protestant. Slaves made up the largest group of non-Christians. A few slaves converted to Christianity in Africa or after they arrived in North America, but most continued to embrace elements of indigenous African religions. Roman Catholics concentrated in Maryland as they had since the seventeenth century, but even there they were outnumbered by Protestants.

The varieties of Protestant faith and practice ranged across an extremely broad spectrum. The thousands of immigrants in the middle colonies and the southern backcountry included militant Baptists and Presbyterians. Huguenots who had fled persecution in Catholic France peopled congregations in several cities. In New England, old-style Puritanism splintered into strands of Congregationalism that differed over fine points of theological doctrine. The Congregational Church was the official established church in New England, and all residents paid taxes for its support. Throughout the plantation South and in urban centers like Charleston, New York, and Philadelphia, prominent colonists belonged to the Anglican Church. The Anglican Church in the South, like the Congregational Church in New England, received support in the form of tax monies. But in both regions, dissenting faiths grew, and in most colonies adherents of other faiths won the right to worship publicly, although the established churches retained official sanction.

Many educated colonists became deists, looking for God's plan in nature more than in the Bible. Deists shared the ideas of eighteenth-century European **Enlightenment** thinkers. Participating in a multifaceted intellectual movement that challenged many conventional ideas, Enlightenment thinkers tended to agree that science and reason could disclose God's laws in the natural order. In the colonies as well as in Europe, Enlightenment ideas encouraged people to study the world around them, to think for themselves, and to ask whether the disorderly appearance of things masked the principles of a deeper, more profound natural order. From New England towns to southern drawing rooms, individuals met to discuss such matters. Philadelphia was the center of these conversations, especially after the formation of the American Philosophical Society in 1769, an outgrowth of an earlier discussion group organized by Benjamin Franklin, who was a deist. The American Philosophical Society fostered communication among leading colonial thinkers; Benjamin Franklin was its first president, Thomas Jefferson its third. Among the purposes of these discussions was to find ways to improve society. Franklin's interest in electricity, stoves, and eyeglasses exemplified the shift of focus among many eighteenth-century colonists from heaven to the here and now.

Most eighteenth-century colonists went to church seldom or not at all, although they probably considered themselves Christians. A minister in Charleston observed that on the Sabbath "the Taverns have more Visitants than the Churches." In the leading colonial cities, church members were a small minority of eligible adults, no more than 10 to 15 percent. Anglican parishes in the South rarely claimed more than one-fifth of eligible adults as members. In some regions of rural New England and the middle colonies, church membership embraced two-thirds of eligible adults, while in other areas only one-quarter of the residents belonged to a church. The dominant faith overall was religious indifference. As a late-eighteenth-century traveler observed, "Religious indifference is imperceptibly disseminated from one end of the continent to the other."

The spread of religious indifference, of deism, of denominational rivalry, and of comfortable backsliding profoundly concerned many Christians. A few despaired that, as one wrote, "religion . . . lay a-dying and ready to expire its last breath of life." To combat what one preacher called the "dead formality" of church services, some ministers set out to convert nonbelievers and to revive the piety of the faithful with a new style of preaching that appealed more to the heart than to the head. Historians have termed this wave of revivals the **Great Awakening**. In Massachusetts during the mid-1730s, the fiery Puritan minister Jonathan Edwards reaped a harvest of souls by reemphasizing traditional Puritan doctrines of humanity's utter depravity and God's vengeful omnipotence. The title of Edwards's most famous sermon, "Sinners in the

> To combat what one preacher called the "dead formality" of church services, some ministers set out to convert nonbelievers and to revive the faithful with preaching that appealed more to the heart than to the head.

George Whitefield

An anonymous artist portrayed George Whitefield preaching, emphasizing the power of his sermons to transport his audience to a revived awareness of divine spirituality. Light from above gleams off Whitefield's forehead. His crossed eyes and faraway gaze suggest that he spoke in a semihypnotic trance. Notice the absence of a Bible at the pulpit. Rather than elaborating on God's word as revealed in Scripture, Whitefield speaks from his own inner awareness. The young woman bathed in light below his hands appears transfixed, her focus not on Whitefield but on some inner realm illuminated by his words. Her eyes and Whitefield's do not meet, yet the artist's use of light suggests that she and Whitefield see the same core of holy Truth. The other people in Whitefield's audience appear not to have achieved this state. They remain intent on Whitefield's words, failing so far to be ignited by the divine spark.

National Portrait Gallery, London.

The most famous revivalist in the eighteenth-century Atlantic world was George Whitefield. An Anglican, Whitefield preached well-worn messages of sin and salvation to large audiences in England using his spellbinding, unforgettable voice. Whitefield visited the North American colonies seven times, staying for more than three years during the mid-1740s and attracting tens of thousands to his sermons, including Benjamin Franklin. Whitefield's preaching transported many in his audience to emotion-choked states of religious ecstasy. About one revival, he wrote, "the bitter cries and groans were enough to pierce the hardest heart. Some of the people were as pale as death; others were wringing their hands; others lying on the ground; others sinking into the arms of their friends; and most lifting their eyes to heaven, and crying to God for mercy. They seemed like persons . . . coming out of their graves to judgment."

Whitefield's successful revivals spawned many lesser imitations. Itinerant preachers, many of them poorly educated, toured the colonial backcountry after midcentury, echoing Whitefield's medium and message as best they could. Educated and established ministers often regarded them with disgust. Bathsheba Kingsley, a member of Jonathan Edwards's flock, preached the revival message informally—as did an unprecedented number of other awakened women throughout the colonies—causing her congregation to brand her a "brawling woman" who had "gone quite out of her place." The revivals awakened and refreshed the spiritual energies of thousands of colonists struggling with the uncertainties and anxieties of eighteenth-century America. The conversions at revivals did not substantially boost the total number of church members, however. After the revivalists moved on, the routines and pressures of everyday existence reasserted their primacy in the lives of many converts. But revivals imparted an important message to colonists, both converted and unconverted. They communicated that every soul mattered, that men and women could choose to be saved, that individuals had the power to make a

Hands of an Angry God," conveys the flavor of his message. In Pennsylvania and New Jersey, Presbyterian William Tennent led revivals dramatizing conventional appeals for spiritual rebirth with accounts of God's miraculous powers—such as raising his son, William Tennent Jr., from the dead.

decision for everlasting life or death. Colonial revivals expressed in religious terms many of the same democratic and egalitarian values expressed in economic terms by colonists' patterns of consumption. One colonist noted the analogy by referring to itinerant revivalists as "Pedlars in divinity." Like consumption, revivals contributed to a set of common experiences that bridged colonial divides of faith, region, class, and status.

Bonds of the British Empire

The plurality of peoples, faiths, and communities that characterized the North American colonies arose from the somewhat haphazard policies of the eighteenth-century British empire. Since the Puritan Revolution of the mid-seventeenth century, British monarchs had valued the colonies' contributions to trade and encouraged their growth and development. Unlike Spain and France—whose policies of excluding Protestants and foreigners kept the population of their North American colonial territories tiny—Britain kept the door to its colonies open to anyone, and tens of thousands of non-British immigrants settled in the North American colonies and raised families. The open door did not extend to trade, however, as the seventeenth-century Navigation Acts restricted colonial trade to British ships and traders. These policies evolved because they served the interests of the monarchy and of influential groups in England and the colonies. The policies also gave the colonists a common framework of political expectations and experiences.

At a minimum, British power defended the colonists from foreign enemies. Each colony organized a militia, and privateers sailed from every port to prey on foreign ships. But the British navy and army bore responsibility for colonial defense. Royal officials warily eyed the small North American settlements of New France and New Spain for signs of threats to the colonies. Alone, neither New France (in present-day Canada, from the St. Lawrence River, around the Great Lakes, and down the Mississippi valley to present-day Louisiana) nor New Spain (in present-day Florida, Alabama, Texas, New Mexico, Arizona, and California) jeopardized British North America, but with Indian allies they could become a potent force that kept colonists on their guard.

Defending the Borderlands of Empire: Indians and French and Spanish Outposts

All along the ragged edge of settlement, colonists encountered Indians. Native Americans' impulse to defend their territory from colonial incursions warred with their desire for trade, which tugged them toward the settlers. As a colonial official observed in 1761, "A modern Indian cannot subsist without Europeans . . . [the European goods that were] only conveniency at first [are] now become necessity." To obtain such necessities as guns, ammunition, clothing, sewing utensils, and much more that was manufactured largely by the British, Indians trapped beaver, deer, and other fur-bearing animals throughout the interior.

> British, French, Spanish, and Dutch traders competed to control the fur trade. Indians took advantage of this competition to improve their own prospects.

Colonial traders and their respective empires competed to control the fur trade (Map 5.4). British, French, Spanish, and Dutch officials monitored the trade to prevent their competitors from deflecting the flow of furs toward their own markets. Indians took advantage of this competition to improve their own prospects, playing one trader and empire off against another. The Iroquois, for example, promised the French exclusive access to the furs and territory of the Great Lakes region and at the same time made the same pledge of exclusive rights to the English. Indian tribes and confederacies also competed among themselves for favored trading rights with one colony or another, a competition colonists encouraged.

The shifting alliances and complex dynamics of the fur trade struck a fragile balance along the frontier. The threat of violence from all sides was ever present, and the threat became reality often enough for all parties to be prepared for the worst. In the Yamasee War of 1715, Yamasee and Creek Indians—with French encouragement—mounted a coordinated attack against colonial settlements in South Carolina and inflicted heavy casualties. The Cherokees, traditional enemies of the Creeks, refused to join the attack. Instead, they protected their access to British trade goods by allying with the colonists and turning the tide of battle, thus triggering a murderous rampage of revenge by the colonists against the Creeks and Yamasees.

Relations between Indians and the colonists differed from colony to colony and from year to

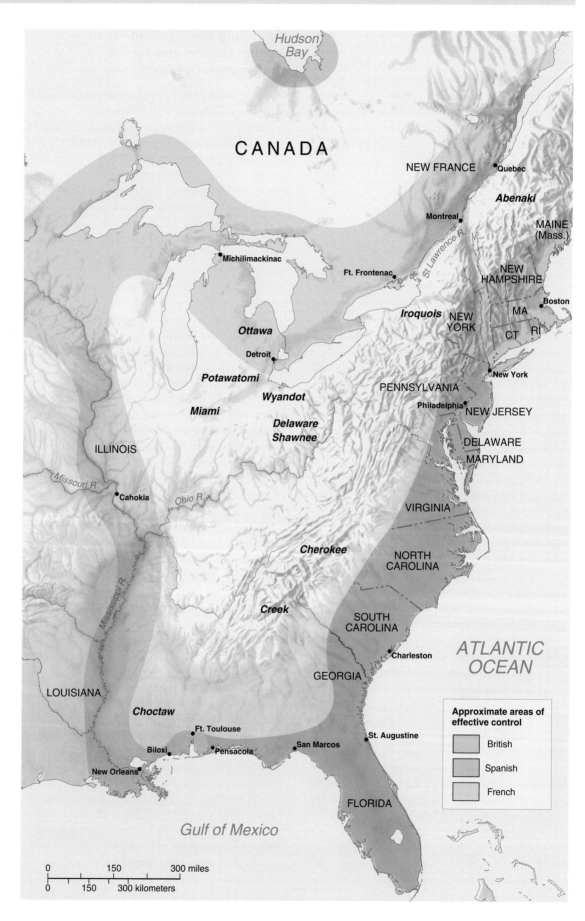

Hudson
Bay

CANADA

NEW FRANCE   •Quebec

Abenaki

Montreal•

MAINE
(Mass.)

NEW
HAMPSHIRE

•Michilimackinac

Ft. Frontenac•

St Lawrence R.

Iroquois   NEW
YORK

MA   •Boston

CT   RI

Ottawa

Detroit•

New York•

Potawatomi

PENNSYLVANIA

Wyandot

Philadelphia•   NEW JERSEY

Miami

Delaware
Shawnee

DELAWARE

MARYLAND

ILLINOIS

Missouri R.

•Cahokia   Ohio R.

VIRGINIA

Cherokee   NORTH
CAROLINA

Mississippi R.

Creek   SOUTH
CAROLINA

Charleston•

ATLANTIC
OCEAN

GEORGIA

LOUISIANA

Choctaw

St. Augustine•

Ft. Toulouse•

Biloxi•   •Pensacola   San Marcos•

New Orleans•

**Approximate areas of
effective control**

British

Spanish

French

FLORIDA

Gulf of Mexico

0   150   300 miles

0   150   300 kilometers

Monterey Presidio
This eighteenth-century portrait of the Monterey Presidio illustrates the military significance of the Spanish outposts in California. The walled enclosure and proximity to the bay (in the background) served defensive purposes, principally against Russian expansion but also against British and French interlopers. The Indian men and women working in the fields and hanging out laundry served to support the soldiers in the presidio. Notice that no Spaniard is pictured at work. Contrast this languid scene with the picture of the Arch Street wharf in Philadelphia (see page 147), where the hustle and bustle of commerce prevailed. At Monterey and elsewhere in Spanish California, the presidios and missions focused on maintaining outposts of empire rather than on developing booming settlements or producing goods for export.
University of California at Berkeley, Bancroft Library.

year. But the colonists' nagging perceptions of menace on the frontier kept them continually hoping for help from the British in keeping the Indians at bay and in maintaining the essential flow of trade. In 1754, the colonists' endemic competition with the French flared into the Seven Years' War (also known as the French and Indian War), which would inflame the frontier for years (see chapter 6). Before the 1760s, neither the colonists nor the British developed a coherent policy toward Indians. But both agreed that Indians made deadly enemies, profitable trading partners, and powerful allies. As a result, the British and the colonists kept an eye on the Spanish Empire to the west and relations with the Indians there.

Indians' potential as allies prompted officials in New Spain to mount a campaign to block Russian access to present-day California by building forts (called *presidios*) and missions. Russian hunters in search of seals and sea otters ventured along the California coast and threatened to become a permanent presence on New Spain's northern frontier.

◀ **MAP 5.4   Zones of Empire in Eastern North America**
British colonies extending westward from the Atlantic coast were much more densely settled than the zones under French, Spanish, or Indian control. The comparatively large number of settlers made British colonists more secure than the relatively few colonists in the vast regions claimed by France and Spain or settlers among the many Indian peoples in the huge area between the Mississippi River and the Appalachian Mountains. Yet British colonists were not powerful enough to dominate the French, Spanish, or Indians. Instead, British colonists had to guard against powerful Indian groups who allied with either the French or the Spanish, since such alliances threatened settlers in the region under British control.

Ambush of Spanish Expedition
This detail from a remarkable hide painting depicts an ambush of a Spanish expedition by French soldiers and their Pawnee and Oto allies in August 1720. Two and a half months earlier, the governor of New Mexico had sent forty-three Spanish soldiers along with sixty Pueblo Indian allies to expel French intruders from the northern borderlands of New Spain. When the expedition reached the confluence of the Platte and Loup rivers in present-day Nebraska, they were surprised by an attack by French, Pawnees, and Otos, who killed thirty-three Spaniards and twelve Pueblos and drove the expedition back to New Mexico. Shortly afterward, an artist—whether Indian or Spanish is unknown—recorded the disastrous ambush of the Spaniards in this painting. The priest in the center of the detail shown here was Father Juan Minguez, the first priest assigned to Albuquerque; he was killed in the ambush. The Indian directly in front of the priest was Joseph Naranjo, who was also killed; he came from the Santa Clara Pueblo. He was the leader of the Spaniards' Pueblo allies and was the son of Domingo Naranjo, a leader of the Pueblo Revolt against the Spaniards in 1680. Museum of New Mexico.

In 1769, an expedition headed by a military man, Gaspar de Portolá, and a Catholic priest, Junípero Serra, traveled north from Mexico to present-day San Diego, where they founded the first California mission, San Diego de Alcalá. They soon journeyed all the way to Monterey, which became the capital of Spanish California. There Portolá established a presidio in 1770 "to defend us from attacks by the Russians," he wrote. The same year Father Serra founded Mission San Carlos Borroméo de Carmelo in Monterey to convert Indians and to recruit them to work to support the soldiers and other officials in the presidio. By 1772, Serra had established other missions (see "American Places," page 165) on the northward path from San Diego to Monterey.

For Indians, the Spaniards' California missions had horrendous consequences, as they had

Spanish Missions in California

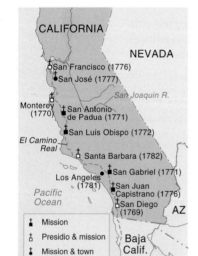

CALIFORNIA
NEVADA
San Francisco (1776)
San José (1777)
San Joaquin R.
Monterey (1770)
San Antonio de Padua (1771)
San Luis Obispo (1772)
El Camino Real
Santa Barbara (1782)
Los Angeles (1781)
San Gabriel (1771)
San Juan Capistrano (1776)
San Diego (1769)
AZ
Baja Calif.
Pacific Ocean

‡ Mission
⌂ Presidio & mission
‡ Mission & town
• Town

elsewhere in the Spanish borderlands. European diseases decimated Indian populations, Spanish soldiers raped Indian women, and missionaries beat Indians and subjected them to near slavery. Indian uprisings against the Spaniards occurred repeatedly (see "Documenting the American Promise," page 166), but the presidios and missions endured as feeble projections of the Spanish Empire along the Pacific coast.

Colonial Politics in the British Empire

British attempts to exercise political power in their colonial governments met with success so long as British officials were on or very near the sea. Colonists acknowledged—although they did not always readily comply with—British authority to collect customs duties, inspect cargoes, and enforce trade regulations. But when royal officials tried to wield their authority on land, in the internal affairs of colonies, they invariably encountered colonial resistance. A governor appointed by the king in each of the nine royal colonies (Rhode Island and Connecticut selected their own governors) or by the proprietors in

AMERICAN PLACES

California Mission Trail

Between 1769 and 1823, Spanish authorities built twenty-one missions in California. The missions usually included a church, a presidio (fort), a school, housing for missionaries, Indians, and soldiers, and various outbuildings. The missions extend from the first one, in San Diego, northward more than 500 miles, beyond the Spanish capital of California at Monterey, where the magnificent Mission San Carlos Borroméo de Carmelo is still an active church, all the way to Sonoma, north of present-day San Francisco.

Visitors today can travel from one mission to another, following in the footsteps of Spanish missionaries, soldiers, and government officials as well as Indians who converted to Christianity and those who resisted. Mission La Purisíma Concepcíon, located north of Santa Barbara near Lompoc, has been restored to its late-eighteenth-century condition. Unlike most of the other missions, which today are in urban settings or are only partially preserved, La Purisíma stands in a rural area that is much like the setting of all the missions in the eighteenth century. Visitors to La Purisíma can tour the chapel, barracks, and other restored buildings and try to imagine how the quiet, bucolic scene of today would have been different in the eighteenth century.

In effect, the California missions established by Junípero Serra and other Franciscans were small islands of Spanish culture surrounded not by villages of Spaniards—as in Spain—but by numerous settlements of California hunter-gatherers who did not worship the Spaniards'

god, speak the Spaniards' language, wear the Spaniards' clothing, or build their houses or places of worship in the Spaniards' style. The missions signified Spaniards' determination to force native Californians to conform to Spanish culture.

The elegant buildings that survive at Mission San Diego and some of the other missions tend to obscure the coercion and brutality that were common features of mission life for Indians. One Spanish soldier praised the work of the missionar-

ies, writing in 1792 that "With flattery and presents [missionaries] attract the savage Indians and persuade them to adhere to life in society and to receive instruction for a knowledge of the Catholic faith, the cultivation of the land, and the arts necessary for making the instruments most needed for farming." Whippings and near enslavement were among the forms of persuasion that missionaries frequently used to bring Indians to the missions and keep them there. It is easy for visitors traveling today from one beautiful mission to another on the California Mission Trail to forget this silent and invisible—but very real—history.

FOR WEB LINKS RELATED TO THIS SITE AND OTHER AMERICAN PLACES, see "PlaceLinks" at bedfordstmartins.com/roark.

Mission San Diego de Alcalá
Courtesy of the Mission San Diego de Alcalá.

Missionaries Report on California Missions

Catholic missionaries sent regular reports to their superiors in Mexico City, New Spain's capital city. The reports described what the missionaries considered their successes in converting pagan Indians—whom they called gentiles—as well as the difficulties caused by the behavior of both Spaniards and Indians.

DOCUMENT 1
Father Luis Jayme
Describes Conditions
at Mission San Diego
de Alcalá, 1772

Father Luis Jayme, a Franciscan missionary, reported on the deplorable behavior of some of the Spanish soldiers at Mission San Diego, who frequently raped Indian women, causing many Indians to resist the efforts of the missionaries.

With reference to the Indians, I wish to say that great progress [in converting Indians] would be made if there was anything to eat and the soldiers would set a good example. We cannot give them anything to eat because what Don Pedro [the governor] has given is not enough to last half a year for the Indians from the Californias who are here. Thus little progress will be made under present conditions. As for the example set by the soldiers, no doubt some of them are good exemplars and deserve to be treated accordingly, but very many of them deserve to be hanged on account of the continuous outrages which they are committing in seizing and raping the women. There is not a single mission where all the gentiles have not been scandalized, and even on the roads, so I have been told. Surely, as the gentiles themselves state, they [the soldiers] are committing a thousand evils, particularly of a sexual nature. . . .

At one of these Indian villages near this mission of San Diego, which said village is very large, and which is on the road to Monterey, the gentiles therein many times have been on the point of coming here to kill us all, and the reason for this is that some soldiers went there and raped their women, and other soldiers who were carrying the mail to Monterey turned their animals into their fields and they ate up their crops. Three other Indian villages . . . [near] here have reported the same thing to me several times. For this reason on several occasions when . . . I have gone to see these Indian villages, as soon as they saw us they fled from their villages and fled to the woods or other remote places. . . . They do this so that the soldiers will not rape their women as they have already done so many times in the past.

No wonder the Indians here were bad when the mission was first founded. To begin with, they did not know why [the Spaniards] had come, unless they wanted to take their lands away from them. Now they all want to be Christians because they know that there is a God who created the heavens and earth and all things, that there is a Hell and Glory, that they have souls, etc., but when the mission was first founded . . . they thought they were like animals, and . . . they were very loath to pray, and they did not want to be Christians at all. . . . [Now] they all know the natural law, which, so I am informed, they have observed as well or better than many Christians elsewhere. They do not have idols; they do not go on drinking sprees; they do not marry relatives; and they have but one wife. The married men sleep with their wives only. . . . Some of the first adults whom we baptized, when we pointed out to them that it was wrong to have sexual intercourse with a woman to whom they were not married, told me that they already knew that, and that among them it was considered to be very bad, and so they do not do so at all. "The soldiers," they told me, "are Christians and, although they know that God will punish them in Hell, do so, having sexual intercourse with

Maryland and Pennsylvania headed the government of each colony. The British envisioned colonial governors as mini-monarchs able to exert influence in the colonies much as the king did in England. But colonial governors were not kings, and the colonies were not England.

Eighty percent of colonial governors had been born in England, not in the colonies. Some governors stayed in England, close to the source of royal patronage, and delegated the grubby details of colonial affairs to subordinates. Even the best-intentioned colonial governors had diffi-

our wives." "We," they said, "although we did not know that God would punish us for that in Hell, considered it to be very bad, and we did not do it, and even less now that we know that God will punish us if we do so." When I heard this, I burst into tears to see how these gentiles were setting an example for us Christians.

DOCUMENT 2
Father Junípero Serra Describes the Indian Revolt at Mission San Diego de Alcalá, 1775

Father Junípero Serra, the founder of many of the California missions, reported to his superiors in Mexico City that an Indian uprising had destroyed Mission San Diego. He recommended rebuilding and urged officials to provide additional soldiers to defend the missions, but not to punish the rebellious Indians.

As we are in the vale of tears, not all the news I have to relate can be pleasant. And so I make no excuses for announcing . . . the tragic news that I have just received of the total destruction of the San Diego Mission, and of the death of the senior of its two religious ministers, called Father Luis Jayme, at the hand of the rebellious gentiles and of the Christian neophytes [Indians who lived in the mission]. All this happened, November 5th, about one or two o'clock at night. The gentiles came together from forty rancherías,

according to information given me, and set fire to the church, after sacking it. They then went to the storehouse, the house where the Fathers lived, the soldiers' barracks, and all the rest of the buildings. They killed a carpenter . . . and a blacksmith. . . . They wounded with their arrows the four soldiers, who alone were on guard at the . . . mission. . . .

And now, after the Father has been killed, the Mission burned, its many and valuable furnishings destroyed, together with the sacred vessels, its paintings, its baptismal, marriage, and funeral records, and all the furnishings for the sacristy, the house, and the farm implements—now the forces [of soldiers] of both presidios [nearby] come together to set things right. . . . What happened was that before they set about reestablishing the Mission, they wanted to . . . lay hands on the guilty ones who were responsible for the burning of the Mission, and the death of the Fathers, and chastise them. The harassed Indians rebelled anew and became more enraged. . . . And so the soldiers there are gathered together in their presidios, and the Indians in their state of heathenism. . . .

While the missionary is alive, let the soldiers guard him, and watch over him, like the pupils of God's very eyes. That is as it should be. . . . But after the missionary has been killed, what can be gained by campaigns [against the rebellious Indians]? Some will say to frighten them and prevent them from killing

others. What I say is that, in order to prevent them from killing others, keep better guard over them than they did over the one who has been killed; and, as to the murderer, let him live, in order that he should be saved—which is the very purpose of our coming here, and the reason which justifies it.

SOURCES: Maynard Geiger, trans. and ed., *Letter of Luís Jayme, O.F.M.: San Diego, October 17, 1772* (Los Angeles, 1970), 38–42.

Antonine Tibesar, O.F.M., ed., *The Writings of Junípero Serra* (Washington, D.C.: 1956), 2:401–07.

QUESTIONS FOR ANALYSIS AND DEBATE

1. In what ways did Jayme and Serra agree about the motivations of Indians in and around Mission San Diego? In what ways did they disagree? How would Serra's recommendations for rebuilding the mission address the problems identified by Jayme that caused the revolt?

2. How did the goals and activities of the Spanish soldiers compare to those of the Catholic missionaries? What accounts for the differences and similarities?

3. How did the religious convictions of Jayme and Serra influence their reports? What might Spanish soldiers or Indians have said about these events? What might they have said about missionaries like Jayme and Serra?

culty developing relations of trust and respect with influential colonists because their terms of office averaged just five years and could be terminated at any time. Colonial governors controlled few patronage positions to secure political friendships in the colonies. The officials who administered the colonial customs service, for example, received their positions through patronage networks centered in England rather than in the hands of colonial governors. In obedience to England, colonial governors fought incessantly with the colonial assemblies. They battled over governors' vetoes of colonial legislation, removal of colonial judges, creation of new courts, dismissal of the representative assemblies, and other local issues. Some governors developed a working relationship with the assemblies. But during the eighteenth century, the assemblies gained the upper hand.

British policies did not clearly define the powers and responsibilities of colonial assemblies. In effect, the assemblies made many of their own rules and established a strong tradition of representative government analogous, in their eyes, to the English Parliament. Voters often returned the same representatives to the assemblies year after year, building continuity in power and leadership that far exceeded that of the governor. By 1720, colonial assemblies had won the power to initiate legislation, including tax laws and authorizations to spend public funds. Although all laws passed by the assemblies (except in Maryland, Rhode Island, and Connecticut) had to be approved by the governor and then by the Board of Trade in England, the difficulties in communication about complex subjects over long distances effectively ratified the assemblies' decisions. Years often passed before laws were repealed, and in the meantime the assemblies' laws prevailed.

The heated political struggles between royal governors and colonial assemblies that occurred throughout the eighteenth century taught colonists a common set of political lessons. They learned to employ traditionally British ideas of representative government to defend their own interests. They learned that power in the British colonies rarely belonged to the British government.

Conclusion: The Dual Identity of British North American Colonists

During the eighteenth century, a society that was both distinctively colonial and distinctively British emerged in British North America. Tens of thousands of immigrants and slaves gave the colonies an unmistakably colonial complexion

and contributed to the colonies' growing population and expanding economy. People of different ethnicities and faiths sought their fortunes in the colonies, where land was cheap, labor was dear, and—as Benjamin Franklin preached—work promised to be rewarding. Indentured servants and redemptioners risked a temporary period of bondage for the potential reward of better opportunities than on the Atlantic's eastern shore. Slaves endured lifetime servitude that they neither chose nor desired but from which their masters greatly benefited.

Identifiably colonial products from New England, the middle colonies, and the southern colonies flowed across the Atlantic. Back came unquestionably British consumer goods along with fashions in ideas, faith, and politics. The bonds of the British Empire required colonists to think of themselves as British subjects and, at the same time, encouraged them to consider their status as colonists.

People of European origin in the North American colonies of Spain and France did not share in the emerging political identity of the British colonists. They also did not participate in the cultural, economic, social, and religious changes experienced by their counterparts in British North America. Unlike the much more numerous colonists in British North America, North American Spanish and French colonists did not develop societies that began to rival the European empires that sponsored and supported them.

By 1750, British colonists in North America could not imagine that their distinctively dual identity—as British and as colonists—would soon become a source of intense conflict. But by 1776, colonists in British North America had to choose whether they were British or American.

FOR ADDITIONAL FIRSTHAND ACCOUNTS OF THIS PERIOD, see Chapter 5 in Michael Johnson, ed., *Reading the American Past,* Third Edition.

TO ASSESS YOUR MASTERY OF THE MATERIAL IN THIS CHAPTER, see the Online Study Guide at bedfordstmartins.com/roark.

FOR WEB LINKS RELATED TO TOPICS IN THIS CHAPTER, see "HistoryLinks," "DocLinks," and "PlaceLinks" at bedfordstmartins.com/roark.

CHRONOLOGY

1702 • Queen Anne's War triggers large German migration to British North American colonies.

1711 • North Carolina founded.

1715 • Yamasee War pits South Carolina colonists against Yamasee and Creek Indians.

1717 • Scots-Irish immigration to American colonies begins to increase.

1721 • *New England Courant* begins publication.

1723 • Benjamin Franklin arrives in Philadelphia.

1730s • Jonathan Edwards leads New England religious revival known as "Great Awakening."

1732 • Georgia founded.

1733 • Benjamin Franklin begins to publish *Poor Richard's Almanack*.

1737 • Penn family exploits "Walking Purchase" to claim extra land from Indians.

1739 • Slave insurrection occurs and is suppressed at Stono, South Carolina.

1740s • George Whitefield preaches revival of religion throughout England and British North America.

• Majority of southern slaves are born in the colonies rather than in Africa.

1741 • New York City officials suspect slave conspiracy and execute 31 slaves.

1745 • Olaudah Equiano born in present-day Nigeria.

1750s • British colonists from Pennsylvania begin to move down Shenandoah Valley into southern backcountry.

• Colonists increasingly become indebted to English merchants.

1754 • Seven Years' War begins in North America pitting France, Britain, and their respective colonists and Indian allies against one another in a military contest for dominance in North America.

1769 • American Philosophical Society founded in Philadelphia.

1770 • Gaspar de Portolá and Junípero Serra establish Mission San Carlos Borroméo de Carmelo and presidio at Monterey, California.

• British North American colonists number over 2 million, almost ten times more than in 1700.

1775 • Indians revolt and destroy San Diego mission.

BIBLIOGRAPHY

Please consult the bibliographies of chapters 2, 3, and 4 for more readings on related topics.

General Works

Douglas Anderson, *The Radical Enlightenment of Benjamin Franklin* (1997).

Richard Aquila, *The Iroquois Restoration: Iroquois Diplomacy on the Colonial Frontier, 1701–1754* (1997).

Bernard Bailyn, *Voyagers to the West: A Passage in the Peopling of America on the Eve of the Revolution* (1986).

Linda Baumgarten, *What Clothes Reveal: The Language of Clothing in Colonial and Federal America* (2002).

Ira Berlin, *Generations of Captivity: A History of African-American Slaves* (2003).

Richard D. Brown, *Knowledge Is Power: The Diffusion of Information in Early America, 1700–1865* (1989).

Jon Butler, *Becoming America: The Revolution before 1776* (2000).

Colin G. Calloway, *New Worlds for All: Indians, Europeans, and the Remaking of Early America* (1997).

A. Roger Ekirch, *Bound for America: The Transportation of British Convicts to the Colonies, 1718–1775* (1987).

Jack P. Greene, *Peripheries and Center: Constitutional Development in the Extended Polities of the British Empire and the United States, 1607–1788* (1986).

Jack P. Greene, *The Intellectual Construction of America: Exceptionalism and Identity from 1492 to 1800* (1993).

Patrick Griffin, *The People with No Name: Ireland's Ulster Scots, America's Scots Irish, and the Creation of a British Atlantic World, 1689–1764* (2001).

Timothy D. Hall, *Contested Boundaries: Itineracy and the Reshaping of the Colonial American Religious World* (1994).

Robert H. Jackson, *Race, Caste, and Status: Indians in Colonial Spanish America* (1999).

Nancy F. Koehn, *The Power of Commerce: Economy and Governance in the First British Empire* (1994).

Frank Lambert, *"Pedlar in Divinity": George Whitefield and the Transatlantic Revivals, 1723–1770* (1994).

Frank Lambert, *Inventing the "Great Awakening"* (1999).

Michael N. McConnell, *A Country Between: The Upper Ohio Valley and Its People, 1724–1774* (1997).

Kerby A. Miller et al., eds., *Irish Immigrants in the Land of Canaan: Letters and Memoirs from Colonial and Revolutionary America, 1675–1815* (2003).

Robert D. Mitchell, *Appalachian Frontiers: Settlement, Society, and Development in the Preindustrial Era* (1991).

Edmund S. Morgan, *Benjamin Franklin* (2002).

Gregory H. Nobles, *American Frontiers: Cultural Encounters and Continental Conquest* (1997).

Mary Beth Norton, *Founding Mothers and Fathers: Gendered Power and the Forming of American Society* (1996).

Alison Gilbert Olson, *Making the Empire Work: London and American Interest Groups, 1690–1790* (1992).

A. G. Roeber, *Palatines, Liberty, and Property: German Lutherans in Colonial British America* (1993).

Sharon V. Salinger, *Taverns and Drinking in Early America* (2002).

Martha Saxton, *Being Good: Women's Moral Values in Early America* (2003).

Michael Schudson, *The Good Citizen: A History of American Civic Life* (1998).

Carole Shammas, *The Pre-Industrial Consumer in England and America* (1990).

David S. Shields, *Civil Tongues and Polite Letters in British America* (1997).

Nancy L. Struna, *People of Prowess: Sport, Leisure, and Labor in Early Anglo-America* (1996).

Laurel Thatcher Ulrich, *The Age of Homespun: Objects and Stories in the Creation of an American Myth* (2001).

Marianne E. Wokeck, *Trade in Strangers: The Beginnings of Mass Migration to North America* (1999).

Stephanie Grauman Wolf, *As Various as Their Land: The Everyday Lives of Eighteenth-Century Americans* (1993).

New England

John L. Brooke, *The Heart of the Commonwealth: Society and Political Culture in Worcester County, Massachusetts, 1713–1861* (1989).

Richard Bushman, *From Puritan to Yankee: Character and the Social Order in Connecticut, 1690–1765* (1967).

David W. Conroy, *In Public Houses: Drink and the Revolution of Authority in Colonial Massachusetts* (1995).

Jay Coughtry, *The Notorious Triangle: Rhode Island and the African Slave Trade, 1700–1807* (1981).

Elaine Forman Crane, *Ebb Tide in New England: Women, Seaports, and Social Change, 1630–1800* (1998).

Christopher Grasso, *A Speaking Aristocracy: Transforming Public Discourse in Eighteenth-Century Connecticut* (1999).

Christine Leigh Heyrman, *Commerce and Culture: The Maritime Communities of Colonial Massachusetts, 1690–1750* (1984).

Phyllis Whitman Hunter, *Purchasing Identity in the Atlantic World: Massachusetts Merchants, 1670–1780* (2001).

Douglas Lamar Jones, *Village and Seaport: Migration and Society in Eighteenth-Century Massachusetts* (1981).

Daniel R. Mandell, *Behind the Frontier: Indians in Eighteenth-Century Eastern Massachusetts* (1996).

George M. Marsden, *Jonathan Edwards: A Life* (2003).

Carolyn Merchant, *Ecological Revolutions: Nature, Gender, and Science in New England* (1989).

Gregory H. Nobles, *Divisions throughout the Whole: Politics and Society in Hampshire County, Massachusetts, 1740–1775* (1983).

Lisa Norling, *Captain Ahab Had a Wife: New England Women and the Whale Fishery, 1720–1870* (2000).

William D. Piersen, *Black Yankees: The Development of an Afro-American Subculture in Eighteenth-Century New England* (1988).

Patricia J. Tracy, *Jonathan Edwards, Pastor: Religion and Society in Eighteenth-Century Northampton* (1979).

Lynne Withey, *Urban Growth in Colonial Rhode Island: Newport and Providence in the Eighteenth Century* (1984).

Middle Colonies

Randall H. Balmer, *A Perfect Babel of Confusion: Dutch Religion and English Culture in the Middle Colonies* (1989).

Thomas J. Davis, *A Rumor of Revolt: The "Great Negro Plot" in Colonial New York* (1985).

Thomas M. Doerflinger, *A Vigorous Spirit of Enterprise: Merchants and Economic Development in Revolutionary Philadelphia* (1986).

Aaron Spencer Fogelman, *Hopeful Journeys: German Immigration, Settlement, and Political Culture in Colonial America, 1717–1775* (1996).

J. William Frost, *A Perfect Freedom: Religious Liberty in Pennsylvania* (1990).

Leslie M. Harris, *In the Shadow of Slavery: African Americans in New York City, 1626–1863* (2003).

Eric Hinderaker, *Elusive Empires: Constructing Colonialism in the Ohio Valley, 1673–1800* (1997).

Peter Charles Hoffer, *The Great New York Conspiracy of 1741: Slavery, Crime, and Colonial Law* (2003).

Jessica Kross, *The Evolution of an American Town: Newtown, New York, 1642–1775* (1983).

Ned C. Landsman, *Scotland and Its First American Colony, 1683–1765* (1985).

Hartmut Lehmann et al., eds. *In Search of Peace and Prosperity: New German Settlements in Eighteenth-Century Europe and America* (2000).

Stephen L. Longenecker, *Piety and Tolerance: Pennsylvania German Religion, 1700–1850* (1994).

Peter C. Mancall, *Valley of Opportunity: Economic Culture along the Upper Susquehanna, 1700–1800* (1991).

Brendan J. McConville, *These Darling Disturbers of the Public Peace: The Struggle for Property and Power in Early New Jersey* (1999).

James H. Merrell, *Into the American Woods: Negotiators on the Pennsylvania Frontier* (1999).

Jane T. Merritt, *At the Crossroads: Indians and Empires on a Mid-Atlantic Frontier, 1700–1763* (2003).

Gary B. Nash and Jean R. Soderlund, *Freedom by Degrees: Emancipation in Pennsylvania and Its Aftermath* (1991).

Benjamin H. Newcomb, *Political Partisanship in the American Middle Colonies, 1700–1776* (1995).

Simon P. Newman, *Embodied History: The Lives of the Poor in Early Philadelphia* (2003).

Sharon V. Salinger, *"To Serve Well and Faithfully": Labor and Indentured Servitude in Pennsylvania, 1682–1800* (1987).

Sally Schwartz, *"A Mixed Multitude": The Struggle for Toleration in Colonial Pennsylvania* (1987).

Mary M. Schweitzer, *Custom and Contract: Household, Government, and the Economy in Colonial Pennsylvania* (1987).

Timothy J. Shannon, *Indians and Colonists at the Crossroads of Empire: The Albany Congress of 1754* (2000).

Beverly Prior Smaby, *The Transformation of Moravian Bethlehem: From Communal Mission to Family Economy* (1988).

Billy G. Smith, *The "Lower Sort": Philadelphia's Laboring People, 1750–1800* (1990).

Merrill D. Smith, *Breaking the Bonds: Marital Discord in Pennsylvania, 1730–1830* (1991).

Jean R. Soderlund, *Quakers and Slavery: A Divided Spirit* (1985).

Peter Thompson, *Rum Punch and Revolution: Taverngoing and Public Life in Eighteenth-Century Philadelphia* (1999).

Alan Tully, *William Penn's Legacy: Politics and Social Structure in Provincial Pennsylvania, 1726–1755* (1977).

Southern Colonies

Gary Clayton Anderson, *The Indian Southwest, 1580–1830: Ethnogenesis and Reinvention* (1999).

Richard R. Beeman, *The Evolution of the Southern Backcountry: A Case Study of Lunenburg County, Virginia, 1746–1832* (1984).

Trevor G. Burnhard, *Creole Gentlemen: The Maryland Elite, 1691–1776* (2002).

Edward J. Cashin, *Lachlan McGillivray, Indian Trader: The Shaping of the Southern Colonial Frontier* (1992).

Edward J. Cashin, *Governor Henry Ellis and the Transformation of British North America* (1994).

David R. Chesnutt, *South Carolina's Expansion into Colonial Georgia, 1720–1765* (1989).

Paul G. E. Clemons, *The Atlantic Economy and Colonial Maryland's Eastern Shore: From Tobacco to Grain* (1980).

Peter A. Coclanis, *The Shadow of a Dream: Economic Life and Death in the South Carolina Low Country, 1670–1920* (1989).

Harry W. Crosby, *Antigua California: Mission and Colony on the Peninsular Frontier, 1697–1768* (1994).

Harold E. Davis, *The Fledgling Province: Social and Cultural Life in Colonial Georgia, 1733–1776* (1976).

A. Roger Ekirch, *Poor Carolina: Politics and Society in Colonial North Carolina, 1729–1776* (1981).

David Hackett Fischer and James C. Kelly, *Bound Away: Virginia and the Westward Movement* (2000).

Sylvia R. Frey and Betty Wood, *Come Shouting to Zion: African American Protestantism in the American South and British Caribbean to 1830* (1998).

Allan Gallay, *The Formation of a Planter Elite: Jonathan Bryan and the Southern Colonial Frontier* (1989).

Michael Angelo Gomez, *Exchanging Our Country Marks: The Transformation of African Identities in the Colonial and Antebellum South* (1998).

Ramón A. Gutiérrez and Richard J. Orsi, eds., *Contested Eden: California before the Gold Rush* (1998).

Gwendolyn Midlo Hall, *Africans in Colonial Louisiana: The Development of Afro-Creole Culture in the Eighteenth Century* (1992).

Rhys Isaac, *The Transformation of Virginia, 1740–1790* (1982).

Robert H. Jackson and Edward Castillo, *Indians, Franciscans, and Spanish Colonization: The Impact of the Mission System on California Indians* (1995).

George Johnson, *The Frontier in the Colonial South: South Carolina Backcountry, 1736–1800* (1997).

Alan L. Karras, *Sojourners in the Sun: Scottish Migrants in Jamaica and the Chesapeake, 1740–1800* (1992).

Marvin L. Michael Kay, *Slavery in North Carolina, 1748–1775* (1995).

Cynthia A. Kierner, *Beyond the Household: Women's Place in the Early South, 1700–1835* (1998).

John Gilman Kolp, *Gentlemen and Freeholders: Electoral Politics and Political Commentary in Colonial Virginia* (1998).

Allan Kulikoff, *Tobacco and Slaves: The Development of Southern Cultures in the Chesapeake, 1680–1800* (1986).

Hugo Prosper Leaming, *Hidden Americans: Maroons of Virginia and the Carolinas* (1995).

Jan Lewis, *The Pursuit of Happiness: Family and Values in Jeffersonian Virginia* (1983).

Philip D. Morgan, *Slave Counterpoint: Black Culture in the Eighteenth-Century Chesapeake and Low Country* (1998).

Michael P. Morris, *The Bringing of Wonder: Trade and the Indians of the Southeast, 1700–1783* (1999).

Michael Mullin, *Africa in America: Slave Acculturation and Resistance in the American South and the British Caribbean, 1736–1831* (1992).

John K. Nelson, *A Blessed Company: Parishes, Parsons, and Parishioners in Anglican Virginia, 1690–1776* (2002).

Robert Olwell, *Masters, Slaves, and Subjects: The Culture of Power in the South Carolina Low Country, 1740–1790* (1998).

Anthony S. Parent, *The Formation of a Slave Society in Virginia, 1660–1740* (2003).

Michael J. Rozbicki, *The Complete Colonial Gentleman: Cultural Legitimacy in Plantation America* (1998).

Jon F. Sensbach, *A Separate Canaan: The Making of an Afro-Moravian World in North Carolina, 1763–1840* (1997).

Marc Simmons, *Hispanic Albuquerque, 1706–1846* (2003).

Daniel Blake Smith, *Inside the Great House: Planter Family Life in Eighteenth-Century Chesapeake Society* (1980).

Mechal Sobel, *The World They Made Together: Black and White Values in Eighteenth-Century Virginia* (1987).

Donna Spindel, *Crime and Society in North Carolina, 1663–1776* (1989).

Daniel B. Thorp, *The Moravian Community in Colonial North Carolina: Pluralism on the Southern Frontier* (1989).

Lorena S. Walsh, *From Calabar to Carter's Grove: The History of a Virginia Slave Community* (1997).

Betty Wood, *The Origins of American Slavery: Freedom and Bondage in the English Colonies* (1997).

PATRICK HENRY'S MAP DESK

Like many of the leading gentry of 1760s Virginia, Patrick Henry pursued land speculation as a way to gain wealth. From 1767 to 1773, he engaged in a half-dozen land ventures, buying up thousands of acres of frontier land in regions now part of Kentucky—purchases that would soon figure in the emerging crisis of empire. This odd little table was Henry's map desk. Its fold-out extensions provided support for the large maps required to represent Virginia's vast western land claims, and its light weight allowed Henry to position it near the best light source in his law office. As is often the case with speculative purchases, Henry's land deals entailed risk: Many of his properties were occupied by the Cherokee, who did not recognize his claim of ownership. The British government, fearing war between Indians and settlers, tried to choke off risky land speculation in 1763 by establishing an imaginary line along the crest of the Appalachian Mountains beyond which settlement was prohibited. But men like Henry continued to buy land cheap in the hopes of selling dear at a later time. As a leading planter and powerful orator, Patrick Henry quickly became a spokesman in the growing imperial struggle with Britain. When he gained election to the Virginia House of Burgesses in 1765, he skillfully maneuvered that assembly into the startling repudiation of British power known as the Virginia Resolves. By 1775 he favored independence from England, a position that eventually would unleash settlers looking to buy land in the West. In 1776, he was elected the first governor of the Commonwealth of Virginia. Patrick Henry ultimately had seventeen children, fourteen of whom survived to adulthood. Through astute land purchases, he managed to establish each with a landed estate.

Courtesy of Scotchtown, photo by Katherine Wetzel.

6

The British Empire and the Colonial Crisis
1754–1775

I N 1771, THOMAS HUTCHINSON became the royal governor of the colony of Massachusetts. Unlike most royal governors, who were British aristocrats sent over by the king for short tours of duty, Hutchinson was a fifth-generation American. A Harvard-educated member of the Massachusetts elite, from a family of successful merchants, Hutchinson had served two decades in the Massachusetts general assembly. In 1758 he was appointed lieutenant governor, and in 1760 he also became chief justice of the colony's highest court. He lived in the finest mansion in Boston. Wealth, power, and influence were his in abundance. He was proud of his connection to the British empire and loyal to his king.

Hutchinson had the misfortune to be a loyal colonial leader during the two very tumultuous decades leading up to the American Revolution. He worked hard to keep the British and colonists aligned in interests, even promoting a plan to unify the colonies into a single defensive unit (the Albany Plan of Union) to ward off Indian wars. The plan of union failed, and a major war ensued—the Seven Years' War, pitting the British and colonists against the French and their Indian allies in the backcountry of the American colonies. When the war ended and the British government began to think about taxing colonists to pay for it, Hutchinson had no doubt that the new British policies were legitimate. Unwise, perhaps, in their specific formulation, but certainly legitimate.

Not everyone in Boston shared his opinion. Fervent, enthusiastic crowds protested against a succession of British taxation policies enacted after 1763—the Sugar Act, the Stamp Act, the Townshend duties, the Tea Act, all landmark events on the road to the American Revolution. But Hutchinson maintained his steadfast loyalty to England. His love of order and tradition inclined him to unconditional support of the British empire, and he was, by nature, a measured and cautious man. "My temper does not incline to enthusiasm," he once wrote.

Privately, he lamented the stupidity of the British acts that provoked trouble, but his sense of duty required him to defend the king's policies, however misguided. Quickly, he became an inspiring villain to the emerging revolutionary movement. Governor Hutchinson came to personify all that was wrong with British and colonial relations. The man not inclined to enthusiasm unleashed popular enthusiasm all around him. He never appreciated that irony.

In another irony, Thomas Hutchinson was actually one of the first Americans to recognize the difficulties of maintaining full rights and privileges

Thomas Hutchinson
The only formal portrait of Thomas Hutchinson still in existence shows an assured young man in ruffles and hair ribbons. Decades of turmoil in Boston failed to puncture his self-confidence. Doubtless he sat for several portraits, as did all the Boston leaders in the 1760s to 1780s, but no other likeness has survived. One portrait hung in his summer house outside Boston, but a revolutionary crowd mutilated it and stabbed out the eyes. In 1775, Hutchinson fled to England, the country he had regarded as his cultural home, only to realize how very American he was.
Courtesy of the Massachusetts Historical Society.

Years' War, which England and its colonies fought together as allies, shook that affection, and imperial policies in the decade following the war (1763–1773) shattered it completely. Over the course of that decade, colonists insistently and repeatedly raised serious questions about American liberties and rights, especially over the issues of taxation and representation. Many came to believe what Thomas Hutchinson could never credit, that a tyrannical Britain had embarked on a course to enslave the colonists by depriving them of their traditional English liberties.

The opposite of **liberty** was slavery, a condition of nonfreedom and of coercion. Political rhetoric about liberty, tyranny, and slavery heated up emotions of white colonists during the many crises of the 1760s and 1770s. But this rhetoric turned out to be a two-edged sword. The call for an end to tyrannical slavery meant one thing when sounded by Boston merchants whose commercial shipping rights had been revoked; the same call meant something quite different in 1775 when sounded by black Americans locked in the bondage of slavery.

All of this was set in motion by the Seven Years' War. The British victory at first fortified loyalty to England, but its aftermath, taxation, stirred up discussions of rights, fueled white colonists' fear of enslavement by king and Parliament, and produced a potent political vocabulary with unexpected consequences.

The Seven Years' War, 1754–1763

For nearly half of the first fifty years of the eighteenth century, England was at war intermittently with France or Spain. Often the colonists in America experienced reverberations from these conflicts, most acutely along the **frontier** in northern New England, which bumped up against New France, an area of French settlement along the St. Lawrence River with population centers at Montreal and Quebec. (New France was also called *Canada* by the French, a borrowed Indian word meaning "settlement.") In the 1750s, international tensions mounted again, but this time over events originating in America. The conflict centered on contested land in the Ohio Valley, variously claimed by Virginians, by Pennsylvanians, by the French in Canada, and by the Indians already living on the land. The re-

for colonists so far from their supreme government, the king and Parliament in England. In 1769, when British troops occupied Boston in an effort to provide civil order, he wrote privately to a friend in England, "There must be an abridgement of what are called English liberties. . . . I doubt whether it is possible to project a system of government in which a colony three thousand miles distant from the parent state shall enjoy all the liberty of the parent state." What he could not imagine was the possibility of giving up the parent state altogether and creating an independent government closer to home.

Thomas Hutchinson was a loyalist; in the 1750s, most English-speaking colonists were affectionately loyal to England. But the Seven

sult was the costly Seven Years' War, which spread in 1756 to encompass much of Europe, the Caribbean, and even India; in its global reach, the war has justly been called by some the first world war. In its American setting, the war actually ran for nine years, not seven, during which British and American soldiers shared the hardships of battle and the glory of victory over the French and their Indian allies. (The conflict in North America is also known as the French and Indian War.) But the immense costs of the war—in money, in deaths, in desires for revenge by losers and even winners—laid the groundwork for the imperial crisis of the 1760s between British leaders and American colonists.

French-English Rivalry in the Ohio Country

In 1753, French soldiers advanced from Canada south into Indian territory in the Ohio Country, a frontier region encompassing present-day western Pennsylvania and eastern Ohio. For several decades, French traders had cultivated alliances with the Indian tribes there, cementing their relationships with gifts in order to facilitate a profitable trade of manufactured goods for beaver furs. Then in the late 1740s, aggressive Pennsylvania traders had pushed into the Ohio Valley and begun to poach on their business, underselling French goods and threatening to reorient Indian loyalties. In response, the French built a series of forts, hoping to create a western barrier to British-American expansion. Their goal was to secure their trade routes, not to open land for French colonial settlement.

The same region was also claimed by Virginia, and in 1747 a group of wealthy Virginians, including the brothers Lawrence and Augustine Washington, formed the Ohio Company and obtained a large **land grant** from the English king. Unlike the French, the Virginians were interested primarily in land acquisition, not fur trading; the exploding English-American population fueled their hopes of profitable resale of

Ohio River Valley, 1753

the western land in the near future. But now a small trading post built by the enterprising Virginians at the forks of the Ohio River (at present-day Pittsburgh) was under threat as an ideal site for a French fort. The royal governor of Virginia, Robert Dinwiddie, himself a shareholder in the Ohio Company, sent a messenger to warn the French that they were trespassing on Virginia land.

The messenger on this dangerous mission was George Washington, younger half-brother of the Ohio Company leaders. Although he was only twenty-one, Washington was an ambitious youth whose imposing height (six feet two) and air of silent competence convinced the governor he could do the job. The middle child in a family of eight, Washington did not stand to inherit great wealth, so he sought to gain public reputation and impress the Virginia elite by volunteering for this perilous duty. Accompanied by six other Virginians (one of whom spoke French), Washington delivered Dinwiddie's message to a French outpost near Lake Erie in late 1753 and returned from his assignment with crucial intelligence about French military strength.

Impressed, Dinwiddie appointed the youth to lead a small military expedition west to assert and, if need be, defend Virginia's claim. Dinwiddie acted with explicit backing from imperial officials in London, who were concerned by the French fortifications and who authorized the Virginia governor "to repell force by force," but only if Virginia troops were attacked first. By early 1754, the French had laid claim to the land at the forks of the Ohio River and had built Fort Duquesne there. Washington's assignment was somehow to chase the French away without being the aggressor and without provoking a larger war.

In spring of 1754, Washington returned to the Ohio Country, this time with 160 armed Virginians aided by Indian allies of the Mingo tribe led by its chief, Tanaghrisson. On an early morning in May, Tanaghrisson and a group of Mingos led a detachment of Washington's soldiers to a small French encampment in the woods. A brief skirmish ensued and fourteen Frenchmen were wounded; who fired the first shot was later a matter of dispute. While Washington struggled to communicate with the

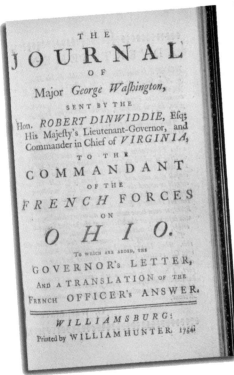

Washington's Journal, 1754

When George Washington returned from his first mission to the French, Governor Dinwiddie asked him to write a full report of what he had seen of the western countryside, of the Indians, and of French troop strength. Washington obliged, writing about 7,000 words in less than two days (about equivalent to a 25-page double-spaced paper). He coolly narrated scenes of personal danger: of traveling in deep snow and freezing temperatures, of falling off a raft into an icy river, of being shot at by a lone Indian. Dinwiddie printed Washington's report, along with his own letter and the French commander's defiant answer, in a 32-page pamphlet; shortly thereafter it was reprinted in London. The governor's aim was to inform Virginians and British leaders about the French threat to the west. But the pamphlet suited Washington's aims as well: At age twenty-two, he became known on both sides of the Atlantic for resolute and rugged courage.

The Huntington Library and Art Collections, San Marino, California.

injured French commander, Tanaghrisson and his men intervened to kill and then scalp the wounded men, including the commander, probably with the aim of enflaming hostilities between the French and colonists.

This sudden massacre violated Washington's instructions to avoid being the aggressor and raised the stakes considerably. Washington, understandably anxious about French retaliation, ordered his men to fortify their position. They dubbed the flimsy structure that they built "Fort Necessity." Reinforcements amounting to several hundred more Virginians arrived; but the Mingos, sensing disaster and displeased by Washington's style of command over them, abandoned the Virginians. (Tanaghrisson later said: "The Colonel was a good-natured man, but had no experience; he took upon him to command the Indians as his slaves, [and] would by no means take advice from the Indians.") In early July, over 600 French soldiers attacked Fort Necessity, aided by tribes the Virginians had as-

sumed were on their side. After a third of the fort's occupants were killed or wounded, Washington surrendered, and the victors sent him back to his governor carrying a message of defeat: The French had no intention of departing from the disputed territory.

The Albany Congress and Intercolonial Defense

Even as Virginians, Frenchmen, and Indians fought and died in the Ohio Country, British imperial leaders were hoping to prevent the

George Washington, by Charles Willson Peale

In 1772, George Washington posed for the artist Charles Willson Peale in his splendid vintage uniform from the Seven Years' War, by then fifteen years in the past. It looks a tight fit. Notice the ornamental gorget hung around his neck, a miniature version of the throat-piece of a medieval suit of armor. Both English and Indian leaders in the eighteenth century often sported gorgets. Peale captured Washington's grandeur in his clothes but not his face, which appears plain, simple, and still very youthful. Washington wrote a friend that he was "in so grave—so sullen a mood" and often so sleepy during the portrait sitting "that I fancy the skill of this gentleman's pencil will be hard put to it, in describing to the world what manner of man I am."

Washington/Custis/Lee Collection, Washington and Lee University, Lexington, Virginia.

Chief Hendrick and John Caldwell

What might it mean when a Mohawk chief dresses in English clothes and a British soldier goes native, and each of them poses for a portrait in attire adopted from the other culture? Dress is a symbol system that conveys status and self-presentation to viewers. Might it also change the way the dresser thinks about himself or herself? Chief Hendrick worked closely with the British in New York to maintain the trade alliance known as the Covenant Chain. In 1740, when he was sixty, he traveled to England, was presented at the royal court, and sat for this portrait. His blue coat, ruffled shirt, three-cornered hat, and cravat are all signs of the well-dressed British gentleman; but he holds a tomahawk in one hand and wampum in the other, and his long white hair is conspicuously uncurled, unlike an eighteenth-century gent's wig. John Caldwell also holds a tomahawk, which goes with his Indian garb: feather headdress, blankets, leggings, and moccasins. During the Revolutionary War, Caldwell was stationed at Fort Detroit, a British garrison that provided aid to tribes in the Ohio Valley battling Americans. Caldwell acquired this Indian outfit for a formal diplomatic mission to the Shawnee in 1780; he took the clothes back to England and wore them for this portrait. Do you think these instances of imitation indicate a willingness to cross cultural boundaries and try to be like, think like, or experience the other culture? Is the co-opting just play or a sign of something deeper?

struggle from turning into a larger war. One obvious strategy was to strengthen British alliances with powerful and seemingly neutral Indian tribes who might otherwise support the French. To this end, British authorities directed the governor of New York to convene a conference drawing delegates from all colonies from Virginia northward.

In June and July of 1754, twenty-four delegates from seven colonies met in Albany, New York; also attending were Iroquois Indians of the Six Nations, a political confederacy of six large tribes inhabiting the central and western parts of what is now the state of New York. Albany had long been the site of periodic meetings that affirmed a trade alliance called the Covenant

Chain, first created in 1692 between New York leaders and Mohawk Indians, the most easterly of the Six Nations tribes. In 1753, the aged and venerable Mohawk leader, Hendrick, accused the English of breaking the Covenant Chain. A prime goal of the Albany Congress was thus to repair trade relations with the Mohawk and enlist their help—or at least their neutrality—against the French threat.

Two delegates at the congress had more ambitious plans. Benjamin Franklin of Pennsylvania and Thomas Hutchinson of Massachusetts, both rising political stars in their home colonies, coauthored the Albany Plan of Union, a document that proposed to provide for colonial defense by instituting a unified but limited government over all the colonies. In the course of the meeting, the Albany delegates learned of George Washington's defeat at Fort Necessity and understood instantly the escalating risk of war with France; they approved the plan. Key features included a president general appointed by the crown, together with a grand council of 48 colonial representatives, which would meet annually to consider questions of war, peace, and trade with the Indians. The writers of the Albany Plan humbly reaffirmed Parliament's authority; this was no bid for enlarged autonomy of the colonies.

To Franklin's surprise, not a single colony approved the Albany Plan. The Massachusetts assembly feared it was "a Design of gaining power over the Colonies," especially the power of taxation. Others objected that it would be impossible to agree on unified policies toward scores of quite different Indian tribes. The British government never backed the Albany Plan either, which perplexed both Franklin and Hutchinson. Instead, British authorities chose to centralize dealings with the Indians by appointing in 1755 two superintendents of Indian affairs, one for the northern and another for the southern colonies, each with exclusive powers to negotiate treaties, trade, and land sales. The superintendent of the northern district was William Johnson, a longtime trading partner and friend of the Mohawk people. This good news for the Mohawks was not welcomed by other tribes of the Iroquois confederacy; they had left the Albany Congress without pledging to help the English battle the French. At this very early point in the Seven Years' War, the Iroquois nations in western New York concluded that the French military presence around the Great Lakes and in the frontier west would help discourage the westward push of American colonists and therefore served their interests.

The War and Its Consequences

By 1755, Washington's frontier skirmish had turned into a major mobilization of British and American troops against the French. At first, the British hoped for quick victory by throwing armies at the French in three strategic places. A large force led by General Edward Braddock, recently arrived from England, was to attack the French at Fort Duquesne in western Pennsylvania; accompanying them would be George Washington's Virginia militia. In Massachusetts, Governor William Shirley aimed his soldiers at Fort Niagara, critically located between Lakes Erie and Ontario. And forces under William Johnson of New York, the new Indian affairs superintendent for the northern colonies, moved north toward Lake Champlain, intending to push the French back to Canada (Map 6.1).

Unfortunately for the British, the French were prepared to fight and had cemented respectful alliances with many Indian tribes from Canada down through the Great Lakes region and into the Ohio Country. In July 1755, General Braddock's large and well-armed force of 2,000 British and Virginia troops (joined by just eight Oneida Indians) marched toward Fort Duquesne, expecting an easy victory with their big guns and overwhelming numbers. One day short of their target, they were encircled in the woods and ambushed by 250 French soldiers and 640 Indian warriors, including Ottawas, Ojibwas, Potawatomis, Shawnees, and Delawares. In the bloody Battle of the Monongahela, named for a nearby river, nearly a thousand on the British side were killed or wounded. Washington was unhurt, though two horses in succession were shot out from under him; General Braddock was killed. Despite the humiliation of defeat, Washington's bravery in battle caused the governor of Virginia to promote him to commander of the Virginia army. At age twenty-two, Washington was beginning to realize his ambitions.

News of Braddock's defeat alarmed the other two British armies, then hacking their way through the dense forests of northern New York, and they retreated from action. For the next two years, the British stumbled badly on the American front. They lacked adequate numbers of soldiers

> To Franklin's surprise, not a single colony approved the Albany Plan. The Massachusetts assembly feared it was "a Design of gaining power over the Colonies," especially the power of taxation.

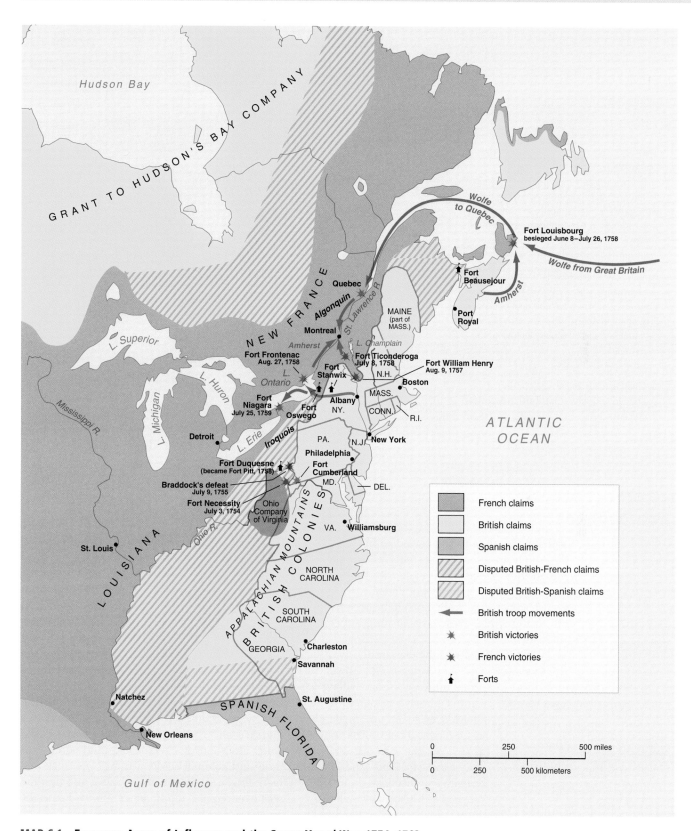

MAP 6.1   European Areas of Influence and the Seven Years' War, 1754–1763

In the mid-eighteenth century, France, England, and Spain claimed vast areas of North America, many of them already inhabited by various Indian peoples. The early flash points of the Seven Years' War were in regions of disputed claims where the French had allied with powerful native groups—the Iroquois and the Algonquian—to put pressure on the westward-moving English.

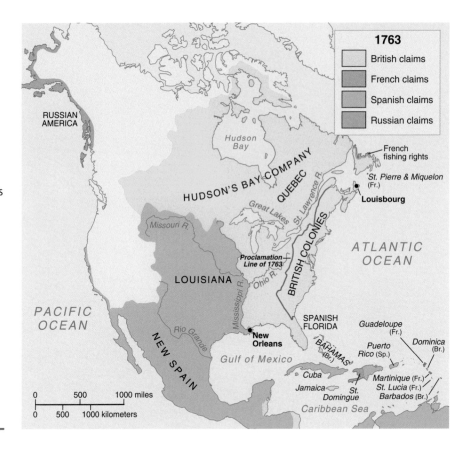

MAP 6.2 North America after the Seven Years' War
In the peace treaty of 1763, France ceded its interior lands but retained fishing rights and islands in the far north and several sugar islands in the Caribbean. Much of France's claim to land called Louisiana went not to England but to Spain.

READING THE MAP: How did European land claims change from 1750 to 1763?
CONNECTIONS: What was the goal of the Proclamation Act of 1763? What was the eventual fate of Louisbourg following the Seven Years' War?

FOR MORE HELP ANALYZING THIS MAP, see the map activity for this chapter in the Online Study Guide at bedfordstmartins .com/roark.

and supplies, and they received scant help from the American colonial assemblies. Nearly all the Indian tribes allied themselves with the French, figuring that the sparsely populated fur-trading French settlements were much to be preferred to the fast-growing, westward-pushing American colonies.

What finally turned the war around was the rise to power in 1757 of William Pitt, England's prime minister, a man willing to commit massive resources to an all-out war to ensure England's victory over France. His strategy led to the capture of Fort Duquesne in 1758 and Forts Niagara and Ticonderoga in 1759. When the British navy sailed up the St. Lawrence River, the French cities of Montreal and Quebec were isolated from help. The decisive victory on the North American continent was the capture of the seemingly invincible fortress city of Quebec in

> England's version of the victory of 1763 awarded all credit to the mighty British army. Colonists read the lessons of the war differently.

September 1759 by the young British general James Wolfe.

The fall of Quebec broke the backbone of the French in North America. The victory was completed by the surrender of the French at Montreal in late 1760. American colonists rejoiced, but the worldwide war was not over yet. Battles continued in the Caribbean, where the French sugar islands Martinique and Guadeloupe fell to the English. Battles raged in Europe, and fighting extended to India. In 1762, the British laid siege to Spanish Cuba because Spain was France's ally in the global conflict. The costly water invasion of Havana required some four thousand colonial soldiers from New York and New England. By the end of 1762, the fighting was over. France and Spain capitulated, and the Treaty of Paris was signed in 1763.

The triumph of victory was sweet but short-lived. The complex peace negotiations reorganized the map of North America but stopped short of providing England with the full spoils of victory. England gained control of Canada, eliminating the French threat from the north and west. English and American title to the eastern half of North America, precisely what England had claimed before the war, was confirmed. But all French territory west of the Mississippi River, including New Orleans, was transferred to Spain as compensation for Spain's assistance to France during the war. Stranger still, Cuba was returned to Spain, and Martinique and Guadeloupe were returned to France (Map 6.2).

In truth, the French islands in the Caribbean were hardly a threat to Americans, for they provided a profitable trade in smuggled molasses. The main threat to the safety of colonists came instead from Indians dismayed by England's victory. The Treaty of Paris completely ignored the Indians and assigned their lands to English rule. With the French gone, the Indians lost the advantage of having two opponents to play off against each other, and they now had to cope with the westward-moving Americans. Indian policy would soon become a serious point of contention between the British government and the colonists.

England's version of the victory of 1763 awarded all credit to the mighty British army. According to this version, ungrateful colonists had provided inadequate support for a war fought to save them from the French. In defiance of British law, the colonists had engaged in smuggling—notably a lively trade in beaver pelts with French fur traders and an illegal molasses trade in the Caribbean. American traders, grumbled the British leaders, were really traitors. William Pitt was convinced that the illegal trade "principally, if not alone, enabled France to sustain and protract this long and expensive war."

Colonists read the lessons of the war differently. American colonial soldiers had turned out in force, they claimed, but the troops had been relegated to grunt work by arrogant British military leaders. Worse yet, they experienced unexpectedly harsh military discipline at British hands, ranging from floggings to executions. One soldier recalled watching three New England soldiers endure whippings of 800 lashes for some "trifling offense" at the hands of the British. At 300 lashes, "the flesh appeared to be entirely whipped from their shoulders, and they hung as mute and motionless as though they had been long since deprived of life." Then a British doctor revived them with "a vial of sharp stuff," saying, "'D__mn you, you can bear it yet'—and then the whipping would commence

again." Americans bristled at stories of British disdain, such as the remark of the impetuous General Wolfe, the British hero of Quebec, who said the American soldiers were "contemptible dogs." General Braddock had foolishly bragged to Benjamin Franklin that "these savages may, indeed, be a formidable enemy to your raw American militia, but upon the king's regular and disciplined troops, sir, it is impossible they should make any impression." Braddock's defeat "gave us Americans," Franklin wrote, "the first suspicion that our exalted ideas of the prowess of British regulars had not been well founded."

The human costs of the war were etched especially sharply in the minds of New England colonists, who had contributed many troops. About one-third of all Massachusetts men between ages fifteen and thirty had seen service. Many families lost loved ones, and this cost would not soon be forgotten. The assault on Havana in Cuba, for example, took the lives of

The Seven Years' War

1692–1750s English and Iroquois create and affirm the Covenant Chain alliance in western New York.

1700–1740s French settlers enjoy exclusive trade with Indians in Ohio Valley.

1747 Ohio Company receives land grant from king of England.

1753 Mohawk chief Hendrick accuses English of breaking the Covenant Chain.

French soldiers advance from Canada into Ohio Country.

George Washington delivers a message telling the French that they are trespassing.

1754 French build Fort Duquesne.

Washington returns to Ohio Country with troops and Mingo allies.

May. Washington, guided by Mingo chief Tanaghrisson, attacks the French.

July. French and Indian soldiers defeat Washington at Fort Necessity.

June–July. Albany Congress convenes.

1755 British authorities appoint two superintendents of Indian affairs.

July. Braddock defeated in the Battle of Monongahela.

1756 William Pitt becomes leader of England's House of Commons.

1758 British capture Fort Duquesne.

1759 British capture Forts Niagara and Ticonderoga.

British capture Quebec.

1760 British capture Montreal.

1762 British capture Cuba.

1763 Treaty of Paris signed.

some 2,000 Americans, half the colonial soldiers who had been sent there.

The enormous expense of the war caused by Pitt's no-holds-barred military strategy cast another huge shadow over the victory. By 1763, England's national debt, double what it had been when Pitt took office, posed a formidable challenge to the next decade of leadership in England.

British Leadership, Indians, and the Proclamation of 1763

In 1760, in the middle of the Seven Years' War, twenty-two-year-old George III came to the British throne, underprepared for his monarchical duties. Timid and insecure, the new king trusted only his tutor, the Earl of Bute, a Scotsman who was an outsider to power circles in London. George III immediately installed Bute as head of his cabinet of ministers. Bute made blunders and did not last long, but in his short time in office he made one very significant decision—to keep a standing army in the mainland colonies even though the last battles there were over in 1760. In both financial and political terms, this was a costly move.

> The ostensible reason for keeping several thousand British troops in America was to maintain the peace between the colonists and the Indians. This was not a misplaced concern.

The ostensible reason for keeping several thousand British troops in America was to maintain the peace between the colonists and the Indians. This was not a misplaced concern. The defeat and withdrawal of the French from North America had left their Indian allies—who did not accept defeat—in a state of alarm. Just three months after the Treaty of Paris was signed in 1763, Pontiac, chief of the Ottawa tribe in the northern Ohio region, attacked the British garrison near Detroit. Six more attacks on forts quickly followed; American settlements were also hit. Joining the Ottawa were tribes from western New York, the Ohio Valley, and the Great Lakes region: the Chippewa, Huron, Potawatomi, Miami, Kickapoo, Mascouten, Wea, Shawnee, Mingo, Delaware, and Seneca. By fall, these tribes had captured every fort west of Detroit,

Pontiac's Uprising, 1763

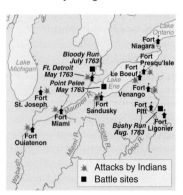

more than 400 British soldiers were dead, and another 2,000 colonists had been killed or taken captive. Pontiac's uprising was quelled in December 1763 by the combined efforts of British and colonial soldiers, but the potential for continued frontier warfare was hardly diminished. (See "Historical Question," page 184.)

To minimize violence, the British government that fall issued an order called the Proclamation of 1763, forbidding colonists to settle west of an imaginary line drawn along the crest of the Appalachian Mountains from Canada in the north to Georgia in the south. The Proclamation chiefly aimed to separate Indians and settlers, but it also was intended to limit trade with Indians to traders licensed by colonial governors, and it forbade private sales of Indian land. The Proclamation's language took care not to identify western lands as belonging to the Indians. Instead, it spoke of Indians "who live under our protection" on "such parts of our Dominions and Territories as, not having been ceded to or purchased by Us, are reserved to them, as their Hunting Grounds." Other parts of the Proclamation of 1763 referred to American colonists and even to the French inhabitants of now-British Canada as "our loving subjects" who could enjoy the blessings of English rights and privileges. In contrast, Indians were clearly rejected as British subjects, described more vaguely as "Tribes of Indians with whom We are connected." Of course, the English were not really well connected with the Indians, nor did they wish connections to form among the tribes. As William Johnson, the superintendent of northern Indian affairs, advised in 1764, "It will be expedient to treat with each nation separately . . . for could they arrive at a perfect union, they must prove very dangerous Neighbours." In Johnson's view, "As long as they Quarrell with one another, we shall be well with them all. And when they are all at Peace, It's the Signal for us to have a good Look out."

The 1763 proclamation line proved nearly impossible to enforce. Surging American population growth had already sent many hundreds of settlers west of the line, and land speculators, such as those of Virginia's Ohio Company, had no desire to lose opportunities for profitable resale of the lands they had been granted more than a decade earlier. Bute's decision to post a standing army in the colonies was thus a cause for concern for western settlers, eastern speculators, and Indian tribes alike.

Silver Medal to Present to Indians
After Pontiac's uprising ended, the British attempted to mend relations with Indian tribes by honoring them with gifts. This silver medal, minted in 1766, displays a profile of King George III on the front and a cozy depiction on the back of an Indian and Briton sharing a smoking peace pipe. The Latin words on the front announce George's name, title, and kingly dominions; the English words on the back would have been equally unintelligible to the recipients of the gift. Imagine a conversation between an Indian chief and an English translator who tries to explain what the slogan "HAPPY WHILE UNITED" might mean. The scene depicted—two men with relaxed, friendly body language—illustrates "HAPPY" and "UNITED." The "WHILE," rooted in a sense of time, temporariness, and contingency, might be tricky to explain. Why?
The American Numismatic Society.

The Sugar and Stamp Acts, 1763–1765

Lord Bute lost power in 1763, and the young King George turned to a succession of leaders throughout the 1760s, searching for a prime minister he could trust. Nearly half a dozen ministers in seven years took their turns formulating policies designed to address one basic, underlying British reality: A huge war debt, amounting to £123 million and growing because of interest due on the loans, needed to be serviced, and the colonists, as British subjects, should help to pay it off. To many Americans, however, that proposition seemed in deep violation of what they perceived to be their rights and liberties as British subjects, and it created resentment that grew and eventually erupted in rebellion. The first provocative revenue acts were the work of Sir George Grenville, prime minister from 1763 to 1765.

Grenville's Sugar Act

To find revenue, George Grenville scrutinized the customs service, a division of the British government responsible for monitoring the flow of ships and collecting duties on specified trade items in both England and America. Grenville found that the salaries of customs officers cost the government four times what was collected in revenue. The shortfall was due in part to bribery and smuggling, so Grenville began to insist on rigorous attention to paperwork and a strict accounting of collected duties.

The hardest duty to enforce was the one imposed by the Molasses Act of 1733—a stiff tax of six pence per gallon on any molasses purchased from non-British sources. The purpose of the tax was to discourage trade with French Caribbean islands and redirect the molasses trade to British sugar islands. But it did not work: French molasses remained cheap and abundant because French **planters** on Martinique and Guadeloupe had no use for it. A by-product of sugar production, molasses was a key ingredient in rum, a drink the French scorned. Rum-loving Americans were eager to buy French molasses, and they had ignored the tax law for decades.

Grenville's ingenious solution to this problem was the Revenue Act of 1764, popularly dubbed the "Sugar Act." It lowered the duty on French molasses to three pence, making it more attractive for shippers to obey the law, and at the same time raised penalties for smuggling. The act appeared to be in the tradition of navigation acts meant to regulate trade, but Grenville's actual intent was to raise revenue. He was using an established form of law for new ends, and he was doing it by the novel means of lowering a duty.

The Sugar Act toughened enforcement policies. From now on, all British naval crews could act as impromptu customs officers, boarding suspicious ships and seizing cargoes found to be in violation. Smugglers caught without proper paperwork would be prosecuted, not in a friendly civil court with a local jury but in a vice-admiralty court located in Halifax, Nova Scotia, where a single judge presided. The implication was that justice would be sure and severe.

How Long Did the Seven Years' War Last in Indian Country?

France was defeated on the North American continent in 1760, and the Treaty of Paris officially ended the global war between France and England in 1763. But there was no lasting peace for the Indian nations of the Ohio Valley and Great Lakes region. In 1761, a Chippewa chief named Minavavana clearly explained why in an ominous speech delivered to a British trader at Fort Michilimackinac, a British outpost guarding the straits of Mackinaw where Lakes Huron and Michigan meet: "Englishman, although you have conquered the French, you have not yet conquered us! We are not your slaves. These lakes, these woods and mountains were left to us by our ancestors. They are our inheritance; and we will part with them to none." Furthermore, Minavavana pointedly noted, "your king has never sent us any presents, nor entered into any treaty with us, wherefore he and we are still at war; and until he does these things we must consider that we have no other father, nor friend, among the white men than the King of France."

Minavavana and other Indians of the region had cause to be alarmed. With the exit of the French, British regiments took over the French-built forts all over the Northwest. Fort Duquesne, renamed Fort Pitt in honor of the British leader who authorized the war-winning strategy, underwent two years of fortification. No one could mistake the new walls—

sixty feet thick at their base, ten at the top—for the external facade of a friendly fur trading post. Nonmilitary Americans were moving into Fort Pitt's neighborhood too, just as Indians had feared they would, crowding out native inhabitants and relying on the military protection of the fort.

Minavavana's complaint about the lack of British presents was a far more serious problem than the British military leaders figured. Gifts exchanged in Indian culture cemented social relationships; they symbolized honor and established obligation. The French over many decades had mastered the subtleties of gift exchange, distributing clothing, textiles, and hats, and receiving calumets (ornamented ceremonial pipe stems) as symbols of friendship. New to the practice, British military leaders often discarded the calumets as trivial trinkets, thereby insulting the givers. Major General Jeffrey Amherst was sometimes willing to offer gifts to particular Indian leaders, positioning the "gift" as a bribe in the British frame of reference. But Amherst saw extensive gift exchange as demeaning to the British, forcing them to pay tribute to people whom he considered inferior. "It is not my intention ever to attempt to gain the friendship of Indians by presents," Amherst declared. The Indian view was the opposite: Generous givers expressed dominance and protection, not subordination, in the act of giving. William Johnson, superintendent of northern

Indian affairs, warned Amherst that he was insulting the Indians, but the imperious Amherst did not listen.

A religious revival in 1760–1761, fueled by the prophetic visions of an Indian leader named Neolin, greatly enhanced the prospects of frontier war in the Northwest. Neolin, of the Delaware tribe, predicted a swift decline for all tribes unless they altered their ways, gave up quarreling with each other, shunned trade in guns, alcohol, and other trade goods, and curbed their overkill of animals for the pelt trade. His preachings spread quickly, gaining credence as the British bungled diplomacy and American settlers continued to penetrate western lands.

A renewal of commitment to Indian ways and the formation of tribal alliances led to open warfare in 1763, called (by the British) Pontiac's Rebellion. (The Indians would not have credited Pontiac with sole leadership; the coordination of the war was the work of many men.) Jeffrey Amherst, never a shrewd observer of Indian relations, flatly declared in April 1763 that reports of impending attack were "Meer Bugbears." But by mid-May, the British commander at Detroit knew the threat was real. Pontiac, chief of the Ottawa, along with Potawatomi and Huron warriors, attacked Fort Detroit and laid siege for two months. In late May, within two weeks of Pontiac's first move, Indians captured four more forts in Ohio, through ruses in which Indians pretending to have peaceful business gained entry to the garrisons. A fifth fort, at Michilimackinac, fell to Ojibwas who seemed to be playing a game of lacrosse near the fort. After several hours of strenuous play, the ball landed near the fort's open gate, and the enthralled British spectators realized too late that the convergence of players on the ball was really a rush

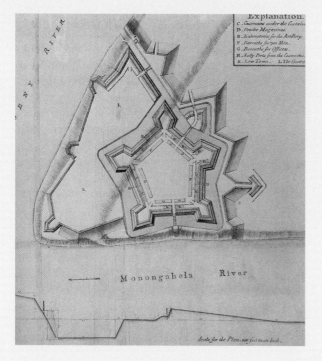

Plan of the New Fort at Pittsburgh
The French Fort Duquesne sat at the strategic forks of the Ohio River on a triangle of land formed by the Allegheny and Monongahela rivers rushing together to create the mighty Ohio. Built in 1754, Fort Duquesne provided a supply depot and a meeting place for the Indian allies of the French. It was the intended target of General Braddock's English army in 1755, but Braddock was forced into battle and soundly defeated a day before his planned attack. In 1758, the British captured an English-speaking man named Johnson along with some Indians taken prisoner. Johnson, an apparent traitor, saved his life by yielding information that Fort Duquesne was greatly undermanned and an easy hit. British and colonial troops sped to attack it; once taken, the fort was blown into rubble. In 1759, this plan for a new fort, named for Prime Minister William Pitt, showed the grand and imposing stronghold with room enough to house 1,000 soldiers inside the thick protective walls. By 1762, the fort was finished, fulfilling Pitt's mandate to "maintain His Majesty's subjects in undisputed possession of the Ohio."

of warriors into the fort. The players seized tomahawks that had been hidden under blankets worn by Indian women on the sidelines. The Ojibwas took the fort.

By the end of June, thirteen British garrisons had either fallen or been evacuated under threat of attack. Yet the British managed to hold on to the three most important forts— Detroit, Niagara, and Pitt—besieged by Indians. At Fort Pitt, two ostensibly friendly Delaware Indians showed up at the end of May to suggest that the British leave to avoid attack. Pitt's commander thanked them but declined their suggestion and sent them on their way with his idea of a gift: two blankets and a handkerchief used by British smallpox patients in the fort. "We hope it will have the desired effect," wrote a militiaman in his diary. Two months later, Jeffrey Amherst suggested to a subordinate that spreading smallpox—a practice akin to later germ warfare—should be considered as a method of war: "We must use Every Strategem in our Power to Reduce them." There is no evidence that the infected blankets ac-

tually propagated smallpox or that Amherst's war strategem was put into greater practice.

From late summer of 1763 into the early months of 1764, Indian country was the scene of tremendous bloodshed. Indians targeted British supply routes and civilian settlements, resulting in several thousand deaths. Two thousand British troops were moved west from points in upper New York and Canada to join the fray. In December, Pennsylvania civilians went on the offensive. Some fifty vigilantes known as the Paxton Boys decided to make war on any Indians they could find. They descended on a peaceful village of friendly Conestoga Indians and murdered and scalped twenty of them. The vigilantes, numbers swelling to 500, next marched on Philadelphia to try to capture and murder some Christian Indians held in protective custody. British troops prevented that, but the unruly Paxton Boys escaped all punishment for their murderous attack on the Conestoga.

In 1764, the rebellion faded. The Indians were short on ammunition;

the British were tired and broke. Amherst's superiors in Britain blamed him for mishandling the conflict, and when he was recalled home, his own soldiers toasted his leaving. Thomas Gage took command and soon distributed gifts profusely among the Indians.

Was the Seven Years' War finally over for the Indians, ten years after it started? If 1764 represents an end, it was only a brief one. Periodic raids and killings punctuated the rest of the 1760s and early 1770s, climaxing in the late 1770s as Indians joined the British to fight the Americans in the Revolutionary War. Warfare and massacres occurred in New England and New York, down to South Carolina and Georgia, and especially in the Ohio Country. The American Revolution eventually ended as well, but the frontier war between Americans and Indians continued on and off— mostly on—until 1815, the end of the War of 1812. Perhaps the Seven Years' War could be called the Sixty-One Years' War, from the Indian point of view.

principally from Americans in the shipping trades inconvenienced by the law.

From the British point of view, the Proclamation of 1763 and the Sugar Act seemed to be reasonable efforts to administer the colonies.

To the Americans, however, the British supervision appeared to be a disturbing intrusion into colonial practices, by which taxes were raised by colonial assemblies composed of elected representatives. Philadelphian Benjamin Franklin, living in London as the agent for Pennsylvania, warned that "two distinct Jurisdictions or Powers of Taxing cannot well subsist together in the same country. If a Tax is propos'd with us, how dare we venture to lay it, as the next Ship perhaps may bring us an Account of some heavy Tax propos'd by you?"

Paper Currency of the 1750s to 1770s

Colonists generally used coins of valued metal for money (British shillings, Spanish doubloons) or else engaged in barter. But during the upheaval of the Seven Years' War, several colonies printed paper money. The currency shown here is laden with words stipulating the legality and value of the money. To discourage counterfeiting, each paper had an elaborate design, a unique handwritten number, and the signature of some authority who vouched for its authenticity. London merchants did not like accepting colonial paper money and prevailed on Parliament to pass a Currency Act in 1764 prohibiting the colonies from printing any, which put a crimp in the colonial economy, always short of coinage. In 1775, the newly established Continental Congress began printing paper money to finance the war. Notice the three-dollar paper at the lower left.

Courtesy of the Decorative & Industrial Arts Collection of the Chicago Historical Society.

The Stamp Act

By his second year in office, Grenville had made almost no dent in the national debt. Continued evasion prevented the Sugar Act from becoming the moneymaker he had hoped it would be. So in February 1765, he escalated his revenue program with the Stamp Act, precipitating a major conflict between England and the colonies over Parliament's right to tax. The Stamp Act imposed a tax on all paper used for various colonial documents—newspapers, pamphlets, court documents, licenses, wills, ships' bills of lading—and required that a special stamp be affixed to the paper proving that the tax had been paid. Unlike the Sugar Act, which regulated trade, the Stamp Act was designed plainly and simply to raise money. It affected nearly everyone who used any taxed paper—newspaper readers, for example—but it fell heaviest on the business and legal communities, heavily reliant on official documents.

Thomas Hutchinson, lieutenant governor of Massachusetts, had warned Grenville that the stamp tax posed difficulties. Aside from the navigation acts, which were intended primarily to regulate trade, Parliament had levied no previous taxes on the colonists. Hutchinson warned that the colonies could reasonably conclude that Parliament had conceded to them the right to tax themselves. On practical grounds, he also urged the British officials to consider whether trade disruptions caused by the Stamp Act might cost

Grenville hoped that his tightening of the customs service and the lowered duties of the Sugar Act would reform American smugglers into law-abiding shippers and in turn generate income for the empire. Unfortunately, the decrease in duty was not sufficient to offset the attractions of smuggling. The vigilant customs officers made bribery harder to accomplish, and several ugly confrontations occurred in port cities such as Newport, Rhode Island, and New York City. Reaction to the Sugar Act foreshadowed questions about England's right to tax Americans, but in 1764 objections to the act came

more than the revenue the act generated. Instead of heeding Hutchinson's fears, Grenville merely delegated the administration of the act to Americans, to avoid the problem of hostility to British enforcers. In each colony, local stamp distributors would be hired at a handsome salary of 8 percent of the revenue collected.

English tradition held that taxes were a gift of the people to their monarch, granted by the people's representatives. This view of taxes as a freely given gift preserved an essential concept of English political theory—the idea that citizens have the liberty to enjoy and use their property without fear of confiscation. The king could not demand money; only the House of Commons could grant it. Grenville quite agreed with the notion of taxation by consent, but he argued that the colonists were already "virtually" represented in Parliament. The House of Commons, he insisted, represented all British subjects, wherever they were.

Colonial leaders emphatically rejected this British view, arguing that **virtual representation** could not withstand the stretch across the Atlantic. The stamp tax itself, levied by a distant Parliament on unwilling colonies, illustrated the problem. "The MINISTER'S virtual representation in Support of the TAX on us is fantastical and frivolous," Maryland inhabitants complained. Daniel Dulany, a Maryland lawyer, wrote a best-selling pamphlet explaining that virtual representation was "a mere cob-web, spread to catch the unwary, and entangle the weak."

Resistance Strategies and Crowd Politics

The Stamp Act was scheduled to take effect on November 1, 1765. News of its passage arrived in the colonies in April 1765, so colonial leaders had seven months to contemplate a response. Governors were unlikely to challenge the law, for most of them owed their office to the king. Instead, the colonial assemblies took the lead; eight of them held discussions on objections to the Stamp Act.

Virginia's assembly, the House of Burgesses, was the first to object. At the very end of its May 1765 session, after two-thirds of the members had gone home, Patrick Henry, a twenty-nine-year-old lawyer and political newcomer, presented a series of resolutions on the Stamp Act that were debated and passed, one by one. They became known as the Virginia Resolves.

Henry's resolutions inched the assembly toward radical opposition to the Stamp Act. The first three stated the obvious: that Virginians were British citizens, that they enjoyed the same rights and privileges as Britons, and that self-taxation was one of those rights. The fourth resolution noted that Virginians had always taxed themselves, through their representatives in the House of Burgesses. The fifth took a radical leap by pushing the other four unexceptional statements to one logical conclusion—that the Virginia assembly alone had the right to tax Virginians.

> The traditional English view of taxes as a gift of the people to their monarch preserved an essential concept of English political theory—the idea that citizens have the liberty to enjoy and use their property without fear of confiscation.

Tax Assessment Book

American colonists routinely paid property taxes to local authorities. This 1772 tax book from Rowley, Massachusetts, records amounts due in pounds, shillings, and pence. The several entries for each name indicate assessments on real estate, personal property, and a poll (head) tax. Notice that two women identified as "Mrs." owe taxes. Since married women by law owned no property, we can conclude that these were widows. What do you think the seven large X marks meant? Why might "Capt Samuel Pike" lack one?

Chicago Historical Society.

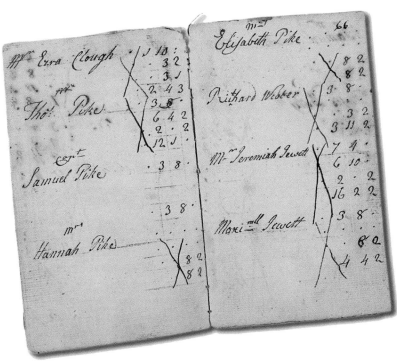

Two more fiery resolutions were debated, but majority support eroded as Henry pressed the logic of his case to the extreme. The sixth resolution denied legitimacy to any tax law originating outside Virginia, and a seventh boldly called anyone who disagreed with these propositions an enemy of Virginia. This was too much for the other representatives. They backed away from resolutions six and seven and later rescinded their vote on number five as well.

Their caution hardly mattered, however, because newspapers in other colonies printed all seven Virginia Resolves, creating the impression that a daring first challenge to the Stamp Act had taken place. As a result, other assemblies were willing to consider even more radical questions, such as: By what authority could Parliament legislate for the colonies without also taxing them? No one disagreed, in 1765, that Parliament had legislative power over the colonists, who were, after all, British subjects. Several assemblies advanced the argument that there was a distinction between *external* taxes, imposed to regulate trade, and *internal* taxes, such as a stamp tax or a property tax, which could only be self-imposed.

Reaction to the Stamp Act ran far deeper than political debate in assemblies. Every person whose livelihood required the use of official paper had to decide whether to comply with the act. Local communities strategized their responses. Should they boycott all paper use? A boycott would keep noncompliance within the law but would be inconvenient; if enough people ceased using stamped paper, the information network dependent on newspapers, the legal system, and business and commerce might grind to a halt. Should communities defy the law and conduct business as usual on unstamped paper, running the risk of fines or jail? A third strategy promised the surest success: destroying the stamped paper or preventing its distribution at the source, before the law took effect, thus ensuring universal noncompliance.

The first organized resistance to the Stamp Act began in Boston, port city and capital of Massachusetts, under the leadership of Samuel Adams, a town politician with a history of opposition to Lieutenant Governor Thomas Hutchinson. Unlike Hutchinson, Adams cared nothing for status, high office, or fine material goods. He was the Harvard-educated son of a Boston brewer, a man with shrewd political instincts and a gift for organizing. He mobilized shopkeepers, master craftsmen, dockworkers, and

***Samuel Adams*, by John Singleton Copley**
Samuel Adams consented to pose for Boston artist John Singleton Copley in 1770. The portrait highlights Adams's face, which projects a dramatic intensity and dominates the bulky body, subdued by dark clothes. Adams stares thoughtfully and silently at the viewer and points to important legal documents before him, including the Massachusetts Charter of 1689. Wealthy merchant John Hancock commissioned the portrait, which hung in his house. Copley painted scores of Boston's leaders in the 1760s, both loyalists and patriots. He maintained neutrality until 1773, when his father-in-law became an official East India tea distributor. Copley's home was threatened by a crowd, and he left for England in 1774. Deposited by the City of Boston, Museum of Fine Arts, Boston.

laborers into a group of protesters who called themselves—and anyone who joined them—Sons of Liberty.

The plan hatched by the Boston Sons of Liberty called for a large street demonstration highlighting a ritualized mock execution designed to convince Andrew Oliver, the stamp distributor, that his personal safety would best be served by resigning. With no stamp distributor, no stamps could be sold. On the morning of August 14, 1765, an effigy of Oliver was found hanging from a tree. In an effort to keep tensions under control, the royal governor of Massachusetts, Francis Bernard, took no action. By evening, a crowd of two to three thousand people paraded Oliver's effigy around town, using it as a prop in short plays demonstrating the dangers of selling stamps, before finally be-heading and burning it. The crowd also pulled down a small building on Oliver's dock, re-ported to be the future stamp office. The flesh-and-blood Oliver stayed in hiding; the next day he resigned his office in a well-publicized an-nouncement.

The demonstration provided lessons for everyone. Oliver learned that stamp distributors would be very unpopular people. Bernard and Hutchinson learned the limitations of their own powers to govern, with no police to call on. The demonstration's leaders learned that street ac-tion was very effective. And hundreds of labor-ers, sailors, and apprentices not only learned what the Stamp Act was all about but also gained pride in their ability to have a decisive impact on politics.

Twelve days later, another crowd action showed how well some of these lessons had been learned. On August 26, a crowd visited the houses of four detested officials. One was a cus-toms officer; two of the others were officers of the admiralty courts, where smugglers were tried; the crowd broke windows and raided wine cellars. The fourth house was the finest dwelling in Massachusetts, owned by the stiff-necked Thomas Hutchinson. Rumors abounded that Hutchinson had urged Grenville to adopt the Stamp Act. Although he had done the opposite, Hutchinson refused to set the record straight, saying curtly, "I am not obliged to give an an-swer to all the questions that may be put me by every lawless person." The crowd attacked his house, and by daybreak only the exterior walls were standing.

The destruction of Hutchinson's house brought a temporary halt to crowd activities in Boston. The Boston town meeting issued a state-ment of sympathy, but a reward of £300 for the arrest and conviction of riot organizers failed to produce a single lead. The Sons of Liberty denied planning the event.

Essentially, the opponents of the Stamp Act in Boston had triumphed; no one volunteered

Andrew Oliver

This portrait shows Bostonian Andrew Oliver at age twenty-two, just a few years after his graduation from Harvard College. The powdered wig and stern look add years to his face; the blousy clothing adds substance to his body. He was fifty-nine and probably even more im-posing in appearance when he ran afoul of the Stamp Act rioters in Boston in 1765.

Collection of the Oliver Family, photo by Clive Russ.

Seal of Andrew Oliver, Lieutenant Governor of Massachusetts Bay

This amethyst seal sug-gests that important business was a routine event for its owner, An-drew Oliver. Long before he became the unfortunate stamp distributor in 1765, Oliver held a succession of offices— overseer of the poor, collector of taxes, member of the provincial council, and secretary of Massachusetts. He thus had many occasions to press the seal into melted wax to authenticate documents. The stone bears the tough-minded motto *Pax Quareritur Bello* (Peace Is Obtained by War), an appropriate maxim for the man willing to become the royal lieutenant governor of Massachusetts in 1770. He re-placed his brother-in-law Thomas Hutchinson, who had moved up to be royal governor.

Collection of the Oliver Family, photo by Clive Russ.

to replace Oliver as distributor. When the Stamp Act took effect on November 1, customs officers were unable to prevent ships lacking properly stamped clearance papers from passing through the harbor. Hutchinson, as chief justice of the Massachusetts court, could not tolerate this defiance of the law, but he could not bring the lawbreakers to justice in his court. So he did the only thing he could do as a principled man: He resigned his judgeship. He remained lieutenant governor, however, and within five years he would agree to become the royal governor.

Liberty and Property

Boston's crowd actions of August sparked similar eruptions by groups calling themselves Sons of Liberty in nearly fifty towns throughout the colonies, and stamp distributors everywhere hastened to resign. One Connecticut distributor was forced by a crowd to throw his hat and powdered wig in the air while shouting a cheer for "Liberty and property!" This man fared better than another Connecticut stamp agent, who was nearly buried alive by Sons of Liberty. Only when the thuds of dirt sounded on his coffin did he have a sudden change of heart, shouting out his resignation to the crowd above. Luckily, he was heard. In Charleston, South Carolina, the stamp distributor resigned after crowds burned effigies and chanted "Liberty! Liberty!"

> The rallying cry "Liberty and property" made perfect sense to many white Americans of all social ranks, who feared that the Stamp Act threatened their traditional right to liberty as British subjects.

Some colonial leaders, disturbed about the riots, hastened to mount a more moderate challenge to parliamentary authority. Twenty-seven delegates representing nine colonial assemblies met in New York City in October 1765 as the Stamp Act Congress. For two weeks, the men hammered out a petition about taxation addressed to the king and Parliament. Their statement closely resembled the first five Virginia Resolves, claiming taxes were "free gifts of the people" that only the people's representatives could give. They dismissed virtual representation: "The people of these colonies are not, and from their local circumstances, cannot be represented in the House of Commons." But the delegates also took great care to affirm their subordination to Parliament and monarch in deferential language. Nevertheless, the Stamp Act Congress, by the mere fact of its meeting, advanced a radical potential, the notion of intercolonial political action.

The rallying cry of "Liberty and property" made perfect sense to many white Americans of all social ranks, who feared that the Stamp Act threatened their traditional right to liberty as British subjects. In this case the liberty in question was the right to be taxed only by representative government. "Liberty and property" came from a trinity of concepts—"life, liberty, property"—that had come to be regarded as the birthright of freeborn British subjects since at least the seventeenth century. A powerful tradition of British political thought invested representative government with the duty to protect individual lives, liberties, and property (possessions or money) against potential abuse by royal authority. Up to 1765, Americans consented to accept Parliament as a body that in some way represented them. But now, in this matter of taxation via stamps, Parliament seemed a distant body that had failed to protect Americans' liberty and property against royal authority.

Alarmed, some Americans began to speak and write about a plot by British leaders to enslave them. The opposite of liberty was slavery, the condition of being under the control of someone else. A Maryland writer warned that if the colonies lost "the right of exemption from all taxes without their consent," that loss would "deprive them of every privilege distinguishing freemen from slaves." In Virginia, a group of planters headed by Richard Henry Lee issued a document called the Westmoreland Resolves, claiming that the Stamp Act was an attempt "to reduce the people of this country to a state of abject and detestable slavery." The opposite meanings of *liberty* and *slavery* were utterly clear to white Americans, but they stopped short of applying similar logic to the half million black Americans they held in bondage. Many blacks, however, could see the contradiction. When a crowd of Charleston blacks paraded with shouts of "Liberty!" just a few months after white Sons of Liberty had done the same, the town militia turned out to break up the demonstration.

Politicians and merchants in England reacted with alarm to the American demonstrations and petitions. Merchants particularly feared trade disruptions and pressured Parliament to repeal the Stamp Act. By late 1765, yet another new minister, the Marquess of Rockingham, headed the king's cabinet. His dilemma was to find a dignified way for Parliament to repeal the act without losing face. George Grenville, author of the Stamp Act, defended his policy and roundly condemned American ingratitude: "When they want the protection of this kingdom, they are always ready to ask for it. . . . The nation has run itself into an immense debt to give them their protection; and now [when] they are called upon to contribute a small share towards the public expence, an expence arising from themselves, they renounce your authority, insult your officers, and break out, I might almost say, into open rebellion."

No doubt many in the British government shared Grenville's anger, but economic considerations won out. In March 1766, Parliament repealed the Stamp Act but passed the Declaratory Act, which asserted Parliament's right to legislate for the colonies "in all cases whatsoever." Perhaps the stamp tax had been inexpedient, but the power to tax—one prime case of a legislative power—was stoutly upheld.

The Townshend Acts and Economic Retaliation, 1767–1770

Rockingham did not last long as prime minister. By the summer of 1766, George III had persuaded William Pitt to resume that position. Pitt appointed Charles Townshend to be chancellor of the exchequer, the chief financial minister. Facing both the old war debt problem and the continuing cost of stationing British troops in America, Townshend turned again to taxation. But his knowledge of the changing political climate in the colonies was limited, and his simple idea to raise revenue turned into a major mistake. In 1768 and 1769, the American colonies were agitated by boycotts of British goods and demonstrations against British policies, even to the point of politicizing women, self-styled "Daughters of Liberty." Boston led the uproar, causing the British to send peacekeeping soldiers to arrest the royal governor. The stage was thus set for the first fatalities in the brewing revolution.

The Townshend Duties

Townshend proposed new taxes in the old form of a navigation act. Officially called the Revenue Act of 1767, it established new duties on tea, glass, lead, paper, and painters' colors imported into the colonies, to be paid by the importer but passed on to consumers in the retail price. A year before, the duty on French molasses had been reduced from three pence to one pence per gallon, and finally the Sugar Act was pulling in a tidy revenue of about £45,000 annually. So it was not unreasonable to suppose that duties on additional trade goods might also improve the cash flow. Townshend assumed that external taxes—that is, duties levied on the transatlantic trade—would be more acceptable to Americans than internal taxes, such as the stamp tax.

The Townshend duties were not especially burdensome, but the principle they embodied—taxation through trade duties—looked different to the colonists in the wake of the Stamp Act crisis. Although Americans once distinguished between external and internal taxes, that distinction was wiped out by an external tax meant only to raise money. John Dickinson, a Philadelphia lawyer, articulated this view in a series of articles titled *Letters from a Farmer in Pennsylvania*, widely reprinted in the winter of 1767–68. "We are taxed without our consent. . . . We are therefore—SLAVES," Dickinson wrote, calling for "a total denial of the power of Parliament to lay upon these colonies any 'tax' whatever."

A controversial provision of the Townshend duties directed that some of the revenue generated would be used to pay the salaries of royal governors. Before 1767, local assemblies set the salaries of their own officials, giving them significant influence over crown-appointed officeholders. Townshend wanted to strengthen the governors' position as well as to curb the growing independence of the assemblies.

In New York, for example, the assembly had refused to enforce a British rule of 1765 called the Quartering Act, which directed the colonies to furnish shelter and provisions for the British army. The assembly argued that the Quartering Act was really a tax measure because it required New Yorkers to pay money by order of Parliament. Townshend came down hard on the New York assembly: He orchestrated a parliamentary order, the New York Suspending Act, which declared all the assembly's acts null and void until it met its obligations to the army. Both measures—

> "We are taxed without our consent. . . . We are therefore—SLAVES," wrote Philadelphia lawyer John Dickinson, calling for "a total denial of the power of Parliament to lay upon these colonies any 'tax' whatever."

the new way to pay royal governors' salaries and the suspension of the governance functions of the New York assembly—struck a chill throughout the colonies. Many wondered if legislative government was at all secure.

The Massachusetts assembly took the lead in protesting the Townshend duties. Samuel Adams, now a member from Boston, argued that any form of parliamentary taxation was unjust because Americans were not represented in Parliament. Further, he argued that the new way to pay governors' salaries subverted the proper relationship between the people and their rulers. The assembly circulated a letter with Adams's arguments to other colonial assemblies and urged their endorsement. As with the Stamp Act Congress of 1765, colonial assemblies were starting to coordinate their protests.

In response to Adams's letter, the new man in charge of colonial affairs in Britain, Lord Hillsborough, instructed the Massachusetts governor, Francis Bernard, to dissolve the assembly if it refused to repudiate the letter. The assembly refused, by a vote of 92 to 17, and Governor Bernard carried out his instruction. In the summer of 1768, Boston was in an uproar.

Nonconsumption and the Daughters of Liberty

The Boston town meeting had already passed resolutions, termed "nonconsumption agreements," calling for a boycott of all British-made goods. Dozens of other towns passed similar resolutions in 1767 and 1768. For example, prohibited purchases in the town of New Haven, Connecticut, included carriages, furniture, hats, clothing, shoes, lace, iron plate, clocks, jewelry, toys, textiles, malt liquors, and cheese. The idea was to encourage home manufacture of such items and to hurt trade with Britain, causing London merchants to pressure Parliament for repeal of the duties.

The nonconsumption agreements were very hard to enforce. With the Stamp Act, there was one hated item, a stamp, and a limited number of official distributors. In contrast, an agreement to shun the purchase of all British goods required attention on many fronts. It also required great personal sacrifice, from buyers and sellers both. Some merchants were wary of nonconsumption because it hurt their pocketbooks, and a few continued to import in readiness for the end of nonconsumption (or to sell on the side to people choosing to ignore nonconsumption). In Boston,

Edenton Tea Ladies
American women in many communities renounced British apparel and tea during the early 1770s. Women in Edenton, North Carolina, publicized their pledge and drew hostile fire in the form of a British cartoon. The cartoon's message is that brazen women who meddle in politics will undermine their femininity. Neglected babies, urinating dogs, wanton sexuality, and mean-looking women are some of the dire consequences, according to the artist. The cartoon works as humor for the British because of the gender inversions it predicts and because of the insult it poses to American men.
Library of Congress.

such merchants found themselves blacklisted in newspapers and broadsides.

A more direct blow to trade came from nonimportation agreements, but getting merchants to agree to stop importing British goods proved even more difficult than enforcing nonconsumption. There was always the risk that merchants in other colonies might continue to trade and thus receive handsome profits if neighboring colonies prohibited trade. Not until late 1768 could Boston merchants agree to suspend trade through a nonimportation agreement lasting from January 1, 1769, to January 1, 1770. Sixty signed the agreement. New York merchants soon followed suit, as did Philadelphia and Charleston merchants in 1769.

Doing without British products, whether luxury goods, tea, or textiles, no doubt was a hardship. But it also presented an opportunity, for many of the British products specified in nonconsumption agreements were household goods traditionally under the control of the "ladies." By 1769, male leaders in the patriot cause clearly understood that women's cooperation in nonconsumption and home manufacture was beneficial to their cause. The Townshend duties thus provided an unparalleled opportunity for encouraging female patriotism. During the Stamp Act crisis, Sons of Liberty took to the streets in protest. During the difficulties of 1768–69, the concept of "Daughters of Liberty" emerged to give shape to a new idea—that women might play a role in public affairs.

Any woman could express affiliation with the colonial protest through conspicuous boycotts of British-made goods. In Boston, over three hundred women signed a petition to abstain from tea, "sickness excepted," in order to "save this abused Country from Ruin and Slavery." A Philadelphia woman inscribed some "patriotic poesy" in praise of women boycotters in her notebook in 1768, ending with the lines, "Stand firmly resolved and bid Grenville to see, That rather than Freedom, we'll part with our Tea." More direct action was taken by a nine-year-old girl visiting the royal governor's house in New Jersey. She took the tea she was offered, curtsied, and tossed the beverage out a nearby window.

Homespun cloth became a prominent symbol of patriotism. A young Boston girl learning to spin called herself "a daughter of liberty," noting that "I chuse to wear as much of our own manufactory as pocible." A stylish matron in Massachusetts who pieced together a patchwork petticoat sewn from dozens of old remnants was deemed exemplary and therefore newsworthy to a Boston newspaper. In the boycott period of 1768–1770, newspapers reported on spinning matches or bees in some sixty New England towns, in which women came together in public to make yarn. Nearly always, the bee was held at the local minister's house, and the yarn produced was charitably handed over to him for distribution to the poor. Newspaper accounts variously called the spinners "Daughters of Liberty" or "Daughters of Industry."

This surge of public spinning was related to the politics of the boycott, which infused traditional women's work with new political purpose. But it is clear that the women spinners were not direct equivalents of the Sons of Liberty. The Sons marched in streets, burned effigies, threatened hated officials, and celebrated anniversaries of their major successes with raucous drinking and feasting in taverns. The Daughters manifested their patriotism

> During the difficulties of 1768–69, the concept of "Daughters of Liberty" emerged to give shape to a new idea—that women might play a role in public affairs.

Spinning Wheel
A lot of skill was needed to spin high-quality thread and yarn. This wheel was used for spinning flax (a plant with a long fibrous stem) into linen thread; it is likely the type used in the politicized 1769 spinning bees in which "Daughters of Liberty" proclaimed their boycott of British textiles. A foot treadle controls the turning of the wheel, and a spindle holds the thread produced. The art of spinning was all in the spinster's hand, which controlled the tension on the thread and the speed of the twisting. The spinning Daughters of Liberty were praised for their virtuous industry. Responding to such praise, one young woman complained, in a Rhode Island newspaper, that young male patriots were deficient in virtue: "Alas! We hear nothing of their working matches, nothing of their concern for the honor of their King or for the safety or liberties of their country"; instead the news is of "nocturnal Carousals and Exploits; of their drinking, gaming & whoring matches; and how they disturb the quiet of honest people."
Smithsonian Institution, Washington, D.C.

quietly, in ways marked by piety, industry, and charity. The difference was due in part to cultural ideals of gender, which prized masculine self-assertion but feminine selflessness. It also was due to class: The Sons were a cross-class alliance, with leaders from the middling orders reliant on men and boys of the lower ranks to fuel their crowds. The Daughters, dusting off spinning wheels and shelving their teapots, were genteel ladies used to buying British goods. The difference between the Sons and Daughters also speaks to two views of how best to challenge authority. Was resistance to British policy most effectively communicated through violent threats and street actions—actions that might border on anarchy? Or were self-discipline and self-sacrifice the better strategies?

On the whole, the anti-British boycotts were a success. Imports fell by more than 40 percent; British merchants felt the pinch and let Parliament know it. In Boston, Lieutenant Governor Hutchinson and his merchant family, prevented from importing or selling goods, also felt the economic pinch. Even more alarming to the rigid man of order and principle was the fact that Boston seemed overrun with anti-British sentiment. The Sons of Liberty staged annual rollicking celebrations of the first Stamp Act riot, and Hutchinson along with Governor Bernard concluded that British troops were necessary to restore order.

Military Occupation and "Massacre" in Boston

In the fall of 1768, three thousand uniformed troops arrived to occupy Boston. The soldiers drilled conspicuously on the Common, played loud music on the Sabbath, and in general grated on the nerves of Bostonians. Although the situation was frequently tense, no major troubles occurred during that winter and through most of 1769. But as January 1, 1770, approached, marking the end of the nonimportation agreement, it was clear that some merchants would no longer engage in the boycott. Thomas Hutchinson's two sons, for example, were both importers hostile to the boycott, and they had already ordered new goods from England. The early months of 1770 were thus bound to be conflict-ridden.

Serious troubles began in January. The shop of the Hutchinson brothers was visited by a crowd that smeared "Hillsborough paint," a potent mixture of human excrement and urine, on the door. In mid-February, a crowd surrounded the house of Ebenezer Richardson, a cranky, low-level customs official. When Richardson panicked and fired his musket to scare off the crowd, he accidentally killed a young boy passing on the street. Although the boy had not been a participant in the demonstration, the Sons of Liberty mounted a massive funeral procession to mark this first instance of violent death in the struggle with England.

For the next week, heightened tensions gripped Boston, and frequent brawls occurred. The climax came on Monday evening, March 5, 1770, when a small crowd taunted a British soldier guarding the customs house. Among other things, he was called a "damned rascally

The Bloody Massacre Perpetrated in King Street, Boston, on March 5, 1770

This mass-produced engraving by Paul Revere sold for six pence a copy. In this patriot version of events, British soldiers fire on an unarmed crowd under orders of their captain. The tranquil dog is an artistic device to signal the crowd's peaceful intent. Crispus Attucks, a black sailor, was among the five killed, but Revere shows only whites among the casualties.

Anne S. K. Brown Military Collection, Brown University Library.

FOR MORE HELP ANALYZING THIS IMAGE, see the visual activity for this chapter in the Online Study Guide at bedfordstmartins.com/roark.

Scoundrel Lobster Son of a Bitch" (the red uniforms of the British were often likened to lobsters). Captain Thomas Preston sent a seven-man guard to join the lone sentry. Meanwhile, the hostile crowd grew, and the nervous soldiers raised their loaded muskets. Onlookers threw snowballs and sticks, heckling and daring the soldiers to fire. Finally one of the soldiers, hit by some object, pulled his trigger. After a short pause, during which someone yelled "Fire!", the other soldiers fired as well. Eleven men in the crowd were hit, five of them fatally.

The Boston Massacre, as the event quickly became known, was over in minutes. In the immediate aftermath, Hutchinson (now acting governor after Bernard's recall to England) showed courage in addressing the crowd from the balcony of the statehouse. By daybreak the next day, he ordered the removal of all the regiments to an island in the harbor to prevent further bloodshed. Hutchinson also jailed Preston and the eight soldiers, as much for their own protection as to appease the townspeople, and promised they would be held for trial.

The Sons of Liberty made sure that the five victims had funerals befitting heroic martyrs. Their bodies lay in state in the town's meeting hall (Faneuil Hall) and then were buried with honors in a cemetery in the center of Boston. (See "American Places," page 197.) Significantly, the one nonwhite victim shared equally in the public's veneration: Crispus Attucks, a sailor and ropemaker in his forties, son of an African man and a Natick Indian woman, a slave in his youth but at the time of his death a free laborer around the Boston docks. Attucks was possibly the first American partisan to die in the American Revolution, and certainly the first African American.

The trial of the eight soldiers was held in the fall of 1770. They were defended by two young Boston attorneys, Samuel Adams's cousin John Adams and Josiah Quincy. Because Adams and Quincy had direct ties to the leadership of the Sons of Liberty, their decision to defend the British soldiers at first seems odd. But John Adams was deeply committed to the idea that even unpopular defendants deserve a fair trial. Samuel Adams respected his cousin's decision to take the case, for there was a tactical benefit as well. It showed that the Boston leadership was not lawless but could be seen as defenders of British liberty and law.

The five-day trial, with dozens of witnesses, resulted in acquittal for Preston and for all but two of the soldiers, who were convicted of manslaughter, branded on the thumbs, and released. Nothing materialized in the trial to indicate a conspiracy or concerted plan, either by the British or by the leaders of the Sons of Liberty, to provoke trouble. To this day, the question of who was responsible for the Boston Massacre remains obscure.

> Among other things, the lone British sentry was called a "damned rascally Scoundrel Lobster Son of a Bitch."

The Tea Party and the Coercive Acts, 1770–1774

In the same week as the Boston Massacre, yet another new British prime minister, Frederick North, acknowledged the decrease in trade caused by the Townshend duties and recommended repeal. A skillful politician, Lord North took office in 1770 and kept it for twelve years; at last King George had stability at the helm. North sought peace with the colonies and prosperity for British merchants, so he persuaded Parliament to remove all the Townshend duties, except the tax on tea, a pointed reminder of Parliament's ultimate power. North hoped to cool tensions without sacrificing principles.

Those few Americans who could not abide the symbolism of the tea tax turned to smuggled Dutch tea. The renewal of trade and the return of cooperation between England and the colonies gave men like Thomas Hutchinson hope that the worst of the crisis was behind them. For nearly two years, peace seemed possible, but signal incidents in 1772 followed by a renewed struggle over the tea tax in 1773 precipitated a full-scale crisis that by 1775 resulted in war.

The Calm before the Storm

Sons of Liberty celebrated the repeal of the Townshend duties, which came not a moment too soon because the political will to maintain nonimportation could not have been sustained much longer. Pent-up demand caused trade to boom in 1770 and 1771. Moreover, the leaders of the popular movement seemed to be losing their power. Samuel Adams, for example, ran for a minor local office in Boston and lost to a conservative merchant.

Then in 1772, several incidents again brought the conflict with England into sharp focus. One was the attacking and burning of the *Gaspée*, a Royal Navy ship pursuing suspected smugglers off the coast of Rhode Island. A royal investigating commission failed to arrest anyone but announced that it would send suspects, if any were found, to England for trial on charges of high treason. This ruling seemed to fly in the face of the traditional English right to trial by a jury of one's peers.

When news of the *Gaspée* investigation spread, it was greeted with disbelief in other colonies. Patrick Henry, Thomas Jefferson, and Richard Henry Lee in the Virginia House of Burgesses proposed that a network of standing committees be established to link the colonies and pass along alarming news. By mid-1773, every colonial assembly except Pennsylvania had such a "committee of correspondence."

Another British action in 1772 furthered the spread of the communications network. Lord North proposed to pay the salaries of superior court justices out of the tea revenue, in a move parallel to Townshend's plan for paying royal governors. The Boston town meeting, alarmed that judges would now be in the pockets of their new paymasters, established a committee of correspondence and urged other towns to do likewise. The first vital message, circulated in December 1772, attacked the judges' salary policy as the latest proof of a British plot to undermine traditional "liberties": unjust taxation, military occupation, massacre, now capped by the subversion of justice. By spring 1773, half the towns in Massachusetts had set up their own committees of correspondence, providing local forums for debate. These committees politicized ordinary townspeople and bypassed the official flow of power and information through the colony's royal government.

The third and final incident that irrevocably shattered the relative calm of the early 1770s was the Tea Act of 1773. Americans had been drinking moderate amounts of English tea and paying the duty without objection, but they were also smuggling large quantities of Dutch tea, cutting into the sales of Britain's East India Company. So Lord North proposed special legislation giving favored status to the East India Company, allow-

> The Boston Sons of Liberty were slower than their compatriots in other cities to act, but their action ultimately provoked alarm as well as alarming reprisals from England.

ing it to sell its tea through special government agents rather than through public auction to independent merchants. The hope was that the price of the East India tea, even with the duty, would then fall below that of the smuggled Dutch tea, motivating Americans to obey the law as well as boosting sales for the East India Company.

Tea in Boston Harbor

In the fall of 1773, news of the Tea Act reached the colonies. Parliamentary legislation to make tea inexpensive struck many colonists as an insidious plot to trick Americans into buying large quantities of the dutied tea. The real goal, some argued, was the increased revenue, which would be used to pay the royal governors and judges. The Tea Act was thus a sudden and painful reminder of Parliament's claim to the power to tax and legislate for the colonies.

As with the Stamp Act and the Townshend duties, the colonists' strategy was crucial. Nonimportation was not a viable option, because the tea trade was too lucrative to expect colonial merchants to give it up willingly. Consumer boycotts of tea had proved ineffective since 1770, chiefly because it was impossible to distinguish between duties tea (the object of the boycott) and smuggled tea (illegal but politically clean) once the tea was in the teapot. Like the Stamp Act, the Tea Act mandated special agents to handle the tea sales, and that requirement pointed to the solution for anti-tea activists. In every port city, revived Sons of Liberty pressured tea agents to resign.

The Boston Sons of Liberty were slow to act at first, but their action—more direct and illegal than actions anywhere else—ultimately provoked alarm as well as alarming reprisals from England. Three ships bearing tea arrived in Boston in late November 1773. They cleared customs and unloaded their other cargoes but not the tea. Sensing the extreme tension, the captains wished to return to England, but because the ships had already entered the harbor, they could not get clearance to leave without first paying the tea duty. Also, there was a time limit on the stay allowed in the harbor. After twenty days, the duty had to be paid or local authorities would confiscate the tea and sell it.

For the full twenty days, pressure built in Boston. Daily mass meetings energized citizens not only from Boston but also from surrounding towns, alerted by the committees of correspon-

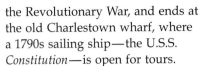

AMERICAN PLACES

The Freedom Trail, Boston, Massachusetts

Visitors to Boston today can relive many of the events leading up to the American Revolution through a walk along the Freedom Trail, a 2.5-mile urban route starting at Boston Common, where British soldiers encamped in 1768. The trail, marked with a red line on the sidewalk, winds around and through the old downtown, passing more than a dozen historic and preserved sites of the Revolutionary era. Among these are the Old Granary Burying Ground, where victims of the Boston Massacre are interred, and the Old State House,

in front of which the Massacre took place and where Governor Thomas Hutchinson addressed the distraught crowds from the balcony. The trail also passes the Old South Church, where Samuel Adams spoke right before British tea was dumped in Boston harbor. The last half of the route passes by Paul Revere's home in the North End, as well as the Old North Church from whence Revere got the famous signal for his midnight ride. The trail then crosses a bridge over the Charles River and passes by Bunker Hill, the site of the second battle in

the Revolutionary War, and ends at the old Charlestown wharf, where a 1790s sailing ship—the U.S.S. *Constitution*—is open for tours.

Although the Freedom Trail has been in existence since 1952, the city it traverses continues to change. Boston has expanded far beyond its 1760s boundaries. Hills were leveled, and the dirt was used to fill in watery bays, creating the neighborhood known as Back Bay. But despite skyscrapers, a train system for public transportation (the "T"), and the "Big Dig" submerging an interstate highway underground, the core of the old city still preserves the footprint of Samuel Adams's town in its narrow curving streets and tiny alleyways.

A hike on the Freedom Trail can trigger the historical imagination. Costumed interpreters lead tours along the path and help re-create the past. The one in this picture kneels in front of Faneuil Hall, the building where Boston's town meetings were held in the 1760s and 1770s and where Samuel Adams and others debated responses to the Sugar Act, the Stamp Act, and other flash points of the pre-Revolutionary decade. Faneuil Hall was built in 1742 and rebuilt after a fire in 1761. It has street-level shops and markets and, on the second floor, a great hall that throughout the nineteenth and twentieth centuries has remained a lecture hall for famous speakers. Its most famous speaker, Adams himself, now stands guard by the building as a large statue—a powerful reminder of the important role Boston and its inhabitants played in the colonial crisis.

FOR WEB LINKS TO THIS SITE AND OTHER AMERICAN PLACES, see "PlaceLinks" at bedfordstmartins.com/roark.

The Freedom Trail
Courtesy Freedom Trail Foundation.

Tossing the Tea
This colored engraving appeared in an English book published in 1789, recounting the history of North America from its earliest settlement to "becoming united, free, and independent states." Men on the ship break into the chests and dump the contents; a few are depicted in Indian disguise, with feathers on their heads or topknots of hair. A large crowd on the shore looks on. The red rowboat is clearly stacked with tea chests, suggesting that some of the raiders were stealing rather than destroying the tea. However, the artist, perhaps careless, shows the rowboat heading toward the ship instead of away. This event was not dubbed the "Tea Party" until the 1830s when a later generation celebrated the illegal destruction of the tea and made heroes out of the few surviving participants, by then men in their eighties and nineties.
Library of Congress.

dence. On the final day, December 16, a large crowd gathered at Old South Church to learn whether Governor Hutchinson would bend the rules. When word arrived that he would not, Samuel Adams declared, "This meeting can do nothing more to save the country." This was a signal to adjourn to the harbor, where between 100 and 150 men, thinly disguised as Indians, their faces darkened with coal, boarded the ships and dumped thousands of pounds of tea into the water while a crowd of 2,000 watched. (See "Documenting the American Promise," page 200.)

The Coercive Acts

Lord North's response was swift and stern. Within three months he persuaded Parliament to issue the first of the Coercive Acts, four laws meant to punish Massachusetts for the destruction of the tea. In America those laws, along

with a fifth one—the Quebec Act—not aimed at Massachusetts alone, were soon known as the Intolerable Acts.

The Boston Port Act closed Boston harbor to all shipping as of June 1, 1774, until the destroyed tea was paid for. England's objective was to bring to a halt the commercial life of the city. The Massachusetts Government Act altered the colony's charter, underscoring Parliament's claim to supremacy over Massachusetts. The royal governor's powers were greatly augmented. The council became an appointive, not elective, body. No town meeting beyond the annual spring election of town selectmen could be held unless the governor expressly permitted it. Not only Boston but every Massachusetts town felt the punitive sting.

The third Coercive Act, the Impartial Administration of Justice Act, stipulated that any royal official accused of a capital crime—for example, Captain Preston and his soldiers at the Boston Massacre—would be tried in a court in England. It did not matter that Preston had gotten a fair trial in Boston. What this act ominously suggested was that down the road more Captain Prestons and soldiers might be firing into unruly crowds.

The Dangers of Neutrality

Reverend Eli Forbes was nearly fifty when his townsmen's revolutionary fervor cost him his job in the central Massachusetts town of Brookfield. In February and March 1775, Forbes's dedication to the anti-British cause was suspect, and despite his twenty-three years of service to the town and a heroic ministry in Canada with wounded troops during the Seven Years' War, his parishioners wanted him out. Forbes thought that ministers should not "meddle much with civil Power," but his congregation thought he meddled on the wrong side. One night, townsmen followed his carriage in the street and hurled stones and epithets at him and his wife. Next, he discovered a bag of feathers and a pot of tar on his doorstep. A church trial and vote at first failed to dismiss him. But when he took the podium to lecture the disciplinary proceedings, a majority to dismiss quickly materialized. Forbes and his wife fled to Boston, to the protection of the British army, and then to Gloucester, a town north of Boston where a married daughter lived. There Forbes eventually resumed the ministry and lived another quarter century in peace. Either Gloucester was a more tolerant town, or Reverend Forbes moderated his political opinions to avoid trouble.

Courtesy of the Society for the Preservation of New England Antiquities, Gift of Bertram K. and Nina Fletcher Little.

The fourth act amended the 1765 Quartering Act and permitted military commanders to lodge soldiers wherever necessary, even in private households. In a related move, Lord North appointed General Thomas Gage, commander of the Royal Army in New York, governor of Massachusetts. Thomas Hutchinson was out, relieved at long last of his duties. Military rule, including soldiers, returned once more to Boston.

Ill-timed, the fifth act—the Quebec Act—had nothing to do with the four Coercive Acts, but it fed American fears. It confirmed the continuation of French civil law, government form, and Catholicism for Quebec—all an affront to **Protestant** New Englanders denied their own representative government. The act also gave Quebec control of disputed lands (and control of the lucrative fur trade) throughout the Ohio Valley, lands also claimed by Virginia, Pennsylvania, Connecticut, and a number of Indian tribes.

The five Intolerable Acts spread alarm among all the colonies. If England could step on Massachusetts and change its charter, suspend government, inaugurate military rule, and on top of that give Ohio to Catholic Quebec, then what liberties were secure? Fearful royal governors in a half-dozen colonies suspended the sitting assemblies, adding to the sense of urgency. Some of the suspended assemblies defiantly continued to meet in new locations. Via the committees of correspondence, colonial leaders arranged to meet in Philadelphia in the fall of 1774 to respond to the crisis.

The First Continental Congress

Most of the statesmen who assembled in Philadelphia in September 1774 in what was later called the First Continental Congress were leaders of the anti-British cause in their home colonies, and many were meeting each other for the first time. The gathering included notables such as Samuel Adams and John Adams from Massachusetts and George Washington and Patrick Henry from Virginia. A few colonies purposely sent men who were cool to provoking a crisis with England, such as Pennsylvania's Joseph Galloway, out of recognition that the best way to keep a foot on the brakes of impending revolt was to not ignore the gathering.

Two difficult tasks confronted the congress: The delegates wanted to agree on exactly what liberties they claimed as English subjects and

The Destruction of the Tea

On the night of December 16, 1773, over 100 men disguised as Indians threw 342 chests of tea into Boston harbor. Here are three accounts by participants close to the action.

DOCUMENT 1
Governor Hutchinson's Account, Published in 1828

In exile in England, Thomas Hutchinson wrote a long history of Massachusetts, which was first published in 1828, decades after his death. In narrating Boston events of the 1760s and 1770s, Hutchinson referred to himself in the third person, but his point of view was definitely weighted toward self-vindication. Here he describes the consequences of his final rejection of a demand by the town meeting that he permit the ship to leave port without paying the tea tax.

It was not expected the governor would comply with the demand; and, before it was possible for the owner of the ship to return . . . with an answer, about fifty men had prepared themselves, and passed by the house where the people were assembled, to the wharf where the vessels lay, being covered with blankets, and making the appearance of Indians. The body of the people remained until they had received the governor's answer; and then, after it had been observed to them, that, every thing else in their power having been done, it now remained to proceed in the only way left . . . the meeting was declared to be dissolved, and the body of the people repaired to the wharf, and sur-rounded the immediate actors, as a guard and security, until they finished their work. In two or three hours, they hoisted out of the holds of the ships, three hundred and forty-two chests of tea, and emptied them into the sea. The governor was unjustly censured by many people in the province, and much abused by the pamphlet and newspaper writers in England, for refusing his pass, which, it was said, would have saved the property thus destroyed; but he would have been justly censured, if he had granted it. He was bound, as all the king's governors were, by oath, faithfully to observe the acts of trade. . . . His granting a pass to a vessel which had not cleared at the custom-house, would have been a direct violation of his oath, by making himself an accessory in the breach of those laws which he had sworn to observe. It was out of his power to have prevented this mischief, without the most imminent hazard of much greater mischief. The tea could have been secured in the town in no other way than by landing marines from the men of war, or bringing to town the regiment which was at the castle, to remove the guards from the ships, and to take their places. This would have brought on a greater convulsion than there was any danger of in 1770, and it would not have been possible . . . for so small a body of troops to have kept possession of the town. Such a measure the governor had no reason to suppose would have been approved of in England. He was not sure of support from any one person in authority. The house of representa-tives openly avowed principles which implied complete independency. The council, appointed by charter to be assisting to him, declared against any advice from which might be inferred an acknowledgment of the authority of parliament in imposing taxes. . . . There was not a justice of peace, sheriff, constable, or peace officer in the province, who would venture to take cognizance of any breach of law, against the general bent of the people.

SOURCE: Thomas Hutchinson, *The History of the Colony and Province of Massachusetts-Bay* (Cambridge, Mass.: Harvard University Press, 1936), 3:311–14.

DOCUMENT 2
George Robert Twelves Hewes's Recollection, Transcribed in 1834

George Robert Twelves Hewes, a thirty-one-year-old Boston shoemaker, was first stirred to political action by witnessing the Boston Massacre. During the struggle over tea, he joined the "Indian" boarding party and found himself thrust into a leadership role, a singular moment of glory that he proudly recounted when he was in his nineties. As one of the last surviving participants of that famous event, he enjoyed enormous celebrity in the 1830s. His life came to symbolize the Revolution's power to lift up the common man and endow him with a sense of political significance.

The commander of the division to which I belonged, as soon as we were on board the ship, appointed me boatswain, and ordered me to go to the captain and demand of him the keys to the hatches and a dozen candles. I made the demand accordingly, and the captain promptly replied, and delivered the articles; but requested me at the same time to do no damage to the ship or rigging. We then were ordered by our commander to open the hatches, and take out all the chests of tea and throw them overboard, and we immediately proceeded to execute his orders; first cutting and splitting the chests with our tomahawks, so as thoroughly to expose them to the effects of the water. In about three hours from the time we went on board, we had thus broken and thrown overboard every tea chest to be found in the ship; while those in the other ships were disposing of the tea in the same way, at the same time. We were surrounded by British armed ships, but no attempt was made to resist us. We then quietly retired to our several places of residence, without having any conversation with each other, or taking any measures to discover who were our associates.

SOURCE: [James Hawkes], *A Retrospect of the Boston Tea-Party, with a Memoir of George R. T. Hewes, a Survivor of the Little Band of Patriots Who Drowned the Tea in Boston Harbour in 1773* (New York, 1834), reprinted in Alfred F. Young, *The Shoemaker and the Tea Party: Memory and the American Revolution* (Boston: Beacon Press, 1999), 44.

DOCUMENT 3
John Adams's Diary Entry of December 17, 1773

John Adams reveled in the bold destruction of the tea in his diary the day after the event. He also gave thought to the legal consequences that might follow, rehearsing the justifications that motivated "the People."

Last Night 3 Cargoes of Bohea Tea were emptied into the Sea. This Morning a Man of War sails.

This is the most magnificent Movement of all. There is a Dignity, a Majesty, a Sublimity, in this last Effort of the Patriots, that I greatly admire. . . . This Destruction of the Tea is so bold, so daring, so firm, intrepid and inflexible, and it must have so important Consequences, and so lasting, that I cant but consider it as an Epocha in History.

This however is but an Attack upon Property. Another similar Exertion of popular Power, may produce the destruction of Lives. Many Persons wish, that as many dead Carcasses were floating in the Harbour, as there are Chests of Tea:—a much less Number of Lives however would remove the Causes of all our Calamities.

The malicious Pleasure with which Hutchinson the Governor, the Consignees of the Tea, and the officers of the Customs, have stood and looked upon the distresses of the People, and their Struggles to get the Tea back to London, and at last the destruction of it, is amazing. Tis hard to believe Persons so hardened and abandoned.

What Measures will the Ministry take, in Consequence of this?—Will they resent it? will they dare to resent it? will they punish Us? How? By quartering Troops upon Us?—by annulling our Charter?—by laying on more duties? By restraining our Trade? By Sacrifice of Individuals, or how.

The Question is whether the Destruction of this Tea was necessary? I apprehend it was absolutely and indispensably so.—They could not send it back, the Governor, Admiral, and Collector and Comptroller would not suffer it. It was in their Power to have saved it—but in no other. It could not get

by the Castle, the Men of War &c. Then there was no other Alternative but to destroy it or let it be landed. To let it be landed, would be giving up the Principle of Taxation by Parliamentary Authority, against which the Continent have struggled for 10 years, it was loosing all our labour for 10 years and subjecting ourselves and our Posterity forever to Egyptian Taskmasters—to Burthens, Indignities, to Ignominy, Reproach and Contempt, to Desolation and Oppression, to Poverty and Servitude.

SOURCE: L. H. Butterfield, ed., *Diary and Autobiography of John Adams* (Cambridge, Mass.: Harvard University Press, 1961), 2:85–86.

QUESTIONS FOR ANALYSIS AND DEBATE

1. Does Thomas Hutchinson persuade you that he had no other option than to refuse to let the ship either leave or land? Why did he reject the use of troops to guard the tea?

2. How might men like Hewes be politicized by hacking open chests of tea?

3. John Adams says that Hutchinson took a malicious pleasure in forcing the tea crisis to its conclusion. Was he right or wrong in your judgment? Why?

4. What is at stake, for John Adams, in the showdown over tea, when he speaks of ten years of struggle by "the Continent" and of poverty and servitude to "Egyptian Taskmasters"? How does he feel about the possibility of deaths in the building struggle?

what powers Parliament held over them, and they needed to make a unified response to the Coercive Acts. Some delegates wanted a total ban on trade with England to force a repeal of the Coercive Acts. Others—especially those from southern colonies heavily dependent on the export of tobacco and rice—opposed halting trade. Samuel Adams and Patrick Henry were eager for a ringing denunciation of all parliamentary control. The conservative Joseph Galloway proposed a plan (quickly defeated) to create a secondary parliament in America to assist the British Parliament in ruling the colonies.

The congress met for seven weeks in Carpenter's Hall in Philadelphia and produced a

declaration of rights couched in traditional language: "We ask only for peace, liberty and security. We wish no diminution of royal prerogatives, we demand no new rights." But, from England's point of view, the rights assumed already to exist were in fact radical. Chief among them was the claim that because Americans were not represented in Parliament, each colonial government had the sole right to legislate for and tax its own people. The one slight concession to England was a carefully worded agreement that the colonists would "cheerfully consent" to trade regulations for the larger good of the empire— so long as trade regulation was not a covert means of raising revenue.

To put pressure on England, the delegates agreed to a staggered and limited boycott of trade—imports prohibited this year, exports the following, and rice totally exempted (to keep South Carolinians happy). To enforce the boycott, they called for a Continental Association, with chapters in each town variously called committees of public safety or of inspection, to monitor all commerce and punish suspected violators of the boycott (sometimes with a bucket of tar and a bag of feathers). Its work done, the congress disbanded in October 1774, with agreement to reconvene the following May.

Many towns and localities heeded the call and established committees of public safety and committees of correspondence. British-authorized government was beginning to break down, being challenged and supplanted by local committees, by the reconstituted colonial assemblies, and by the Continental Congress itself. All these became functioning political bodies without any formal constitutional authority. British officials did not recognize them as legitimate, but many Americans who supported the patriot cause instantly accepted them. A key reason for the stability of such unauthorized bodies throughout the Revolutionary period was that they were composed of the same men, by and large, who had composed the official bodies that were now disbanded.

England's severe reaction to Boston's destruction of the tea finally succeeded in making many colonists from New Hampshire to Georgia realize that the problems of British rule went far beyond questions of taxation. The Coercive Acts infringed on liberty and denied self-government; they could not be ignored. With one colony already subordinated to military rule and a British army at the ready in Boston, the threat of a general war was at the doorstep.

Tarring and Feathering Cartoon
In 1774, a Boston crowd tarred and feathered customs collector John Malcolm as punishment for extorting money from shippers. This ritualized humiliation involved stripping a man, painting him with hot tar, and dipping him in chicken feathers. Local committees of public safety often used threats of this treatment as a weapon to enforce boycotts; actual tarring and feathering was not a common occurrence. This cartoon, of English origin, is hostile to Americans, who are shown with cruelly gleeful faces, forcing tea down Malcolm's throat. The Liberty Tree has become a gallows; posted to it is the Stamp Act, upside down. The dumping of tea in the harbor is shown in the background.
Courtesy of the John Carter Brown Library at Brown University.

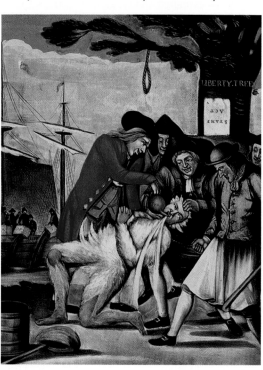

Domestic Insurrections, 1774–1775

Before the Second Continental Congress could meet, war broke out in Massachusetts. General Thomas Gage, military commander and the new royal governor, at first thought he faced a domestic insurrection that could be quieted with only a show of force. But the rebels saw things differently: They were defending their homes and liberties against an intrusive power bent on enslaving them. To the south, a different and inverted version of the same story began to unfold, as thousands of enslaved black men and women seized an unprecedented opportunity to mount a different kind of insurrection—against planter-patriots who looked over their shoulders uneasily whenever they called out for liberty from the British.

Lexington and Concord

Over the winter of 1774–75 Americans pressed on with boycotts. Optimists hoped to effect a repeal of the Coercive Acts; pessimists started stockpiling arms and ammunition. In Massachusetts, gunpowder and shot were secretly stored, and militia units known as minutemen prepared to respond on a minute's notice to any threat from the British troops in Boston.

Thomas Gage soon realized how desperate the British position was. The people, Gage wrote Lord North, were "numerous, worked up to a fury, and not a Boston rabble but the freeholders and farmers of the country." Gage requested twenty thousand reinforcements. He also strongly advised repeal of the Coercive Acts. Leaders in England, however, could not bring themselves to admit failure. Instead, they ordered Gage in mid-April 1775 to arrest the troublemakers immediately, before the Americans got better organized.

Gage quickly planned a surprise attack on a suspected ammunition storage site at Concord, a village about eighteen miles west of Boston (Map 6.3). Near midnight on April 18, 1775, British soldiers moved west across the Charles River. Boston silversmith Paul Revere and William Dawes, a tanner, raced ahead to alert the

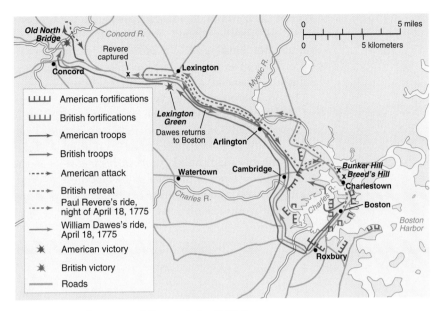

MAP 6.3   Lexington and Concord, April 1775

Under pressure from England, some 900 British forces at Boston staged a raid on a suspected rebel arms supply in Concord, Massachusetts, starting the first battle of the Revolutionary War. The routes of two early warning scouts are marked. Paul Revere went by boat from Boston to Charlestown and then continued by horse through Medford to Lexington, while William Dawes casually passed British sentries guarding the only land route out of Boston, a land bridge called the Neck, and then rode his horse full speed to Lexington. Revere and Dawes reached Samuel Adams and John Hancock, guests in a Lexington home, and urged them to flee to avoid capture. The two then went on to Concord, to warn residents of the impending attack.

READING THE MAP: William Dawes was, like Paul Revere, a messenger who raced ahead of British troops to warn the minutemen of British plans for raiding their supply of weapons. How did Dawes's route differ from Revere's? What kinds of terrain and potential dangers did each man face during his ride, according to the map?

CONNECTIONS: Why might it matter who shot first on the Lexington Green? What is at stake for each side in claiming the other shot first?

FOR MORE HELP ANALYZING THIS MAP, see the map activity for this chapter in the Online Study Guide at bedfordstmartins.com/roark.

minutemen. When the soldiers got to Lexington, a village five miles east of Concord, they were met by some seventy armed men assembled on the village green. The British commander barked out, "Lay down your arms, you damned rebels and disperse." The militiamen hesitated and began to comply, turning to leave the green. Then someone—nobody knows who—fired. In the next two minutes, more firing left eight Americans dead and ten wounded.

The British units continued their march to Concord, any pretense of surprise gone. Three companies of minutemen nervously occupied the

center of Concord but offered no challenge to the British as they searched in vain for the ammunition. Finally, at Old North Bridge in Concord, troops and minutemen exchanged shots, killing two Americans and three British soldiers.

By now both sides were very apprehensive. The British had failed to find the expected arms storage, and the Americans had failed to stop their raid. As the British returned to Boston along a narrow road, militia units in hiding attacked from the sides of the road in the bloodiest fighting of the day. In the end, 273 British soldiers were wounded or dead; the toll for the Americans stood at about 95. It was April 19, 1775, and the war had begun.

Rebelling against Slavery

News of the battles of Lexington and Concord spread rapidly. Within eight days, Virginians had heard of the fighting, and, as Thomas Jefferson reflected, "A phrenzy of revenge seems to have seized all ranks of people." The royal governor of Virginia, Lord Dunmore, removed a large quantity of gunpowder from the Williamsburg powder house and put it on a ship in the dead of

---

British Troops in Concord Center
In this contemporary engraving by Amos Doolittle, based on a painting done on the spot by Ralph Earl, two British officers seek the high ground of the cemetery in Concord, Massachusetts, to orient themselves to the unfamiliar town at around 9 A.M. on April 19, 1775. Their troops march in formation, fresh from the skirmish at Lexington. American militiamen had amassed at the Old North Bridge, off to the right about a mile from the town center. The officer with the telescope is undoubtedly scanning for them.
Miriam and Ira D. Wallah Division of Art, Prints and Photographs, The New York Public Library. Astor, Lenox and Tilden Foundations.

night, out of reach of any frenzied Virginians. Next, he threatened to arm slaves, if necessary, to ward off attacks by colonists.

This was an effective threat; Dunmore understood full well how to produce panic among the planters. He did not act on his warning until November 1775, when he issued an official proclamation promising freedom to defecting slaves who would fight for the British. His offer was limited to able-bodied men. Although Dunmore wanted to scare the planters, he had no intention of liberating all slaves or of starting a real slave rebellion. Female, young, and elderly slaves were not welcome behind British lines, and many were sent back to face irate masters. Astute blacks noticed that Dunmore neglected to free his own slaves. A Virginia barber named Caesar declared that "he did not know any one foolish enough to believe him [Dunmore], for if he intended to do so, he ought first to set his own free."

Not surprisingly, Lord Dunmore's proclamation was not reported in southern newspapers. Blacks, however, did not depend on newspapers for their information. John Adams was assured by southern delegates to the Continental Congress that Dunmore's decree would quickly draw 20,000 slaves in South Carolina because "the Negroes have a wonderful art of communicating Intellience among themselves; it will run several hundreds of miles in a week or fortnight." White planters sped the news along themselves by publicizing Dunmore's inflammatory decree as a means of unifying anti-British sentiment and recruiting whites into the militia. A South Carolina planter foresaw that the proclamation would "more effectively . . . work an eternal separation between Great Britain and the Colonies,—than any other expedient, which could possibly be thought of."

By December 1775, around 2,000 slaves in Virginia had fled to Lord Dunmore, who armed them and called them his "Ethiopian Regiment." Camp diseases quickly set in: dysentery, typhoid fever, and worst of all, smallpox. When Dunmore sailed for England in mid-1776, he took just 300 black survivors with him. But the association of freedom with the British authorities had been established, and throughout the war, thousands more southern slaves made bold to run away as soon as they heard the British army was approaching.

In the northern colonies as well, slaves clearly recognized the evolving political struggle with England as an ideal moment to bid for freedom. A twenty-one-year-old Boston domestic

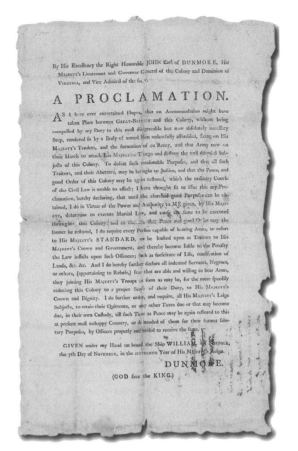

Lord Dunmore's Proclamation
In November 1775, Lord Dunmore of Virginia offered freedom to "all indented Servants, Negroes, or others (appertaining to Rebels)" who would help put down the rebellion. Dunmore issued multiple printed copies in broadside form from the safety of a ship anchored at Norfolk, Virginia.
Special Collections, University of Virginia, Alderman Library.

slave employed biting sarcasm in a 1774 newspaper essay to call attention to the hypocrisy of local slave owners: "How well the Cry for Liberty, and the reverse Disposition for exercise of oppressive Power over others agree,— I humbly think it does not require the Penetration of a Philosopher to Determine." This extraordinary young woman, Phillis Wheatley, had already gained international recognition through a book of poems, endorsed by Governor Thomas Hutchinson and Boston merchant  John Hancock and published in London in 1773. Possibly neither man fully appreciated the irony of his endorsement, however, for Wheatley's poems spoke of "Fair Freedom" as the "Goddess long desir'd" by Africans enslaved in America.

Slaves clearly recognized the evolving political struggle with England as an ideal moment to bid for freedom.

At the urging of his wife, Wheatley's master freed the young poet in 1775.

Wheatley's poetic ideas about freedom found concrete expression among other discontented groups. Some slaves in Boston petitioned Thomas Gage, promising to fight for the British if he would liberate them. Gage turned them down. In Ulster County, New York, along the Hudson River, two blacks were overheard discussing gunpowder, and thus a plot unraveled that involved at least twenty slaves in four villages discovered to have ammunition stashed away.

In Maryland, soon after the news of the Lexington battle arrived, blacks exhibited impatience with their status as slaves, causing one Maryland planter to report that "the insolence of the Negroes in this county is come to such a height, that we are under a necessity of disarming them. . . . We took about eighty guns, some bayonets, swords, etc." In North Carolina, a planned uprising was uncovered and scores of slaves were arrested; ironically, it was the revolutionary committee of public safety that ordered the whippings to punish this quest for liberty.

By 1783, when the Revolutionary War ended, as many as 80,000 blacks had voted against slavery with their feet by seeking refuge with the British army. (As a percentage of all slaves in the thirteen colonies, the number might very roughly have been 10 percent.) Most failed to achieve the liberation they were seeking. The British generally used them for menial labor; and disease, especially smallpox, devastated encampments of runaways. But several thousand persisted through the war and later, under the protection of the British army, left America to start new lives of freedom in Canada's Nova Scotia or Africa's Sierra Leone.

Conclusion: How Far Does Liberty Go?

The Seven Years' War set the stage for the imperial crisis of the 1760s and 1770s by creating distrust between England and its colonies and by running up a huge deficit in the British treasury. The years from 1763 to 1775 brought repeated attempts by the British government to subordinate the colonies into taxpaying partners in the larger

scheme of empire. The Sugar and Stamp Acts, the Townshend duties, the Tea Act, which culminated in the Coercive Acts, all demonstrated the British view that Americans were subject to parliamentary control.

American resistance grew slowly but steadily over those years. In 1765, loyalist Thomas Hutchinson shared with patriot Samuel Adams the belief that it was exceedingly unwise for England to assert a right to taxation, because Parliament did not adequately represent Americans. But by temperament and office, Hutchinson had to uphold British policy; Adams, in contrast, protested the policy and made political activists out of thousands in the process. Through crowd actions, congresses, and petitions to Britain by colonial assemblies, many Americans gravitated to the Adams position and became radicals in a struggle against British authority.

By 1775, events propelled many Americans to the conclusion that a concerted effort was afoot to deprive them of all their liberties, the most important of which were the right to self-taxation, the right to live free of an occupying army, and their right to self-rule. Hundreds of minutemen converged on Concord, prepared to die for these American liberties. April 19 marked the start of their rebellion.

Another rebellion under way in 1775 was doomed to be short-circuited. Black Americans who had experienced actual slavery listened to shouts of "Liberty!" from white crowds and appropriated the language of revolution swirling around them that spoke to their deepest needs and hopes. Defiance of authority was indeed contagious.

The emerging leaders of the patriot cause were mindful of a delicate balance they felt they had to strike. To energize the American public about the crisis with England, they had to politicize masses of men—and eventually women too—and infuse them with a keen sense of their rights and liberties. But in so doing, they became fearful of the unintended consequences of teaching a vocabulary of rights and liberties. They worried that the rhetoric of enslavement might go too far.

The question of how far the crisis could be stretched before something snapped was largely unexamined in 1765. Patriot leaders in that year wanted a correction, a restoration of an ancient liberty of self-taxation that Parliament seemed to be ignoring. But events from 1765 to 1775 convinced many that a return to the old ways was impossible. Challenging Parliament's right to tax had led, step by step, to challenging Parliament's right to legislate over the colonies in any matter. If Parliament's sovereignty was set aside, then who actually had authority over the American colonies? By 1775, with the outbreak of fighting and the specter of slave rebellions, American leaders turned to the king for the answer to that question.

FOR ADDITIONAL FIRSTHAND ACCOUNTS OF THIS PERIOD, see Chapter 6 in Michael Johnson, ed., *Reading the American Past,* Third Edition.

TO ASSESS YOUR MASTERY OF THE MATERIAL IN THIS CHAPTER, see the Online Study Guide at bedfordstmartins.com/roark.

FOR WEB LINKS RELATED TO TOPICS IN THIS CHAPTER, see "HistoryLinks," "DocLinks," and "PlaceLinks" at bedfordstmartins.com/roark.

CHRONOLOGY

1747 • Ohio Company of Virginia formed, raising hopes of colonist land speculation in territory controlled by French and Indians.

1754 • Seven Years' War begins in North America.
• Albany Congress proposes Plan of Union and courts Iroquois support; the plan is never implemented.

1755 • French and Indians defeat General Braddock in western Pennsylvania.

1756 • William Pitt, prime minister in Britain, fully commits to war effort against France.

1759 • Quebec falls to British.

1760 • Montreal falls to British in the last Seven Years' War battle in North America.
• George III becomes British king.

1763 • Treaty of Paris ends Seven Years' War; hostilities between British and Indians in Ohio Valley and Great Lakes region continue.
• Pontiac's uprising brings destruction to western forts and frontier settlements.
• Paxton Boys massacre friendly Indians in Pennsylvania.
• Proclamation of 1763 forbids colonial settlement west of Appalachians.

1764 • Parliament enacts Revenue (Sugar) Act, lowering tax on foreign molasses to promote compliance with trade duty.

1765 • Parliament enacts Stamp Act, imposing tax on documents and other papers in colonies and raising complaints of taxation without representation.
• Patrick Henry presents Virginia Resolves, opposing Stamp Act.
• Crowd actions fomented by Sons of Liberty intimidate local stamp distributors into resignations.
• Stamp Act Congress meets in New York City.

1766 • Parliament repeals Stamp Act and passes Declaratory Act, which asserts Parliament's right to pass laws affecting the colonies.

1767 • Parliament enacts Townshend duties, imposing revenue-raising taxes on tea, paper, glass, and other products imported to the colonies; colonists respond with boycotts.

1768 • British station troops in Boston to restore order.

1769 • Merchants in Boston and other cities sign nonimportation agreements.
• "Daughters of Liberty" formed.

1770 • Boston Massacre ignites outrage among Sons of Liberty.
• Parliament repeals Townshend duties.

1772 • British navy ship *Gaspée* attacked and burned, an action considered treason by British authorities.
• Committees of correspondence formed to speed communication between colonies.

1773 • Parliament passes Tea Act, lowering price of tea to encourage Americans to purchase legal English rather than smuggled Dutch tea.
• Dumping of tea in Boston harbor.

1774 • As punishment for destruction of tea, Parliament passes Coercive Acts (Intolerable Acts): Boston Port Act; Massachusetts Government Act; Impartial Administration of Justice Act; an amendment to the 1765 Quartering Act; and Quebec Act.
• Alarm about the attack on liberties in Massachusetts spreads throughout colonies.
• First Continental Congress meets; Continental Association formed.

1775 • Battles of Lexington and Concord spark the Revolutionary War.
• Virginia's Lord Dunmore promises freedom to defecting slaves.

BIBLIOGRAPHY

General Works

John R. Alden, *A History of the American Revolution* (1989).

Edward Countryman, *The American Revolution* (1985).

Marc Egnal, *A Mighty Empire: The Origins of the American Revolution* (1988).

Francis Jennings, *The Creation of America through Revolution to Empire* (2000).

Merrill Jensen, *The Founding of a Nation: A History of the American Revolution, 1763–1776* (1968).

A. J. Langguth, *Patriots: The Men Who Started the American Revolution* (1989).

James Kirby Martin, *In the Course of Human Events: An Interpretive Exploration of the American Revolution* (1979).

Robert Middlekauff, *The Glorious Cause: The American Revolution, 1763–1789* (1982).

Edmund S. Morgan, *The Challenge of the American Revolution* (1976).

Gordon Wood, *The Radicalism of the American Revolution* (1992).

Alfred F. Young, *The American Revolution: Explorations in the History of American Radicalism* (1976).

Native Americans and the Seven Years' War

Fred Anderson, *A People's Army: Massachusetts Soldiers and Society in the Seven Years' War* (1984).

Fred Anderson, *Crucible of War: The Seven Years' War and the Fate of Empire in British North America, 1754–1766* (2000).

Colin G. Calloway, ed., *The World Turned Upside Down: Indian Voices from Early America* (1994).

Greg Evans Dowd, *War under Heaven: Pontiac, the Indian Nations and the British Empire* (2002).

Francis Jennings, *Empire of Fortune: Crowns, Colonies, and Tribes in the Seven Years' War in America* (1988).

Douglas E. Leach, *Roots of Conflict: British Armed Forces and Colonial Americans, 1677–1763* (1986).

Daniel Martson, David Martson, and Robert O'Neill, *The Seven Years' War* (2001).

Michael N. McConnell, *A Country Between: The Upper Ohio Valley and Its Peoples, 1724–1774* (1992).

James H. Merrell, *Into the American Woods: Negotiators on the Pennsylvania Frontier* (1999).

Jane T. Merritt, *At the Crossroads: Indians and Empires on a Mid-Atlantic Frontier, 1700–1763* (2003).

Timothy J. Shannon, *Indians and Colonists at the Crossroads of Empire: The Albany Congress of 1754* (1999).

Ian K. Steele, *Warpaths: Invasions of North America* (1994).

Richard White, *The Middle Ground: Indians, Empires, and Republics in the Great Lakes Region, 1650–1815* (1991).

The British View of Empire

Bernard Bailyn, *The Origins of American Politics* (1968).

John L. Bullion, *A Great and Necessary Measure: George Grenville and the Genesis of the Stamp Act, 1763–1765* (1983).

Don Cook, *The Long Fuse: How England Lost the American Colonies, 1760–1785* (1996).

Jack P. Greene, *Peripheries and Center: Constitutional Development in the Extended Politics of the British Empire and the United States, 1607–1788* (1986).

James A. Henretta, *"Salutary Neglect": Colonial Administration under the Duke of Newcastle* (1972).

Michael Kammen, *A Rope of Sand: Colonial Agents, British Politics, and the American Revolution* (1968).

Michael Kammen, *Empire and Interest: The American Colonies and the Politics of Mercantilism* (1970).

Philip Lawson, *George Grenville: A Political Life* (1984).

Alison Gilbert Olson, *Making the Empire Work: London and American Interest Groups, 1690–1790* (1992).

Alan Rogers, *Empire and Liberty: American Resistance to British Authority, 1755–1763* (1974).

The Revolutionary Crisis of the 1760s and 1770s

David Ammerman, *In the Common Cause: American Response to the Coercive Acts of 1774* (1975).

Bernard Bailyn, *The Ideological Origins of the American Revolution* (1967).

Bernard Bailyn, *The Ordeal of Thomas Hutchinson* (1974).

Bernard Bailyn, *Faces of Revolution: Personalities and Themes in the Struggle for American Independence* (1990).

Richard R. Beeman, *Patrick Henry* (1974).

Ruth H. Bloch, *Visionary Republic: Millennial Themes in American Thought, 1775–1800* (1985).

John L. Brooke, *The Heart of the Commonwealth: Society and Political Culture in Worcester County, Massachusetts, 1713–1861* (1989).

John E. Ferling, *The First of Men: A Life of George Washington* (1988).

David Hackett Fischer, *Paul Revere's Ride* (1994).

Jay Fliegelman, *Prodigals and Pilgrims: The American Revolution against Patriarchal Authority, 1750–1800* (1982).

Dirk Hoerder, *Crowd Action in Revolutionary Massachusetts, 1765–1780* (1977).

Woody Holton, *Forced Founders: Indians, Debtors, Slaves, and the Making of the American Revolution in Virginia* (1999).

Marjoleine Kars, *Breaking Loose Together: The Regulator Rebellion in Pre-Revolutionary North Carolina* (2002).

Thomas A. Lewis, *For King and Country: The Maturing of George Washington, 1748–1760* (1993).

Pauline Maier, *From Resistance to Revolution: Colonial Radicals and the Development of American Opposition to Britain, 1765–1776* (1972).

Pauline Maier, *The Old Revolutionaries: Political Lives in the Age of Samuel Adams* (1980).

Edmund S. Morgan, *The Genius of George Washington* (1980).

Edmund S. Morgan, *Inventing the People: The Rise of Popular Sovereignty in England and America* (1988).

Edmund S. Morgan, *Benjamin Franklin* (2002).

Edmund S. Morgan and Helen M. Morgan, *The Stamp Act Crisis: Prologue to Revolution* (1962).

Gary B. Nash, *The Urban Crucible: Social Change, Political Consciousness, and the Origins of the American Revolution* (1979).

Peter Shaw, *American Patriots and the Rituals of Revolution* (1981).

John W. Tyler, *Smugglers and Patriots: Boston Merchants and the Advent of the American Revolution* (1986).

Ann Fairfax Withington, *Toward a More Perfect Union: Virtue and the Formation of American Republics* (1991).

Alfred F. Young, *The Shoemaker and the Tea Party: Memory and the American Revolution* (1999).

Hiller B. Zobel, *The Boston Massacre* (1970).

Women

Richard Buel and Joy Day Buel, *The Way of Duty: A Woman and Her Family in Revolutionary America* (1984).

Joan Gundersen, *To Be Useful to the World: Women in Revolutionary America, 1740–1790* (1996).

Ronald Hoffman and Peter J. Albert, eds., *Women in the Age of the American Revolution* (1989).

Linda Kerber, *Women of the Republic: Intellect and Ideology in Revolutionary America* (1980).

Mary Beth Norton, *Liberty's Daughters: The Revolutionary Experience of American Women, 1750–1800* (1980).

Slavery

Ira Berlin and Ronald Hoffman, *Slavery and Freedom in the Age of the American Revolution* (1983).

Jeffrey Crow, *The Black Experience in Revolutionary North Carolina* (1977).

David Brion Davis, *The Problem of Slavery in the Age of Revolution, 1770–1823* (1975).

Sylvia Frey, *Water from the Rock: Black Resistance in a Revolutionary Age* (1991).

Winthrop D. Jordan, *White over Black: American Attitudes toward the Negro, 1550–1812* (1968).

Sidney Kaplan and Emma Nogrady Kaplan, *The Black Presence in the Era of the American Revolution* (1989).

Duncan J. Macleod, *Slavery, Race, and the American Revolution* (1974).

Philip Morgan, *Slave Counterpoint: Black Culture in the Eighteenth-Century Chesapeake and Low Country* (1998).

Donald L. Robinson, *Slavery in the Structure of American Politics, 1765–1820* (1971).

Regional Studies

Richard R. Beeman, *The Evolution of the Southern Backcountry: A Case Study of Lunenburg County, Virginia, 1746–1832* (1984).

T. H. Breen, *Tobacco Culture: The Mentality of the Great Tidewater Planters on the Eve of the American Revolution* (1985).

Richard D. Brown, *Revolutionary Politics in Massachusetts: The Boston Committee of Correspondence and the Towns, 1772–1774* (1970).

Edward Countryman, *A People in Revolution: The American Revolution and Political Society in New York, 1760–1790* (1981).

A. Roger Ekirch, *"Poor Carolina": Politics and Society in North Carolina, 1729–1776* (1981).

Paul Gilje, *Road to Mobocracy: Popular Disorder in New York City, 1763–1834* (1987).

Robert A. Gross, *The Minutemen and Their World* (1976).

Ronald Hoffman, *A Spirit of Dissension: Economics, Politics, and the Revolution in Maryland* (1973).

Rhys Isaac, *The Transformation of Virginia, 1740–1790* (1982).

Stephen E. Lucas, *Portents of Rebellion: Rhetoric and Revolution in Philadelphia, 1765–1776* (1976).

William Pencak, *Politics and Revolution in Provincial Massachusetts* (1981).

Bruce A. Ragsdale, *A Planters' Republic: The Search for Economic Independence in Revolutionary Virginia* (1996).

Steven Rossman, *Arms, Country, and Class: The Philadelphia Militia and the "Lower Sort" during the American Revolution* (1987).

Albert H. Tillson, *Gentry and Common Folk: Political Culture on a Virginia Frontier, 1740–1789* (1991).

CONTINENTAL ARMY UNIFORM WORN AT THE SIEGE OF FORT STANWIX, 1777

In 1775, the Continental Congress faced the daunting prospect of fielding an army to fight the largest military force in the world. Money was scarce, soldiers were hastily trained and short of equipment, and uniforms were hard to come by. (Many were purchased from France.) At the start of the war, ordinary enlisted men often wore brown work clothes, and while this gave them a unified look, it did not allow for easy categorization of soldiers by their unit. When Washington finally issued dress specifications, he chose the color already preferred by many officers—dark blue— and then specified the variety of colors to be used for the facings and linings of the coat to establish the rank and the unit of each soldier. Officers especially needed distinctive clothing, to distinguish them from ordinary soldiers and also from other officers, so that military hierarchy could be maintained at all times. The coat pictured here belonged to a brigadier general, Peter Gansevoort Jr., who was twenty-eight in 1777 and in command of Fort Stanwix in the Mohawk River valley of New York. The coat has a buff-colored lining (seen inside the coattails) and bright red facings on the collar, the lapel, and the cuffs, marking him as a New York soldier. The color of the shoulder ribbons reveals Gansevoort's rank; the ribbons could be easily replaced with a new color, enabling a man to ascend in rank without having to get a new coat.

National Museum of American History, Smithsonian Institution, Washington, D.C.

The War for America
1775–1783

ABIGAIL ADAMS WAS IMPATIENT for American independence. While her husband, John, was away in Philadelphia as a member of the Second Continental Congress, Abigail tended house and farm in Braintree, Massachusetts, just south of British-occupied Boston. She had four young children to look after, and in addition to her feminine duties, such as cooking, sewing, and making soap, she also had to shoulder masculine duties in her husband's absence—hiring farm help, managing rental property, selling the crop. John wrote to her often, approving of the fine "Farmeress" who was conducting his business so well. She replied, conveying news of the family along with shrewd commentary on revolutionary politics. In December 1775, she chastised the congress for being too timid and urged that independence be declared. A few months later, she astutely observed to John that southern slave owners might shrink from a war in the name of **liberty**: "I have sometimes been ready to think that the passion for Liberty cannot be Equally strong in the Breasts of those who have been accustomed to deprive their fellow Creatures of theirs."

"I long to hear that you have declared an independency," she wrote in March 1776. "And by the way in the new Code of Laws which I suppose it will be necessary for you to make I desire you would Remember the Ladies, and be more generous and favourable to them than your ancestors." If Abigail was politically precocious in favoring independence and questioning slave owners' devotion to liberty, she was positively visionary in this extraordinary plea to her husband to "Remember the Ladies." "Do not put such unlimited power into the hands of the Husbands," she advised. "Remember all Men would be tyrants if they could." Abigail had put her finger on another form of tyranny that was rarely remarked on in her society: that of men over women. "If particular care and attention is not paid to the Ladies," she jokingly threatened, "we are determined to foment a Rebellion, and will not hold ourselves bound by any Laws in which we have no voice, or Representation."

John Adams dismissed his wife's provocative idea as a "saucy" suggestion: "As to your extraordinary Code of Laws, I cannot but Laugh." The Revolution had perhaps unleashed discontent among other dependent groups, he allowed; children, apprentices, students, Indians, and blacks had grown "disobedient" and "insolent." "But your Letter was the first Intimation that another Tribe more numerous and powerful than all the rest were grown discontented." Men were too smart to repeal their "Masculine Systems," John assured her, for otherwise they would find themselves living under a "despotism of the petticoat."

This clever exchange between husband and wife in 1776 says much about the cautious, limited radicalism of the American Revolution. Both John and

Abigail Adams
Abigail Smith Adams was twenty-two when she sat for this pastel portrait in 1766. A wife for two years and a mother for one, Adams exhibits a steady, intelligent gaze. Pearls and a lace collar anchor her femininity, while her facial expression projects a confidence and maturity not often credited to young women of the 1760s.
Courtesy of the Massachusetts Historical Society ©.

Abigail Adams understood (Abigail probably far more than John) that ungluing the hierarchical bond between the king and his subjects potentially unglued other kinds of social inequalities. John was surely joking in listing the groups made unruly in the spirit of a challenge to authority, for children, apprentices, and students were hardly rebellious in the 1770s. But it would soon prove to be an uncomfortable joke, because Indians and blacks did take up the cause of their own liberty during the Revolution, and the great majority of them saw their liberty best served by joining the British side in the war.

Though Abigail Adams was impatient for independence, many other Americans feared separation from Britain. What kind of civilized country had no king? Who, if not Britain, would protect Americans from the French and Spanish? How could the colonies possibly win a war against the most powerful military machine on the globe? Reconciliation, not independence, was favored by many.

Members of the Continental Congress, whether they were pro-independence like John Adams or more cautiously hoping for reconciliation, had their hands full in 1775 and 1776. The war had already begun, and it fell to the congress to raise an army, finance it, and explore diplomatic alliances with foreign countries. In part a classic war with professional armies and textbook battles, the Revolutionary War was also a civil war in America, at times even a brutal **guerrilla war**, of committed rebels versus loyalists.

In one glorious moment, the congress issued a ringing statement about how social hierarchy would be rearranged in America after submission to the king was undone. That was on July 4, 1776, when the Declaration of Independence asserted that "all men are created equal." But this striking phrase went completely unremarked in the two days of congressional debate spent tinkering with the language of the Declaration. The solvent to dissolve social inequalities in America was created at that moment, but none of the men at the congress, or even Abigail Adams up in Braintree, fully realized it at the time.

The Second Continental Congress

On May 10, 1775, nearly one month after the fighting at Lexington and Concord, the Second Continental Congress assembled in Philadelphia. The congress immediately set to work on two crucial and seemingly contradictory tasks: to raise and supply an army and to explore reconciliation with England. To do the former, they needed soldiers and a commander to come to the aid of the Massachusetts militiamen, they needed money, and they needed to work out a declaration of war. To do the latter, however, they needed diplomacy to approach the king. But the king was not receptive, and by 1776, as the war progressed and hopes of reconciliation faded, delegates at the congress began to ponder the treasonous act of declaring independence—said by some to be plain common sense.

Assuming Political and Military Authority

Like members of the First Continental Congress (see chapter 6), the delegates to the second were well-established figures in their home colonies, but they still had to learn to know and trust each other; they did not always agree. The Adams cousins John and Samuel defined the radical end of the spectrum, favoring independence. John Dickinson of Pennsylvania, no longer the eager revolutionary who had dashed off *Letters from a Farmer* back in 1767, was now a moderate, seeking reconciliation with England. Benjamin Franklin, fresh off a ship from an eleven-year residence in England, was feared by some to be a British spy. Mutual suspicions flourished easily when the undertaking was so dangerous, opinions were so varied, and a misstep could spell disaster.

Most of the delegates were not yet prepared to break with England. Several legislatures instructed their delegates to oppose independence. Some felt that government without a monarchical element was unworkable, while others feared it might be suicidal to lose England's protection against the traditional enemies, France and Spain. Colonies that traded actively with England feared undermining their economies. Nor were the vast majority of ordinary Americans able to envision independence from the British monarchy. From the Stamp Act of 1765 to the Coercive Acts of 1774 (see chapter 6), the constitutional struggle with England had turned on the issue of parliamentary power. During that decade, almost no one had questioned the legitimacy of the monarchy.

In mid-1775, the few men at the Continental Congress who did think that independence was desirable were, not surprisingly, from Massachusetts. Their colony had been stripped of civil government under the Coercive Acts, and their capital was occupied by the British army. Even so, those men knew that it was premature to push for a break with England. John Adams wrote to Abigail in June 1775: "America is a great, unwieldy body. Its progress must be slow. It is like a large fleet sailing under convoy. The fleetest sailors must wait for the dullest and slowest."

As slow as the American colonies were in sailing toward political independence, they needed to take swift action to coordinate a military defense, for the Massachusetts countryside was under threat of further attack. Even the hes-itant moderates in the congress agreed that a military buildup was necessary. Around the country, militia units from New York to Georgia collected arms and drilled on village greens in anticipation. (See "The Promise of Technology," page 214.) On June 14, the congress voted to create the Continental army. Choosing the commander in chief offered an opportunity to demonstrate that this was no local war of a single rebellious colony. The congress bypassed Artemas Ward from Massachusetts, a veteran of the Seven Years' War, who was already commanding the soldiers massed around Boston. The congress instead chose George Washington, also an experienced war veteran but preferable precisely because he was from a colony five hundred miles to the south of the fighting. His appointment sent the clear message to England that there was widespread commitment to war beyond New England.

Next the congress drew up a document titled "A Declaration on the Causes and Necessity of Taking Up Arms," which rehearsed familiar arguments about the tyranny of Parliament and the need to defend traditional English liberties. This declaration was first drafted by a young Virginia **planter**, Thomas Jefferson, a newcomer to the congress and a radical on the question of independence. The moderate John Dickinson, fearing that the declaration would offend England and rule out reconciliation, was allowed to rewrite it; however, he still left much of Jefferson's highly charged language about choosing "to die freemen rather than to live slaves." Even a man as reluctant for independence as Dickinson acknowledged the necessity of military defense against an invading army.

To pay for the military buildup, the congress authorized a currency issue of $2 million. The Continental dollars were merely paper; they did not represent gold or silver, for the congress owned no precious metals. The delegates somewhat naively expected that the currency would be accepted as valuable on trust as it spread in the population through the hands of soldiers, farmers, munitions suppliers, and beyond.

In just two months, the Second Continental Congress had created an army, declared war, and issued its own currency. It had taken on the major functions of a legitimate government, both

> From the Stamp Act of 1765 to the Coercive Acts of 1774, the constitutional struggle with England had turned on the issue of parliamentary power. Almost no one had questioned the legitimacy of the monarchy.

Arming the Soldiers: Muskets and Rifles

How combat-ready was the American side in the Revolutionary War? Were there adequate numbers of firearms along with men trained in their use? These lively and important questions have recently generated sharp debate among historians. A book published in 2000 argued that gun ownership was surprisingly rare in the 1770s, occurring in only one out of seven households. This finding did not square with historians' largely untested assumption that a militia-based defense system implied that virtually all households contained a gun. The ensuing controversy quickly became a firestorm, involving activists on both sides of the modern gun-control debate as well as historians. In consequence, the examination of evidence and methods to evaluate gun ownership has been considerably sharpened.

What were eighteenth-century guns like? There were guns called fowling pieces that fired shot (small pellets), useful for hunting ducks and wild turkeys as food and small game such as raccoons and squirrels. For larger game, and for warfare purposes, muskets were the preferred weapon. Muskets were a sixteenth-century invention, featuring by the mid-eighteenth century an improved flinklock ignition system in which the trigger released a spring-held cock that caused a hammer to strike a flint, creating sparks. The sparks set off a small charge in a priming pan leading directly to a larger explosion in the barrel. To load the gun, a shooter first put it on half-cock to prevent an accidental firing. He next put a small quantity of powder (carried in a powder horn) in the priming pan and closed it, poured more powder down the smooth gun barrel, dropped in the projectile—usually a one-ounce lead ball—and then wadded paper down the barrel with a ramrod to hold the loose ball in place. He then raised the gun to firing position, put it on full cock, and fired. The whole procedure took highly experienced shooters from 45 to 90 seconds.

The range of muskets extended only about 50 to 100 yards. They were notoriously inaccurate, because of the poor fit between ball and barrel and the considerable kick produced by firing, which interfered with aiming. Far more accurate were longer-barreled rifles, used in frontier regions where big-game hunting was more common. The interior of a rifle barrel carried spiral grooves that imparted spin to the ball as it traversed the barrel, stabilizing and lengthening its flight, and enabling expert marksmen to hit small targets at 150 or 200 yards. Yet for militia use, muskets were preferred over rifles. Rifles took twice as long to load and fire, and their longer barrels made them unwieldy for soldiers on the march. Inaccurate muskets were quite deadly enough when fired by a group of soldiers in unison at targets 50 yards away.

How many American men actually owned fowling pieces, muskets, or rifles? A partial answer can be gleaned from probate inventories, many thousands of which exist in state archives. Inventories listed a decedent's possessions, to facilitate inheritance practice and to make sure creditors were paid off. Yet these sources are fraught with thorny problems. For one thing, they are often not complete: If few inventories itemized clothing, can we conclude the decedents went nude? If no firearm is listed, can we conclude the decedent *never* owned a gun? Clearly not. Probate inventories were made only for a subset of dead property owners, primarily for the use of creditors and heirs, so they are biased by age (older), sex (male), and wealth (more).

Despite complexities, scholars have worked with probate inventories to establish a baseline figure for gun ownership. It takes sophistication with statistical sampling technique as well as ability to read old handwriting to use the evidence, since the thousands of inventories cannot all be read. Recent careful studies based on this source yield estimates on overall gun ownership that range from 40 to 50 percent of all probated estates in the 1770s.

A second way to assess gun ownership is to look at the arms procurement experiences of state legislatures and the Continental Congress as they geared up for war. In the early months of 1775, New England patriot leaders had a keen interest to know how many armed soldiers could be mobilized in the event of war. One scholar has located militia returns from thirty towns in Massachusetts, New Hampshire, and Rhode Island. Scattered returns from other states exist in archives. At their most complete, these records form a census of soldiers and equipment taken on a militia training day. A particularly detailed list from Salem,

Massachusetts, notes against each man's name his ownership of a firelock, a bayonet, a sword, a pouch, a cartouche box, a cartridge, a flint, lead balls, gunpowder, a knapsack, and priming wires. Salem's list appears to support the conclusion that 100 percent of adult men owned guns, yet the scholar seeking to calculate gun ownership must ask: Who is not on this list? Who failed to report to the muster exercise? This careful study concludes that in 1775, roughly three quarters of all men age sixteen to sixty in New England owned guns.

These high rates of ownership are not matched by a final kind of evidence: reports from militia officers to state legislatures complaining of being underarmed. A New Hampshire captain complained of his unit's plight in June 1775: "We are in want of both arms and ammunition. There is but very little, nor none worth mentioning—perhaps one pound of powder to twenty men, and not one-half our men have arms." A militia officer in Pennsylvania noted that men who owned high-quality muskets and rifles were often reluctant to report for active duty with them unless assured they would be reimbursed in the event of loss of the valuable possession. A Prussian general who volunteered his expertise to the Continental army arrived at Valley Forge in 1778 and was shocked to find "muskets, carbines, fowling pieces, and rifles" all in the same

company of troops. Lack of uniformity in guns posed considerable problems for supplying appropriate ammunition. While this evidence seems to point to an underarmed soldiery, the opposite evidence— militia captains who failed to register complaints—did not leave a corresponding paper trail for historians. Historians must take care not to be misled by stray documents or quotations that may be atypical.

The Continental Congress knew more guns were needed, certainly. Before 1774, American artisans imported British-made gunlocks, the central firing mechanism, and added the wooden stock and iron barrel to produce muskets. But in October 1774, the British Parliament, anticipating trouble, prohibited all gunlock and firearm exports to the colonies. Congress then turned to French and Dutch suppliers to purchase gunlocks, gunpowder, and finished muskets.

Muskets and even fowling pieces worked well enough for the Revolutionary War, where similarly armed combatants engaged in massed, synchronized firing at close range. In individual use, however, muskets were clumsy, inaccurate, and hence not highly lethal. High rates of musket ownership did not translate to high rates of successful homicide or accidental deaths by shooting. But sixty years after the Revolution, all that changed with the

advent of machine-tooled firearms such as the Colt revolver and the Remington rifle. These new repeat-fire weapons were cheaper, more accurate, and far more deadly. Comparing ownership rates of muskets with that of revolvers—or assault weapons—across time may not be the most meaningful path to understanding this country's historic relationship with guns.

Powder Horn

James Pike, a twenty-three-year-old New England militiaman, made and then personalized this powder horn, a hollow cow's horn capped on both ends with leather. The stopper was designed to be pulled off by the teeth, so the hands of the user would be free to hold the musket barrel and pour the powder. Pike's carvings suggest his motivation for fighting. Above his name he depicts a scene dated April 19, 1775, in which British soldiers, labeled "the Aggressors," fire through the Liberty Tree at "Provincials, Defending." Pike was not at Lexington or Concord; his first combat experience came two months later at the battle of Bunker Hill, where he saw his brother killed and was himself wounded in the shoulder.
Chicago Historical Society.

Committee of Safety Musket

This gun was one of the small number of American-made muskets produced in 1775 in a German region of Pennsylvania where blacksmith shops were numerous. The smithy forged and fashioned the gun barrel and attached it to an imported gunlock, the mechanism over the trigger. A wooden stock completed the design.
York County Historical Society.

military and financial, without any legal basis for its authority, for it had not—and would not for a full year—declare independence from the authority of the king.

Pursuing Both War and Peace

The battle of Bunker Hill was a British victory, but an expensive one. As General Clinton later remarked, "It was a dear bought victory; another such would have ruined us."

Three days after the congress voted to raise the Continental army, one of the bloodiest battles of the Revolution occurred. The British commander in Boston, Thomas Gage, had recently received troop reinforcements, three talented generals (William Howe, John Burgoyne, and Henry Clinton), and new instructions to root out the rebels around Boston. But before Gage could take the offensive, the Americans fortified the hilly terrain of Charlestown, a peninsula just north of Boston, on the night of June 16, 1775.

The British generals could have nipped off the peninsula where it met the mainland, to box in the Americans. But General Howe insisted on a bold frontal assault, sending his 2,500 soldiers across the water and up the hill in an intimidating but potentially costly attack. The American troops, 1,400 strong, listened to the British drummers pacing the uphill march and held their fire until the British were about twenty yards away. At that distance, the musket volley was sure and deadly, and the British turned back. Twice more General Howe sent his men up the hill and received the same blast of firepower; each time they had to step around the bodies of men felled in the previous attempts.

On the third assault, the British took the hill, mainly because the American ammunition supply gave out, and the defenders quickly retreated. The battle of Bunker Hill was thus a British victory, but an expensive one. The dead numbered 226 on the British side, with more than 800 wounded; the Americans suffered 140 dead, 271 wounded, and 30 captured. As General Clinton later remarked, "It was a dear bought victory; another such would have ruined us."

Instead of pursuing the fleeing Americans, Howe pulled his

army back to Boston, unwilling to risk more raids into the countryside. If the British had had any grasp of the basic instability of the American units gathered around Boston, they might have pushed westward and perhaps decisively defeated the core of the Continental army in its infancy. Instead they hung back in Boston, dependent on British naval vessels for their food and supplies, abandoning the town without a fight nine months later. Howe used the time in Boston to inoculate his army against smallpox, because a new epidemic of the deadly disease was spreading in port cities along the Atlantic. Inoculation worked by producing a light but real (and therefore risky) case of smallpox, followed by lifelong immunity. Howe's instinct here was right: From 1775 to 1782, the years coinciding with the American Revolution, some 130,000 people on the American continent, most of them Indians, died of smallpox.

A week after Bunker Hill, General Washington arrived to take charge of the new Continental army. He found enthusiastic but undisciplined troops. Sanitation was an unknown concept, with inadequate latrines fouling the campground. Drunkenness on duty was common. Soldiers apparently came and went at will. The amazed general attributed the disarray to the New England custom of letting militia units elect their own officers, a custom he felt undermined deference. A captain from a Connecticut regiment was spotted shaving one of his own men, an inappropriate gesture of personal service by a superior officer. But in civilian life the captain was a barber; he had been elected an officer by the men of his town, who saw nothing strange in his practicing his trade in the camp. Washington quickly imposed more hierarchy and authority. "Discipline is the soul of the army," he stated.

While military plans moved forward, the Second Continental Congress pursued its second, contradictory objective, reconciliation with England. Delegates from the middle colonies (Pennsylvania, Delaware, and New York), whose merchants depended on trade with England, urged that channels for negotiation remain open. In July 1775, congressional moderates led by John Dickinson engineered an appeal to the king called the Olive Branch Petition. The petition affirmed loyalty to the monarchy and blamed all the troubles on the king's ministers and on Parliament. It proposed that the American colonial assemblies be recognized as individual parliaments, under the umbrella of the monarchy. That Dickinson himself could write both the

The Battle of Bunker Hill, 1775

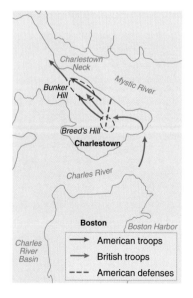

An Exact View of the Late Battle at Charlestown, June 17th 1775

This dramatic panorama is the earliest visual representation of the battle of Bunker Hill. On sale to the public six weeks after the battle, the engraving shows Charlestown in flames (center back) and British and American soldiers in fixed formation firing muskets at each other. The Americans, to the left, are dug in along the crest of the hill; British casualties have begun to mount up. The artist, Bernard Romans, was a noted cartographer, military engineer, linguist, and mathematician. Born in the Netherlands, he came to America as a British-paid surveyor, but he took the American side in the Revolution. His maps of war zones were bought by Americans eager to track the geography of war. His large depiction of Bunker Hill, produced in multiple copies, some of which were hand-colored like this one, likely decorated many a patriot's wall. It was advertised for sale in newspapers in Philadelphia and Virginia, and a half-size copy was engraved and inserted in an issue of *The Pennsylvania Magazine*, a monthly periodical edited by Thomas Paine. One ad for the picture promised that "Every well-wisher to this country cannot but delight in seeing a plan of the ground on which our brave American Army conquered the British Ministerial Forces." Technically the British won the battle by taking the hill, but that was not the story told by this picture.

Colonial Williamsburg Foundation.

George Washington's Camp Chest

This portable camp chest (or mess kit) belonged to George Washington during the Revolutionary War. The wooden box, covered in leather and lined with wool fabric, held an elaborate setup neatly collapsed into a small space: four tin pots with detached handles, five tin plates, three tin platters, two tin boxes, two knives, three forks, eight glass bottles with cork stoppers, salt and pepper shakers, and a woolen sack with six compartments. The chest also contained a tinder box, which held kindling and a flint for starting a fire, and a gridiron (or grate) with collapsed legs for cooking over the fire. Washington—or, more likely, a subordinate preparing his food—would have used this chest when the army was on the move. It was an officer's chest, presented to the general by a Philadelphia merchant in 1776; enlisted men would have had something much more basic, if anything. Washington saved the chest for two decades after the war. After his death it was auctioned off and donated to the federal government by the new owner. It is now owned by the Smithsonian Institution in Washington, D.C.

National Museum of American History, Smithsonian Institution, Behring Center.

"Declaration on the Causes and Necessity of Taking Up Arms" and the Olive Branch Petition within a few days of each other shows how ambivalent the American position was in the summer of 1775.

By late fall 1775, however, reconciliation was out of the question. King George rejected the Olive Branch Petition and heatedly condemned the Americans, calling them rebels and traitors. Thereafter it was hard to maintain the illusion that ministers and not the king himself were to blame for the conflict.

Thomas Paine and the Case for Independence

Pressure for independence started to mount in January 1776, when a pamphlet titled *Common Sense* appeared in Philadelphia. Thomas Paine, its author, was an English **artisan** and coffee-house intellectual who had befriended Benjamin Franklin in London. He came to America in the fall of 1774 with letters of introduction from Franklin to several Philadelphia printers. He landed a job with *The Pennsylvania Magazine* and

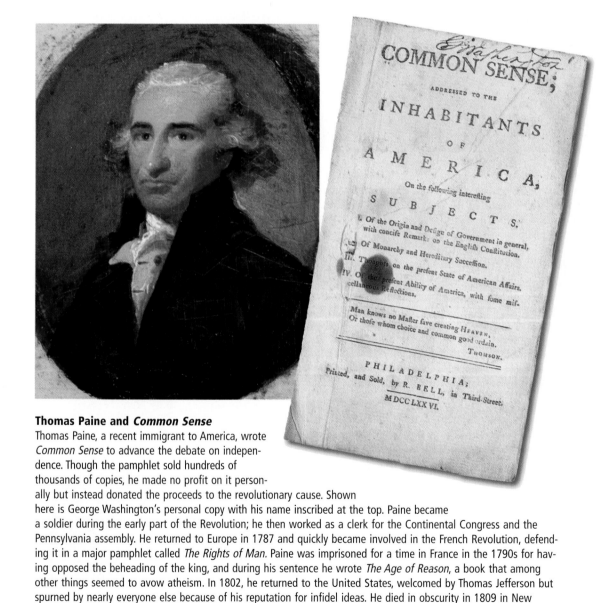

Thomas Paine and *Common Sense*
Thomas Paine, a recent immigrant to America, wrote *Common Sense* to advance the debate on independence. Though the pamphlet sold hundreds of thousands of copies, he made no profit on it personally but instead donated the proceeds to the revolutionary cause. Shown here is George Washington's personal copy with his name inscribed at the top. Paine became a soldier during the early part of the Revolution; he then worked as a clerk for the Continental Congress and the Pennsylvania assembly. He returned to Europe in 1787 and quickly became involved in the French Revolution, defending it in a major pamphlet called *The Rights of Man*. Paine was imprisoned for a time in France in the 1790s for having opposed the beheading of the king, and during his sentence he wrote *The Age of Reason*, a book that among other things seemed to avow atheism. In 1802, he returned to the United States, welcomed by Thomas Jefferson but spurned by nearly everyone else because of his reputation for infidel ideas. He died in obscurity in 1809 in New Rochelle, New York, and a Manhattan newspaper unfairly summarized his life by saying, "He had lived long, did some good and much harm."
Book: Boston Athenaeum; portrait: Monticello/Thomas Jefferson Memorial Foundation, Inc.

soon met delegates from the Second Continental Congress. With their encouragement, he wrote *Common Sense* to lay out a lively and compelling case for complete independence.

In simple yet forceful language, Paine elaborated on the absurdities of the British monarchy. Why should one man, by accident of birth, claim extensive power over others? he asked. A king might be foolish or wicked. "One of the strongest natural proofs of the folly of hereditary right in kings," Paine wrote, "is that nature disapproves it; otherwise she would not so frequently turn it into ridicule by giving mankind *an ass for a lion*." Calling the king of England an ass broke through the automatic deference most Americans still had for the monarchy. To replace monarchy, Paine advocated **republican** government, based on the consent of the people. Rulers, according to Paine, were only representatives of the people, and the best form of government relied on frequent elections to achieve the most direct **democracy** possible.

Paine's pamphlet sold more than 150,000 copies in a matter of weeks. Newspapers reprinted it; men read it aloud in taverns and coffeehouses; John Adams sent a copy to Abigail Adams, who passed it around to neighbors. Another of John Adams's correspondents wrote him in late February that many New Englanders desired an official declaration of independence. Middle and southern colonies, under no immediate threat of violence, remained cautious.

One factor hastening official independence was the prospect of an alliance with France, Britain's archrival. France was willing to provide military supplies as well as naval power, but not without firm assurance that the Americans would separate from England. News that the British were negotiating for German mercenary soldiers further solidified support for independence. By May, all but four colonies were agitating for a declaration. The holdouts were Pennsylvania, Maryland, New York, and South Carolina, the latter two containing large loyalist populations. An exasperated Virginian wrote to his friend in the congress, "For God's sake, why do you dawdle in the Congress so strangely? Why do you not at once declare yourself a separate independent state?" But a more pessimistic southerner feared that independence

Jefferson's Laptop Writing Desk

On a long stagecoach ride from Virginia to Philadelphia in May 1776, thirty-three-year-old Thomas Jefferson sketched out a design for a portable laptop writing desk. On arrival, he hired a Philadelphia cabinetmaker to produce it in mahogany. The adjustable book rest shown here (notice the notches) could also unfold on its hinges to create a large writing surface. Pens, quills, ink, and paper were stored below; the desk weighed five pounds. Here Jefferson penned rough drafts of the Declaration of Independence. Near the end of his life, he gave the desk to his granddaughter's husband, expressing the hope that it might become esteemed for its connection to the Declaration. The man replied that he would revere the desk as something "no longer inanimate, and mute, but as something to be interrogated and caressed." In 1876, it was a featured exhibit at a centennial exhibition in Philadelphia honoring the independence of the nation.

National Museum of American History, Smithsonian Institution, Washington, D.C.

was "in truth a delusive bait which men inconsiderably snatch at, without knowing the hook to which it is affixed."

In early June, Richard Henry Lee of the Virginia delegation introduced a resolution calling for independence. The moderates still commanded enough support to postpone a vote on the measure until July, so they could go home and consult about this extreme step. In the meantime, the congress appointed a committee, with Thomas Jefferson and others, to draft a longer document setting out the case for independence.

On July 2, after intense politicking, all but one state voted for independence; New York abstained. The congress then turned to the document drafted by Thomas Jefferson and his committee. Jefferson began with a preamble that articulated philosophical principles about natural rights, equality, the right of revolution, and the consent of the governed as the only true basis for government. He then listed more than two dozen grievances against King George. The congress merely glanced at the political philosophy, finding nothing exceptional in it; the ideas about natural rights and the consent of the governed were seen as "self-evident truths," just as the document claimed. In itself, this absence of comment showed a remarkable transformation in political thinking since the end of the Seven Years' War. The single phrase declaring the natural equality of "all men" was also passed over without comment; no one elaborated on its radical implications.

For two days, the congress wrangled over the list of grievances, especially the issue of slavery. Jefferson had included an impassioned statement blaming the king for slavery, which delegates from Georgia and South Carolina struck out. They had no intention of denouncing their labor system as an evil practice. But the congress let stand another of Jefferson's fervent grievances, blaming the king for mobilizing "the merciless Indian Savages" into bloody **frontier** warfare.

On July 4, the amendments to Jefferson's text were complete and the congress formally adopted the document. (See appendix, page A-1.) Nearly a month later, on August 2, the delegates gathered to sign the official parchment copy, handwritten by an exacting scribe. Four men, including John Dickinson, declined to sign; several others "signed with regret . . . and with many doubts," according to John Adams. The document was then printed, widely distributed, and read aloud in celebrations everywhere. A crowd in New York listened to a public reading of it and then toppled a lead statue of George III on horseback to melt it down for bullets. On July 15, the New York delegation switched from abstention to endorsement, making the vote on independence truly unanimous.

Printed copies of the Declaration of Independence did not include the signers' names, for they had committed treason, a crime punishable by death. On the day of signing, they indulged in gallows humor. When Benjamin Franklin paused before signing to look over the document, John Hancock of Massachusetts teased him, "Come, come, sir. We must be unanimous. No pulling different ways. We must all hang together." Franklin replied, "Indeed we must all hang together. Otherwise we shall most assuredly hang separately."

> Printed copies of the Declaration of Independence did not include the signers' names, for they had committed treason, a crime punishable by death.

The First Year of War, 1775–1776

Both sides had cause to approach the war for America with uneasiness. The Americans, with only inexperienced and undertrained militias, opposed the mightiest military power in the world, and many thought it was foolhardy to expect victory. Further, pockets of loyalism remained strong; the country was not united. But the British faced serious obstacles as well. Their utter disdain for the fighting abilities of the Americans had to be reevaluated in light of their costly Bunker Hill victory. The logistics of supplying an army with food across three thousand miles of water were daunting. And since the British goal was to regain allegiance, not to destroy and conquer, the army was often constrained in its actions. These patterns—undertrained American troops and British troops strangely unwilling to press their advantage—played out repeatedly in the first year of war when the Americans invaded Canada, the British invaded New York, and the two sides chased each other up and down the length of New Jersey.

The American Military Forces

Americans claimed that the initial months of war were purely defensive, triggered by the British army's invasion. But quickly the war also became a rebellion, an overthrowing of long-established authority. As both defenders and rebels, Americans were generally highly motivated to fight, and the potential manpower that could be mobilized was in theory very great.

From the earliest decades of settlement, local defense in the colonies rested with a militia requiring participation from nearly every able-bodied man over age sixteen. When the main threat to public safety was the occasional Indian attack, the local militia made sense. But such attacks were now mostly limited to the frontier. Southern militias trained with potential slave rebellions in mind, but these too were rare. The annual muster day in most communities had evolved into a holiday of drinking, marching, and perhaps shooting practice with small fowling guns or muskets.

Militias were best suited to limited engagements, when a local community was under immediate attack. They were not appropriate for extended wars requiring military campaigns far from home. In forming the Continental army, the congress set enlistment at one year, but army leaders soon learned that that was not enough time to train soldiers and carry out campaigns. A three-year enlistment earned a new soldier a $20 bonus, while men who committed for the duration of the war were promised a postwar **land grant** of one hundred acres. To make this in-

Black Revolutionary War Sailor
The fledgling American navy recruited blacks from the beginning of the war, because there was a pool of experienced black sailors to draw from. They were mainly hired as ordinary seamen, though a few were pilots of ships. Their names are preserved in crew lists; rarely, however, were their likenesses preserved. This 1780 portrait by an unknown artist shows an unnamed man in dress uniform, sword and scabbard at hand, with a ship in view to establish his naval connection.
Collection of A. A. McBurney.

ducement effective, of course, recruits had to believe that the Americans would win. By early 1777, the army was the largest it would ever be. Over the course of the war, some 231,000 men spent time in military service, amounting to roughly one-quarter of the white male population over age sixteen.

Women also served in the Continental army. They were needed to do the daily cooking and washing, and after battle they nursed the wounded. The British army established a ratio of one woman to every ten men; in the Continental army, the ratio was set at one woman to fifteen men. Close to 20,000 women served in the war, probably most of them wives of men in service. Children tagged along as well, and babies were born in the camps and on the road.

Black Americans were at first excluded from the Continental army, a rule that slave owner George Washington made as commander in chief. But as manpower needs increased, the northern states began to welcome free blacks into service; even slaves could serve, with their masters' permission. About 5,000 black men served in the Revolutionary War on the rebel side, nearly all from the northern states. Black Continental soldiers sometimes were segregated into separate units; two battalions from Rhode Island were entirely black. Just under three hundred blacks joined regiments from Connecticut. While some of these were **draftees**, others were clearly inspired by the ideals of freedom being voiced in a war against tyranny. For example, twenty-three blacks gave "Liberty," "Freedom," or "Freeman" as their surname at the time of enlistment. (Southern slaves did not join the Continental army; in large numbers they chose to run to the British instead.)

Military service helped to politicize Americans during the early stages of the war. In early 1776, independence was a risky idea, potentially treasonous. But as the war heated up and recruiters demanded commitment, some Americans discovered that apathy had its dangers as well. Anyone who refused to serve ran the risk of being called a traitor to the cause. Military service established one's credentials as a patriot; it became a prime way of defining and demonstrating political allegiance.

The American army was at times raw and inexperienced and much of the time woefully undermanned. It never had the precision and discipline of European professional armies. But it was never as bad as the British continually assumed. The British were to learn that it was a serious mistake to underrate the enemy.

> Close to 20,000 women served during the war. Children tagged along as well, and babies were born in the camps and on the road.

The British Strategy

The American strategy was relatively straightforward—to repulse and defeat an invading army. The British strategy was not nearly so clear. England wanted to put down a rebellion and restore monarchical power in the colonies, but the question was how to accomplish this. A decisive defeat of the Continental army was essential but not sufficient to end the rebellion, for the British would still have to contend with an armed and highly motivated insurgent population.

Furthermore, there was no single political nerve center whose capture would spell certain victory. The Continental Congress moved from place to place, staying just out of reach of the British. During the course of the war, the British captured and for a time occupied every major port city—Boston, New York, Newport, Philadelphia, and Charleston—essential for receiving their constant caravan of supply ships. But capturing them brought no serious loss to the Americans, 95 percent of whom lived in the countryside.

England's delicate task was to restore the old governments, not to destroy an enemy country. Hence, the British generals were usually reluctant to ravage the countryside, confiscate food, or burn villages and towns. There were thirteen distinct political entities to capture, pacify, and then restore to the crown, and they stretched in a long line from New Hampshire to Georgia. Clearly a large land army was required for the job. Without the willingness to seize food from the locals, such an army needed hundreds of supply ships that could keep several months' worth of food in storage. Another ingredient of the British strategy was the untested assumption that many Americans remained loyal to the king and would come to their aid. Without substantial numbers of loyal subjects, the plan to restore old royal governments made no sense.

The overall British plan was a divide-and-conquer approach, focusing first on New York, the state judged to harbor the greatest number of loyal subjects. New York offered a geographic advantage as well: Control of the Hudson River would allow the British to isolate those troublesome New Englanders. British armies could descend from Canada and move up from New York City along the Hudson River into western Massachusetts. Squeezed between a naval blockade on the eastern coast and army raids in the west, Massachusetts could be driven to surrender. New Jersey and Pennsylvania would fall in line, the British thought, due to loyalist strength. Virginia was a problem, like Massachusetts, but the British were confident that the Carolinas would help them isolate and subdue Virginia.

Quebec, New York, and New Jersey

In late 1775, an American expedition was swiftly launched to capture the British cities Montreal and Quebec before British reinforcements could arrive. This offensive was a clear sign that the war was not purely a reaction to the invasion of

Massachusetts. The two cities were symbolic as well as strategic goals, having been sites of bloody contest in the French-British wars of the 1740s and 1750s (see chapter 6). A force of New York Continentals commanded by General Richard Montgomery took Montreal easily in September 1775 and then advanced on Quebec. Meanwhile, a second contingent of Continentals led by Colonel Benedict Arnold moved north through Maine to Quebec, a punishing trek through mountainous country drenched in late fall freezing rain with woefully inadequate supplies; many men died. Arnold's determination to get to Quebec was heroic, but in human costs the campaign was a tragedy. Arnold and Montgomery jointly attacked Quebec in December but failed to take the city (Map 7.1). Worse yet, they encountered smallpox, which killed more men than had been felled by the British.

The main action of the first year of war came not in Canada, however, but in New York, so crucial to England. In August 1776, some 45,000 British troops (including 8,000 German mercenaries, called Hessians) landed south of New York City, under the command of General Howe. General Washington had anticipated that New York would be Howe's target and had moved his army, numbering about 20,000, south from Massachusetts. The Battle of Long Island, in late August 1776, pitted the well-trained British redcoats (common slang referring to the red British uniforms) against a very green Continental army. Howe attacked, inflicting many casualties

MAP 7.1   The War in the North, 1775–1778 ▶
After the early battles in Massachusetts in 1775, rebel forces invaded Canada but failed to capture Quebec. A large British army landed in New York in August 1776, turning New Jersey into a continual site of battle in 1777 and 1778. Burgoyne arrived to secure Canada and made his attempt to pinch off New England along the Hudson River line, but he was stopped at Saratoga in 1777 in the key battle of the early war years.

READING THE MAP: Which general's troops traveled the farthest in each of these years: 1775, 1776, and 1777? How did the availability of water routes affect British and American strategy?

CONNECTIONS: Why did the French wait until early 1778 to join American forces against the British? What did they hope to gain from participating in the war?

FOR MORE HELP ANALYZING THIS MAP, see the map activity for this chapter in the Online Study Guide at bedfordstmartins.com/roark.

(1,500 dead and wounded) and spreading panic among the American soldiers, who fled under fire to the eastern edge of Long Island. Howe failed to press forward, however, perhaps re-membering the costly victory of Bunker Hill, and in the meantime Washington evacuated his troops to Manhattan Island in the dead of a foggy night.

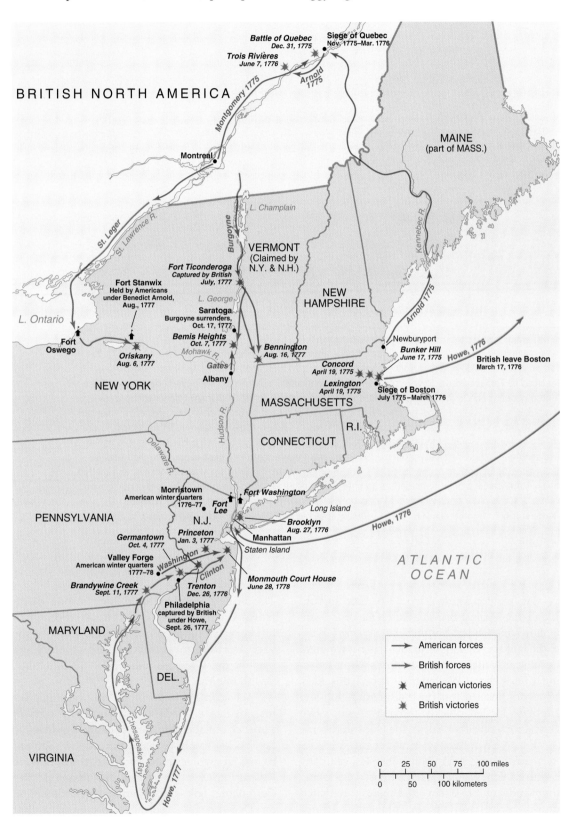

BRITISH NORTH AMERICA

Battle of Quebec
Dec. 31, 1775
Siege of Quebec
Nov. 1775–Mar. 1776
Trois Rivières
June 7, 1776

Montgomery 1775
Arnold 1775

MAINE
(part of MASS.)

Montreal

L. Champlain

Burgoyne

VERMONT
(Claimed by
N.Y. & N.H.)

Kennebec R.

Fort Ticonderoga
Captured by British
July, 1777

Fort Stanwix
Held by Americans
under Benedict Arnold,
Aug., 1777

L. George

NEW
HAMPSHIRE

Arnold 1775

St. Leger
St. Lawrence R.

L. Ontario

Saratoga
Burgoyne surrenders,
Oct. 17, 1777

Fort
Oswego

Oriskany
Aug. 6, 1777

Bemis Heights
Oct. 7, 1777

Mohawk R.

Gates

Bennington
Aug. 16, 1777

Newburyport
Bunker Hill
June 17, 1775

Howe, 1776

British leave Boston
March 17, 1776

Concord
April 19, 1775

NEW YORK

Albany

Lexington
April 19, 1775

Siege of Boston
July 1775–March 1776

MASSACHUSETTS

Hudson R.

R.I.

CONNECTICUT

Delaware R.

Morristown
American winter quarters
1776–77

Fort
Lee

Fort Washington

Long Island

PENNSYLVANIA

N.J.

Princeton
Jan. 3, 1777

Brooklyn
Aug. 27, 1776

Howe, 1776

Germantown
Oct. 4, 1777

Manhattan

Valley Forge
American winter quarters
1777–78

Washington

Staten Island

ATLANTIC
OCEAN

Clinton

Brandywine Creek
Sept. 11, 1777

Trenton
Dec. 26, 1776

Monmouth Court House
June 28, 1778

Philadelphia
captured by British
under Howe,
Sept. 26, 1777

MARYLAND

DEL.

Chesapeake Bay

VIRGINIA

Howe, 1777

→ American forces
→ British forces
✷ American victories
✷ British victories

0   25   50   75   100 miles
0   50   100 kilometers

"A View of the Attack against Fort Washington"
An eyewitness sketched this scene of British troops attacking Fort Washington in mid-November 1775. The fort, manned by 3,000 American soldiers, sat on well-secured high ground over the Hudson River; it was matched by Fort Lee on the New Jersey side, also a Continental stronghold. (The modern-day George Washington Bridge connects the approximate sites of the two forts.) A British lieutenant colonel at the scene wrote home that "we could not be masters of York Island or indeed secure of New York" while the Americans held the fort. Yet taking it was dangerous. The boatloads of soldiers could not land under protective cover of their own fire because of "the shortness of artillery," and the open boats and steep hillside denuded of leaves allowed American gunners easy pickings. "So smart was the fire that the Sailors abandoned their oars & hid themselves in the bottom of the Boats," the British officer wrote. The British prevailed, however, and the fort finally surrendered, prompting the officer to note, "This secures all York Island to us. We took a number of cannons, stores of all kinds with two Months provisions & likewise took the heart of the rebels."

The Phelps Stokes Collection, Miriam and Ira D. Wallach Division of Art, Prints, and Photographs, The New York Public Library. Astor, Lenox, and Tilden Foundations.

Washington knew it would be hard to hold Manhattan against British attack. One of his generals recommended burning the city; two-thirds of the buildings belonged to loyalists anyway, and burning it would prevent the British from housing troops there. Washington vetoed this idea, preferring instead to strip it of ammunition and supplies. He left quickly, moving north to two critical forts on either side of the Hudson River.

For two months, the armies engaged in limited skirmishing, but in November, Howe finally captured Fort Washington and Fort Lee, taking thousands of prisoners. Washington retreated quickly across New Jersey into Pennsylvania.

The British army followed him; at one point, Howe was only one hour behind Washington, but he rested his men for a day and widened the gap. As Howe moved through New Jersey, the Continental Congress, meeting in Philadelphia, fled to Baltimore.

Yet again, Howe unaccountably failed to press his advantage. Had he attacked Washington's army at Philadelphia, he probably would have taken the city. Instead he parked his German troops in winter quarters along the Delaware River. Perhaps he knew that many of the Continental soldiers' enlistment periods ended on December 31, so he felt confident that the Americans would not attack him. But he was wrong. On December 25 near midnight, as a storm of sleet and hail rained down, Washington stealthily moved his large army across the icy Delaware River and in the early morning made a quick capture of the unsuspecting German soldiers encamped at Trenton. This impressive victory did much to restore the sagging morale of the patriot side. For the next two weeks, Washington remained on the offensive, capturing supplies in a clever attack on British units at Princeton on January 3. Soon he was safe in Morristown, in northern New Jersey, where he settled his troops for the winter, a season when eighteenth-century armies in snowy climates generally stayed put, out of harm's way. Finally Washington had time enough to do as Howe had done, to administer mass smallpox inoculations and see his men through the abbreviated course of the disease. Future recruits would also face inoculation.

All in all, in the first year of declared war, the rebellious Americans had a few isolated moments to feel proud of but also much to worry about. The very inexperienced Continental army had barely hung on in the New York campaign. Washington had shown exceptional daring as well as admirable restraint, but what really saved the Americans may have been the repeated reluctance of the British to follow through militarily when they had the advantage.

The Home Front

Battlefields alone did not determine the outcome of the war. Struggles on the home front were equally important. In 1776, each community contained small numbers of highly committed people on both sides and far larger numbers who were uncertain about whether independence was worth a war. The contest for the allegiance of the many neutrals thus was a major factor, and both persuasion and force were used. Revolutionaries who took control of local government often used it to punish loyalists and intimidate neutrals. On their side, loyalists worked to reestablish British authority. The struggle to secure political allegiance was complicated greatly by the wartime instability of the economy. The creative financing of the fledgling government brought hardships as well as opportunities, forcing Americans to confront new manifestations of virtue and corruption.

Patriotism at the Local Level

Committees of correspondence, of public safety, and of inspection dominated the political landscape in patriot communities. These committees took on more than customary local governance; they enforced boycotts, picked army draftees, and policed suspected traitors. They sometimes invaded homes to search for contraband goods such as British tea or textiles.

Loyalists were dismayed by what seemed to them to be arbitrary power taken on by patriots. A man in Westchester, New York, described his response to intrusions by committees: "Choose your committee or suffer it to be chosen by a half

Rhode Island Regiment Flag

In the absence of an official American flag, regiments often commissioned their own symbolic banners. Almost certainly the elaborate stitchery and even the design work of this Rhode Island artillery company flag came from female hands wielding needle and thread. There were thus dozens, not just one, "Betsy Ross," the legendary Philadelphia woman credited with designing the prototype of the Stars and Stripes. A popular 1770s flag theme portrayed a coiled rattlesnake paired with the slogan "Don't Tread on Me." Such a flag conveyed a dire warning and a clear point of view about who had started the war in America: The rattler, uniquely American, was deadly only when aroused or provoked. This 1775 flag offers an unusual variant, using the more formal "do not" instead of "don't." The slogan endures today, showing up on state license plates and as lyrics in popular songs. Notice as well another nearly familiar motto: "In God We Hope." It precedes by almost a century the Civil War–era origins of the modern-day motto on U.S. coinage, "In God We Trust."

Collection of Mr. and Mrs. Boleslaw Mastai.

dozen fools in your neighborhood—open your doors to them—let them examine your tea-cannisters and molasses-jugs, and your wives' and daughters' petty coats—bow and cringe and tremble and quake—fall down and worship our sovereign lord the mob. . . . Should any pragmatical committee-gentleman come to my house and give himself airs, I shall show him the door, and if he does not soon take himself away, a good hickory cudgel shall teach him better manners." Oppressive or not, the local committees of safety and of inspection were rarely challenged. Their persuasive powers convinced many middle-of-the-road citizens that neutrality was not a comfortable option.

> Local committees of safety and of inspection convinced many middle-of-the-road citizens that neutrality was not a comfortable option.

Another group new to political life—white women—increasingly demonstrated a capacity for patriotism at the local level as wartime hardships dramatically altered their work routines. Like Abigail Adams on her Braintree farm, many wives with husbands away on military or political service took on masculine duties. Their increased competence to tend farms and make business decisions encouraged some to assert competence in political matters as well. Eliza Wilkinson managed a plantation on the South Carolina coast and talked revolutionary politics with her women friends. "None were greater politicians than the several knots of ladies who met together," she remarked, alert to the unusual turn female conversations had taken. "We commenced perfect statesmen."

Women from prominent Philadelphia families went a step beyond political talk to action. In 1780, they formed the Ladies Association, going door to door collecting a substantial sum of money to help support the Continental soldiers. A published broadside, "The Sentiments of an American Woman," defended their female patriotism. "The time is arrived to display the same sentiments which animated us at the beginning of the Revolution, when we renounced the use of teas [and] when our republican and laborious hands spun the flax."

The Loyalists

Between 20 and 30 percent of the American population remained openly loyal to the British monarchy in 1776, and another 20 to 40 percent could be described as neutral. Such a large population base could have sustained the British empire in America, if only the British army leaders had known how to use it (Map 7.2). In general, loyalists were people who still felt strong cultural and economic ties to the British empire and who believed that American prosperity and stability depended on British rule and on a government anchored by monarchy and aristocracy. Perhaps most of all, they feared democratic tyranny. Like Abigail Adams, they understood that dissolving the automatic respect that subjects had for their king could lead to a society in which hierarchy came unglued. Adams wel-

Joseph Brant
The Mohawk leader Thayendanegea, called Joseph Brant by Americans, had been educated in English ways at Eleazar Wheelock's New England school (which became Dartmouth College in 1769). In 1775, the thirty-four-year-old Brant traveled to England with another warrior to negotiate Mohawk support for the British. While there, he had his portrait painted by the English artist George Romney. Notice that Brant wears a metal gorget around his neck over his English shirt, along with Indian armbands, sash, and headdress. A gorget was a symbolic piece of armor, a shrunken version of a throatpiece from the feudal days of metal-clad knights. Many military men, both white and Indian, wore gorgets when they dressed formally for portraits—or for war.
National Gallery of Canada.

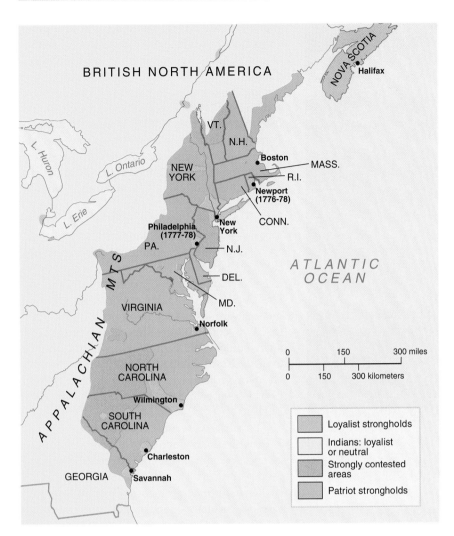

MAP 7.2 **Loyalist Strength and Rebel Support**
The exact number of loyalists can never be known. No one could have made an accurate count at the time; in addition, political allegiance often shifted with the winds. This map shows the regions of loyalist strength on which the British relied—most significantly the lower Hudson valley and the Carolina Piedmont.

READING THE MAP: Which forces were stronger, those loyal to Britain or those rebelling? (Consider size of areas, centers of population, and vital port locations.) What areas were contested? If the contested areas ultimately sided with the British, how would the balance of power change?

CONNECTIONS: Who was more likely to be a loyalist, and why? How many loyalists left the United States? Where did they go?

FOR MORE HELP ANALYZING THIS MAP, see the map activity for this chapter in the Online Study Guide at bedfordstmartins.com/roark.

comed this chance to identify tyranny in unequal power relations, as between men and women; loyalists feared it. Patriots seemed to them to be unscrupulous, violent, self-interested men who simply wanted power for themselves.

The most visible and dedicated loyalists (also called Tories by their enemies) were royal officials, not only top officeholders like Thomas Hutchinson in Massachusetts but also local judges and customs officers. Wealthy merchants with commercial ties to England gravitated toward loyalism to maintain the trade protections of navigation acts and the British navy. Conservative urban lawyers admired the stability of British law and order. Some colonists chose loyalism simply to oppose traditional adversaries. For example, backcountry farmers in the Carolinas tended to be loyalists out of resentment over the political and economic power of the lowlands gentry, who were largely on the

patriot side. And of course southern slaves had their own resentments against the white slave-owning class and looked to Britain for hope of freedom.

Many Indian tribes attempted to maintain neutrality at the start of the war, seeing the conflict as a civil war between English and American brothers. But eventually most were drawn in, many taking the British side. The powerful Iroquois confederacy divided: Mohawk, Cayuga, Seneca, and Onondaga peoples lined up with the British; the Oneida and Tuscarora aided the Americans. One young literate and Christianized Mohawk leader, Thayendanegea (known also by his English name, Joseph Brant), had worked closely with the British Indian agent William Johnson in the 1760s; Brant's sister Molly was for some years Johnson's domestic partner (an acknowledged common-law wife but without the formalities of British marriage).

Death of Jane McCrea

This 1804 painting by John Vanderlyn memorializes the martyr legend of Jane McCrea. McCrea lived with her patriot family in northern New York, and in July 1777 she fled to join her fiancé, a loyalist fighting with Burgoyne's army. She was murdered en route, allegedly by Iroquois allies of the British. The American general Horatio Gates sent Burgoyne an accusatory letter. "The miserable fate of Miss McCrea was particularly aggravated by her being dressed to meet her promised husband," Gates wrote, "but she met her murderers employed by you." Gates skillfully used the story of the vulnerable, innocent maiden dressed in alluring clothes as propaganda to inspire his soldiers' drive for victory at Saratoga. Vanderlyn's work, and other similar pictorial representations, emphasized McCrea's helplessness and sexuality. Had McCrea been a man, her flight would have been traitorous. Why this different treatment of a woman?

Wadsworth Atheneum, Hartford.

Johnson died in 1774, and Brant traveled from New York to England in 1775 to meet King George to complain about American settlers cheating his people of their land. "It is very hard when we have let the King's subjects have so much of our lands for so little value," he wrote, "they should want to cheat us in this manner of the small spots we have left for our women and children to live on. We are tired out in making complaints & getting no redress." Brant pledged Indian support for the king in exchange for protection from encroaching settlers. In western Pennsylvania and Ohio, parts of the Shawnee and Delaware tribes started out pro-American but shifted to the British side by 1779 in the face of repeated betrayals by American settlers and soldiers.

Pockets of loyalism thus existed everywhere—in the middle colonies, in the backcountry of the southern colonies, and out beyond the Appalachian Mountains in Indian country. Even New England towns at the heart of turmoil, like Concord, Massachusetts, had a small and increasingly silenced core of loyalists who refused to countenance armed revolution. Loyalists could even lurk within patriot families: On occasion, husbands and wives, fathers and sons disagreed completely on the war. (See "Documenting the American Promise," page 230.)

Loyalists were most vocal between 1774 and 1776, when the possibility of a full-scale rebellion against England was still uncertain. Loyalists used pamphlets, broadsides, and newspapers to challenge the emerging patriot side. In New York City, 547 loyalists signed and circulated a broadside titled "A Declaration of Dependence," in rebuttal to the congress's July 4 declaration, denouncing this "most unnatural, unprovoked Rebellion that ever disgraced the annals of Time."

Speeches delivered by ministers in the pulpit and others at open-air meetings bolstered the loyalist cause. At a backcountry rally in South Carolina in 1775, a loyalist warned listeners of the superior might of the British army and of the damage to trade that war would bring. Most effectively, he played on white farmers' resentment of coastal planters' wealth and political power: It is ironic, he said, that "the charge of our intending to enslave you should come oftenest from the mouths of those lawyers who in your southern provinces, at least, have long made you slaves to themselves."

Who Is a Traitor?

The rough treatment that loyalists experienced at the hands of the revolutionaries seemed to substantiate their worst fears. In June 1775, the First

Continental Congress passed a resolution declaring loyalists to be traitors. Over the next year, state laws defined as treason acts such as joining or provisioning the British army, saying or printing anything that undermined patriot morale, or discouraging men from enlisting in the Continental army. Punishments ranged from house arrest and suspension of voting privileges to confiscation of property and deportation. And sometimes self-appointed committees of Tory-hunters bypassed the judicial niceties and terrorized loyalists, raiding their houses or tarring and feathering them.

A question rarely asked in the heat of the revolutionary moment was whether the wives of loyalists were traitors as well. When loyalist families fled the country, property held in the name of the family patriarch was then confiscated. But what if the wife stayed? One Connecticut woman brought witnesses to testify that she was "a steady and true and faithful friend to the American states in opposition to her husband, who has been of quite a different character." In such cases, the court typically allowed the woman to keep one-third of the property, the amount she was due if widowed, and confiscated the rest. But even when the wife fled with her husband, was she necessarily a traitor? If he insisted, was she not obligated to go? Such questions came up in several lawsuits after the Revolution, when descendants of refugee loyalists sued to regain property that had entered the family through the mother's inheritance. In one well-publicized Massachusetts case in 1805, the outcome confirmed the traditional view of women as political blank slates. The American son of loyalist refugee Anna Martin recovered her property on the grounds that she had no independent will to be a loyalist.

Tarring and feathering, property confiscation, deportation, terrorism—to the loyalists, such denials of liberty of conscience and of freedom to own private property proved that democratic tyranny was more to be feared than the monarchical variety. A Boston loyalist, Mather Byles, aptly expressed this point: "They call me a brainless Tory, but tell me . . . which is better—to be ruled by one tyrant three thousand miles away, or by three thousand tyrants not a mile away?" Byles was soon sentenced to deportation.

Throughout the war, probably 7,000 to 8,000 loyalists fled to England, and 28,000 found closer haven in Canada. But many chose to remain in the new United States and tried to swing with the changing political winds. In some instances, that proved difficult. In New Jersey, for example, 3,000 Jerseyites felt protected (or scared) enough by the occupying British army in 1776 to swear an oath of allegiance to the king. But then General Howe drew back to New York City, leaving them to the mercy of local patriot committees. British strategy depended on using loyalists to hold occupied territory, but the New Jersey experience showed just how poorly that strategy was carried out.

Financial Instability and Corruption

Wars cost money—for arms and ammunition, for food and uniforms, for soldiers' pay. The Continental Congress printed money, but its value quickly deteriorated because the congress held no reserves of gold or silver to back the currency. In practice, it was worth only what buyers and sellers agreed it was worth. When the dollar eventually bottomed out at one-fortieth of its face value, a loaf of bread that once sold for two and a half cents then sold for a dollar. States too were printing their own paper money to pay for wartime expenses, further complicating the economy.

Soon the congress had to resort to other means to procure supplies and labor. One method was to borrow **hard money** (gold or silver coins, not paper) from wealthy men in exchange for certificates of debt (public securities) promising repayment with interest. The certificates of debt were similar to present-day **government bonds**. To pay soldiers, the congress issued land grant certificates, written promises of acreage usually located in frontier areas such as central Maine or eastern Ohio. Both the public securities and the land grant certificates quickly became forms of negotiable currency. A soldier with no cash, for example, could sell his land grant certificate to get food for his family. These certificates fluctuated in value, mainly depreciating.

Depreciating currency inevitably led to rising prices, as sellers compensated for the falling value of the money. The wartime economy of the late 1770s, with its unreliable currency and price inflation, was extremely demoralizing to Americans everywhere. In 1778, in an effort to impose some stability, local committees of public

> The wartime economy of the late 1770s, with its unreliable currency and price inflation, was extremely demoralizing to Americans everywhere.

Families Divide over the Revolution

Generalizing about rebels versus loyalists is a complex historical task. Sometimes categorizing by class, race, and geographical descriptors helps explain the split. But beyond economic interests or cultural politics, sometimes the loyalist-patriot split cut across families—and cut deeply. These documents reveal men and women divided with loved ones over wartime allegiance.

DOCUMENT 1
A Loyalist Wife Writes to Her Patriot Husband, 1778

Mary Gould Almy, wife and mother, lived in Newport, Rhode Island, an island town occupied by the British army in 1778. She was a Quaker and loyalist, in contrast to her Anglican husband, Benjamin Almy, who joined the American army. Mary wrote to Benjamin in September 1778, sending him her account of the month-long siege of the town by the French fleet and American troops.

September 02, 1778.   Once more, my dear Mr. Almy, I am permitted to write you. . . . I am to give you an account of what passes during the siege; but first let me tell you, it will be done with spirit, for my dislike to the nation that you call your friends, is the same as when you knew me, knowing there is no confidence to be placed in them. . . .

[The 1st day]: At nine in the morning a signal was made for a fleet in sight; at ten o'clock was discovered the number to be eleven large ships . . . the French fleet. . . .

With a distressed heart, I endeavor to comfort my poor children by saying, that they would not come in till morning, and then began to secure my papers and plate in the ground.

[The 9th day]: Heavens! what a scene of wretchedness before this once happy and flourishing island. . . . Neither sleep to my eyes, nor slumber to my eyelids, this night; but judge you, what preparation could I make, had I been endowed with as much presence of mind as ever woman was; six children hanging around me, the little girls crying out, "Mamma, will they kill us?" The boys endeavor to put on an air of manliness, and strive to assist, but slip up to the girls, in a whisper, "Who do you think will hurt you? Ain't your papa coming with them?" Indeed this cut me to the soul.

[The 18th day]: Still carting, still fortifying; your people encroaching nearer, throwing up new works every night. Our people beholding it every morning, with wonder and astonishment. And really, Mr. Almy, my curiosity was so great, as to wish to behold the entrenchment that I supposed you were behind; . . . Believe me, my dear friend, never was a poor soul more to be pitied, such different agitations as by turns took hold upon me. Wishing most ardently to call home my wanderer, at the same time, filled with resentment against those he calls his friends.

[The 24th day]: They kept up a smart firing till two o'clock, and then they began to bury the dead and bring in the wounded. . . . The horrors of that day will never be quite

out of my remembrance. I quitted company and hid myself to mourn in silence, for the wickedness of my country. Never was a heart more differently agitated than mine. Some of my good friends in the front of the battle here; and Heaven only knows how many of the other side. . . . At last I shut myself from the family, to implore Heaven to protect you, and keep you from imprisonment and death.

SOURCE: *Mrs. Almy's Journal: Siege of Newport, R.I., August 1778* (Newport, R.I.: Newport Historical Pub. Co., 1881, pp. 19–31). Available online in select college libraries in the electronic database *North American Women's Letters and Diaries*, Alexander Street Press.

DOCUMENT 2
Patriot Benjamin Franklin and Loyalist Son William Correspond, 1784

Benjamin Franklin was a member of the Continental Congress and a special envoy to France on behalf of the American rebels. Franklin's son, William, stayed loyal to the crown. William was Benjamin's illegitimate son; the mother's identity has never been known. Franklin raised him from infancy in his own family in Philadelphia and took William to England in 1757 for four years when he was a colonial agent for Pennsylvania. Thanks to his father, William acquired connections at court and in 1762, at age thirty-one, was appointed the royal governor of New Jersey, a post he held until 1776. When the war began, he was declared a traitor to the patriot cause and placed under house arrest. Father and son did not communicate for the next nine years, even when William was confined in a Connecticut prison for eight months. During this time, Benjamin took charge of William's oldest son, himself an illegitimate child born before William's legal marriage. In 1783 William returned to England. In 1784 he wrote to his father, then in Paris, asking for a meeting of reconciliation. He did not apologize for his loyalism.

Dear and honored Father,
Ever since the termination of the unhappy contest between Great Britain and America, I have been anxious to write to you, and to endeavor to revive that affectionate intercourse and connection which, until the commencement of the late troubles, had been the pride and happiness of my life. . . . There are narrow illiberal Minds in all Parties. In that which I took, and on whose Account I have so much suffered, there have not been wanting some who have insinuated that my Conduct has been founded on Collusion with you, that one of us might succeed whichever Party should prevail. Similar Collusions, they say, were known to have existed between Father and Son during the civil Wars in England and Scotland. The Falsity of such Insinuation in our Case you well know, and I am happy that I can with Confidence appeal not only to you but to my God, that I have uniformly acted from a strong Sense of what I conceived my Duty to my King, and Regard to my Country, required. If I have been mistaken, I cannot help it. It is an Error of Judgment what the maturest Reflection I am capable of cannot rectify; and I verily believe were the same Circumstances to occur again Tomorrow, my Conduct would be exactly similar to what it was heretofore.

The father replied:

Dear Son,
I received your letter of the 22nd past, and am glad to find that you desire to revive the affectionate Intercourse, that formerly existed between us. It will be very agreeable to me; indeed nothing has ever hurt me so much and affected me with such keen Sensations, as to find myself deserted in my old age by my only Son; and not only deserted, but to find him taking up Arms against me, in a Cause, wherein my good Fame, Fortune and Life were all at Stake. You conceived, you say, that your Duty to your King and regard for your Country requir'd this. I ought not to blame you for differing in Sentiment with me in Public Affairs. We are Men, all subject to errors. Our opinions are not in our own Power; they are form'd and govern'd much by Circumstances, that are often as inexplicable as they are irresistible. Your Situation was such that few would have censured your remaining Neuter, *tho' there are Natural Duties which preceded political ones, and cannot be extinguish'd by them.*

This is a disagreeable Subject. I drop it. And we will endeavor, as you propose mutually to forget what has happened relating to it, as well as we can. I send your Son over to pay his Duty to you. You will find him much improv'd. He is greatly esteem'd and belov'd in this Country, and will make his Way anywhere. It is my Desire, that he should study the Law, as the necessary Part of Knowledge for a public Man, and profitable if he should have occasion to practise it. . . . I shall be glad to see you when convenient, but would not have you come here at present. You may confide to your son the Family Affairs you wished to confer upon with me, for he is discreet. And I trust, that you will prudently avoid introducing him to Company, that it may be improper for him to be seen with. . . . Wishing you Health, and more happiness than it seems you have lately experienced, I remain your affectionate father,

B. Franklin

SOURCE: Courtesy of the American Philosophical Society, <www.amphilsoc.org>.

DOCUMENT 3
Two Oneida Brothers Confront Their Different Allegiances, 1779

Mary Jemison is the source for this story of two Oneida brothers on different sides of the war. Jemison was captured as a girl during the Seven Years' War and adopted into the Seneca tribe of western New York, where she remained for life. When she was eighty, her narrative was taken down and published. In this story, some Oneida warriors siding with the British capture two Indians guiding General Sullivan's 1779 campaign of terror in central New York. One of the conquerors recognizes his own brother.

Envy and revenge glared in the features of the conquering savage, as he advanced to his brother (the prisoner) in all the haughtiness of Indian pride, heightened by a sense of power, and addressed him in the following manner:

"Brother, you have merited death! The hatchet or the war-club shall finish your career! When I begged of you to follow me in the fortunes of war, you was deaf to my cries—you spurned my entreaties!

"Brother! You have merited death and shall have your deserts! When the rebels raised their hatchets to fight their good master, you sharpened your knife, you brightened your rifle and led on our foes to the fields of our fathers! You have merited

(continued)

(continued)

death and shall die by our hands! When those rebels had drove us from the fields of our fathers to seek out new homes, it was you who could dare to step forth as their pilot, and conduct them even to the doors of our wigwams, to butcher our children and put us to death! No crime can be greater! But though you have merited death and shall die on this spot, my hands shall not be stained in the blood of a brother! *Who will strike?*"

Little Beard, who was standing by, as soon as the speech was ended, struck the prisoner on the head with his tomahawk, and dispatched him at once.

SOURCE: James E. Seaver, *A narrative of the life of Mrs. Mary Jemison, who was taken by the Indians, in the year 1755, when only about twelve years of age, and has continued to reside amongst them to the present time* (1824), chapter VII, Project Gutenberg, <http://www.ibiblio.org/gutenberg/etext04/jemsn10.txt> (accessed January 14, 2004).

DOCUMENT 4
Petition from a Wife Deserted by a Tory Husband, 1783

Margaret Brisbane's husband James, of Charleston, South Carolina, was a loyalist throughout the war. The state legislature banished him and confiscated his estate; her petition of 1783 was an effort to recover some property to support herself and her children. Her petition was rejected, but three years later her sons recovered their father's property.

The Petition of Margerett Brisbane Humbly Sheweth

That she . . . intermarried with Mr. James Brisbane, formerly of this State; A Gentleman, whose political sentiments differed from those of his fellow Citizens, which, induced him to quit this Country, at a very early period, in this unhappy Contest. The part he has taken, has, unfortunately, drawn on him the heavy displeasure of the Legislature. . . . And your petitioner, apprehensive least this honorable House, under an Idea of Retaliation, or, from political motives, may think proper, to send away from this Country, the Unfortunate & distressed Wives & Children of those persons who have become so obnoxious, has taken the Liberty of requesting that she may be considered, not only in the view of a wife, but that of a Mother. . . .

[She] flatters herself with hopes, that when the House reflects on the weak and Defenceless Situation of woman & children, who are not the promoters of the War, nor, from their Sphere in Life, can possibly be disadvantageous to the contest; and whose Opinions seldom avail, and do not frequently operate on the Judgment of Men; when they recollect this, and are informed that her Sentiments *with regard to the present Contest* never coincided with, but were always contrary to her Husbands. . . . That they will take into Consideration the facts above set forth, and extend its benevolence towards her, by permitting her to remain in this Country . . . and by granting some part of that property, which she once considered, as, in some degree, her own, and ultimately, as the inheritance of her now destitute Children.

SOURCE: Cynthia A. Kierner, *Southern Women in Revolution, 1776–1800: Personal and Political Narratives* (Columbia: University of South Carolina Press, 1998), 174–75.

QUESTIONS FOR ANALYSIS AND DEBATE

1. Why is Mary Almy "cut to the soul" by the remarks of her sons? She is frightened for her husband's safety. Is she also angry with him? Why or why not?

2. What does Benjamin Franklin mean by the emphasized words *"Natural Duties"*? Do you think Franklin really believed his son was entitled to his own political opinions on the Revolutionary War? What factors help explain why William remained loyal to the crown?

3. Why does the Oneida warrior believe his brother merits death?

4. Is Margaret Brisbane's claim of allegiance to the American cause compelling? Can you imagine what a more successful petition might contain?

---

safety began to fix prices on goods such as flour, bread, and other essentials for short periods. Inevitably, some Americans turned this unstable situation to their advantage. Money that fell fast in value needed to be spent quickly; being in debt was suddenly advantageous because the debt could be repaid in devalued currency. A brisk black market sprang up in prohibited luxury imports, such as tea, sugar, textiles, and wines, even though these items came from Britain. A New Hampshire delegate to the congress denounced the extravagance that flew in the face of the virtuous homespun association agreements of just a few years before: "We are a crooked and perverse generation, longing for the fineries and follies of those Egyptian task masters from whom we have so lately freed ourselves."

The Campaigns of 1777–1779: The North and West

In early 1777, the Continental army had a bleak road ahead. General Washington had shown considerable skill in avoiding outright defeat, but the minor victories in New Jersey lent only faint optimism to the American side. The British moved large numbers of soldiers into Quebec, readying their plan to isolate New England from the rest of the colonies by taking control of the Hudson River. Their attack moving down from the north drew the American Continental army up into central New York, polarizing Indian tribes of the Iroquois nation and turning the Mohawk Valley into a bloody war zone. By 1779, tribes in western New York and in Indian country in the Ohio Valley were fully involved in the Revolutionary War; most sided with the British and against the Americans. The Americans had some success in this period, such as the victory at Saratoga, but the involvement of Indians and the continuing strength of the British forced the American government to look toward France for help.

Burgoyne's Army and the Battle of Saratoga

In 1777, General John Burgoyne assumed command of a British army of 7,800 soldiers in Canada and began the northern squeeze on the Hudson River valley. His goal was to capture Albany, a town 150 miles north of New York City near the intersection of the Hudson and Mohawk rivers (see Map 7.1). Traveling with Burgoyne and his soldiers were a thousand assorted "camp followers" (cooks, laundresses, musicians) and some 400 Indian warriors and scouts. This large force did not travel light, requiring food supplies not only for 9,200 people but also for the more than 400 horses needed to haul heavy artillery. Burgoyne also carted thirty trunks of personal belongings,  including fine wines and elegant clothing.

In July, Burgoyne captured Fort Ticonderoga with ease. Some 3,000 American troops stationed there spotted the approaching British and, low on food and supplies, abandoned the fort without a fight. The British continued to move south, but the large army moved slowly on primitive roads through heavily forested land. Burgoyne

A Soldier's Canteen
This wooden canteen belonged to Noah Allen, whose name and regiment number are carved into the side. Allen was from the Sixth Continental Regiment from Massachusetts. Almost no piece of equipment surpassed in importance the soldier's canteen.
Fort Ticonderoga Museum.

lost a month hacking his way down the road, and meanwhile his supply lines back to Canada were severely stretched. Soldiers sent out to forage for food were beaten back by local militia units.

The logical second step in isolating New England should have been to advance troops up the Hudson from New York City to meet Burgoyne. American surveillance indicated that General Howe in Manhattan was readying his men for a major move in August 1777. George Washington, watching from New Jersey, was astonished to see Howe's men sail south; Howe had decided to try to capture Philadelphia.

The third prong of the British strategy involved bringing troops—regular British soldiers along with German mercenary soldiers hired by England—from Montreal to the Great Lakes and thence east along the Mohawk River in central New York. The 800 troops were joined by some 800 Mohawks and Senecas of the Iroquois confederacy, and these in turn were aided by loyalists native to the Mohawk Valley who had taken up arms for the king. The British believed that a large enclave of Palatine Germans living in the Mohawk Valley would be heavily loyalist, so they expected little trouble getting to Albany. These Germans were descendants of some 10,000 migrants who came to New York around 1710 from the Palatinate, a region of Germany near the Rhine River.

A hundred miles west of their goal, in August 1777, the British encountered American Continental army soldiers at Fort Stanwix, reinforced by hundreds of Palatine German militiamen and their Oneida Indian allies. Led by the Mohawk Joseph Brant, the Senecas and Mohawks ambushed the Germans and the Oneidas in a narrow ravine called Oriskany and inflicted extremely heavy losses: 500 out of 800 men on the American side were killed or mortally wounded. On Brant's side, about 90 warriors were killed. But Fort Stanwix held back the

British regulars and Seneca and eventually sent them into retreat (see Map 7.1). The Oriskany and Fort Stanwix battles were very deadly; they were also complexly multiethnic, pitting Indians against Indians, German Americans against German mercenaries, New York patriots against neighboring New York loyalists, and English Americans against the British.

The British retreat at Fort Stanwix deprived General Burgoyne of the additional troops he expected to carry out his Hudson River strategy. Camped at a small village called Saratoga, he was isolated with food supplies dwindling and men deserting. His adversary at Albany, General Horatio Gates, began moving 7,000 Continental soldiers toward him. Burgoyne decided to attack first because every day his army was weakening. In this first attack, the British prevailed, but at the great cost of 600 dead or wounded redcoats. Three weeks later, an American attack on Burgoyne's forces at Saratoga cost the British another 600 men and most of their cannons. Burgoyne finally surrendered to the American forces at Saratoga on October 17, 1777.

Americans on the side of the rebellion were jubilant. After Saratoga, the first decisive victory for the Continental army, a popular dance called "General Burgoyne's Surrender" swept through the country, and bookies in the major cities set odds at five to one that the war would be won in six months.

General Howe, meanwhile, had succeeded in occupying Philadelphia in September 1777. Figuring that the Saratoga loss was balanced by the capture of Philadelphia, the British government proposed a negotiated settlement—not including independence—to end the war. The American side refused.

American optimism in the winter of 1777–78 was not well founded. Spirits ran high, but supplies of arms and food ran precariously low. Washington moved his troops into winter quarters at Valley Forge, a day's march west of occupied Philadelphia, where they stayed from December to June. (See "American Places,"

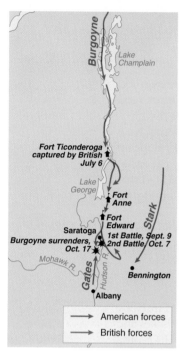

The Battle of Saratoga, 1777

Burgoyne

Lake Champlain

Fort Ticonderoga captured by British July 6

Lake George

Fort Anne

Fort Edward

Saratoga
Burgoyne surrenders, Oct. 17

1st Battle, Sept. 9
2nd Battle, Oct. 7

Mohawk R.

Bennington

Stark

Hudson R.

Gates

Albany

→ American forces
→ British forces

> For native tribes, the war was not about taxation, representation, or monarchical rule; it was about independence, freedom, and land.

page 235.) Quartered in drafty huts, the men lacked blankets, boots, and stockings. Washington complained to the congress that nearly 3,000 of his men were "unfit for duty because they are bare foot and otherwise naked"; without blankets, large numbers were forced to "set up all Night by fires, instead of taking comfortable rest in a natural way." Food was also scarce. Local farms had produced adequate grain that year, but Washington was sure that the farmers were selling it to the British, who could pay with the king's silver.

Evidence of corruption and profiteering was abundant. Army suppliers too often provided defective food, clothing, and gunpowder. Washington's men unfolded a shipment of blankets only to discover that they were a quarter of their customary size. Teamsters who hauled barrels of preserved salted meat might drain out the brine to lighten their load and then refill the barrels later, allowing the meat to rot in transit. Selfishness and greed seemed to infect the American side. As one Continental officer said, "The people at home are destroying the Army by their conduct much faster than Howe and all his army can possibly do by fighting us."

The War in the West: Indian Country

Burgoyne's defeat in the fall of 1777 and Washington's long stay at Valley Forge up to June 1778 might suggest that the war paused for a time; and it did, on the Atlantic coast. But in the interior western areas—the Mohawk Valley, the Ohio Valley, and Kentucky—the war of Indians against the American pro-independence side was heating up. For native tribes, the war was not about taxation, representation, or monarchical rule; it was about independence, freedom, and land.

The ambush and slaughter at Oriskany in August 1777 marked the beginning of three years of near-constant terror for all the inhabitants of the Mohawk Valley. Loyalists and Indians together engaged in many small raids on farms and villages throughout the spring and summer of 1778, killing and capturing the residents. In retaliation, American militiamen destroyed the Indian village of Joseph Brant, called Onaquaga, thought to be the headquarters for many hundreds of Iroquoian warriors. Most of the village residents fled the day before the at-

Valley Forge National Historical Park, Valley Forge, Pennsylvania

From December 1777 to June 1778, 12,000 Continental army soldiers camped at Valley Forge, 18 miles northwest of British-occupied Philadelphia. The soldiers felled trees and built a thousand rough huts, like the one pictured here, for winter quarters. Wood for huts and firewood was plentiful, but nothing else was. Severe hardship afflicted the army, making Valley Forge famous to future generations as a glorious symbol of American sacrifice and patriotic determination. At the time it did not seem at all glorious. Washington had to conceal his troops' hardships for fear of letting the British know how weakened his army really was.

Food was always inadequate. Standard rations dwindled for a time to "firecake," a tasteless pancake made of flour and water. In one week in February there were no food rations at all. Clothing was even harder to procure, and men went barefoot and in rags in the cold winter months. Disease flourished. Some 2,000 men died of dysentery, pneumonia, and other contagious illnesses. Not everyone could cope with such sacrifice. Official records show that 8 or 10 men deserted every day, totaling 2,000 desertions over the six months. Yet 8,000 men did not desert or die; they stayed and suffered, out of dedication to the cause.

Spring finally came, as did Baron Friedrich von Steuben, a Prussian general who arrived from Europe to begin formal training of the troops. American officers did not inspire their men to obey; the baron sharply corrected that. He inaugurated constant drill parades, overseeing the men himself, gaining their respect through his competence and authority. He worked a near miracle, transforming both officers and men into a model of military discipline. Before the baron's arrival, ran a common joke, an enlisted man might call his commanding officer "a Chuckleheaded Son of a bitch" if he disliked an order. After training by von Steuben, the soldier would instead say "Damn your orders sir." Clearly, neither the Prussian baron nor the severe winter drained all the spunk out of the American recruits.

Valley Forge was preserved as a historical park in 1893 and became part of the National Park Service in 1977. Visitors can tour Washington's headquarters and several re-created log huts. If their visit is well timed, they can experience the snow and bone-chilling cold that created misery in February 1778. The Park Service wisely does not try to re-create all of the harsh conditions of the camp, but it provides ample information to help visitors tap their own imagination.

FOR WEB LINKS RELATED TO THIS SITE AND OTHER AMERICAN PLACES, see "PlaceLinks" at bedfordstmartins.com/roark.

Reenactors in Winter at Valley Forge
Courtesy Valley Forge National Historical Park.

tack, but some children in hiding were killed. A month later, in November, Brant's warriors attacked the town of Cherry Valley, killing 32 townspeople and 16 soldiers and taking 71 people captive.

The following summer, General Washington authorized a campaign to wreak "total destruction and devastation" on all the Iroquoian villages of central New York. Some 4,500 Continental army troops under the command of General John Sullivan carried out a deliberate campaign of terror in late summer and fall of 1779. Forty Indian towns met with total obliteration; the soldiers looted and torched the dwellings, then burned cornfields and fruit orchards. In a few towns, women and children were slaughtered; but in most, the inhabitants managed to escape, fleeing to the British at Fort Niagara. Thousands of Indian refugees, sick and starving, camped around the fort in one of the most miserable winters on record.

Much farther to the west, beyond Fort Pitt, another complex story unfolded, of alliances and betrayals between American militiamen and Indians. Some 150,000 native peoples lived between the Appalachian Mountains and the Mississippi River. By 1779, it was clear to the multitudes of Indian tribes that neutrality was not a viable option. Most sided with the British, who maintained a major garrison at Fort Detroit. But a portion of the Shawnee and Delaware tribes for a time actively sought peace with the Americans.

In mid-1778, a Delaware leader named White Eyes negotiated a treaty with the Americans at Fort Pitt, pledging Indian support in the war in exchange for supplies and trade goods. But supplies and goods were not forthcoming, and escalating violence began to undermine the agreement. That fall, American soldiers in Ohio captured and killed two friendly Shawnee chiefs, Cornstalk and Red Hawk. The Continental Congress hastened to apologize, as did the governors of Pennsylvania and Virginia, but the soldiers who stood trial for the murders were acquitted. Two months later, White Eyes, still nominally an ally and informant for the Americans, died under mysterious circumstances, almost certainly murdered by militiamen. Despite Indian professions of support, American military leaders repeatedly had trouble honoring distinctions between allied and enemy Indians.

The frontier war zone extended from western North Carolina into the area later called Tennessee, where in 1779 militias attacked Cherokee settlements, destroying thirty-six villages and burning fields and livestock. In Kentucky, Indian raiders from north of the Ohio River who had allied with the British stationed at Fort Detroit repeatedly attacked white settlements, such as Boonesborough, that had sprouted up in defiance of the Proclamation of 1763 (Map 7.3; see also chapter 6). In retaliation, a young Virginian, George Rogers Clark, led Kentucky militiamen into what is now Illinois, his men attacking and taking the British (formerly French) fort at Kaskaskia. Clark's men wore hunting shirts and breech cloths, native clothing, but their native dress was not a sign of solidarity with Indians. When they attacked British-held Fort Vincennes, in 1779, Clark's troops tomahawked Indian captives and threw their still-live bodies in the river in a gory spectacle witnessed by the redcoats. "To excel them in barbarity is the only way to make war upon Indians," Clark announced. And, he might have added, a good way to terrorize the British soldiers as well.

By 1780, very few Indians remained neutral. Clark's and other violent raids drove Indians into the hills, into starvation, and into the arms of the British at Detroit and Niagara, or into the arms of the Spanish, who still held much of the land west of the Mississippi River. Said one officer on the Sullivan campaign, "Their nests are destroyed but the birds are still on the wing." For those who stayed near their native lands, chaos and confusion prevailed.

Rare as it was, Indian support for the American side occasionally emerged out of a strategic sense that the Americans were unstoppable in their westward pressure and that it was better to work out an alliance than to lose in a war. But American treatment of even friendly Indians showed that there really was no winning strategy to be had for the Indians.

The French Alliance

On their own, the Americans could not have defeated England, and the western pressure from hostile Indians magnified their task. Essential help arrived as a result of the victory at Saratoga, which convinced the French to enter the war; a formal alliance was signed in February 1778. France recognized the United States as an independent nation and promised full military and commercial support throughout the war. Most crucial was the French navy, which could chal-

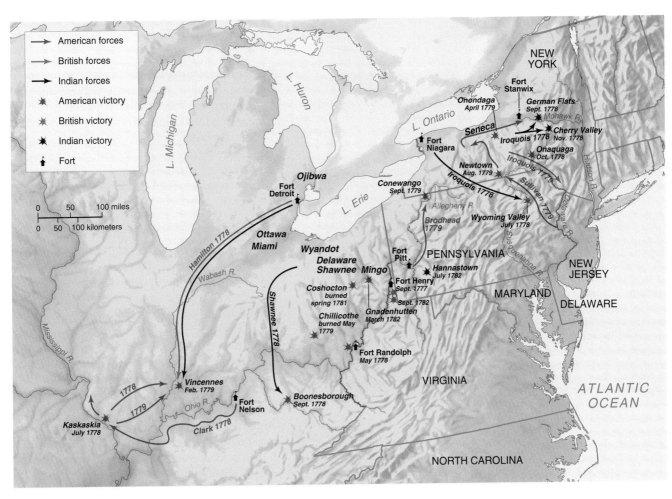

MAP 7.3 The War in the West, 1778–1782
The American Revolution involved many Indian tribes, most of them supporting the British side. Iroquois with British aid attacked American towns in New York's Mohawk Valley throughout 1778. In 1779 the Continental army marched on 40 Iroquois villages in central New York and destroyed them. Shawnee and Delaware to the west of Fort Pitt tangled with American militia units in 1779, while tribes supported by the British at Fort Detroit conducted raids on Kentucky settlers who hit back with raids of their own. George Rogers Clark led Kentucky militiamen against Indians in the Illinois region. Sporadic fighting continued in the West through 1782, ending with Indian attacks on Hannastown, Pennsylvania, and Fort Henry on the Ohio River. By the late 1780s, occasional fighting resumed, sparked by American settlers pressing west onto Indian lands.

lenge England's transatlantic shipment of supplies and troops.

Although France had been waiting for a promising American victory to justify a formal declaration of war, since 1776 the French had been providing aid to the Americans in the form of cannons, muskets, gunpowder, and highly trained military advisers. Still, monarchical France was understandably cautious about endorsing a democratic revolution attacking the principles of kingship. For France, the main attraction of an alliance was the opportunity it pro-

vided to defeat England, its archrival. A victory would also open pathways to trade and perhaps result in France acquiring the coveted British West Indies. Even American defeat would not be a full disaster for France if the war lasted many years and drained England of men and money.

French support materialized slowly. The navy arrived off the coast of Virginia in July 1778 but then went south to the West

> On their own, the Americans could not have defeated England. The victory at Saratoga convinced the French to enter the war.

Pulpit of the Reverend Samuel Cooper

From this pulpit in the Brattle Street Congregational Church in Boston, the Reverend Samuel Cooper departed from his customary apolitical sermons one day in 1778 to announce that a letter from his friend Benjamin Franklin in Paris declared that France had officially entered the war on the American side. This long-awaited news was very welcome to his congregation. Cooper had deep sympathies with the American side. Like many Bostonians, he had fled his city while the British army occupied it, returning when they left in 1776. Cooper's church had been taken over as a temporary barracks for British soldiers. The elegant mahogany pulpit was spared any defacement by the redcoats because it was covered in a wooden casing.
Courtesy of the Society for the Preservation of New England Antiquities.

Indies to defend the French sugar-producing islands. French help would prove indispensable to the American victory, but the alliance's first months brought no dramatic victories, and some Americans grumbled that the partnership would prove worthless.

The Southern Strategy and the End of the War

When France joined the war, some British officials wondered whether the fight was worth continuing. A troop commander, arguing for an immediate negotiated settlement, shrewdly observed that "we are far from an anticipated peace, because the bitterness of the rebels is too widespread, and in regions where we are masters the rebellious spirit is still in them. The land is too large, and there are too many people. The more land we win, the weaker our army gets in the field." The commander of the British navy argued for abandoning the war, and even Lord

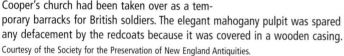

White southerners feared that all-out war might unleash violence from slaves seizing the moment to claim freedom.

North, the prime minister, agreed. But the king was determined to crush the rebellion, and he encouraged a new strategy for victory focusing on the southern colonies, thought to be more persuadably loyalist. It was a brilliant but desperate plan, and ultimately unsuccessful, as the king learned that southern colonists were not all that loyal and in fact were willing to engage in guerrilla warfare against the British. The southern strategy thus led to a British defeat at Yorktown and the end of the war.

Georgia and South Carolina

The new strategy called for British forces to abandon New England and focus on the South. The southern region had valuable crops—tobacco, rice, and indigo—worth keeping under the British flag. Also, the large slave population was a powerful destabilizing factor from which the British hoped to benefit. White southerners feared that all-out war might unleash violence from slaves seizing the moment to claim freedom. Living in Georgia and the Carolinas were large numbers of loyalists likely to support Britain's war effort. The British hoped to recapture the southern colonies one by one, restore the loyalists to power, and then move north to the more problematic middle colonies, saving prickly New England for last.

Georgia, the first target, fell at the end of December 1778 (Map 7.4). A small army of British soldiers occupied Savannah and Augusta, and a new royal governor and loyalist assembly were quickly installed. Taking Georgia was easy because the bulk of the Continental army was in New York and New Jersey, keeping an eye on General Henry Clinton, Howe's replacement as commander in chief, and the French were in the West Indies. The British in Georgia quickly organized twenty loyal militia units, and 1,400 Georgians swore an oath of allegiance to the king. So far, the southern strategy looked as if it might work.

The next target was South Carolina. General Clinton moved British troops south from New York by sea, while the Continental army raised 2,500 soldiers from southern states and 2,000 local militiamen and put them in Charleston to defend it. For five weeks in early 1780, the British laid siege to the city, which finally surrendered in mid-May 1780, sending 3,300 American soldiers, a tremendous loss, into British captivity. Again, the king's new strategy seemed to be on target.

Clinton returned to New York, leaving the task of pacifying the rest of South Carolina to General Charles Cornwallis and 4,000 troops. The boldest of all the British generals in the war for America, Lord Cornwallis quickly moved into action. He chased out the remaining Continental army units and established military control of South Carolina by midsummer 1780. He purged rebels from government office and disarmed potential rebel militias. The export of South Carolina's main crop, rice, resumed, and as in Georgia, pardons were offered to Carolinians who swore loyalty oaths to the crown and then proved their loyalty by taking up arms for the British.

In August 1780, the Continental army was ready to strike back at Cornwallis. General Gates, the hero of the Battle of Saratoga, arrived in South Carolina with more than 3,000 troops, some of them experienced army units and others militiamen with little battlefield experience. They met Cornwallis's army at Camden, South Carolina, on August 16 (see Map 7.4). Gates put the militiamen into the center of the battle. At the sight of the approaching enemy cavalry, they panicked; men threw down unfired muskets and ran. When regiment leaders tried to regroup the next day, only 700 showed up; the rest were dead, captured, or still in flight. Camden was a devastating defeat; prospects seemed very grim for the Americans.

Britain's southern strategy succeeded in 1780 in part because of information about American troop movements secretly passed on to the British by an American traitor: Benedict Arnold. The hero of several American battles, Arnold was a brilliant military talent but also a deeply insecure man who never felt he got his due, in either honor or financial reward. Sometime in 1779, he opened secret negotiations

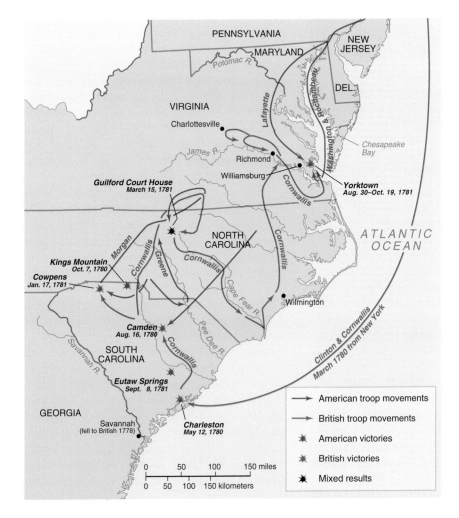

MAP 7.4   The War in the South, 1780–1781

After taking Charleston in May 1780, the British advanced into South Carolina and the foothill region of North Carolina, leaving a bloody civil war in their wake. When the American general Horatio Gates and his men fumbled and fled from the humiliating Battle of Camden, Gates was replaced by General Nathaniel Greene and General Daniel Morgan, who pulled off major successes at King's Mountain and Cowpens. The British general Cornwallis then moved north and invaded Virginia but was bottled up and finally overpowered at Yorktown in the fall of 1781.

Benedict Arnold
This portrait shows Benedict Arnold in 1776, when he was the hero of the Quebec campaign. Probably the final straw for Arnold came when he failed to earn a promotion while men he considered inferior were elevated to higher rank.

Anne S. K. Brown Military Collection, Providence, R.I.

of turncoat southern Tories, panic like that of the terrified soldiers at Camden. But instead of symbolizing all that was troubling about the American side of the war, the treachery of Arnold was publically and ritually denounced—in parades, broadsides, and cartoons—in a kind of displacement of the anxieties of the moment. Vilifying Arnold allowed Americans to stake out a wide distance between themselves and dastardly conduct. It inspired a renewal of patriotism at a particularly low moment.

The Other Southern War: Guerrillas

Shock over Gates's defeat at Camden and Arnold's treason revitalized rebel support in western South Carolina, an area that Cornwallis believed to be pacified and loyal. The backcountry of the South soon became the site of guerrilla warfare. In hit-and-run attacks, both sides burned and ravaged not only opponents' property but the property of anyone claiming to be neutral. Loyalist militia units organized by the British were met by fierce rebel militia units who figured they had little to lose. In South Carolina, some six thousand men became active partisan fighters, and they entered into at least twenty-six engagements with loyalist units. Some were classic battles, but on other occasions the fighters were more like bandits than soldiers. Guerrilla warfare soon spread to Georgia and North Carolina. Both sides committed murders and atrocities and plundered property, clear deviations from standard military practice.

The success of Britain's southern strategy depended on sufficient loyalist strength to hold reconquered territory as Cornwallis's army moved north. The backcountry guerrilla war proved that loyalist support was far weaker than the British had supposed. The Americans won few major battles in the South, but they ultimately succeeded by harassing the British forces and thus preventing them from foraging for food. Cornwallis moved into North Carolina in the fall of 1780, not because he thought South Carolina was secure—it was not—but because the North Carolinians were supplying the South Carolina rebels with arms and men (see Map 7.4). Then news of a massacre on October 7 of loyalist units in western South Carolina at King's Mountain, at the hands of 1,400 frontier riflemen, sent him hurrying back. The British were stretched too thin to hold on to even two of their onetime colonies.

with General Clinton in New York, trading information for money and hinting that he could deliver far more of value. When General Washington made him commander of West Point, a new fort sixty miles north of New York City on the Hudson River, Arnold's plan crystallized. West Point controlled the Hudson; its easy capture by the British might well have meant victory in the war.

Arnold's plot to sell a West Point victory to the British was foiled when Americans captured the man carrying plans of the fort's defense from Arnold to Clinton. News of Arnold's treason created shock waves. Arnold represented all of the patriots' worst fears about themselves: greedy self-interest like that of the war profiteers, the unprincipled abandonment of war aims like that

A French Officer's View of the French Blockade
Pierre Joseph Jeunot, a young naval officer, sketched the lines of British and French ships shortly before they clashed at the Battle of the Chesapeake Capes, at the entrance to Chesapeake Bay on September 5, 1781. More than two dozen French ships sealed the bay and the York River, preventing the escape of Cornwallis's army at Yorktown. Jeunot showed some ships in action, totally obscured by the impenetrable smoke of the fired cannons.
The Huntington Library & Arts Collections, San Marino, California.

Surrender at Yorktown

In early 1781, the war was going very badly for the British. Their defeat at King's Mountain was quickly followed by a second major defeat, the Battle of Cowpens in South Carolina in January 1781, where local militia units backed by Continental soldiers bested the British army. Meanwhile, Cornwallis had pushed further north into Virginia, where he captured Williamsburg in June and sent a raiding party to Charlottesville, the town hosting Virginia's revolutionary government. The British seized members of the Virginia assembly but failed to capture Governor Thomas Jefferson, who escaped the soldiers by a mere ten minutes. (More than a dozen of Jefferson's slaves chose this moment to seek refuge with the British.) These minor victories allowed Cornwallis to imagine that he was gaining the upper hand in Virginia. On instructions from General Henry Clinton in New York City,

Cornwallis took over Yorktown, Virginia, near Chesapeake Bay, to prepare for the arrival of British ships.

What tipped the balance of power in the war was the arrival, finally, of French military support. A large French army under the command of the Comte de Rochambeau had joined General Washington in Rhode Island in mid-1780. News that a fleet of warships had sailed from France in the spring of 1781 set in motion Washington's plan to defeat the British. The fleet, commanded by the Comte de Grasse, was bound for the Chesapeake Bay, so Washington and Rochambeau fixed their attention on Virginia. Bypassing New York (where Clinton had been expecting an attack), thousands of American and French soldiers headed south in August 1781, traveling on four separate roads to confuse the British.

When British navy ships arrived to defend the Chesapeake, they found that the French navy had already taken control of it. A five-day naval battle in early September sent the British ships limping away and left the French navy in clear control of the Virginia and North Carolina coasts. This proved to be the decisive factor in ending the war, because it eliminated the possibility of reinforcements for Cornwallis's army, dug in at Yorktown, and made rescue by the British navy impossible.

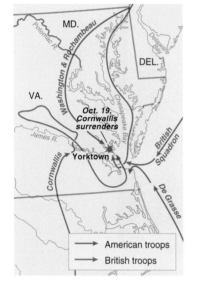

Siege of Yorktown, 1781

On land, General Cornwallis and his 7,500 troops faced a combined French and American army numbering over 16,000. For twelve days, the Americans and French bombarded the British fortifications at Yorktown; Cornwallis ran low on food and ammunition. An American observer keeping a diary noted that "the enemy, from want of forage, are killing off their horses in great numbers. Six or seven hundred of these valuable animals have been killed, and their carcasses are almost continually floating down the river." Realizing escape was impossible, Cornwallis signaled his intention to surrender. On October 19, 1781, he formally capitulated.

What began as a promising southern strategy in 1778 turned into a discouraging defeat by 1781. British attacks in the South had energized American resistance, as did the timely exposure of Benedict Arnold's treason. The arrival of the French fleet sealed the fate of Cornwallis at Yorktown, and the military war quickly came to a halt.

The Losers and the Winners

The surrender at Yorktown proved to be the end of the war with England, but it took some time for the principal combatants to realize that. Frontier areas in Kentucky, Ohio, and Illinois still blazed with battles and sieges. The peace treaty was nearly two years in the making, and in the meantime both American and British armies remained in the field in case the treaty fell through. King George clung to the idea of pursuing the war, but sentiment favoring a formal peace was growing in Parliament. The war had become

> The first article of the peace treaty went to the heart of the matter: "His Britannic Majesty acknowledges the said United States to be free Sovereign and independent States."

unpopular among the British citizenry in general, and support for it dwindled until finally the king had to realize it was over.

It took six months for the American commissioners—Benjamin Franklin, John Adams, and John Jay of New York—and their British and French counterparts to negotiate the three-way settlement in Paris. In November 1782, eighty-two articles of peace were agreed to. The first article went to the heart of the matter: "His Britannic Majesty acknowledges the said United States to be free Sovereign and independent States." Other articles set the western boundary of the new country at the Mississippi River and guaranteed that creditors on both sides could collect debts owed them in sterling money, a provision especially important to British merchants. England agreed to withdraw its troops quickly; more than a decade later, this promise still had not been fully kept. The final, official peace treaty—the Treaty of Paris—was signed on September 2, 1783.

Like the Treaty of Paris at the end of the Seven Years' War, this Treaty of Paris failed to recognize the Indians as players in the conflict. As one American told the Shawnee people, "Your Fathers the English have made Peace with us for themselves, but forgot you their Children, who Fought with them, and neglected you like Bastards." Indian lands were assigned to the victors as though they were uninhabited. Some Indian refugees fled west into present-day Missouri and Arkansas, and others, such as Joseph Brant's Mohawks, relocated to Canada. But significant numbers remained within the new United States, occupying their traditional homelands in areas west and north of the Ohio River. For them, the Treaty of 1783 brought no peace at all; their longer war against the Americans would extend at least until 1795 and for some, to 1813. Their ally, Britain, conceded defeat, but the Indians did not.

When the treaty was finally signed, the British began their evacuation of New York, Charleston, and Savannah, a process complicated by the sheer numbers involved—soldiers, fearful loyalists, and runaway slaves by the thousands. In New York City, more than 27,000 soldiers and 30,000 loyalists sailed on hundreds of ships for England in late fall 1783. In a final act of mischief, on the November day when the last ships left, the losing side raised the British flag at the southern tip of Manhattan, cut away the ropes used to hoist it, and greased the flagpole.

"The Ballance of Power," 1780
This cartoon was published in England soon after Spain and the Netherlands declared an alliance with France to support the war in America. On the left, Britannia, a female figure representing Great Britain, cannot be moved by all the lightweights combined on the right side of the scale. France wears a ruffled shirt, Spain has a feather in his hat, and a Dutch boy has just hopped on, saying, "I'll do anything for money." The forlorn Indian maiden, the standard icon representing America in the eighteenth century, sits on the scale, head in hand, wailing, "My Ingratitude is Justly Punished." The poem printed below the cartoon predicts that "The Americans too will with Britons unite." This fanciful prediction was punctured nine months after it appeared, when the British surrendered to the Americans and the French at Yorktown in 1781.

Print Collection, Miriam and Ira D. Wallach Division of Art, Prints, and Photographs, the New York Public Library. Astor, Lenox and Tilden Foundations.

FOR MORE HELP ANALYZING THIS IMAGE, see the visual activity for this chapter in the Online Study Guide at bedfordstmartins.com/roark.

Conclusion: Why the British Lost

The British began the war for America convinced that they could not lose. They had the strongest and best-trained army and navy in the world; they were familiar with the American landscape from the Seven Years' War; they outnumbered their opponents in uniform; they had the willing warrior-power of most of the native tribes of the backcountry; and they easily captured every port city of consequence in America. Probably one-fifth of the population was loyalist, and another two-fifths were undecided. Why, then, did the British lose?

One continuing problem the British faced was the uncertainty of supplies. Unwilling to ravage the countryside, the army depended on a steady stream of supply ships from home. Insecurity about food helps explain the repeated reluctance of Howe and Clinton to pursue the Continental army aggressively.

A second obstacle to British success was their continual misuse of loyalist energies. Any plan to repacify the colonies required the cooperation of the loyalists as well as new support from the many neutrals. But again and again, the British failed to back the loyalists, leaving them to the mercy of vengeful rebels. In the South, they allowed loyalist militias to engage in vicious guerrilla warfare that drove away potential converts among the rest of the population.

The French alliance looms large in any explanation of the British defeat. The artillery and ammunition the French supplied even before 1778 were critical necessities for the Continental army. In 1780, the French army brought a fresh infusion of troops to a war-weary America, and the French navy made the Yorktown victory possible. The major naval defeat in the Chesapeake, just before the Yorktown siege, dissolved the pro-war spirit in England and forced the king to concede defeat.

Finally, the British abdicated civil power in the colonies in 1775 and 1776, when royal officials were forced to flee to safety, and they never really regained it. For nearly seven years, of necessity the Americans created their own government structures, from the Continental Congress to local committees and militias. Staffed by many who before 1775 had been the political elites, these new government agencies had remarkably little trouble establishing their authority to rule. The basic British goal—to turn back the clock to imperial rule—receded into impossibility as the war dragged on.

The war for America had taken five and a half years to fight, from Lexington to Yorktown;

negotiations and the evacuation took two more. It profoundly disrupted the lives of Americans everywhere. It was a war for independence from England, but it was more. It was a war that required men and women to think about politics and the legitimacy of authority. The precise disagreement with England about representation and political participation had profound implications for the kinds of governance the Americans would adopt, both in the moment of emergency and in the longer run of the late 1770s and early 1780s when states began to write their constitutions. The rhetoric employed to justify the revolution against England put words such as *liberty, tyranny, slavery, independence,* and *equality* into common usage. These words carried far deeper meanings than a mere complaint over taxation without representation. As Abigail Adams and others saw, the Revolution unleashed a dynamic of equality and liberty. That it was largely unintended and unwanted by the revolutionary leaders of 1776 made it all the more potent a force in American life in the decades to come.

FOR ADDITIONAL FIRSTHAND ACCOUNTS OF THIS PERIOD, see Chapter 7 in Michael Johnson, ed., *Reading the American Past,* Third Edition.

TO ASSESS YOUR MASTERY OF THE MATERIAL IN THIS CHAPTER, see the Online Study Guide at bedfordstmartins.com/roark.

FOR WEB LINKS RELATED TO TOPICS IN THIS CHAPTER, see "HistoryLinks," "DocLinks," and "PlaceLinks" at bedfordstmartins.com/roark.

CHRONOLOGY

1775
- Second Continental Congress convenes in Philadelphia and creates Continental army.
- British win Battle 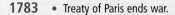 of Bunker Hill, though at a great cost.
- Congress offers Olive Branch Petition to King George; he rejects it.

1776
- American forces assault Quebec and lose.
- Thomas Paine's *Common Sense* creates sensation over idea of independence from Britain.
- British evacuate Boston to avoid entrapment and further dangerous encounters with American troops.
- **July 4.** Congress adopts Declaration of Independence.
- Massive British forces land on Long Island and take Manhattan.

1777
- American army winters at Morristown, New Jersey, and gets inoculated against smallpox.
- General Burgoyne takes Fort Ticonderoga for British.
- Ambush by Mohawk, Seneca, and British at Oriskany inflicts heavy losses on Americans.
- Americans hold Fort Stanwix, depriving Burgoyne's army of additional troops.
- General Howe and the British occupy Philadelphia.
- Burgoyne surrenders at Saratoga; France encouraged to enter war.
- General Washington camps Contiental army for six months in Valley Forge, Pennsylvania, where army endures extreme hardship.

1778
- France enters war on American side.
- Terrorizing warfare strikes both sides in Mohawk Valley of New York.
- American militiamen destroy Mohawk Joseph Brant's village.
- Delaware leader White Eyes negotiates a treaty with the Americans at Fort Pitt.
- Americans murder Shawnee chiefs Cornstalk and Red Hawk; Delaware chief White Eyes mysteriously dies.
- Savannah, Georgia, falls to British.

1779
- Militias attack Cherokee settlements in North Carolina and Tennessee.
- Skirmishes in South Carolina and Georgia.
- General Sullivan's campaign destroys 40 Indian towns in New York.
- George Rogers Clark's militia takes Forts Kaskaskia and Vincennes in the West.
- British evacuate Newport.

1780
- Philadelphia Ladies Association raises money for soldiers.
- Charleston, South Carolina, falls to British.
- Comte de Rochambeau arrives at Newport, bringing much-needed French army.
- British victory at Battle of Camden, South Carolina, dims hopes for Americans.
- Benedict Arnold's treasonous plot to betray West Point to the British exposed.
- Guerrilla warfare between loyalists and rebels starts in South Carolina and spreads to Georgia and North Carolina.
- American victory at Battle of King's Mountain, South Carolina, results in heavy loyalist casualties.

1781
- American victory at Battle of Cowpens, South Carolina.
- British forces led by General Cornwallis push into Virginia and capture Williamsburg.
- Cornwallis occupies Yorktown, Virginia.
- French fleet blockades Chesapeake Bay.
- Cornwallis surrenders at Yorktown and concedes British defeat in the Revolutionary War.

1783
- Treaty of Paris ends war.
- United States gains all land to the Mississippi River from British; Indians living on much of that land not consulted.

BIBLIOGRAPHY

General Works

Benson Bobrick, *Angel in the Whirlwind: The Triumph of the American Revolution* (1997).

Edward Countryman, *The American Revolution* (1985).

Don Higginbotham, *The War of Independence: Military Attitudes, Policies, and Practices, 1763–1789* (1983).

Don Higginbotham, *War and Society in Revolutionary America: The Wider Dimensions of Conflict* (1988).

Ronald Hoffman and Peter J. Albert, *Arms and Independence: The Military Character of the American Revolution* (1984).

Mark V. Kwasny, *Washington's Partisan War, 1775–1783* (1996).

Piers Mackesy, *The War for America, 1775–1783* (1964).

Ray Raphael, *A People's History of the American Revolution: How Common People Shaped the Fight for Independence* (2001).

Charles Royster, *A Revolutionary People at War: The Continental Army and American Character, 1775–1783* (1979).

Geoffrey Scheer, *Rebels and Redcoats: The American Revolution through the Eyes of Those Who Fought and Lived It* (1988).

John Shy, *A People Numerous and Armed: Reflections on the Military Struggle for American Independence* (rev. ed., 1990).

James L. Stokesbury, *A Short History of the American Revolution* (1991).

The Wartime Confederation

John Alden, *George Washington* (1984).

H. W. Brands, *The First American: The Life and Times of Benjamin Franklin* (2000).

Joseph J. Ellis, *Passionate Sage: The Character and Legacy of John Adams* (1993).

John E. Ferling, *John Adams: A Life* (1992).

John E. Ferling, *Setting the World Ablaze: Washington, Adams, Jefferson, and the American Revolution* (2000).

Jay Fliegelman, *Declaring Independence: Jefferson, Natural Language, and the Culture of Performance* (1993).

Eric Foner, *Tom Paine and Revolutionary America* (1976).

Edith Gelles, *Portia: The World of Abigail Adams* (1992).

James H. Hutson, *John Adams and the Diplomacy of the American Revolution* (1980).

Allen Jayne, *Jefferson's Declaration of Independence: Origins, Philosophy and Theology* (1998).

Pauline Maier, *American Scripture: Making the Declaration of Independence* (1997).

Jackson Turner Main, *The Sovereign States, 1775–1783* (1973).

David McCullough, *John Adams* (2001).

Edmund S. Morgan, *Benjamin Franklin* (2002).

Jack N. Rakove, *The Beginnings of National Politics: An Interpretive History of the Continental Congress* (1979).

Sheila L. Skemp, *William Franklin, Son of a Patriot, Servant of a King* (1990).

Henry Wiencek, *An Imperfect God: George Washington, His Slaves, and the Creation of America* (2003).

Garry Wills, *Inventing America: Jefferson's Declaration of Independence* (1978).

Lynne Withey, *Dearest Friend: A Life of Abigail Adams* (1981).

The Loyalists

Wallace Brown, *The Good Americans: The Loyalists in the American Revolution* (1969).

Robert M. Calhoon, *The Loyalists of Revolutionary America* (1973).

Robert M. Calhoon, *The Loyalist Perception and Other Essays* (1989).

John E. Ferling, *The Loyalist Mind: Joseph Galloway and the American Revolution* (1977).

Malcolm Frieberg, *Prelude to Purgatory: Thomas Hutchinson in Provincial Massachusetts Politics, 1760–1770* (1990).

Adele Hast, *Loyalism in Revolutionary Virginia* (1982).

William N. Nelson, *The American Tory* (1961).

Mary Beth Norton, *The British-American: The Loyalist Exiles in England, 1774–1789* (1972).

William Pencak, *America's Burke: The Mind of Thomas Hutchinson* (1982).

Janice Potter, *The Liberty We Seek: Loyalist Ideology in Colonial New York and Massachusetts* (1983).

James W. St. G. Walker, *The Black Loyalists: The Search for a Promised Land in Nova Scotia and Sierra Leone, 1783–1870* (1976).

The War in the North

Michael A. Bellesiles, *Revolutionary Outlaws: Ethan Allen and the Struggle for Independence on the Early American Frontier* (1993).

W. Jeffrey Bolster, *Black Jacks: African American Seamen in the Age of Sail* (1998).

Clare Brandt, *The Man in the Mirror: A Life of Benedict Arnold* (1994).

Richard Buel Jr., *Dear Liberty: Connecticut's Mobilization for the Revolutionary War* (1980).

E. Wayne Carp, *To Starve the Army at Pleasure: Continental Army Administration and American Political Culture, 1775–1783* (1984).

Edward Countryman, *A People in Revolution: The American Revolution and Political Society in New York, 1760–1790* (1981).

John C. Dann, ed., *The Revolution Remembered: Eyewitness Accounts of the War for Independence* (1980).

William M. Fowler Jr., *Rebels under Sail: The American Navy during the Revolution* (1976).

Francis S. Fox, *Sweet Land of Liberty: The Ordeal of the American Revolution in Northampton County, Pennsylvania* (2000).

Sylvia Frey, *The British Soldier in America: A Social History of Military Life in the Revolutionary Period* (1965).

Robert Gross, *The Minutemen and Their World* (1976).

Ira D. Gruber, *The Howe Brothers and the American Revolution* (1972).

Richard J. Hargrove Jr., *General John Burgoyne* (1983).

Sidney Kaplan and Emma Nogrady Kaplan, *The Black Presence in the Era of the American Revolution* (1989).

Richard M. Ketchum, *Saratoga: Turning Point of America's Revolutionary War* (1997).

Arthur S. Lefkowitz, *The Long Retreat: The Calamitous American Defense of New Jersey, 1776* (1999).

Donald R. Lennon and Charles E. Bennett, *A Quest for Glory: Robert Howe and the American Revolution* (1991).

David G. Martin, *The Philadelphia Campaign: June 1777–1778* (2003).

James Kirby Martin, *Benedict Arnold, Revolutionary Hero: An American Warrior Reconsidered* (1997).

James Kirby Martin and Edward Mark Lender, *A Respectable Army: The Military Origins of the Republic, 1763–1789* (1982).

David B. Mattern, *Benjamin Lincoln and the American Revolution* (1995).

Holly A. Mayer, *Belonging to the Army: Camp Followers and Community during the American Revolution* (1996).

Dave R. Palmer, *The Way of the Fox: American Strategy in the War for America, 1775–1783* (1975).

Gary A. Puckrein, *The Black Regiment in the American Revolution* (1978).

Ray Raphael, *The First American Revolution, before Lexington and Concord* (2002).

John Shy, *Toward Lexington: The Role of the British Army in the Coming of the American Revolution* (1965).

Evan Thomas, *John Paul Jones: Sailor, Hero, Father of the American Navy* (2003).

John A. Tilley, *The British Navy and the American Revolution* (1987).

John E. Walsh, *The Execution of Major André* (2001).

Donald Wallace White, *A Village at War: Chatham, New Jersey, and the American Revolution* (1979).

Robert K. Wright Jr., *The Continental Army* (1983).

The War in Indian Country

Colin G. Calloway, *The American Revolution in Indian Country: Crisis and Diversity in Native American Communities* (1995).

Gregory E. Dowd, *A Spirited Resistance: The North American Indian Struggle for Unity, 1745–1815* (1992).

Joseph R. Fischer, *A Well-Executed Failure: The Sullivan Campaign against the Iroquois, July–September 1779* (1997).

Barbara Graymont, *The Iroquois in the American Revolution* (1972).

Lowell Hayes Harrison, *George Rogers Clark and the War in the West* (2001).

Isabel T. Kelsay, *Joseph Brant, 1743–1807* (1984).

Diplomacy

Jonathan R. Dull, *A Diplomatic History of the American Revolution* (1985).

R. Ernest Dupuy et al., *The American Revolution: A Global War* (1977).

Ronald Hoffman and Peter Albert, eds., *Peace and the Peacemakers: The Treaty of 1783* (1986).

Reginald Horsman, *The Diplomacy of the New Republic, 1776–1815* (1985).

James H. Hutson, *John Adams and the Diplomacy of the American Revolution* (1980).

Lee Kennett, *The French Forces in America, 1780–1783* (1977).

The Southern Strategy

Lawrence E. Babits, *A Devil of a Whipping: The Battle of Cowpens* (1998).

W. Arthur Bowler, *Logistics and the Failure of the British Army in America, 1775–1783* (1975).

Jeffrey J. Crow and Larry Tise, eds., *The Southern Experience in the American Revolution* (1978).

John Ferling, ed., *The World Turned Upside Down: The American Victory in the War of Independence* (1988).

M. Thomas Hatley, *The Dividing Paths: Cherokees and South Carolinians through the Era of Revolution* (1993).

W. Robert Higgins, ed., *The Revolutionary War in the South* (1979).

Ronald Hoffman, Thad W. Tate, and Peter J. Albert, eds., *An Uncivil War: The Southern Backcountry during the American Revolution* (1985).

Marjoleine Kars, *Breaking Loose Together: The Regulator Rebellion in Pre-Revolutionary North Carolina* (2002).

Henry Lumpkin, *From Savannah to Yorktown* (1981).

Jerome J. Nadelhaft, *The Disorders of War: The Revolution in South Carolina* (1981).

James H. O'Donnell III, *Southern Indians in the American Revolution* (1973).

John S. Pancake, *This Destructive War: The British Campaign in the Carolinas, 1780–1782* (1985).

Hugh Rankin, *The North Carolina Continentals* (1971).

John E. Selby, *The Revolution in Virginia, 1775–1783* (1988).

Timothy Silver, *A New Face on the Countryside: Indians, Colonists, and Slaves in South Atlantic Forests, 1500–1800* (1990).

Russell F. Weigley, *The Partisan War: The South Carolina Campaign of 1780–1782* (1970).

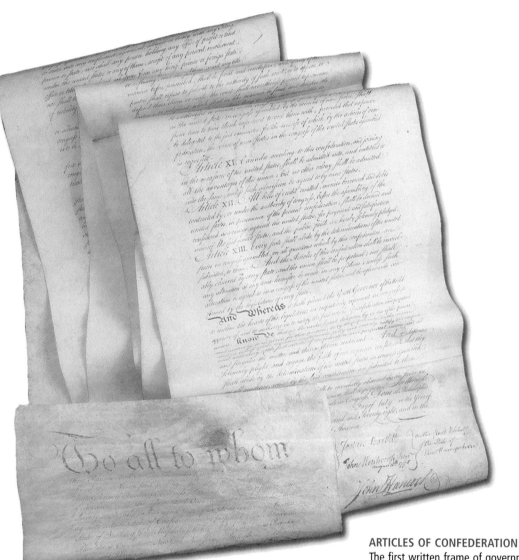

ARTICLES OF CONFEDERATION

The first written frame of government that bound together the thirteen rebelling colonies was called the Articles of Confederation. Delegates to the Second Continental Congress hammered out the plan over many months in 1776 and 1777, working on it when there was time free from the more pressing problems of pursuing the war. Once the congress agreed on it, the plan was printed and distributed to state legislatures for ratification, a process that took nearly five years because it required the assent of all thirteen. After ratification, in February 1781, this parchment copy became the official original version. As was often done with significant manuscript documents, a professional scribe wrote the opening words of the Articles in very large print, to proclaim the news. How does "To all to whom" compare with such famous opening words as "In Congress, July 4, 1776" (the start of the Declaration of Independence) and "We the people" (the start of the U.S. Constitution, which replaced the Articles in 1788)? Do you think "To all to whom" would have become a slogan or catchphrase had the Articles persisted as the country's sacred text? Why or why not?

National Archives.

Building a Republic
1775–1789

JAMES MADISON GRADUATED from Princeton College in New Jersey in 1771, not knowing what to do next with his life. Certainly the twenty-year-old had an easy fallback position. As the firstborn son of a wealthy plantation owner, he could return home to the foothills of Virginia and wait to inherit substantial land and a large force of slaves. But James was an intensely studious young man, uninterested in farming and reluctant to leave the collegiate environment. Five years at boarding school had given him fluency in Greek, Latin, French, and mathematics, and three years at Princeton acquainted him with the great thinkers, both ancient and modern. Driven by a thirst for learning, young Madison slept only five hours a night, perhaps undermining his health. Protesting that he was too ill to travel, he hung around Princeton six months after graduation.

In 1772, he returned home, still adrift. He tried studying law, but his unimpressive oratorical talents discouraged him. Political theory greatly attracted him, and he swapped reading lists and ideas about political theory by letter with a Princeton classmate, prolonging his student life. While Madison struggled for direction, the powerful winds before the storm of the American Revolution swirled through the colonies; the youth's drifting would abruptly end. In May 1774, Madison traveled north to deliver his brother to boarding school and was in Philadelphia when the startling news broke that Britain had closed the port of Boston in retaliation for the destruction of the tea. Turbulent protests over the Coercive Acts turned him into a committed revolutionary.

Back in Virginia, Madison joined his father on the newly formed committee of public safety. For a few days in early 1775, the twenty-four-year-old took up musket practice, but his continued poor health ruled out the soldier's life, and he quickly gave it up. His special contribution to the Revolution lay along a different path. In spring 1776, Madison was elected to the Virginia Convention, an extra-legal assembly replacing the defunct royal government. The convention's main task was to hammer out a state constitution featuring revolutionary goals such as frequent elections and a limited executive power. Shy, self-effacing, and still learning the ropes, Madison mostly stayed on the sidelines. Still, Virginia's elder statesmen noted the young man's logical, thoughtful contributions. When his county failed to return him to the assembly in the next election, he was appointed to the governor's council, where he spent two years gaining experience helping to manage a wartime government.

In early 1780, Madison represented Virginia in the Continental Congress. Not quite twenty-nine, unmarried, and supported by his father's money, Madison was free of the burdens that made distant political service difficult for so many others. He stayed in the North for three years, working with men such as Alexander Hamilton of New York and Robert Morris of Pennsylvania as the congress wrestled with the chaotic economy and the ever-precarious war effort. In one crisis Madison's negotiating skills proved crucial: He broke the deadlock over the ratification of the Articles of Confederation by arranging for the cession of Virginia's vast western lands. Those lands would soon appear on maps as the Northwest Territory, calling forth a series of western land ordinances planned out by Madison's friend Thomas Jefferson that were the shining example of promise and high hopes for the future of the new confederation government. But more often, service in the congress proved frustrating to Madison because the confederation government seemed to lack essential powers, chief among them the power to tax.

Madison resumed a seat in the Virginia state assembly in 1784. But he did not retreat to a local point of view, as so many other state politicians of the decade did. The difficult economic times and hardships created by heavy state taxation programs—which in Massachusetts led to a full-fledged rebellion against state government—spurred Madison to pursue means to strengthen the government of the thirteen new states. He worked hard to bring about an all-state convention in Philadelphia in the late spring of 1787, where he took the lead in steering the delegates to a complete rewrite of the structure of the na-

tional government, investing it with considerably greater powers. True to form, Madison spent the months before the convention in feverish study of the great thinkers he had read in college, searching out the best way to constitute a government on **republican** principles. His lifelong passion for scholarly study, seasoned by a dozen years of energetic political experience, paid off handsomely. The United States Constitution was the result.

By the end of the 1780s, James Madison had had his finger in every kind of political pie, on the local, state, confederation, and finally national level. He had transformed himself from a directionless and solitary youth into one of the leading political thinkers of the Revolutionary period. His personal history over the 1780s was deeply entwined with the path of the emerging United States.

The Articles of Confederation

For five years after declaring independence, the Second Continental Congress continued to meet in Philadelphia and other cities without any formal constitutional basis. Delegates first had to work out a plan of government that embodied Revolutionary principles. With monarchy gone, where would sovereignty lie? What would be the nature of representation? Who would hold the power of taxation? Who should vote; who

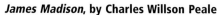

James Madison, by Charles Willson Peale

A short and slight man, James Madison appeared younger than he was. This miniature portrait, made in 1783 when he was thirty-two, shows him with natural hair (no wig) and a boyishly smooth face. Madison commissioned the portrait on the occasion of his first serious romance. The Philadelphia artist Charles Willson Peale painted matching miniatures of Madison and his fiancée, Kitty Floyd, the sixteen-year-old daughter of a New York delegate in the Continental Congress. Madison and his Virginia friend Thomas Jefferson both boarded with the Floyd family while the congress met in Philadelphia. Jefferson, a very recent widower, encouraged the shy Madison and assured him that Kitty "will render you happier than you can possibly be in a single state." Madison's portrait was mounted in a brooch (note the pin sticking out on the right) so that his lady love might wear it on her person; the back of the brooch held a neatly plaited lock of Madison's hair. The companion miniature of Kitty no longer holds a lock of her hair, if it ever did, for Kitty soon jilted Madison for a suave younger man and returned the Madison miniature to the grieving bachelor. Eleven years later, Madison tried romance again when New York congressman Aaron Burr introduced him to a Virginia widow named Dolley Payne Todd, seventeen years his junior. Madison was forty-three and Dolley was twenty-six; they married four months after meeting.

Library of Congress.

should rule? And exactly who were "the people" anyway? The resulting plan, called the Articles of Confederation, proved to be surprisingly difficult to implement, mainly because the thirteen states had serious disagreements about how to manage lands to the west whose political ownership was contested. Once the Articles were finally ratified and the confederation was formally constituted, that arena of government seemed to many to be far less relevant or interesting than the state governments.

Congress and Confederation

The Second Continental Congress assumed power in May 1775, when the British attack on Lexington and Concord required a unified colonial response (see chapter 7). Only as the delegates fashioned the Declaration of Independence a year later did they consider the need for a written document that would specify what powers the congress had and by what authority it existed. It finally fell to John Dickinson, the moderate conciliator from Pennsylvania, to chair the committee entrusted with the important task of drafting such a document.

Dickinson's draft of the Articles of Confederation reveals that the delegates, unified by their opposition to England, agreed on key government powers: pursuing war and peace, conducting foreign relations, regulating trade, and running a postal service. But there was serious disagreement about the powers of congress over the western boundaries of the states. Virginia and Connecticut, for example, had old colonial charters that located their western boundaries many hundreds of miles to the west. States without extensive land claims wanted to redraw those colonial boundaries. Dickinson's draft granted the congress final authority on this and many other matters.

For over a year, the congress tinkered with the Articles; its energies were far more consumed by the war. A final version of the document emerged only in November 1777, departing from the Dickinson draft in defining the Union as a loose confederation of states. Gone was the provision giving the congress control of state boundaries and western lands. Each state retained all powers and rights not expressly delegated to the congress, and the Union was characterized as "a firm league of friendship" existing mainly to foster a common defense. There was no national executive (that is, no president) and no national judiciary.

The structure of the government paralleled that of the existing Continental Congress. The congress was composed of two to seven delegates from each state, selected annually by the state legislatures and prohibited from serving more than three years out of any six. The actual number of delegates was not critical, since each state delegation cast a single vote.

Routine decisions in the congress required a simple majority of seven states; for momentous decisions, such as declaring war, nine states needed to agree. To approve or amend the Articles required the unanimous consent both of the thirteen state delegations and of the thirteen state legislatures. The congressional delegates undoubtedly thought they were guaranteeing that no individual state could be railroaded by the other twelve in fundamental constitutional matters. But what this requirement really did was to hamstring the government. One state could—and did—hold the rest of the country hostage to its demands.

On the delicate question of deriving revenue to run the government, specifically to finance the war, the Articles provided an ingenious but ultimately troublesome solution. Each state was to contribute in proportion to the property value of the state's land. Large and populous states would give more than small or sparsely populated states. The actual taxes would be levied by the state legislatures, not by the congress, to preserve the Revolution's principle of taxation only by direct representation. However, no mechanism was created to compel states to contribute their fair share.

The lack of centralized authority in the confederation government was exactly what many state leaders wanted in the late 1770s. A league of states with rotating personnel, no executive branch, no power of taxation, and a requirement of unanimity for any major change seemed to be a good way to avoid the potential tyranny of government. But right away, the inherent weaknesses of these features became apparent.

> With monarchy gone, where would sovereignty lie? What would be the nature of representation? And exactly who were "the people" anyway?

The Problem of Western Lands

Once approved by the congress in 1777, the Articles of Confederation had to be approved unanimously by the state legislatures. Newspapers published the plan, but there was

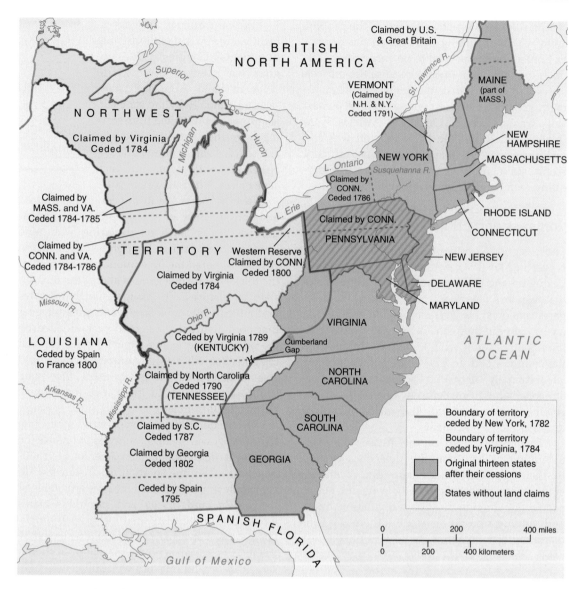

MAP 8.1   Cession of Western Lands, 1782–1802
The thirteen new states found it hard to ratify the Articles of Confederation without settling their conflicting land claims in the west, an area larger than the original states and occupied by Indian tribes. The five states objecting to the Articles' silence over western lands policy were Maryland, Delaware, New Jersey, Rhode Island, and Pennsylvania.

READING THE MAP: Which states had the largest claims on western territory? What disputed territory became the fourteenth state?

CONNECTIONS: In what context did the first dispute regarding western lands arise? How was it resolved? Does the map suggest a reason why Pennsylvania, a large state, joined the four much smaller states on this issue?

FOR MORE HELP ANALYZING THIS MAP, see the map activity for this chapter in the Online Study Guide at
bedfordstmartins.com/roark.

little public discussion because the war monopolized the news.

The approval process stalled for five years, principally due to sharply conflicting ideas about how to deal with lands west of the existing states and east of the Mississippi River. Five states, all lacking prior land claims—Maryland,

Delaware, New Jersey, Rhode Island, and Pennsylvania—insisted that the congress control those lands as a national domain that would eventually constitute new states. The other eight states refused to yield their colonial-era claims and opposed giving the congress power to alter boundaries (Map 8.1). In all the heated debate, few seemed to remember that those same western lands were inhabited by many thousands of Indians not party to the disputes.

The eight land-claiming states were ready to sign the Articles of Confederation in 1777. Rhode Island, Pennsylvania, and New Jersey eventually capitulated and signed, "not from a Conviction of the Equality and Justness of it," said a New Jersey delegate, "but merely from an absolute Necessity there was of complying to save the Continent." But Delaware and Maryland continued to hold out, insisting on a national domain policy. In 1779, the disputants finally compromised: Any land a state volunteered to relinquish would become the national domain. The logjam finally broke in 1781, when congressmen James Madison and Thomas Jefferson ceded all of Virginia's huge land claim, except the area that later became West Virginia. The compromise undercut Virginia's economic interests but made sense in terms of republican principles. Both Madison and Jefferson recognized that such a large area as Virginia claimed could not really be governed successfully because the seat of state government would be too far from its citizens to represent them adequately. With Virginia's concession, the Articles were at last unanimously approved.

The western lands issue demonstrated that powerful interests divided the thirteen new states. The apparent unity of purpose inspired by fighting the war against England papered over sizable cracks in the new confederation.

Running the New Government

No fanfare greeted the long-awaited inauguration of the new government. The congress continued to sputter along, its problems far from solved by the signing of the Articles. The lack of a quorum often hampered day-to-day activities. The Articles required representation from seven states to conduct business, and a minimum of two men from each state's delegation. But some days, fewer than fourteen men in total showed up. State legislatures were slow to select delegates, and many of those appointed were reluctant to attend, especially if they had wives and children at home. Absenteeism was a constant problem. Consequently, some of the most effective and committed delegates were young bachelors like James Madison and men in their fifties and sixties whose families were grown, like Samuel Adams. Other delegates came for very short terms, barely learning the business of the congress before they were on their way home.

Many active politicians preferred to devote their energies to their state governments, especially when the congress seemed deadlocked or, worse, irrelevant. It also did not help that the congress had no permanent home. During the war, when the British army threatened Philadelphia, the congress relocated to small Pennsylvania towns such as Lancaster and York and then to Baltimore. After hostilities ceased, the congress moved from Trenton to Princeton to Annapolis to New York City.

To address the difficulties of an inefficient congress, executive departments of war, finance, and foreign affairs were created to handle purely administrative functions. When the department heads were ambitious—as was Robert Morris, a wealthy Philadelphia merchant who served as superintendent of finance—they could exercise considerable executive power. The Articles of Confederation had deliberately refrained from setting up an executive branch, but a modest one was being invented by necessity.

Because of the pressing needs of running a war machine, the confederation government got a slow start on writing its plan of government, and then the difficulties over ownership of western lands slowed ratification for years. By the time the Articles were fully functioning, yet another problem emerged. Much more exciting political work was going on at the state level, especially during the creative burst of state constitution writing in the late 1770s. Before 1776, the cream of political talent in the country was attracted to the Continental Congress, but between 1776 and 1780 the talent flowed instead to the state governments.

> No fanfare greeted the long-awaited inauguration of the new government. The congress continued to sputter along, its problems far from solved by the signing of the Articles.

The Sovereign States

In the first decade of independence, the states were sovereign and all-powerful. Relatively few functions, like that of declaring war and peace, had been transferred to the confederation government. As Americans discarded their English identity, they thought of themselves instead as Virginians or New Yorkers or Rhode Islanders. Familiar and close to home, state government claimed the allegiance of citizens and became the arena in which the Revolution's innovations would first be tried. States defined who was a voter, and they also defined who would be free. The question of slavery quickly became a front-burner issue, as all the states were forced to grapple with squaring revolutionary ideals with lifelong bondage for African Americans. Northern states had more success with this than did the southern, where slavery was deeply entrenched in the economy.

The State Constitutions

In May 1776, the congress in Philadelphia recommended that all states draw up constitutions based on "the authority of the people." By 1778, ten had produced documents spelling out the **liberties,** rights, and obligations of citizens and rulers, and three more (Connecticut, Massachusetts, and Rhode Island) adopted and updated their original colonial charters. Americans felt they had been injured by the unwritten nature of British political traditions; liberties they had assumed were theirs had been denied them. They wanted a written contract whose basic principles could not be easily altered by the government in power at the moment. Having been denied unwritten British liberties, Americans wanted written contracts that guaranteed basic principles.

A shared feature of all the state constitutions was the conviction that government ultimately rests on the consent of the governed. Political writers in the late 1770s embraced the concept of republicanism as the underpinning of the new governments. Republicanism meant more than popular elections and representative institutions. For some, republicanism invoked a way of thinking about who leaders should be—autonomous, virtuous citizens who placed civic values above private interests. For others, it suggested direct **democracy,** with nothing standing in the way of the will of the people. For all, it meant government that promoted the people's welfare.

Widespread agreement about the virtues of republicanism went hand in hand with the idea that republics could succeed only in relatively small units. A government run for and by the people had to be near at hand, so the people could make sure their interests were being served. Distant governments could easily become tyrannical; that was the lesson of the 1760s.

It followed, then, that the best form of government was one that allowed maximum voice

to the people. Nearly every state continued the colonial practice of a two-chamber assembly but greatly augmented the powers of the lower house. Two states, Pennsylvania and Georgia, did away with the upper house altogether, believing—as had Thomas Paine in *Common Sense*—that an upper house usually was an aristocratic and therefore undesirable check on the powers of the democratic lower house. Virtually all of the state constitutions severely limited the powers of the governor, identified in most people's minds with the royal governor of colonial days. Governors could no longer convene or dismiss legislatures at will, veto legislation, or buy loyalty through land grants or job patronage. Most states also restricted the governor's term to one year and limited eligibility for reelection. Pennsylvania and Georgia went so far as to abolish the office of governor.

Daily governance of each state rested with the lower house, whose most important decisions were economic: printing, borrowing, taxing, and spending money to finance each state's war effort. Most states made their lower houses very responsive to popular majorities, with annual elections and guaranteed rotation in office. If a representative displeased his constituents, he could be out of office in a matter of months. James Madison's second attempt to win election to the Virginia assembly offers an example. After only one year in office, the fledgling politician was defeated in 1777; he was sure he lost because he failed to campaign in the traditional style with the abundant liquor and glad-handing that his constituents had come to expect. Shy and retiring, Madison was not capable of electioneering in this manner. His series of increasingly significant political posts from 1778 to 1787 all came as a result of appointment, not popular election.

Six of the state constitutions included bills of rights, lists of basic individual liberties that governments could not abridge. Virginia debated and passed the first bill of rights in June 1776, and many of the other states borrowed from it. Its language also bears a close resemblance to the wording of the Declaration of Independence, which Thomas Jefferson was drafting that same June in Philadelphia: "That all men are by nature equally free and independent, and have certain inherent rights, of which, when they enter into a state of society, they cannot by any compact deprive or divest their posterity; namely, the enjoyment of life and liberty, with the means of acquiring and possessing property, and pursuing and obtaining happiness and safety." Along with these inherent rights went more specific rights to freedom of speech, freedom of the press, and trial by jury.

Who Are "the People"?

When the Continental Congress called for state constitutions based on "the authority of the people," and when the Virginia bill of rights granted "all men" certain rights, who was meant by "the people"? Who exactly were the citizens of this new country, and how far would the principle of democratic government extend? Different people answered these questions differently, but in the 1770s certain limits to full political participation by all Americans were widely agreed upon.

One limit was defined by property. The idea prevailed everywhere that the propertied classes were the only legitimate participants in government. In nearly every state, candidates for the highest offices—the governorship and membership in the upper house—needed to meet substantial property qualifications. In Maryland, for example, a candidate for governor had to be worth £5,000, quite a large sum of money. Voters in Maryland had to own fifty acres of land or £30, a sum that screened out perhaps one-third of adult white males. In the most democratic state, Pennsylvania, voters and candidates alike needed only to be taxpayers—that is, to own enough property to owe taxes.

The justification for restricting political participation to property owners was so widely accepted that it rarely needed to be explained. Only property owners were presumed to possess the necessary independence of mind to make wise political choices. Are not propertyless men, asked John Adams, "too little acquainted with public affairs to form a right judgment, and too dependent upon other men to have a will of their own?" Adams and others assumed that only property owners would feel a keen sense of community and thus be able to think clearly about the public interest. Besides, it did not seem right to give a propertyless man a voice in decisions to levy taxes if he was not going to be paying taxes himself.

Property qualifications probably disfranchised from one-quarter to one-half of adult white males in all the states. Not all of them took their nonvoter status quietly. One Maryland man wondered what was so special about being worth £30: "Every poor man has a life, a personal liberty, and a right to his earnings; and is in danger of being injured by government in a variety

of ways." Why then restrict such a man from voting for his representatives? Others pointed out that propertyless men were fighting and dying in the Revolutionary War; surely they were expressing an active concern about politics. A very few radical voices challenged the notion that owning property transformed men into good citizens. Perhaps it did the opposite: The richest men might well be greedy and selfish and therefore bad citizens. But ideas like this were clearly outside the mainstream. The writers of the new constitutions, themselves men of property, viewed the Revolution as an effort to guarantee people the right to own property and to prevent unjust governments from appropriating it through taxation.

> Who exactly were the citizens of this new country, and how far would the principle of democratic government extend? Different people answered these questions differently.

Another exclusion from voting—women—was so ingrained that very few stopped to question it. Yet the logic of allowing propertied females to vote did occur to at least two well-placed women, who raised the issue with their male relatives. Abigail Adams wrote to John in 1782 that "Even in the freest countrys our property is subject to the controul and disposal of our partners, to whom the Laws have given a sovereign Authority. Deprived of a voice in Legislation, obliged to submit to those Laws which are imposed upon us, is it not sufficient to make us indifferent to the publick Welfare?" A wealthy Virginia widow named Hannah Corbin wrote to her brother, Richard Henry Lee, to complain of her taxation without the corresponding representation. Her letter no longer exists, but his reply does: "You complain that widows are not represented, and that being temporary possessors of the estates, ought not to be liable to the tax." Yet, he continued, women would be "out of character . . . to press into those tumultuous assemblies of men where the business of choosing representatives is conducted."

Only three states bothered to specify that voters had to be male, so powerful was the unspoken assumption that only men could vote. Still, in one state, small numbers of women began to turn out at the polls in the 1780s. New Jersey's constitution of 1776 enfranchised all free inhabitants worth over £50, language that in theory opened the door to free blacks as well as unmarried women who met the property requirement. (Married women owned no property, for by law their husbands held title to

A Possible Voter in Essex County, New Jersey
Mrs. Elizabeth Alexander Stevens was married to John Stevens, a New Jersey delegate to the Continental Congress in 1783. Widowed in 1792, she would have then been eligible to vote in state elections according to New Jersey's unique enfranchisement of property-holding women. Mrs. Stevens's family was a prominent one. Her father had been surveyor general of New Jersey and New York; her husband was active in politics and was secretary to the governor of New York. Her son, John Stevens, was the inventor of steamboat and locomotive innovations; her daughter Mary married Robert R. Livingston of New York, also a delegate to the Continental Congress and a man who later built a fortune in steamboating. Essex County, where Elizabeth Stevens lived, was said to be the place where female suffrage was exercised most actively. This portrait, done around 1793–1794, represents the most likely face of that rare bird, the eighteenth-century female voter. The widow Stevens died in 1799, before suffrage was redefined to be the exclusive right of males.
New Jersey Historical Society.

everything; few free blacks would meet the property qualification.) Little fanfare accompanied this radical shift, and some historians have inferred that the inclusion of unmarried women and blacks was an accidental oversight. Yet other parts of the **suffrage** clause pertaining to residency and property were extensively debated when it was put in the state constitution, and no

objections were raised at that time to its gender- and race-free language. Thus other historians have concluded that the law was intentionally inclusive. In 1790, a revised election law used the words *he or she* in reference to voters, thus making woman suffrage explicit. As one New Jersey legislator declared, "Our Constitution gives this right to maids or widows *black or white*."

In 1790, only about 1,000 free black adults of both sexes lived in New Jersey, a state with a population of 184,000. The number of unmarried adult white women was probably also small, and most of them probably were widows. In view of the property requirement, the voter bloc enfranchised under this law could not have been decisive in elections. Still, this highly unusual situation lasted until 1807, when a new state law specifically disfranchised both blacks and women. Henceforth, independence of mind, that essential precondition of voting, was redefined to be sex- and race-specific.

In the 1780s, voting everywhere was class-specific. John Adams urged the framers of the Massachusetts constitution not even to discuss the scope of suffrage but simply to adopt the traditional colonial property qualifications. If suffrage is brought up for debate, he warned, "there will be no end of it. New claims will arise; women will demand a vote; lads from twelve to twenty-one will think their rights not enough attended to; and every man who has not a farthing, will demand an equal voice with any other." Adams was astute enough to anticipate complaints about excluding women, youth, and poor men from political life, but it did not even occur to him to worry about another group: slaves.

Equality and Slavery

Restrictions on political participation did not mean that propertyless people enjoyed no civil rights and liberties. The various state bills of rights applied to all individuals who had, as the Virginia bill so carefully phrased it, "enter[ed] into a state of society." No matter how poor, a free person was entitled to life, liberty, property, and freedom of conscience. Unfree people, however, were another matter. Their status was legally controlled by the states, and with thirteen of them, variation was possible.

The author of the Virginia bill of rights was George Mason, a plantation owner with 118 slaves. When he penned the sentence "all men are by nature equally free and independent," he did not have his slaves in mind; he meant that Americans were the equals of the British and could not be denied the liberties of British citizens. Other Virginia legislators, however, worried that the words could be construed to apply to slaves. These aristocratic slaveholders were finally put at ease by the addition of the phrase that rights belonged only to people who had entered civil society. As one wrote, with relief, "Slaves, not being constituent members of our society, could never pretend to any benefit from such a maxim."

One month later, the Declaration of Independence used essentially the same phrase about equality, this time without the modifying

Paul Cuffe's Silhouette

Captain Paul Cuffe of Martha's Vineyard, off the Massachusetts coast, was the son of a Wampanoag Indian woman and an African man who had purchased his own freedom from a Quaker owner. Cuffe studied navigation and went to sea at age sixteen during the American Revolution, enduring several months of imprisonment by the British. After the war, he and his brother petitioned for tax relief, a move that foreshadowed Cuffe's life of dedication to racial issues. In his thirty-year career as a shipbuilder and master mariner, Cuffe traveled extensively. By 1812, when this engraving with silhouette was made, Cuffe had explored the African country of Sierra Leone as a possible site for resettlement of American blacks and had met with African kings, English dukes, and an American president. Library of Congress.

clause about entering society. Two state constitutions, for Pennsylvania and Massachusetts, also included the inspiring language about equality, again without limiting it as in Virginia. In Massachusetts, where the state constitution was sent around to be ratified town by town, the town of Hardwick suggested that the sentence on equality be reworded to read "All men, whites and blacks, are born free and equal." The suggestion fell on deaf ears.

The only other state to draft language about equality was Vermont, whose 1777 constitution explicitly made slavery illegal and based its logic on the equality phrase. (Vermont had almost no slaves within its borders. Its statehood was not recognized until 1791 because New York and New Hampshire, each of which claimed the Vermont land as its own, had many friends in the Continental Congress.) Reluctance to include equality language in other state bills of rights and constitutions probably means that its radical implication for the institution of slavery was beginning to be recognized.

Yet inevitably, after 1776, the ideals of the Revolution about natural equality and liberty began to erode the institution of slavery. Sometimes enslaved blacks led the challenge. (See "Documenting the American Promise," page 258.) In 1777, several Massachusetts slaves petitioned the state legislature, claiming a "natural & unalienable right to that freedom which the great Parent of the Universe hath bestowed equally on all mankind." They modestly asked for freedom for their children at age twenty-one and were turned down. In 1779, similar petitions in Connecticut and New Hampshire met with no success. Seven Massachusetts freemen, including the mariner brothers Paul and John Cuffe, refused to pay taxes for three years on the grounds that they could not vote and so were not represented. The Cuffe brothers landed in jail in 1780 for tax evasion, but their petition to the state

> Reluctance to include equality language in state bills of rights and constitutions probably means that its radical implication for the institution of slavery was beginning to be recognized.

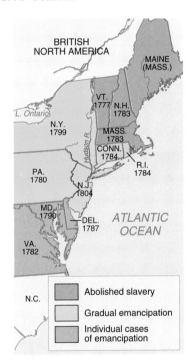

Legal Changes to Slavery, 1777–1804

Blacks Petition for Freedom and Rights

I n the 1780s, a language of rights and liberty was in the air and on many lips. Extraordinary times encouraged extraordinary actions, and enslaved as well as newly freed African Americans everywhere felt emboldened to make bids to enlarge their own liberty. Brand-new state governments held out the potential for revolutionary change in legal and social relations, encouraging some blacks to take up their pens to petition for various freedoms. To be effective, petitions generally needed to beg or persuade rather than assert. Notice the kinds of argument made by these three sets of petitioners, the ways they describe themselves, and the promises they make about how they will use their hoped-for freedom.

DOCUMENT 1
Four Men Petition the Massachusetts Assembly for Their Freedom, 1773

Massachusetts law in the 1770s allowed even slaves to present petitions to the government. These four enslaved men arranged for a printing of their petition so they could send a separate copy to each town representative instead of submitting a single copy to the assembly. (The document was entirely set in type except the last word—Thompson—which was written in by hand.) Making a separate appeal to each representative was perhaps a way to maximize the impact of the petition.

Boston, April 20th, 1773
Sir, The efforts made by the legislative of this province in their last sessions to free themselves from

slavery, gave us, who are in that deplorable state, a high degree of satisfaction. We expect great things from men who have made such a noble stand against the designs of their fellow-men to enslave them. We cannot but wish and hope Sir, that you will have the same grand object, we mean civil and religious liberty, in view in your next session. The divine spirit of freedom, seems to fire every humane breast on this continent, except such as are bribed to assist in executing the execrable plan.

We are very sensible that it would be highly detrimental to our present masters, if we were allowed to demand all that of right belongs to us for past services; this we disclaim. Even the Spaniards, who have not those sublime ideas of freedom that English men have, are conscious that they have no right to all the services of their fellow-men, we mean the Africans, whom they have purchased with their money; therefore they allow them one day in a week to work for themselves, to enable them to earn money to purchase the residue of their time, which they have a right to demand in such portions as they are able to pay for (a due appraizement of their services being first made, which always stands at the purchase money). We do not pretend to dictate to you Sir, or to the Honorable Assembly, of which you are a member. We acknowledge our obligations to you for what you have already done, but as the people of this province seem to be actuated by the principles of equity and justice, we cannot but expect your house will

again take our deplorable case into serious consideration, and give us that ample relief which, as men, we have a natural right to.

But since the wise and righteous governor of the universe, has permitted our fellow men to make us slaves, we bow in submission to him, and determine to behave in such a manner as that we may have reason to expect the divine approbation of, and assistance in, our peaceable and lawful attempts to gain our freedom.

We are willing to submit to such regulations and laws, as may be made relative to us, until we leave the province, which we determine to do as soon as we can, from our joynt labours procure money to transport ourselves to some part of the Coast of Africa, where we propose a settlement. We are very desirous that you should have instructions relative to us, from your town, therefore we pray you to communicate this letter to them, and ask this favor for us.

In behalf of our fellow slaves in this province, and by order of their Committee.

Peter Bestes,
Sambo Freeman,
Felix Holbrook,
Chester Joie.
For the Representative of the town of Thompson.

SOURCE: Herbert Aptheker, ed., *A Documentary History of the Negro People in the United States* (New York: Citadel Press, 1968), 1:7–8. Copyright © by Citadel Press. Reprinted with permission.

DOCUMENT 2
Paul and John Cuffe Protest Taxation in Massachusetts, 1780

After judicial emancipation in Massachusetts, Paul and John Cuffe, *together with five other freed men from the town of Dartmouth, sent this petition to the Massachusetts legislature.*

To the Honouerable Councel and House of Representatives in General Court assembled for the State of the Massachusetts Bay in New England—March 14th AD 1780—

The petition of several poor Negroes & molattoes who are Inhabitant of the Town of Dartmouth Humbly Sheweth—That we being Chiefly of the African Extract and by Reason of Long Bondag and hard Slavery we have been deprived of Injoying the Profits of our Labouer or the advantage of Inheriting Estates from our Parents as our Neighbouers the white peopel do haveing some of us not long Injoyed our own freedom & yet of late, Contrary to the invariable Custom & Practice of the Country we have been & now are Taxed both in our Polls and that small Pittance of Estate which through much hard Labour & Industry we have got together to Sustain our selves & families withal—We apprehand it therefore to be hard usag and will doubtless if Continued will Reduce us to a State of Beggary whereby we shall become a Berthan to others if not timely prevented by the Interposition of your Justice & power & yor Petitioners farther sheweth that we apprehand ourselves to be Aggreeved, in that while we are not allowed the Privilage of freemen of the State having no vote or Influence in the Election of those that Tax us yet many of our Colour (as is well known) have cheerfully Entered the field of Battle in the defence of the Common Cause and that (as we conceive) against a similar Exertion of Power (in Regard to taxation) too well Known to need a recital in this place—

That these the Most honouerable Court we Humbley Beseech they would take this into Considerration and Let us aside from Paying tax or taxes or cause us to Be Cleaired for we ever have Been a people that was fair from all these thing ever since the days of our four fathers and therefore we take it as aheard ship that we should be so delt By now in these Difficulty times for there is not to exceed more then five or six that hath a cow in this town and theirfore in our Distress we send unto the peaceableness of thee people and the mercy of God that we may be Releaved for we are not alowed in voating in the town meating in nur to chuse an oficer Neither their was not one ever heard in the active Court of the General Asembly the poor Dispised miserable Black people, & we have not an equal chance with white people neither by Sear nur by Land therefore we take it as a heard ship that poor old Negroes should be Rated which have been in Bondage some thirty some forty and some fifty years and now just got their Liberty some by going into the serviese and some by going to Sea and others by good fortan and also poor Distressed mungrels which have no larning and no land. . . . Neither where to put their head but some shelter them selves into an old rotten hut which thy dogs would not lay in.

Therefore we pray that these may give no offence at all By no means But that thee most Honouerable Court will take it in to consideration as if it were their own case for we think it as to be a heard ship that we should be assessed and not be a lowed as we may say to Eat Bread therefore we Humbley Beg and pray thee to plead our Case for us with thy people O God; that those who have the rule in their hands

may be mercyfull unto the poor and needy give unto those who ask of thee and he that would Borrow of thee turn not away empty. . . . Neither with lieing Lips therefore we think that we may be clear from being called tories tho some few of our Colour hath Rebelled and Done Wickedly however we think that there is more of our Collour gone into the wars according to the Number of them into the Respepiktive towns then any other nation here. . . . We most humbley Request therefore that you would take our unhappy Case into your serious Consideration and in your wisdom and Power grant us Relief from Taxation while under our Present depressed Circumstances and your poor Petioners as in duty bound shall ever pray &c.

SOURCE: Herbert Aptheker, ed., *A Documentary History of the Negro People in the United States* (New York: Citadel Press, 1968), 1:15–16. Copyright © 1968 by Citadel Press. Reprinted with permission.

DOCUMENT 3
The Connecticut Assembly Answers a Petition from a Husband and Wife, 1789

Fifteen years after their loyalist owner fled the country, this black couple petitioned the state assembly to clarify their legal status. After a hearing, the assembly reviewed the evidence and granted them and their children freedom.

Upon the Petition of Cesar a Negro and Lowis his Wife both of Hebron in the County of Tolland Shewing to this Assembly that by the Laws of this State they were Slaves to the Revd Samuel Peters lateof said Hebron but now of the City of

(continued)

London in Great Britain who left Said Hebron in Septembr 1774 and hath ever since remained in the Kingdom of Great Britain, and that the Petitioners have during the absence of the said Peters been at Liberty to provide for themselves, and that the Petitioners now have eight Children, which they have by their Industry maintained in a decent Manner, and the Petitioners in April 1784, wrote to the said Peters then at London requesting that he would give to the Petitioners and their Children their Freedom. And that the said Peters in answer to the request of the Petitioners on the 26th Day of July 1784 Wrote a Letter to the Petitioners declaring his willingness to grant the request of the Petitioners if it was in his Power, but supposed that the Petitioners were Claimed by the State of Connecticut as forfeited by the said Peters to said State, and that some Persons have lately been endeavouring to sell the Petitioners and their Children out of this State, and that the Petitioners are in continual fear of being secretly taken with their Children and sold out of this State to some foreign Country. Praying that they and their said eight Children may be emancipated and declared free from the said Peters as per Petition on File, And upon the Tryal of said Cause and a full hearing of the said Petition and the Evidence produced to support the same, it appears that the said Peters by his Letter dated at London the 26th Day of July 1784, to the Petitioners in answer to their request that he has in said Letter declared that he is willing to emancipate the Petitioners and their Children, and that he would do all in his Power to effect the same.

Whereupon it is Resolved by this Assembly that the Petitioners and their said eight Children be and they are hereby emancipated and declared free from the said Peters and all others from by or under his former Claim to the Petitioners and their said eight Children as Slaves.

SOURCE: Herbert Aptheker, ed., *A Documentary History of the Negro People in the United States* (New York: Citadel Press, 1968), 1:21–22. Copyright © 1968 by Citadel Press. Reprinted with permission.

QUESTIONS FOR ANALYSIS AND DEBATE

1. What do the four Massachusetts petitioners mean when they congratulate the state legislators for their recent efforts "to free themselves from slavery"? Are they contradictory when they claim a natural right "as men" to relief from slavery but then also "bow in submission" to the "governor of the universe" who has allowed their slavery? What is it they "disclaim" out of consideration to their present masters? Why do they raise the case of a Spanish version of slavery?

2. Is the Cuffe petition essentially a call for "no taxation without representation"? Does it differ from the revolutionaries' stand on taxation in relation to Britain? Do the petitioners want representation—or relief from taxation? Why do they mention their military service?

3. Why do you think the Connecticut couple waited until 1784 to contact their former owner, who had left in 1774? Who might be scaring the family with threats to sell them out of state? What is the basis of their petition to the state government? On what grounds were they finally freed? How might you account for the assembly's additional five-year delay to arrive at this decision in 1789?

4. What can you conclude about the options available to northern blacks to secure freedom or rights under law? Are the petitioners confident about their rights, or about the outcome they expect? How have they had to shape their petitions to appeal to an all-white legislature? Do you see instances of subtle irony or sarcasm employed?

---

legislature spurred the extension of suffrage to taxpaying free blacks in that state.

Another way to bring the issue before lawmakers was to sue in court. In 1781, a Massachusetts slave named Quok Walker charged his master with assault and battery, arguing that he was a free man under the state constitution's assertion that "all men are born free and equal." Walker won and was set free, a decision confirmed in an appeal to the state's superior court in 1783. Several similar cases followed, and by 1789 slavery had been effectively abolished by judicial decision in Massachusetts.

In other northern states, untold numbers of blacks simply ran away from owners and claimed their freedom, sometimes with the help of sympathetic whites. One estimate holds that more than half of young slave men in Philadelphia took flight in the 1780s and joined the ranks of free blacks. By 1790, free blacks outnumbered slaves in Pennsylvania by nearly a factor of two.

Pennsylvania was the first state to legislate an end to slavery by statute, in 1780. Yet the law provided for very gradual **emancipation**: Only infants born to a slave mother on or after March 1, 1780, would be freed, but not until age twenty-eight. That meant that no current slave in Pennsylvania would gain freedom until 1808, and that well into the nineteenth century some blacks—those born before 1780—would still be slaves. (Not until 1847 did Pennsylvania fully abolish slavery.) Rhode Island and Connecticut adopted gradual emancipation laws in 1784. In 1785, New York expanded the terms under which individual owners could free slaves, but only in 1799 did the state adopt a gradual emancipation law; New Jersey followed suit in 1804. These were the two northern states with the largest number of slaves: New York in 1800 with 20,000 and New Jersey, more than 12,000. In contrast, Pennsylvania had just 1,700. Gradual emancipation illustrates the tension between radical and conservative implications of republican ideology. Republican government protected people's liberties and property, yet slaves were both people and property. Gradual emancipation balanced the civil rights of blacks and the property rights of their owners by delaying the promise of freedom.

South of Pennsylvania, in Delaware, Maryland, and Virginia, where slavery was so important to the economy, general emancipation bills were rejected. All three states, however, eased legal restrictions and allowed individual acts of emancipation for adult slaves below the age of forty-five, under new manumission laws passed in 1782 (Virginia), 1787 (Delaware), and 1790 (Maryland). By 1790, close to 10,000 newly freed Virginia slaves had formed local free black communities complete with schools and churches.

In the deep South—the Carolinas and Georgia—freedom for slaves was unthinkable for whites. Yet more than 10,000 slaves from South Carolina achieved freedom in 1783 by leaving with the British army from Charleston, and another 6,000 set sail under the British flag from Savannah, Georgia. This was by far the largest emancipation of blacks in the entire country. Some went to Canada, some to England, and a small number to Sierra Leone, on the west coast of Africa. In addition, many hundreds of ex-slaves took refuge with Seminole and Creek Indians, becoming permanent members of their communities in Spanish Florida and western Georgia.

Black Loyalists in Canada
This rare sketch from 1788 shows an ordinary day laborer: a black woodcutter who came to Nova Scotia in the migration of black loyalists. Over 3,000 black refugees from the American Revolution arrived in northeastern Canada between 1783 and 1785. Very few were able to acquire land, and after 1786 the British authorities stopped provisioning them. Most, like the man pictured here, were forced to become servants or day laborers for whites. Low wages created dissatisfaction, and racial tensions broke loose in a riot. In 1791–1792, nearly a third of the black refugees in Nova Scotia left for Sierra Leone in west Africa, where British officials promised them land ownership and opportunities for self rule. In 1798, a refugee from South Carolina named Boston King published a memoir of his experiences joining the British during the Revolution, living in Nova Scotia, and traveling on to Sierra Leone; his rich account is one of the few existing personal narratives of black loyalism.
William Booth, National Archives of Canada C-401621.

Although emancipation affected fewer blacks in the North than in the South, simply because there were far fewer of them there to begin with, its symbolic importance was enormous. Every state from Pennsylvania northward acknowledged that slavery was fundamentally inconsistent with revolutionary ideology; "all men are created equal" was beginning to acquire real force as a basic principle. On some level, southerners also understood this, but their inability to imagine a free biracial society prevented them from taking much action. George Washington owned 390 slaves and freed not one of them in the 1780s, even when his friend the French general Lafayette urged him to do so as a model for others. In his will, written in 1799, the now guilt-stricken Washington provided for the eventual freedom of his slaves—but only after his wife, Martha, died. (One year after his death, Martha Washington freed them all, preferring loss of income to the uneasy situation of her life being her slaves' only barrier to freedom.) From the 1780s on, the North was associated with freedom and the South with slavery. This geographical pattern would have profound consequences for the next two centuries of American history.

The Critical Period

From 1781 to 1786, a sense of crisis gripped some of the revolutionary leaders who feared the Articles of Confederation were too weak. But others defended the Articles as the best guarantee of individual liberty, because real governance occurred at the state level, closer to the people. Political theorizing about the proper relation among citizen, state, and confederation remained active and controversial throughout the decade as Americans confronted questions of finance, territorial expansion, and civil disorder.

Financial Chaos and Paper Money

Seven years of war produced a chaotic economy in the 1780s. The confederation and the individual states had run up huge war debts, financed by printing paper money and borrowing from private sources. Some $400 to $500 million in paper currency had been injected into the economy, and prices and wages fluctuated wildly. Private debt and rapid expenditure flourished, as people quickly bought what goods they could with the depreciating currency. Newspapers bemoaned the rampant spending on imported items—hats, silks, china, tea—indulged in even by ordinary people. In many localities, legal suits between debtors and creditors quadrupled over prewar levels. A laborer in central Massachusetts, William Manning, described the economic trouble brewing: "With the prices of labor and produce falling very fast, creditors began calling for old debts and saying that they would not take payment in paper money. . . . Property was selling almost every day by execution [court-ordered foreclosures] for less than half its value. The jails were crowded with debtors." A serious postwar depression settled in by the mid-1780s and did not lift until the 1790s.

The confederation government itself was in a terrible financial fix. Continental dollars had lost almost all value: It took 146 of them to buy what one dollar had bought in 1775. Desperate times required desperate measures. The congress turned to Robert Morris, a merchant and newly reelected delegate from Pennsylvania, appointing him superintendent of finance. Six years earlier, the wealthy Morris had procured from Europe much-needed muskets for the army, which were shipped to his private firm in crates disguised as routine merchandise. Morris had resigned from the congress in 1778 under suspicion that he had unfairly profited from his public service efforts; indeed, he had left public life many thousands of dollars richer than he had entered it. Nevertheless, the congress called on him from 1781 to 1784 to apply his considerable talent to the confederation's economic problems.

To augment the government's revenue, Morris first proposed a 5 percent import tax (called an impost). Since there was no authority in the Articles of Confederation for such a tax, Morris's plan required an amendment to the Articles approved unanimously by the thirteen states. But unanimous agreement was impossible. States with bustling ports already collected taxes on imports and were loath to share that income. Rhode Island, with its active wharves at Newport and Providence, absolutely refused. When Morris pushed the impost amendment again late in 1783, it was New York (whose premier port had just been freed from British occupation) that refused.

Morris's next idea was the creation of the Bank of North America. This private bank, located in Philadelphia, would enjoy a special relationship with the confederation, holding the government's **hard money** (insofar as there was any) as well as private deposits, and providing the government with short-term loans. The bank's contribution to economic stability came in the form of banknotes, pieces of paper inscribed with a dollar value. Unlike the Continental dollars of the early war days, these banknotes were backed by hard money in the bank's vaults and thus would not depreciate. Morris hoped this form of money would retain value; Congress agreed and voted to approve the bank in 1781.

But the bank had limited success curing the confederation's economic woes. In the short run, the bank supplied the government with currency that held its value, but it issued so little that the impact was very small. The bank mainly en-

Philadelphia Almshouse
The city almshouse occupied a block on Spruce Street between Tenth and Eleventh Streets in Philadelphia. Built in 1767 to provide greater capacity than the prior almshouse, it was run by a city board called the Guardians of the Poor and financed by a city poor tax. It offered temporary housing and care for indigents unable to support themselves, many of whom were children, unwed mothers, or mentally disturbed people. A neighboring building named the House of Employment sheltered able-bodied poor who were forced to work in exchange for food and shelter.
Rare Book Department, The Free Library of Philadelphia.

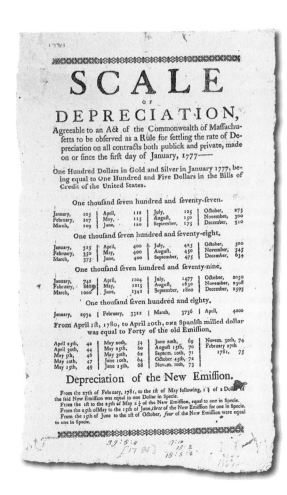

riched Morris and three close associates, who owned a large part of the bank's stock.

If Morris could not resuscitate the economy in the 1780s, probably no one could have done it. Because the Articles of Confederation reserved most economic functions to the states, the congress was helpless to tax trade, control inflation, curb the flow of state-issued paper money, or pay the mounting public debt. But the confederation had acquired one source of enormous potential wealth: the huge territory ceded by

Scale of Depreciation
This chart shows the monthly value of U.S. Continental dollars from January 1777 to February 1781, as stipulated by the government of Massachusetts. For example, in March 1780, 3,736 Continental dollars equaled the buying power of $100 in gold or silver based on values of the dollar in January 1777. By April 1780, the same value of hard money required $4,000 Continentals. Such a chart was needed when debtors and creditors settled accounts contracted at one time and paid off later in greatly depreciated dollars. How easy would you find it to keep your head above water in an economy with such fast currency depreciation? What level of arithmetic and chart-reading skills were required? Notice the handwritten figuring at the bottom of the chart. Do these arithmetic operations look familiar to you?
Courtesy, American Antiquarian Society.

Virginia, which in 1784 became the national domain. With American settlers resuming their westward pressure at the end of the Revolutionary War, there was need to plan for the orderly sale and distribution of that land.

Land Ordinances and the Northwest Territory

> Jefferson's aim was to encourage rapid and democratic settlement, to build a nation of freeholders, and to avoid speculative frenzy.

The Continental Congress appointed Thomas Jefferson to draft a national domain policy. Jefferson proposed dividing the territory north of the Ohio River and east of the Mississippi—called the Northwest Territory—into ten new states, each divided into townships ten miles square. He at first advocated giving the land to settlers, rather than selling it, on the grounds that the improved lands would so enrich the country through future property taxes that there was no need to make the settlers pay twice. Jefferson's aim was to encourage rapid and democratic settlement of the land, to build a nation of freeholders (as opposed to renters), and to avoid speculative frenzy. Jefferson also insisted that the new states have representative governments equal in status to those of the original states once they reached a certain population. Most boldly of all, Jefferson's draft prohibited slavery in the ten new states.

The congress adopted parts of Jefferson's plan in the Ordinance of 1784: the rectangular grid, the ten states, and the guarantee of self-government and eventual statehood. What the congress found too radical was the proposal to give away the land; the national domain was the confederation's only source of independent wealth. The slavery prohibition also failed, by a vote of seven to six states.

A year later, the congress refined and revised the legislation to set up procedures for surveying, mapping, and selling the land. The Ordinance of 1785 called for a rectilinear survey of the national domain (Map 8.2). On paper, the plan seemed to guarantee precision: There were to be walkable townships six miles square, each containing thirty-six perfect one-mile-square sections. Each section was to contain 640 acres, enough for four family farms, and one lot in each township was to be set aside for educational purposes. The 1785 ordinance reduced Jefferson's plan for ten rectangular states down to a less specific three to five states with boundaries conforming to natural geographic features such as the Great Lakes and major rivers instead of to abstractly drawn survey lines. But within the future states, the unrelentingly rectilinear survey lines ran straight over hills and mountains and through rivers and lakes, reducing all property to mappable squares.

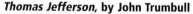

Thomas Jefferson, by John Trumbull

This miniature shows Thomas Jefferson at age forty-five, during his years as a diplomat in Paris. The American artist John Trumbull visited France in 1788 and painted Jefferson's likeness in this five-by-four-inch format so he could later copy it into his planned large canvas depicting the signing of the Declaration of Independence. Jefferson requested three replicas of the miniature to bestow as gifts. One went to his daughter Martha, another to an American woman in London, and the third to Maria Cosway, a British artist with whom Jefferson shared an intense infatuation during his stay in France. A widower, Jefferson never remarried, but a scandal over his private life erupted in 1802, when a journalist charged that he had fathered several children by his slave Sally Hemings. In 1998, a careful DNA study concluded that uniquely marked Jefferson Y-chromosomes were common to male descendants in both the Hemings and Jefferson lines. The DNA evidence, when combined with historical evidence about Jefferson's whereabouts at the start of each of Hemings's six pregnancies, makes it extremely likely that Jefferson fathered some or perhaps all of her children. What cannot be known is the nature of the relationship between the two. Was it coerced or voluntary, or somewhere in between? In all his voluminous writings, Jefferson left no comment about Sally Hemings, and the record on her side is entirely mute.

Monticello/Thomas Jefferson Memorial Foundation, Inc.

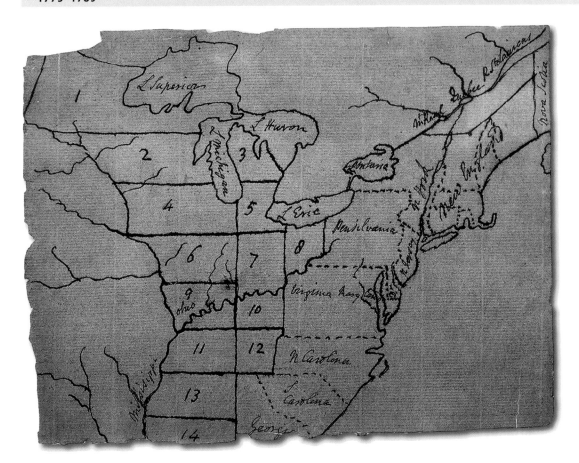

Jefferson's Map of the Northwest Territory
Thomas Jefferson sketched out borders for ten new states in his initial plan for the Northwest Territory in 1784. Straight lines and right angles held a strong appeal for him. But such regularity ignored inconvenient geographic features such as rivers and even more inconvenient political features such as Indian territorial claims, most unlikely to be ceded by treaty in orderly blocks. Jefferson also submitted ten distinctive names for the states. Number 9, for example, was Polypotamia, "land of many rivers" in Greek.
William L. Clements Library.

For more help analyzing this image, see the visual activity for this chapter in the Online Study Guide at bedfordstmartins.com/roark.

The 1785 ordinance decreed that land sales would occur by public auction. The minimum price was set at one dollar an acre, but market forces could drive up the prices of the most desirable land. Two further restrictions applied: Land was to be sold in minimum parcels of 640 acres each, and payment had to be in hard money or in certificates of debt from Revolutionary days. This effectively meant that the land's first owners would be prosperous speculators, men who had the large sum of $640 on hand or who had bought up quantities of certificates of debt at bargain prices. The grid of invariant squares further enhanced speculation, because owners could buy and sell exactly mapped parcels of land without

ever setting foot on the acreage. The commodification of land had been taken to a new level.

Speculators usually held the land for resale rather than inhabiting it. Thus they avoided direct contact with the most serious obstacle to settlement: the dozens of Indian tribes that claimed the land as their own. Treaties signed at Fort Stanwix in 1784 and Fort McIntosh in 1785 coerced partial cessions of land from Iroquois, Delaware, Huron, and Miami tribes. Then in 1786, a united Indian meeting near Detroit issued an ultimatum: No cession would be valid without unanimous consent. The Indians advised the United States to "prevent your surveyors and other people from coming upon our side

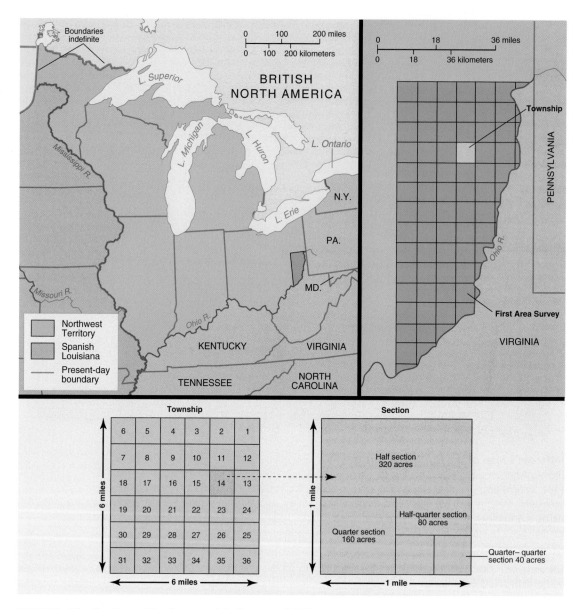

MAP 8.2   The Northwest Territory and Ordinance of 1785
Surveyors mapping the eastern edge of the Northwest Territory followed the Ordinance of 1785, using the stars as well as poles and chains (standard surveying equipment) to run long boundary lines. The result was a blanket of six-mile-square townships, subdivided into one-mile squares each containing sixteen 40-acre farms.

of the Ohio river." For two more decades, violent Indian wars in Ohio and Indiana would continue to impede white settlement (see chapter 9).

In 1787, a third land act, called the Northwest Ordinance, went well beyond the first two to specify the exact mechanism by which settled territories would advance to statehood, "on an equal footing with original states." Three stages of development were identified. First, a sparsely settled territory would be gov-

erned by officials appointed by the congress, and they in turn could adopt a legal code and appoint local magistrates as needed to administer justice. When the white male population of voting age and landowning status (fifty acres) reached 5,000, the territory could elect its own legislature and send a nonvoting delegate to the congress. When the population of voting citizens reached 60,000, they could write a state constitution and apply for full admission to the Union.

At all three territorial stages, the inhabitants were subject to taxation to support the Union, in the same manner as were the original states.

The Northwest Ordinance of 1787 was one of the most important pieces of legislation passed by the confederation government. It ensured that the new United States, so recently released from colonial dependency, would not itself become a colonial power—at least not with respect to white citizens. The mechanism it established allowed for the successful and orderly expansion of the United States across the continent in the next century.

Nonwhites were not forgotten or neglected in the 1787 ordinance. The brief document acknowledged the Indian presence in the Northwest Territory and promised that "the utmost good faith shall always be observed towards the Indians; their lands and property shall never be taken from them without their consent; and, in their property, rights, and liberty, they shall never be invaded or disturbed, unless in just and lawful wars authorized by Congress." The 1787 ordinance further pledged that "laws founded in justice and humanity, shall from time to time be made for preventing wrongs being

A Survey Plat of William Few's Land in Georgia

An anonymous artist illustrates the traditional metes-and-bounds surveying technique in this charming land plat (or map) drawn in 1784, in which chains and compasses measured out the boundaries of property. These 887 acres along a river bottom in Georgia were owned by the wealthy William Few. Two surveyors pictured at the upper right measure out land with chains of standard length; compass readings (such as N30 W50) indicate the direction of the lines being measured from one fixed point to the next. Note that the fixed points are not actually permanent; they are poplar, oak, hickory, and maple trees. In the metes-and-bounds technique, large stones might also serve that function. In contrast, Jefferson's 1785 plan to map out the Northwest Territory in perfect squares represented a revolutionary approach to land measurement. His rectilinear system called for surveying by the stars to run long baseline or meridian lines over hundreds of miles; subdivisions of land, defined by straight lines and right angles, could then be drawn on maps with a ruler and protractor, irrespective of rivers, trees, rocks, or steep hillsides. William Few of Georgia could buy a rich river bottom with the metes-and-bounds system of property division; Jefferson's plan aimed to democratize and simplify land measurement, which meant that valuable geographic features might well be divided.

Georgia Division of Archives and History, Office of Secretary of State.

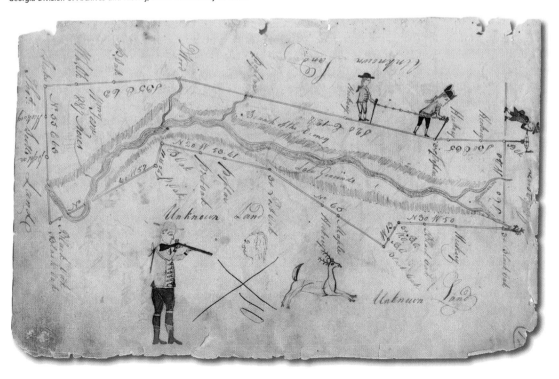

done to them, and for preserving peace and friendship with them." These promises were full of noble intentions, but they were not generally honored in the decades to come.

Jefferson's original suggestion to prohibit slavery in the Northwest Territories resurfaced in the 1787 ordinance, and it passed this time without debate. But the document acknowledged and supported slavery's existence in the South, in the assurance that fugitive southern slaves caught north of the Ohio River would be returned to their owners. Southerners could thus vote for the prohibition on slavery, secure in the knowledge that it applied only north of the Ohio; plenty of territory south of the river and west of Georgia and the Carolinas was still available for the spread of slavery. Still, the prohibition of slavery in the Northwest Territory perpetuated the dynamic of gradual emancipation in the North: A North-South sectionalism, based on slavery, was slowly taking shape.

Shays's Rebellion, 1786–1787

Without an impost amendment, and with the land sales of the Northwest Territory projected but not yet realized, the confederation turned to the states in the 1780s to contribute revenue voluntarily. Struggling with their own war debts, most state legislatures were reluctant to tax their constituents too heavily. Massachusetts, however, had a tough-minded, fiscally conservative legislature, dominated by the coastal commercial centers, which wanted to retire the state debt by raising taxes. Worse yet, it insisted that taxes be paid in hard money, not cheap paper. For four years, the state legislature exacted property and poll (or head) taxes; farmers in the western two-thirds of the state found it increasingly difficult to comply.

> Western farmers had learned from the American Revolution how to resist oppressive taxation.

Western farmers had learned from the American Revolution how to resist oppressive taxation. From 1782, they sent petitions to the state legislature, voicing their grievances. In July 1786, when the legislature adjourned yet again without addressing the farmers' complaints, a series of conventions was quickly organized. At one such convention, representing fifty towns, dissidents called for revisions to the state constitution that would promote democracy, eliminate the elite upper house, and move the capital farther west in the state.

Still not being heard in Boston, the dissidents targeted the most visible symbol of state authority in their regions, the county courts. In the fall of 1786, armed men numbering two or three thousand marched on courthouses in six Massachusetts counties and closed them down. Bewildered judges were forced to sign agreements not to hold court until the state constitution was revised or replaced. Sympathetic local militias did little or nothing to stop these activities. The insurgents were not predominantly poor or debt-ridden farmers; they included veteran soldiers and officers in the Continental army as well as leaders of their towns, men who thought the state government had fallen into the hands of a tyrannical few and ceased to be responsive to the interests of the many. One of several leaders was a farmer and one-time captain in the army, Daniel Shays, from the town of Pelham.

The governor of Massachusetts, James Bowdoin, who had once organized protests against British taxes, now characterized the western dissidents as illegal rebels. He villified Shays as the chief leader, and a Boston newspaper claimed Shays planned to burn Boston to the ground and overthrow the government, clearly an overreaction. Another former radical, Samuel Adams, took the extreme position that "the man who dares rebel against the laws of a republic ought to suffer death." These aging revolutionaries had given little thought to the possibility that popular majorities, embodied in a state legislature, could seem to be just as oppressive as monarchs. The dissidents challenged the assumption that popularly elected governments would always be fair and just.

Members of the Continental Congress grew worried that the situation in Massachusetts was spinning out of control. In October, the congress issued plans to triple the size of the federal army, calling for 660 new recruits from Massachusetts and another 560 from New England; but fewer than 100 enlisted in the troubled state. So Governor Bowdoin raised a private army, gaining the services of some 3,000 by paying them bounties provided by donations from a small wealthy circle of Boston merchants (who were later repaid by the state).

In January 1787, the insurgents learned of the private army marching their way, and 1,500 of them moved swiftly to capture a federal armory in Springfield to gain weapons. But a militia band loyal to the state government beat them to the weapons facility and met their attack with gunfire; four rebels were killed and another

Silver Bowl for an Anti-Shays General
Members of the militia of Springfield in western Massachusetts presented their leader, General William Shepard, with this silver bowl to honor his victory over the insurgents in Shays's Rebellion. Presentational silver conveyed a double message. It announced gratitude and praise in engraved words, and it transmitted considerable monetary value in the silver itself. General Shepard could display his trophy on a shelf, use it as a punch bowl, will it to descendants to keep his famous moment alive in memory, or melt it down in hard times. Shepard's is not the only name commemorated on the bowl; Shays's name appears in the last line, there for the ages to remember.
Yale University Art Gallery, Mabel Brady Garvan Collection.

twenty wounded. The final and bloodless encounter came at Petersham, where Bowdoin's army surprised the rebels on a freezing February morning and took 150 prisoners; the others fled into the woods. Shays took off for Canada and other leaders left the state, but more than 1,000 dissidents were rounded up and jailed.

In the end, only two men were executed for rebellion; sixteen more were sentenced to hang but were reprieved, sometimes at the last moment on the gallows. Some 4,000 men gained leniency by confessing their misconduct and swearing an oath of allegiance to the state. A special Disqualification Act prohibited the penitent rebels from voting, holding public office, serving on juries, working as schoolmasters, or operating taverns for up to three years, a period shortened to a year for those demonstrating good behavior.

Shays's Rebellion caused leaders throughout the country to worry about the confedera-

Shays's Rebellion, 1786–1787

Map showing locations including Williamstown, Greenfield, Deerfield, Petersham, BERKSHIRE COUNTY, Pelham, WORCESTER COUNTY, Hatfield, Lenox, Northampton, Hadley, Paxton, Stockbridge, Belchertown, Worcester, Great Barrington, HAMPSHIRE COUNTY, Springfield, Sturbridge, Westfield.

✳ Attacks by Shays's followers

✳ Encounters between Shays's and government forces

tion's ability to handle civil disorder. Massachusetts newspapers made it seem that bloody mob rule had nearly succeeded; perhaps, some feared, similar "combustibles" in other states were awaiting the spark that would set off a dreadful political conflagration. New York lawyer and diplomat John Jay wrote to George Washington, "Our affairs seem to lead to some crisis, some revolution—something I cannot foresee or conjecture. I am uneasy and apprehensive; more so than during the war." Benjamin Franklin, in his eighties, shrewdly observed that in 1776 Americans had feared "an excess of power in the rulers," but now the problem was "a defect of obedience" in the subjects. Among such leaders, the sense of crisis in the confederation had greatly deepened.

The United States Constitution

Shays's Rebellion provoked an odd mixture of fear and hope that the government under the Articles of Confederation was losing its grip on power. A small circle of Virginians decided to try one last time to augment the powers granted to the government by the Articles. Their call for a meeting to discuss trade regulation led, more quickly than they could have imagined in 1786, to a total reworking of the national government.

From Annapolis to Philadelphia

The Virginians took their lead from James Madison, now thirty-five and a member of the Virginia assembly. Madison convinced the congress of the confederation government to allow a meeting of delegates at Annapolis, Maryland, in September 1786, to try again to revise the trade regulation powers of the Articles. But only five states participated. Like Madison, the dozen men who attended sensed an impending crisis, and they rescheduled the meeting for Philadelphia in May 1787. (See "American Places," page 271.) The congress reluctantly endorsed the Philadelphia meeting and tried to limit its scope to "the sole and express purpose of revising the Articles of

Confederation." But at least one representative at the Annapolis meeting had far more ambitious plans. Alexander Hamilton of New York hoped the Philadelphia meeting would do whatever was necessary to strengthen the federal government.

Alexander Hamilton by character was suited for such bold steps. The illegitimate son of

City Tavern

Philadelphia's City Tavern, built in 1773, became a favorite gathering place for political delegates who traveled to that city for continental congresses. Taverns provided important public meeting spaces for business and social functions; they were critical nodes on the information network of the day, the place to learn news from travelers, newspapers, or local gossip. John Adams called the City Tavern "the most genteel one in America." Here, in the Long Room on the second floor, delegates toasted each other on the anniversary of the Declaration of Independence on July 4, 1777. The men who wrote the Constitution in the summer of 1787 took meals and drinks there. This engraving and others like it aided in the complete reconstruction of the tavern on its original site in the 1970s; today it is open to the public as a period restaurant, complete with staff in costume.

Rare Book Department, The Free Library of Philadelphia.

a poor mother in the West Indies, Hamilton trained as a bookkeeper and prospered under the intellectual mentorship of a local minister. In 1773, the bright lad greatly impressed an American trader, who sent him to New York City for a college education. Hamilton soon got swept up in the military enthusiasm of 1776 and by 1777 had joined George Washington's staff, serving at the general's side through much of the Revolution. After the war, he studied law, married into a New York merchant family, and sat in the Continental Congress for two years. Despite his stigmatized and impoverished childhood, the aspiring Hamilton identified with the elite classes and their fear of democratic disorder.

The fifty-five men who assembled at Philadelphia in May 1787 to consider the shortcomings of the Articles of Confederation were generally those most concerned about weaknesses in the present government. Few attended who were opposed to revising the Articles. Patrick Henry, author of the Virginia Resolves in 1765 and more recently state governor, refused to go, saying he "smelled a rat." Rhode Island refused to send delegates. Two New York representatives left in dismay in the middle of the convention, leaving Hamilton as the sole New York delegate.

This gathering of white men included no **artisans** or day laborers or even farmers of middling wealth. Two-thirds of the delegates were lawyers. The majority had served in the confederation congress and knew its strengths and weaknesses; fully half had been officers in the Continental army. Seven men had been governors of their states and knew firsthand the frustrations of thwarted executive power. A few elder statesmen attended, such as Benjamin Franklin and George Washington, but on the whole, the delegates were young, like Madison and Hamilton.

The Virginia and New Jersey Plans

The convention worked in secrecy, so the men could freely explore alternatives without fear that their honest opinions would come back to haunt them. The Virginia delegation first laid out a fifteen-point plan for a complete restructuring of the government. This Virginia Plan was a total repudiation of the principle of a confederation of states. Largely the work of Madison, the plan set out a three-branch government composed of a two-chamber legislature, a powerful executive, and a judiciary. It practically eliminated the

AMERICAN PLACES

Independence Park, Philadelphia, Pennsylvania

Philadelphia Independence Park
Independence National Historic Park.

In the 1780s, Philadelphia was the largest city in America, with over 30,000 inhabitants. With many hotels and taverns and a convenient location (equidistant from Boston and Williamsburg, each 300 miles away), there is little wonder that it became the preferred meeting site for Revolutionary-era congresses.

Nine eighteenth-century buildings in downtown Philadelphia are open to visitors at the 45-acre Independence National Historical Park, established in 1948. The main attraction is Independence Hall (shown here), where both the Declaration of Independence and the U.S. Constitution were debated and signed.

Nearby is Carpenter's Hall, built as a meeting hall for a trade guild (a skilled labor union), where the First Continental Congress met in 1774. Congress Hall, built in 1787, housed the U.S. House and Senate through the 1790s.

Although the focus at Independence Park is understandably on those important congresses, the site reveals much more about Revolutionary-era life. Typical of late-eighteenth-century cities, the neighborhood around Independence Hall was both commercial and residential and mixed by class. A mansion owned by the financier Robert Morris became the residence of Presidents Washington and John Adams in the 1790s; it no longer exists. A more modest house (open for tours) was home to Dolley Payne Todd (future wife of James Madison), whose first husband and child died in the yellow fever epidemic that killed over 4,000 Philadelphians in 1793. Much smaller houses once lined the streets around Independence Hall and were home and shop to working-class shoemakers, potters, and at least two African American women who peddled fruit tarts.

Today, nearly a million visitors each year stroll the grounds of this historic park, perhaps without realizing that until the 1940s the grassy areas were crowded with structures. **Archaeological** digs have produced upwards of 30,000 items—pieces of pottery, bones, buttons, household utensils, toys, and chamber pots, even a shoe with leather still flexible after two centuries, preserved by moisture at the bottom of a buried well. These **artifacts** help remind historians and tourists that even at a time of momentous political change, most Americans still went about their daily lives.

FOR WEB LINKS RELATED TO THIS SITE AND OTHER AMERICAN PLACES, see "PlaceLinks" at bedfordstmartins.com/roark.

The Pennsylvania Statehouse
The constitutional convention assembled at the Pennsylvania statehouse to sweat out the summer of 1787. Despite the heat, the delegates nailed the windows shut to eliminate the chance of being heard by eavesdroppers, so intent were they on secrecy. The statehouse, built in the 1740s to house the colony's assembly, accommodated the Continental Congress at various times in the 1770s and 1780s. The building is now called Independence Hall, in honor of the signing of the Declaration of Independence within its walls in 1776.
Historical Society of Pennsylvania.

voices of the smaller states by pegging representation in both houses of the congress to population. The theory was that government operated directly on people, not on states. Among the breathtaking powers assigned to the congress were the rights to veto state legislation and to coerce states militarily to obey national laws. To prevent the congress from having absolute power, the executive and judiciary could jointly veto its actions.

In mid-June, delegates from New Jersey, Connecticut, Delaware, and New Hampshire—all small states—unveiled an alternative proposal. The New Jersey Plan, as it was called, maintained the existing single-house congress of the Articles of Confederation in which each state had one vote. Acknowledging the need for an executive, it created a plural presidency to be shared by three men elected by the congress

from among its membership. Where it sharply departed from the existing government was in the sweeping powers it gave to the congress: the right to tax, to regulate trade, and to use force on unruly state governments. In favoring national power over **states' rights,** it aligned itself with the Virginia Plan. But the New Jersey Plan retained the confederation principle that the national government was to be an assembly of states, not of people.

For two weeks, delegates debated the two plans, focusing on the key issue of representation. The small-state delegates conceded that one house in a two-house legislature could be apportioned by population, but they would never agree that both houses could be. Madison was equally vehement about bypassing representation by state, which he viewed as the fundamental flaw in the Articles.

The debate seemed deadlocked, and for a while the convention was "on the verge of dissolution, scarce held together by the strength of a hair," according to one delegate. Only in mid-July did the so-called Great Compromise break the stalemate and produce the basic structural features of the emerging United States Constitution. Proponents of the competing plans agreed on a bicameral legislature. Representation in the lower house, the House of Representatives, would be apportioned by population, and representation in the upper house, the Senate, would come from all the states equally. Instead of one vote per state in the upper house, as in the New Jersey Plan, the compromise provided two senators who voted independently.

Representation by population turned out to be an ambiguous concept once it was subjected to rigorous discussion. Who counted? Were slaves, for example, people or property? As people, they would add weight to the southern delegations in the House of Representatives, but as property they would add to the tax burdens of those states. What emerged was the compromise known as the three-fifths clause: All free persons plus "three-fifths of all other Persons" constituted the numerical base for the apportionment of representatives.

Using "all other Persons" as a substitute for "slaves" indicates the discomfort delegates felt in acknowledging in the Constitution the existence of slavery. The words *slave* and *slavery* appear nowhere in the document, but slavery figured in two other places besides the three-fifths clause. Trade regulation, for example, a power of the new House of Representatives, naturally included regulation of the slave trade. In euphemistic language, a compromise between southern and northern states specified that "the Migration or Importation of such Persons as any of the States now shall think proper to admit, shall not be prohibited by the Congress prior to the Year one thousand eight hundred and eight." A third provision guaranteed the return of fugitive slaves: "No person, held to Service or Labour in one State, under the Laws thereof, escaping into another, shall, in Consequence of any Law or Regulation therein, be discharged from such Service or Labour but shall be delivered up on Claim of the party to whom such Service or Labour may be due." Slavery was nowhere named, but it was recognized, guaranteed, and thereby perpetuated by the U.S. Constitution.

Plenty of fine-tuning followed the Great Compromise of mid-July, but the most difficult problem, representation, had been solved. The small states worked to consolidate power in the Senate, where their weight would be proportionately greater than in the lower house, and Madison slowly recovered from his initial crushing sense of defeat. He had entered the convention convinced that the major flaw in the old government was that it had relied on unreliable states, and he feared that the Great Compromise perpetuated that flaw. But as the respective powers of the House and Senate were hammered out, he lent his support to the package as the most reasonable of political outcomes.

Democracy versus Republicanism

The delegates in Philadelphia made a distinction between *democracy* and *republicanism* new to American political vocabulary. Pure democracy was now taken to be a dangerous thing. As a Massachusetts delegate put it, "the evils we experience flow from the excess of democracy." The delegates still favored republican institutions, but they created a government that gave direct voice to the people only in the House and that granted a check on that voice to the Senate, a body of men elected not by direct popular vote but by the state legislatures. Senators served for six years, with no limit on reelection; they were protected from the whims of democratic majorities, and their long terms fostered experience and maturity in office.

Similarly, the presidency evolved into a powerful office out of the reach of direct democracy. The delegates devised an electoral college whose only function was to elect the president and vice president. Each state's legislature would choose the electors, whose number was the sum of representatives and senators for the state, an interesting melding of the two principles of representation. The president thus would owe his office not to the Congress, the states, or the people, but to a temporary assemblage of distinguished citizens who could vote their own judgment on the candidates.

The framers had developed a far more complex form of federal government than that provided by the Articles of Confederation. To curb the excesses of democracy, they devised a government with limits and checks on all three branches of government. They set forth a powerful president who could veto Congress, but they gave Congress power to override presidential vetoes. They set up a national judiciary to settle disputes between states and citizens of different states. They made the other branches of government as independent from the other branches as they could, by basing election on different universes of voters—voting citizens, state legislators, the electoral college.

> The words *slave* and *slavery* appear nowhere in the document, but slavery was recognized, guaranteed, and thereby perpetuated by the U.S. Constitution.

The convention carefully listed the powers of Congress and of the president. The president could initiate policy, propose legislation, and veto acts of Congress; he could command the military and direct foreign policy; and he could appoint the entire judiciary, subject to Senate approval. Congress held the purse strings: the power to levy taxes, to regulate trade, and to coin money and control the currency. States were expressly forbidden to issue paper money. Two more powers of Congress—to "provide for the common defence and general Welfare" of the country and "to make all laws which shall be necessary and proper" for carrying out its powers—provided elastic language that came closest to Madison's wish to grant sweeping powers to the new government.

The Constitution was a product of lengthy debate and compromise; no one was entirely satisfied with every line. Madison himself, who soon became its staunchest defender, remained unsure that the most serious flaws of the Articles had been expunged. But when the final vote was taken at the Philadelphia convention in September 1787, only three dissenters refused to endorse the document. The thirty-nine who signed it (thirteen others had gone home early) no doubt wondered how to sell this plan, with its powerful executive and Congress and its deliberate limits on pure democracy, to the American public. The Constitution specified a mechanism for ratification that avoided the dilemma faced earlier by the confederation government: Nine states, not all thirteen, had to ratify it, and special ratifying conventions elected only for that purpose, not state legislatures, would make the crucial decision.

Ratification of the Constitution

Had a popular vote been taken on the Constitution in the fall of 1787, it would probably have been rejected. In the three most populous states—Virginia, Massachusetts, and New York—substantial majorities opposed a powerful new national government. North Carolina and Rhode Island refused to call ratifying conventions. Seven of the eight re-

MAP 8.3   Ratification of the Constitution, 1788–1790

Populated areas cast votes for delegates to state ratification conventions. This map shows Antifederalist strength generally concentrated in backcountry, noncoastal, and nonurban areas, but with significant exceptions (for example, Rhode Island).

READING THE MAP: Where was Federalist opinion concentrated? How did the distribution of Federalist and Antifederalist sentiment affect the order of state ratifications of the Constitution?
CONNECTIONS: What objections did Antifederalists have to the new United States Constitution? How did their locations affect their view of the Federalist argument?

FOR MORE HELP ANALYZING THIS MAP, see the map activity for this chapter in the Online Study Guide at bedfordstmartins.com/roark.

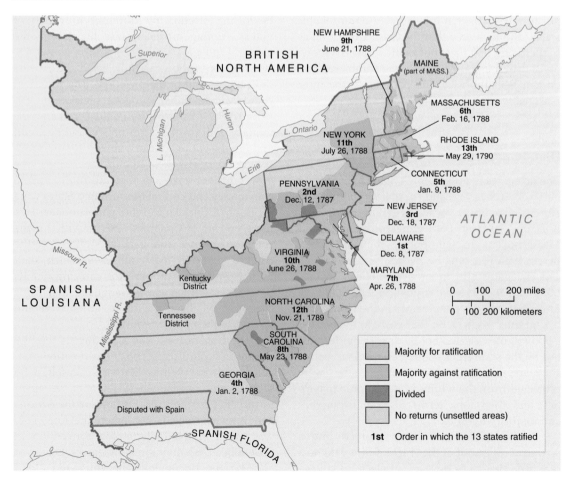

maining states were easy victories for the Constitution, but securing the approval of the ninth proved difficult. Pro-Constitution forces, called Federalists, had to strategize very shrewdly to defeat anti-Constitution forces, who were called Antifederalists.

The Federalists

Proponents of the Constitution moved into action swiftly. To silence the criticism that they had gone beyond their charge (which indeed they had), they sent the document to the congress. Congress withheld explicit approval but resolved to send the Constitution to the states for their consideration. The pro-Constitution forces shrewdly secured another advantage by calling themselves "Federalists." By all logic, this label was more suitable for the backers of the confederation concept, because the Latin root of the word *federal* means "league." Their opponents became known as "Antifederalists," a label that made them sound defensive and negative, lacking a program of their own.

The Federalists targeted the states most likely to ratify quickly, to gain momentum. Delaware provided unanimous ratification by early December, before the Antifederalists had even begun to campaign. Pennsylvania, New Jersey, and Georgia followed within a month (Map 8.3). In the latter two states, voter turnout was extremely low; apathy favored the Federalists. Delaware and New Jersey were small states surrounded by more powerful neighbors; a government that would regulate trade and set taxes according to population was an attractive proposition. Georgia sought the protection that a stronger national government would afford against hostile Indians and Spanish Florida to the south. "If a weak State with the Indians on its back and the Spaniards on its flank does not see the necessity of a General Government there must I think be wickedness or insanity in the way," said Federalist George Washington.

Another three easy victories came in Connecticut, Maryland, and South Carolina. As in Pennsylvania, merchants, lawyers, and urban artisans in general favored the new Constitution, as did large landowners and slaveholders. This tendency for the established political elite to be Federalist enhanced the prospects of victory, for Federalists already had power disproportionate to their numbers. Antifederalists in these states

Bed Curtain
This fabric, made into a bed curtain, was manufactured in England for sale in the American market around 1785. In repeating pattern it depicts two heroes of the new young country. One row shows George Washington standing majestically at the front of a chariot drawn by panthers. The alternate row depicts Benjamin Franklin dressed in a humble fur cap (his trademark) leading Miss Liberty forward. The British government may have lost the war, but the British textile industry was determined not to lose business.
Colonial Williamsburg Foundation.

tended to be rural, western, and noncommercial, men whose access to news was limited and whose participation in state government was tenuous. (See "Historical Question," page 276.)

Was the New United States a Christian Country?

Rebecca Samuel, a Jewish resident of Virginia, conveyed her excitement about the new U.S. Constitution when she wrote her German parents in 1791 that finally "Jew and Gentile are as one" in the realm of politics and citizenship. Other voices were distinctly less approving. An Antifederalist pamphlet warned that the pope could become president; another feared that "a Turk, a Jew, a Roman Catholic, and what is worse than all, a Universalist, may be President."

The document that produced such wildly different readings was indeed remarkable in its handling of religion. The Constitution did not invoke Christianity as a state religion. It made no reference to an almighty being, and it specifically promised, in Article 6, section 3, that "no religious test shall ever be required as a qualification to any office or public trust under the United States." The six largest congregations of Jews—numbering about two thousand and located in Newport, New York, Philadelphia, Baltimore, Charleston, and Savannah—were delighted with this nearly unprecedented statement of political equality and wrote George Washington to express their hearty thanks.

But more than a few Christian leaders were stunned at the Constitution's near silence on religion. It seemed to represent a complete turnabout from the state constitutions of the 1770s and 1780s. A New Yorker warned that "should the Citizens of America be as irreligious as her Constitution, we will have reason to tremble, lest the Governor of the universe . . . crush us to atoms." A delegate to North Carolina's ratifying convention played on anti-immigrant fears by predicting that the Constitution was "an invitation for Jews and pagans of every kind to come among us." A concerned Presbyterian minister asked Alexander Hamilton why religion was not in the Constitution. Hamilton reportedly quipped, "Indeed, Doctor, we forgot it."

Measured against the practices of state governments, Hamilton's observation is hardly credible. The men who wrote and debated the state and federal constitutions from 1775 to 1787 actively thought about principles of inclusion and exclusion when they defined citizenship, voting rights, and officeholding. They carefully considered property ownership, race, gender, and age in formulating rules about who could participate.

And they also thought about religious qualifications.

Most leaders of the 1780s took for granted that Christianity was the one true faith and the essential foundation of morality. All but two state constitutions assumed the primacy of **Protestantism,** and one-third of them collected public taxes to support Christian churches. Every state but New York required a Christian oath as a condition for officeholding. Every member of Pennsylvania's legislature swore to "acknowledge the Scripture of the Old and New Testament to be given by divine inspiration." North Carolina's rule was even more restrictive, since it omitted Catholics: "No person who shall deny the being of God or the truth of the Protestant religion, or the divine authority of the Old or New Testaments" could hold office. In South Carolina all voters had to be Protestants.

Other common political practices affirmed that the United States was a Christian country. Governors proclaimed days of public thanksgiving in the name of the Holy Trinity. Chaplains led legislatures in Christian prayer. Jurors and witnesses in court swore Christian oaths. New England states passed Sabbath laws prohibiting all work or travel on Sunday. Blasphemy laws punished people who cursed the Christian God or Jesus.

Close to half the state constitutions included the right to freedom of religion as an explicit guarantee. But freedom of religion meant only that difference would be tolerated; it did not guarantee political equality. How then did the U.S. Constitution come to be such a break from the im-

mediate past? Had the framers really just forgotten about religion?

Not James Madison of Virginia. Madison arrived at the 1787 convention fresh from a hard-won victory in Virginia to establish religious liberty. At the end of 1786, he had finally secured passage of a bill written by Thomas Jefferson seven years earlier called the Virginia Statute of Religious Freedom. "All men shall be free to profess, and by argument to maintain, their opinions in matters of religion, and that the same shall in no wise diminish, enlarge, or affect their civil capacities," the bill read. Madison had convinced both the Episcopalians and the Baptist dissenters, at war with each other over state support, that to grant either or both churches tax money would be to concede to the state the authority to endorse one religion—and by implication to crush another. The statute separated church from state

to protect religion. Further, it went beyond mere toleration to guarantee that religious choice was independent of civil rights.

In Madison's judgment, it was best for the U.S. Constitution to say as little as possible about religion, especially since state laws reflected a variety of positions. When Antifederalists demanded a bill of rights, Madison drew up a list for the first Congress to consider. Two items dealt with religion, but only one was approved. One became part of the First Amendment: "Congress shall make no law respecting an establishment of religion, or prohibiting the free exercise thereof." In a stroke, Madison set religious worship and the privileging of any one church beyond Congress's power. Significantly, his second proposal failed to pass: "No State shall violate the equal rights of conscience." Evidently, the states wanted to be

able to keep their Christian-only rules without federal interference. Different faiths would be tolerated—but not guaranteed equal standing. And the very same session of Congress proceeded to hire Christian chaplains and proclaim days of thanksgiving.

Gradually, states deleted restrictive laws, but as late as 1840 Jews still could not hold public office in four states. Into the twentieth century, some states maintained Sunday laws that forced business closings on the Christian Sabbath, working enormous hardship on those whose religion required Saturday closings. The guarantee of freedom of religion was embedded in state and federal founding documents in the 1770s and 1780s, but it has taken many years to fulfill Jefferson's vision of what true religious liberty means: the freedom for religious belief to be independent of civil status.

Massachusetts was the only early state that gave the Federalists difficulty. The vote to select the ratification delegates decidedly favored the Antifederalists, whose strength lay in the western areas of the state, home to Shays's Rebellion. One rural delegate from Worcester County voiced widely shared suspicions: "These lawyers and men of learning and money men that talk so finely, and gloss over matters so smoothly, to make us poor illiterate people swallow down the pill, expect to get into Congress themselves; they expect to be the managers of the Constitution and get all the power and all the money into their own hands, and then they will swallow up all us little folks." Nevertheless, the Antifederalist lead was slowly eroded by a vigorous newspaper campaign. In the end, the Federalists won by a very slim margin and only with promises that amendments to the Constitution would be taken up in the first Congress.

By May 1788, eight states had ratified; only one more was needed. North Carolina and Rhode Island were hopeless for the Federalist cause, and New Hampshire seemed nearly as bleak. More worrisome was the failure to win over the largest and most important states, Virginia and New York.

The Antifederalists

Antifederalists were a composite group, united mainly in their desire to block the Constitution. Although much Antifederalist strength came from backcountry areas long suspicious of eastern elites, many Antifederalist leaders came from the same social background as Federalist leaders; economic class alone did not differentiate them. Antifederalism also drew strength in states already on sure economic footing, like New York, that could afford to remain independent. Probably the biggest appeal of antifederalism lay in the long-nurtured fear that distant power might infringe on people's liberties. The language of the earlier revolutionary movement was not easily forgotten.

But by the time eight states had ratified, the Antifederalists faced a far harder task than they had once imagined. First, they were no longer defending the status quo, now that the momentum lay with the Federalists. Second, it was difficult to defend the confederation government with its admitted flaws. Even so, they remained genuinely fearful that the new government would be too distant from the people and could thus become corrupt or tyrannical. "The difficulty, if not impracticability, of exercising the equal and equitable powers of government by a single legislature over an extent of territory that reaches from the Mississippi to the western lakes, and from them to the Atlantic ocean, is an insuperable objection to the adoption of the new system," wrote one articulate Antifederalist in a compelling and much-read political pamphlet by "A Columbia Patriot." The Columbia Patriot was the alias for Mercy Otis Warren, a Massachusetts woman whose father, brother, and husband had all been active leaders in the revolutionary movement in Boston.

The new government was indeed distant. In the proposed House of Representatives, the only directly democratic element of the Constitution, one member represented some 30,000 people. How could that member really know or communicate with his whole constituency, the Antifederalists wondered. In contrast, one wrote, "The members of our state legislatures are annually elected—they are subject to instructions—they are chosen within small circles—they are sent but a small distance from their respective homes. Their conduct is constantly known to their constituents. They frequently see, and are seen, by the men whose servants they are."

The Antifederalists also worried that elected representatives would always be members of the elite. Such men "will be ignorant of the sentiments of the middling and much more of the lower class of citizens, strangers to their ability, unacquainted with their wants, difficulties, and distress," worried a Maryland man. None of this would be a problem under a confederation system, according to the Antifederalists, because real power would continue to reside in the state governments.

The Federalists generally agreed that the elite would be favored for election to the House of Representatives, not to mention the Senate and the presidency. That was precisely what they hoped. Federalists wanted power to flow to intelligent, virtuous, public-spirited leaders like themselves. They did not envision a government constituted of every class of people. "Fools and knaves have voice enough in government already," argued a New York Federalist, without being guaranteed representation in proportion

> Probably the biggest appeal of antifederalism lay in the long-nurtured fear that distant power might infringe on people's liberties. The language of the Revolution was not easily forgotten.

to the total population of fools. Alexander Hamilton claimed that mechanics and laborers preferred to have their social betters represent them. Antifederalists challenged the notion that any class could be sufficiently selfless to rule disinterestedly for others. One, calling himself "Brutus" in a newspaper article, complained that "in reality, there will be no part of the people represented, but the rich, even in that branch of the legislature, which is called the democratic. . . . It will literally be a government in the hands of the few to oppress and plunder the many."

Antifederalists fretted over many specific features of the Constitution. It prohibited state-issued paper money. It regulated the time and place of congressional elections, leading to fears that only one inconvenient polling place might be authorized, to disfranchise rural voters. The most widespread objection to the Constitution was its lack of any guarantees of individual liberties in a bill of rights, like those contained in many state constitutions. This glaring omission made many Antifederalists exceedingly uneasy.

Despite Federalist campaigns in the large states, it was a small state—New Hampshire—that provided the decisive ninth vote for ratification, on June 21, 1788. Federalists there succeeded in getting the convention postponed from February to June and in the interim conducted an intense and successful lobbying effort on specific delegates.

The Big Holdouts: Virginia and New York

Four states still remained outside the new union, and a glance at a map demonstrated the necessity of pressing the Federalist case in the two largest, Virginia and New York (see Map 8.2). Though Virginia was home to Madison and Washington, an influential Antifederalist group led by Patrick Henry and George Mason made the outcome uncertain. Mason had been present throughout the Philadelphia convention and was one of the three delegates who refused to sign the Constitution; this made him an especially effective opponent. The Federalists finally won his support by proposing twenty specific amendments—some of which would protect individual liberties—that the new government would promise to consider. By a 10-vote margin, out of 168 votes cast, the Federalists got their ratification in Virginia.

New York voters tended to antifederalism out of a sense that a state so large and powerful need not relinquish so much authority to the new federal government. But New York was also home to some of the most persuasive Federalists. Starting in October 1787, Alexander Hamilton collaborated with James Madison and New York lawyer John Jay on a series of eighty-five essays on the political philosophy of the new Constitution, published in New York newspapers and later republished as *The Federalist*. The essays brilliantly set out the failures of the Articles of Confederation and offered an analysis of the complex nature of federalism. In one of the most compelling essays, number 10, Madison challenged the Antifederalists' heartfelt conviction that republican government had to be small-scale. Madison argued that a large and diverse population was itself a guarantee of liberty. In a national government, no single faction could ever be large enough to subvert the freedom of other groups. "Extend the sphere, and you take in a greater variety of parties and interests; you make it less probable that a majority of the whole will have a common motive to invade the rights of other citizens," Madison asserted. He called it "a republican remedy for the diseases most incident to republican government."

At New York's ratifying convention, Antifederalists predominated, some fearful that an extended republic would fail, others worried that individual liberties were endangered. But impassioned debate and lobbying—plus the dramatic news of Virginia's ratification—finally tipped the balance to the Federalists. Still, the Antifederalists' approval of the document was delivered with a list of twenty-four individual rights they hoped would be protected and thirty-three structural changes they hoped to see in the Constitution. New York's ratification assured the solidity and legitimacy of the new government. It took another year and a half for Antifederalists in North Carolina to come around. Fiercely independent Rhode Island held out until May 1790, and even then it ratified by only a two-vote margin.

In less than twelve months, the U.S. Constitution was both written and ratified. (See appendix, page A-4.) An amazingly short time by twentieth-century standards, it is even more remarkable for the late eighteenth century, with its horse-powered transportation and hand-printed communications. The Federalists had faced a formidable task, but by building momentum and assuring consideration of a **Bill of Rights,** they did indeed carry the day.

Conclusion: The "Republican Remedy"

Thus ended one of the most intellectually tumultuous and creative decades in American history. American leaders experimented with ideas and drew up plans to embody their evolving and conflicting notions of how a society and a government ought to be formulated. There was widespread agreement that government should derive its power and authority from the people, but there was fierce disagreement over the degree of democracy—the amount of direct control of government by the people—that would be workable in American society.

The decade began in 1776 with a confederation government that could barely be ratified because of its requirement of unanimity, but there was no reaching unanimity on the western lands, on the impost amendment, or on the proper way to respond to unfair taxation in a republican state. The new Constitution offered a different approach to these problems by loosening the grip of impossible unanimity and by embracing the ideas of a heterogeneous public life and a carefully balanced government that together would prevent any one part of the public from tyrannizing another. The genius of James Madison was to anticipate that diversity of opinion was not only an unavoidable reality but a hidden strength of the new society beginning to take shape. This is what he meant in his tenth Federalist essay when he spoke of the "republican remedy" for the troubles most likely to befall a government where the people are the source of authority.

Despite Madison's optimism, political differences remained keen and worrisome to many. The Federalists still hoped for a society in which leaders of exceptional wisdom would discern the best path for public policy. They looked backward to a society of hierarchy, rank, and benevolent rule by an aristocracy of talent, but they created a government with forward-looking **checks and balances** as a guard against corruption, which they figured would most likely emanate from the people. The Antifederalists also looked backward, but to an old order of small-scale direct democracy and local control, where virtuous people kept a close eye on potentially corruptible rulers. Antifederalists feared a national government led by distant, self-interested leaders who needed to be held in check. In the 1790s, these two conceptions of republicanism and of leadership would be tested in real life.

FOR ADDITIONAL FIRSTHAND ACCOUNTS OF THIS PERIOD, see Chapter 8 in Michael Johnson, ed., *Reading the American Past,* Third Edition.

TO ASSESS YOUR MASTERY OF THE MATERIAL IN THIS CHAPTER, see the Online Study Guide at bedfordstmartins.com/roark.

FOR WEB LINKS RELATED TO TOPICS IN THIS CHAPTER, see "HistoryLinks," "DocLinks," and "PlaceLinks" at bedfordstmartins.com/roark.

CHRONOLOGY

1775 • Second Continental Congress meets and takes over direction of the war.

1776 • Virginia adopts state bill of rights.

1777 • Congress approves final draft of Articles of Confederation and sends it to states; controversies over western lands hold up ratification for five years.

1778 • State constitutions completed.

1780 • Pennsylvania institutes gradual emancipation.
• Cuffe brothers' petition to Massachusetts legislature results in extension of suffrage in Massachusetts to taxpaying free blacks.

1781 • Articles of Confederation ratified.
• Creation of executive departments; Robert Morris appointed superintendent of finance.
• Congress charters Bank of North America in an attempt to create stable currency, but bank has only a small impact.
• Slave Quok Walker successfully sues for freedom in Massachusetts.

1782 • Virginia relaxes state manumission law.

1783 • Treaty of Paris signed, ending the Revolutionary War.

1784 • Gradual emancipation laws passed in Rhode Island and Connecticut.
• Treaty of Fort Stanwix cedes Iroquois land to U.S. confederation government.

1786 • Virginia adopts Statute of Religious Freedom.
• Daniel Shays and fellow rebels challenge Massachusetts government, spreading fears that neither state nor central government can put down rebellions.
• Annapolis meeting proposes convention to revise Articles of Confederation.

1787 • Shays's Rebellion crushed in Massachusetts.
• Northwest Ordinance allows self-government and prohibits slavery in Northwest Territory.
• Delaware provides manumission law.
• Constitutional convention meets in Philadelphia.

1788 • U.S. Constitution ratified after vigorous campaign by Federalists.

1790 • Maryland provides manumission law.

1799 • Gradual emancipation law passed in New York.

1804 • Gradual emancipation law passed in New Jersey.

BIBLIOGRAPHY

General Works

Lance Banning, *The Sacred Fire of Liberty: James Madison and the Founding of the Federal Republic* (1995).
Jacob E. Cooke, *Alexander Hamilton* (1982).
Joseph J. Ellis, *After the Revolution: Profiles of Early American Culture* (1979).
Merrill Jensen, *The New Nation: A History of the United States during the Confederation, 1781–1789* (1950).
Ralph Ketcham, *James Madison: A Biography* (1971).
Edmund S. Morgan, *Inventing the People: The Rise of Popular Sovereignty in England and America* (1988).
Richard B. Morris, *The Forging of the Union, 1781–1789* (1987).
Peter S. Onuf and Cathy D. Matson, *A Union of Interests: Political and Economic Thought in Revolutionary America* (1990).
John Phillip Reid, *The Concept of Liberty in the Age of the American Revolution* (1988).
Robert E. Shalhope, *The Roots of Democracy: American Thought and Culture, 1760–1800* (1990).

Gordon Wood, *The Creation of the American Republic, 1776–1787* (1969).
Alfred F. Young, ed., *Beyond the American Revolution: Explorations in the History of American Radicalism* (1993).

The Confederation Government

Joseph L. Davis, *Sectionalism in American Politics, 1774–1787* (1977).
Daniel M. Friedenberg, *Life, Liberty, and the Pursuit of Land: The Plunder of Early America* (1992).
J. James Henderson, *Party Politics in the Continental Congress* (1974).
Merrill Jensen, *The Articles of Confederation: An Interpretation of the Social-Constitutional History of the American Revolution, 1774–1781* (1940).
Jackson Turner Main, *Political Parties before the Constitution* (1973).
Peter S. Onuf, *Statehood and Union: A History of the Northwest Ordinance* (1987).

Jack N. Rakove, *The Beginnings of National Politics: An Interpretive History of the Continental Congress* (1979).

Rosemarie Zagarri, *The Politics of Size: Representation in the United States, 1776–1850* (1987).

The Sovereign States

Willi Paul Adams, *The First American Constitutions: Republican Ideology and the Making of the State Constitutions in the Revolutionary Era* (1980).

Van Beck Hall, *Politics without Parties: Massachusetts, 1780–1791* (1972).

Ronald Hoffman and Peter J. Albert, eds., *Sovereign States in an Age of Uncertainty* (1981).

Marc W. Kruman, *Between Authority and Liberty: State Constitution Making in Revolutionary America* (1997).

Jackson Turner Main, *The Sovereign States, 1775–1783* (1973).

Richard P. McCormick, *Experiment in Independence: New Jersey in the Critical Period, 1781–1789* (1950).

Alfred Young, *The Democratic-Republicans of New York: The Origins, 1763–1797* (1967).

Citizenship

Ira Berlin, *Many Thousands Gone: The First Two Centuries of Slavery in North America* (1998).

Robert Dinkin, *Voting in Revolutionary America* (1982).

Linda K. Kerber, *Women of the Republic: Intellect and Ideology in Revolutionary America* (1980).

Linda K. Kerber, *No Constitutional Right to Be Ladies: Women and the Obligations of Citizenship* (1998).

James H. Kettner, *The Development of American Citizenship, 1608–1870* (1978).

Joanne Pope Melish, *Disowning Slavery: Gradual Emancipation and "Race" in New England, 1780–1860* (1998).

Gary B. Nash and Jean R. Sonderlund, *Freedom by Degrees: Emancipation in Pennsylvania and Its Aftermath* (1991).

Marylynn Salmon, *Women and the Law of Property in Early America* (1986).

Rogers M. Smith, *Civic Ideals: Conflicting Visions of Citizenship in U.S. History* (1997).

Rosemarie Zagarri, *A Woman's Dilemma: Mercy Otis Warren and the American Revolution* (1995).

The Critical Period

William G. Anderson, *The Price of Liberty: The Public Debt of the American Revolution* (1983).

Robert A. Becker, *Revolution, Reform, and the Politics of American Taxation, 1763–1783* (1980).

John L. Brooke, *The Heart of the Commonwealth: Society and Political Culture in Worcester County, Massachusetts, 1713–1861* (1989).

E. James Ferguson, *The Power of the Purse: A History of American Public Finance, 1776–1790* (1961).

Robert A. Gross, ed., *In Debt to Shays: The Bicentennial of an Agrarian Rebellion* (1993).

James R. Morrill, *The Practice and Politics of Fiat Finance: North Carolina in the Confederation, 1783–1789* (1969).

Leonard L. Richards, *Shays's Rebellion: The American Revolution's Final Battle* (2002).

David P. Szatmary, *Shays' Rebellion: The Making of an Agrarian Insurrection* (1980).

Alan Taylor, *Liberty Men and Great Proprietors: The Revolutionary Settlement on the Maine Frontier, 1760–1820* (1990).

The Constitution and Ratification

John K. Alexander, *The Selling of the Constitutional Convention: A History of News Coverage* (1990).

Lance Banning, *The Sacred Fire of Liberty: James Madison and the Founding of the Federal Republic* (1995).

Charles Beard, *An Economic Interpretation of the Constitution* (1913).

Richard Beeman, Stephen Botein, and Edward C. Carter II, eds., *Beyond Confederation: Origins of the Constitution and American National Identity* (1987).

Herman Belz, Ronald Hoffman, and Peter J. Albert, eds., *To Form a More Perfect Union: The Critical Ideas of the Constitution* (1992).

Richard B. Bernstein and Kym S. Rice, *Are We to Be a Nation? The Making of the Constitution* (1987).

Stephen R. Boyd, *The Politics of Opposition: Antifederalists and the Acceptance of the Constitution* (1979).

M. E. Bradford, *Original Intentions: On the Making and Ratification of the United States Constitution* (1993).

Richard Brookhiser, *Gentleman Revolutionary: Gouverneur Morris, the Rake Who Wrote the Constitution* (2003).

Robert E. Brown, *Charles Beard and the Constitution* (1956).

Roger H. Brown, *Redeeming the Republic: Federalists, Taxation, and the Origins of the Constitution* (1993).

Christopher Collier and James Lincoln Collier, *Decision in Philadelphia: The Constitutional Convention of 1787* (1987).

Patrick T. Conley and John P. Kaminski, eds., *The Bill of Rights and the States: The Colonial and Revolutionary Origins of American Liberties* (1992).

Saul Cornell, *The Other Founders: Anti-Federalism and the Dissenting Tradition in America, 1788–1828* (1999).

Linda Grant DePauw, *The Eleventh Pillar: New York State and the Federal Constitution* (1966).

Michael Allen Gillespie and Michael Lienesch, eds., *Ratifying the Constitution* (1989).

John P. Kaminski and Richard Leffler, *Federalists and Antifederalists: The Debate over the Constitution* (1998).

Michael Kammen, *A Machine That Would Go of Itself: The Constitution in American Culture* (1986).

Cecelia M. Kenyon, *Men of Little Faith: Selected Writings by Cecelia Kenyon* (2003).

Ralph Ketcham, *Framed for Posterity: The Enduring Philosophy of the Constitution* (1993).

Peter B. Knupfer, *The Union as It Is: Constitutional Unionism and Sectional Compromise, 1787–1861* (1991).

Leonard W. Levy and Dennis J. Mahoney, eds., *The Framing and Ratification of the Constitution* (1987).

Jackson Turner Main, *The Antifederalists: Critics of the Constitution, 1781–1788* (1961).

Elizabeth P. McCaughey, *Government by Choice: Inventing the United States Constitution* (1987).

Forrest McDonald, *We the People: The Economic Origins of the Constitution* (1958).

William Lee Miller, *The Business of May Next: James Madison and the Founding* (1992).

Richard B. Morris, *Witnesses at the Creation: Hamilton, Madison, Jay, and the Constitution* (1985).

Ellen Franken Paul and Howard Dickman, eds., *Liberty, Property, and the Foundations of the American Constitution* (1989).

Jack N. Rakove, *James Madison and the Creation of the American Republic* (1990).

Jack N. Rakove, *Original Meanings: Politics and Ideas in the Making of the Constitution* (1996).

John Phillip Reid, *Constitutional History of the American Revolution: The Authority of Rights* (1986).

William H. Riker, *The Strategy of Rhetoric: Campaigning for the American Constitution* (1996).

Robert A. Rutland, *The Ordeal of the Constitution: The Antifederalists and the Ratification Struggle of 1787–1788* (1966).

Stephen L. Schechter, *The Reluctant Pillar: New York and the Adoption of the Federal Constitution* (1985).

Bernard Schwartz, *The Great Rights of Mankind: A History of the American Bill of Rights* (1992).

Garry Wills, *Explaining America: The Federalist* (1981).

Religion

Ruth H. Bloch, *Visionary Republic: Millennial Themes in American Thought, 1756–1800* (1985).

Morton Borden, *Jews, Turks, and Infidels* (1984).

Thomas E. Buckley, *Church and State in Revolutionary Virginia, 1776–1787* (1977).

Jon Butler, *Awash in a Sea of Faith: Christianizing the American People* (1990).

Naomi W. Cohen, *Jews in Christian America: The Pursuit of Religious Equality* (1992).

Thomas J. Curry, *The First Freedoms: Church and State in America to the Passage of the First Amendment* (1986).

Nathan O. Hatch, *The Sacred Cause of Liberty: Republican Thought and the Millennium in Revolutionary New England* (1977).

Nathan O. Hatch, *The Democratization of American Christianity* (1989).

Ronald Hoffman and Peter Albert, eds., *Religion in a Revolutionary Age* (1994).

Rhys Isaac, *The Transformation of Virginia, 1740–1790* (1982).

Leonard W. Levy, *The Establishment Clause: Religion and the First Amendment* (1994).

Jacob Marcus, *United States Jewry, 1776–1985* (1989).

William G. McLoughlin, *New England Dissent, 1630–1833: The Baptists and the Separation of Church and State* (1971).

William Lee Miller, *The First Liberty: Religion and the American Republic* (1986).

Sally Schwartz, *A Mixed Multitude: The Struggle for Toleration in Colonial Pennsylvania* (1987).

WASHINGTON STANDS OUTSIDE OF TIME
A French clockmaker and artist produced this piece of Washington memorabilia after the death of the president. Washington's trim figure, rendered in gilt bronze, sports a spiffy uniform complete with fringed epaulets. One gloved hand rests on a sword; the other holds a rolled parchment, offered up in front of an eagle, the symbol of America's strength. Below the eagle a familiar motto is inscribed: "E Pluribus Unum" — "Out of many, one" — a reference to the political unity of the sovereign states. Below the clock is a motto about Washington that was first uttered in his funeral eulogy: "First in War, First in Peace, and First in the Hearts of his Countrymen." Death elevated Washington to celebrity status, and Americans immortalized him in many souvenirs.

The Warner Collection of Gulf States Paper Corporation.

The New Nation Takes Form

1789–1800

ALEXANDER HAMILTON, the first secretary of the United States Treasury, faced a challenge in June 1790. The new Constitution provided powers of taxation and an explicit promise to honor the large debt dating from the Revolutionary War, but it fell to the bright young treasury secretary to propose a concrete plan to finance the debt. Hamilton's idea was to roll over the old and nearly worthless federal debt certificates into new, valuable certificates that carried the same dollar amounts but paid guaranteed interest and were backed by the new government. That much had proved somewhat controversial, but Hamilton went a step further and proposed adding all the states' debts still outstanding to the federal debt. Such large-scale debt consolidation (called *assumption* at the time) struck some other politicians as expensive, unnecessary, plainly unfair, and, worst of all, possibly a power grab by the new government to subordinate the states. Hamilton's bold plan was deadlocked in Congress.

Hamilton's chief opponent on the debt question was his onetime ally James Madison, now a member of the first federal Congress, which had convened in New York City. Together, these two had created the intellectual underpinnings of federalism by writing the *Federalist* essays during the ratification of the Constitution. But now the collaborators took opposite sides; the trust between them had eroded. Madison feared that Virginians, who had responsibly paid down the debt of their own state, would be taxed to pay the debts of other states. He also had strong misgivings about the whole debt plan because of the way it rewarded speculators who had bought the old debt at a steep discount in anticipation of its being fully repaid. Greedy speculators, Madison claimed, "are still exploring the interior & distant parts of the Union in order to take advantage of the holders." Through strenuous politicking, Madison had stalled out Hamilton's plan.

At this first crisis point—one of many to come in the 1790s—a solution arrived thanks to the hospitality of Thomas Jefferson, the secretary of state. Deeply worried about the stability of the Union, Jefferson invited Hamilton and Madison to dinner at his New York residence, and over good food and candlelight Hamilton secured the reluctant Madison's promise to restrain his opposition. In return, Hamilton pledged to back efforts to locate the nation's new capital city in the South, along the Potomac River, an outcome that was sure to please Virginians. In early July, Congress voted for the Potomac site, and in late July, Congress passed the debt package, assumption and all.

Alexander Hamilton
Alexander Hamilton was brash, confident, handsome, and audacious. Through force of personality, he had overcome what was for his era and culture a double obstacle in life, being born in obscurity and bastardy on the small West Indies island of Nevis. His mother died when he was thirteen, and five years later he had made his way to the mainland colony of New York and managed to charm his way into elite circles. He attended college, served in the Continental army, earned George Washington's uncommon admiration, and helped to write and ratify the Constitution. Along the way, he married Betsey Schuyler, whose father was one of the richest men in New York. He posed for this portrait by John Trumbull in 1792, at the age of thirty-seven and at the height of his power.
Yale University Art Gallery.

Far from being a cozy agreement-by-handshake, this momentous political deal points up the fears and fragility that haunted the new government in its first years of existence. Jefferson and Madison feared that Hamilton's funding plan would not only reward the wrong sort of men but bind them by financial ties to the government. Jefferson later wrote that the deal he and Madison struck "was unjust, and was acquiesced in merely from a fear of disunion, while our government was still in its infant state." They feared "disunion" when they heard fellow Virginians comparing Hamilton's assumption plan to the unjust parliamentary taxation that had started the Revolutionary War. Their solution was to do what it took to get the capital city situated in their own region, the better to watch it and influence it.

From 1790 to 1800, the "Founding Fathers" of the Revolution and Constitution era became keen competitors and sometimes bitter rivals. Part of the problem arose from clashing personalities. Hamilton's charm no longer worked with Madison, and it had never worked with John Adams, the new vice president, who privately called Hamilton "the bastard brat of a Scotch pedlar," and worse, a brat characterized by "disappointed Ambition and unbridled malice and revenge." Abigail Adams thought Hamilton a second Napoleon Bonaparte, an uncomplimentary reference to the belligerent leader of war-torn France. Late in his life, Madison was asked why he deserted Hamilton, his onetime ally, and Madison replied, "Colonel Hamilton deserted me."

Some of the rivalry stemmed from serious differences in political philosophy. Hamilton assumed that government was safest when in the hands of "the rich, the wise, and the good," three words that to him summarized one group: America's commercial elite. For Hamilton, economic and political power naturally belonged together, creating an energetic force for economic growth. Jefferson and Madison, in contrast, assumed the country's future lay with those whose wealth was tied to the land. Agrarian values ran deep with them, and they were suspicious of get-rich-quick speculators and financiers.

And finally, the breakup of the old Federalist alliance arose out of different loyalties and orientations toward Europe. Hamilton was an unabashed admirer of everything British, while Jefferson was enchanted by France, where he had lived in the 1780s. These loyalties governed foreign relations in the late 1790s, when the United States was in a war or near war with both of these overseas rivals.

The personal and political antagonisms of this first generation of American leaders left their marks on the young country. No one was prepared for the intense and passionate polarization that emerged over economic and foreign policy. The disagreements were articulated around particular events and policies: taxation and the public debt, a new farmers' rebellion in a western region, economic policies favoring commercial development, a treaty with England, a rebellion in Haiti, and a quasi-war with France that led to severe strictures on ideas of sedition and free speech. But at their heart, these disagreements arose out of opposing ideological stances on the value of **democracy**, the nature of leadership, and the limits of federal power. About the only major policy development that did not replicate or intensify these antagonisms among political leaders was Indian policy in the new republic.

By 1800, the oppositional politics ripening between Hamiltonian and Jeffersonian politicians would begin to crystallize into political parties, the Federalists and the Republicans. To the men of that day, this appeared to be an unhappy development.

The Search for Stability

Political parties were not part of the Constitution's plan for government. James Madison had argued in *The Federalist* in 1788 that a superior feature of the national government was precisely that the country's extensive size would prevent small, selfish factions from becoming dangerously dominant. Parties were thought of as destructive political forces, and their development was unanticipated and unwelcome. Only in future decades would American politicians come to realize that parties serve to organize conflict, legitimize disagreement, and mediate among competing political strategies.

Leaders in the early 1790s instead sought ways to heal divisions of the 1780s and bring unity to the country. Widespread veneration for President Washington provided one powerful source of stability. People trusted him to initiate the untested and perhaps elastic powers of the presidency. Congress quickly agreed on passage of the **Bill of Rights** in 1791, which pleased many Antifederalist critics. And the private virtue of women was mobilized to bolster the public virtue of male citizens; **republicanism** was forcing a rethinking of women's relation to the state.

Washington Inaugurates the Government

The election of George Washington in February 1789 was quick work, the tallying of the unanimous votes by the electoral college a mere formality. Washington, everyone's first choice, perfectly embodied the republican ideal of disinterested, public-spirited leadership. Indeed, he cultivated that image through such astute ceremonies as the dramatic surrender of his sword to the Continental Congress at the end of the war, symbolizing the subservience of military power to the law.

With attractive modesty, Washington at first feigned reluctance to accept the presidency. He wrote his wartime confidant, Alexander

> George Washington perfectly embodied the republican ideal of disinterested, public-spirited leadership.

Liverpool Souvenir Pitcher, 1789
A British pottery manufacturer produced this commemorative pitcher for the American market to capture sales at the time of George Washington's inauguration in 1789. The design shows Liberty as a woman dressed in a golden gown, her liberty cap on a pole, holding a laurel wreath (signifying classical honors) over Washington's head. Fifteen labeled links encircle the scene, representing the states. Yet in 1789, only eleven states had ratified the Constitution. No doubt the Liverpool manufacturer hoped to improve sales by maximizing the territory included. What two states are named beyond the original thirteen? Commemorative pitchers, jugs, and mugs were a commonplace article of consumer culture produced in Britain for specialized markets.
Smithsonian Institute, Washington, D.C.

Hamilton, for advice: Could he hesitate to accept but then ultimately take the office, without seeming to be too ambitious? Hamilton replied that he must accept the office; public sentiment was universally for it.

Once in the presidency, Washington carefully calculated his moves, knowing that with every step he was setting a precedent and any misstep could be dangerous for the fragile new government. How kingly should a president be? Congress debated the proper form of address, and the various options under consideration reveal a range of thought about how lofty executive leadership should be. Suggestions included such titles as "His Highness, the President of the United States of America and Protector of Their Liberties" and "His Majesty, the President"; Washington was known to favor "His High Mightiness." But in the end, republican simplicity prevailed. The final version was simply "President of the United States of America," and the established form of address became "Mr. President," a subdued yet dignified title in a society where only property-owning adult white males could presume to be called "Mister."

Washington's genius in establishing the presidency lay in his capacity for implanting his own reputation for integrity into the office itself. He was not a brilliant thinker, nor was he a shrewd political strategist. He was not even a particularly congenial man. In the political language of the day, he was virtuous. He remained aloof, resolute, and dignified, to the point of appearing wooden at times. He really preferred being a farmer, home at Mount Vernon, his Virginia plantation. (See "American Places," page 289.) But as president, he encouraged pomp and ceremony to create respect for the office, traveling with no fewer than six horses drawing his coach, hosting formal balls, and surrounding himself with servants in livery. He even held weekly levees, as European monarchs did, hour-long audiences granted to distinguished visitors (and including women), at which Washington appeared attired in black velvet, with a feathered hat and a polished sword. The president and his guests bowed, avoiding the egalitarian familiarity of handshakes. But he always managed, perhaps just barely, to avoid the extreme of royal splendor.

Washington chose talented and experienced men to preside over the newly created departments of war, treasury, and state. Yet deep philosophical differences separated key appointees. For the Department of War,

Washington chose General Henry Knox, former secretary of war in the confederation government. For the Treasury—an especially tough job in view of revenue conflicts during the Confederation (see chapter 8)—the president picked Alexander Hamilton of New York, known for his general brilliance and financial astuteness. To lead the Department of State, the foreign policy arm of the executive branch, Washington chose Thomas Jefferson, a master of the intricacy of diplomatic relations, who was then serving as minister to France. For attorney general Washington picked Edmund Randolph, a Virginian who had attended the Constitutional Convention but had turned Antifederalist during ratification. For chief justice of the Supreme Court, Washington designated John Jay, the New York lawyer who, along with Madison and Hamilton, had vigorously defended the Constitution in *The Federalist*.

Washington liked and trusted all these men, and by 1793, in his second term, he was meeting regularly with them, thereby establishing the precedent of a presidential cabinet. (Vice President John Adams did not join these meetings; his only official duty was to preside over the Senate, a job he found "a punishment" because he could not actually participate in legislative debates. He complained to his wife, Abigail, "My country has in its wisdom contrived for me the most insignificant office.") No one anticipated that two decades of party turbulence would emerge from the brilliant but explosive mix of Washington's first cabinet.

The Bill of Rights

An early order of business in the First Congress was the passage of a Bill of Rights. Seven states had ratified the Constitution on the condition that guarantees of individual liberties and limitations to federal power be incorporated into the founding document. James Madison and other Federalists of 1787 had thought an enumeration of rights unnecessary, but in 1789 Madison, now a member of Congress, understood that healing the divisions of the 1780s was of prime importance. "It will be a desirable thing to extinguish from the bosom of every member of the community," Madison said in his speech proposing his list of amendments, "any apprehensions that there are those among his countrymen who wish to deprive them of the liberty for which they valiantly fought and honorably bled."

Mount Vernon, Virginia

When George Washington became president in 1789, he left his rural Virginia home for New York, the capital city, feeling like "a culprit who is going to the place of his execution, so unwilling am I, in the evening of a life nearly consumed in public cares, to quit a peaceful abode for an Ocean of difficulties." Washington had spent over thirty years improving that peaceful abode, Mount Vernon, along the Potomac River, and during his presidency he retreated to it whenever he could.

Washington had inherited the 2,000-acre plantation (a farm with a modest house) from a half-brother in the late 1750s, and as soon as his duties in the Seven Years' War were concluded, he set to work transforming the property. He designed another story to give the house two and a half floors, and he directed workers to renovate the exterior walls using pine boards spackled with sand and painted to look like stone. He also altered the entrance road, creating a dramatic vista down a long grassy mall for a visitor's first glimpse of the house; at that distance, the pine board really looked like the stones of a British manor.

When Martha Dandridge Custis, a young widow, married Washington in 1759, she brought to Mount Vernon two small children, a large fortune, and many slaves. The new money allowed Washington to enhance the building and decorating plans. Consulting a British architectural design book, he chose paint colors and wood paneling that reflected upper-class taste from England, a country he never visited. When the remodel was finally finished, the house contained 9,000 square feet, with nine bedrooms and plenty of space for the constant visits of friends, relations, and political dignitaries.

The mansion's grounds also were carefully planned, with formal gardens and practical kitchen gardens. There were the ordinary outbuildings: kitchen, storehouse, smokehouse, icehouse, privies, washhouse, and stable. More unusual was a large greenhouse, still standing, where exotic plants such as orange trees could be nurtured in a controlled climate. Two brick wings off the greenhouse were slave quarters, housing a portion of the several hundred slaves Washington owned.

When he was not a soldier or a statesman, George Washington preferred to think of himself as a farmer—up at dawn, surveying his acreage, his overseers, and his slaves. Farming it was, but on a grand scale. Washington aspired to, and achieved, the life of a country gentleman. Today one can glimpse Washington's life as gentleman farmer by visiting the accurately restored buildings and grounds, which are maintained by the Mount Vernon Ladies' Association.

For Web links related to this site and other American Places, see "PlaceLinks" at bedfordstmartins.com/roark.

A Reenactor at Mount Vernon
Courtesy of Mount Vernon Ladies' Association.

Madison pulled much of his wording of rights directly from the language of various state constitutions with bills of rights. He enumerated guarantees of freedom of speech, press, and religion; the right to petition and assemble, the right to be free from unwarranted searches and seizures. One amendment asserted the right to keep and bear arms in support of a "well-regulated militia," to which Madison added, "but no person religiously scrupulous of bearing arms, shall be compelled to render military service in person." That provision for what a later century would call "conscientious objector" status failed to gain acceptance in Congress.

In September 1789, Congress approved a set of twelve amendments and sent them to the states for approval; ten were eventually ratified. Amendments One through Eight dealt with individual liberties, and Nine and Ten concerned the boundary between federal and state authority. (See the amendments to the U.S. Constitution in the appendix, page A-12.) One of the proposed amendments that failed of passage suggested a formula for fine-tuning the ratio of representation as population grew; the other required that any congressional pay raise voted in would not take effect until after the next election (not until 1992 did this amendment— the Twenty-seventh—pass). The process of state ratification took another two years, but there was no serious doubt about the outcome.

> Republican ideals cast motherhood in a new light by claiming significant maternal influence on the future male citizenry.

Still, not everyone was entirely satisfied. State ratifying conventions had submitted some eighty proposed amendments. Congress never considered proposals to change the structural details of the new government, and Madison had no intention of reopening debates about the length of the president's term or the power to levy excise taxes.

Significantly, no one complained about one striking omission in the Bill of Rights: the right to vote. Only much later was voting seen as a fundamental **liberty** requiring protection by constitutional amendment—indeed, by four amendments. The 1788 Constitution deliberately left definition of voters to the states, which set differing property qualifications. Any uniform federal voting law would run the double risk of excluding—or including—people who could already vote in some state elections with unusual voting statutes: for example, the unmar-

ried women worth over £50 who were allowed to vote in New Jersey, at first perhaps by oversight but in 1790 by an explicit election statute using *he or she* (see chapter 8, page 256). Voter qualification remained a state decision, and no other state followed New Jersey's lead.

The Republican Wife and Mother

The general exclusion of women from political activity did not mean they had no civic role or responsibility. A flood of periodical articles of the 1790s by both male and female writers reevaluated courtship, marriage, and motherhood in light of republican ideals and found ways to enlist white, literate women in the cause of the republican experiment in government. Tyrannical power in the ruler, whether king or husband, was now declared a thing of the past. Affection, not duty, bound wives to their husbands and citizens to their government. In republican marriages, the writers claimed, women had the capacity to reform the morals and manners of men. A male commencement speaker at a girl's school promised the graduates that "the solidity and stability of the liberties of your country rest with you; since Liberty is never sure, 'till Virtue reigns triumphant. . . . While you thus keep our country virtuous, you maintain its independence."

Until the 1790s, public virtue was strictly a masculine quality. But another sort of virtue loomed in importance: sexual chastity, a private asset prized as a feminine quality. Essayists of the 1790s explicitly advised young women to use sexual virtue to increase public virtue in men. "Love and courtship . . . invest a lady with more authority than in any other situation that falls to the lot of human beings," one male essayist proclaimed. A young woman at boarding school wrote in an essay, "Were all women rational, unaffected, and virtuous, coxcombs, flatterers and libertines would no longer exist." If women spurned selfish suitors, they could promote good morals more than any social institution could, essayists promised.

Republican ideals also cast motherhood in a new light. Throughout the 1790s, advocates legitimized female education, still a controversial proposition, through the claim of significant maternal influence on the future male citizenry. Benjamin Rush, a Pennsylvania physician and educator, called for female education because "our ladies should be qualified . . . in instructing their sons in the principles of liberty and government." A series of published essays by Judith

Republican Womanhood: Judith Sargent Murray
The twenty-one-year-old in this portrait became known eighteen years later as America's foremost public spokeswoman for the idea of woman's equality to man. Judith Sargent Murray frequently wrote essays for the *Massachusetts Magazine* under the pen name "Constantia." In "On the Equality of the Sexes," published in 1790, she confidently asserted that women had "natural powers" of mind fully the equal of men's. Murray, the wife of a Universalist minister, wrote plays that were performed on the Boston stage, and in 1798 she published her collected "Constantia" essays in a book titled *The Gleaner;* George Washington and John Adams each bought a copy. Murray is the only woman of her era to keep an indexed letter book, containing copies of nearly two thousand of her own letters written over her lifetime.

John Singleton Copley, *Portrait of Mrs. John Stevens* (Judith Sargent, later Mrs. John Murray), 1770–1772, oil on canvas, 50 × 40 inches, Terra Foundation for the Arts, Daniel J. Terra Art Acquisition Endowment Fund, 2000.6; photograph courtesy of Terra Foundation for the Arts, Chicago.

Sargent Murray of Massachusetts favored education that would remake women into self-confident, competent, rational beings, poised to become the equals of men. Her first essay, published in 1790, was boldly titled "On the Equality of the Sexes." A subsequent essay on education asserted that educated women "will accustom themselves to reflection; they will investigate accurately, and reason will point their conclusion; Yet they will not be assuming; the characteristic trait [sweetness] will still remain." Even Murray had to dress her advanced ideas in the cloak of

republican motherhood, assuring that female education would not destroy women's compliant, domestic character.

Although women's obligations as wives and mothers were now infused with political meaning, traditional gender relations remained unaltered. (For the relatively few American voices that raised questions about what rights women might have, see "Beyond America's Borders," page 292.) The analogy between marriage and civil society worked precisely because of the self-subordination inherent in the term *virtue.* Men should put the public good first, before selfish desires, just as women must put their husbands and families first, before themselves. Women might gain literacy and knowledge, but only in the service of improved domestic duty. Many of the essayists took care to caution wives that they must still defer to their husbands. In Federalist America, wives and citizens alike should feel affection for and trust in their rulers; neither should ever rebel.

Hamilton's Economic Policies

The new government had the lucky break to be launched in flush economic times. Compared to the severe financial instability of the 1780s, the 1790s brimmed with opportunity and prosperity, as seen in increased agricultural trade, transportation, and banking improvements. In 1790, the federal government moved from New York City to Philadelphia, a more central location with a substantial mercantile class. There, Alexander Hamilton, the secretary of the treasury, embarked on his innovative and controversial programs designed to solidify the government's economic base.

Agriculture, Transportation, and Banking

Dramatic increases in the international price of grain in the 1790s motivated American farmers to boost agricultural production for the export trade. Europe's rising population needed grain, and the French Revolutionary and Napoleonic Wars that engulfed Europe for some dozen years after 1793 severely compromised production there. From the Connecticut River valley to the Chesapeake,

France, England, and Woman's Rights in the 1790s

During the 1770s and 1780s in America, only rarely did anyone wonder about rights for women. Abigail Adams's letter to husband John in 1776, asking him to "remember the ladies" when writing new laws, stayed a private document for a century. Boycotts by Daughters of Liberty did not challenge gender hierarchy, nor did New Jersey's handful of women voters. Simply replacing a monarchy with a republic did not, in America, lead to an immediate or substantial challenge to women's subordinate status. It was influence from abroad, not at home, that initially sparked Americans' ideas about women's place in society.

In France between 1789 and 1793, the revolution against monarchy enlarged ideas about citizenship and led some women to argue for the concept of the *citoyenne*, the female citizen. Women's political clubs such as the Society of Republican Revolutionary Women in Paris sent petitions and gave speeches to the National Assembly, demanding education, voting rights, and a curbing of the paternal and marital powers of men over women. In 1791, Frenchwoman Olympe de Gouges rewrote the male revolutionaries' document *The Rights of Man* into *The Rights of Woman,* asserting that "All women are born free and remain equal to men in rights." Another prominent woman, Théroigne de Méricourt, held a feminist salon, marched around Paris in masculine riding attire, and took part in an attack on a palace. Her vision went beyond political rights to the social customs that dictated women's subordination: "It is time for women to break out of the shameful incompetence in which men's ignorance, pride, and injustice have so long held us captive."

While voting rights for French women never passed in that era, the male National Assembly reformed French civil and family law in the early 1790s. Marriage was removed from the control of the church, divorce was legalized, and the age of majority for women was lowered. A far-reaching advance in inheritance law *required* division of a patriarch's estate among all his children, regardless of age, sex, and even legitimacy. Henceforth daughters could inherit along with sons; no longer did a woman from a family of means need to marry money—or indeed, to marry at all. In contrast, most American states imported traditional English family law virtually unchanged into their lawbooks.

French **feminism** traveled across the channel to England and directly inspired a talented woman named Mary Wollstonecraft. In 1792 she published *A Vindication of the Rights of Woman,* arguing for the intellectual equality of the sexes, economic independence for women, and participation in representative government. Most radically, she called marriage legalized prostitution.

Wollstonecraft's book created a sensation in America. Excerpts appeared immediately in Philadelphia and Boston periodicals, bookstores stocked the London edition, and by 1795 there were three American reprints. Some women readers were cautious. A sixty-year-old Philadelphian, Elizabeth Drinker, reflected in her diary that "In very many of her sentiments, she, as some of our friends say, *speaks my mind;* in some others, I do not altogether coincide with her. I am not for quite so much independence." Other women embraced Wollstonecraft's ideas. A woman much younger than Drinker, Priscilla Mason, gave a biting commencement address at the new Young Ladies' Academy in Philadelphia in 1794 and took Wollstonecraft as her departure for a rousing speech condemning "the high and mighty lords"—men—who had denied women education and professional opportunities in church, law, and politics. "Happily, a more liberal way of thinking begins to prevail. . . . Let us by suitable education, qualify ourselves for those high departments," and, she concluded with unwarranted optimism, "they will open before us." Many women's letters report lively debates stimulated by *A Vindication of the Rights of Woman.*

Male readers' responses were varied as well. Aaron Burr, a senator from New York, called the book "a work of genius." A Fourth of July speaker in New Jersey in 1793 proclaimed that "the Rights of Woman are no longer strange sounds to an American ear," and he hoped they would soon be embedded in state law codes. A more negative orator on that same holiday in New York argued that woman's rights really meant a woman's duty "to submit to the control of that government she has voluntarily chosen," namely the government of a husband. And a New Hampshire July Fourth orator advanced this tart joke: "Every man, by the Constitution, is born with an equal right to be elected to the highest office. And every woman is born with an equal right to be the wife of the most eminent man." For some, it was clearly hard to think seriously about gender equality.

The notion of equal rights for women had a long incubation period in the United States. In the 1790s, ideas of equality were too closely associated with the radicalism of the French Revolution, a divisive topic in America; and soon revelations of Wollstonecraft's unconventional personal life as an unwed mother dampened enthusiasm for her pioneering book. Not until the 1830s and 1840s would there be a new generation of women, led by Sarah Grimké, raising questions of sex equality anew (see chapter 11, page 377, and chapter 12, page 428). Most Americans of the 1790s preferred a moderate stance, praising women's contribution to civil society through their influence on family—the "Republican motherhood" concept, histo-

rians have called it. While this fell far short of an egalitarian claim to rights, it did justify—and this was no small gain—women's formal education. A young woman speaker at a Fourth of July picnic in Connecticut in 1799 summed it up perfectly to her all-female audience: "As mothers, wives, sisters, and daughters, we may all be important, [and] teach our little boys, the inestimable value of Freedom, how to blend and harmonize the natural and social rights of man, and as early impressions are indelible, thus assist our dear country, to be as glorious in maintaining, as it was great in gaining her immortal independence."

BIBLIOGRAPHY

Jane Abray, "Feminism in the French Revolution," *American Historical Review* 80 (1975).

Harriet Branson Applewhite and Darline G. Levy, eds. *Women and Politics in the Age of the Democratic Revolution* (1990).

Susan Branson, *These Fiery Frenchified Dames: Women and Political Culture in Early National Philadelphia* (2001).

Linda Kerber, *Women of the Republic: Intellect and Ideology in Revolutionary America* (1980).

Barbara Taylor, *Mary Wollstonecraft and the Feminist Imagination* (2003).

Rosemarie Zagarri, "The Rights of Man and Woman in Post-Revolutionary America," *William and Mary Quarterly* 55 (1998).

FRONTISPIECE.

Thackara & Vallance sculp.

Publish'd at Philad.ᵃ Dec.ʳ 1ˢᵗ 1792.

Woman's Rights in the *Lady's Magazine* of 1792

This frontispiece, appearing in the first volume of the Philadelphia periodical the *Lady's Magazine and Repository of Entertaining Knowledge,* accompanied excerpts from Mary Wollstonecraft's *Vindication.* (The editor was a literary man, Charles Brockden Brown.) The caption identified the kneeling figure as "the Genius of the *Lady's Magazine,*" accompanied by "the Genius of Emulation" carrying a trumpet and a laurel wreath. (*Genius* here meant a spirit; *emulation* meant ambition to excel, now an obsolete usage. Thus the genius of emulation was the spirit of ambition—women's ambition in this case.) The spirit representing the *Lady's Magazine* kneels before Liberty, identified by her liberty cap on a poll, and presents a paper titled "RIGHTS OF WOMAN." Study the objects below Liberty: two books, a musical instrument, artist's paints, a globe, and a page of geometrical shapes. The kneeling figure seems to gesture toward them. What do they suggest about the nature of the "rights of woman" this picture endorses?

Library Company of Philadelphia.

farmers responded by planting more wheat. The increase in overseas grain trade generated a host of new jobs in related areas as the number of millers, coopers, dockworkers, and ship and wagon builders expanded.

Cotton production in the southern states also underwent a boom, spurred by market demand and a mechanical invention. Limited amounts of smooth-seed cotton had long been grown in the low-lying coastal areas of the South, but this variety of cotton did not prosper in the drier, inland regions. Green-seed cotton grew well inland, but it contained many rough seeds that adhered tenaciously to the cotton fibers, making it very labor-intensive to clean. In 1793, a Yale graduate named Eli Whitney, visiting a Georgia plantation, invented the cotton gin, a device to separate out the seeds. Use of the gin increased cotton production, from 138,000 pounds in 1792 to 35 million in 1800. Most of it was shipped to English factories to be made into textiles.

A surge of road building helped propel the prosperous economy. Only one continuous and improved road existed before 1790, the Post Road running for 1,600 miles from Maine to Georgia near the coast. This was joined, in 1794, by the Lancaster Turnpike, the first private toll road in the nation, connecting Philadelphia with Lancaster, Pennsylvania. Soon another turnpike connected Boston with Albany, New York, and continued west. Private companies chartered by state governments financed and built these and other turnpikes and collected fees from all vehicles. Farther inland, a major road extended southwest down the Shenandoah Valley, while another road linked Richmond, Virginia, with the Tennessee towns of Knoxville and Nashville.

By 1800, a dense network of dirt, gravel, or plank roadways connected cities and towns in southern New England and the Middle Atlantic states, while isolated roadways and old Indian trails fanned out to the west. Commercial stage lines connected major eastern cities, offering four-day travel time between New York and Boston and an exhausting but speedy one-and-one-half-day trip between New York and Philadelphia (Map 9.1). In 1790, only three stage-

Major Roads in the 1790s

coach companies operated out of Boston, but by 1800 there were twenty-four. Transport of goods by road was still expensive per mile compared to water transport on navigable rivers or along the coast, but at least it was possible.

A third development signaling economic resurgence was the growth of commercial banking. During the 1790s, the number of banks nationwide multiplied tenfold, from three to twenty-nine in 1800. Banks drew in money chiefly through the sale of stock. They then made loans in the form of banknotes, paper currency backed by the gold and silver paid in by stockholders. Because they issued two or three times as much money in banknotes as they held in **hard money**, banks were really creating new money for the economy.

Bridge Toll Sign, 1796

This sign lists an amazing variety of tolls charged for crossing a bridge over the Connecticut River between Cornish, New Hampshire, and Windsor, Vermont, in 1796. Owners of bridges and toll roads collected fees from users of their privately built right-of-ways. Can you deduce any principle of pricing in this list? Is the list exhaustive? What if a boy with a dog attempted to cross the bridge? Do you imagine there were traffic jams at the tollgate? New Hampshire Historical Society.

MAP 9.1 **Travel Times from New York City in 1800**
Notice that travel out of New York extends over a much greater distance in the first week than in subsequent weeks. River corridors in the West and East speeded up travel—but only if one were going downriver. Also notice that travel by sea (north and south along the coast) was much faster than land travel.

READING THE MAP: Compare this map to the map of "Major Roads in the 1790s" (page 294) and to Map 9.2. What physical and cultural elements account for the slower travel times west of Pittsburgh?

CONNECTIONS: Why did Americans in the 1790s become so interested in traveling long distances? How did travel times affect the American economy?

FOR MORE HELP ANALYZING THIS MAP, see the map activity for this chapter in the Online Study Guide at bedfordstmartins.com/roark.

The Public Debt and Taxes

The upturn in the economy, plus the new taxation powers of the government, suggested that the government might soon be able to repay its debts, amounting to some $52 million owed to foreign and domestic creditors. The debt dated from the difficult war years, when the government needed supplies and manpower but had no independent source of revenue. Many of the certificates of debt had been issued to soldiers as their pay. In the 1780s, those certificates had fallen in value, reflecting the widespread belief that the confederation government could never make good on them. The Constitution promised that "all debts contracted and engagements entered into, before the adoption of this Constitution, shall be as valid against the United States" under the new government as under the old. But how valid, exactly, would that be?

Alexander Hamilton's answer, elaborated in his *Report on Public Credit* in January 1790, was that the debt be funded—but not repaid immediately—at full value. This meant that old certificates of debt would be rolled over into new bonds, which would earn interest until retired several years later. There would still be a public debt, but it would be secure, supported by citizens' confidence in the new government. The bonds would circulate, injecting new valuable money into the economy. "A national debt if not excessive will be to us a national blessing; it will be a powerfull cement of our union," Hamilton wrote to a financier.

A large part of the old debt had been bought up cheaply by speculators in the late 1780s, and Hamilton's report touched off more rapid purchasing by men in the know. (Hamilton held none of the debt personally, but his father-in-law, Philip Schuyler, held $60,000 worth at face

The Return for SOUTH CAROLINA having been made since the foregoing Schedule was originally printed, the whole Enumeration is here given complete, except for the N. Western Territory, of which no Return has yet been published.

DISTICTS	Free white Males of 16 years and upwards, including heads of families.	Free white Males under 16 years.	Free white Females, including heads of families.	All other free persons.	Slaves.	Total.
Vermont	22435	22328	40505	255	16	85539
N. Hampshire	36086	34851	70160	630	158	141885
Maine	24384	24748	46870	538	NONE	96540
Massachusetts	95453	87289	190582	5463	NONE	378787
Rhode Island	16019	15799	32652	3407	948	68825
Connecticut	60523	54403	117448	2808	2764	237946
New York	83700	78122	152320	4654	21324	340120
New Jersey	45251	41416	83287	2762	11423	184139
Pennsylvania	110788	106948	206363	6537	3737	434373
Delaware	11783	12143	22384	3899	8887	59094
Maryland	55915	51339	101395	8043	103036	319728
Virginia	110936	116135	215046	12866	292627	747610
Kentucky	15154	17057	28922	114	12430	73677
N. Carolina	69988	77506	140710	4975	100572	393751
S. Carolina	35576	37722	66880	1801	107094	249073
Georgia	13103	14044	25739	398	29264	82548
	807094	791850	1541263	59150	694280	3893635

Total number of Inhabitants of the United States exclusive of S. Western and N. Territory.	Free white Males of 21 years and upwards.	Free white Males under 21 years of age.	Free white Females.	All other free persons.	Slaves.	Total.
S. W. territory	6271	10277	15365	361	3417	35691
N. Ditto						

1790 Census Page

This page provides a published tally of the final results of the first federal census of 1790, mandated by the U.S. Constitution as a means by which representation in Congress and proportional taxation on the states would be determined. Notice the choice of 5 classifications for the count: free white males over 16, free white males under 16, free white women, all other free persons, and slaves. To implement the Constitution's three-fifths clause (counting slaves as three-fifths of a person), slaves had to be counted separately from all free persons. Separating white males into two broad age groups at 16 allows for a measure of military strength, surely something important for the government to gauge at a time of continuing and threatened Indian wars. Why separate males from females? Who does "all other free persons" mean? Which northern states still have slaves? Which state is the largest in population? Which largest in white population?

U.S. Census Bureau.

value.) These investors would now have a direct financial stake in the new government, support that Hamilton regarded as essential to the country's stability. He was also providing those same men with more than $40 million released for new investment, a distinct improvement over the old depreciated bonds, which had circulated in daily transactions at a fraction of their face value.

If the *Report on Public Credit* had gone only this far, it would have been only somewhat controversial. But Hamilton took a much bolder step by augmenting the debt with another $25 million still owed by state governments to individuals. All the states had obtained supplies during the war by issuing IOUs to farmers, merchants, and moneylenders. Some states, such as Virginia and New York, had paid off these debts entirely, while others, like Massachusetts, had partially paid them through heavy taxation of the inhabitants. About half the states had made little headway. Hamilton called for the federal government to assume these state debts and add them to the federal debt, in effect consolidating federal power over the states.

Congressman James Madison objected to putting windfall profits in the pockets of speculators. He proposed instead a complex scheme to pay both the original holders of the federal debt and the speculators, each at a fair fraction of the total. He also strenuously objected to assumption of all the states' debts. A large debt was dangerous, Madison warned, especially because it would lead to high taxation. But he lost the vote in Congress. Madison and Hamilton, so recently allies in writing *The Federalist,* were becoming opponents. Secretary of State Jefferson also was fearful of Hamilton's proposals. "No man is more ardently intent to see the public debt soon and sacredly paid off than I am. This exactly marks the difference between Colonel Hamilton's views and mine, that I would wish the debt paid tomorrow; he wishes it never to be paid, but always to be a thing where with to corrupt and manage the legislature." Eventually, Madison and Jefferson compromised with Hamilton on the assumption of state debts; in exchange, a decision favoring Virginians was reached to locate the nation's capital on the banks of the Potomac River, on the border shared by Virginia and Maryland. (See "Historical Question," page 298.)

The First Bank of the United States and the *Report on Manufactures*

The second and third major elements of Hamilton's economic plan were his proposal for a national Bank of the United States and his program to encourage domestic manufacturing. Believing that banks were the "nurseries of national wealth," Hamilton modeled his plan on the Bank of England, a private corporation that worked primarily for the public good. In

Bill of Sale for Wallpaper and a Wallpapered Chest

Wallpaper manufacturing flourished in the United States in the 1790s. After years of importing English and French wallpaper, Americans began to buy from the dozen or so new enterprises springing up in Boston and Philadelphia. These companies produced cheap yet attractive coverings for plastered walls. On the left is a bill of sale from the Appleton Prentiss manufactory of Boston, showing the 1791 purchase of five batches of rolls of paper and borders, perhaps intended for five rooms of a house. Can you decode the calculations of the price? (Hint: pounds, shillings, pence.) This customer gets a 10 percent deduction at the end; can you guess why? Below is a trunk decorated with wallpaper; not all wallpaper ended up on walls.

Courtesy of the Society for the Preservation of New England Antiquities.

Hamilton's plan, 20 percent of the bank's stock would be bought by the federal government. In effect, the bank would become the fiscal agent of the new government, holding and handling its revenues derived from import duties, land sales, and various other taxes. The other 80 percent of the bank's capital would come from private investors, who could buy stock in the bank with either hard money (silver or gold) or federal securities. Because of its size and the privilege of being the only national bank, the bank would help stabilize the economy by exerting prudent control over credit, interest rates, and the value of the currency. The bank had twenty-five directors, five appointed by the government and the other twenty chosen from the bank's stockholders, sure to be merchants from the world of high finance.

Concerned that the bank would give a handful of rich men undue influence over the economy, Madison tried but failed to stop the plan in Congress. Jefferson advised Washington that the Constitution did not permit Congress to charter banks. Hamilton, however, argued that the Constitution listed certain powers to regulate commerce ending with a broad grant of the right "to make all laws which shall be necessary and proper for carrying into execution the foregoing powers." Washington agreed with Hamilton and signed the Bank of the United States into law in February 1791, providing it with a charter to operate for twenty years. When the bank's privately held stock went on sale in New York City in July, it sold out in a few hours, touching off an immediate mania of speculation in resale. A discouraged Madison reported that "the Coffee House is an eternal buzz with the gamblers," some of them self-interested congressmen intent on "public plunder."

The third component of Hamilton's plan was issued in December 1791 in the *Report on Manufactures*, a proposal to encourage the production of American-made goods. Manufacturing was in its infancy in 1790, the result of years of dependence on British imports. Hamilton recognized that a balanced and self-reliant economy required the United States to produce its own cloth and iron products. His plan mobilized the new powers of the federal government to impose tariffs and grant subsidies to encourage the

How Did Washington, D.C., Become the Federal Capital?

Why didn't Boston, Philadelphia, or New York City become the capital of the United States? The great cities of London and Paris were great precisely because political power was situated at the heart of commerce and culture in those European countries. Although much smaller in scale, several American cities boasted elegant houses, cultural institutions, lively economies, newspapers, food markets, taverns, coffeehouses, and stagecoach and shipping lines—nearly everything necessary to accommodate the political elites who would be running the new government. Instead, the infant United States chose marshy, vacant acreage along the Maryland shore of the Potomac River for its permanent capital.

While the choice of that particular site was by no means inevitable, the country's leaders agreed that there should be only one site. During the war years, the Continental Congress had jumped around many times, from Philadelphia, Lancaster, and York in Pennsylvania to Princeton and Trenton in New Jersey, and down to Baltimore, often on the run from the British army. Even after the war, the Congress continued to circulate, meeting in Trenton, in Annapolis and Georgetown in Maryland, and finally in

New York City. When the confederation government commissioned an equestrian statue of George Washington to inspire and dignify its meetings, a humorist suggested that the marble horse be fitted with wheels so it could be towed from place to place.

For some, a floating capital symbolized the precarious status of the confederation. But the alternative, a fixed location, put the federal government at the mercy of the particular state it sat in. If irate citizens stormed the congress, as had happened once in Philadelphia in 1783, could the local state militia always be counted on to protect it? The writers of the Constitution thus came up with a novel solution. They decided to locate the capital on land not controlled by any state. The 1788 Constitution specified a square district, not exceeding ten miles on a side, where Congress would have sole jurisdiction; but it deferred the complicated choice of the exact site to the First Congress.

In 1790, more than forty cities and towns clamored for consideration, from Kingston and Newburgh in New York's Hudson River valley down to Richmond and Williamsburg in Virginia. Eleven contenders clustered along the Delaware River between New Jersey and Pennsylva-

nia, roughly the demographic center of the country. Six more sites fell in the interior of Pennsylvania, along the Susquehanna River, each claiming to be the future geographic center as the country grew westward. Another eleven locations dotted the Potomac River from Chesapeake Bay to the Appalachians. Clearly, river transportation figured heavily in all these plans, and investors in canal and river navigation companies took special notice.

The First Congress struggled to reconcile private interests, regional jealousies, and genuine dilemmas of citizen access. A Pennsylvania proposal naming a Susquehanna River site finally passed the House but not the Senate. Virginians held out for the Potomac, drawing objections from New Englanders fearful of disease-laden southern swamps. Philadelphians insisted that their city, the premier cultural and economic center of America, was the only logical choice. In short, the situation was at a stalemate.

Another, unrelated stalemate obstructed Congress in early 1790. Alexander Hamilton presented Congress with his controversial plan to fund the public debt by assuming state debts. James Madison objected and wrested the necessary votes from Hamilton—at first.

Hamilton approached Robert Morris of Pennsylvania to propose a deal: If Morris would deliver votes for Hamilton's assumption plan, the influential Hamilton would back a capital site in Pennsylvania. But Morris could not command enough congressional votes, so Hamilton next approached Thomas Jefferson, secretary of state, who invited him to dinner with James Madison. There the three reached agreement:

enough southern votes for assumption in exchange for a Potomac River site. Madison could not bring himself to vote for assumption, but he rounded up the necessary votes from men representing districts along the river. In the final bill, Philadelphia was named the interim capital until 1800, by which time a site on the Potomac River, to be selected by President Washington, would be constructed and open for business. Robert Morris gloated that the Virginians had been tricked; he felt sure that Philadelphia's charms would ensnare the government permanently. Assumption quickly passed, by six votes.

Washington, drawing on his surveying expertise, took another year to select the hill-banked plain east of Georgetown, after scouting far up the river. No matter what location he chose, the Potomac Company—a canal-building enterprise of which Washington himself was president and principal investor—stood to benefit, but this was not considered a conflict of interest in the 1790s. Indeed, Washington had extensive landholdings up the Potomac and into the Ohio Valley, so the decision to site the capital on the Potomac River was much to his personal benefit. What made the Potomac advantageous both for a capital site and for investment in navigation was that it penetrated the farthest inland of any East Coast river, traversing the lowest point in the Appalachian Mountains. Washington's scouting trips convinced him that with short portages, water routes

Plan for Washington, D.C., on a Handkerchief
In 1791 and 1792, the pressure was high to get a detailed map of the proposed capital city into circulation so that prospective land buyers could be lined up. Finally a Philadelphia engraving firm produced this plan of the future city with each block numbered. It was reproduced on large handkerchiefs in an early marketing strategy to entice buyers. The actual site in 1792 consisted of fields and marshes.
Library of Congress.

could connect Chesapeake Bay to western Pennsylvania and beyond to the Ohio and Mississippi rivers.

Next, the rural site had to be purchased from the Maryland farmers who owned it. Washington and Jefferson purposely deployed surveyors in widely scattered locations up and down the river, to keep local owners from guessing where the government center would finally rest within the district—and thus to keep a lid on land prices. The president also deputized friends to pur-

chase the land, "as if for yourselves, and to conduct your propositions so as to excite no suspicion that they are on behalf of the public."

Washington then hired a French-born master designer to plan the capital. Pierre L'Enfant, an architect living in New York City, mapped out a grid of streets slashed dramatically by wide diagonal boulevards. L'Enfant envisioned a mall surrounded by grand government buildings. The rest of his map showed small lots intended for private buyers, who, it was hoped, would provide housing and services for the government population. The proceeds of the land sales would fund construction, so that a city could be built without having to draw on the U.S. Treasury at all.

In the end, the capital landed in the South because a major east-west river was there and because the South had crucial votes to trade on the assumption bill. Washington, D.C., represented the geographic but not the demographic center of the thirteen states. Its placement exerted a southern tug on the federal government, augmented by the fact that five of the first seven presidents were southerners. In all the political horse trading over choosing the site, nobody thought it worthy to note that the capital of the Republic sat in the heart of a slave society. But it would turn out to be of major significance some sixty years later, when the capital of President Abraham Lincoln's Union was surrounded by slavery, with many of its inhabitants of doubtful loyalty to the Union.

growth of local manufacturing. Hamilton had to be careful not to undercut his important merchant allies who traded with England and generated over half the government's income. A high tariff would either seriously dampen that trade or force merchants into smuggling. So Hamilton favored a moderate tariff, with extra bounties paid to American manufacturers to encourage production. The *Report on Manufactures* was the one Hamiltonian plan that was not approved by Congress.

The Whiskey Rebellion

Hamilton's plan to restore public credit required new taxation measures to meet the interest payments on a national debt swollen to some $77 million. Hamilton did not propose raising import duties, in deference to the merchant class, whose favor he sought; nor did he propose land taxes, which would have put the biggest burden on the nation's wealthiest landowners. Instead, he convinced Congress in 1791 to pass a 25 percent excise tax on whiskey, to be paid by farmers when they brought their grain to the distillery, then passed on to individual whiskey consumers in the form of higher prices. Members of Congress from eastern areas favored the tax—especially those from New England, where the favorite drink was rum, an imported beverage already taxed under the import laws. A New Hampshire representative pointed out that the country would be "drinking down the national debt," an idea he evidently found acceptable.

Not surprisingly, the new excise tax proved very unpopular with cash-short grain farmers in the western regions and whiskey drinkers everywhere. In 1791, farmers in the western parts of Pennsylvania, Virginia, Maryland, and the Carolinas and throughout Kentucky forcefully conveyed to Congress their resentment of Hamilton's tax. One farmer complained that he already paid half his grain to the local distillery for distilling his rye, and now the distiller was taking the new whiskey tax out of the farmer's remaining half. This "reduces the balance to less than one-third of the original quantity. If this is not an oppressive tax, I am at a loss to describe what is so." Congress responded with modest modifications to the tax in 1792; but even so, discontent was rampant.

> The Whiskey Rebellion presented an opportunity for the new federal government to flex its muscles and stand up to civil disorder.

Simple evasion of the law was the most common response; the tax proved hard to collect. Renewing painful humiliation rituals of revolutionary days, crowds tarred and feathered federal tax collectors, while some distilleries underreported their production. Four counties in Pennsylvania established committees of correspondence and held assemblies to carry their message to Congress. President Washington issued a warning that the protests had to stop, and for a time things cooled down. Still, noncompliance continued, and an embarassed Hamilton had to admit that the revenue was far less than anticipated. But rather than abandon the law, he tightened up the prosecution of tax evaders.

In western Pennsylvania, Hamilton had one ally, a stubborn tax collector named John Neville, who refused to quit even after a group of spirited farmers burned him in effigy. In May 1794, Neville filed charges against seventy-five farmers and distillers for tax evasion. In July, he and a federal marshal were ambushed in Allegheny County by a group of forty men, and then Neville's house was burned to the ground by a crowd estimated at five hundred; one man in the crowd was killed. At the end of July, 7,000 farmers planned a march—or perhaps an attack, some thought—on Pittsburgh to protest the hated tax.

The governor of Pennsylvania refused to call out the militia, preferring to allow arrests and judicial authority to handle illegal acts. In response, Washington nationalized the Pennsylvania militia and set out, with Hamilton at his side urging him on, at the head of 13,000 soldiers. (This event remains the only time in the country's history when a president in military uniform has led an army in anticipated action.) A worried Philadelphia newspaper criticized the show of force: "Shall Pennsylvania be converted into a human slaughter house because the dignity of the United States will not admit of conciliatory measures? Shall torrents of blood be spilled to support an odious excise system?" But in the end, no blood was spilled. By the time the army arrived in late September, the demonstrators had evaporated. No battles were fought, and no fire was exchanged. Twenty men were rounded up as rebels and charged with high treason, but only two were convicted, and both were soon pardoned by Washington.

Had the government overreacted? Thomas Jefferson thought so; he saw the event as a replay of Shays's Rebellion of 1786, when a protest against government taxation had been met with unreasonable government force (see chapter 8).

George Washington Reviewing Troops, 1795
This painting envisions President Washington reviewing army troops at Fort Cumberland, in western Maryland, at the start of the Whiskey Rebellion. Washington did lead an army into western Pennsylvania and very likely did inspect his men at attention from the heights of a horse, but the scene is an artist's reconstruction. The soldiers stretch in lines far to the right horizon; note all the tents on a distant hill. The artist, Frederick Kemmelmeyer, was a German emigrant living in Baltimore. He painted portrait miniatures and signage for a living.

The Metropolitan Museum of Art, Gift of Edgar William and Bernice Chrysler Garbisch, 1963 (63.201.1). Photograph © 1983 the Metropolitan Museum of Art.

The rebel farmers agreed; they felt entitled to resort to protest and demonstration in the face of oppressive taxation. Hamilton and Washington, however, thought laws passed by a republican government must be obeyed. The Whiskey Rebellion presented an opportunity for the new federal government to flex its muscles and stand up to civil disorder.

Conflicts West, East, and South

While the whiskey rebels challenged federal leadership from within the country, disorder threatened the United States from external sources as well. From 1790 onward, serious trouble brewed in three directions. To the west, a powerful confederation of Indian tribes in the Ohio Country resisted white encroachment, resulting in a brutal war. At the same time, conflicts between the major European powers forced Americans to take sides and nearly thrust the country into another war, this time across the Atlantic. And to the south, a Caribbean slave rebellion raised fears that racial war would be imported to the United States. Despite these conflicts, and the grave threats they posed to the young country, Washington won reelection to the presidency unanimously in the fall of 1792.

To the West: The Indians

By the Treaty of Paris of 1783, England had given up all land east of the Mississippi River to the United States—but without consulting its one-time allies, the Indian tribes who inhabited

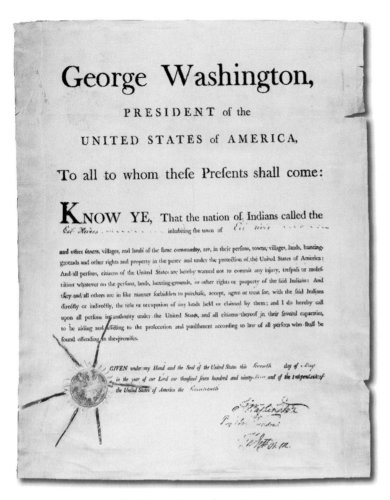

Washington's Proclamation Protecting Indian Territory

The president's name, in bold print, prefaces a warning that American citizens were forbidden to injure Indians or trespass on their lands in the Northwest Territory. When the federal government signed treaties with tribes ceding land, it often guaranteed protections for land not ceded. This poster of 1793, designed to be tacked up on trees, announced federal protection for Indians around the Eel River in Ohio. Such warnings were not very effective, however. Washington wrote in 1796, "I believe scarcely any thing short of a Chinese Wall, or line of Troops will restrain Land Jobbers, and the Incroachment of Settlers, upon Indian Territory."

The Huntington Library and Art Collections, San Marino, California.

25,000 square miles of that territory. When the Indians learned of the treaty terms, they expressed astonishment. "They told me they never could believe that our king could pretend to cede to America what was not his own to give," the British commander at Fort Niagara wrote of the Iroquois. In Ohio, British Indian agents assured the Shawnee and Delaware peoples that England had relinquished only political control to the United States and the Indians still had the right to occupy the land over the claims of American settlers. Further, British troops still occupied a half dozen forts in the northwest. Such confusion and misrepresentation aggravated an already volatile situation.

A doubled American population, from two million in 1770 to nearly four million in 1790, created an insistent pressure for western land. Several thousand settlers a year moved down the Ohio River in the mid-1780s, some bound for Kentucky on the south bank of the river, but many others eyeing the fresh forests and fields to the north, in Indian country. By the late 1780s, government land sales in eastern Ohio commenced (Map 9.2). But actual settlement proved costly, as bloody **frontier** raids and skirmishes broke out between settlers and Indians.

Meanwhile, the western half of Ohio, where white settlers did not yet dare to go, was subjected to military incursions by the U.S. army. Fort Washington, built on the Ohio River in 1789 at the site of present-day Cincinnati, became the command post for three major invasions of Indian country. General Josiah Harmar, under orders from Secretary of War Henry Knox to subdue the Indians of western Ohio, marched with 1,400 men into Ohio's northwest region in the fall of 1790, burning Indian villages. His inexperienced troops were ambushed by Miami and Shawnee Indians led by their chiefs Little Turtle and Blue Jacket; one in eight of Harmar's men was killed.

Harmar's defeat—so humiliating that Harmar was court-martialed—led to renewed efforts to clear Ohio for permanent American settlement. General Arthur St. Clair, the military governor of the entire Northwest Territory, had earlier tried peaceful tactics, signing treaties with Indians for land in eastern Ohio—dubious treaties, as it happened, since the Indian negotiators were not chiefs authorized to yield land. In the wake of Harmar's defeat, St. Clair geared up for further military action. In the fall of 1791, he led more than 2,000 men (accompanied by 200 women camp followers) north from Fort Washington to engage in battle with Miami and Shawnee Indians. A month of cold weather spurred many desertions. His force reduced to about 1,400 men, St. Clair set up camp near the headwaters of the Wabash River in northwestern Ohio. The next morning at dawn, November 4, some thousand Miami Indians led by Little

Turtle staged a surprise attack. The ferocious battle was a disaster for the Americans, 55 percent of whom were dead or wounded before noon; only three of the women escaped alive. "The savages seemed not to fear anything we could do," wrote an officer afterward. "They could skip out of reach of bayonet and return, as they pleased. The ground was literally covered with the dead. . . . It appeared as if the officers had been singled out, as a very great proportion fell. The men being thus left with few officers, became fearful, despaired of success, gave up the fight." The Indians captured valuable weaponry, scalped and dismembered the dying, and pursued fleeing survivors for miles. With more than 900 lives lost, it was the most stunning American loss in the entire history of the U.S.-Indian wars. President Washington fumed that St. Clair "was worse than a murderer" and demanded his resignation. Grisly tales of St. Clair's defeat became instantly infamous, increasing, if this were possible, the level of sheer terror that Americans brought to their confrontations with the Indians.

Washington responded by doubling the American military presence in Ohio and appointing a new commander, General Anthony Wayne of Pennsylvania, nicknamed "Mad Anthony" for his headstrong, hard-drinking style of leadership. About the Ohio natives Wayne wrote, "I have always been of the opinion that we never should have a permanent peace with those Indians until they were made to experience our superiority." With some 3,500 men, Wayne established two new military camps, Fort Greenville and Fort Recovery, deep in Indian territory in western Ohio, the latter on the site of St.

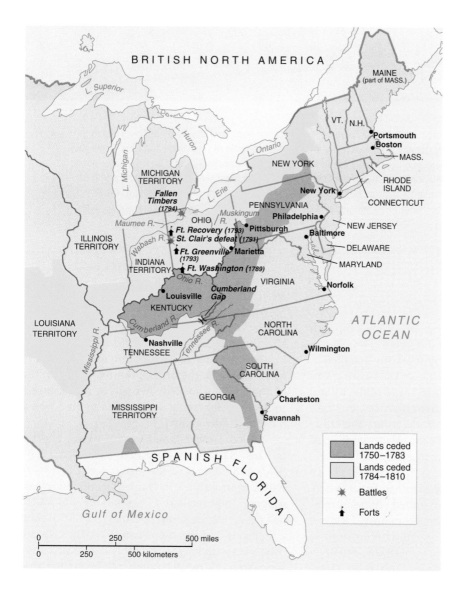

MAP 9.2 Western Expansion and Indian Land Cessions to 1810
By the first decade of the nineteenth century, the period of intense Indian wars had resulted in significant cessions of land to the U.S. government by treaty.

READING THE MAP: Locate the Appalachians. What line of 1763 ran along the mountains? What was that line's purpose, and how well was that purpose met?
CONNECTIONS: How much did the population of the United States grow between 1750 and 1790? How did this growth affect western settlement?

FOR MORE HELP ANALYZING THIS MAP, see the map activity for this chapter in the Online Study Guide at bedfordstmartins.com/roark.

Treaty of Greenville, 1795
This painting by an unknown artist of the 1790s purports to depict the signing of the Treaty of Greenville in 1795. The treaty was signed by General Anthony Wayne and Chief Little Turtle of the Miami and Chief Tarhe the Crane of the Wyandot. An American officer kneels in the front, apparently writing on paper on his knee—not a likely posture in which to draft a formal treaty. One Indian of the three pictured seems to be gesturing with emphasis, as if to dictate to the writing American, but in fact, the treaty's terms were most favorable to the Americans. Many Indians from a dozen Ohio tribes congregated at the signing of the treaty; this picture shows unrealistically open spaces and very few Indians.
Chicago Historical Society.

Clair's defeat. Wayne's men had to pick through skeletal remains to build the fort.

Throughout 1794 Wayne's army engaged in skirmishes with Shawnee, Delaware, and Miami Indians. Chief Little Turtle of the Miami tribe advised negotiation; in his view, Wayne's large army looked overpowering. But Blue Jacket of the Shawnees counseled continued warfare, and his view prevailed. The decisive action came in August 1794 at the Battle of Fallen Timbers, near the Maumee River where a recent tornado had felled many trees. The confederated Indians—mainly Ottawa, Potawatomi, and Delaware, numbering around 800—first ambushed the Americans, but they were underarmed, many having only toma-

hawks. Wayne's well-disciplined troops made effective use of their guns and bayonets, causing the Indians to take flight to nearby Fort Miami, held by the British. But the former allies of the Indians locked their gates and refused protection. Surviving Indians fled to the woods, their ranks decimated.

Fallen Timbers was a major defeat for the Indians. The Americans had destroyed cornfields and villages on the march north, and with winter approaching, the Indians' confidence was sapped. They reentered negotiations in a much less powerful bargaining position. In 1795, about a thousand Indians representing nearly a dozen tribes met with Wayne and other American emissaries to work out the Treaty of Greenville. The

Americans offered $25,000 worth of treaty goods (calico shirts, axes, knives, blankets, kettles, mirrors, ribbons, thimbles, and abundant wine and liquor casks) and promised additional shipments every year. The government's idea was to create a dependency on American goods to keep the Indians friendly. In exchange, the Indians ceded most of Ohio to the Americans; only the northwest region of the territory was reserved solely for the Indians.

The treaty brought peace to the region, but it did not bring back a peaceful life to the Indians. The annual allowance from the United States too often came in the form of liquor. "More of us have died since the Treaty of Greenville than we lost by the years of war before, and it is all owing to the introduction of liquor among us," said Chief Little Turtle in 1800. "This liquor that they introduce into our country is more to be feared than the gun and tomahawk."

Across the Atlantic: France and England

While Indian battles engaged the American military, another war overseas had to be closely watched. Since 1789, a violent revolution had been raging in France. At first, the general American reaction was positive, for it was flattering to think that the American Revolution had inspired imitation in France. Monarchy and privilege were overthrown in the name of republicanism; towns throughout America celebrated the victory of the French people with civic feasts and public festivities.

But news of the beheading of King Louis XVI quickly dampened the uncritical enthusiasm for everything French. Those who fondly remembered the excitement and risk of the American Revolution were still likely to regard France with optimism. However, the reluctant revolutionaries of the 1770s and 1780s, who had worried about excessive democracy and social upheaval in America, deplored the far greater violence occurring in the name of republicanism as France in 1793 moved into the Reign of Terror, characterized by a bloody surge of executions of counterrevolutionaries.

In the United States, support for the French Revolution could remain a matter of personal conviction until 1793, when England and France fell to fighting in what were called the Napoleonic Wars and loyalty to France versus loyalty to England became a critical foreign policy ques-

tion. France had helped America substantially during the American Revolution, and the confederation government had signed an alliance in 1778 promising aid if France were ever under attack. Americans optimistic about the eventual outcome of the French Revolution wanted to deliver on that promise. But others, including those shaken by the guillotining of thousands of French people as well as those with strong commercial ties to England, sought ways to stay neutral.

In May 1793, President Washington issued a Neutrality Proclamation with friendly assurances to both sides. But tensions at home flared in response to official neutrality. "The cause of France is the cause of man, and neutrality is desertion," wrote H. H. Brackenridge, a western Pennsylvanian, voicing the sentiments of thousands. Dozens of pro-French political clubs called Democratic or Republican Societies sprang up around the country. The societies mobilized farmers and mechanics, issued circular letters, injected pro-French and anti-British feelings into local elections, and in general heightened popular participation and public interest in foreign policy. The activities of these societies disturbed Washington and Hamilton intensely, for they encouraged opposition to the policies of the president.

The Neutrality Proclamation was in theory a fine idea, in view of Washington's goal of staying out of European wars. Yet American ships continued to trade between the French West Indies and France, and in late 1793 and early 1794, the English expressed their displeasure by halting more than three hundred of these vessels near the West Indies, capturing their cargoes and impressing (illegally seizing) their crews. Clearly, something had to be done to assert American power.

President Washington sent John Jay, the chief justice of the Supreme Court and a man of strong pro-British sentiments, to England to negotiate commercial relations in the British West Indies, secure compensation for the seized cargoes, and stop the impressment of sailors. In addition, Jay was supposed to resolve several longstanding problems dating from the end of the Revolution. Southern **planters** wanted reimbursement for the slaves lured away by the British army during the war, and western settlers wanted England to vacate the western forts still

> Support for the French Revolution could remain a matter of personal conviction until 1793, when England and France went to war.

occupied—twelve years after the end of the Revolution—because of their strategic proximity to the Indian fur trade.

Jay returned from his diplomatic mission in 1795 with a treaty that no one could love. First, the treaty made no direct provision for the captured cargoes, impressed seamen, or the lost property in slaves. Second, it granted the British eighteen more months to withdraw from the western forts while guaranteeing them continued rights in the fur trade. (Even with the delay, the provision disheartened the Indians just then negotiating the Treaty of Greenville out in Ohio; it was a significant factor in their decision to make peace.) Finally, the Jay Treaty called for repayment with interest of the debts that some American planters still owed to British firms dating from the Revolutionary War. In exchange for such generous terms, Jay secured limited trading rights in the West Indies and agreement that some issues—boundary disputes with Canada, the damage and loss claims of the shipowners—would be decided later by arbitration commissions.

The Senate debated the treaty in secrecy, knowing how explosive its terms would be, and passed it by a vote of twenty to ten. President Washington signed it, but with misgivings. When newspapers published the terms of the treaty, powerful opposition emerged from Maine to Georgia. In Massachusetts, graffiti appeared on a wall: "Damn John Jay! Damn everyone who won't damn John Jay! Damn everyone who won't stay up all night damning John Jay!" Bonfires in many places burned effigies of Jay and copies of the treaty. A newspaper in New Jersey used accessible gender imagery to explain to its readers the implications of the Jay Treaty:

> The nation has been secretly, I will not say treacherously, divorced from France, and most clandestinely married to Great Britain: we are taken from the embraces of a loving wife, and find ourselves in the arms of a destestable and abandoned whore, covered with crimes, rottenness, and corruption.

When Alexander Hamilton appeared at a public meeting in New York City to defend the treaty, he was hissed and booed, and several stones were thrown at him. Within days he was challenging opponents to fights, but no one took up his challenge.

Some representatives in the House, led by Madison, tried to undermine the Senate's approval by insisting on a separate vote on the funding provisions of the treaty, on the grounds that the House controlled all money bills. Finally, in 1796, the House approved funds to implement the various commissions mandated by the treaty, but by only a three-vote margin. The cleavage of votes in both houses of Congress divided along the same lines as the Hamilton-Jefferson split on economic policy. This was the most bitter political split yet in the country's short history.

To the South: The Haitian Revolution

In addition to the Indian wars in Ohio and the European wars across the Atlantic, a third bloody conflict to the south polarized and even terrorized many Americans in the 1790s. The western third of the large Caribbean island of Hispaniola, just to the east of Cuba, became engulfed in revolution starting in 1791. The eastern portion of the island was a Spanish colony called Santo Domingo; the western part, in bloody conflagration, was the French Saint Domingue.

Haitian Revolution, 1790–1804

War raged there for over a decade, resulting in the birth of the Republic of Haiti in 1804, distinguished as the first and only independent black state to arise out of a successful slave revolution.

The Haitian Revolution was a complex event involving many participants, including the diverse local population and, eventually, three European countries. Some 30,000 whites ruled the island in 1790, running sugar and coffee plantations with close to half a million slaves, two-thirds of them of African birth. The white French colonists were not the only plantation owners, however. About 28,000 free coloreds (*gens de couleur*) of mixed race also lived in Saint Domingue; they owned one-third of the island's plantations and nearly a quarter of the slave labor force. Despite their economic status, the free coloreds were barred from political power; but they aspired to it.

The French Revolution of 1789 was the immediate catalyst for rebellion in this already tense society. First, white colonists challenged the white royalist government in an effort to link Saint Domingue with the new revolutionary government in France. Next the free coloreds rebelled in 1791, demanding equal civil rights with the whites. No sooner was this revolt viciously suppressed than another part of the island exploded as thousands of slaves armed with machetes and torches wreaked devastation and slaughter. In 1793, the civil war escalated to include French, Spanish, and British troops fighting the inhabitants and also each other. Slaves led by Toussaint L'Ouverture in alliance with Spain occupied the northern regions of the island, leaving a thousand plantations in ruins and tens of thousands of people dead. Thousands of whites and free coloreds, along with some of their slaves, fled to Spanish Louisiana and southern cities of the United States.

White Americans followed the revolution in fascinated horror through newspapers and refugees' accounts. A few sympathized with the impulse for liberty, but many more shuddered at the violent atrocities. White refugees were welcomed in Charleston, Norfolk, and Richmond; but French-speaking blacks, whether free or slave, were eventually barred from entry in all southern states except Virginia. White Southerners clearly feared that violent black insurrection might be imported from Haiti into their own society.

Many black American slaves also followed the revolution, hearing about it from dockworkers, from black sailors, from anxious whites who spoke of it over dinner or at the tavern, where blacks waited on table, and from the French blacks themselves, arriving in Virginia ports in significant numbers after 1793. Amazing news— the success of a first ever, massive revolution by slaves—traveled quickly in this oral culture. Whites complained of behaviors that might prefigure plots and conspiracies, such as increased insolence and higher runaway rates among slaves.

The Haitian Revolution provoked naked fear of race war in white southern Americans. Jefferson, agonizing over the contagion of liberty in 1797, wrote another Virginia slaveholder that "if something is not done, and soon done, we shall be the murderers of our own children . . . ; the revolutionary storm, now sweeping the globe, will be upon us, and happy if we make timely provision to give it an easy passage over our land. From the present state of things in Europe and America, the day which brings our combustion must be near at hand; and only a single spark is wanting to make that day to-morrow." Jefferson's cataclysmic fears were not shared by New Englanders. Timothy Pickering of Massachusetts, in Washington's cabinet since 1795, chastised the inconsistent Jefferson for supporting French revolutionaries while condemning black Haitians fighting for freedom, just because they had "a skin not colored like our own." Not that Pickering supported either type of violent revolutionary—he did not. But he and his political allies, soon to be called the Federalists, were far more willing to contemplate trade and diplomatic relations with the emerging black republic of Haiti.

> White Southerners clearly feared that violent black insurrection might be imported from Haiti into their own society.

Federalists and Republicans

By the mid-1790s, the polarization of opinions on the French Revolution, on Haiti, on the Jay Treaty, and on Hamilton's economic plans had led to two distinct and consistent rival political groups: Federalists and Republicans. Politicians and newspapers adopted these labels, words that summarized conflicting ideologies and principles; they did not yet describe full-fledged political parties, which were still thought to be a sign of failure of the experiment in government. Washington's decision not to seek a third term opened the floodgates to serious partisan electioneering in the presidential and congressional elections of 1796. Although Federalist John Adams emerged the victor, his single term in office was very acrimonious as party strife accelerated over failed diplomacy in France, which brought the United States to the brink of war. Pro-war and antiwar antagonism created a major crisis in the young country over political free speech, militarism, and fears of sedition and treason.

The Election of 1796

Washington struggled to appear to be above party politics, and in his farewell address of September 1796 he stressed the need to maintain a "unity of government" reflecting a unified body politic. He also urged the country to "steer

Washington's Farewell Address Printed on a Textile, 1806

This small square of fabric, suitable for framing or tacking to the wall, was one of many items that served to immortalize Washington as the benevolent savior of the young Republic. Known well by close associates as a man with ordinary human failings—one Federalist member of his last cabinet complained that he was "vain and weak and ignorant"—Washington in death became a demigod, a genius of inspired leadership and faultless integrity. This 1806 textile features the final paragraph of Washington's 1796 farewell address, one highlighting his modesty and self-deprecation. At the bottom, the American eagle and the British lion flank two sailing ships (one close, one far off) under the words "Commercial Union." The textile picture, then, was an implicit criticism of the new president, Thomas Jefferson, whose leadership was producing deteriorating relations with Britain that would finally result in the War of 1812.

Collection of Janice L. and David J. Frent.

persuasion and intrigue. Bruised by his conflicts with Hamilton, Jefferson had resigned as secretary of state in 1793 and retreated to Monticello, his home in Virginia. Adams's job as vice president kept him closer to the political action, but his personality often put people off. He was temperamental, thin-skinned, and quick to take offense.

The leading Federalists and Republicans informally caucused to choose candidates. The Federalists picked Thomas Pinckney of South Carolina to run with Adams; the Republicans settled on Aaron Burr of New York to pair with Jefferson. The Constitution did not anticipate parties and tickets. Instead, each electoral college voter could cast two votes for any two candidates, but on only one ballot. The top vote-getter became president and the next highest assumed the vice presidency. (This procedural flaw was corrected by the Twelfth Amendment, adopted in 1804.) With only one ballot, careful maneuver-

John Adams

In 1793, a year after the youthful secretary of the treasury Alexander Hamilton posed for him (see page 286), John Trumbull painted Vice President John Adams, then age fifty-eight. A friend once listed Adams's shortcomings as a politician: "He can't dance, drink, game, flatter, promise, dress, swear with gentlemen, and small talk and flirt with the ladies."

National Portrait Gallery, Smithsonian Institution/Art Resources, NY.

clear of permanent alliances with any portion of the foreign world." The leading contenders for his position, John Adams of Massachusetts and Thomas Jefferson of Virginia, in theory agreed with him, but around them raged a party contest split along pro-English versus pro-French lines.

Adams and Jefferson were not adept politicians in the modern sense, skilled in the arts of

ing was required to make sure the chief rivals for the presidency did not land in the top two spots.

Into that maneuverable moment stepped Alexander Hamilton. No longer in the cabinet, Hamilton had returned to his law practice in 1795, but he kept a firm hand on political developments. Hamilton did not trust Adams; he preferred Pinckney, and he tried to influence electors to throw their support to the South Carolinian. But his plan backfired: Adams was elected president with 71 electoral votes, and Jefferson came in second with 68 and thus became vice president. Pinckney got 59 votes, while Burr trailed with 30.

Adams's inaugural speech pledged neutrality in foreign affairs and respect for the French people, which made Republicans hopeful. To please Federalists, Adams retained three cabinet members from Washington's administration—the secretaries of state, treasury, and war. But the three were Hamilton loyalists, passing on Hamilton's judgments and advice as their own to the unwitting Adams. Vice President Jefferson extended a conciliatory arm to Adams when the two old friends met in Philadelphia, still the capital. They even took temporary lodging in the same boardinghouse as if expecting to work closely together. But the Hamiltonian cabinet ruined the honeymoon. Jefferson's advice was spurned, and he withdrew from active counsel of the president.

The XYZ Affair

Foreign policy lay at the heart of the rift between Adams and Jefferson and between Federalists and Republicans. If the Jay Treaty heated American tempers initially, the French response in 1797 was like oil added to the fire. Adams's one-term presidency was a perpetual crisis.

France read the Jay Treaty as the Republicans did: as a document giving so many concessions to the British that it made the United States a British satellite. In retaliation, France abandoned the terms of its 1778 wartime alliance with the United States and allowed French privateers—armed private vessels—to detain American ships carrying British goods. By March 1797, more than 300 American vessels had been seized. In a related move, in the winter of 1796–97, France refused to recognize a new minister sent by President Washington, Charles Cotesworth Pinckney.

To avenge these insults, Federalists started murmuring openly about war with France.

"The Ladies Patriotic Song," 1799
This sheet music invests women with the power to inspire soldiers and sailors in the undeclared war with France. The second verse begins: "What Hero will Beauty's soft influence disprove / What Sword will not start, urg'd by Honour and Love / Columbia's fair Daughters will bless with their charms / The generous in Peace—The Triumphant in Arms." The song was published in Boston, a staunchly Federalist city in the heart of New England federalism. Would you expect to see a song like this published in Charlottesville, Virginia, Thomas Jefferson's home town? Chicago Historical Society.

Adams preferred negotiations and dispatched a three-man commission to France in the fall of 1797. At the same time, the president recommended new expenditures for military defense; negotiations needed to be backed by military preparedness. Congress agreed and approved the construction of three new naval frigates. When the three commissioners arrived in Paris, French officials would not receive them. Finally the French minister of foreign affairs, Talleyrand, sent three French agents, unnamed and later known to the American public as X, Y, and Z, to the American commissioners with the recommendation that $250,000 might grease the wheels of diplomacy and that a $12 million loan to the French government would be the price of a peace treaty. Incensed by Talleyrand's suggestion of a bribe, the three American commissioners departed to inform the president.

> Foreign policy lay at the heart of the rift between Adams and Jefferson and between Federalists and Republicans. If the Jay Treaty heated American tempers initially, the XYZ affair was like oil added to the fire.

Cartoon of the Matthew Lyon Fight in Congress
The political tensions of 1798 were not merely intellectual. A February session in Congress degenerated from name-calling to a brawl. Roger Griswold, a Connecticut Federalist, called Matthew Lyon, a Vermont Republican, a coward. Lyon responded with some well-aimed spit, the first departure from the gentle-man's code of honor. Griswold responded by raising his cane to Lyon, whereupon Lyon grabbed nearby fire tongs to beat back his assailant. Madison wrote to Jefferson that the two should have dueled: "No man ought to reproach another with cowardice, who is not ready to give proof of his own courage" by negotiating a duel, the honorable way to avenge insults in Virginia's planter class. But Lyon, a Scots-Irish immigrant, did not come from a class or culture that cultivated the art of the duel; rough-and-tumble fighting was his first response to insult. What is the picture on the wall of the House chambers?
Library of Congress.

For more help analyzing this image, see the visual activity for this chapter in the Online Study Guide at bedfordstmartins.com/roark.

Americans reacted to the XYZ affair with shock and anger. Even staunch pro-French Republicans began to reevaluate their allegiance. The Federalist-dominated Congress appropri-ated money for an army of 10,000 soldiers. It re-pealed all prior treaties with France, and in 1798 twenty naval warships launched the United States into its first undeclared war, now called the Quasi-War by historians to underscore its un-certain legal status. The main scene of action was the Caribbean, where more than 100 French pri-vateers were captured.

There was no home-front unity in this time of undeclared war; antagonism only intensified between Federalists and Republicans. Because there seemed to be very little chance of a land in-vasion by France, leading Republicans feared, with some justification, that the Federalists' real aim might be to raise the army to threaten do-mestic dissenters. Some claimed that Hamilton had masterminded the army buildup and was lobbying to be second in command, behind the aging Washington. President Adams was in-creasingly mistrustful, but his cabinet backed the military buildup, and Adams was too weak politically to prevail. He was, moreover, beginning to suspect that his cabinet was more loyal to Hamilton than to the presidency.

Republican newspapers heaped abuse on Adams. Pro-French mobs roamed the capital city, and Adams, fearing for his personal safety, stocked weapons in his presidential quarters. Federalists too went on the offensive. In Newburyport, Massachusetts, they lit a huge bonfire, burning issues of the state's Republican newspapers. One Federalist editor ominously declared that "he who is not for us is against us." Officers in a New York militia unit drank a menacing toast on July 4, 1798: "One and but one party in the United States."

The Alien and Sedition Acts

With tempers so dangerously high, and fears that political dissent was perhaps akin to treason, Federalist leaders moved to muffle the opposition. In mid-1798, Congress hammered out a Sedition Act that mandated a heavy fine or a jail sentence for anyone engaged in conspiracies or revolts or convicted of speaking or writing anything that defamed the president or Congress. Criticisms of government leaders were now criminal utterances. (See "Documenting the American Promise," page 312.)

Congress also passed two Alien Acts. The first extended the waiting period for an alien to achieve citizenship from five to fourteen years and required all aliens to register with the federal government. The second empowered the president in time of war to deport or imprison without trial any foreigner suspected of being a danger to the United States. The clear intent of the alien laws was to harass French immigrants already in the United States and discourage others from coming.

The main targets of the Sedition Act were Republican newspaper editors who were free and abusive in their criticism of the Adams administration. One Federalist in Congress justified his vote for the law: "Let gentlemen look at certain papers printed in this city and elsewhere, and ask themselves whether an unwarrantable and dangerous combination does not exist to overturn and ruin the government by publishing the most shameless falsehoods against the representatives of the people." In all, twenty-five men, almost all newspaper editors, were charged with sedition; twelve were convicted.

Republicans strongly opposed the Alien and Sedition Acts on the grounds that they were in conflict with the Bill of Rights, but they did not have the votes to revoke the acts in Congress, nor could the federal judiciary, dominated by Federalist judges, be counted on to challenge them. Jefferson and Madison turned to the state legislatures, the only other competing political arena, to press their opposition. Each man drafted a set of resolutions condemning the acts and had the legislatures of Virginia and Kentucky present them to the federal government in late fall 1798. The Virginia and Kentucky Resolutions tested the novel argument that state legislatures have the right to judge the constitutionality of federal laws and to **nullify** laws that infringe on the liberties of the people as defined in the Bill of Rights. The resolutions made little dent in the Alien and Sedition Acts, but the idea of a state's right to nullify federal law did not disappear. It surfaced several times in decades to come, most notably in a major tariff dispute in 1832 and in the sectional arguments that led to the Civil War.

Amid all the war hysteria and sedition fears in 1798, President Adams regained his balance. He was uncharacteristically restrained in pursuing opponents under the Sedition Act, and he finally refused to declare war on France, despite the wishes of extreme Federalists. No doubt he was beginning to realize how much he had been the dupe of Hamilton. He also shrewdly realized that France was not in fact eager for war and that a peaceful settlement might be close at hand. In January 1799, a peace initiative from France arrived in the form of a letter assuring Adams that diplomatic channels were open again and that new commissioners would be welcomed in France. Adams accepted this overture and appointed a new negotiator. By late 1799, the Quasi-War with France had subsided; but in responding to the French initiative, Adams lost the support of a significant part of his own party and sealed his fate as the first one-term president of the United States.

The election of 1800 was openly organized along party lines. The self-designated national leaders of each group met to handpick their candidates for president and vice president. Adams's chief opponent was Thomas Jefferson. When the election was finally over, President Jefferson mounted the inaugural platform to

> Republicans strongly opposed the Alien and Sedition Acts on the grounds that they were in conflict with the Bill of Rights.

The Crisis of 1798: Sedition

As President John Adams inched toward an undeclared war with France, criticism of his foreign policy reached an all-time high. Newspaper editors and politicians favorable to France blasted him with such intemperate language that his supporters feared the United States could be pushed to the brink of civil war. Federalists in Congress tried to muffle the opposition by criminalizing seditious words, believing it the only path to preserve the country. Republicans just redoubled their opposition.

DOCUMENT 1
Abigail Adams Complains of Sedition, 1798

Throughout the spring of 1798, a beleaguered Abigail Adams complained repeatedly in confidential letters to her sister Mary Cranch about the need for a sedition law to put a stop to the political criticisms of her husband, the president, by Benjamin Bache, pro-French editor of the Philadelphia Aurora.

(April 26): . . . Yet dairingly do the vile incendaries keep up in Baches paper the most wicked and base, voilent & caluminiating abuse—It was formerly considerd as leveld against the Government, but now it . . . insults the Majesty of the Sovereign People. But nothing will have an Effect untill congress pass a Sedition Bill. . . . (April 28): . . . we are now wonderfully popular except with Bache & Co who in his paper calls the President old, querilous, Bald, blind, cripled, Toothless

Adams. (May 10): . . . This Bache is cursing & abusing daily. If that fellow . . . is not surpressd, we shall come to a civil war. (May 26): . . . I wish the Laws of our Country were competant to punish the stirer up of sedition, the writer and Printer of base and unfounded calumny. This would contribute as much to the Peace and harmony of our Country as any measure. . . . (June 19): . . . in any other Country Bache & all his papers would have been seazd and ought to be here, but congress are dilly dallying about passing a Bill enabling the President to seize suspisious persons, and their papers. (June 23): . . . I wish our Legislature would set the example & make a sedition act, to hold in order the base Newspaper calumniators. In this State, you could not get a verdict, if a prosecution was to be commenced.

SOURCE: Stewart Mitchell, ed., *New Letters of Abigail Adams, 1788–1801* (Boston: Houghton Mifflin, 1947), 165, 167, 172, 179, 193, 196.

DOCUMENT 2
The Sedition Act of 1798

On July 14, 1798, Congress approved a bill making sedition with malicious intent a crime.

SECTION 1. . . . if any persons shall unlawfully combine or conspire together, with intent to oppose any measure or measures of the government of the United States . . . , or to impede the operation of any law of the United States, or to intimidate

or prevent any person holding . . . office in or under the government of the United States, from undertaking, performing or executing his trust or duty, and if any person or persons, with intent as aforesaid, shall counsel, advise or attempt to procure any insurrection, riot, unlawful assembly, or combination . . . , he or they shall be deemed guilty of a high misdemeanor, and on conviction . . . shall be punished by a fine not exceeding five thousand dollars, and by imprisonment during a term not less than six months nor exceeding five years. . . .

SEC. 2. . . . if any person shall write, print, utter or publish, or shall cause or procure to be written, printed, uttered or published . . . , any false, scandalous and malicious writing or writings against the government of the United States, or either house of the Congress of the United States, or the President of the United States, with intent to defame the said government . . . or to bring them . . . into contempt or disrepute; or to excite against them . . . the hatred of the good people of the United States . . . , or to aid, encourage or abet any hostile designs of any foreign nation against the United States . . . , then such person, being thereof convicted thereof . . . shall be punished by a fine not exceeding two thousand dollars, and by imprisonment not exceeding two years.

DOCUMENT 3
Matthew Lyon Criticizes John Adams, 1798

Matthew Lyon, a member of Congress from Vermont, published this criticism of President Adams in a letter to the editor of Spooner's Vermont Journal *(July 31, 1798). It became the first of three counts against him in a sedition* *trial. Lyon drew a four-month sentence and a fine of $1,000. From jail he ran for reelection to Congress—and won.*

As to the Executive, when I shall see the efforts of that power bent on the promotion of the comfort, the happiness, and the accommodation of the people, that Executive shall have my zealous and uniform support. But when I see every consideration of the public welfare swallowed up in a continual grasp for power, in an unbounded thirst for ridiculous pomp, foolish adulation, or selfish avarice; when I shall behold men of real merit daily turned out of office for no other cause but independence of sentiment; when I shall see men of firmness, merit, years, abilities, and experience, discarded on their application for office, for fear they possess that independence; and men of meanness preferred for the ease with which they take up and advocate opinions, the consequence of which they know but little of; when I shall see the sacred name of religion employed as a State engine to make mankind hate and persecute one another, I shall not be their humble advocate.

SOURCE: Matthew Lyon, Letter in *Spooner's Vermont Journal*, July 31, 1798. Quoted in Aleine Austin, *Matthew Lyon: New Man of the Democratic Revolution, 1749–1822* (University Park: Pennsylvania State University Press, 1981), 108–09.

DOCUMENT 4
James Bayard Defends the Law, 1799

James Bayard, a Federalist representative from Delaware, led the charge in the House to expel Matthew Lyon from his seat in Congress. Bayard argued that Lyon was guilty of subverting the government.

This Government . . . depends for its existence upon the good will of the people. That good will is maintained by their good opinion. But, how is that good opinion to be preserved, if wicked and unprincipled men, men of inordinate and desperate ambition, are allowed to state facts to the people which are not true, which they know at the time to be false, and which are stated with the criminal intention of bringing the Government into disrepute among the people? This was falsely and deceitfully stealing public opinion; it was a felony of the worst and most dangerous nature.

SOURCE: *Annals of Congress* (1799). Quoted in Richard Buel, *Securing the Revolution: Ideology in American Politics* (Ithaca, N.Y.: Cornell University Press, 1972), 256.

DOCUMENT 5
The Virginia Resolution, December 24, 1798

James Madison drafted the Virginia Resolution and had a trusted ally present it to the Virginia legislature, which was dominated by Republicans. (Jefferson did the same for Kentucky.) The Virginia document denounces the Alien and Sedition Acts and declares that states have the right to "interpose" to stop unconstitutional actions by the federal government.

RESOLVED . . . That this assembly most solemnly declares a warm attachment to the Union of the States, to maintain which it pledges all its powers; and that for this end, it is their duty to watch over and oppose every infraction of those principles which constitute the only basis of that Union, because a faithful observance of them, can alone secure its existence and the public happiness.

That this Assembly doth explicitly and peremptorily declare, that it views the powers of the federal government, as resulting from the compact, to which the states are parties; as limited by the plain sense and intention of the instrument constituting the compact; as no further valid that they are authorized by the grants enumerated in that compact; and that in case of a deliberate, palpable, and dangerous exercise of other powers, not granted by the said compact, the states who are parties thereto, have the right, and are in duty bound, to interpose for arresting the progress of the evil, and for maintaining within their respective limits, the authorities, rights and liberties appertaining to them. . . .

That the General Assembly doth particularly protest against the palpable and alarming infractions of the Constitution, in the two late cases of the "Alien and Sedition Acts" . . . ; the first of which exercises a power no where delegated to the federal government . . . ; and the other of which acts, exercises in like manner, a power not delegated by the constitution, but on the contrary, expressly and positively forbidden by one of the amendments thereto; a power, which more than any other, ought to produce universal alarm, because it is levelled against that right of freely examining public characters and measures, and of free communication among the people thereon, which has ever been justly deemed, the only effectual guardian of every other right.

SOURCE: Avalon Project, Yale Law School, 1996, <www.yale.edu/lawweb/avalon/virres.htm>.

(continued)

(continued)

QUESTIONS FOR ANALYSIS
AND DEBATE

1. Why did Federalists believe a Sedition Act was necessary? What exactly was the threat, according to Abigail Adams? According to James Bayard? What threat is implied by the wording of the act?

2. Does Matthew Lyon's criticism of President Adams rise to the level of threat that Federalists feared? How do you explain his guilty verdict? His reelection to Congress?

3. What might Madison have meant by "interpose" as the desired action by states? What could states actually do?

4. How would Adams and Bayard square the Sedition Act with the First Amendment's protection of free speech? Did critics of the law invoke freedom of speech and press?

5. Which side had the stronger argument in 1798–1799? Do you think there should be limits on what can be said publicly about high government officials? Why or why not?

announce, "We are all republicans, we are all federalists," an appealing rhetoric of harmony appropriate to an inaugural address. But his formulation perpetuated a denial of the validity of party politics, a denial that ran deep in the founding generation of political leaders.

Conclusion: Parties Nonetheless

American political leaders began operating the new government in 1789 with great hopes to unify the country and to overcome selfish factionalism. The enormous popularity of, and trust in, President Washington was the central foundation for that hope, and Washington did not disappoint, becoming a model Mr. President with a good blend of integrity and authority. Stability was further aided by easy passage of the Bill of Rights (to appease Antifederalists) and by attention to cultivating a virtuous citizenry of upright men supported and rewarded by republican womanhood. Yet the hopes of the honeymoon period soon turned to worries and then fears as major political disagreements flared up.

At the core of the conflict was a group of talented men—Hamilton, Madison, Jefferson, and Adams—so recently allies but now opponents. They diverged over Hamilton's economic program, over relations with the British and the Jay Treaty, over the French and Haitian revolutions, and over preparedness for war abroad and free speech rights at home. Hamilton was perhaps the driving force in these conflicts, but the antagonism was not about mere personality. Parties were taking shape, not around individuals but around principles, such as ideas about what constitutes enlightened leadership, how powerful should the federal government be, who is the best ally in Europe, and when does oppositional political speech turn into treason. The Federalists were pro-British, pro-commerce, and ever alarmed about the potential excesses of democracy. The Republicans celebrated, up to a point, the radical republicanism of France and found the Sedition Act an alarming example of the old Antifederalists' worst nightmare.

When Jefferson, then, in his inaugural address of 1800 offered his conciliatory assurance that Americans were at the same time "all republicans" and "all federalists," he probably mystified some listeners. Possibly he meant to suggest that both groups shared two basic ideas—the value of republican government, in which power derived from the people, and the value of the unique federal system of shared governance structured by the Constitution. But by 1800, these two words defined competing philosophies of government. Jefferson's speech was spoken aloud; his listeners could not hear the presence or absence of capital letters. To at least some of his listeners, Jefferson's assertion of harmony across party lines could only have seemed bizarre. For the next two decades, these two parties would battle each other, both fearing that the success of the other might bring the demise of the country. And for the next two decades, leaders continued to worry that party spirit itself was a bad thing.

For **ADDITIONAL FIRSTHAND ACCOUNTS OF THIS PERIOD,** see Chapter 9 in Michael Johnson, ed., *Reading the American Past,* Third Edition.

To **ASSESS YOUR MASTERY OF THE MATERIAL IN THIS CHAPTER,** see the Online Study Guide at bedfordstmartins.com/ roark.

For **WEB LINKS RELATED TO TOPICS IN THIS CHAPTER,** see "HistoryLinks," "DocLinks," and "PlaceLinks" at bedfordstmartins.com/roark.

CHRONOLOGY

1789
- George Washington inaugurated first president.
- French Revolution begins, causing celebration in America.
- First Congress meets in New York City.
- Fort Washington erected in western Ohio as command post for invasions of Indian country.

1790
- Alexander Hamilton issues his *Report on Public Credit,* and Congress approves his plan for funding the federal debt and assuming states' debts.
- Congress approves Potomac River site for U.S. capital.
- Federal government moves from New York to Philadelphia.
- Judith Sargent Murray publishes "On the Equality of the Sexes."
- New Jersey election law specifically refers to state voters as *he or she.*
- General Josiah Harmar's defeat by Shawnee and Miami Indians in Ohio leads to his recall and court-martial.

1791
- Bill of Rights ratified by states.
- Hamilton proposes and Congress charters the Bank of the United States.
- General Arthur St. Clair's forces defeated by Ohio Indians in worst loss ever by Americans in Indian wars.
- Congress passes whiskey tax.
- Haitian Revolution begins and raises fears of race wars in U.S. South.
- Hamilton issues his *Report on Manufactures,* proposing tariffs to encourage American manufacturing.

1793
- Washington's second term begins.
- Napoleonic Wars break out between France and England.
- Washington issues Neutrality Proclamation over war between France and England.
- Reign of Terror in France throws deep chill over American admiration of French Revolution.
- Eli Whitney invents cotton gin, leading to large rise in agricultural production of cotton in the South.

1794
- Farmers stage Whiskey Rebellion in western Pennsylvania, causing President Washington to lead U.S. army west to break it up.
- Lancaster Turnpike, first private toll road, constructed in Pennsylvania.

1795
- Treaty of Greenville cedes most Indian land in Ohio to United States.
- Jay Treaty settles little with England and causes much popular protest in the United States.

1796
- Federalist John Adams elected second president, Thomas Jefferson vice president.

1797
- XYZ affair in France insults U.S. honor and leads to preparations for war with France.

1798
- Quasi-War with France erupts, resulting in capture of French ships in the Caribbean.
- Congress passes Alien and Sedition Acts to suppress pro-French, anti-Adams sentiments.
- Virginia and Kentucky Resolutions press for states' rights in judging constitutionality of federal laws.

1800
- Republican Thomas Jefferson elected third president.

BIBLIOGRAPHY

General Works

Bernard Bailyn, *To Begin the World Anew: The Genius and Ambiguities of the American Founders* (2003).

Doron Ben-Atar and Barbara B. Oberg, eds., *Federalists Reconsidered* (1998).

Richard Buel, *Securing the Revolution: Ideology in American Politics, 1789–1815* (1972).

William Nisbet Chambers, *Political Parties in a New Nation: The American Experience, 1776–1809* (1963).

David P. Currie, *The Constitution in Congress: The Federalist Period, 1789–1801* (1997).

Stanley Elkins and Eric McKitrick, *The Age of Federalism: The Early American Republic, 1788–1800* (1993).

Joseph J. Ellis, *Founding Fathers: The Revolutionary Generation* (2000).

John E. Ferling, *A Leap in the Dark: The Struggle to Create the American Republic* (2003).

Marshall Foletta, *Coming to Terms with Democracy: Federalist Intellectuals and the Shaping of an American Culture* (2001).

Joanne B. Freeman, *Affairs of Honor: National Politics in the New Republic* (2001).

John F. Hoadley, *Origins of American Political Parties, 1789–1803* (1986).

Ronald Hoffman and Peter J. Albert, eds., *Launching the "Extended Republic": The Federalist Era* (1996).

Donald R. Kennon, ed., *A Republic for the Ages: The United States Capitol and the Political Culture in the Early Republic* (1999).

Ralph Ketcham, *Presidents above Party: The First American Presidency, 1789–1829* (1984).

David McCullough, *John Adams* (2001).

John R. Nelson, *Liberty and Property: Political Economy and Policymaking in the New Nation, 1789–1812* (1987).

James Rogers Sharp, *American Politics in the Early Republic: The New Nation in Crisis* (1993).

Larry E. Tise, *The American Counterrevolution: A Retreat from Liberty, 1783–1800* (1999).

David Waldstreicher, *In the Midst of Perpetual Fetes: The Making of American Nationalism, 1776–1820* (1997).

Washington's Administration

Carl Abbott, *Political Terrain: Washington, D.C., from Tidewater Town to Global Metropolis* (1999).

Akhil Reed Amar, *The Bill of Rights: Creation and Reconstruction* (2000).

Bob Arnebeck, *Through a Fiery Trial: Building Washington, 1790–1800* (1991).

Kenneth R. Bowling, *Politics in the First Congress, 1789–1791* (1990).

Kenneth R. Bowling, *The Creation of Washington, D.C.: The Idea and Location of the American Capital* (1991).

Steven R. Boyd, ed., *The Whiskey Rebellion: Past and Present Perspectives* (1985).

Jerry A. Clouse, *The Whiskey Rebellion: Southwestern Pennsylvania's Frontier People Test the American Constitution* (1995).

James T. Flexner, *George Washington and the New Nation, 1783–1793* (1970).

James T. Flexner, *George Washington: Anguish and Farewell, 1793–1799* (1972).

Robert F. Jones, *George Washington: Ordinary Man, Extraordinary Leader* (2002).

Forrest McDonald, *The American Presidency: An Intellectual History* (1994).

Robert A. Rutland, *The Birth of the Bill of Rights, 1776–1791* (1991).

Thomas P. Slaughter, *The Whiskey Rebellion: Frontier Epilogue to the American Revolution* (1986).

Henry Wiencek, *An Imperfect God: George Washington, His Slaves, and the Creation of America* (2003).

The Economy and Hamilton's Program

Joyce Appleby, *Capitalism and a New Social Order: The Republican Vision of the 1790s* (1984).

Richard Brookhiser, *Alexander Hamilton, American* (2000).

Christopher Clark, *The Roots of Rural Capitalism: Western Massachusetts, 1780–1860* (1990).

Jacob E. Cooke, *Alexander Hamilton* (1982).

Paul A. Gilje, ed., *Wages of Independence: Capitalism in the Early American Republic* (1997).

James A. Henretta, *The Origins of American Capitalism: Collected Essays* (1991).

Joan Jensen, *Loosening the Bonds: Mid-Atlantic Farm Women, 1750–1850* (1986).

Lawrence S. Kaplan, *Alexander Hamilton: Ambivalent Anglophile* (2002).

Allan Kulikoff, *The Agrarian Origins of American Capitalism* (1992).

James Lemon, *The Best Poor Man's Country: A Geographical Study of Early Southeastern Pennsylvania* (1972).

Forrest McDonald, *Alexander Hamilton: A Biography* (1982).

Winifred Rothenberg, *From Market-Places to a Market Economy: The Transformation of Rural Massachusetts, 1750–1850* (1992).

Herbert E. Sloan, *Principle and Interest: Thomas Jefferson and the Problem of Debt* (1995).

Society and Culture

Richard D. Brown, *Knowledge Is Power: The Diffusion of Information in Early America, 1700–1865* (1989).

Patricia Cline Cohen, *A Calculating People: The Spread of Numeracy in Early America* (1999).

Nancy Cott, *The Bonds of Womanhood: Women's Sphere in New England, 1780–1835* (1977).

Cathy N. Davidson, *Revolution and the Word: The Rise of the Novel in America* (1986).

Emory Elliott, *Revolutionary Writers: Literature and Authority in the New Republic, 1725–1810* (1982).

Richard R. John, *Spreading the News: The American Postal System from Franklin to Morse* (1996).

Richard B. Kielbowicz, *News in the Mail: The Press, the Post Office, and Public Information, 1700–1860* (1989).

Sheila L. Skemp, *Judith Sargent Murray: A Brief Biography with Documents* (1998).

Indians and the Frontier

Robert F. Berkhofer Jr., *Salvation and the Savage: An Analysis of Protestant Missions and American Indian Response, 1787–1862* (1965).

Colin G. Calloway, *Crown and Calumet: British-Indian Relations, 1783–1815* (1987).

Andrew R. L. Cayton, *Frontier Republic: Ideology and Politics in the Ohio Country, 1780–1825* (1989).

Gregory E. Dowd, *A Spirited Resistance: The North American Indian Struggle for Unity, 1745–1815* (1992).

R. Douglas Hurt, *The Ohio Frontier: Crucible of the Old Northwest, 1720–1830* (1998).

Francis Paul Prucha, *American Indian Policy in the Formative Years: The Indian Trade and Intercourse Acts, 1780–1834* (1962).

Malcolm J. Rohrbough, *The Transappalachian Frontier: People, Societies, and Institutions, 1775–1850* (1978).

Wiley Sword, *President Washington's Indian War: The Struggle for the Old Northwest, 1790–1795* (1985).

Richard White, *The Middle Ground: Indians, Empires, and Republics in the Great Lakes Region, 1650–1815* (1991).

Foreign Relations

Albert H. Bowman, *The Struggle for Neutrality: Franco-American Diplomacy during the Federalist Era* (1974).

Jerald A. Combs, *The Jay Treaty: Political Battleground of the Founding Fathers* (1970).

Alexander DeConde, *The Quasi-War: The Politics and Diplomacy of the Undeclared War with France, 1797–1801* (1966).

Carolyn E. Fick, *The Making of Haiti: The Saint Domingue Revolution from Below* (1991).

David Barry Gaspar and David Patrick Geggus, eds., *A Turbulent Time: The French Revolution and the Greater Caribbean* (1997).

Peter P. Hill, *French Perceptions of the Early American Republic, 1783–1793* (1988).

Daniel G. Lang, *Foreign Policy in the Early Republic* (1985).

Martin Ros, *Night of Fire: The Black Napoleon and the Battle for Haiti* (1993).

William Stinchcombe, *The XYZ Affair* (1981).

Richard J. Twomey, *Jacobins and Jeffersonians: Anglo-American Radicalism in the United States, 1790–1820* (1989).

Federalists and Republicans

Ralph A. Brown, *The Presidency of John Adams* (1975).

Noble Cunningham, *The Jeffersonian Republicans: The Formation of Party Organization, 1789–1801* (1957).

Larry D. Eldridge, *A Distant Heritage: The Growth of Free Speech in Early America* (1994).

Joseph J. Ellis, *Passionate Sage: The Character and Legacy of John Adams* (1993).

John Ferling, *John Adams: A Life* (1992).

Richard Hofstadter, *The Idea of a Party System: The Rise of Legitimate Opposition in the United States, 1780–1840* (1969).

Richard H. Kohn, *Eagle and Sword: The Federalists and the Creation of the Military Establishment in America, 1783–1802* (1975).

Leonard Levy, *The Emergence of a Free Press* (1985).

Drew McCoy, *The Elusive Republic: Political Economy in Jeffersonian America* (1980).

Jeffrey L. Pasley, *The Tyranny of Printers: Newspaper Politics in the Early American Republic* (2001).

James Morton Smith, *Freedom's Fetters: The Alien and Sedition Laws and American Civil Liberties* (1966).

John Zvesper, *Political Philosophy and Rhetoric: A Study of the Origins of American Party Politics* (1977).

State Histories

Richard R. Beeman, *The Old Dominion and the New Nation, 1788–1801* (1972).

Andrew R. L. Cayton, *Frontier Indiana* (1996).

Paul Goodman, *The Democratic-Republicans of Massachusetts* (1964).

Christopher Grasso, *A Speaking Aristocracy: Transforming Public Discourse in Eighteenth-Century Connecticut* (1999).

Norman Risjord, *Chesapeake Politics, 1781–1800* (1978).

Charles Steffen, *The Mechanics of Baltimore: Workers and Politics in the Age of Revolution, 1763–1812* (1984).

Alan Taylor, *Liberty Men and Great Proprietors: The Revolutionary Settlement on the Maine Frontier, 1760–1820* (1990).

Alfred Young, *The Democratic-Republicans of New York: The Origins, 1763–1797* (1967).

A JEFFERSON FAN

Ladies' fans became increasingly popular fashion accessories in the late eighteenth and early nineteenth centuries, equally useful for communication and cooling. This folding fan of vellum and carved ivory, made in the early 1800s, features a medallion portrait of President Thomas Jefferson. Carried by the ribbon on a woman's wrist, the fan could be flicked open to announce a partisan political statement. Fans and other handheld articles such as parasols and handkerchiefs expanded the repertoire of nonverbal expression for women, who by the custom and training of the time were expected to be less assertive than men in mixed-sex conversation. Many emotions and messages—from modesty, coyness, and flirtatiousness to anger, irritability, and boredom—could be communicated by the expert deployment of this delicate emblem of femininity. Women learned the conventions of fluttering the fan by close observation and perhaps by explicit training.

Collection of David J. and Janice L. Frent.

Republicans in Power

1800–1824

THE NAME TECUMSEH translates to "Shooting Star," a fitting name for the Shawnee chief who reached meteoric heights of fame among Indians during Thomas Jefferson's presidency. From Canada to Georgia and west to the Mississippi, Tecumseh was accounted a charismatic leader. White Americans praised (and feared) him as a would-be Moses of the Indians. Graceful, eloquent, compelling, magnetic, astute: Tecumseh was all these and more, a gifted natural leader, equal parts politician and warrior.

Tecumseh was born in 1768 into a family of six sons and one daughter in the Ohio Country. His parents had migrated there around 1760 from the South along with hundreds of Shawnees. The Northwest Territory had become home to some dozen Indian tribes, several of them recent migrants from points east and south. But now Ohio was a battleground in the struggle with the Big Knives, as the Shawnee people called the Americans, producing perpetual conflict from the Revolution to the 1790s Indian wars. Tecumseh's childhood was marked by repeated violence and the loss of his father and two brothers in battle. Five times between 1774 and 1782 the boy fled raids by American soldiers that left his homes in flames and his villages destroyed. When he was ten, his widowed mother returned to the South, leaving her remaining children in the care of an aunt.

The establishment of the United States government brought no peace to the Indians' country. George Washington's administration could not stem the flow of eager but foolhardy American settlers floating down the Ohio River on flatboats, and the youthful Tecumseh honed his warrior skills by ambushing those pioneers. He did not take part in the Indians' 1791 dramatic victory over General St. Clair's army, but he fought at the Battle of Fallen Timbers, a major Indian defeat. He avoided the 1795 negotiations of the Treaty of Greenville, in which a half dozen dispirited tribes ceded much of Ohio to the Big Knives. With frustration he watched as seven additional treaties between 1802 and 1805 whittled away more Indian land.

Some Indians, resigned and tired, looked for ways to accommodate to new realities, taking up farming, trade, and even intermarriage with the Big Knives. Others spent their treaty payments on deadly alcohol. Tecumseh's younger brother Tenskwatawa led an embittered life of idleness and drink. But Tecumseh rejected assimilation and inebriation and embarked on a campaign to return his people to their ancient ways. Donning traditional animal-skin garb, he traveled around the Great Lakes area, persuading tribes to join his pan-Indian confederacy. The American territorial governor of Indiana, William Henry Harrison, reported, "For four years he has been in constant motion. You see him today on the Wabash, and in a short time hear of him on the shores of Lake Erie or Michigan, or on the banks of the Mississippi, and

Tecumseh
Several portraits of Tecumseh exist, but they all present a different visage, and none of them enjoys verified authenticity. This one perhaps comes closest: It is an 1848 engraving adapted from an earlier drawing that no longer exists, sketched by a French trader in Indiana named Pierre Le Dru in a live sitting with the Indian leader in 1808. The engraver has given Tecumseh a British army officer's uniform, showing that he fought on the British side in the War of 1812. Notice the head covering and the medallion around the neck, marking Tecumseh's Indian identity.
Library of Congress.

wherever he goes he makes an impression favorable to his purpose." In 1811, he toured the South, visiting tribes from Mississippi to Georgia while an especially brilliant comet illuminated the night sky. The human Shooting Star understood that only a powerful alliance of Indians could block the path of the westward-moving Big Knives.

Tecumseh's once-dissolute brother joined his campaign after a close brush with death in 1805. Tenskwatawa miraculously revived and recounted a startling vision, a meeting with the Master of Life. Renaming himself the Prophet, Tenskwatawa urged Indians everywhere to return to tradition. He preached that the white Americans were children of the Evil Spirit, des-

tined to be destroyed. Headquartered at a new village called Prophetstown, located in present-day Indiana along Tippecanoe Creek, Tecumseh and his brother pledged a potent blend of spiritual regeneration and political unity that attracted thousands of followers. Governor Harrison admired and feared Tecumseh, calling him "one of those uncommon geniuses which spring up occasionally to produce revolutions."

President Jefferson worried about Tecumseh as well. Although his first term in office was marked by notable successes, such as the Louisiana Purchase and the Lewis and Clark expedition, Jefferson's second term brought the storm clouds of impending war generated by a worrisome Indian-English alliance. That war eventually came in 1812, during President Madison's term. It was partly fought over issues similar to those of the late 1790s: insults over international shipping rights, the capture of vessels, and impressment of sailors. But it was also a product of tensions with Indians in the West in renewed coalition with England, occupying land coveted by westward-moving Americans.

Tecumseh's confederacy delivered 800 warriors to augment British military strength in Canada. Unfortunately for the Indians, the British concentrated on protecting Canada, not the Indians' country. Tecumseh died on Canadian soil at the Battle of the Thames in the fall of 1813, defending Canada against an army led by American general William Henry Harrison. In the end, the War of 1812 settled little between the Americans and the British, but it was tragically conclusive for the Indians. No Indian leader with the star power of Tecumseh would emerge again east of the Mississippi.

The briefly unified Indian confederacy under Tecumseh had no counterpart in the young Republic's confederation of states, where widespread unity and enthusiasm behind a single leader proved impossible to achieve. Republicans did battle with Federalists during the Jefferson and Madison administrations, but then Federalists doomed their party by opposing the War of 1812 and after 1815 ceased to be a major force in political life. The next two presidents, James Monroe and John Quincy Adams, congratulated themselves on the Federalists' demise and Republican unity, but in fact divisions within their party were extensive. Wives of politicians increasingly inserted themselves into this dissonant mix, managing men's politicking and jockeying for power in the Capitol, enabling their husbands to appear above the fray and maintain the fiction of a non-factionalized state. That it was a fiction became sharply apparent in the most serious political crisis of this period, the Missouri Compromise of 1820.

Jefferson Assumes Power, 1800–1801

The nerve-wracking election of 1800, decided in the House of Representatives, enhanced fears that party divisions born in the 1790s would ruin the country. A panicky Federalist newspaper in Connecticut predicted that Jefferson's victory would produce civil war and usher in an immoral reign of "murder, robbery, rape, adultery and incest," leading to a "nation black with crimes," its "soil soaked with blood."

Nothing nearly so drastic or revolutionary occurred. Jefferson later called his election the "revolution of 1800," by which he meant his thorough yet peaceful repudiation of the monarchical power of the Federalists. He first had to deal with a set of midnight appointments made by John Adams as he vacated office, an instance demonstrating keen Federalist mistrust but also leading to the important legal principle of judicial review. Meanwhile, quite a different "revolution of 1800" nearly materialized when a literate Virginia slave named Gabriel followed the scurrilous rhetoric of the presidential campaign and plotted his own rebellion, figuring it might succeed when white men were so badly divided. Gabriel was wrong, but his plot added greatly to the turbulence of 1800–1801.

Jefferson indeed did radically transform the presidency, away from the Federalists' vision of a powerful, even regal, executive branch to republican simplicity and limited government. Yet even Jefferson found that circumstances sometimes required him to draw on the expansive powers of the presidency.

Election by the House

Jefferson's election in 1800 was a cliff-hanger. It was no surprise that his Federalist opponent, John Adams, lost. Adams's diplomatic overtures to France had angered many in his own party, and Alexander Hamilton's abusive scorn of Adams doomed him to defeat. But the Republican voters in the electoral college slipped up, giving equal numbers of votes to Jefferson and his run-

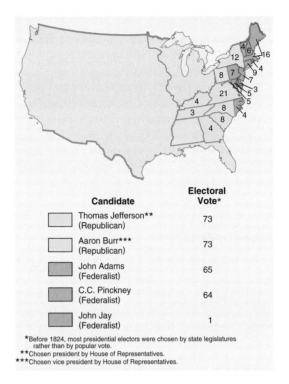

Candidate	Electoral Vote*
Thomas Jefferson** (Republican)	73
Aaron Burr*** (Republican)	73
John Adams (Federalist)	65
C.C. Pinckney (Federalist)	64
John Jay (Federalist)	1

*Before 1824, most presidential electors were chosen by state legislatures rather than by popular vote.
**Chosen president by House of Representatives.
***Chosen vice president by House of Representatives.

MAP 10.1   The Election of 1800

ning mate, Senator Aaron Burr of New York, an outcome possible because of the single balloting to choose both president and vice president (Map 10.1). (The Twelfth Amendment to the Constitution, adopted four years later, provided for distinct ballots for the two offices to fix this problem.) Burr, driven by ambition and vanity, declined to concede the presidency to Jefferson. So the election moved to the Federalist-dominated House of Representatives for decision.

In February 1801, the House met to choose. Each state delegation commanded one vote, and the winner needed nine votes. Some Federalists preferred Burr, believing his character flaws made him more susceptible to Federalist pressure. "His very selfishness prevents his entertaining any mischievous predilections for foreign nations," wrote one senator privately. But Hamilton, although no friend to Jefferson, recognized that the high-strung and arrogant Burr would be more dangerous in the presidency than Jefferson, with his hated but steady habits of **republicanism**. Jefferson was a fanatic and a "contemptible hypocrite" in Hamilton's opinion, but at least he was not corrupt. Jefferson had the votes of eight states on the first ballot; it took thirty-six more ballots and six days to get a ninth vote (and also a tenth) in his column. In the end, anti-Burr Federalist representatives in three states abstained from voting to allow Jefferson the victory without actually having to cast a ballot for him.

The election of 1800 demonstrated a remarkable feature of the new constitutional government. No matter how hard fought the campaign, this election showed that leadership of the nation could shift from one group to a distinctly different group in a peaceful transfer of power effected by ballots, not bullets.

Gabriel's Rebellion

As the country struggled over its white leadership crisis, a twenty-four-year-old blacksmith named Gabriel plotted his own revolution of 1800 in Virginia. Gabriel, the slave of Thomas Prosser, recruited hundreds of co-conspirators from five counties. Inspired by the Haitian Revolution (see chapter 9), and perhaps directly informed of it by French slaves new to the Richmond area, Gabriel and his followers planned to march on the state capitol at Richmond, set diversionary fires, capture an arsenal, and take the governor, James Monroe, hostage. Gabriel intended to spare Methodists and Quakers, known to hold antislavery views, and he also expected Indians and "the poor white people" of Richmond to join him. Taking seriously the Federalist rhetoric about Republican Francophiles, Gabriel assumed that the pro-French (and thus **liberty**-loving) Republican governor Monroe might prove sympathetic to the rebels' cause.

Gabriel's revolt never materialized. A massive thunderstorm scuttled it on the appointed day in August, and a few nervous slaves spilled the secret. Within days, scores of implicated conspirators were jailed and brought to trial. One of the accused, Jack Ditcher, declared in court, "We have as much right to fight for our liberty as any men." Another jailed rebel compared himself to the most venerated icon of the early Republic: "I have nothing more to offer than what General Washington would have had to offer, had he been taken by the British and put to trial by them." Such talk invoking the specter of a black George Washington worried James Monroe and Thomas Jefferson.

> As the country struggled over its white leadership crisis, a twenty-four-year-old blacksmith named Gabriel plotted his own revolution of 1800 in Virginia.

Persistent rumors implicated two white Frenchmen in the plot. If that connection had been established, it would have strengthened Federalist claims that the slave insurrections were a logical outcome of Republican slogans about liberty and equality. Meanwhile, Virginia judges were keeping the Richmond gallows busy. Over September and October, 27 black men were hanged for contemplating rebellion. Finally, Jefferson advised Monroe that the hangings had gone far enough and that deportation was a better alternative. "The world at large will forever condemn us if we indulge a principle of revenge," Jefferson wrote Monroe.

Gabriel's near-rebellion failed, but it scared Virginia politicians into a serious—but secret—effort to identify a site to which future troublesome slaves could be deported. In 1801, the Virginia legislature pressed the federal government for help because deportation required cooperation with a foreign power. Though sympathetic to this effort, Jefferson let the idea drop. Deporting insubordinate slaves to Sierra Leone in Africa or to some Spanish colony west of the Mississippi would perhaps reduce tensions in Virginia, but it might also encourage defiance because the eventual payoff was freedom.

The Jeffersonian Vision of Republican Simplicity

Jefferson sidestepped the problem of slavery and turned his attention to establishing a mode of governing that presented a clear contrast to that of the Federalists. On inauguration day, held for the first time in the village optimistically called Washington City, he walked to the new Capitol building to be sworn in, shunning the pageantry of a horse-drawn carriage and an entourage of attendants. His clothes were rustic, not dressy: green breeches and gray woolen stockings. A disdainful Federalist later remarked, "Everyone knew, of course, that he had a fine French wardrobe of damask waistcoats, frilled shirts, and silk stockings." But Jefferson's aim was to strike the tone of republican simplicity.

Once in office, he continued to emphasize unfussy frugality. He scaled back on Federalist building plans for Washington City and cut the government budget. He continued to wear plain clothes, appearing "neglected but not slovenly," according to one onlooker. He cultivated a casual style, wearing slippers to greet important guests, avoiding the formality of state parties and liveried servants. Jefferson's studied carelessness was very deliberate.

Martha Washington and Abigail Adams had received the wives of government figures at formal weekly teas, thereby helping to create and cement social relations in the governing class. But Jefferson, a long-term widower, abolished female gatherings and avoided the women of Washington City. He abandoned George Washington's tradition of weekly levees, scaling back open-house receptions to just two a year, on New Year's Day and July 4. His preferred social event was the small dinner party with carefully chosen politicos seated at one round table, a table shape that guaranteed nonhierarchical seating plus the certainty that no conversation could escape the president's ears. Generally his guest list was either entirely Republican or entirely Federalist, and in both cases usually entirely male. At these intimate dinners, the president demonstrated his version of statecraft, exercising influence and strengthening informal relationships that would help him to govern.

Jefferson's paramount goal was to scale back the federal exercise of power and promote policies that would foster the independence of ordinary American citizens. Jefferson was no Antifederalist. He had supported the Constitution in 1788, although he had qualms about the unrestricted reelection allowed to the president. But events of the 1790s had caused him to worry about the stretching of powers in the executive branch. Jefferson had watched with distrust as Hamilton led the Federalists to fund the public debt, establish a national bank, and secure commercial ties with England (see chapter 9). The Hamiltonian program seemed to Jefferson to be promoting the interests of money-hungry speculators at the expense of the rest of the country. Jefferson was not at all anticommerce. But financial schemes that seemed merely to allow rich men to become richer, without enhancing the vast and natural productivity of America, were corrupt and worthless, he believed, and their promotion had no authority under the Constitution. In Jefferson's vision, the source of

true liberty in America was the independent farmer, someone who owned and worked his land both for himself and for the market.

Jefferson set out to dismantle Federalist innovations. He reduced the size of the army by a third, leaving only three thousand soldiers, and he cut back the navy from twenty-five to seven ships. Peacetime defense, he felt, should rest with "a well-disciplined militia," not a standing army. With the consent of Congress, he abolished all federal internal taxes based on population or on whiskey. A national tax on population had been tried just once, in 1798, and proved as burdensome and expensive as taking a census. It was far more feasible to derive government revenue solely from customs duties and from the sale of west-

> In Jefferson's vision, the source of true liberty in America was the independent farmer, someone who owned and worked his land both for himself and for the market.

Jefferson's Red Waistcoat
During his presidency, Jefferson often wore this red silk waistcoat as informal daywear. The garment had a velvet collar, woolen sleeves, and a thick lining made from recycled cotton and wool stockings. The thrifty Jefferson preferred to conserve firewood by wearing layers of warm clothes. A senator visiting in 1802 reported in dismay that the president was "dressed, or rather undressed, with an old brown coat, red waistcoat, old corduroy small clothes, much soiled, woolen hose, and slippers without heels." Another guest in 1804 found him wearing the red waistcoat, green velveteen breeches with pearl buttons, and "slippers down at the heels" that made him look like an ordinary farmer. Such colorful clothing in silk and velveteen carries dressy or feminine connotations in the twenty-first century, but it did not in 1800. Jefferson put on silk stockings and clean linen for fancy dinner parties; and when he lived in Paris in the 1780s, he wore an elaborately embroidered silk waistcoat under a greatcoat trimmed with gold lace. But in the 1800s, he used simple, colorful clothes to make a point about republican manners.
Courtesy of Monticello. Photo by Colonial Williamsburg.

Jefferson's Duplicating Machine

Jefferson wrote tens of thousands of letters over his lifetime. For some years he kept copies of his work by using a patented slow-drying ink and special tissue paper obtained in England. The very thin tissue could be pressed against a manuscript page whose ink was still wet and then carefully peeled off to create a copy. In 1804, Jefferson acquired his first polygraph or duplicating machine, which could produce four identical copies of a handwritten page. No doubt the stepped-up business of the presidency (and his small clerical staff) made this machine very useful. Patented by an Englishman and a Philadelphian in 1803, the polygraph linked up to five pens using rods in three dimensions. The motion of the first pen, held in Jefferson's hand, was perfectly mimicked by the rest of the pens poised over tautly held paper.

National Museum of American History, Smithsonian Institution, Behring Center.

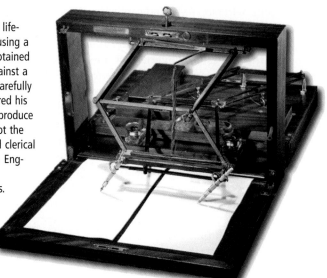

ern lands. This maneuver was of particular benefit to the South, because the three-fifths clause of the Constitution counted slaves for both representation and taxation. Now the South could enjoy its extra weight in the House of Representatives without the threat of extra taxes. By the end of his first term, Jefferson had deeply reduced Hamilton's cherished national debt.

A properly limited federal government, according to Jefferson, was responsible merely for running a postal system, maintaining the federal courts, staffing lighthouses, collecting customs duties, and conducting a census once every ten years. Government jobs were kept to a minimum. The president had just one private secretary, a young man named Meriwether Lewis, to help with his correspondence, and Jefferson paid him out of his own pocket. (Another 14 servants performed domestic and valet chores for the president, and they were also paid—or owned—by Jefferson.) The Department of State employed only 8 people: Secretary James Madison, 6 clerks, and a messenger. The Treasury Department was by far the largest unit, with 73 revenue commissioners, auditors, and clerks, plus 2 watchmen. The entire payroll of the executive branch amounted to a mere 130 people in 1801.

The Judiciary and the Midnight Judges

There was one set of government workers not under Jefferson's control to appoint. His predecessor, John Adams, seized the short time between his election defeat and Jefferson's inauguration to appoint 217 Federalist men to various judicial, diplomatic, and military posts.

Most of this windfall of appointments came to Adams as a result of the Judiciary Act of 1801, passed in the final month of his presidency. Its predecessor, the Judiciary Act of 1789, had established a six-man Supreme Court and six circuit courts. The new law authorized sixteen circuit courts, each headed by a new judge. The fast-acting Adams could appoint sixteen judges with lifetime tenure, plus dozens more state attorneys, marshals, and clerks for each court. The 1801 act also reduced the Supreme Court from six to five justices. Adams had recently appointed solidly Federalist Virginian John Marshall to a vacant sixth seat, but once the 1801 act became law, a future president would not be able to fill the next empty seat.

In the last weeks of February 1801, Adams and Marshall worked feverishly to secure agreements from the new appointees. In view of the slowness of mail, achieving 217 acceptances was astonishing. The two men were at work until 9 P.M. on the last night Adams was president, signing and delivering commissions (appointment papers) to the new officeholders.

The hasty selection of Federalist "midnight judges" infuriated the Republicans. Jefferson, upon taking office, immediately canceled the nonjudicial appointments that lacked tenure and refused to honor the few appointments that had not yet been delivered. One of them was addressed to William Marbury, who soon decided to sue the new secretary of state, James Madison, for failure to make good on the appointment.

This action gave rise to a landmark Supreme Court case, *Marbury v. Madison*, decided in 1803. The Court, presided over by John Marshall, ruled that although Marbury's commission was valid and the new president should have delivered it, the Court could not compel him to do so. What made the case significant was little noted at the time: The Court found that the grounds of Marbury's suit, resting in the Judiciary Act of 1789, were in conflict with the Constitution. For the first time, the Court acted to disallow a law on the grounds that it was unconstitutional. John Marshall quietly established the concept of judicial review; the Supreme Court in effect assumed the legal authority to **nullify** acts judged in conflict with the Constitution.

Jefferson's Presidency

The reach of the *Marbury* decision went largely unnoticed in 1803 because the president and Congress were preoccupied with foreign policy problems. The rise of Napoleon to power in France brought France and England into open warfare again in 1803, and these renewed foreign tensions created unexpected opportunities and challenges for Jefferson's administration. On the opportunity side, Jefferson's envoys in France negotiated the spectacular purchase of the Louisiana Territory, and explorers Meriwether Lewis and William Clark set out on a cross-country expedition to the Pacific Northwest coast. On the challenge side, pirates threatened American ships off the north coast of Africa, and British and French naval forces nipped at American ships—and American honor—in the Atlantic Ocean.

The Promise of the West: The Louisiana Purchase and the Lewis and Clark Expedition

Up through the Seven Years' War (see chapter 6), France claimed but only lightly settled a large expanse of land west of the Mississippi River, then lost it to Spain in the 1763 Treaty of Paris. Spain never sent adequate forces to control or settle the land, and Spanish power in North America remained precarious everywhere outside New Orleans.

In the 1770s to 1790s, American farming families were settling Kentucky and Tennessee, along rivers emptying into the upper Mississippi. For a time, the Spanish governor of New Orleans granted free navigational rights on that major river to the Americans, who shipped their agricultural produce south for sale in New Orleans and points beyond. Spain even encouraged American settlements on the western side of the river, in Spanish territory, in an effort to augment the population. By 1801, Americans made up a sizable minority of the population around the lower Mississippi. Publicly, Jefferson protested the luring of Americans into Spanish territory, but privately he welcomed it as a first move in a potential appropriation of territory immediately west of the Mississippi. He wrote, "I wish a hundred thousand of our inhabitants would accept the invitation; it will be the means of delivering to us peaceably, what may otherwise cost us a war."

Jefferson's fears of war were not unrealistic. In 1802, the Spanish governor revoked American shipping privileges through or past New Orleans. Congressmen began muttering about taking the city by force. Talk of war, especially in Federalist newspapers, became commonplace.

In the same year, rumors reached Jefferson that Spain had struck a secret bargain with France to hand over a large part of Spain's trans-Mississippi territory to Napoleon in exchange for some land in Italy. Spain had proved a weak western neighbor, but France was another story. Jefferson was so alarmed that he instructed Robert R. Livingston, America's minister in France, to try to buy New Orleans. At first the French denied they owned the city, but when Livingston hinted that the United States might simply seize it if buying was not an option, the French negotiator suddenly asked him to name his price for the entire Louisiana Territory, from the Gulf of Mexico north to Canada. Livingston stalled, and the Frenchman made suggestions: $125 million? $60 million? Livingston shrewdly stalled some more, and within days the French sold the entire territory for the bargain price of $15 million (Map 10.2). The French, motivated sellers, needed cash because of impending war with England and the recent failure, despite twenty thousand troops, to prevent Haitian independence.

Jefferson and most of Congress were delighted with the outcome of the diplomatic mission. Still, Jefferson had some qualms about the Louisiana Purchase. The price was right, and the enormous territory fulfilled Jefferson's dream of abundant farmland for future generations. But by what authority in the Constitution could he justify the purchase? His frequent criti-

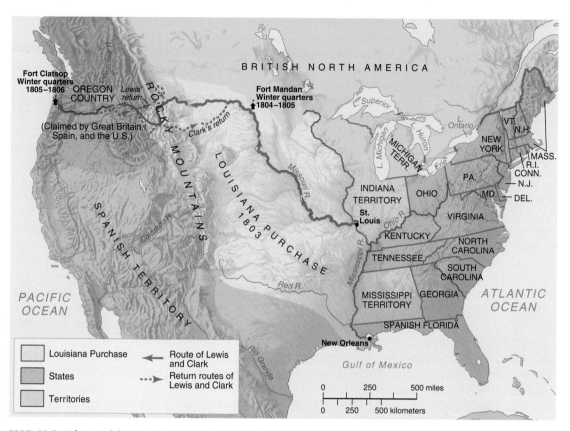

MAP 10.2   The Louisiana Purchase and the Lewis and Clark Expedition
Robert Livingston's bargain buy of 1803 far exceeded his initial assignment, to acquire the city of New Orleans. New England Federalists, worried that their geographically based power in the federal government would someday be eclipsed by the West, voted against the purchase. The Indians who inhabited the vast region, unaware that their land had been claimed by either the French or the Americans, got their first look at Anglo-American and African American men when the Lewis and Clark expedition came exploring in 1804–1806.

READING THE MAP: What natural boundaries defined the Louisiana Purchase? How did the size of the newly acquired territory compare to the existing land area of American states and territories?
CONNECTIONS: What political events in Europe created the opportunity for the Jefferson administration to purchase Louisiana? What constitutional obstacles to expansion did Jefferson have to contend with? How did the American acquisition of the Louisiana territory affect Spain's hold on North America?

FOR MORE HELP ANALYZING THIS MAP, see the map activity for this chapter in the Online Study Guide at
bedfordstmartins.com/roark.

Even before the Louisiana Purchase, Jefferson had eyed the trans-Mississippi West with intense curiosity.

cism of the Hamiltonian stretching of the Constitution came back to haunt him. His legal reasoning told him he needed a constitutional amendment to authorize the addition of territory; more expedient minds told him the treaty-making powers of the president were sufficient. Expediency won out. In late 1803, the American army took formal control of the Louisiana Territory, and the United States was now 828,000 square miles larger.

Even before the Louisiana Purchase, Jefferson had eyed the trans-Mississippi West with intense curiosity. In early 1803, he had arranged congressional funding for a secret scientific and military mission into Spanish and Indian territory. Jefferson appointed twenty-eight-year-old Meriwether Lewis, his personal secretary, to head the expedition, instructing him to investigate Indian cultures, to collect plant and animal specimens, and to chart the geography of the West.

Grizzly Bear Claw Necklace

Lewis and Clark collected hundreds of Indian artifacts on their expedition, but until December 2003 only six were known to still exist. Then this grizzly bear claw necklace unexpectedly turned up at Harvard University's Peabody Museum of Archaeology and Ethnology, stored by mistake in a South Pacific collection. Curators instantly recognized it as a necklace missing since 1899 that had been part of a Lewis and Clark museum exhibit in the mid-nineteenth century. In their expedition journal, the famed explorers noted seeing bear claw necklaces on Shoshone warriors in the Rocky Mountains; possibly one of these warriors gave his necklace to the travelers. The 38 impressive claws, each 3 to 4 inches long, are strung together by rawhide thongs; the necklace required at least two grizzly bears. Male grizzlies are large—6 to 7 feet tall, 500 to 900 pounds—and aggressive. What would it be like to wear this necklace? Whether spiritual or physical, it seems certain that a sense of power was bestowed on the wearer.

Peabody Museum of Archaeology and Ethnology, Harvard University.

Congress had more traditional goals in mind: The expedition was to scout locations for military posts, open commercial agreements for the fur trade, and locate any possible waterway between the east and west coasts.

For his co-leader, Lewis chose Kentuckian William Clark, a fellow veteran of the 1790s Indian wars. Together they handpicked a crew of forty-five, including expert rivermen, gunsmiths, hunters, interpreters, a cook, and a slave named York, who belonged to Clark. The explorers left St. Louis in the spring of 1804, working their way northwest up the Missouri River. They camped for the winter at a Mandan village in what is now central North Dakota. (See "American Places," page 329.) The Mandan Indians were familiar with British and French traders from Canada, but the black man York created a sensation. Reportedly, Indians rubbed moistened fingers over the man's skin to see if the color was painted on.

The following spring, the explorers headed west, aided by a French trapper accompanied by his wife, a sixteen-year-old Indian woman named Sacajawea, and their baby. Sacajawea's presence was to prove unexpectedly helpful. Indian tribes encountered en route withdrew their suspicion that the Americans were hostile because, as Lewis wrote in his journal, "no woman ever accompanies a war party of Indians in this quarter."

The Lewis and Clark expedition reached the Pacific Ocean at the mouth of the Columbia River in November 1805. When Lewis and Clark returned home the following year, they were greeted as national heroes. They had established favorable relations with dozens of Indian tribes; they had collected invaluable information on the peoples, soils, plants, animals, and geography of the West; and they had inspired a nation of restless explorers and solitary imitators.

Challenges Overseas: The Barbary Wars

The inspiring opportunity of westward exploration was matched at the same time by a frustrating challenge overseas. From 1801 to 1805, the United States was drawn into belligerent exchanges off the north coast of Africa that featured hijacked ships and captured crews. For well over a century, four Arabic settlements on the Barbary coast—Morocco, Algiers, Tunis, and Tripoli—controlled shipping traffic through the Mediterranean by means of privateering. Swift vessels overtook merchant ships, plundered the cargoes, and captured the crews for ransom. Most European states spared their ships by paying tribute—an annual sum of money—to secure safe passage. When American ships flew under the British flag, up to 1776, they were protected. But once independent, the United States also began to pay tribute, by the mid-1790s, on the order of $50,000 to the leader of each state.

In 1801, the pasha (military head) of Tripoli demanded a large increase in his tribute. Jefferson had long thought such payments were extortion, and his response was to send four warships to Tripoli. A rallying slogan backed Jefferson: "Millions for defense, not one cent for

The Burning of the Frigate *Philadelphia* **in Tripoli Harbor**
The American frigate *Philadelphia* went down in flames in the harbor of Tripoli on the North African coast in 1804. The man responsible became an instant hero in America: a young naval commander named Stephen Decatur, who pulled off a stealth mission into the Tripoli harbor at night in order to destroy the ship. North African sailors, called "Barbary pirates" in the United States, had captured the American warship and planned to refurbish it as their own vessel of war, but Decatur foiled that plan. Nicolino Calyo, an Italian-born American, made this painting several decades after the 1804 event.
The Mariners Museum, Newport News, Virginia.

tribute." In response, the pasha declared war on the United States.

From 1801 to 1803, American ships blockaded Tripoli and Tunis with only partial success and offered escort protection to passing American merchant ships. Only a few skirmishes ensued. Then, in late 1803, the first major action by the United States floundered: the USS *Philadelphia*, a large frigate, ran aground near the Tripoli harbor. Its 300-man crew was captured, along with the ship, which greatly augmented Tripoli's naval strength.

Several months later, the Americans retaliated. Seventy men led by the young navy lieutenant Stephen Decatur sailed into the harbor after dark with an Arabic-speaking pilot to fool harbor sentries. They drew up to the *Philadelphia*, boarded it, set it on fire, and escaped. Decatur was an instant hero in America.

In summer of 1804, the U.S. forces attacked Tripoli, destroying enemy vessels, firing on the city, and also offering ransom for the captured *Philadelphia* sailors. The pasha resisted, holding out for more money, until he learned that fresh U.S. forces, aided by Egyptian and Turkish mercenaries, were headed toward Tripoli. The pasha then entered treaty negotiations, accepting $60,000 for the prisoners and agreeing to forgo tribute. One significant clause of the treaty stipulated that "no pretext arising from Religious Opinions" should interrupt good relations since the United States has "no character of enmity against the Laws, Religion or Tranquility of Musselmen" (that is, Muslims).

Fort Mandan, Washburn, North Dakota

Along the upper Missouri River, the Lewis and Clark expedition arrived at a major center of Indian trade composed of five Mandan and Hidatsa villages with a population of over 4,000. An early snowfall signaled a long winter for 1804–05, so the men built rough wooden cabins surrounded by a palisade (a fence of pointed stakes). The fort provided some degree of protection against the frigid air of a northern plains winter, but it fell far short of the dwellings of the local Indians, who were warmer in their round earth lodges with central fireplaces.

The expedition rested at the fort for five months. To develop a reliable map for the projected journey west, Meriwether Lewis "separately and carefully" interviewed many Indian traders arriving at the Mandan villages. New members joined the expedition at Mandan: the French Canadian trader Toussaint Charbonneau, his young wife Sacajawea, and their baby, born in one of these cabins in February 1805. The new mother was a Shoshone Indian captured by Hidatsas at about age ten from her tribe five hundred miles to the west. Lewis anticipated that her language skill would prove helpful when they reached the Rocky Mountains. Still, the translation chain was tenuous: Sacajawea rendered Shoshone into Hidatsa to Charbonneau, who trans-

lated it into French to a bilingual expedition member, who then delivered it in English to Lewis and Clark.

The long winter wait at Fort Mandan allowed for sociability with the locals. The Americans had a fiddle, and Indians attending a New Year's Day party were "much pleased at the Danceing of our men," wrote William Clark; "I ordered my black Servent to Dance which amused the Croud Verry much, and somewhat astonished them, that So large a man should be active." Social events like these at Fort Mandan helped to restore the spirits of Lewis and Clark's men, something that proved useful as they set off to continue their remarkable journey in the spring.

Today visitors to the Fort Mandan site can relive the past through a fully reconstructed replica of the original fort, complete with furnished rooms adorned with the type of equipment and other trappings members of the expedition would have brought with them. Run by the North Dakota Lewis & Clark Bicentennial Foundation, the site, located on the Lewis & Clark National Historic Trail in Washburn, North Dakota, includes a visitors' center showcasing a variety of related exhibits and on-site interpreters who provide educational programs and tours of the fort year-round.

FOR WEB LINKS RELATED TO THIS SITE AND OTHER AMERICAN PLACES, see "PlaceLinks" at bedfordstmartins.com/roark.

Reconstruction of Lewis and Clark's Winter Quarters
Lewis & Clark National Historic Trail.

Although the tribute system with other Barbary states would not end until 1812, when frigates returned to the Mediterranean for further skirmishes, none of this affected the election of 1804, which proved an easy triumph for Jefferson. The Federalist candidate, Charles Cotesworth Pinckney of South Carolina, secured only 14 votes in the electoral college, in contrast to 162 for the president. Just months before the election, the Federalists had lost their shrewdest statesman: Alexander Hamilton, called by some "the brains of the Federalist Party," was tragically killed in a duel with Aaron Burr. (See "Historical Question," page 332.) Republicans would hold the presidency for another twenty years.

More Maritime Troubles: Impressment and Embargo

The Barbary coast was not the only trouble spot for Americans. When France and England resumed war in 1803, each warned America not to aid the other. Britain acted on these threats in 1806, stopping American ships, inspecting cargoes for military aid to France, and seizing suspected deserters from the British navy, along with not a few Americans. Ultimately, 2,500 sailors were swept up—impressed—by the British. Jefferson and the American public were outraged.

One incident made the usually cautious Jefferson nearly belligerent. In June 1807, an American ship, the *Chesapeake*, harboring some British deserters, was ordered to stop by a British frigate, the *Leopard*. The *Chesapeake* refused, and the *Leopard* opened fire, killing three Americans—right at the mouth of Chesapeake Bay, well within U.S. territory. Before this incident, Jefferson had convinced Congress to pass nonimportation laws banning a select list of British-made goods as a strategy for putting pressure on Britain. But now Jefferson and Secretary of State James Madison pushed the idea of total embargo, prohibiting American ships from engaging in trade with any foreign port. The Embargo Act passed by Congress in December 1807 was surely a drastic measure but one meant to forestall a

The *Chesapeake* Incident, June 22, 1807

greater crisis, all-out war. The goal was to make England suffer, and all trade to foreign ports was banned to make sure no ships could engage in secret trading with England through secondary ports. Jefferson was convinced that England needed America's agricultural products far more than America needed British goods. He also was wary of Federalist shipowners who might circumvent the ban.

The Embargo Act of 1807 was a total disaster. From 1790 to 1807, U.S. exports had increased fivefold; the new law brought commerce to a standstill. In New England, the heart of the shipping industry, unemployment rose. Grain plummeted in value, river traffic halted, tobacco rotted in the South, and cotton went unpicked. Protest petitions flooded Washington. The federal government suffered too, for import duties were a significant source of revenue. Jefferson's Republicans paid political costs as well. The Federalist Party, in danger of fading away after its weak showing in 1804, began to revive.

The Madisons in the White House

In mid-1808, Jefferson indicated that he would not run for a third term. Secretary of State James Madison got the nod from Republican caucuses—informal political groups that orchestrated the selection of candidates for state and local elections. Federalist caucuses chose Charles Cotesworth Pinckney again. Pinckney did much better than in 1804; he received 47 electoral votes, nearly half Madison's total. Support for the Federalists remained centered in the New England states, but Republicans still held the balance of power nationwide.

As president, Madison continued Jefferson's policy of economic pressure on England and France with a modified embargo, but he broke new ground in the domestic management of the executive office, with the aid of his astute and talented wife, Dolley Madison. Under her leadership, the president's house became the White House—something close to a palace, but a palace many Americans were welcome to visit. Under his leadership, the country went to war in 1812 with England and with Tecumseh's warrior confederacy. In 1814, British forces burned the White House and Capitol building nearly to the ground.

Women in Washington City

In her first eight years in Washington as wife of the highest-ranked cabinet officer, Dolley Madison had developed elaborate social networks that, in the absence of any Mrs. Jefferson, constituted the uppermost level of female politicking in the highly political city. Though women could not vote and supposedly left politics to men, the women of Washington took on several critical and overtly political functions that greased the wheels of the affairs of state. Through dinners, balls, receptions, and the intricate custom of "calling," in which men and women paid brief visits or left calling cards at each other's houses, a regularized social network developed that facilitated cohesion among the governing classes and provided avenues of preferment for jobs and for advancement. It was not uncommon for women in this social set to write letters of introduction or recommendation for men seeking government work. Hostessing was therefore no trivial or leisured business: Washington women mediated the webs of personal connections (as well as the gossip networks) that influenced the patronage system of the federal government.

Upon her husband's election, Dolley Madison, called by some the "presidentress," struck a balance between queenliness and republican openness. She dressed the part in resplendent clothes, choosing a plumed velvet turban for her headdress at her husband's inauguration. She swiftly redesigned three large and newly elegant rooms in the executive mansion and opened them to evening parties once a week. George and Martha Washington's levees had been stiff, brief affairs with few guests accomplishing little more than bows and curtsies. In contrast, the Madisons' drawing-room parties went on for hours with scores and even hundreds of guests standing, milling about, talking, and eating. Nicknamed "Mrs. Madison's crush" or "squeeze," the weekly party required an invitation or letter of introduction to attend, if one did not already know the Madisons. Evidently this was not a highly restrictive requirement. Members of Congress, cabinet officers, distinguished guests, envoys from foreign countries, important travelers, all these and their womenfolk attended with regularity. Even those who hated parties—or this party in particular—still attended. Mrs. Madison's "squeeze" was an essential event for gaining political access, trading information, and establishing the kinds of informal channels that smooth the governing process.

In 1810–1811, Dolley Madison's house acquired the unofficial nickname "White House," probably a reference to the building's light sandstone exterior. The fact that the house received a nickname is significant: This was not a palace named after a royal family or duchy, nor was it an unnamed private residence meant simply to shelter a president when off duty and out of sight. It was the people's house, and, said a Baltimore newspaper in 1810, "'White house' may be considered the 'people's name.'" People came in very large numbers to the weekly parties, experiencing simultaneously the splendor of the executive mansion and the atmosphere of republicanism that made it accessible to so many. Dolley Madison, ever an enormous political

Dolley Madison

The "presidentress" of the Madison administration sat for this official portrait in 1804. Mrs. Madison here wears an empire-style dress, at the height of French fashion in 1804 and worn by many women at the coronation of the emperor Napoleon in Paris. The hallmarks of an empire dress were light fabric in muslin or chiffon, short sleeves, a high waistline from which the fabric fell straight to the ground, and usually a low open neckline as shown here. The artist, Gilbert Stuart, made a companion likeness of James Madison, and the two portraits hung in the drawing room of Madison's Virginia estate, Montpelier.

Courtesy of the Pennsylvania Academy of the Fine Arts, Philadelphia.

How Could a Vice President Get Away with Murder?

On July 11, 1804, the vice president of the United States, Aaron Burr, shot Alexander Hamilton, the architect of the Federalist Party, in a duel on a narrow ledge below the cliffs of Weehawken, New Jersey, across the Hudson River from New York City. The pistol blast tore through a rib, demolished Hamilton's liver, and splintered his spine. The forty-seven-year-old Hamilton died the next day, in agonizing pain.

How could it happen that a sitting vice president and a prominent political leader could put themselves at such risk? Why did men who made their living by the legal system go outside the law and turn to the centuries-old ritual of the duel? Here were two eminent attorneys, skilled in the legalistic negotiations meant to substitute for violent resolution of disputes, firing .54-caliber hair-trigger weapons at ten paces. Did anyone try to stop them? How did the public react? Was Hamilton's death a criminal act? How could Burr continue to fulfill his federal office, presiding over the U.S. Senate?

Burr challenged Hamilton in late June after learning from a newspaper report that Hamilton "looked upon Mr. Burr to be a dangerous man, and one who ought not be trusted with the reins of government." Burr knew that Hamilton had long held a very low opinion of him and had never hesitated to say so in private, but now his private disparagement had made its way into print. Compounding the insult were political consequences: Burr was sure that Hamilton's remark had cost him election to the governorship of New York.

Quite possibly he was right. Knowing that Jefferson planned to dump him from the federal ticket in the 1804 election, Burr decided to run for New York's highest office; his opponent was an obscure Republican judge. Burr's success depended on the support of the old Federalist leadership in the state. Up to the eve of the election, he appeared to have it—until Hamilton's remark was circulated.

So on June 18, Burr challenged Hamilton to a duel if he did not disavow his comment. Over the next three weeks, the men exchanged several letters clarifying the nature of the insult that aggrieved Burr. Hamilton the lawyer evasively quibbled over words, causing Burr finally to rail against his focus on syntax and grammar. At heart, Hamilton could not deny the insult, nor could he spurn the challenge without injury to his reputation for integrity and bravery. Both Burr and Hamilton were locked in a highly ritualized procedure meant to uphold a gentleman's code of honor.

In accordance with the code of dueling, each man had a trusted "second" who helped frame and deliver the letters and finally assisted at the duel site. Only a handful of close friends knew of the challenge, and no one tried to stop it. Hamilton did not tell his wife. He wrote her a tender farewell letter the night before, to be opened in the event of his death. He knew full well the pain dueling brought to loved ones, for three years earlier, his nineteen-year-old son Philip had been killed in a duel at the same ledge at Weehawken, as a result of hotheaded words exchanged at a New York theater. Even when Hamilton's wife was called to her husband's deathbed, she was first told he had terrible spasms from an illness. Women were completely shut out of the masculine world of dueling.

News of Hamilton's death spread quickly in New York and then throughout the nation. On the day of the funeral, church bells tolled continuously and New York merchants shut down all business. Thousands joined the procession, and the city council declared a six-week mourning period. Burr fled to Philadelphia, fearing retribution by the crowd.

Response in the South was subdued. Dueling was fully accepted there as an extralegal remedy for insult, and Burr's grievance fit perfectly the sense of violated honor that legitimated duels. In addition, Southerners had never been particularly fond of the Federalist Hamilton.

Northern newspapers, in contrast, expressed indignation over the illegal duel and the tragic death of so prominent a man. Many northern states had criminalized dueling recently, treating a challenge as a misdemeanor and a dueling death as a homicide. After death, the body of the loser of an illegal duel could be subjected to one final indignity—being buried without a coffin, having a stake driven through the body, being strung up in public until the body rotted, or (more horrible still at that time) being donated to medical students for dissection. Such prescribed mutilation of the dead showed that northern lawmakers themselves participated in the code of honor by using threats of postmortem humiliation to discourage dueling. Hamilton's body was spared such a fate. But two ministers in succession refused to administer Holy Communion to him in his dying hours because he was a duelist; finally, one relented.

The public demanded to know the reasons for the duel, so the seconds prepared the correspondence between the principals for publication. A coroner's jury in New York soon indicted the vice president on misdemeanor charges for issuing a challenge; a grand jury in New Jersey indicted him for murder. By that time, Burr was a fugitive from justice, hiding out with sympathetic friends in South Carolina.

But not for long. Amazingly, he returned to Washington, D.C., in November 1804 to resume presiding over the Senate, a role he continued to assume until his vice presidential term ended in March 1805. Federalists snubbed him, but eleven Republican senators petitioned New Jersey to drop its indictment on the grounds that "civilized nations" do not treat dueling deaths as "common murders." New Jersey did not pursue the murder charge. Burr freely visited New Jersey and New York for three more decades, paying no penalty for killing Hamilton.

Few would doubt that Burr was a scoundrel, albeit a brilliant one. A few years later, he was indicted for treason against the U.S. government in a presumed plot to break off part

***Aaron Burr,* by John Vanderlyn**
Aaron Burr was fifty-three years old when the New York artist John Vanderlyn painted this portrait in 1809, five years after the Burr-Hamilton duel.
Collection of The New-York Historical Society.

of the United States and start his own country in the Southwest. (He dodged that bullet too, in a spectacular trial presided over by John Marshall, chief justice of the Supreme Court.) Hamilton certainly thought Burr a scoundrel, and when that opinion reached print, Burr had cause to defend his honor under the etiquette of dueling. The accuracy of Hamilton's charge was of absolutely no account. Dueling redressed questions of honor, not questions of fact.

Dueling continued to be a feature of southern society for many more decades, but in the North the custom became extremely rare by the 1820s, helped into obscurity by the disrepute of Hamilton's death and by the rise of a legalistic society that preferred evidence, interrogation, and monetary judgments to avenge injury.

Pistols from the Burr-Hamilton Duel
Alexander Hamilton's brother-in-law John B. Church purchased this pair of dueling pistols in London in 1797. Church used them once in a duel with Aaron Burr, occasioned by Church's calling Burr a scoundrel in public; neither man was hurt. Hamilton's son Philip borrowed them for his own fatal duel. When Burr challenged Hamilton, the latter also turned to John Church for the weapons. The guns stayed in the Church family until 1930, when they were given to the Chase Manhattan Bank in New York City, chartered in 1799 as the Manhattan Company. (Burr, Church, and Hamilton all served on the bank's board of directors.) When the pistols were cleaned in 1874, a hidden hair trigger came to light. Each gun could be cocked by moving the trigger forward one-eighth inch; then only a half-pound pull, instead of ten pounds, was needed to fire each gun. Hamilton gained no advantage from the hair trigger, if he knew of it.
Courtesy of Chase Manhattan Archives.

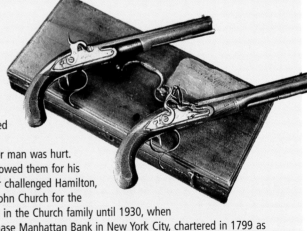

asset to her rather shy husband, understood well the symbolic function of inventing this new White House to create power and legitimacy for the presidency.

Indian Troubles in the West

While the Madisons cemented alliances at home, difficulties with England and France overseas and Indians in the old Northwest continued to increase. The Shawnee chief Tecumseh actively solidified his confederacy, while far northern tribes renewed ties with supportive British agents and fur traders in Canada, a potential source of food and weapons. If the United States embarked on a war with England, there would clearly be serious repercussions on the **frontier**.

> A fundamental part of Tecumseh's message was the assertion that all Indian lands were held in common by all the tribes.

Shifting demographics raised the stakes for both sides. The 1810 census counted some 230,000 Americans living in Ohio, only seven years after statehood. Another 40,000 Americans inhabited the territories of Indiana, Illinois, and Michigan. The Indian population of the entire region (the old Northwest Territory) was much smaller, probably about 70,000, a number unknown (because uncounted) to the Americans but certainly gauged by Tecumseh during his extensive travels.

Up to 1805, Indiana's territorial governor, William Henry Harrison, had negotiated a series of treaties in a divide-and-conquer strategy extracting Indian lands for paltry payments. But with the rise to power of Tecumseh and his brother Tenskwatawa, the Prophet, Harrison's strategy became harder to carry out. A fundamental part of Tecumseh's message was the assertion that all Indian lands were held in common by all the tribes:

> No tribe has the right to sell, even to each other, much less to strangers. . . . Sell a country! Why not sell the air, the great sea, as well as the earth? Didn't the Great Spirit make them all for the use of his children? The way, the only way to stop this evil is for the red man to unite in claiming a common and equal right in the land, as it was first, and should be now, for it was never divided.

Taking advantage of Tecumseh's absence on a recruiting trip, Harrison assembled leaders of the Potawatomi, Miami, and Delaware tribes to negotiate the Treaty of Fort Wayne in 1809. As required, Harrison first sought approval from President Madison, who authorized negotiations so long as all "who have or pretend right to these lands" were party to the agreement. Harrison sidestepped that requirement, working instead with chiefs who in some cases had no pretense of claims to the land in question, along the Wabash River in southern Indiana. After promising (falsely) that this was the last cession of land the United States would seek, Harrison secured three million acres at about two cents per acre (Map 10.3).

When he returned, Tecumseh was furious with both Harrison and the tribal leaders. Leaving his brother in charge at Prophetstown on Tippecanoe Creek, the Shawnee chief left on a trip to seek alliances in the South. Harrison then decided to attack Prophetstown with one thousand men. The two-hour battle resulted in the deaths of 62 Americans and 40 Indians before the

Tenskwatawa

Tenskwatawa, the Shawnee Prophet, and his brother Tecumseh led the spiritual and political efforts of a number of Indian tribes to resist land-hungry Americans moving west in the decade before the War of 1812. The Prophet is shown in a portrait by George Catlin with beaded necklaces, metal arm- and wristbands, and earrings. Compare the metal gorget here with the one worn by Joseph Brant (page 226).
National Museum of American Art, Washington, D.C./Art Resource, NY.

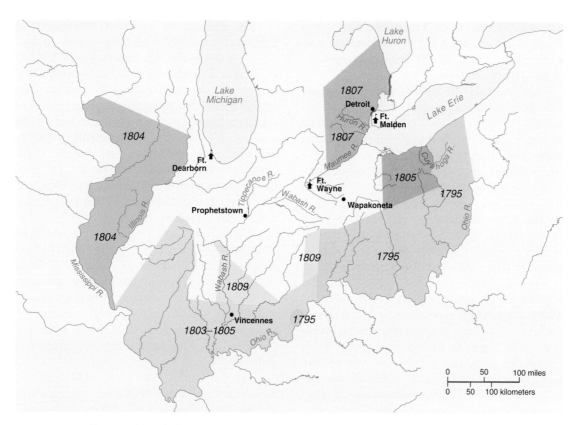

MAP 10.3 Indian Lands Ceded by Treaties in the Old Northwest Territory, 1795–1809
The Treaty of Greenville (1795) transferred two-thirds of Ohio to the Americans. For more than a decade there-after, by negotiating with Indians whose authority to speak for their tribes was often unclear or dubious, officials such as William Henry Harrison managed to acquire vast tracts along the Ohio and up the Mississippi rivers.
"Land Cessions in the Old Northwest, 1795–1809." From *Tecumseh: A Life* by John Sugden. Copyright 1997 by John Sugden. Reprinted with the permission of Henry Holt and Company LLC.

Prophet's forces fled the town, which Harrison's men set on fire. The November 1811 Battle of Tippecanoe was heralded as a glorious victory for the Americans; the Prophet Tenskwata-wa's magical powers were sharply diminished among his people and he lost influ-ence. But Tecumseh was now more determined than ever to unite Indians to hold back the Americans.

The War of 1812

The Indian conflicts in the Northwest Territory in 1811 soon merged into the wider conflict with England now known as the War of 1812.

Battle of Tippecanoe, 1811

Between 1809 and 1812, President Madison teetered between declar-ing England or France the prime enemy, as attacks by both countries on American ships continued. In 1809, Congress had replaced Jef-ferson's stringent embargo with the Non-Intercourse Act, which pro-hibited trade only with England and France and their colonies, thus opening up other trade routes to di-minish the anguish of shippers, farmers, and **planters**. In 1810, the Non-Intercourse Act expired, and Congress replaced it with a law that permitted direct trade with ei-ther France or England, whichever first promised to stop harassing American ships. Napoleon seized the initiative and declared that France would comply. Madison too hastily accepted this offer, reopened trade with France, and notified England that he intended to reinstate the embargo in the spring of 1811 unless England rescinded its search-and-seizure policy.

Unfortunately for Madison, the duplicitous French continued to seize American ships and sailors. Furthermore, the British made no move to stop impressments or to repeal trade restrictions, and Madison was forced to reactivate the embargo, much to the great displeasure of the New England shipping industry. In 1811, the country was seriously divided and in a deep quandary. To some, the United States seemed, appropriately, on the verge of war—though with France or England was not clear. To others, war with either meant disaster for commerce.

A new Congress, elected in the fall of 1810, arrived in Washington in March 1811 as Madison's embargo took effect. Several dozen of the new and much younger Republican members were eager to avenge the insults from abroad. In particular, Henry Clay, thirty-four, from Kentucky, and John C. Calhoun, twenty-nine, from South Carolina, became the center of a group informally known as the **War Hawks**. They saluted Harrison's Tippecanoe victory and urged the country to war. Mostly lawyers by profession, they came from the West and South, and they welcomed a war with England both to legitimize attacks on the Indians and to bring an end to impressment. Many were also expansionists, looking to occupy Florida and threaten Canada. And they captured prominent posts in Congress from which to wield influence. Henry Clay was elected Speaker of the House, an extraordinary honor for a young newcomer. John C. Calhoun won a seat on the Foreign Relations Committee. The War Hawks approved major defense expenditures; the army, for example, quadrupled in size.

In June 1812, Congress declared war on Great Britain in a vote that divided on sectional lines: New England and some Middle Atlantic states opposed the war, while the South and West were strongly for it. Ironically, Great Britain had just announced it would stop the search and seizure of American ships. But the war momentum would not be slowed. The Foreign Relations Committee issued an elaborate justification titled *Report on the Causes and Reasons for War,* written mainly by Calhoun and containing extravagant language about Britain's "lust for power," "unbounded tyranny," and "mad ambition." These were fighting words in a war that was in large measure about insult and honor.

The War Hawks proposed an invasion of Canada, confidently predicting victory in four weeks. Instead, the war lasted two and a half years, and Canada never fell. The northern invasion turned out to be a series of strategic blunders that revealed the grave unpreparedness of the United States for war. The combined British and Indian forces were unexpectedly powerful, and the United States made no attempt at the outset to create a naval presence on the Great Lakes. Detroit quickly fell, as did Fort Dearborn (site of the future Chicago). By the fall of 1812, the outlook was grim.

Worse, the New England states dragged their feet in raising troops, while New England merchants carried on illegal trade with Great Britain. Britain encouraged friendly overtures with New England, hoping to create dissension among the Americans. New Englanders drank India tea in Liverpool cups while President Madison fumed in Washington about Federalist disloyalty.

The presidential election in 1812 solidified Federalist discontent with the war. Madison was opposed by DeWitt Clinton of New York, nominally Republican but able to attract the Federalist vote. He picked up all of New England's electoral votes, with the exception of Vermont's, and also took New York, New Jersey, and part of Maryland. Madison won in the electoral college, 128 to 89, but his margin of victory was considerably smaller than in 1808.

In late 1812 and early 1813, the tide began to turn in the Americans' favor. First came some reassuring victories at sea. Then Americans attacked York (now Toronto), the capital of Upper Canada, and burned it in April 1813. A few months later, Commodore Oliver Hazard Perry defeated the British fleet at the western end of Lake Erie. Emboldened, General Harrison drove an army into Canada from Detroit and in October 1813 defeated the British and Indians at the Battle of the Thames, where Tecumseh met his death (Map 10.4).

Indians in the South who had allied with Tecumseh's confederacy were also plunged into all-out war. Some fifty villages containing around 10,000 Creek Indians in the southern region of Mississippi Territory put up a spirited fight against American militia troops for ten months in 1813–1814. Even without Tecumseh's recruitment trip of 1811 or the War of 1812, the Creeks had grievances aplenty, sparked by American settlers moving into their territory along the rivers of the future Alabama. Aided by

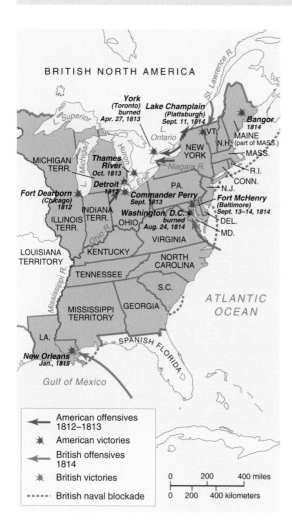

MAP 10.4 The War of 1812
During the War of 1812, battles were fought along the border of Canada and in the Chesapeake region. The most important American victory came in New Orleans, two weeks after peace had been agreed to in England.

worker removed the Declaration of Independence to safety. Dolley Madison, with dinner for guests on the fire (see "The Promise of Technology," page 338), fled with her husband's papers and a portrait of George Washington. Five thousand British troops entered the city and began torching government buildings. British commanders ate Mrs. Madison's meal before burning her house; they also burned the Capitol, a newspaper office, some dockyards, and a well-stocked arsenal. August 24 was a very low moment for the American side.

Instead of trying to hold the city, the British headed north for Baltimore and attacked it on September 11, 1814. A fierce defense by the Maryland militia and a steady barrage of gunfire from Fort McHenry in the harbor kept them at bay. The firing continued until midnight, motivating Francis Scott Key to compose a poem he called "The Star-Spangled Banner" the next day. The British pulled back, unwilling to try to take the city.

September 1814 brought another powerful British offensive. Marching from Canada into New York State, the British seemed to have every advantage—trained soldiers, superior artillery, cavalry. But a series of mistakes cost them a naval skirmish at Plattsburgh on Lake Champlain and also cost them their nerve, and they retreated to Canada. The withdrawal was a decisive military event, for British leaders in England, hearing of the retreat, concluded that incursions by land into the United States would be expensive and difficult.

This point was confirmed when a large British army landed in lower Louisiana and encountered General Andrew Jackson and his militia just outside New Orleans in early January 1815. Jackson's forces dramatically carried the day. The British suffered between 2,000 and 3,000 casualties, the Americans fewer than 80. Jackson became an instant hero. The Battle of New Orleans was the most glorious and decisive victory the

> The Battle of New Orleans was the most glorious and decisive victory the Americans had experienced. Ironically, negotiators in Europe had already signed a peace agreement.

guns provided by Spanish agents living in the panhandle of Spanish Florida, the Creeks mounted a strong defense. But the Creek War was suddenly over in March 1814, when a general named Andrew Jackson led 2,500 Tennessee militiamen in a bloody attack called the Battle of Horseshoe Bend. Jackson's militia killed more than 550 Indians, and several hundred more died trying to escape across a river. Later that year, General Jackson extracted a treaty from the defeated Creeks relinquishing thousands of square miles of their land to the United States.

Washington City Burns: The British Offensive

In August 1814, British ships sailed into Chesapeake Bay, throwing the capital into a panic. Families evacuated, banks hid their money, and government clerks carted away boxes of important papers. One State Department

Stoves Transform Cooking

The cookstove, one of the most underrated achievements of the technology of daily life, fundamentally changed the way men and women labored to put food on the table. Its slow development can be traced in the nearly one thousand patents registered between 1815 and 1850 by inventors tinkering to control heat, devise convenient cooking surfaces, and improve fuel efficiency.

Before 1815, nearly all household cooking was accomplished in wood-burning fireplaces. Daily fires used for cooking and heating consumed immense amounts of wood; in cold climates, a household might require 40 cords of wood per year. Supplying each cord (a pile measuring 4-by-4-by-8 feet) was laborious men's work; the difficult and dangerous tasks of cooking and maintaining the fire fell to women. Great skill was needed to time the peak heat to coordinate with the varying temperature needs of baking, stewing, and roasting. Muscles and stamina were required to hoist 20-pound iron pots and cauldrons onto the hooks that suspended them over the fire. Cooks worked dangerously close to open flames when tending a roasting joint of meat on a spit or raking smaller fires out of the large one to heat frying skillets set on trivets on the hearth. Women wearing long skirts risked clothing fires, and children running about sometimes collided with hot pots and burning logs at floor level. The heavy lifting and exposure to the blasting heat, especially uncomfortable on hot summer days, exacted a toll on every cook.

In 1744, Benjamin Franklin developed a heating stove that enclosed a wood fire on three sides in a small cast-iron box, which radiated heat to the room. (The open fourth side allowed a pleasing view of the dancing flames.) The Franklin stove cut fuel costs, but it did not catch on for another half century as an alternative to heating by fireplace. Its inadequate venting of smoke was one problem, not fixed until the 1790s. Further, cast iron was expensive and wood was cheap, and the Franklin stove offered no provision for cooking. As long as wood remained affordable, Americans preferred the look of a log fire and the taste of food cooked over one.

Then, between 1800 and 1815, a serious fuel shortage driven by the depletion of forests caused wood prices to double along the eastern coast. At the same time, domestic iron manufacturing started to flourish, encouraged by Jefferson's shipping embargo and the War of 1812.

With wood rising and iron falling in price, the conditions were right for the start of serious cookstove manufacture. Many inventors got to work.

The cast iron contraptions advertised around 1815 were larger than the Franklin stove and had a flat surface on top where pots and pans could be heated by the fire burning below. One challenge was to find a simple way to modulate the fire by varying the amount of air feeding it, through better design of the damper system. Dampers were valves or movable plates that controlled the draft of air to the fire and hence the rate of combustion. A related challenge was to manage the temperatures of the cooking spaces and surfaces. This could be done by moving pots around, by raising and lowering the grate that held the logs inside the firebox, or even by using cranks to rotate the fire.

Most of the new stoves raised the cooking surface nearly to waist level, offering relief from the backbreaking labor required by fireplace cookery. They fully enclosed the fire, minimizing the risk of clothing fires; they prevented sparks from jumping on floors and carpets; and they piped sooty air with combustion pollutants out of the house. For all these reasons, stove cooking was a great advance in safety.

New stoves changed not only the way people cooked but the way they ate. On a hearth, separate dishes

Americans had experienced. Ironically, negotiators in Europe had signed a peace agreement two weeks earlier.

The Treaty of Ghent, signed in December 1814, settled few of the surface issues that had led to war. Neither country could claim victory, and no land changed hands. Instead, the treaty reflected a mutual agreement to give up certain goals. The Americans yielded on impressment and gave up any claim to Canada; and the

An Early Cookstove

A stove of the 1820s, patented by W. T. James, sits in this reconstructed historical site adjacent to the fireplace it has replaced. A stovepipe vents combustion fumes out the old chimney; a large flat surface over the fire provides a cooktop, shown here with a copper pot and a teakettle whose extremely large base speeds water to a boil. The round container on the lower ledge of the stove is a reflector oven, called a "tin kitchen," first used with fireplaces and then adapted for cookstoves. A spit inside held meat, and a crank (visible on the end) was used to turn the food. Put against the fire, the tin oven cooked its contents by direct and reflected heat, while the round bottom preserved the meat juices. In this scene, the old fireplace is bricked up and used for storing wood for the stove. Householders of the 1820s would have seen this setup as a highly modern convenience, with improvements in safety, fuel efficiency, and heat control.

Old Sturbridge Village.

The cookstove changed home labor for both men and women. It shrank men's role in meal preparation by curtailing the work of procuring wood. No such reduction occurred for women, however. Replacing the hours of careful fire-tending that women had once done were hours spent maintaining and cleaning stoves—removing ashes, cleaning soot from flues and dampers, and blacking the entire stove weekly with a thick paste to keep it from rusting.

From 1815 to the mid-nineteenth century, the cookstove was a work in progress; the many imperfections in the initial designs sent inventors back to the workbench again and again to try to perfect this new cooking system. Nonetheless, women wanted stoves for their safety and convenience, and men liked them for their fuel efficiency. In the late 1840s, the widespread popularity of cookstoves became evident along wagon trails heading west. Many families had packed up their stoves for the trip—evidence they embraced the new style of cooking—but had to abandon them along the way when forced to lighten their loads. One traveling teenager wrote that "we heard great talk of things being thrown away on the road but we saw little that was any good excepting stoves and there were plenty of them." Cookstoves had become America's first popular "consumer durable."

required separate fires, so cooks generally limited meals to one-pot stews. Using the new stoves, cooks could prepare several different dishes with just one fire, and meals became more varied. However, not everyone was pleased. Many complained that the convenience of stoves came at the price of food quality. Oven-baked meat was nearly universally regarded as less savory than meat roasted over a fire, and in flavor and crustiness oven-baked bread did not measure up to bread baked in the brick chamber of a fireplace wall. Nonetheless, convenience triumphed.

British agreed to abandon aid to Indians. Nothing was said about shipping rights. The most concrete result was a plan for a commission to determine the exact boundary between the United States and Canada.

Antiwar New England Federalists did not feel triumphant at the war's ambiguous conclusion. Instead they felt disgrace because of a meeting convened in Hartford, Connecticut, in December 1814. Politicians at the Hartford Convention

Remains of the President's House

This watercolor sketch documents the burning of the White House in Washington in August 1814, when the British attacked the city. The light-colored walls still stand, but the interior has been gutted by the fire. Some British engaged in plundering that night. Shown here is James Madison's personal medicine chest, taken by a British soldier back to England. A descendent of his returned the wartime souvenir in 1939 to President Franklin D. Roosevelt.

Watercolor: Library of Congress; medicine chest: FDR Library.

its grip, and within a few years its presence even in New England was reduced to a shadow.

No one really won the War of 1812. Americans celebrated as though they had, however, with parades and fireworks. The war gave rise to a new spirit of **nationalism**. The paranoia over British tyranny evident in the 1812 declaration of war was laid to rest, replaced by pride in a more equal relationship with the old mother country. Indeed, in 1817 the two countries signed the Rush-Bagot disarmament treaty (named after its two negotiators), which limited each country to a total of four naval vessels, each with just a single cannon, to patrol the vast watery border between them. The Rush-Bagot treaty was perhaps the most successful disarmament treaty for a century to come.

The biggest winners in the War of 1812 were the young men, once called War Hawks, who took up the banner of the Republican Party and carried it in new, expansive directions. These young politicians favored trade, western expansion, internal improvements, and the energetic development of new economic markets. The biggest losers of the war were the Indians. Tecumseh was dead, the Prophet discredited, the prospects of an Indian confederacy dashed, the Creeks' large homeland seized, and the British protectors gone.

discussed the possible secession of New England from the Union. They also proposed amending the Constitution to abolish the three-fifths clause as a basis of representation; to specify that congressional powers to pass embargoes, admit states, or declare war should require a two-thirds vote instead of a simple majority; and to limit the president to one term and prohibit successive presidents from the same state. The cumulative effect of these proposals would have been to reduce the South's political power and break the lock of the Virginia dynasty on national office. New England wanted to assure that no one sectional party could again lead the country into war against the clear interests of another. Coming just as peace was achieved, however, the Hartford Convention suddenly looked very unpatriotic. The Federalist Party never recovered

Women's Status in the Early Republic

With the model of Dolley Madison, the able "presidentress," so prominently before the public, and the memory of the 1790s debate over education for motherhood not yet erased (see chapter 9), it might be expected that the first three decades of the nineteenth century would provide new arenas of social change for women. One that definitely did permit tangible advancement was that of female schooling, which continued to expand. The spread of basic public education for children up to age twelve, so vital to the production of citizens in a **democratic** state, routinely included girls as well as boys; by

1830, female literacy and numeracy were rapidly rising. Further, between 1790 and 1830, some 400 female academies were founded, providing the opportunity for adolescent girls of genteel families to move beyond the rudiments of reading and writing to such subjects as history, rhetoric, natural philosophy, arithmetic, and French. But other arenas and institutions central to the shaping of women's lives—laws, marriage, and church—showed either no change or only incremental change. State legislatures and the courts grappled with the legal dependency of married white women in a country whose defining characteristic was independence, while religious organizations struggled to redefine the role of women in church governance. If, in the end, there was no giant step forward for women in these decades, it is still significant that these questions were raised at all.

Women and the Law

The Anglo-American view of women, implanted in British common law, was that wives had no independent legal or political personhood. The legal doctrine of *feme covert* (covered woman) held that a wife's civic life was completely subsumed by her husband's. A wife was obligated to obey her husband; her property was his, her domestic and sexual services were his, and even their children were legally his. Women had no right to keep their wages, to make contracts, or to sue or be sued. Any crime committed by a wife in the presence of her husband was chargeable to him, with two exceptions: treason against the state and keeping a brothel. The fundamental assumption of coverture was that husbands did—and ought to—control their wives.

State legislatures generally passed up the opportunity to rewrite the laws of domestic relations even though they redrafted other British laws in light of republican principles. The standard treatise on family law, published in 1816 and consulted by lawyers everywhere as a summary of the best legal thinking on marriage, was titled *The Law of Baron and Feme*—that is "lord and woman." The title perfectly captured how lawyers framed husband-wife power relations. Lawyers never paused to defend, much less to challenge, the assumption that unequal power relations lay at the heart of marriage. An occasional woman offered a challenge in print, as in this 1801 example from an anonymous Connecticut author writing *The Female Advocate:*

Home and Away: The New Boarding School
These two engravings show "before" and "after" pictures of a young woman circa 1820 whose family enrolled her in one of the new female academies that were springing up by the scores in the decades after 1800. What seem to be the family's expectations as they send her off? How is she changed when she returns? Did she acquire a practical or an ornamental education? Notice the various emblems of women's household work. What do these pictures reveal about the options for young women in this period? Is the artist, John Lewis Krimmel, making a joke? Or does this picture betray anxieties about women's education? Krimmel himself was a Philadelphia painter who worked as a drawing master at a girls' academy.
Library Company of Philadelphia.

"Must woman have no law but her husband? Has she not a rational nature, as well as the man? And is she not equally accountable for the improvement or misuse of her judgment?"

The one aspect of family law that did change in the early Republic was divorce. Before the Revolution, only New England jurisdictions recognized a limited right to divorce; by 1820, every state except South Carolina did so. This was a major symbolic crack in the traditional assumption that marriage was lifelong and indissoluble. However, divorce was uncommon and difficult and in many states could be obtained only by petition to the state's legislature, a daunting obstacle for many ordinary people. A mutual wish to terminate a marriage was never sufficient grounds for legal divorce. A New York judge affirmed that "it would be aiming a deadly blow at public morals to decree a dissolution of the marriage contract merely because the parties requested it. Divorces should never be allowed, except for the protection of the innocent party, and for the punishment of the guilty." States upheld the institution of marriage both to protect persons they thought of as naturally dependent (women and children) and to regulate the use and inheritance of property. (Unofficial self-divorce, desertion, and bigamy were remedies that ordinary people sometimes chose to get around the strictness of marriage law. But powerful social sanctions against such behavior usually prevailed.) Legal enforcement of marriage as an unequal relationship played a major role in maintaining gender inequality in the nineteenth century.

Single adult women could own and convey property, make contracts, initiate suits, and pay taxes. They could not vote (except in New Jersey before 1807), serve on juries, or practice law, so their civil status was limited. Single women's economic status was often limited as well, by custom as much as by law. Unless they had inherited adequate property or could live with married siblings, single adult women in the early Republic were very often poor.

None of the legal institutions that structured white gender relations applied to black slaves. As property themselves, slaves could not freely consent to any contractual obligations, including marriage. The protective features of state-sponsored unions were thus denied to black men and women in slavery, who were controlled by a more powerful authority, the slave owner. But this also meant that slave unions did not establish unequal power relations between partners, backed by the force of law, as did marriages among the free.

Women and Church Governance

In most **Protestant** denominations around 1800, white women made up the majority of congregants, as they had for some time. Yet the church hierarchy—ordained ministers and elders—was exclusively male, and the governance of most denominations rested in men's hands.

There were some exceptions, however. In several small **evangelical** groups, notably Baptist congregations in New England that had been strongly affected by the **Great Awakening**, women served along with men on church governance committees, where they decided admission of new members, voted on the hiring of ministers, and even debated doctrinal points.

Women and the Church: Jemima Wilkinson
Jemima Wilkinson, the "Publick Universal Friend," in an early woodcut, wears a clerical collar and body-obscuring robe, in keeping with the claim that the former Jemima was now a person without sex or gender. Her hair is pulled back tight on her head and curled at the neck in a masculine style of the 1790s. Did she become masculinized, or did she truly transcend gender?
Rhode Island Historical Society.

Quakers, too, had a history of recognizing women's spiritual talents. Quaker women who felt a special call were accorded the status of minister, which meant they were capable of leading and speaking in Quaker meetings. Separate men's and women's committees heard disciplinary cases and formulated Quaker policy.

Between 1790 and 1820, a small and highly unusual set of women emerged who actively engaged in open preaching. Most were from Freewill Baptist groups centered in New England and upstate New York. Some were from small Methodist sects, and others rejected any formal religious affiliation. Probably fewer than a hundred such women existed, but several dozen traveled beyond their local communities, creating converts and controversy. They spoke from the heart, without prepared speeches, often exhibiting trances and claiming to exhort (counsel or warn) rather than to preach. None of these women were ordained ministers with official credentials to preach or perform baptisms.

Perhaps the most well-known exhorting woman was Jemima Wilkinson, who called herself the "Publick Universal Friend." After a near-death experience from high fever in 1776, Wilkinson proclaimed her body no longer female *or* male but the incarnation of the "Spirit of Light." She dressed in men's clothes, wore her hair in a masculine style, shunned gender-specific pronouns, and preached openly in Rhode Island and Philadelphia. In the early nineteenth century, Wilkinson withdrew with more than 250 followers, to a settlement called New Jerusalem in western New York. Her fame was sustained by periodic newspaper articles that fed public curiosity about her lifelong transvestism and her unfeminine forcefulness.

As more women exhorters cropped up, their behavior came under increasing fire. A Baptist periodical in Massachusetts printed frequent reminders of the biblical prohibition "Let your women learn to keep silence in the churches" (1 Corinthians 14:34). Female preachers well knew such scriptural passages and were ready with biblical interpretations of their own, as in Deborah Peirce's 1820 pamphlet *A Scriptural Vindication of Female Preaching, Prophesying, or Exhortation.*

The decades from 1790 to the 1820s marked a period of unusual confusion, ferment, and creativity in American religion. New denominations blossomed, new styles of religiosity gripped adherents, and an extensive periodical press devoted to religion popularized all manner of theological and institutional innovations. Congregations increasingly attracted vibrant female participation, often eclipsing the percentage of male congregants. In such a climate, the age-old tradition of gender subordination came into question here and there among the most radically democratic of the churches. But the presumption of male authority over women was deeply entrenched in American culture. Even denominations that had allowed women to participate in church governance began to pull back, and most churches reinstated patterns of hierarchy along gender lines. In church as in state, top leadership remained completely in male hands.

Monroe and Adams

With the elections of 1816 and 1820, Virginians continued their long hold on the presidency. In 1816, James Monroe beat Federalist Rufus King of New York by 183 electoral votes to 34. When Monroe was reelected in 1820 with all but one electoral vote, the national presence of the Federalists was fully eclipsed. The unanimity of the 1820 election did not necessarily reflect voter satisfaction with the status quo, however, for barely one-quarter of eligible voters bothered to cast ballots.

The collapse of the Federalist Party led one over-optimistic newspaper to dub Monroe's first term the "Era of Good Feelings," as though a one-party government would of course be harmonious. The harmony turned out to be very short-lived. Monroe and his aloof wife Elizabeth sharply curtailed regular social affairs in the White House and returned to a 1790s style of high formality in the events that remained. Mrs. Monroe even shunned the practice of formal calling. But instead of closing down the avenues for social cohesion that Dolley Madison had enlarged, the Monroes' chilliness drove the hard work of social network building into different channels. Ill feelings were further displayed in a major sectional crisis over the admission of Missouri to the Union, and foreign policy questions animated sharp disagreements as well. The election of 1824 brought forth an abundance of candidates, all claiming to be Republicans; the winner was John Quincy Adams, in an election decided by the House of Representatives—and, many believed, maybe by a backroom bargain. A one-party political system was put to the test of practical circumstances; it failed and then fractured.

The Missouri Compromise

In February 1819, Missouri applied for statehood. Since 1815, four other states had joined the Union (Indiana, Mississippi, Illinois, and Alabama), following the blueprint laid out by the Northwest Ordinance of 1787. But Missouri posed a problem. Although much of its area was on the same latitude as Illinois, its territorial population was already one-sixth slave, consisting of 10,000 African Americans brought there by southern white planters.

> Just as southern economic power rested on slave labor, southern political power drew extra strength from the slave population, which was counted as three-fifths of the free population for purposes of representation.

Missouri's unusual combination of geography and demography led a New York representative in Congress, James Tallmadge Jr., to propose two amendments to the statehood bill. The first stipulated that slaves born in Missouri after statehood would be free at age twenty-five, and the second declared that no new slaves could be imported into the state. Tallmadge modeled the first amendment on New York's gradual **emancipation** law of 1799. It did not strip slave owners of their current property, and it allowed them full use of the labor of newborn slaves well into their prime productive years. Still, Southerners in Congress loudly protested the amendments. Although gradual emancipation protected slave owners from immediate financial loss, in the long run it made Missouri a free state, tipping the national balance of power between free and slave states. Just as southern economic power rested on slave labor, southern political power drew extra strength from the slave population, when three-fifths of all slaves were added to the count of all whites to determine representation in Congress. In 1820, the South had seventeen additional seats in the House of Representatives based on slave population.

Both of Tallmadge's amendments passed in the House, but by a close and sharply sectional vote of North against South (with a few northern Republicans taking the side of the South). The ferocious debate led a Georgia representative to observe that the question had started "a fire which all the waters of the ocean could not extinguish. It can be extinguished only in blood." The Senate, with an even number of slave and free states, voted down the amendments; some free border states joined the proslavery line. Missouri statehood was postponed for the next congressional term.

In 1820, a compromise emerged in the Senate. Maine, once a part of Massachusetts, applied for statehood, balancing against Missouri as a slave state. The Senate further agreed that

Eli Terry's Pillar and Scroll Clock

Before the 1790s, sundials and church bells answered most timekeeping needs; clocks were objects of art, not utility. The Connecticut clockmaker Eli Terry realized that affordable clocks might change all that. First he switched from brass to wood for the clock's internal movement, and then he designed machinery to mass-produce the parts, achieving the first successful system of "interchangeable parts" and turning out thousands of clocks a year. In 1814, Terry developed this inexpensive compact clock and sold tens of thousands over the next dozen years. Affordable clocks revolutionized timekeeping, enabling workers to arrive before the factory bell and travelers to make stagecoach and canal boat departure times. Employers could demand punctuality, a moral virtue made possible by the pervasiveness of clocks. For good or ill, clocks did not merely measure time; they helped speed up the pace of life.

American Clock & Watch Museum, Bristol, CT. Photo by C. R. Lang Photography.

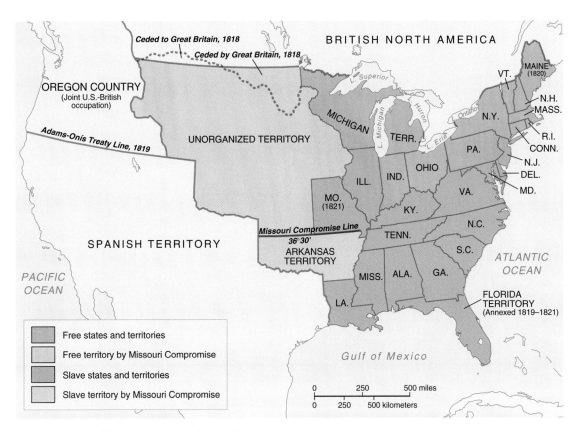

OREGON COUNTRY
(Joint U.S.-British occupation)

Ceded to Great Britain, 1818

Ceded by Great Britain, 1818

BRITISH NORTH AMERICA

Adams-Onís Treaty Line, 1819

UNORGANIZED TERRITORY

SPANISH TERRITORY

Missouri Compromise Line 36° 30'

ARKANSAS TERRITORY

PACIFIC OCEAN

MICHIGAN TERR.

MO. (1821)

ILL. IND. OHIO

KY.

TENN.

LA.

MISS. ALA. GA.

VT.

MAINE (1820)

N.H.

MASS.

N.Y.

PA.

R.I.

CONN.

N.J.

DEL.

MD.

VA.

N.C.

S.C.

ATLANTIC OCEAN

FLORIDA TERRITORY (Annexed 1819–1821)

Gulf of Mexico

Free states and territories

Free territory by Missouri Compromise

Slave states and territories

Slave territory by Missouri Compromise

0   250   500 miles
0   250   500 kilometers

MAP 10.5   The Missouri Compromise, 1820
After a difficult battle in Congress, Missouri entered the Union in 1821 as part of a package of compromises. Maine was admitted as a free state to balance slavery in Missouri, and a line drawn at latitude 36°30' put most of the rest of the Louisiana Territory off limits to slavery in the future.

READING THE MAP: How many free and how many slave states were there prior to the Missouri Compromise? What did the admission of Missouri as a slave state threaten to do?
CONNECTIONS: Who precipitated the crisis over Missouri, what did he propose, and where did the idea come from? Who proposed the Missouri Compromise, and who benefited from it?

FOR MORE HELP ANALYZING THIS IMAGE, see the map activity for this chapter in the Online Study Guide at bedfordstmartins.com/roark.

the southern boundary of Missouri—latitude 36°30'—extended west, would become the permanent line dividing slave from free states (Map 10.5). The House also approved the compromise, thanks to expert deal brokering by Kentucky's Henry Clay, who earned the nickname the "Great Pacificator" for his superb negotiating skills. The North secured a large area where federal prohibition of slavery was guaranteed and also got Maine as a counterbalance to Missouri. The South got Missouri without any interference with slavery. The whole package passed only because seventeen northern representatives in the House decided that minimizing sectional conflict was in the best interests of the United States and so voted with the South.

President Monroe and Thomas Jefferson at first worried that the Missouri crisis would reinvigorate the Federalist Party as the party of the North. But even ex-Federalists agreed that the split between free and slave states was too dangerous a fault line to be permitted to become a shaper of national politics. When new parties did develop in the 1830s, they took pains to bridge geography, each party developing a presence in both North and South. Monroe and Jefferson also worried about the future of slavery. Each understood slavery to be deeply

A View of St. Louis from an Illinois Town, 1835
Just fifteen years after the Missouri Compromise, St. Louis was already a booming city, having gotten its start in the eighteenth century as a French fur-trading village. It was incorporated as a town in 1809 and chartered as a city in 1822. In this 1835 view, commercial buildings and steamships line the riverfront; a ferry on the Illinois shore prepares to transport travelers across the Mississippi River. Black laborers (in the foreground) handle loading tasks. The Illinois side is a free state; Missouri, where the ferry lands, is a slave state.
A View of St. Louis from an Illinois Town, 1835: Private collection.

FOR MORE HELP ANALYZING THIS IMAGE, see the visual activity for this chapter in the Online Study Guide at
bedfordstmartins.com/roark.

problematic, but, as Jefferson said, "We have the wolf by the ears, and we can neither hold him, nor safely let him go. Justice is in one scale, and self-preservation in the other."

The Monroe Doctrine

New foreign policy challenges arose even as Congress struggled with the slavery issue. In 1816, American troops led by General Andrew Jackson invaded Spanish Florida in search of Seminole Indians welcoming and harboring escaped slaves. Once there, Jackson declared himself the commander of northern Florida, demonstrating his power in 1818 by executing two British men who he claimed were dangerous enemies. In asserting rule over the territory,

and surely in executing the two British subjects on Spanish land, Jackson had gone too far. Privately, President Monroe was distressed and pondered court-martialing Jackson, prevented only by Jackson's immense popularity as the hero of the Battle of New Orleans. Instead, John Quincy Adams, the secretary of state, negotiated with Spain the Adams-Onís Treaty, which delivered Florida to the United States in 1819. In exchange, the Americans agreed to abandon any claim to Texas or Cuba; Southerners viewed this as a large concession, having eyed both places as potential acquisitions for future slave states.

Spain at that moment was preoccupied with its colonies in South America. One after another—Chile, Colombia, Peru, and finally

Mexico—declared itself independent in the early 1820s. To discourage Spain or France from reconquering these colonies, Monroe formulated a declaration of principles on South America. Incorporated into his annual message to Congress in December 1823, the declaration became known in later years as the **Monroe Doctrine**. The president warned that "the American Continents, by the free and independent condition which they have assumed and maintain, are henceforth not to be considered as subjects for future colonization by any European power." Any attempt to interfere in the Western Hemisphere would be regarded as "the manifestation of an unfriendly disposition towards the United States." In exchange for noninterference by Europeans, Monroe pledged that the United States would stay out of European struggles. He articulated these policy goals without any real force to back them up. Realistically, the American navy could not defend Chile or Peru against Spain or France. Monroe did not even have the backing of Congress for his statement; it was merely his idea of a sound policy laid out in a public message.

The Election of 1824

Monroe's attempt at a nonpartisan administration was the last of its kind, a fitting throwback to eighteenth-century ideals, led by the last president to wear a powdered wig and knee breeches. Monroe's cabinet contained men of sharply different philosophies, all calling themselves Republicans. Secretary of State John Quincy Adams represented the urban Northeast; South Carolinian John C. Calhoun spoke for the planter aristocracy as secretary of war; and William H. Crawford of Georgia, secretary of the treasury, was a proponent of Jeffersonian **states' rights** and limited federal power. Even before the end of Monroe's first term, these men and others began to maneuver for the election of 1824.

Election Sewing or Trinket Boxes from 1824
Women could mark their partiality to a presidential candidate by purchasing a sewing box emblazoned with the face of their choice. On the left is a box with John Quincy Adams's picture inside the cover, created with a lithographic process just coming into wide use in the 1820s that made possible the production of thousands of pictures from a single master stone plate. (Wood and copper plates, the earlier technology, produced prints numbering only in the hundreds before deteriorating under pressure.) The top of the Adams box carries a velvet pincushion printed with the slogan "BE FIRM FOR ADAMS." A competing box on the right puts Andrew Jackson's likeness under glass on the top of the cover. The lithographic portrait is hand colored with watercolors. Notice that Jackson is shown in his military uniform with the title of general and a rather younger-looking face than he actually had in 1824.
Collection of Janice L. and David J. Frent.

Crucially helping them to maneuver were their wives, who accomplished some of the work of modern campaign managers through assiduous courting of men—and women—of influence. The parties not thrown by Mrs. Monroe were now thrown all over town by women whose husbands were jockeying for political favor. Louisa Catherine Adams, for example, remodeled her house and had parties every Tuesday night for guests numbering in the hundreds. (At one party she learned before her husband did that the Adams-Onís Treaty he had negotiated had been formally approved by Spain.) Adams lacked charm—"I am a man of reserved, cold, austere, and forbidding manners" he once wrote—but his abundantly charming (and hardworking) wife more than made up for that. She attended to the etiquette of social calls, sometimes making two dozen in one morning, and counted sixty-eight members of Congress as her regular Tuesday guests.

Since 1800, the congressional caucus of each party had met to identify and lend its considerable but still informal support to its party's leading candidate. In 1824, with only one party alive—and alive with five serious candidates—the caucus system splintered. Since such a large number of candidates reduced the chance of anyone securing a majority in the electoral college, many expected that the final election would be decided by the House of Representatives. Having sixty-eight members of the House on one's regular guest list was thus smart politics.

> The 1824 election was the first presidential contest in which candidates' popularity with ordinary voters could be measured.

John Quincy Adams (and Louisa Catherine) very much wanted the presidency, an ambition fed by John's sense of rising to his father's accomplishment. Furthermore, since 1800 every president had once been secretary of state; Adams was the heir apparent, or so he thought. Henry Clay, Speaker of the House, also was a declared candidate. A man of vast congressional experience, he had engaged in high-level diplomacy, having accompanied Adams to Ghent to negotiate the 1814 peace treaty with Britain. The Kentuckian put forth a set of policies he called the American System, a package of protective tariffs to promote manufacturing and federal expenditures for extensive internal improvements, such as roads and canals. William Crawford, of the Treasury Department, was a favorite of Republicans from the big states of Virginia and

New York; despite suffering an incapacitating stroke in mid-1824, he remained their favorite. South Carolinian John C. Calhoun, a lawyer as well as a planter, was another serious contender, having served in Congress and in several cabinets. Like Clay, he favored internal improvements and protective tariffs, which he figured would gain him support in northern states.

The final candidate was an outsider and a latecomer: General Andrew Jackson of Tennessee. Jackson had much less national political experience than the others, having served one year in the House and two in the Senate. His fame rested on his reputation as a military leader, but that was sufficient to gain him a huge following, much to the surprise of the experienced politicians. In early 1824, on the anniversary of the Battle of New Orleans, the Adamses had thrown a spectacular ball with five hundred guests in honor of General Jackson. No doubt John Quincy Adams hoped that some of Jackson's charisma would rub off on him; he was not yet thinking of Jackson as a rival for office. But later in 1824, Jackson supporters put his name in play, and voters in the West and South reacted with enthusiasm. Calhoun soon dropped out of the race and shifted his attention to winning the vice presidency.

The 1824 election was the first presidential contest in which candidates' popularity with ordinary voters could be measured. Recent changes in state constitutions gave voters in all but six states the power to choose electors for the electoral college. (Before, state legislatures had held this power.) Jackson was by far the most popular candidate with voters. He won more than 153,000 votes, while Adams was second with 109,000; Clay won 47,000 votes, and the debilitated Crawford garnered 46,600. This was not a large voter turnout, probably amounting to only a quarter of adult white males. Many more voters participated regularly in local and state elections, where the real political action generally lay.

In the electoral college, Jackson received 99 votes, Adams 84, Crawford 41, and Clay 37 (Map 10.6). Jackson did not have a majority, so the election was thrown into the House of Representatives, for the second (and last) time in American history. Each state delegation had one vote; according to the Twelfth Amendment to the Constitution, passed in 1804, only the top three candidates could enter the runoff. Thus Henry Clay was out of the race and in a position to bestow his support on another candidate.

Jackson's supporters later characterized the election of 1824 as the "corrupt bargain." Clay backed Adams, and Adams won by one vote in the House. Clay's support made sense on several levels. Despite strong mutual dislike, he and Adams agreed on issues such as federal support to build roads and canals, and Clay was uneasy with Jackson's volatile temperament and un-stated political views and with Crawford's diminished capacity. What made Clay's decision look "corrupt" was that immediately after the election, Adams offered to appoint Clay secretary of state—and Clay accepted.

In the weeks before the vote in the House, rumors of such a deal had been denied by Adams and Clay supporters, confident that the two archenemies could never cooperate. There probably was no concrete bargain; Adams's subsequent cabinet appointments demonstrated his lack of political astuteness. But Andrew Jackson felt that the election had been stolen from him, and he wrote bitterly that "the Judas of the West has closed the contract and will receive the thirty pieces of silver."

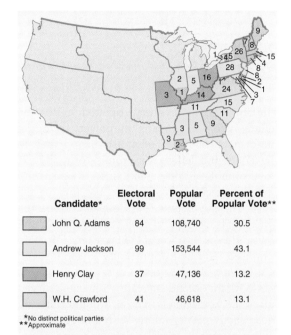

Candidate*	Electoral Vote	Popular Vote	Percent of Popular Vote**
John Q. Adams	84	108,740	30.5
Andrew Jackson	99	153,544	43.1
Henry Clay	37	47,136	13.2
W.H. Crawford	41	46,618	13.1

*No distinct political parties
**Approximate

Note: Because no candidate garnered a majority in the electoral college, the election was decided in the House of Representatives. Although Clay was eliminated from the running, as Speaker of the House he influenced the final decision in favor of Adams.

MAP 10.6 The Election of 1824

The Adams Administration

John Quincy Adams, like his father, was a one-term president. His career had been built on diplomacy, not electoral politics, and, despite his wife's deft experience in the art of political influence, his own political horse sense was not well developed. His cabinet choices welcomed his opposition into his inner circle. He asked Crawford to stay on in the Treasury, and he retained an openly pro-Jackson postmaster general, even though that position controlled thousands of nationwide patronage appointments. Most amazingly, he asked Jackson to become secretary of war. With Calhoun as vice president (elected without opposition by the electoral college) and Clay at the State Department, the whole argumentative crew would have been thrust into the executive branch. Crawford and Jackson had the good sense to decline the appointments.

Adams had lofty ideas for federal action during his presidency, and the plan he put before Congress was so sweeping that it took Henry Clay aback. Adams called for federally built roads, canals, and harbors. He proposed a national university in Washington as well as government-sponsored scientific research. He wanted to build observatories to advance astronomical

knowledge and to promote precision in time-keeping, and he backed a decimal-based system of weights and measures. In all these endeavors, Adams believed he was continuing the Jefferson and Madison legacy, using the powers of government to advance knowledge. But his opponents feared he was too Hamiltonian, using federal power inappropriately to advance commercial interests.

Whether he was more truly Federalist or Republican was a moot point, however. Lacking the give-and-take political skills required to gain congressional support, Adams was unable to implement much of his program. He scorned the idea of courting voters to gain support and using the patronage system to enhance his power. He often made appointments (to posts such as customs collectors) to placate enemies rather than reward friends. A story of a toast offered to the president may well have been mythical, but as humorous folklore it made the rounds during his term and came to summarize Adams's precarious hold on leadership. A dignitary raised a glass and pledged, "May he strike confusion to his foes . . . ," to which another voice scornfully chimed in, "as he has already done to his friends."

Conclusion: Republican Simplicity Becomes Complex

The nineteenth century opened with the Jeffersonian Republicans in power, trying to undo much of what Federalists had created in the 1790s. But Jefferson's promise of a simpler government—limited in size, scope, and power—quickly gave way to the lure of the West. The Lewis and Clark expedition excited armchair travelers and real travelers alike, and the sudden acquisition of the Louisiana Purchase promised land and opportunity to settlers. But Southerners and Northerners moving into Missouri, the second state after Louisiana carved out of the Louisiana Purchase, brought differing ideas about slavery (along with a large number of slaves), greatly complicating the country's political future with the burning issues central to the crisis over Missouri statehood.

Jeffersonian simplicity also gave way in the face of increasing antagonism both from foreign nations and from Indian nations. Jefferson and his successor Madison met it with a combination of embargoes, treaties, and military action. Battles with Indians blended into the major engagement with England, the War of 1812—a war motivated less by concrete economic or political issues than by questions of honor. Its conclusion at the Battle of New Orleans allowed Americans the illusion that they had fought a second war of independence.

If the War of 1812 seemed a second war of independence for the whites, how much more so was it for the Indians, who lost both times. Tecumseh's vision of an unprecedentedly large confederacy of Indian tribes that would halt western expansion by white Americans was cut short by the war and by his death. Without British support, the Indians probably could not have successfully challenged for long the westward dynamic of American settlement. But British support came at a time when Canada was under attack, and the British valued their own defense more than they valued their promises to help the Indians.

The war elevated to national prominence General Andrew Jackson, whose sudden popularity with voters in the 1824 election surprised traditional politicians—and their politically astute wives—and threw the one-party rule of Republicans into a tailspin. John Quincy Adams barely occupied his office in 1825 before the election campaign of 1828 was off and running. Appeals to the people—the mass of white male voters—would be the hallmark of all elections after 1824. It was a game Adams could not easily play.

Politics in this entire period was a game that women could not play either. Except for the political wives of Washington, women, whether white or free black, had no place in government. While male legislatures maintained women's *feme covert* status, keeping wives dependent on husbands, a few women found a pathway to greater personal autonomy through religion. Meanwhile, the routine inclusion of girls in public schools and the steady spread of female academies planted seeds that would blossom into a major transformation of gender in the 1830s and 1840s.

The War of 1812 started another chain of events that would prove momentous in later decades. Jefferson's long embargo and Madison's wartime trade stoppages gave strong encouragement to American manufacturing, momentarily protected from competition with English factories. When peace returned in 1815, the years of independent development burst forth into a period of sustained economic growth that continued nearly unabated into the mid-nineteenth century.

FOR ADDITIONAL FIRSTHAND ACCOUNTS OF THIS PERIOD, see Chapter 10 in Michael Johnson, ed., *Reading the American Past,* Third Edition.

TO ASSESS YOUR MASTERY OF THE MATERIAL IN THIS CHAPTER, see the Online Study Guide at bedfordstmartins.com/roark.

FOR WEB LINKS RELATED TO TOPICS IN THIS CHAPTER, see "HistoryLinks," "DocLinks," and "PlaceLinks" at bedfordstmartins.com/roark.

CHRONOLOGY

1789 • Judiciary Act establishes six Supreme Court justices, who preside over six circuit courts.

1800 • Thomas Jefferson and Aaron Burr tie in electoral college.
• Gabriel's slave rebellion in Virginia tries but fails to exploit white electoral crisis.

1801 • Judiciary Act reduces Supreme Court justices to five and allows for sixteen circuit courts and circuit court judges.
• House of Representatives elects Jefferson president after 36 ballots.

1803 • Supreme Court in *Marbury v. Madison* establishes concept of judicial review.
• England and France place embargoes on American shipping.
• United States purchases Louisiana Territory from France for $15 million.

1804 • Jefferson elected to a second term.
• Burr-Hamilton duel ends in Alexander Hamilton's death.

1804–1806
• Lewis and Clark expedition goes to the Pacific and inspires ideas of western expansion.

1807 • New Jersey revises the law to exclude women and blacks from voting.
• British attack and search *Chesapeake* in Chesapeake Bay.
• Embargo Act forbids American ships from engaging in trade with any foreign port.

1808 • James Madison elected president; Dolley Madison soon dubbed "presidentress."

1809 • Treaty of Fort Wayne cedes 3 million acres of Indian land in Indiana Territory to United States.
• Non-Intercourse Act forbids American trade with England, France, and their colonies.

1811 • William Henry Harrison's troops win Battle of Tippecanoe, destroying Prophetstown in Indiana Territory and breaking Tenskwatawa's power.

1812 • United States declares war on Great Britain.
• Madison elected to a second term.

1813 • Tecumseh dies at Battle of the Thames.

1814 • British attack Washington, D.C., burning White House and Capitol.
• Treaty of Ghent ends War of 1812.
• New England Federalists at Hartford Convention consider secession and look unpatriotic.

1815 • Andrew Jackson's forces win Battle of New Orleans.

1816 • James Monroe elected president.

1819 • Spain cedes Florida to United States in Adams-Onís Treaty.

1820 • Missouri Compromise admits Missouri as slave state and Maine as free state, ending the most serious North-South political crisis in the early Republic.
• Monroe elected to a second term.

1823 • Monroe Doctrine asserts independence of Western Hemisphere from European intervention.

1824 • John Quincy Adams becomes president in "corrupt bargain" election.

BIBLIOGRAPHY

General Works

Lance Banning, *The Jeffersonian Persuasion: Evolution of a Party Ideology* (1978).

Saul Cornell, *The Other Founders: Anti-Federalism and the Dissenting Tradition in America, 1788–1828* (1999).

Noble E. Cunningham, *In Pursuit of Reason: The Life of Thomas Jefferson* (1987).

Ralph Ketcham, *Presidents above Party: The First American Presidency, 1789–1829* (1984).

David Waldstreicher, *In the Midst of Perpetual Fetes: The Making of American Nationalism, 1776–1820* (1997).

Stephen Watts, *The Republic Reborn: War and the Making of Liberal America, 1790–1820* (1987).

Republicans and Federalists

Doron S. Ben-Atar, *The Origins of Jeffersonian Commercial Policy and Diplomacy* (1993).

James Broussard, *The Southern Federalists, 1800–1816* (1978).

Noble E. Cunningham, *The Jeffersonian Republicans in Power: Party Operations, 1801–1809* (1963).

Alexander DeConde, *This Affair of Louisiana* (1976).

Joseph J. Ellis, *American Sphinx: The Character of Thomas Jefferson* (1997).

Richard E. Ellis, *The Jeffersonian Crisis: Courts and Politics in the Young Republic* (1971).

David Hackett Fischer, *The Revolution of American Conservatism: The Federalist Party in the Era of Jeffersonian Democracy* (1965).

Marshall Fotella, *Coming to Terms with Democracy: Federalist Intellectuals and the Shaping of an American Culture* (2001).

Joanne B. Freeman, *Affairs of Honor: National Politics in the New Republic* (2001).

Annette Gordon-Reed, *Thomas Jefferson and Sally Hemings: An American Controversy* (1997).

Morton J. Horwitz, *The Transformation of American Law, 1780–1860* (1977).

Herbert A. Johnson, *The Chief Justiceship of John Marshall, 1801–1835* (1997).

Lawrence S. Kaplan, "Entangling Alliances with None": American Foreign Policy in the Age of Jefferson* (1987).

Jon Kukla, *A Wilderness So Immense: The Louisiana Purchase and the Destiny of America* (2003).

Jan Ellen Lewis and Peter S. Onuf, eds., *Sally Hemings and Thomas Jefferson: History, Memory, and Civic Culture* (1999).

Milton Lomask, *Aaron Burr* (1982).

Dumas Malone, *Jefferson the President: First Term, 1801–1805* (1970).

Dumas Malone, *Jefferson the President: Second Term, 1805–1809* (1974).

Richard K. Matthews, *The Radical Politics of Thomas Jefferson: A Revisionist View* (1984).

Drew R. McCoy, *The Elusive Republic: Political Economy in Jeffersonian America* (1980).

Drew R. McCoy, *The Last of the Fathers: James Madison and the Republican Legacy* (1989).

R. Kent Newmyer, *The Supreme Court under Marshall and Taney* (1986).

Peter Onuf, ed., *Jeffersonian Legacies* (1993).

Merrill Peterson, *Thomas Jefferson and the New Nation: A Biography* (1970).

Arnold A. Rogow, *A Fatal Friendship: Alexander Hamilton and Aaron Burr* (1998).

Robert A. Rutland, *The Presidency of James Madison* (1990).

Thomas C. Shevory, ed., *John Marshall's Achievement: Law, Politics, and Constitutional Interpretations* (1989).

Jack M. Sosin, *The Aristocracy of the Long Robe: The Origins of Judicial Review in America* (1989).

Francis N. Stites, *John Marshall: Defender of the Constitution* (1981).

Robert W. Tucker, *Empire of Liberty: The Statecraft of Thomas Jefferson* (1990).

G. E. White, *The Marshall Court and Cultural Change, 1815–1835* (1988).

Lewis and Clark and the West

Stephen E. Ambrose, *Undaunted Courage: Meriwether Lewis, Thomas Jefferson, and the Opening of the American West* (1996).

Albert Furtwangler, *Acts of Discovery: Visions of America in the Lewis and Clark Journals* (1993).

David Freeman Hawke, *Those Tremendous Mountains: The Story of the Lewis and Clark Expedition* (1980).

James P. Ronda, *Lewis and Clark among the Indians* (1984).

Foreign Policy and the War of 1812

James M. Banner, *To the Hartford Convention: The Federalists and the Origins of Party Politics in Massachusetts, 1789–1815* (1969).

Carl Benn, *The Iroquois in the War of 1812* (1998).

Pierre Berton, *The Invasion of Canada* (1980).

Harry L. Coles, *The War of 1812* (1965).

Ronald L. Hatzenbuehler and Robert L. Ivie, *Congress Declares War: Rhetoric, Leadership, and Partisanship in the Early Republic* (1983).

Donald R. Hickey, *The War of 1812: A Forgotten Conflict* (1989).

Reginald Horsman, *The Causes of the War of 1812* (1962).

Linda K. Kerber, *Federalists in Dissent: Imagery and Ideology in Jeffersonian America* (1970).

C. Edward Skeen, *Citizen Soldiers in the War of 1812* (1999).

Burton Spivak, *Jefferson's English Crisis: Commerce, Embargo, and the Republican Revolution* (1979).

J. C. A. Stagg, *Mr. Madison's War: Politics, Diplomacy, and Warfare in the Early American Republic, 1783–1830* (1983).

Slavery

David Brion Davis, *The Problem of Slavery in the Age of Revolution, 1770–1823* (1975).

Douglas Egerton, *Gabriel's Rebellion* (1993).

Sylvia Frey, *Water from the Rock* (1991).

James Oliver Horton and Lois E. Horton, *In Hope of Liberty: Culture, Community, and Protest among Northern Free Blacks, 1700–1860* (1997).

Robert McColley, *Slavery and Jeffersonian Virginia* (1964).

Gary B. Nash, *Forging Freedom: The Formation of Philadelphia's Black Community, 1720–1840* (1988).

Donald L. Robinson, *Slavery in the Structure of American Politics, 1765–1820* (1971).

James Sidbury, *Ploughshares into Swords: Race, Rebellion, and Identity in Gabriel's Virginia* (1997).

Shane White, *Somewhat More Independent: The End of Slavery in New York City, 1710–1810* (1991).

Native Americans

Henry Warner Bowden, *American Indians and Christian Missions: Studies in Cultural Conflict* (1981).

Christopher Densmore, *Red Jacket: Iroquois Diplomat and Orator* (1999).

Gregory E. Dowd, *A Spirited Resistance: The North American Indian Struggle for Unity, 1745–1815* (1992).

R. David Edmunds, *The Shawnee Prophet* (1983).

R. David Edmunds, *Tecumseh and the Quest for Indian Leadership* (1984).

Bil Gilbert, *God Gave Us This Country: Tekamthi and the First American Civil War* (1989).

H. S. Halbert and T. H. Ball, *The Creek War of 1813 and 1814* (1969).

William G. McLoughlin, *Cherokees and Missionaries, 1789–1839* (1984).

James Merrell, *The Indians' New World: Catawbas and Their Neighbors from European Contact through the Era of Removal* (1989).

Paul Francis Prucha, *The Great Father: The United States Government and the American Indians* (1984).

Bernard W. Sheehan, *Seeds of Extinction: Jeffersonian Philanthropy and the American Indians* (1973).

John Sugden, *Tecumseh: A Life* (1997).

Richard White, *The Middle Ground: Indians, Empires, and Republics in the Great Lakes Region, 1650–1815* (1991).

Women, Marriage, and Religion

Catherine Allgor, *Parlor Politics: In Which the Ladies of Washington Help Build a City and a Government* (2000).

Norma Basch, *In the Eyes of the Law: Women, Marriage, and Property in Nineteenth-Century New York* (1982).

Norma Basch, *Framing American Divorce: From the Revolutionary Generation to the Victorians* (1999).

Catherine A. Brekus, *Strangers and Pilgrims: Female Preaching in America, 1740–1845* (1998).

Jon Butler, *Awash in a Sea of Faith: Christianizing the American People* (1990).

Nancy Cott, *Public Vows: A History of Marriage and the Nation* (2001).

Philip Greven, *The Protestant Temperament: Patterns of Child-Rearing, Religious Experience, and the Self in Early America* (1977).

Michael Grossberg, *Governing the Hearth: Law and the Family in Nineteenth-Century America* (1985).

Hendrik Hartog, *Man and Wife in America: A History* (2000).

Nathan Hatch, *The Democratization of American Christianity* (1989).

Nancy Isenberg, *Sex and Citizenship in Antebellum America* (1998).

Susan Juster, *Disorderly Women: Sexual Politics and Evangelicalism in Revolutionary New England* (1994).

Linda Kerber, *Women of the Republic* (1980).

Jan Lewis, *The Pursuit of Happiness: Family and Values in Jefferson's Virginia* (1983).

Carla Pestana, *Quakers and Baptists in Colonial Massachusetts* (1991).

Marylynn Salmon, *Women and the Law of Property in Early America* (1986).

Suzanne R. Thurman, *"O Sisters Ain't You Happy?": Gender, Family, and Community among the Harvard and Shirley Shakers, 1781–1918* (2002).

Laurel Thatcher Ulrich, *A Midwife's Tale: The Life of Martha Ballard, Based on Her Diary, 1786–1812* (1990).

Monroe and Adams Presidencies

Harry Ammon, *James Monroe: The Quest for National Identity* (1971).

Noble E. Cunningham Jr., *The Presidency of James Monroe* (1996).

George Dangerfield, *The Era of Good Feelings* (1952).

Don E. Fehrenbacher, *The South and Three Sectional Crises* (1980).

Mary W. M. Hargreaves, *The Presidency of John Quincy Adams* (1986).

Shaw Livermore, *The Twilight of Federalism: The Disintegration of the Federalist Party, 1815–1830* (1962).

Ernest R. May, *The Making of the Monroe Doctrine* (1975).

Paul C. Nagel, *John Quincy Adams: A Public Life, a Private Life* (1997).

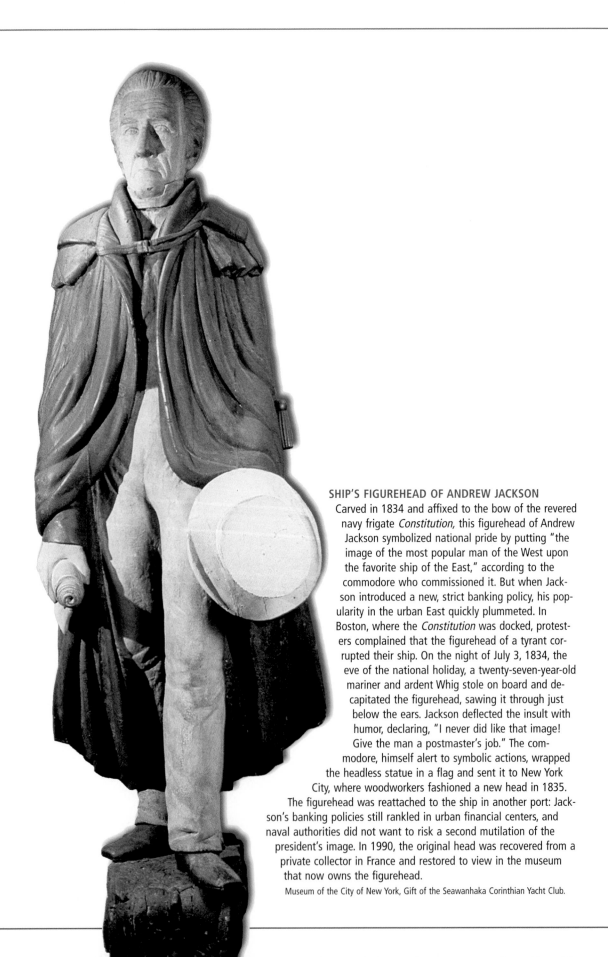

SHIP'S FIGUREHEAD OF ANDREW JACKSON

Carved in 1834 and affixed to the bow of the revered navy frigate *Constitution,* this figurehead of Andrew Jackson symbolized national pride by putting "the image of the most popular man of the West upon the favorite ship of the East," according to the commodore who commissioned it. But when Jackson introduced a new, strict banking policy, his popularity in the urban East quickly plummeted. In Boston, where the *Constitution* was docked, protesters complained that the figurehead of a tyrant corrupted their ship. On the night of July 3, 1834, the eve of the national holiday, a twenty-seven-year-old mariner and ardent Whig stole on board and decapitated the figurehead, sawing it through just below the ears. Jackson deflected the insult with humor, declaring, "I never did like that image! Give the man a postmaster's job." The commodore, himself alert to symbolic actions, wrapped the headless statue in a flag and sent it to New York City, where woodworkers fashioned a new head in 1835. The figurehead was reattached to the ship in another port: Jackson's banking policies still rankled in urban financial centers, and naval authorities did not want to risk a second mutilation of the president's image. In 1990, the original head was recovered from a private collector in France and restored to view in the museum that now owns the figurehead.

Museum of the City of New York, Gift of the Seawanhaka Corinthian Yacht Club.

The Expanding Republic

1815–1840

PRESIDENT ANDREW JACKSON was the dominant figure of his age, yet his precarious childhood little foretold the fame, fortune, and influence he would enjoy in the years after 1815. Jackson was born in the Carolina backcountry in 1767. His Scots-Irish father had recently died, leaving a poor, struggling mother to support three small boys. During the Revolution, Andrew followed his brothers into the militia, where both died of disease, as did his mother. Orphaned at fourteen, Jackson drifted around, drinking, gambling, and brawling.

But at seventeen, his prospects improved. He studied under a lawyer for three years and then moved to Nashville, a **frontier** community full of opportunities for a young man with legal training and an aggressive temperament. He became a public prosecutor, married into a leading family, and acquired land and slaves. When Tennessee became a state in 1796, Jackson, then twenty-nine, was elected to Congress for a single term.

Jackson captured national attention in 1815 by leading the victory at the Battle of New Orleans. With little else to celebrate about the War of 1812, many Americans seized on the Tennessee general as the champion of the day. Songs, broadsides, and an admiring biography set him up as the original self-made man, the parentless child magically responsible for his own destiny. Jackson seemed to have created himself, a gritty, forceful personality extracting opportunities from the dynamic, turbulent frontier.

Jackson was more than a man of action, however. He was also strong-willed, reckless, and quick to anger, impulsively challenging men to duels, sometimes on slight pretexts. In one legendary fight in 1806, Jackson deliberately let his opponent, an expert marksman, shoot first. The bullet hit him in a rib, but Jackson masked all sign of injury under a loose cloak and immobile face. He then took careful aim at the astonished man and killed him. Such steely courage chilled his political opponents.

Jackson's image as a tough frontier hero set him apart from the learned and privileged gentlemen from Virginia and Massachusetts who had occupied the presidency up to 1828. When he lost the 1824 election to John Quincy Adams, an infuriated Jackson vowed to fight a rematch. He won in 1828 and again in 1832, capturing large majorities. His appeal stretched across the urban working classes of the East, frontier voters of the West, and slaveholders in the South, who all saw something of themselves in Jackson. Once elected, he brought a combative style to politics and enlarged the powers of the presidency.

The confidence and even recklessness of Jackson's personality mirrored the new confidence of American society in the years after 1815. An entrepreneurial spirit gripped the country, producing a market revolution of unprecedented scale. Old social hierarchies eroded; ordinary men dreamed of moving high on the ladder of success, just as Jackson had done. Stunning advances in transportation and economic productivity fueled such dreams and propelled thousands to move west or to cities. Urban growth and technological change fostered the diffusion of a distinctive and vibrant public culture, spread through newspapers and the spoken word. The development of rapid print allowed popular opinions to coalesce and intensify; Jackson's sudden nationwide celebrity was a case in point.

Expanded communication transformed politics dramatically. Sharp disagreements over the best way to promote individual **liberty**, economic opportunity, and national prosperity in the new market economy defined key differences between Jackson and Adams and the parties they gave rise to in the 1830s. The process of party formation brought new habits of political participation and party loyalty to many thousands more adult white males. Religion became democratized as well: A nationwide **evangelical** revival brought its adherents the certainty that salvation and perfection were now available to all.

As president from 1829 to 1837, Jackson presided over all these changes, fighting some and supporting others in his vigorous and volatile way. As with his own stubborn person-

MAP 11.1 Routes of Transportation in 1840

By the 1830s, transportation advances had cut travel times significantly. Goods and people could move from New York City to Buffalo, New York, in four days by way of the Erie Canal, a trip that took two weeks by road in 1800. A trip from New York to New Orleans that took four weeks in 1800 could be accomplished in less than half that time on steamboats in the western rivers.

READING THE MAP: In what parts of the country were canals built most extensively? Were most of them within a single state's borders, or did they encourage interstate travel and shipping? **CONNECTIONS:** What impact did the Erie Canal have on the development of New York City? How did improvements in transportation affect urbanization in other parts of the country?

FOR MORE HELP ANALYZING THIS MAP, see the map activity for this chapter in the Online Study Guide at bedfordstmartins.com/roark.

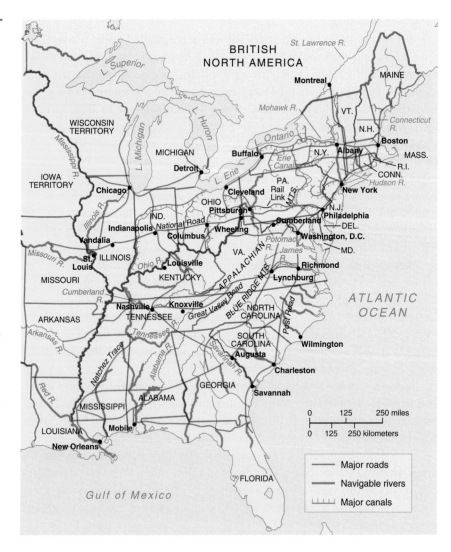

ality, there was a dark underside to the confidence and expansiveness of American society. Steamboats blew up, banks and businesses periodically collapsed, alcoholism rates soared, Indians were killed or relocated farther west, and slavery continued to expand. The brash confidence that turned some people into rugged, self-promoting, Jackson-like individuals inspired others to think about the human costs of rapid economic expansion and thus about reforming society in dramatic ways. The common denominator was a faith that people and societies can shape their own destinies.

The Market Revolution

The return of peace in 1815 unleashed powerful forces that revolutionized the organization of the economy. Spectacular changes in transportation facilitated the movement of commodities, information, and people, while textile mills and other factories created many new jobs, especially for young unmarried women. Innovations in banking, legal practices, and tariff policies promoted swift economic growth.

This was not yet an industrial revolution but a market revolution, fueled by traditional sources—water, wood, beasts of burden, and human muscle. What was new was the accelerated pace of economic activity and the scale of distribution of goods. Men and women were drawn out of old patterns of rural self-sufficiency into the wider realm of national market relations. At the same time, the nation's money supply enlarged considerably, leading to speculative investments in commerce, manufacturing, transportation, and land. The new nature and scale of production and consumption changed Americans' economic behavior, leading to raised expectations of material improvement. But in 1819 and again in 1837, serious crashes of the economy punctured those optimistic expectations.

Improvements in Transportation

Before 1815, transportation in the United States was slow and expensive; it cost as much to ship freight over thirty miles of domestic roads as it did to send the same cargo across the Atlantic Ocean. The fastest stagecoach trip from Boston to New York took an uncomfortable four days. But between 1815 and 1840, networks of roads, canals, steamboats, and finally railroads dramatically raised the speed and lowered the cost of travel (Map 11.1). Andrew Jackson spent weeks walking and riding west to Nashville in the 1790s along old Indian trails, but when he returned east in 1829, the new president traveled by steamboat and turnpike to Washington, D.C., in a matter of days.

Improved transportation moved goods and products into much wider markets. It moved people too, broadening the horizons of passengers on business and pleasure trips and allowing youth to take up new employment in cities or factory towns. Transportation also facilitated the flow of political and other information through heavy traffic in newspapers, periodicals, and books.

Enhanced public transport was expensive and produced uneven economic benefits, so administrations from Jefferson to Monroe were reluctant to fund it with federal dollars. Only the National Road, begun in 1806, was government sponsored. By 1818, it extended from Baltimore to Wheeling, in western Virginia. Instead, private investors pooled resources and chartered stagecoach, canal, steamboat, and railroad companies, receiving significant aid from state governments in the form of subsidies and guarantees of **monopoly** rights. Turnpike and roadway mileage dramatically increased after 1815, reducing the cost of land shipment of goods. Stagecoach lines proliferated in an extensive network of passenger corridors dense in the populated East and fanning out to the Mississippi River. Travel time on main routes was cut in half; Boston to New York now took two days.

Water travel was similarly transformed. In 1807, Robert Fulton's steam-propelled boat, the *Clermont*, churned upstream on the Hudson River from New York City to Albany in thirty-two hours, touching off a steamboat craze. In 1820, a dozen boats left New York City daily, and scores more operated on midwestern rivers and the Great Lakes. A voyager on one of the first steamboats to go down the Mississippi reported that the Chickasaw Indians called the vessel a "fire canoe" and considered it "an omen of evil." By the early 1830s, steamboat travel in the East was routine, and more than seven hundred steamboats were in operation on the Ohio and Mississippi rivers. A journey upriver from New Orleans to Louisville, Kentucky, took only one week.

Steamboats were not benign advances, however. The urgency to cut travel time led to

> The new nature and scale of production and consumption changed Americans' behavior, attitudes, and expectations.

Early Steamboats

Steamboats revolutionized travel in the early nineteenth century. The basic technology consisted of an engine powered by the steam from a boiler heated by a wood-burning furnace. The steam first collected in a cylinder and then cooled and condensed to create a vacuum that drove a piston, which in turn propelled a paddlewheel mounted at the side or the stern of the boat. From the 1780s to 1807, several inventors sought the ideal combination of engine size, boat size, and paddlewheel type. Robert Fulton's *Clermont* of 1807 was not the first American steamboat, but it was the first long-distance, commercially successful endeavor.

Two advantages marked Fulton's effort: He imported a superior British-made engine, a low-pressure model built with many precision parts, and he formed a partnership with New York businessman Robert R. Livingston. Livingston had acquired from the New York state legislature in 1798 the right to a twenty-year monopoly on all steam transportation on the Hudson River, on the condition that he produce a boat capable of traveling four miles per hour upriver. The *Clermont* met that test.

In 1811, Fulton and Livingston launched the first steamboat on the Mississippi River. Their low-pressure engine, operating at about two pounds per square inch of pressure

in the cylinder, failed to maneuver against the river's shifting currents and many obstructions. A high-pressure steam engine developed by Delaware entrepreneur Oliver Evans proved far more suitable. Generating pressures from eighty to one hundred pounds per square inch, it required 30 percent more fuel, but at that time wood was plentiful along western waterways. By the 1830s, there were many hundreds of boats on the Mississippi, the Ohio, and the lower Missouri rivers, run by companies competing to reduce travel time. An upriver trip from New Orleans to Louisville that took nearly a month in the 1810s took less than a week in the 1830s. The American traveling public fell in love with steamboats for their speed and power.

Steamboats offered luxury as well as speed. They often were floating palaces, carrying several hundred passengers and providing swank accommodations to ladies and gentlemen paying first-class fares. A few boats had private cabins, but most often there were two large rooms, one for each sex, filled with chairs that converted to beds. (The separation of sexes answered an important need in addition to bodily modesty: Women travelers often expressed their disgust over the spit-drenched carpets in the men's cabin.) Dining rooms with elegant appointments served elaborate meals. Many

steamboats had gambling rooms as well. Low-fare passengers, typically men, occupied the lower decks, finding sleeping space out in the open or in crowded berths in public rooms. Often these men were pressed into service loading wood at the frequent fueling stops.

The fire and smoke of a steamboat proved awesome and even terrifying to many. An older gent making his first trip in 1836 wrote that "I went on board, and passing the fireroom, where they were just firing up, I stopped, with unfeigned horror, and asked myself if, indeed, I was prepared to die!" But many others were enthralled by the unprecedented power represented by the belching smoke. Impromptu boat racing became a popular sport. A German traveler identified a competitive streak in American passengers: "When two steamboats happen to get alongside each other, the passengers will encourage the captains to run a race. . . . The boilers intended for a pressure of only 100 pounds per square inch, are by the accelerated generation of steam, exposed to a pressure of 150, and even 200 pounds, and this goes sometimes so far, that the trials end with an explosion."

Steamboats were far from safe. Between 1811 and 1851, accidents destroyed nearly 1,000 boats—a third of all steam vessels built in that period. More than half the sinkings resulted from underwater debris that penetrated hulls. Fires, too, were fearsome hazards in wooden boats that commonly carried highly combustible cargoes, such as raw cotton in burlap bags. The development of

overstoked furnaces, sudden boiler explosions, and terrible mass fatalities. (See "The Promise of Technology," on this page.) Another huge cost, to the environment, was the deforestation brought by steamboats, which had to load fuel—"wood up"—every twenty miles or so. By the 1830s the banks of main rivers were denuded of trees, and forests miles in from the rivers fell to the ax.

LEXINGTON

Awful Conflagration of the Steam boat LEXINGTON *In Long Island Sound on Monday Eve.ª Jan.ʸ 13ᵗʰ 1840, by which melancholy occurrence ; over 100 PERSONS PERISHED.*

"The Awful Conflagration of the Steamboat *Lexington* in Long Island Sound," 1840

The *Lexington* was six years old in 1840 and equipped with many extra safety features, such as a fire engine and pump, but with only three lifeboats. The lifeboats could accommodate only half of the passengers; they were quickly swamped in the emergency and rendered useless. Only four people survived; many of the 139 victims froze to death in the icy January waters. Consider this lithograph as a commodity made for sale in many thousands of copies: Who would buy this kind of artistic production?

The Mariners Museum, Newport News, VA.

sheet metal, which strengthened hulls and protected wooden surfaces near the smokestacks from sparks, was a major safety advance.

Boiler explosions were the most horrifying cause of accidents. By far the greatest loss of life came from scalding steam, flying wreckage, and fire, which could engulf a boat in a matter of minutes. In the 1830s alone, 89 boiler explosions caused 861 deaths and many more injuries. The cause of explosion was often mysterious: Was it excessive steam pressure or weak metal? Exactly how much pressure could plate iron fastened with rivets really withstand? Did a dangerous or explosive gas develop in the boiler when the water level fell too low? Or was the principal cause human error—reckless or drunk pilots (none of them licensed) or captains bent on breaking speed records?

And who was responsible for public safety? When the three-week-old *Moselle* blew up near Cincinnati in 1838, with the loss of 150 lives, a citizen's committee fixed blame on the twenty-eight-year-old captain, who had ordered the fires stoked with pitch and the safety valves shut to build up a bigger head of steam. "Such disasters have their foundation in the present mammoth evil of our country, an inordinate love of gain," said the committee. "We are not satisfied with getting rich, but we must get rich in a day. We are not satisfied with traveling at a speed of ten miles an hour, but we must fly. Such is the effect of competition that everything must be done cheap; boiler iron must be cheap, traveling must be done cheap, freight must be cheap, yet everything must be speedy. A steamboat must establish a reputation of a few minutes 'swifter' in a hundred miles than others, before she can make fortunes fast enough to satisfy the owners."

In 1830, the federal government awarded a grant to the Franklin Institute of Philadelphia to study the causes of boiler explosions. But not until 1852 did public safety become a federal responsibility with the passage of regulations by Congress mandating steamboat inspections. After the Civil War, affordable sheet steel and the development of new welding techniques produced boilers that were much stronger and safer.

Steamboats burned large amounts of wood, transferring the carbon stored in trees into the atmosphere, creating America's first signficant air pollution.

Canals were another major innovation of the transportation revolution. These shallow highways of water (sometimes just four feet deep) allowed passage for barges and boats pulled by

View of the Erie Canal at Lockport
The Erie Canal struck many as the eighth wonder of the world when it was completed in 1825, not only for its length of 350 miles but also for its impressive elevation. Eighty-three locks were required to move canal boats over the combined ascent and descent of 680 feet. The biggest challenge of the entire route came at Lockport, 20 miles northeast of Buffalo, where the canal had to traverse a steep escarpment of rocky slate. Work crews—mostly immigrant Irishmen—used gunpowder and grueling physical labor to blast out a deep artificial gorge into the cliff; note the raw cut rock on the left. Next, five double locks were constructed to move boats in stages up and down the 60-foot elevation. Pedestrians would take the stairs that separate the locks, while barge animals would take the towpath on the far side. Even with double locks, this passage surely created bottlenecks in traffic on the canal. So, not surprisingly, a village grew here to service waiting passengers and crews; its name, Lockport, was probably an obvious choice.
Library of Congress.

horses or mules trudging on a towpath beside the canal. Travel speed was slow, under five miles per hour, but the economy came from increased loads. The low-friction water allowed one horse to pull a fifty-ton barge. In winter, canals froze over and became smooth stump- and rock-free highways for sleighs.

Pennsylvania in 1815 and New York in 1817 commenced major state-sponsored canal enterprises. Pennsylvania's Schuylkill Canal stretched from Philadelphia 108 miles west into the state when it was completed in 1826. It was overshadowed by the impressive Erie Canal in New York, finished in 1825, stretching 350 miles between Albany on the Hudson River and Buffalo on Lake Erie. The canal was a waterbridge linking the port of New York City with the entire Northwest Territory. Wheat and flour moved east, textiles and other goods moved west, and passengers went in both directions. By the 1830s, the cost of shipping by canal fell to less than a tenth of the cost of overland transport, and New York City quickly blossomed into the premier commercial city in the United States.

In the 1830s, private railroad companies began to give canals stiff competition, and by the mid-1840s the canal-building era was over. (However, use of the canals for freight continued well into the twentieth century.) The nation's first railroad, the Baltimore and Ohio, laid thirteen miles of track in 1829. During the 1830s, three thousand more miles of track materialized nationwide, the result of a speculative fever in railroad construction master-minded by bankers, locomotive manufacturers, and state legislators, who provided subsidies, charters, and land rights-of-way. Rail lines in the 1830s were generally short, on the order of twenty to one hundred miles; they were not yet an efficient distribution system for goods. But passengers flocked to experience the marvelous travel speeds of fifteen to twenty miles per hour, enduring the frightful noise and cascades of cinders that rained on them.

Taken together, the advances in transportation by the 1830s were little short of revolutionary. They made possible an economic and cultural unification of the United States, connecting far-flung rural outposts with the broader currents of social change.

Factories, Workingwomen, and Wage Labor

Transportation advances promoted a rapid expansion of manufacturing after 1815. Teamsters and bargemen hauled consumer products such as shoes, textiles, clocks, and books into nationwide distribution. Some of the gain in manufacturing, especially in the textile industry, came from the development of water-driven machinery, built near fast-coursing rivers. (The steam power harnessed for steamboats and railroads had limited application in industry until the 1840s.) Much of the new manufacturing involved a reorganization of production, still using the power and skill of human hands, as well as improved mechanical devices. Both mechanized and manual manufacturing pulled young women into the labor market for the first time and greatly enlarged the segment of the population earning a living by selling labor for hourly wages.

The earliest factory, built by British immigrant Samuel Slater in Pawtucket, Rhode Island, in the 1790s, featured a mechanical spinning machine that produced thread and yarn. By 1815, nearly 170 spinning mills dotted lower New England, along streams and rivers. Unlike English

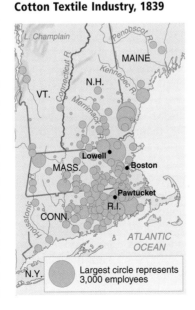

Cotton Textile Industry, 1839

Largest circle represents 3,000 employees

manufacturing cities, where entire families worked in low-wage, health-threatening factories, American factories targeted young women as employees, cheap to hire because of their limited employment options. Mill girls would retire to marriage, replaced by fresh recruits earning a beginner's wage. There would thus be no class of permanent poor clustered around factories, and factory labor would remain cheap.

In 1821, a group of Boston entrepreneurs founded the town of Lowell, on the Merrimack River, where all aspects of cloth production—carding, fulling, spinning, weaving, and dyeing—were centralized. By 1830, the eight mills in Lowell employed more than 5,000 young women, most of them sixteen to twenty-three years old. A key innovation was the close moral supervision of the female workers, who lived in company-owned boardinghouses with housemothers, four to six girls per bedroom. Corporation rules required regular church attendance and prohibited card playing, drinking, and unsupervised courtship; dorm lockdown came at 10 P.M. Typical mill workers averaged $2 to $3 for a seventy-hour workweek, more than a seamstress or domestic servant could earn but less than a young man's wages. The job consisted of tending noisy power looms in large rooms kept hot and humid, ideal for thread but not for people. (See "American Places," page 363.)

Despite the discomforts, young women left farms and flocked to factory towns in the hope of gaining more autonomy. They welcomed the unprecedented if still limited personal freedom of living in an all-female social space, away from parents and domestic tasks and with pay in their pockets. In Lowell, the women could engage in evening self-improvement activities, such as attending lectures or writing for the company's periodical, *The Lowell Offering*.

In the mid-1830s, worldwide changes in the cotton market impelled mill owners to speed up

> The mill workers welcomed the unprecedented if still limited personal freedom of living in an all-female social space, away from parents and domestic tasks and with pay in their pockets.

Mill Worker Tending a Power Loom, 1850
This daguerreotype—the earliest form of photograph (see page 482)—shows a young woman weaver tending a power loom in a textile mill. Her main task was to replace the spindle of thread when it ran out, by reloading a new spindle into the shuttle. The close-up shows a shuttle next to spindles of pink and blue thread. The factory operative also had to be constantly alert for sudden breaks in the wrap yarn which then required a fast shut-down of the loom and a quick repair of the thread. In the 1830s, women weavers generally tended two machines at a time; in the 1840s, some companies increased the workload to four.
Mill worker: American Textile History Museum; shuttle with spindle: Picture Research Consultants & Archives.

work and lower wages. The workers protested, emboldened by their communal living arrangements and by their relative independence from the job as temporary employees. In 1834 and again in 1836, hundreds of women at Lowell went out on strike. All over New England, female mill workers led strikes and formed unions. Women at a mill in Dover, New Hampshire, in 1834 denounced their owners for trying to turn them into "slaves": "However freely the epithet of 'factory slaves' may be bestowed upon us, we will never deserve it by a base and cringing submission to proud wealth or haughty insolence." Their assertiveness surprised many; but ultimately their easy replaceability undermined their bargaining power, and owners in the 1840s began to shift to immigrant families as their labor source.

Other manufacturing enterprises of the 1820s and 1830s, such as shoemaking, employed women in ever larger numbers. New modes of organizing the work allowed the manufacturers to step up production, control wastage and quality, and lower wages by subdividing the tasks and by hiring women, including wives. Male workers cut leather and made soles. The stitching of the upper part of the shoe, called shoebinding, became women's work, performed at home so that it could mesh with domestic chores. Although their wages were lower than men's, shoebinder wives contributed earned cash to family income.

In the economically turbulent 1830s, the new shoe entrepreneurs cut shoebinder wages. Unlike the mill workers in factories, women shoebinders worked in isolation, a serious hindrance to organized protest. In Lynn, Massachusetts, a major shoemaking center, women turned to other female networks, mainly churches, as sites for

AMERICAN PLACES

Lowell National Historic Park, Lowell, Massachusetts

L owell was America's first planned factory town. Eight large textile mills and hundreds of boardinghouses provided work and housing for the unprecedented concentration of 5,000 female factory operatives who lived there in the 1830s. These mill girls pioneered several experiences entirely new to young American women. Freed from the watchful scrutiny (as well as kindly protection) of parents, they slept in dormitories, lived by the clock backed up by the insistent factory bell, and worked very long hours in deafening machine rooms. They also earned cash wages, escaped domestic drudgery, and made new friends. Little wonder that Lowell quickly became a showcase city, to which European and American tourists flocked to see water-powered manufacturing free of smoke and a novel labor force seemingly free of poverty and vice.

In the twenty-first century, tourists still arrive at Lowell to experience the historic restoration of several of the old mills. The Boott Cotton Mills Museum features a room with eighty-eight power looms. In the 1830s, similar looms were driven by the power of the coursing Merrimack River diverted into nearly six miles of canals that threaded their way around and under the manufacturing buildings. A few of the power looms in Boott Mills stay in operation as tourists walk through the room, experiencing the incredible din and roar of that early machinery. National Park Service rangers hand out earplugs—something that mill workers of the 1830s must have improvised somehow. But the discomfort went beyond noise: Workers spoke of the constant vibration of the work rooms.

Next to Boott Mills is a restored boardinghouse where crowded tables are set for a swift midday meal. Factory timetables show that a mere 35 minutes was allowed for this break, including travel time to and from the boardinghouse and bathroom time. This was the only official break of what was a 12-hour workday yearlong. In upstairs bedrooms, two double beds accommodated four to six roommates per room.

Lowell remained an active textile town until the 1930s, but the labor force changed over time. As wages fell and other occupations (such as teaching) opened to women, fewer New England girls came to Lowell. Their places were taken by Irish girls and then by entire Irish families in the 1850s, then by Poles and other immigrant groups. Aging mills were not modernized, and in the early twentieth century, textile producers moved operations to the South, where labor tended to be nonunion and thus cheaper. In the 1920s and 1930s, the Lowell factories started to close, and urban decay set in, accelerated by the Great Depression. The gritty Lowell of the mid-twentieth century has now come back to a semblance of its former self, as a scrubbed-up stop on the circuit of early American historical sites.

FOR WEB LINKS RELATED TO THIS SITE AND OTHER AMERICAN PLACES, see "PlaceLinks" at bedfordstmartins.com/roark.

Boott Mills
Kevin Harkins.

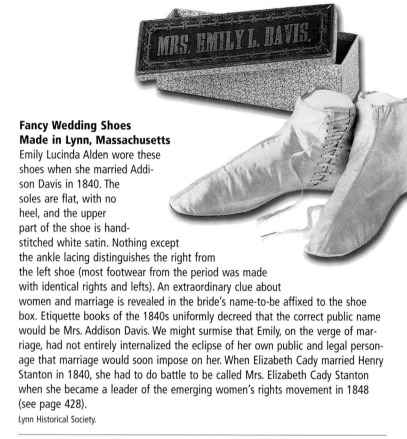

**Fancy Wedding Shoes
Made in Lynn, Massachusetts**
Emily Lucinda Alden wore these
shoes when she married Addison Davis in 1840. The
soles are flat, with no
heel, and the upper
part of the shoe is hand-
stitched white satin. Nothing except
the ankle lacing distinguishes the right from
the left shoe (most footwear from the period was made
with identical rights and lefts). An extraordinary clue about
women and marriage is revealed in the bride's name-to-be affixed to the shoe
box. Etiquette books of the 1840s uniformly decreed that the correct public name
would be Mrs. Addison Davis. We might surmise that Emily, on the verge of marriage, had not entirely internalized the eclipse of her own public and legal person-
age that marriage would soon impose on her. When Elizabeth Cady married Henry
Stanton in 1840, she had to do battle to be called Mrs. Elizabeth Cady Stanton
when she became a leader of the emerging women's rights movement in 1848
(see page 428).
Lynn Historical Society.

meetings and to religious newspapers as forums
for communication. The Lynn shoebinders who
demanded higher wages in 1834 built on a
collective sense of themselves as women even
though they did not share daily work lives.
"Equal rights should be extended to all—to the
weaker sex as well as the stronger," they wrote in
a document forming the Female Society of Lynn.

In the end, the Lynn shoebinders' protests
failed to achieve wage increases. Isolated workers all over New England continued to accept
low wages, and even in Lynn, many women
shied away from organized protest, preferring to
situate their work in the context of family duty
(helping their menfolk to finish shoes) instead of
market relations.

Bankers and Lawyers

Entrepreneurs like the Lowell factory owners
relied on innovations in the banking system to
finance their ventures. The number of state-
chartered banks in the United States more than
doubled in the boom years 1814–1816, from
fewer than 90 to 208; by 1830, there were 330, and

hundreds more by 1840. Banks stimulated the
economy by making loans to merchants and
manufacturers and by enlarging the money supply. Borrowers were issued loans in the form of
banknotes—certificates unique to each bank.

Borrowers used the notes exactly as they
used money, for all transactions. Neither
federal nor state governments issued paper
money, so banknotes became the currency
of the country.

In theory, a note could always be
traded in at a bank for its **hard-money**
equivalent in gold or silver (a transaction
known as "specie payment"). A note from a
solid local bank might be worth exactly what it
was written for, but if a note came from a distant
or questionable bank, its value would be dis-
counted by a fraction. Buying and selling banknotes in Jacksonian America surely required
knowledge and caution. Not surprisingly, counterfeiting flourished under these conditions.

Bankers exercised great power over the economy, deciding who would get loans and what the
discount rates would be. The most powerful
bankers sat on the board of directors for the second Bank of the United States, headquartered in
Philadelphia. (The first Bank of the United States,
chartered in 1791, had lapsed in 1811.) The second
Bank of the United States, with eighteen branches
throughout the country, opened for business in
1816 under a twenty-year charter. The rechartering of this bank would prove to be a major issue
in Andrew Jackson's reelection campaign in 1832.

Accompanying the market revolution was a
revolution in commercial law, fashioned by
politicians to enhance the prospects of private investment. By 1820, most representatives in the
U.S. Congress were lawyers, and a similar wave
of legal professionals moved into state politics.
Starting in 1811, states rewrote laws of incorporation (the chartering of businesses by states),
and the number of corporations expanded
rapidly, from about twenty in 1800 to eighteen
hundred by 1817. Incorporation protected individual investors from being held liable for corporate financial debts. State lawmakers also
wrote laws of eminent domain, empowering
states to buy land for roads and canals, even
from unwilling sellers. They drafted legislation
on contributory negligence, relieving employers
from responsibility for workplace injuries. In
such ways, entrepreneurial lawyers of the 1820s
and 1830s created the legal foundation for an
economy that gave priority to ambitious individuals interested in maximizing their own wealth.

Not everyone applauded these developments. Andrew Jackson, himself a skillful lawyer-turned-politician, spoke for a large and mistrustful segment of the population when he warned about the abuses of power "which the moneyed interest derives from a paper currency which they are able to control, from the multitude of corporations with exclusive privileges which they have succeeded in obtaining in the different states, and which are employed altogether for their benefit." Jacksonians believed that ending government-granted privileges was the way to maximize individual liberty and economic opportunity.

Booms and Busts

One aspect of the economy that the lawyer-politicians could not control was the threat of financial collapse. The boom years from 1815 to 1818 exhibited a volatility that resulted in the first sharp, large-scale economic downturn in U.S. history, a depression that Americans called a "panic"; the pattern was repeated in the 1830s. Rapidly rising consumer demand stimulated rising prices for goods, and speculative investment opportunities with high payoffs abounded—in bank stocks, western land sales, urban real estate, and commodities markets. Steep inflation made some people wealthy but created hardships for workers on fixed incomes.

When the bubble burst in 1819, the overnight rich suddenly became the overnight poor. Some suspected that a precipitating cause of the panic of 1819 was the second Bank of the United States. For too long, the bank had neglected to exercise control over state banks, many of which had suspended specie payments—the exchange of gold or silver for banknotes—in their eagerness to make loans and expand the economic bubble. Then, in mid-1818, the Bank of the United States started to call in its loans and insisted that state banks do likewise. The contraction of the money supply created tremors throughout the economy, a foretaste of the catastrophe to come.

What made the crunch worse was a parallel financial crisis in Europe in the spring of 1819. Overseas prices of cotton, tobacco, and wheat plummeted by more than 50 percent. Now when the Bank of the United States and state banks tried to call in their outstanding loans, debtors involved in the commodities trade could not pay. The number of business and personal bankruptcies skyrocketed. The intricate web of credit and debt relationships meant that almost everyone with even a toehold in the new commercial economy was affected by the panic of 1819. Thousands of Americans lost their savings and property, and unemployment estimates suggest that a half million people lost their jobs.

Recovery from the panic of 1819 took several years. Unemployment rates fell, but bitterness lingered, ready to be mobilized by politicians in the decades to come. The dangers of a system dependent on extensive credit were now clear: In one memorable, folksy formulation that circulated around 1820, a farmer was said to compare credit to "a man pissing in his breeches on a cold day to keep his arse warm—very comfortable at first but I dare say . . . you know how it feels afterwards."

By the mid-1820s, the booming economy was back on track, driven by increases in productivity and consumer demand for goods, an accelerating international trade, and a restless and calculating people moving goods, human labor, and investment capital in expanding circles of commerce. But an undercurrent of anxiety about rapid economic change continued to shape the political views of many Americans.

The Spread of Democracy

Just as the market revolution held out the promise, if not the reality, of economic opportunity for anyone who worked hard, the political transformation of the 1830s held out the promise of political opportunity for hundreds of thousands of new voters. Between 1829 and 1837, the years of Andrew Jackson's presidency, the second American party system took shape, although not until 1836 would the parties have distinct names and consistent programs that transcended the particular personalities running for office. Over those years, more men could and did vote, responding to new methods of arousing voter interest. In 1828, Jackson's charismatic personality defined his party, and the election against

> Jacksonians believed that ending government-granted privileges was the way to maximize individual liberty and economic opportunity.

> Just as the market revolution held out the promise, if not the reality, of economic opportunity for anyone who worked hard, the political transformation of the 1830s held out the promise of political opportunity for hundreds of thousands of new voters.

John Quincy Adams was particularly personal, fought over questions of moral character. Once in office, Jackson identified his supporters as the ordinary citizens arrayed against the special power elite, or **democracy** versus aristocracy in Jackson's terminology. A lasting contribution of the Jackson years was the notion that politicians had to appear to have the common touch in an era when popularity with voters drove the electoral process.

Popular Politics and Partisan Identity

The election of 1828 was the first presidential contest in which popular votes determined the outcome. In twenty-two out of twenty-four states, voters—not state legislatures—chose the electors in the electoral college; each elector was committed in advance to a particular candidate. More than a million voters participated, three times the number in 1824 and nearly half the electorate, reflecting the high stakes that voters perceived in the Adams-Jackson rematch. Throughout the 1830s, the number of voters rose to all-time highs. This increase resulted partly from relaxed voting restrictions; by the mid-1830s, all but three states allowed universal white male **suffrage,** without property qualifications. But the higher turnout—over 70 percent in some states—also indicated increased political interest.

The 1828 election inaugurated new campaign styles as well. State-level candidates routinely gave speeches to woo the voters, appearing at rallies, picnics, and banquets. Adams and Jackson still declined such activities as too undignified; but Henry Clay of Kentucky, campaigning for Adams, earned the nickname "Barbecue Orator." Campaign rhetoric, under the necessity to create popular appeal, became more informal and even blunt. The Jackson camp established many Hickory Clubs, trading on Jackson's popular nickname, "Old Hickory," from a common Tennessee tree suggesting resilience and toughness. (Jackson was the first presidential candidate to have an affectionate and widely used nickname.)

Partisan newspapers defined issues and publicized political personalities as never before. Party leaders judiciously dispensed subsidies and other favors to secure the loyalties of papers,

> The campaign of 1828 was the first national election in which scandal and character questions reigned supreme.

even in remote towns and villages. In New York State, where party development was most advanced, a pro-Jackson group called the Bucktails controlled fifty weekly publications. Stories from the leading Jacksonian paper in Washington, D.C., were reprinted two days later in a Boston or Cincinnati paper, as fast as the mail stage could carry them. Presidential campaigns were now coordinated in a national arena.

Parties declined to adopt official names in 1828, still honoring the fiction of Republican Party unity. Instead, they called themselves the Jackson party or the Adams party. By the 1832 election, labels began to appear. Adams's political heir, Henry Clay, represented the National Republicans; Jackson's supporters called themselves Democratic Republicans. The National Republicans favored federal action to promote commercial development; the Democratic Republicans promised to be responsive to the will of the majority. By 1834, a few state-level National Republicans had changed their name to the Whig Party, a term that was in common use by 1836, the same year that Jackson's party became simply the Democrats. Thus, Whig and Democrat crystallized as names only at the end of an eight-year evolution.

The Election of 1828 and the Character Issue

The campaign of 1828 was the first national election in which scandal and character questions reigned supreme. John Quincy Adams was vilified by his opponents as an elitist, bookish academic, perhaps even a monarchist. Critics pointed to Adams's White House billiard table and ivory chess set as symbols of his aristocratic degeneracy along with the "corrupt bargain" of 1824, the alleged election deal between Adams and Henry Clay (see chapter 10). The Adams men returned fire with fire. They played on Jackson's fatherless childhood to portray him as the bastard son of a prostitute. Worse, the cloudy circumstances around his marriage to Rachel Donelson Robards in 1791 gave rise to the story that Jackson was a seducer and an adulterer, having married a woman whose divorce from her first husband was not entirely legal. Pro-Adams newspapers howled that Jackson was sinful and impulsive, while portraying Adams as pious, learned, and virtuous.

Editors in favor of Adams played up Jackson's notorious violent temper, evidenced by the many duels, brawls, and canings they

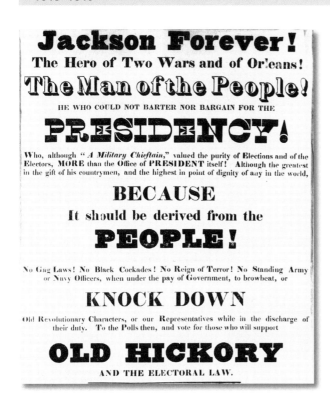

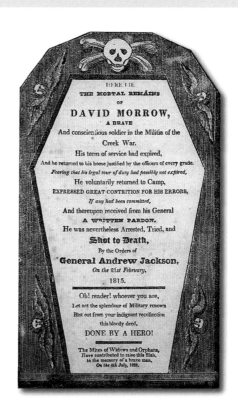

Campaign Posters from 1828

The campaign poster on the left praises Andrew Jackson as a war hero and "man of the people" and reminds readers that Jackson, who won the largest popular vote in 1824, did not stoop to bargain for the presidency, as presumably John Q. Adams did in his dealing with Henry Clay. (What "two wars" does the poster refer to?) The campaign poster at right, with ominous tombstone and coffin graphics, accuses Jackson of the unjustified killing of a Kentucky militiaman (one of six executed) during the Creek War in 1815. The text implores readers to think of the "hero" as a man capable of "bloody deeds."

Pro-Jackson broadside: © Collection of the New-York Historical Society; anti-Jackson broadside: Smithsonian Institute, Washington, D.C.

could recount. Jackson men used the same stories to project Old Hickory as a tough frontier hero who knew how to command obedience. As for learning, Jackson's rough frontier education gave him a "natural sense," wrote a Boston editor, which "can never be acquired by reading books—it can only be acquired, in perfection, by reading men."

These stories were not smoke screens to obscure the "real" issues in the election. They became real issues themselves because voters used them to comprehend the kind of public officer each man would make. Character issues conveyed in shorthand larger questions about morality, honor, and discipline; Jackson and Adams presented two radically different styles of masculinity.

Jackson won a sweeping victory, with 56 percent of the popular vote and 178 electoral votes, compared with Adams's 83 (Map 11.2).

MAP 11.2   The Election of 1828

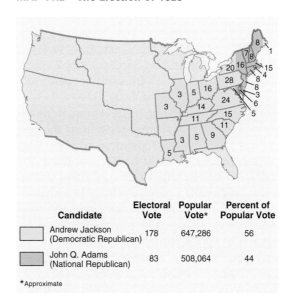

Candidate	Electoral Vote	Popular Vote*	Percent of Popular Vote
Andrew Jackson (Democratic Republican)	178	647,286	56
John Q. Adams (National Republican)	83	508,064	44

*Approximate

President Jackson's Kitchen Cabinet
Early in his administration, Jackson fell out with most of his official cabinet—largely over a social crisis provoked by the wives of cabinet officers. So Jackson turned to a set of close friends, quickly dubbed the Kitchen Cabinet by the press, for advice, for patronage decisions, and even for the drafting of official papers. Several were newspapermen; one was an old Tennessee friend, William B. Lewis, who moved into the White House with Jackson. Martin Van Buren was also in this inner circle. This cartoon purports to show a meeting of the Kitchen Cabinet: raucous, argumentative, violently employing the tools of women's work. How does its pointed message reflect the new partisan politics of the time?
Granger Collection.

contentious, energetic party (the Democrats) ready to embrace liberty-loving individualism.

Jackson's Democratic Agenda

Before the inauguration in March 1829, Rachel Jackson died. The president, certain that the ugly campaign had hastened her death, went into deep mourning. His depression was worsened by constant pain from the 1806 bullet still lodged in his chest and by mercury poisoning from the medicines he took. Sixty-two years old, he carried only 140 pounds on his six-foot-one frame. His adversaries doubted he would make it to a second term. His supporters, however, went wild at the inauguration. Thousands cheered his ten-minute inaugural address, the shortest in history. An open reception at the White House turned into a near riot as well-wishers jammed the premises, used windows as doors, stood on furniture for a better view of the great man, and broke thousands of dollars' worth of china and glasses.

During his presidency, Jackson continued to offer unprecedented hospitality to the public. Twenty spittoons newly installed in the East Room of the White House accommodated the tobacco spit of the throngs that arrived daily to see the president. The courteous Jackson, committed to his image as the president of the "common man," held audience with unannounced visitors throughout his two terms.

Jackson's cabinet appointments marked a departure. Past presidents had tried to lessen party conflict by including men of different factions in their cabinets, but Jackson would have only Jackson loyalists, a political tactic followed by most later presidents. The most important position, secretary of state, he offered to Martin Van Buren, one of the shrewdest politicians of the day and newly elected governor of New York.

Jackson put new stress on party allegiance throughout the federal government. As a candidate he promised to remove corrupt federal ap-

> The courteous Jackson, committed to his image as the president of the "common man," held audience with unannounced visitors throughout his two terms.

The victor took most of the South and West and carried Pennsylvania and New York as well. Jackson's vice president was John C. Calhoun, who had just served as vice president under Adams but had broken with Adams's policies.

After 1828, national politicians no longer deplored the existence of political parties. They were coming to see that parties mobilized and delivered voters, sharpened candidates' differences, and created party loyalty that surpassed loyalty to individual candidates and elections. Adams and Jackson clearly symbolized and defined for voters the competing ideas of the emerging parties: a moralistic, top-down party (the Whigs) ready to make major decisions to promote economic growth competing against a

pointees; as president he went further and removed competent civil servants as well on a newly asserted principle of rotation in office. There were some ten thousand civil servants on the federal payroll: ambassadors, judges, auditors, customs collectors, land office registrars, and thousands of local postmasters, clerks, and deputy clerks. In the end, Jackson removed fewer than one-tenth of these employees, so there was no clean sweep of the federal bureaucracy. But when he made replacement appointments, he made sure to reward party loyalists. "To the victor belong the spoils," said a Democratic senator from New York, expressing approval of patronage-driven appointments. Jackson's approach to civil service employment got tagged the **spoils system**; it was a concept the president strenuously defended.

Jackson's agenda quickly emerged once he was in office. Like Jefferson, he favored a limited federal government. Fearing that intervention in the economy inevitably favored some groups at the expense of others, he opposed federal support of transportation and grants of monopolies and charters that privileged wealthy investors. Like Jefferson, he anticipated rapid settlement of the country's interior, where land sales would spread economic democracy to settlers. Thus, establishing a federal policy to remove the Indians had high priority. Unlike Jefferson, however, Jackson exercised full presidential powers over Congress; a limited government did not mean a limited presidency. In 1830, he vetoed a highway project in Maysville, Kentucky— Henry Clay's home state—that Congress had voted to support with federal dollars. The Maysville Road veto articulated Jackson's principled stand that citizens' federal tax dollars could only be spent on projects of a "general, not local" character. In all, Jackson used the veto twelve times; all previous presidents had exercised that right a total of nine times.

Cultural Shifts

Despite differences on the best or fairest way to enhance commercial development, Jackson's Democratic Republicans and Henry Clay's National Republicans shared enthusiasm for the outcome—a growing, booming economy. For increasing numbers of families, especially in the highly commercialized Northeast, the standard of living rose, consumption patterns changed, and the nature and location of work altered.

All of these changes had a direct impact on the roles and duties of men and women and on the training of youth for the economy of the future. New ideas about gender relations in a commercial economy surfaced in printed material and in public behavior. In Jacksonian America, a widely shared public culture came into being, originating within the new commercial classes and spreading rapidly through rising levels of literacy and an explosion of print.

The Family and Separate Spheres

The centerpiece of new ideas about gender relations was the notion that husbands found their status and authority in the new world of work, leaving wives to tend the hearth and home. Sermons, advice books, periodicals, and novels reinforced the idea that men and women inhabited **separate spheres** and had separate duties. "To woman it belongs . . . to elevate the intellectual character of her household [and] to kindle the fires of mental activity in childhood," wrote Mrs. A. J. Graves in a popular book titled *Advice to American Women*. For men, in contrast, "the absorbing passion for gain, and the pressing demands of business, engross their whole attention." In particular, the home, now the exclusive domain of women, was sentimentalized as the source of intimacy, love, and safety, a refuge from the cruel and competitive world of market relations.

> The home, now the exclusive domain of women, was sentimentalized as a refuge from the cruel and competitive world of market relations.

Some new aspects of society gave substance to this formulation of separate spheres. Men's work was undergoing profound change after 1815, especially in the manufacturing Northeast and in urban areas both large—Boston, New York, Cincinnati— and small—Buffalo, Cleveland, Chicago. Increasingly, men's jobs brought cash to the household. Farmers and tradesmen sold products in a market, and bankers, bookkeepers, shoemakers, and canal diggers got pay envelopes. Furthermore, many men performed jobs outside of the home, at an office or store. For men who were not farmers, work indeed seemed newly disconnected from the home.

A woman's domestic role was more complicated than the cultural prescriptions indicated. Although the vast majority of married white women did not hold paying jobs, the home continued to be a site of time-consuming labor. But

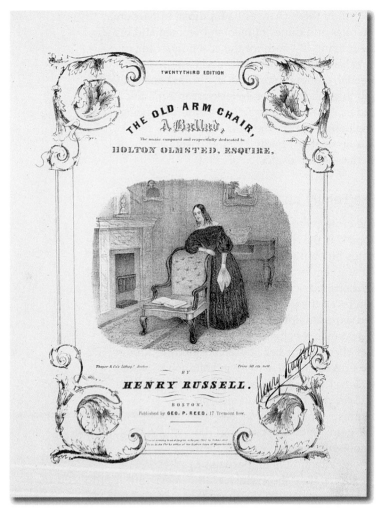

Sheet Music Cover from 1840
Popular songs in the early nineteenth century circulated in the form of sheet music, usually consisting of a cover picture and three pages of music scored for the piano. This lithographed cover illustrates a sentimental ballad called "The Old Arm Chair." A sad woman in black with handkerchief in hand stands behind an empty chair of a departed family member who has in all likelihood just died. (Note the piano behind her.) The armchair with open book (to suggest a very recent and perhaps somehow *temporary* departure) appeared in cemeteries as a sentimentalized stone monument over graves. Online sheet music collections allow a new form of downloading music: A pianist can print the scores and play hundreds of mawkish pop tunes from the 1830s and 1840s. The Library of Congress maintains a large collection at <http://memory.loc.gov/ammem/sm2html/sm2home.html>.
Collection of Lynn Wenzel.

for shoebinding, hatmaking, or needlework done at home. Even among the most comfortable classes, the market intruded whenever wives hired domestic servants to perform the heavy household tasks no true lady would consider doing, such as laundry. Most middle- and upper-income families hired servants; households striving to meet a respectable level of class display simply could not be run on the labor of one woman. Wives in the poorer classes of society, including most free black wives, did not have the luxury of husbands earning adequate wages; for them, work as servants or laundresses helped augment family income.

These idealized notions about the sentimental, noncommercial, feminine home and the masculine world of work gained acceptance in the 1830s (and well beyond) because of the cultural dominance of the middle and upper classes of the Northeast, expressed through books and periodical publications. The doctrine of separate spheres unambiguously defined masculinity and femininity: Men were to achieve a sense of manhood through work and pay; women established a sense of femininity through duty to the home and family and service to others. The convenient fiction of this formulation of gender difference helped smooth the path for the first generation of Americans experiencing the market revolution. The doctrine of separate spheres ordained that men would absorb and display the values appropriate to the market economy—competition, acquisitiveness—and women would exemplify and foster traditional, noncommercial values of virtuous service to family and community. Both men and women of the middle classes benefited from this bargain: Men were set free to pursue wealth, and women gained moral authority within the home. Beyond white families of the middle and upper classes, however, these new gender ideals had limited applicability. Despite their apparent dominance in printed material of the period, they were never all-pervasive.

The Education and Training of Youth

The market economy with its new expectations for men and women required fresh methods of training youth of both sexes. The generation that came of age in the 1820s and 1830s had opportunities for education and work unparalleled in previous eras, at least for white children in the middling classes and above. Northern states

the advice books treated household tasks as loving familial duties; housework as *work* was thereby rendered invisible in an economy that evaluated work by how much cash it generated.

In reality, wives directly contributed to family income in many ways. Some took in boarders, while others engaged in outwork, earning pay

adopted public schooling between 1790 and the 1820s, and in the 1820s and 1830s southern states followed suit. The curriculum produced pupils who were able, by age twelve or fourteen, to read, write, and participate in marketplace calculations. Remarkably, girls usually received the same basic education as boys. Literacy rates for white females climbed dramatically, rivaling the rates for white males for the first time.

The fact that taxpayers paid for children's education created an incentive to seek an inexpensive teaching force. By the 1830s, school districts began replacing male teachers with young females. Like mill workers, teachers were in their late teens and regarded the work as temporary. Often these female teachers had attended private female academies, hundreds of which were spread over all states of the Union. Starting in the 1830s, states from Massachusetts to Kentucky began to open teacher training schools ("normal" schools) exclusively for women students, because, as a Massachusetts report put it, "females can be educated cheaper, quicker, and better, and will teach cheaper after they are qualified." With the exception of Oberlin College in Ohio, no other colleges admitted women until after the Civil War, but a handful of private "female seminaries" established a rigorous curriculum that rivaled that of the best men's colleges. Three of the most prominent were the Troy Seminary in New

> The generation that came of age in the 1820s and 1830s had opportunities for education and work unparalleled in previous eras.

Women Graduates of Oberlin College, Class of 1855
Oberlin College was founded in Ohio by evangelical and abolitionist activists in the 1830s. It admitted white and black men and women, although in the early years the black students were all male and the women students were all white. Admission was not exactly equal: The women entered a separate Ladies' Department. By 1855, as this daguerreotype shows, black women had integrated the Ladies' Department. The two older women with bonnets were the principal and a member of the board. The students wear the latest fashion: dark taffeta dresses with sloping shoulders and a tight bodice topped by detachable white lace collars. Hair fashions were similarly uniform for women of all ages throughout the 1850s: a central part, hair dressed with oil and lustrously coiled over the ears. Compare these women with the mill woman pictured on page 362. What differences do you see?
Oberlin College Archives, Oberlin, Ohio.

York, founded by Emma Willard in 1821; the Hartford Seminary in Connecticut, founded by Catharine Beecher in 1822; and Mount Holyoke in Massachusetts, founded by Mary Lyon in 1837. These women educators argued that women made better teachers than men: "If men have more knowledge, they have less talent at communicating it. Nor have they the patience, the long-suffering, and gentleness necessary to superintend the formation of character," said the author Harriet Beecher Stowe, who taught at her sister's Hartford school.

Male youths leaving public school faced two paths. A small percentage continued at private boys' academies (numbering in the several hundreds nationwide), and a far smaller number entered the country's two dozen colleges. More typically, boys left school at fourteen to apprentice to a specific trade or to seek business careers in entry-level clerkships, abundant in the growing urban centers. Young girls also headed for mill towns or for the cities in unprecedented numbers, seeking work in the expanding service sector as seamstresses and domestic servants.

Changes in patterns of youth employment and training meant that large numbers of youngsters in the 1830s and later escaped the watchful eyes of their families. Moralists fretted about the dangers of unsupervised youth, and, following the lead of the Lowell mill owners, some established apprentices' libraries and uplifting lecture series to keep young people honorably occupied. Advice books published by the hundreds instructed youth in the virtues of hard work and delayed gratification.

Public Life, the Press, and Popular Amusements

Many new forms of inexpensive reading matter and public entertainment competed with the moralistic messages for youth. Innovations in printing technology as well as rising literacy rates created a brisk market in the 1830s for publications appealing to popular tastes: adventure and mystery pamphlets, romance novels, and penny press newspapers. In cities, theaters were nightly magnets for audiences in the thousands.

In the 1790s, fewer than ninety newspapers, each printing a few thousand copies per issue, provided news of current events. By 1830, there were eight hundred papers, sixty-five of them urban dailies, and in the 1830s the most successful of these, the innovative penny press papers, gained circulations of ten to twenty thousand copies daily. Such huge print runs were made possible by the development of steam-driven rotary presses with automatic paper feed devices replacing the old-style handpresses. Six-cent papers covered politics, banking, and shipping news; the one-cent ("penny") papers featured breezy political coverage, irreverent editorializing on current events, and crime reporting. Issued in eastern cities, the penny papers extended their influence throughout the nation, facilitated by a regular system of newspaper exchange by means of the postal system. Town and village papers reprinted the snappy political editorials and sensationalized crime stories, putting very undeferential ideas into the heads of readers new to politics.

Newspapers were not the only new medium for spreading a shared American culture. Starting in the 1820s, traveling lecturers crisscrossed the country, bringing entertainment and instruction to small-town audiences. Speakers gave dramatic readings of plays or poetry or lectured on history, current events, popular science, or controversial topics such as advanced female education or anatomy and physiology. Theater also blossomed in the 1830s, providing urban Americans with their most common form of shared entertainment, featuring Shakespearean plays, melodramas, and the newly popular minstrelsy, a musical comedy first performed in 1831 by white performers with blackened faces.

The popularity of theaters exemplified a general cultural turn toward the celebration of brilliant public speech. In this golden age of oration, actors, lawyers, politicians, and ministers could hold crowds spellbound for hours with their flawless elocution and elegant turns of phrase. Criminal trials, for example, were very short by modern standards, but the lawyers' closing arguments might consume many hours, with crowds of spectators hanging on every word. Senator Daniel Webster of Massachusetts was the acknowledged genius of political oration. At a Webster speech commemorating the Pilgrims' arrival, one man in a crowd of

TABLE 11.1	THE GROWTH OF NEWSPAPERS, 1820–1840			
	1820	*1830*	*1835*	*1840*
U.S. population (in millions)	9.6	12.8	15.0	17.1
Number of newspapers published	500	800	1,200	1,400
Daily newspapers	42	65	___	138

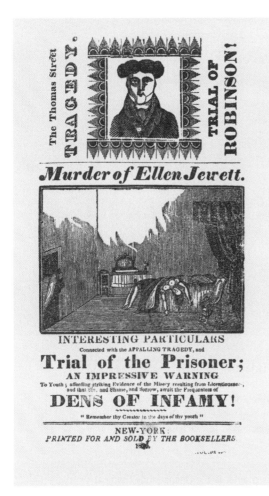

Lurid Cover of a Crime Pamphlet, New York
Cheap and easy printing in the early nineteenth century gave rise to new genres of popular reading matter, including a large pamphlet literature detailing horrific murder stories that invited readers to contemplate the nature of evil. This woodcut cover from 1836 promises to reveal the "interesting particulars" of the murder of Ellen Jewett, a New York City prostitute axed to death in her brothel bed. The pamphlet claims to constitute "an impressive warning" to youth about the tragedies of "dens of infamy." But the crude picture of the female corpse, with bare legs and breasts fully exposed, suggests that alternative, less moralistic readings of the same material were certainly possible for the purchasers.
William L. Clements Library.

Democracy and Religion

Oratorically gifted ministers had work aplenty in the 1820s and 1830s. An unprecedented revival of evangelical religion peaked in that period, after gathering two decades of momentum in states across the North and the Upper South. Known as the **Second Great Awakening**, the outpouring of religious fervor changed the shape of American **Protestantism**. The heart of the evangelical message was that salvation was available to anyone willing to eradicate individual sin and accept faith in God's grace. Just as universal male suffrage allowed all white men to vote, democratized religion offered salvation to all who chose to embrace it.

> Just as universal male suffrage allowed all white men to vote, democratized religion offered salvation to all who chose to embrace it.

Among the most serious adherents of evangelical Protestantism were men and women of the new merchant classes whose self-discipline in pursuing market ambitions meshed well with the message of self-discipline in pursuit of spiritual perfection. Not content with individual perfection, many of these men and women sought to perfect society as well, by defining excessive alcohol consumption, nonmarital sex, and slavery as the three major evils of modern life in need of correction.

The Second Great Awakening

The earliest manifestations of fervent piety marking the start of the Second Great Awakening appeared in 1801 in Kentucky. A crowd of ten thousand people camped out on a hillside at Cane Ridge for a revival meeting that lasted several weeks. By the 1810s and 1820s, "camp meetings" had spread to the Atlantic seaboard states, finding especially enthusiastic audiences in western New York and Pennsylvania. The outdoor settings permitted huge attendance, which itself intensified the emotional impact of the experience. "For more than a half mile, I could see people on their knees before God in humble prayer," recalled one Cane Ridge worshipper.

The gatherings attracted women and men hungry for a more immediate access to spiritual peace, one not requiring years of soul-searching. Ministers adopted an emotional style and invited an immediate experience of conversion and salvation. One eyewitness at a revival reported that

fifteen hundred recalled that "three or four times I thought my temples would burst with the gush of blood." Ministers with gifted tongues could in the space of an evening transform crowds of skeptics into believers. Skillful speakers demanded and generally got attentive listeners.

Charles G. Finney and His Broadway Tabernacle

The Reverend Charles G. Finney (shown here in a portrait done in 1834) took his evangelical movement to New York City in the early 1830s, operating first out of a renovated theater. In 1836, the Broadway Tabernacle was built for his pastorate. In its use of space, the tabernacle resembled a theater more than a traditional church, but in one respect it departed radically from one very theaterlike tradition of churches—the custom of charging pew rents. In effect, most churches required worshippers to purchase their seats. Finney, in contrast, insisted that all seats in his house were free, unreserved, and open to all.

Oberlin College Archives, Oberlin, Ohio.

For more help analyzing this image, see the visual activity for this chapter in the Online Study Guide at bedfordstmartins.com/roark.

"some of the people were singing, others praying, some crying for mercy. . . . At one time I saw at least five hundred swept down in a moment as if a battery of a thousand guns had been opened upon them, and then immediately followed shrieks and shouts that rent the very heavens."

From 1800 to 1820, church membership doubled in the United States, much of it among the evangelical groups. Methodists, Baptists, and Presbyterians formed the core of the new movement; Episcopalians, Congregationalists, Unitarians, Dutch Reformed, Lutherans, and Catholics maintained strong skepticism about the emotional enthusiasm. Women more than men were attracted to the evangelical movement, and wives and mothers typically recruited husbands and sons to join them.

The leading exemplar of the Second Great Awakening was a lawyer-turned-minister. Charles Grandison Finney lived in western New York, where the completion of the Erie Canal in

1825 fundamentally altered the social and economic landscape overnight. Towns swelled with new inhabitants who brought in remarkable prosperity along with other, less admirable side effects, such as prostitution, drinking, and gaming. Finney saw New York canal towns as especially ripe for evangelical awakening. In Rochester, New York, he sustained a six-month revival through the winter of 1830, generating thousands of new converts.

Finney's message was directed primarily at women and men of the business classes, and, true to his training, he couched it in legal metaphors. "The world is divided into two great political parties," he announced—the party of Satan and the party of Jehovah. "Ministers should labor with sinners, as a lawyer does with a jury . . . ; and the sinner should weigh his arguments, and make up his mind as upon oath and for his life, and give a verdict upon the spot." Finney's sermons reached national distribution through the religious press. He argued that a reign of Christian perfection loomed, one that required a public-spirited outreach to the less than perfect to foster their salvation. Evangelicals promoted Sunday schools to bring piety to children; they battled to end mail delivery, to stop public transport, and to close shops on Sundays to honor the Sabbath. Many women formed missionary societies, which distributed millions of Bibles and religious tracts. Through such avenues, evangelical religion offered women expanded spheres of influence.

In 1832, Finney moved to New York City and renovated a disreputable theater into a Free Presbyterian church. His dynamic, theatrical performances were taken down by scribes and published in the *New York Evangelist,* a weekly paper of national distribution. Finney adopted tactics of Jacksonian-era politicians—publicity, argumentation, rallies, and speeches—to sell his cause. His object, he said, was to get Americans to "vote in the Lord Jesus Christ as the governor of the Universe."

The Temperance Movement and the Campaign for Moral Reform

The evangelical disposition—a combination of faith, energy, self-discipline, and righteousness—animated vigorous campaigns to eliminate alcohol abuse and eradicate sexual sin. Millions of Americans took the temperance pledge to abstain from strong drink, and thousands became involved in efforts to end prostitution.

Alcohol consumption had risen steadily in the decades up to 1830, when the average person over age thirteen consumed an astonishing 9 gallons of hard liquor plus around 30 gallons of hard cider, beer, and wine per year. To a degree, consumption of bottled, fermented drinks made sense in view of unsafe urban water sources and the lack of reliable refrigeration. However, alcohol abuse was on the rise.

All classes imbibed. A lively saloon culture fostered masculine camaraderie along with extensive alcohol consumption among laborers, and a new style of binge drinking alarmed older proponents of moderate consumption. In elite homes, the after-dinner whiskey or sherry was commonplace. Colleges before 1820 routinely served students a pint of ale with meals, and the army and navy included rum in the standard daily ration.

Organized opposition to drinking first surfaced in the 1810s among health and religious re-

formers. In 1826, Lyman Beecher, a Connecticut minister of an "awakened" church, founded the American Temperance Society, which held that drinking led to poverty, idleness, crime, and family violence. Adopting the methods of evangelical ministers, temperance lecturers traveled the country expounding the damage of drink; by 1833, some six thousand local affiliates of the American Temperance Society boasted more than a million members. Middle-class drinking began a steep decline. One powerful tool of persuasion was the temperance pledge, which many manufacturers and business owners began to require of employees.

In 1836, leaders of the **temperance movement** regrouped into a new society, the American Temperance Union, which demanded total abstinence of its adherents. The intensified war against alcohol moved beyond individual moral suasion into the realm of politics, as reformers sought to deny taverns liquor licenses. By 1845, temperance advocates had put an impressive dent in alcohol consumption, which diminished to one-quarter of the per capita consumption of 1830. In 1851, Maine became the first state to ban entirely the manufacture and sale of all alcoholic beverages.

More controversial than temperance was a social movement called "moral reform," which first aimed at public morals in general but quickly narrowed to a campaign to eradicate sexual sin, especially prostitution. In 1833, a group of Finneyite women started the New York Female Moral Reform Society. Its members insisted that uncontrolled male sexual expression posed a serious threat to society

The Cold Water Army Fan
This fan was a keepsake for children enlisted in the Reverend Thomas Hunt's Cold Water Army of 1836, which advocated abstinence from alcohol. Hunt, a Presbyterian, figured that preventing children from beginning to drink would be an effective strategy against future alcoholism: "Prevention is better than cure" was his motto.
Museum of American Political Life.

in general and to women in particular. The society's nationally distributed newspaper, the *Advocate of Moral Reform,* was the first major paper in the country that was written, edited, and typeset by women. Columns were devoted to first-person tales of woe and to advice about curbing sexual sin. The women reformers condemned men who visited brothels or who seduced innocent victims. Within five years, more than four thousand auxiliary groups of women members had sprung up, mostly in New England, New York, Pennsylvania, and Ohio.

In its analysis of the causes of licentiousness and its conviction that women had a duty to speak out about unspeakable things, the Moral Reform Society pushed the limits of what even the men in the evangelical movement could tolerate. Yet they did not regard themselves as radicals. They were simply pursuing the logic of a gender system that defined home protection and morality as women's special sphere and a religious conviction that called for the eradication of sin.

Organizing against Slavery

> Even more radical than temperance and moral reform was the movement in the 1830s to abolish the sin of slavery.

More radical still was the movement in the 1830s to abolish the sin of slavery. The only previous antislavery organization, the American Colonization Society, had been founded in 1817 by some Maryland and Virginia **planters** to promote gradual individual **emancipation** of slaves followed by **colonization** in Africa (see page 430). By the early 1820s, several thousand ex-slaves had been transported to Liberia on the West African coast. But not surprisingly, newly freed men and women were often not eager to emigrate; their African roots were three or more generations in the past. Emigration to Africa proved to be so gradual (and expensive) as to have a negligible impact on American slavery.

At the end of the 1820s, northern challenges to slavery surfaced with increasing frequency and resolve, beginning in the free black communities of Boston, Philadelphia, and New York. In 1829, a Boston printer named David Walker published *Appeal . . . to the Coloured Citizens of the World,* which condemned racism, invoked the egalitarian language of the Declaration of Independence, and hinted at racial violence if whites did not change their prejudiced ways. In 1830, a ten-day National Negro Convention met in Philadelphia, the first of three decades of such meetings. At that inaugural event, forty blacks from nine states met to discuss the racism of American society and to found the "American Society of Free People of Colour for improving their condition in the United States; for purchasing lands; and for the establishment of a settlement in the Province of Canada." In 1832, a twenty-eight-year-old black woman, Maria Stewart, delivered public lectures for black audiences in Boston on slavery and racial prejudice. While her arguments against slavery were welcomed, her voice—that of a woman—created problems even among her sympathetic audiences. Few American-born women had yet engaged in public speaking beyond theatrical performances or religious prophesizing. (See "Documenting the American Promise," page 378.) Stewart was breaking a social taboo, an offense made worse by her statements suggesting black women should rise above housework: "How long shall the fair daughters of Africa be compelled to bury their minds and talents beneath a load of iron pots and kettles?" She retired from the platform in 1833 but took up writing and published her lectures in a national publication called the *Liberator,* giving them much wider circulation.

The *Liberator,* founded in 1831 in Boston, took antislavery agitation to new heights. Its founder and editor, an uncompromising twenty-six-year-old white printer named William Lloyd Garrison, advocated immediate abolition of slavery:

> On this subject, I do not wish to think, or speak, or write, with moderation. No! No! Tell a man whose house is on fire to give a moderate alarm; tell him to moderately rescue his wife from the hands of the ravisher; tell the mother to gradually extricate her babe from the fire into which it has fallen;—but urge me not to use moderation in a cause like the present.

In 1832, Garrison supporters started the New England Anti-Slavery Society; Philadelphia and New York started similar groups in 1833. Soon there were a dozen antislavery newspapers, along with scores of antislavery lecturers spreading the word and inspiring the formation of new local societies, which grew to number 1,300 by 1837. Entirely confined to the North, their membership totaled a quarter of a million men and women.

Many white Northerners were not prepared to embrace the abolitionist call for emancipation, immediate or gradual. They might oppose slavery as a blot on the country's ideals or as a rival to the **free-labor** system of the North, but at the same time most white Northerners remained antiblack and therefore antiabolition. From 1834 to 1838, there were more than a hundred eruptions of serious mob violence against abolitionists or free blacks. On one occasion, antislavery headquarters in Philadelphia and a black church and orphanage were burned to the ground; in another incident, Illinois abolitionist editor Elijah Lovejoy was killed by a rioting crowd attempting to destroy his printing press.

Women played a prominent role in abolition, just as they did in moral reform and evangelical religion. (See "Beyond America's Borders," page 380.) They formed women's auxiliaries and engaged in fund-raising to support lecturers in the field. They circulated antislavery petitions, presented to the U.S. Congress with tens of thousands of signatures. Garrison particularly welcomed women's activity. When a southern plantation daughter named Angelina Grimké wrote him about her personal repugnance for slavery, Garrison published the letter in the *Liberator* and brought her overnight fame. Grimké and her older sister Sarah quickly became lecturers for the antislavery movement and started a speaking tour to women's groups in Massachusetts in 1837. The Grimkés' powerful eyewitness speeches attracted men as well, causing leaders of the Congregational Church in Massachusetts to warn all Congregational ministers not to let the Grimké sisters use their pulpits. Like Maria Stewart, the Grimkés had violated a gender norm by presuming to instruct men.

In the late 1830s, the cause of abolition divided the nation as no other issue did. Even among the abolitionists, significant divisions emerged. The Grimké sisters, radicalized by the public reaction to their speaking tour, began to write and speak about woman's rights. They were opposed by moderate abolitionists who were unwilling to mix a new and controversial issue about women with their first cause, the rights of blacks. A few radical men, like Garrison, embraced women's rights fully, working to get women leadership positions in the national antislavery group.

The many men and women active in reform movements in the 1830s found their initial inspiration in evangelical Protestantism's dual message: Salvation was open to all, and society needed to be perfected. Their activist mentality squared well with the interventionist tendencies of the party forming in opposition to Andrew Jackson's Democrats. On the whole, reformers gravitated to the Whig Party.

Abolitionist Purses
Female antislavery societies raised many thousands of dollars to support the abolitionist cause by selling handcrafted items at giant antislavery fairs. Toys, infant clothes, quilts, caps and collars, purses, needlebooks, wax flowers, inlaid boxes: The list was endless. Items were often emblazoned with abolitionist mottoes, such as "Let My People Go," "Liberty," and "Loose the Bonds of Wickedness." These pink silk drawstring bags were decorated with pictures of the hapless slave woman, an object of compassion. Dollars raised at these fairs supported the travels of abolitionist speakers as well as the publication and distribution of many antislavery books and articles.
The Daughters of the American Revolution Museum, Washington, D.C. Gift of Mrs. Erwin L. Broecker.

Jackson Defines the Democratic Party

In his eight years in office, Andrew Jackson worked to implement his vision of a politics of opportunity for all white men. He also greatly enhanced the power of the presidency. To open more land east of the Mississippi River for white settlement, he favored the relocation of all the eastern Indian peoples. He had a dramatic confrontation with John C. Calhoun and South Carolina when that state tried to nullify the tariff of 1828. Disapproving of all government-granted privilege, Jackson challenged what he called the "monster" Bank of the United States and took it

American Women Speak Out in Public

Public speaking was strictly a masculine prerogative up to the 1830s. Only actresses on the stage and a handful of religious women who claimed to be passive instruments of God's voice escaped criticism for breaking this firm gender barrier, thought to have ancient biblical sanction in 1 Corinthians 14:33–39, which commands women to keep silent in the church. Maria Stewart, a young African American widow in Boston, was probably the first American woman to lecture on social issues. A few years later, Angelina Grimké and her sister Sarah staged a lecture tour on abolition, paving the way for Mary S. Gove a year later to offer a lecture series on women's health. All these women endured stiff criticism, but the barrier was broken, leading to a cascade of women speakers in the 1840s and 1850s.

DOCUMENT 1
Maria Stewart Addresses the Afric-American Female Intelligence Society of America, 1832

In 1832 Maria Stewart commenced public lecturing to black audiences of both sexes in Boston. She stressed racial uplift through Christian values, diligent parenting, education, discipline, and ambition. In this speech to an audience of black women, Stewart acknowledged criticism of her lectures and justified her course of action as one inspired by religion.

The frowns of the world shall never discourage me, nor its smiles flatter me; for with the help of God, I am resolved to withstand the fiery darts of the devil, and the assaults of wicked men. . . . The only motive that has prompted me to raise my voice in your behalf, my friends, is because I have discovered that religion is held in low repute among some of us. . . . I am a strong advocate for the cause of God, and for the cause of freedom. . . . Suffer me, then, to express my sentiments but this once . . . and then hereafter let me sink into oblivion, and let my name die in forgetfulness.

. . . my soul has been so discouraged within me, that I have almost been induced to exclaim, "Would to God that my tongue hereafter might cleave to the roof of my mouth, and become silent forever!" and then I have felt that the Christian has no time to be idle, and I must be active, knowing that the night of death cometh, in which no man can work.

O woman, woman! upon you I call; for upon your exertions almost entirely depends whether the rising generation shall be any thing more than we have been or not. O woman, woman! your example is powerful, your influence great; it extends over your husbands and over your children, and throughout the circle of your acquaintance. Then let me exhort you to cultivate among yourselves a spirit of Christian love and unity. . . . And O, my God, I beseech thee to grant that the nations of the earth may hiss at us no longer!

SOURCE: Maria Stewart lectures, African American History, 1 March 2004, <http://afroamhistory.about.com/library/blmaria_stewart_intelligencesociety.htm>

DOCUMENT 2
Angelina Grimké Writes a Friend about Speaking to a "Mixed" Audience, 1837

The Grimké sisters' speaking tour of 1837 caused a sensation in Massachusetts. Raised in a South Carolina slave-owning family, the white sisters abhorred slavery and fled north. Their firsthand experience of the system made them especially compelling abolitionist speakers. By June, men as well as women were coming to their public talks, giving them a "mixed" or "promiscuous" audience. Grimké writes her friend Jane Smith about stage fright.

In the evening of the same day [June 21], addressed our first large mixed audience [in Lynn]. about 1000 present. Great openness to hear & ease in speaking. 22d. Held another in Lynn, but in a smaller house, so that it was crowded to excess. About 600 seated. Many went away, about 100 stood around the door, & we were told that on each window on the outside stood three men with their heads above the lowered sash. Very easy speaking indeed. 23d. held a meeting here [Danvers]. About 200 out—a few of the brethren. Very hard speaking. . . . And now thou will want to know how we feel about all these things. . . . Whilst in the act of speaking I am favored to forget little "I" entirely & to feel altogether hid behind the great cause I am pleading. Were it not for this feeling, I know not how I could face such audiences without embarrassment.

It is wonderful to us how the way has been opened for us to address mixed audiences, for most sects here are greatly opposed to public speaking for women, but curiosity in many & real interest in the AS [anti-slavery] cause in others induce the attendance of our meetings. When they are over, we feel as if we had nothing to do with the results. We cast our burden upon the Lord, & feel an inexpressible relief until the approach of another meeting produces an exercise & sense of responsibility which becomes at times almost insupportable. At some meetings I have really felt sick until I rose to speak. But our health has been good & we bear the exertion of body & exercise of mind wonderfully. Our compass of voice has astonished us, for we can fill a house containing 1000 persons with ease. . . .

SOURCE: Kathryn Kish Sklar, *Women's Rights Emerges within the Antislavery Movement, 1830–1870: A Brief History with Documents* (Boston: Bedford/St. Martin's, 2000), 115–16.

DOCUMENT 3
A Massachusetts Minister
Rebukes the Grimkés, July 1837

Jonathan Stearns, a Presbyterian minister in Newburyport, Massachusetts, devoted a sermon to female public speaking. His ideas accorded with a "Pastoral Letter" issued also in July by the leadership of the Massachusetts Congregational Association, warning ministers not to open their pulpits for antislavery meetings featuring the Grimké sisters. Stearns outlined woman's rightful spheres of influence—home, benevolence and charity work, religion—and argued that women were not *inferior to men but rather* different. *He then rehearsed the biblical prohibitions that forbade women from speaking in church or instructing their husbands—prohibitions that, he argued, elevated women, gave them influence over men, and kept them modest and delicate.*

Let her lay aside delicacy, and her influence over our sex is gone. And for what object would she make such sacrifices? That she may do good more extensively? Then she sadly mistakes her vocation. But why then? That she may see her name blazoned on the rolls of fame, and hear the shouts of delighted assemblies, applauding her eloquence? That she may place her own sex on a fancied equality with men, obtain the satisfaction of calling herself independent, and occupy a station in life which she can never adorn? For this would she sacrifice the almost magic power, which, in her own proper sphere she now wields over the destinies of the word? . . . That there are ladies who are capable of public debate, who could make their voice heard from end to end of the church and the senate house, that there are those who might bear a favorable comparison with others as eloquent orators, and who might speak to better edification than most of those on whom the office has hitherto devolved, I am not disposed to deny. The question is not in regard to *ability,* but to *decency,* to order, to Christian *propriety.*

SOURCE: Jonathan F. Stearns, "Female Influence, and the True Christian Mode of Its Exercise: A Discourse Delivered in the First Presbyterian Church in Newburyport, July 30, 1837," in Aileen S. Kraditor, ed., *Up from the Pedestal, Selected Writings in the History of American Feminism* (Chicago: University of Chicago Press, 1968), 47–50.

DOCUMENT 4
Mary Gove Lectures on
Health Reform and Sex, 1838

The Grimké lecture tour of 1837 emboldened other women to take up public speaking. Mary S. Gove, a self-trained medical practitioner from Lynn, Massachusetts, launched her career as a lecturer on women's anatomy and physiology in 1838. Her lectures on corsets and on sex were particularly controversial, even though she restricted her audience for the latter lecture to married women only. In this letter, Anna Breed, a Quaker woman from Lynn, writes Abigail Kelley about the local reaction to Gove's first series. The lecture on tight lacing drew 2,000 listeners in Boston.

Thou has probably heard of M. S. Gove's success in her new sphere. I have attended three of her lectures which were both edifying and interesting. The first that I heard was upon the formation of bones—the 2nd upon their situations, number, and wonderful use—3d The evils of tight lacing—an excellent lecture—she has according to my estimation, very correct views of the effects of that horrid practice. I think Abby, thou would be much interested in her lectures; she appears better than I ever saw her in any other situation. She is censured, ridiculed, and misrepresented, of course; but as she has a pretty good share of independence, I think she will not be much affected by the [sa]rcasms inflicted upon her. I have never before seen so intelligent looking a company of women together in this place as we met there. She is giving a second course to a large audience in Boston.

SOURCE: Anna Breed to Abigail Kelley, November 1838, Abigail Kelley Foster Papers, American Antiquarian Society, Worcester, MA.

QUESTIONS FOR ANALYSIS
AND DEBATE

1. What did Reverend Stearns identify as the chief social ill that would follow if women were allowed to lecture in public? What would women lose? What might men lose?

2. Stearns condemns female ambition and ego. Do you think Stewart, Grimké, or Gove exhibit female ambition? What do you think motivated each one to lecture?

3. How much do you think the *subject matter* of the lectures would influence the degree of criticism each woman experienced? Can you discern strategies that any of these speakers adopted to try to ward off criticism?

Transatlantic Abolition

Lucretia Coffin Mott
Lucretia Coffin was born in 1793 in a Quaker community of Nantucket, Massachusetts. She later recalled the influence of British abolitionists in her formative years: "My sympathy was early enlisted for the poor slave by the class books read in our schools, and the pictures of the slave-ships as presented by [Thomas] Clarkson." She married James Mott of Philadelphia in 1811, and by the mid-1820s both Motts endorsed boycotts of slave products (sugar, cotton), a particular hardship for James, a cloth merchant, who only sold wool thereafter. Lucretia Mott was a prime mover in the Philadelphia Female Anti-Slavery Society, founded in 1833, and she gave her first public lecture on slavery to an all-female audience in May 1837. In 1840 she was one of eight American women chosen to attend the World Antislavery Convention, presided over by the octogenarian Clarkson, whose work had early inspired her. Though the women were rejected as delegates on account of their sex, Mott made the most of the meeting's networking opportunities. For years after 1840, she was a steady correspondent with English and Irish abolitionists.
Chicago Historical Society.

Abolitionism blossomed in the United States in the 1830s, but its roots stretched back to the 1780s, both in the northern states and in Europe. Developments on both sides of the Atlantic reinforced each other, leading to a transatlantic antislavery movement with shared ideas and strategies, shared activists, shared songs, and, eventually, shared victories.

An important source of antislavery sentiment derived from the Quaker religion, with its deep convictions of human equality, so, not surprisingly, antislavery activism first spread along established Quaker networks in England, Ireland, and the United States, propelled by traveling ministers and religious pamphlet literature. In Pennsylvania, Quakers launched the Pennsylvania Society for Promoting the Abolition of Slavery, which non-Quakers Benjamin Franklin and Thomas Paine also joined. Founded in 1784, the Society worked to end slavery in that state and also petitioned the confederation congress—unsuccessfully—to put an end to American participation in the international slave trade. Quaker counterparts in the British cities of London and Plymouth formed antislavery societies that same year and embarked on a drive to ban England's transatlantic traffic in humans. A French group, the Société des Amis des Noirs (Society of the Friends of

Blacks) sprang up in Paris in 1788. All three groups agreed that ending the overseas commerce was the critical first step in ending slavery.

The English Quakers were initially the most successful in mounting a public campaign. From 1787 to 1791, the Society for Effecting the Abolition of the Slave Trade amassed thousands of signatures on petitions and organized a boycott of slave-produced sugar from the British West Indies, a boycott said to have involved 300,000 Britons. Women, the traditional cooks of English families, were essential to that effort. In 1789, the Society scored a publicity coup by publishing two chilling illustrations of cross-sectioned slaving ships stacked with human cargo, the dark, near-naked bodies packed like sardines in each ship's hold. These images, reprinted by the thousands, created a sensation. The Reverend Thomas Clarkson of the Society distributed them in Paris and in northern U.S. cities along with a book he wrote detailing the shipboard tortures inflicted on slaves by the use of shackles, handcuffs, whips, and branding irons. The Society mobilized the resulting groundswell of antislavery sentiment to pressure Parliament. A sympathetic member of that body, the Methodist William Wilburforce, brought the anti–slave trade issue to a debate and vote in 1791; it lost.

American Quakers approached the first federal Congress, meeting in New York in 1790, with petitions requesting an immediate end to the slave trade. This caused some puzzlement at first, because the U.S. Constitution contained a clause prohibiting the federal government from banning the "Importation of Such Persons as any of the States now existing shall think proper to admit" (that is, slaves) before the year 1808. Congressmen banished the Quaker petitions to a committee. The next day, a bolder Quaker petition, endorsed by the venerated Benjamin Franklin, arrived requesting an end to slavery as well as to the slave trade and suggesting how to accomplish it.

The petitioners urged Congress to invoke the constitutional provision that empowered the government to make all laws "necessary and proper" to ensure the "general welfare" of the country, arguing that "Liberty for all Negroes" was crucial to the general welfare. This petition triggered the first debate in the new government on slavery. As in England, the outcome did not bode well for slaves: By a close vote (29 to 25), Congress not only rejected this move for emancipation but also clarified its view—in a precedent-setting resolution—that slavery was under the sole regulation of the states where it existed.

Over the next three decades, the antislavery cause in Britain and in America moved forward in piece-meal fashion. Efforts to ban the slave trade in England came to parliamentary votes in 1805 and again in 1807, when a law forbidding English ships to carry Africans into slavery finally passed. (The British law was not perfect, however; it levied a fine of £100 per slave on any English captain caught with illegal cargo, creating a grim incentive for captains to shove people overboard if they faced challenge by the British navy.) A year later, in 1808, the United States also banned the slave trade, meeting the constitutional time limit. What made for relatively easy passage at this time was the burgeoning natural increase of the African American population. Older slave states supported the international ban because it increased the value of their native-born slave population, which could be sold and transported to points west in the interstate slave trade.

British antislavery opinion took a new tack in the 1820s, when women became active and pushed beyond the ban on trade. Quaker widow Elizabeth Heyrick authored *Immediate not Gradual Abolition* in 1824, triggering the formation of scores of all-women societies. A massive petition campaign again bombarded Parliament, and of the 1.3 million signatures submitted in 1833, 30 percent were women's. In 1833, Parliament finally passed the Abolition of Slavery Act, which freed all slave children under age six and gradually phased out slavery for everyone older during a four-year apprenticeship. The act also provided financial compensation for owners (£20 million), a key proviso made possible by the relatively small number of slaveowners in the British slaveholding colonies.

Description of a Slave Ship

This powerful and often-reprinted image combined a precise technical rendering of a British ship (normally evoking pride in Britons) with the horrors of a crowded mass of dark human flesh.

Peabody Essex Museum, Salem, MA.

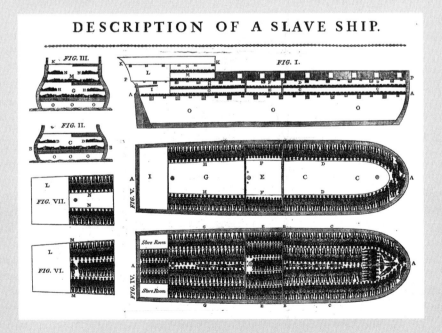

DESCRIPTION OF A SLAVE SHIP.

(continued)

(continued)

American abolitionists were also heating up the struggle in the 1830s, and as in Britain, women's involvement was accelerating. The Grimké sisters were only the most visible part of women's new activism. Many hundreds of women joined Female Anti-Slavery organizations and held fairs where they sold handmade goods to raise money to promote the abolitionist cause. Both women and men abolitionists from both sides of the Atlantic traveled overseas to meet their counterparts abroad. In one worrisome moment, a Boston crowd threatened to lynch British abolitionist George Thompson and his host, William Lloyd Garrison, the editor of the *Liberator.*

British and American abolitionists came together in full force at the World Antislavery Convention, held in London in 1840. Among the 409 delegates were Clarkson, who presided, Garrison, and Philadelphia Quaker Lucretia Mott, a lifelong antislavery activist. A half dozen French delegates attended, 53 others were Americans, and the rest were from Britain and the West Indies. Only about a quarter of the attendees were Quakers. Ten days of meetings produced speeches and fact-finding reports on slavery worldwide, captured in a 600-page book detailing the proceedings. Economic and religious strategies were debated, and a plan was hatched to inform America about how British emancipation had worked. Memorials were sent to governments, and each governor of a southern U.S. state was targeted with a letter condemning the interstate slave trade. The delegates closed their meeting, exhilarated by the idea of their international congress to move toward international solutions to an international problem.

BIBLIOGRAPHY

David Brion Davis, *The Problem of Slavery in the Age of Revolution, 1770–1823* (1975).

Seymour Drescher, *The Mighty Experiment: Free Labor versus Slavery in British Emancipation* (2002).

Julie Roy Jeffrey, *The Great Silent Army of Abolition: Ordinary Women in the Antislavery Movement* (1998).

James Stewart, *Holy Warriors: The Abolitionists and American Slavery* (1976).

David Turley, *The Culture of English Antislavery, 1780–1860* (1991).

Marcus Wood, *Blind Memory: Visual Representations of Slavery in England and America, 1780–1865* (2000).

down to defeat. Jackson's legacy to his successor, Martin Van Buren, was a Democratic Party strong enough to withstand the passing of the Old Hickory. But another of his legacies was the most severe economic contraction yet to hit the U.S. economy, the panic of 1837. Although the panic was not solely Jackson's doing, it was a fitting ending to a decade of rambunctious speculation and expansion.

Indian Policy and the Trail of Tears

Jackson declared in his first annual message that removing Indians to territory west of the Mississippi was the only way to save them.

Probably nothing defined Jackson's presidency more than his efforts to "solve" what he saw as the Indian problem. Many thousands of Indians lived in the South and the old Northwest; indeed, not a few lived in New England and New York. Jackson, who had gained his national reputation fighting the Creek in 1814 and the Seminole in 1816–1817, declared in 1829 in his first annual message to Congress that removing Indians to territory west of the Mississippi was the only way to save them. White civilization destroyed Indian resources and thus doomed the Indians: "That this fate surely awaits them if they remain within the limits of the states does not admit of a doubt. Humanity and national honor demand that every effort should be made to avert so great a calamity." Jackson never publicly wavered from this seemingly noble theme, returning to it in his next seven annual messages.

Prior administrations had tried different policies. Starting in 1819, Congress granted $10,000 a year to various missionary associations eager to "civilize" native peoples by converting them to Christianity. The assimilationist program also included teaching Indians English literacy and agricultural practices. Missionaries also promoted white gender customs, but Indian women were reluctant to embrace practices that accorded them less power than their tribal system did. The federal government had also pursued aggressive treaty making with many tribes, dealing with the Indians as if they were foreign nations. (See chapter 10, pages 334–35.)

Privately, Andrew Jackson thought it was "absurd" to treat the Indians as foreigners. In his view, they were subjects of the United States. Jackson also did not approve of assimilation; that way lay extinction, he said. In his 1833 annual message to Congress he wrote, "They have neither the intelligence, the industry, the moral habits, nor the desire of improvement which are essential. . . . Established in the midst of a superior race . . . they must necessarily yield to the force of circumstances and ere long disappear." Congress backed Jackson's goal and passed the Indian Removal Act of 1830, appropriating $500,000 to relocate eastern tribes to land west of the Mississippi River. About 100 million acres of eastern land would be vacated for eventual white settlement under this act authorizing ethnic expulsion (Map 11.3).

For northern tribes, their numbers diminished by years of war, gradual removal was already well under way. But not all the Indians went quietly. In 1832 in western Illinois, Black Hawk, a leader of the Sauk and Fox Indians who had fought with Tecumseh in the War of 1812 (see chapter 10, page 336), resisted. Volunteer militias attacked and chased the Indians into

---

MAP 11.3 Indian Removal and the Trail of Tears

The federal government under President Andrew Jackson pursued a vigorous policy of Indian removal in the 1830s. Tribes were forcibly moved west to land known as Indian Territory (in present-day Oklahoma). As many as a quarter of the Cherokee Indians died in 1838 on the route known as the Trail of Tears.

READING THE MAP: From which states were most of the Native Americans removed? Through which states did the Trail of Tears go?
CONNECTIONS: Before Jackson's presidency, how did the federal government view Native Americans, and what policy initiatives were undertaken by the government and private groups? How did Jackson change the government's Native American policies?

FOR MORE HELP ANALYZING THIS MAP, see the map activity for this chapter in the Online Study Guide at bedfordstmartins.com/roark.

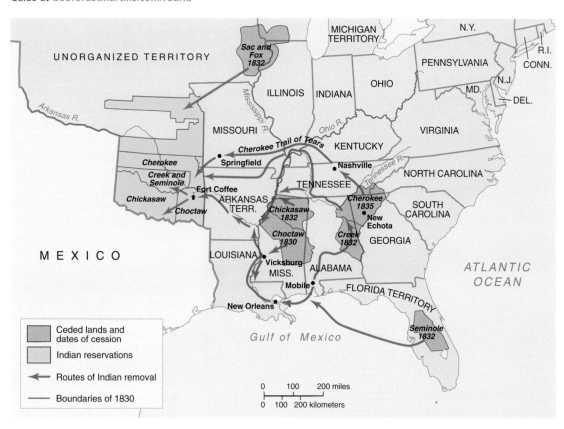

southern Wisconsin, where, after several skirmishes and a deadly battle, Black Hawk was captured and some 400 of his people were massacred.

Southern tribes proved even more resistant to removal. The powerful Creek, Chickasaw, Choctaw, and Cherokee tribes refused to relocate. A second Seminole War in Florida broke out as the Indians there—a mixture of Seminoles and escaped black slaves who had intermarried with the tribe—took up arms against relocation in 1836–1837.

The Cherokee of Georgia responded with a unique legal challenge to being treated as subjects. More than any other southern tribe, the 17,000 Cherokee had incorporated white political and economic practices into their tribal life. Spurred by dedicated missionaries, they had adopted written laws, culminating in 1827 in

Cherokee Phoenix
Around 1820, Sequoyah, about forty-five years old and nephew of a Cherokee chief, invented written symbols to convey the Cherokee language. Each symbol represented a syllable of sound. In 1828, the Cherokees in New Echota, Georgia, ordered custom-made type embodying the new symbols and began printing a newspaper, the *Cherokee Phoenix*, the first newspaper published by Native Americans, printed in both English and Cherokee.

Special Collections Division, Georgetown University Library, Washington, D.C.

a constitution closely modeled on the U.S. Constitution. Some two hundred of the wealthiest Cherokees had intermarried with whites and had adopted white styles of housing, dress, and cotton agriculture, including the ownership of more than a thousand slaves. They had developed a written alphabet and published a newspaper as well as Christian prayerbooks in their language.

In 1831, after Georgia announced it would subject the Indians to state law and seize their property, the Cherokee tribe appealed to the U.S. Supreme Court to restrain Georgia. Chief Justice John Marshall found for Georgia on the grounds that the Cherokee did not have standing to sue. When Georgia jailed two missionaries under an 1830 state law forbidding missionary aid to Indians without permission, the Cherokee brought suit again, fronting one of the missionaries as plaintiff. In the 1832 case, *Worcester v. Georgia,* the Supreme Court upheld the territorial sovereignty of the Cherokee, recognizing their existence as "a distinct community, occupying its own territory, in which the laws of Georgia can have no force." Ignoring the Supreme Court's decision, an angry President Jackson pressed the Cherokee for removal west. "If they now refuse to accept the liberal terms offered, they can only be liable for whatever evils and difficulties may arise. I feel conscious of having done my duty to my red children."

The Cherokee tribe remained in Georgia for two more years without significant violence. Then in 1835, a small, unauthorized part of the tribe signed a treaty ceding all the tribal land—a large piece of northern Georgia—to the state in exchange for $5 million and equal acreage west of Arkansas. Georgia rapidly sold the land to whites. Cherokee chief John Ross, backed by several thousand Cherokees, petitioned the U.S. Congress to ignore the bogus treaty. "By the stipulations of this instrument," he wrote, "we are stripped of every attribute of freedom and eligibility for legal self-defence. Our property may be plundered before our eyes; violence may be committed on our persons; even our

Choctaw Indian Sash, 1820s
The pattern of beadwork on wool marks this sash as
Choctaw handiwork. A sash like this one, which is 46
inches long, was worn diagonally across the chest. Its
sharply contrasting colors and vivid design could be seen
at a distance, allowing for quick identification of tribal
members. The Choctaw lived in Mississippi and were one
of the five southern Indian nations that were subjected to
Andrew Jackson's removal policy in the 1830s.
Peabody Essex Museum, Salem, MA.

lives may be taken away. . . . We are denational-
ized; we are disfranchised."

Most Cherokees refused to move, so in May
1838, the deadline for voluntary evacuation, federal troops sent by Jackson's successor, Martin
Van Buren, arrived to deport them. Under armed
guard, the Cherokees embarked on a 1,200-mile
journey that came to be called the Trail of Tears.
A newspaperman in Kentucky described the
forced march: "Even aged females, apparently,
nearly ready to drop into the grave, were travel-

ing with heavy burdens attached to the back. . . .
They buried fourteen to fifteen at every stopping
place." Nearly a quarter of the Cherokees died
en route from the hardship. Survivors joined
the fifteen thousand Creek, twelve thousand
Choctaw, five thousand Chickasaw, and several
thousand Seminole Indians also forcibly relocated to "Indian Territory" (which became, in
1907, the state of Oklahoma).

In his farewell address to the nation in 1837,
Jackson again professed his belief about the benefit of Indian removal: "This unhappy race . . .
are now placed in a situation where we may well
hope that they will share in the blessings of civilization and be saved from the degradation and
destruction to which they were rapidly hastening while they remained in the states." Possibly
Jackson genuinely believed that exile to the West
was necessary to save Indian cultures from destruction. But for the forcibly removed tribes, the
costs of relocation were high.

The Tariff of Abominations and Nullification

Jackson's Indian policy happened to harmonize
with the principle of **states' rights**: The president
supported Georgia's right to ignore the Supreme
Court decision in *Worcester v. Georgia*. But in another pressing question of states' rights, Jackson
contested South Carolina's attempt to ignore federal tariff policy.

Federal tariffs as high as 33 percent on imports such as textiles and iron goods had been
passed in 1816 and again in 1824, in an effort to
favor new American manufactures and shelter
them from foreign competition as well as to raise
federal revenue. Some southern congressmen
opposed the steep tariffs, fearing they would decrease overseas shipping and hurt the South's
cotton export. During John Quincy Adams's administration (1825–1829), tariff policy generated
heated debate. In 1828, Congress passed a revised tariff that came to be known as the Tariff of
Abominations. A bundle of conflicting duties—
some as high as 50 percent—the legislation had
provisions that pleased and angered every economic and sectional interest. Assembled mostly
by southern congressmen, who loaded it with
duties on raw materials needed by New
England, it also contained protectionist elements
favored by northern manufacturers.

South Carolina in particular suffered from
the Tariff of Abominations. Worldwide prices for
cotton were already in sharp decline in the late

1820s, and the further depression of shipping caused by the high tariffs hurt the South's export market. In 1828, a group of South Carolina politicians headed by John C. Calhoun drew up a statement outlining a doctrine called **nullification**. The Union, they argued, was a confederation of states that had yielded some but not all power to the federal government. When Congress overstepped its powers, states had the right to nullify Congress's acts; as precedents they pointed to the Virginia and Kentucky Resolutions of 1798, which had attempted to invalidate the Alien and Sedition Acts (see chapter 9). Congress had erred in using tariff policy as an instrument to benefit specific industries, the South Carolinians claimed; tariffs should be used only to raise revenue.

On assuming the presidency in 1829, Jackson ignored the South Carolina statement of nullification and shut out Calhoun, his new vice president, from influence or power. Tariff revisions in early 1832 brought little relief to the South. Sensing futility, Calhoun resigned from the vice presidency in 1832 and accepted election by the South Carolina legislature to a seat in the U.S. Senate, where he could better argue his state's antitariff stance. Strained to their limit, the South Carolina leaders took the radical step of declaring the federal tariffs to be null and void in their state as of February 1, 1833. Finally, the constitutional crisis was out in the open.

Opting for a dramatic confrontation, Jackson sent armed ships to Charleston's harbor and threatened to invade the state. He pushed through Congress a bill, called the Force Bill, defining the Carolina stance as treason and authorizing military action to collect federal tariffs. At the same time, Congress moved quickly to pass a revised tariff more acceptable to the South. The conciliating Senator Henry Clay rallied support for a moderate bill that gradually reduced tariffs down to the 1816 level. On March 1, 1833, Congress passed both the new tariff and the Force Bill. South Carolina responded by withdrawing its nullification of the old tariff—and then nullifying the Force Bill. It was a symbolic gesture, since Jackson's show of muscle was no longer necessary. Both sides were satisfied with the immediate outcome. Federal power had prevailed over a dangerous assertion of states' rights, and South Carolina got the lower tariff it wanted.

Yet the question of federal power versus states' rights was far from settled. The implied threat behind nullification was secession, a position articulated in 1832 by some South Carolinians whose concerns went beyond tariff policy. The growing voice of antislavery activism in the North threatened the South's economic system. If and when a northern-dominated federal government decided to end slavery, the South Carolinians thought, the South must have the right to remove itself from the Union.

The Bank War and the Panic of 1837

Along with the tariff and nullification, President Jackson had another political battle on his hands, over the Bank of the United States. After riding out the panic of 1819, the bank finally prospered. It handled the federal government's deposits, extended credit and loans, and issued banknotes—by 1830 the most stable currency in the country. Now having twenty-nine branches, it benefited the whole nation. Jackson, however, did not find the bank's functions sufficiently valuable to offset his criticism of the concept of a national bank. In his first two annual messages to Congress, in 1829 and 1830, Jackson claimed that the bank concentrated undue economic power in the hands of a few.

National Republican (Whig) senators Daniel Webster and Henry Clay decided to force the issue. They convinced the bank to apply for charter renewal in 1832, well before the fall election, even though the existing charter ran until 1836. They fully expected that Congress's renewal would force Jackson to follow through on his rhetoric with a veto, that the unpopular veto would cause Jackson to lose the election, and that the bank would survive on an override vote from a new Congress swept into power on the anti-Jackson tide.

At first the plan seemed to work. The bank applied for rechartering, Congress voted to renew, and Jackson, angry over being manipulated, issued his veto. But it was a brilliantly written veto, full of fierce language about the privileges of the moneyed elite who oppress the democratic masses in order to enrich themselves. "Many of our rich men have not been content with equal protection and equal benefits, but have besought us to make them richer by act of Congress," Jackson wrote.

Clay and his supporters found Jackson's economic ideas so absurd and his language of class antagonism so shocking that they distributed thousands of copies of the bank veto as campaign material for their own party. A confident Henry Clay headed his party's ticket for the presidency. But the plan backfired. Jackson's

Fistfight between Old Hickory and Bully Nick
This 1834 cartoon represents President Andrew Jackson squaring off to fight Nicholas Biddle, the director of the Bank of the United States. Pugilism as a semiprofessional sport gained great popularity in the 1830s. The joke here is that the aged Jackson and the aristocratic Biddle would strip to revealing tight pants and engage in open combat. To Biddle's left are his seconds, Daniel Webster and Henry Clay; behind the president is his vice president, Martin Van Buren. Whiskey and port wine lubricate the action.
The Library Company of Philadelphia.

translation of the bank controversy into a language of class antagonism and egalitarian ideals strongly resonated with many Americans. Old Hickory won the election easily, gaining 55 percent of the popular vote and a lopsided electoral college vote of 219 to 49. The Jackson party still controlled Congress, so no override was possible. The second Bank of the United States would cease to exist after 1836.

Jackson, however, wanted to destroy the bank sooner. Calling it a "monster," he ordered the sizable federal deposits to be removed from its vaults and redeposited into favored "pet banks," Democratic-leaning state banks throughout the country. In retaliation, the Bank of the United States raised interest rates and called in loans. This action caused a brief decline

in the economy in 1833 and actually enhanced Jackson's claim that the bank was too powerful for the good of the country.

Unleashed and unregulated, the economy in 1834 went into high gear. Perhaps only a small part of the problem arose from irresponsible banking practices. Just at this moment, an excess of silver from Mexican mines made its way into American banks, giving bankers license to print ever more banknotes. Inflation soared from 1834 to 1837; prices of basic goods rose more than 50 percent. States quickly chartered many hundreds of new private banks. Each bank issued its own banknotes and set

> Jackson's translation of the bank controversy into a language of class antagonism and egalitarian ideals strongly resonated with many Americans.

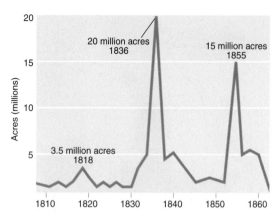

FIGURE 11.1   Western Land Sales, 1810–1860
Land sales peaked in the 1810s, 1830s, and 1850s as Americans rushed to speculate in western lands sold by the federal government. The surges in 1818 and 1836 demonstrate the volatile, speculative economy that suddenly collapsed in the panics of 1819 and 1837.

interest rates as high as the market would bear. Entrepreneurs borrowed and invested money, much of it funneled into privately financed railroads and canals.

The market in western land sales heated up. In 1834, about 4.5 million acres of the public domain had been sold, the highest annual volume since the peak year 1819; by 1836, the total reached an astonishing 20 million acres (Figure 11.1). Some of this was southern land in Mississippi and Louisiana, which slave owners rushed to bring under cultivation, but much more was in the North, where land offices were deluged with buyers. The Jackson administration worried that the purchasers were overwhelmingly eastern capitalists, land speculators instead of self-reliant **yeoman** farmers who intended to settle on the land.

In one respect, the economy attained an admirable goal: The national debt disappeared, and, for the first and only time in American  history, from 1835 to 1837, the government had a monetary surplus. But much of it consisted of questionable bank currencies— "bloated, diseased" currencies, in Jackson's vivid terminology. Jackson decided to restrain the economy. In 1836, the Treasury Department issued the Specie Circular, an order that public land could be purchased only with hard money, federally coined gold and silver. In response, bankers started to reduce their loans, fearing a general contraction

of the economy. Compounding the difficulty, the Bank of England also now insisted on hard-money payments for American loans, which had grown large since 1831 because of a trade imbalance. Failures in various crop markets, a downturn in cotton prices on the international market, and the silver glut, all unrelated to Jackson's fiscal policies, fed the growing economic crisis.

The familiar events of the panic of 1819 unfolded again, with terrifying rapidity. In April 1837, a wave of bank and business failures ensued, and the credit market tumbled like a house of cards. The Specie Circular was only one precipitating cause, but the Whig Party held it and Jackson responsible for the depression. For more than five years after the panic of 1837, the United States suffered from economic hard times.

Van Buren's One-Term Presidency

The election of 1836, which preceded the panic by six months, demonstrated the transformation of the Democrats from coalition to party. Jackson's personality had stamped the elections of 1824, 1828, and 1832. By 1836, the party apparatus was sufficiently developed to support itself. Local and state committees existed throughout the country. Democratic candidates ran in every state election, succeeding even in old Federalist states like Maine and New Hampshire. More than four hundred newspapers declared themselves Democratic. In 1836, the Democrats repeated an innovation begun in 1832: holding a national convention. They nominated Vice President Martin Van Buren of New York for president.

Sophisticated party organization was Martin Van Buren's specialty. Nicknamed the "Little Magician" for his consummate political skills, the New Yorker had built his career by pioneering many of the loyalty-enhancing techniques the Democrats used in the 1830s. After serving as senator and then governor, he became Jackson's secretary of state in 1828. Four years later he replaced Calhoun as Jackson's running mate. His eight years in the volatile Jackson administration required the full measure of his political deftness as he sought repeatedly to save Jackson from both his enemies and his own obstinacy.

Van Buren was a backroom politician, not a popular public figure, and the Whigs hoped that he might be defeatable. In many states, Whigs had captured high office in 1834, shedding the awkward National Republican label and developing statewide organizations to rival those of the Democrats. However, no figure commanded nationwide support. The result was that three candidates opposed Van Buren in 1836, each with a solid regional base. Senator Daniel Webster of Massachusetts could deliver New England; Senator Hugh Lawson White of Tennessee attracted proslavery, pro-Jackson, but anti–Van Buren voters in the South; and the aging General William Henry Harrison of Indiana, memorable for his Indian war heroics in 1811, pulled in the western, anti-Indian vote. Not one of the three candidates could have won the presidency, but together they came close to denying Van Buren a majority vote. Their combined strength drew many Whigs into office at the state level. In the end, Van Buren had 170 electoral votes, while the other three received a total of 113.

Van Buren took office in March 1837, and a month later the panic hit. The new president called a special session of Congress to consider creating an independent treasury system to fulfill some of the functions of the defunct Bank of the United States. Such a system, funded by government deposits, would deal only in hard money, forcing commercial banks to restrict their issuance of paper currency. Equally important, the new system would not make loans and would thus avoid the danger of speculative meddling in the economy. In short, an independent treasury system could exert a powerful moderating influence on inflation and the credit market without itself being directly involved in the market. But Van Buren encountered strong resistance in Congress, even from Democrats. The treasury system finally won approval in 1840; by then, however, Van Buren's chances of a second term in office were virtually nil. With federal bank policy at a stalemate, the four years had proved to be tumultuous for the economy.

In 1840, the Whigs settled on William Henry Harrison, sixty-seven, to oppose Van Buren. The campaign drew on voter involvement as no presidential campaign ever had. The Whigs borrowed tricks from the Democrats: Harrison was touted as a common man born in a log cabin (in reality he was born on a Virginia plantation), and raucus campaign parades featured toy log cabins held aloft. His Indian-fighting days, now thirty years behind him, were played up to give him a Jacksonian aura. Whigs staged festive rallies all over the country, drumming up mass appeal with candlelight parades and song shows. Women partici-

pated in Whig campaign rallies as never before. Some 78 percent of eligible voters cast ballots—the highest percentage ever in American history. Harrison took 53 percent of the popular vote and won a resounding 234 electoral college votes to Van Buren's 60. A Democratic editor lamented, "We have taught them how to conquer us!"

Conclusion: The Age of Jackson or the Era of Reform?

Harrison's election marked the close of a decade that brought the common man and democracy into the forefront of American politics. The same forces that propelled Jacksonian politics also laid the groundwork for the first large wave of American reform activity cresting in the 1830s. Jacksonian Democrats and reform-minded Whigs were on opposite sides of politics, but both were products of vast and important changes marking the 1830s.

One of the most significant of those changes was the economic transformation of the period. Revolutionary advances in transportation put goods and people in circulation, drawing the rural backcountry to the densely settled East Coast and propelling the growth of urban centers. Entrepreneurs figured out new ways to harness the power of water to drive manufacturing. Trade and banking mushroomed, and western lands once occupied by Indians were auctioned off in a landslide of sales. As one religious periodical put it, the country was marked by the "overstrained pursuit of wealth." Two economic downturns, the panics of 1819 and 1837, offered sobering but easily forgotten lessons about where speculative fever can lead.

With increased economic opportunity came increased public involvement in politics. Andrew Jackson symbolized the age for many. His fame as an aggressive general, Indian fighter, champion of the common man, and defender of slavery attracted voters to an emergent Democratic Party that championed personal liberty, free competition, and egalitarian opportunity for all white men.

Jackson's constituency was challenged by a small but vocal segment of the population troubled by serious moral problems that Jacksonians preferred to ignore. Reformers drew sustenance from the message of the Second

Great Awakening: that all men and women are free to choose salvation, and that personal *and* societal sins can be overcome. Reformers targeted personal vices (illicit sex, intemperance) and social problems (prostitution, poverty, and slavery), confident that a perfect world was attainable. Reformers who could vote tended to vote Whig. But of course a lot of reformers—women imbued with a combined sense of benevolence and urgent duty—could not vote at all. Reformers joined forces with evangelicals and wealthy lawyers and merchants North or South who appreciated a national bank and protective tariffs. The Whig Party was the party of activist moralism and state-sponsored entrepreneurship.

National politics in the 1830s were more heated and divisive than at any other time since the 1790s. The new party system of Democrats and Whigs cut far deeper into the electorate than had the previous system of Federalists and Republicans. Stagecoaches and steamboats carried newspapers with their political coverage from the city to the backwoods, politicizing voters who now understood what they might gain or lose under the competing economic policies of the two parties. Politics acquired immediacy and excitement, causing four out of five white men to cast ballots in 1840.

High rates of voter participation would continue into the 1840s and 1850s because politics remained the arena where difficult choices about economic development and social change were contested. Unprecedented urban growth, westward expansion, and early industrialism marked those decades, sustaining the Jacksonian-Whig split in the electorate. But other new challenges not easily dealt with by those two parties—critiques of slavery, concerns for free labor, and an emerging protest against women's second-class citizenship—complicated the political scene of the 1840s, leading to third-party movements that splintered from the two parties of the 1830s. One of these third parties, called the Republican Party, would achieve dominance in 1860 with the election of an Illinois lawyer, Abraham Lincoln, to the presidency.

FOR ADDITIONAL FIRSTHAND ACCOUNTS OF THIS PERIOD, see Chapter 11 in Michael Johnson, ed., *Reading the American Past,* Third Edition.

TO ASSESS YOUR MASTERY OF THE MATERIAL IN THIS CHAPTER, see the Online Study Guide at bedfordstmartins.com/roark.

FOR WEB LINKS RELATED TO TOPICS IN THIS CHAPTER, see "HistoryLinks," "DocLinks," and "PlaceLinks" at bedfordstmartins.com/roark.

CHRONOLOGY

1807 • Robert Fulton develops first commercially successful steamboat, *Clermont.*

1816 • Congress charters second Bank of the United States for twenty years.
• Congress imposes high import tariff on foreign textiles to stimulate American textile manufacturing.

1817 • American Colonization Society founded to promote gradual emancipation and removal of African Americans to Liberia.

1818 • National Road links Baltimore and Wheeling, in western Virginia.

1819 • Economic panic grips nation—the first major short depression.

1821 • Boston entrepreneurs start to build mills with power looms at Lowell, Massachusetts.

1824 • Congress increases tariff on foreign imports.

1825 • Erie Canal spans 350 miles in New York State, in effect linking New York City with Great Lakes.

1826 • American Temperance Society, founded in Connecticut, encourages temperance pledges from working-class laborers as condition of employment.
• Schuylkill Canal—108 miles long—opens in Pennsylvania.

1828 • Congress passes Tariff of Abominations, setting the stage for South Carolina's nullification of federal law.

- Democrat Andrew Jackson elected president.

1829
- David Walker's *Appeal . . . to the Coloured Citizens of the World* published in Boston.
- Baltimore and Ohio Railroad, the first U.S. railroad, lays 13 miles of track.

1830
- Indian Removal Act appropriates money to relocate Indian tribes west of Mississippi River.
- First National Negro Convention meets in Philadelphia to discuss status of free blacks in the North; such conventions continue for three decades.

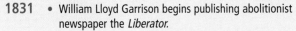

1831
- William Lloyd Garrison begins publishing abolitionist newspaper the *Liberator.*
- Charles G. Finney stages evangelical revival in Rochester, New York, taking Second Great Awakening mainstream to the new business classes.
- U.S. Supreme Court fails to prevent Georgia from subjecting Cherokee Indians to state laws.

1832
- Chief Black Hawk and Sauk and Fox Indians lose war against American militias in Illinois and Wisconsin.
- U.S. Supreme Court in *Worcester v. Georgia* recognizes Cherokees as distinct community outside legal jurisdiction of Georgia.
- Jackson vetoes Bank of the United States charter, gaining greater popularity and momentum for victory in the fall election; Henry Clay greatly surprised.

- Maria Stewart of Boston becomes one of the first American women to speak in public lectures on social issues.
- New England Anti-Slavery Society founded—the start of an organized and sustained antislavery movement.
- Andrew Jackson elected to a second term.

1833
- Nullification crisis: South Carolina declares federal tariffs void in the state.
- New York and Philadelphia antislavery societies founded.
- New York Female Moral Reform Society founded, with goal to curb male sexual excess.

1834–1836
- Female mill workers strike in Lowell, Massachusetts, protesting wage cuts and work speedups—the first major labor strike in U.S. history.

1836
- Jackson issues Specie Circular, requiring use of hard money to purchase public lands; start of contraction of the economy.
- Democrat Martin Van Buren elected president.

1837
- Economic panic.

1838
- Trail of Tears—Cherokees forced to relocate west.

1840
- Whig William Henry Harrison elected president.

BIBLIOGRAPHY

General Works

Daniel Feller, *The Jacksonian Promise: America, 1815–1840* (1995).
Michael F. Holt, *Political Parties and American Political Development from the Age of Jackson to the Age of Lincoln* (1992).
Merrill D. Peterson, *The Great Triumvirate: Webster, Clay, and Calhoun* (1987).
Charles G. Sellers, *The Market Revolution: Jacksonian America, 1815–1846* (1991).
Harry L. Watson, *Liberty and Power: The Politics of Jacksonian America* (1990).
Robert H. Wiebe, *The Opening of American Society: From the Adoption of the Constitution to the Eve of Disunion* (1984).

The Market Revolution

Elizabeth Blackmar, *Manhattan for Rent, 1785–1850* (1989).
Mary H. Blewett, *Men, Women, and Work: Class, Gender, and Protest in the New England Shoe Industry, 1780–1910* (1988).

Jeanne Boydston, *Home and Work: Housework, Wages, and the Ideology of Labor in the Early Republic* (1990).
Christopher Clark, *The Roots of Rural Capitalism: Worcester, Massachusetts, 1780–1860* (1990).
Alan Dawley, *Class and Community: The Industrial Revolution in Lynn* (1976).
Thomas Dublin, *Women at Work: The Transformation of Work and Community in Lowell, Massachusetts, 1826–1860* (1979).
Thomas Dublin, *Transforming Women's Work: New England Lives in the Industrial Revolution* (1994).
Tony A. Freyer, *Producers versus Capitalists: Constitutional Conflict in Antebellum America* (1994).
Paul A. Gilje, ed., *Wages of Independence: Capitalism in the Early Republic* (1997).
Jonathan A. Glickstein, *Anxiety: Wages, Competition, and Degraded Labor in the Antebellum United States* (2002).
Erik F. Haites, James Mak, and Gary M. Walton, *Western River Transportation: The Era of Early Internal Development, 1800–1860* (1975).

Morton J. Horwitz, *The Transformation of American Law, 1780–1860* (1977).

Bruce Laurie, *Artisans into Workers: Labor in Nineteenth-Century America* (1989).

John D. Majewski, *A House Dividing: Economic Development in Pennsylvania and Virginia before the Civil War* (2000).

Otto Mayr and Robert C. Post, eds., *Yankee Enterprise: The Rise of the American System of Manufactures* (1981).

Lawrence A. Peskin, *Manufacturing Revolution: The Intellectual Origins of Early American Industry* (2003).

Ronald E. Shaw, *Erie Water West: A History of the Erie Canal, 1792–1854* (1990).

Carol Sheriff, *The Artificial River: The Erie Canal and the Paradox of Progress, 1817–1862* (1996).

Richard B. Stott, *Workers in the Metropolis: Class, Ethnicity, and Youth in Antebellum New York City* (1990).

Christopher L. Tomlins, *Law, Labor, and Ideology in the Early American Republic* (1993).

Barbara Tucker, *Samuel Slater and the Origins of the American Textile Industry, 1790–1860* (1984).

The Spread of Democracy

Andrew Burstein, *The Passions of Andrew Jackson* (2003).

Marshall Foletta, *Coming to Terms with Democracy: Federalist Intellectuals and the Shaping of an American Culture* (2001).

Ronald P. Formisano, *The Birth of Mass Political Parties: Michigan, 1827–1861* (1971).

Paul Goodman, *Towards a Christian Republic: Antimasonry and the Great Transition in New England, 1826–1836* (1988).

Daniel W. Howe, *The Political Culture of the American Whigs* (1980).

Lawrence Frederick Kohl, *The Politics of Individualism: Parties and the American Character in the Jacksonian Era* (1989).

Robert V. Remini, *Andrew Jackson and the Course of American Freedom, 1822–1832* (1981).

Robert V. Remini, *The Life of Andrew Jackson* (2001).

Alexander Saxton, *The Rise and Fall of the White Republic: Class Politics and Mass Culture in Nineteenth-Century America* (1990).

Sean Wilentz, *Chants Democratic: New York City and the Rise of the American Working Class, 1788–1850* (1984).

Culture and Society

Gerald J. Baldasty, *The Commercialization of News in the Nineteenth Century* (1992).

Stuart M. Blumin, *The Emergence of the Middle Class: Social Experience in the American City, 1760–1900* (1989).

Richard L. Bushman, *The Refinement of America: Persons, Houses, Cities* (1992).

Kenneth Cmiel, *Democratic Eloquence: The Fight over Popular Speech in Nineteenth-Century America* (1990).

Patricia Cline Cohen, *The Murder of Helen Jewett: The Life and Death of a Prostitute in Nineteenth-Century New York* (1998).

Faye E. Dudden, *Women in the American Theatre: Actresses and Audiences, 1790–1870* (1994).

Ann Fabian, *Card-Sharps, Dream Books, and Bucket Shops: Gambling in Nineteenth-Century America* (1990).

Timothy J. Gilfoyle, *City of Eros: New York City, Prostitution, and the Commercialization of Sex, 1790–1920* (1992).

Karen Halttunen, *Confidence Men and Painted Women: A Study of Middle-Class Culture in America, 1830–1870* (1982).

Shawn Johansen, *Family Men: Middle-Class Fatherhood in Early Industrializing America* (2001).

Richard R. John, *Spreading the News: The American Postal System from Franklin to Morse* (1995).

Carl F. Kaestle, *Pillars of the Republic: Common Schools and American Society, 1780–1860* (1983).

John F. Kasson, *Rudeness and Civility: Manners in Nineteenth-Century America* (1990).

Lawrence W. Levine, *Highbrow/Lowbrow: The Emergence of Cultural Hierarchy in America* (1988).

Louis P. Masur, *1831: Year of Eclipse* (2001).

Lewis Perry, *Boats against the Current: American Culture between Revolution and Modernity, 1820–1860* (1993).

E. Anthony Rotundo, *American Manhood: Transformations in Masculinity from the Revolution to the Modern Era* (1993).

Mary P. Ryan, *Women in Public: Between Banners and Ballots, 1825–1880* (1990).

Carroll Smith-Rosenberg, *Disorderly Conduct: Visions of Gender in Victorian America* (1985).

Christine Stansell, *City of Women: Sex and Class in New York, 1789–1860* (1986).

Richard B. Stott, *Workers in the Metropolis: Class, Ethnicity, and Youth in Antebellum New York City* (1990).

Alan Taylor, *William Cooper's Town: Power and Persuasion on the Frontier of the Early American Republic* (1995).

Ronald J. Zboray, *A Fictive People: Antebellum Development and the American Reading Public* (1993).

Reform and Religion

Robert Abzug, *Cosmos Crumbling: American Reform and the Religious Imagination* (1994).

R. J. M. Blackett, *Building an Antislavery Wall: Black Americans in the Atlantic Abolitionist Movement, 1830–1860* (1983).

Ellen Eslinger, *Citizens of Zion: The Social Origins of Camp Meeting Revivalism* (1999).

Lawrence J. Friedman, *Gregarious Saints: Self and Community in American Abolitionism, 1830–1870* (1982).

Lori D. Ginzberg, *Women and the Work of Benevolence: Morality, Politics, and Class in the Nineteenth-Century United States* (1990).

Charles E. Hambrick-Stowe, *Charles G. Finney and the Spirit of American Evangelicalism* (1996).

Stanley Harrold, *The Abolitionists and the South, 1831–1861* (1995).

Stanley Harrold, *Subversives: Antislavery Community in Washington, D.C., 1828–1865* (2003).

Nathan O. Hatch, *The Democratization of American Christianity* (1989).

Nancy A. Hewitt, *Women's Activism and Social Change: Rochester, New York, 1822–1872* (1984).

Christine Leigh Heyrman, *Southern Cross: The Beginnings of the Bible Belt* (1997).

Donald M. Jacobs, ed., *Courage and Conscience: Black and White Abolitionists in Boston* (1993).

Julie Roy Jeffrey, *The Great Silent Army of Abolitionism: Ordinary Women in the Antislavery Movement* (1998).

Paul E. Johnson, *A Shopkeeper's Millennium: Society and Revivals in Rochester, New York, 1815–1837* (1978).

Paul E. Johnson and Sean Wilentz, *The Kingdom of Matthias* (1994).

Katharine Du Pré Lumpkin, *The Emancipation of Angelina Grimké* (1974).

Steven Mintz, *Moralists and Modernizers: America's Pre–Civil War Reformers* (1995).

Richard S. Newman, *The Transformation of American Abolitionism: Fighting Slavery in the Early Republic* (2002).

Jane and William H. Pease, *They Who Would Be Free: Blacks' Search for Freedom, 1830–1861* (1990).

Benjamin Quarles, *Black Abolitionists* (1969).

Mary P. Ryan, *Cradle of the Middle Class: The Family in Oneida County, New York, 1790–1865* (1981).

Ian Tyrrell, *Sobering Up: From Temperance to Prohibition in Antebellum America, 1800–1860* (1979).

Jean Fagan Yellin and John C. Van Horne, eds., *The Abolitionist Sisterhood: Women's Political Culture in Antebellum America* (1994).

Jacksonian Politics

Irving H. Bartlett, *John C. Calhoun: A Biography* (1993).

Maurice G. Baxter, *Henry Clay and the American System* (1995).

Hendrik Booraem, *Young Hickory: The Making of Andrew Jackson* (2001).

Donald B. Cole, *The Presidency of Andrew Jackson* (1993).

Richard E. Ellis, *The Union at Risk: Jacksonian Democracy, States' Rights, and the Nullification Crisis* (1987).

Daniel Feller, *The Public Lands in Jacksonian Politics* (1984).

William W. Freehling, *Prelude to Civil War: The Nullification Controversy in South Carolina, 1816–1836* (1965).

Michael F. Holt, *The Rise and Fall of the American Whig Party: Jacksonian Politics and the Onset of the Civil War* (1999).

Peter B. Knupfer, *The Union as It Is: Constitutional Unionism and Sectional Compromise, 1787–1861* (1991).

Richard B. Latner, *The Presidency of Andrew Jackson: White House Politics, 1829–1837* (1979).

John Niven, *Martin Van Buren: The Romantic Age of American Politics* (1983).

John Niven, *John C. Calhoun and the Price of Union: A Biography* (1988).

Lynn Hudson Parsons, *John Quincy Adams* (1998).

Robert V. Remini, *Henry Clay: Statesman for the Union* (1991).

Robert V. Remini, *Daniel Webster: The Man and His Time* (1997).

Leonard Richards, *The Life and Times of Congressman John Quincy Adams* (1986).

Native Americans

William H. Anderson, *Cherokee Removal: Before and After* (1991).

John A. Andrew, *From Revivals to Removal: Jeremiah Evarts, the Cherokee Nation, and the Search for the Soul of America* (1992).

Black Hawk, *Black Hawk's Autobiography* (1999).

John Drinnan, *Facing West: The Metaphysics of Indian Hating and Empire Building* (1981).

John Ehle, *Trail of Tears: The Rise and Fall of the Cherokee Nation* (1997).

David S. Heidler and Jeanne T. Heidler, *Old Hickory's War: Andrew Jackson and the Quest for Empire* (1996).

Roger L. Nichols, *Black Hawk and the Warrior's Path* (1992).

Sean Michael O'Brien, *In Bitterness and in Tears: Andrew Jackson's Destruction of the Creeks and Seminoles* (2003).

Theda Perdue, *Cherokee Women: Gender and Culture Change, 1700–1835* (1998).

Theda Perdue and Michael D. Green, eds., *The Cherokee Removal: A Brief History with Documents* (1995).

Robert V. Remini, *Andrew Jackson and His Indian Wars* (2001).

Michael Paul Rogin, *Fathers and Children: Andrew Jackson and the Subjugation of the American Indian* (1975).

Anders Stephanson, *Manifest Destiny: American Expansionism and the Empire of Right* (1996).

Anthony F. C. Wallace, *The Long, Bitter Trail: Andrew Jackson and the Indians* (1993).

Philip Weeks, *Farewell, My Nation: The American Indian and the United States, 1820–1890* (1990).

J. Leitch Wright, *The Only Land They Knew: The Tragic Story of the American Indians in the Old South* (1981).

GOLD NUGGETS
Gold! Nuggets like these scooped from a California river drove
Easterners crazy with excitement. A quarter of a million people joined
the great rush for western riches in the five years after gold's discovery in 1848. Men from the East and around the world sought to escape
routine jobs and mundane lives by "making their pile" in California.
The carnival that was the gold rush fulfilled the hopes of only a
few, but the rest participated in one of the great adventures of the
nineteenth-century and rarely regretted their experiences.
The Oakland Museum.

The New West and Free North

1840–1860

EARLY IN NOVEMBER 1842, Abraham Lincoln and his new wife, Mary, moved into their first home in Springfield, Illinois, a rented room measuring eight by fourteen feet on the second floor of the Globe Tavern, the nicest place Abraham had ever lived. A busy blacksmith shop next door filled the Lincolns' room with the clanging of iron being pounded into horseshoes, hinges, and other useful shapes. Mary Todd Lincoln had grown up in Lexington, Kentucky, attended by slaves in the elegant home of her father, a prosperous merchant, banker, and politician. The small, noisy room above the Globe Tavern was the worst place she had ever lived. Fewer than twenty years later, in March 1861, the Lincolns moved into what would prove to be their last home, the presidential mansion in Washington, D.C. Abraham Lincoln climbed from the Globe Tavern to the White House by relentless work, unslaked ambition, and immense talent, traits he had honed since boyhood.

Born in a Kentucky log cabin in 1809, Lincoln grew up on small, struggling farms as his family moved westward. His father, Thomas, moved to Kentucky from Virginia, where he had been born, and he never learned to read or, as Abraham explained, "never did more in the way of writing than to bunglingly sign his own name." Lincoln's mother, Nancy, could neither read nor write. In December 1816, Thomas Lincoln moved his young family out of Kentucky, crossing the Ohio River to the Indiana wilderness. They lived for two frozen months in a crude lean-to only partially enclosed by limbs and bushes while Thomas, a skilled carpenter, built a new cabin. On the Indiana farmstead, Abraham learned the arts of agriculture practiced by families throughout the nation. Although only eight years old, Abraham "had an axe put into his hands at once" and used it "almost constantly" for the next fifteen years, he recalled. He worked for neighbors for twenty-five cents a day and gave the money to his father. When he could be spared from work, the boy attended school, less than a year in all. "There was absolutely nothing to excite ambition for education," Lincoln recollected. In contrast, Mary Todd, his future wife, received ten years of schooling in Lexington's best academies for young women.

By 1830, Thomas Lincoln decided to move farther west and start over again. The Lincolns hitched up the family oxen and headed two hundred miles west to central Illinois, and there they built another log cabin. The next spring Thomas Lincoln moved once again, and this time Abraham stayed behind and set out on his own, a "friendless, uneducated, penniless boy," as he described himself.

Abraham Lincoln's Hat
Abraham Lincoln wore this stovepipe hat, made of beaver pelt, during his years as president of the United States. Stovepipe hats were worn by established, respectable, middle-class men in the 1850s. Workingmen and farmers would have felt out of place wearing such a hat, except perhaps on special occasions like weddings or funerals. Growing up in Kentucky, Indiana, and Illinois, Lincoln may have seen stovepipe hats on the leading men of his community, but he probably never owned one until he became an aspiring Illinois lawyer and politician. Wearing such a hat was a mark that one had achieved a certain success in life, in Lincoln's case the enormous social distance he had traveled from his backwoods origins to the White House. But even as president he continued a backwoods practice he had begun as a young postmaster in New Salem, Illinois, using his hat as a place to store letters and papers. Lincoln's law partner William Herndon termed Lincoln's hat "an extraordinary receptacle [that] served as his desk and memorandum book."
Smithsonian Institution, Washington, D.C.

By dogged striving, Lincoln gained an education and the respect of his Illinois neighbors, although a steady income eluded him for years. He and Mary received help from her father. Shortly after their marriage, he gave the young couple eighty acres of land and promised them a yearly allowance of about $1,100 for six years, helping them to move out of their room above the Globe Tavern. Lincoln eventually built a thriving law practice in Springfield and served in the Illinois legislature and then in Congress. His political activity and hard-driving ambition ultimately catapulted him into the White House, the first president to be born west of the Appalachian Mountains.

Like Lincoln, millions of Americans believed they could make something of themselves, whatever their origins, so long as they were willing to work. Individuals who refused to work—who were lazy, improvident, or foolish—had only themselves to blame if they failed. Work was a prerequisite for success, not a guarantee. The promise of rewards from hard work spurred efforts that shaped the contours of America, pushing the boundaries of the nation south to the Rio Grande, north to the Great Lakes, and ever westward from Indiana, Illinois, Iowa, and Kansas to Texas, Oregon, California, and the Pacific Ocean. During his presidency, Lincoln himself talked about moving to California at the end of his term. The economic, political, and geographic expansion that Lincoln exemplified raised anew the question of whether slavery should also move west, the question that Lincoln and other Americans confronted again and again following the Mexican War, yet another outgrowth of the nation's ceaseless westward movement.

The Westward Movement

Westward expansion was nothing new in American history, but the 1840s ushered in a new era of rapid westward movement. Until then, the overwhelming majority of Americans lived east of the Mississippi River. To the west, Native Americans inhabited the plains, prairies, and deserts to the rugged coasts of the Pacific. The British claimed Oregon Country, and the Mexican flag flew over the vast expanse of the Southwest. But by 1850, the boundaries of the United States stretched to the Pacific, and the nation had more than doubled its size. By 1860, the great migration had carried four million Americans west of the Mississippi River.

Thomas Jefferson, John Quincy Adams, and other government officials had helped clear the way for the march across the continent by aggressively acquiring territory in the west. The nation's revolution in transportation and communication, its swelling population, and its booming economy propelled the westward surge. But the emigrants themselves conquered the continent. Shock troops of the American empire, **frontier** settlers craving land took the soil and then, with the exception of the Mormons in Deseret, lobbied their government to follow them with the flag. The human cost of westward expansion was high. The young Mexican nation suffered a humiliating defeat and the loss of half its territory. Two centuries of Indian wars east of the Mississippi ended during the 1830s, but the old, fierce struggle between native inhabitants and invaders continued for another half century in the West.

> By 1850, the boundaries of the United States stretched to the Pacific, and the nation had more than doubled its size.

Manifest Destiny

Most Americans believed that the superiority of their institutions and white culture bestowed on them a God-given right to spread their civilization across the continent. They imagined the West as a howling wilderness, empty and undeveloped. If they recognized Indians and Mexicans at all, they dismissed them as primitive drags on progress who would have to be redeemed, shoved aside, or exterminated. The sense of uniqueness and mission was as old as the Puritans, but by the 1840s the conviction of superiority had been bolstered by the United States's amazing success. The West needed the civilizing power of the hammer and plow, the ballot box and pulpit, that had transformed the East, most Americans believed.

In 1845, New York journalist John L. O'Sullivan coined the term **manifest destiny** as the latest justification for white settlers to take the land they coveted. Although O'Sullivan was only an armchair expansionist, he took second place to no one in his passion for conquest of the West. He called on Americans to resist any foreign power—British, French, or Mexican—that attempted to thwart "the fulfillment of our manifest destiny to overspread the continent allotted

In the Mountains, **Albert Bierstadt, 1867**
Born and trained in Germany, Albert Bierstadt visited the American West for the first time in 1859 with a U.S. government expedition searching for shortcuts along the Oregon Trail. The Rocky Mountains captured his imagination. He portrays a new Eden, an epic landscape of spectacular beauty that silently beckons a restless, questing young nation. Bountiful, empty, lacking any marks of civilization, Bierstadt's West shimmers in a golden light, a kind of divine sanction of manifest destiny. The writer Mark Twain claimed that Bierstadt's landscapes were more beautiful than even the Creator's, but he lamented that the artist strayed from factual accuracy. Indeed, Bierstadt painted his dramatic images back in his New York studio (or even in Europe), where he was less interested in accuracy than in creating a romantic visual metaphor for America's national potential.
The Wadsworth Atheneum, Hartford. Gift of John J. Morgan in memory of his mother, Juliet Pierpont Morgan.

by Providence for the free development of our yearly multiplying millions . . . [and] for the development of the great experiment of liberty and federative self-government entrusted to us." Almost overnight, the magic phrase *manifest destiny* swept the nation and provided an ideological shield for conquering the West.

As important as national pride and racial arrogance were to manifest destiny, economic gain made up its core. Land hunger drew hundreds of thousands of average Americans westward. Some politicians, moreover, had become convinced that national prosperity depended on capturing the rich trade of the Far East. To trade with Asia, the United States needed the Pacific coast ports that stretched from San Francisco to Puget Sound. No one was more eager to extend American trade in the Pacific than Missouri's Senator Thomas Hart Benton. "The sun of civilization must shine across the sea: socially and commercially," he declared. The United States and Asia must "talk together, and trade together. Commerce is a great civilizer." In the 1840s, American economic expansion came wrapped in the rhetoric of uplift and civilization.

Plains Indians and Trails West in the 1840s and 1850s

Oregon and the Overland Trail

Oregon Country—a vast region bounded on the west by the Pacific, on the east by the Rockies, on the south by the forty-second parallel, and on the north by Russian Alaska—caused the pulse of American expansionists to race (Map 12.1). But Americans were not alone in hungrily eyeing the Pacific Northwest. The British traced their interest—and their rights—to the voyage of Sir Francis Drake, who, they argued, discovered the Oregon coast in 1579. Americans matched the British assertion with historic claims of their own. Unable to agree on ownership, the United States and Great Britain decided in 1818 on "joint occupation" that would leave Oregon "free and open" to settlement by both countries. A handful of American fur traders and "mountain men" roamed the region in the 1820s, but in the 1830s and 1840s expansionists made Oregon Country an early target of manifest destiny.

By the late 1830s, settlers began to trickle along the Oregon Trail, following a path blazed by the mountain men. The first wagon trains hit the trail in 1841, and by 1843 about 1,000 emigrants a year set out from Independence, Missouri. By 1869, when the first transcontinental railroad was completed, something like 350,000 migrants had traveled west to the Pacific in wagon trains.

Emigrants encountered Plains Indians, whose cultures differed markedly from those of the Eastern Woodland tribes (see chapter 1). The quarter of a million Native Americans who populated the area between the Rocky Mountains and the Mississippi River defy easy generalization. Some were farmers who lived peaceful, sedentary lives, but a majority of Plains Indians—the Sioux, Cheyenne, Shoshone, and Arapaho of the central Plains and the Kiowa, Wichita, Apache, and Comanche in the Southwest—were horse-mounted, nomadic, nonagricultural peoples whose warriors symbolized the "savage Indian" in the minds of whites.

Horses, which had been brought to North America by Spaniards in the sixteenth century, permitted the Plains tribes to become highly mobile hunters of buffalo. In time, they came to depend on buffalo for most of their food, clothing, shelter, and fuel. As they followed the huge herds over the plains, these peoples bumped into one another. Competition and warfare became crucial components of their way of life. Young men were introduced to the art of war early, learning to ride ponies at breakneck speed while firing off arrows and, later, rifles with astounding accuracy. "A Comanche on his feet is out of his element," observed George Catlin, an artist of the West, "but the moment he lays his hands upon his horse, his *face* even becomes handsome, and he gracefully flies away like a different being."

Plains Indians struck fear in the hearts of whites on the wagon trains. But Native Americans had far more to fear from whites. Indians killed fewer than 400 emigrants on the trail between 1840 and 1860, while whites proved to be deadly to the Indians. Even though

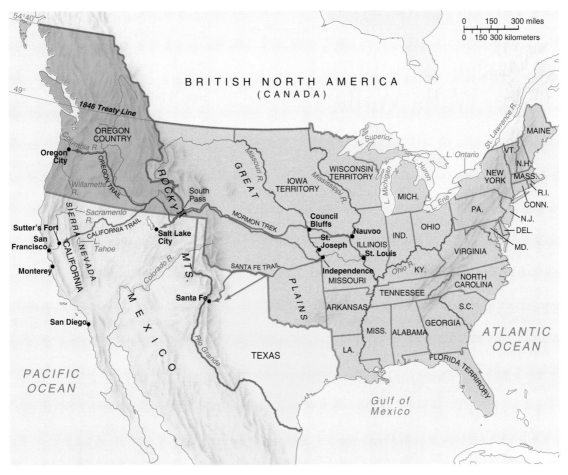

MAP 12.1   Trails to the West
In the 1830s, wagon trains began snaking their way to the Southwest and the Pacific coast. Deep ruts, some of which can still be seen today, soon marked the most popular routes.

they were usually just passing through on their way to the Pacific Slope, whites brought alcohol and disease, especially epidemics of smallpox, measles, cholera, and scarlet fever. Moreover, whites killed the buffalo, often slaughtering them for sport. Buffalo still numbered some twelve million in 1860, but the herds were shrinking rapidly, intensifying conflict among the Plains Indians.

As the number of wagon trains increased, emigrants insisted that the federal government provide them more protection. The government responded by constructing a chain of forts along the Oregon Trail. More important, the United States adopted a new Indian policy: "concentration." The government rescinded the "permanent" buffer it had granted the Indians west of the ninety-fifth meridian, which was only two or three hundred miles west of the Mississippi River. Then, in 1851, it called the Plains tribes to a conference at Fort Laramie, Wyoming. Some ten thousand Dakota, Sioux, Arapaho, Cheyenne, Crow, and other Indians showed up, hopeful that something could be done to protect them from the ravages of the wagon trains. Instead, U.S. government negotiators persuaded the chiefs to sign agreements that cleared a wide corridor for wagon trains by restricting Native Americans to specific areas that whites promised they would never violate. This policy of concentration became the seedbed for the subsequent policy of reservations. But whites would not keep out of Indian territory, and Indians would not easily give up their traditional ways of life. (See "American Places," page 400.) Competition meant warfare for decades to come.

> Whites would not keep out of Indian territory, and Indians would not easily give up their traditional ways of life.

AMERICAN PLACES

Whitman Mission National Historic Site, Walla Walla, Washington

In 1836, Marcus and Narcissa Whitman, Presbyterian missionaries from New York, joined a group of fur trappers bound for Oregon Country. Scores of other missionaries would follow, but Narcissa Whitman was one of the first two white women to cross the continent overland. Settling among the Cayuse Indians near present-day Walla Walla, Washington, the Whitmans established a mission station to promote Christianity and "civilization." Their efforts created tensions with the Cayuse, especially in the 1840s when the mission became a stop for wagon trains traveling the Oregon Trail. The newcomers slaughtered game, took Indian land, and inadvertently brought disease. When a measles outbreak in 1847 killed nearly half of the local Cayuse, the survivors blamed the whites and attacked the mission, killing the Whitmans and eleven others. News of the murders shocked the nation and prompted Congress to make Oregon a U.S. territory. It also reinforced in easterners' imaginations links between Indians, heathenism, violence, and the West.

Since 1936, the National Park Service has managed the 98-acre Whitman Mission site. Visitors can walk a portion of the old Oregon Trail, which runs through the property. The foundations of the original buildings are visible, and outdoor exhibits revive for visitors the feel of the mission in the 1840s. The Cayuse called the area Waiilatpu, "Place of the Rye Grass," and the Park Service has restored the natural grasses to the site. The Whitman Mission also preserves the grave of the thirteen individuals who were killed. Two of the thirteen, John and Frank Sager, were members of the remarkable Sager family of seven children who arrived at the mission in 1844. The children were orphaned on the Oregon Trail and adopted by Marcus and Narcissa Whitman. The 1847 attack orphaned the five surviving Sagers a second time. The Sager story reminds us of the risks families took when they struck out on the Oregon Trail. The Whitman site exemplifies the violence that so often accompanied the clash of cultures and interests between U.S. citizens and Native Americans in the West.

FOR WEB LINKS RELATED TO THIS SITE AND OTHER AMERICAN PLACES, see "PlaceLinks" at bedfordstmartins.com/roark.

Whitman Mission Reenactors on the Oregon Trail
Whitman Mission National Historic Site.

Still, Indians threatened emigrants less than life on the trail did. The men, women, and children who headed west each spring could count on at least six months of grueling travel. With nearly two thousand miles to go and traveling no more than fifteen miles a day, the pioneers endured parching heat, drought, treacherous rivers, disease, physical and emotional exhaustion, and, if the snows closed the mountain passes before they got through, freezing and starvation. Women sometimes faced the dangers of trailside childbirth. It was said that a person could walk from Missouri to the Pacific stepping only on the graves of those who had died heading west.

Everyone experienced hardships on the trail, but no one felt the burden quite as much as the women. Because husbands usually made the decision to pull up stakes and go west, many wives went involuntarily. One miserable woman, trying to keep her children dry in a rainstorm and to calm them as they listened to Indian shouts, wondered "what had possessed my husband, anyway, that he should have thought of bringing us away out through this God forsaken country." Men viewed the privation as a necessary step to land of their own and an independent life; women tended to judge it by the homes, kin, and friends they had left behind to take up what one called "this wild goose chase."

When men reached Oregon, they usually liked what they found. Oregon is "one of the greatest countries in the world," Richard R. Howard declared. From "the Cascade mountains to the Pacific, the whole country can be cultivated." When women reached Oregon, they found a wilderness. "I had all I could do to keep from asking George to turn around and bring me back home," one woman wrote to her mother in Missouri. Neighbors were few and far between, and the isolation weighed heavily. Moreover, things were in a "primitive state." One young wife set up housekeeping with her new husband with only one stew kettle and three knives. Necessity blurred the traditional division between men's and women's work. "I am maid of all traids," one busy woman remarked in 1853. Work seemed unending. "I am a very old woman," remarked twenty-nine-year-old Sarah Everett. "My face is thin sunken and wrinkled, my hands bony withered and hard." As another settler observed, "A woman that can not endure almost as much as a horse has no business here."

Kee-O-Kuk, the Watchful Fox, Chief of the Tribe, George Catlin, 1835
In the 1830s, Pennsylvania-born artist George Catlin traveled the West painting Native American portraits, rituals, and landscapes. Although not the first artist to paint Indians, he was the first to portray them in their own environments and one of the few to present them as human beings, not savages. Convinced that western Indian cultures would soon disappear, Catlin sought to document Indian life through hundreds of paintings and prints. Keokuk, chief of the Sac and Fox, struggled with the warrior Black Hawk about the proper strategy for dealing with whites. Black Hawk fought American expansion; Keokuk believed war was fruitless and signed over land in Illinois, Missouri, and Wisconsin.
Smithsonian American Art Institution, Washington, D.C. Gift of Mrs. Joseph Harrison Jr.

Despite the ordeal of the trail and the difficulties of starting from scratch, emigrants kept coming. By 1845, Oregon counted 5,000 American settlers. And from the beginning, they clamored for the protection of the U.S. government.

The Mormon Exodus

Not every wagon train heading west was bound for the Pacific Slope. One remarkable group of religious emigrants chose to settle in the heart of the arid West. Halting near the Great Salt Lake in what was then Mexican territory, the Mormons deliberately chose the remote site as a refuge. After years of persecution in the East, they fled west to find religious freedom and communal security.

In 1830, Joseph Smith Jr., who was only twenty-four, published *The Book of Mormon* and founded the Church of Jesus Christ of Latter-Day Saints (the Mormons). A decade earlier, the upstate New York farm boy had begun to have visions and revelations that were followed, he

Pioneer Family on the Trail West
In 1860, W. G. Chamberlain photographed these unidentified travelers momentarily at rest by the upper Arkansas River in Colorado. We do not know their fates, but we can hope that they fared better than the Sager family: Henry, Naomi, and their six children, who set out from St. Joseph, Missouri, in 1844. "Father," one of Henry and Naomi's daughters remembered, "was one of those restless men who are not content to remain in one place long at a time. [He] had been talking of going to Texas. But mother, hearing much said about the healthfulness of Oregon, preferred to go there." Still far from Oregon, Henry Sager died of fever; twenty-six days later, Naomi died, leaving seven children, the last delivered on the trail. The Sager children, under the care of other families in the wagon train, pressed on. After traveling 2,000 miles in seven months, the migrants arrived in Oregon, where Marcus and Narcissa Whitman, whose own daughter had drowned, adopted all seven of the Sager children.
Denver Public Library, Western History Division # F3226.

FOR MORE HELP ANALYZING THIS IMAGE, see the visual activity for this chapter in the Online Study Guide at bedfordstmartins.com/roark.

said, by a visit from an angel who led him to golden tablets buried near his home. With the aid of magic stones, Smith translated the mysterious language on the tablets. What was revealed was *The Book of Mormon*. It told the story of an ancient Christian civilization in the New World and predicted the appearance of an American prophet who would reestablish Jesus Christ's undefiled kingdom in America. Converts, attracted to the promise of a pure faith in the midst of **antebellum** America's social turmoil and rampant materialism, flocked to the new church.

Neighbors branded Mormons heretics, and persecution drove Smith and his followers from New York to Ohio, then to Missouri, and finally in 1839 to Nauvoo, Illinois, where they built a prosperous community of fifteen thousand. But dissenters within the church accused Smith of advocating plural marriage (polygamy) and published an exposé of the practice. Non-Mormons caught wind of the controversy and eventually arrested Smith and his brother. On June 27, 1844, a mob stormed the jail and shot both men dead.

The embattled church turned to an extraordinary new leader, Brigham Young, who immediately began to plan the exodus of his people from Illinois. In 1846, traveling in 3,700 wagons, 12,000 Mormons made their way to eastern Iowa; the following year they arrived at their new home beside the Great Salt Lake. Young described the region as a barren waste, "the paradise of the lizard, the cricket and the rattlesnake." Within ten years, however, the Mormons developed an extensive irrigation system and made the desert bloom. They accomplished the feat through cooperative labor, not the individualistic and competitive enterprise common among most emigrants. Under the stern leadership of Young and other church leaders, the Mormons built a thriving community.

In 1850, only three years after its founding, Deseret, as the Mormons called their kingdom, became annexed to the United States as Utah Territory. But what focused the nation's attention on the Latter-Day Saints was the announcement by Brigham Young in 1852 that many Mormons practiced polygamy. Although only one Mormon man in five had more than one wife (Young had twenty-three), Young's public statement caused an outcry that forced the U.S. government to establish its authority in Utah. In 1857, 2,500 U.S. troops invaded Salt Lake City in what was known as the Mormon War. The bloodless occupation illustrates that most Americans viewed the Mormons as a threat to American morality, law, and institutions. The invasion did not dislodge the Mormon Church from its central place in Utah, however, and for years to come most Americans perceived the Mormon settlement as a strange and suitably isolated place.

The Mexican Borderlands

In the Mexican Southwest, westward-moving Anglo-American pioneers confronted northern-moving Spanish-speaking frontiersmen. On this frontier of brush country, deserts, and mountains, as elsewhere, national cultures, interests, and aspirations collided. Since 1821, when Mexico won its independence from Spain, the Mexican flag had flown over the vast expanse that stretched from the Gulf of Mexico to the Pacific and from Oregon Country to Guatemala (Map 12.2). Mexico's borders remained ill defined, and its northern provinces were sparsely populated. Moreover, severe problems plagued the young nation: civil wars, economic crises, quarrels with the Roman Catholic Church, and devastating raids by the Comanche, Apache, and Kiowa. Mexico found it increasingly difficult to defend its borderlands, especially when faced with a northern neighbor convinced of its superiority and bent on territorial acquisition.

The American assault began quietly. In the 1820s, Anglo-American trappers, traders, and settlers drifted into Mexico's far northern provinces and discovered that their newly independent neighbor was eager for American business. Santa Fe, a remote outpost in the province of New Mexico, became a magnet for American enterprise. Each spring, American traders gathered at Independence, Missouri, for the long trek southwest along the Santa Fe Trail (see Map 12.1). They crammed their wagons with inexpensive American manufactured goods and returned home with Mexican silver, furs, and mules.

The Mexican province of Texas attracted a flood of Americans who had settlement, not long-distance trade, on their minds (see Map 12.2). The Mexican government, which wanted

> In the Mexican Southwest, Anglo-American pioneers confronted Spanish-speaking frontiersmen. On this frontier as elsewhere, cultures, interests, and aspirations collided.

MAP 12.2 Texas and Mexico in the 1830s

As Americans spilled into lightly populated and loosely governed northern Mexico, Texas and then other Mexican provinces became contested territory.

Surveying Texas Land, **Theodore Gentilz, c. 1844**
Land has always bred conflict in Texas. The new republic (1836–1845) wrestled with a confusing variety of Spanish, Mexican, and Texas claims, surveys, and titles. In this painting, Theodore Gentilz portrays the efforts of surveyor John James to settle thorny landownership issues. Five years later, Texas
governor P. H. Bell could still observe: "There is no subject which addresses itself more forcibly . . .
than that of settling upon a secure and permanent basis the land titles of the country."
Courtesy Mr. Larry Sheerin.

to populate and develop its northern territory, granted the American Stephen F. Austin a huge tract of land along the Brazos River, and in the 1820s he became the first Anglo-American *empre-sario* (colonization agent) in Texas. Land was cheap—only ten cents an acre—and thousands of farmers poured across the border. Most of the migrants were Southerners, who brought cotton and slaves with them. By 1835, the American settlers had established a thriving plantation economy and numbered—free and slave— thirty-five thousand, while the *Tejano* (Spanish-speaking) population was less than eight thousand. Most Anglo-American settlers were not Roman Catholic, did not speak Spanish, and cared little about assimilating into a culture that

was so different from their own. In 1829, the Mexican government sought to halt further immigration by outlawing slavery, which it hoped would make Texas less attractive. The settlers sidestepped the decree by calling their slaves servants, but settlers had other grievances, most significantly the puny voice they had in local government. General Antonio López de Santa Anna all but extinguished that voice when he seized political power and concentrated authority in Mexico City.

Faced with what they considered tyranny, the Texan settlers rebelled and declared the independent Republic of Texas. Santa Anna ordered the Mexican army northward and in February 1836 arrived at the outskirts of San Antonio.

The rebels, who included the Tennessee frontiersman David Crockett and the Louisiana adventurer James Bowie, as well as a number of Tejanos, took refuge in a former Franciscan mission known as the Alamo. When Santa Anna's siege failed, he sent wave after wave of his 4,000-man army crashing against the walls until the attackers finally broke through and killed all 187 defenders. A few weeks later in the small town of Goliad, Mexican forces surrounded and captured a garrison of Texans. Following orders from Santa Anna, Mexican firing squads executed more than 300 of the men as "pirates." Then in April 1836 at San Jacinto, General Sam Houston's army adopted the massacre at Goliad as a battle cry and produced a crushing defeat of Santa Anna's troops. Texans had succeeded in establishing their Lone Star Republic, and the following year the United States recognized the independence of Texas from Mexico.

Texas War for Independence, 1836

The distant Mexican province of California also caught the eye of a few Anglo-Americans. In 1824, in an effort to increase Mexican migration to thinly settled California, the Mexican government granted *ranchos*—huge estates devoted to cattle raising—to new settlers. *Rancheros* ruled over near-feudal empires worked by Indians whose condition sometimes approached that of slaves. Not satisfied, *rancheros* coveted the vast lands controlled by the Franciscan missions. In 1834, they persuaded the Mexican government to confiscate the missions and make their lands available to new settlement, a development that accelerated the decline of California Indians. Devastated by disease, the Indians, who numbered approximately 300,000 when the Spanish arrived in 1769, declined to half that number by 1846.

Despite the efforts of the Mexican government, California in 1840 counted a population of only 7,000 Mexican settlers. Non-Mexican settlers numbered only 380, but among them were Americans who championed manifest destiny. Thomas O. Larkin, a prosperous merchant, John Marsh, a successful *ranchero* in the San Joaquin Valley, and others became boosters who sought to attract Americans from Oregon Country to California. The first overland party arrived in California in 1841. Thereafter, wagon after wagon followed the California Trail, which forked off from the Oregon Trail near the Snake River and led through the Sierra Nevada at Lake Tahoe (see Map 12.1). As the trickle of Americans became a river, Mexican officials grew alarmed, for as a New York newspaper put it in 1845, "Let the tide of emigration flow toward California and the American population will soon be sufficiently numerous to play the Texas game." Only a few Americans in California looked forward to separatist war, but many dreamed of living again under the American flag.

The U.S. government made no secret of its desire to acquire California. In 1835, President Andrew Jackson tried to purchase it. In 1842, Commodore Thomas Catesby Jones, hearing a rumor that the United States and Mexico were at war, seized the port of Monterey and ran up the American flag. The red-faced officer promptly ran it down again when he learned of his error, but his actions left no doubt about Washington's intentions. In 1846, American settlers in the Sacramento Valley took matters into their own hands. Prodded by John C. Frémont, a former army captain and explorer who had arrived in December 1845 with a party of sixty buckskin-clad frontiersmen spoiling for a fight, the Californians raised an independence movement known as the Bear Flag Revolt. By then, James K. Polk, a champion of expansion, sat in the White House.

Expansion and the Mexican-American War

Although emigrants acted as the advance guard of American empire, there was nothing automatic about the U.S. annexation of territory in the West. Acquiring territory required political action, and in the 1840s the difficult problems of Texas, Oregon, and the Mexican borderlands intruded into national politics. The politics of expansion became entangled with sectionalism and the slavery question and thrust the United States into dangerous diplomatic crises with Great Britain and Mexico.

Aggravation between Mexico and the United States escalated to open antagonism in 1845 when the United States annexed Texas. Absorbing territory still claimed by Mexico ruptured diplomatic relations between the two countries and set the stage for war. But it was President James K. Polk's insistence on having Mexico's other northern provinces that made war certain. The war was not as easy as Polk anticipated, but it ended in American victory and the acquisition of a new American West.

The Politics of Expansion

The complicated issues of westward expansion and the nation's boundaries ended up on the desk of John Tyler when he became president in April 1841. The Whig William Henry Harrison had been elected president in 1840 but died one month after taking office. Tyler, nominally a Whig but actually a Democrat in his political convictions, spent much of his administration beating back Henry Clay's efforts to turn the Whig Party's American System—protective tariffs, a national bank, and internal improvements—into law. But the issue that stirred Tyler's blood, and that of much of the nation, was Texas. Texans had sought admission to the Union almost since winning their independence from Mexico in 1836. Tyler, an ardent expansionist, understood that Texas was a dangerous issue: Any suggestion of adding another slave state to the Union would bring many Northerners to a boil. Annexing Texas also risked precipitating war because Mexico had never relinquished its claim to its lost province.

Cold-shouldered by the United States, Texans explored Great Britain's interest in recognition. Britain was eager to keep Texas independent. In Britain's eyes, Texas provided a buffer against American expansion and also a new market for English manufactured goods. American officials worried that Britain's real objective was to add Texas to the British

> Texas was a dangerous issue: Any suggestion of adding another slave state to the Union would bring many Northerners to a boil.

Empire. Southerners knew that if Britain, the leading abolitionist power in the world, gained Texas, the westward expansion of slavery would end. This volatile mix of threat, fear, and opportunity convinced Tyler to risk negotiations with Texas, and he worked vigorously to annex the republic before his term expired. His efforts pushed Texas and the slavery issue to the center of national politics.

In April 1844, after months of secret negotiations between Texas and the Tyler administration, Secretary of State John C. Calhoun laid an annexation treaty before the Senate. But when Calhoun linked annexation to the defense of slavery, he doomed the treaty. Howls of protest erupted across the North. Michigan politician Lewis Cass described Calhoun's proposal as an "avalanche." In Massachusetts, future senator Charles Sumner deplored the "insidious" plan to annex Texas and carve from it "great slaveholding states." The Senate soundly rejected the treaty, and it appeared that Tyler had succeeded only in inflaming sectional conflict.

The issue of Texas had not died down by the 1844 elections. Henry Clay looked forward to receiving the Whig presidential nomination and waging his campaign on the old Whig economic principles that Tyler had frustrated. In an effort to appeal to northern voters, Clay came out against the immediate annexation of Texas. "Annexation and war with Mexico are identical," he declared. When news of Clay's statement reached Andrew Jackson at his plantation in Tennessee, he chuckled, "Clay [is] a dead political Duck." In Jackson's shrewd judgment, no man who opposed annexation could be elected president. Nevertheless, the Whig Party nominated Clay.

The Democrats chose Tennessean James K. Polk, who was as strong for the annexation of Texas as Clay was against it. To make Texas annexation palatable to Northerners, the Democrats shrewdly yoked Texas to Oregon, thus tapping the desire for expansion in the free states of the North as well in the slave states of the South. The Democratic platform called for the "reannexation of Texas" and the "reoccupation of Oregon." The suggestion that the United States was merely reasserting existing rights was poor history but good politics. According to the Democratic formula, the annexation of Texas would not give an advantage to slavery and the South; instead, linked to Oregon, Texas would expand America to the advantage of the entire nation.

During the campaign, Clay finally recognized the groundswell for expansion, and he waffled, hinting that under certain circumstances he might accept annexation. His retreat won little support in the South and succeeded only in alienating antislavery opinion in the North. James G. Birney, the candidate of the fledgling Liberty Party, picked up the votes of thousands of disillusioned Clay supporters. In the November election, Polk received 170 electoral votes and Clay 105. New York's 35 electoral votes proved critical to Clay's defeat. A shift of just one-third of Birney's 15,000 votes to Clay would have given Clay the state and the presidency.

On March 4, 1845, James K. Polk, at age forty-nine, became the youngest president in the nation's history. In his inaugural address, he offered a ringing reaffirmation of aggressive **nationalism** and manifest destiny. "This heaven-favored land," Polk declared, enjoyed the "most admirable and wisest system of well-regulated self-government . . . ever devised by human minds." And he asked, "Who shall assign limits to the achievements of free minds and free hands under the protection of this glorious Union?"

The nation did not have to wait for Polk's inauguration to see results from his victory. One month after the election, President Tyler announced that the triumph of the Democratic Party provided a mandate for the annexation of Texas "promptly and immediately." In February 1845, after a fierce debate between antislavery and proslavery forces, Congress approved a joint resolution offering the Republic of Texas admission to the United States. Texas entered as the fifteenth slave state.

Tyler delivered Texas, but Polk had promised Oregon, too. Westerners particularly demanded that the new president make good on the Democrats' pledge—"Fifty-four Forty or Fight"—that is, all of Oregon, right up to Alaska (54°40' was the southern latitude of Russian Alaska). But Polk was close to war with Mexico and could not afford a simultaneous war with Britain over U.S. claims in Canada. After the initial bluster, therefore, Polk muted the all-of-Oregon refrain and renewed an old offer to divide Oregon along the forty-ninth parallel. When Britain accepted the compromise, some cried betrayal, but most Americans celebrated the agreement that gave the nation an enormous territory peacefully. Besides, when the Senate finally approved the treaty in June 1846, the United States and Mexico were already at war.

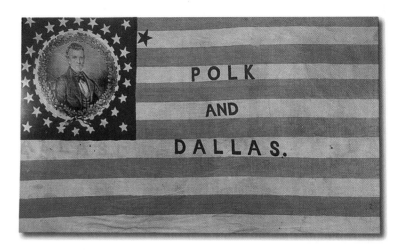

Polk and Dallas Banner, 1844
In 1844, Democratic presidential nominee James K. Polk and vice presidential nominee George M. Dallas campaigned under this cotton banner. The extra star spilling over into the red and white stripes symbolizes Polk's vigorous support for annexing the huge slave republic of Texas, which had declared independence from Mexico eight years earlier. Henry Clay, Polk's Whig opponent, ran under a banner that was similar but conspicuously lacked the additional star.
Collection of Janice L. and David J. Frent.

The Mexican-American War, 1846–1848

From the day he entered the White House, Polk craved Mexico's remaining northern provinces: California and New Mexico, land that today makes up California, Nevada, and Utah, most of New Mexico and Arizona, and parts of Wyoming and Colorado. Polk hoped to buy the territory, but the Mexicans refused to sell. Furious, Polk concluded that military force would be needed to realize the United States's manifest destiny.

Polk had already ordered General Zachary Taylor to march his 4,000-man army of occupation of Texas from its position on the Nueces River, the southern boundary of Texas according to the Mexicans, 150 miles south, to the banks of the Rio Grande, the boundary claimed by Texans (Map 12.3). Viewing the American advance as aggression, the Mexican general in Matamoros ordered Taylor back to the Nueces. Taylor refused, and on April 25 Mexican cavalry attacked a party of American soldiers, killing or wounding sixteen and capturing the rest. Even before news of the battle arrived in Washington, Polk had already obtained his cabinet's approval of a war message.

On May 11, 1846, the president told Congress, "Mexico has passed the boundary of the United States, has invaded our territory, and shed American blood upon American soil." Thus "war exists, and, notwithstanding all our efforts to avoid it, exists by the act of Mexico herself." Two days later, Congress passed a declaration of war and began raising an army. Despite years of saber rattling toward Mexico and Britain, the U.S. army was pitifully small, only 8,600 soldiers. Faced with the nation's first foreign war, against a Mexican army that numbered more than 30,000, Polk called for volunteers. Of the men who rushed to the colors, 40 percent were immigrants and a third of them were illiterate. Eventually, more than 112,000 white Americans (blacks were banned) joined the army to fight in Mexico.

Despite the outpouring of support, the war divided the nation. Northern Whigs in particular loudly condemned the war as the unwarranted bullying of a weak nation by its greedy expansionist neighbor. The Massachusetts legislature declared that the war was being fought for the "triple object of

> Despite the outpouring of support, the Mexican-American War divided the nation.

extending slavery, of strengthening the slave power, and of obtaining control of the free states." On January 12, 1848, a gangly freshman Whig representative from Illinois rose from his back-row seat in the House of Representatives to deliver his first important speech in Congress. Before Abraham Lincoln sat down, he had questioned Polk's intelligence, honesty, and sanity. The president simply ignored the upstart representative, but antislavery, antiwar Whigs kept up the attack throughout the conflict. In their effort to undercut national support, they labeled it "Mr. Polk's War."

Since most Americans backed the war, it was not really Polk's war, but the president acted as if it were. Although he had no military experience, he directed the war personally. Working eighteen hours a day, Polk established overall strategy and oversaw the details of military campaigns. He planned a short war in which U.S. armies would occupy Mexico's northern provinces and defeat the Mexican army in a decisive battle or two, after which Mexico would sue for peace and the United States would keep the territory its armies occupied.

At first, Polk's strategy seemed to work. In May 1846, Zachary Taylor's troops drove south from the Rio Grande and routed the Mexican army, first on the plain of Palo Alto and then in vicious hand-to-hand fighting in a palm-filled ravine known as Resaca de la Palma (see Map 12.3). "Old Rough and Ready," as Taylor was af-

Shako Hat

American soldiers fighting in the Mexican-American War were a colorful lot. U.S. army regulars wore as a dress uniform a dark blue wool tailcoat and sky-blue wool trousers, topped with the shako, a full-dress cap made of leather, crowned with black feathers, and adorned with a decorative plate showing the eagle spreading its wings—the symbol of manifest destiny.

One veteran criticized the army for "dressing up men within an inch of their lives, until they looked more like a flock of eastern flamingos . . . than the descendants of the race of men who fought and bled to establish civil liberty and republican simplicity in our country." General Winfield Scott—his men nicknamed him "Old Fuss and Feathers"—expected his troops to follow "regulations of dress, hair, whiskers, and so forth." Other commanders, most notably General Zachary Taylor, were notoriously lax, especially for volunteer troops, who were required to furnish their own uniforms. One junior officer serving under Taylor observed: "We wear all kinds of uniforms here, each one to his taste, some shirtsleeves, some white, some purple, some fancy jackets and all colors of cottonelle pants, some straw and some Quaker hats, and that is just the way, too, that our fellows went into battle."

Chicago Historical Society.

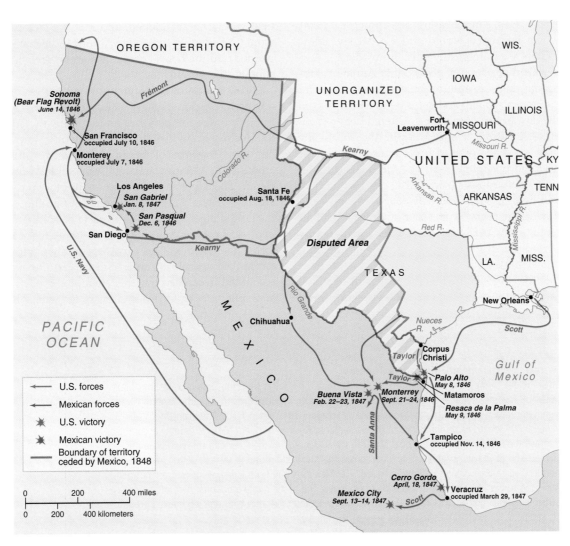

MAP 12.3   The Mexican War, 1846–1848
American and Mexican soldiers skirmished across much of northern Mexico, but the major battles took place between the Rio Grande and Mexico City.

fectionately known among his adoring troops, became an instant war hero. Polk rewarded Taylor for his victories by making him commander of the Mexican campaign.

A second prong of the campaign to occupy Mexico's northern provinces centered on Colonel Stephen Watts Kearny, who led a 1,700-man army from Missouri into New Mexico. Without firing a shot, U.S. forces took Santa Fe in August 1846. Kearny promptly proclaimed New Mexico U.S. territory. Polk ordered him on to California. On the trail, Kearny met Kit Carson, part of John C. Frémont's buckskin army. Carson mistakenly informed him that California was al-

ready secured. Pushing on with only 300 troops, Kearny three months later marched into San Diego and into a major Mexican rebellion against American rule. In January 1847, after several clashes and severe losses, the U.S. forces occupied Los Angeles. California and New Mexico were in American hands.

By then, Taylor had driven deep into the interior of Mexico. In September 1846, after a five-day siege and house-to-house fighting, he took the fortified city of Monterrey. With reinforcements and fresh supplies, Taylor pushed his 5,000 troops southwest, where the Mexican hero of the Alamo, General Antonio López de Santa

Anna, was concentrating an army of 21,000, which he hoped would strike a decisive blow against the numerically inferior invaders.

On February 23, 1847, Santa Anna's troops began their assault at Buena Vista. Superior American artillery and accurate musket fire won the day, but the Americans suffered heavy casualties, including Henry Clay Jr., the son of the man who had opposed Texas annexation for fear it would precipitate war. The Mexicans suffered even greater losses (some 3,400 dead, wounded, and missing compared with 650 Americans), and during the night Santa Anna withdrew his battered army from the battlefield, much to the "profound disgust of the troops," one Mexican officer remembered. "They are filled with grief that they were going to lose the benefit of all the sacrifices that they had made; that the conquered field would be abandoned, and that the victory would be given to the enemy." Retreat, he complained, fed the belief "that it was impossible to conquer the Americans."

The series of uninterrupted victories in northern Mexico certainly fed the American troops' sense of superiority and very nearly led to a feeling of invincibility. "No American force has ever thought of being defeated by any amount of Mexican troops," one soldier declared. The Americans worried about other hazards, however. "I can assure you that fighting is the least dangerous & arduous part of a soldier's life," one young man said. Letters home told of torturous marches across arid wastes alive with tarantulas, scorpions, and rattlesnakes. Others recounted dysentery, malaria, smallpox, cholera, and yellow fever. One out of every ten U.S. sol-

Battala del Sacramento, **Michaud y Thomas**

Most images of the Mexican-American War were created by artists from the United States, but Mexicans also recorded the war. In this hand-colored lithograph, Mexican artist Michaud y Thomas offers his interpretation of the battle that took place in February 1847 when 1,100 American troops engaged 3,000 Mexicans on the banks of the Sacramento River in northern Mexico. Thomas accurately portrays the first moments of the bold Mexican cavalry charge at the American center, but he neglects to finish the story. American artillery forced the Mexican lancers to retreat, with "great confusion in their ranks." When the fighting ended, 700 Mexicans had been killed, wounded, or captured. American forces lost one man killed and six wounded. The battle made a national hero of the American commander, Colonel Alexander Doniphan, who watched the battle with one leg hooked around his saddle horn, whittling a stick in full view of the enemy.

Yale Collection of Western Americana, Beinecke Rare Book and Manuscript Library.

diers died while in Mexico. Of the 13,000 American soldiers who died (some 50,000 Mexicans died), fewer than 2,000 fell to Mexican bullets and shells. Disease killed most of the others. Medicine was so primitive and conditions so harsh that army doctors could do little. As a Tennessee man observed, "nearly all who take sick die."

Victory in Mexico

Although Americans won battle after battle, President Polk's strategy misfired. Despite its loss of territory and men, Mexico determinedly refused to trade land for peace. One American soldier captured the Mexican mood: "They cannot submit to be deprived of California after the loss of Texas, and nothing but the conquest of their Capital will force them to such a humiliation." Polk had arrived at the same conclusion. Zachary Taylor had not proved decisive enough for Polk, and the president tapped another general to carry the war to Mexico City. While Taylor occupied the north, General Winfield Scott would land his army on the Gulf coast of Mexico and march 250 miles inland to the capital. Polk's plan entailed enormous risk; it meant that Scott would have to cut himself off from supplies and lead his men deep into enemy country against a much larger army.

After months of careful planning and the skillful coordination of army and navy, an amphibious landing on March 9, 1847, near Vera Cruz put some 10,000 American troops ashore by midnight without the loss of a single life. After eighty-eight hours of furious shelling, Vera Cruz surrendered. Scott immediately began preparations for the march west. Transportation alone posed enormous problems. His army required 9,300 wagons and 17,000 pack mules, 500,000 bushels of oats and corn, and 100 pounds of blister ointment before it could begin the mountainous journey. In early April 1847, the army moved out, following the path that had been trodden more than three centuries earlier by Hernán Cortés to "the halls of the Montezumas" (see chapter 2).

Meanwhile, after the frightful defeat at Buena Vista, Santa Anna had returned to Mexico City. He rallied his ragged troops and marched them east to set a trap for Scott in the mountain pass at Cerro Gordo. Knifing through Mexican lines, the Americans almost captured Santa Anna, who fled the field on foot. So complete was the victory that Scott gloated to Taylor,

Mexican Family
This family had its portrait taken in 1847, in the middle of the war. Where were the adult males? Mexican civilians were vulnerable to atrocities committed by the invading army. Volunteers, a large portion of American troops, received little training and resisted discipline. The "lawless Volunteers stop at no outrage," Brigadier General William Worth declared. "Innocent blood has been basely, cowardly, and barbarously shed in cold blood." Generals Zachary Taylor and Winfield Scott gradually tamed the volunteers with stern military justice.
Amon Carter Museum of Western Art.

"Mexico no longer has an army." But Santa Anna, ever resilient, again rallied the Mexican army. Some 30,000 troops took up defensive positions on the outskirts of Mexico City. They hurriedly began melting down church bells to cast new cannon.

In August, Scott began his assault on the Mexican capital. The fighting proved the most brutal of the war. Santa Anna backed his army into the city, fighting each step of the way. At the Battle of Churubusco, the Mexicans took 4,000 casualties in a single day and the Americans more than 1,000. At the castle of Chapultepec, American troops scaled the walls and fought the Mexican defenders hand to hand. After Chapultepec, Mexico City officials persuaded Santa Anna to evacuate the city to save it from destruction, and on September 14, 1847, General Winfield Scott rode in triumphantly. The ancient capital of the Aztecs had fallen once again to an invading army.

With Mexico City in U.S. hands, Polk sent Nicholas P. Trist, the chief clerk in the State Department, to Mexico to negotiate the peace. On February 2, 1848, Trist and Mexican officials signed the Treaty of Guadalupe Hidalgo. Mexico agreed to give up all claims to Texas north of the Rio Grande and to cede the provinces of New Mexico and California—more than 500,000 square miles—to the United States (see Map 12.3). The United States agreed to pay Mexico $15 million and to assume $3.25 million in claims that American citizens had against Mexico. Some Americans clamored for all of Mexico, others for less, but in March 1848 the Senate ratified the treaty by a vote of thirty-eight to fourteen. The last American soldiers left Mexico a few months later.

Golden California

The American triumph in the war had enormous consequences for both Mexico and the United States. Less than three-quarters of a century after its founding, the United States had achieved its self-proclaimed manifest destiny to stretch from the Atlantic to the Pacific (Map 12.4). The United States would enter the industrial age with vast new natural resources and a two-ocean economy, while Mexico suffered sharply diminished economic opportunities. Moreover, with the northern half of Mexico in American hands, California gold poured into American and not Mexican pockets.

On a cold January morning in 1848, just weeks before the formal transfer of territory, James Marshall discovered gold in the American River in the foothills of the Sierra Nevada. The flakes he found set off the California gold rush, one of the wildest mining stampedes in the world's history. Between 1849 and 1852, more than 250,000 "forty-niners," as the would-be miners were known, descended on the Golden State. In less than two years, Marshall's discovery transformed California from foreign territory to statehood.

Americans did not find it surprising that the discovery coincided with American acquisition. "God kept that coast for a people of the Pilgrim blood," one minister intoned. "He would not permit any other to be fully developed there." But news of gold quickly spread around the world. Soon a polyglot swirl of races and nationalities bent on getting rich arrived in California, where the forty-niners remade the quiet world of Mexican ranches into a raucous, roaring mining and town economy. (See "Historical Question," page 414.)

Forty-niners rarely had much money or mining experience, but as one witness observed, "No capital is required to obtain this gold, as the laboring man wants nothing but his pick, shovel, and tin pan, with which to dig and wash the gravel; and many frequently pick gold out of the crevices of rock with their butcher knives in pieces from one to six ounces." But life in the gold fields was nasty, brutish, and often short. Men faced abysmal living conditions, some living in holes and brush lean-tos. They also faced diseases such as cholera and scurvy, exorbitant prices for food and services (eggs sold for a dollar apiece), deadly encounters with claim jumpers, and endless backbreaking labor. Still, an individual with gold in his pocket could find temporary relief in the saloons, card games, dog fights, gambling dens, and brothels that flourished in the mining camps.

At first, news of the gold strike turned the city of San Francisco, on the coast, into a ghost town as men raced to the foothills. New arrivals, who sailed into the port by the thousands, abandoned five hundred ships when passengers and crews struck out for the gold fields. "The whole country from San Francisco to Los Angeles, and from the seashore to the base of the Sierra Nevada, resounds to the sordid cry *gold!* GOLD!! **GOLD!!!**" observed one newspaper, "while the field is left half planted, the house half built, and everything neglected but the manufacture of shovels and pickaxes." By 1853, however, San Francisco had grown into a raw, booming urban settlement of 50,000 and depended as much on gold as did the mining camps inland. The city suffered from overcrowding, fire, crime, and violence, like all the towns that dotted the San Joaquin and Sacramento valleys, but enterprising individuals had learned that there was money to be made tending to the needs of the miners. Hotels, saloons, restaurants, laundries, and shops and stores of all kinds exchanged services for miners' gold.

As wild as the mining camps were, San Francisco was no tamer. In 1851, an association called the Committee of Vigilance determined to bring order to the city. Members pledged that "no thief, burglar, incendiary or assassin shall escape punishment, either by the quibbles of the

> The American triumph in the Mexican-American War had enormous consequences. Less than three-quarters of a century after its founding, the United States stretched from the Atlantic to the Pacific.

law, the insecurity of prisons, the carelessness or corruption of the police, or a laxity of those who pretended to administer justice." Lynchings soon proved that the Committee meant business. In time, merchants, **artisans,** and professionals made the city their home and brought their families from back east. Theaters sprouted and gunfights in the streets declined, but many years would pass before anyone tamed San Francisco.

Establishing civic order on a turbulent frontier was made more difficult by the welter of nationalities, ethnicities, and races drawn to California and by Anglo bigotry. The Chinese attracted special scrutiny from the white majority. By 1851, there were 25,000 Chinese in California, and their religion, language, dress, queues (long pigtails), eating habits, and opium convinced

many Anglos that they were not fit citizens of the Golden State. As early as 1852, opponents demanded a halt to Chinese immigration. Chinese leaders in San Francisco fought back. While admitting deep cultural differences, they insisted that "in the important matters we are good men. We honor our parents; we take care of our children; we are industrious and peaceable; we trade much; we are trusted for small and large sums; we pay our debts; and are honest, and of course must tell the truth." Their protestations, however, offered little protection, and racial violence braided with forty-niner optimism and energy.

Westward expansion did not stop at the California shore. By midcentury, California's ports were connected to a vast trade network in the Pacific, where American seafarers and

MAP 12.4   Territorial Expansion by 1860
Less than a century after its founding, the United States had spread from the Atlantic seaboard to the Pacific Ocean. War, purchase, and diplomacy had gained a continent.

READING THE MAP: List the countries from which the United States acquired land. Which nation lost the most land because of U.S. expansion?

CONNECTIONS: Who coined the phrase *manifest destiny*? When? What does it mean? What areas targeted for expansion were the subjects of debate during the presidential campaign of 1844?

FOR MORE HELP ANALYZING THIS MAP, see the map activity for this chapter in the Online Study Guide at bedfordstmartins.com/roark.

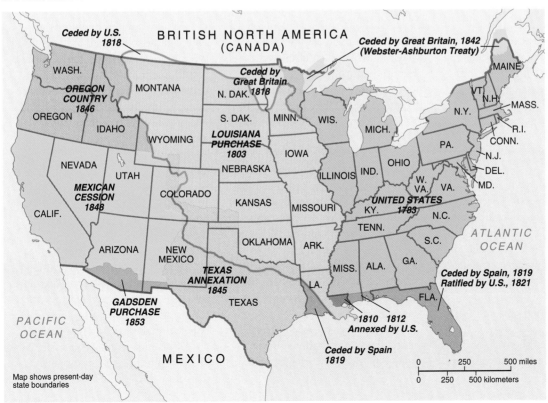

Who Rushed for California Gold?

When news of James Marshall's discovery reached the East in the fall of 1848, gold proved irresistible. Newspapers went crazy with stories about prospectors who extracted half a pan of gold from every pan of gravel they scooped from western streams. Soon, cities reverberated with men singing:

Oh Susannah, don't you cry for me;
I'm gone to California with my
wash-bowl on my knee.

Scores of ships sailed from East Coast ports, headed either around South America to San Francisco or across the Gulf of Mexico to Panama, where the passengers made their way by foot and canoe to the Pacific coast and waited for a ship to carry them north. Even larger numbers of gold seekers took riverboats to the Missouri River and then set out in wagons, on horseback, or by foot for the West.

Young men everywhere contracted gold fever. As stories of California gold circled the globe, Chinese and Germans, Mexicans and Irish, Australians and French, Chileans and Italians, and people of dozens of other nationalities set out to strike it rich. Louisa Knapp Clappe, wife of a minister and one of the few women in gold country, remarked that when she walked through Indian Bar, the little mining town where she lived, she heard English, French, Spanish, German, Italian, Kanaka (Hawaiian), Asian Indian, and American Indian languages. Hangtown, Hell's Delight, Gouge Eye, and a hundred other crude mining camps became temporary home to a diverse throng of nationalities and peoples.

One of the largest groups of new arrivals was the Chinese. Between 1848 and 1854, Chinese men numbering 45,000 (but almost no Chinese women) arrived in California. Most considered themselves "sojourners," temporary residents who planned to return home as soon as their savings allowed. The majority came under a Chinese-controlled contract labor system in which each immigrant worked out the cost of his transportation. In the early years, most became wage laborers in mining. By the 1860s, they dominated railroad construction in the West. Ninety percent of the Central Pacific Railroad's 10,000 workers were Chinese. The Chinese also made up nearly half of San Francisco's labor force, working in the shoe, tobacco, woolen, laundry, and sewing trades. By 1870, the Chinese population had grown to 63,200, including 4,500 women. They constituted nearly 10 percent of the state's people and 25 percent of its wage-earning force.

The presence of peoples from around the world shattered the Anglo-American dream of a racially and ethnically homogeneous West, but ethnic diversity did nothing to increase the tolerance of Anglo-American prospectors. In their eyes, no "foreigner" had a right to dig for gold. In 1850, the California legislature passed the Foreign Miners' Tax Law, which levied high taxes on non-Americans to drive them from the gold fields, except as hired laborers working on claims owned by Americans. Stubborn foreign miners were sometimes hauled before "Judge Lynch." Among the earliest victims of lynching in the gold fields were a Frenchman and a Chilean.

Anglo-Americans considered the Chinese devious and unassimilable. They also feared that hard-working, self-denying Chinese labor would undercut white labor and drive it from the country. As a consequence, the Chinese were segregated residentially and occupationally and made ineligible for citizenship. Along with blacks and Indians, Chinese were denied public education and the right to testify in court. In addition to exclusion, they suffered from violence. Mobs drove them from Eureka, Truckee, and other mining towns.

American prospectors swamped the *Californios*, Spanish and Mexican settlers who had lived in California for generations. Soon after the American takeover, raging prejudice and discriminatory laws pushed Hispanic *rancheros*, professionals,

Gold Mountain
This hardworking young man is wearing the typical dress of Chinese laborers, a blue cotton shirt and baggy pants. We cannot tell if a queue is hanging down his back. He bears the heavy tools of his trade of placer (surface) mining but still manages a smile. Although he probably did not strike it rich in Gum Sam (Gold Mountain), he did find a new world and a new way of life.
Nevada Historical Society.

merchants, and artisans into the ranks of unskilled labor. Americans took their land even though the U.S. government had pledged to protect Mexican and Spanish land titles after the cession of 1848. Anglo forty-niners branded Spanish-speaking miners, even native-born Californios, "foreigners" and drove them from the diggings. Mariano Vallejo, a leading Californio, said of the forty-niners: "The good ones were few and the wicked many."

For Native Americans, the gold rush was a catastrophe. Numbering about 150,000 in 1848, the Indian population of California fell to 25,000 in 1856. Californios had exploited the native peoples, but the forty-niners wanted to eradicate them. Starvation, disease, and a declining birthrate took a heavy toll. Indians

also fell victim to wholesale murder. "That a war of extermination will continue to be waged between the two races until the Indian race becomes extinct must be expected," declared California governor Peter W. Burnett in 1851. The nineteenth-century historian Hubert Howe Bancroft described white behavior toward Indians during the gold rush as "one of the last human hunts of civilization, and the basest and most brutal of them all." To survive, Indians moved to the most remote areas of the state and tried to stay out of the way.

The forty-niners created dazzling wealth—in 1852, 81 million ounces of gold, nearly half of the world's production. Only a few prospectors—of whatever race and nationality—struck it rich, however.

The era of the prospector panning in streams quickly gave way to corporate-owned deep-shaft mining. The larger the scale of mining operations became, the smaller were the opportunities for individual miners. Most forty-niners eventually took up farming or opened small businesses or worked for wages for the corporations that pushed them out. But because of gold, an avalanche of people had roared into California. Anglo-Americans were most numerous, and Anglo dominance developed early. But the gold rush also brought a rainbow of nationalities. Anglo-American ascendancy *and* ethnic and racial diversity in the West both count among the most significant legacies of the gold rush. But because Anglo-Americans made the rules, not everyone shared equally.

merchants traded furs, hides and tallow, and lumber and participated in whaling and the China trade. But as California's first congressional representative observed, the state was separated "by thousands of miles of plains, deserts, and almost impossible mountains" from the rest of the Union. Dreamers talked about a railroad that would someday connect the Golden State with the booming agriculture and thriving industry of the East.

Economic and Industrial Evolution

During the 1840s and 1850s, Americans lived amid profound economic transformation that had been under way since the start of the nineteenth century. By 1860, the nation's population numbered over 31 million. Since 1800, the total output of the U.S. economy had multiplied twelvefold. Four fundamental changes in American society fueled this phenomenal economic growth.

First, millions of Americans—Abraham Lincoln among them—left their farms, swelling the urban population, although farmers still made up 80 percent of the nation's population by 1860. Second, more and more Americans were working in factories, almost 20 percent of the labor force by 1860. This trend contributed to the nation's economic growth because, in general, factory workers were twice as productive (in output per unit of labor input) as agricultural workers.

A third fundamental change was the shift from water to steam as a source of energy, which permitted factories to be more productive. Beginning around 1840, steam became harnessed to manufacturing, but the transition was slow, delayed by the continued effectiveness of water and animal power. By 1850, for example, animal and human muscles still provided thirty-three times more energy for manufacturing than steam. During the 1830s, extensive mining began in Pennsylvania coal fields, and massive quantities of coal became available for industrial fuel. Coal provided heat to power steam engines in factories, railroads, and ships.

> While cities, factories, and steam engines multiplied throughout the nation—especially in the North and West—the roots of the United States's economic growth lay in agriculture.

A fourth fundamental change propelling America's industrial development was the rise in agricultural productivity (defined as crop output per unit of labor input), which nearly doubled during Lincoln's lifetime. More than any other single factor, this dramatic increase spurred the economic growth of the era. While cities, factories, and steam engines multiplied throughout the nation—especially in the North and West—the roots of the United States's economic growth lay in agriculture.

This cascade of interrelated developments—steam, coal, factories, cities, railroads, and farms—was beginning to transform the American economy by the 1850s. Historians often refer to this transformation as an industrial revolution. However, the profound changes occurring in these years did not cause a revolutionary discontinuity in the economy or society. The United States remained overwhelmingly agricultural. Old methods of production continued alongside the new. The process that the American economy underwent before 1860 might best be termed "industrial evolution."

Agriculture and Land Policy

It may seem odd to consider an ax a basic agricultural tool, like a hoe or a shovel, yet farmers needed axes. A French traveler observed that Americans had "a general feeling of hatred against trees" and taught their children "at an early age to use the axe against the trees, their enemies." Although the traveler exaggerated, his observation contained an important truth. Forests impeded agriculture. With axes—Lincoln termed them "that most useful instrument"—farmers leveled trees, cleared land for planting, and built cabins, fences, and barns.

The amount of physical labor required to convert unimproved land to cultivated fields limited agricultural productivity. Energy that might have gone to growing crops went instead to clearing land. But as farmers pushed westward, they encountered thinner forests and eventually the Midwest's comparatively treeless prairie, where they could spend less time with an ax and more time with a plow or hoe. Rich prairie soils gave somewhat higher crop yields than eastern farms, and farmers migrated to the Midwest by the tens of thousands between 1830 and 1860. The population of Indiana, Illinois, Michigan, Wisconsin, and Iowa exploded tenfold, growing from 500,000 in 1830 to more than 5 million by 1860, four times faster than the

Harvesting Grain with Cradles
This late-nineteenth-century painting shows the grain harvest during the mid-nineteenth century at Bishop Hill, Illinois, a Swedish community where the artist, Olof Krans, and his parents settled in 1850. The men swing cradles, slowly cutting a swath through the grain; the women gather the cut grain into sheaves to be hauled away later for threshing. Bishop Hill, a well-organized community, could call upon the labor of a large number of men and women at harvest time. Most farmers had only a few family members and a hired hand or two to help with the harvest. Notice that although the grain field appears level enough to be ideal for a mechanical reaper, all the work is done by hand; no machine is in sight.
Bishop Hill State Historic Site, Illinois Historic Preservation Agency.

growth of the nation as a whole. During the 1850s, Illinois added more people than any other state in the Union.

Labor-saving improvements in farm implements also hiked agricultural productivity. The cast-iron plow in use since the 1820s proved too weak for the thick turf and dense soil of the midwestern prairie. In 1837, John Deere patented a strong, smooth steel plow that sliced through prairie soil so cleanly that farmers called it the "singing plow." Deere's company became the leading plow manufacturer in the Midwest, turning out more than ten thousand plows a year by the late 1850s. By 1860, the energy for plowing still came from two- and four-legged animals, but better plows permitted that energy to break more ground and plant more crops.

Improvements in wheat harvesting also multiplied farmers' productivity. In 1850, most farmers harvested wheat by hand, cutting two or three acres a day with backbreaking labor. Tinkerers throughout the nation tried to fashion a mechanical reaper that would make the wheat harvest easier and quicker. Cyrus McCormick and others experimented with designs until the late 1840s, when mechanical reapers began to appear in American wheat fields. A McCormick reaper that cost between $100 and $150 allowed a farmer to harvest up to twelve acres a day. By 1860, about eighty thousand reapers had been sold. Although reapers represented the cutting edge of agricultural technology, they still had to be powered by a horse or an ox. Most farmers continued to cut their grain by hand. Neither reapers nor plows increased the yield of a given acre of cultivated land. Instead, they allowed more land to be brought into cultivation: The labor that farmers saved could be used to plow and plant more land. Access to fresh, uncultivated land allowed farmers to double the corn and wheat harvests between 1840 and 1860.

The agricultural productivity that fueled the nation's economy was an outgrowth of federal land policy. Up to 1860, the United States continued to be land-rich and labor-poor. During the nineteenth century, the nation became a great deal richer in land, acquiring more than a billion acres with the Louisiana Purchase (see chapter 10) and the annexation of Florida, Oregon, and vast territories following the Mexican War. The federal government made the land available for purchase to attract settlers and to generate revenues. Although federal land cost only $1.25 an acre, millions of Americans could not afford to pay $50 for a forty-acre farm. They squatted on unclaimed federal land and carved out a farm that they neither rented nor owned. Many poor farmers never accumulated enough money to purchase the land on which they squatted, and eventually they moved elsewhere, often to squat again on unclaimed federal land.

In addition to aiding small farmers, government land policy enriched wily speculators who found ways to claim large tracts of the most desirable plots and sell them to settlers at a generous markup. Nonetheless, by making land available to millions of ordinary people, the federal government achieved the goal of attracting settlers to the new territories in the West, which in due course joined the Union as new states. Above all, federal land policy created the basic precondition for the increase in agricultural productivity that underlay the nation's impressive economic growth.

Manufacturing and Mechanization

Changes in manufacturing arose in the context of the nation's land-rich, labor-poor economy. England and other European countries had land-poor, labor-rich economies; there, meager opportunities in agriculture kept factory laborers plentiful and wages low. In the United States, western expansion and government land policies buoyed agriculture, keeping millions of people on the farm and thereby limiting the supply of workers for manufacturing and elevating

Railroads captured Americans' imaginations because they seemed to break the bonds of nature.

wages. Because of this relative shortage of workers, manufacturers searched constantly for ways to save labor.

Mechanization marched forward as quickly as manufacturers could turn innovative ideas into workable combinations of gears, levers, screws, and pulleys. Outside the textile industry (see chapter 11), homegrown machines set the pace. The practice of manufacturing and then assembling interchangeable parts spread from gun making to other industries and became known as the "American system." Clock makers used it; sewing machine makers used it; even ax makers used it. Mechanization became so integral to American manufacturing that some machinists specialized in what was called the machine tool industry, which made machines that made parts for other machines.

Manufacturing and agriculture meshed into a dynamic national economy. New England led the nation in manufacturing, shipping products such as clocks, guns, and axes west and south, while commodities such as wheat, pork, whiskey, tobacco, and cotton moved north and east. Manufacturers specialized in producing for the gigantic domestic market rather than for export. British goods dominated the international market and, on the whole, were cheaper and better than American-made products. U.S. manufacturers supported tariffs to minimize British competition, but their best protection from British competitors was to strive harder to please their American customers, the vast majority of whom were farmers.

Throughout American manufacturing, hand labor continued to be essential despite advances in mechanization. Even in heavily mechanized industries, factories remained fairly small; few had more than twenty or thirty employees. The industrial evolution under way before 1860 would quicken later in the nineteenth century; railroads were a harbinger of that future.

Railroads: Breaking the Bonds of Nature

Railroads incorporated the most advanced developments of the age. A Swedish visitor in 1849 noticed that American schoolboys constantly doodled sketches of locomotives, always belching smoke and steam, always in motion. Why did railroads capture Americans' imaginations? They seemed to break the bonds of nature. When

Railroad Travel

In addition to carrying people and goods more quickly and reliably than ever before, railroads also brought many Americans face-to-face for the first time with machinery that was much larger and more powerful than any human being. This painting of a train leaving Rochester, New York, in 1852 contrasts the size and power of human beings and machines. The huge, lovingly portrayed, steam-belching locomotive is barely held back by some unseen brake against which the massive engine strains, ready to pull the long train through the columns of the station, out of the past and into the future. The people, in contrast, appear indistinct, passive, and dependent. Except for the two women and child in the foreground, the people face backward, and all of them avoid looking directly at the locomotive. The painting evokes the way the almost incomprehensible power of the railroads dwarfed human effort.

Rochester Historical Society.

canals and rivers froze in winter or became impassable during summer droughts, trains steamed ahead. When becalmed sailing ships went nowhere, locomotives kept on chugging, averaging over twenty miles an hour during the 1850s. Above all, railroads offered cities not blessed with canals or navigable rivers a way to compete for the trade of the countryside.

By 1850, trains steamed along nine thousand miles of track, almost two-thirds of it in New England and the Middle Atlantic states. By 1860, several railroads had crossed the Mississippi River to link frontier farmers to the nation's 30,000 miles of track, approximately as much as in all the rest of the world combined (Map 12.5). (In 1857, for example, France had

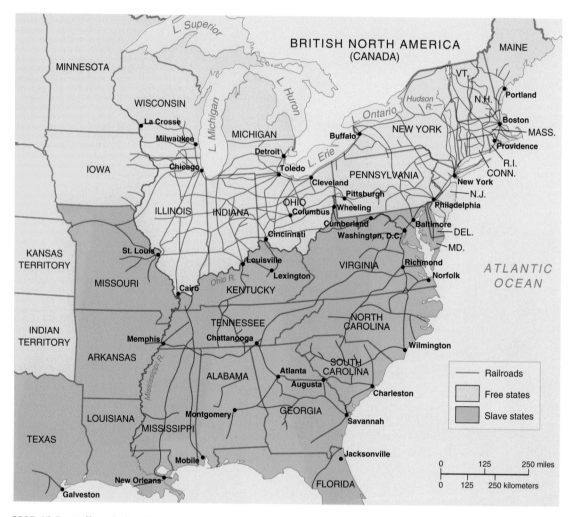

MAP 12.5   Railroads in 1860
Railroads were a crucial component of the revolutions in transportation and communications that transformed nineteenth-century America. The railroad system reflected the differences that had developed in the economies of the North and South.

READING THE MAP: In which sections of the country were most of the railroad tracks laid by the middle of the nineteenth century? What cities served as the busiest railroad hubs?
CONNECTIONS: How did the expansion of railroad networks affect the American economy? Why was the U.S. government willing to grant more than twenty million acres of public land to the private corporations that ran the railroads?

FOR MORE HELP ANALYZING THIS MAP, see the map activity for this chapter in the Online Study Guide at bedfordstmartins.com/roark.

3,700 miles of track; England and Wales had a total of 6,400 miles.) Chicago stood at the hub of eleven railroads, including the Illinois Central, the longest railroad anywhere. This massive expansion of railroads helped the United States catapult into position as the world's second leading industrial power, behind Great Britain.

In addition to speeding transportation, railroads propelled the growth of the iron and coal industries, both vital to railroad construction and operation. Iron production grew five times faster than the population during the decades up to 1860, in part to meet the demand for rails, wheels, axles, locomotives, and heavy, gravity-defying iron bridges. Railroads also stimulated the fledgling telegraph industry (see "The Promise of Technology," page 422). In 1844, Samuel F. B. Morse persuasively demonstrated the potential of his telegraph by transmitting a series of dots and dashes that instantly conveyed an electronic message along forty miles of wire strung between Washington and Baltimore. By 1861, more than fifty thousand miles of wire stretched across the continent to the Pacific, often alongside railroad tracks. Telegraphy made railroads safer and more efficient, swiftly signaling whether tracks were clear.

Almost all railroads were built and owned by private corporations rather than by governments. Undergirding these private investments was massive government aid, especially federal **land grants**. Up to 1850, the federal government had granted a total of seven million acres of federal land to various turnpike, highway, and canal projects. In that year, Illinois senator Stephen A. Douglas obtained congressional approval for a precedent-setting grant to railroads of 6 square miles of federal land for each mile of track laid. Railroad companies quickly lined up congressional support for other lucrative land deals. By 1860, Congress had granted railroads more than twenty million acres of federal lands, establishing a generous policy that would last for decades.

The railroad boom of the 1850s signaled the growing industrial might of the American economy. But railroads, like other industries, succeeded because they served farms as well as cities. And older forms of transportation remained significant. By 1857, for example, trains carried only about one-third of the mail; most of the rest still went by stagecoach or horseback. In 1860, most Americans were still far more familiar with four-legged horses than with iron horses.

The economy of the 1840s and 1850s linked an expanding, westward-moving population by muscles, animals, and farms as well as machines, steam, railroads, and cities. Abraham Lincoln split rails as a young man and defended railroad corporations as a successful attorney. His upward mobility illustrated the direction of economic change and the opportunities that change offered to enterprising individuals.

Free Labor: Promise and Reality

The nation's impressive economic performance did not reward all Americans equally. Native-born white men tended to do better than immigrants. With few exceptions, women were excluded from the opportunities open to men. Tens of thousands of women worked as seamstresses, laundresses, domestic servants, factory hands, and teachers but had little opportunity to aspire to higher-paying jobs. In the North and West, slavery was slowly eliminated in the half century after the American Revolution, but most free African Americans there found themselves relegated to dead-end jobs as laborers and servants. Discrimination against immigrants, women, and free blacks did not trouble most white men. With certain notable exceptions, they considered it proper and just.

The Free-Labor Ideal: Freedom plus Labor

During the 1840s and 1850s, leaders throughout the North and West emphasized a set of ideas that seemed to explain why the changes under way in their society benefited some more than others. They referred again and again to the advantages of what they termed **free labor**. (The word *free* referred to laborers who were not slaves; it did not mean laborers who worked for nothing.) By the 1850s, free-labor ideas described a social and economic ideal that accounted for both the successes and the shortcomings of the economy and society taking shape in the North and West.

Free-labor spokesmen celebrated hard work, self-reliance, and independence. They proclaimed that the door to success was open not just to those who inherited wealth or status but also to self-made men like Abraham Lincoln. Lincoln himself declared, "Free labor—the just and generous, and prosperous system, which opens the way for all—gives hope to all, and energy, and progress, and improvement of condition to all." The free-labor system, Lincoln argued, permitted farmers and artisans to enjoy the products of their own labor and also benefited wage workers. Ultimately, the free-labor system made it possible for hired laborers to become independent property owners, proponents argued. "The prudent, penniless beginner in the world," Lincoln asserted, "labors for wages awhile, saves a surplus with which to buy tools or land, for himself; then labors on his own account another while, and at length hires another new beginner to help him." Wage labor was the first rung on the ladder toward self-employment and, eventually, to hiring others.

> Free-labor spokesmen proclaimed that the door to success was open not just to those who inherited wealth or status but also to self-made men like Abraham Lincoln.

The Telegraph: The "Wonder Working Wire"

The telegraph played as important a role as the railroad in opening the West and uniting the nation. Telegraph wires often paralleled railroad lines, and the two developments were allies in the nineteenth-century communications revolution. Both delivered what nineteenth-century Americans craved—speed and efficiency and the ability to overcome vast distances.

Samuel F. B. Morse is credited with inventing the telegraph because of his patent of June 20, 1840, but, as is the case with many inventions, the assumption of "one man, one invention" exaggerates the contribution of a single individual. The telegraph grew out of scientific knowledge gradually acquired in the eighteenth and nineteenth centuries by a number of scientists, especially André Ampère of France, Alessandro Volta of Italy, and Joseph Henry of the United States, who pioneered in the field of electromagnetism and experimented with sending electrical signals through wires.

Morse was no scientist—he was an acclaimed painter—but beginning in the early 1830s he devoted himself to creating a machine that transmitted messages electrically. As one contemporary observed, Morse's talent consisted of "combining and applying the discoveries of others in the invention of a particular instrument and process for telegraphic purposes." This was no small achievement. In addition, Morse's system depended on a code he devised that represented each letter and number with dots and dashes. With a series of taps on a telegraph key, operators sent short and long pulses of electricity—a dash was three times as long as a dot. At the receiver's end, the code was originally written out by an electrically activated stylus on a moving strip of paper and then read off. But soon skilled operators found that by listening to the taps they could interpret the message and write it down. The Morse code became the universal language of the telegraph.

The breakthrough moment for Morse's invention came in 1842 when Congress voted $30,000 to build an experimental line between Washington and Baltimore. Four years earlier, a congressional report had declared that if Morse's invention succeeded, "space will be, to all practical purposes of information, completely annihilated between the States of the Union," and Congress was eager to find out if it would work. With the federal subsidy, Morse strung the line, and from the Supreme Court in Washington on May 22, 1844, he tapped out a biblical phrase. In Baltimore, forty-one miles away, a receiver transcribed: "What hath God wrought!" The trial was a stunning technical success, and it was also a public relations coup, for the entire nation stood awed by the speed and precision of the "wonder working wire."

The telegraph spread almost as swiftly as news of its existence. By 1846, most eastern cities were connected by telegraph. By 1850, of the states east of the Mississippi River, only Florida remained without it. More than fifty thousand miles of wires webbed the nation by 1861 when the telegraph reached California. Despite the cost—initially, an astronomical $1 a word—the line between San Francisco and the East chattered with dots and dashes.

The telegraph obliterated distance, and cheap, efficient, and fast communication changed American businesses, newspapers, government, and everyday life. Telegraphs made it possible to synchronize clocks, which in turn allowed railroads to run safely according to precise schedules. Businesses of every kind could send and receive information and orders almost instantaneously. Investors from across the country could learn the latest stock

---

The free-labor ideal affirmed an egalitarian vision of human potential. Lincoln and other spokesmen stressed the importance of universal education to permit "heads and hands [to] cooperate as friends." Throughout the North and West, communities supported public schools to make the rudiments of learning available to young children. By 1860, many cities and towns boasted that up to 80 percent of children ages seven to thirteen attended school at least for a few weeks each year. In rural areas, where the labor of children was more difficult to spare,

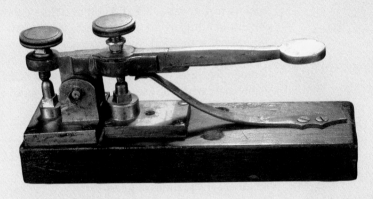

Telegraph Transmitter
This is Samuel Morse's telegraph key, the one that sent the first telegraph in 1844.
Division of Political History, Smithsonian Institution, Washington, D.C.

Telegraph Receiver
Early receivers pressed dots and dashes into a moving paper strip attached to the machine.
Division of Political History, Smithsonian Institution, Washington, D.C.

prices from the New York Stock Exchange. In 1852, an English visitor reported:

> If, on the arrival of an European mail at one of the northern ports, the news from Europe report that the supply of cotton or of corn is inadequate to meet the existing demand, almost before the vessel can be moored intelligence is spread by the Electric Telegraph, and the merchants and shippers of New Orleans are busied in the preparation of freights, or the corn-factors of St. Louis and Chicago, in the far west, are emptying their granaries and forwarding their contents by rail or by canal to the Atlantic ports.

Newspapers could gather information from around the country and have it in the headlines within hours.

As early as 1848, Americans followed the war in Mexico not from reports brought by messengers on horseback or on ships but by the magical wire. After 1866, when an underwater transatlantic cable linked Europe and the United States, the federal government used the telegraph to monitor international affairs and to respond swiftly to crises. On a personal level, families scattered across the continent could communicate more quickly than letter writing allowed. The telegraph met the needs of the vigorous, sprawling nation.

It is one thing to conceive of and build an innovative device. It is another to develop the idea into a profitable business. Unlike Eli Whitney, the unlucky inventor of the cotton gin, Morse was a skilled entrepreneur who grew rich from his invention. Patent rights, which he defended vigorously and successfully, allowed the Morse telegraph to dominate the United States and most of the non-British world. Morse's technology made him wealthy and worked powerfully to draw the far-flung young nation together, even as it began to pull apart politically.

schools typically enrolled no more than half the school-age children. Lessons included more than arithmetic, penmanship, and a smattering of other subjects. Teachers—most of whom were young women—and textbooks drummed into students the virtues of the free-labor system: self-reliance, discipline, and, above all, hard work. "Remember that all the ignorance, degradation, and misery in the world is the result of indolence and vice," one textbook intoned. Free-labor ideology, whether in school or out, emphasized labor as much as freedom.

Miner with Pick, Pan, and Shovel
This young man exhibits the spirit of individual effort that was the foundation of free labor ideals. Posing with a pick and shovel to loosen gold-bearing deposits and a pan to wash away debris, the man appears determined to succeed as a miner by his own muscle and sweat. Hard work with these tools, the picture suggests, promises deserved rewards and maybe riches.
Collection of Matthew Isenburg.

Economic Inequality

The free-labor ideal made sense to many Americans, especially in the North and West, because it seemed to describe their own experience. Lincoln frequently referred to his humble beginnings as a hired laborer and implicitly invited his listeners to consider how far he had come. In 1860, his wealth of $17,000 easily placed him in the top 5 percent of the population. The opportunities presented by the expanding economy made a few men much, much richer. In 1860, the nation had about forty millionaires, including Cyrus McCormick, whose wealth exceeded $2 million. Most Americans, however, measured success in far more modest terms. The average wealth of adult white men in the North in 1860 barely topped $2,000. Only about a quarter of American men possessed that much.

Nearly half had no wealth at all; about 60 percent owned no land. It is difficult to estimate the wealth of adult white women because property possessed by married women was normally considered to belong to their husbands, but certainly women had less wealth than men. Free African Americans had still less; 90 percent were propertyless.

Free-labor spokesmen considered these economic inequalities a natural outgrowth of freedom, the inevitable result of some individuals being more able, more willing to work, and luckier. These inequalities suggest, however, the gap between the promise and the performance of the free-labor ideal. Economic growth permitted many men to move from being landless squatters to landowning farmers and from being hired laborers to independent, self-employed producers. But many more Americans remained behind, landless and working for wages. Even those who realized their aspirations had a precarious hold on their independence; bad debts, crop failure, sickness, or death could quickly eliminate a family's gains.

Seeking out new opportunities in pursuit of free-labor ideals created restless social and geographic mobility. Commonly up to two-thirds of the residents of a rural area moved every decade, and the population turnover in cities was even greater. Such constant comings and goings weakened community ties to neighbors and friends and threw individuals even more on their own resources for help in times of trouble. Abraham Lincoln managed to get out of the log cabin in which he grew up, but memories of his life in that log cabin—with its economic insecurities and educational deficiencies, with his illiterate mother and semiliterate father—remained with him, reminding him how far he had come and how few were able to come so far.

Immigrants and the Free-Labor Ladder

The risks and uncertainties of free labor did not deter millions of immigrants from entering the United States during the 1840s and 1850s. Almost 4.5 million immigrants arrived between 1840 and 1860, six times more than had come during the previous two decades (Figure 12.1). The half-million immigrants who came in 1854 accounted for nearly 2 percent of the entire U.S. population, a higher proportion than in any other single year of the nation's history. By 1860, foreign-born residents made up about one-

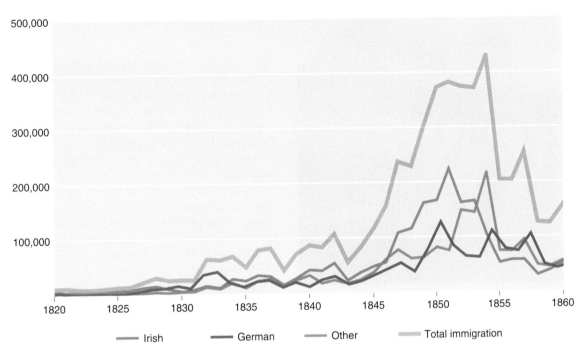

FIGURE 12.1 Antebellum Immigration, 1820–1860
After increasing gradually for several decades, immigration shot up in the mid-1840s. Between 1848 and 1860, nearly 3.5 million immigrants entered the United States.

eighth of the U.S. population, a fraction that held steady well into the twentieth century.

Nearly three out of four of the immigrants who arrived between 1840 and 1860 came from Germany or Ireland. The vast majority of the 1.4 million Germans who entered the United States during these years were skilled tradesmen and their families. They left Germany to escape deteriorating economic conditions and to seize opportunities offered by the expanding American economy. Skilled artisans had little difficulty finding work in the United States. German butchers, bakers, beer makers, carpenters, shopkeepers, machinists, and others tended to congregate in cities, particularly in the Midwest. Roughly a quarter of German immigrants were farmers, most of whom scattered throughout the Midwest, although some settled in Texas. On the whole, German Americans settled into that middle stratum of sturdy independent producers celebrated by free-labor spokesmen; relatively few Germans occupied the bottom rung of the free-labor ladder as wage laborers or domestic servants.

Irish immigrants, in contrast, entered at the bottom of the free-labor ladder and had difficulty climbing up. Nearly 1.7 million Irish immi-grants arrived between 1840 and 1860, nearly all of them desperately poor and often weakened by hunger and disease. Potato blight struck Ireland in 1845 and returned repeatedly in subsequent years, spreading a catastrophic famine throughout the island. Many of the lucky ones, half-starved, crowded into the holds of ships and set out for America, where they congregated in northeastern cities. As one immigrant group declared, "All we want is to get out of Ireland; we must be better anywhere than here." Death trailed after them. So many died crossing the Atlantic that ships from Ireland were often termed "coffin ships."

Roughly three out of four Irish immigrants worked as laborers or domestic servants. Irish men dug canals, loaded ships, laid railroad track, and took what other work they could find. Irish women hired out to cook, wash and iron, mind children, and clean house. Almost all Irish immigrants were Catholic, a fact that set them apart from the overwhelmingly **Protestant** native-born residents. Many natives regarded the Irish as hard-drinking, obstreperous,

> The risks and uncertainties of free labor did not deter millions of immigrants from entering the United States during the 1840s and 1850s.

Eviction of Irish Tenant
An Irish tenant (the seated man with crossed arms) and his family (two barefoot boys are shown) are evicted; their few pieces of furniture have been piled outside the cottage. The landlord or his agent (the man near the doorway) has brought four armed police to force the tenant to leave. Evictions like this were common in Ireland in the mid-nineteenth century. Poverty and human suffering pushed many Irish immigrants to the United States.
Lawrence Collection, National Library of Ireland.

half-civilized folk. Such views lay behind the discrimination that often excluded Irish immigrants from better jobs. Job announcements commonly stated, "No Irish need apply." Despite such prejudices, native residents hired Irish immigrants because they accepted low pay and worked hard.

In America's labor-poor economy, Irish laborers could earn in one day wages that would require several weeks' work in Ireland, if work could be found there. In America, one immigrant explained in 1853, there was "plenty of work and plenty of wages plenty to eat and no land lords thats enough what more does a man want." But some immigrants wanted more, especially respect and decent working conditions. One immigrant complained that he was "a slave for the Americans as the generality of the Irish . . . are."

Such testimony illustrates that the free-labor system, whether for immigrants or native-born laborers, often did not live up to the optimistic vision outlined by Abraham Lincoln and others. Many wage laborers could not realistically aspire to become independent, self-sufficient property holders, despite the claims of free-labor proponents.

Reforming Self and Society

The emphasis on self-discipline and individual effort at the core of the free-labor ideal pervaded America in the 1840s and 1850s. Many Americans believed that insufficient self-control caused the major social problems of the era. **Evangelical** Protestants struggled to control individuals' propensity to sin, and **temperance** advocates exhorted drinkers to control their urge for alcohol. In the midst of the worldly disruptions of geographic expansion and economic change, evangelicals brought more Americans than ever before into churches. Historians estimate that church members accounted for about one-third of the American population by midcentury. Most Americans remained outside churches, as did Abraham Lincoln. But the influence of evangelical religion reached far beyond those who belonged to churches. The evangelical temperament—a conviction of righteousness coupled with energy, self-discipline, and faith that the world could be improved—animated most reformers.

A few activists pointed out that certain fundamental injustices lay beyond the reach of individual self-control. Transcendentalists and utopians believed that perfection could be attained only by rejecting the competitive values of the larger society. Women's rights activists and abolitionists sought to reverse the subordination of women and to eliminate the enslavement of blacks by changing laws and social institutions as well as attitudes and customs. They confronted the daunting challenge of repudiating widespread assumptions about male supremacy and white supremacy and somehow subverting the entrenched institutions that reinforced those assumptions: the family and slavery.

The Pursuit of Perfection: Transcendentalists and Utopians

A group of New England writers that came to be known as transcendentalists believed that individuals should conform neither to the dictates of the materialistic world nor to the dogma of formal religion. Instead, people should look within themselves for truth and guidance. The leading transcendentalist, Ralph Waldo Emerson—an essayist, poet, and lecturer—proclaimed that the power of the solitary individual was nearly limitless. Henry David Thoreau, Margaret Fuller, and other transcendentalists agreed with Emerson that "if the single man plant himself indomitably on his instincts, and there abide, the huge world will come round to him." In many ways, transcendentalism represented less an alternative to the values of mainstream society than an exaggerated form of the rampant individualism of the age.

Unlike transcendentalists who sought to turn inward, a few reformers tried to change the world by organizing utopian communities as alternatives to prevailing social arrangements. Although these communities never attracted more than a few thousand people, the activities of their members demonstrated both dissatisfaction with the larger society and their efforts to realize their visions of perfection. Some communities functioned as retreats for those who did not want to sever ties with the larger society. Brook Farm, organized in 1841 in West Roxbury, Massachusetts, briefly provided a haven for a few literary and artistic New Englanders trying to balance bookish pursuits with manual labor.

Other communities set out to become models of perfection that they hoped would point the way toward a better life for everyone. During the 1840s, more than two dozen communities—principally in New York, New Jersey, Pennsylvania, and Ohio—organized around the ideas of Charles Fourier, a French critic of contemporary society. Members of Fourierist phalanxes, as these communities were called, believed that individualism and competition were evils that denied the basic truth that "men . . . are brothers and not competitors." Fourierist phalanxes tried to replace competition with harmonious cooperation based on communal ownership of property. Members were supposed to work not because they had to but because their work was satisfying and fulfilling. One former member recalled that "there was plenty of discussion, and an abundance of variety, which is called the spice of life. This spice however constituted the greater part of the fare, as we sometimes had scarcely anything to eat." Such complaints signaled the failure of the Fourierist communities to achieve their ambitious goals. Few survived more than two or three years.

The Oneida community went beyond the Fourierist notion of communalism. John Humphrey Noyes, the charismatic leader of Oneida, believed that individuals who had achieved salvation were literally without sin but the larger society's commitment to private property made even saints greedy and selfish. Noyes believed that the root of private property lay in marriage, in men's conviction that their wives were their exclusive property. Drawing from a substantial inheritance, Noyes organized the Oneida community in New York in 1848 to practice what he called "complex marriage." Sexual intercourse was permitted between any man and woman in the community who had been saved. Noyes usually reserved for himself the duties of "first husband," introducing sanctified young virgins to

Mary Cragin, Oneida Woman

A founding member of the Oneida community, Mary Cragin had a passionate sexual relationship with John Humphrey Noyes even before the community was organized. Within the bounds of complex marriage as practiced by the Oneidans, Cragin's magnetic sexuality made her a favorite partner of many men. In her journal, she confessed that "every evil passion was very strong in me from my childhood, sexual desire, love of dress and admiration, deceit, anger, pride." Oneida, however, transformed evil passion to holy piety. Cragin wrote, "In view of [God's] goodness to me and of his desire that I should let him fill me with himself, I yield and offer myself, to be penetrated by his spirit, and desire that love and gratitude may inspire my heart so that I shall sympathize with his pleasure in the thing, before my personal pleasure begins, knowing that it will increase my capability for happiness." Oneida's sexual practices were considered outrageous and sinful by almost all other Americans. Even Oneidans did not agree with all of Noyes's ideas about sex. "There is no reason why [sex] should not be done in public as much as music and dancing," he declared. It would display the art of sex, he explained, and watching "would give pleasure to a great many of the older people who now have nothing to do with the matter." Nonetheless, public sex never caught on among Oneidans.

Oneida Community Mansion House.

Elizabeth Cady Stanton
Women's rights leader Elizabeth Cady Stanton, pictured here with her sons, knew firsthand the joys and frustrations of domestic life. Like other women's rights activists, she sought to expand women's political, moral, and social responsibilities beyond the confines of hearth and home.
Collection of Rhoda Jenkins.

> In 1848, about one hundred reformers led by Elizabeth Cady Stanton and Lucretia Mott gathered at Seneca Falls, New York, for the first national women's rights convention in the United States.

complex marriage. To prevent a population explosion and to promote health and self-control, Noyes insisted that Oneida men practice "male continence," sexual intercourse without ejaculation. Noyes also required all members to relinquish their economic property to the community, which developed a lucrative business manufacturing animal traps. Oneida's sexual and economic communalism attracted several hundred members, but most of their neighbors considered Oneidans adulterers, blasphemers, and worse. Yet the practices

that set Oneida apart from its mainstream neighbors strengthened the community, and it survived long after the Civil War.

Women's Rights Activists

Women participated in the many reform activities that grew out of evangelical churches. Women church members outnumbered men two to one and worked to put their religious ideas into practice by joining peace, temperance, antislavery, and other societies. Involvement in reform organizations gave a few women activists practical experience in such political arts as speaking in public, running a meeting, drafting resolutions, and circulating petitions. Along with such experience came confidence. The abolitionist Lydia Maria Child pointed out in 1841 that "those who urged women to become missionaries and form tract societies . . . have changed the household utensil to a living energetic being and they have no spell to turn it into a broom again."

In 1848, about one hundred reformers led by Elizabeth Cady Stanton and Lucretia Mott gathered at Seneca Falls, New York, for the first national women's rights convention in the United States. The Seneca Falls Declaration of Sentiments proclaimed that "the history of mankind is a history of repeated injuries and usurpations on the part of man toward woman, having in direct object the establishment of an absolute tyranny over her." In the style of the Declaration of Independence (see appendix, page A-1), the Seneca Falls Declaration listed the ways in which women had been discriminated against. Through the tyranny of male supremacy, men "endeavored in every way that [they] could to destroy her confidence in her own powers, to lessen her self-respect, and to make her willing to lead a dependent and abject life." The Declaration demanded that women "have immediate admission to all the rights and privileges which belong to them as citizens of the United States," particularly the "inalienable right to the elective franchise."

Nearly two dozen other women's rights conventions assembled before 1860, repeatedly calling for **suffrage**. But they had difficulty receiving a respectful hearing, much less obtaining legislative action. No state came close to permitting women to vote. Politicians and editorialists hooted at the idea. Everyone knew, they sneered, that a woman's place was in the home, rearing her children and civilizing her man. Nonetheless, the Seneca Falls Declaration served as a pathbreaking manifesto of dissent against male supremacy and of support for woman suffrage, which would become the focus of the women's rights movement during the next seventy years.

Abolitionists and the American Ideal

During the 1840s and 1850s, abolitionists continued to struggle to draw the nation's attention to the plight of slaves and the need for emancipation. Former slaves such as Frederick Douglass, Henry Bibb, and Sojourner Truth lectured to reform audiences throughout the North about the cruelties of slavery. Abolitionists published newspapers, held conventions, and petitioned Congress. But they never attracted a mass following among white Americans. Many white Northerners became convinced that slavery was wrong, but they still believed that blacks were inferior. Many other white Northerners shared the common view of white Southerners that slavery was necessary and even desirable. The geographic expansion of the nation during the 1840s offered abolitionists an opportunity to link their unpopular ideal to a goal that many white Northerners found much more attractive— limiting the geographic expansion of slavery, an issue that moved to the center of national politics during the 1850s (see chapter 14).

Black leaders rose to prominence in the abolitionist movement during the 1840s and 1850s. African Americans had actively opposed slavery for decades, but a new generation of leaders came to the forefront in these years. Frederick Douglass, Henry Highland Garnet, William Wells Brown, Martin R. Delany, and others became impatient with white abolitionists' appeals to the conscience of the white majority. Garnet proclaimed in 1843 that slaves should rise in insurrection against their masters, an idea that alienated almost all white people. To express their own uncompromising ideas, black abolitionists founded their own newspapers and held their own antislavery conventions, although they still cooperated with sympathetic whites.

The commitment of black abolitionists to battling slavery grew out of their own experiences with white supremacy. The 250,000 free African Americans in the North and West constituted less than 2 percent of the total population. They confronted the humiliations of racial discrimination in virtually every arena of daily life: at work, at school, at church, in shops, in the streets, on

Abolitionist Meeting

This rare daguerreotype was made by Ezra Greenleaf Weld in August 1850 at an abolitionist meeting in Cazenovia, New York. Frederick Douglass, who had escaped from slavery in Maryland twelve years earlier, is seated on the platform next to the woman at the table. One of the nation's most brilliant and eloquent abolitionists, Douglass also supported equal rights for women. The man immediately behind Douglass gesturing with his outstretched arm is Gerrit Smith, a wealthy New Yorker and militant abolitionist whose funds supported many reform activities. Notice the two black women in similar clothing on either side of Smith and the white woman next to Douglass. Most white Americans considered such voluntary racial proximity scandalous and promiscuous. What messages did abolitionists attempt to convey by attending such protest meetings? Collection of the J. Paul Getty Museum, Malibu, CA.

trains, in hotels. Only four states (Maine, Massachusetts, New Hampshire, and Vermont) permitted black men to vote; New York imposed a special property-holding requirement on black—but not white—voters, effectively excluding most black men from the **franchise**. The pervasive racial discrimination both handicapped and energized black abolitionists. Some

Back to Africa: The United States in Liberia

In the first half of the nineteenth century, thousands of free African Americans returned to Africa. In Liberia, they established a beachhead for American culture, one that clearly remains alive today. American-sounding names (the county of Maryland), American institutions (Masonic lodges), a red, white, and blue flag patterned on the Stars and Stripes, and a restaurant that advertises Maryland-style fried chicken make it impossible to forget the American origins of this modern-day West African nation.

In 1817, white men with a range of motives founded the American Colonization Society to transport black Americans to Africa. Some colonizationists sympathized with America's oppressed blacks and urged them to return to Africa, their "natural home," to escape racism, improve their lot in life, and help "civilize" an entire continent. Other colonizationists wanted to rid the United States of what they considered a "useless, pernicious, and dangerous" people. Whatever their motivation, colonizationists agreed that the two races could not live together and that blacks should leave. Aware that British antislavery forces had founded Sierra Leone in West Africa as a haven for freed slaves a generation earlier, the Society purchased land to the south from African chiefs. They named it Liberia, after **liberty**, and its capital Monrovia, after President James Monroe.

Between 1820, when it shipped the first settlers to Liberia, and the start of the American Civil War in 1861, the Society sent approximately 12,000 African Americans to Africa. Some 7,000 were slaves whose masters freed them (often because they were favorites or kin) on the condition that they leave America, and some 5,000 were free blacks who chose to go because they had lost hope of achieving equality in the United States. John Russwurm was one such free black who accepted the Society's invitation because he concluded that blacks in America could never overcome "the odium of [an] inferior and degraded caste." The overwhelming majority of free blacks claimed America as their country and decided to make their stand at home. Frederick Douglass spoke for them in 1849 when he denounced colonizationists: "Shame upon the guilty wretches that dare propose . . . such a proposition. We live here—have lived here—have a right to live here, and mean to live here."

American settlers in Liberia found life even harder there than at home. Land along the coast was swampy, covered with forests, and often lacked fresh water. The Society never had enough funds to support the settlers adequately, and even though former masters provided some assistance, the newcomers faced shortages of basic necessities. Moreover, settlers and Africans clashed as the Americans pushed inland, taking land, killing game, and attacking slave traders who kidnapped or bought people to ship as laborers to Cuba and Brazil. The outpost somehow managed to survive, but many emigrants did not. In the first two decades of settlement, "African fever," most likely malaria, killed about one-quarter of the settlers.

In time, the settlers established a foothold, and life grew a little less precarious. They learned to farm without their horses and mules, which could not survive African diseases, and they began trading coffee, sugar, and palm oil. They stabilized the boundaries of the colony, controlling some 250 miles of coastline to a depth of 40 or 50 miles. But by the 1840s, the American Colonization Society was nearly bankrupt. When the U.S. government refused to assume sovereignty of the private colony, the Society demanded that the settlers proclaim independence. In 1847, a few thousand North American immigrants announced the Republic of Liberia and took control of a substantial piece of Africa and several hundred thousand Africans.

The settlers had fled America, but rather than cast off American culture, they clung to it, straining every muscle to rebuild American lives, without slavery and white supremacy, in Africa. As far as possible, they retained American habits in food, dress, manners, and housing. Liberia produced abundant crops of millet, yams, cassava, and pawpaw, but the settlers maintained a taste for flour, pork, and dried fruit, which they imported when they could. Settlers established American institutions, including public schools, fraternal organizations, and temperance societies. Most important, they promoted their evangelical Christian faith by building Methodist and Baptist churches everywhere they settled. Most newcomers felt a profound missionary urge to carry "the blessed Gospel" to the land of their forefathers.

Despite their African heritage, settlers felt little kinship with Africans. The newcomers displayed a strong sense of superiority and engaged in what they considered a

Liberian Crowds Await the U.S. President
In April 1978, Americans and Liberians await the arrival of President Jimmy Carter at the airport outside Monrovia. Flying side by side, the two national flags offer dramatic evidence of the American origins and continuing influence of the United States on Liberian history.
© Wally McNamee/Corbis.

providential effort to "civilize and uplift." "It is something to think that these people are calld [sic] our ancestors," Peyton Skipwith, an ex-slave from Virginia, declared. "In my present thinking if we have any ancestors they could not have been like these hostile tribes . . . for you may . . . do all you can for them and they still will be your enemy." Settlers labored to maintain the distinctions between themselves and the Gola, Kru, and Vai peoples who surrounded them. Africa was populated, Matilda Skipwith insisted, with "the most savage, & blud thirsty people I ever saw." But opposition to Africans did not mean that the African American settler community was united. Settlers carried with them old tensions and divisions, especially those between the free-born and slave-born. Light-skinned free-born African Americans often arrived with more money, education, and skills, and they quickly enjoyed greater wealth and political power.

The settlers did, however, agree that they had found in Africa what they had primarily come for—dignity and freedom. Despite the continuing heartache of leaving family behind and the stubborn reality of physical hardship, they refused to return to America. In 1848, one African American declared, "I will never consent to leave the country . . . for this is the only place where a colored person can enjoy his liberty, for there exists no prejudice of color in this country, and every man is free and equal."

In the second half of the nineteenth century, when European powers sliced Africa into colonies, Liberia managed to retain its political independence. But in the 1920s an American corporation, the Firestone Rubber Company, made Liberia a kind of economic colony. Today, Liberians of American descent comprise only about 5 percent of Liberia's population, but they continue to wield disproportionate power. Only in 1946 did the dominant Americo-Liberians allow indigenous people to vote.

In 1980, the African majority rose up in bloody rebellion against the still-Americanized Liberian elite. Years of civil war have largely wrecked the country, trapping its people in fear and starvation.

Contemporary Liberia

Liberians have implored the United States, which some call "big brother," to recognize its historic connections with the African nation and fulfill what they see as its continuing responsibilities by intervening with peacekeeping forces. Black Americans in the twentieth century developed a close sense of kinship with Africa, particularly in the 1950s and 1960s when they sensed the interconnectedness of freedom struggles on both sides of the Atlantic, but the U.S. government has been slower to acknowledge historic ties. In August 2003, following a bloody uprising in Liberia and intense pressure from the international community for swift action, the Bush administration successfully pressured President Charles Taylor into resigning his office, and sent in a token handful of troops to keep the peace. Nevertheless, the U.S. government continues to resist the argument that the United States has a special relationship with Liberia.

BIBLIOGRAPHY

David Eltis, *Economic Growth and the Ending of the Transatlantic Slave Trade* (1987).

James H. Meriwether, *Proudly We Can Be Africans: Black Americans and Africa, 1935–1961* (2002).

Floyd J. Miller, *The Search for a Black Nationality: Black Emigration and Colonization, 1787–1863* (1975).

Randall M. Miller, ed., *Dear Master: Letters of a Slave Family* (1978).

Tom W. Shick, *Behold the Promised Land: A History of Afro-American Settler Society in Nineteenth-Century Liberia* (1977).

Philip J. Staudenraus, *The African Colonization Movement, 1816–1865* (1961).

Richard West, *Back to Africa: A History of Sierra Leone and Liberia* (1970).

Bell I. Wiley, ed., *Slaves No More: Letters from Liberia, 1833–1869* (1980).

cooperated with the American Colonization Society's efforts to send freed slaves and other black Americans to Liberia in west Africa (see "Beyond America's Borders," page 430). Other black American leaders organized campaigns against segregation, particularly in transportation and education. Their most notable success came in 1855 when Massachusetts integrated public schools. Elsewhere white supremacy continued unabated.

Outside the public spotlight, free African Americans in the North and West contributed to the antislavery cause by quietly aiding fugitive slaves. Harriet Tubman escaped from slavery in Maryland in 1849 and repeatedly risked her freedom and her life to return to the South to escort slaves to freedom. When the opportunity arose, free blacks in the North provided fugitive slaves with food, a safe place to rest, and a helping hand. This "underground railroad" ran mainly through black neighborhoods, black churches, and black homes, an outgrowth of the anti-slavery sentiment and opposition to white supremacy that unified nearly all African Americans in the North.

Conclusion: Free Labor, Free Men

In the 1840s, diplomacy and war handed the United States 1.2 million square miles and more than 1,000 miles of Pacific coastline. California almost immediately rewarded its new owners with mountains of gold. To most Americans, vast geographical expansion seemed to be the natural companion of a stunning economic transformation. A cluster of interrelated developments—steam power, railroads, and the growing mechanization of agriculture and manufacturing—resulted in greater productivity, a burst of output from farms and factories, and prosperity for many.

To Northerners, industrial evolution confirmed the choice they had made to eliminate slavery and to promote free labor as the key to independence, equality, and prosperity. Millions of Northerners, like Abraham Lincoln, could point to personal experience as evidence of the practical truth of the free-labor ideal. But millions of others had different stories to tell. Rather than producing economic equality, the free-labor system saw wealth and poverty continue to rub shoulders. Instead of social independence, more than half of the nation's free-labor workforce toiled for someone else by 1860. Free-labor enthusiasts denied that the problems were built into the system. They argued that most social ills—including poverty and dependency—sprang from individual deficiencies. Consequently, reformers usually focused on the lack of self-control and discipline, on sin and alcohol. They denied that free labor meant exploitation. They argued that slaves, not free workers, suffered. White Southerners, in contrast, pitied northern free workers, not slaves.

By the 1840s, the nation was half slave and half free, and each region was animated by economic interests, cultural values, and political aims that were antithetical to those of the other. Not even the victory over Mexico could bridge the deepening differences between North and South.

FOR ADDITIONAL FIRSTHAND ACCOUNTS OF THIS PERIOD, see Chapter 12 in Michael Johnson, ed., *Reading the American Past*, Third Edition.

TO ASSESS YOUR MASTERY OF THE MATERIAL IN THIS CHAPTER, see the Online Study Guide at bedfordstmartins.com/roark.

FOR WEB LINKS RELATED TO TOPICS IN THIS CHAPTER, see "HistoryLinks," "DocLinks," and "PlaceLinks" at bedfordstmartins.com/roark.

CHRONOLOGY

1836 • Texas declares independence from Mexico.

1837 • John Deere patents his steel plow.

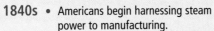

1840s • Americans begin harnessing steam power to manufacturing.

• Cyrus McCormick and others create practical mechanical reapers.

1841 • First wagon trains head west on Oregon Trail.

• Vice President John Tyler becomes president when William Henry Harrison dies in office after one month.

1844 • Democrat James K. Polk elected president on platform calling for annexation of Texas and Oregon.

• Samuel F. B. Morse invents telegraph.

1845 • Term *manifest destiny* coined by New York journalist John L. O'Sullivan; used as justification for Anglo-American settlers to take land in West.

• United States annexes Texas, which enters Union as slave state.

1846 • Bear Flag Revolt, independence movement to secede from Mexico, takes place in California.

• Congress declares war on Mexico.

• United States and Great Britain agree to divide Oregon Country at forty-ninth parallel.

1847 • Brigham Young leads advance party of Mormons to Great Salt Lake in Utah.

1848 • Treaty of Guadalupe Hidalgo ends Mexican War: Mexico gives up all claims to Texas north of Rio Grande and cedes provinces of New Mexico and California to United States.

• Oneida community organized in New York.

• First U.S. women's rights convention takes place at Seneca Falls, New York.

1849 • California gold rush begins.

• Harriet Tubman escapes from slavery in Maryland.

1850 • Mormon community of Deseret annexed to United States as Utah Territory.

1851 • Conference in Laramie, Wyoming, between U.S. government and Plains tribes marks beginning of government policy of forcing Indians onto reservations.

1855 • Massachusetts integrates public schools as result of campaigns led by African Americans.

BIBLIOGRAPHY

General Works

Glenn C. Altschuler and Stuart M. Blumin, *Rude Republic: Americans and Their Politics in the Nineteenth Century* (2000).

Stuart Bruchey, *Enterprise: The Dynamic Economy of a Free People* (1990).

David B. Danbom, *Born in the Country: A History of Rural America* (1995).

David Herbert Donald, *Lincoln* (1995).

John Mack Faragher, *Sugar Creek: Life on the Illinois Frontier* (1986).

Lori D. Ginzberg, *Women and the Work of Benevolence: Morality, Politics, and Class in the Nineteenth-Century United States* (1990).

Jon Gjerde, *The Minds of the West: Ethnocultural Evolution in the Rural Middle West, 1830–1917* (1997).

Nathan O. Hatch, *The Democratization of American Christianity* (1991).

Helen Lefkowitz Horowitz, *Rereading Sex: Battles over Sexual Knowledge and Suppression in Nineteenth-Century America* (2002).

Bruce Laurie, *Artisans into Workers: Labor in Nineteenth-Century America* (1989).

Patricia Nelson Limerick, *The Legacy of Conquest: The Unbroken Past of the American West* (1987).

Malcolm Rohrbough, *Days of Gold: The California Gold Rush and the American Nation* (1997).

Mark Voss-Hubbard, *Beyond Party: Cultures of Antipartisanship in Northern Politics before the Civil War* (2002).

Richard White, *"It's Your Misfortune and None of My Own": A New History of the American West* (1993).

Kenneth J. Winkle, *The Young Eagle: The Rise of Abraham Lincoln* (2001).

Politics and Expansion

Leonard J. Arrington and Davis Bitton, *The Mormon Experience: A History of the Latter-Day Saints* (1979).

Richard A. Bartlett, *The New Country: A Social History of the American Frontier, 1776–1890* (1974).

William A. Bowen, *The Willamette Valley: Migration and Settlement on the Oregon Frontier* (1978).

Gene Brack, *Mexico Views Manifest Destiny, 1821–1846: An Essay on the Origins of the Mexican War* (1975).

Mark M. Carroll, *Homesteads Ungovernable: Families, Sex, Race, and Law in Frontier Texas, 1823–1860* (2001).

Tom Chaffin, *Pathfinder: John Charles Frémont and the Course of American Empire* (2002).

Donald E. Chipman, *Spanish Texas, 1519–1821* (1992).

Arnoldo De Leon, *The Tejano Community, 1836–1900* (1982).

William Dusinberre, *Slavemaster President: The Double Career of James Polk* (2003).

John Mack Faragher, *Women and Men on the Overland Trail* (1979).

James R. Gibson, *Farming the Frontier: The Agricultural Opening of the Oregon Country, 1786–1846* (1985).

William H. Goetzmann, *New Lands, New Men: America and the Second Great Age of Discovery* (1986).

Thomas R. Hietala, *Manifest Design: Anxious Aggrandizement in Late Jacksonian America* (rev. ed., 2002).

Reginald Horsman, *Race and Manifest Destiny: The Origins of American Racial Anglo-Saxonism* (1981).

Stephen G. Hyslop, *Bound for Santa Fe: The Road to New Mexico and the American Conquest, 1806–1848* (2002).

Julie Roy Jeffrey, *Frontier Women: The Trans-Mississippi West, 1840–1880* (1979).

D. W. Meinig, *The Shaping of America: A Geographical Perspective on 500 Years of History*, vol. 2, *Continental America, 1800–1867* (1993).

Frederick Merk, *Manifest Destiny and Mission in American History: A Reinterpretation* (1963).

David Montejano, *Anglos and Mexicans in the Making of Texas, 1836–1986* (1987).

Gregory H. Nobles, *American Frontiers: Cultural Encounters and Continental Conquest* (1997).

David M. Pletcher, *The Diplomacy of Annexation: Texas, Oregon, and the Mexican War* (1973).

Glenda Riley, *The Female Frontier: A Comparative View of Women on the Prairie and the Plains* (1988).

Randy Roberts and James L. Olson, *A Line in the Sand: The Alamo in Blood and Memory* (2001).

Malcolm J. Rohrbough, *The Trans-Appalachian Frontier* (1978).

Joel H. Silbey, *The American Political Nation, 1838–1915* (1991).

John D. Unruh, *The Plains Across: The Overland Emigrants and the Trans-Mississippi West, 1840–1860* (1979).

David J. Weber, *The Mexican Frontier, 1821–1846: The American Southwest under Mexico* (1982).

Sanford Wexler, ed., *Westward Expansion: An Eyewitness History* (1991).

The Mexican War and California Gold

Jajia Aarim-Heriot, *Chinese Immigrants, African Americans, and Racial Anxiety in the United States, 1848–82* (2003).

K. Jack Bauer, *The Mexican War, 1846–1848* (1974).

Peter J. Blodgett, *Land of Golden Dreams: California in the Gold Rush Decade, 1848–1858* (1999).

H. W. Brands, *The Age of Gold: The California Gold Rush and the New American Dream* (2002).

Yong Chen, *Chinese San Francisco, 1850–1943: A Trans-Pacific Community* (2000).

Seymour V. Conner and Odie B. Faulk, *North America Divided: The Mexican War, 1846–1848* (1971).

John S. D. Eisenhower, *So Far from God: The U.S. War with Mexico, 1846–1848* (1989).

Donald S. Frazier, ed., *The United States and Mexico at War: Nineteenth-Century Expansionism and Conflict* (1998).

William S. Greever, *Bonanza West: The Story of the Western Mining Rushes, 1848–1900* (1963).

Albert L. Hurtado, *Indian Survival on the California Frontier* (1988).

Albert L. Hurtado, *Intimate Frontiers: Sex, Gender, and Culture in Old California* (1999).

Robert H. Jackson and Edward Castillo, *Indians, Franciscans, and Spanish Colonization: The Impact of the Mission System on California Indians* (1995).

Robert W. Johannsen, *To the Halls of the Montezumas: The Mexican War in the American Imagination* (1985).

David Alan Johnson, *Founding the Far West: California, Oregon, and Nevada, 1840–1890* (1992).

Susan Lee Johnson, *Roaring Camp: The Social World of the California Gold Rush* (2000).

Ernest M. Lander Jr., *Reluctant Imperialists: Calhoun, the South Carolinians, and the Mexican War* (1980).

Rudolph M. Lapp, *Blacks in Gold Rush California* (1977).

Ward McAfee and J. Cordell Robinson, eds., *Origins of the Mexican War: A Documentary Source Book*, 2 vols. (1982).

James M. McCaffrey, *Army of Manifest Destiny: The American Soldier in the Mexican War, 1846–1848* (1992).

Charles J. McClain, *In Search of Equality: The Chinese Struggle against Discrimination in Nineteenth-Century America* (1994).

Kenneth N. Owens, *Riches for All: The California Gold Rush and the World* (2002).

Rodman W. Paul, *Mining Frontiers of the Far West, 1848–1880* (1963).

Ramón Eduardo Ruiz, ed., *The Mexican War: Was It Manifest Destiny?* (1963).

Richard Bruce Winders, *Mr. Polk's Army: The American Military Experience in the Mexican War* (1997).

The Economy and Free Labor

Edward J. Balleisen, *Navigating Failure: Bankruptcy and Commercial Society in Antebellum America* (2001).

Howard Bodenhorn, *A History of Banking in Antebellum America: Financial Markets and Economic Development in an Era of Nation Building* (2000).

James Dilts, *The Great Road: The Building of the Baltimore and Ohio, the Nation's First Railroad, 1828–1853* (2003).

J. Matthew Gallman, *Receiving Erin's Children: Philadelphia, Liverpool, and the Irish Famine Migration, 1854–1855* (2000).

Jonathan A. Glickstein, *Concepts of Free Labor in Antebellum America* (1991).

Jonathan A. Glickstein, *American Exceptionalism, American Anxiety: Wages, Competition, and Degraded Labor in the Antebellum United States* (2002).

Brooke Hindle and Steven Lubar, *Engines of Change: The American Industrial Revolution, 1790–1860* (1986).

Donald R. Hoke, *Ingenious Yankees: The Rise of the American System of Manufactures in the Private Sector* (1990).

David A. Hounshell, *From the American System to Mass Production, 1800–1932: The Development of Manufacturing Technology in the United States* (1984).

Reeve Huston, *Land and Freedom: Rural Society, Popular Protest, and Party Politics in Antebellum New York* (2000).

Paul Israel, *From Machine Shop to Industrial Laboratory: Telegraphy and the Changing Context of American Invention, 1830–1920* (1992).

Allan Kulikoff, *The Agrarian Origins of American Capitalism* (1992).

Amy Schrager Lang, *Syntax of Class: Writing Inequality in Nineteenth-Century America* (2003).

Edward Laxton, *The Famine Ships: The Irish Exodus to America* (1998).

Robert A. Margo, *Wages and Labor Markets in the United States, 1820–1860* (2000).

Jonathan Prude, *The Coming of Industrial Order: Town and Factory Life in Rural Massachusetts, 1810–1860* (1983).

W. J. Rorabaugh, *The Craft Apprentice: From Franklin to the Machine Age in America* (1986).

Antebellum Culture and Reform

Norman Basch, *In the Eyes of the Law: Women, Marriage, and Property in Nineteenth-Century New York* (1982).

Stuart Blumin, *The Emergence of the Middle Class: Social Experience in the American City, 1790–1900* (1989).

Jeanne Boydston, *Home and Work: Housework, Wages, and the Ideology of Labor in the Early Republic* (1990).

Bruce Dorsey, *Reforming Men and Women: Gender in the City* (2002).

Ellen Carol DuBois, *Feminism and Suffrage: The Emergence of an Independent Women's Suffrage Movement in America, 1848–1869* (1978).

David F. Ericson, *The Debate over Slavery: Antislavery and Proslavery Liberalism in Antebellum America* (2001).

Robert Fanuzzi, *Abolition's Public Sphere* (2003).

Joseph P. Ferrie, *Yankeys Now: Immigrants in the Antebellum United States, 1840–1860* (1999).

Lawrence Foster, *Women, Family, and Utopia: Communal Experiments of the Shakers, the Oneida Community, and the Mormons* (1991).

Rhoda Golden Freeman, *The Free Negro in New York City in the Era before the Civil War* (1994).

Kathryn Glover, *The Fugitives' Gibraltar: Escaping Slaves and Abolition in New Bedford, Massachusetts* (2001).

Paul Goodman, *Of One Blood: Abolitionism and the Origins of Racial Equality* (1998).

Karen Halttunen, *Confidence Men and Painted Women: A Study of Middle-Class Culture in America, 1830–1870* (1982).

Debra Gold Hansen, *Strained Sisterhood: Gender and Class in the Boston Female Anti-Slavery Society* (1993).

Stephen John Hartnett, *Democratic Dissent and the Cultural Fictions of Antebellum America* (2002).

David Henkin, *City Reading: Written Words and Public Spaces in Antebellum New York* (1999).

Nancy A. Hewitt, *Women's Activism and Social Change: Rochester, New York, 1822–1872* (1984).

Leo P. Himel, *Children of Wrath: New School Calvinism and Antebellum Reform* (1998).

Sylvia D. Hoffert, *When Hens Crow: The Women's Rights Movement in Antebellum America* (1995).

James O. Horton and Lois E. Horton, *In Hope of Liberty: Culture, Community, and Protest among Northern Free Blacks, 1700–1860* (1998).

Nancy Isenberg, *Sex and Citizenship in Antebellum America* (1998).

Julie Roy Jeffrey, *The Great Silent Army of Abolitionism: Ordinary Women in the Antislavery Movement* (1998).

Joan M. Jensen, *Loosening the Bonds: Mid-Atlantic Farm Women, 1750–1850* (1986).

Carl F. Kaestle, *Pillars of the Republic: Common Schools and American Society, 1780–1860* (1983).

Spencer Klaw, *Without Sin: The Life and Death of the Oneida Community* (1993).

Isabelle Lehuu, *Carnival on the Page: Popular Print Media in Antebellum America* (2000).

Timothy Mahoney, *Provincial Lives: Middle-Class Experience in the Antebellum Middle West* (1999).

Henry Mayer, *All on Fire: William Lloyd Garrison and the Abolition of Slavery* (1998).

William J. McFeely, *Frederick Douglass* (1991).

Kerby A. Miller, *Emigrants and Exiles: Ireland and the Irish Exodus to North America* (1985).

Steven Mintz, *Moralists and Modernizers: America's Pre–Civil War Reformers* (1995).

Richard S. Newman, *The Transformation of American Abolitionism: Fighting Slavery in the Early Republic* (2002).

John W. Quist, *Restless Visionaries: The Social Roots of Antebellum Reform in Alabama and Michigan* (1998).

Patrick Rael, *Black Identity and Black Protest in the Antebellum North* (2002).

Mary P. Ryan, *Civic Wars: Democracy and Public Life in the American City during the Nineteenth Century* (1998).

Susan M. Ryan, *The Grammar of Good Intentions: Race and the Antebellum Culture of Benevolence* (2003).

Mark S. Schantz, *Piety in Providence: Class Dimensions of Religious Experience in Antebellum Rhode Island* (2000).

John Stauffer, *The Black Hearts of Men: Radical Abolitionists and the Transformation of Race* (2002).

Daniel W. Stowell, *In Tender Consideration: Women, Families, and the Law in Abraham Lincoln's Illinois* (2002).

Albert J. Von Frank, *The Trials of Anthony Burns: Freedom and Slavery in Emerson's Boston* (1998).

Edward L. Widmer, *Young America: The Flowering of Democracy in New York City* (1998).

Shirley Yee, *Black Women Abolitionists: A Study in Activism, 1828–1860* (1992).

Jean Fagan Yellin, *Women and Sisters: The Antislavery Feminists in American Culture* (1989).

Susan Zaeske, *Signatures of Citizenship: Petitioning, Antislavery, and Women's Political Identity* (2003).

CLAY JUG

This ceramic water cooler, made in about 1840, is attributed to Thomas Chandler, a famous potter of Edgefield District, South Carolina. The relatively fine clothes of the African American man and woman portrayed on the vessel suggest that they are house servants. On the wall of the home of Alexander Stephens in Crawfordsville, Georgia, an intriguing letter from Stephens states that two of his favorite slaves are getting married and orders the plantation manager to butcher a hog for their wedding. This cooler, with its portrait of a couple, a hog, and a jug, way have been commissioned by Stephens to commemorate the union.

Potters made vessels to be used—to hold water and food. Analysis of the form, decoration, and glazes of southern pottery suggests a blend of European, African, and Native American ceramic traditions. Some pottery went beyond the utilitarian and became art. The most renowned slave potter was an Edgefield man named Dave, who skillfully fashioned huge vessels, inscribed poems on their surfaces, and proudly and boldly signed them "Dave the potter."

13

The Slave South
1820–1860

NAT TURNER WAS BORN A SLAVE in Southampton County, Virginia, in October 1800. People in his neighborhood claimed that he had always been different. His parents noticed special marks on his body, which they said were signs that he was "intended for some great purpose." His master said that he learned to read without being taught. As an adolescent, he adopted an austere lifestyle of Christian devotion and fasting. In his twenties, he received visits from the "Spirit," the same spirit, he believed, that had spoken to the ancient prophets. In time, Nat Turner began to interpret these things to mean that God had appointed him an instrument of divine vengeance for the sin of slaveholding.

In the early morning of August 22, 1831, he set out with six trusted friends—Hark, Henry, Sam, Nelson, Will, and Jack—to punish slave owners and free their suffering slaves. Turner struck the first blow, an ax to the head of his master, Joseph Travis. The rebels killed all of the white men, women, and children they encountered in each household they attacked. By noon, they had visited eleven farms and slaughtered fifty-seven whites and, along the way, added fifty or sixty men to their army. Word spread quickly, however, and soon the militia and hundreds of local whites gathered. By the next day, whites had captured or killed all of the rebels, except Nat Turner, who successfully hid out for about ten weeks before being captured in nearby woods. Within a week, he was tried, convicted, and executed. By then, forty-five slaves had stood trial, twenty had been convicted and hanged, and another ten had been transported from Virginia. Frenzied whites had killed another hundred or more blacks—insurgents and innocent bystanders—in their counterattack against the rebellion.

Virginia's governor John Floyd asked how Turner's band of "assassins and murderers" could have assaulted the "unsuspecting and defenseless" citizens of "one of the fairest counties in the Commonwealth." White Virginians prided themselves on having the "mildest" slavery in the South, but sixty black rebels on a rampage challenged the comforting theory of the contented slave. Nonetheless, whites found explanations that allowed them to feel safer. They placed the blame on outside agitators. In 1829, David Walker, a freeborn black man living in Boston, had published his *Appeal . . . to the Coloured Citizens of the World*, an invitation to slaves to rise up in bloody rebellion, and copies had fallen into the hands of Virginia slaves. Moreover, on January 1, 1831, in Boston, William Lloyd Garrison, the Massachusetts abolitionist, had published the first issue of *Liberator,* his fiery newspaper. White Virginians also dismissed the rebellion's leader, Nat Turner, as insane. "He is a complete fanatic, or plays his part admirably," wrote Thomas R. Gray, the lawyer who was assigned to defend Turner.

labor, Southerners spread slavery, cotton, and plantations. Geographic expansion meant that slavery became more vigorous and profitable than ever, embraced more people, and increased the South's political power. **Antebellum** Southerners included diverse peoples who at times found themselves at odds with one another— not only slaves and free people, but also women and men; Indians, Africans, and Europeans; and aristocrats and common folk. Nevertheless, beneath this diversity of Southerners, there was also forming a distinctively southern society and culture. The South became a slave society, and most white Southerners were proud of it.

The Growing Distinctiveness of the South

From the earliest settlements, inhabitants of southern colonies had shared a great deal with northern colonists. Most whites in both sections were British and **Protestant**, and they spoke a common language, even if a regional twang or drawl flavored their speech. They shared an exuberant pride in their victorious revolution against British rule. The creation of the new nation under the Constitution in 1789 forged strong political ties that bound all Americans. In the nineteenth century, the beginnings of a national economy fostered economic interdependence and communication across regional boundaries. White Americans everywhere celebrated the achievements of the prosperous young nation, and they looked forward to its seemingly boundless future.

Despite these national similarities, Southerners and Northerners grew increasingly different. The French political observer Alexis de Tocqueville believed he knew why. "I could easily prove," he asserted in 1831, "that almost all the differences which may be noticed between the character of the Americans in the Southern and Northern states have originated in slavery." Slavery made the South different, and it was the differences between the North and the South, not the similarities, that came to shape antebellum American history.

Cotton Kingdom, Slave Empire

In the first half of the nineteenth century, legions of Americans migrated west. In the South, the stampede began after the Creek War of 1813–14,

Nat Turner
There are no known contemporary images of Nat Turner. This imagined portrait comes from William Still's *The Underground Railroad* (1872). Meeting secretly at night deep in a forest and thus well out of earshot of whites, an intense Turner passionately tries to convince four other slaves to join him in rebellion. What do their faces reveal? What considerations do you suppose entered their calculations about whether to join Turner? Significantly perhaps, they are holding work tools, not arms.
Library of Congress.

In the months following the insurrection, white Virginians debated the future of slavery in their state. While some expressed substantial doubts, the Virginia legislature reaffirmed the state's determination to beat back threats to white supremacy. Delegates passed a raft of laws strengthening the institution of slavery and further restricting free blacks. A thirty-year-old professor at the College of William and Mary, Thomas R. Dew, published a vigorous defense of slavery that became the bible of Southerners' proslavery arguments. More than ever, the nation was divided along the "Mason-Dixon line," the surveyors' mark that in colonial times had established the boundary between Maryland and Pennsylvania but half a century later divided the free North and slave South.

Black slavery increasingly dominated the South and shaped it into a distinctive region. In the decades after 1820, Southerners, like Northerners, raced westward, but unlike Northerners who spread small farms and free

> Slavery made the South different, and it was the differences between the North and the South, not the similarities, that came to shape antebellum American history.

which divested the Creek Nation of 24 million acres and initiated the government campaign to remove Indian people living east of the Mississippi River to the West (see chapters 10 and 11). Eager slaveholders seeking virgin acreage for new plantations, struggling farmers looking for patches of good land for small farms, herders and drovers pushing their hogs and cattle toward fresh pastures— anyone who was restless and ambitious felt the pull of Indian land. Southerners pushed westward relentlessly, until by midcentury the South encompassed nearly a million square miles, much of it planted in cotton.

Frontier Land Opened by Indian Removal, 1830s

The South's climate and geography were ideally suited for the cultivation of cotton. As Southerners advanced nearly a thousand miles west from the Atlantic, they encountered a variety of terrain, soil, and weather, but the cotton seeds they carried with them proved very adaptable. They grew in the sandy plains of the tidewater along the Atlantic, in the red clay of the piedmont east of the Blue Ridge and Appalachian Mountains, and especially in the rich soils of the black belt (named for the dark color of the soil in Georgia and Alabama) and of the alluvial deltas of the Mississippi Valley. Cotton requires two hundred frost-free days from planting to picking and prefers rains that are plentiful in spring and lighter in fall, conditions found in much of the South. By the 1830s, cotton fields stretched from southern Virginia to central Texas. Heavy westward migration led to statehood for Arkansas in 1836 and for Texas and Florida in 1845. Production soared, from 300,000 bales in 1830 to nearly 5 million in 1860, and by 1860 the South produced three-fourths of the world's supply. The South— especially that tier of states from

South Carolina west to Texas known as the Lower South— had become the cotton kingdom (Map 13.1).

The cotton kingdom was also a slave empire. The South's cotton boom rested on the backs of slaves, who grew 75 percent of the crop on plantations, toiling in gangs in broad fields under the direct supervision of whites. As cotton agriculture expanded westward, whites shipped more than 300,000 slaves out of the old seaboard states. Some slaves accompanied masters who were leaving behind worn-out, eroded plantations, but at least two-thirds were victims of a brutal but thriving domestic slave trade. Traders advertised for slaves who were "hearty and well made" and marched black men, women, and children hundreds of miles to the new plantation regions of the Lower South. Cotton, slaves, and plantations moved west together.

Slave Traders: Sold to Tennessee

Slave trading—or "Negro speculation," as it was called by contemporaries—was a booming business in the antebellum South. This color drawing by Lewis Miller portrays slaves walking from Virginia to Tennessee under the watchful eyes of professional slave traders. A few children accompany the adults, some of whom may be their parents. Forced migrations almost always resulted in the separation of black family members.
Abby Aldrich Rockefeller Folk Art Center, Williamsburg, VA.

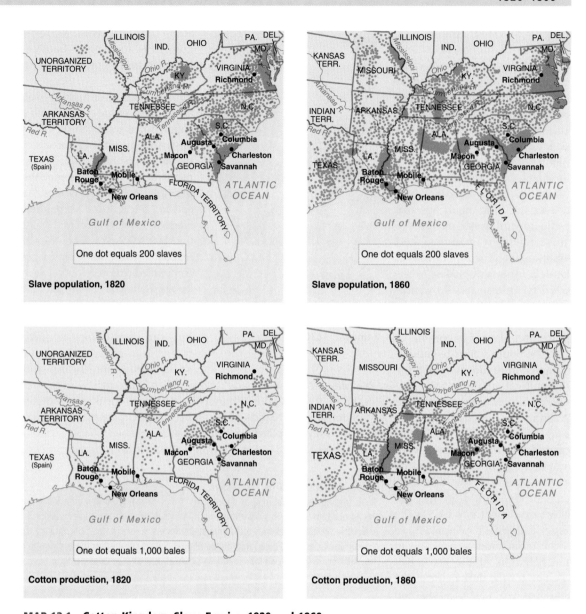

MAP 13.1   Cotton Kingdom, Slave Empire: 1820 and 1860
As the production of cotton soared, the slave population increased dramatically. Slaves continued to toil in tobacco and rice fields along the Atlantic seaboard, but increasingly they worked on cotton plantations in Alabama, Mississippi, and Louisiana.

READING THE MAP: Where was slavery most prevalent in 1820? In 1860? How did the spread of slavery compare with the spread of cotton?
CONNECTIONS: How much of the world's cotton was produced in the American South in 1860? While most slaves worked in agriculture, how else were slaves employed?

FOR MORE HELP ANALYZING THESE MAPS, see the map activity for this chapter in the Online Study Guide at bedfordstmartins.com/roark.

The slave population grew enormously. Southern slaves numbered fewer than 700,000 in 1790, about 2 million in 1830, and over 4 million by 1860, an increase of almost 600 percent in seven decades. By 1860, the South contained more slaves than all the other slave societies in the New World combined. The extraordinary growth was not the result of the importation of slaves, which was outlawed in 1808. Instead, the slave population grew through natural reproduction. By the nineteenth century, most slaves were native-born Southerners.

The South in Black and White

By 1860, one in every three Southerners was black (more than 4 million blacks and 8 million whites). In the Lower South, the proportion was higher, for whites and blacks lived there in almost equal numbers. In Mississippi and South Carolina, blacks were the majority (Figure 13.1). The contrast with the North was striking: In 1860, only one Northerner in 76 was black (about 250,000 blacks to 19 million whites).

The presence of large numbers of African Americans had profound consequences for the South. Southern culture—language, food, music, religion, and even accents—was in part shaped by blacks. But the most direct consequence of the South's biracialism was the response it stimulated in the region's white majority. Southern whites were dedicated to white supremacy. Northern whites believed in racial superiority, too, but they lived in a society in which blacks made up barely more than 1 percent of the population. Their commitment to white supremacy lacked the intensity and urgency increasingly felt by white Southerners. White Southerners lived among millions of blacks, whom they simultaneously despised and feared. They despised blacks because they considered them members of an inferior race, further degraded by their status as slaves. They feared blacks because they realized that slaves had every reason to hate them and to seek to end their oppression, as Nat Turner had, by any means necessary.

Attacks on slavery after 1820—from blacks and a handful of white antislavery advocates within the South and from abolitionists without— jolted southern slaveholders into a distressing

> The presence of large numbers of African Americans had profound consequences for the South. Southern culture— language, food, music, religion, and even accents—was in part shaped by blacks.

FIGURE 13.1 Black and White Populations in the South, 1860
Blacks represented a much larger fraction of the population in the South than in the North, but considerable variation existed from state to state. Only one Missourian in ten, for example, was black, while Mississippi and South Carolina had black majorities. States in the Upper South were "whiter" than states in the Lower South, despite the Upper South's greater number of free blacks.

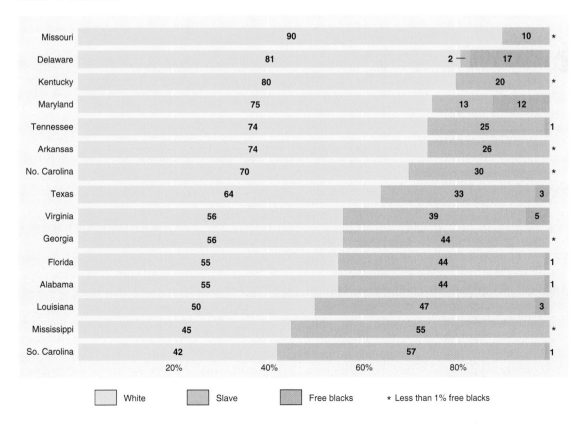

THE FRUITS OF AMALGAMATION.

The Fruits of Amalgamation

White Southerners and Northerners alike generally agreed that giving blacks equal rights would lead to miscegenation (also known as "amalgamation"). In this lithograph from 1839, Edward W. Clay of Philadelphia attacked abolitionists by imagining the outcome of their misguided campaign. He drew a beautiful white woman with her two black children, one suckling at her breast while her dark-skinned, ridiculously overdressed husband, resting his feet in his wife's lap, reads an abolitionist newspaper. The couple is attended by a white servant. Another interracial couple—perhaps the man is abolitionist William Lloyd Garrison himself—has come calling. Hanging on the wall is a picture entitled *Othello & Desdemona*, based on the popular play *Othello*, a tragic tale about a couple who crossed the color line. A black and a white dog play indiscriminately on the floor. Abolitionists denied the charge of amalgamation and pointed to the lasciviousness of southern slaveholders as the true source of miscegenation in antebellum America.

Courtesy, American Antiquarian Society.

awareness that they lived in a dangerous and fragile world. In response, southern leaders initiated fresh efforts to strengthen slavery. State legislatures constructed elaborate slave codes that required the total submission of slaves to their masters and to white society in general. As the Louisiana code stated, a slave "owes his master . . . a respect without bounds, and an absolute obedience." The laws underlined the authority of all whites, not just masters. Any white could "correct" slaves who did not stay "in their place."

Intellectuals joined legislators in the campaign to strengthen slavery. The South's academics, writers, and clergy constructed a proslavery argument that sought to unify the region's whites around slavery and provide ammunition for the emerging war of words with northern abolitionists. Under the intellectuals' tutelage, the white South gradually moved away from defending slavery as a "necessary evil"—the halfhearted argument popular in Jefferson's day—and toward a full-throated, aggressive defense of slavery as a "positive good." John C. Calhoun declared that in the states where slavery had been abolished "the condition of the African, instead of being improved, has become worse," while in the slave states the Africans "have improved greatly in every respect."

Slavery's champions employed every imaginable defense. The law protected slavery, they declared, for slaves were legal property. And wasn't the security of property the bedrock of American **liberty**? They also used historical evidence to endorse slavery. Weren't the great civilizations—such as those of the Hebrews, Greeks, and Romans—slave societies? They argued that the Bible, properly interpreted, also sanctioned slavery. Old Testament patriarchs owned slaves, they observed, and in the New Testament Paul returned the runaway slave Onesimus to his master. Some proslavery spokesmen went on the offensive and attacked the economy and society of the North. George Fitzhugh of Virginia argued that behind the North's grand slogans—**free labor**, individualism, and egalitarianism—lay a heartless philosophy: "Every man for himself, and the devil take the hindmost." Gouging capitalists exploited wage workers unmercifully, Fitzhugh said, and he contrasted the vicious capitalist-laborer relationship with the humane relations that he claimed prevailed between masters and slaves because slaves were valuable capital that masters sought to protect.

Since slavery was a condition that white Southerners reserved exclusively for African Americans, the heart of the defense of slavery rested on claims of black inferiority. Black enslavement was both necessary and proper, antebellum defenders argued, because Africans were inferior beings. Rather than exploitative, slavery was a mass civilizing effort by caring whites that lifted lowly blacks from barbarism and savagery, taught them disciplined work, and converted them to soul-saving Christianity. According to Virginian Thomas R. Dew, most slaves were grateful. He declared that "the slaves of a good master are his warmest, most constant, and most devoted friends."

Black slavery encouraged whites to unify around race rather than to divide by class. The grubbiest, most tobacco-stained white man could proudly proclaim his superiority to all blacks and his equality with the most refined southern patrician. Because slaves were not recognized as citizens in the South, Georgia attorney Thomas R. R. Cobb observed, every white Southerner "feels that he belongs to an elevated class. It matters not that he is no slaveholder; he is not of the inferior race; he is a freeborn citizen." Consequently, the "poorest meets the richest as an equal; sits at his table with him; salutes him as a neighbor; meets him in every public assembly, and stands on the same social platform." In the South, Cobb boasted, "there is no war of classes."

In reality, slavery did not create perfect harmony among whites or ease every strain along class lines. But by providing every antebellum white Southerner symbolic membership in the ruling class, racial slavery helped whites bridge differences in wealth, education, and culture. Slavery meant white dominance, white superiority, and white equality.

The Plantation Economy

As important as slavery was in unifying white Southerners, only about one-quarter of the white population lived in slaveholding families. A majority of slaveholders owned fewer than five slaves. Only about 12 percent of slave owners owned twenty or more, the number of slaves that historians consider necessary to distinguish a **planter** from a farmer. Although hugely outnumbered, planters nevertheless dominated the southern economy. In 1860, 52 percent of the South's slaves lived and worked on plantations. Plantation slaves produced more than 75 percent of the South's export crops, the backbone of the region's economy. Although slavery was dying elsewhere in the New World, slave plantations increasingly dominated southern agriculture.

The South's major cash crops—tobacco, sugar, rice, and cotton—grew on plantations (Map 13.2). Tobacco was the original plantation crop in North America, but by the nineteenth century tobacco had shifted westward from the Chesapeake to Tennessee and Kentucky. Work in the tobacco fields was labor-intensive. Most phases of the process—planting, transplanting, thinning, picking off caterpillars, cutting, drying, packing—required field hands to stoop or bend down in painful labor.

Large-scale sugar production began in 1795, when Étienne de Boré built a modern sugar mill in what is today New Orleans. Labor on sugarcane

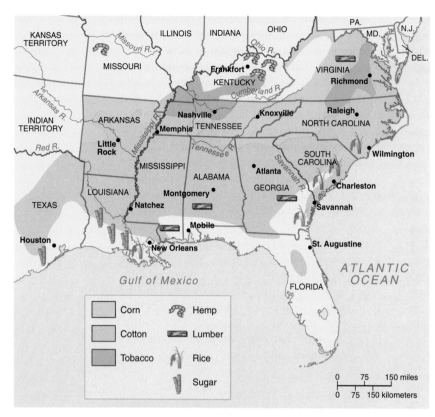

MAP 13.2 The Agricultural Economy of the South, 1860
Cotton dominated the South's agricultural economy, but the region grew a variety of crops and was largely self-sufficient in foodstuffs.

READING THE MAP: In what type of geographical areas were rice and sugar grown in 1860? After cotton, what crop commanded the greatest agricultural area in the South? In which region of the South was this crop predominantly found?
CONNECTIONS: What role did the South play in the U.S. economy in 1860? How did the economy of the South differ from that of the North?

FOR MORE HELP ANALYZING THIS MAP, see the map activity for this chapter in the Online Study Guide at bedfordstmartins.com/roark.

> If tobacco, sugar, and rice were the princes of plantation agriculture, cotton was king.

meant danger and extreme discomfort. Working in water and mud in the heat of a Carolina summer regularly threatened slaves with malaria, yellow fever, and other diseases. Rice cultivation required huge numbers of slaves to plant, cultivate, and harvest rice, as well as to maintain the canals, dikes, and gates necessary to flood the fields with water and then drain them. As a consequence, blacks accounted for 90 percent of the population in the coastal area.

If tobacco, sugar, and rice were the princes of plantation agriculture, cotton was king. Cotton became commercially significant after the advent of Eli Whitney's cotton gin in 1793. (See "The Promise of Technology," page 448.) By the early years of the nineteenth century, cotton had begun to dominate the southern economy. Cotton was relatively easy to grow and took little capital to get started—just enough for land, seed, and simple tools. Thus, small farmers as well as planters grew the white fluffy stuff. While hardscrabble Mississippi farmer Jessup Snopes grew half a bale of cotton in 1859, fellow Mississippian Frederick Stanton, who owned a plantation of more than 15,000 prime acres and hundreds of slaves, produced 3,054 bales. Although farmers far outnumbered planters, slave labor meant that plantations were responsible for producing three-quarters of the South's cotton.

For major slaveholders, then, the Old South's economy was productive and profitable. Further, plantation slavery benefited the national economy. By 1840, cotton alone accounted for more than 60 percent of the nation's exports. Soaring international demand meant eager buyers for every pound that southern cotton growers produced. Much of the profit from sales of cotton overseas returned to planters, but some went to northern middlemen who bought, sold, insured, warehoused, and shipped cotton to the mills in Great Britain and elsewhere. As one New York merchant observed, "Cotton has enriched all through whose hands it has passed." As middlemen invested their profits in the burgeoning northern economy, industrial development received a burst of much-needed capital. Furthermore, southern plantations benefited northern industry by providing an important market for textiles, agricul-

plantations was reputed to be the most physically demanding in the antebellum South. During the fall, slaves worked eighteen hours a day to cut the cane and haul it to the sugar mill, where they would grind and boil it. So hard was the slaves' task that one visitor concluded that "nothing but 'involuntary servitude' could go through the toil and suffering required to produce sugar." Sugar plantations were confined almost entirely to Louisiana.

Commercial rice production began in the seventeenth century, and like sugar, rice was confined to a small geographic area, a narrow strip of coast stretching from the Carolinas into Georgia. For slaves, rice

tural tools, and other manufactured goods.

The economies of the North and the South steadily diverged. While the North developed a mixed economy—agriculture, commerce, and manufacturing—the South remained overwhelmingly agricultural. Since planters were earning healthy profits, they saw little reason to diversify. Moreover, planters knew that if the South followed the path blazed by the North, manufacturing would mean the rise of a southern urban, industrial working class without direct ties to slavery or the plantation. Would city-dwelling factory workers accept rural planter rule and give their hearty support to slavery, or would they view slaves as unfair competition and favor free labor, as northern workers did? Planters did not want to find out. Year after year, they funneled the profits they earned from land and slaves back into more land and slaves.

With its capital flowing into agriculture, the South did not develop many factories. By 1860, only 10 percent of the nation's industrial workers lived in the South. Indiana and Illinois, two midwestern states known for agriculture, had more capital invested in industry than the seven Lower South states, including Louisiana with its sugar mills. Some cotton mills sprang up, but the region that produced 100 percent of the nation's cotton manufactured less than 7 percent of its cotton textiles.

Without significant economic diversification, the South developed fewer cities than the North (Map 13.3). In 1860, it was the least urban region in the country. While nearly 37 percent of New England's population lived in cities, less than 12 percent of Southerners were urban dwellers. That figure would have been dramatically smaller without Maryland's 34 percent urban population (because of Baltimore) and Louisiana's 26 percent (because of New Orleans). In fact, nine southern states counted 5 percent or fewer of their people in cities.

Not only were cities less common in the South, but they were also different from those in the North. They were mostly port cities on the

The *Henry Frank*, New Orleans
The steamboat *Henry Frank* sits dangerously overloaded with cotton bales at the New Orleans levee in 1854. The banner flying from the flagstaff indicates that captains boasted about the number of bales their boats carried. The magnitude of the cotton trade in the South's largest city and major port is difficult to capture. Six years earlier, a visitor, Solon Robinson, had expressed awe: "It must be seen to be believed; and even then, it will require an active mind to comprehend acres of cotton bales standing upon the levee, while miles of drays [carts] are constantly taking it off to the cotton presses. . . . Boats are constantly arriving, so piled up with cotton, that the lower tier of bales on deck are in the water." Amid the mountains of cotton, few Southerners doubted that cotton was king.
Historic New Orleans Collection.

periphery of the region and busy principally with exporting the agricultural products of plantations in the interior. Urban merchants provided agriculture with indispensable services, such as hauling, insuring, and selling cotton, rice, and sugar, but as the tail on the plantation dog, southern cities did not become nationally significant manufacturing centers or important independent centers of social and economic innovation. Southern cities could also claim something no northern city desired—140,000 slaves in 1860. Urban slaves sometimes made up half of a southern city's population, and they worked in nearly every conceivable occupation, helping the southern economy thrive.

Because the South had so few cities and industrial jobs, it attracted relatively small numbers of European immigrants. Seeking economic

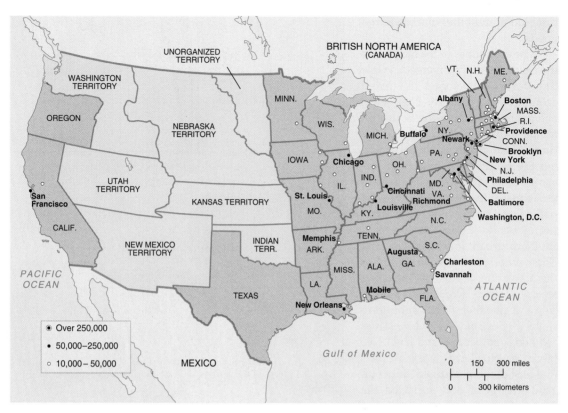

MAP 13.3 Major Cities in 1860
By 1860, northern cities were more numerous and larger than southern cities. In the slave states, cities
were usually seaports or river ports that served the needs of agriculture, especially cotton.

Immigrants as a Percentage of State Populations, 1860

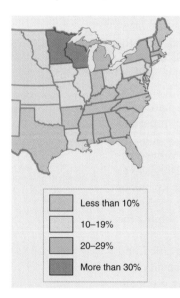

Less than 10%
10–19%
20–29%
More than 30%

opportunity, not competition with slaves (whose labor would keep wages low), immigrants steered well north of the South's slave-dominated, agricultural economy. In 1860, 13 percent of all Americans were foreign-born. But in nine of the fifteen slave states, only 2 percent or fewer were born abroad. Immigrants who did venture below the Mason-Dixon line concentrated in cities, just as they did in the North.

Not every Southerner celebrated the region's plantation economy. Critics railed against the excessive commitment to cotton and slaves and bemoaned what one called the "deplorable scarcity" of factories. Diversification, reformers promised, would make the South not only economically independent but more prosperous as well. State governments encouraged economic diversifica-

tion and development by helping to create banking systems that supplied credit for a wide range of projects, industrial as well as agricultural. Alabama constructed its first railroad in 1830 just five years after Englishmen built the world's first modern railroad and only three years after the inauguration of the first railroad in America. Thirty years later, 9,280 miles of track spanned the South.

But encouragement of a diversified economy had clear limits. State governments failed to create some of the essential services modern economies require. By midcentury, for example, no southern legislature had created a statewide public school system. Consequently, the South's illiteracy rate for whites topped 20 percent. Dominant slaveholders failed to see any benefit in educating the region's labor force, especially with their tax money. Despite the flurry of railroad building, the South's mileage in 1860 was less than half that of the North. Moreover, while railroads crisscrossed the North carrying manufactured goods as well as agricultural products, most railroads in the South ran from port cities back into farming areas and were built to export staple crops (see Map 12.5, page 420).

Northerners claimed that slavery was an outmoded and doomed labor system, but few Southerners perceived economic weakness in their region. In fact, the planters' pockets were never fuller than at the end of the 1850s. Compared with Northerners, Southerners invested less of their capital in industry, transportation, and public education. Planters' decisions to reinvest in staple agriculture ensured the momentum of the plantation economy and the political and social relationships rooted in it.

Masters, Mistresses, and the Big House

Nowhere was the contrast between northern and southern life more vivid than on the plantations of the South. Located on a patchwork of cleared fields and dense forests, a plantation typically included a "big house" and slave quarters. Scattered about were numerous outbuildings, each with a special function. Near the big house were the kitchen, storehouse, smokehouse (for curing and preserving meat), and hen coop. More distant were the barns, toolsheds, **artisans'** workshops, and overseer's house. Large plantations sometimes had additional buildings such as an infirmary and a chapel for slaves. Depending on the crop, there was a tobacco shed, a rice mill, a sugar refinery, or a cotton gin house. Lavish or plain, plantations everywhere had an underlying similarity (Figure 13.2).

The plantation was the home of masters, mistresses, and slaves. Slavery shaped the lives of all the plantation's inhabitants, from work to leisure activities, but it affected each differently. A hierarchy of rigid roles and duties governed relationships. Presiding was the master, who ruled his wife, children, and slaves, none of whom had many legal rights and all of whom were designated by the state as dependents under his dominion and protection.

Plantation Masters

The work relationship between plantation master and slave was organized quite simply. While smaller planters supervised the labor of their slaves themselves, larger planters often hired overseers who went to the fields with the slaves, leaving planters free to concentrate on marketing,

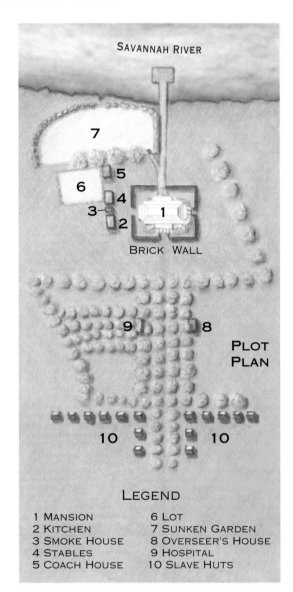

FIGURE 13.2 A Southern Plantation
Slavery determined how masters laid out their plantations, where they situated their "big houses" and slave quarters, and what kinds of buildings they constructed. This model of the Hermitage, the mansion built in 1830 for Henry McAlpin, a Georgia rice planter, shows the overseer's house poised in the grove of oak trees halfway between the owner's mansion and the slave huts. The placement of the mansion at the end of an extended road leading up from the river underscored McAlpin's affluence and authority.

Adapted from *Back of the Big House: The Architecture of Plantation Slavery* by John Michael Vlach. Copyright © 1993 by the University of North Carolina Press. Original illustration property of the Historic American Buildings Survey, a division of the National Park Service.

finance, and general plantation affairs. Planters also found time to escape to town to discuss the weather, to the courthouse and legislature to debate politics, and to the woods to hunt and fish.

The Cotton Gin: Engine of the South

In 1792, a young New Englander accepted a position as tutor to the children of a Georgia planter. The teaching post did not work out, but Eli Whitney stayed on at the Savannah River plantation of Mrs. Catherine Greene, widow of Nathanael Greene, hero of the American Revolution. On September 11, 1793, Whitney wrote his sister: "I have . . . heard much said of the extreme difficulty of ginning cotton. That is, separating it from its seed." He had met "a number of respectable Gentlemen at Mrs Greene's who all agreed that if a machine could be invented which would clean the cotton with expedition, it would be a great thing both to the country and the inventor." Whitney was a Yale graduate who could read Latin, but he was also a practical man, and he turned his attention to the problem.

Cotton gins (the word *gin* is short for *engine*) already existed in 1793. One model in which cotton was fed between two rollers to squeeze out the seeds operated efficiently on the sea-island cotton that grew on the South Carolina and Georgia coasts. But the variety of cotton that grew inland—green seed, or short staple—was filled with seeds that clung to the fiber like ticks to the skin. Many a pioneer family spent long winter evenings seated around the fire tediously plucking the fluff from each seed. The little cotton produced by evenings of handpicking got made up into homespun on family spinning wheels and handlooms.

The problem of sticky seeds attracted the attention of mechanics from India to Santo Domingo, but it was Whitney who succeeded in building a simple little device for separating cotton from the seeds—wire teeth set in a wooden cylinder that, when rotated, reached through narrow slats to pull cotton fibers away from the seeds while a brush swept the fibers from the revolving teeth. It was crude, but news of the invention spread like wildfire. Just days later, the South Carolina planter Pierce Butler wrote a friend, "There is a young Man at Mrs Greene's in Georgia, who has made a Cotton Ginn that with two Boys cleans of the green seed cotton 64 pds of clean cotton in about 9 hours." Planters understood that Whitney's invention would break the bottleneck in the commercial production of cotton. They also understood that his invention would allow them to produce vast amounts of clean cotton and satisfy the cotton-hungry English market. Eager to cash in on his invention, Whitney rushed back to

Increasingly in the nineteenth century, planters characterized their mastery in terms of what they called "Christian guardianship" and what historians have called **paternalism**. The concept of paternalism denied that the form of slavery practiced in the South was brutal and exploitative. Instead, it defined slavery as a set of reciprocal obligations between masters and slaves. In exchange for the slaves' labor and obedience, masters provided basic care and necessary guidance. To northern claims that they were tyrants and exploiters, slaveholders responded that they were stewards and guardians. As owners of blacks, masters argued, they had the heavy responsibility of caring for a childlike, dependent people. In 1814, Thomas Jefferson captured the essence of the advancing ideal: "We should endeavor, with those whom fortune has thrown on our hands, to feed & clothe them well, protect them from ill usage, require such reasonable labor only as is performed voluntarily by freemen, and be led by no repugnancies to abdicate them, and our duties to them." A South Carolina rice planter insisted, "I manage them as my children."

Paternalism was part propaganda and part self-delusion. But it was more. Slavery in the South reached its zenith in the nineteenth cen-

Connecticut, where he took out a patent and began manufacturing cotton gins.

Planters clamored for the machines, and southern craftsmen who understood Whitney's basic design could reproduce it (and enlarge and improve it) without looking at a model or drawing. No mere patent could stop them, and nothing could force them to pay Whitney royalties. The Patent Act of 1793 stressed that proof of invention and proof of infringement were the burden of the inventor. Although Whitney's gin was pirated time and again, he found that it was difficult and costly to gain proof. At one time Whitney had more than sixty lawsuits pending, and the revenue from his gin factory in New Haven could scarcely keep up with his legal bills.

While Whitney made little money from the cotton gin, planters profited hugely. Cotton quickly pushed out indigo, then tobacco, as

The Cotton Gin
By the 1790s, the English had succeeded in mechanizing the manufacture of cotton cloth, but they were unable to get enough raw cotton. The South could grow cotton in unimaginable quantities, but cotton stuck to seeds was useless in English textile mills. In 1793, Eli Whitney, a Northerner who was living on a Savannah River plantation, built a simple device for separating the cotton from the seed. Widespread use of the cotton gin broke the bottleneck in the commercial production of cotton and eventually bound millions of African Americans to slavery.
Smithsonian Institution, Washington, D.C.

the southern interior's major cash crop. In just a few years, the gin helped transform the entire economy of the South. The commercial production of cotton bound millions of African Americans to perpetual slavery. For them, the promise of this particular piece of technology proved tragically hollow. Whitney's invention also spawned a cotton industry that changed the face of northern Britain and New England as mill towns sprang up everywhere. The cotton mills of Lancashire and Lowell brought cotton cloth within reach of everyone. Before the gin, the world was clothed in flax and wool, and cotton fabrics were luxury items. After the gin, cotton soon became the poor people's cloth.

The great nineteenth-century British historian Lord Macaulay hardly exaggerated when he declared: "What Peter the Great did to make Russia dominant, Eli Whitney's invention of the cotton gin has more than equaled in relation to the power and progress of the United States."

tury, after the nation closed its external slave trade. Masters increasingly recognized slaves as valuable assets to be maintained, and they realized that the expansion of the slave labor force could come only from natural reproduction. The rising price of slaves led one planter to declare in 1849 that "it behooves those who own them to make them last as long as possible." Another planter instructed his overseer to pay attention to "whatever tends to promote their health and render them prolific."

One consequence of this paternalism and economic self-interest was a small improvement in slaves' welfare. Diet improved, although nineteenth-century slaves still mainly ate fatty pork and cornmeal. Housing improved, although the cabins still had cracks large enough, slaves said, for cats to slip through. Clothing improved, although slaves seldom received much more than two crude outfits a year and perhaps a pair of cheap shoes. In the fields, workdays remained sunup to sundown, but planters often provided a rest period in the heat of the day. And most owners ceased the colonial practices of punishing slaves by branding and mutilation.

Paternalism should not be mistaken for "Ol' Massa"'s kindness and goodwill. It encouraged

Southern Man with Children and Their Mammy
Obviously prosperous and looking like a man accustomed to giving orders and being obeyed, this patriarch poses around 1848 with his young daughters and their nurse. The black woman is clearly a servant, a status indicated by her race and her attire. Why does she appear in the daguerreotype? The absent mother may be dead. Her death might account for the inclusion of the African American woman in the family circle. In any case, her presence signals her importance in the household. Fathers left the raising of children to mothers and nurses.
Collection of the J. Paul Getty Museum, Malibu, CA.

better treatment because it made economic sense to provide at least minimal care for valuable slaves. Nor did paternalism require that planters put aside their whips. They could flail away and still claim that they were only fulfilling their responsibilities as guardians of their naturally lazy and at times insubordinate dependents. The law in southern states gave masters nearly "uncontrolled authority over the body" of the slave, according to the North Carolina judge Thomas Ruffin. Paternalism offered slaves some protection against the most brutal punishments, but whipping remained the planters' essential coercion. (See "Historical Question," page 452.)

Paternalism never won universal acceptance among planters, but by the nineteenth century it had become a kind of communal standard. With its notion that slavery imposed on masters a burden and a duty, paternalism provided slaveholders with a means of legitimizing their rule. But it also provided some slaves with leverage over the conditions of their lives. Slaves learned to

manipulate a slaveholder's need to see himself as a good and decent master. To avoid a reputation as a cruel tyrant, planters sometimes negotiated with slaves, rather than just resorting to the whip. Small garden plots in which they could work for themselves after their day in the fields or a few days off and a dance when they had gathered the last of the cotton were among the concessions slaves sometimes won from masters who were seeking to confirm their status as benevolent paternalists.

The Virginia statesman Edmund Randolph argued that slavery created in white southern men a "quick and acute sense of personal liberty" and a "disdain for every abridgement of personal independence." Indeed, prickly individualism and aggressive independence became crucial features of the southern concept of honor. Social standing, political advancement, and even self-esteem rested on an honorable reputation. Defending honor became a male passion. Andrew Jackson's mother reportedly told her son, "Never tell a lie, nor take what is not your own, nor sue anybody for slander or assault and battery. *Always settle them cases yourself.*" Southern boys were expected to master the "manly" arts, and among planters such advice sometimes led to duels. Dueling arrived from Europe in the eighteenth century. It died out in the North, but in the South, even after legislatures banned it, gentlemen continued to defend their honor with pistols at ten paces.

Southerners also expected an honorable gentleman to be a proper patriarch. Nowhere in America was masculine power more accentuated. Slavery buttressed the power of husbands and fathers. Planters described plantations as households that incorporated both their "white and black families." And planters brooked no opposition from any of their dependents. The master's absolute dominion sometimes led to **miscegenation**, the sexual mixing of the races. Laws prohibited interracial sex, and some masters practiced self-restraint. Others merely urged discretion. How many trips masters and their sons made to slave cabins is impossible to tell, but as long as slavery gave white men extraordinary power, slave women were forced to submit to the sexual appetites of the men who ruled them.

Individualistic impulses were strong among planters, but duty to family was paramount. In time, as the children of one elite family married the children of another, ties of blood and kinship as well as ideology and economic interest linked

AMERICAN PLACES

Middleton Place, Charleston, South Carolina

The Grounds of Middleton Place
The Middleton Place Foundation, Charleston, South Carolina.

Situated a few miles north of Charleston on the Ashley River, Middleton Place exemplifies the taste, pride, and wealth of eighteenth-century South Carolina planters. Like many plantation homes of that era, the main house faces the river, the highway for shipping rice, South Carolina's principal crop. Visitors arriving by boat were certain to be impressed by the spectacular view of the house and grounds from the water.

In 1741, Henry Middleton married Mary Williams, who brought as her dowry the house and plantation that became Middleton Place. One of the wealthiest and most politically powerful men in the colony of South Carolina, in 1774 Henry Middleton was elected president of the First Continental Congress. Between 1741 and the Civil War, four generations of Middletons sustained the family's economic and political standing by producing

tons of rice and a host of political leaders, including a signer of the Declaration of Independence, a governor of the state, and a signer of South Carolina's ordinance of secession.

Soon after Henry Middleton acquired the property in 1741, he began constructing lavish formal gardens, laid out in the grand classic European style that emphasized geometry and symmetry. According to family lore, it took a hundred slaves ten years to complete the sixty-five acres of broad terraces, walkways, artificial ponds, and sweeping vistas of the river and marshlands beyond. In 1857, a visitor observed: "In its natural and artificial beauty and elegance, Middleton Place comes nearer than any place I have seen in America to the Italian villas, which I visited, or saw, near Rome."

During the Civil War, federal troops burned much of the brick, three-story main residence, and in 1886 an earthquake largely completed the destruction, leaving only one wing of the elegant old home standing. The twentieth-century restoration of the remaining structure and the extensive gardens gives visitors a stunning impression of how the eighteenth-century South's plantation gentry lived. Missing, however, are the cabins of the generations of slaves who labored their lives away producing rice and maintaining the beauty of Middleton Place.

FOR WEB LINKS RELATED TO THIS SITE AND OTHER AMERICAN PLACES, see "PlaceLinks" at bedfordstmartins.com/roark.

planters to one another. Conscious of what they shared as slaveholders, planters worked together to defend their common interests. The values of the big house—slavery, honor, male domination—washed over the boundaries of plantations and flooded all of southern life.

Plantation Mistresses

Like their northern counterparts, southern ladies were expected to possess feminine virtues of piety, purity, chastity, and obedience within the context of marriage, motherhood, and domesticity.

How Often Were Slaves Whipped?

As important as this question is to historians, and obviously was to slaves, we have very little reliable evidence on the frequency of whipping. We know from white sources that whipping was the prescribed method of physical punishment on most antebellum plantations. Masters' instructions to overseers authorized whippings and often set limits on the number of strokes an overseer could administer. Some planters allowed fifteen lashes, some fifty, and some one hundred. But slave owners' instructions, as revealing as they are, tell us more about the severity of beatings than their frequency.

Remembrances of former slaves confirm that whipping was widespread and frequent. In the 1930s, a government program gathered testimony from more than 2,300 elderly African Americans about their experiences as slaves. Their accounts offered grisly evidence of the cruelty of slavery. "You say how did our Master treat his slaves?" asked one woman. "Scandalous, they treated them just like dogs." She was herself whipped "till the blood dripped to the ground." A few slaves remembered kind masters and never personally felt the sting of the lash. Bert Strong was one such slave, but he also recalled hearing slaves on other farms "hollering when they get beat." He said, "They beat them till it a pity." Beatings occurred often, but how often?

A remarkably systematic record of whippings over a sustained period of time comes from the diary of Bennet H. Barrow, the master of Highland plantation in West Feliciana Parish, Louisiana. For a twenty-three-month period in 1840–1841, Barrow meticulously recorded every whipping he administered or ordered. On most large plantations, overseers handled the business of day-to-day management, but in 1838 Barrow concluded that overseers were "good for nothing" and "a perfect nuisance." He dismissed his white overseer and, assisted only by a black driver, began managing his own plantation.

What does the Barrow evidence show? In 1840, according to the federal census, Barrow owned 129 slaves. In the twenty-three-month period, Barrow recorded 160 whippings. That means that, on the average, a slave was whipped every four and a half days. Sixty of the 77 slaves who worked in the fields were whipped at least once. Most of the 17 field slaves who escaped being beaten were children and pregnant women. Eighty percent of male cotton pickers and 70 percent of female cotton pickers were whipped at least once in this period. Dave Barley received eight floggings, more than any other Barrow slave, and Patience received six whippings, more than any other female slave.

In most instances, Barrow recorded not only the fact of a whipping but also its cause. All sorts of "misconduct," "rascallity," and "disorderly acts" made Barrow reach for his whip. The provocations included family quarrels in the slave quarters, impudence, running away, and failure to keep curfew. But nearly 80 percent of the acts he recorded were related to poor work. Barrow gave beatings for "not picking as well as he can," for picking "very trashy cotton," and for failing to pick the prescribed weight of cotton. One slave claimed to have lost his eyesight and for months refused to work until Barrow "gave him 25 cuts yesterday morning & ordered him to work Blind or not."

Whippings should not be mistaken for spankings. Some planters used whips that raised welts, caused blisters, and bruised. Others resorted to rawhide and cowhide whips that broke the skin, caused scarring, and sometimes permanently maimed. Occasionally, slaves were beaten to death. Whipping was not Barrow's only means of inflicting pain. His diary mentions confining slaves to a plantation jail, putting them in chains, shooting them, breaking a "sword cane" over one slave's head, having slaves mauled by dogs, placing them in stocks, "staking down" slaves for hours, "hand sawing" them, holding their heads under water, and a variety of punishments intending to ridicule

Southerners also expected ladies to exemplify all that was best in plantation society. Countless toasts praised the southern lady as the perfect complement to her husband, the patriarch. She was physically weak, "formed only for the less laborious occupations," and thus dependent on male protection. To gain this protection, she was naturally modest and delicate, possessed beauty and grace, and cultivated refinement and charm.

But for women, the image of the lady, which rigidly prescribed proper character and behavior, was no blessing. Chivalry—the South's romantic ideal of male-female relationships—glorified the lady while it subordinated her. Chivalry's

and to shame, including making men wear women's clothing and do "women's work," such as the laundry. Still, Barrow's preferred instrument of punishment was the whip.

On the Barrow plantation, as on many others, whipping was public. Victims were often tied to a stake in the quarters, and the other slaves were made to watch. In a real sense, the entire slave population on the plantation experienced a whipping every four and a half days. Even though some never felt the lash personally, all were familiar with its terror and agony.

Was whipping effective? Did it produce a hardworking, efficient, and conscientious labor force? Not according to Barrow's own record. No evidence indicates that whipping changed the slaves' behavior. What Barrow considered bad work continued. Unabated whipping is itself evidence of the failure of punishment to achieve the master's will. Slaves knew the rules. Yet they continued to act "badly." And they continued to suffer. It was a gruesome drama—the master seeking from his slaves hard labor and slaves denying their master what he most wanted, day after day.

Did Barrow whip with the same frequency as other planters? We simply do not know. As much as we would like to answer the question precisely, because of the lack of quantifiable evidence we will never know exactly how often whippings occurred. Still, the Barrow evidence allows us to speculate profitably on the frequency of whipping by large planters. We do know that Barrow

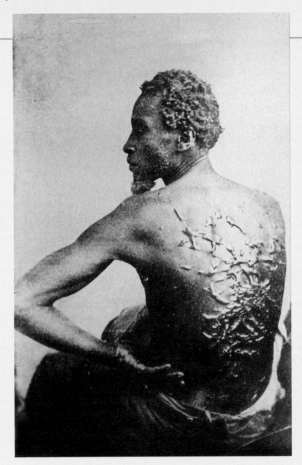

Gordon
This photograph of Gordon, a runaway slave from Baton Rouge, Louisiana, was taken on April 2, 1863, and sent home from the Civil War by Frederick W. Mercer, an assistant surgeon with the Forty-seventh Massachusetts Regiment. Mercer examined four hundred other runaways and found many "to be as badly lacerated." Masters claimed that they whipped only when they had to and only as hard as they had to, but slave testimony and photographic evidence refute their defense of slavery as a benign institution.
Courtesy of the Massachusetts Historical Society.

did not consider himself a cruel man. He bitterly denounced his neighbor as "the most cruel Master i ever knew of" for castrating three of his slaves. Moreover, Barrow had dispensed with the overseers in part because of their "brutal feelings" toward slaves. Like most whites, he believed that the lash was essential to get work done. He used it no more than he believed absolutely necessary.

Most masters, including Barrow, tried to encourage work with promises of small gifts and brief holidays, but punishment was their most important motivator. We will never know if the typical slave was beaten

once a year as on the Barrow plantation, but the admittedly scanty evidence suggests that on large plantations the whip fell on someone's back every few days.

And former slaves remembered. More than a half century after emancipation, their sharpest recollections usually involved punishment. They remembered the pain, the injustice, and their bitter resentment. They evaluated their former masters according to how frequently they reached for the whip. According to one former slave, "some was good and some was bad, and about the most of them was bad."

underlying assumptions about the weakness of women and the protective authority of men resembled the paternalistic defense of slavery. Indeed, the most articulate spokesmen for slavery also vigorously defended the subordination of women. George Fitzhugh, for example, insisted that "a woman, like children, has but one right and that is the right to protection. The right to protection involves the obligation to obey. A husband, a lord and master, nature designed for every woman. . . . If she be obedient she stands little danger of maltreatment." Just as the slaveholder's mastery was written into law, so too were the paramount rights of husbands.

Once married, women found divorce almost impossible.

Daughters of planters confronted chivalry's demands at an early age. Their educations aimed at fitting them to become southern ladies. At their private boarding schools they read literature, learned languages, and struggled to master the requisite drawing-room arts. Elite women began courting at a young age and married early. Kate Carney exaggerated only slightly when she wrote in her diary: "Today, I am seventeen, getting quite old, and am not married." Elizabeth Ruffin, who was about the same age, complained of being pushed into a wedding. Everyone, she said, seemed determined to "deter me from all the anticipated horrors of *old-maidenhood*." Some young women hesitated, realizing that marriage meant turning their fates over to their husbands. One mother warned her daughter: "A single life has fewer troubles; but then it is not the one for which our maker designed us." When they married, elite women made enormous efforts to live up to their region's lofty ideal.

Proslavery ideologues claimed that slavery freed white women from drudgery. Surrounded "by her domestics," declared Thomas Roderick

Bird Store, 626 Royal Street, New Orleans

Most elite white women in the antebellum South lived isolated existences on rural plantations. But some lived in cities, where others visited them from time to time, and going shopping was a prominent feature of such visits. Teenager Gertrude Clanton, who lived in Augusta, Georgia, wore store-bought clothes that she described endlessly in letters to her friends. Here a wealthy mother and daughter shop for a pet in a New Orleans bird store. The attentive proprietor and attractive shop provide everything they need—birds, cages, bird food, even an inviting couch and blanket in case they want to rest before moving on. Elite white women themselves were, in a way, like birds kept in golden cages. Could it be that they were attracted to the thought of owning birds of their own, something they could care for, train, and control?

Historic New Orleans Collection.

Tools of a Plantation Mistress: Key Basket and Keys
Almost every plantation mistress supervised the big house's storerooms and oversaw the distribution of the supplies kept there. To protect the goods from sticky-fingered house servants, each mistress kept the supplies under lock and key and carried the keys with her. The large five-inch key would have opened a door, and the four smaller keys on a ring would have opened boxes that held valuable foodstuffs such as sugar and tea. Throughout the day, slaves came to the mistress for access to household goods: "I keep all the keys and if anything is wanted they are obliged to come to me," one white woman declared.
Basket: Courtesy June Lambert; Keys: Valentine Museum, Cook Collection.

Dew, "she ceases to be a mere beast of burden" and "becomes the cheering and animating center of the family circle." In fact, however, the ideal of the southern lady clashed with the daily reality of the plantation mistress. Rather than being freed from labor by servants, she discovered that having servants required her to work long hours. Like her husband, the mistress had managerial responsibilities. She managed the big house, directly supervising as many as a dozen servants. But unlike her husband, the mistress had no overseer. All house servants answered directly to her. She assigned them tasks each morning, directed their work throughout the day, and punished them when she found fault. In addition to supervising a complex household, she had responsibility for the henhouse and dairy. And on some plantations, she directed the slave hospital and nursery and rationed supplies for the slave quarters. Women also bore the dangers of childbearing and responsibilities of child rearing. Southern ladies did not often lead lives of leisure.

Whereas masters used their status as slaveholders as a springboard into public affairs, the mistress's life was circumscribed by the plantation. Masters left the plantation when they pleased, but plantation mistresses needed chaperones to travel. When they could, they went to church, but women spent most days on the plantation, where they often became lonely. In 1853, Mary Kendall wrote how much she enjoyed her sister's letter: "For about three weeks I did not have the pleasure of seeing one white female face, there being no white family except our own upon the plantation." In their few leisure hours, plantation mistresses read and wrote letters, but they preferred the company of friends. Grand parties and balls occasionally broke the daily routine, but the burden of planning and supervising the preparation of the food and drink fell to the mistress.

As members of slaveholding families, mistresses lived privileged lives. But they also had significant grounds for discontent, and a few independent-minded women protested. No feature of plantation life generated more rage and anguish among mistresses than miscegenation. Mary Boykin Chesnut of Camden, South Carolina, wrote in her diary, "ours is a monstrous system, a wrong and iniquity. Like the patriarchs of old, our men live all in one house with their wives and their concubines; and the mulattos one sees in every family partly resemble the white children. Any lady is ready to tell you who is the father of all the mulatto children in everybody's household but her own. Those, she seems to think drop from the clouds."

> Out of eyesight and earshot of the big house, slaves drew together and built lives of their own.

But most planters' wives, including Mary Boykin Chesnut, found ways to accept slavery. After all, the mistress's world rested on slaves, just as the master's did. By acknowledging the realities of male power, mistresses enjoyed the rewards of their class and race. These rewards came at a price. Still, the heaviest burdens of slavery fell not on those who lived in the big house but on those who toiled to support it.

Slaves and the Quarters

On most plantations, only a few hundred yards separated the big house and the slave quarters. The distance was short enough to assure whites easy access to the labor of blacks. Yet the distance was great enough to provide slaves with some privacy. Out of eyesight and earshot of the big house, slaves drew together and built lives of their own. They created families, worshipped God, and developed an African American community.

The Price of Blood
This 1868 painting by T. S. Noble depicts a transaction between a slave trader and a rich planter. The trader nervously pretends to study the contract, while the planter waits impatiently for the completion of the sale. The planter's mulatto son, who is being sold, looks away. The children of white men and slave women were property and could be sold by the father/master. The tragedy of miscegenation, however, extended beyond the son shown here. Who is absent from the painting? Whose marriage has been betrayed? Who else's son is being sold away?
Morris Museum of Art, Augusta, GA.

FOR MORE HELP ANALYZING THIS IMAGE, see the visual activity for this chapter in the Online Study Guide at bedfordstmartins.com/roark.

Despite the rise of plantations, a substantial minority of slaves lived and worked elsewhere. Most labored on small farms, where they wielded a hoe alongside another slave or two and perhaps their master. But by 1860, almost half a million slaves (one in eight) did not work in agriculture at all. Some were employed in towns and cities as domestics, day laborers, bakers, barbers, tailors, and more. Others, far from urban centers, toiled as fishermen, lumbermen, railroad workers, and deckhands and stokers on riverboats. Slavery was a flexible labor system, and slaves could be found in virtually every skilled and unskilled occupation throughout the South, including the region's factories. Nevertheless, a majority of slaves (52 percent) counted plantations as their homes and workplaces.

Work

Slaves understood clearly the motive for their enslavement. As ex-slave Albert Todd recalled, "Work was a religion we was taught." Indeed, all slaves who were capable of productive labor worked. Young children were introduced to the world of work as early as age five or six. Ex-slave Carrie Hudson recalled that children who were "knee high to a duck" were sent to the fields to carry water to thirsty workers or to protect ripening crops from hungry birds. Others helped in the slave nursery, caring for children even younger than themselves, or in the big house, where they swept floors or shooed flies in the dining room. When slave boys and girls reached the age of eleven or twelve, masters sent most of them to the fields, where they learned farmwork by laboring alongside their parents. After a lifetime of labor, old women left the fields to care for the small children and spin yarn and old men moved on to mind livestock and clean stables.

The overwhelming majority of all plantation slaves in 1860 were field hands. Planters sometimes assigned men and women to separate gangs, the women working at lighter tasks and the men doing the heavy work of clearing and breaking the land. But women also did heavy work. "I had to work hard," Nancy Boudry remembered, and "plow and go and split wood just like a man." Although the daily tasks of slaves differed according to the crop, the backbreaking labor and the monotonous year-round routines made for grim similarity. As one ex-slave observed, on the plantation the "history of one day is the history of every day."

Nancy Fort, House Servant
This rare portrait of a slave woman at the turn of the nineteenth century depicts a strong and dignified person. Some individuals who worked in domestic service took pride in their superior status and identified more with the master than with their fellow slaves. "Honey, I wan't no common eve'day slave," one former servant recalled proudly. "I [helped] de white folks in de big house." But intense interaction with whites did not necessarily breed affection. Most domestic servants remained bound to the slave quarters by ties of kinship and friendship as well as by common oppression.
Courtesy of Georgia Department of Archives and History.

A few slaves (only one or two in every ten) became house servants. And nearly all of those who did (nine of ten) were women. There, under the critical eye of the white mistress, they cooked, cleaned house, babysat, washed clothes, and did the dozens of other tasks the master and mistress required. House servants enjoyed certain advantages over field hands, such as somewhat less physically demanding work and better food, but working in the big house had significant drawbacks. House servants were constantly on call, with no time that was entirely their own. Since no servant could please constantly, most bore the brunt of white frustration and rage. Ex-slave Jacob Branch of Texas remembered, "My poor mama! Every washday old Missy give her a beating."

Even rarer than house servants were skilled artisans. In the cotton South, no more than one slave in twenty (almost all men) worked in a skilled trade. Most were blacksmiths and carpenters, but slaves also worked as masons, mechanics, millers, and shoemakers. When a slave artisan's labor was not needed on the plantation, masters would often send the slave to work in the neighborhood as hired help. Slave craftsmen took pride in their skills and often exhibited the independence of spirit that caused slaveholder James H. Hammond of South Carolina to declare in disgust that when a slave became a skilled artisan, "he is more than half freed." Skilled slave fathers often taught their crafts to their sons. "My pappy was one of the black smiths and worked in the shop," John Mathews remembered. "I had to help my pappy in the shop when I was a child and I learnt how to beat out the iron and make wagon tires, and make plows."

Rarest of all slave occupations was that of slave driver. Probably no more than one male slave in a hundred worked in this capacity. These

Haywood Dixon, Slave Carpenter

In this 1854 daguerreotype, Dixon (1826–c. 1889), a slave carpenter who worked in Greene County, North Carolina, poses with a symbol of his craft, the carpenter's square. When work was slow on the home plantation, masters could hire out their skilled artisans to neighbors who needed a carpenter, blacksmith, or mason.
Collection of William L. Murphy.

men were well named, for their primary task was driving other slaves to work harder in the fields. In some drivers' hands, the whip never rested. Ex-slave Jane Johnson of South Carolina called her driver the "meanest man, white or black, I ever see." But other drivers showed all the restraint they could. "Ole Gabe didn't like that whippin' business," West Turner of Virginia remembered. "When Marsa was there, he would lay it on 'cause he had to. But when old Marsa wasn't lookin', he never would beat them slaves."

Normally, slaves worked from what they called "can to can't," from "can see" in the morning to "can't see" at night. Even with a break at noon for a meal and rest, it made for a long day. For slaves, Lewis Young recalled, "work, work, work, 'twas all they do."

Family, Religion, and Community

From dawn to dusk, slaves worked for the master, but at night, when the labor was done, and all day Sundays and usually Saturday afternoons, slaves were left largely to themselves. Bone tired perhaps, they nonetheless used the time and space to develop and enjoy what mattered most: family, religion, and community.

In the quarters, slaves lived lives that their masters were hardly aware of. Temporarily leaving the master-slave relationship at their cabin doors, slaves became husbands and wives, mothers and fathers, sons and daughters, preachers and singers, storytellers and conjurers. Over the generations, they created a community and a culture of their own that buoyed them up during long hours in the fields and brought them joy and hope in the few hours they had to themselves.

One of the most important consequences of the slaves' limited autonomy was the preservation and persistence of the family. Perhaps the most serious charge abolitionists leveled against slavery was that it wrecked black family life, a telling indictment in a society that put family at the heart of decent society. Slaveholders sometimes agreed that blacks had no family life, but they placed the blame on the slaves themselves, claiming that blacks chose to lead licentious, promiscuous lives.

Contrary to both abolitionists' and slaveholders' claims, the black family survived slavery. Indeed, family was the chief fact of life in the quarters. Although owners increasingly encouraged the creation and maintenance of families, slave family life grew primarily from slaves' own commitment. No laws recognized slave marriage, and therefore no master or slave was legally obligated to honor the bond. Nevertheless, plantation records show that slave marriages were often long-lasting. Young men and women in the slave quarters fell in love, married, and set up housekeeping in cabins of their own. The primary cause of the ending of slave marriages was death, just as it was in white families. But the second most frequent cause of the end of slave marriages was the sale of the husband or wife, something no white family ever had to fear. Precise figures are unavailable, but one scholar estimates that in the years 1820 to 1860, sales destroyed 300,000 slave marriages.

In 1858, a South Carolina slave named Abream Scriven wrote a letter to his wife, who lived on a neighboring plantation. "My dear wife," he began, "I take the pleasure of writing you . . . with much regret to inform you I am Sold to man by the name of Peterson, a Treader and Stays in New Orleans." Scriven promised to send some things when he got to his new home in Louisiana, but he admitted that he was not sure how he would "get them to you and my children." He asked his wife to "give my love to my father and mother and tell them good Bye for me. And if we shall not meet in this world I hope to meet in heaven. . . . My dear wife for you and my children my pen cannot express the griffe I feel to be parted from you all." Finally, he closed with words that no master would have permitted in a slave's marriage vows: "I remain your truly husband until Death." While there can be no doubt about Abream Scriven's love for the family he was forced to leave behind, it remains clear that slavery represented a massive assault on family life in the quarters.

Not all fathers could live with their children—some men like Scriven married women on neighboring plantations—but plantation records reveal that slave fathers often managed to create significant roles for themselves within their families. Despite their inability to fulfill the traditional roles of provider and protector, they gained status by doing what they could to help

Slave Quarter, South Carolina
On large plantations, several score of African Americans lived in cabins that were often arranged along what slaves called "the street." The dwellings in this image by Civil War photographer George N. Barnard of a South Carolina plantation were better built than the typical rickety, one-room, dirt-floored slave cabin. Almost certainly posed, this photograph shows the inhabitants of the slave quarter—little children playing in the dirt, girls and women sitting on the steps talking and working at something, older boys and men driving carts and wagons. During the daylight hours of the workweek, when most men and women labored in the fields, the quarter was mostly empty. At night and on Sundays, it was a busy place.
Collection of the New-York Historical Society.

their families. Slave fathers and mothers divided responsibilities in the quarters along traditional gender lines: Women cooked, sewed, and cleaned, while men hunted, raised hogs, cultivated a garden, and made furniture for the cabin. Slaves held both their mothers and their fathers in high esteem, grateful for the small bits of refuge their parents provided from the rigors of slavery when they were children.

Like families, religion also provided slaves with a refuge and a reason for living. Beginning about the time of the American Revolution, Protestant **evangelical** sects, particularly the

Baptists and Methodists, began trying to convert slaves from their African beliefs. Evangelicals offered an emotional "religion of the heart" to which blacks (and many whites as well) responded enthusiastically. By the mid-nineteenth century, perhaps as many as one-quarter of all slaves claimed church membership, and many of the rest would not have objected to being called Christians.

Planters began promoting Christianity in the quarters because they came to see the slaves' salvation as part of their obligation and to believe that religion made slaves more obedient. Certainly, the Christianity that masters broadcast to slaves emphasized the meeker virtues and admonished them to obey their masters. South Carolina slaveholder Charles Colcock Jones, the leading missionary to the slaves, published his *Catechism for Colored Persons* in 1834. In it, he instructed slaves "to count their Masters 'worthy of all honour,' as those whom God has placed over them in this world." But slaves laughed up their sleeves at such messages. "That old white preacher just was telling us slaves to be good to our masters," one ex-slave chuckled. "We ain't cared a bit about that stuff he was telling us 'cause we wanted to sing, pray, and serve God in our own way."

> Slaves created a Christianity that served their needs, not the masters'. Rather than obedience, their faith emphasized justice. They believed that God kept score and that the accounts of this world would be settled in the next.

Meeting in their cabins or secretly in the woods, slaves created an African American Christianity that served their needs, not the masters'. Beginning in the 1830s, laws prohibited teaching slaves to read, but a few slaves could read enough to struggle with the Bible. With the help of black preachers, they interpreted the Christian message themselves. Rather than obedience, their faith emphasized justice. Nat Turner felt himself to be an avenging angel who would punish whites and end bondage. More often, slaves believed that God kept score and that the accounts of this world would be settled in the next. "The idea of a revolution in the conditions of the whites and blacks is the cornerstone" of the slaves' religion, recalled ex-slave Charles Ball. But the slaves' faith also spoke to their experiences in this world. In the Old Testament they discovered Moses, who delivered his people from slavery, and in the New Testament they found Jesus, who offered salvation to all and thereby established the equality of all people. Jesus' message of equality provided a potent antidote to the planters' claim that blacks were an inferior people whom God condemned to slavery, and it became a crucial buttress to the slaves' self-esteem.

Christianity did not entirely drive out traditional African beliefs. Even slaves who were Christians sometimes continued to believe that conjurers, witches, and spirits possessed the power to injure and protect. Moreover, their Christian music, preaching, and rituals showed the influence of Africa, as did many of the slaves' secular activities, such as wood carving, quilt making, and storytelling. But by the mid-nineteenth century, black Christianity had assumed a central place in slaves' quest for freedom. In the words of one spiritual: "O my Lord delivered Daniel/O why not deliver me too?"

Gourd Fiddle
Found in St. Mary's County, Maryland, this slave-made gourd fiddle is an example of the many musical instruments that African Americans crafted and played throughout the South. Henry Wright, an ex-slave from Georgia, remembered: "I made a fiddle out of a large sized gourd—a long wooden handle was used as a neck, and the hair from a horse's tail was used for the bow. The strings were made of catgut." A hybrid of African and European elements, this fiddle offers material evidence of the cultural transformation of African slaves. Although Africans lost much in their forced journey to the Americas, Africa remained in their cultural memory. Black men and women drew on the traditions of their homeland and the South to create something new—an African American culture. Music, a crucial component of that sustaining culture, provided slaves with a creative outlet and relief from the rigors of slavery.
Smithsonian Institution/Aldo Tutino/Folio, Inc.

Resistance and Rebellion

Slaves did not suffer slavery passively. They were, as whites said, "troublesome property." Slaves understood that accommodation to what they could not change was the price of survival, but in a hundred ways they protested their bondage. Theoretically, the master was all-powerful and the slave powerless. But sustained by their families, religion, and community, slaves engaged in day-to-day resistance against their enslavers.

The spectrum of slave resistance ranged from mild to extreme. Telling a pointed story by the fireside in a slave cabin was probably the mildest form of protest. But when the weak got the better of the strong, as they did in tales of Br'er Rabbit and Br'er Fox (*Br'er* is a contraction of *Brother*), listeners could enjoy the thrill of a vicarious victory over their masters. Protest in the fields was more active than that around firesides. Slaves were particularly inventive in resisting their master's demand that they work. They dragged their feet getting to the fields, put rocks in their cotton bags before putting them on the scale to be weighed, feigned illness, and pretended to be so thickheaded that they could not understand the simplest instruction. Slaves broke so many handles on their hoes that owners outfitted the hoes with oversized handles. Slaves so mistreated the work animals that masters switched from horses to mules, which could absorb more abuse. While slaves worked hard in the master's fields, they also sabotaged his interests.

Running away, a widespread form of protest, particularly angered masters. By escaping the plantation, runaways denied masters what they wanted most from their slaves—work. Sometimes runaways sought the ultimate prize: freedom in the North or in Canada. Over the decades, thousands of slaves, almost all from the Upper South, made it. But escape from the Lower South was almost impossible, except in Texas, where several hundred slaves found freedom by slipping across the Mexican border. But the overwhelming majority of runaways could hope only to escape for a few weeks. They usually stayed close to their plantation, keeping to the deep woods or swamps and slipping back into the quarters at night to get food. "Lying out," as it was known, usually ended when the runaway, worn out and ragged, gave up or was finally chased down by slave-hunting dogs.

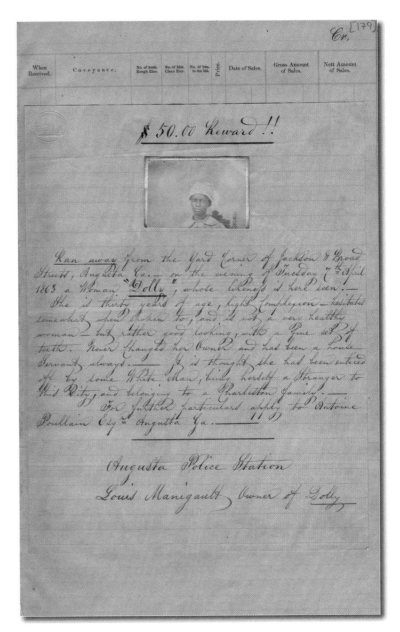

"$50 Reward"

Runaway slaves were as common as thunderstorms in the South. Slave owners often employed notices—reward posters like this one and newspaper advertisements—to recover their property. Typically, notices provide precise information about the runaway's physical appearance—size, age, color, build, scars, and hairstyle—and clothing, since slaves often fled with only the clothes on their backs. Notices frequently mentioned the slave's personality and speech habits as well. Here, according to her owner, prominent rice planter Louis Manigault, Dolly was slow to repond when spoken to. Manigault apparently could not accept that a trusted house servant would flee on her own, and thus he suggests that "some white man" had enticed her away. But Manigault also notes that Dolly was new to Augusta, which may suggest that she was seeking to reunite with her family on the coast after Manigault had moved his white family and house servants inland seeking safety during the Civil War. What distinguishes this runaway notice from almost all others is Dolly's photograph. Manigault had apparently rewarded this favorite servant with a photograph, and then he used it to track her down.

Manigault Papers, Southern Historical Collection, North Carolina Collection, The Library of the University of North Carolina, Chapel Hill, collection #P484.

While resistance was common, outright rebellion—a violent assault on slavery by large numbers of slaves—was very rare. The scarcity of revolts is not evidence of the slaves' contentedness, however. Rather, conditions gave rebels almost no chance of success. By 1860, whites in the South outnumbered blacks two to one and were heavily armed. Moreover, communication between plantations was difficult, and the South provided little protective wilderness into which rebels could retreat and defend themselves. Organized rebellion in the American South, as Nat Turner's experience showed, was virtual suicide.

Despite the rarity of slave revolts, whites believed that they were surrounded by conspiracies to rebel. In 1822, whites in Charleston accused Denmark Vesey, a free black carpenter, of conspiring with plantation slaves to storm the city arsenal, capture its weapons, kill any white who stood in the way, and set fire to the city. The authorities rounded up scores of suspects, who, prodded by torture and the threat of death, implicated others in the plot "to riot in blood, outrage, and rapine." Although the city fathers never found any weapons and Vesey and most of the accused steadfastly denied the charges of conspiracy, officials hanged thirty-five black men, including Denmark Vesey, and banished another thirty-seven blacks from the state.

Although masters often boasted that their slaves were "instinctively contented," steady resistance and occasional rebellion proved otherwise. Slaves did not have the power to end their bondage, but by asserting themselves, they affirmed their humanity and worth. By resisting their masters' will, slaves became actors in the plantation drama, helping to establish limits beyond which planters and overseers hesitated to go.

It would be false to the historical record to minimize what the lack of freedom meant to slaves. Because the essence of slavery was the inability to shape one's own life, slavery blunted and thwarted African Americans' hopes and aspirations. Slavery broke some and crippled others. But slavery's destructive power had to contend with the resiliency of the human spirit. Slaves fought back physically, culturally, and spiritually. They not only survived bondage, but they created in the quarter a vibrant African American culture and community that sustained them through more than two centuries of slavery and after.

Black and Free: On the Middle Ground

Not every black Southerner was a slave. In 1860, some 260,000 (approximately 6 percent) of the region's 4.1 million African Americans were free (see Figure 13.1). What is surprising is not that their numbers were small but that they existed at all. "Free black" seemed increasingly a contradiction to most white Southerners. According to the emerging racial thinking, blacks were supposed to be slaves; only whites were supposed to be free. Blacks who were free did not fit neatly into the South's idealized social order. They stood out, and whites made them more and more objects of scrutiny and scorn. Free blacks realized that they stood precariously between slavery and full freedom, on what a young free black artisan in Charleston in 1848 characterized as "a middle ground." But they made the most of their freedom, and some managed significant success despite the restrictions placed on them by southern society.

Precarious Freedom

Free blacks were rare in the colonial era, but their numbers swelled after the Revolution, when the natural rights philosophy of the Declaration of Independence and the egalitarian message of evangelical Protestantism joined to challenge slavery. Although probably not more than one slaveholder in a hundred freed his slaves, a brief flurry of **emancipation** visited the Upper South, where the ideological assault on slavery coincided with a deep depression in the tobacco economy. Other planters permitted favorite slaves to work after hours to accumulate money with which to buy their freedom. By 1810, free blacks numbered more than 100,000 and had become the fastest-growing element of the southern population. Burgeoning numbers of free blacks worried white Southerners, who, because of the cotton boom, wanted desperately to see more slaves, not more free blacks.

In the 1820s and 1830s, state legislatures acted to stem the growth of the free black population and to shrink the liberty of those blacks who had already gained their freedom. Laws denied masters the right to free their slaves. Other laws humiliated and restricted free blacks by subjecting them to special taxes, requiring them to register annually with the state or to choose a white guardian, prohibiting them from interstate travel, denying them the right to have schools and to participate in politics, and requiring them to carry "freedom papers" to prove they were not slaves. Increasingly, whites subjected free blacks to many of the same laws as slaves. They could not testify under oath in a court of law or serve on juries. They were liable to punishment meted out to slaves such as whipping and the treadmill. Like slaves, free blacks were forbidden to strike whites, even to defend themselves. "Free negroes belong to a degraded caste of society," a South Carolina judge summed up in 1848. "They are in no respect on a perfect equality with the white man. . . . They ought, by law, to be compelled to demean themselves as inferiors."

The elaborate system of regulations confined most free African Americans to a constricted life of poverty and dependence. Typically, free blacks were rural, uneducated, unskilled agricultural laborers and domestic servants, scrambling to find work and eke out a living. Opportunities of all kinds—for work, education, community—were slim. Planters looked on free blacks as degraded parasites, likely to set a bad example for slaves. They believed that free blacks subverted the racial subordination that was the essence of slavery.

Achievement despite Restrictions

Despite increasingly harsh laws and stepped-up persecution, free African Americans made the most of the advantages their status offered. Unlike slaves, free blacks could legally marry. They could protect their families from arbitrary disruption and pass on their heritage of freedom to their children. Freedom also meant that they could choose occupations and own property. For most, these economic rights proved only theoretical, for whites allowed most free blacks few opportunities. Unlike whites, a majority of the antebellum South's free blacks remained propertyless.

Still, some free blacks escaped the poverty and degradation whites thrust on them. Particularly in urban areas—especially the cities of Charleston, Mobile, and New Orleans—a small elite of free blacks developed and even flourished. Urban whites enforced many of the restrictive laws only sporadically, allowing free blacks room to maneuver. The elite consisted overwhelmingly of light-skinned African Americans who worked at skilled trades, as tailors, carpenters, mechanics, and the like. Their

Freedom Paper
This legal document attests to the free status of the Rev. John F. Cook of Washington, D.C., his daughter Mary, and his son George. Cook was a free black man who kept his "freedom paper" in this watertight tin, which he probably carried with him at all times. Free blacks had to be prepared to prove their free status any time a white man challenged them, for southern law presumed that a black person was a slave unless he or she could prove otherwise. Without such proof, blacks risked enslavement.
Moorland-Spingarn Research Center, Howard University, Washington, D.C.

customers were prominent whites—planters, merchants, and judges—who appreciated their able, respectful service. The free black elite operated schools for their children and traveled in and out of their states, despite laws forbidding both activities. They worshiped with whites (in separate seating) in the finest churches and lived scattered about in white neighborhoods, not in ghettos. And like elite whites, some owned slaves. Blacks could own blacks because, despite all of the restrictions whites placed on free African Americans, whites did not deny them the right to own property, which in the South included human property. Of the 3,200 black slaveholders (barely 1 percent of the free black population), most owned only a few slaves, who were sometimes family members whom they could not legally free. But others owned slaves in large numbers and exploited them for labor.

One such free black slave owner was William Ellison of South Carolina. Ellison was born a slave in 1790, but in 1816 he bought his freedom and moved to a thriving plantation district about one hundred miles north of Charleston. He set up business as a cotton gin maker, a trade he had learned as a slave, and by 1835 he was prosperous enough to purchase the home of a former governor of the state. By the time of his death in 1861, he had become a cotton planter, with sixty-three slaves and an 800-acre plantation.

Most free blacks neither became slaveholders like Ellison nor sought to raise a slave rebellion, as whites accused Denmark Vesey of doing. Rather, most free blacks simply tried to preserve their freedom, which was under increasing attack from planters who wanted to eliminate or enslave them and from white artisans who coveted their jobs. For their part, free blacks clung to their precarious freedom by seeking to impress whites with their reliability, economic contribution, and good behavior.

The Cotton Belt

The Plain Folk

Like most free blacks, most whites in the South did not own slaves, not even one. In 1860, more than 6 million of the South's 8 million whites lived in slaveless households. Some slaveless whites lived in cities and worked as artisans, mechanics, and traders. Others lived in the country but worked outside agriculture as storekeepers, parsons, and schoolteachers. But the majority of "plain folk" were small farmers. Perhaps three out of four were **yeomen**, small farmers who owned their own land. As in the North, farm ownership provided a family with an economic foundation, social respectability, and political standing. Unlike their northern counterparts, however, southern yeomen lived in a region whose economy and society were increasingly dominated by unfree labor.

In an important sense, the South had more than one white yeomanry. The huge southern landscape provided space enough for two yeoman societies, separated roughly along geographical lines. Yeomen throughout the South

had a good deal in common, but the life of a small farm family in the plantation belt—the flatlands that spread from South Carolina to east Texas—differed from the life of one in the upcountry—the area of hills and mountains. And some rural slaveless whites were not yeomen; they owned no land at all and were often desperately poor.

Plantation Belt Yeomen

Plantation belt yeomen lived within the orbit of the planter class. Small farms actually outnumbered plantations in that great arc of fertile cotton land that spread from South Carolina to east Texas, but they were dwarfed in importance. Small farmers grew food crops, particularly corn, but like planters, yeomen devoted a significant portion of their land to growing cotton. With only family labor to draw upon, however, they produced only a few 400-pound bales each year, whereas large planters measured their crop in hundreds of bales. The small farmers' cotton tied them to planters. Unable to afford cotton gins or baling presses of their own, they relied on helpful neighborhood slave owners to gin and bale their small crops. With no link to merchants in the port cities, plantation belt yeomen turned to better-connected planters to ship and sell their cotton.

A dense network of relationships laced small farmers and planters together in patterns of reciprocity and mutual obligation. A planter might send his slaves to help a newcomer build a house or a sick farmer get in his crop. He hired out surplus slaves to ambitious yeomen who wanted to expand cotton production. He sometimes chose his overseers from among the sons of local farm families. Plantation mistresses sometimes nursed ailing neighbors. Family ties could span class lines, making rich and poor kin as well as neighbors. Yeomen shared the planters' commitment to white supremacy and actively defended black subordination. Rural counties required adult white males to ride in slave patrols, which nightly scoured country roads to make certain that no slaves were moving about without permission. On Sundays, plantation dwellers and plain folk came together

***Gathering Corn in Virginia,* c. 1870**
In this romanticized agricultural scene, painter Felix O. C. Darley depicts members of a white farm family gathering its harvest by hand. A young black drover, who before the Civil War would have been the property of the white man or would have been rented by him from a neighboring planter, steadies the team of oxen while another man fills the wagon. Sitting before the bundled stalks, the couple shucks the ripened ears of corn. The happy moment is made complete by playful and dozing children and a sleeping dog. In reality, growing corn was hard work. Even yeomen who grew considerable cotton also grew lots of corn, usually producing about twice the corn they needed for their families and livestock and marketing the rest. The artist, however, is less concerned with realism than with extolling rural family labor as virtuous and noble. Darley surrounds the southern yeomen with an aura of republican independence, dignity, and freedom.
Warner Collection of Gulf States Paper Corporation.

in church to worship and afterward lingered to gossip and to transact small business.

Plantation belt yeomen may have envied, and at times even resented, wealthy slaveholders, but in general small farmers learned to accommodate. Planters made accommodation easier by going out of their way to provide necessary services, behave as good neighbors, and avoid direct exploitation of slaveless whites in their community. As a consequence, rather than raging at the oppression of the planter regime, the typical plantation belt yeoman sought entry into it. He dreamed of adding acreage to his farm, buying a few slaves of his own, retiring from fieldwork, and perhaps even joining his prosperous neighbors on their shady verandas for a cool drink.

Upcountry Yeomen

By contrast, the hills and mountains of the South resisted the penetration of slavery and plantations. In the western parts of Virginia, North Carolina, and South Carolina, northern Georgia and Alabama, and eastern Tennessee and Kentucky, the higher elevation, colder climate,

Upcountry of the South

rugged terrain, and poor transportation made it difficult for commercial agriculture to make headway. As a result, yeomen dominated these isolated areas, and planters and slaves were scarce.

At the core of this distinctive upcountry society was the independent farm family working its own patch of land; raising hogs, cattle, and sheep; and seeking self-sufficiency and independence. Toward that end, all members of the family worked, their tasks depending on their sex and age. Husbands labored in the fields, and with their sons they cleared, plowed, planted, and cultivated primarily food crops—corn, wheat, sweet potatoes, and perhaps some fruit. Although pressed into field labor at harvest time, wives and daughters of upcountry yeomen, like those of plantation belt yeomen, worked in and about the cabin most of the year. One upcountry farmer remembered that his mother "worked in the house cooking, spinning, weaving [and doing] patchwork." Women also tended the vegetable garden, kept a cow and some chickens, preserved foods, cleaned their homes, fed their families, and cared for their children. Male and female tasks were equally crucial to the farm's success, but as in other white southern households, the domestic sphere was subordinated to the will of the male patriarch.

> At the core of this distinctive upcountry society was the independent farm family working its own patch of land and seeking self-sufficiency and independence.

The typical upcountry yeoman also grew a little cotton or tobacco, but production for home consumption was more important than production for the market. Not much currency changed hands in the upcountry. Credit was common, as was barter. A yeoman might trade his small cotton or tobacco crop to a country storeowner for a little salt, lead shot, needles, and nails. Or he might swap extra sweet potatoes with the blacksmith for a plow or with the tanner for leather. Networks of exchange and mutual assistance tied individual homesteads to the larger community. Farm families also joined together in logrolling, house- and barn-raising, and cornhusking.

Yeomen did not have the upcountry entirely to themselves. Even the hills had some plantations and slaves. But they existed in much smaller numbers than in the plantation belt. Most upcountry counties were less than a quarter black, whereas counties in the plantation belt were more than half black. The few upcountry folks who owned slaves usually had only two or three. As a result, slaveholders had much less direct social and economic power, and yeomen had more. But yeoman domination did not mean that the upcountry opposed slavery. As long as they were free to lead their own lives, upcountry plain folk defended slavery and white supremacy just as staunchly as did other white Southerners.

Poor Whites

The South's white majority constituted a sturdy yeomanry—hardworking, landholding small farmers. But Northerners believed that slavery had produced a misshapen society that condemned all slaveless whites to poverty, brutality, and backwardness. The British antislavery advocate J. E. Cairnes charged that the South harbored "three classes . . .—the slaves on whom devolves all the regular industry, the slaveholders who reap all its fruits, and an idle and lawless rabble who live dispersed over vast plains little removed from absolute barbarism." Critics called this third class a variety of derogatory names: hillbillies, crackers, rednecks, and poor white trash. Poor whites were not just whites who were poor, according to these claims. The label carried a moral as well as a material meaning. Poor whites were supposedly ignorant and inbred, sick in body, and degenerate in culture. Even slaves were known to chant: "I'd rather be a nigger an' plow ol' Beck / Than a white hillbilly with a long red neck."

A fraction of the white population of the South was poor, rather than the majority, as the critics of the South's social structure claimed. Perhaps one in four white farmers was landless. Some lived as tenants, renting land and struggling to make a go of it. Others scratched out a living by herding pigs and cattle. And still others worked for wages—ditching, mining, logging, and laying track for railroads. A Georgian remembered that his "father worked by the day when ever he could get work." Poor white men gained a reputation for unruly behavior and spontaneous violence. One visitor claimed that a "bowie-knife was a universal, and a pistol a not at all unusual, companion." But unlike the planter class, with its carefully delineated rules for dueling, poor whites were more likely to engage in ear-biting, eye-gouging free-for-alls to preserve their masculine honor. Observers also claimed that poor whites were lazy, but visitors often mistook physical disability for laziness, for in the South's warm, wet climate, barefooted people sometimes contracted hookworm, pellagra, and other debilitating diseases.

Although impoverished, most poor white Southerners were not degenerate. They sat at the bottom of the white pecking order, but they had not lost heart or ambition. Most were ambitious people scratching to survive and aspiring to climb into the yeomanry. The Lipscomb family illustrates the possibility of upward mobility. In 1845, Smith and Sally Lipscomb and their children abandoned their tired land in South Carolina for Benton County, Alabama. "Benton is a mountainous country but ther is a heep of good levil land to tend in it," Smith wrote back to his brother. Alabama, Smith said, "will be better for the rising generation if not for ourselves but I think it will be the best for us all that live any length of time." Indeed, primitive living conditions made life precarious. All of the Lipscombs fell ill, but all recovered, and the entire family went to work. Because they had no money to buy land, they squatted on seven unoccupied acres. With the help of neighbors, they built a 22-by-24-foot cabin, a detached kitchen, and two stables. From daylight to dark, Smith and his sons worked the land. Nature cooperated, and they produced enough food for the table and several bales of cotton. The women worked as hard in the cabin, and Sally contributed to the family's income by selling homemade shirts and socks. In time, the Lipscombs bought land of their own and joined the Hebron Baptist Church, completing their transformation to respectable yeomen.

Many poor whites succeeded in climbing the economic ladder, but in the 1850s upward mobility slowed. The cotton boom of that decade caused planters to expand their operations, driving the price of land beyond the reach of poor families. Whether they gained their own land or not, however, most poor whites shared a great deal in common with yeomen, including their culture.

The Culture of the Plain Folk

Situated on scattered farms and in tiny villages, rural plain folk lived isolated, local lives. Bad roads and a lack of newspapers meant that everyday life revolved around family, a handful of neighbors, the local church, and perhaps a country store. Work occupied most hours, but plain folk still found time for pleasure. "Dancing they are all fond of," a visitor to the backcountry of North Carolina discovered, "especially when they can get a fiddle, or bagpipe." They also loved their tobacco. One visitor complained that the "use of tobacco is almost universal." Men smoked and chewed (and spat), while women dipped snuff. Some plain folk also showed a fondness for liquor, especially whiskey. But the truly universal pastimes among men and boys were fishing and hunting. A traveler in Mississippi recalled that his host sent "two of his sons, little fellows that looked almost too small to shoulder a gun," for food. "One went off towards the river and the other struck into the forest, and in a few hours we were feasting on delicious venison, trout and turtle."

Plain folk did not usually associate "book learning" with the basic needs of life. A northern woman visiting the South in the 1850s observed, "Education is not extended to the masses here as at the North." Private academies charged fees that yeomen could not afford, and public schools were scarce. Even where public schools existed, terms were short, only about 50 or 60 days a year compared with 100 to 150 days in the North. Although most people managed to pick up a basic knowledge of the "three R's," approximately one southern white man in five was illiterate in 1860, and the rate for white women was even higher. "People here prefer talking to reading," a Virginian remarked. Telling stories, reciting ballads, and singing hymns were important activities in yeoman culture.

Plain folk everywhere spent more hours in revival tents than in classrooms. By no means were all rural whites religious, but many were, and the most characteristic feature of their evangelical Christian faith was the revival. The greatest of the early-nineteenth-century revivals occurred in 1801 at Cane Ridge, Kentucky, where some 20,000 people gathered to listen to a host of evangelical preachers who spoke day and night for a week. Ministers sought to convert and save souls by bringing individuals to a personal conviction of sin. Revivalism crossed denominational

> Although impoverished, most poor white Southerners were ambitious people scratching to survive and aspiring to climb into the yeomanry.

***A Baptising on the South Branch of the Potomac near Franklin, Virginia* (detail), 1844**
In 1844, noted painter William Thompson Russell Smith undertook a geological expedition to Virginia, and there he encountered a rural baptism. Primarily a landscape painter, Smith portrayed the human figures as minor characters. If one of the participants had sketched the baptism, he or she might have emphasized the human drama, the emotional pitch of what was for evangelical Christians throughout the South a profound religious moment.
The Charleston Renaissance Gallery, Robert M. Hicklin Jr., Inc., Charleston, South Carolina.

ernments. As a result, they received significant benefits. Nonslaveholding whites were concerned mainly with preserving their liberties and keeping their taxes low. Collectively, they asked government for little of an economic nature, and they received little.

Slaveholders sometimes worried about nonslaveholders' loyalty to slavery, but since the eighteenth century, the mass of whites had accepted the planters' argument that the existing social order served *all* Southerners' interests. Slavery compensated every white man—no matter how poor—with membership in the South's white ruling class. It also provided the means by which nonslaveholders might someday advance into the ranks of the planters. White men in the South fought furiously about many things, but the majority agreed that they should take land from Indians, promote agriculture, uphold white supremacy and masculine privilege, and defend slavery from its enemies.

The Democratization of the Political Arena

The political reforms that swept the nation in the first half of the nineteenth century reached deeply into the South. Southern politics became democratic politics—for white men. Southerners eliminated the wealth and property requirements that had once restricted political participation. By the early 1850s, every state had extended **suffrage** to all white males who were at least twenty-one years of age. Most southern states also removed the property requirements for holding state offices. In addition, increasing numbers of local and state officials—justices of the peace, judges, militia officers, and others—were chosen by the voters. To be sure, undemocratic features lingered. Plantation districts still wielded disproportionate power in several state legislatures. Nevertheless, southern politics took place within an increasingly democratic political structure.

White male suffrage ushered in an era of vigorous electoral competition. Eager voters rushed to the polls to exercise their new rights. In South Carolina, for example, in the 1810 election—the last election with voting restrictions in place—only 43 percent of white men cast ballots. In 1824, a remarkable 76 percent of white men voted. High turnouts became a hallmark of southern electoral politics. Candidates crisscrossed their electoral districts, speaking to voters who demanded stirring oratory and also

lines; Baptists and Methodists adopted it wholeheartedly and by midcentury had become the South's largest religious groups. By emphasizing free choice and individual worth, the plain folk's religion was hopeful and affirming. Hymns and spirituals provided guides to right and wrong—praising humility and steadfastness, condemning drunkenness and profanity. Above all, hymns spoke of eventual release from worldly sorrows and the assurance of eternal salvation.

The Politics of Slavery

By the mid-nineteenth century, all southern white men—aristocrats and plain folk alike—had gained access to the arena of politics. Like every other significant feature of southern society, politics reflected slavery's power. Even after the South's politics became **democratic** in form for the white male population, political power remained unevenly distributed. The nonslaveholding white majority wielded less political power than their numbers indicated. The slaveholding white minority wielded more. Self-conscious, cohesive, and with a well-developed sense of class interest, slaveholders busied themselves with party politics, campaigns, and officeholding and made demands of state gov-

> By the early 1850s, southern politics became democratic politics—for white men.

good entertainment—barbecues and bands, rum and races. In the South, it seemed, "everybody talked politics everywhere," even the "illiterate and shoeless."

As politics became aggressively democratic in the South and across the nation, it also grew fiercely partisan. From the 1830s to the 1850s, Whigs and Democrats battled for the electorate's favor. In the South, both parties presented themselves as the plain white folk's best friend. All candidates declared their fervent commitment to **republican** equality and pledged to defend the people's liberty. Each party sought to portray the other as a collection of rich, snobbish, selfish men who had antidemocratic designs up their silk sleeves. Each, in turn, claimed for itself the mantle of humble "servant of the people."

The Whig and Democratic parties sought to serve the people differently, however. Southern Whigs tended, as Whigs did elsewhere in the nation, to favor government intervention in the economy, and Democrats tended to oppose it. Whigs generally backed state support of banks, railroads, and corporations, arguing that government aid would stimulate the economy, enlarge opportunity, and thus increase the general welfare. Democrats emphasized the threat to individual liberty that government intervention posed, claiming that granting favors to special economic interests would result in concentrated power, which would in turn jeopardize the common man's opportunity and equality. Beginning with the panic of 1837, the parties clashed repeatedly on concrete economic and financial issues.

Planter Power

Whether Whig or Democrat, southern officeholders were likely to be slave owners. The power slaveholders exerted over slaves did not translate directly into political authority over whites, however. In the nineteenth century, political power could be won only at the ballot box, and almost everywhere nonslaveholders were in the majority. Yet year after year, proud and noisily egalitarian common men elected wealthy slaveholders.

Over time, slaveholders increased their power in state legislatures. By 1860, the percentage of slave owners in state legislatures ranged from 41 percent in Missouri to nearly 86 percent in North Carolina (Table 13.1). Legislators not only tended to own slaves—they often owned large numbers. The percentage of planters (indi-

viduals with twenty or more slaves) in southern legislatures in 1860 ranged from 5.3 percent in Missouri to 55.4 percent in South Carolina. In North Carolina, where only 3 percent of the state's white families belonged to the planter class, 36.6 percent of the legislature were planters. The democratization of politics in the nineteenth century meant that more ordinary citizens participated in elections, but yeomen and artisans remained rare sights in the halls of southern legislatures.

Upper-class dominance of southern politics reflected the elite's success in persuading the white majority that what was good for slaveholders was also good for them. The South had, on the whole, done well by the plain folk. Most had farms of their own. They participated as equals in a democratic political system. They enjoyed an elevated social status, above all blacks and in theory equal to all other whites. They commanded patriarchal authority over their households. And as long as slavery existed, they could dream of joining the planter class, of rising above the drudgery of field labor. Slaveless white men found much to celebrate in the slave South.

Most slaveholders took pains to win the plain folk's trust and to nurture their respect. In the plantation districts especially, where slaveholders and nonslaveholders lived side by side,

TABLE 13.1	PERCENT OF SLAVEHOLDERS AND PLANTERS IN SOUTHERN LEGISLATURES, 1860	
Legislature	Slaveholders	Planters*
Virginia	67.3%	24.2%
Maryland	53.4	19.3
North Carolina	85.8	36.6
Kentucky	60.6	8.4
Tennessee	66.0	14.0
Missouri	41.2	5.3
Arkansas	42.0	13.0
South Carolina	81.7	55.4
Georgia	71.6	29.0
Florida	55.4	20.0
Alabama	76.3	40.8
Mississippi	73.4	49.5
Louisiana	63.8	23.5
Texas	54.1	18.1

*Planters: Owned 20 or more slaves.

Source: Adapted from Ralph A. Wooster, *The People in Power: Courthouse and Statehouse in the Lower South, 1850–1860* (1969), 41; Wooster, *Politicians, Planters, and Plain Folks: Courthouse and Statehouse in the Upper South* (1975), 40. Courtesy of the University of Tennessee Press.

planters learned that flexing their economic muscle was a poor way to win the political allegiance of common men. Instead, they developed a lighter touch, fully attentive to their own interests but aware of the personal feelings of poorer whites. One South Carolinian told his wealthy neighbor that he had a bright political future because he never thought himself "too good to sit down & talk to a poor man." South Carolinian Mary Boykin Chesnut complained about the fawning attention her slaveholding husband showed to poor men, including one who had "mud sticking up through his toes."

Smart candidates found ways to convince wary plain folk of their democratic convictions and egalitarian sentiments, whether they were genuine or not. When young John A. Quitman ran for a seat in the Mississippi legislature, he amazed a boisterous crowd of small farmers at one campaign stop by not only entering but winning contests in jumping, boxing, wrestling, and sprinting. For his finale he outshot the area's champion marksman. Then, demonstrating his deft political touch, he gave his prize, a fat ox, to the defeated rifleman. The electorate showed its approval by sending Quitman to the state capital. When Walter L. Steele ran for a seat in the North Carolina legislature in 1846, he commented sarcastically to a friend that he was "busily engaged in proving to the people, the soundness of my political faith, and the purity of my personal character & playing fool to a considerable extent, as you know, all candidates are obliged to do." He detested pandering to the electorate, but he had learned to speak with "a candied tongue."

The massive representation of slaveholders ensured that southern legislatures would make every effort to preserve their interests. Georgia politics show how well planters protected themselves in the political struggle. In 1850, about half of the state's revenues came from taxes on slave property, the characteristic form of planter wealth. However, the tax rate on slaves was trifling, only about one-fifth the rate on land. Moreover, planters benefited far more than other social groups from public spending: Financing railroads—which carried cotton to market—was the largest state expenditure. The legislature also established low tax rates on land, the characteristic form of yeoman wealth, which meant that the typical yeoman's annual tax bill was small. Still, relative to their wealth, large slaveholders paid less than did other whites. Relative to their numbers, they got more in return. A sym-

pathetic slaveholding legislature protected planters' interests and gave the impression of protecting the small farmers' interests as well.

The South's elite protected slavery in other ways. In the 1830s, whites decided that slavery was too important to debate. "So interwoven is [slavery] with our interest, our manners, our climate and our very being," one man declared in 1833, "that no change can ever possibly be effected without a civil commotion from which the heart of a patriot must turn with horror." To end free speech on the slavery question, slavery's critics were dismissed from college faculties, driven from pulpits, and hounded from political life. Sometimes they fell victim to vigilantes and mob violence. One could defend slavery; one could even delicately suggest mild reforms. But no Southerner could safely call slavery evil or advocate its destruction.

In the antebellum South, therefore, the rise of the common man occurred alongside the continuing, even growing, power of the planter class. Rather than pitting slaveholders against nonslaveholders, elections remained an effective means of binding the region's whites together. Elections affirmed the sovereignty of white men, whether planter or plain folk, and the subordination of African Americans. Those twin themes played well among white women as well. Although unable to vote, white women supported equality for whites and slavery for blacks. In the antebellum South, the politics of slavery helped knit together all of white society.

Conclusion: A Slave Society

By the early nineteenth century, northern states had either abolished slavery or put it on the road to extinction while southern states were aggressively building the largest slave society in the New World. Regional differences increased over time, not merely because the South became more and more dominated by slavery, but also because developments in the North rapidly propelled it in a very different direction.

In 1860, one-third of the South's population was enslaved. Bondage saddled blacks with enormous physical and spiritual burdens: hard labor, poor treatment, broken families, and most important, the denial of freedom itself. Although degraded and exploited, they were not defeated. Out of African memories and New World realities, blacks created a life-affirming African

American culture that sustained and strengthened them. Their families, religion, and community provided antidotes to white racist ideas and even to white power. Defined as property, they refused to be reduced to things. Perceived as inferior beings, they rejected the notion that they were natural slaves. Slaves engaged in a war of wills with masters who sought their labor while the slaves sought to live dignified, autonomous lives.

Much more than racial slavery contributed to the South's distinctiveness and to the loyalty and regional identification of its whites. White Southerners felt strong attachments to local communities, to extended families, to personal, face-to-face relationships, to rural life, to evangelical Protestantism, and to codes of honor and chivalry, among other things. But slavery was crucial to the South's economy, society, culture, and politics, as well as to its developing sectional consciousness. After the 1830s, the South was not merely a society with slaves; it was a slave society. Little disturbed the white consensus south of the Mason-Dixon line that racial slavery was necessary and just. By making all blacks a pariah

class, all whites gained a measure of equality and harmony.

Racism did not erase stress along class lines. Nor did the other features of southern life that helped confine class tensions: the wide availability of land, rapid economic mobility, the democratic nature of political life, patriarchal power among white men, the shrewd behavior of slaveholders toward poorer whites, kinship ties between rich and poor, and rural traditions. Anxious slaveholders continued to worry that yeomen would defect from the proslavery consensus. But during the 1850s, a far more ominous division emerged—between the "slave states" and the "free states."

FOR ADDITIONAL FIRSTHAND ACCOUNTS OF THIS PERIOD, see Chapter 13 in Michael Johnson, ed., *Reading the American Past*, Third Edition.

TO ASSESS YOUR MASTERY OF THE MATERIAL IN THIS CHAPTER, see the Online Study Guide at bedfordstmartins.com/roark.

FOR WEB LINKS RELATED TO TOPICS IN THIS CHAPTER, see "HistoryLinks," "DocLinks," and "PlaceLinks" at bedfordstmartins.com/roark.

CHRONOLOGY

1808 • External slave trade outlawed.

1813–1814 • Creek War opens 24 million acres of Indian land to southern settlement in the West.

1810s–1850s • Suffrage gradually extended throughout South to white males over twenty-one years of age.

1820s–1830s • Southern legislatures enact slave codes to strengthen slavery.
• Southern legislatures enact laws to restrict growth of free black population and to limit freedom of free blacks.
• Southern intellectuals begin to fashion systematic defense of slavery.

1820–1860 • Cotton production soars from about 300,000 bales to nearly 5 million bales.

1822 • Denmark Vesey executed for conspiring to lead a slave rebellion in South Carolina.

1829 • David Walker publishes *Appeal . . . to the Coloured Citizens of the World*.

1830 • U.S. Census reveals southern slaves number approximately 2 million.

1831 • Nat Turner's slave rebellion occurs in Virginia.
• William Lloyd Garrison publishes the first issue of *Liberator*, his abolitionist newspaper, in Boston.

1834 • Charles Colcock Jones publishes *Catechism for Colored Persons*.

1836 • Arkansas admitted to the Union as a slave state.

1840 • Cotton accounts for more than 60 percent of the nation's exports.

1845 • Texas and Florida admitted to the Union as slave states.

1860 • U.S. Census reveals that southern slaves number more than 4 million, one-third of the South's population.

BIBLIOGRAPHY

General Works

John B. Boles, *The South through Time: A History of an American Region* (2nd ed., 1999).
W. J. Cash, *The Mind of the South* (1941).
William J. Cooper Jr. and Thomas E. Terrill, *The American South: A History* (2nd ed., 1996).
Carl N. Degler, *Place over Time: The Continuity of Southern Distinctiveness* (1977).
Peter Kolchin, *A Sphinx on the American Land: The Nineteenth-Century South in Comparative Perspective* (2003).
James Oakes, *Slavery and Freedom: An Interpretation of the Old South* (1990).

The Economy

Fred Bateman and Thomas Weiss, *A Deplorable Scarcity: The Failure of Industrialization in the Slave Economy* (1981).
David L. Carlton and Peter A. Coclanis, *The South, the Nation, and the World: Perspectives on Southern Economic Development* (2003).
Daniel S. Dupre, *Transforming the Cotton Frontier: Madison County, Alabama, 1800–1840* (1997).
Robert W. Fogel, *Without Consent or Contract: The Rise and Fall of American Slavery* (1989).
Sam B. Hilliard, *Atlas of Antebellum Southern Agriculture* (1984).
John Majewski, *A House Dividing: Economic Development in Pennsylvania and Virginia before the Civil War* (2000).
Joseph P. Reidy, *From Slavery to Agrarian Capitalism in the Cotton Plantation South: Central Georgia, 1800–1880* (1992).
Larry Schweikart, *Banking in the American South from the Age of Jackson to Reconstruction* (1987).
Harold D. Woodman, *King Cotton and His Retainers: Financing and Marketing the Cotton Crop of the South, 1800–1925* (1968).
Gavin Wright, *The Political Economy of the Cotton South: Households, Markets, and Wealth in the Nineteenth Century* (1978).

Slaveholders

Jane T. Censer, *North Carolina Planters and Their Children, 1800–1860* (1984).
Catherine Clinton, *The Plantation Mistress: Woman's World in the Old South* (1982).
Drew G. Faust, *James Henry Hammond and the Old South: A Design for Mastery* (1982).
Elizabeth Fox-Genovese, *Within the Plantation Household: Black and White Women of the Old South* (1988).
Eugene D. Genovese, *The World the Slaveholders Made: Two Essays in Interpretation* (1969).
James David Miller, *South by Southwest: Planter Emigration and Identity in the Slave South* (2002).
James Oakes, *The Ruling Race: A History of American Slaveholders* (1982).
Anne F. Scott, *The Southern Lady: From Pedestal to Politics, 1830–1930* (1970).
Steven M. Stowe, *Intimacy and Power in the Old South: Ritual in the Lives of the Planters* (1987).
Michael Tadman, *Speculators and Slaves: Masters, Traders, and Slaves in the Old South* (1989).
Marli F. Weiner, *Mistresses and Slaves: Plantation Women in South Carolina, 1830–1880* (1998).
Jeffrey Robert Young, *Domesticating Slavery: The Master Class in Georgia and South Carolina, 1670–1837* (1999).

Slaves, Slavery, and Race Relations

GENERAL WORKS

Ira Berlin, *Generations of Captivity: A History of African-American Slaves* (2003).
John W. Blassingame, *The Slave Community: Plantation Life in the Antebellum South* (1972).
Carl N. Degler, *Neither Black nor White: Slavery and Race Relations in Brazil and the United States* (1971).
George M. Fredrickson, *The Black Image in the White Mind: The Debate on Afro-American Character and Destiny, 1817–1914* (1971).
George M. Fredrickson, *The Arrogance of Race: Historical Perspectives on Slavery, Racism, and Social Inequality* (1988).
Eugene D. Genovese, *Roll, Jordan, Roll: The World the Slaves Made* (1974).
Peter Kolchin, *American Slavery, 1619–1877* (1993).
Elise Lemire, *"Miscegenation": Making Race in America* (2002).
George P. Rawick, ed., *The American Slave: A Composite Autobiography*, 41 vols. (1972–1979).
Willie Lee Rose, ed., *A Documentary History of Slavery in North America* (1976).
Kenneth M. Stampp, *The Peculiar Institution: Slavery in the Antebellum South* (1956).
Sterling Stuckey, *Slave Culture: Nationalist Theory and the Foundations of Black America* (1987).

IMPORTANT ASPECTS OF SLAVERY

Wilma A. Dunaway, *The African-American Family in Slavery and Emancipation* (2002).
Sharla M. Fett, *Working Cures: Healing, Health, and Power on Southern Slave Plantations* (2002).
John Hope Franklin and Loren Schweninger, *Runaway Slaves: Rebels on the Plantation* (1999).
David Barry Gaspar and Darlene Clark Hine, eds., *More Than Chattel: Black Women and Slavery in the Americas* (1996).
Eugene D. Genovese, *From Rebellion to Revolution: Afro-American Slave Revolts in the Making of the Modern World* (1979).
Kenneth S. Greenberg, ed., *Nat Turner: A Slave Rebellion in History and Memory* (2002).
Herbert G. Gutman, *The Black Family in Slavery and Freedom, 1750–1925* (1976).
Walter Johnson, *Soul by Soul: Life inside the Antebellum Slave Market* (1999).
Ann Patton Malone, *Sweet Chariot: Slavery, Family, and Household Structure in Nineteenth-Century Louisiana* (1992).
Thomas D. Morris, *Southern Slavery and the Law, 1619–1860* (1996).
Dylan C. Penningroth, *The Claims of Kinfolk: African American Property and Community in the Nineteenth-Century South* (2003).
Albert J. Raboteau, *Slave Religion: The "Invisible Institution" in the Antebellum South* (1978).
Judith Kelleher Schafer, *Becoming Free, Remaining Free: Manumission and Enslavement in New Orleans, 1846–1862* (2002).
Marie Jenkins Schwartz, *Born in Bondage: Growing Up Enslaved in the Antebellum South* (2000).
Brenda E. Stevenson, *Life in Black and White: Family and Community in the Slave South* (1996).
William L. Van Deburg, *The Slave Drivers: Black Agricultural Labor Supervisors in the Antebellum South* (1979).
Richard C. Wade, *Slavery in the Cities: The South, 1820–1860* (1964).
Deborah G. White, *Ar'n't I a Woman? Female Slaves in the Plantation South* (1985).

STATE AND LOCAL STUDIES

Edward E. Baptist, *Creating an Old South: Middle Florida's Plantation Frontier before the Civil War* (2002).

Randolph B. Campbell, *An Empire for Slavery: The Peculiar Institution in Texas, 1821–1865* (1989).

Margaret W. Creel, *"A Peculiar People": Slave Religion and Community-Culture among the Gullahs* (1988).

Charles B. Dew, *Bond of Iron: Master and Slave at Buffalo Forge* (1994).

Barbara J. Fields, *Slavery and Freedom on the Middle Ground: Maryland during the Nineteenth Century* (1985).

John C. Inscoe, *Mountain Masters, Slavery, and the Sectional Crisis in Western North Carolina* (1989).

Charles W. Joyner, *Down by the Riverside: A South Carolina Slave Community* (1984).

Melton A. McLaurin, *Celia, a Slave* (1991).

SOCIETY AND CULTURE

Edward L. Ayers, *Vengeance and Justice: Crime and Punishment in the Nineteenth-Century American South* (1984).

Peter W. Bardaglio, *Reconstructing the Household: Families, Sex, and the Law in the Nineteenth-Century South* (1995).

Ira Berlin, *Slaves without Masters: The Free Negro in the Antebellum South* (1974).

Charles C. Bolton and Scott P. Culclasure, eds., *The Confessions of Edward Isham: A Poor White Life of the Old South* (1998).

Orville Vernon Burton, *In My Father's House Are Many Mansions: Family and Community in Edgefield, South Carolina* (1985).

Victoria E. Bynum, *Unruly Women: The Politics of Social and Sexual Control in the Old South* (1992).

Bruce Collins, *White Society in the Antebellum South* (1985).

John Patrick Daly, *When Slavery Was Called Freedom: Evangelicalism, Proslavery, and the Causes of the Civil War* (2002).

Susanna Delfino and Michele Gillespie, eds., *Neither Lady nor Slave: Working Women of the Old South* (2002).

Neil Foley, *The White Scourge: Mexicans, Blacks, and Poor Whites in Texas Cotton Culture* (1997).

Sally E. Hadden, *Slave Patrols: Law and Violence in Virginia and the Carolinas* (2001).

Steven Hahn, *The Roots of Southern Populism: Yeoman Farmers and the Transformation of the Georgia Upcountry, 1850–1890* (1983).

J. William Harris, *Plain Folk and Gentry in a Slave Society: White Liberty and Black Slavery in Augusta's Hinterlands* (1985).

Christine Leigh Heyrman, *Southern Cross: The Beginnings of the Bible Belt* (1997).

Samuel C. Hyde Jr., ed., *Plain Folk of the South Revisited* (1997).

Michael P. Johnson and James L. Roark, *Black Masters: A Free Family of Color in the Old South* (1984).

Robert C. Kenser, *Kinship and Neighborhood in a Southern Community: Orange County, North Carolina, 1849–1881* (1987).

Suzanne Lebsock, *The Free Women of Petersburg: Status and Culture in a Southern Town, 1784–1860* (1984).

Stephanie McCurry, *Masters of Small Worlds: Yeoman Households, Gender Relations, and the Political Culture of the Antebellum South Carolina Low Country* (1995).

Christopher Morris, *Becoming Southern: The Evolution of a Way of Life, Warren County and Vicksburg, Mississippi, 1770–1860* (1995).

John Solomon Otto, *The Southern Frontiers, 1607–1860* (1989).

Christopher H. Owen, *The Sacred Flame of Love: Methodism and Society in Nineteenth-Century Georgia* (1998).

Nicolas W. Proctor, *Bathed in Blood: Hunting and Mastery in the Old South* (2002).

Mark M. Smith, *Mastered by the Clock: Time, Slavery, and Freedom in the American South* (1997).

Mitchell Snay, *Gospel of Disunion: Religion and Separatism in the Antebellum South* (1993).

Randy J. Sparks, *On Jordan's Stormy Banks: Evangelicalism in Mississippi, 1773–1876* (1994).

Christopher Waldrep, *Roots of Disorder: Race and Criminal Justice in the American South, 1817–80* (1998).

Bertram Wyatt-Brown, *Southern Honor: Ethics and Behavior in the Old South* (1982).

POLITICS AND POLITICAL CULTURE

Anthony Gene Carey, *Parties, Slavery, and the Union in Antebellum Georgia* (1997).

William J. Cooper Jr., *Liberty and Slavery: Southern Politics to 1860* (1983).

Lacy K. Ford Jr., *Origins of Southern Radicalism: The South Carolina Upcountry, 1800–1860* (1988).

Robert E. May, *John A. Quitman: Old South Crusader* (1985).

John N. Sacher, *A Perfect War of Politics: Parties, Politicians, and Democracy in Louisiana, 1824–1861* (2003).

Craig M. Simpson, *A Good Southerner: The Life of Henry A. Wise of Virginia* (1985).

J. Mills Thornton III, *Politics and Power in a Slave Society: Alabama, 1800–1860* (1978).

Elizabeth R. Varon, *We Mean to Be Counted: White Women and Politics in Antebellum Virginia* (1998).

Peter Wallenstein, *From the Slave South to New South: Public Policy in Nineteenth-Century Georgia* (1987).

Ralph A. Wooster, *The People in Power: Courthouse and Statehouse in the Lower South, 1850–1860* (1969).

Ralph A. Wooster, *Politicians, Planters, and Plain Folks: Courthouse and Statehouse in the Upper South, 1850–1860* (1975).

JOHN BROWN'S PIKES
Scorning what he called "milk-and-water" abolitionists who only talked about slavery, John Brown favored "action!" In 1859 when he brought his abolitionist war to Virginia, he carried with him 950 pikes, handsome but deadly spears made by a Connecticut blacksmith, which he expected to put into the hands of rebelling slaves. Bloody pikes, he thought, would end slavery in America. After Brown's failure at Harpers Ferry, townspeople sold many of the weapons as souvenirs.
Chicago Historical Society.

The House Divided

1846–1861

Other than twenty children, John Brown did not have much to show for his life in 1859. Grizzled, gnarled, and fifty-nine years old, he had for decades lived like a nomad, hauling his large family back and forth across six states as he tried desperately to better himself. He turned his hand to farming, raising sheep, running a tannery, and selling wool, but failure followed failure. The world had given John Brown some hard licks, but it had not budged his conviction that slavery was wrong and ought to be destroyed. He had learned to hate slavery at his father's knee, and in the wake of the fighting that erupted over the issue in Kansas in the 1850s, his beliefs turned violent. On May 24, 1856, he led an eight-man antislavery posse in the midnight slaughter of five allegedly proslavery men at Pottawatomie, Kansas. He told Mahala Doyle, whose husband and two oldest sons he killed, that if a man stood between him and what he thought right, he would take that man's life as calmly as he would eat breakfast.

After the killings, Brown slipped out of Kansas and reemerged in the East. More than ever, he was a man on fire for abolition. He spent thirty months begging money from New England abolitionists to support his vague plan for military operations against slavery. He captivated the genteel easterners, particularly the Boston elite. They were awed by his iron-willed determination and courage, but most could not accept violence. "These men are all talk," Brown declared. "What is needed is action—action!" But the hypnotic-eyed Brown convinced a handful that God had touched him for a great purpose, and they donated enough for him to gather a small band of antislavery warriors.

On the night of October 16, 1859, John Brown took his war against slavery into the South. With only twenty-one men, including five African Americans, he invaded Harpers Ferry, Virginia. His band quickly seized the town's armory and rifle works, but the invaders were immediately surrounded, first by local militia and then by Colonel Robert E. Lee, who commanded the U.S. troops in the area. When Brown refused to surrender, federal soldiers charged with bayonets. Seventeen men, two of whom were slaves, lost their lives. Although a few of Brown's raiders escaped, federal forces killed ten (including two of his sons) and captured seven, among them Brown.

"When I strike, the bees will begin to swarm," Brown told Frederick Douglass a few months before the raid. As slaves rushed to Harpers Ferry, Brown planned to arm them with the pikes he carried with him and with weapons stolen from the armory. They would then fight a war of liberation. Brown, however, neglected to inform the slaves that he had arrived in Harpers Ferry, and the few who knew of his arrival wanted nothing to do

John Brown
In this 1859 photograph, John Brown appears respectable, even statesmanlike, but contemporaries debated his mental state and moral character, and the debate has raged ever since. Critics argue that he was a bloody terrorist, a religious fanatic who believed that he was touched by God for a great purpose, one for which he was willing to die. Admirers see a resolute and selfless hero, a rare white man who believed that black people were the equals of whites, a reformer who recognized that moral suasion would not end slavery in America.
National Portrait Gallery, Smithsonian Institution/Art Resource, NY.

with his enterprise. "It was not a slave insurrection," Abraham Lincoln observed. "It was an attempt by white men to get up a revolt among slaves, in which the slaves refused to participate. In fact, it was so absurd that the slaves, with all their ignorance, saw plainly enough it could not succeed."

Although Brown's raid ended in utter defeat, white Southerners viewed it as proof of their growing suspicion that Northerners actively sought to incite slaves in bloody rebellion. For more than a decade, Northerners and Southerners had accused one another of hostile intentions, and by 1859, emotions were raw. Sectional tension was as old as the United States, but hostility had escalated to unprecedented heights with the outbreak of war with Mexico in May 1846, provoked by President Polk's desire to add northern Mexican lands to U.S. territory in the West (see chapter 12). Only three months after the war began, national expansion and the slavery issue intersected when Representative David Wilmot introduced a bill to prohibit slavery from any territory that might be acquired as a result of the war. After that, the problem of slavery in the territories became the principal wedge that divided the nation.

"Mexico is to us the forbidden fruit," South Carolina senator John C. Calhoun declared at the war's outset. "The penalty of eating it [is] to subject our institutions to political death." For a decade and a half, the slavery issue intertwined with the fate of former Mexican land, poisoning

national political debate. Slavery proved powerful enough to transform party politics into sectional politics. Rather than Whigs and Democrats confronting one another across party lines, Northerners and Southerners eyed one another hostilely across the Mason-Dixon line. Sectional politics encouraged the South's separatist impulses. A fitful tendency before the Mexican War, southern separatism gained strength with each confrontation. As the nation lurched from crisis to crisis, southern disaffection and alienation mounted, and support for compromise and conciliation eroded. The era began with a crisis of Union and ended with the Union in even graver peril. As Abraham Lincoln predicted in 1858, "A house divided against itself cannot stand."

The Bitter Fruits of War

Between 1846 and 1848, the nation grew by 1.2 million square miles, an incredible two-thirds. By 1850, the gold rush had transformed the sleepy **frontier** of California into a booming, thriving economy (see chapter 12). The 1850s witnessed new "rushes," for gold in Colorado and silver in Nevada's Comstock Lode. Hundreds of thou-

Vischer's Views of California
This illustrated title page from *Vischer's Views of California*, a book intended for curious Easterners, dramatizes (and exaggerates) the gargantuan size of California's redwoods by portraying microscopic individuals walking on the stump of a cut tree. Some Easterners were awed by nature's bounty in the West; others calculated the board feet in a single tree. Images such as this inspired hundred of thousands of individuals to dream of life in the West.
Yale Collection of American Literature, Beinecke Rare Book Room and Manuscript Library, Yale University.

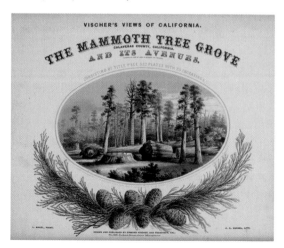

sands of people from around the world flocked west, particularly to the Pacific Slope, where they produced a vibrant agriculture as well as tons of gold and silver. The phenomenal dynamism of the West demanded the attention of the federal government. It quickly became clear that Northerners and Southerners had very different visions of the West, particularly the place of slavery in its future. As slavery in the western territories became the preeminent issue in national politics, Americans came to understand that the nation's fate rested on finding a solution.

Congress had faced the question of slavery in the national territories before the Mexican-American War, but history provided contradictory precedents. In 1787, Congress passed the Northwest Ordinance, which banned slavery in territory north of the Ohio River. In 1803, when the United States acquired the Louisiana Territory, where slavery was already legal, Congress allowed slavery to remain. As part of the Missouri Compromise of 1820, Congress voted to prohibit slavery in part of the territory and allow it in the rest. In 1846, when it appeared that the war with Mexico would mean new territory for the United States, politicians put on the table a variety of different plans; but when the war ended in 1848, Congress had made no headway in solving the great issue of slavery in the western territories. In 1850, after four years of strife, Congress patched together a settlement, one that Americans hoped would be permanent.

The Wilmot Proviso and the Expansion of Slavery

In the years leading up to the Civil War, Americans focused not on slavery where it existed but on the possibility that slavery might expand into areas where it did not exist. Except for a few abolitionists who strove to uproot slavery wherever they found it, most Americans agreed that the Constitution had left the issue of slavery to the individual states to decide. Northern states had done away with slavery, while southern states had retained it. But what about slavery in the nation's territories? The Constitution stated that "Congress shall have power to . . . make all needful rules and regulations respecting the territory . . . belonging to the United States." The debate between North and South about slavery, then, turned toward Congress and the definition of its authority over western lands.

The spark for the national debate was provided in August 1846 by a young Democratic

representative from Pennsylvania, David Wilmot, who proposed that Congress bar slavery from all lands acquired in the war with Mexico. Wilmot explained that the Mexicans had already abolished slavery in their country, adding, "God forbid that we should be the means of planting this institution upon it."

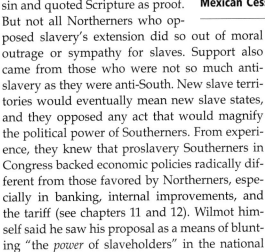

Mexican Cession, 1848

Regardless of party affiliation, Northerners lined up behind Wilmot's effort to stop the spread of slavery. Some supported **free soil**, by which they meant territory from which slavery would be prohibited, on the basis of principle. They denounced slavery as a sin and quoted Scripture as proof. But not all Northerners who opposed slavery's extension did so out of moral outrage or sympathy for slaves. Support also came from those who were not so much anti-slavery as they were anti-South. New slave territories would eventually mean new slave states, and they opposed any act that would magnify the political power of Southerners. From experience, they knew that proslavery Southerners in Congress backed economic policies radically different from those favored by Northerners, especially in banking, internal improvements, and the tariff (see chapters 11 and 12). Wilmot himself said he saw his proposal as a means of blunting "the *power* of slaveholders" in the national government.

Further support for "free soil" came from Northerners who were hostile to African Americans and wanted to reserve new lands for whites. Wilmot understood what one Indiana man put bluntly: "The American people are emphatically a *Negro-hating* people." Wilmot himself had blatantly encouraged racist support when he declared, "I would preserve for free white labor a fair country, a rich inheritance, where the sons of toil, of my own race and own color, can live without the disgrace which association with negro slavery brings upon free labor." It is no wonder that some called the Wilmot Proviso the White Man's Proviso.

While the specter of new slave territory alarmed most Northerners, the thought that slavery might be excluded outraged almost all white Southerners. **Yeoman** and **planter** alike regarded the West as a ladder for economic and social opportunity. In addition, they agreed that the exclusion of slavery was a slap in the face. An Alabaman observed that at least half of the American soldiers in Mexico were Southerners. "When the war-worn soldier returns home," he asked, "is he to be told that he cannot carry his property to the country won by his blood?"

Southern leaders also approached the territorial issue with an eye on political clout. They understood the need for political parity with the North to protect the South's interests, especially slavery. The need never seemed more urgent than in the 1840s, when the North's population and wealth were booming. James Henry Hammond of South Carolina predicted that ten new states would be carved from the acquired Mexican land. If free soil won, the North would "ride over us rough shod" in Congress, he claimed. "Our only safety is in *equality* of POWER."

In the nation's capital, the two sides squared off. Because Northerners had a majority in the House, they easily passed the Wilmot Proviso over the united opposition of Southerners. In the Senate, John C. Calhoun of South Carolina denied that Congress had constitutional authority to exclude slavery from the nation's territories. He argued in 1847 that the territories were the "joint and common property" of all the states, that Congress could not justly deprive any state of equal rights in the territories, and that Congress therefore could not bar citizens of one state from migrating with their property (including slaves) to the territories. Whereas Wilmot demanded that Congress slam shut the door to slavery, Calhoun called on Congress to hold the door wide open. Because slave states in the Senate outnumbered free states fifteen to fourteen, southern senators successfully stopped the proviso.

Senator Lewis Cass of Michigan offered a compromise between these extremes. He proposed the doctrine of **popular sovereignty**, by which he meant letting the people who actually settled the territories decide for themselves slavery's fate. This solution, Cass argued, sat squarely in the American tradition of **democracy** and local self-government. It had the added attraction of removing the incendiary issue of the expansion of slavery from the nation's capital and lodging it in distant, sleepy territorial legislatures, where it would excite fewer passions.

The plan's most attractive feature was its ambiguity about the precise moment when settlers could determine slavery's fate. Northern advocates believed that the decision on slavery could be made as soon as the first territorial legislature assembled. With free-soil majorities likely because of the North's greater population, they would shut the door to slavery almost before the first slave arrived. Southern supporters declared that popular sovereignty guaranteed that slavery would be unrestricted throughout the entire settlement period. Only at the very end, when settlers in the territory drew up a constitution and applied for statehood, could they decide the issue of slavery or freedom. By then, slavery would have sunk deep roots. As long as the matter of timing remained vague, popular sovereignty provided some Northerners and some Southerners with common ground.

When Congress ended its session in 1848, no plan had won a majority in both houses. Northerners who demanded no new slave territory anywhere, ever, and Southerners who demanded free entry for their slave property into all territories, or else, staked out their extreme positions. Unresolved in Congress, the territorial question naturally became an issue in the presidential election of 1848.

The Election of 1848

The Democratic and Whig parties were both hurting in 1848. The territorial debate revealed free-soil factions in both parties. Antislavery northern Democrats challenged Democratic President Polk and the dominant southern element of their party. Northern Whigs split between an antislavery group called Conscience Whigs and a more **conservative** group called Cotton Whigs (many of them were textile mill owners), who sought compromise to hold the party together. Conscience Whigs denounced the evil alliance of northern "lords of the loom" and southern "lords of the lash" and threatened to bolt the party.

When President Polk—worn out, ailing, and unable to unite the Democratic Party—chose not to seek reelection, the Democratic convention nominated Lewis Cass of Michigan, the man most closely associated with popular sovereignty. But, in an effort to keep peace between the proslavery and antislavery factions within the party, the Democrats adopted a platform that avoided a firm position on slavery in the territories. The Whigs followed a different strategy in their effort to patch the fissure within their party over slavery. They nominated a Mexican War hero, General Zachary Taylor. The Whigs bet that the combination of a military hero and total silence on the central issue facing the country would carry the day, so they declined to adopt a

General Taylor Cigar Case
This papier-mâché cigar case portrays General Zachary Taylor, Whig presidential candidate in 1848, in a colorful scene from the Mexican War. Shown here as a dashing, elegant officer, Taylor was in fact a short, thickset, and roughly dressed Indian fighter who had spent his career commanding small frontier garrisons. The inscription reminds voters that Taylor was a victor in the first four battles fought in the war and directs attention away from the fact that in politics he was a rank amateur.
Collection of Janice L. and David J. Frent.

party platform. Taylor, who owned more than 100 slaves on plantations in Mississippi and Louisiana, was hailed by Georgia politician Robert Toombs as a "Southern man, a slaveholder, a cotton planter."

Antislavery Whigs balked and looked for an alternative. The time seemed ripe for a major political realignment. Senator Charles Sumner called for "one grand Northern party of Freedom," and in the summer of 1848 antislavery Whigs and antislavery Democrats founded the Free-Soil Party. Nearly 15,000 noisy Free-Soilers gathered in Buffalo, New York, where they  welded the factions together by nominating a Democrat, Martin Van Buren, for president and a Whig, Charles Francis Adams, for vice president. The platform boldly proclaimed, "Free soil, free speech, free labor, and free men."

The November election dashed the hopes of the Free-Soilers. Although they succeeded in making slavery the campaign's central issue, they did not carry a single state. The major parties went through contortions to present their candidates favorably in both North and South, and their evasions succeeded. As one disappointed Free-Soiler observed: "During the last Presidential canvas, it was hard to find in the free States an opponent of slavery prohibition." Taylor won the all-important electoral vote, 163 to 127, carrying eight of the fifteen slave states and seven of the fifteen free states (Map 14.1). (Wisconsin had entered the Union earlier in 1848 as the fifteenth free state.) Northern voters proved they were not yet ready for Sumner's "one grand Northern party of Freedom," but the struggle over slavery in the territories had shaken the major parties badly.

Debate and Compromise

Zachary Taylor entered the White House in March 1849 and almost immediately shocked the nation. The slaveholding Southerner championed a free-soil solution to the problem of western land. The discovery of gold and the rush of 1849 made the existing military rule of California and New Mexico pitifully inadequate and the need for competent civil government urgent. Believing that he could avoid further sectional strife if California and New Mexico skipped the territorial stage, he sent agents west to persuade the settlers to frame constitutions and apply for admission to the Union as states. Predominately antislavery, the settlers began writing free-state constitutions. "For the first time," Mississippian Jefferson Davis lamented, "we are about permanently to destroy the balance of power between the sections."

MAP 14.1 The Election of 1848

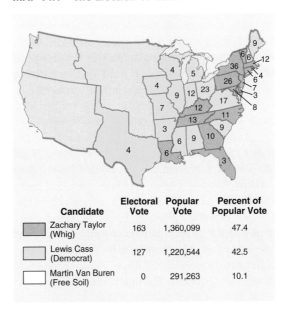

Candidate	Electoral Vote	Popular Vote	Percent of Popular Vote
Zachary Taylor (Whig)	163	1,360,099	47.4
Lewis Cass (Democrat)	127	1,220,544	42.5
Martin Van Buren (Free Soil)	0	291,263	10.1

When Congress convened in December 1849, anxious citizens packed the galleries, eager for the "Great Debate." They witnessed what proved to be one of the longest, most contentious, and most significant sessions in the history of Congress.

When Congress convened in December 1849, anxious citizens packed the galleries, eager for the "Great Debate." They witnessed what proved to be one of the longest, most contentious, and most significant sessions in the history of Congress. Foremost was the territorial issue. President Taylor urged Congress to admit California as a free state immediately and to admit New Mexico, which lagged behind a few months, as soon as it applied. Southerners exploded. In their eyes, Taylor had betrayed his region. Southerners who would "consent to be thus degraded and enslaved," a North Carolinian declared, "ought to be whipped through their fields by their own negroes."

Into this rancorous scene stepped Henry Clay, recently returned to the Senate by his home state of Kentucky. His reputation preceded him: the "Great Pacificator," master of accommodation, architect of Union-saving compromises in the Missouri and **nullification** crises. "Mr. President," Clay declared when he took the floor on January 29, 1850, "I hold in my hand a series of resolutions which I desire to submit to the consideration of this body. Taken together, in combination, they propose an amicable arrangement of all questions in controversy between the free and slave states, growing out of the subject of slavery." Clay's comprehensive plan sought to balance the interests of the slave and free states. Admit California as a free state, he proposed, but organize the rest of the Southwest without restrictions on slavery. Require Texas to abandon its claim to parts of New Mexico, but compensate it by assuming its preannexation debt. Abolish the domestic slave trade in Washington, D.C., but confirm slavery itself in the nation's capital. Reassert Congress's lack of authority to interfere with the interstate slave trade. And enact a more effective fugitive slave law.

Antislavery advocates and "fire-eaters" (as radical Southerners who urged secession from the Union were called) savaged Clay's plan. Senator Salmon Chase of Ohio ridiculed it as "sentiment for the North, substance for the South." Senator Henry S. Foote of Mississippi denounced it as more offensive to the South than the speeches of abolitionists William Lloyd Garrison, Wendell Phillips, and Frederick Douglass combined. The most ominous response came from Calhoun, who rose from his sickbed to charge that unending northern agitation on the slavery question had "snapped" many of the "cords which bind these states together in one common Union . . . and has greatly weakened all the others." Calhoun argued that the fragile political unity of North and South depended on continued equal representation in the Senate, which Clay's plan for a free California destroyed. "As things now stand," he said in February 1850, the South "cannot with safety remain in the Union."

After Clay and Calhoun had spoken, it was time for the third member of the "great triumvirate," Senator Daniel Webster of Massachusetts, to address the Senate. Like Clay, Webster sought to build a constituency for compromise. Admitting that the South had complaints that required attention, he argued forcefully that secession from the Union would mean civil war.

John C. Calhoun
Hollow-cheeked and dark-eyed in this 1850 daguerreotype by Mathew Brady, Calhoun had only months to live. Still, his passion and indomitable will come through. British writer Harriet Martineau once described the champion of southern rights as "the cast-iron man who looks as if he had never been born and could never be extinguished."
National Portrait Gallery, Smithsonian Institution/Art Resource, NY.

He appealed for an end to reckless proposals and, to the dismay of many Northerners, mentioned by name the Wilmot Proviso. A legal ban on slavery in the territories was unnecessary, he said, because the harsh climate effectively prohibited the expansion of cotton and slaves into the new American Southwest.

Free-soil forces recoiled from what they saw as Webster's desertion. In Boston, the clergyman and abolitionist Theodore Parker could only conclude that "the Southern men" must have offered Webster the presidency. In Washington, Senator William H. Seward of New York responded that Webster's and Clay's compromise with slavery was "radically wrong and essentially vicious." He flatly rejected Calhoun's argument that Congress lacked constitutional authority to exclude slavery from the territories. In any case, Seward said, in the most sensational moment in his address, there was a "higher law than the Constitution"—the law of God—to ensure freedom in all the public domain. Claiming that God was a Free-Soiler did nothing to cool the superheated atmosphere of Washington or to quiet rumblings across the nation.

In May, a Senate committee (with the tireless Clay at its head) reported a bill that joined Clay's resolutions into a single comprehensive package, known as the Omnibus Bill because it was a vehicle on which "every sort of passenger" could ride. Clay bet that a majority of Congress wanted compromise and that even though the omnibus contained items that individuals disliked, each would vote for the package to gain an overall settlement of sectional issues. But the omnibus strategy backfired. Free-Soilers and proslavery Southerners would support separate parts of Clay's bill, but they would not endorse the whole. After making seventy speeches to defend his plan, Clay saw it go down to defeat.

Fortunately for those who favored a settlement, Senator Stephen A. Douglas, a rising Democratic star from Illinois, stepped into Clay's shoes. Rejecting the omnibus strategy, he broke the bill into its various parts and skillfully ushered each through Congress. The agreement Douglas won in September 1850 was very much the one Clay had proposed in January. California entered the Union as a free state. New Mexico and Utah became territories in which the ques-

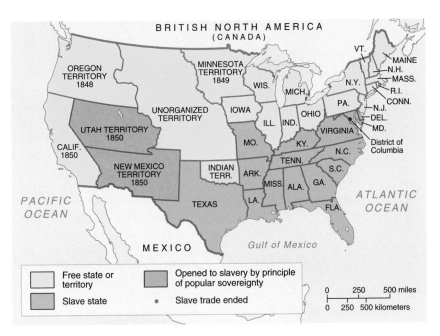

MAP 14.2 The Compromise of 1850
The patched-together sectional agreement was both clumsy and unstable. Few Americans— in either the North or South—supported all five parts of the Compromise.

tion of slavery would be decided by popular sovereignty. Texas accepted its present-day boundary with New Mexico and received $10 million from the federal government. Congress ended the slave trade in the District of Columbia but enacted a more stringent fugitive slave law. In September, Millard Fillmore, who had become president when Zachary Taylor died suddenly in July, signed each bill, collectively known as the Compromise of 1850, into law (Map 14.2; see also "The Promise of Technology," page 482).

Actually, the Compromise of 1850 was not a true compromise at all. Douglas's parliamentary skill, not a spirit of conciliation, led to legislative success. Only by nimbly allying a small group of true compromisers with larger blocs of Northerners and Southerners who voted along sectional lines did Douglas gain a majority for each separate measure. Still, the nation breathed a sigh of relief, for the Compromise preserved the Union and peace for the moment. Daniel Webster declared, "we have gone through the most important crisis that has occurred since the foundation of the Government." But others recognized that the Compromise scarcely touched the deeper conflict over slavery. Free-Soiler Salmon Chase correctly observed, "The question of slavery in the territories has been avoided. It has not been settled."

Daguerreotypes: The "Sunbeam Art"

Early in the nineteenth century, several Europeans working separately discovered that the shadow of an object falling on a chemically treated surface remained after the light source was removed. In the late 1830s, Frenchman Louis Daguerre learned how to keep the "shadow" from fading. News of Daguerre's success in fixing an image arrived in New York City in the spring of 1839.

As Americans found, photography was not for amateurs. The daguerreotype photographic process was cumbersome and messy. Initially, a photographer's equipment included a large wooden box, glass lens, copper plates coated with silver, vials of chemicals, and fire for heat. Because picture taking required several minutes of exposure, candid shots were impossible. To ease the strain of sitting immobile for so long while facing the camera, an American photographer invented a vise to clamp the sitter's head from behind. The process tested patience and often led to photographs that captured grimaces and pained scowls.

Despite their considerable shortcomings, daguerreotypes were an instant success. Samuel Morris, the first American to see a daguerreotype, exclaimed, "The exquisite minuteness of the delineation cannot be conceived. No painting or engraving ever approached it." Another awed observer declared that the daguerreotype was a "perfect transcript of the thing itself." The hyperrealism of the images spooked country people, some of whom suspected magic. But by the early 1840s, photography was a booming business. Itinerant photographers rode the rural and small-town circuit, while in the cities photographic galleries sprang up. In 1850, one observer declared, "In our great cities a Daguerreotypist is to be found in almost every square; and there is scarce a county in the states that has not one or more of those industrious individuals busy at work catching 'the shadow' ere the 'substance fade.'"

Ordinary citizens could not afford to have their portraits painted, and thus few working people owned personal likenesses. Compared to paintings, daguerreotypes were cheap, and at midcentury one reporter claimed that "it is hard to find a man who has not gone through the operator's hands from once to half-a-dozen times, or who has not the shadowy faces of his wife & children done up in purple morocco and velvet. . . . Truly the sunbeam art is a most wonderful one, and the public feel it a great benefit." In the 1850s, the rage for photographs meant that Americans were buying millions of images each year. The new technology met the needs of a culture undergoing vast and rapid change. People kept their precious daguerreotypes in safe places, thankful that this "camera magic" preserved families so often parted by distance or death.

No early American photographer was more important than Mathew Brady. In 1844, he opened the Daguerrean Miniature Gallery at Broadway and Fulton Street in New York City. He sought to bend photography from merely personal to political ends. Brady declared that "from the first, I regarded myself as under obligation to my country to preserve the faces of its historic men and mothers." Seeing himself as a kind of historian of the nation, he shot portraits of distinguished citizens—presidents, congressmen, senators, and statesmen—as well as everyday people who walked into his gallery. Likenesses of illustrious Americans reflected Brady's devotion to the country, and he hoped that they would inspire patriotism in others.

The Sectional Balance Undone

With the words "final settlement" still resounding through the halls of Congress like a magical phrase, the Compromise of 1850 began to come apart. The thread that unraveled the Compromise was not slavery in the Southwest, the crux of the original disagreement, but runaway slaves in New England, a part of the settlement that had previously received relatively little attention. Instead of restoring calm, the Compromise brought the horrors of slavery into the North.

The Palmer Family
Although sitters had to remain still for long periods, early masters of the daguerreotype managed to create memorable photographic portraits. This 1845 photograph by Marcus Aurelius Root is obviously posed and formal but is not painfully somber and stiff. Instead, it captures the conviviality of the family—the Palmers, Quaker abolitionists of Philadelphia—and reaches beyond mere likeness to delve into individual character and personality.
Wm. B. Becker Collection/American Museum of Photography.

Americans—twelve portraits of famous statesmen, including John C. Calhoun, Daniel Webster, and Henry Clay. Anxiety framed the project. At that moment, Washington was embroiled in bitter sectional controversy, and the United States stood on the brink of disintegration. Accurate, realistic images of eminent public men, Brady figured, would capture the "genius" of the nation and rally citizens to their beleaguered Republic. The *Gallery* was a nonpartisan, nonsectional gesture that sought to embrace Whigs and Democrats, Northerners and Southerners, and to urge them to overcome the disuniting elements in American life. The magic of daguerreotypes, Brady thought, would help bind citizens more directly, more personally to living statesmen and to the country they symbolized.

Technology, even technology married to art, could not save the nation. But such was the promise of early photography that some believed it might. Like Webster and Clay, the *Gallery* pleaded for compromise and national unity. Brady hoped that the new technology of photography would serve as a moral agent furthering political reconciliation and peace. By 1860, however, daguerreotypes had all but disappeared from American life, replaced by more efficient photographic processes, and the Union remained imperiled.

His elegant establishment was renowned as a meeting place where people of all classes mingled freely. "People used to stroll in there in those days," a writer remembered, "to see what new celebrity had been added to the little collection, and the last new portrait at Brady's was a standing topic of conversation."

In 1850, Brady sought to extend the public-spirited message of his photographs beyond his shop. He published *The Gallery of Illustrious*

Millions of Northerners who had never seen a runaway slave confronted slavery in the early 1850s. Harriet Beecher Stowe's *Uncle Tom's Cabin*, a novel that vividly depicted the brutality and heartlessness of the South's "peculiar institution," aroused passions so deep that many found goodwill toward white Southerners nearly impossible. But no popular uprising forced Congress to reopen the slavery controversy: Politicians did it themselves. Four years after Congress delicately stitched the sectional compromise together, it ripped the threads out. Once again it posed the question of slavery in the territories, the deadliest of all sectional issues.

The Fugitive Slave Act

The Fugitive Slave Act proved the most explosive of the Compromise measures. The issue of runaways was as old as the Constitution, which contained a provision for the return of any "person held to service or labor in one state" who escaped to another. In 1793, a federal law gave muscle to the provision by authorizing slave owners to enter other states to recapture their slave property. Proclaiming the 1793 law a license to kidnap free blacks, northern states in the 1830s began passing "personal liberty laws" that provided fugitives with some protection.

Some northern communities also formed vigilance committees to help runaways and to obstruct white Southerners who came north to reclaim them. Each year, a few hundred slaves escaped into free states and found friendly northern "conductors" who put them aboard the "underground railroad," which was not a railroad at all but a series of secret "stations" (hideouts) on the way to Canada. Harriet Tubman, an escaped slave from Maryland, returned to the South more than a dozen times and guided more than 300 slaves to freedom.

Furious about northern interference, Southerners in 1850 insisted on the stricter fugitive

The Modern Medea

In 1855, a slave family—Robert Garner, his twenty-two-year-old wife Margaret, their four children, and his parents—fled Kentucky. Archibald Gaines, Margaret's owner, tracked them to a cabin in Ohio. Thinking that all was lost and that her children would be returned to slavery, Margaret seized a butcher knife and cut the throat of her two-year-old daughter. She was turning on her other children when slave catchers burst in and captured her. Garner's child-murder electrified the nation. Abolitionists claimed that the act revealed the horror of slavery and the tragic heroism of slave mothers. Defenders of slavery argued that the deed proved that slaves were savages.

In 1867, Thomas Satterwhite Noble painted a defiant Margaret Garner standing over the bodies of two boys. Noble's departure from history was demanded by his allusion to Greek myth about Medea killing her two children to spite her husband. In 1988, Toni Morrison's novel *Beloved,* drawing on the Garner tragedy, was awarded a Pulitzer Prize.

Harper's Weekly, May 18, 1867/ Picture Research Consultants & Archives.

slave law that was passed as part of the Compromise. To seize an alleged slave, a slave-holder or his agent simply had to appear before a commissioner and swear that the runaway was his. The commissioner earned $10 for every black returned to slavery but only $5 for those set free. Most galling to Northerners, the law stipulated that all citizens were expected to assist officials in apprehending runaways.

Theodore Parker, the clergyman and aboli-tionist, denounced the law as "a hateful statute of kidnappers" and headed a Boston vigilance committee that openly violated it. In February 1851, an angry crowd overpowered federal mar-shals and snatched a runaway named Shadrach from a courtroom, put him on the underground railroad, and whisked him off to Montreal, Canada. Three years later when another Boston crowd rushed the courthouse in a failed attempt to rescue Anthony Burns, who had recently fled slavery in Richmond, a guard was shot dead. A judge sentenced Burns to be returned to slavery in Virginia. Martha Russell was among the angry crowd that observed him being escorted to the ship. "Did you ever feel every drop of blood in you boiling and seething, throbbing and burn-ing, until it seemed you should suffocate?" she asked. "I have felt all this today. I have seen that poor slave, Anthony Burns, carried back into slavery!"

To white Southerners, it seemed that fanatics of the "higher law" creed had whipped Northerners into a frenzy of massive resistance. Actually, the overwhelming majority of fugitives claimed before federal commissioners were reenslaved and shipped south peacefully. Spectacular rescues such as the one that saved Shadrach and tried to save Burns were rare. But brutal enforcement of the unpopular law had a radicalizing effect in the North, particularly in New England. And to Southerners it seemed that Northerners had betrayed the Compromise. "The continued existence of the United States as one nation," warned the *Southern Literary Messenger*, "depends upon the full and faithful execution of the Fugitive Slave Bill."

Uncle Tom's Cabin

The spectacle of shackled African Americans being herded south seared the conscience of every Northerner who witnessed such a scene. But even more Northerners were turned against slavery by a fictional account, a novel. Harriet Beecher Stowe, a Northerner who had never

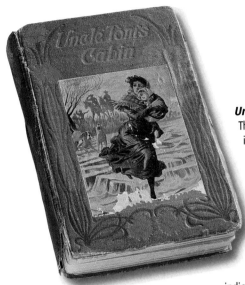

Uncle Tom's Cabin
The cover drawing on this early illustrated edition of Harriet Beecher Stowe's novel shows a runaway slave mother rac-ing across ice floes to es-cape dogs and slave catch-ers. During the 1850s, at least ten individuals, including Harriet Beecher Stowe herself, dramatized the novel. Stowe's moral indictment of slavery translated well to the stage. Scenes of Eliza crossing the ice with bloodhounds in pursuit, the cruelty of Simon Legree, and Little Eva borne to heaven on puffy clouds gripped the imagination of audiences in America and Britain and fueled the growing antislavery crusade.
Picture Research Consultants & Archives.

seen a plantation, made the South's slaves into flesh-and-blood human beings almost more real than life.

The daughter of evangelist Lyman Beecher and member of a famous clan of preachers, teachers, and reformers, Stowe despised the slave catchers and wrote to expose the sin of slavery. Serialized in a leading magazine in 1851 and then published as a book in 1852, *Uncle Tom's Cabin, or Life among the Lowly* became a blockbuster hit and sold 300,000 copies in its first year and more than 2 million copies within ten years. Her characters leaped from the page. Here was the gentle slave Uncle Tom, a Christian saint who forgave those who beat him to death; the courageous slave Eliza, who fled with her child across the frozen Ohio River; and the fiendish overseer Simon Legree, whose Louisiana planta-tion was a nightmare of torture and death. Herself the mother of seven children, Stowe aimed her most powerful blows at slavery's de-structive impact on the family. Her character Eliza succeeds in keeping her son from being sold away, but other mothers are not so fortu-nate. When told that her infant has been sold, Lucy drowns herself. Driven half mad by the sale of a son and daughter, Cassy decides "never again [to] let a child live to grow up!" She gives her third child an opiate and watches as "he slept to death."

Responses to *Uncle Tom's Cabin* depended on geography. What Northerners accepted as truth, Southerners denounced as slander.

Responses to *Uncle Tom's Cabin* depended on geography. In the North, common people and literary giants alike shed tears and sang its praises. The poet John Greenleaf Whittier sent "ten thousand thanks for thy immortal book"; the poet Henry Wadsworth Longfellow judged it "one of the greatest triumphs recorded in literary history." What Northerners accepted as truth, Southerners denounced as slander. Virginian George F. Holmes proclaimed Stowe a member of the "Woman's Rights" and "Higher Law" schools and dismissed the novel as a work of "intense fanaticism." Unfortunately, he said, this "maze of misinterpretation" had filled those who knew nothing about slavery "with hatred for that institution and those who uphold it." Although it is impossible to measure precisely the impact of a novel on public opinion, *Uncle Tom's Cabin* clearly helped to crystallize northern sentiment against slavery and to confirm white Southerners' suspicion that they no longer had any sympathy in the free states.

Other writers—ex-slaves who knew life in slave cabins firsthand—also produced stinging indictments of slavery. Solomon Northup's compelling *Twelve Years a Slave* (1853) sold 27,000 copies in two years, and the powerful *Narrative of the Life of Frederick Douglass, as Told by Himself* (1845) eventually sold more than 30,000 copies. But no work touched the North's conscience like the novel by the woman who had never set foot on a plantation. A decade after its publication, when Stowe visited Abraham Lincoln at the White House, he reportedly said, "So you are the little woman who wrote the book that made this great war."

The Kansas-Nebraska Act

As national elections approached in 1852, Democrats and Whigs sought to close the sectional rifts that had opened within their parties. For their presidential nominee, the Democrats turned to Franklin Pierce of New Hampshire. Pierce's most valuable asset was his well-known sympathy with southern views on public issues. His leanings caused northern critics to include

him among the "doughfaces," northern men malleable enough to champion southern causes. The Whigs were less successful in bridging differences. Adopting the formula that had proved successful in 1848, they chose another Mexican War hero, General Winfield Scott of Virginia. But the Whigs were hopelessly divided between their northern and southern factions and suffered a humiliating defeat. The Democrat Pierce carried twenty-seven states to Scott's four, 254 electoral votes to 42 (Table 14.1). In the afterglow of the Compromise of 1850, the Free-Soil Party lost almost half of the voters who had turned to it in the tumultuous atmosphere of 1848.

Eager to leave the sectional controversy behind, the new president turned swiftly to foreign expansion. **Manifest destiny** remained robust. (See "Beyond America's Borders," page 490.) Pierce's major objective was Cuba, which was owned by Spain and in which slavery flourished, but Pierce's clumsy diplomatic efforts galvanized antislavery Northerners, who blocked Cuba's acquisition to keep more slave territory from entering the Union. Pierce's fortunes improved in Mexico. In 1853, he sent diplomat James Gadsden to negotiate a $15 million purchase of some 30,000 square miles of territory south of the Gila River in present-day Arizona and New Mexico. The Gadsden Purchase stemmed from the dream of a transcontinental railroad to California and Pierce's desire for a southern route through Mexican territory. The booming population of the Pacific coast made it obvious that the vast, loose-jointed republic needed a railroad to bind it together. Talk of a railroad ignited rivalries in cities from New Orleans to Chicago as they maneuvered to become the eastern terminus. Thus, the desire for a transcontinental railroad evolved into a sectional contest, which by the 1850s inevitably involved slavery.

No one played the railroad game more enthusiastically than Illinois's Democratic senator Stephen A. Douglas, who was an energetic spokesman for western economic development. He badly wanted the transcontinental railroad for Chicago and his home state, and his chairmanship of the Senate Committee on Territories provided him with an opportunity. Any railroad that ran west from Chicago would pass through

Gadsden Purchase of 1853

a region that Congress in 1830 had designated a "permanent" Indian reserve. Douglas proposed giving this vast area between the Missouri River and the Rocky Mountains an Indian name, Nebraska, and then nullifying Indian titles and throwing the Indians out. Once the region achieved territorial status, whites could survey and sell the land, establish civil government, and build a railroad.

Congress's promise to the Indians did not cause Douglas to hesitate, but another of its promises did. Nebraska lay within the Louisiana Purchase north of latitude 36°30' and, according to the Missouri Compromise of 1820, was closed to slavery (see chapter 10). Since Douglas could not count on New England to back western economic development, he needed southern votes

TABLE 14.1	THE ELECTION OF 1852		
Candidate	Electoral Vote	Popular Vote	Percent of Popular Vote
Franklin Pierce (Democrat)	254	1,601,117	50.9
Winfield Scott (Whig)	42	1,385,453	44.1
John P. Hale (Free-Soil)	0	155,825	5.0

to pass his Nebraska legislation. But Southerners had no incentive to create another free territory or to help a northern city win the transcontinental railroad. Southerners, however, agreed to help organize Nebraska for a price: nothing less than repeal of the Missouri Compromise. Southerners insisted that Congress organize Nebraska according to popular sovereignty. That meant giving slavery a chance in the Nebraska Territory and reopening the dangerous issue of slavery expansion, which Douglas himself had so ably helped to resolve only four years earlier.

In January 1854, Douglas introduced his bill to organize the Nebraska Territory, leaving to the settlers themselves the decision about slavery. At southern insistence, and even though he knew it would "raise a hell of a storm," Douglas added an explicit repeal of the Missouri Compromise. Indeed, the Nebraska bill raised a storm of controversy. Free-Soilers branded Douglas's plan "a gross violation of a sacred pledge" and an "atrocious plot" to transform free land into a "dreary region of despotism, inhabited by masters and slaves."

Undaunted, Douglas skillfully shepherded the explosive bill through Congress in May 1854. Nine-tenths of all southern members (Whigs and Democrats) and half of the northern Democrats cast votes in favor. Like Douglas, most northern Democrats believed that popular sovereignty would make Nebraska free territory. Ominously, however, half of the northern Democrats broke with their party and opposed the bill. In its final form, the Kansas-Nebraska Act divided the huge territory in two: Nebraska west of the free state of Iowa and Kansas west of the slave state of Missouri (Map 14.3). With this act, the government pushed the Plains Indians farther west, making way for railroads and farmers.

Papago Indians

Major William Emory's Mexican boundary survey of the early 1850s provided Americans with glimpses of a little-known southwestern frontier. In this drawing, Papago Indian women in Arizona Territory use sticks to knock down cactus fruit.

The Center for American History, The University of Texas at Austin.

MAP 14.3   The Kansas-Nebraska Act, 1854
Americans hardly thought twice about dispossessing the Indians of lands guaranteed them by treaty, but many worried about the outcome of repealing the Missouri Compromise and opening up lands to slavery.

READING THE MAP: How many slave states and how many free states does the map show? Estimate the percentage of territory likely to be settled by slaveholders.
CONNECTIONS: Who would be more likely to support changes in government legislation to discontinue the Missouri Compromise, slaveholders or free-soil advocates? Why?

FOR MORE HELP ANALYZING THIS MAP, see the map activity for this chapter in the Online Study Guide at bedfordstmartins.com/roark.

Realignment of the Party System

The Kansas-Nebraska Act marked a fateful escalation of the sectional conflict. Douglas's controversial measure had several consequences, none more crucial than the realignment of the nation's political parties. Since the rise of the Whigs in the early 1830s, Whigs and Democrats had organized and channeled political conflict in the nation. This party system dampened sectionalism and strengthened the Union. To achieve national political power, Whigs and Democrats had to retain strength in both North and South. Strong northern and southern wings required that each party compromise and find positions acceptable to both wings.

The Kansas-Nebraska controversy shattered this stabilizing political system. In place of two national parties with bisectional strength, the mid-1850s witnessed the development of one party heavily dominated by one section and another party entirely limited to the other section. Rather than "national" parties, the country had what one critic disdainfully called "geographic" parties. Parties now had the advantage of sharpening ideological and policy differences between the sections; they no longer muffled moral issues, like slavery. But the new party system also

thwarted political compromise and instead promoted political polarization and further jeopardized the Union.

The Old Parties: Whigs and Democrats

Distress signals could be heard from the Whig camp as early as the Mexican-American War, when members clashed over the future of slavery in annexed Mexican lands. But the disintegration of the party dated from 1849–1850, when southern Whigs watched in stunned amazement as Whig president Zachary Taylor sponsored a plan for a free California. Thereafter, Southerners left the party in droves. The slavery issue also confounded northern Whigs, but antislavery forces were clearly dominant in the North. By 1852, the Whig Party could please its southern wing or its northern wing but not both. The Whigs' miserable showing in the election of 1852 made clear that they were no longer a strong national party. By 1856, after more than two decades of contesting the Democrats, they were hardly a party at all (Map 14.4).

The decline and eventual collapse of the Whig Party left the Democrats as the country's only national party. Although the Democrats were not immune to the disruptive pressures of the territorial question, they discovered in

1846–1861

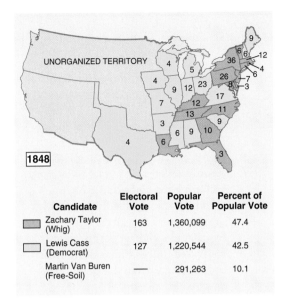

Candidate	Electoral Vote	Popular Vote	Percent of Popular Vote
Zachary Taylor (Whig)	163	1,360,099	47.4
Lewis Cass (Democrat)	127	1,220,544	42.5
Martin Van Buren (Free-Soil)	—	291,263	10.1

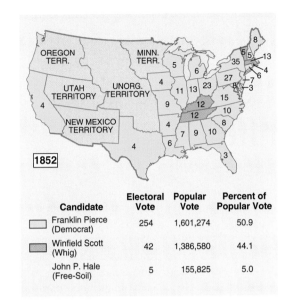

Candidate	Electoral Vote	Popular Vote	Percent of Popular Vote
Franklin Pierce (Democrat)	254	1,601,274	50.9
Winfield Scott (Whig)	42	1,386,580	44.1
John P. Hale (Free-Soil)	5	155,825	5.0

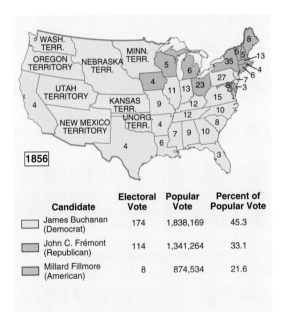

Candidate	Electoral Vote	Popular Vote	Percent of Popular Vote
James Buchanan (Democrat)	174	1,838,169	45.3
John C. Frémont (Republican)	114	1,341,264	33.1
Millard Fillmore (American)	8	874,534	21.6

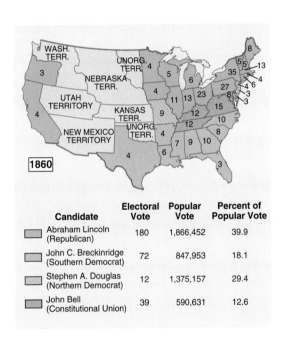

Candidate	Electoral Vote	Popular Vote	Percent of Popular Vote
Abraham Lincoln (Republican)	180	1,866,452	39.9
John C. Breckinridge (Southern Democrat)	72	847,953	18.1
Stephen A. Douglas (Northern Democrat)	12	1,375,157	29.4
John Bell (Constitutional Union)	39	590,631	12.6

MAP 14.4 Political Realignment, 1848–1860

In 1848, slavery and sectionalism began hammering the country's party system. The Whig Party was an early casualty. By 1860, national parties—those that contended for votes in both North and South—had been replaced by regional parties.

READING THE MAP: Which states did the Democrats pick up in the 1852 election over the previous election? Which of the states won in 1852 were lost to the Democrats in 1856? Describe the general geographical location of the states won by the Republicans in 1860 over the 1856 election.

CONNECTIONS: In the 1860 election, which party benefited the most from the addition of western and midwestern states added to the Union since 1848? Why would these states choose to back the Republicans over the Democrats?

FOR MORE HELP ANALYZING THIS MAP, see the map activity for this chapter in the Online Study Guide at bedfordstmartins.com/roark.

Filibusters: The Underside of Manifest Destiny

Each year the citizens of Caborca, Mexico, a small town in the northern state of Sonora, celebrate the defeat there in 1857 of an American army. The invaders did not wear the uniform of the U.S. army but marched as a private army, the "Arizona Colonization Company." Their commander, Henry A. Crabb, a Mississippian who followed the gold rush to California, saw fresh opportunity in the civil disorder that reigned south of the border. Fierce fighting between Mexicans and Apache and Yaqui Indians made life precarious in Sonora and prompted division among the Mexicans. When the governor of Sonora faced an insurrection, he invited Crabb, who was married to a Sonoran woman, to help him repress his enemies in exchange for mineral rights and land.

Crabb marched his band of sixty-eight heavily armed ex-miners south from Los Angeles into Mexico. But by the time the Americans arrived, the governor had put down the insurgency, and he turned on the invaders. Every American except one died either in battle or at the hands of Mexican firing squads. Crabb's head was preserved in alcohol and placed on display as a symbol of victory.

Henry Crabb was one of thousands of American adventurers, known as "filibusters" (from Spanish *filibustero*, meaning "freebooter" or "pirate"), who in the mid-nineteenth century joined private armies that invaded foreign countries in North America, Central America, South America, and the Caribbean. Although these expeditions were illegal and violated the U.S. Neutrality Act of 1818, private American armies attacked Canada, Mexico, Ecuador, Honduras, Cuba, and Nicaragua and planned invasions of places as far away as the Hawaiian kingdom. The federal government occasionally winked at the actions of filibusters, but more often it cracked down, fearful that private invasions would jeopardize legitimate diplomatic efforts to promote trade and acquire territory.

Filibusters joined invading armies for a variety of reasons ranging from personal gain to validating manhood. Many saw themselves as carrying on the work of manifest destiny, extending America's reach beyond Texas, California, and Oregon, the prizes of the 1830s and 1840s. In addition, during the 1840s and 1850s when Northerners grew increasingly intent on containing slavery's spread to the North and West, Southerners joined filibustering expeditions to expand slavery to the south beyond U.S. borders. Although filibusters came from all regions of the country, their greatest numbers and support came from the proslavery forces of the South. The leading proslavery ideologue, George Fitzhugh, sought to blunt criticism of filibustering by defending it through historical comparison: "They who condemn the modern filibuster, to be consistent, must also condemn the discoverers and settlers of America, of the East Indies of Holland, and of the Indian and Pacific Oceans." Such arguments, deeply rooted in manifest destiny, failed to convince many, including the ambassador from Costa Rica, who called filibustering America's "social cancer." Northerners claimed (with some justification) that filibustering was a southern campaign to extend "the empire of the lash."

One of the most vigorous filibusters to appeal to southern interests was not an American: Narciso Lopez was a Venezuelan-born Cuban who dedicated himself to the liberation of Cuba from Spanish rule. In his first attempt in 1849, he recruited an army of several hundred would-be liberators but got no farther than New York harbor, where U.S. marshals intercepted his fleet. Thereafter, he resolved to "rest his hopes on the men of the bold West and chivalric South." Lopez claimed that Spain was planning to free Cuba's slaves, and he told Southerners that "self-preservation" demanded that they seize the island. When Governor John Quitman of Mississippi joined his scheme, Lopez shifted his headquarters to New Orleans. Early in 1850, Lopez and an army of more than 500 landed on the northwest coast of Cuba, but Spanish troops quickly drove them off. Two months later, with 450 troops, he tried again. This time, the Spanish crushed the invasion, killing 200 filibusters, shipping 160 prisoners to Spain, executing 50 invaders by firing squad, and publicly garroting Lopez. John Quitman gathered another army of several thousand, but federal authorities seized one of his ships and ended the threat to Cuba.

Filibustering in Nicaragua

In this image of a pitched battle in Nicaragua in 1856, Costa Ricans on foot fight American filibusters on horseback. Costa Rican soldiers and their Central American allies defeated William Walker's *filibusteros* in 1857, but before then the Pierce administration had extended diplomatic recognition to Walker's regime, and white Southerners had cheered Walker's attempt to "introduce civilization" in Nicaragua and to develop its rich resources "with slave labor."

London Illustrated Times, May 24, 1856.

The most successful of all filibusters was William Walker of Tennessee, a restless dreamer who longed for an empire of his own south of the border. Walker cut his filibustering teeth with expeditions to Baja California and Sonora, but when they failed, he turned to Central America. He believed that Southerners paid too much attention to Kansas and that instead they should expand slavery in tropical America. In May 1855, Walker and an army of fifty-six men sailed from San Francisco to the west coast of Nicaragua. Two thousand reinforcements and a civil war in Nicaragua gave Walker his victory. He had himself proclaimed president, legalized slavery, and called on Southerners to come raise cotton, sugar, and coffee in "a magnificent country." Hundreds of Southerners took up **land grants**, but Walker's regime survived only until 1857, when a coalition of Central American countries allied with the Nicaraguans and sent Walker packing. Walker doggedly launched four other attacks on Nicaragua; then in 1860, Honduran forces captured and shot him.

Filibustering had lost steam by 1861, but the battle-hardened adventurers found new employment in the armies of the Civil War, particularly in the service of the Confederate military. The Confederacy paid a diplomatic price for its association with filibustering, however. The Guatemalan minister Antonio Jose de Irisarri declared that there was "no foreign Nation which can have less cause for sympathy with the enemies of the American Union, than the Republics of Central America, because from the Southern States were set on foot those filibustering expeditions." No Central American state recognized Confederate independence.

A century and more later, the peoples of Central America and the Caribbean, like the inhabitants of Sonora, harbor bitter memories of filibusters' private wars of **imperialism** and honor those who fought off American advances. When U.S. marines occupied Nicaragua in the 1920s, insurgents found inspiration in their country's defeat of William Walker's army of freebooters eighty years earlier. In 1951, on the centennial of Lopez's invasion, Cubans erected a monument at the very spot where his ill-fated army came ashore. Costa Ricans celebrate Juan Santamaria as their national martyr for his courage in battling William Walker. Memories of the invasions by nineteenth-century filibusters set the stage for anti-American sentiment in Latin America that lingers to this day.

BIBLIOGRAPHY

Charles H. Brown, *Agents of Manifest Destiny: The Lives and Times of the Filibusters* (1980).

John Hope Franklin, *The Militant South, 1800–1861* (1956).

Robert E. May, *The Southern Dream of a Caribbean Empire, 1854–1861* (1973).

Robert E. May, *Manifest Destiny's Underworld: Filibustering in Antebellum America* (2002).

Frank L. Owsley, *Filibusters and Expansionists: Jeffersonian Manifest Destiny, 1800–1821* (1997).

William Walker, *The War in Nicaragua* (1860).

popular sovereignty a doctrine that many Democrats could support. Even so, popular sovereignty very nearly undid the party as well. When Stephen Douglas applied the doctrine to the part of the Louisiana Purchase where slavery had been barred, he divided northern Democrats and destroyed the dominance of the Democratic Party in the free states. After 1854, the Democrats became a southern-dominated party.

Nevertheless, the Democrats, unlike the Whigs, remained a national political organization throughout the 1850s. Gains in the South more than balanced Democratic losses in the North. During the decade, Democrats elected two presidents and won majorities in Congress in almost every election. But holding on to national power required the party to maintain northern and southern wings, which in turn required the Democrats to avoid the issue of the expansion of slavery.

The breakup of the Whigs and the disaffection of significant numbers of northern Democrats set many Americans politically adrift. As they searched for new political harbors, Americans found that the death of the old party system created a multitude of fresh political alternatives. The question was which party would attract the drifters.

Know-Nothing Banner

Convinced that the incendiary issue of slavery had blinded Americans to the greater dangers of uncontrolled immigration and foreign influence, the Know-Nothing Party in 1856 ran Millard Fillmore for president. There is more than a little irony in this banner's appeal to "Native Americans" to stem the invasion from abroad. Know-Nothings meant native-born Americans, but bona fide Native Americans, American Indians, also faced an invasion and to them it made little difference whether the aggressors were fresh off the boat or born in the U.S.A.
Milwaukee County Historical Society.

The New Parties: Know-Nothings and Republicans

Dozens of new political organizations vied for voters' attention. Out of the confusion two emerged as true contenders. One grew out of the slavery controversy, a spontaneous coalition of indignant antislavery Northerners. The other arose from an entirely different split in American society, between Roman Catholic immigrants and native **Protestants**.

The tidal wave of immigrants that broke over America from 1845 to 1855 produced a nasty backlash among Protestant Americans, who believed that the American Republic was about to drown in a sea of Roman Catholics from Ireland and Germany (see Figure 12.1, page 425). The new arrivals encountered economic prejudice, ethnic hostility, and religious antagonism. Most immigrants who entered American politics became Democrats because they perceived that party as more tolerant of newcomers than were the Whigs. But in the 1850s they met sharp political opposition when **nativists** (individuals who were anti-immigrant) began to organize, first into secret fraternal societies and then into a political party. Recruits swore never to vote for either foreign-born or Roman Catholic candidates and not to reveal any information about the organization. When questioned, they said: "I know nothing." Officially, they were named the American Party, but most Americans called them Know-Nothings.

The Know-Nothings exploded onto the political stage in 1854 and 1855 with a series of dazzling successes. They captured state legislatures in the Northeast, West, and South and claimed dozens of seats in Congress. Their greatest triumph came in Massachusetts, a favorite destination for the Irish. Know-Nothings elected the Massachusetts governor, all of the state senators, all but two of the state representatives, and all of the congressmen. The American Party attracted both Democrats and Whigs, but with their party crumbling, more Whigs responded to the attraction. Members of both traditional parties described the phenomenal success of the Know-Nothings as a "tornado," a "hurricane," or "a freak of political insanity." By 1855, an observer might reasonably have concluded that the Know-Nothings had emerged as the successor to the Whigs.

Know-Nothings were not the only new party making noise. One of the new antislavery organizations provoked by the Kansas-Nebraska Act called itself Republican. Republicans attempted to unite under their banner all the dissidents and political orphans—Whigs, Free-Soilers, anti-Nebraska Democrats, even Know-Nothings—who opposed the extension of slavery into any territory of the United States.

The Republican creed tapped into the basic beliefs and values of the northern public. Slave labor and free labor, Republicans argued, had spawned two incompatible civilizations. In the South, slavery degraded the dignity of white labor by associating work with blacks and servility. Three-quarters of the South's white population, claimed one Republican, "retire to the outskirts of civilization, where they live a semi-savage life, sinking deeper and more hopelessly into barbarism with every succeeding generation." Republicans argued that slavery repressed every Southerner except planter aristocrats. They warned that those insatiable slave lords, whom antislavery Northerners called the "Slave Power"—were conspiring through their control of the Democratic Party to expand slavery, subvert liberty, and undermine the Constitution. Only if slavery were restricted to the South, Republicans believed, could the system of **free labor** flourish elsewhere. The ideal of free labor respected the dignity of work and provided anyone willing to toil an opportunity for a decent living and for advancement (see chapter 12).

In the North, one Republican declared in 1854, "every man holds his fortune in his own right arm; and his position in society, in life, is to be tested by his own individual character." Free of slavery, the western territories would provide vast economic opportunity for free men. These powerful images of **liberty** and free labor attracted a wide range of Northerners to the Republican cause.

The Election of 1856

By the mid-1850s, the Know-Nothings had emerged as the principal champions of nativism, the Republicans as the primary advocates of the antislavery position. But the election of 1856 revealed that the Republicans had become the Democrats' main challenger and slavery in the territories the election's only issue. The Know-Nothings came apart when party leaders insisted on a platform that endorsed the Kansas-Nebraska Act. Most Northerners walked out. The Know-Nothings who remained nominated ex-president Millard Fillmore.

The Republicans, in contrast, adopted a platform that focused almost exclusively on "making

The Realignment of Political Parties

Whig Party

1848 Whig Party divides into two factions over slavery; Whigs adopt no platform and nominate war hero Zachary Taylor, who is elected president.

1852 Whigs nominate war hero General Winfield Scott for president; deep divisions in party result in humiliating loss.

1856 Shattered by sectionalism, Whig Party fields no presidential candidate.

Democratic Party

1848 President Polk declines to run again. Democratic Party nominates Lewis Cass, the man most closely associated with popular sovereignty, but the party avoids firm platform position on expansion of slavery.

1852 To bridge the rift in the party, Democrats nominate a northern war veteran with southern views, Franklin Pierce, for president; he wins with 50.9 percent of popular vote.

1856 Democrat James Buchanan elected president on an ambiguous platform; his prosouthern actions in office alienate northern branch of the party.

1860 Democrats split into northern Democrats and southern Democrats, and each group fields its own presidential candidate.

Free-Soil Party

1848 Breakaway antislavery Democrats and antislavery Whigs found Free-Soil Party. Free-Soil presidential candidate takes 10.1 percent of popular vote, mainly from Whigs.

1852 Support for Free-Soil Party ebbs in wake of Compromise of 1850; Free-Soil presidential candidate wins only 5 percent of popular vote.

American (Know-Nothing) Party

1851 The anti-immigrant American (Know-Nothing) Party formed.

1854–1855 American Party succeeds in state elections and attracts votes from northern and southern Whigs in congressional elections.

1856 Know-Nothing presidential candidate wins only the state of Maryland and subsequently disbands.

Republican Party

1854 Republican Party formed to oppose the expansion of slavery in the territories; it attracts northern Whigs, northern Democrats, and Free-Soilers.

1856 Republican presidential candidate wins all but five of the northern states, establishing the Republicans as the main challenger to the Democrats.

1860 Republican Abraham Lincoln wins all of the northern states except New Jersey and is elected president in four-way race against the divided Democrats and the southern Constitutional Union Party.

every territory free." When they labeled slavery a "relic of barbarism," Republicans signaled that they had written off the South. For president, they nominated the dashing soldier and California adventurer John C. Frémont, "Pathfinder of the West." Frémont lacked political credentials, but political know-how resided in his wife, Jessie, who, as a daughter of Senator Thomas Hart Benton of Missouri, knew the political map as well as her husband knew western trails. Although careful to maintain a proper public image, the vivacious young mother and antislavery zealot helped draw ordinary women into electoral politics. (See "Documenting the American Promise," page 498.)

The Democrats, successful in 1852 in bridging sectional differences by nominating a northern man with southern principles, chose another "doughface," James Buchanan of Pennsylvania. The Democrats took refuge in the ambiguity of popular sovereignty and portrayed Republicans as extremists ("Black Republican Abolitionists") whose support for the Wilmot Proviso risked pushing the South out of the Union.

The Democratic strategy helped carry the day for Buchanan, but Frémont did astonishingly well. Buchanan won 174 electoral votes against Frémont's 114 and Fillmore's 8. Campaigning under the banner "Free soil, Free men, Fremont," the Republican carried all but five of the states north of the Mason-Dixon line. The election made clear that the Whigs had disintegrated, that the Know-Nothings would not ride nativism to national power, and that the Democrats were badly strained (see Map 14.4). But the big news was what the press called the "glorious defeat" of the Republicans. Despite being a brand-new party and purely sectional, Republicans seriously challenged other parties for national power. Sectionalism had fashioned a new party system, one that spelled danger for the Republic (Figure 14.1). Indeed, war had already broken out between proslavery and antislavery forces in distant Kansas Territory.

Freedom under Siege

The "glorious defeat" of the Republicans meant that the second party in the new two-party system was entirely sectional. Without a southern wing, the Republican Party had no need to compromise, to conciliate, to keep Southerners happy. Indeed, Republicans organized around the premise that the slaveholding South provided a profound threat to "free soil, free labor, and free men."

Events in Kansas Territory in the mid-1850s provided the young Republican organization with an enormous boost and help explain its strong showing in the election of 1856. Kansas reeled with violence between settlers with northern and settlers with southern sympathies. Republicans argued that the violence was southern in origin. They claimed that the Kansas frontier opened a window to southern values and intentions. Republicans also pointed to the brutal beating by a Southerner of a respected northern senator on the floor of Congress. Even the Supreme Court, in the Republicans' view, reflected the South's drive toward tyranny and minority rule. Then, in 1858, the issues dividing North and South received an extraordinary airing

John and Jessie Frémont Poster
The election of 1856 marked the first time a candidate's wife appeared on campaign items. Smart and ambitious, Jessie Benton Frémont made the breakthrough. In this poster—made from paper letters and figures cut from an English hunting print—Jessie and her husband, John C. Frémont, Republican Party presidential nominee, ride spirited horses. The scene emphasizes their youth (John was 43 and Jessie 31), their vigor, and their outdoor exuberance. Jessie helped plan Frémont's campaign, coauthored his election biography, and drew northern women into political activity as never before. "What a shame that women can't vote!" declared abolitionist Lydia Maria Child. "We'd carry 'our Jessie' into the White House on our shoulders, wouldn't we." Critics of Jessie's violation of women's traditional sphere ridiculed both Frémonts. A man who met the couple in San Francisco pronounced her "the better man of the two." Jessie Frémont was, as Abraham Lincoln observed ambivalently, "quite a female politician."
Museum of American Political Life.

in a senatorial contest in Illinois, when the nation's foremost Democrat debated a resourceful Republican.

"Bleeding Kansas"

Three days after the House of Representatives approved the Kansas-Nebraska Act in 1854, Senator William H. Seward of New York boldly challenged the South. "Come on then, Gentlemen of the Slave States," he cried, "since there is no escaping your challenge, I accept it in behalf of the cause of freedom. We will engage in competition for the virgin soil of Kansas, and God give the victory to the side which is stronger in numbers as it is in right." Because of Stephen Douglas, popular sovereignty would determine whether Kansas became slave or free. No one really expected New Mexico and Utah, with their harsh landscapes, to become slave states when Congress instituted popular sovereignty there in 1850. But many believed Kansas could go either way. Free-state and slave-state settlers each sought majorities at the ballot box, claimed God's blessing, and kept their rifles ready. In theory, popular sovereignty meant an orderly tallying of ballots. In Kansas, however, elections became violent events.

In the North, emigrant aid societies sprang up to promote settlement from the free states. The most famous, the New England Emigrant Aid Company, sponsored some 1,240 settlers in 1854 and 1855. In the South, tiny rural communities from Virginia to Texas raised money to support proslavery settlers. Missourians, already bordered on the east by the free state of Illinois and on the north by the free state of Iowa, especially thought it important to secure Kansas for slavery.

Thousands of hell-for-leather frontiersmen from Missouri, egged on by Missouri senator David Rice Atchison, invaded Kansas. "There are eleven hundred coming over from Platte

Fraudulent Voting in Kansas

This drawing is a northern indictment of the corruption of popular sovereignty by Missourians. Rough frontier types, with pistols and knives tucked into their belts, rush to get free whiskey and then line up at the polling place, whose sign, DOWN WITH THE ABOLITIONISTS, indicates that they voted the proslavery ticket.

Kansas State Historical Society.

FOR MORE HELP ANALYZING THIS IMAGE, see the visual activity for this chapter in the Online Study Guide at bedfordstmartins.com/roark.

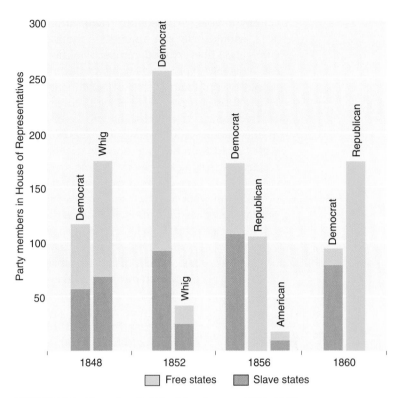

FIGURE 14.1 Changing Political Landscape, 1848–1860
The polarization of American politics between the free states and slave states occurred in little more than a decade.

County to vote," Atchison reported, "and if that ain't enough we can send five thousand— enough to kill every God-damned abolitionist in the Territory." Not surprisingly, proslavery candidates swept the elections in November 1854. When Kansas's first territorial legislature met, it enacted some of the most severe proslavery laws in the nation. Antislavery men, for example, were barred from holding office or serving on juries. Assisting a runaway became a capital offense. Ever-pliant President Pierce endorsed the work of the fraudulently elected proslavery legislature. Free-soil Kansans did not. They elected their own legislature, which promptly banned both slaves and free blacks from the territory. Organized into two rival governments and armed to the teeth, Kansans verged on civil war.

Fighting broke out on the morning of May 21, 1856, when a mob of several hundred proslavery men entered the town of Lawrence, the center of free-state settlement. Only one man died— a proslavery raider who was killed when a burning wall collapsed—but the "Sack of Lawrence," as free-soil forces called it, inflamed northern opinion. Elsewhere in Kansas, news of events in Lawrence provoked John Brown, a free-soil settler, to "fight fire with fire." Announcing that "it was better that a score of bad men should die than that one man who came here to make Kansas a Free State should be driven out," he led the posse that massacred five allegedly proslavery settlers along the Pottawatomie Creek. After that, **guerrilla war** engulfed the territory.

By providing graphic evidence of a dangerously aggressive Slave Power, "Bleeding Kansas" further hardened opinions in the antislavery North and West and gave the fledgling Republican Party fresh ammunition. The Republicans received additional encouragement from an event that occurred in the national capital. On May 19 and 20, 1856, Senator Charles Sumner of Massachusetts delivered a scathing speech entitled "The Crime against Kansas." He damned the administration, the South, and proslavery Kansans. He also indulged in a scalding personal attack on the elderly South Carolina senator Andrew P. Butler, whom Sumner de-

"Bleeding Kansas," 1850s

scribed as a "Don Quixote" who had taken as his mistress "the harlot, slavery."

Preston Brooks, a young South Carolina member of the House and a kinsman of Butler, felt compelled to defend the honor of both his aged relative and his state. On May 22, armed with a walking cane, Brooks entered the Senate, where he found Sumner working at his desk. He began beating Sumner over the head with his cane, and within a minute, Sumner lay bleeding and unconscious on the Senate floor. Brooks resigned his seat in the House, only to be promptly reelected. In the North, the southern hero became an archvillain. Like "Bleeding Kansas," "Bleeding Sumner" provided the Republican Party with a potent symbol of the South's twisted and violent "civilization."

The *Dred Scott* Decision

Political debate over slavery in the territories became so heated in part because the Constitution lacked precision on the issue. Only the Supreme Court speaks definitively about the meaning of the Constitution; in 1857, in the case of *Dred Scott v. Sandford,* the Court announced its judgment of the matter, but its decision demonstrated that it enjoyed no special immunity from the sectional and partisan passions that convulsed the land.

In 1833, John Emerson, an army doctor, bought the slave Dred Scott in St. Louis, Missouri, and took him as his personal servant to Fort Armstrong, Illinois. Two years later, Scott accompanied Emerson when he was transferred to Fort Snelling in Wisconsin Territory. Emerson eventually returned Scott to St. Louis, where in 1846, Scott, with the help of white friends, sued to prove that he, his wife Harriet, and their two daughters, Eliza and Lizzie, were legally entitled to their freedom. Scott based his claim on his travels and residences. He argued that living in Illinois, a free state, and Wisconsin, a free territory according to the Missouri Compromise of 1820, had made his family free. And they remained free even after returning to Missouri, a slave state.

In 1857, eleven years after the Scotts first sued for freedom, the U.S. Supreme Court ruled in the case. The Court saw the case as an opportunity to settle once and for all the vexing question of slavery in the territories. Chief Justice Roger B. Taney hated Republicans and detested

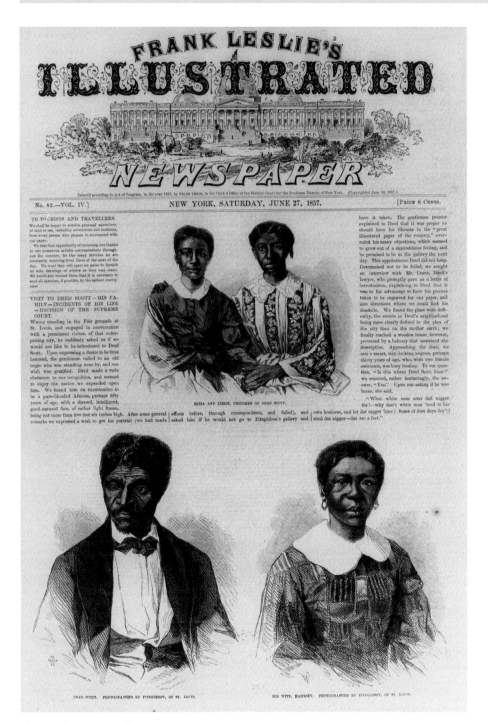

The Dred Scott Family

The *Dred Scott* case in 1857 not only produced a fierce political storm but also fueled enormous curiosity about the family suing for freedom. The correspondent for the popular *Frank Leslie's Illustrated* met Dred Scott in St. Louis and reported: "We found him on examination to be a pure-blooded African, perhaps fifty years of age, with a shrewd, intelligent, good-natured face, of rather light frame, being not more than five feet six inches high." Northerners wanted to see all of the Scotts: Harriet, who was a slave when Dred Scott married her in Wisconsin Territory in about 1836; daughter Eliza, who was born in 1838 on board a ship traveling in free territory north of Missouri; and daughter Lizzie, born after the Scotts returned to St. Louis.

Library of Congress.

Women's Politics

Although women could not vote before the Civil War, they nevertheless participated in public political activity. Hundreds of thousands of women exercised their right of petition and sought through petition campaigns to influence Congress and exert political influence. Uncle Tom's Cabin, Harriet Beecher Stowe's searing indictment of slavery, galvanized support for the Republican Party's campaign against the extension of slavery. Throughout her life, Jessie Benton Frémont sought unabashedly to affect politics, even as she sought to fulfill her domestic roles as wife and mother. She, like many other women, wrote to men of influence on behalf of her husband. "Do not suppose Sir, that I lightly interfere in a matter properly belonging to men," she began a letter to President James Polk, "but in the absence of Mr. Frémont I attend to his affairs at his request." During the 1850s, she became one of her husband's principal political analysts and advisers.

DOCUMENT 1
Jessie Benton Frémont's Letter to Elizabeth Blair Lee, 1856

On October 20, 1856, Jessie Frémont offered a clear-eyed interpretation of the significance of the Republican Party's paper-thin but devastating loss in the October 14 Pennsylvania state election.

I heartily regret the defeat we have met and do not look for things to change for the better. The Democrats will follow up their advantage with the courage of success & our forces are unorganized and just now surprised and inactive. I wish the cause had triumphed. I do wish Mr. Frémont had been the one to administer the bitter dose of subjection to the South for he has the coolness & nerve to do it just as it needs to be done—without passion & without sympathy—as coldly as a surgeon over a hospital patient would he have cut off their right hand Kansas from the old unhealthy southern body. . . . Tell your Father he must come to us for example & comfort in November for I don't think we will wear any but black feathers this year.

SOURCE: Pamela Herr and Mary Lee Spence, eds., *The Letters of Jessie Benton Frémont* (Urbana: University of Illinois Press, 1993), 140.

DOCUMENT 2
Harriot K. Hunt's Letter "to . . . [the] Treasurer, and the Assessors, and other Authorities of the city of Boston, and the Citizens generally," 1852

Some activist women challenged the domesticity that Stowe and Frémont hon-

ored, arguing that women's equality depended on their liberation from tradition. These women attended women's rights conventions, signed petitions asking legislators to change laws that discriminated against women, and worked to put the ideas of equal rights into practice in their personal lives. Harriot K. Hunt protested having to pay taxes when she was prohibited from voting. A physician who had practiced medicine in Boston since 1835, Hunt had been refused admission to Harvard Medical School and finally received her medical degree in 1853 from the Female Medical College of Philadelphia.*

Harriot K. Hunt, physician, a native and permanent resident of the city of Boston, and for many years a taxpayer therein, in making payment of her city taxes for the coming year, begs leave to protest against the injustice and inequality of levying taxes upon women, and at the same time refusing them any voice or vote in the imposition and expenditure of the same. The only classes of male persons required to pay taxes, and not at the same time allowed the privilege of voting, are aliens and minors. The objection in the case of aliens is their supposed want of interest in our institutions and knowledge of them. The objection in the case of minors, is the want of sufficient understanding. These objections can not apply to women, natives of the city, all of whose property interests are here, and who have accumulated, by their own sagacity and

racial equality, and the Court's majority decision, which he wrote, reflected those prejudices. First, the Court ruled that Dred Scott could not legally claim violation of his constitutional rights because he was not a citizen of the United States. In 1787, when the Constitution was written, Taney said, blacks "had for more than a century before been regarded as beings of an inferior order . . . so far inferior, that they had no rights which the white man was bound to respect." Second, the laws of Dred Scott's home state, Missouri, determined his status, and thus his travels in free areas did not make him free. Third, Congress's power to make "all needful rules and regulations"

industry, the very property on which they are taxed. But this is not all; the alien, by going through the forms of naturalization, the minor on coming of age, obtain the right of voting; and so long as they continue to pay a mere poll-tax of a dollar and a half, they may continue to exercise it, though so ignorant as not to be able to sign their names, or read the very votes they put into the ballot-boxes. Even drunkards, felons, idiots, and lunatics, if men, may still enjoy that right of voting to which no woman, however large the amount of taxes she pays, however respectable her character, or useful her life, can ever attain. Wherein, your remonstrant would inquire, is the justice, equality, or wisdom of this?

Source: Elizabeth Cady Stanton, Susan B. Anthony, and Matilda Joslyn Gage, eds., *History of Woman Suffrage*, vol. 1 (New York: Fowler & Wells, 1881), 259.

DOCUMENT 3
Lucy Stone–Henry B. Blackwell
Marriage Agreement, 1855

Marriage typically made women legally inferior to their husbands, but women's rights activists refashioned marriage vows to honor equality rather than subordination. When women's rights leader Lucy Stone married Henry B. Blackwell in 1855, both signed the following statement.

While acknowledging our mutual affection by publicly assuming the re-

lationship of husband and wife, yet in justice to ourselves and a great principle, we deem it a duty to declare that this act on our part implies no sanction of, nor promise of voluntary obedience to such of the present laws of marriage, as refuse to recognize the wife as an independent, rational being, while they confer upon the husband an injurious and unnatural superiority, investing him with legal powers which no honorable man would exercise, and which no man should possess. We protest especially against the laws which give to the husband:

1. The custody of the wife's person.
2. The exclusive control and guardianship of their children.
3. The sole ownership of her personal [property], and use of her real estate. . . .
4. The absolute right to the product of her industry.
5. Also against laws which give to the widower so much larger and more permanent an interest in the property of his deceased wife, than they give to the widow in that of the deceased husband.
6. Finally, against the whole system by which "the legal existence of the wife is suspended during marriage," so that in most States, she neither has a legal part in the choice of her residence, nor can she make a will, nor sue or be sued in her own name, nor inherit property.

We believe that personal independence and equal human rights can never be forfeited, except for crime; that marriage should be an equal and permanent partnership, and so recognized by law; that until it is so recognized, married partners should provide against the radical injustice of present laws, by every means in their power. . . .

Thus reverencing law, we enter our protest against rules and customs which are unworthy of the name, since they violate justice, the essence of law.

(signed) Henry B. Blackwell
Lucy Stone

Source: Elizabeth Cady Stanton, Susan B. Anthony, and Matilda Joslyn Gage, eds., *History of Woman Suffrage*, vol. 1 (New York: Fowler & Wells, 1881), 260–61.

QUESTIONS FOR ANALYSIS AND DEBATE

1. Jessie Frémont did not interpret the Republican defeat in Pennsylvania in 1856 as a "glorious defeat." Can you suggest possible reasons why she did not?
2. On what grounds, according to Harriot Hunt, should women be accorded the vote? Do you agree with her argument? Why or why not?
3. What legal disabilities for women was the marriage contract of Henry Blackwell and Lucy Stone designed to overcome?

for the territories did not include the right to prohibit slavery. The Court then explicitly declared the Missouri Compromise unconstitutional, even though it had already been voided by the Kansas-Nebraska Act.

Republicans exploded in rage at the Taney Court's extreme proslavery position. By declar-

ing the Missouri Compromise unconstitutional, the decision nullified the underlying precept of federal exclusion of slavery in the territories and cut the ground out from under the Republican Party. Moreover, as the *New York Tribune* lamented, the decision cleared the way for "all our Territories . . . to be ripened into Slave States."

Particularly frightening to African Americans in the North was the Court's declaration that blacks were not citizens and had no rights. Black leader Frederick Douglass predicted that "the National Conscience" would soon overturn this dangerous and undemocratic ruling.

The Republican rebuttal to the *Dred Scott* ruling relied heavily on the brilliant dissenting opinion of Justice Benjamin R. Curtis. Scott *was* a citizen of the United States, Curtis argued. At the time of the writing of the Constitution, free black men could vote in five states and participated in the ratification process. Scott *was* free: Because slavery was prohibited in Wisconsin, the "involuntary servitude of a slave, coming into the Territory with his master, should cease to exist." And the Missouri Compromise *was* constitutional. The Founders had meant exactly what they said: Congress had the power to make "*all* needful rules and regulations" for the territories, including barring slavery.

Rejecting such arguments, a seven-to-two majority of the justices validated the most extreme statement of the South's territorial rights. John C. Calhoun's claim that Congress had no authority to exclude slavery became the law of the land. While southern Democrats cheered, northern Democrats feared that the *Dred Scott* decision would annihilate not just the Missouri Compromise but popular sovereignty as well. If Congress itself lacked the authority to exclude slavery, how could a mere territorial government assume that right? The Kansas-Nebraska Act had opened the territory to popular sovereignty, and now, contrary to Stephen A. Douglas's promise, it appeared that Free-Soilers would not be able to keep slavery out, and that no one could legally exclude slavery until the moment of statehood. By draining nearly the last drop of ambiguity out of popular sovereignty, the *Dred Scott* decision jeopardized the ability of the Democratic Party to hold its northern and southern wings together.

The *Dred Scott* decision actually strengthened the young Republican Party. That "outrageous" decision, one Republican said, was "the best thing that could have happened." It gave evidence for the Republicans' claim that a hostile Slave Power conspired against northern liberties. Only the capture of the Supreme Court by

> While southern Democrats cheered, northern Democrats feared that the *Dred Scott* decision annihilated not just the Wilmot Proviso but popular sovereignty as well.

the "slavocracy," Republicans argued, could explain the tortured and historically inaccurate *Dred Scott* decision. As for Dred Scott, although the Court rejected his suit, he did in the end gain his freedom. In May 1857, Taylor Blow, the son of his first owner, purchased and freed Scott and his family. On September 17, 1858, Dred Scott died in obscurity. Nevertheless, his case played a key role in changing the political landscape and bringing new Republican politicians to the fore.

Prairie Republican: Abraham Lincoln

The re-igniting of sectional flames provided Republican politicians, including Abraham Lincoln of Illinois, with fresh challenges and fresh opportunities. Lincoln had long since put behind him his hardscrabble log-cabin beginnings in Kentucky and Indiana. At the time of the *Dred Scott* decision, he lived in a fine two-story house in Springfield. (See "American Places, page 503.") He brought in enough business from the Illinois Central Railroad to be known as the "railroad lawyer," and by virtue of his marriage into a well-to-do family and his successful law practice, he associated with men and women of reputation and standing.

The law provided Lincoln's living, but politics was his life. "His ambition was a little engine that knew no rest," observed his law partner William Herndon. At age twenty-six, he served his first term in the Illinois state legislature. Between 1847 and 1849, he enjoyed his only term in the House of Representatives, where he fired away at "Mr. Polk's War" and cast dozens of votes for free soil but otherwise served inconspicuously. When he returned to Springfield, he pitched into his law practice but kept his eye fixed on public office.

But, like Whigs everywhere in the mid-1850s, Lincoln had no political home. His credo—opposition to "the *extension* of slavery"—made the Democrats an impossible choice. Because the Republicans chose free soil as their principal tenet, in 1856 Lincoln joined the party. Convinced that slavery was a "monstrous injustice," a "great moral wrong," and an "unqualified evil to the negro, the white man, and the State," Lincoln condemned Douglas's Kansas-Nebraska Act of 1854 for giving slavery a new life. He accepted that the Constitution permitted slavery in those states where it existed, but he believed that the Founders had planned to contain its spread. Penned in, Lincoln believed, plantation slavery would exhaust southern soil,

Discussing the News
Newspapers permitted midwesterners to keep up-to-date. Here a farmer takes a break from cutting firewood to debate the latest news with his friends. He is so engrossed that he ignores the little girl tugging at his pants leg and trying to get him to notice the woman waving in the doorway. Men like these increasingly accepted Lincoln's portrait of the Republican Party as the guardian of the common people's liberty and economic opportunity. When Lincoln claimed that southern slaveholders threatened free labor and democracy, the midwestern farmers listened.

and in time Southerners would have no choice but to end slavery themselves. In Lincoln's opinion, by providing fresh land in the territories, Douglas had put slavery "on the high road to extension and perpetuity."

Just as Lincoln staked out the middle ground of antislavery opinion, he held what were, for his times, moderate racial views. Like a majority of Republicans, Lincoln defended black humanity without challenging white supremacy. He denounced slavery as immoral and believed that it should end, but he also viewed black equality as impractical and unachievable. "Negroes have natural rights . . . as other men have," he said, "although they cannot enjoy them here." Insurmountable white prejudice made it

impossible to extend full citizenship and equality to blacks in America, he believed. Freeing blacks and allowing them to remain in this country would lead to race war. In Lincoln's mind, social stability and black progress required that slavery end and that blacks leave the country.

Lincoln envisioned the western territories as "places for poor people to go to, and better their conditions." The "*free* labor system," he said, "opens the way for all—gives hope to all, and energy, and progress, and improvement of condition to all." Lincoln believed that the expansion of slave labor threatened free men's basic freedom to succeed. He became persuaded that slaveholders were engaging in an aggressive and dangerous conspiracy to nationalize slavery. As evidence, he pointed both to the Kansas-Nebraska Act, which repealed the restriction on slavery's advance in the territories, and to the *Dred Scott* decision, which denied Congress the right to impose fresh restrictions. The next step, Lincoln warned, would be "another Supreme Court decision, declaring that the Constitution of the United States does not permit a State to exclude slavery from its limits." Unless the citizens of Illinois woke up, he warned, the Supreme Court would make "Illinois a slave State."

In Lincoln's view, the nation could not "endure, permanently half slave and half free." Either opponents of slavery would arrest its spread and place it on the "course of ultimate extinction," or its advocates would push it forward until it became legal in "*all* the States, *old* as well as *new*—*North* as well as *South*." Lincoln's convictions that slavery was wrong, that Congress must stop its spread, and that it must be put on the road to extinction formed the core of the Republican ideology. Although Lincoln had not held public office in the 1850s, by 1858 he had so impressed his fellow Republicans in Illinois with his speeches and other statements about major national issues that they chose him to challenge the nation's premier Democrat, who was seeking reelection to the U.S. Senate.

The Lincoln-Douglas Debates

When Stephen Douglas learned that the Republican Abraham Lincoln would be his opponent for the Senate, he confided in a fellow Democrat: "He is the strong man of the party—full of wit, facts, dates—and the best stump speaker, with his droll ways and dry jokes, in the West. He is as honest as he is shrewd, and if I beat him my victory will be hardly won."

Not only did Douglas have to contend with a formidable foe, but he also carried the weight of a burden not of his own making. The previous year, the nation's economy experienced a sharp downturn. Prices plummeted, thousands of businesses failed, and unemployment rose. Although Illinois suffered less than the Northeast, Douglas the Democrat had to go before the voters in 1858 as a member of the party whose policies stood accused of causing the "panic" of 1857.

> Lincoln and Douglas debated, often brilliantly, the central issue before the country: slavery and freedom.

Douglas's response to another crisis in 1857, however, helped shore up his standing with his constituents. Proslavery forces in Kansas met in the town of Lecompton, drafted a proslavery constitution, and applied for statehood. Everyone knew that Free-Soilers outnumbered proslavery settlers by at least two to one, but President Buchanan instructed Congress to admit Kansas as the sixteenth slave state. Republicans denounced the "Lecompton swindle." Douglas broke with the Democratic administration and came out against the proslavery constitution, not because it accepted slavery but because it violated the principle of democratic rule. Congress killed the Lecompton bill. (When Kansans reconsidered the Lecompton constitution in an honest election, they rejected it six to one. Kansas entered the Union in 1861 as a free state.) In coming out against the Lecompton constitution, Douglas declared his independence from the South and, he hoped, made himself acceptable at home.

A relative unknown and a decided underdog in the Illinois election, Lincoln challenged the incumbent Douglas to debate him face-to-face. Douglas agreed, and the two met in seven communities for what would become a legendary series of debates. To the thousands who stood straining to see and hear, they must have seemed an odd pair. Douglas was five feet four inches tall, broad, and stocky; Lincoln was six feet four inches tall, angular, and lean. Douglas was in perpetual motion, darting across the platform, shouting, and jabbing the air. Lincoln stood still and spoke deliberately. Douglas wore the latest fashion and dazzled audiences with his flashy vests. Lincoln wore good suits but managed to look rumpled anyway. Their differences in physical appearance and style, however, were of little importance. They showed the citizens of Illinois (and much of the nation because of widespread press coverage) the difference between an anti-Lecompton Democrat and a true Republican. They debated, often brilliantly, the central issue before the country: slavery and freedom.

Lincoln badgered Douglas with the question of whether he favored the spread of slavery. He tried to force Douglas into the damaging admission that the Supreme Court had repudiated Douglas's own territorial solution, popular sovereignty. In the debate at Freeport, Illinois, Douglas admitted that settlers could not now pass legislation barring slavery, but he argued

AMERICAN PLACES

Lincoln Home National Historic Site, Springfield, Illinois

Abraham Lincoln's Home in Springfield, Illinois
Lincoln Home National Historic Site.

In 1844, Abraham Lincoln, who was born in a one-room, dirt-floored log cabin, and Mary Todd Lincoln, who was born in a fourteen-room southern mansion, moved into this Springfield, Illinois, home. It was the only home that Lincoln ever owned, and today visitors can easily imagine Lincoln's domestic life while he was still the "railroad lawyer" from Illinois.

Three of the Lincolns' four sons were born here, and one, Eddie, died here. When Lincoln was elected president in 1860, he and Mary decided to rent rather than to sell their house, expecting to return after the presidency. After Lincoln's assassination, however, Mary said that she "could not bear to return to the scenes of the happiest times in my life without my family," and she never lived in the house again. In 1887, Lincoln's only surviving son, Robert, gave the house to the state of Illinois, which in time donated it to the nation.

The National Park Service restored the house to its 1860 appearance. Springfield had become the capital of Illinois only in 1839, and pigs, chickens, and cattle still roamed the streets in Lincoln's time. Improvements during the seventeen years the Lincolns lived in the house reflected both their growing family and his rising income. The nicest room is the formal parlor, where the Lincolns entertained and where on May 19, 1860, Republican leaders asked Lincoln to run for the presidency. Family members spent most of their time in the sitting room. At six foot four inches, Lincoln found the furniture uncomfortable and often sprawled on the floor with the children, dog, and cats. One visitor described the rooms as "elegantly and comfortably furnished." Another said that the home was "handsome, but not pretentious." As long as he lived here, Lincoln chopped wood, lit the fires in the morning, brushed the horse, and milked the cow. Although the Lincolns employed servants, the successful railroad lawyer had obviously not entirely forgotten his hardscrabble beginnings.

For Web links related to this site and other American Places, see "PlaceLinks" at bedfordstmartins.com/roark.

---

that they could ban slavery just as effectively by not passing protective laws. Without "appropriate police regulations and local legislation," such as those found in slave states, he explained, slavery could not live a day, an hour. Southerners condemned Douglas's "Freeport Doctrine" and charged him with trying to steal the victory they had gained with the *Dred Scott* decision. Lincoln chastised his opponent for his "don't care" atti-

tude about slavery, for "blowing out the moral lights around us."

Douglas worked the racial issue. He called Lincoln an abolitionist and an egalitarian enamored with "our colored brethren." Put on the defensive, Lincoln came close to staking out positions on abolition and race that were as conservative as Douglas's. Lincoln reiterated his belief that slavery enjoyed constitutional protection where it existed. He also reaffirmed his faith in white rule: "I will say, then, that I am not, nor ever have been, in favor of bringing about in any way the social and political equality of the white and black race." But unlike Douglas, who told racist jokes and spit out racial epithets, Lincoln was no negrophobe. He always tried to steer the debate back to what he considered the true issue: the morality and future of slavery. "Slavery is wrong," Lincoln repeated, because "a man has the right to the fruits of his own labor."

As Douglas predicted, the election was hard-fought. It was also closely contested. Until the adoption of the Seventeenth Amendment in 1911, citizens voted for state legislators, who in turn selected U.S. senators. Since Democrats won a slight majority in the Illinois legislature, the members returned Douglas to the Senate. But the debates thrust Lincoln, the prairie Republican, into the national spotlight.

The Union Collapses

Lincoln's thesis that the "slavocracy" conspired to make slavery a national institution now seems exaggerated. But from the northern perspective, the Kansas-Nebraska Act, the Brooks-Sumner affair, the *Dred Scott* decision, and the Lecompton constitution amounted to irrefutable evidence of the South's aggressiveness. Southerners, of course, saw things differently. They were the ones who were under siege and had grievances, they declared. Signs were everywhere, they argued, that the North planned to use its numerical advantage to attack slavery, and not just in the territories. Republicans had loudly denounced the *Dred Scott* decision and made it clear that they were unwilling to accept the Supreme Court's ruling as the last word on the issue of slavery expansion. After John Brown attempted to incite a slave insurrection in Virginia in 1859, Southerners argued that Northerners had also proved themselves unwilling to be bound by Christian decency and reverence for life.

Threats of secession increasingly laced the sectional debate. Talk of leaving the Union had been heard for years, but until the final crisis, Southerners had used secession as a ploy to gain concessions within the Union, not to destroy it. Then the 1850s delivered powerful blows to Southerners' confidence that they could remain Americans and protect slavery. And when the

Republican Party won the White House in 1860, many Southerners concluded that they would have to leave.

The Aftermath of John Brown's Raid

If John Brown had been killed during his raid on Harpers Ferry in 1859, his impact on history would probably have been minor. But he lived and stood trial for treason, murder, and incitement of slave insurrection. "To hang a fanatic is to make a martyr of him and fledge another brood of the same sort," cautioned one newspaper, but on December 2, 1859, the state of Virginia executed Brown. In life, Brown was a ne'er-do-well, but he died with courage, dignity, and composure. At his trial, he told the court: "If it is deemed necessary that I should forfeit my life for the furtherance of the ends of justice, and mingle my blood further with the blood of . . . millions in this slave country whose rights are disregarded by wicked, cruel, and unjust enactments, I say, let it be done." When he left his cell the morning of his hanging, he passed a message to one of his guards. "I John Brown am now quite *certain*," it read, "that the crimes of this *guilty land will* never be purged *away*; but with Blood."

Northerners had at first denounced Brown's raid at Harpers Ferry as dangerous fanaticism and perhaps even the work of a madman. But after Brown's heroic death, denunciation gave way to grudging respect. Some Northerners even celebrated John Brown. The abolitionist author Lydia Maria Child declared, "What a splendid martyrdom. The scaffold will be as glorious as the Cross of Calvary." Writer and philosopher Henry David Thoreau also likened Brown to Christ and concluded, "he is an angel of light." Some abolitionists went beyond canonizing Brown to explicitly endorse Brown's resort to violence. Abolitionist William Lloyd Garrison, who usually professed pacifism, announced, "I am prepared to say 'success to every slave insurrection at the South and in every country.'"

Most Northerners did not advocate bloody rebellion, however. Like Lincoln, they concluded that Brown's noble antislavery ideals could not "excuse violence, bloodshed, and treason." Still, when many in the North marked the day of John Brown's execution with tolling bells, hymns, and prayer vigils, white Southerners were beside themselves with rage.

***John Brown Going to His Hanging*, Horace Pippin, 1942**
The grandparents of Horace Pippin, a Pennsylvania artist, were slaves. His grandmother witnessed the hanging of John Brown, and here Pippin recalls the scene she so often described to him. He uses a muted palette to establish the bleak setting and to tell the grim story, but he manages to convey a striking intensity nevertheless. Historically accurate, the painting depicts Brown tied and sitting erect on his coffin, passing resolutely before the silent, staring white men. The black woman in the lower right corner is presumably Pippin's grandmother.

Romare Bearden, a leading twentieth-century African American artist, recalled the central place of John Brown in black memory: "Lincoln and John Brown were as much a part of the actuality of the Afro-American experience, as were the domino games and the hoe cakes for Sunday morning breakfast. I vividly recall the yearly commemorations for John Brown and see my grandfather reading Brown's last speech to the court, which was a regular part of the ceremony at Pittsburgh's Shiloh Baptist Church."

Pennsylvania Academy of Fine Arts, Philadelphia. John Lambert Fund.

In Philadelphia, more than 250 medical students from the South were so appalled by what they witnessed that they marched to the railroad station and boarded a train to Richmond. In Mississippi, a planter disgusted with northern sympathy denounced Brown as a bloodthirsty fiend whose mission was "to incite slaves to murder helpless women and children." Southerners everywhere contemplated what they had in common with people who "regard John Brown as a martyr and a Christian hero, rather than a murderer and robber." Many Southerners concluded that, like Brown, Northerners were eager to see slavery washed away in a river of blood. Georgia senator Robert Toombs announced solemnly that Southerners must "never permit this Federal government to pass into the traitorous hands of the black Republican party." At that moment, the presidential election was only months away.

Republican Victory in 1860

Anxieties provoked by John Brown's raid flared for months as southern whites feverishly searched for abolitionists and whipped, tarred and feathered, and sometimes hanged those they suspected. Moreover, other events in the eleven months between Brown's hanging and the presidential election heightened sectional hostility and estrangement. A southern business convention meeting in Nashville shocked the country (including many Southerners) by calling for the reopening of the African slave trade, closed since 1808 and considered an abomination everywhere in the Western world. Chief Justice Taney provoked new indignation when the Supreme Court ruled northern personal liberty laws unconstitutional and reaffirmed the Fugitive Slave Act.

Then, in February 1860, the normally routine business of electing a Speaker of the House threatened to turn bloody as Democrats and Republicans battled over control of the office. After two months of acrimonious debate left the House deadlocked, one congressman observed that the "only persons who do not have a revolver and a knife are those who have two revolvers." The House averted a shootout when a few Know-Nothings finally joined the Republicans to elect an old Whig. Finally, Mississippian Jefferson Davis demanded that the Senate adopt a federal slave code for the territories, a goal of extreme proslavery Southerners for several years. Not only was Congress powerless to block slavery's spread, he argued, but it was obligated to offer slavery all "needful protection."

When Democrats converged on Charleston for their convention in April 1860, Southerners gave notice that they intended to make their extreme position on the territories binding party doctrine. Southern fire-eaters denounced Stephen Douglas and demanded a platform that included federal protection of slavery in the territories. But northern Democrats knew that northern voters would not stomach a federal slave code. When two platforms—one with a federal slave code and one with popular sovereignty—came before the delegates, popular sovereignty won. Representatives from the entire Lower South and Arkansas stomped out of the convention. The remaining delegates adjourned to meet a few weeks later in Baltimore, where they nominated Douglas for president and adopted a platform that advocated little beyond congressional noninterference in the territories.

When southern Democrats met, they nominated Vice President John C. Breckinridge of Kentucky for president and approved a platform with a federal slave code. But southern moderates refused to support Breckinridge and the fire-eaters. Senator John J. Crittenden of Kentucky and others formed a new party to provide voters a Unionist choice. Instead of adopting a platform and confronting the slavery question, the Constitutional Union Party merely approved a vague resolution pledging "to recognize no political principle other than *the Constitution . . . the Union . . . and the Enforcement of the Laws*." For president they picked former senator John Bell of Tennessee.

The Republicans smelled victory. Four years earlier they had enjoyed "glorious defeat" by a Democratic Party that had since broken up. Still, Republicans estimated that they needed to carry nearly all the free states to win. In 1856, they were essentially a one-idea party. In 1860, the Republicans expanded their platform beyond antislavery opinion. They hoped that free homesteads, a protective tariff, a transcontinental railroad, and a guarantee of immigrant political rights would provide an economic and social agenda broad enough to unify the North. While recommitting themselves to stopping the spread of slavery, they also denounced John Brown's raid as "among the gravest of crimes" and confirmed the security of slavery in the South.

Republicans cast about for a moderate candidate to go with their evenhanded platform. The foremost Republican, William H. Seward, had made enemies with his radical "higher law" doctrine and "irrepressible conflict" speech. Lincoln, however, since bursting onto the national scene in 1858 had demonstrated his clear purpose, good judgment, and solid Republican credentials. That, and his residence in Illinois, a crucial state, made him attractive to the party. Masterful maneuvering by Lincoln's managers converted his status as the second choice of many convention delegates into a majority on the third ballot. Defeated by Douglas in a state contest less than two years earlier, Lincoln now stood ready to take him on for the presidency.

The election of 1860 was like none other in American politics. It took place in the midst of the nation's severest crisis. Four major candidates crowded the presidential field. Rather than a four-cornered contest, however, the election

Abraham Lincoln
Lincoln actively sought the Republican presidential nomination in 1860. When in New York City to give a political address, he had his photograph taken by Mathew Brady. "While I was there I was taken to one of the places where they get up such things," Lincoln explained, sounding more innocent than he was, "and I suppose they got my shadow, and can multiply copies indefinitely." Multiply they did. Copies of the dignified photograph of Lincoln soon replaced the less flattering drawings. Later, Lincoln credited his victory to his New York speech and to Mathew Brady.
The Lincoln Museum, Fort Wayne, Indiana. Photo: #0-17; drawing: #2024.

broke into two contests, each with two candidates. In the North, Lincoln faced Douglas; in the South, Breckinridge confronted Bell. Southerners did not even permit Lincoln's name to appear on the ballot in ten of the fifteen slave states, so outrageous did they consider the Republican Party.

An unprecedented number of voters cast ballots on November 6, 1860. Approximately 82 percent of eligible northern men and nearly 70 percent of eligible southern men went to the polls. Lincoln swept all of the eighteen free states except New Jersey, which split its electoral votes between him and Douglas. While Lincoln received only 39 percent of the popular vote, he won easily in the electoral balloting, gaining 180 votes, 28 more than he needed for victory. Lincoln did not win because his opposition was splintered. Even if the votes of his three opponents had been combined, Lincoln would still have won. He won because 99 percent of his votes were concentrated in the free states, which contained a majority of electoral votes. Ominously, however, Breckinridge, running on a southern-rights platform, won the entire Lower South plus Delaware, Maryland, and North Carolina. Two fully sectionalized parties swept their regions, but the northern one won the presidency (Map 14.5).

Secession Winter

The telegraphs had barely stopped tapping out the news of Lincoln's victory when anxious Southerners began reappraising the value of the

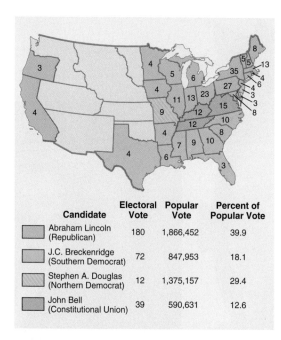

Candidate	Electoral Vote	Popular Vote	Percent of Popular Vote
Abraham Lincoln (Republican)	180	1,866,452	39.9
J.C. Breckenridge (Southern Democrat)	72	847,953	18.1
Stephen A. Douglas (Northern Democrat)	12	1,375,157	29.4
John Bell (Constitutional Union)	39	590,631	12.6

MAP 14.5 The Election of 1860

started than controlled," he warned. "I consider slavery much more secure in the Union than out of it."

Secessionists emphasized the urgency of the moment and the dangers of delay. No Southerner should mistake Republican intentions, they argued. "Mr. Lincoln and his party assert that this doctrine of equality applies to the negro," former Georgia governor Howell Cobb declared, "and necessarily there can exist no such thing as property in our equals." Lincoln's election without a single electoral vote from the South meant that Southerners were unable to defend themselves within the Union, Cobb argued. Why wait, he asked, for Lincoln to appoint Republican judges, marshals, customs collectors, and postmasters to federal posts throughout the South? Each would become an abolitionist emissary, he warned. As for war, there would be none. The Union was a voluntary compact, and Lincoln would not coerce patriotism. If Northerners did resist with force, secessionists argued, the conflict would be brief, for one southern woodsman could whip five of Lincoln's greasy mechanics.

For all their differences, southern whites were generally united in their determination to defend slavery, to take slave property into the territories, and to squeeze from the North an admission that they were good and decent people. They disagreed about whether the mere presence of a Republican in the White House made it necessary to exercise what they considered a legitimate right to secede.

The debate about what to do was briefest in South Carolina. It seceded from the Union on December 20, 1860. By February 1861, the six other deep South states marched in South Carolina's footsteps. Only South Carolinians voted overwhelmingly in favor of secession, however; elsewhere, the vote was close. In general, the nonslaveholding inhabitants of the Piedmont and mountain counties, where slaves were relatively few, displayed the greatest attachment to the Union. Slaveholders spearheaded secession. On February 4, representatives from South Carolina, Georgia, Florida, Alabama, Mississippi, Louisiana, and Texas met in Montgomery, Alabama, where three days later they celebrated the birth of the Confederate States of America. Jefferson

Union. Although Breckinridge had carried the South, a vote for "southern rights" was not necessarily a vote for secession. In fact, Breckinridge steadfastly denied that he was a secession candidate. Besides, slightly more than half of the Southerners who had voted cast ballots for Douglas and Bell, two stout defenders of the Union. During the winter of 1860–61, Southerners debated what to do.

Southern Unionists tried to calm the fears that Lincoln's election triggered. Let the dust settle, they pleaded. Extremists in both sections, they argued, had created the crisis. Former congressman Alexander Stephens of Georgia eloquently defended the Union. He asked what Lincoln had done to justify something as extreme as secession. Had he not promised to respect slavery where it existed? In Stephens's judgment, the fire-eater cure would be worse than the Republican disease. Secession might lead to war, which would loosen the hinges of southern society, possibly even open the door to slave insurrection or a revolt by nonslaveholding whites. "Revolutions are much easier

Secession of the Lower South, December 1860–February 1861

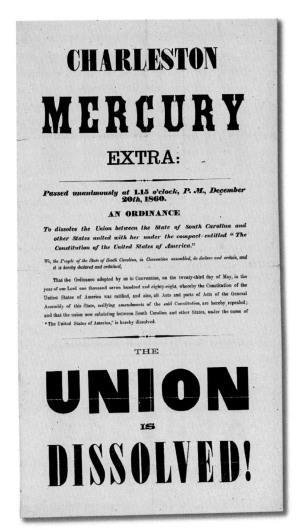

"The Union Is Dissolved!"
On December 20, 1860, the *Charleston Mercury* put out this special edition of the paper to celebrate South Carolina's secession from the Union. Six weeks earlier, upon hearing the news that Lincoln had won the presidency, it had predicted as much. "The tea has been thrown overboard," the *Mercury* announced. "The revolution of 1860 has been initiated."
Chicago Historical Society.

Davis became president, and Alexander Stephens, who had spoken so eloquently about the dangers of revolution, became vice president.

Lincoln's election had split the Union. Now secession split the South. Seven slave states seceded during the winter, but eight did not. Citizens of the Upper South debated just as furiously whether the South could defend itself better inside or outside the Union, but they came down opposite the Lower South, at least for the moment. The fact was that the Upper South had a smaller stake in slavery. Just over half as many white families in the Upper South held slaves (21 percent) as did those in the Lower South (37 percent). Slaves represented twice as large a percentage of the population in the Lower South (48 percent) as in the Upper South (23 percent). Consequently, whites in the Upper South had fewer fears that Republican ascendancy meant economic catastrophe, racial war, and social chaos. Lincoln would need to do more than just be elected to provoke them into secession.

The nation had to wait until March 4, 1861, when Lincoln took office to see what he would do. (Presidents-elect waited four months to take office until 1933, when the Twentieth Amendment to the Constitution shifted the inauguration forward to January 20.) After his election, Lincoln chose to stay in Springfield and to say nothing. "Lame-duck" president James Buchanan sat in Washington and did nothing. Buchanan firmly denied the constitutionality of secession but also denied that he had power to resist it. Buchanan demonstrated, William H. Seward said mockingly, that "it is the President's duty to enforce the laws, unless somebody opposes him." In Congress, efforts at cobbling together a peace-saving compromise came to nothing.

In his inaugural address, Lincoln began with reassurances to the South. He had "no lawful right" to interfere with slavery where it existed, he said again, adding for emphasis that he had "no inclination to do so." There would be "no invasion—no using of force against or among the people anywhere." In filling federal posts, he would not "force obnoxious strangers" on the South. Conciliatory toward Southerners, Lincoln proved inflexible about the Union. The Union, he declared, is "perpetual." Secession was "anarchy" and "legally void." The Constitution required him to execute the law "in all the States." He would hold federal property, collect federal duties, and deliver the mails.

The decision for civil war or peace rested in the South's hands, Lincoln warned. "You can have no conflict, without being yourselves the aggressors. *You* have no oath registered in Heaven to destroy the government, while *I* shall have the most solemn one to 'preserve, protect, and defend' it." What Southerners in Charleston held in their hands at that very moment were the cords for firing the cannons aimed at the federal garrison at Fort Sumter.

> Lincoln's election had split the Union. Now secession split the South.

Conclusion: Slavery, Free Labor, and the Failure of Political Compromise

As their economies, societies, and cultures diverged in the nineteenth century, Northerners and Southerners increasingly expressed different concepts of the American promise and the role of slavery within it. Their differences crystallized into political form in 1846 when David Wilmot proposed banning slavery in any territory won in the Mexican-American War. "As if by magic," a Boston newspaper observed, "it brought to a head the great question that is about to divide the American people." Discovery of gold and other precious metals in the West added urgency to the controversy over slavery in the territories. Although Congress attempted to address the issue with the Compromise of 1850, the Fugitive Slave Act provision quickly brought discontent and mistrust of the compromise in both free and slave states. Matters worsened with the 1852 publication of *Uncle Tom's Cabin*, which further hardened northern sentiments against slavery and confirmed southern suspicions of northern ill will. The bloody violence that erupted in Kansas in 1856 and the incendiary *Dred Scott* decision in 1857 further eroded hope for a solution to this heated question.

During the extended crisis of the Union that stretched from 1846 to 1861, the slavery question braided with national politics. As the traditional Whig and Democratic parties struggled with fallout from the slavery issue, new parties, most notably the Republican Party, emerged. Although the nation fixed its attention on the expansion of slavery, from the beginning both Northerners and Southerners recognized that the controversy had less to do with slavery in the territories than with the future of slavery in America.

For more than seventy years, imaginative statesmen had found compromises that accepted slavery and preserved the Union. Citizens on both sides of the Mason-Dixon line took enormous pride in the national experiment in **republican** democracy and few gave up the experiment easily. But as each section grew increasingly committed to its labor system and the promise it provided, Americans discovered that accommodation had limits. In 1859, John Brown's militant antislavery had pushed white Southerners to the edge. In 1860, Lincoln's election convinced whites in the deep South that slavery and the society they had built on it were at risk in the Union, and they seceded. In his inaugural, Lincoln pleaded, "We are not enemies but friends. We must not be enemies." By then, however, the deep South had ceased to sing what he called "the chorus of the Union." It remained to be seen whether disunion would mean war.

FOR ADDITIONAL FIRSTHAND ACCOUNTS OF THIS PERIOD, see Chapter 14 in Michael Johnson, ed., *Reading the American Past,* Third Edition.

TO ASSESS YOUR MASTERY OF THE MATERIAL IN THIS CHAPTER, see the Online Study Guide at bedfordstmartins.com/roark.

FOR WEB LINKS RELATED TO TOPICS IN THIS CHAPTER, see "HistoryLinks," "DocLinks," and "PlaceLinks" at bedfordstmartins.com/roark.

CHRONOLOGY **511**

1846–1861

CHRONOLOGY

1820 • Missouri Compromise divides Louisiana Purchase between slave and free territory.

1846 • Wilmot Proviso proposes barring slavery from all lands acquired in Mexican War.

1847 • Senator John C. Calhoun challenges Wilmot Proviso on constitutional grounds, stating that Congress has no power to exclude slavery from territories.

• Senator Lewis Cass offers compromise of "popular sovereignty," allowing people of territories to determine fate of slavery.

1848 • Opponents of expansion of slavery found Free-Soil Party.

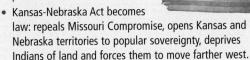

• Whig General Zachary Taylor elected president.

1849 • California Gold Rush leads thousands to the West, further fueling the debate over slavery in the territories.

1850 • Vice President Millard Fillmore becomes president upon death of Zachary Taylor.

• Senator Stephen Douglas's compromise bills (Compromise of 1850) become law: California admitted to the Union as a free state; Utah and New Mexico organized as territories with the status of slavery deliberately left uncertain; fugitive slave law strengthened.

1850s • Vigilance committees in North resist Fugitive Slave Act.

1852 • Harriet Beecher Stowe's *Uncle Tom's Cabin* published in book form.

• Democrat Franklin Pierce elected president.

1853 • Gadsden Purchase adds 30,000 square miles of territory in present-day Arizona and New Mexico.

1854 • American Party (Know-Nothings) emerges, advocating nativist positions.

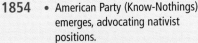

• Kansas-Nebraska Act becomes law: repeals Missouri Compromise, opens Kansas and Nebraska territories to popular sovereignty, deprives Indians of land and forces them to move farther west.

• Republican Party emerges, opposing extension of slavery into territories.

1856 • Proslavery and antislavery forces clash in "Bleeding Kansas."

• Preston Brooks of South Carolina assaults Charles Sumner of Massachusetts on Senate floor.

• John Brown leads massacre of proslavery men in Pottawatomie, Kansas.

• Democrat James Buchanan elected president; Republicans suffer "glorious defeat."

1857 • In *Dred Scott* decision, U.S. Supreme Court rules that African Americans have no constitutional rights, that Congress cannot exclude slavery in the territories, and that the Missouri Compromise is unconstitutional.

• Congress rejects Kansas's proslavery Lecompton constitution.

• Nation experiences economic downturn—the panic of 1857.

1858 • Abraham Lincoln and Stephen A. Douglas debate slavery; Douglas defeats Lincoln for Illinois Senate seat.

1859 • John Brown's attempt to foment slave uprising in Harpers Ferry, Virginia, further alienates South and moves nation toward war.

1860 • Republican Abraham Lincoln elected president in four-way race that divides electorate along sectional lines.

• South Carolina secedes from Union.

1861 • Six other deep South states secede.

• The seven seceded states form the Confederate States of America.

• Lincoln takes office.

BIBLIOGRAPHY

General Works

John Ashworth, *Slavery, Capitalism, and Politics in the Antebellum Republic* (1995).

Don E. Fehrenbacher, *The Slaveholding Republic: An Account of the United States Government's Relations to Slavery* (2001).

Eric Foner, *Politics and Ideology in the Age of the Civil War* (1980).

Michael F. Holt, *Political Parties and American Political Development from the Age of Jackson to the Age of Lincoln* (1992).

Michael F. Holt, *The Rise and Fall of the American Whig Party: Jacksonian Politics and the Onset of the Civil War* (1999).

Bruce C. Levine, *Half Slave and Half Free: The Roots of Civil War* (1992).

John D. Majewski, *A House Dividing: Economic Development in Pennsylvania and Virginia before the Civil War* (2000).

James M. McPherson, *Ordeal by Fire: The Civil War and Reconstruction* (1982).

Allan Nevins, *Ordeal of the Union*, 2 vols. (1947).

Allan Nevins, *The Emergence of Lincoln*, 2 vols. (1950).

Roy F. Nichols, *Disruption of American Democracy* (1948).

Merrill D. Peterson, *The Great Triumvirate: Webster, Clay, and Calhoun* (1987).

David M. Potter, *The Impending Crisis, 1848–1861* (1976).

Leonard Richards, *The Slave Power: The Free North and Southern Domination, 1780–1860* (2000).

Richard Sewell, *A House Divided: Sectionalism and Civil War, 1848–1865* (1988).

Kenneth M. Stampp, ed., *The Imperiled Union: Essays on the Background of the Civil War* (1980).

Kenneth M. Stampp, ed., *The Causes of the Civil War* (rev. ed., 1991).

Mark W. Summers, *The Plundering Generation: Corruption and the Crisis of the Union, 1849–1861* (1987).

Slavery in the Territories

Paul H. Bergeron, *The Presidency of James K. Polk* (1987).

Eugene H. Berwanger, *The Frontier against Slavery: Western Anti-Negro Prejudice and the Slavery Extension Controversy* (1967).

Don E. Fehrenbacher, *The Dred Scott Case: Its Significance in American Law and Politics* (1978).

Paul Finkelman, *An Imperfect Union: Slavery, Federalism, and Comity* (1981).

Holman Hamilton, *Prologue to Conflict: The Crisis and Compromise of 1850* (1964).

Robert W. Johannsen, *The Frontier, the Union, and Stephen A. Douglas* (1989).

Chaplain W. Morrison, *Democratic Politics and Sectionalism: The Wilmot Proviso Controversy* (1967).

James A. Rawley, *Race and Politics: "Bleeding Kansas" and the Coming of the Civil War* (1969).

Kenneth M. Stampp, *America in 1857: A Nation on the Brink* (1990).

Gerald W. Wolff, *The Kansas-Nebraska Bill: Party, Section, and the Coming of the Civil War* (1977).

Northern Sectionalism

Richard H. Abbott, *Cotton and Capital: Boston Businessmen and Antislavery Reform, 1854–1868* (1991).

Tyler Anbinder, *Nativism and Slavery: The Northern Know Nothings and the Politics of the 1850s* (1992).

Jean H. Baker, *Affairs of Party: The Political Culture of Northern Democrats in the Mid-Nineteenth Century* (1983).

Dale Baum, *The Civil War Party System: The Case of Massachusetts, 1848–1876* (1984).

R. J. M. Blackett, *Building an Antislavery Wall: Black Americans in the Atlantic Abolitionist Movement, 1830–1860* (1983).

Frederick J. Blue, *The Free Soilers: Third Party Politics, 1848–1854* (1973).

Stanley W. Campbell, *The Slave Catchers: Enforcement of the Fugitive Slave Law, 1850–1860* (1970).

Tom Chaffin, *Pathfinder: John Charles Frémont and the Course of American Empire* (2002).

Gary Lee Collison, *Shadrach Minkins: From Fugitive Slave to Citizen* (1997).

Robert F. Dalzell Jr., *Daniel Webster and the Trial of American Nationalism, 1843–1852* (1972).

David H. Donald, *Charles Sumner and the Coming of the Civil War* (1960).

Robert R. Dykstra, *Bright Radical Star: Black Freedom and White Supremacy on the Hawkeye Frontier* (1993).

Don E. Fehrenbacher, *Prelude to Greatness: Lincoln in the 1850s* (1962).

Eric Foner, *Free Soil, Free Labor, Free Men: The Ideology of the Republican Party before the Civil War* (1970).

George B. Forgie, *Patricide in the House Divided: A Psychological Interpretation of Lincoln and His Age* (1979).

Ronald P. Formisano, *The Birth of Mass Political Parties: Michigan, 1827–1861* (1971).

William E. Gienapp, *The Origins of the Republican Party, 1852–1856* (1987).

Thomas F. Gossett, *"Uncle Tom's Cabin" and American Culture* (1985).

Len Gougeon, *Virtue's Hero: Emerson, Antislavery, and Reform* (1990).

Susan-Mary Grant, *North over South: Northern Nationalism and American Identity in the Antebellum Era* (2000).

David Grimsted, *American Mobbing, 1828–1865: Toward Civil War* (1998).

Stanley Harrold, *Subversives: Antislavery Community in Washington, D.C., 1828–1865* (2002).

Joan D. Hedrick, *Harriet Beecher Stowe: A Life* (1994).

Pamela Herr, *Jessie Benton Frémont: A Biography* (1987).

Pamela Herr and Mary Lee Spence, eds., *The Letters of Jessie Benton Frémont* (1993).

Nancy Isenberg, *Sex and Citizenship in Antebellum America* (1998).

Robert W. Johannsen, *Lincoln, the South, and Slavery: The Political Dimension* (1991).

Bruce C. Levine, *The Spirit of 1848: German Immigrants, Labor Conflict, and the Coming of the Civil War* (1992).

William S. McFeely, *Frederick Douglass* (1991).

John R. McKivigan, *The War against Proslavery Religion: Abolitionism and the Northern Churches, 1830–1865* (1984).

Thomas D. Morris, *Free Men All: The Personal Liberty Laws of the North, 1780–1861* (1974).

Stephen B. Oates, *To Purge This Land with Blood: A Biography of John Brown* (2nd ed., 1984).

Merrill D. Peterson, *John Brown: The Legend Revisited* (2002).

James A. Rawley, *Race and Politics: "Bleeding Kansas" and the Coming of the Civil War* (1969).

Richard H. Sewell, *Ballots for Freedom: Antislavery Politics in the United States, 1837–1860* (1976).

Thomas P. Slaughter, *Bloody Dawn: The Christiana Riot and Racial Violence in the Antebellum North* (1991).

James Brewer Stewart, *Holy Warriors: The Abolitionists and American Slavery* (1976).

James Brewer Stewart, *Wendell Phillips, Liberty's Hero* (1986).

Hans L. Trefousse, *The Radical Republicans: Lincoln's Vanguard for Racial Justice* (1969).

Wendy Hamand Venet, *Neither Ballots nor Bullets: Women Abolitionists and the Civil War* (1991).

Albert J. Von Frank, *The Trials of Anthony Burns: Freedom and Slavery in Emerson's Boston* (1998).

Ronald G. Walters, *The Antislavery Appeal: American Abolitionism after 1830* (1976).

Douglas L. Wilson, *Honor's Voice: The Transformation of Abraham Lincoln* (1998).

Susan Zaeske, *Signatures of Citizenship: Petitioning, Antislavery, and Women's Political Identity* (2003).

David Zarefsky, *Lincoln, Douglas, and Slavery: In the Crucible of Public Debate* (1990).

Southern Sectionalism

William L. Barney, *The Road to Secession: A New Perspective on the Old South* (1972).

Irving H. Bartlett, *John C. Calhoun: A Biography* (1993).

Tom Chaffin, *Fatal Glory: Narciso López and the First Clandestine U.S. War against Cuba* (1996).

William J. Cooper Jr., *The South and the Politics of Slavery, 1828–1856* (1978).

John Patrick Daly, *When Slavery Was Called Freedom: Evangelicalism, Proslavery, and the Causes of the Civil War* (2002).

Drew Gilpin Faust, *James Henry Hammond and the Old South: A Design for Mastery* (1982).

Don E. Fehrenbacher, *The South and Three Sectional Crises* (1980).

Lacy K. Ford Jr., *Origins of Southern Radicalism: The South Carolina Upcountry, 1800–1860* (1988).

William W. Freehling, *The Road to Disunion*, vol. 1, *Secessionists at Bay, 1776–1854* (1990).

Vicki Vaughn Johnson, *The Men and the Vision of the Southern Commercial Conventions, 1845–1871* (1992).

Robert E. May, *The Southern Dream of a Caribbean Empire, 1854–1861* (1973).

John Niven, *John C. Calhoun and the Price of Union: A Biography* (1988).

Christopher J. Olsen, *Political Culture and Secession in Mississippi: Masculinity, Honor, and the Antiparty Tradition, 1830–1860* (2002).

David M. Potter, *The South and the Sectional Conflict* (1968).

Manisha Sinha, *The Counterrevolution of Slavery: Politics and Ideology in Antebellum South Carolina* (2000).

Mitchell Snay, *Gospel of Disunion: Religion and Separatism in the Antebellum South* (1993).

J. Mills Thornton III, *Politics and Power in a Slave Society: Alabama, 1800–1860* (1978).

Eric H. Walther, *The Fire-Eaters* (1992).

Secession

William L. Barney, *The Secessionist Impulse: Alabama and Mississippi in 1860* (1974).

Walter L. Buenger, *Secession and the Union in Texas* (1984).

Steven A. Channing, *Crisis of Fear: Secession in South Carolina* (1970).

Daniel W. Crofts, *Reluctant Confederates: Upper South Unionists in the Secession Crisis* (1989).

Charles B. Dew, *Apostles of Disunion: Southern Secession Commissioners and the Causes of the Civil War* (2001).

James L. Huston, *The Panic of 1857 and the Coming of the Civil War* (1987).

Michael P. Johnson, *Toward a Patriarchal Republic: The Secession of Georgia* (1977).

William A. Link, *Roots of Secession: Slavery and Politics in Antebellum Virginia* (2002).

David M. Potter, *Lincoln and His Party in the Secession Crisis* (1942).

Lorman A. Ratner and Dwight L. Teeter Jr., *Fanatics and Fire-Eaters: Newspapers and the Coming of the Civil War* (2003).

Kenneth M. Stampp, *And the War Came: The North and the Secession Crisis, 1860–61* (1960).

James M. Woods, *Rebellion and Realignment: Arkansas's Road to Secession* (1987).

Ralph A. Wooster, *The Secession Conventions of the South* (1962).

FORT SUMTER STARS AND STRIPES
This U.S. flag flew over Fort Sumter throughout the Confederate bombardment that initiated the Civil War on April 12, 1861. Shrapnel from thirty-three hours of cannon fire shredded the flag, but when the Union major Robert Anderson surrendered on April 13, he and his men marched out of the fort under this tattered banner. The governor of South Carolina cheered what he called the humbling of the flag of the United States. Northerners bridled at this insult, and within days flags sprouted across the Union. The Civil War stitched the flag and American nationalism together and made the Stars and Stripes the powerful symbol it is today. When Anderson returned to Fort Sumter in April 1865, he triumphantly raised this very flag.
Confederate Museum, United Daughters of the Confederacy.

CHAPTER 15

The Crucible of War
1861–1865

O N THE RAINY NIGHT OF SEPTEMBER 21, 1862, in Wilmington, North Carolina, twenty-four-year-old William Gould and seven other black men crowded into a small boat on Cape Fear River and quietly pushed away from the dock. Knowing that the authorities would sound the alarm for eight runaway slaves at daybreak, they rowed hard throughout the night. By dawn, the runaways had traveled twenty-eight miles to where the river flowed into the Atlantic Ocean. No longer concerned about being detected, they raised their sail and plunged into the swells. They made for the Union navy patrolling offshore to disrupt the flow of goods in and out of Wilmington, a major Confederate port. At 10:30 that morning, the U.S.S. *Cambridge* spied the sail and took the men aboard.

Astonishingly, on the same day that Gould reached the federal ship, President Abraham Lincoln announced to his cabinet in Washington, D.C., that he intended to issue a proclamation of **emancipation** freeing slaves in the Confederate states. Because the proclamation would not take effect until January 1863, Gould was not legally free in the eyes of the U.S. government. But the U.S. navy, suffering from a shortage of sailors, cared little about the formal status of runaway slaves. And within days of setting foot on the *Cambridge*, all eight runaways became sailors "for three years," Gould said, "first taking the Oath of Allegiance to the Government of Uncle Samuel."

Unlike most slaves, William Gould could read and write, and he began making almost daily entries in a remarkable diary, apparently the only diary kept during the war by a sailor who had been a slave. Much of Gould's naval experience was indistinguishable from that of white sailors. He found duty on a ship in the blockading squadron both boring and exhilarating. He often recorded "All hands painting, cleaning," and "Cruised as usual." But long days of tedious work were sometimes interrupted by the sighting of a ship on the horizon and a frantic "period of daring exploit" as enemies locked in combat. When the *Cambridge* closed on one Confederate vessel, Gould declared that "we told them good morning in the shape of a shot." In one five-day period in 1862, his ship and two other blockaders captured four blockade runners and ran another aground.

In October 1863, Gould transferred to the U.S.S. *Niagara* and sailed for European waters to search for Confederate cruisers abroad. "We are expecting a fight," he confided, "but who will be the victors remains to be seen." The *Niagara* did not engage the enemy in Europe, but when a sister ship, the U.S.S. *Kearsarge*, caught up with and sent to the bottom the *Alabama*, an infamous Confederate raider, Gould declared that his crew was "as delighted and as proud of the deed as if they had done it themselves."

Newly Recruited Contrabands, 1862
The U.S. navy recruited men with little regard for status or color. Blacks initially served only as coal heavers, cooks, and stewards, but within a year, some black sailors joined their ships' gun crews. As this photograph of newly recruited ex-slaves reveals, naval service was not limited to young men.
Courtesy of the New Hampshire Historical Society.

Despite having much in common with white sailors, Gould's Civil War experience was shaped by his race. Most whites fought to preserve their government and society, but most black men in the Union military saw service as an opportunity to fight slavery. From the beginning, Gould linked freedom and Union, which he called "the holiest of all causes."

Even though the navy treated black sailors better than the army treated black soldiers, Gould witnessed a number of racial incidents. "There was A malee [melee] on Deck between the white and colard men," he declared. Later, when a black regiment came aboard, "they were treated verry rough by the crew." White sailors "refused to let them eat off the mess pans and calld them all kinds of names[;] . . . in all they was treated shamefully." Recording another incident, Gould stated, "This Morning four or fiv[e] white fellows beat Jerry Jones (co[lored]). He was stabd in his left shoulder. Verry bad."

Still, Gould was proud of his service in the navy and carefully traced the progress of racial equality during the war. On shore leave in 1863, he cheered the "20th Regmt of U.S. (collard [colored]) Volunteers, the first collard Regement raised in New York pronounce[d] by all to be A splendid Regement." In March 1865, he celebrated the "passage of an amendment of the Con[sti]tution prohibiting slavery througho[ut] the United States." And a month later, he thrilled to the "Glad Tidings that the Stars and Stripe[s] had been planted over the Capital of the D—nd Confederacy by the invincible Grant." He added, we must not forget the "Mayrters to the cau[se] of Right and Equality."

Many slaves like the eight runaways from Wilmington took the first steps toward making the war a contest for freedom. Early in the war, black abolitionist Frederick Douglass challenged the friends of freedom to "*be up and doing;—now is your time.*" Although Southerners believed that the North threatened slavery, few Northerners agreed that their fight against disunion marked the beginning of the end of slavery. For eighteen months, Union soldiers fought solely to uphold the Constitution and preserve the nation. But in 1863, the northern war effort took on a dual purpose: to save the Union and to free the slaves.

Even if the Civil War had not touched slavery, the conflict still would have transformed America. As the world's first modern war, it mobilized the entire populations of North and South, harnessed the productive capacities of both economies, and produced battles that fielded 200,000 soldiers and created casualties in the tens of thousands. The carnage lasted four years and cost the nation an estimated 633,000 lives, nearly as many as in all of its other wars before and after combined. The war helped mold the modern American nation-state. The federal government emerged with new power and responsibility over national life. War furthered the emergence of a modern industrializing nation. It tore families apart and pushed women into new work and roles. But because the war to preserve the Union also became a war to destroy slavery, the northern victory had truly revolutionary meaning. Defeat and emancipation destroyed the slave society of the Old South and gave birth to a different southern society.

Years later, remembering the Civil War years, Frederick Douglass said, "It is something to couple one's name with great occasions." It *was* something—for William Gould and millions of other Americans. Whether they fought for the Confederacy or the Union, whether they labored behind the lines to supply Yankee or rebel soldiers, whether they prayed for the safe return of Northerners or Southerners, all Americans experienced the crucible of war. But the war affected no group more than the four million African Americans who saw its beginning as slaves and emerged as free people.

"And the War Came"

New to high office, Abraham Lincoln faced the worst crisis in the history of the nation: the threat of disunion. Lincoln revealed his strategy on March 4, 1861, in his inaugural address, which he carefully crafted to combine firmness and conciliation. First, he sought to stop the contagion of secession. Eight of the fifteen slave states had said "no" to disunion, but they remained suspicious and skittish. Lincoln wanted to avoid any act that would push the Upper South (North Carolina, Virginia, Maryland, Delaware, Kentucky, Tennessee, Missouri, and Arkansas) into leaving. Second, he sought to buy time so that emotions could cool in the deep South. By reassuring South Carolina, Georgia, Florida, Alabama, Mississippi, Louisiana, and Texas that the Republicans would not abolish slavery, Lincoln believed that Unionists there would assert themselves and overturn the secession decision. Always, Lincoln expressed his uncompromising will to oppose secession and to uphold the Union.

His counterpart, Jefferson Davis, fully intended to establish the Confederate States of America as an independent republic. To achieve permanence, Davis had to sustain the secession fever that had carried the deep South out of the Union. Even if the deep South held firm, however, the Confederacy would remain weak without additional states. Davis watched for opportunities to add new stars to the Confederate flag.

Neither man sought war. Both wanted to achieve their objectives peacefully. But as Lincoln later observed, "Both parties deprecated war, but one of them would *make* war rather than let the nation survive, and the other would *accept* war rather than let it perish. And the war came."

Attack on Fort Sumter

Fort Sumter's thick brick walls rose forty feet above the tiny island on which it perched at the entrance to Charleston harbor. Major Robert Anderson and some eighty U.S. soldiers occupied what Confederates claimed as their property. The fort with its American flag became a hated symbol of the nation that Southerners had abandoned, and they wanted federal troops out. Sumter was also a symbol to Northerners, a beacon affirming federal sovereignty in the seceded states.

The situation at Fort Sumter presented Lincoln with hard choices. Ordering the fort's evacuation would play well in the Upper South, whose edgy slave states threatened to bolt to the Confederacy if Lincoln resorted to military force to resolve the secession crisis. But yielding the fort would make it appear that Lincoln accepted the Confederacy's existence. He decided to hold Fort Sumter. But to do so, he had to provision it, for Anderson was running dangerously short of food. In the first week of April 1861, Lincoln authorized a peaceful expedition to bring supplies, but not military reinforcements, to the fort. The president understood that he risked war, but his plan honored his inaugural promises to defend federal property and to avoid using military force unless first attacked. Masterfully, Lincoln had shifted the fateful decision of war or peace to Jefferson Davis.

On April 9, Jefferson Davis and his cabinet met to consider the situation in Charleston harbor. The territorial integrity of the Confederacy demanded the end of the federal presence, Davis argued. But his secretary of state, Robert Toombs of Georgia, pleaded against military action. "Mr. President," he declared, "at this time it is suicide, murder, and will lose us every friend at the North. You will wantonly strike a hornet's nest which extends from mountain to ocean, and legions now quiet will swarm out and sting us to death." Davis rejected Toombs's prophecy and sent word to General Pierre Gustave T. Beauregard, the Louisianan commanding Confederate troops in Charleston, to take the fort before the relief expedition arrived. Thirty-three hours of bombardment on April 12 and 13 reduced the fort to rubble. Miraculously, not a single Union soldier died. On April 14, with the fort ablaze, Major Anderson offered his surrender and lowered the U.S. flag. The Confederates had Fort Sumter, but they also had war.

The response of the free states was thunderous. On April 15, Lincoln called for 75,000 militiamen to serve for ninety days to put down the rebellion, but several times that number rushed to defend the flag. Democrats responded as fervently as Republicans. Stephen A. Douglas, the recently defeated Democratic candidate for president, pledged his support. "There are only two sides to the question," he told a massive crowd in Chicago. "Every man must be for the United States or against it. There can be no

> The fort with its American flag became a hated symbol of the nation that Southerners had abandoned. Sumter was also a symbol to Northerners, a beacon affirming federal sovereignty in the seceded states.

Fort Sumter after the Bombardment
Located on an artificial island inside the entrance to Charleston harbor, Fort Sumter had walls eight to twelve feet thick. The fort was so undermanned that when Confederate shells began raining down on April 12, U.S. troops could answer back with only a few of the fort's forty-eight guns. Confederate artillery lobbed more than 4,000 rounds. Cannonballs pulverized the walls, while hot shot ignited the wooden buildings inside.
Minnesota Historical Society.

with the Confederate States and sink or swim with them."

Some found the choice excruciating. Robert E. Lee, a career military officer and the son of one of Virginia's oldest families, denounced secession in the deep South as the work of cotton-state hotheads. "I can anticipate no greater calamity for the country than a dissolution of the Union," he told his son in January 1861. Still, he said, "a Union that can only be maintained by swords and bayonets . . . has no charm for me." When Virginia left the Union in April, Lee went with his state and resigned from the U.S. army and declared, "Save in defense of my native State, I never desire again to draw my sword." But his beloved state offered no sanctuary for his tortured allegiances. Richmond would soon be the capital of the Confederacy; Virginia would be a battlefield, and Lee would again command military forces.

One by one the other states of the Upper South jumped off the fence. Within weeks, Arkansas, Tennessee, and North Carolina had followed Virginia's lead (Map 15.1). But in the border states of Delaware, Maryland, Kentucky, and Missouri, Unionism triumphed. Only in Delaware, where slaves accounted for less than 2 percent of the population, was the victory easy. In Maryland, Unionism needed a helping hand. Rather than allow the state to secede and make Washington, D.C., a federal island in a Confederate sea, Lincoln suspended the writ of habeas corpus, essentially setting aside constitutional guarantees that protect citizens from illegal and arbitrary arrest and detention, and he ordered U.S. troops into Baltimore, essentially placing the city under military arrest. Maryland's legislature, frightened by the federal invasion and aware of the strength of Union sentiment in the state's western counties, rejected secession.

The struggle turned violent in the West. In Missouri, Unionists won a narrow victory, but southern-sympathizing **guerrilla** bands roamed the state for the duration of the conflict, wreaking bloody havoc on civilians and soldiers alike. In Kentucky as in Missouri, Unionists barely defeated secession, and a prosouthern minority claimed that the state had severed ties with the Union. The Confederacy was not particularly fastidious in counting votes and eagerly made Missouri and Kentucky the twelfth and thirteenth stars on the Confederate flag.

Throughout the border states, but especially in Kentucky, the Civil War was truly a "brother's war." Seven of Henry Clay's grandsons fought: four for the Confederacy and three for the

neutrals in this war, *only patriots—or traitors.*" No one faced more acutely the dilemma of loyalty than the men and women of the Upper South.

The Upper South Chooses Sides

The Upper South faced a horrendous choice: either to fight against the Lower South or to fight against the Union. Many who only months earlier had rejected secession now embraced the Confederacy. To oppose southern independence was one thing; to fight fellow Southerners another. Thousands felt betrayed, believing that Lincoln had promised to achieve a peaceful reunion by waiting patiently for Unionists to retake power in the seceding states. One man furiously denounced the conflict as a "politician's war," conceding that "this is no time now to discuss the causes, but it is the duty of all who regard Southern institutions of value to side with the South, make common cause

> Throughout the border states, but especially in Kentucky, the Civil War was truly a "brother's war."

MAP 15.1 Secession, 1860–1861
After Lincoln's election, the fifteen slave states debated what to do. Seven states quickly left the Union, four left after the firing on Fort Sumter, and four remained loyal to the Union.

Union. Lincoln understood that the border states—particularly Kentucky—not only contained indispensable resources, population, and wealth but also controlled major rivers and railroads. "I think to lose Kentucky is nearly the same as to lose the whole game," Lincoln said. "Kentucky gone, we can not hold Missouri, nor, as I think, Maryland. These all against us, . . . we would as well consent to separation at once."

In the end, only eleven of the fifteen slave states joined the Confederate States of America. Moreover, the four seceding Upper South states contained significant numbers of people who felt little affection for the Confederacy. Dissatisfaction was so rife in the western counties of Virginia that in 1863 citizens there voted to create the separate state of West Virginia, loyal to the Union. Still, the acquisition of four new Confederate states greatly strengthened the cause of southern independence.

The Combatants

Although fierce struggle continued in the border states and in some areas within the seceding states, most whites in the South chose to defend the Confederacy. Only slaveholders had a direct economic stake in preserving slavery (estimated at some $3 billion in 1860), but most whites de-

fended the institution and the way of life they had built on it. The degraded and subjugated status of blacks was the basis of elevated status for even the most humble whites. "It matters not whether slaves be actually owned by many or by few," one Southerner declared. "It is enough that one simply belongs to the superior and ruling race, to secure consideration and respect." Moreover, Yankee "aggression" was no longer a secessionist's abstraction; it was real, and it was at the South's door. Most southern whites equated the secession of 1861 with the declaration of independence from tyrannical British rule in 1776. As one Georgia woman observed, Southerners wanted "nothing from the North but—*to be let alone*—and *they*, a people like ourselves whose republican independence was won by a rebellion, whose liberty was achieved by a secession, to think that they should attempt to coerce us—the idea is preposterous."

For Northerners, rebel "treason" threatened to destroy the best government on earth. The South's failure to accept the **democratic** election of a president and its firing on the nation's flag challenged the rule of law, the authority of the Constitution, and the ability of the people to govern themselves. As an Indiana soldier told his wife, a "good government is the best thing on earth. Property is nothing without it, because it is not protected; a family is nothing without it, because they cannot be educated." Lincoln captured the special magnetism of the Union cause when he called it "a People's contest," one in which America's promise "to elevate the condition of man" hung in the balance.

Men rallied behind their separate battle flags, fully convinced that they were in the right and that God was on their side. While both sides claimed the lion's share of virtue, no one could argue that the South's resources and forces equaled the North's. A glance at the census figures contradicted such a notion. Yankees took heart at their superior power, but the rebels believed they had advantages that nullified every northern strength. Both sides mobilized swiftly in the spring and summer of 1861, and each devised what it believed would be a winning military and diplomatic strategy.

How They Expected to Win

The balance sheet of northern and southern resources reveals enormous advantages for the Union (Figure 15.1). The twenty-three states remaining in the Union had a population of 22.3

million; the eleven Confederate states had a population of only 9.1 million, of whom 3.67 million (40 percent) were slaves. The North's economic advantages were even more overwhelming. The North manufactured more than 90 percent of the nation's industrial goods. It produced 13 times as much textiles as the South, 16 times as much iron, 32 times as many firearms, and so on. So mismatched were North and South that the question becomes why the South made war at all. Was not the South's cause lost before Confederates lobbed the first rounds at Fort Sumter? The answer quite simply is "no." Southerners expected to win—for some good reasons—and they came very close to doing so.

Southerners believed that they would triumph because of their region's just cause, superior civilization, and unsurpassed character. They bucked the military odds, but hadn't the **liberty**-loving colonists in 1776 also done so? "Britain could not conquer three million," a Louisianan proclaimed, and "the world cannot conquer the South." How could anyone doubt the outcome of a contest between lean, hard, country-born rebel warriors defending family, property, and liberty, and soft, flabby, citified Yankee mechanics waging an unconstitutional war of aggression and subjugation?

The South's confidence also rested on its estimation of the economic clout of its principal crop, cotton. Southerners believed that northern prosperity depended on the South's cotton. It followed then that without cotton, New England textile mills would stand idle. And without southern **planters** purchasing northern manufactured goods, northern factories would drown in their own unsold goods. And without the foreign exchange earned by the overseas sales of cotton, the financial structure of the entire Yankee nation would collapse. A Virginian spoke for most Confederates when he declared that in the South's ability to "withhold the benefits of our trade, we hold a power over the North more powerful than a powerful army in the field."

Cotton would also make Europe a powerful ally of the Confederacy, Southerners reasoned. After all, they said, England's economy (and to a lesser degree France's) depended on cotton. Of the 900 million pounds of cotton

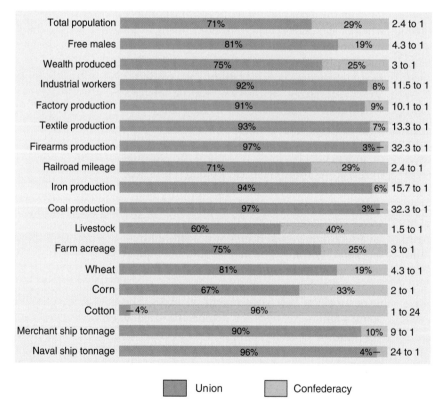

	Union	Confederacy	Ratio
Total population	71%	29%	2.4 to 1
Free males	81%	19%	4.3 to 1
Wealth produced	75%	25%	3 to 1
Industrial workers	92%	8%	11.5 to 1
Factory production	91%	9%	10.1 to 1
Textile production	93%	7%	13.3 to 1
Firearms production	97%	3%	32.3 to 1
Railroad mileage	71%	29%	2.4 to 1
Iron production	94%	6%	15.7 to 1
Coal production	97%	3%	32.3 to 1
Livestock	60%	40%	1.5 to 1
Farm acreage	75%	25%	3 to 1
Wheat	81%	19%	4.3 to 1
Corn	67%	33%	2 to 1
Cotton	4%	96%	1 to 24
Merchant ship tonnage	90%	10%	9 to 1
Naval ship tonnage	96%	4%	24 to 1

Union   Confederacy

FIGURE 15.1 Resources of the Union and Confederacy
The Union's enormous statistical advantages failed to convince Confederates that their cause was doomed.

Bridge on the Orange and Alexandria Railroad
Confederate forces burned southern railroads and bridges to slow Union advances, cut federal supply lines, and protect Confederate retreats. West Point–trained Herman Haupt, seen here inspecting a rebuilt bridge, was in charge of the Union's efforts at railroad construction and repair. Although railroads were used as an instrument of war in the Crimea in the 1850s, it was during the Civil War that railroads took on revolutionary importance. Railroads helped set new standards of overland mobility, rapid maneuver, and concentration of forces.
Library of Congress.

England imported annually, more than 700 million came from the South. If the supply were interrupted, sheer economic need would make England (and perhaps France) a Confederate ally. And because the British navy ruled the seas, the North would find Britain a formidable foe.

Southerners' confidence may seem naive today, but even tough-minded European military observers picked the South to win. Offsetting the North's power was the South's expanse. The North, Europeans predicted, could not conquer the vast territory (750,000 square miles) extending from the Potomac to the Rio Grande, with rugged terrain and bad roads. To defeat the South, the Union would need to raise a massive invading army, supply it with huge quantities of provisions and arms, and protect supply lines that would stretch farther than any in modern history.

Indeed, the South enjoyed major advantages, and the Confederacy devised a military strategy to exploit them. Jefferson Davis called it an "offensive-defensive" strategy. It recognized that a Union victory required the North to defeat and subjugate the South but a Confederate victory required only that the South stay at home, blunt invasions, avoid battles that risked annihilating its army, and outlast the North's will to fight. When an opportunity presented itself, the South would strike the invaders. Like the American colonists, the South could win independence by not losing the war.

If the North did nothing, the South would by default establish

> The Confederacy devised an "offensive-defensive" strategy. Victory required only that the South stay at home, blunt invasions, avoid battles that risked annihilating its army, and outlast the North's will to fight.

itself as a sovereign nation. The Lincoln administration therefore adopted an offensive strategy. On April 19, four days after the president issued the proclamation calling for a militia to put down the rebellion, he issued another proclamation declaring a naval blockade of the Confederacy. He sought to deny the Confederacy the advantages offered by its most valuable commodity—cotton. Without the sale of cotton abroad, the South would have far fewer dollars to pay for war goods. Even before the North could mount an effective blockade, however, Jefferson Davis decided voluntarily to cease exporting cotton. He wanted to create a cotton "famine" that would enfeeble the northern economy and precipitate European intervention. But the cotton famine Davis created devastated the South, not the North, and left Europe on the diplomatic sidelines.

Southerners were not the only ones with illusions. Lincoln's call-up of 75,000 men for ninety days illustrates his inability to foresee the magnitude and duration of the war. He and most other Americans thought of war in terms of their most recent experience, the Mexican-American War of the 1840s. In Mexico, fighting had taken place between relatively small armies, had cost relatively few lives, and had inflicted only light damage on the countryside. Americans on the eve of the Civil War could not know that four ghastly years of bloodletting lay ahead.

Lincoln and Davis Mobilize

Mobilization required effective political leadership, and at first glance the South appeared to have the advantage. A gentleman from a Mississippi planter family, Jefferson Davis brought to the Confederate presidency a distinguished political career, including experience in the U.S. Senate. He was also a West Point graduate, a combat veteran and authentic hero of the Mexican-American War, and a former secretary of war. Dignified and erect, with "a jaw sawed in steel," Davis appeared to be everything a nation could want in a wartime leader.

In contrast, Abraham Lincoln brought to the White House one lackluster term in the House of Representatives and almost no administrative experience, and his sole brush with anything

> In Lincoln, the North got far more than met the eye. He proved himself a master politician and a superb leader.

military was as a captain in the militia in the Black Hawk War, a brief struggle in Illinois in 1832 in which whites expelled the last Indians from the state. Lincoln later joked about his service in the Black Hawk War as the time when he survived bloody encounters with mosquitoes and led raids on wild onion patches. The lanky, disheveled Illinois lawyer-politician looked anything but military or presidential in his bearing, and even his friends feared that he was in over his head.

Davis, however, proved to be less than he appeared. Although he worked hard and was fervently dedicated to the Confederate cause, Davis possessed little capacity for broad military strategy yet intervened often in military affairs. He was an even less able political leader. Quarrelsome and proud, he had an acid tongue that made enemies the Confederacy could ill afford. He insisted on dealing with every scrap of paper that came across his desk, and he grew increasingly unbending and dogmatic. The Confederacy's intimidating problems might have defeated an even more talented leader, however. For example, **state sovereignty**, which was enshrined in the Confederate constitution, made Davis's task of organizing a new nation and fighting a war difficult in the extreme.

With Lincoln, in contrast, the North got far more than met the eye. He proved himself a master politician and a superb leader. He never allowed personal feelings to get in the way of his objectives. When forming his cabinet, for example, Lincoln shrewdly appointed representatives of every Republican faction, men who were often his chief rivals and critics. He appointed Salmon P. Chase secretary of the treasury, knowing that Chase had presidential ambitions. As secretary of state, he chose his chief opponent for the Republican nomination in 1860, William H. Seward, who mistakenly expected to twist Lincoln around his little finger and formulate policy himself. Despite his civilian background, Lincoln displayed an innate understanding of military strategy. In time, no one was more crucial in mapping the Union war plan. Further, Lincoln wrote beautifully and through letters and speeches reached out to the North's people, helping to galvanize them in defense of the nation he called "the last best hope of earth."

Guided by Lincoln and Davis, the North and South began gathering their armies. Southerners had to build almost everything from scratch, and Northerners had to mobilize their superior numbers and industrial resources for war. In 1861,

Minié Ball

The Union army was one of the best equipped armies in history. None of its weaponry proved more vital than a French innovation: Captain Claude Minié's new bullet. In 1848, Minié created an inch-long slug that was rammed down a rifled barrel and would spin at great speed as it left the muzzle. The spin gave the bullet greater distance and accuracy than bullets fired from smoothbore weapons. When the war began, most soldiers carried smoothbore muskets; but by 1863, infantry on both sides fought with rifles. Bullets caused more than 90 percent of battle wounds, and minié balls proved extremely destructive to human bodies on impact.

Picture Research Consultants & Archives.

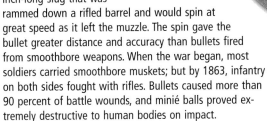

before the war, the puny federal army numbered only 16,000 men, most of them scattered over the West subjugating Indians. One-third of the officers followed the example of the Virginian Robert E. Lee, resigning their commissions and heading south. The U.S. navy was in better shape. Forty-two ships were in service, and a large merchant marine would in time provide more ships and sailors for the Union cause. The Confederate navy was never a match for the Union fleet, and thus the South pinned its hopes on its armies.

From the beginning, the South exhibited more enthusiasm than ability to provide its soldiers with supplies and transportation. The Confederacy made prodigious efforts to build new factories to produce tents, blankets, shoes, and its gray uniforms, but many rebel soldiers slept in the open air without proper clothes and sometimes without shoes. Even when factories managed to produce what the soldiers needed, southern railroads—constructed to connect plantations with ports—often could not deliver the goods. And in each year of the war, more railroads were captured, destroyed, or left in disrepair. Food production proved less of a problem, but food sometimes rotted before it reached the soldiers. The one bright spot was the Confederacy's Ordnance Bureau, headed by Josiah Gorgas, a near miracle worker when it came to manufacturing gunpower, cannon, and rifles. In April 1864, Gorgas proudly observed:

"Where three years ago we were not making a gun, a pistol nor a sabre, no shot nor shell . . . — a pound of powder—we now make all these in quantities to meet the demands of our large armies."

Recruiting and supplying huge armies required enormous public spending. Before the war, the federal government's tiny income had come primarily from tariff duties and the sale of public lands. Massive wartime expenditures made new revenues imperative. At first, both North and South sold war bonds, which essentially were loans from patriotic citizens. In addition, both Union and Confederacy turned to taxes. The North raised one-fifth of its wartime revenue from taxes; the South raised only one-twentieth. Eventually, both sides began printing paper money. Inflation soared, but the South suffered more because it financed a greater part of its wartime costs through the printing press. Prices in the North rose by about 80 percent during the war, while inflation in the South topped 9,000 percent.

Within months of the bombardment of Fort Sumter, both sides had found men to fight and people to supply and support them. But the underlying strength of the northern economy gave the Union the decided advantage. With their military and industrial muscles beginning to ripple, Northerners became itchy for action. They wanted an invasion that once and for all would smash the rebellion. Horace Greeley's *New York Tribune* began to chant: "Forward to Richmond! Forward to Richmond!"

Battling It Out, 1861–1862

During the first year and a half of the war, armies fought major campaigns in both East and West. Because the rival capitals—Richmond and Washington, D.C.—were only ninety miles apart and each was threatened more than once with capture, the eastern campaign was especially dramatic and commanded public attention. But the battles in the West proved more decisive. As Yankee and rebel armies pounded each other on land, the navies of each side fought on the seas and in the rivers of the South, and Confederate and U.S. diplomats competed for advantage in the corridors of power in Europe. All the while, casualty lists in both South and North reached appalling lengths.

Stalemate in the Eastern Theater

Lincoln appointed Mexican-American War veteran Irvin McDowell to be commanding general of the Union army assembling outside Washington. McDowell had no thought of taking his raw recruits into battle during the summer of 1861, but Lincoln ordered him to prepare his 35,000 greenhorn troops for an attack on the 20,000 Confederates defending Manassas, a railroad junction in Virginia about thirty miles southwest of Washington.

On July 21, the Union army forded Bull Run, a branch of the Potomac River, and engaged the southern forces effectively (Map 15.2). But fast-moving southern reinforcements blunted the Union attack and then counterattacked. What began as an orderly Union retreat turned

---

MAP 15.2   The Civil War, 1861–1862

While eyes focused on the eastern theater, especially the 90-mile stretch of land between the U.S. capital at Washington and the Confederate capital at Richmond, Union troops were winning strategic victories in the West.

READING THE MAP: In which states did the Confederacy and the Union each win the most battles in this period? Which side used or followed water routes most for troop movements and attacks?

CONNECTIONS: Which major cities in the South and West fell to Union troops in 1862? Which strategic area did those Confederate losses place in Union hands? How did this outcome affect the later movement of troops and supplies?

FOR MORE HELP ANALYZING THIS MAP, see the visual activity for this chapter in the Online Study Guide at bedfordstmartins.com/roark.

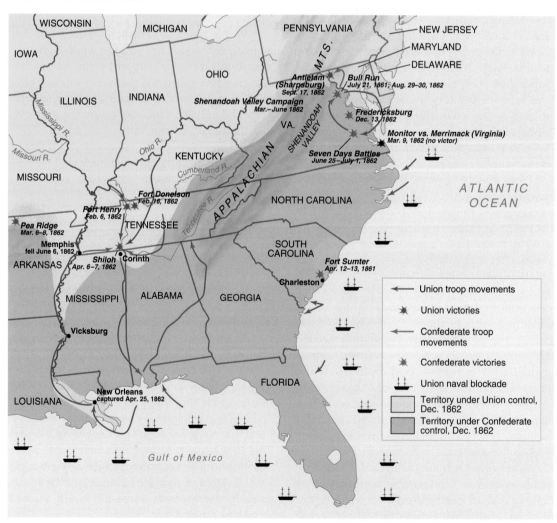

into a panicky stampede. Demoralized federal troops ran over shocked civilians as the soldiers raced back to Washington.

By Civil War standards, casualties (wounded and dead) at Bull Run (or Manassas, as Southerners called the battle) were light: about 2,000 Confederates and 1,600 Federals. The significance of the battle lay in the lessons Northerners and Southerners drew from it. For Southerners, it confirmed the superiority of rebel fighting men and the inevitability of Confederate nationhood. Manassas was *"one of the decisive battles of the world,"* a Georgian proclaimed. It *"has* secured our independence." While victory elevated southern pride, defeat sobered Northerners. It was a major setback, admitted the *New York Tribune,* but "Let us go to work, then, with a will." Bull Run taught Lincoln that victory would be neither quick nor easy.

The Battle of Savage's Station, **Robert Knox Sneden, 1862**
In 1862, thirty-year-old Robert Sneden joined the Fortieth New York Volunteers and soon found himself in Virginia, part of George McClellan's peninsula campaign. A gifted artist in watercolor as well as an eloquent writer, Sneden captures here an early Confederate assault in what became known as the Seven Days Battle. "The immense open space in front of Savage's [house] was densely thronged with wagon trains, artillery, caissons, ammunition trains, and moving troops," Sneden observed. The "storm of lead was continuous and deadly on the approaching lines of the Rebels. They bravely rushed up, however, to within twenty feet of our artillery, when bushels of grape and canister from the cannon laid them low in rows." Over the next three years, Sneden produced hundreds of vivid drawings and eventually thousands of pages of remembrance, providing one of the most complete accounts of a Union soldier's Civil War experience.
© 1996, Lora Robbins Collection of Virginia Art, Virginia Historical Society.

Within four days of the disaster, the president signed bills authorizing the enlistment of one million men for three years.

Lincoln also found a new general, replacing McDowell with young George B. McClellan. Born in Philadelphia of well-to-do parents, educated in the best schools before graduating from West Point second in his class, the thirty-four-year-old McClellan believed that he was a great soldier and that Lincoln was a dunce, the "original Gorilla." A superb administrator and organizer, McClellan came to Washington as commander of the newly named Army of the Potomac. In the months following his appointment, McClellan energetically whipped his dispirited army into shape but was reluctant to send his soldiers into battle. For all his energy, McClellan lacked decisiveness. Lincoln wanted a general who would advance, take risks, and fight, but McClellan went into winter quarters without budging from the banks of the Potomac. "If General McClellan does not want to use the army I would like to *borrow* it," Lincoln declared in frustration.

Finally, in May 1862, McClellan launched his long-awaited offensive. He transported his highly polished army, now 130,000 strong, down the Chesapeake Bay to the mouth of the James River and began moving up the Yorktown peninsula toward Richmond. McClellan took two and a half months to advance a mere sixty-five miles. When he was within six miles of the Confederate capital, the Confederate general Joseph Johnston hit him like a hammer. In the assault, Johnston was wounded and was replaced by Robert E. Lee, the reluctant Confederate, who would become the South's most celebrated general. Lee named his command the Army of Northern Virginia.

The contrast between Lee and McClellan could hardly have been greater. McClellan brimmed with conceit and braggadocio; Lee was courteous and reserved. On the battlefield, McClellan grew timid and irresolute, and Lee became audaciously, even recklessly, aggressive. And Lee had at his side in the peninsula campaign military men of real talent: General Thomas J. Jackson, nicknamed "Stonewall" for

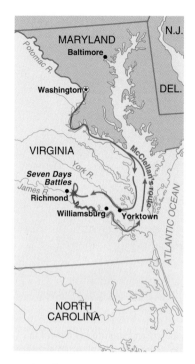

Peninsula Campaign, 1862

holding the line at Manassas, and James E. B. (Jeb) Stuart, a dashing twenty-nine-year-old cavalry commander who rode circles around Yankee troops.

Lee's assault initiated the Seven Days Battle (June 25–July 1) and began McClellan's march back down the peninsula. By the time McClellan reached the water and the safety of the Union navy, 30,000 men from both sides had died or been wounded. Although Southerners suffered twice the casualties of Northerners, Lee had saved Richmond and achieved a strategic success. Lincoln wired McClellan to abandon the peninsula campaign and replaced him with General John Pope.

In August, north of Richmond, Pope had his own rendezvous with Lee. At the Second Battle of Bull Run, Lee's smaller army battered Pope's forces and sent them scurrying back to Washington. Lincoln ordered Pope to Minnesota to pacify Indians and again put McClellan in command. Lincoln had not changed his mind about McClellan's capacity as a warrior. But he reluctantly acknowl-

edged that "If he can't fight himself, he excels in making others ready to fight."

Lee could fight, and sensing that he had the enemy on the ropes, he sought to land the knockout punch. Lee pushed the Army of Northern Virginia across the Potomac and invaded Maryland. A victory on northern soil would dislodge Maryland from the Union, Lee reasoned, and might even cause Lincoln to sue for peace. On September 17, 1862, McClellan's forces finally engaged Lee's army at Antietam Creek (see Map 15.2). (See "American Places," page 527.) Earlier, a Union soldier had found a copy of Lee's orders to his army wrapped around some cigars dropped by a careless Confederate officer, so McClellan had a clear picture of Lee's position. McClellan's characteristic caution, however, cost him the opportunity to destroy the opposing army. Still, he did severe damage. With "solid shot . . . cracking skulls like eggshells," according to one observer, the armies went after each other. By nightfall, 6,000 men lay dead or dying on the battlefield, and 17,000 more had been wounded. The Battle of Antietam would be the bloodiest day of the war. Instead of being the war-winning fight Lee had anticipated when he came north, Antietam sent the battered Army of North Virginia limping back home. McClellan claimed to have saved the North, but Lincoln again removed him from command of the Army of the Potomac and appointed General Ambrose Burnside.

Although bloodied, Lee remained alert for an opportunity to punish the enemy. In December, Burnside provided that chance. At Fredericksburg, Virginia, Burnside's 122,000 Union troops faced 78,500 Confederates dug in behind a stone wall on the heights above the Rappahannock River. Half a mile of open

The Dead of Antietam
In October 1862, Mathew Brady opened at his New York gallery an exhibition that shocked the nation. Entitled "The Dead of Antietam," the exhibition consisted of ninety-five photographs and presented the battlefield as the soldiers saw it. This photograph shows the bodies of Confederate troops lined up for burial. Among the thousands of visitors to the exhibit was a reporter for the *New York Times*, who observed: "Mr. Brady has done something to bring to us the terrible reality and earnestness of the war. If he has not brought bodies and laid them in our door-yards and along [our] streets, he has done something very like it."
Library of Congress.

AMERICAN PLACES

Antietam National Battlefield, Sharpsburg, Maryland

Bloody Lane
Antietam National Battefield.

Fresh from their victory at Second Manassas, General Robert E. Lee's troops reached Sharpsburg, Maryland, on September 15 and took up positions on the low ridge that runs along the western side of Antietam Creek. General George McClellan's army arrived on the east side of the creek that same day. On the morning of September 17, McClellan's troops attacked Lee's lines.

General Joseph "Fighting Joe" Hooker's men rushed forward, pouring into a cornfield, "loading and firing with demoniacal fury and shouting and laughing hysterically." So intense was the firing, Hooker remembered, that quickly "every stalk of corn in the . . . field was cut as closely as could have been done with a knife." Rival soldiers surged back and forth. According to some accounts, the field changed hands fifteen times before the Yankees prevailed.

A little to the south of Miller's Cornfield, Confederate troops concentrated in a 800-yard sunken road, worn down over the years by heavy wagons hauling grain. The well-protected rebels repelled four Union assaults. "For three hours and thirty minutes," a Union officer remembered, "the battle raged incessantly, without either party giving way." In the early afternoon, northern troops finally routed the rebels, but by then some 6,400 killed and mortally wounded soldiers lay along the sunken road, known thereafter as Bloody Lane.

South of Bloody Lane, Union general Ambrose E. Burnside's 12,000 men struggled to cross a 12-foot-wide bridge over Antietam Creek while 450 Georgia sharpshooters in a wooded bluff overlooking the bridge poured down lethal fire. Late in the day, Burnside's troops forced their way across and cleared out the Georgia defenders.

The fighting ended when night fell. The next morning, a Pennsylvania soldier wrote: "No tongue can tell, no mind can conceive, no pen portray the horrible sights I witnessed." Antietam proved to be one of the critical turning points in the Civil War. The U.S. army stopped the Confederacy's first invasion of the North, and the victory provided Lincoln an opportunity to transform the war for Union into a crusade for freedom. A national site since 1890, the Antietam battlefield offers visitors access to Miller's Cornfield, Bloody Lane, and "Burnside's Bridge," killing fields that silently testify to the fighting on that awful day.

FOR WEB LINKS RELATED TO THIS SITE AND OTHER AMERICAN PLACES, see "PlaceLinks" at bedfordstmartins.com/roark.

ground separated the armies. "A chicken could not live on that field when we open on it," a Confederate artillery officer predicted. Yet Burnside ordered a frontal assault. Wave after wave of Union soldiers crashed against impregnable defenses. When the shooting finally ceased, the Federals counted nearly 13,000 casualties, the Confederates fewer than 5,000. The Battle of Fredericksburg was one of the Union's worst defeats. As 1862 ended, the North seemed no nearer to ending the rebellion than it had been when the war began. Rather than checkmate, military struggle in the East had reached stalemate.

Union Victories in the Western Theater

While most eyes focused on events in the East, the decisive early encounters of the war were taking place to the west, between the Appalachian Mountains and the Ozarks (see Map 15.2). The West's rivers—the Mississippi, the Tennessee, and the Cumberland—became the keys to the military situation. Looking northward along the three rivers, Southerners spied Missouri and Kentucky, states they claimed but did not control. Looking southward, Northerners saw that they would split Arkansas, Louisiana, and Texas from the Confederacy if they controlled the Mississippi River. The Cumberland and Tennessee rivers penetrated Tennessee, one of the Confederacy's main producers of food, mules, and iron—all vital resources.

> While most eyes focused on events in the East, the decisive early encounters of the war were taking place to the West between the Appalachian Mountains and the Ozarks.

Before the Federals could march on Tennessee, they needed to secure Missouri to the west. Union troops commanded by General Samuel R. Curtis swept across Missouri to the northwestern border of Arkansas. There, in March 1862 at Pea Ridge, they encountered General Earl Van Dorn's 16,000-man Confederate army, which included three regiments of Indians from the Five Civilized Nations in Indian Territory. Although Native Americans fought on both sides during the war, in this battle the Indians, mostly Cherokees, sided with the South because they hoped that the Confederacy would grant them more independence than had the United States. Curtis's victory at the Battle of Pea Ridge left Missouri free of Confederate troops and opened much of Arkansas to federal advance. But Missouri was not free of Confederate guerrillas. Guerrilla bands led by the notorious William Clarke Quantrill and "Bloody Bill" Anderson burned, tortured, scalped, and murdered Union civilians and soldiers until the final year of the war.

Farther west, Confederate armies sought to fulfill Jefferson Davis's vision of a slaveholding empire stretching all the way to the Pacific and even into Mexico. Both the Confederacy and the Union recognized the immense value of the gold and silver mines of California, Nevada, and Colorado. A quick strike by Texas troops had taken Sante Fe, New Mexico, in the winter of 1861–62. Then in March 1862, a band of

Native American Recruits
Both the Union and the Confederacy sought soldiers from tribes in Indian Territory. Here a Union recruiter swears in Indian recruits, but it was the Confederacy that signed treaties with the so-called Five Civilized Tribes—the Choctaw, Chickasaw, Creek, Seminole, and Cherokee—in 1861. Confederates promised to assume the financial obligations of the old treaties with the United States, guarantee slavery, respect the independence of the tribes, and permit the tribes to send delegates to Richmond. John Ross, chief of the Cherokee Nation, prayed that he had chosen the right side. "We are in the situation of a man standing upon a low naked spot of ground," he said, "with the water rising all around him. . . . The tide carries by him, in its mad course, a drifting log. . . . By refusing it he is a doomed man. By seizing hold of it he has a chance for his life." Several thousand Indians fought in blue and in gray uniforms. In some battles in Arkansas, Indians fought Indians.
Wisconsin Historical Society.

Colorado miners ambushed and crushed southern forces at Glorieta Pass, outside Santa Fe. One rebel soldier described the Unionists as "regular demons, that iron and lead had no effect upon, in the shape of Pike's Peakers from the Denver City Gold mines." (The Coloradans were commanded by Colonel John M. Chivington, who later shocked the nation in November 1864 when his volunteers massacred some 500 Cheyenne and Arapaho—primarily women and children—peacefully camped at Sand Creek, Colorado.) Confederate military failures in the far West in 1862 meant that there would be no Confederate empire beyond Texas.

Battle of Glorieta Pass, 1862

The principal western battles took place in Tennessee, where General Ulysses S. Grant emerged as the key northern commander. Grant had graduated from West Point and served bravely in Mexico. When the Civil War began, he was a thirty-nine-year-old dry-goods clerk in Galena, Illinois. Gentle at home, he became pugnacious on the battlefield. "The art of war is simple," he said. "Find out where your enemy is, get at him as soon as you can and strike him as hard as you can, and keep moving on." Grant's philosophy of war as annihilation would take a huge toll in human life, but it played to the North's strength: superiority in manpower. In his old uniform and slouch hat, with his tired, sad, nondescript face, Grant did not look much like a general. But Lincoln, who did not look much like a president, learned his worth. Later, to critics who wanted the president to sack Grant because of his drinking, Lincoln would say: "*I can't spare this man. He fights.*"

In February 1862, operating in tandem with U.S. navy gunboats, Grant captured Fort Henry on the Tennessee River and Fort Donelson on the Cumberland (see Map 15.2). Defeat forced the Confederates to withdraw from all of Kentucky and most of Tennessee. Grant pushed after the retreating rebels. On April 6, General Albert Sidney Johnston's army surprised him at Shiloh Church in Tennessee. Grant's troops were badly mauled the first day, but Grant remained cool and brought up reinforcements throughout the night. The next morning, the Union army counterattacked, driving the Confederates before it. The Battle of Shiloh was terribly costly to both

sides; there were 20,000 casualties, among them General Johnston. Grant later said that after Shiloh he "gave up all idea of saving the Union except by complete conquest."

Although no one knew it at the time, Shiloh inflicted a mortal wound to the Confederacy's bid to control the theater of operations in the West. In short order, the Yankees captured the strategic town of Corinth, Mississippi, the river city of Memphis, and the South's largest city, New Orleans. By the end of 1862, the far West and most—but not all—of the Mississippi valley lay in Union hands. At the same time, the outcome of the struggle in another theater of war was also becoming clearer.

War and Diplomacy in the Atlantic Theater

At the beginning of the war, with a blockade fleet of only about three dozen ships and more than 3,500 miles of southern coastline to patrol, the U.S. navy faced an impossible task. At first, rebel merchant ships slipped in and out of southern

Major Battles of the Civil War, 1861–1862

April 12–13, 1861	Attack on Fort Sumter
July 21, 1861	First Battle of Bull Run (Manassas)
February 6, 1862	Battle of Fort Henry
February 16, 1862	Battle of Fort Donelson
March 9, 1862	Battle of the *Merrimack* (the *Virginia*) and the *Monitor*
March 26, 1862	Battle of Glorieta Pass
March 28, 1862	Battle of Pea Ridge
May–July 1862	McClellan's peninsula campaign
April 6–7, 1862	Battle of Shiloh
June 6, 1862	Fall of Memphis
June 25–July 1, 1862	Seven Days Battles
August 29–30, 1862	Second Battle of Bull Run (Manassas)
September 17, 1862	Battle of Antietam
December 13, 1862	Battle of Fredericksburg

ports nearly at will. Taking on cargoes in the Caribbean, the sleek, fast blockade runners brought in vital supplies—guns and medicine—and also small quantities of luxury goods such as tea and liquor. But with the U.S. navy commissioning a new blockader almost weekly, the naval fleet eventually numbered 150 ships on duty, and the Union navy dramatically improved its score.

Unable to build a conventional navy equal to the expanding U.S. fleet, the Confederates experimented with a radical new maritime design: the ironclad warship. At Norfolk, Virginia, they layered the wooden hull of the frigate *Merrimack* with two-inch-thick armor plate. Rechristened *Virginia*, the ship steamed out in March 1862 to engage the wooden ships enforcing the federal blockade (see Map 15.2). Within a few hours, it sank two large federal ships, killing at least 240 Union sailors. The following morning, when the *Virginia* returned to finish off the federal blockaders, it was challenged by the *Monitor*, a federal ironclad that had arrived from Brooklyn during the night. The *Monitor*, a ship of even more radical design than the *Virginia*, was topped with a revolving turret containing two eleven-inch guns. On March 9, the two ships hurled shells at each other for two hours, but neither could penetrate the other's armor and the battle ended in a draw.

The Confederacy never found a way to break the Union blockade, despite exploring many naval innovations, including a new underwater vessel—the submarine. (See "The Promise of Technology," page 532.) Each month the Union fleet tightened its noose. By 1863, the South had abandoned its embargo policy and desperately wanted to ship cotton to pay for imports of the arms, bullets, shoes, and uniforms it needed to fight the war. But the growing effectiveness of the federal blockade, a southern naval officer observed, "shut the Confederacy out from the world, deprived it of supplies, weakened its military and naval strength." By 1865, the blockaders were intercepting about half of the southern ships attempting to break through.

What Confederates could not achieve on saltwater, they sought to achieve through foreign policy. According to their theory of King Cotton, cotton-starved European nations had no choice but to break the Union blockade and recognize the

> According to the theory of King Cotton, cotton-starved European nations had no choice but to break the Union blockade and recognize the Confederacy.

Confederacy. Britain and France briefly discussed joint action to lift the blockade in 1862 but rejected the notion. Some European nations granted the Confederacy "belligerent" status, which enabled it to buy goods and build ships in European ports, but none recognized the Confederate States of America as a nation, a bold act that probably would have drawn them into war with the United States.

King Cotton diplomacy failed for several reasons. A bumper cotton crop in 1860 meant that the warehouses of British textile manufacturers bulged with surplus cotton throughout 1861. In 1862, when Europe began to feel the pinch of a cotton shortage, manufacturers found new sources in Egypt and India. In addition, the development of a brisk trade between the Union and Britain—British war materiel for American grain and flour—helped offset the decline in textiles and encouraged Britain to remain neutral.

Europe's temptation to intervene disappeared for good in 1862. Union military successes on the rivers of the West made Britain and France think twice about linking their fates to the Confederacy. And in September 1862, five days after the northern victory at Antietam, Lincoln announced a new policy that made an alliance with the Confederacy an alliance with slavery, an alliance the French and British were not willing to make.

Union *and* Freedom

For a year and a half, Lincoln insisted that the abolition of slavery was not a northern war aim; the war, he said, was strictly to save the Union. But despite Lincoln's repeated pronouncements, the war for union became a war for African American freedom. Each month the conflict dragged on, it became clearer that the Confederate war machine depended heavily on slavery. Rebel armies used slaves to build fortifications, haul materiel, tend horses, and perform camp chores. On the home front, slaves labored in ironworks and shipyards, and they grew the food that fed both soldiers and civilians. Slavery undergirded the Confederacy as certainly as it had the Old South. In the field among Union military commanders, in the halls of Congress, and in the White House, the truth gradually came into focus: To defeat the Confederacy, the North would have to destroy slavery. "I am a slow walker," Lincoln said, "but I never walk back."

From Slaves to Contraband

Personally, Lincoln detested human bondage, but as president he felt compelled to act prudently in the interests of the Union. He doubted his right under the Constitution to tamper with the "domestic institutions" of any state, even states in rebellion. An astute politician, Lincoln worked within the limits of public opinion, and in 1861 he believed those limits were tight. The issue of black freedom was particularly explosive in the loyal border states, where slaveholders threatened to jump into the arms of the Confederacy at even the hint of emancipation. Black freedom also raised alarms in the free states. The Democratic Party gave notice that emancipation would kill the bipartisan alliance and make the war strictly a Republican affair. Democrats were as passionate for union as Republicans, but they marched under the banner "The Constitution As It Is, the Union As It Was."

Moreover, many white Northerners were not about to risk their lives to satisfy abolitionist "fanaticism." "We Won't Fight to Free the Nigger," one popular banner read. They feared that emancipation would propel "two or three million semi-savages" northward, where they would crowd into white neighborhoods, compete for white jobs, and mix with white "sons and daughters." A surge of anti-emancipation, antiblack sentiment, then, threatened to dislodge the loyal slave states from the Union, alienate the Democratic Party, deplete the armies, and perhaps even spark race warfare.

Yet proponents of emancipation pressed Lincoln as relentlessly as the anti-emancipation forces. Abolitionists argued that by seceding, Southerners had forfeited their right to the protection of the Constitution, and that Lincoln could—as the price of their treason—legally confiscate their property in slaves. When Lincoln refused, abolitionists scalded him. Frederick Douglass labeled him "the miserable tool of traitors and rebels." Abolitionists won increasing numbers of converts during the war, especially among the radical faction of the Republican Party.

The Republican-dominated Congress refused to leave slavery policy entirely in Lincoln's hands. In August 1861, Congress approved the Confiscation Act, which allowed the seizure of any slave employed directly by the Confederate military. The House and the Senate also fulfilled the **free-soil** dream of prohibiting slavery in the territories and abolished slavery in Washington, D.C. Democrats and border-state representatives voted against even these mild measures, but little by little, Congress displayed a stiffening of attitude as it cast about for a just and practical slavery policy.

Slaves, not politicians, became the most insistent force for emancipation. By escaping their masters by the tens of thousands and running away to Union lines, they forced slavery on the North's wartime agenda. Union officials could not ignore the flood of fugitives, and runaways precipitated a series of momentous decisions by the army, Congress, and the president. Were the runaways really free, or were they still slaves who, according to the fugitive slave law, had to be returned to their masters? At first, most Yankee military officers believed that administration policy required them to send the

> Slaves, not politicians, became the most insistent force for emancipation. By escaping their masters by the tens of thousands and running away to Union lines, they forced slavery on the North's wartime agenda.

Contrabands

These refugees from slavery crossed the Rappahannock River in Virginia in August 1862 to seek sanctuary with a federal army. Most slaves fled with little more than the clothes on their backs, but not all escaped slavery empty-handed. The oxen, wagon, and goods seen here could have been procured by a number of means—purchased during slavery, "borrowed" from the former master, or gathered during flight. Refugees who possessed draft animals and a wagon had much more economic opportunity than those who had only their labor to sell.

Library of Congress.

C.S.S. *H. L. Hunley*: The First Successful Submarine

The Confederacy had no navy when it came into being in 1861, and without major shipyards, it could not build a naval fleet to match that of the Union. As the federal blockade of southern ports gradually began to strangle Confederate shipping, Southerners were forced to innovate in naval technology: the ironclad, floating mines called torpedoes, and, most spectacular of all, the submarine.

On the bone-chilling night of February 17, 1864, a lookout aboard the U.S.S. *Housatonic*, the largest ship among the Union blockaders off Charleston, noticed something in the water. It might have been a log or a porpoise, but he was jumpy because of rumors of a Confederate secret weapon roaming the ocean, something Union sailors called the "infernal machine." The lookout sounded the alarm. The *Housatonic*'s cannons could not target something so low in the water, and the ship's crew soon discovered that rifle and revolver rounds would not stop it.

Just below the surface of the Atlantic, eight sweating men at hand cranks propelled their peculiar vessel—a submarine named C.S.S. *H. L. Hunley*—toward the Union blockader. The *Hunley* rammed a 135-pound explosive, which was lashed to a spar protruding from its bow, into the *Housatonic* below the waterline, then quickly backed away as a 150-foot detonation rope played out. Within seconds, an explosion ripped the big Union ship. The *Housatonic* quickly sank, the first ship ever sunk by a submarine. Five sailors lost their lives. The *Hunley* then surfaced, and crew members flashed a light to their comrades on the shore to signal a successful mission. Minutes later, the *Hunley* and its crew vanished without a trace.

Three years of trial-and-error experimentation and wartime innovation produced the *Hunley*. Shortly after the war began, a group of New Orleans engineers and investors, including H. L. Hunley, imagined a new kind of ship: an underwater vessel that would defend the city from assault by the U.S. navy. First, they built the *Pioneer*, a cigar-shaped submarine with a crew of two, but in

April 1862, Admiral David Farragut's fleet captured New Orleans before the *Pioneer* could go into action. Hunley and his partners moved their operations to Mobile, where they built a second underwater ship, the *American Diver*, with a four-man crew. The builders experimented with propelling the submarine with an electromagnetic engine, but when the device failed to generate enough power, they returned to the hand-crank design. Stormy seas sank the *American Diver* in February 1863. Within weeks, the civilian builders, now joined by the Confederate military, began work on a third submarine, the *H. L. Hunley*.

A sleek, 40-foot version of previous efforts, the *Hunley* was an engineering marvel that exhibited both sophisticated technology and primitive features. Ballast tanks at each end of the hull could be flooded to submerge the vessel and emptied to raise it to the surface. Two lateral fins, or adjustable dive planes, regulated the ship's underwater depth. The captain steered the sub with a vertical rod attached to the rudder. A 4,000-pound keel ensured that the ship would remain upright as it slipped through the water. Eight men, squeezed into a space no more than four feet high, turned a crankshaft connected to a propeller. The ship had two towers with manholes secured by hatch covers fitted with watertight rubber gaskets that the crew secured from inside. Each

fugitives back. But Union armies needed laborers, and some officers accepted the runaways and put them to work. At Fort Monroe, Virginia, General Benjamin F. Butler not only refused to turn them over to their owners but also provided them with a new status. He called them "contraband of war," meaning "confiscated property."

Congress made Butler's practice national policy in March 1862 when it forbade the practice of returning fugitive slaves to their masters. Slaves were still not legally free, but there was a tilt toward emancipation.

Gradually, Lincoln's policy of noninterference with slavery crumbled. To calm Northerners'

***The C.S.S.* H. L. Hunley *at Charleston, 6 December 1863*, Conrad Wise Chapman**
This striking image of the *Hunley* makes clear why General P. G. T. Beauregard felt compelled to explain to men who were considering volunteering for its crew the "desperately hazardous nature of the service required." The artist contrasts the grim reality of the submarine with the beautiful (and safe) sailboat in the distance.
Museum of the Confederacy.

teen men, including H. L. Hunley himself. The sinkings were apparently caused by accidents, not design flaws. After the second accident, however, Beauregard declared, "I can have nothing more to do with that submarine boat. It is more dangerous to those who use it than the enemy." But Charleston's plight caused him to raise the sub and man it with an all-volunteer crew. The *Hunley* did no more damage after its destruction of the *Housatonic* in 1864, when it sank for a third and final time for unknown reasons. No submarine would sink an enemy ship until World War I, more than a half century later.

Much of what we know about the world's first successful submarine comes from discovery of the *Hunley* in May 1995, four miles off Sullivan's Island, South Carolina, in thirty feet of water and under three feet of sand. One marine **archaeologist** described it as the "find of the century." Raised in August 2000 and deposited in a large steel tank filled with 55,000 gallons of cold fresh water to protect it from further deterioration, the *Hunley* is today the object of intensive investigation; scientists and historians are successfully teasing evidence of its past from its remains. Essentially a time capsule, the *Hunley* has not yet given an answer to the question of why it did not return safely to Charleston harbor, but investigators are closing in on the answer.

tower had small round windows. The vessel was equipped with a kind of snorkel for air, but because it never worked, the sub had to surface every half hour or so for fresh air. The *Hunley* also was outfitted with a mercury depth gauge, a compass, and a single wax candle, which provided not only light but a warning

when the oxygen level became dangerously low.

Desperate to break the Union blockade in Charleston, General P. G. T. Beauregard ordered the *Hunley* loaded on a train and shipped from Mobile to Charleston harbor. Test runs began immediately, and the sub sank twice, with the loss of thir-

racial fears, which he considered the chief obstacle to Union acceptance of emancipation, Lincoln offered **colonization**, the deportation of African Americans from the United States to Haiti, Panama, or elsewhere. (For earlier colonization efforts in Liberia, see pages 430–31.) In the summer of 1862, he defended colonization to a dele-

gation of black visitors to the White House. He told them that deep-seated racial prejudice made it impossible for blacks to achieve equality in this country. An African American from Philadelphia spoke for the group when he told the president, "This is our country as much as it is yours, and we will not leave it." Congress voted a small amount of money to underwrite colonization, but after one miserable experiment on a small island in the Caribbean, practical limitations and black opposition sank further efforts.

While Lincoln was developing his own initiatives, he snuffed out actions that he believed would jeopardize northern unity. He was particularly alert to Union commanders who tried to dictate slavery policy from the field. In August 1861, when John C. Frémont, former Republican presidential nominee and now commander of federal troops in Missouri, impetuously freed the slaves belonging to Missouri rebels, Lincoln forced the general to revoke his edict and then removed him from command. The following May, when General David Hunter issued a proclamation freeing the slaves in Georgia, South Carolina, and Florida, Lincoln countermanded his order. Events moved so rapidly, however, that Lincoln found it impossible to control federal policy on slavery.

> Lincoln described emancipation as an "act of justice," but it was the lengthening casualty lists that finally brought him around.

From Contraband to Free People

On August 22, 1862, Lincoln replied to an angry abolitionist who demanded that he go after slavery. "My paramount objective in this struggle *is* to save the Union," Lincoln said deliberately, "and is *not* either to save or destroy slavery. If I could save the Union without freeing *any* slave I would do it, and if I could save it by freeing *all* the slaves I would do it; and if I could save it by freeing some and leaving others alone I would also do that." At first glance, it seemed a restatement of his old position: that union was the North's sole objective. But what marked it as a radical departure was Lincoln's refusal to say that slavery was untouchable. Instead, he said that he would emancipate every slave if doing so would preserve the Union.

By the summer of 1862, events were tumbling rapidly toward emancipation. On July 17, Congress adopted a second Confiscation Act. The first had confiscated slaves employed by the Confederate military; the second declared all slaves of rebel masters "forever free of their servitude." In theory, this breathtaking measure freed most of the slaves in the Confederacy, for slaveholders formed the backbone of the rebellion. Congress had traveled far since the war

began. Lincoln had too. On July 21, the president informed his cabinet that he was ready "to take some definitive steps in respect to military action and slavery." The next day, he read a draft of a preliminary emancipation proclamation that promised to free *all* slaves in the seceding states on January 1, 1863.

Lincoln described emancipation as an "act of justice," but it was the lengthening casualty lists that finally brought him around. Emancipation, he declared, was "a military necessity, absolutely essential to the preservation of the Union." Only freeing the slaves would "strike at the heart of the rebellion." His cabinet favored Lincoln's plan but advised him to wait for a military victory before announcing it so that critics would not call it an act of desperation. On September 22, after Antietam, he promised freedom to all slaves in all areas still in rebellion on January 1, 1863.

The limitations of the proclamation—it exempted the loyal border states and Union-occupied areas of the Confederacy—caused some to ridicule the act. The *London Times* observed cynically, "Where he has no power Mr. Lincoln will set the negroes free, where he retains power he will consider them as slaves." But Lincoln had no power to free slaves in loyal states, and invading Union armies would liberate slaves in the Confederacy as they advanced.

By presenting emancipation as a "military necessity," Lincoln hoped he had disarmed his **conservative** critics. Emancipation would deprive the Confederacy of valuable slave laborers, shorten the war, and thus save lives. Democrats, however, exploded with rage. They charged that the "shrieking and howling abolitionist faction" had captured the White House and made it "a nigger war." The fall 1862 congressional elections were only weeks away, and Democrats sought to make political hay out of Lincoln's action. War-weariness probably had as much to do with the results as emancipation, but Democrats gained thirty-four congressional seats. House Democrats quickly proposed a resolution branding emancipation "a high crime against the Constitution." The Republicans, who maintained narrow majorities in both houses of Congress, beat it back.

As promised, on New Year's Day 1863, Lincoln issued the final Emancipation Proclamation. In addition to freeing the slaves in the states that were in rebellion, the edict also committed the federal government to the fullest use of African Americans to defeat the Confederate enemy.

War of Black Liberation

Even before Lincoln proclaimed freedom a Union war aim, African Americans in the North had volunteered to fight. But the War Department, doubtful of their abilities and fearful of white reaction to serving side by side with them, refused to make black men soldiers. Instead, the army employed black men as manual laborers; black women sometimes found employment as laundresses and cooks. The navy, however, from the outset accepted blacks, including runaway slaves like William Gould, as sailors. They usually served in noncombatant roles, but within months a few blacks served on gun crews.

As the Union experienced manpower shortages, Northerners gradually and reluctantly turned to African Americans to fill the Union army's blue uniforms. With the Militia Act of July 1862, Congress authorized enrolling blacks in "any military or naval service for which they may be found competent." Lingering resistance to black military service largely disappeared in 1863. After the Emancipation Proclamation, whites—like it or not—were fighting and dying for black freedom, and few were likely to insist that blacks remain out of harm's way behind the lines. Indeed, rather than resist black military participation, whites insisted that blacks share the danger, especially after March 1863, when Congress resorted to the **draft** to fill the Union army.

Black soldiers discovered that the military was far from color-blind. The Union army established segregated black regiments, paid black soldiers $10 per month rather than the $13 it paid to whites, refused blacks the opportunity to become commissioned officers, punished blacks as if they were slaves, and assigned blacks to labor battalions rather than to combat units. But nothing deterred black recruits. When the war ended, 179,000 African American men had served in the Union military, approximately 10 percent of the army total. An astounding 71 percent of black men ages eighteen to forty-five in the free states wore Union blue, a participation rate that was substantially higher than that of white men. More than 130,000 black soldiers came from the slave states, perhaps 100,000 of them ex-slaves.

In time, whites allowed blacks to put down their shovels and to shoulder rifles. At the battles of Port Hudson and Milliken's Bend on the Mississippi River and at Fort Wagner in Charleston harbor, black courage under fire

Guard Detail of the 107th U.S. Colored Infantry, Arlington, Virginia, 1865
A white man's war when it began, the Civil War eventually gained color, as this photograph of the soldiers of the 107th U.S. Colored Infantry attests. The Lincoln administration was slow to accept black soldiers, in part because of lingering doubts about their ability to fight. Colonel Thomas W. Higginson, a white Massachusetts clergyman and abolitionist, commanded the First South Carolina Infantry, which was made up of former slaves. After his regiment's first skirmish with Confederate troops, Higginson celebrated his men's courage: "No officer in this regiment now doubts that the key to the successful prosecution of this war lies in the unlimited employment of black troops. . . . Instead of leaving their homes and families to fight they are fighting for their homes and families." After the spring of 1863, the federal government did all it could to maximize the number of black soldiers. Eventually, ex-slaves and free blacks filled 145 Union regiments. Throughout the war, however, policy required that blacks serve under white commissioned officers.
© Bettmann/Corbis.

finally dispelled notions that African Americans could not fight. More than 38,000 black soldiers died in the Civil War, a mortality rate that was higher than that of white troops. Blacks played a crucial role in the triumph of the Union and the destruction of slavery in the South.

The South at War

By seceding, Southerners brought on themselves a firestorm of unimaginable fury. Monstrous losses on the battlefields nearly bled the Confederacy to death. White Southerners on the home front also suffered, even at the hands of their own government. Efforts by the Davis administration in Richmond to centralize power to fight the war effectively convinced some men and women that the Confederacy had betrayed them. Wartime economic changes hurt everyone, some more than others. By 1863, planters and

yeomen who had stood together began to drift apart. Most disturbing of all, slaves became open participants in the destruction of slavery and the Confederacy.

Revolution from Above

As one Confederate general observed, Southerners were engaged in a total war "in which the whole population and the whole production . . . are to be put on a war footing, where every institution is to be made auxiliary to war." When Jefferson Davis became president of the Confederacy in 1861, he faced the task of building an army and navy from scratch, supplying them from factories that were scarce and anemic, and paying for it all from a treasury that did not exist. Building the army proved easiest. Hundreds of officers defected from the U.S. army, and hundreds of thousands of eager young rebels volunteered to follow them. Very quickly, the Confederacy developed formidable striking power.

The Confederacy's economy and finances proved tougher. Because of the Union blockade, the government had no choice but to build an industrial sector itself. Government-owned clothing and shoe factories, mines, arsenals, and powder works "sprung up almost like magic," according to one Mississippian. In addition, the government harnessed private companies, such as the huge Tredegar Iron Works in Richmond, to the war effort. The financial task proved most difficult because Southerners had invested their

capital in land and slaves, which Confederate officials found difficult to tap for the war effort. Richmond came up with a mix of bonds, taxes, and paper money to finance the war.

Despite its bold measures, however, the Davis administration failed to transform the slave-labor, staple-producing agricultural economy into a modern industrial one. The Confederacy manufactured much more than most people imagined possible, but it never produced all that the South needed. Each month, the gap between the North's and the South's production widened. Moreover, the flood of paper money coming from Richmond caused debilitating inflation. By 1863, Charlestonians paid ten times more for food than they had paid at the start of the war. By Christmas 1864, a Confederate soldier's monthly pay no longer bought a pair of socks.

Richmond's war-making effort meant that government intruded in unprecedented ways into the private lives of Confederate citizens. In April 1862, the Confederate Congress passed the first **conscription** (draft) law in American history. All able-bodied white males between the ages of eighteen and thirty-five (later seventeen and fifty) were liable to serve in the rebel army for three years. The Confederate government adopted a policy of impressment, which allowed officials to confiscate food, horses, wagons, and whatever else they wanted from private citizens and to pay for them at below-market rates. After March 1863, the Confederacy also legally impressed slaves, employing them as military laborers. In addition, Richmond took control of the South's railroads and shipping.

The war necessitated much of the government's unprecedented behavior, but citizens found it arbitrary and inequitable. Richmond's

Confederate Soldiers and Their Slaves
Soldiers of the Seventh Tennessee Cavalry pose with their slaves. Many slaveholders took "body servants" with them to war. These slaves cooked, washed, and cleaned for the white soldiers. In 1861, James H. Langhorne reported to his sister: "Peter . . . is charmed with being with me & 'being a soldier.' I gave him my old uniform overcoat & he says he is going to have his picture taken . . . to send to the servants." Do you think Peter was "puttin' on ol' massa" or just glad to be free of plantation labor?
Daguerreotype courtesy of Tom Farish. Photographed by Michael Latil.

FOR MORE HELP ANALYZING THIS IMAGE, see the visual activity for this chapter in the Online Study Guide at bedfordstmartins.com/roark.

centralizing efforts ran head-on into the South's traditional values of **states' rights** and unfettered individualism. The states lashed out at what Georgia governor Joseph E. Brown denounced as the "dangerous usurpation by Congress of the reserved right of the States." Richmond and the states struggled for control of money, supplies, and soldiers, with damaging consequences for the war effort. Individual citizens also remembered that Davis had promised to defend southern "liberty" against Republican "despotism." In time, Southerners named Jefferson Davis as the politician they hated most, after Lincoln.

Hardship Below

Hardships were widespread, but they fell most heavily on the poor. Inflation, for example, threatened the poor with starvation. Salt—necessary for preserving meat—shot up from $2 to $60 a bag during the first year of the war. Flour that cost three or four cents a pound in 1861 cost thirty-five cents in 1863. The draft depopulated yeoman farms of men, leaving the women and children

The Texas Brigade in Camp, 1861

Rebel soldiers who did not have slave servants to attend them spent much of their time doing what these four members of the Texas Brigade are doing—chores. Standing in front of their winter quarters near Dumfries, Virginia, the Texans are busy washing dishes, washing clothes, chopping firewood, and cooking. The soldier with the skillet displays the cornbread he has just cooked. Confederate troops ate salted meat and cornbread more than anything else. A federal officer marching through an abandoned rebel camp near Sharpsburg, Maryland, in 1862 recalled that "huge corn cakes, 2 inches thick and 12 to 15 inches wide, lay in piles and were kicked along the road by our men." Southerners learned to appreciate anything on their plates, but soldiers grew very tired of the old standbys. "If any person offers me cornbread after this war comes to a close," a Louisianan declared just before Lee's surrender, "I shall probably tell him to—go to hell!"

Atlanta History Center, Austin Public Library; Museum of the Confederacy.

to grow what they ate. A rampaging army, a drought, a sickness, a lame mule—any one calamity could cost a family a vital crop. When farm wives succeeded in bringing in a harvest, government agents took 10 percent of it as a "tax-in-kind" on agriculture. Like inflation, shortages also afflicted the entire population, but the rich lost luxuries while the poor lost necessities. In the spring of 1863, bread riots broke out in a dozen cities and villages across the South. In Richmond, a mob of nearly a thousand hungry women broke into shops and took what they needed.

Severe deprivation had powerful consequences. One southern leader observed in November 1862, "Men cannot be expected to fight for the Government that permits their wives & children to starve." A few wealthy individuals shared their bounty, the Confederacy

made some efforts at social welfare, and the states did even more; but every effort fell short. In late 1864, one desperate farm wife told her husband: "I have always been proud of you, and since your connection with the Confederate army, I have been prouder of you than ever before. I would not have you do anything wrong for the world, but before God, Edward, unless you come home, we must die." By some estimates, when the war ended, one-third of the soldiers had already gone home. A Mississippi deserter explained, "We are poor men and are willing to defend our country but our families [come] first." (See "Documenting the American Promise," page 538.)

The Confederacy also failed to persuade the suffering white majority that the war's burdens were being shared equally. Instead, yeomen saw a profound inequality of sacrifice. They called it

Home and Country

Husbands fighting for the Confederacy and wives back home exchanged countless letters during the war. They wrote movingly of family, hardships, and battles, and they shared their deepest loves and fears. Their letters, which were uncensored, often revealed the conflicting tugs of home and country.

Christian Marion Epperly and his wife, Mary Epperly, lived in the Blue Ridge Mountains of Virginia. Although neither was an ardent secessionist, Marion entered the army as a private early in 1862. He saw action in the eastern and western theaters of the war. He hated army life and longed for his wife and children. Mary was equally heartsick without Marion. The couple's letters reveal their limited schooling, but more important they show how plain folks wrestled with the tangled issues of personal and political loyalties and obligations.

DOCUMENT 1
Letter from Chickahominy Creek, Virginia, May 16, 1862

During the peninsula campaign in Virginia, as Union general George B. McClellan was approaching the Confederate capital of Richmond, Marion wrote to Mary from near the action.

I think the people will be bound to suffer for something to eat[;] the grain is all destroid and nearly all the fenses is burnt up from yorktown to Richmond: it looks distressing just to travel along the road: the wheat up waist hi some of it and horses and cattle has eat the most of it to the ground and I think the yankees will make a finish of the ballans [balance] that is left but the[y] cant doo much more damage than our army did[;] our own men killed all the cattle and hogs & sheep that the farmers had[,] even took ther chickens[;] every thing is totally destroid in this part of the State[.] I don't think the yankeys could doo much wors if they had a chanse[.]

I hope and pray this awful war will soon come to a close some way or another[,] any way to get pease in the world wonst more[;] it seems to me I had drather be at home and live on bred and water than to have this war hanging over us but I pray god pease will soon be made[.] I dont think the war can last long.

DOCUMENT 2
Letter from Camp near Bells Bridge, Tennessee, August 15, 1863

By the summer of 1863, Marion's regiment had moved to Tennessee, where he notices increasing war weariness, desertions, and disillusionment with the Confederacy.

You don't know how glad I would be if I was just thar with you this morning to see the sun rise over the hills in Virginia again[,] for everry thing seames so sad and desolate here this morning; it seames like the absens of dear friends and the present condition of things has brought deep refletion and sadnes upon everry heart, and [men] are growing weary and getting out of heart and leaving the Army everry day. I cant tell wheather it will be for the better or wheather it will make things wors: but I hope it is a way god has provided to bring this war and time of sorrow to an end and to give us pease in our land again: Thoug I believe the south first started on a just course but our own wickedness and disobedians has brought us to what we are and I firmly believe wee will be bound to give up to subjugation[.] I don't think the south will stand much longer, and I am sorrow to say it for wee will be a ruined people while time ma [may] last, but wee ought to submit to any thing to have this awwful war ended.

DOCUMENT 3
Letter from Floyd County, Virginia, August 16, 1863

Mary longs for peace and argues that desertion will end the war.

Oh how much beter satisfied would I be if you was just hear with me this beatiful Sabath morning. I feel as if my troubles on earth would all be over if you was just at home to stay wonst more[,] but god sent it upon us and we will have to bear with it the best we can but I do pray that he may soon end this destressing time some way[.] I would be willing for it to end most any way just so it would end[.] Dear Marion I think if the head men dont soon end this war that the soldiers will for they are runing way from down east by hundreds[;] they was five hundard went though hear last weak and well armed and they say they wont go back any more and I dont blame them for it[.] I wish they would all runaway and these head men would be oblige to fight it out but as long as they can stay at home and speculate off of the poor soulders they dont care how long the war lasts[.] Serious Smith wrote a leter the 9 of this month and he wrote that they had to pay 15 dolars for a bushel of taters . . . how can the poor soulders make out and only get a leven [eleven] dolars a month[?] He wrote that they sawd very hard times down thare and had a heap of hard fighting to do[;] they had a fight the 1 and 4 of this month and he wrote that thare was five wounded and more killed and they was expecting a fight every hour.

DOCUMENT 4
Letter from Floyd County, Virginia, December 4, 1863

Mary tells Marion that the Confederacy's new conscription law has thrown their neighborhood into turmoil.

It seams like things [are in] such a uproar that I cant keep my mind together long a nuff to write a leter as it aut to be wrote[;] people has never bin in such a uproar and confusion hear since the war as they are now[;] thare is orders now to take up every man between the age of 17 and 50 that hasent reported and if they hant [aren't] able to walk they have to hall them. . . . Dear Husban I expect they will pass a law yet to take the wimen for they have taken all the men and children almost ded and alive and the next I read I recon will be for the wiman. Dear Marion hour Country has got in a turable fix[;] thare is nothing but sorow and destress in this world any more[;] when I set and study about it and think if I could just take you and my dear litle children with me to heaven I would be willing to do to day but Dear Husban wee was born in this world to see trouble and wee will have to put up with it the best wee can and pray for a beter day to come which I hope is not fare off.

DOCUMENT 5
Letter from Outskirts of Dalton, Georgia, March 25, 1864

As his regiment is backing toward Atlanta, trying to fend off Sherman, Marion considers what has gone wrong with the Confederacy.

I dont think it will last much longer if the souldiers doo what they say they will doo[;] they are all verry tired of this war and the way it is carried on[.] I think wee all have stud it about as long as we can unless our leading men dos a heap better than they ever have yet: if they wer God fearing men I would think wee would prosper but so long as they [seek] the Bottom of a Whiskey Barl and frolick around bad places just so long we will hafto fight and suffer. . . . we was all Born in a free land and I think wee ought to stil be free and not be bound down wors than slaves[;] we wonst had a union and was living happy and had all man can wish for[;] now we are cut off from that union and what are wee nothing but a ruend people as long as we shal live . . . dissatisfaction and wickedness all over the south[;] may God show us our errors and put us in the rite way and Bring us Back to our old union again.

DOCUMENT 6
Letter from Floyd County, Virginia, March 24, 1865

Mary expects a Yankee victory and says again that Confederate soldiers can end the war by deserting. Despite his doubts about the Confederacy and continued affection for the Union, Marion left the army without authorization only once, and after a few weeks at home in 1863, he returned to his regiment. Like many

disillusioned soldiers, he fought in the rebel army to the very end.

Dear Marion they are looking every day for the yankees to take Richmond and Linchburg and I do wish from my hart that they had it now for I am not afrade of the yankeys treating us any worse nor not half as bad as our own men dos for they have taking all the men or tride to take all that is any acout [account] and are now taking the horses. . . . How much worse could the yankeys do than that[?] . . . It lais in the souldires hands now to make pease and I do wish that they may make it soon[;] our strongest sesess [secessionists] hear say that wee are whiped and they have nown [known] it for some time but was ashame to own it.

Source: Christian M. Epperly Correspondence, Gilder Lehrman Collection, Pierpont Morgan Library, New York.

QUESTIONS FOR ANALYSIS AND DEBATE

1. For Marion and Mary Epperly, what explains the suffering of the South in the Civil War? How do they each see the matter differently?

2. How does Marion contrast life in the Union with life in the Confederacy?

3. In what ways does the Epperlys' perspective on the Confederacy reflect their social position as plain folk in Virginia society?

4. Marion makes clear why he had such affection for his home; he is much less clear about why he fought for the Confederacy. What might some of his reasons have been?

> Yeomen saw a profound inequality of sacrifice. They called it "a rich man's war and a poor man's fight," and they had evidence.

"a rich man's war and a poor man's fight," and they had evidence. The original draft law permitted a man who had money to hire a substitute to take his place. Moreover, the "twenty-Negro law" exempted one white man on every plantation with twenty or more slaves. The government intended this law to provide protection for white women and to see that slaves tended the crops, but yeomen perceived it as rich men evading military service. A slaveless Mississippian complained to his governor about stay-at-home planters who sent their slaves into the fields to grow cotton while in plain view "poor soldiers' wives are plowing with *their own* hands to make a subsistence for themselves and children—while their husbands are suffering, bleeding and dying for their country." In fact, most slaveholders went off to war, but the extreme suffering of common folk and the relative immunity of planters fueled class animosity.

The Richmond government hoped that the crucible of war would mold a region into a nation. Officials and others worked tirelessly to promote a vibrant southern **nationalism** that, as one Confederate politician said, would "excite in our citizens an ardent and enduring attachment to our Government and its institutions." Clergymen assured their congregations that God had blessed slavery and the new nation. Jefferson Davis asked citizens to observe national days of fasting and prayer. Patriotic songwriters, poets, authors, and artists extolled southern culture. But it proved difficult to create a united slave republic in the midst of all-out war. Efforts to build consensus never succeeded in winning over thousands of die-hard Unionists. And friction between yeomen and planters increased rather than decreased. The war also threatened to rip the southern social fabric along its racial seam.

The Disintegration of Slavery

The legal destruction of slavery was the product of presidential proclamation, congressional legislation, and eventually constitutional amendment, but the practical destruction of slavery was the product of war, what Lincoln called war's "friction and abrasion." War exposed the flimsy nature of planter **paternalism** and the illusion of slave contentment. Rather than laboring faithfully, protecting their white folks, and

Maria Isabella ("Belle") Boyd, Spy
Most white southern women, in addition to keeping their families fed and safe, served the Confederate cause by sewing uniforms, knitting socks, rolling bandages, and nursing the sick and wounded. But Belle Boyd became a spy. Only seventeen when the war broke out, she became in the words of a northern journalist "insanely devoted to the rebel cause." Her first act for the Confederacy came on July 3, 1861, when she shot a drunken federal soldier who barged into her Virginia home and insulted her mother. Her relations with occupying northern troops improved, and soon this compelling young woman was eavesdropping on officers' conversations and slipping messages to Confederate armies. Boyd's information handed Stonewall Jackson an easy victory at Front Royal, Virginia, in May 1862. "I thank you," the general wrote Boyd, ". . . for the immense service that you have rendered your country today." Imprisoned several times for spying, Boyd took up a theatrical career when the war ended.
Courtesy Warren Rifles Confederate Museum, Front Royal, VA.

hiding the mistress's silver from marauding Yankees, slaves took advantage of the upheaval to reach for freedom. Some half a million of the South's four million slaves ran away to northern military lines. More than 100,000 men fled bondage, took up arms as federal soldiers and sailors, and attacked slavery directly. Other men and women stayed in the slave quarters, where they staked their claim to more freedom.

In dozens of ways, the war disrupted the routine, organization, and discipline of bondage. Almost immediately, for example, it called the master away, leaving white women to assume additional managerial responsibilities. But neither plantation mistresses nor masters could maintain traditional standards of slave discipline in wartime.

In large parts of the South, the balance of power between master and slave gradually shifted. Slaveholders complained about the slaves' "demoralization" and "betrayal." Slaves got to the fields late, worked indifferently, and quit early. Some slaveholders responded violently; most saw no alternative but to strike bargains—offering gifts or part of the crop—to keep slaves at home and at work. An Alabama woman reported that she "begged . . . what little is done." Changes in slave behavior shocked slaveholders. They had prided themselves on "knowing" their slaves, and they learned that they did not know them at all. When the war began, a North Carolina woman praised her slaves as "diligent and respectful." When it ended, she said, "As to the idea of a *faithful servant, it is all a fiction.*"

As military action increasingly sliced through the South's farms and plantations, some slaveholders fled, leaving behind their slaves. Many more took their slaves with them, but flight meant additional chaos and offered slaves new opportunities to resist bondage. Whites' greatest fear—retaliatory violence—rarely occurred. Instead, slaves undermined white mastery and expanded control over their own lives.

The North at War

Because rebel armies generally operated within the Confederate borders, most of the North was untouched by fighting. But Northerners could not avoid being touched by war. Almost every family had a son, a husband, a brother in uniform. Moreover, this war—a total war—blurred the distinction between home front and battlefield. As in the South, men marched off to fight, but preserving the country, either Union or Confederacy, was also women's work. For civilians as well as soldiers, for women as well as men, war was transforming.

The need to build and fuel the Union war machine boosted the northern economy. The North sent nearly 2 million men into the military and still increased production in almost every area. But because the rewards and burdens of patriotism were not evenly distributed, the North experienced sharp, even violent, divisions. Workers confronted employers, whites confronted blacks, and Democrats confronted Republicans. Still, Northerners on the home front remained fervently attached to the ideals of **free labor** and the Union.

The Government and the Economy

When the war began, the United States had no national banking system, no national currency, and no federal income or excise taxes. But the secession of eleven slave states cut the Democrats' strength in Congress in half and destroyed their capacity to resist Republican economic programs. The Legal Tender Act of February 1862 created a national currency, paper money that Northerners called "greenbacks." With passage of the National Banking Act in February 1863, Congress created a system of national banks that by the 1870s had largely replaced the **antebellum** system of decentralized state banks. Congress also enacted a series of sweeping tax laws that encompassed everything from incomes to liquor to billiard tables. The Internal Revenue Act created the Bureau of Internal Revenue to collect taxes. In addition, Congress enacted a higher tariff to increase revenues and protect manufacturers against foreign competition. By revolutionizing the country's banking, monetary, and tax structures, the Republicans generated enormous economic power.

> The secession of eleven slave states cut the Democrats' strength in Congress in half and destroyed their capacity to resist Republican economic programs.

Some of the Republicans' wartime legislation was designed to integrate the West more thoroughly into the Union. In May 1862, Congress approved the Homestead Act, which offered public land—limited to 160 acres to prevent the spread of plantations—to settlers who would live and labor on it. The Homestead Act bolstered western loyalty and in time resulted in more than a million new farms. The passage of the Pacific Railroad Act in July 1862 provided massive federal assistance for building a transcontinental railroad that ran from Omaha to San Francisco when completed in 1869. Congress

Union Ordnance, Yorktown, Virginia
As the North successfully harnessed its enormous industrial capacity to the needs of war, cannon, mortars, and shells poured out of its factories. A fraction of that abundance is seen here in 1862 at Yorktown, ready for transportation to Union troops in the field. Two years later, Abraham Lincoln observed that the Union was "gaining strength, and may if need be maintain the contest indefinitely. . . . Material resources are now more complete and abundant than ever. . . . The national resources are unexhausted, and, as we believe, inexhaustible."
Library of Congress.

For more help analyzing this image, see the visual activity for this chapter in the Online Study Guide at bedfordstmartins.com/roark.

further bound East and West by subsidizing the Pony Express mail service and a transcontinental telegraph.

Two additional initiatives had long-term consequences for agriculture and industry. Congress created a Department of Agriculture and passed the Land-Grant College Act (also known as the Morrill Act after its sponsor, Representative Justin Morrill of Vermont), which set aside public lands to support universities that emphasized "agriculture and mechanical arts." Republicans defended their wartime legislation by arguing that additional economic muscle meant increased military might. Initiatives from

the Lincoln administration in Washington immeasurably strengthened the North's effort to win the war, but they were also permanently changing the nation.

Women and Work on the Home Front

More than a million farm men were called to the military, so farm women added men's chores to their own. "I met more women driving teams on the road and saw more at work in the fields than men," a visitor to Iowa reported in the fall of 1862. Rising production figures testified to their success in plowing, planting, and harvesting. Rapid mechanization assisted farm women in their new roles. Cyrus McCormick sold 165,000 of his reapers during the war years. The combination of high prices for farm products and increased production ensured that war and prosperity joined hands in the rural North.

A few industries, such as textiles (which depended on southern cotton), declined during the war, but many more grew. Huge profits prompted one Pennsylvania ironmaster to remark, "I am in no hurry for peace." With orders pouring in and a million nonfarm workers siphoned off into the military, unemployment declined and wages often rose. The boom proved friendlier to owners than to workers, however. Inflation and taxes cut so deeply into their paychecks that workers' standard of living actually fell.

Women in cities also stepped into jobs vacated by men, particularly in manufacturing, and also into essentially new occupations such as government secretaries and clerks. Many had no choice because they could not make ends meet on their husbands' army pay. Women made up about one-quarter of the manufacturing workforce when the war began and one-third when it ended. As more and more women entered the workforce, employers cut wages. By 1864, New York seamstresses working fourteen-hour days earned only an average of $1.54 a week. Cincinnati seamstresses complained to Abraham Lincoln that their wages were not enough "to sustain life." Urban workers resorted increasingly to strikes to wrench decent salaries from their employers, but their protests rarely succeeded. Nevertheless, tough times failed to undermine the patriotism of most workers, who took pride in their contribution to northern victory.

Middle-class white women were expected to be homebodies, and hundreds of thousands of them contributed to the war effort in traditional ways. Like southern white women, they sewed, wrapped bandages, and sold homemade goods at local fairs to raise money to aid the soldiers. Other women expressed their patriotism in an untraditional way—as wartime nurses. Thousands of women on both sides defied prejudices about female delicacy and volunteered to nurse the wounded. Many of the northern female volunteers worked through the U.S.

U.S. Sanitary Commission, Brandy Station, Virginia, 1863
The burden of caring for millions of Union soldiers was more than the government could shoulder. Private initiative in the form of the U.S. Sanitary Commission brought additional medical attention to the Union wounded and boosted the comfort and morale of soldiers in the camps. Volunteers like these northern women standing in front of the Commission's headquarters in Brandy Station, Virginia, offered soldiers some of the comforts of home—clean socks, new blankets, and fresh fruit. Do you suppose that the freshly painted white picket fence surrounding their building had symbolic value? If so, what did it symbolize?
National Archives.

Sanitary Commission, a civilian organization that bought and distributed clothing, food, and medicine and recruited doctors and nurses. Nursing meant working in the midst of unspeakable sights, sounds, and smells, but it often brought profound satisfaction. Katherine Wormeley of Rhode Island, who served three months as a volunteer nurse on a hospital ship in 1862, recorded in her diary, "We all know in our hearts that it is thorough enjoyment to be here—it is life."

Some volunteers went on to become paid military nurses. For example, Dorothea Dix, well known for her efforts to reform insane asylums, was named superintendent of female nurses in April 1861. Eventually, some 3,000 women served under her. Most nurses worked in hospitals behind the battle lines, but some, like Clara Barton, who later founded the American Red Cross, worked in battlefield units. At Antietam, as Barton was giving a wounded man a drink, a bullet ripped through her sleeve, striking and killing the soldier. Women who served in the war went on to lead the postwar movement to establish training schools for female nurses.

Politics and Dissent

At first, the bustle of economic and military mobilization seemed to silence politics; Democrats supported the Union as fervently as Republicans. But bipartisan unity did not last. Within a year, Democrats were labeling the Republican administration a "reign of terror," and Republicans were calling Democrats the party of "Dixie, Davis, and the Devil." Year by year, Republican policy pushed the Democrats toward a dangerous alienation. Republicans emancipated the slaves, subsidized private business, and expanded federal power at every turn. The Lincoln administration argued that the war required a loose interpretation of the Constitution, to which the Democrats countered, "The Constitution is as binding in war as in peace."

In September 1862, in an effort to stifle opposition to the war, Lincoln placed under military arrest any person who discouraged enlistments, resisted the draft, or engaged in "disloyal" practices. Before the war ended, his administration had imprisoned nearly 14,000 individuals, most in the border states. The campaign fell short of a reign of terror, for the majority of the prisoners

> At first, the bustle of economic and military mobilization seemed to silence politics. But bipartisan unity did not last.

were not northern Democratic opponents but Confederates, blockade runners, and citizens of foreign countries, and most of those arrested gained quick release. Still, the administration's heavy-handed tactics did suppress free speech.

When the Republican-dominated Congress enacted the draft law in March 1863, Democrats had another grievance. Grim news from the battlefields had dried up the stream of volunteers, and the North, like the South a year earlier, turned to military conscription to fill the ranks. The law required that all men between the ages of twenty and forty-five enroll and make themselves available for a lottery, which would decide who went to war. What poor men found particularly galling were provisions that allowed a draftee to hire a substitute or simply to pay a $300 fee and get out of his military obligation. As in the South, common folk could be heard chanting, "A rich man's war and a poor man's fight."

Linking the draft and emancipation, Democrats argued that Republicans employed an unconstitutional means (the draft) to achieve an unconstitutional end (emancipation). In the summer of 1863, antidraft, antiblack mobs went on rampages in northern cities. In July, New York City experienced an explosion of unprecedented proportions. Solidly Democratic Irish workingmen—crowded into stinking, disease-ridden tenements, gouged by inflation, enraged by the inequities of the draft, and dead set against fighting to free blacks—erupted in four days of rioting. By the time police and soldiers restored order, at least 105 people, most of them black, lay dead, and the Colored Orphan Asylum was a smoking ruin.

The riots stunned black Northerners, but the racist mobs failed to achieve their purpose: the subordination of African Americans. Free black leaders had lobbied aggressively for emancipation, and after Lincoln's proclamation they fanned out over the North agitating for equality. They won some small wartime successes. Illinois and Iowa overturned laws that had excluded blacks from entering those states. Illinois and Ohio began permitting blacks to testify in court. But defeat was more common. Indiana, for example, continued to forbid blacks to vote, testify, and attend public schools, and additional blacks were

not allowed to enter the state. Significant progress toward black equality would have to wait until the war ended.

Grinding Out Victory, 1863–1865

In the early months of 1863, the Union's prospects looked bleak, and the Confederate cause stood at high tide. Then in July 1863, the tide began to turn. The military man most responsible for this shift was Ulysses S. Grant. Lifted from obscurity by his successes in the West in 1862 and 1863, Grant became the "great man of the day," one man observed in July 1864, "perhaps of the age." Elevated to supreme command, Grant knit together a powerful war machine that integrated a sophisticated command structure, modern technology, and complex logistics and supply systems. But the arithmetic of this plain man remained unchanged: Killing more of the enemy than he kills of you equaled "the complete overthrow of the rebellion."

The North ground out the victory, battle by bloody battle. The balance tipped in the Union's favor in 1863, but if the Confederacy was beaten, Southerners clearly did not know it. The fighting reached new levels of ferocity in the last two years of the war. As national elections approached in the fall of 1864, a discouraged Lincoln expected a war-weary North to make him a one-term president. Instead, northern voters declared their willingness to continue the war in the defense of the ideals of union and freedom.

Vicksburg and Gettysburg

Perched on the bluffs above the eastern bank of the Mississippi River, Vicksburg, Mississippi, bristled with cannons and dared Yankee ships to try to pass. This Confederate stronghold stood between Union forces and complete control of the river. Impenetrable terrain made the city impossible to take from the north. To get his army south of

Vicksburg Campaign, 1863

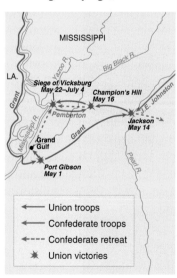

Vicksburg, Grant marched it down the swampy western bank of the Mississippi. Union forces crossed the Mississippi River, marched north more than one hundred miles, and attacked the city. The Confederates beat back the assault, and in May, Grant decided to lay siege to the city and starve out the enemy. Civilian residents of Vicksburg moved into caves to escape the incessant Union bombardment, and as the siege dragged on, they had to eat mules and rats to survive.

After six weeks, the siege had the desired effect. On July 4, 1863, nearly 30,000 rebels marched out of Vicksburg, stacked their arms, and surrendered unconditionally. A Yankee captain wrote home to his wife: "The backbone of the Rebellion is this day broken. The Confederacy is divided. . . . Vicksburg is ours. The Mississippi River is opened, and Gen. Grant is to be our next President."

On the same Fourth of July that a grateful nation received the news of Vicksburg, word arrived that Union forces had crushed General Lee at Gettysburg, Pennsylvania (Map 15.3). Lee's triumph in early May at Chancellorsville, Virginia, over Joseph "Fighting Joe" Hooker had revived his confidence, even though the battle cost him his favorite commander, the incomparable Stonewall Jackson, accidentally shot in the dark by his own troops.

Emboldened by the victory at Chancellorsville and hoping to relieve Virginia of the burden of the fighting, Lee and his 75,000-man Army of Northern Virginia invaded Pennsylvania in June. On June 28, the Army of the Potomac, under its new commander, General George G. Meade, moved quickly to intercept the Confederate force. Advance units of both armies met at the small town of Gettysburg, where Union forces occupied the high ground. Three days of furious fighting involving 165,000 soldiers could not dislodge the Federals from the ridges and hills. Lee ached for a decisive victory, and on July 3 he ordered a major assault against the

Major Battles of the Civil War, 1863–1865

May 1–4, 1863	Battle of Chancellorsville
July 1–3, 1863	Battle of Gettysburg
July 4, 1863	Fall of Vicksburg
September 16–20, 1863	Battle of Chickamauga
November 23–25, 1863	Battle of Chattanooga
May 5–7, 1864	Battle of the Wilderness
May 7–19, 1864	Battle of Spotsylvania Court House
June 3, 1864	Battle of Cold Harbor
June 27, 1864	Battle of Kennesaw Mountain
September 2, 1864	Fall of Atlanta
November–December 1864	Sheridan sacks Shenandoah Valley Sherman's March to the Sea
December 15–16, 1864	Battle of Nashville
December 22, 1864	Fall of Savannah
April 2–3, 1865	Fall of Petersburg and Richmond
April 9, 1865	Lee surrenders at Appomattox Court House

Union center on Cemetery Ridge. Open, rolling fields provided the dug-in Yankees with three-quarters of a mile of clear vision, and they raked the mile-wide line of Confederate soldiers under General George E. Pickett with cannon and rifle fire. Time and again, the rebels closed ranks and raced forward, until finally their momentum failed. Gettysburg cost Lee more than one-third of his army—28,000 casualties. "It's all my fault," he lamented. In a drenching rain on the night of July 4, 1863, he marched his battered army back to Virginia.

The twin disasters at Vicksburg and Gettysburg proved to be the turning point of the war. The Confederacy could not replace the nearly 60,000 soldiers who were captured, wounded, or killed. Lee never launched another major offensive north of the Mason-Dixon line. It is hindsight, however, that permits us to see the pair of battles as decisive. At the time, the Confederacy still controlled the heartland of the South, and Lee,

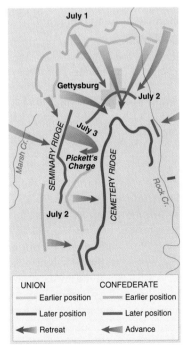

Battle of Gettysburg, July 1–3, 1863

July 1

Gettysburg

July 2

SEMINARY RIDGE

Marsh Cr.

July 3

Pickett's Charge

CEMETERY RIDGE

Rock Cr.

July 2

UNION	CONFEDERATE
Earlier position	Earlier position
Later position	Later position
Retreat	Advance

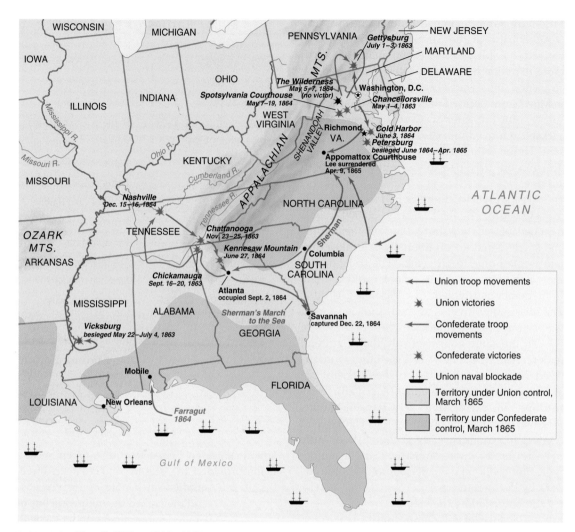

MAP 15.3   The Civil War, 1863–1865
Ulysses S. Grant's victory at Vicksburg divided the Confederacy at the Mississippi River. William Tecumseh Sherman's march from Chattanooga to Savannah divided it again. In northern Virginia, Robert E. Lee fought fiercely, but Grant's larger, better-supplied armies prevailed.

READING THE MAP: Describe the difference between Union and Confederate naval capacity. Were the battles shown on the map fought primarily in Union-controlled or Confederate-controlled territory (look at the land areas on the map)?

CONNECTIONS: Did former slaves serve in the Civil War? If so, on which side, and what did they do?

FOR MORE HELP ANALYZING THIS MAP, see the map activity for this chapter in the Online Study Guide at bedfordstmartins.com/roark.

---

back on the defensive in Virginia, still had a vicious sting. War-weariness threatened to erode the North's will to win before Union armies could destroy the Confederacy's ability to go on.

Grant Takes Command

Toward the end of September 1863, Union general William Rosecrans placed his army in a dangerous situation in Chattanooga, Tennessee, where he had retreated after taking a whipping

at the Battle of Chickamauga earlier in the month (see Map 15.3). Rebels surrounded the disorganized bluecoats and threatened to starve them into submission. Ulysses S. Grant, whom Lincoln had made commander of Union forces between the Mississippi River and the Appalachians, arrived in Chattanooga in October. Within weeks, he opened an effective supply line, broke the siege, and then (largely because Union troops disobeyed orders and charged wildly up Missionary Ridge) routed the Confederate army.

The victory at Chattanooga on November 25 had immense strategic value. It opened the door to Georgia. It also confirmed Lincoln's estimation of Grant. In March 1864, the president asked Grant to come east to become the general in chief of all Union armies.

In Washington, Grant implemented his grand strategy for a war of annihilation. He ordered a series of simultaneous assaults from Virginia to Louisiana. Two actions proved more significant than the others. In one, General William Tecumseh Sherman, whom Grant appointed his successor to command the western armies, plunged southeast toward Atlanta. In the other, Grant, who took control of the Army of the Potomac, went head-to-head with Lee for almost four straight weeks in Virginia.

Grant and Lee met in the first week of May 1864 in northern Virginia at the Wilderness, a dense tangle of scrub oaks and small pines that proved to be Lee's ally, for it helped offset the Yankees' numerical superiority. Often unable to see more than ten paces, the armies pounded away at each other until approximately 18,000 Yankees and 11,000 rebels had fallen. The savagery of the Battle of the Wilderness did not compare with that at Spotsylvania Court House a few days later. Frenzied men fought hand to hand for eighteen hours in the rain. One veteran remembered men "piled upon each other in some places four layers deep, exhibiting every ghastly phase of mutilation." Spotsylvania cost Grant another 18,000 casualties and Lee 10,000, but the Yankee bulldog would not let go. Grant kept moving and tangled with Lee again at Cold Harbor, where he suffered 13,000 additional casualties to Lee's 5,000. (See "Historical Question," page 548.)

Twice as many Union soldiers as rebel soldiers died in four weeks of fighting in Virginia in May and June. Yet Grant did not consider himself defeated. Because Lee had only half the number of troops, he lost proportionally as many men as Grant. Grant knew that the South could not replace the losses. Moreover, the campaign carried Grant to the outskirts of Petersburg, just south of Richmond, the Confederate capital. Most of the major railroad lines supplying Richmond ran through Petersburg, so Lee had little choice but to defend the city. Grant abandoned the costly tactic of the frontal assault and began a siege that immobilized both armies and dragged on for nine months.

There was no pause in Sherman's invasion of Georgia. Grant had instructed Sherman to

Grant at Cold Harbor
Seated next to his chief of staff, John A. Rawlins, at his Cold Harbor, Virginia, headquarters, Ulysses S. Grant plots his next move against Robert E. Lee. On June 3, 1864, Grant ordered frontal assaults against entrenched Confederate forces, resulting in enormous Union losses. "I am disgusted with the generalship displayed," young Brigadier General Emory Upton exclaimed. "Our men have, in many cases, been foolishly and wantonly slaughtered." Years later, Grant said that he regretted the assault at Cold Harbor, but in 1864 he kept pushing toward Richmond.
Chicago Historical Society.

"get into the interior of the enemy's country as far as you can, inflicting all the damage you can against their War resources." In early May, Sherman moved 100,000 men south against the

Why Did So Many Soldiers Die?

From 1861 to 1865, Americans killed Americans on a scale never before seen. Not until the First World War, a half century later, would the world match (and surpass) the killing fields at Shiloh, Antietam, and Gettysburg (Figure 15.2). Why were the Civil War totals so horrendous? Why did 260,000 rebel soldiers and 373,000 Union soldiers die?

By the mid-nineteenth century, the balance between the ability to kill and the ability to save lives had tipped disastrously toward death. The sheer size of the armies—some battles involved more than 200,000 soldiers—ensured that battlefields would turn red with blood. Moreover, armies fought with antiquated strategy. In the generals' eyes, the ideal soldier remained the veteran of Napoleonic warfare, a man trained to advance with his comrades in a compact, close-order formation. Theory also emphasized frontal assaults. In classrooms at West Point and on the high plains of Mexico in the 1840s, men who would one day be officers in rival armies learned that infantry advancing shoulder to shoulder, supported by artillery, carried the day.

By the 1860s, modern technology had made such strategy appallingly deadly. Weapons with rifled barrels (that is, with spiral grooves cut into the bore) were replacing smoothbore muskets and cannon. Whereas muskets had an effective range of only about eighty yards, rifles propelled spinning bul-

lets four times as far. The rifle's greater range and accuracy, and rifled cannons firing canisters filled with flesh-ripping, bone-breaking steel shot, made sitting ducks of charging infantry units and gave an enormous advantage to entrenched defensive forces. As a result, battles

took thousands of lives in a single day. On July 2, 1862, the morning after the battle at Malvern Hill in eastern Virginia, a Union officer surveyed the scene: "Over 5,000 dead and wounded men were on the ground . . . enough were alive and moving to give to the field a singular crawling effect."

Wounded soldiers often lay on battlefields for hours, sometimes days, without water or care of any kind. When the Civil War began, no one anticipated casualty lists with thousands of names. Union and

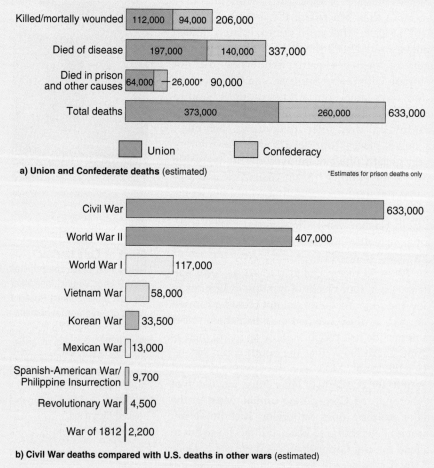

a) **Union and Confederate deaths** (estimated)   *Estimates for prison deaths only

b) **Civil War deaths compared with U.S. deaths in other wars** (estimated)

FIGURE 15.2 Civil War Deaths
The loss of life in the Civil War was almost equal to the losses in all other American wars.

Wounded Men at Savage's Station
Misery did not end when the cannon ceased firing. This heap of mangled humanity was but a fraction of the cost of General George McClellan's campaign on the Virginia peninsula in 1862.
Library of Congress.

Doctor's Surgical Kit
With simple instruments like these, not unlike the tools of the butcher's trade, northern and southern surgeons performed approximately 60,000 amputations. Approximately 45,000 of the amputees survived.
Chicago Historical Society.

Confederate medical departments could not cope with skirmishes, much less large-scale battles. They had no ambulance corps to remove the wounded from the scene. They had no field hospitals. Early in the war, someone in the U.S. Quartermaster Department, which was responsible for constructing Union hospitals, responded to demands that it do something to improve the care of the wounded by saying: "Men need guns, not beds." Only the shock of massive casualties compelled reform. A lack of resources meant that the South lagged behind the North, but gradually both North and South organized effective ambulance corps, built hospitals, and hired trained surgeons and nurses.

Soldiers did not always count speedy transportation to a field hospital as a blessing. As one Union soldier said, "I had rather risk a battle than the Hospitals." Real danger lurked behind the lines. While the technology of killing advanced to very high standards, medicine remained primitive. Physicians gained a reputation as butchers, and soldiers dreaded the operating table more than they did entrenched riflemen. Serious wounds to a leg or an arm usually meant amputation, the best way doctors knew to save lives. After major battles, surgeons worked among piles of severed limbs.

(continued)

(continued)

A wounded man's real enemy was not doctors' callousness but medical ignorance. Physicians had almost no knowledge of the cause and transmission of disease or the benefits of antiseptics. Not aware of basic germ theory, they spread infection almost every time they operated. Doctors wore the same bloody smocks for days and washed their hands and their scalpels and saws in buckets of dirty water. When they had difficulty threading their needles, they wet the thread with their own saliva. Soldiers often did not survive amputations, not because of the operation but because of the infection that inevitably followed. Of the Union soldiers whose legs were amputated above the knee, more than half died. A Union doctor discovered in 1864 that bromine (previously used in combination with other elements as a sedative) arrested gangrene, but the best that most amputees could hope for was maggots, which ate dead flesh on the stump and thus inhibited the spread of infection. During the Civil War, nearly one of every five wounded rebel soldiers died, and one of every six Yankees. A century later, in Vietnam, the proportion of deaths was one wounded American soldier in four hundred.

Soldiers who avoided battlefield wounds and hospital infections still faced sickness. Deadly diseases swept through crowded army camps, where latrines were often dangerously close to drinking-water supplies. The principal killers were dysentery and typhoid, but pneumonia and malaria also cut down thousands. Doctors did what they could, but often their treatments only added to the misery. They prescribed doses of turpentine for patients with typhoid, they fought respiratory problems with mustard plasters, and they attacked intestinal disorders by blistering the skin with sulfuric acid.

Thousands of female nurses, including Dorothea Dix, Clara Barton, and Juliet Ann Opie Hopkins, improved the wounded men's odds and alleviated their suffering. Civilian relief agencies, such as the U.S. Sanitary Commission and the Women's Relief Society of the Confederacy, promoted hygiene in army camps and made some headway. Nevertheless, as Figure 15.2 shows, disease killed nearly twice as many soldiers as did combat. Many who died of disease were prisoners of war. Approximately 30,000 Northerners died in Confederate prisons, and approximately 26,000 Southerners died in Union prisons. No northern prison, however, could equal the horror of Andersonville in southern Georgia. In August 1864, about 33,000 emaciated men lived in unspeakable conditions in a 26-acre barren stockade with no shelter except what the prisoners were able to construct. More than 13,000 perished.

In the end, 633,000 northern and southern soldiers died, a staggering toll.

65,000 rebels in the rugged mountains of northern Georgia. Skillful maneuvering, constant skirmishing, and one pitched battle, at Kennesaw Mountain at the end of June, brought Sherman to Atlanta, which fell on September 2.

Sherman was only warming up. Intending to "make Georgia howl," he marched out of Atlanta on November 15 with 62,000 battle-hardened veterans, heading for Savannah, 285 miles away on the Atlantic coast. Federal troops cut a swath from twenty-five to sixty miles wide. One veteran remembered, "[We] destroyed all we could not eat, stole their niggers, burned their cotton & gins, spilled their sorghum, burned & twisted their R. Roads and raised Hell generally." Sherman's "March to the Sea" aimed at destroying the will of the southern people. A few weeks earlier, General Philip H. Sheridan had carried out his own scorched-earth campaign in the Shenandoah Valley, complying with Grant's order to turn the valley into "a barren waste . . . so that crows flying over it for the balance of this season will have to carry their provender [food] with them." When Sherman's troops entered an undefended Savannah in the third week of December, the general telegraphed Lincoln that he had "a Christmas gift" for him. A month earlier, Union voters had bestowed on the president an even greater gift.

The Election of 1864

In the fall, white men in the Union states turned to the election of a president. Never before had a nation held general elections in the midst of war. "We can not have free government without elections," Lincoln explained, "and if the rebellion could force us to forgo or postpone a national

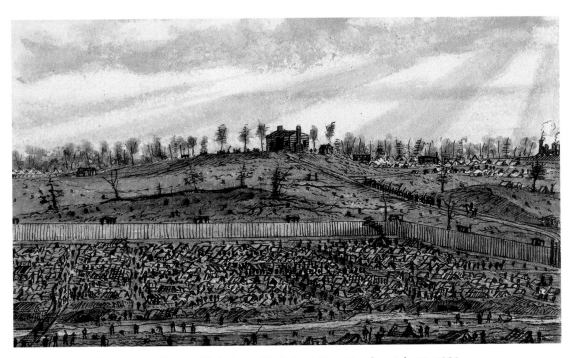

***R. K. Sneden's Shanty at Andersonville Prison, GA**, Robert Knox Sneden, July 15, 1864*
The train carrying prisoner-of-war Robert Sneden arrived at Andersonville on the last day of February
1864 as the Confederates were completing the stockade that surrounded their newest prison. Soon the
sixteen and a half acres in southwestern Georgia were crammed with humanity. By June, the prison area
had to be extended to 26.5 acres. Its 33,000 Union prisoners made Andersonville the fifth largest city in
the Confederacy. A talented watercolorist, Sneden sketched this scene while a captive and touched it up
later. Smallpox, dysentery, scurvy, malnutrition, and infections took the lives of thousands. "The flies are
now here in millions," Sneden observed. "Everything is covered with them, dense swarms like a cloud
settle on the pile of dead which are daily seen near the gates. The ground in the thickest part settled in
the camp is fairly alive and moves with maggots or lice! The filthy swamp undulates like small waves
with them, while the insufferable stench nearly takes away one's breath!"

election, it might fairly claim to have already conquered and ruined us." Lincoln's determination to hold elections is especially noteworthy because the Democratic Party smelled victory. With Sherman temporarily checked outside Atlanta and Grant bogged down in the siege of Petersburg, the Union war effort had stalled during the summer, and frustration had settled over the North. Rankled by inflation, the draft, the attack on civil liberties, and the commitment to blacks, Northerners appeared ready for a change. Lincoln himself concluded in the gloomy summer of 1864, "It seems exceedingly probable that this administration will not be reelected."

Democrats were badly divided, however. "Peace" Democrats insisted on an armistice, while "war" Democrats supported the conflict but opposed Republican means of fighting it.

The party tried to paper over the chasm by nominating a war candidate, General George McClellan, but adopting a peace platform that demanded that "immediate efforts be made for a cessation of hostilities." Republicans denounced the peace plank as a sellout that "virtually proposed to surrender the country to the rebels in arms against us."

Lincoln was no shoo-in for renomination, much less reelection. Conservatives believed he had acted precipitously in emancipating the slaves, and radicals criticized him for moving too slowly to free them and for failing to champion black equality. But frightened by the strength of the peace Democrats, the Republican

> "We can not have free government without elections," Lincoln explained, "and if the rebellion could force us to forgo or postpone a national election, it might fairly claim to have already conquered and ruined us."

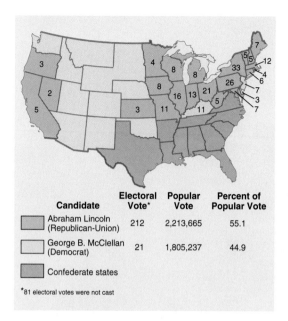

Candidate	Electoral Vote*	Popular Vote	Percent of Popular Vote
Abraham Lincoln (Republican-Union)	212	2,213,665	55.1
George B. McClellan (Democrat)	21	1,805,237	44.9
Confederate states			

*81 electoral votes were not cast

MAP 15.4   The Election of 1864

Party stuck with Lincoln. In an effort to reach out to the largest number of voters, however, the Republicans made two changes. First, they chose the new name, the Union Party, making it easier for prowar Democrats to embrace Lincoln. Second, they chose a new vice presidential candidate, Andrew Johnson of Tennessee, a Southerner who was an uncompromising Unionist.

The capture of Atlanta on September 2 turned the political tide in favor of the Republicans. Lincoln received 55 percent of the popular vote, but his electoral margin was a whopping 212 to McClellan's 21 (Map 15.4). The Republicans also stormed back in the congressional elections, gaining large margins over the Democrats in the Senate and the House. The Union Party bristled with factions, but they united for a resounding victory, one that gave Lincoln a mandate to continue the war until slavery and the Confederacy were dead.

The Confederacy Collapses

As 1865 dawned, military disaster littered the Confederate landscape. With the destruction of John B. Hood's army at Nashville in December 1864, the interior of the Confederacy lay in Yankee hands (see Map 15.3). Sherman's troops, resting momentarily in Savannah, eyed South Carolina hungrily. Farther north, Grant had Lee's army pinned down in Petersburg, just a

Ruins of Richmond
A Union soldier and a small boy wearing a Union cap contemplate the silence and devastation of the Confederacy's capital. On their way out of the city on the evening of April 2, 1865, Confederate demolition squads set fire to tobacco warehouses and ammunition dumps. Huge explosions tore holes in the city, and windswept fires destroyed much of what was left standing. As one Confederate observed, "The old war-scarred city seemed to prefer annihilation to conquest."
Library of Congress.

few miles from Richmond. Southerners took out their frustration and bitterness on their president. Kinder than most, Alexander Stephens, vice president of the Confederacy, likened Jefferson Davis to "my poor old blind and deaf dog."

In the final months of the war, more and more Confederates turned their backs on the rebellion. News from the battlefields made it difficult not to conclude that the Yankees had beaten them. Soldiers' wives begged their husbands to return home to keep their families from starving, and the stream of deserters became a flood. In most cases, white Southerners lost the will to continue, not so much because they lost faith in independence but because they had been battered into submission. Despite all the divisions and conflicts within the Confederacy and the loss of heart in the final months, white Southerners had shown remarkable endurance for their cause. Half of the 900,000 Confederate soldiers had been killed or wounded, and ragged, hungry women and children had sacrificed for four years. Confederates exhibited astounding staying power through the bloodiest war then known to history.

The end came with a rush. On February 1, 1865, Sherman's troops stormed out of Savannah into South Carolina, the "cradle of the Confederacy." Before Sherman could push through North Carolina and arrive at the rear of Lee's army at Petersburg, where he expected to crush the Confederates between his hammer and Grant's anvil, Lee abandoned the city. Davis fled Richmond, and the capital city of the Confederacy fell a few days later. Grant pursued Lee for one hundred miles, until Lee surrendered on April 9, 1865, in a farmhouse near the village of Appomattox Court House, Virginia. The beaten general arrived wearing an immaculate full-dress uniform, complete with sash and sword; the victor wore his usual mud-splattered private's outfit. Grant offered generous peace terms. He allowed Lee's men to return home and to keep their horses to help "put in a crop to carry themselves and their families through the next winter." With Lee gone, the remaining Confederate armies lost hope and gave up within two weeks. After four years, the war was over.

The day after Lee's surrender, a brass band led a happy crowd of three thousand to the White House, where they pleaded with Lincoln for a speech. He begged off and asked the band to strike up "Dixie." He knew that the rebels had claimed the tune as their own, he said, but it was one of his favorites, and now he was taking it back. The crowd roared its approval, and the band played "Dixie," following it with "Yankee Doodle." No one was more relieved than Lincoln that the war was over, but his celebration was re-

Robert E. Lee and Friends, Mathew Brady, 1865
One week after the surrender at Appomattox Court House, Robert E. Lee, again wearing his uniform, sat for this portrait by Mathew Brady, the country's most famous photographer. Lee is joined by his eldest son, Major General George Washington Custis Lee, left, and Lieutenant Colonel Walter H. Taylor, a longtime aide. Lee's sober, worn expression reflects four hard years of war and his final defeat. Already a matchless hero to white Southerners, Lee was well on his way toward saintly immortality. In 1868, one woman described Lee as "bathed in the white light which falls directly upon him from the smile of an approving and sustaining God."
Museum of the Confederacy.

strained. He told his cabinet that his postwar burdens would weigh almost as heavily as those of wartime.

Seeking distraction, Lincoln attended Ford's Theatre on the evening of Good Friday, April 14, 1865. While he and his wife, Mary, enjoyed *Our American Cousin*, a British comedy, John Wilkes Booth, an actor with southern sympathies, slipped into the president's box and shot Lincoln in the head. He died at 7:22 the following morning. Vice President Andrew Johnson became president. The man who had led the nation through the war would not lead it during the postwar search for a just peace.

Conclusion: The Second American Revolution

A transformed nation emerged from the crucible of war. Antebellum America was decentralized politically and loosely integrated economically. To bend the resources of the country to a Union victory, Congress enacted legislation that reshaped the nation's political and economic character. It created national currency and banking systems, and turned to free land, a transcontinental railroad, and miles of telegraph lines to bind the West to the rest of the nation. Congress also adopted policies that established the sovereignty of the federal government and permanently increased its power. To the average citizen before the war, Washington meant the post office and little more; during the war years, the federal government drafted, taxed, and judged Americans in unprecedented ways. The massive changes brought about by war—the creation of a national government, a national economy, and a national spirit—led one historian to call the American Civil War the "Second American Revolution."

The Civil War also had a profound effect on individual lives. When the war began in 1861, millions of men dropped their hoes, hammers, and pencils, put on blue or gray uniforms, and fought and suffered for what they passionately believed was right. The war disrupted families, leaving most women at home with additional responsibilities while offering new opportunities to others for wartime work in factories, offices, and hospitals. It offered blacks new and more effective ways to resist slavery and agitate for equality; for nearly 200,000 black men it provided the opportunity to fight for their freedom, as William Gould did.

The war also devastated the South. Three-fourths of southern white men of military age served in the Confederate army, and at least half of them were captured, wounded, or killed or died of disease. The war destroyed two-fifths of the South's livestock, wrecked half of the farm machinery, and blackened dozens of cities and towns. The immediate impact of the war on the North was more paradoxical. Putting down the slaveholders' rebellion cost the North a heavy price: 373,000 lives. But rather than devastating the land, war set the countryside and cities humming with business activity. The radical shift in power from South to North signaled a new direction in American development: the long decline of agriculture and the rise of industrial capitalism.

Most revolutionary of all, the war ended slavery. Ironically, the South's war to preserve slavery killed it. Ex-slaves like William Gould dedicated their wartime service to its destruction. Because slavery was both a labor and a racial system, the institution was entangled in almost every aspect of southern life. Slavery's uprooting inevitably meant fundamental change. But the full meaning of abolition remained unclear in 1865. Determining the new economic, political, and social status of four million ex-slaves would be the principal task of reconstruction.

FOR ADDITIONAL FIRSTHAND ACCOUNTS OF THIS PERIOD, see Chapter 15 in Michael Johnson, ed., *Reading the American Past,* Third Edition.

TO ASSESS YOUR MASTERY OF THE MATERIAL IN THIS CHAPTER, see the Online Study Guide at bedfordstmartins.com/roark.

FOR WEB LINKS RELATED TO TOPICS IN THIS CHAPTER, see "HistoryLinks," "DocLinks," and "PlaceLinks" at bedfordstmartins.com/roark.

CHRONOLOGY

1861
- **April.** Confederate attack on Fort Sumter opens the Civil War.

- Union nurse Dorothea Dix named superintendent of female nurses.
- **April–May.** Four Upper South states secede and join Confederacy.
- **July.** Union forces routed in First Battle of Bull Run at Manassas, Virginia, the first major clash of war.
- **August.** Congress approves first Confiscation Act, which allows seizure of any slave employed by Confederate military.

1862
- **February.** Legal Tender Act creates first national currency—paper money called "greenbacks."
- Union forces under General Grant capture Fort Henry and Fort Donelson and drive Confederates from Kentucky and most of Tennessee.
- **March.** Defeat at Glorieta Pass helps convince Confederates to abandon their dream of a southwestern slaveholding empire.

- Union victory at Battle of Pea Ridge clears Missouri of Confederate troops and opens Arkansas to federal advance.
- **April.** Battle of Shiloh in Tennessee ends Confederate bid to control Mississippi Valley.
- Confederate Congress passes first draft law in American history.
- **May.** Homestead Act offers western land to people willing to live and labor on it.
- **May–July.** General McClellan's Union forces defeated during Virginia peninsula campaign.
- **July.** Congress approves second Confiscation Act, freeing all slaves of rebel masters.

- Congress passes Militia Act, authorizing enrollment of blacks in Union military.

- **September.** Battle of Antietam stops General Lee's advance into Maryland.
- Lincoln announces preliminary emancipation proclamation.

1863
- **January.** Emancipation Proclamation becomes law, freeing slaves in areas still in rebellion.

- **February.** National Banking Act creates system of national banks.
- **March.** Congress authorizes draft.
- **July.** Vicksburg falls to Union forces, effectively cutting Confederacy in two along Mississippi River.
- Battle of Gettysburg costs Lee more than one-third of his army.
- Antidraft riots sweep New York City.

1864
- **March.** Grant appointed general in chief of all Union forces.
- **May–June.** Grant's forces engage Confederates in Virginia in bloodiest fighting of war, from Wilderness campaign to beginnings of siege of Petersburg.

- **September.** Atlanta falls to Union forces under General Sherman.
- **November.** Lincoln elected to a second term.
- **December.** General Sherman occupies Savannah after scorched-earth campaign in Georgia.

1865
- **April 9.** Lee surrenders to Grant at Appomattox Court House, Virginia, bringing Civil War to an end.
- **April 14.** John Wilkes Booth shoots Lincoln at Ford's Theatre in Washington.

- **April 15.** Lincoln dies.
- Vice President Andrew Johnson becomes president.

BIBLIOGRAPHY

General Works

Jean Harvey Baker, David Herbert Donald, and Michael F. Holt, *The Civil War and Reconstruction* (2001).

James M. McPherson, *Battle Cry of Freedom: The Civil War Era* (1988).

James M. McPherson and William J. Cooper Jr., *Writing the Civil War: The Quest to Understand* (1998).

Allan Nevins, *The War for the Union*, 4 vols. (1959–1971).

Roger L. Ransom, *Conflict and Compromise: The Political Economy of Slavery, Emancipation, and the American Civil War* (1989).

Russell F. Weigley, *A Great Civil War: A Military and Political History, 1861–1865* (2000).

LeeAnn Whites, *The Civil War as a Crisis in Gender* (2000).

The Combatants

Michael Barton, *Goodmen, the Character of Civil War Soldiers* (1981).

Richard E. Beringer et al., *Why the South Lost the Civil War* (1986).

Stephen W. Berry II, *All That Makes a Man: Love and Ambition in the Civil War South* (2003).

Gabor S. Boritt, ed., *Why the Confederacy Lost* (1992).

Catherine Clinton and Nina Silber, eds., *Divided Houses: Gender and the Civil War* (1992).

Richard Nelson Current, *Lincoln's Loyalists: Union Soldiers from the Confederacy* (1992).

David Herbert Donald, *Lincoln* (1995).

David Herbert Donald, ed., *Why the North Won the Civil War* (1960).

Lesley J. Gordon, *General George E. Pickett in Life and Legend* (1998).

William B. Gould IV, ed., *Diary of a Contraband: The Civil War Passage of a Black Sailor* (2002).

Gerald F. Linderman, *Embattled Courage: The Experience of Combat in the American Civil War* (1987).

John F. Marszalek, *Sherman: A Soldier's Passion for Order* (1993).

James Marten, *The Children's Civil War* (1998).

William S. McFeely, *Grant: A Biography* (1981).

James M. McPherson, *What They Fought For, 1861–1865* (1994).

Randall M. Miller, Harry S. Stout, and Charles Reagan Wilson, eds., *Religion and the American Civil War* (1998).

Reid Mitchell, *Civil War Soldiers: Their Expectations and Their Experiences* (1988).

Reid Mitchell, *The Vacant Chair: The Northern Soldier Leaves Home* (1993).

Mark E. Neely Jr., *The Last Best Hope of Earth: Abraham Lincoln and the Promise of America* (1993).

Alan T. Nolan, *Lee Considered: General Robert E. Lee and Civil War History* (1991).

Stephen B. Oates, *A Woman of Valor: Clara Barton and the Civil War* (1994).

James I. Robertson Jr., *Soldiers Blue and Gray* (1988).

Stephen W. Sears, *George B. McClellan: The Young Napoleon* (1988).

Brooks D. Simpson, *Ulysses S. Grant: Triumph over Adversity, 1822–1865* (2000).

Emory M. Thomas, *Robert E. Lee: A Biography* (1995).

Bell I. Wiley, *The Life of Johnny Reb: The Common Soldier of the Confederacy* (1943).

Bell I. Wiley, *The Life of Billy Yank: The Common Soldier of the Union* (1952).

C. Vann Woodward, ed., *Mary Chesnut's Civil War* (1981).

Military History

Gabor S. Boritt, ed., *Lincoln's Generals* (1994).

Robert M. Browning Jr., *Success Is All That Was Expected: The South Atlantic Blockading Squadron during the Civil War* (2002).

Bruce Catton, *The Centennial History of the Civil War*, 3 vols. (1961–1965).

Michael Fellman, *Inside War: The Guerrilla Conflict in Missouri during the American Civil War* (1989).

Joseph T. Glatthaar, *The March to the Sea and Beyond: Sherman's Troops in the Savannah and Carolinas Campaigns* (1985).

Mark Grimsley, *The Hard Hand of War: Union Military Policy toward Southern Civilians, 1861–1865* (1995).

Herman Hattaway and Archer Jones, *How the North Won: A Military History of the Civil War* (1983).

Archer Jones, *Civil War Command and Strategy: The Process of Victory and Defeat* (1992).

Alvin M. Josephy Jr., *The Civil War in the American West* (1991).

George C. Rable, *Fredericksburg! Fredericksburg!* (2002).

Charles Royster, *The Destructive War: William Tecumseh Sherman, Stonewall Jackson, and the Americans* (1991).

Stephen W. Sears, *Landscape Turned Red: The Battle of Antietam* (1983).

Steven E. Woodworth, *Davis and Lee at War* (1995).

Union and Freedom

Herman Belz, *Emancipation and Equal Rights: Politics and Constitutionalism during the Civil War Era* (1978).

Ira Berlin et al., eds., *Freedom: A Documentary History of Emancipation, 1861–1867*, 4 vols. (1982–1993).

David W. Blight, *Frederick Douglass's Civil War: Keeping Faith in Jubilee* (1989).

Dudley Taylor Cornish, *The Sable Arm: Black Troops in the Union Army, 1861–1865* (1987).

LaWanda Cox, *Lincoln and Black Freedom: A Study in Presidential Leadership* (1981).

Louis S. Gerteis, *From Contraband to Freedman: Federal Policy toward Southern Blacks, 1861–1865* (1973).

Joseph T. Glatthaar, *Forged in Battle: The Civil War Alliance of Black Soldiers and White Officers* (1990).

Waldo E. Martin Jr., *The Mind of Frederick Douglass* (1984).

William S. McFeely, *Frederick Douglass* (1991).

James M. McPherson, *Abraham Lincoln and the Second American Revolution* (1990).

Clarence L. Mohr, *On the Threshold of Freedom: Masters and Slaves in Civil War Georgia* (1986).

Steven J. Ramold, *Slaves, Sailors, Citizens: African Americans in the Union Navy* (2002).

Edwin S. Redkey, ed., *A Grand Army of Black Men: Letters from African-American Soldiers in the Union Army, 1861–1865* (1992).

C. Peter Ripley, *Slaves and Freedmen in Civil War Louisiana* (1976).

C. Peter Ripley, ed., *Witness for Freedom: African American Voices on Race, Slavery, and Emancipation* (1993).

The South at War

Stephen V. Ash, *When the Yankees Came: Conflict and Chaos in the Occupied South, 1861–1865* (1995).

William A. Blair, *Virginia's Private War: Feeding Body and Soul in the Confederacy, 1861–1865* (1998).

William J. Cooper, *Jefferson Davis, American* (2000).

Mary A. DeCredico, *Patriotism for Profit: Georgia's Urban Entrepreneurs and the Confederate War Effort* (1990).

Charles B. Dew, *Ironmaker to the Confederacy: Joseph R. Anderson and the Tredegar Iron Works* (1966).

Wayne K. Durrill, *War of Another Kind: A Southern Community in the Great Rebellion* (1990).

Paul D. Escott, *After Secession: Jefferson Davis and the Failure of Confederate Nationalism* (1978).

Drew Gilpin Faust, *The Creation of Confederate Nationalism: Ideology and Identity in the Civil War South* (1988).

Drew Gilpin Faust, *Mothers of Invention: Women of the Slaveholding South in the American Civil War* (1996).

Noralee Frankel, *Freedom's Women: Black Women and Families in Civil War Era Mississippi* (1999).

William W. Freehling, *The South vs. the South: How Anti-Confederate Southerners Shaped the Course of the Civil War* (2001).

Ernest B. Furgurson, *Ashes of Glory: Richmond at War* (1996).

Gary W. Gallagher, *The Confederate War* (1997).

Charles M. Hubbard, *The Burden of Confederate Diplomacy* (1998).

John C. Inscoe and Gordon B. McKinney, *The Heart of Confederate Appalachia: Western North Carolina in the Civil War* (2000).

Ervin L. Jordan Jr., *Black Confederates and Afro-Yankees in Civil War Virginia* (1995).

Mark E. Neely Jr., *Southern Rights: Political Prisoners and the Myth of Confederate Constitutionalism* (1999).

John Solomon Otto, *Southern Agriculture during the Civil War Era, 1860–1880* (1994).

Philip Shaw Paludan, *Victims: A True Story of the Civil War* (1981).

George C. Rable, *Civil Wars: Women and the Crisis of Southern Nationalism* (1989).

George C. Rable, *The Confederate Republic: A Revolution against Politics* (1994).

James L. Roark, *Masters without Slaves: Southern Planters in the Civil War and Reconstruction* (1977).

Daniel E. Sutherland, *Seasons of War: The Ordeal of a Confederate Community, 1861–1865* (1995).

Emory M. Thomas, *The Confederate Nation, 1861–1865* (1979).

Steven Elliott Tripp, *Yankee Town, Southern City: Race and Class Relations in Civil War Lynchburg* (1997).

Stephen R. Wise, *Lifeline of the Confederacy: Blockade Running during the Civil War* (1988).

The North at War

Iver Bernstein, *The New York City Draft Riots: Their Significance for American Society and Politics in the Age of the Civil War* (1990).

George M. Fredrickson, *The Inner Civil War: Northern Intellectuals and the Crisis of the Union* (1965).

Judith Ann Giesberg, *Civil War Sisterhood: The U.S. Sanitary Commission and Women's Politics in Transition* (2000).

Earl J. Hess, *Liberty, Virtue, and Progress: Northerners and Their War for the Union* (1988).

Howard Jones, *Abraham Lincoln and a New Birth of Freedom: The Union and Slavery in the Diplomacy of the Civil War* (1999).

Theodore J. Karamanski, *Rally 'Round the Flag: Chicago and the Civil War* (1993).

Ernest A. McKay, *The Civil War and New York City* (1990).

James H. Moorhead, *American Apocalypse: Yankee Protestants and the Civil War, 1860–1869* (1978).

Mark E. Neely Jr., *The Fate of Liberty: Abraham Lincoln and Civil Liberties* (1991).

Philip Shaw Paludan, *"A People's Contest": The Union and Civil War, 1861–1865* (1988).

Philip Shaw Paludan, *The Presidency of Abraham Lincoln* (1994).

Heather Cox Richardson, *The Greatest Nation of the Earth: Republican Economic Policies during the Civil War* (1997).

Joel H. Silby, *A Respectable Minority: The Democratic Party in the Civil War Era, 1860–1868* (1977).

Amy Dru Stanley, *From Bondage to Contract: Wage Labor, Marriage, and the Market in the Age of Slave Emancipation* (1998).

CARPETBAG

A carpetbag was a nineteenth-
century suitcase made from carpet, often brightly
colored. Applied first to wildcat bankers on the western frontier, "carpetbagger" was a derogatory name for rootless and penniless adventurers
who could carry everything they owned in a single carpetbag. Critics of Republican administrations in the South hurled the name "carpetbaggers" at white Northerners who
moved South during reconstruction and became active in politics. According to white
Southerners, carpetbaggers exploited gullible ex-slaves to gain power and wealth. In
fact, many Northerners who came to the South joined with blacks and some southern
whites to form Republican state and local governments that were among the most
progressive anywhere in the nineteenth century.

Private Collection/Picture Research Consultants & Archives.

Reconstruction
1863–1877

"**Y**ORK DISAPPEARED on yesterday morning," David Golightly Harris
noted in his journal on June 6, 1865. "I suppose that he has gone to
the yankey. I wish they would give him a good whipping & hasten
him back." York, a black field hand, had once belonged to Harris, a white
slaveholder in Spartanburg District, South Carolina. When York disappeared,
the war had been over for two months, and York was a free man. In Harris's
mind, however, simply declaring York free did not make him so. In July,
Harris noted that another field hand, Old Will, had left "to try to enjoy the
freedom the Yankey's have promised the negroes." Two weeks later, black
freedom still seemed in doubt. "There is much talk about freeing the negroes.
Some are said already to have freed them," Harris declared. But Harris had
not freed anyone. He did not inform his former slaves of their freedom until
federal military authorities required him to. "*Freed the Negroes*," he declared
on August 16, four months after Appomattox and more than two and a half
years after the Emancipation Proclamation.

Like many ex-slaveholders, Harris had trouble coming to grips with
emancipation. "Family well, Horses well, Cattle well, Hogs well & everything else are well so far as I know, if it was not for the free negroes," Harris
wrote on September 17. "On their account everything is turned upside down.
So much so that we do not know what to do with our land, nor who to hire if
we want it worked. . . . We are in the midst of troublesome times & do not
know what will turn up." Harris had owned ten slaves, and now he faced
what seemed to him an insoluble problem. He needed blacks to cultivate his
farm, but like most whites he did not believe that African Americans would
work much when free. Some kind of compulsion would be needed. But slavery was gone, leaving the South upside down. White men in Harris's neighborhood sought to set it straight again. "In this district several negroes have
been badly whipped & several have been hung by some unknown persons,"
he noted in November. "This has a tendency to keep them in their proper
bounds & make them more humble." But the violence did not keep ex-slaves
from acting like free people. On Christmas Day 1865, Harris recorded, "The
negroes leave today to hunt themselves a new home while we will be left to
wait upon ourselves."

Across the South, ex-masters predicted that emancipation would mean
economic collapse and social anarchy. Carl Schurz, a Union general who undertook a fact-finding mission to the former Confederate states in the summer
of 1865, encountered this dire prediction often enough to conclude that the
Civil War was a "revolution but half accomplished." Northern victory had
freed the slaves, but it had not changed former slaveholders' minds about the
need for slavery. Left to themselves, Schurz believed, whites would "introduce

some new system of forced labor, not perhaps exactly slavery in its old form but something similar to it." To defend their freedom, blacks would need federal protection, land of their own, and voting rights, Schurz concluded. Until whites "cut loose from the past, it will be a dangerous experiment to put Southern society upon its own legs." Schurz discovered that the end of the war did not mean the beginning of peace. Instead, the nation entered one of its most chaotic and conflicted eras—Reconstruction, an era that would define the status of the defeated South within the Union and the meaning of freedom for ex-slaves.

The status of the South and the contours of black freedom were determined in the nation's capital, where the federal government played an active role, but also in the state legislatures and county seats of the South and through the active participation of blacks themselves. On farms and plantations from Virginia to Texas, ex-slaves like York and Old Will struggled to become free people, while whites like David Golightly Harris clung to the Old South. In the midst of the racial flux and chaos, a small band of crusading women sought to achieve gender equality. The years of reconstruction witnessed an enormous struggle to determine the consequences of Confederate defeat and emancipation. In the end, white Southerners prevailed. Their **New South** was a very different South from the one to which whites like David Golightly Harris wished to return.

Wartime Reconstruction

Reconstruction did not wait for the end of war. As the odds of a northern victory increased, thinking about reunification quickened. Immediately, a question arose: Who had authority to devise a plan for reconstructing the Union? Lincoln believed firmly that reconstruction was a matter of executive responsibility. Congress just as firmly asserted its jurisdiction. Fueling the argument about who had authority to set the terms of reconstruction were significant differences about the terms themselves. Lincoln's primary aim was the restoration of national unity, which he sought through a program of speedy, forgiving political reconciliation. Congress feared that the president's program amounted to restoring the old southern ruling class to power. It wanted greater assurances of white loyalty and greater guarantees of black rights.

Black Woman in Cotton Fields, Thomasville, Georgia

Few images of everyday black women during the Reconstruction era survive. This photograph was taken in 1895, but it nevertheless goes to the heart of the labor struggle after the Civil War. Before emancipation black women worked in the fields, and after emancipation white landlords wanted them to continue working there. Freedom allowed some women to escape field labor, but not this Georgian, who probably worked to survive. The photograph reveals a strong person with a clear sense of who she is. Though worn to protect her head and body from the fierce heat, her intricately wrapped headdress dramatically expresses her individuality. Her bare feet also reveal something about her life.

William Gladstone.

In their eagerness to formulate a plan for political reunification, neither Lincoln nor Congress gave much attention to the South's land and labor problems. But as the war rapidly eroded slavery and traditional plantation agriculture, Yankee military commanders in the Union-occupied areas of the Confederacy had no choice but to oversee the emergence of a new labor system.

"To Bind Up the Nation's Wounds"

On March 4, 1865, President Abraham Lincoln delivered his second inaugural address. He surveyed the history of the long, deadly war and then looked ahead to peace. "With malice toward none; with charity for all; with firmness in the right, as God gives us to see the right," Lincoln said, "let us strive on to finish the work we are in; to bind up the nation's wounds . . . to do all which may achieve and cherish a just, and a lasting peace." Lincoln had contemplated reunion for nearly two years. Deep compassion for the enemy guided his thinking about peace. But kindness is not the key to understanding Lincoln's program. His reconstruction plan aimed primarily at shortening the war and ending slavery.

In his Proclamation of Amnesty and Reconstruction, issued in December 1863, Lincoln offered a full pardon to rebels willing to renounce secession and to accept the abolition of slavery. (Pardons were valuable because they restored all property, except slaves, and full political rights.) His offer excluded several groups of Confederates, such as high-ranking civilian and military officers. When only 10 percent of the men who had been qualified voters in 1860 had taken an oath of allegiance, they could organize a new state government. Lincoln's plan did not require ex-rebels to extend social or political rights to ex-slaves, nor did it anticipate a program of long-term federal assistance to freedmen. Clearly, the president sought to restore the broken Union, not to reform it.

Lincoln's easy terms enraged abolitionists like Bostonian Wendell Phillips, who charged that the president "makes the negro's freedom a mere sham." He "is willing that the negro should be free but seeks nothing else for him," Phillips declared. He compared Lincoln to the most passive of the Civil War generals: "What McClellan was on the battlefield—'Do as little hurt as possible!'—Lincoln is in civil affairs—'Make as little change as possible!'" Phillips and other northern radicals called instead for a thorough overhaul of southern society. Their ideas proved to be too drastic for most Republicans during the war years, but Congress agreed that Lincoln's plan was inadequate. In July 1864, Congress put forward a plan of its own.

Congressman Henry Winter Davis of Maryland and Senator Benjamin Wade of Ohio jointly sponsored a bill that threw out Lincoln's "10 percent plan" and demanded that at least half of the voters in a conquered rebel state take the oath of allegiance before reconstruction could begin. Moreover, the Wade-Davis bill banned ex-Confederates from participating in the drafting of new state constitutions. Finally, the bill guaranteed the equality of freedmen before the law. Congress's reconstruction would be neither as quick nor as forgiving as Lincoln's. Still, the Wade-Davis bill angered radicals because it did not include a provision for black **suffrage**. When Lincoln exercised his right not to sign the bill and let it die instead, Wade and Davis published a manifesto charging the president with usurpation of power. They warned Lincoln to confine himself to "his executive duties—to obey and execute, not make the laws—to suppress by arms armed rebellion, and leave political organization to Congress."

Undeterred, Lincoln continued to nurture the formation of loyal state governments under his own plan. Four states—Louisiana, Arkansas, Tennessee, and Virginia—fulfilled the president's requirements, but Congress refused to seat representatives from the "Lincoln states." In his last public address in April 1865, Lincoln defended his plan but for the first time expressed publicly his endorsement of suffrage for southern blacks, at least "the very intelligent, and . . . those who serve our cause as soldiers." The announcement demonstrated that Lincoln's thinking about reconstruction was still evolving. Four days later, he was dead.

> Clearly, the president sought to restore the broken Union, not to reform it.

Land and Labor

Lincoln's thinking about how to deal with the South's systems of land and labor was still undeveloped when he died, but of all the problems raised by emancipation, none proved more critical. As federal armies proceeded to invade and occupy the Confederacy during the war, hundreds of thousands of slaves became free workers. Northern occupation also meant that Union armies controlled vast territories where legal title to land had become unclear. The wartime Confiscation Acts punished "traitors" by taking away their property. The question of what to do with federally occupied land and how to organize labor on it engaged former slaves, former slaveholders, Union military commanders, and federal government officials long before the war ended.

Up and down the Mississippi Valley, occupying federal troops announced a new labor code. The code required slaveholders to sign contracts with ex-slaves and to pay wages. It also obligated employers to provide food, housing, and medical care. It outlawed whipping, but it reserved to the army the right to discipline blacks who refused to work. The code required black laborers to enter into contracts, work diligently, and remain subordinate and obedient. Military leaders clearly had no intention of promoting a social or economic revolution. Instead, they sought with wage labor to restore plantation agriculture. The effort resulted in a hybrid system that one contemporary called "compulsory free labor," something that satisfied no one. Depending on one's point of view, it provided either too little or too much of a break with the past.

> The wartime system of "compulsory free labor" satisfied no one. Depending on one's point of view, it provided either too little or too much of a break with the past.

Planters complained because the new system fell short of slavery. Blacks could not be "transformed by proclamation," a Louisiana sugar planter warned. Yet under the new system, blacks "are expected to perform their new obligations without coercion, & without the fear of punishment which is essential to stimulate the idle and correct the vicious." Without the right to whip, he argued, the new labor system did not have a chance.

African Americans found the new regime too reminiscent of slavery to be called **free labor**. Of its many shortcomings, none disappointed ex-slaves more than the failure to provide them land of their own. "What's the use of being free if you don't own land enough to be buried in?" one man asked. Freedmen believed they had a moral right to land because they and their ancestors had worked it without compensation for more than two centuries. Moreover, several wartime developments led them to believe that the federal government planned to undergird black freedom with landownership.

In January 1865, General William T. Sherman set aside part of the coast south of Charleston for black settlement. He devised the plan to relieve himself of the burden of thousands of impoverished blacks who trailed desperately after his army. By June 1865, some 40,000 freedmen sat on 400,000 acres of "Sherman land." In addition, in March 1865, Congress passed a bill establishing the Bureau of Refugees, Freedmen, and Abandoned Lands. The Freedmen's Bureau, as it was called, distributed food and clothing to destitute Southerners and eased the transition of blacks from slaves to free persons. Congress also authorized the agency to divide abandoned and confiscated land into 40-acre plots, to rent them to freedmen, and eventually to sell them "with such title as the United States can convey." By June 1865, the bureau had situated nearly 10,000 black families on a half million acres abandoned by fleeing planters. Hundreds of thousands of other ex-slaves eagerly anticipated farms of their own.

Despite the flurry of activity, wartime reconstruction settled nothing. Two years of controversy failed to produce agreement about whether the president or Congress had the authority to devise and direct policy or what proper policy should be. Clearly, the nation faced dilemmas almost as trying as those of the war.

The African American Quest for Autonomy

Ex-slaves never had any doubt about what they wanted freedom to mean. They had only to contemplate what they had been denied as slaves. (See "Documenting the American Promise," page 564.) Slaves had to remain on their plantations; freedom allowed blacks to go wherever they pleased. Thus, in the first heady weeks after emancipation, freedmen often abandoned their plantations just to see what was on the other side of the hill. Slaves had to be at work in the fields by dawn; freedom permitted blacks to taste the formerly forbidden pleasure of sleeping through a sunrise. Freedmen also tested the etiquette of racial subordination. "Lizzie's maid passed me today when I was coming from church *without speaking to me*," huffed one plantation mistress.

To whites, emancipation looked like pure anarchy. Without the discipline of slavery, they said, blacks reverted to their natural condition: lazy, irresponsible, and wild. Actually, these former slaves were experimenting with freedom, but they could not long afford to roam the countryside, neglect work, and casually provoke whites. Soon, most were back on plantations, at work in the fields and kitchens.

But other items on ex-slaves' agenda of freedom endured. Freedmen did not easily give up their quest for economic independence. "The way we can best take care of ourselves is to have land," a delegation of South Carolina blacks told General Sherman in 1865, "and turn it and till it by our own labor." Another group of former slaves from South Carolina declared that they wanted land, "not a Master or owner[,] Neither a driver with his Whip." In addition, slavery had deliberately kept blacks illiterate, and freedmen emerged from slavery eager to read and write. "I wishes the Childern all in School," an ex-slave and Union army veteran asserted. "It is beter for them then to be their Surveing a mistes [mistress]."

Moreover, bondage had denied slaves secure family lives, and the restoration of their families became a persistent black aspiration. As a consequence, thousands of black men and women took to the roads in 1865 to look for relations who had been sold away or to free those who were being held illegally as slaves. A black soldier from Missouri wrote his daughters that he was coming for them. "I will have you if it cost me my life," he declared. "Your Miss Kitty said that I tried to steal you," he told them. "But I'll let her know that god never intended for a man to steal his own flesh and blood." And he swore that "if she meets me with ten thousand soldiers, she [will] meet her enemy."

Another hunger that freedom permitted African Americans to satisfy was independent worship. Under slavery, blacks had often prayed with whites in biracial churches. Intent on religious independence, blacks greeted freedom with a mass exodus from white churches. Some joined the newly established southern branches of all-black northern churches, such as the African Methodist Episcopal Church. Others formed black versions of the major southern denominations, Baptists and Methodists. Slaves had comprehended their tribulations through the lens of their deeply felt Christian faith, and freedmen continued to interpret the events of the Civil War and reconstruction as people of faith. One black woman

Washington Miller and Family
After the Civil War, thousands of ex-slaves whose marriages had no legal standing under slavery rushed to formalize their unions. Natchez, Mississippi, home of cotton millionaires before the war, became the home of many black families after the war. Most ex-slaves worked as house servants, laundresses, gardeners, cooks, and day laborers, but some gained real economic independence. The proud and respectable Washington Miller family represents the achievement of middle-class African Americans. This sensitive photograph is the work of Henry C. Norman, a white Georgian who arrived in Natchez about 1870. Over the next four decades, Norman made thousands of photographs of the black and white citizens who visited his studio.
Collection of Thomas H. Gandy and Joan W. Gandy.

thanked Lincoln for the Emancipation Proclamation, declaring, "When you are dead and in Heaven, in a thousand years that action of yours will make the Angels sing your praises I know it."

Presidential Reconstruction

Abraham Lincoln died on April 15, 1865, just hours after John Wilkes Booth shot him at a Washington, D.C., theater. Chief Justice Salmon P. Chase immediately administered the oath of office to Vice President Andrew Johnson of Tennessee. Congress had adjourned in March, which meant that legislators were away from

The Meaning of Freedom

On New Year's Day 1863, President Abraham Lincoln issued the Emancipation Proclamation. It states that "all persons held as slaves" within the states still in rebellion "are, and henceforward shall be, free." Although the Proclamation in and of itself did not free any slaves, it transformed the character of the war. Despite often intolerable conditions, black people focused on the possibilities of freedom.

DOCUMENT 1
Letter from John Q. A. Dennis to Edwin M. Stanton, July 26, 1864

John Q. A. Dennis, formerly a slave in Maryland, wrote to ask Secretary of War Edwin M. Stanton for help in reuniting his family.

Boston
Dear Sir I am Glad that I have the Honour to Write you afew line I have been in troble for about four yars my Dear wife was taken from me Nov 19th 1859 and left me with three Children and I being a Slave At the time Could Not do Anny thing for the poor little Children for my master it was took me Carry me some forty mile from them So I Could Not do for them and the man that they live with half feed them and half Cloth them & beat them like dogs & when I was admitted to go to see them it use to brake my heart & Now I say again I am Glad to have the honour to write to you to see if you Can Do Anny thing for me or for my poor little Children I was keap in Slavy untell last Novr 1863. then the Good

lord sent the Cornel borne [federal Colonel William Birney?] Down their in Marland in worsester Co So as I have been recently freed I have but letle to live on but I am Striveing Dear Sir but what I went too know of you Sir is it possible for me to go & take my Children from those men that keep them in Savery if it is possible will you pleas give me a permit from your hand then I think they would let them go. . . .

Hon sir will you please excuse my Miserable writeing & answer me as soon as you can I want get the little Children out of Slavery, I being Criple would like to know of you also if I Cant be permited to rase a Shool Down there & on what turm I Could be admited to Do so No more At present Dear Hon Sir

SOURCE: Ira Berlin, Joseph P. Reidy, and Leslie S. Rowland, eds., *Freedom: A Documentary History of Emancipation, 1861–1867*, ser. 1, vol. 1, *The Destruction of Slavery* (Cambridge: Cambridge University Press, 1985), 386.

DOCUMENT 2
Report from Reverend A. B. Randall, February 28, 1865

Freedom prompted ex-slaves to seek legal marriages, which under slavery had been impossible. Writing from Little Rock, Arkansas, to the adjutant general of the Union army, A. B. Randall, the white chaplain of a black regiment, affirmed the importance of marriage to freed slaves and emphasized their conviction that emancipation was only the first step toward full freedom.

Weddings, just now, are very popular, and abundant among the Colored People. They have just learned, of the Special Order No. 15. of Gen Thomas [Adjutant General Lorenzo Thomas] by which, they may not only be lawfully married, but have their Marriage Certificates, Recorded; in a book furnished by the Government. This is most desirable. . . . Those who were captured . . . at Ivy's Ford, on the 17th of January, by Col Brooks, had their Marriage Certificates, taken from them; and destroyed; and then were roundly cursed, for having such papers in their posession. I have married, during the month, at this Post; Twenty five couples; mostly, those, who have families; & have been living together for years. I try to dissuade single men, who are soldiers, from marrying, till their time of enlistment is out: as that course seems to me, to be most judicious.

The Colord People here, generally consider, this war not only; their exodus, from bondage; but the road, to Responsibility; Competency; and an honorable Citizenship—God grant that their hopes and expectations may be fully realized.

SOURCE: Ira Berlin, Joseph P. Reidy, and Leslie S. Rowland, eds., *Freedom: A Documentary History of Emancipation, 1861–1867*, ser. 2, *The Black Military Experience* (Cambridge: Cambridge University Press, 1982), 712.

DOCUMENT 3
Petition "to the Union Convention of Tennessee Assembled in the Capitol at Nashville," January 9, 1865

Early efforts at political reconstruction prompted petitions from former slaves

demanding civil and political rights. In January 1865, black Tennesseans petitioned a convention of white Unionists debating the reorganization of state government.

We the undersigned petitioners, American citizens of African descent, natives and residents of Tennessee, and devoted friends of the great National cause, do most respectfully ask a patient hearing of your honorable body in regard to matters deeply affecting the future condition of our unfortunate and long suffering race.

First of all, however, we would say that words are too weak to tell how profoundly grateful we are to the Federal Government for the good work of freedom which it is gradually carrying forward; and for the Emancipation Proclamation which has set free all the slaves in some of the rebellious States, as well as many of the slaves in Tennessee. . . .

We claim freedom, as our natural right, and ask that in harmony and co-operation with the nation at large, you should cut up by the roots the system of slavery, which is not only a wrong to us, but the source of all the evil which at present afflicts the State. For slavery, corrupt itself, corrupted nearly all, also, around it, so that it has influenced nearly all the slave States to rebel against the Federal Government, in order to set up a government of pirates under which slavery might be perpetrated.

In the contest between the nation and slavery, our unfortunate people have sided, by instinct, with the former. We have little fortune to devote to the national cause, for a hard fate has hitherto forced us to live in poverty, but we do devote to its success, our hopes, our toils, our whole heart, our sacred honor, and our lives. We will work, pray, live, and, if need be, die for the Union, as cheerfully as ever a white patriot died for his country. The color of our skin does not lessen in the least degree, our love either for God or for the land of our birth. . . .

We know the burdens of citizenship, and are ready to bear them. We know the duties of the good citizen, and are ready to perform them cheerfully, and would ask to be put in a position in which we can discharge them more effectually. . . .

This is a democracy—a government of the people. It should aim to make every man, without regard to the color of his skin, the amount of his wealth, or the character of his religious faith, feel personally interested in its welfare. Every man who lives under the Government should feel that it is his property, his treasure, the bulwark and defence of himself and his family, his pearl of great price, which he must preserve, protect, and defend faithfully at all times, on all occasions, in every possible manner.

This is not a Democratic Government if a numerous, law-abiding, industrious, and useful class of citizens, born and bred on the soil, are to be treated as aliens and enemies, as an inferior degraded class, who must have no voice in the Government which they support, protect and defend, with all their heart, soul, mind, and body, both in peace and war. . . .

The possibility that the negro suffrage proposition may shock popular prejudice at first sight, is not a conclusive argument against its wisdom and policy. No proposition ever met with more furious or general opposition than the one to enlist colored soldiers in the United States army. The opponents of the measure exclaimed on all hands that the negro was a coward; that he would not fight; that one white man, with a whip in his hand could put to flight a regiment of them; that the experiment would end in the utter rout and ruin of the Federal army. Yet the colored man has fought so well, on almost every occasion, that the rebel government is prevented, only by its fears and distrust of being able to force him to fight for slavery as well as he fights against it, from putting half a million of negroes into its ranks.

The Government has asked the colored man to fight for its preservation and gladly has he done it. It can afford to trust him with a vote as safely as it trusted him with a bayonet.

SOURCE: Ira Berlin, Joseph P. Reidy, and Leslie S. Rowland, eds., *Freedom: A Documentary History of Emancipation, 1861–1867*, ser. 2, *The Black Military Experience* (Cambridge: Cambridge University Press, 1982), 811–16.

QUESTIONS FOR ANALYSIS AND DEBATE

1. How does John Q. A. Dennis interpret his responsibility as a father?
2. Why do you think ex-slaves wanted their marriages legalized?
3. Why, according to petitioners to the Union Convention of Tennessee, did blacks deserve voting rights?

Washington when Lincoln was killed. They would not reconvene until December. Throughout the summer and fall, therefore, the "accidental president" made critical decisions about the future of the South without congressional input. Like Lincoln, Johnson believed that responsibility for restoring the Union lay with the president. With dizzying speed, he drew up and executed a plan of reconstruction.

Congress returned to the capital in December to find that, as far as the president and former Confederates were concerned, reconstruction was already decided. To most Republicans, Johnson's modest demands of ex-rebels made a mockery of the sacrifice of Union soldiers. Instead of honoring the dead by providing the nation with "a new birth of freedom," as Lincoln had promised in the 1863 speech at Gettysburg, Johnson had acted as midwife to the rebirth of the Old South. He had achieved political reunification at the cost of black **liberty**. To let his program stand, Republican legislators said, would mean that the North's dead had indeed died in vain. They proceeded to dismantle it and substitute a program of their own, one that southern whites found ways to resist.

Johnson's Program of Reconciliation

Born in 1808 in Raleigh, North Carolina, Andrew Johnson was the son of poor, illiterate parents. Unable to afford to send her son to school, Johnson's widowed mother apprenticed him to a tailor. Self-educated and ambitious, he later worked as a tailor in Tennessee, accumulated a fortune in land, acquired five slaves, and built a career in politics championing the South's common white people and assailing its "illegitimate, swaggering, bastard, scrub aristocracy." The only senator from a Confederate state to remain loyal to the Union, Johnson held the planter class responsible for secession. Less than two weeks before he became president, he made it clear what he would do to planters if he ever had the chance: "I would arrest them—I would try them—I would convict them and I would hang them."

Despite such statements, Johnson was no friend of northern radicals. A southern Democrat all his life, Johnson occupied the White House only because the Republican Party in 1864 had needed to broaden its appeal to loyal, Union-supporting Democrats. Johnson favored traditional Democratic causes, vigorously defending **states' rights** (but not secession) and opposing Republican efforts to expand the power of the federal government. He voted against almost every federal appropriation, including a bill to pave the streets of Washington.

Mount Zion Baptist Church, San Antonio, Texas, 1877
Freedom from bondage permitted blacks to flee white ministers and white churches, to "come out from under the yoke," as one ex-slave put it. Former slave Nancy Williams recalled: "Ole white preachers used to talk wid dey tongues widdout sayin' nothin', but Jesus told us slaves to talk wid our hearts." When slavery ended, African Americans worshipped as their hearts dictated. This large, well-dressed congregation standing in front of its substantial church building in San Antonio, Texas, demonstrates how successful some freedmen were in building churches of their own.
Institute of Texas Cultures, San Antonio, Texas.

Johnson had also been a steadfast defender of slavery. He had owned slaves until 1862, when Tennessee rebels, angry at his Unionism, confiscated them. He only grudgingly accepted emancipation. When he did, it was more because he hated planters than sympathized with slaves. "Damn the negroes," he said. "I am fighting those traitorous aristocrats, their masters." At a time when the nation faced its moment of truth regarding black Americans, the new president harbored unshakable racist convictions. Africans, Johnson said, were "inferior to the white man in point of intellect—better calculated in physical structure to undergo drudgery and hardship."

Johnson presented his plan of reconstruction as a continuation of Lincoln's plan, and in some ways it was. Like Lincoln, he stressed reconciliation between the Union and the defeated Confederacy and rapid restoration of civil government in the South. Like Lincoln, he offered to pardon most, but not all, ex-rebels. Johnson recognized the state governments created by Lincoln but set out his own requirements for restoring the rebel states to the Union. All that the citizens of a state had to do was to renounce the right of secession, deny that the debts of the Confederacy were legal and binding, and ratify the Thirteenth Amendment abolishing slavery, which became part of the Constitution in December 1865. Johnson's plan ignored Lincoln's acceptance near the end of his life of some form of limited black voting.

Johnson's eagerness to normalize relations with southern states and his lack of sympathy for blacks also led him to instruct military and government officials to return to pardoned ex-Confederates all confiscated and abandoned land, even if it was in the hands of freedmen. Reformers were shocked. They had expected the president's vendetta against planters to mean the permanent confiscation of the South's plantations and the distribution of the land to loyal freedmen. Instead, his instructions canceled the promising beginnings made by General Sherman and the Freedmen's Bureau to settle blacks on land of their own. As one freedman observed, "Things was hurt by Mr. Lincoln getting killed."

Southern Resistance and Black Codes

In the summer of 1865, delegates across the South gathered to draw up the new state constitutions required by Johnson's plan of reconstruction.

The Black Codes

Titled "Selling a Freeman to Pay His Fine at Monticello, Florida," this 1867 drawing from a northern magazine equates the black codes with the reinstitution of slavery. The laws stopped short of reenslavement but sharply restricted blacks' freedom. In Florida, as in other southern states, certain acts, such as breaking a labor contract, were made criminal offenses, the penalty for which could be involuntary plantation labor for a year.

Library of Congress.

Although they had been defeated, whites clearly had not been subdued. Rather than take their medicine, delegates choked on even the president's mild requirements. Refusing to declare their secession ordinances null and void, the South Carolina and Georgia conventions merely "repudiated" their ordinances, preserving in principle their right to secede. In addition, South Carolina and Mississippi refused to disown their Confederate war debts. Finally, Mississippi rejected the Thirteenth Amendment outright, and Alabama rejected it in part. Despite these defiant acts, Johnson did not demand that Southerners comply with his lenient terms. By failing to draw a hard line, he rekindled southern resistance. White Southerners began to think that by standing up for themselves they—not victorious Northerners—would shape the transition from slavery to freedom. In the fall of 1865, newly elected southern legislators set out to reverse what they considered the "retreat into barbarism" that followed emancipation.

State governments across the South adopted a series of laws known as *black codes*. Emancipation had brought freedmen important rights that they had lacked as slaves—to own property, make contracts, marry legally, and sue and be sued in court. The black codes made a travesty of freedom. They sought to keep blacks subordinate to whites by subjecting blacks to every sort of discrimination. Several states made it illegal for blacks to own a gun. Mississippi made insulting gestures and language by blacks a criminal offense. The codes barred blacks from jury duty. Not a single southern state granted any black—no matter how educated, wealthy, or refined—the right to vote.

> Emancipation had brought freedmen important rights that they had lacked as slaves—to own property, to make contracts, to marry legally. The black codes made a travesty of freedom.

At the core of the black codes, however, lay the matter of labor. Faced with the death of slavery and the disintegration of plantations, legislators sought to hustle freedmen back into traditional roles to restore the old plantation economy. South Carolina attempted to limit blacks to either farmwork or domestic service by requiring them to pay annual taxes of $10 to $100 to work in any other occupation. Mississippi declared that blacks who did not possess written evidence of employment could be declared vagrants and be subject to fines or involuntary plantation labor. Most states allowed judges to bind certain black children—orphans and others whose parents they deemed unable to support them—to white employers. Under these so-called apprenticeship laws, courts bound thousands of black children to work for planter "guardians."

Johnson refused to intervene decisively. A staunch defender of states' rights, he believed that the citizens of every state, even those citizens who had attempted to destroy the Union, should be free to write their own constitutions and laws. Moreover, since Johnson was as eager as other white Southerners to restore white supremacy and black subordination, the black codes did not offend him.

But Johnson also followed the path that he believed would offer him the greatest political return. A **conservative** Tennessee Democrat at the head of a northern Republican Party, he began to look southward for political allies. Despite tough talk about punishing traitors, he personally pardoned 14,000 wealthy or high-ranking ex-Confederates. By pardoning planters and Confederate officials, by acquiescing in the South's black codes, and by accepting the new

southern governments even when they failed to satisfy his minimal demands, he won useful friends.

If Northerners had any doubts about the mood of the South, they evaporated in the elections of 1865. To represent them in Congress, white Southerners chose former Confederates, not loyal Unionists. Of the eighty senators and representatives they sent to Washington, fifteen had served in the Confederate army, ten of them as generals. Another sixteen had served in civil and judicial posts in the Confederacy. Nine others had served in the Confederate Congress. One—Alexander Stephens—had been vice president of the Confederacy. In December, this remarkable group arrived on the steps of the nation's Capitol building to be seated in Congress. As one Georgian remarked: "It looked as though Richmond had moved to Washington."

Expansion of Federal Authority and Black Rights

Southerners had blundered monumentally. They had assumed that what Andrew Johnson was willing to accept, the northern public and Congress would accept as well. But southern intransigence compelled even moderate Republicans to conclude that ex-rebels were a "generation of vipers," still dangerous and untrustworthy. So angry were northern Republicans with the rebels that the federal government refused to supply artificial limbs to disabled Southerners, as they did for Union veterans (see "The Promise of Technology," page 570).

The black codes in particular soured moderate Republicans on the South. The codes became a symbol of southern intentions not to accept the verdict of the battlefields but instead to "restore all of slavery but its name." Northerners were hardly saints when it came to racial justice, but black freedom had become a hallowed war aim. "We tell the white men of Mississippi," the *Chicago Tribune* roared, "that the men of the North will convert the State of Mississippi into a frog pond before they will allow such laws to disgrace one foot of the soil in which the bones of our soldiers sleep and over which the flag of freedom waves."

Moderates represented the mainstream of the Republican Party and wanted only assurance that slavery and treason were dead. They did not champion black equality or the confiscation of plantations or black voting, as did the Radicals, a minority faction within the Republican Party. In December 1865, however, when Congress convened in Washington, it became clear that southern obstinacy had succeeded in forging unity (at least temporarily) among Republican factions. Exercising Congress's right to determine the qualifications of its members, Republicans refused to seat the southern representatives. Rather than accept Johnson's claim that the "work of restoration" was done, Congress challenged his executive power. Congressional Republicans enjoyed a three-to-one majority over the Democrats, and if they could agree on a program of reconstruction, they could easily pass legislation and even override presidential vetoes.

The moderates took the initiative. Senator Lyman Trumbull of Illinois declared that the president's policy of trusting southern whites proved that the ex-slave would "be tyrannized over, abused, and virtually reenslaved without some legislation by the nation for his protection." Early in 1866, the moderates produced two bills that strengthened the federal shield. The first, the Freedmen's Bureau bill, prolonged the life of the agency established by the previous Congress. Since the end of the war, it had distributed food, supervised labor contracts, and sponsored schools for freedmen. Arguing that the Constitution never contemplated a "system for the support of indigent persons," President Andrew Johnson vetoed the Freedmen's Bureau bill. Congress failed by a narrow margin to override the president's veto.

Johnson's veto galvanized nearly unanimous Republican support for the moderates' second measure, the Civil Rights Act. Designed to nullify the black codes, it affirmed the rights of blacks to enjoy "full and equal benefit of all laws and proceedings for the security of person and property as is enjoyed by white citizens." The act boldly required the end of legal discrimination in state laws and represented an extraordinary expansion of black rights and federal

Confederate Flag Dress
While politicians in Washington, D.C., debated the future of the South, white Southerners were coming to grips with the meaning of Confederate defeat. They began to refer to their failure to secede from the Union as the "Lost Cause." They enshrined the memory of certain former Confederates, especially Robert E. Lee, whose nobility and courage represented the white South's image of itself, and they made a fetish of the Confederate flag. White Southerners incorporated symbols of the Lost Cause into their daily lives. This dress, made from material embossed with the rebel flag, did double duty. It both memorialized the Confederacy and, through the sale of the cloth, raised funds for the Confederate Soldiers' Home in Richmond, Virginia.
Valentine Museum, Cook Collection.

authority. The president argued that the civil rights bill amounted to an "unconstitutional invasion of states' rights" and vetoed it. In essence, he denied that the federal government possessed authority to protect the civil rights of blacks.

The president did not have the final word. In April 1866, an incensed Republican Party again pushed the civil rights bill through Congress and overrode the presidential veto. In July, it passed another Freedmen's Bureau bill and overrode Johnson's veto. For the first time in American history, Congress had overridden presidential vetoes of major legislation. As a worried South Carolinian observed, Johnson had succeeded in uniting the Republicans and probably touched off "a fight this fall such as has never been seen."

Congressional Reconstruction

By the summer of 1866, President Andrew Johnson and Congress had dropped their gloves and stood toe to toe in a bare-knuckled contest

Filling the "Empty Sleeve": Artificial Limbs

Industrial and technological developments that made the Civil War so destructive also came to the aid of maimed veterans during national reconstruction. The minié ball, a new kind of ammunition used in the war, proved extremely destructive to human flesh. In attempts to save lives, northern and southern surgeons performed approximately 60,000 amputations. Confederate nurse Kate Cummings observed that in her hospital amputations were so common that they were "scarcely noticed." Approximately 45,000 of the amputees survived, and as the nation began reconstructing the Union, it also sought the literal reconstruction of disabled veterans.

Once their wounds had healed, most amputees were eager to fill an empty sleeve or pant leg with an artificial limb. The federal government provided limbs to those who had fought for the Union, and individual southern states provided limbs for Confederate veterans. Innovations in design and production began during the war and accelerated sharply as the enormous demand produced a surge of interest in prosthetic technology. In the 15 years before the war, 34 patents were issued for artificial limbs and assisting devices; in the 12 years from the beginning of the war to 1873, 133 patents for limbs were issued, nearly a 300 percent increase. As Oliver Wendell Holmes Jr., an army veteran and future Supreme Court justice, observed, if "war unmakes legs," then "human skill must supply their places."

The search for a functional, lightweight, artificial limb drew on a number of advancing fields, including photography, physiology, physics, mathematics, and psychology. For example, in 1859 photographers in Edinburgh and New York succeeded in taking a rapid succession of fast-speed pictures of pedestrians and breaking their strides down into minute parts. Photographs of individuals frozen in mid-step provided new information about human movement that helped make better artificial limbs.

The application of photography is but one example of the growing application of science and technology to the alleviation of human suffering in the second half of the nineteenth century. As excited designers sought to overcome problems of noise, weight, appearance, and discomfort, artificial limbs advanced quickly from crude peg legs to hollow willow legs with movable ankles that simulated the natural motions of the foot. Newly invented vulcanized rubber (called India rubber) increased strength and flexibility and allowed disabled veterans to dispense with metal bolts and springs in their new limbs. Limb makers sought to erase the line between nature and technology, to merge "bodies with machines," as one manufacturer promised. One doctor boasted: "In our time, limb-making has been carried to such a state of perfection that both in form and function they so completely resemble the natural extremity that those who wear them pass unobserved and unrecognized in walks of business and pleasure." He exaggerated, for the artificial limbs of the 1860s were crude by today's standards, but they did represent significant technological advances.

Less than two years after the war, the manufacture of artificial limbs was, according to Oliver Wendell Holmes Jr., "a great and active branch of history." Before the war, locksmiths, gunsmiths, toolmakers, harness makers, and cabinetmakers had made peg legs and artificial arms individually as sidelines to their principal tasks. After the war, the great demand for

---

unprecedented in American history. Johnson made it clear that he would not budge on either constitutional issues or policy. Moderate Republicans made a major effort to resolve the dilemma of reconstruction by amending the Constitution. But the obstinacy of Johnson and white Southerners pushed Republican moderates ever closer to the Radicals and to acceptance of additional federal intervention in the South. In time, white men in Congress debated whether to give the ballot to black men. Outside of Congress, blacks raised their voices on behalf of color-blind voting rights, while women argued to make voting sex-blind as well.

artificial limbs prompted businesses to apply industrial manufacturing processes to limbs. Soon American factories—high-volume, mechanized, and uniform—were producing untold numbers of sewing machines, bicycles, and typewriters—as well as artificial limbs.

The postwar business of prosthesis was highly competitive. With the federal and state governments placing large, lucrative orders, dozens of manufacturers entered the market. Very quickly, buyers could choose from among English, French, German, and American models. With so many choices, men had to be persuaded that one leg was better than another. Aggressive advertising campaigns announced the new products. Northern manufacturers used government military and pension registration rolls to mail brochures directly to the homes of Union veterans. Manufacturers in New York, Philadelphia, and Boston established dazzling showrooms on major shopping streets and sponsored "cripple races" to test and promote their products.

Politics sometimes affected opinions about artificial limbs and about which product to choose. Southern manufacturers proclaimed that they

"Before and After"

These photographic images of a veteran showing the results of two amputations and wearing his artificial legs come from the back of an A. A. Marks business card in about 1878. This manufacturer of artificial limbs sent a clear message: Marks legs make maimed men whole again. Marks promised that, thus restored, the wounded man would be the "equal of his fellowmen in every employment of life."

Warshaw Collection, National Museum of American History, Smithsonian Institution.

were "a home manufacturer" and were more deserving of contracts from former Confederate states than were their northern competitors. Former Confederate general John B. Hood made a controversial admission when he declared that his "Yankee leg was the best of all." Another disabled Southerner, however, disliked his northern-manufactured leg, which, he concluded, "like the majority of Yankee inventions proved to be a 'humbug.'"

Disabled veterans were likely to find their postwar struggle to obtain work, to overcome stigma, and to regain their confidence almost as difficult as their battlefield experiences. Some manufacturers of prosthetics attempted, through a combination of technology and psychology, to help them. Each year in New York City, for example, manufacturers sponsored a left-handed penmanship contest to encourage men who had lost their right arms to learn to write with their left hands. Well into the twentieth century, veterans' "empty sleeve" remained both a badge of courage and a sign of permanent loss, a wound national reconstruction could never heal.

The Fourteenth Amendment and Escalating Violence

In April 1866, Republican moderates introduced the Fourteenth Amendment to the Constitution. Congress passed it in June, and two years later it gained the necessary ratification of three-fourths of the states. The most important provisions of this complex amendment made all native-born or naturalized persons American citizens and prohibited states from abridging the "privileges and immunities" of citizens, depriving them of "life, liberty, or property without due process of law," and denying them "equal protection of the laws."

By making blacks national citizens, the Fourteenth Amendment provided a national guarantee of equality before the law. In essence, it protected the rights of citizens against violation by their own state governments.

By making blacks national citizens, the amendment nullified the *Dred Scott* decision of 1857 and provided a national guarantee of equality before the law. In essence, it protected the rights of citizens against violation by their own state governments.

The Fourteenth Amendment also dealt with voting rights. Rather than explicitly granting the vote to black men, as Radicals wanted, the amendment gave Congress the right to reduce the congressional representation of states that withheld suffrage from some of its adult male population. In other words, white Southerners could either allow black men to vote or see their representation in Washington slashed.

The Republicans drafted the Fourteenth Amendment to their benefit. If southern whites granted voting rights to freedmen, the Republican Party, entirely a northern party, would gain valuable black votes, establish a wing in the South, and secure its national power. But if whites refused, representation of southern Democrats would plunge, and Republicans would still gain political power. Although whites in the North were largely hostile to voting rights for blacks too, northern states could continue to withhold suffrage and not suffer in Washington, for the black populations in the North were too small to count in figuring representation. To Radicals, the Fourteenth Amendment's voting provision was "hypocritical" and a "swindle."

The suffrage provisions in the amendment completely ignored the small band of politicized and energized women who had emerged from the war demanding "the ballot for the two disenfranchised classes, negroes and women." Founding the American Equal Rights Association in 1866, Susan B. Anthony and Elizabeth Cady Stanton lobbied for "a government by the people, and the whole people; for the people and the whole people." They felt betrayed when their old antislavery allies, who now occupied positions of national power, proved to be fickle and refused to work for their goals. "It was the Negro's hour," Frederick Douglass later

The Fourteenth Amendment's suffrage provisions completely ignored the small band of politicized and energized women who had emerged from the war demanding "the ballot for two disenfranchised classes, negroes and women."

explained. The Republican Party had to avoid anything that might jeopardize black gains, Charles Sumner declared. He suggested that woman suffrage could be "the great question of the future."

The Fourteenth Amendment dashed women's expectations. It provided for punishment of any state that excluded voters on the basis of race but not on the basis of sex. The amendment also introduced the word *male* into the Constitution when it referred to a citizen's right to vote. Stanton had predicted that "if that word 'male' be inserted, it will take us a century at least to get it out."

Despite women's objections, Tennessee approved the Fourteenth Amendment in July, and Congress promptly welcomed the state's representatives and senators back. Had Johnson counseled other southern states to ratify this relatively mild amendment and warned them that they faced the fury of an outraged Republican Party if they refused, they might have listened. Instead, Johnson advised Southerners to reject the Fourteenth Amendment and to rely on him to trounce the Republicans in the fall congressional elections.

Johnson had decided to make the Fourteenth Amendment the overriding issue of the 1866 congressional elections and to gather its white opponents into a new conservative party, the National Union Party. In August, his supporters met in Philadelphia. Democrats came, but most Republicans did not. Johnson was unable to draw disgruntled Republicans; his previous actions had united the Republican Party against him.

The president's strategy had suffered a setback two weeks earlier when whites in several southern cities went on rampages against blacks. It was less an outbreak of violence than an escalation of the violence that had never ceased. In New Orleans, a mob assaulted delegates to a black suffrage convention, and 34 blacks died. In Memphis, white mobs hurtled through the black sections of town and killed at least 46 people. The slaughter shocked Northerners and renewed skepticism about Johnson's claim that southern whites could be trusted. "Who doubts that the Freedmen's Bureau ought to be abolished forthwith," a New Yorker observed sarcastically, "and the blacks remitted to the paternal care of their old masters, who 'understand the nigger, you know, a great deal better than the Yankees can.'"

The 1866 election resulted in an overwhelming Republican victory in which the party re-

Memphis Riots, May 1866

On May 1, 1866, two carriages, one driven by a white man and the other by a black man, collided on a busy Memphis street. This minor incident spiraled into three days of bloody racial violence in which dozens of blacks and two whites died. Racial friction was common in postwar Memphis, and white newspapers routinely heaped abuse on black citizens. "Would to God they were back in Africa, or some other seaport town," the *Memphis Argus* shouted two days before the riot erupted, "anywhere but here." South Memphis, pictured in this lithograph from *Harper's Weekly*, was a shantytown where the families of black soldiers stationed at nearby Fort Pickering lived. The army commander refused to send troops to protect soldiers' families and property, and white mobs ran wild.

Library of Congress.

tained its three-to-one congressional majority over Democrats. Johnson had bet that Northerners would not support federal protection of black rights. He expected a racist backlash to blast the Republican Party. But the Fourteenth Amendment was not radical enough to drive Republican voters into Johnson's camp, and the war was still fresh in northern minds. As one Republican explained, southern whites "with all their intelligence were traitors, the blacks with all their ignorance were loyal."

Radical Reconstruction and Military Rule

The elections of 1866 should have taught southern whites the folly of relying on Andrew Johnson as a guide through the thicket of reconstruction. But when Johnson continued to urge Southerners toward rejection of the Fourteenth Amendment, every southern state except

Tennessee voted it down. "The last one of the sinful ten," thundered Representative James A. Garfield of Ohio, "has flung back into our teeth the magnanimous offer of a generous nation." In the void created by the South's rejection of the moderates' program, the Radicals seized the initiative.

Each act of defiance by southern whites had boosted the standing of the Radicals within the Republican Party. At the Radical core was a small group of men who had cut their political teeth on the **antebellum** campaign against slavery, who had goaded Lincoln toward making the war a crusade for freedom, and who had carried into the postwar period the conviction that only federal power could protect the rights of the freedmen. Except for freedmen themselves, no one did more to make freedom the "mighty moral question of the age." Men like Senator Charles Sumner, that pompous but sincere Massachusetts crusader, and Thaddeus Stevens, the caustic representative from Pennsylvania, did not speak with a single voice, but they united in calling for civil and political equality. They insisted on extending to ex-slaves the same opportunities that northern working people enjoyed under the free-labor system. The southern states were "like clay in the hands of the potter," Stevens declared in January 1867, and he called on Congress to begin reconstruction all over again.

In March 1867, moderates joined the Radicals to overturn the Johnson state governments and initiate military rule of the South. The Military Reconstruction Act (and three subsequent acts) divided the ten unreconstructed Confederate states into five military districts. Congress placed a Union general in charge of each district and instructed him to "suppress insurrection, disorder, and violence" and to begin political reform. After the military had completed voter registration, which would include black men and exclude all those barred by the Fourteenth Amendment from holding public office, voters in each state would elect delegates to conventions that would draw up new state constitutions. Each constitution would guarantee black suffrage. When the voters of each state had approved the constitution and the state legislature had ratified the Fourteenth Amendment, the state could submit its work to Congress. If Congress approved, the state's senators and representatives could be seated, and political reunification would be accomplished.

Radicals proclaimed the provision for black suffrage "a prodigious triumph." The doggedness of the Radicals and of African Americans, and the pigheadedness of Johnson and the white South, swept the Republican Party far beyond the limited suffrage provisions of the Fourteenth Amendment. Republicans finally agreed with Sumner that only the voting power of ex-slaves could bring about a permanent revolution in the South. Indeed, suffrage provided blacks with a powerful instrument of change and self-protection. When combined with

Reconstruction Military Districts, 1867

> The doggedness of the Radicals and of African Americans, and the pigheadedness of Johnson and the white South, swept the Republican Party far beyond the limited suffrage provisions of the Fourteenth Amendment.

the disfranchisement of thousands of ex-rebels, it promised to cripple any neo-Confederate resurgence and guarantee Republican state governments in the South.

Despite its bold suffrage provision, the Military Reconstruction Act of 1867 disappointed those who advocated the confiscation and redistribution of southern plantations to ex-slaves. Among the most distressed was Thaddeus Stevens, who believed that at bottom reconstruction was an economic problem. He agreed wholeheartedly with the ex-slave who said, "Give us our own land and we take care of ourselves, but without land, the old masters can hire us or starve us, as they please." But most Republicans believed they had already provided blacks with the critical tools: equal legal rights and the ballot. If blacks were to get forty acres, they would have to gain the land themselves.

Declaring that he would rather sever his right arm than sign such a formula for "anarchy and chaos," Andrew Johnson vetoed the Military Reconstruction Act. Congress overrode his veto the very same day, dramatizing the shift in power from the executive to the legislative branch of government. With the passage of the Reconstruction Acts of 1867, congressional reconstruction was virtually completed. Congress had left whites owning most of the South's land but, in a radical departure, had given black men the ballot. More than any other provision, black suffrage justifies the term "radical reconstruction." In 1867, the nation began an unprecedented experiment in interracial democracy—at least in the South, for Congress's plan did not touch the North. Soon the former Confederate states would become the primary theater for political struggle. But before the spotlight swung away from Washington, the president and Congress had one more scene to play.

Impeaching a President

Despite his defeats, Andrew Johnson had no intention of yielding control of reconstruction. In a dozen ways he sabotaged Congress's will and encouraged white belligerence and resistance. He issued a flood of pardons to undermine efforts at political and economic change. He waged war against the Freedmen's Bureau by removing officers who sympathized too fully with ex-slaves. And he replaced Union generals eager to enforce Congress's Reconstruction Acts with conservative men eager to defeat them. Johnson claimed that he was merely defending the "violated Constitution." At bottom, however, the president subverted congressional reconstruction to protect southern whites from what he considered the horrors of "Negro domination."

When Congress realized that overriding Johnson's vetoes did not ensure that Congress got its way, it attempted to tie the president's hands. Congress required that all orders to field commanders pass through the General of the Army, Ulysses S. Grant, who Congress believed was sympathetic to southern freedmen, southern Unionists, and Republicans. It also enacted the Tenure of Office Act in 1867, which required the approval of the Senate for the removal of any government official who had been appointed with Senate consent. Congress intended the Tenure of Office Act to protect Secretary of War Edwin M. Stanton, the last remaining friend of radical reconstruction in Johnson's cabinet. Some Republicans, however, believed that nothing less than getting rid of Johnson could save reconstruction, and they initiated a crusade to impeach the president and remove him from office.

As long as Johnson refrained from breaking a law, **impeachment** remained a faint hope. According to the Constitution, the House of Representatives can impeach and the Senate can try any federal official for "treason, bribery, or other high crimes and misdemeanors." Radicals argued that Johnson's abuse of constitutional powers and his failure to fulfill constitutional obligations were impeachable offenses, but moderates interpreted the constitutional provision to mean violation of criminal statutes. Then in August 1867, Johnson suspended Secretary of War Stanton from office. As required by the Tenure of Office Act, the president requested the Senate to consent to the dismissal. When the Senate balked, Johnson removed Stanton anyway. "Is the President crazy, or only drunk?" asked a dumbfounded Republican moderate. "I'm afraid his doings will make us all favor impeachment."

News of Johnson's open defiance of the law convinced every Republican in the House to vote for a resolution impeaching the president. Supreme Court Chief

Andrew Johnson, with Additions
This dignified portrait by Currier and Ives of President Andrew Johnson appeared in 1868, the year of his impeachment trial. The portrait was apparently amended by a disgruntled citizen. Johnson's vetoes of several reconstruction measures passed by Congress caused his opponents to charge him with arrogant monarchical behavior. Johnson preferred the unamended image—that of a plain and sturdy statesman.
Museum of American Political Life.

Justice Salmon Chase presided over the Senate trial, which lasted from March until May 1868. Chase refused to allow Johnson's opponents to raise broad issues of misuse of power and forced them to argue their case exclusively on the narrow legal grounds of Johnson's removal of Stanton. Johnson's lawyers argued that he had not committed a criminal offense, that the Tenure of Office Act was unconstitutional, and that in any case it did not apply to Stanton, who had been appointed by Lincoln. When the critical vote came, seven moderate Republicans broke with their party and joined the Democrats in voting not guilty. With 35 in favor and 19 opposed, the impeachment forces fell one vote short of the two-thirds needed to convict.

Johnson survived but did not come through the ordeal unscathed. After his trial he called a truce, and for the remaining ten months of his term congressional reconstruction proceeded unhindered by presidential interference. Without interference from Johnson, Congress revisited the suffrage issue.

The Fifteenth Amendment and Women's Demands

In February 1869, Republicans passed the Fifteenth Amendment to the Constitution. The amendment prohibited states from depriving any citizen of the right to vote because of "race, color, or previous condition of servitude." The Reconstruction Acts of 1867 already required black suffrage in the South; the Fifteenth Amendment extended black voting to the entire

Major Reconstruction Legislation, 1865–1875

1865

Thirteenth Amendment (ratified 1865)	Abolishes slavery.

1865 and 1866

Freedmen's Bureau Acts	Establish the Freedmen's Bureau to distribute food and clothing to destitute Southerners and help freedmen with labor contracts and schooling.
Civil Rights Act of 1866	Affirms the rights of blacks to enjoy "full and equal benefit of all laws and proceedings for the security of person and property as is enjoyed by white citizens" and effectively requires the end of legal discrimination in state laws.
Fourteenth Amendment (ratified 1868)	Makes native-born blacks citizens and guarantees all citizens "equal protection of the laws." Threatens to reduce representatives of a state that denies suffrage to any of its male inhabitants.

1867

Military Reconstruction Acts	Impose military rule in the South, establish rules for readmission of ex-Confederate states to the Union, and require those states to guarantee the vote to black men.

1869

Fifteenth Amendment (ratified 1870)	Prohibits racial discrimination in voting rights in all states in the nation.

1875

Civil Rights Act of 1875	Outlaws racial discrimination in transportation, public accommodations, and juries.

nation. Partisan advantage played an important role in the amendment's passage. Gains by northern Democrats in the 1868 elections worried Republicans, and black voters now represented the balance of power in several northern states. By giving ballots to northern blacks, Republicans could lessen their political vulnerability. As one Republican congressman observed, "Party expediency and exact justice coincide for once."

Some Republicans, however, found the final wording of the Fifteenth Amendment "lame and halting." Rather than absolutely guaranteeing the right to vote, the amendment merely prohibited exclusion on grounds of race. The distinction would prove to be significant. In time, inventive white Southerners would devise tests of literacy and property and other apparently nonracial measures that would effectively disfranchise blacks yet not violate the Fifteenth Amendment. But an amendment that fully guaranteed the right to vote courted defeat outside the South. Rising antiforeign sentiment—against the Chinese in California and against European immigrants in the Northeast—caused states to resist giving up total control of suffrage requirements. The limits of the proposed amendment made it appealing. In March 1870, after three-fourths of the states had ratified it, the Fifteenth Amendment became part of the Constitution. Republicans generally breathed a sigh of relief, confident that black suffrage was "the last great point that remained to be settled of the issues of the war."

Woman suffrage advocates, however, were sorely disappointed with the Fifteenth Amendment's failure to extend voting rights to women. Although women fought hard to include the word *sex* (as they had fought hard to keep the word *male* out of the Fourteenth Amendment), the amendment denied states the right to forbid suffrage only on the basis of race. Elizabeth Cady Stanton and Susan B. Anthony condemned the Republicans' "negro first" strategy and concluded that woman "must not put her trust in man."

The Fifteenth Amendment severed the early **feminist** movement from its abolitionist roots. Over the next several decades, women would establish an independent suffrage crusade that drew millions of women into political life. But in 1869 northern Republicans took enough satisfaction in the Fifteenth Amendment to promptly scratch the "Negro question" from the agenda of national politics. Even that steadfast crusader for

Susan B. Anthony

Like many outspoken suffragists, Anthony, depicted here in 1852, began her public career working on behalf of temperance and abolition. But she grew tired of laboring under the direction of male clergymen—"white orthodox little saints," she called them—who controlled the reform movements and who routinely dismissed the opinions of women. Anthony's continued passion for other causes—improving working conditions for labor, for example—led some conservatives to oppose women's political rights because they equated the suffragist cause with radicalism in general. Women could not easily overcome such views, and the long struggle for the vote eventually drew millions of women into public life.

Susan B. Anthony House, Inc.

equality, Wendell Phillips, concluded that the black man now held "sufficient shield in his own hands. . . . Whatever he suffers will be largely now, and in future, his own fault." Reformers like Phillips had no idea of the violent struggles that lay ahead.

The Struggle in the South

Northerners believed they had discharged their responsibilities with the Reconstruction Acts and the amendments to the Constitution, but Southerners knew that the battle had just begun. Black suffrage and large-scale rebel disfranchise-

ment that came with congressional reconstruction had destroyed traditional southern politics and established the foundation for the rise of the Republican Party in the South. Gathering together outsiders and outcasts, southern Republicans won elections, wrote new state constitutions, and formed new state governments.

Challenging the established class for political control was dangerous business. Equally dangerous were the confrontations that took place on farms and plantations across the South. In the countryside, blacks sought to give practical, everyday meaning to their newly won legal and political equality. But ex-masters like David Golightly Harris and other whites had their own ideas about the social and economic arrangements that should replace slave labor and the old plantation economy. Freedom remained contested territory, and Southerners fought pitched battles with one another to determine the contours of their postemancipation world.

Freedmen, Yankees, and Yeomen

African Americans made up the majority of southern Republicans. Freedmen realized that without the ballot they were almost powerless, and they threw themselves into the suffrage campaign. Southern black men gained voting rights in 1867, and within months nearly every eligible black man had registered to vote. Almost all registered as Republicans, grateful to the party that had freed them and given them the **franchise**. Black women, like white women, remained disfranchised but mobilized along with black men. They attended political rallies and parades and in the 1868 presidential election bravely wore buttons supporting the Republican candidate, former Union general Ulysses S. Grant. Southern blacks did not have identical political priorities, but they united in their desire for education and equal treatment before the laws.

Northern whites who decided to make the South their home after the war were a second element of the South's Republican Party. Conservative white Southerners called any northern migrant a "carpetbagger," a man so poor that he could pack all his earthly belongings in a single carpet-sided suitcase and swoop southward like a buzzard to "fatten on our misfortunes." But most Northerners who moved south were restless, relatively well-educated young men, often former Union officers and Freedmen's Bureau agents who looked upon the South as they did the West—as a promising place to make a living. They expected that a South without slavery would prosper, and they wanted to be part of it. Northerners in the southern Republican Party consistently supported programs that encouraged vigorous economic development along the lines of the northern free-labor model.

Southern whites made up the third element of the Republican Party in the South. Approximately one out of four white Southerners voted Republican. The other three cursed those who did. They condemned southern-born white Republicans as traitors to their region and their race and called them "scalawags," a term for runty horses and low-down, good-for-nothing rascals. **Yeoman** farmers accounted for the vast majority of white Republicans in the South. Some were Unionists who emerged from the war with bitter memories of Confederate persecution. Others were small farmers who welcomed the Republican Party because it promised to end favoritism toward the interests of plantation owners who had dominated southern politics before the war. Yeomen usually supported initiatives for public schools and for expanding economic opportunity in the South.

The Republican Party in the South, then, was made up of freedmen, Yankees, and yeomen—an improbable coalition. The mix of races, regions, and classes inevitably meant friction as each group maneuvered to define the party. But Reconstruction represents an extraordinary moment in American politics: Through the Republican Party, blacks and whites joined together to pursue political change. Formally, of course, only men participated in politics—casting ballots and holding offices—but women also played parts in the political struggle by joining in parades and rallies, attending stump speeches, and even campaigning.

> Reconstruction represents an extraordinary moment in American politics: Through the Republican Party, blacks and whites joined together to pursue political change.

Reconstruction politics was not for cowards. Activity on behalf of Republicans in particular took courage. Most whites in the South condemned the entire political process as illegitimate and felt justified in doing whatever they could to stamp out Republicanism. Violence against blacks—the "white terror"—took brutal institutional form in 1866 with the formation in Tennessee of the Ku Klux Klan, a social club of Confederate veterans that quickly developed into a paramilitary organization armed against Republicans. The Klan went on a rampage of whipping, hanging, shooting, burning, and throat-cutting to defeat reconstruction and restore white supremacy. (See "Historical Question," page 580.) Rapid demobilization of the Union army after the war left only 20,000 troops to patrol the entire South, a vast territory. Without effective military protection, southern Republicans had to take care of themselves.

Republican Rule

The Reconstruction Acts required southern states to draw up new constitutions before they could be readmitted to Congress. Beginning in the fall of 1867, southern states held elections for delegates to state constitutional conventions. About 40 percent of the white electorate stayed home because they had been disfranchised or because they had decided to boycott politics. Republicans won three-fourths of the seats. About 15 percent of the Republican delegates to the conventions were Northerners who had moved south, 25 percent were African Americans, and 60 percent were white Southerners. As a British visitor observed, the delegate elections reflected "the mighty revolution that had taken place in America." But Democrats described the state conventions as zoos of "baboons, monkeys, mules . . . and other jackasses." In fact, the conventions brought together serious, purposeful men who hammered out the legal framework for a new order.

The reconstruction constitutions introduced two broad categories of changes in the South: those that reduced aristocratic privilege and increased **democratic** equality and those that expanded the state's responsibility for the general welfare. In the first category, the constitutions adopted universal male suffrage, abolished property qualifications for holding office, and made more offices elective and fewer appointed. In the second category, they enacted prison reform; made the state responsible for caring for orphans, the insane, and the deaf and mute; and aided debtors by exempting their homes from seizure.

These forward-looking state constitutions provided blueprints for a new South but stopped short of the specific reforms advocated by some southern Republicans. Despite the wishes of virtually every former slave, no southern constitution confiscated and redistributed land. And despite the prediction of Unionists that unless all

Congressman John R. Lynch
Although whites almost always maintained control of reconstruction politics, over 600 blacks served in legislatures in the South. Ex-slaves made up the majority of the black legislators. The Union army freed John R. Lynch of Mississippi, and he gained an education at a Natchez freedmen's school. Lynch (1847–1939) was only twenty-four when he became speaker of Mississippi's house of representatives. In 1872, he joined six other African Americans in Congress in Washington, D.C., where in support of civil rights legislation he described his personal experience of being forced to occupy railroad smoking cars with gamblers and drunks. After reconstruction ended, Lynch practiced law and wrote a history of the reconstruction legislatures, which, he argued, were the "best governments those States ever had." Natchez photographer Henry C. Norman took this powerful photograph, probably in the early 1870s.
Collection of Thomas H. Gandy and Joan W. Gandy.

Republican voters were black men, more than four out of five Republican officeholders were white. Southerners sent fourteen black congressmen and two black senators to Washington, but only 6 percent of Southerners in Congress during reconstruction were black (Figure 16.1). With the exception of South Carolina, where blacks briefly held a majority in one house of the legislature, no state experienced "Negro rule," despite black majorities in the populations of three states.

In almost every state, voters ratified the new constitutions and swept Republicans into power. After ratifying the Fourteenth Amendment, the former Confederate states were readmitted to Congress. Southern Republicans then turned to a staggering array of problems. Wartime destruction—burned cities, shattered bridges, broken levees—still littered the landscape. The South's share of the nation's wealth had fallen from 30 to only 12 percent. Manufacturing limped along at a fraction of prewar levels, agricultural production remained anemic, and the region's railroads had hardly advanced from the devastated condition in which Union armies had left them. Without the efforts of the Freedmen's Bureau, black and white Southerners would have starved. Making matters worse, racial harassment and reactionary violence dogged Southerners who sought reform. In this desperate

FIGURE 16.1 Southern Congressional Delegations, 1865–1877
The statistics contradict the myth of black domination of congressional representation during Reconstruction.

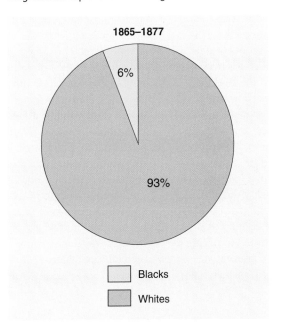

former Confederates were banned from politics they would storm back and wreck reconstruction, no state constitution disfranchised ex-rebels wholesale.

Democrats, however, were blind to the limits of the Republican program. They thought they faced wild revolution. According to Democrats, Republican victories initiated "black and tan" (ex-slave and mulatto) governments across the South. But the claims of "Negro domination" had almost no validity. While four out of five

What Did the Ku Klux Klan Really Want?

In the summer of 1866, six Confederate veterans in Pulaski, Tennessee, founded the Ku Klux Klan. Borrowing oaths and rituals from a college fraternity, the young men innocently sought fun and fellowship in a social club. But they quickly tired of playing pranks on one another and shifted to more serious matters. By the spring of 1868, when congressional reconstruction went into effect, new groups, or "dens," of the Ku Klux Klan had sprouted throughout the South.

According to former Confederate general and Georgia Democratic politician John B. Gordon, the Klan owed its popularity to the "instinct of self-preservation . . . the sense of insecurity and danger, particularly in those neighborhoods where the Negro population largely predominated." Everywhere whites looked, he said, they saw "great crime." Republican politicians organized ignorant freedmen and marched them to the polls, where they blighted honest government. Ex-slaves drove overseers from plantations and claimed the land for themselves. Black robbers and rapists made white women cower behind barred doors. It was necessary, Gordon declared, "in order to protect our families from outrage and preserve our own lives, to have something that we could regard as a brotherhood—a combination of the best men of the country, to act purely in self-defense." According to Gordon and other conservative white Southerners, Klansmen were

good men who stepped forward to do their duty—men who wanted nothing more than to guard their families and defend decent society from the assaults of degraded ex-slaves and a vindictive Republican Party.

Behind the Klan's high-minded and self-justifying rhetoric, however, lay another agenda, revealed in members' actions. Klansmen embarked on a campaign to reverse history. Garbed in robes and hoods, Klansmen engaged in hit-and-run **guerrilla warfare** against free labor, civil equality, and political democracy. They aimed to terrorize their enemies—ex-slaves and white Republicans—into submission. As the South's chief terrorist organization between 1868 and 1871, the Klan whipped, burned, and shot in the name of white supremacy. Changes in four particular areas of southern life proved flash points for Klan violence: racial etiquette, education, labor, and politics.

Klansmen punished blacks and whites whom they considered guilty of breaking the Old South's racial code. The Klan considered "impudence" a punishable offense. Asked to define "impudence" before a congressional investigating committee, one white opponent of the Klan responded: "Well, it is considered impudence for a negro not to be polite to a white man—not to pull off his hat and bow and scrape to a white man, as was done formerly." Klansmen whipped blacks for crimes that ranged from speaking disrespectfully

and refusing to yield the sidewalk to raising a good crop and dressing well. Black women who "dress up and fix up like ladies" risked a midnight visit from the Klan. The Ku Klux Klan sought to restore racial subordination in every aspect of private and public life.

Klansmen also took aim at black education. White men, especially those with little schooling, found the sight of blacks in classrooms hard to stomach. Schools were easy targets, and scores of them went up in flames. Teachers, male and female, were flogged, or worse. Klansmen drove northern-born teacher Alonzo B. Corliss from North Carolina for "teaching niggers and making them like white men." In Cross Plains, Alabama, the Klan hanged an Irish-born teacher along with four black men. But not just ill-educated whites opposed black education. Planters wanted ex-slaves back in the fields, not at desks. Each student meant one less laborer. In 1869, an Alabama newspaper reported the burning of a black school and observed that it should be "a warning for them to stick hereafter to 'de shovel and de hoe,' and let their dirty-backed primers go."

Planters turned to the Klan as part of their effort to preserve plantation agriculture and restore labor discipline. An Alabama white admitted that in his area, the Klan was "intended principally for the negroes who failed to work." Masked bands "punished Negroes whose landlords had complained of them." Sharecroppers who disputed their share at "settling up time" risked a visit from the night riders. Klansmen murdered a Georgia blacksmith who refused to do additional work for a white man until he was paid for a previous job. It was dangerous for freedmen to consider changing employers. "If we got out looking for some other place to go," an ex-slave from Texas remembered, "them KKK they would tend to Mister negro good and plenty." In Marengo County, Alabama, when the Klan heard that some local blacks were planning to leave, "the disguised men went to them and told them if they undertook it they would be killed on their way." Whites had decided that they would not be "deprived of their labor."

Above all, the Klan terrorized state and local Republican leaders and voters. Klansmen became the military arm of the Democratic Party. They drove blacks from the polls on election day and terrorized black officeholders. Klansmen gave Andrew Flowers, a black politician in Chattanooga, a brutal beating and told him that they "did not intend any nigger to hold office in the United States." Jack Dupree, president of the Republican Club in Monroe County, Mississippi, a man known to "speak his mind," had his throat cut and was disemboweled while his wife was forced to watch.

Between 1868 and 1871, political violence reached astounding levels. Arkansas experienced nearly 300 political killings in the three months before the fall elections in 1868. Little Rock's U.S. congressman, J. M. Hinds, was one of the victims. Louisiana was even bloodier. Between the local elections in the spring of 1868 and the presidential election in the fall, Louisiana experienced more than 1,000 killings. Political violence often proved effective. In Georgia, Republican presidential candidate Ulysses S. Grant received no votes at all in 1868 in eleven counties, despite black majorities. The Klan murdered three

Ku Klux Klan Robe and Hood
The white robes that we associate with the Ku Klux Klan are a twentieth-century phenomenon. In the Reconstruction era, Klansmen donned robes of various designs and colors. Joseph Boyce Stewart of Lincoln County, Tennessee, wore this robe of brown and white linen. The robe's fancy trimming and the elaborate hat make it highly unlikely that Stewart sewed the costume himself. Women did not participate in midnight raids, but mothers, wives, and daughters of Klansmen often shared their reactionary vision and did what they could to bring about the triumph of white supremacy.

Photograph courtesy of the Chicago Historical Society, Hope B. McCormick Costume Center. Worn by Joseph Boyce Stewart, Lincoln County, TN, c. 1866. Gift of W. G. Dithmer.

scalawag members of the Georgia legislature and drove ten others from their homes. As one Georgia Republican commented after a Klan attack: "We don't call them Democrats, we call them southern murderers."

It proved hard to arrest Klansmen and harder still to convict them. "If a white man kills a colored man in any of the counties of this State," observed a Florida sheriff, "you cannot convict him." By 1871, the death toll had reached thousands. Federal intervention—in the Ku Klux Klan Acts of 1870 and 1871—signaled an end to much of the Klan's power but not to counterrevolutionary violence in the South. Other groups continued the terror.

context, Republicans struggled to breathe life into their new state governments.

Republican activity focused on three areas—education, civil rights, and economic development. Every state inaugurated a system of public education and began building schools and training teachers. Before the Civil War, whites had deliberately kept slaves illiterate, and planter-dominated governments rarely spent tax money to educate the children of yeomen. By 1875, half of Mississippi's and South Carolina's eligible children (the majority of whom were black) were attending school. Despite underfunding and dilapidated facilities, literacy rates rose sharply. Although public schools were racially segregated, education remained for many blacks a tangible, deeply satisfying benefit of freedom and Republican rule. Freedmen looked upon schools as "first proof of their *independence*."

State legislatures also attacked racial discrimination and defended civil rights. Republicans especially resisted efforts to segregate blacks from whites in public transportation. Mississippi levied fines of up to $1,000 and three years in jail for railroads, steamboats, hotels, and theaters that denied "full and equal rights" to all citizens. But passing color-blind laws was one thing; enforcing them was another. Despite the law, segregation—later called **Jim Crow**—developed at white insistence and became a feature of southern life long before the end of the Reconstruction era.

Republican governments also launched ambitious programs of economic development. They envisioned a South of diversified agriculture, roaring factories, and booming towns. Republican legislatures chartered scores of banks and industrial companies, appropriated funds to fix ruined levees and to drain swamps, and went on a railroad-building binge. These efforts fell far short of solving the South's economic troubles, however. Republican spending to stimulate economic growth also meant rising taxes and enormous debt that drained funds from schools and other programs.

The southern Republicans' record, then, was mixed. To their credit, the biracial Republican coalition had taken up an ambitious agenda to change the South under trying circumstances. Money was scarce, the Democrats kept up a constant drumbeat of harassment, and factionalism threatened the Republican Party from within. However, corruption infected Republican governments in the South. Public morality reached new lows everywhere in the nation after the Civil War, and the chaos and disruption of the postwar South proved fertile soil for bribery, fraud, and influence peddling. Despite problems and shortcomings, however, the Republican Party made headway in its efforts to purge the South of aristocratic privilege and racist oppression. Republican governments had less success in overthrowing the long-established white oppression of black farm laborers in the rural South.

> Despite the law, segregation developed at white insistence and became a feature of southern life long before the end of the Reconstruction era.

One-Cent Primer

"The people are hungry and thirsty after knowledge," a former slave observed after the Civil War. Future African American leader Booker T. Washington remembered "a whole race trying to go to school. Few were too young, and none too old, to make the attempt to learn." Inexpensive elementary textbooks (this eight-page primer cost a penny) offered ex-slaves the basic elements of literacy. For people long forbidden to learn to read and write, literacy symbolized freedom and allowed the deeply religious to experience the joy of Bible reading. It also permitted African Americans to understand labor agreements, sign contracts, and participate knowledgeably in politics. *Gladstone Collection.*

White Landlords, Black Sharecroppers

In the countryside, clashes occurred daily between ex-slaves who wished to take control of their working lives and ex-masters who wanted to reinstitute old ways. Except for having to put down the whip and pay subsistence wages, planters had not been required to offer many concessions to emancipation. They continued to believe that African Americans were inherently lazy and would not work without coercion. Whites moved quickly to restore the antebellum world of work gangs, white overseers, field labor for black women and children, clustered cabins, minimal personal freedom, and even whipping whenever they could get away with it.

Ex-slaves resisted every effort to roll back the clock. They argued that if any class could be described as "lazy," it was the planters, who, as one ex-slave noted, "lived in idleness all their lives on stolen labor." Land of their own would anchor their economic independence, they believed, and do much to end planters' interference in their personal lives. They could then, for example, make their own decisions about whether women and children would labor in the fields. Indeed, within months after the war, perhaps one-third of black women abandoned field labor to work on chores in their own cabins just as poor white women did. With freedom to decide how to use family time, hundreds of thousands of black children enrolled in school. But landownership proved to be beyond the reach of most blacks once the federal government abandoned plans to redistribute Confederate property. Without land, ex-slaves had little choice but to work on plantations.

Although they were forced to return to the planters' fields, freedmen resisted efforts to restore slavelike conditions. In his South Carolina neighborhood, David Golightly Harris discovered that few freedmen were "willing to hire by the day, month or year." Instead of working for wages, "the negroes all seem disposed to rent land," which would increase their independence from whites. By rejecting wage labor, by striking, and by abandoning the most reactionary employers, blacks sought to force concessions. Out of this tug-of-war between white landlords and black laborers emerged a new system of southern agriculture.

Sharecropping was a compromise that offered both ex-masters and ex-slaves something but satisfied neither. Under the new system,

Black Family, 1870s
"If a man got to go crost de riber, and he can't git a boat, he take a log," a South Carolina freedman declared after President Andrew Johnson allowed planters to repossess their land. "If I can't own de land, I'll hire or lease land, but I won't contract." Determined to "set up for himself," almost every freedman in the cotton South preferred the economic independence and personal freedom of sharecropping to the dependency of wage labor. The members of this black family posed in front of their dilapidated home are clearly proud and undefeated, but optimism was hard to sustain in the postwar rural South. "We thought we was goin' to be richer than the white folks," recalled a former slave in Texas, "cause we was stronger and knowed how to work, and the whites didn't and they didn't have us to work for them anymore. But it didn't turn out that way."
Roll, Jordan, Roll by Doris Ullman 1933.

planters divided their cotton plantations into small farms of twenty-five to thirty acres that freedmen rented, paying with a share of each year's crop, usually two-thirds. Sharecropping gave blacks more freedom than the system of wages and labor gangs and released them from the day-to-day supervision of whites. Black families abandoned the old slave quarters and scattered over plantations, building separate cabins for themselves on the patches of land they rented (Map 16.1). Black families now decided who would work, for how long, and how hard. Still, most blacks remained dependent on white landlords, who had the power to expel them at the end of each growing season. For planters, sharecropping offered a way to resume agricultural production, but it did not allow them to restore the old plantation system or to administer whatever discipline they considered necessary.

> Sharecropping was a compromise that offered both ex-masters and ex-slaves something but satisfied neither.

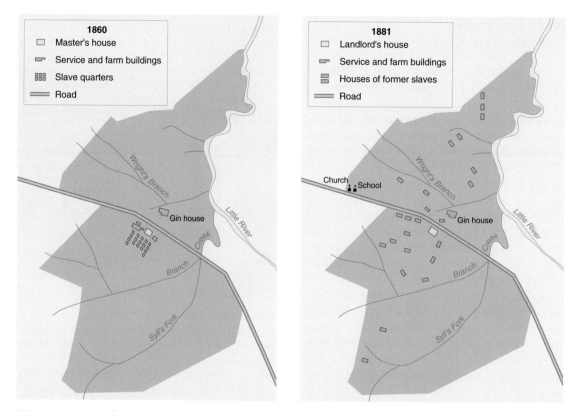

MAP 16.1   A Southern Plantation in 1860 and 1881
These maps of the Barrow plantation in Georgia illustrate some of the ways in which ex-slaves expressed their freedom. Freed men and women deserted the clustered living quarters behind the master's house, scattered over the plantation, built family cabins, and farmed rented land. The former Barrow slaves also worked together to build a school and a church.

READING THE MAP: Compare the number and size of the slave quarters in 1860 with the homes of the former slaves in 1881. How do they differ? Which buildings were prominently located along the road in 1860, and which could be found along the road in 1881?
CONNECTIONS: How might the former master feel about the new configuration of buildings on the plantation in 1881? In what ways did the new system of sharecropping replicate the old system of plantation agriculture? In what ways was it different?

FOR MORE HELP ANALYZING THIS MAP, see the map activity for this chapter in the Online Study Guide at bedfordstmartins.com/roark.

Sharecropping introduced a new figure—the country merchant—into the agricultural equation. Landlords supplied sharecroppers with land, mules, seeds, and tools, but blacks also needed credit so they could obtain essential food and clothing before they harvested their crops. Thousands of merchants at small crossroads stores sprang up to offer credit. Under an arrangement called a crop lien, a local merchant would advance goods to a sharecropper in exchange for a *lien*, or legal claim, on the farmer's future crop. Some merchants charged exorbitant rates of interest, as much as 60 percent, on the goods they sold. At the end of the growing season, after the landlord had taken two-thirds of the farmer's crop for rent, the merchant would consult his ledger to see how much the sharecropper owed him. Often, the farmer's debt to the merchant exceeded the income he received from his remaining one-third of the crop. Empty-handed, the farmer would have no choice but to borrow more from the merchant and begin the cycle all over again.

An experiment at first, sharecropping spread quickly and soon dominated the cotton South. By 1870, the work gang system, direct white supervision, and clustered black living quarters were fading memories. Sharecropping quickly ensnared small white farmers as well as black farmers. Lien merchants forced tenants to plant cotton, which was easy to sell, instead of food crops. The result was excessive production of cotton and a disastrous decline in food production in the South after the Civil War. The new sharecropping system of agriculture took shape just as the political power of Republicans in the South began to buckle under Democratic pressure.

Reconstruction Collapses

By 1870, after a decade of engagement with the public issues of war and reconstruction, Northerners wanted to turn to their own affairs and put "the southern problem" behind them. Increasingly, practical, business-minded men came to the forefront of the Republican Party, replacing the band of reformers and idealists who had been prominent in the 1860s. While northern commitment to defend black freedom eroded, southern commitment to white supremacy intensified. Without northern protection, southern Republicans were no match for the Democrats' economic coercion, political corruption, and bloody violence. One by one, Republican state governments fell in the South. The election of 1876 both confirmed and completed the collapse of reconstruction.

Grant's Troubled Presidency

In 1868, the Republican Party's presidential nomination went to Ulysses S. Grant, the man who at the start of the Civil War was a clerk in his father's general store and at the end was the nation's leading general. As the republic's foremost hero and a supporter of congressional reconstruction, Grant was the obvious choice. His Democratic opponent, Horatio Seymour of New York, ran on a platform that blasted congressional reconstruction as "a flagrant usurpation of power . . . unconstitutional, revolutionary, and void." The Republicans answered by "waving the **bloody shirt**"; that is, they reminded voters that the Democrats were "the party of rebellion," the party that stubbornly resisted a just peace. During the campaign, the Ku Klux Klan erupted in a reign of terror, murdering hundreds of southern Republicans. Violence in the South cost Grant votes, but he gained a narrow 309,000-vote margin in the popular vote and a substantial victory (214 votes to 80) in the electoral college (Map 16.2).

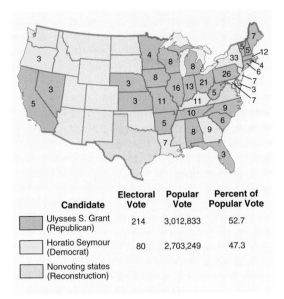

Candidate	Electoral Vote	Popular Vote	Percent of Popular Vote
Ulysses S. Grant (Republican)	214	3,012,833	52.7
Horatio Seymour (Democrat)	80	2,703,249	47.3
Nonvoting states (Reconstruction)			

MAP 16.2   The Election of 1868

Grant hoped to forge a policy that secured both sectional reconciliation and justice for blacks. But he took office at a time when a majority of white Northerners had grown weary of the "Southern Question" and were increasingly willing to let southern whites manage their own affairs. Moreover, Grant was not as good a president as he was a general. The talents he had demonstrated on the battlefield—decisiveness, clarity, and resolution—were less obvious in the White House. Able advisers might have helped, but he surrounded himself with fumbling kinfolk and old cronies from his army days. He also made a string of dubious appointments that led to a series of damaging scandals. Charges of corruption tainted his vice president, Schuyler Colfax, and brought down his secretary of war and secretary of the navy as well as his private secretary. Grant's dogged loyalty to liars and cheats only compounded the damage. While never personally implicated in any scandal, Grant was aggravatingly naive and his administration filled with rot.

Anti-Grant Republicans grew increasingly disgusted and in 1872 bolted and launched the Liberal Party. The Liberals condemned the Grant regime of graft and corruption. To clean up the mess, they proposed ending the **spoils system**, by which victorious parties rewarded loyal workers with public office, and replacing it with a nonpartisan **civil service** commission that would oversee competitive examinations for appointment to office. Moreover, they demanded that the federal government remove its troops from the South and restore "home rule" (southern white control). Democrats especially liked the Liberals' southern policy, and the Democratic Party endorsed the Liberal presidential candidate, Horace Greeley, the longtime editor of the *New York Tribune*. However, the nation still felt enormous affection for the man who had saved the Union and in 1872 re-elected Grant with 56 percent of the popular vote.

Grant was not without accomplishments during his eight years as president. In 1872, Hamilton Fish, Grant's secretary of state, skillfully orchestrated a peaceful settlement of the U.S. claim against Great Britain for wartime damages caused by British-built Confederate ships. But Grant's great passion in foreign affairs—

Grant's Proposed Annexation of Santo Domingo

annexation of Santo Domingo in the Caribbean—ended in failure. Grant argued that the acquisition of this tropical land would permit the United States to expand its trade and simultaneously provide a new home for the South's blacks, who were so desperately harassed by the Klan. Aggressive foreign policy had not originated with the Grant administration. Lincoln and Johnson's secretary of state, William H. Seward, had thwarted French efforts to set up a puppet empire under Maximilian in Mexico, and his purchase of Alaska ("Seward's Ice Box") from Russia in 1867 for only $7 million had fired Grant's **imperialist** ambition. But in the end, Grant could not marshal the votes needed in Congress to approve the treaty of annexation of Santo Domingo. Issues closer to home preoccupied Congress and undermined Grant's initiatives.

Northern Resolve Withers

Grant understood that most Northerners had grown weary of reconstruction. Northern businessmen who wanted to invest in the South believed that recurrent federal intrusion was itself a major cause of instability in the region. A growing number of northern Republican leaders began to question the wisdom of their party's alliance with the South's lower classes—its small farmers and sharecroppers. Grant's secretary of the interior, Jacob D. Cox of Ohio, proposed allying with the "thinking and influential native southerners . . . the intelligent, well-to-do, and controlling class."

Northerners increasingly wanted to shift their attention from reconstruction to other issues, especially after the nation slipped into a devastating economic depression in 1873. More than eighteen thousand businesses collapsed, and more than a million workers lost their jobs. The old issues of reconstruction, however, would not go away. When southern Republicans pleaded for federal protection from Klan violence, Congress enacted three laws in 1870 and 1871 that were intended to break the back of white terrorism. The severest of the three, the Ku Klux Klan Act (1871), made interference with

Grant and Scandal

In this anti-Grant cartoon, Thomas Nast, the nation's most celebrated political cartoonist, shows the president falling headfirst into the barrel of fraud and corruption that tainted his administration. During Grant's eight years in the White House, many members of his administration failed him. Sometimes duped, sometimes merely loyal, Grant stubbornly defended wrongdoers, even to the point of perjuring himself to keep an aide out of jail.
Library of Congress.

For more help analyzing this image, see the visual activity for this chapter in the Online Study Guide at bedfordstmartins.com/roark.

voting rights a felony and authorized the use of the army to enforce it. Intrepid federal marshals arrested thousands of Klansmen suspected of violently depriving citizens of the right to vote. The government came close to destroying the Klan but did not end terrorism against blacks. Congress also passed the Civil Rights Act of 1875, which boldly outlawed racial discrimination in transportation, public accommodations, and juries. But federal authorities did little to enforce the law, and segregated facilities remained the rule throughout the South.

The retreat from reconstruction had begun in 1868 with Grant's election. Grant genuinely wanted to see blacks' civil and political rights protected, but he felt uneasy about an open-ended commitment that seemed to ignore constitutional limitations on federal power. In May 1872, Congress restored the right of officeholding to all but three hundred ex-rebels. By the early 1870s, reform had lost its principal spokesmen to death or defeat at the polls. Many Republicans concluded that the quest for black equality was mistaken or hopelessly naive. In the opinion of many, traditional white leaders offered the best hope for honesty, order, and prosperity in the South.

Underlying the North's abandonment of reconstruction was unyielding racial prejudice. During the war, Northerners had learned to accept black freedom, but deep-seated prejudice prevented many from equating freedom with equality. Even the actions they took on behalf of blacks often served partisan political advantage. Northerners generally supported Indiana senator Thomas A. Hendricks's declaration that "this is a white man's Government, made by the white man for the white man."

The U.S. Supreme Court also did its part to undermine reconstruction. In the 1870s, a series of Court decisions significantly weakened the federal government's ability to protect black Southerners under the Fourteenth and Fifteenth Amendments. In the *Slaughterhouse* Cases (1873), the Court distinguished between national and state citizenship and ruled that the Fourteenth Amendment protected only those rights that stemmed from the federal government, such as voting in federal elections and interstate travel. Since the Court decided that most rights derived from the states, it sharply curtailed the federal government's authority to protect black citizens. Even more devastating, the *United States v. Cruikshank* ruling (1876) said that the reconstruction amendments gave Congress power to leg-

islate against discrimination only by states, not by individuals. The "suppression of ordinary crime," such as assault, remained a state responsibility. The Supreme Court did not declare reconstruction unconstitutional but gradually undermined its legal foundation.

The mood of the North had found political expression in the election of 1874, when for the first time in eighteen years the Democrats gained control of the House of Representatives. As one Republican observed, the people had grown tired of the "negro question, with all its complications, and the reconstruction of Southern States, with all its interminable embroilments." Reconstruction had come apart. Congress gradually abandoned it. President Grant grew increasingly unwilling to enforce it. The Supreme Court busily denied the constitutionality of significant

---

Is This a Republican Form of Government?
In this powerful 1876 drawing, Thomas Nast depicts the end of reconstruction as the tragedy it was. As white supremacists in the South piled up more and more bodies, supporters of civil rights accused the Grant administration of failing to protect black Southerners and legitimately elected governments. They pointed specifically to the constitutional requirement that "the United States shall guarantee to every State in this Union a republican form of government, and shall protect each of them . . . against domestic violence" (Article IV, section 4).
Library of Congress.

parts of it. And the people sent unmistakable messages that they were tired of it. Rather than defend reconstruction from its southern enemies, Northerners steadily backed away from the challenge. After the early 1870s, southern blacks faced the forces of reaction largely on their own.

White Supremacy Triumphs

Republican state and local governments in the South attracted more bitterness and hatred than any other political regimes in American history. In the eyes of the majority of whites, each day of Republican rule produced fresh insults: Black militiamen patrolled town streets, black laborers negotiated contracts with former masters, black maids stood up to former mistresses, black voters cast ballots, and black legislators enacted laws. The northern retreat from reconstruction permitted southern Democrats to harness this white rage to politics. Taking the name "Redeemers," they promised to replace "bayonet rule" (some federal troops continued to be stationed in the South) with "home rule." They branded Republican governments a carnival of extravagance, waste, and fraud and promised that honest, thrifty Democrats would supplant the irresponsible tax-and-spend Republicans. Above all, Redeemers swore to save southern civilization from a descent into African "barbarism" and "negro rule." As one man put it, "We must render this either a white man's government, or convert the land into a Negro man's cemetery."

> Redeemers swore to save southern civilization from a descent into African "barbarism" and "negro rule."

By the early 1870s, Democrats understood that race was their most potent weapon. They adopted a two-pronged racial strategy to overthrow Republican governments. First, they sought to polarize the parties around color; then they relentlessly intimidated black voters. They went about gathering all the South's white voters into the Democratic Party, leaving the Republicans to depend on blacks. The "straight-out" appeal to whites promised great advantage because whites made up a majority of the population in every southern state except Mississippi, South Carolina, and Louisiana.

Democrats employed several devices to dislodge whites from the Republican Party. First and foremost, they fanned the flames of racial

"White Man's Country"

White supremacy emerged as a central tenet of the Democratic Party before the Civil War, and Democrats kept up a vicious racist attack on Republicans as long as reconstruction lasted. On this silk ribbon from the 1868 presidential election between Republican Ulysses S. Grant and his Democratic opponent, New York governor Horatio Seymour, the Democrats openly declare their racial goal. During the campaign, Democratic vice presidential nominee Francis P. Blair Jr. promised that a Seymour victory would restore "white people" to power by declaring the reconstruction governments in the South "null and void." The Democrats' promotion of white supremacy reached new levels of shrillness in the 1870s, when northern support for reconstruction began to waver.

Collection of Janice L. and David J. Frent.

prejudice. In South Carolina, a Democrat crowed that his party appealed to the "proud Caucasian race, whose sovereignty on earth God has proclaimed." Ostracism also proved effective. Local newspapers published the names of whites who kept company with blacks. So complete was the ostracism that one of its victims said, "No white man can live in the South in the future and act with any other than the Democratic party unless he is willing and prepared to live a life of social isolation."

In addition, Democrats exploited the severe economic plight of small white farmers by blaming it on Republican financial policy. Government spending soared during reconstruction, and small farmers saw their tax burden skyrocket. When cotton prices fell by nearly 50 percent in the 1870s, yeomen farmers found cash in short supply. In South Carolina, David Golightly Harris observed, "This is tax time. We are nearly all on our head about them. They are so high & so little money to pay with." Golightly and other farmers without enough cash to pay their taxes began "selling every egg and chicken they can get." In 1871, Mississippi reported that one-seventh of the state's land—3.3 million acres—had been forfeited for nonpayment of taxes. The small farmers' economic distress had a racial dimension. Because few freedmen succeeded in acquiring land, they rarely paid taxes. In Georgia in 1874, blacks made up 45 percent of the population but paid only 2 percent of the taxes. From the perspective of a small white farmer, Republican rule meant not only that he was paying more taxes but that he was paying them to aid blacks. Democrats asked whether it was not time for hard-pressed yeomen to join the white man's party.

If racial pride, social isolation, and Republican financial policies proved insufficient to drive yeomen from the Republican Party, Democrats turned to terrorism. "Night riders" targeted white Republicans as well as blacks for murder and assassination. "A dead Radical is very harmless," South Carolina Democratic leader Martin Gary told his followers. By the early 1870s, then, only a fraction of southern whites any longer professed allegiance to the party of Lincoln. Racial polarization became a reality as rich and poor whites united against southern Republicanism.

The second prong of Democratic strategy—intimidation of black voters—proved equally devastating. Antiblack political violence escalated to unprecedented levels. In 1873 in Louisiana, a clash between black militiamen and gun-toting whites killed two white men and an estimated seventy black men. Ruthless whites slaughtered half of the black men after they surrendered. Although the federal government indicted more than one hundred white men, local juries failed to convict a single one of them. This regime of violent intimidation prompted some blacks to move to the North and West in search of a better life (see "American Places," page 590).

Even before adopting the all-out white supremacist tactics of the 1870s, Democrats had already taken control of the governments of Virginia, Tennessee, and North Carolina. The new campaign brought fresh gains. The Redeemers retook Georgia in 1871, Texas in 1873, and Arkansas and Alabama in 1874. In 1876, Mississippi fell. Mississippi was a scene of open, unrelenting, and often savage intimidation of black voters and their few re-

maining white allies. As the state election approached in 1876, Governor Adelbert Ames appealed to Washington for federal troops to control the violence, only to hear from the attorney general that the "whole public are tired of these annual autumnal outbreaks in the South." Abandoned, Mississippi Republicans succumbed to the Democratic onslaught in the fall elections. By 1876, only three Republican state governments—in Florida, Louisiana, and South Carolina—survived (Map 16.3).

An Election and a Compromise

The centennial year of 1876 witnessed one of the most tumultuous elections in American history. Its chaos and confusion provided a fitting conclusion to the experiment known as Reconstruction. The election took place in November, but not until March 2 of the following year, at 4 A.M., did the nation know who would be

---

MAP 16.3 The Reconstruction of the South
Myth has it that Republican rule of the former Confederacy was not only harsh but long. In most states, however, conservative southern whites stormed back into power in a few months or a very few years. By the election of 1876, Republican governments could be found in only three states. And they soon fell.

READING THE MAP: List in chronological order the readmission of the former Confederate states to the Union. Which states reestablished conservative governments most quickly?
CONNECTIONS: What did the former Confederate states need to do in order to be readmitted to the Union? How did reestablished conservative governments react to reconstruction?

FOR MORE HELP ANALYZING THIS MAP, see the map activity for this chapter in the Online Study Guide at bedfordstmartins.com/roark.

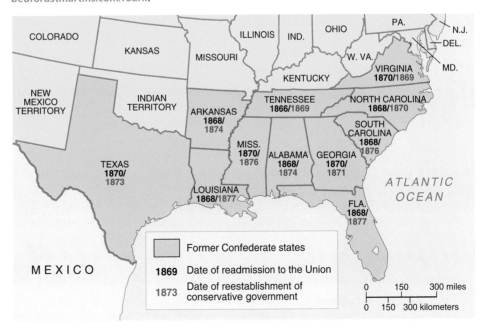

AMERICAN PLACES

Nicodemus National Historic Site, Nicodemus, Kansas

Former slaves hoped that emancipation would usher in an age of equal rights and bountiful opportunity in the South. But when racial violence and oppression overwhelmed the promises of freedom, some African Americans concluded that to find security and prosperity they would have to leave.

Town and land promoters lured millions of Americans westward after the Civil War, and southern blacks particularly were drawn to Kansas, the land of the fiery abolitionist John Brown, where there was ample free or cheap federal land and, they hoped,

a fresh start. In 1877 thirty blacks from Kentucky founded the town of Nicodemus, and within a year another 550 settlers joined them. For a "Promised Land," the treeless and apparently desolate Kansas prairie did not look very promising. Willina Hickman, who arrived in 1878, remembered that the men in her party began shouting when they approached Nicodemus: "Where is Nicodemus? I don't see it yet." Hickman recalled, "My husband pointed out various smokes coming out of the ground and said, 'That is Nicodemus.' The families lived in dugouts. . . . The scenery

was not at all inviting, and I began to cry."

Briefly living "like prairie dogs," by the mid-1880s the strong-willed settlers had built a prosperous town. They could boast of two newspapers, two pharmacies, three general stores, several churches, a number of small hotels, a school, an ice cream parlor, a bank, a livery stable, a blacksmith shop, and many homes. But only a railroad could assure long-term economic success. When the Union Pacific bypassed Nicodemus in 1887, the town's fate was sealed. Population dwindled, until the town had only sixteen inhabitants in 1950. In 1996, Congress established Nicodemus National Historic Site, and today the National Park Service preserves the town's five remaining historic structures—First Baptist Church, the African Methodist Episcopal Church, the St. Francis Hotel, the school, and the town hall.

Nicodemus is the only remaining western town planned and settled by African Americans during the Reconstruction era. Visitors to Nicodemus today can learn more about the town and the history of blacks in the West through interpretative exhibits at the visitors' center. Walking tours of the five historic buildings offer physical testament to the mainstays of this community—religion, business, education, and government. In addition, every July, descendants from around the nation return to celebrate "Homecoming" and to remember their southern ancestors who went west.

FOR WEB LINKS RELATED TO THIS SITE AND OTHER AMERICAN PLACES, see "PlaceLinks" at bedfordstmartins.com/roark.

Homecoming in Nicodemus
Nicodemus National Historic Site.

inaugurated president on March 4. For four months the country suffered through a constitutional and political crisis. Sixteen years after Lincoln's election, Americans feared that a presidential contest would again precipitate civil war.

The Democrats had nominated New York's reform governor, Samuel J. Tilden, who immediately targeted the corruption of the Grant administration and the despotism of Republican reconstruction. The Republicans put forward a reformer of their own, Rutherford B. Hayes, governor of Ohio. Privately, Hayes considered "bayonet rule" a mistake but concluded that waving the "bloody shirt"—that is, reminding voters that the Democrats were the "party of rebellion"—remained the Republicans' best political strategy.

On election day, Tilden tallied 4,300,000 votes to Hayes's 4,036,000. But in the all-important electoral college, Tilden fell one vote short of the majority required for victory. The electoral votes of three states—South Carolina, Louisiana, and Florida, the only remaining Republican governments in the South—remained in doubt because both Republicans and Democrats in those states claimed victory and submitted electoral votes supporting their candidates. To win, Tilden needed only one of the nineteen contested votes. Hayes had to have all of them.

Congress had to decide who had actually won the elections in the three southern states and thus who would be president. The Constitution provided no guidance for this situation. Moreover, Democrats controlled the House, and Republicans controlled the Senate. To break the deadlock, Congress created a special electoral commission to arbitrate the disputed returns. A cumbersome compromise, the commission was made up of five representatives (two Republicans, three Democrats), five senators (two Democrats, three Republicans), and five justices of the Supreme Court (two Republicans, two Democrats, and David Davis, who was considered an independent). Before the commission could meet, the Illinois legislature elected Davis to the Senate, and his place on the commission was filled with a Republican. All of the commissioners voted the straight party line, giving every state to the Republican Hayes and putting him over the top in electoral votes (Map 16.4).

Some outraged Democrats vowed to resist Hayes's victory. Rumors flew of an impending coup and renewed civil war. But the impasse was broken when negotiations behind the scenes between Hayes's lieutenants and some moderate

"Reading Election Bulletin by Gaslight"
Throughout the nation in November 1876, eager citizens gathered on street corners at night to catch the latest news about the presidential election. When Democrats and Republicans disputed the returns, anxiety and anger mounted. With Samuel J. Tilden well ahead in the popular count, some Democrats began chanting "Tilden or War." Tilden received letters declaring that thousands of "well armed men" stood ready to march on Washington. In Columbia, Ohio, a bullet shattered a window in the home of Rutherford B. Hayes as his family sat down to dinner. Violent rhetoric and action badly frightened a nation with fresh memories of a disastrous civil war, and for four long months it remained unclear whether the nation would peacefully inaugurate a new president.
Granger Collection.

southern Democrats resulted in an informal understanding, known as the Compromise of 1877. In exchange for a Democratic promise not to block Hayes's inauguration and to deal fairly with the freedmen, Hayes vowed not to use the army to uphold the remaining Republican regimes in the South. The South would also gain substantial federal subsidies for internal

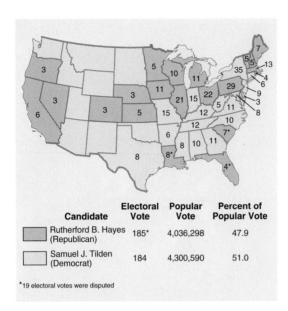

Candidate	Electoral Vote	Popular Vote	Percent of Popular Vote
Rutherford B. Hayes (Republican)	185*	4,036,298	47.9
Samuel J. Tilden (Democrat)	184	4,300,590	51.0

*19 electoral votes were disputed

MAP 16.4   The Election of 1876

improvements. Two days later, the nation celebrated Hayes's peaceful inauguration.

Stubborn Tilden supporters bemoaned the "stolen election" and damned "His Fraudulency," Rutherford B. Hayes. Old-guard Radicals such as William Lloyd Garrison denounced Hayes's bargain as a "policy of compromise, of credulity, of weakness, of subserviency, of surrender." But the nation as a whole celebrated, for the Republic had weathered a grave crisis. The last three Republican state governments in the South fell quickly once Hayes abandoned them and withdrew the U.S. army. Reconstruction came to an end.

Conclusion: "A Revolution But Half Accomplished"

In 1865, when General Carl Schurz visited the South, he discovered "a revolution but half accomplished." War and defeat had not prepared the South for an easy transition from slavery to free labor, from white racial despotism to equal justice, and from white political **monopoly** to biracial democracy. Ex-masters like David Golightly Harris had trouble seeing former slaves like York and Old Will as free people. The old elite wanted to get "things back as near to slavery as possible," Schurz reported, while ex-slaves and whites who had lacked power in the slave regime were eager to exploit the revolutionary implications of defeat and emancipation.

The northern-dominated Republican Congress pushed the revolution along. Although it refused to provide an economic underpinning to black freedom, through constitutional amendments Congress required defeated Confederates to accept legal equality and share political power with black men. Congress was not willing to extend such power to women. Conservative whites fought ferociously to recover their power and privilege. When they regained control of politics through the Democratic Party, they used the power of the state, along with private violence, to wipe out many of the gains of reconstruction. So successful were the reactionaries that one observer concluded that the North had won the war but the South had won the peace.

The Redeemer counterrevolution, however, did not mean a return to slavery. Northern victory in the Civil War ensured abolition, and ex-slaves gained the freedom to not be whipped or sold, to send their children to school, to worship in their own churches, and to work independently on their own rented farms. The lives of impoverished sharecroppers overflowed with hardships, but even sharecropping provided more autonomy and economic welfare than bondage had. It was limited freedom, to be sure, but it was not slavery.

The Civil War and emancipation set in motion the most profound upheaval in the nation's history, and nothing whites did entirely erased its revolutionary impact. War destroyed the richest and largest slave society in the New World, and abolition overturned the social and economic order that had dominated the region for nearly two centuries. The world of masters and slaves succumbed to that of landlords and sharecroppers, a world in which old lines of racial dominance continued, though with greater freedom for blacks. War also served as midwife for the birth of a modern nation-state. For the first time sovereignty rested uncontested in the federal government, and Washington increased its role in national affairs. When the South returned to the Union, it did so as a junior partner. The victorious North now possessed the power to establish the nation's direction, and the North set the nation's compass toward the expansion of industrial capitalism.

Still, despite massive changes, the Civil War remained only a "half accomplished" revolution. The nation did not fulfill the promises that it seemed to hold out to black Americans at war's end, and thus Reconstruction represents a tragedy of enormous proportions. Southern Democrats bludgeoned Republican governments just as northern interest in reconstruction faded. The failure to protect blacks and guarantee their rights had enduring consequences. Almost a century after Reconstruction, the nation would embark on what one observer called a "second reconstruction," another effort to fulfill nineteenth-century promises. The solid achievements of the Thirteenth, Fourteenth, and Fifteenth Amendments to the Constitution would provide a legal foundation for the renewed commitment. It is worth remembering, though, that it was only the failure of the first reconstruction that made a modern civil rights movement necessary.

FOR ADDITIONAL FIRSTHAND ACCOUNTS OF THIS PERIOD, see Chapter 16 in Michael Johnson, ed., *Reading the American Past,* Third Edition.

TO ASSESS YOUR MASTERY OF THE MATERIAL IN THIS CHAPTER, see the Online Study Guide at bedfordstmartins.com/roark.

FOR WEB LINKS RELATED TO TOPICS IN THIS CHAPTER, see "HistoryLinks," "DocLinks," and "PlaceLinks" at bedfordstmartins.com/roark.

CHRONOLOGY

1863
- President Lincoln issues Proclamation of Amnesty and Reconstruction.

1864
- Wade-Davis bill offers more stringent plan for reconstruction.

1865
- General William T. Sherman sets aside land in South Carolina for black settlement.
- Congress establishes Freedmen's Bureau.
- Lincoln sworn in for second term as president.
- Lincoln shot, dies on April 15, succeeded by Vice President Andrew Johnson.
- Johnson presents his plan of reconstruction to restore ex-Confederate states to the Union; terms include restoration of confiscated lands, thus canceling distribution of land to freedmen.
- Southern state legislatures enact discriminatory black codes.
- Thirteenth Amendment, which abolishes slavery, becomes part of Constitution.

1866
- Congress approves Fourteenth Amendment, making native-born blacks American citizens and guaranteeing all American citizens "equal protection of the laws" (amendment becomes part of Constitution in 1868).
- Overriding presidential veto, Congress passes Civil Rights Act prohibiting discrimination by states.
- Susan B. Anthony and Elizabeth Cady Stanton found Equal Rights Association to lobby for the vote for women.
- Overriding presidential veto, Congress extends Freedmen's Bureau.
- Ku Klux Klan founded in Tennessee.
- Republicans triumph over Johnson's Democrats in congressional elections.

1867
- Overriding presidential veto, Congress passes Military Reconstruction Act, imposing military rule on South and requiring southern states to guarantee the vote to black men.
- Congress passes Tenure of Office Act, requiring Senate approval for removal of officials appointed with Senate consent.

1868
- Senate impeachment trial of President Johnson results in acquittal.
- Ulysses S. Grant elected president.

1869
- Congress approves Fifteenth Amendment, prohibiting racial discrimination in voting rights in all states (amendment becomes part of Constitution in 1870).

1871
- Congress enacts Ku Klux Klan Act in effort to end white terrorism in South.

1872
- Anti-Grant Republicans form Liberal Party and demand an end to government corruption.
- President Grant elected to a second term.

1873
- Economic depression sets in for remainder of decade.
- Supreme Court decision in *Slaughterhouse* cases limits government authority to protect black citizens.

1874
- Elections return Democratic majority to House of Representatives.

1875
- Civil Rights Act outlaws racial discrimination; federal authorities do little to enforce it.

1876
- Supreme Court in *United States v. Cruikshank* rules Congress may legislate against discrimination by states, not by individuals, thus weakening federal ability to protect black citizens.

1877
- Special congressional commission awards disputed electoral votes to Republican Rutherford B. Hayes, making him president of United States. Hayes agrees to pull military out of South, ending Reconstruction.

BIBLIOGRAPHY

General Works

David Herbert Donald, Jean H. Baker, and Michael F. Holt, *The Civil War and Reconstruction* (2000).

W. E. B. Du Bois, *Black Reconstruction, 1860–1880* (1935).

Eric Foner, *Reconstruction: America's Unfinished Revolution* (1988).

John Hope Franklin, *Reconstruction after the Civil War* (1961).

Susan-Mary Grant and Peter J. Parish, *Legacy of Disunion: The Enduring Significance of the American Civil War* (2003).

James M. McPherson, *Ordeal by Fire: The Civil War and Reconstruction* (3rd ed., 2000).

Paul A. Shackel, *Memory in Black and White: Race, Commemoration, and the Post-Bellum Landscape* (2003).

Kenneth M. Stampp, *The Era of Reconstruction, 1865–1877* (1965).

Wartime Reconstruction

Richard H. Abbott, *The Republican Party and the South, 1855–1877: The First Southern Strategy* (1986).

Herman Belz, *Emancipation and Equal Rights: Politics and Constitutionalism in the Civil War Era* (1978).

Louis S. Gerteis, *From Contraband to Freedman: Federal Policy toward Southern Blacks, 1861–1865* (1973).

William S. McFeely, *Yankee Stepfather: General O. O. Howard and the Freedmen* (1968).

James M. McPherson, *The Struggle for Equality: Abolitionists and the Negro in the Civil War and Reconstruction* (1964).

Willie Lee Rose, *Rehearsal for Reconstruction: The Port Royal Experiment* (1964).

Brooks D. Simpson, *Let Us Have Peace: Ulysses S. Grant and the Politics of War and Reconstruction, 1861–1868* (1991).

The Meaning of Freedom

James D. Anderson, *The Education of Blacks in the South, 1860–1935* (1988).

Ira Berlin et al., eds., *Freedom: A Documentary History of Emancipation, 1861–1867*, 4 vols. to date (1982–).

Edmund L. Drago, *Black Politicians and Reconstruction in Georgia: A Splendid Failure* (1982).

Russell Duncan, *Freedom's Shore: Tunis Campbell and the Georgia Freedmen* (1986).

Barbara J. Fields, *Slavery and Freedom on the Middle Ground: Maryland during the Nineteenth Century* (1985).

Michael W. Fitzgerald, *The Union League Movement in the Deep South: Politics and Agricultural Change during Reconstruction* (1989).

Eric Foner, *Nothing but Freedom: Emancipation and Its Legacy* (1983).

Janet Sharp Hermann, *The Pursuit of a Dream* (1981).

Thomas C. Holt, *Black over White: Negro Political Leadership in South Carolina during Reconstruction* (1977).

Peter Kolchin, *First Freedom: The Responses of Alabama's Blacks to Emancipation and Reconstruction* (1972).

Leon F. Litwack, *Been in the Storm So Long: The Aftermath of Slavery* (1979).

William E. Montgomery, *Under Their Own Vine and Fig Tree: The African-American Church in the South, 1865–1900* (1992).

Lynda J. Morgan, *Emancipation in Virginia's Tobacco Belt, 1850–1870* (1992).

Robert Morris, *Reading, 'Riting and Reconstruction* (1981).

Howard N. Rabinowitz, *Race Relations in the Urban South, 1865–1890* (1978).

Roger L. Ransom and Richard Sutch, *One Kind of Freedom: The Economic Consequences of Emancipation* (1977).

C. Peter Ripley, *Slaves and Freedmen in Civil War Louisiana* (1976).

Julie Saville, *The Work of Reconstruction: From Slave to Wage Laborer in South Carolina, 1860–1870* (1994).

Clarence E. Walker, *A Rock in a Weary Land: The African Methodist Episcopal Church during the Civil War and Reconstruction* (1982).

Joel Williamson, *After Slavery: The Negro in South Carolina during Reconstruction, 1861–1877* (1965).

Joel Williamson, *The Crucible of Race: Black/White Relations in the American South since Emancipation* (1984).

The Politics of Reconstruction

Michael Les Benedict, *The Impeachment and Trial of Andrew Johnson* (1973).

Michael Les Benedict, *A Compromise of Principle: Congressional Republicans and Reconstruction* (1974).

Richard F. Bensel, *Yankee Leviathan: The Origins of Central State Authority in America, 1859–1877* (1990).

Michael Kent Curtis, *No State Shall Abridge: The Fourteenth Amendment and the Bill of Rights* (1986).

David H. Donald, *Charles Sumner and the Rights of Man* (1970).

Ellen Carol DuBois, *Feminism and Suffrage: The Emergence of an Independent Women's Movement in America* (1978).

William Gillette, *The Right to Vote: Politics and the Passage of the Fifteenth Amendment* (1965).

Victor B. Howard, *Religion and the Radical Republican Movement, 1860–1870* (1990).

Harold M. Hyman, *A More Perfect Union: The Impact of the Civil War and Reconstruction on the Constitution* (1973).

Michael L. Lanza, *Agrarianism and Reconstruction Politics: The Southern Homestead Act* (1990).

William S. McFeely, *Grant: A Biography* (1981).

Eric L. McKitrick, *Andrew Johnson and Reconstruction* (1960).

James C. Mohr, ed., *Radical Republicans in the North: State Politics during Reconstruction* (1976).

David Montgomery, *Beyond Equality: Labor and the Radical Republicans, 1862–1872* (1967).

William E. Nelson, *The Fourteenth Amendment: From Political Principle to Judicial Doctrine* (1988).

James E. Sefton, *Andrew Johnson and the Uses of Constitutional Power* (1980).

Joel H. Sibley, *A Respectable Minority: The Democratic Party in the Civil War Era, 1860–1868* (1977).

Hans L. Trefousse, *Andrew Johnson: A Biography* (1989).

The Struggle in the South

Stephen V. Ash, *Middle Tennessee Society Transformed, 1860–1870: War and Peace in the Upper South* (1988).

James Alex Baggett, *The Scalawags: Southern Dissenters in the Civil War and Reconstruction* (2003).

Dwight B. Billings Jr., *Planters and the Making of a "New South": Class, Politics, and Development in North Carolina, 1865–1900* (1979).

Randolph B. Campbell, *A Southern Community in Crisis: Harrison County, Texas, 1850–1880* (1983).

Dan T. Carter, *When the War Was Over: The Failure of Self-Reconstruction in the South, 1865–1867* (1985).

Jane Turner Censer, *The Reconstruction of White Southern Woman-hood, 1865–1895* (2003).

Paul A. Cimbala, *Under the Guardianship of the Nation: The Freedmen's Bureau and the Reconstruction of Georgia, 1865–1870* (1997).

Barry A. Crouch, *The Freedmen's Bureau and Black Texans* (1992).

Richard N. Current, *Those Terrible Carpetbaggers: A Reinterpretation* (1988).

Jane E. Dailey, *Before Jim Crow: The Politics of Race in Post-Emancipation Virginia* (2000).

Laura F. Edwards, *Gendered Strife and Confusion: The Political Culture of Reconstruction* (1997).

W. McKee Evans, *Ballots and Fence Rails: Reconstruction on the Lower Cape Fear* (1966).

Gaines Foster, *Ghosts of the Confederacy: Defeat of the Lost Cause and the Emergence of the New South, 1865 to 1913* (1987).

Steven Hahn, *The Roots of Southern Populism: Yeoman Farmers and the Transformation of the Georgia Upcountry, 1850–1890* (1983).

William C. Harris, *Day of the Carpetbagger: Republican Reconstruction in Mississippi* (1979).

Elizabeth Jacoway, *Yankee Missionaries in the South: The Penn School Experiment* (1980).

Jacqueline Jones, *Soldiers of Light and Love: Northern Teachers and Georgia Blacks, 1865–1873* (1980).

Robert C. Kenzer, *Kinship and Neighborhood in a Southern Community: Orange County, North Carolina, 1849–1881* (1987).

Richard G. Lowe, *Republicans and Reconstruction in Virginia, 1865–1870* (1991).

Scott Reynolds Nelson, *Iron Confederacies: Southern Railways, Klan Violence, and Reconstruction* (1999).

Donald G. Nieman, *To Set the Law in Motion: The Freedmen's Bureau and the Legal Rights of Blacks, 1865–1868* (1979).

Michael Perman, *Reunion without Compromise: The South and Reconstruction, 1865–1868* (1973).

Michael Perman, *The Road to Redemption: Southern Politics, 1869–1879* (1984).

Lawrence N. Powell, *New Masters: Northern Planters during the Civil War and Reconstruction* (1980).

George C. Rable, *But There Was No Peace: The Role of Violence in the Politics of Reconstruction* (1984).

Philip N. Racine, ed., *Piedmont Farmer: The Journals of David Golightly Harris, 1855–1870* (1990).

James L. Roark, *Masters without Slaves: Southern Planters in the Civil War and Reconstruction* (1977).

John C. Rodrigue, *Reconstruction in the Cane Fields: From Slavery to Free Labor in Louisiana's Sugar Parishes, 1862–1880* (2001).

Crandall A. Shifflett, *Patronage and Poverty in the Tobacco South: Louisa County, Virginia, 1860–1900* (1982).

James M. Smallwood, Barry A. Crouch, and Larry Peacock, *Murder and Mayhem: The War of Reconstruction in Texas* (2003).

Mark W. Summers, *Railroads, Reconstruction, and the Gospel of Prosperity: Aid under the Radical Republicans, 1865–1877* (1984).

Allen Trelease, *White Terror: The Ku Klux Klan Conspiracy and Southern Reconstruction* (1971).

Ted Tunnell, *Crucible of Reconstruction: War, Radicalism, and Race in Louisiana, 1862–1877* (1984).

Peter Wallenstein, *From Slave South to New South: Public Policy in Nineteenth-Century Georgia* (1987).

Michael Wayne, *The Reshaping of Plantation Society: The Natchez District, 1860–1880* (1983).

Jonathan M. Wiener, *Social Origins of the New South, 1860–1885* (1978).

Sara Woolfolk Wiggins, *The Scalawag in Alabama Politics, 1865–1881* (1977).

Gavin Wright, *Old South, New South: Revolutions in the Southern Economy since the Civil War* (1986).

The Collapse of Reconstruction

William Gillette, *Retreat from Reconstruction, 1869–1879* (1979).

Otto H. Olsen, ed., *Reconstruction and Redemption in the South: An Assessment* (1980).

Ian Polakoff, *The Politics of Inertia: The Election of 1876 and the End of Reconstruction* (1973).

Terry L. Seip, *The South Returns to Congress: Men, Economic Measures, and Intersectional Relationships, 1868–1879* (1983).

John G. Sproat, *"The Best Men": Liberal Reformers in the Gilded Age* (1968).

Mark W. Summers, *The Era of Good Stealings* (1993).

Margaret S. Thompson, *The "Spider Web": Congress and Lobbying in the Age of Grant* (1985).

C. Vann Woodward, *Reunion and Reaction: The Compromise of 1877 and the End of Reconstruction* (1951).

Documents

For additional documents see the DocLinks feature at bedfordstmartins.com/roark.

THE DECLARATION OF INDEPENDENCE

In Congress, July 4, 1776,

THE UNANIMOUS DECLARATION OF THE
THIRTEEN UNITED STATES OF AMERICA

When in the course of human events, it becomes necessary for one people to dissolve the political bands which have connected them with another, and to assume, among the powers of the earth, the separate and equal station to which the laws of nature and of nature's God entitle them, a decent respect to the opinions of mankind requires that they should declare the causes which impel them to the separation.

We hold these truths to be self-evident, that all men are created equal; that they are endowed by their Creator with certain unalienable rights; that among these, are life, liberty, and the pursuit of happiness. That, to secure these rights, governments are instituted among men, deriving their just powers from the consent of the governed; that, whenever any form of government becomes destructive of these ends, it is the right of the people to alter or to abolish it, and to institute a new government, laying its foundation on such principles, and organizing its powers in such form, as to them shall seem most likely to effect their safety and happiness. Prudence, indeed, will dictate that governments long established, should not be changed for light and transient causes; and, accordingly, all experience hath shown, that mankind are more disposed to suffer, while evils are sufferable, than to right themselves by abolishing the forms to which they are accustomed. But, when a long train of abuses and usurpations, pursuing invariably the same object, evinces a design to reduce them under absolute despotism, it is their right, it is their duty, to throw off such government and to provide new guards for their future security. Such has been the patient sufferance of these colonies, and such is now the necessity which constrains them to alter their former systems of government. The history of the present King of Great Britain is a history of repeated injuries and usurpations, all having, in direct object, the establishment of an absolute tyranny over these States. To prove this, let facts be submitted to a candid world:

He has refused his assent to laws the most wholesome and necessary for the public good.

He has forbidden his governors to pass laws of immediate and pressing importance, unless suspended in their operation till his assent should be obtained; and, when so suspended, he has utterly neglected to attend to them.

He has refused to pass other laws for the accommodation of large districts of people, unless those people would relinquish the right of representation in the legislature; a right inestimable to them, and formidable to tyrants only.

He has called together legislative bodies at places unusual, uncomfortable, and distant from the depository of their public records, for the sole purpose of fatiguing them into compliance with his measures.

He has dissolved representative houses repeatedly for opposing, with manly firmness, his invasions on the rights of the people.

He has refused, for a long time after such dissolutions, to cause others to be elected; whereby the legislative powers, incapable of annihilation, have returned to the people at large for their exercise; the state remaining in the mean-time exposed to all the danger of invasion from without, and convulsions within.

He has endeavoured to prevent the population of these States; for that purpose, obstructing the laws for naturalization of foreigners, refusing to pass others to encourage their migration hither, and raising the conditions of new appropriations of lands.

He has obstructed the administration of justice, by refusing his assent to laws for establishing judiciary powers.

He has made judges dependent on his will alone, for the tenure of their offices, and the amount and payment of their salaries.

He has erected a multitude of new offices, and sent hither swarms of officers to harass our people, and eat out their substance.

He has kept among us, in times of peace, standing armies, without the consent of our legislature.

He has affected to render the military independent of, and superior to, the civil power.

He has combined, with others, to subject us to a jurisdiction foreign to our Constitution, and unacknowledged by our laws; giving his assent to their acts of pretended legislation:

For quartering large bodies of armed troops among us:

For protecting them by a mock trial, from punishment, for any murders which they should commit on the inhabitants of these States:

For cutting off our trade with all parts of the world:

For imposing taxes on us without our consent:

For depriving us, in many cases, of the benefit of trial by jury:

For transporting us beyond seas to be tried for pretended offences:

For abolishing the free system of English laws in a neighboring province, establishing therein an arbitrary government, and enlarging its boundaries, so as to render it at once an example and fit instrument for introducing the same absolute rule into these colonies:

For taking away our charters, abolishing our most valuable laws, and altering, fundamentally, the powers of our governments:

For suspending our own legislatures, and declaring themselves invested with power to legislate for us in all cases whatsoever.

He has abdicated government here, by declaring us out of his protection, and waging war against us.

He has plundered our seas, ravaged our coasts, burnt our towns, and destroyed the lives of our people.

He is, at this time, transporting large armies of foreign mercenaries to complete the works of death, desolation, and tyranny, already begun, with circumstances of cruelty and perfidy scarcely paralleled in the most barbarous ages, and totally unworthy the head of a civilized nation.

He has constrained our fellow citizens, taken captive on the high seas, to bear arms against their country, to become the executioners of their friends, and brethren, or to fall themselves by their hands.

He has excited domestic insurrections amongst us, and has endeavored to bring on the inhabitants of our frontiers, the merciless Indian savages, whose known rule of warfare is an undistinguished destruction of all ages, sexes, and conditions.

In every stage of these oppressions, we have petitioned for redress; in the most humble terms; our repeated petitions have been answered only by repeated injury. A prince, whose character is thus marked by every act which may define a tyrant, is unfit to be the ruler of a free people.

Nor have we been wanting in attention to our British brethren. We have warned them, from time to time, of attempts made by their legislature to extend an unwarrantable jurisdiction over us. We have reminded them of the circumstances of our emigration and settlement here. We have appealed to their native justice and magnanimity, and we have conjured them, by the ties of our common kindred, to disavow these usurpations, which would inevitably interrupt our connections and correspondence. They, too, have been deaf to the voice of justice and consanguinity. We must, therefore, acquiesce in the necessity which denounces our separation, and hold them as we hold the rest of mankind, enemies in war, in peace, friends.

We, therefore, the representatives of the United States of America, in general Congress assembled, appealing to the Supreme Judge of the world for the rectitude of our intentions, do, in the name, and by authority of the good people of these colonies, solemnly publish and declare, that these united colonies are, and of right ought to be, free and independent states: that they are absolved from all allegiance to the British Crown, and that all political connection between them and the state of Great Britain is, and ought to be, totally dissolved; and that, as free and independent states, they have full power to levy war, conclude peace, contract alliances, establish commerce, and to do all other acts and things which independent states may of right do. And, for the support of this declaration, with a firm reliance on the protection of Divine Providence, we mutually pledge to each other our lives, our fortunes, and our sacred honor.

The foregoing Declaration was, by order of Congress, engrossed, and signed by the following members:

JOHN HANCOCK

New Hampshire	New York
Josiah Bartlett	William Floyd
William Whipple	Phillip Livingston
Matthew Thornton	Francis Lewis
	Lewis Morris

Massachusetts Bay	New Jersey
Samuel Adams	Richard Stockton
John Adams	John Witherspoon
Robert Treat Paine	Francis Hopkinson
Elbridge Gerry	John Hart
	Abraham Clark

Rhode Island	Pennsylvania
Stephen Hopkins	Robert Morris
William Ellery	Benjamin Rush
	Benjamin Franklin
	John Morton

Connecticut	George Clymer
Roger Sherman	James Smith
Samuel Huntington	George Taylor
William Williams	James Wilson
Oliver Wolcott	George Ross

Delaware	North Carolina	Virginia	Georgia
Caesar Rodney	William Hooper	George Wythe	Button Gwinnett
George Read	Joseph Hewes	Richard Henry Lee	Lyman Hall
Thomas M'Kean	John Penn	Thomas Jefferson	George Walton
		Benjamin Harrison	
Maryland	**South Carolina**	Thomas Nelson, Jr.	
Samuel Chase	Edward Rutledge	Francis Lightfoot Lee	
William Paca	Thomas Heyward, Jr.	Carter Braxton	
Thomas Stone	Thomas Lynch, Jr.		
Charles Carroll,	Arthur Middleton		
of Carrollton			

Resolved, That copies of the Declaration be sent to the several assemblies, conventions, and committees, or councils of safety, and to the several commanding officers of the continental troops; that it be proclaimed in each of the United States, at the head of the army.

THE ARTICLES OF CONFEDERATION AND PERPETUAL UNION

Agreed to in Congress, November 15, 1777.
Ratified March 1781.

BETWEEN THE STATES OF NEW HAMPSHIRE, MASSACHU-SETTS BAY, RHODE ISLAND AND PROVIDENCE PLANTA-TIONS, CONNECTICUT, NEW YORK, NEW JERSEY, PENN-SYLVANIA, DELAWARE, MARYLAND, VIRGINIA, NORTH CAROLINA, SOUTH CAROLINA, GEORGIA.*

Article 1

The stile of this confederacy shall be "The United States of America."

Article 2

Each State retains its sovereignty, freedom and inde-pendence, and every power, jurisdiction, and right, which is not by this confederation expressly dele-gated to the United States, in Congress assembled.

Article 3

The said states hereby severally enter into a firm league of friendship with each other for their com-mon defence, the security of their liberties and their mutual and general welfare; binding themselves to assist each other against all force offered to, or at-tacks made upon them, or any of them, on account of religion, sovereignty, trade, or any other pretence whatever.

*This copy of the final draft of the Articles of Confederation is taken from the *Journals,* 9:907–925, November 15, 1777.

Article 4

The better to secure and perpetuate mutual friend-ship and intercourse among the people of the dif-ferent states in this union, the free inhabitants of each of these states, paupers, vagabonds, and fugi-tives from justice excepted, shall be entitled to all privileges and immunities of free citizens in the several states; and the people of each State shall have free ingress and regress to and from any other State, and shall enjoy therein all the privileges of trade and commerce, subject to the same duties, im-positions, and restrictions, as the inhabitants thereof respectively; provided, that such restric-tions shall not extend so far as to prevent the re-moval of property, imported into any State, to any other State of which the owner is an inhabitant; provided also, that no imposition, duties, or restric-tion, shall be laid by any State on the property of the United States, or either of them.

If any person guilty of, or charged with treason, felony, or other high misdemeanor in any State, shall flee from justice and be found in any of the United States, he shall, upon demand of the gover-nor or executive power of the State from which he fled, be delivered up and removed to the State hav-ing jurisdiction of his offence.

Full faith and credit shall be given in each of these states to the records, acts, and judicial proceed-ings of the courts and magistrates of every other State.

Article 5

For the more convenient management of the general interests of the United States, delegates shall be an-nually appointed, in such manner as the legislature of each State shall direct, to meet in Congress, on the 1st Monday in November in every year, with a power reserved to each State to recall its delegates, or any of them, at any time within the year, and to send others in their stead for the remainder of the year.

No State shall be represented in Congress by less than two, nor by more than seven members; and no person shall be capable of being a delegate for more than three years in any term of six years; nor shall any person, being a delegate, be capable of holding any office under the United States, for which he, or any other for his benefit, receives any salary, fees, or emolument of any kind.

Each State shall maintain its own delegates in a meeting of the states, and while they act as members of the committee of the states.

In determining questions in the United States, in Congress assembled, each State shall have one vote.

Freedom of speech and debate in Congress shall not be impeached or questioned in any court or place out of Congress: and the members of Congress shall be protected in their persons from arrests and imprisonments, during the time of their going to and from, and attendance on Congress, except for treason, felony, or breach of the peace.

Article 6

No State, without the consent of the United States, in Congress assembled, shall send any embassy to, or receive any embassy from, or enter into any conference, agreement, alliance, or treaty with any king, prince, or state; nor shall any person, holding any office of profit or trust under the United States, or any of them, accept of any present, emolument, office or title, of any kind whatever, from any king, prince, or foreign state; nor shall the United States, in Congress assembled, or any of them, grant any title of nobility.

No two or more states shall enter into any treaty, confederation, or alliance, whatever, between them, without the consent of the United States, in Congress assembled, specifying accurately the purposes for which the same is to be entered into, and how long it shall continue.

No state shall lay any imposts or duties which may interfere with any stipulations in treaties entered into by the United States, in Congress assembled, with any king, prince, or state, in pursuance of any treaties already proposed by Congress to the courts of France and Spain.

No vessels of war shall be kept up in time of peace by any State, except such number only as shall be deemed necessary by the United States, in Congress assembled, for the defence of such State or its trade; nor shall any body of forces be kept up by any State, in time of peace, except such number

only as, in the judgment of the United States, in Congress assembled, shall be deemed requisite to garrison the forts necessary for the defence of such State; but every State shall always keep up a well regulated and disciplined militia, sufficiently armed and accoutred, and shall provide, and constantly have ready for use, in public stores, a due number of field pieces and tents, and a proper quantity of arms, ammunition and camp equipage.

No State shall engage in any war without the consent of the United States, in Congress assembled, unless such State be actually invaded by enemies, or shall have received certain advice of a resolution being formed by some nation of Indians to invade such State, and the danger is so imminent as not to admit of a delay till the United States, in Congress assembled, can be consulted; nor shall any State grant commissions to any ships or vessels of war, nor letters of marque or reprisal, except it be after a declaration of war by the United States, in Congress assembled, and then only against the kingdom or state, and the subjects thereof, against which war has been so declared, and under such regulations as shall be established by the United States, in Congress assembled, unless such State be infested by pirates, in which case vessels of war may be fitted out for that occasion, and kept so long as the danger shall continue, or until the United States, in Congress assembled, shall determine otherwise.

Article 7

When land forces are raised by any State for the common defence, all officers of or under the rank of colonel, shall be appointed by the legislature of each State respectively, by whom such forces shall be raised, or in such manner as such State shall direct; and all vacancies shall be filled up by the State which first made the appointment.

Article 8

All charges of war and all other expences, that shall be incurred for the common defence or general welfare, and allowed by the United States, in Congress assembled, shall be defrayed out of a common treasury, which shall be supplied by the several states, in proportion to the value of all land within each State, granted to or surveyed for any person, as such land and the buildings and improvements thereon shall be estimated according to such mode as the United States, in Congress assembled, shall, from time to time, direct and appoint.

The taxes for paying that proportion shall be laid and levied by the authority and direction of the legislatures of the several states, within the time agreed upon by the United States, in Congress assembled.

Article 9

The United States, in Congress assembled, shall have the sole and exclusive right and power of determining on peace and war, except in the cases mentioned in the 6th article; of sending and receiving ambassadors; entering into treaties and alliances, provided that no treaty of commerce shall be made, whereby the legislative power of the respective states shall be restrained from imposing such imposts and duties on foreigners as their own people are subjected to, or from prohibiting the exportation or importation of any species of goods or commodities whatsoever; of establishing rules for deciding, in all cases, what captures on land or water shall be legal, and in what manner prizes, taken by land or naval forces in the service of the United States, shall be divided or appropriated; of granting letters of marque and reprisal in times of peace; appointing courts for the trial of piracies and felonies committed on the high seas, and establishing courts for receiving and determining, finally, appeals in all cases of captures; provided, that no member of Congress shall be appointed a judge of any of the said courts.

The United States, in Congress assembled, shall also be the last resort on appeal in all disputes and differences now subsisting, or that hereafter may arise between two or more states concerning boundary, jurisdiction or any other cause whatever; which authority shall always be exercised in the manner following: whenever the legislative or executive authority, or lawful agent of any State, in controversy with another, shall present a petition to Congress, stating the matter in question, and praying for a hearing, notice thereof shall be given, by order of Congress, to the legislative or executive authority of the other State in controversy, and a day assigned for the appearance of the parties by their lawful agents, who shall then be directed to appoint, by joint consent, commissioners or judges to constitute a court for hearing and determining the matter in question; but, if they cannot agree, Congress shall name three persons out of each of the United States, and from the list of such persons each party shall alternately strike out one, the petitioners beginning, until the number shall be reduced to thirteen; and from that number not less than seven, nor more than nine names, as Congress shall direct, shall, in the presence of Congress, be drawn out by lot; and the persons whose names shall be so drawn, or any five of them, shall be commissioners or judges to hear and finally determine the controversy, so always as a major part of the judges who shall hear the cause shall agree in the determination; and if either party shall neglect to attend at the day appointed, without shewing reasons which Congress shall judge sufficient, or, being present, shall refuse to strike, the Congress shall proceed to nominate three persons out of each State, and the secretary of Congress shall strike in behalf of such party absent or refusing; and the judgment and sentence of the court to be appointed, in the manner before prescribed, shall be final and conclusive; and if any of the parties shall refuse to submit to the authority of such court, or to appear or defend their claim or cause, the court shall nevertheless proceed to pronounce sentence or judgment, which shall, in like manner, be final and decisive, the judgment or sentence and other proceedings begin, in either case, transmitted to Congress, and lodged among the acts of Congress for the security of the parties concerned: provided, that every commissioner, before he sits in judgment, shall take an oath, to be administered by one of the judges of the supreme or superior court of the State where the cause shall be tried, "well and truly to hear and determine the matter in question, according to the best of his judgment, without favour, affection, or hope of reward:" provided, also, that no State shall be deprived of territory for the benefit of the United States.

All controversies concerning the private right of soil, claimed under different grants of two or more states, whose jurisdictions, as they may respect such lands and the states which passed such grants, are adjusted, the said grants, or either of them, being at the same time claimed to have originated antecedent to such settlement of jurisdiction, shall, on the petition of either party to the Congress of the United States, be finally determined, as near as may be, in the same manner as is before prescribed for deciding disputes respecting territorial jurisdiction between different states.

The United States, in Congress assembled, shall also have the sole and exclusive right and power of regulating the alloy and value of coin struck by their own authority, or by that of the respective states; fixing the standard of weights and measures throughout the United States; regulating the trade and managing all affairs with the Indians not members of any of the states; provided that the legislative right of any State within its own limits be not infringed or violated; establishing and regulating post offices from one State to another throughout all the United States, and exacting such postage on the papers passing through the same as may be requisite to defray the expences of the said office; appointing all officers of the land forces in the service of the United States, excepting regimental officers; appointing all the officers of the naval forces, and commissioning all officers whatever in the service of the United States; making rules for the government and regulation of the said land and naval forces, and directing their operations.

The United States, in Congress assembled, shall have authority to appoint a committee to sit in the recess of Congress, to be denominated "a Committee of the States," and to consist of one delegate from each State, and to appoint such other committees and civil officers as may be necessary for managing the general affairs of the United States, under their direction; to appoint one of their number to preside; provided that no person be allowed to serve in the office of president more than one year in any term of three years; to ascertain the necessary sums of money to be raised for the service of the United States, and to appropriate and apply the same for defraying the public expences; to borrow money or emit bills on the credit of the United States, transmitting, every half year, to the respective states, an account of the sums of money so borrowed or emitted; to build and equip a navy; to agree upon the number of land forces, and to make requisitions from each State for its quota, in proportion to the number of white inhabitants in such State; which requisitions shall be binding; and thereupon, the legislature of each State shall appoint the regimental officers, raise the men, and cloathe, arm, and equip them in a soldier-like manner, at the expence of the United States; and the officers and men so cloathed, armed, and equipped, shall march to the place appointed and within the time agreed on by the United States, in Congress assembled; but if the United States, in Congress assembled, shall, on consideration of circumstances, judge proper that any State should not raise men, or should raise a smaller number than its quota, and that any other State should raise a greater number of men than the quota thereof, such extra number shall be raised, officered, cloathed, armed, and equipped in the same manner as the quota of such State, unless the legislature of such State shall judge that such extra number cannot be safely spared out of the same, in which case they shall raise, officer, cloathe, arm, and equip as many of such extra number as they judge can be safely spared. And the officers and men so cloathed, armed, and equipped, shall march to the place appointed and within the time agreed on by the United States, in Congress assembled.

The United States, in Congress assembled, shall never engage in a war, nor grant letters of marque and reprisal in time of peace, nor enter into any treaties or alliances, nor coin money, nor regulate the value thereof, nor ascertain the sums and expences necessary for the defence and welfare of the United States, or any of them: nor emit bills, nor borrow money on the credit of the United States, nor appropriate money, nor agree upon the number of vessels of war to be built or purchased, or the number of land or sea forces to be raised, nor appoint a commander in chief of the army or navy, unless nine states assent to the same; nor shall a question on any other point, except for adjourning from day to day, be determined, unless by the votes of a majority of the United States, in Congress assembled.

The Congress of the United States shall have power to adjourn to any time within the year, and to any place within the United States, so that no period of adjournment be for a longer duration than the space of six months, and shall publish the journal of their proceedings monthly, except such parts thereof, relating to treaties, alliances or military operations, as, in their judgment, require secrecy; and the yeas and nays of the delegates of each State on any question shall be entered on the journal, when it is desired by any delegate; and the delegates of a State, or any of them, at his, or their request, shall be furnished with a transcript of the said journal, except such parts as are above excepted, to lay before the legislatures of the several states.

Article 10

The committee of the states, or any nine of them, shall be authorized to execute, in the recess of Congress, such of the powers of Congress as the United States, in Congress assembled, by the consent of nine states, shall, from time to time, think expedient to vest them with; provided, that no power be delegated to the said committee, for the exercise of which, by the articles of confederation, the voice of nine states, in the Congress of the United States assembled, is requisite.

Article 11

Canada acceding to this confederation, and joining in the measures of the United States, shall be admitted into and entitled to all the advantages of this union; but no other colony shall be admitted into the same, unless such admission be agreed to by nine states.

Article 12

All bills of credit emitted, monies borrowed and debts contracted by, or under the authority of Congress before the assembling of the United States, in pursuance of the present confederation, shall be deemed and considered as a charge against the United States, for payment and satisfaction whereof the said United States and the public faith are hereby solemnly pledged.

Article 13

Every State shall abide by the determinations of the United States, in Congress assembled, on all questions which, by this confederation, are submitted to them. And the articles of this confederation shall be inviolably observed by every State, and the union shall be perpetual; nor shall any alteration at any time hereafter be made in any of them, unless such alteration be agreed to in a Congress of the United States, and be afterwards confirmed by the legislatures of every State.

These articles shall be proposed to the legislatures of all the United States, to be considered, and if approved of by them, they are advised to authorize their delegates to ratify the same in the Congress of the United States; which being done, the same shall become conclusive.

THE CONSTITUTION OF THE UNITED STATES*

Agreed to by Philadelphia Convention, September 17, 1787. Implemented March 4, 1789.

Preamble

We the people of the United States, in order to form a more perfect union, establish justice, insure domestic tranquility, provide for the common defense, promote the general welfare, and secure the blessings of liberty to ourselves and our posterity, do ordain and establish this Constitution for the United States of America.

Article I

Section 1   All legislative powers herein granted shall be vested in a Congress of the United States, which shall consist of a Senate and a House of Representatives.

Section 2   The House of Representatives shall be composed of members chosen every second year by the people of the several States, and the electors in each State shall have the qualifications requisite for electors of the most numerous branch of the State Legislature.

No person shall be a Representative who shall not have attained to the age of twenty-five years, and been seven years a citizen of the United States, and who shall not, when elected, be an inhabitant of that State in which he shall be chosen.

Representatives and direct taxes shall be apportioned among the several States which may be included within this Union, according to their respective numbers, *which shall be determined by adding to the whole number of free persons, including those bound to service for a term of years and excluding Indians not taxed, three-fifths of all other persons.* The actual enumeration shall be made within three years after the first meeting of the Congress of the United States, and within every subsequent term of ten years, in such manner as they shall by law direct. The number of Representatives shall not exceed one for every thirty thousand, but each State shall have at least one Representative; *and until such enumeration shall be made, the State of New Hampshire shall be entitled to choose three, Massachusetts eight, Rhode Island and Providence Plantations one, Connecticut five, New York six, New Jersey four, Pennsylvania eight, Delaware one, Maryland six, Virginia ten, North Carolina five, South Carolina five, and Georgia three.*

When vacancies happen in the representation from any State, the Executive authority thereof shall issue writs of election to fill such vacancies.

The House of Representatives shall choose their Speaker and other officers; and shall have the sole power of impeachment.

Section 3   The Senate of the United States shall be composed of two Senators from each State, *chosen by the legislature thereof,* for six years; and each Senator shall have one vote.

Immediately after they shall be assembled in consequence of the first election, they shall be divided as equally as may be into three classes. The seats of the Senators of the first class shall be vacated at the expiration of the second year, of the second class at the expiration of the fourth year, and of the third class at the expiration of the sixth year, so that one-third may be chosen every second year; *and if vacancies happen by resignation or otherwise, during the recess of the legislature of any State, the Executive thereof may make temporary appointments until the next meeting of the legislature, which shall then fill such vacancies.*

No person shall be a Senator who shall not have attained to the age of thirty years, and been nine years a citizen of the United States, and who shall not, when elected, be an inhabitant of that State for which he shall be chosen.

The Vice-President of the United States shall be President of the Senate, but shall have no vote, unless they be equally divided.

The Senate shall choose their other officers, and also a President *pro tempore*, in the absence of the Vice-President, or when he shall exercise the office of President of the United States.

The Senate shall have the sole power to try all impeachments. When sitting for that purpose, they shall be on oath or affirmation. When the President of the United States is tried, the Chief Justice shall preside: and no person shall be convicted without the concurrence of two-thirds of the members present.

Judgment in cases of impeachment shall not extend further than to removal from the office, and disqualification to hold and enjoy any office of honor, trust or profit under the United States: but the party convicted shall nevertheless be liable and subject to indictment, trial, judgment and punishment, according to law.

Section 4   The times, places and manner of holding elections for Senators and Representatives shall be prescribed in each State by the legislature thereof; but the Congress may at any time by law make or alter such regulations, except as to the places of choosing Senators.

The Congress shall assemble at least once in every year, and such meeting *shall be on the first*

---

*Passages no longer in effect are in italic type.

Monday in December, unless they shall by law appoint a different day.

Section 5 Each house shall be the judge of the elections, returns and qualifications of its own members, and a majority of each shall constitute a quorum to do business; but a smaller number may adjourn from day to day, and may be authorized to compel the attendance of absent members, in such manner, and under such penalties, as each house may provide.

Each house may determine the rules of its proceedings, punish its members for disorderly behavior, and with the concurrence of two-thirds, expel a member.

Each house shall keep a journal of its proceedings, and from time to time publish the same, excepting such parts as may in their judgment require secrecy; and the yeas and nays of the members of either house on any question shall, at the desire of one-fifth of those present, be entered on the journal.

Neither house, during the session of Congress, shall, without the consent of the other, adjourn for more than three days, nor to any other place than that in which the two houses shall be sitting.

Section 6 The Senators and Representatives shall receive a compensation for their services, to be ascertained by law and paid out of the treasury of the United States. They shall in all cases except treason, felony and breach of the peace, be privileged from arrest during their attendance at the session of their respective houses, and in going to and returning from the same; and for any speech or debate in either house, they shall not be questioned in any other place.

No Senator or Representative shall, during the time for which he was elected, be appointed to any civil office under the authority of the United States, which shall have been created, or the emoluments whereof shall have been increased, during such time; and no person holding any office under the United States shall be a member of either house during his continuance in office.

Section 7 All bills for raising revenue shall originate in the House of Representatives; but the Senate may propose or concur with amendments as on other bills.

Every bill which shall have passed the House of Representatives and the Senate, shall, before it become a law, be presented to the President of the United States; if he approve he shall sign it, but if not he shall return it with objections to that house in which it shall have originated, who shall enter the objections at large on their journal, and proceed to reconsider it. If after such reconsideration two-thirds of that house shall agree to pass the bill, it shall be sent, together with the objections, to the other house, by which it shall likewise be reconsidered, and, if approved by two-thirds of that house,

it shall become a law. But in all such cases the votes of both houses shall be determined by yeas and nays, and the names of the persons voting for and against the bill shall be entered on the journal of each house respectively. If any bill shall not be returned by the President within ten days (Sundays excepted) after it shall have been presented to him, the same shall be a law, in like manner as if he had signed it, unless the Congress by their adjournment prevent its return, in which case it shall not be a law.

Every order, resolution, or vote to which the concurrence of the Senate and House of Representatives may be necessary (except on a question of adjournment) shall be presented to the President of the United States; and before the same shall take effect, shall be approved by him, or being disapproved by him, shall be repassed by two-thirds of the Senate and House of Representatives, according to the rules and limitations prescribed in the case of a bill.

Section 8 The Congress shall have power

To lay and collect taxes, duties, imposts, and excises, to pay the debts and provide for the common defense and general welfare of the United States; but all duties, imposts and excises shall be uniform throughout the United States;

To borrow money on the credit of the United States;

To regulate commerce with foreign nations, and among the several States, and with the Indian tribes;

To establish an uniform rule of naturalization, and uniform laws on the subject of bankruptcies throughout the United States;

To coin money, regulate the value thereof, and of foreign coin, and fix the standard of weights and measures;

To provide for the punishment of counterfeiting the securities and current coin of the United States;

To establish post offices and post roads;

To promote the progress of science and useful arts by securing for limited times to authors and inventors the exclusive right to their respective writings and discoveries;

To constitute tribunals inferior to the Supreme Court;

To define and punish piracies and felonies committed on the high seas and offences against the law of nations;

To declare war, grant letters of marque and reprisal, and make rules concerning captures on land and water;

To raise and support armies, but no appropriation of money to that use shall be for a longer term than two years;

To provide and maintain a navy;

To make rules for the government and regulation of the land and naval forces;

THE CONSTITUTION OF THE UNITED STATES

To provide for calling forth the militia to execute the laws of the Union, suppress insurrections and repel invasions;

To provide for organizing, arming, and disciplining the militia, and for governing such part of them as may be employed in the service of the United States, reserving to the States respectively the appointment of the officers, and the authority of training the militia according to the discipline prescribed by Congress;

To exercise exclusive legislation in all cases whatsoever, over such district (not exceeding ten miles square) as may, by cession of particular States, and the acceptance of Congress, become the seat of the government of the United States, and to exercise like authority over all places purchased by the consent of the legislature of the State, in which the same shall be, for erection of forts, magazines, arsenals, dock-yards, and other needful buildings;—and

To make all laws which shall be necessary and proper for carrying into execution the foregoing powers, and all other powers vested by this Constitution in the government of the United States, or in any department or officer thereof.

Section 9 *The migration or importation of such persons as any of the States now existing shall think proper to admit shall not be prohibited by the Congress prior to the year one thousand eight hundred and eight; but a tax or duty may be imposed on such importation, not exceeding ten dollars for each person.*

The privilege of the writ of habeas corpus shall not be suspended, unless when in cases of rebellion or invasion the public safety may require it.

No bill of attainder or ex post facto law shall be passed.

No capitation, or other direct, tax shall be laid, unless in proportion to the census or enumeration herein before directed to be taken.

No tax or duty shall be laid on articles exported from any State.

No preference shall be given by any regulation of commerce or revenue to the ports of one State over those of another; nor shall vessels bound to, or from, one State be obliged to enter, clear, or pay duties in another.

No money shall be drawn from the treasury, but in consequence of appropriations made by law; and a regular statement and account of the receipts and expenditures of all public money shall be published from time to time.

No title of nobility shall be granted by the United States: and no person holding any office of profit or trust under them, shall, without the consent of the Congress, accept of any present, emolument, office, or title, of any kind whatever, from any king, prince, or foreign state.

Section 10 No State shall enter into any treaty, alliance, or confederation; grant letters of marque and reprisal; coin money; emit bills of credit; make anything but gold and silver coin a tender in payment of debts; pass any bill of attainder, ex post facto law, or law impairing the obligation of contracts, or grant any title of nobility.

No State shall, without the consent of Congress, lay any imposts or duties on imports or exports, except what may be absolutely necessary for executing its inspection laws: and the net produce of all duties and imposts, laid by any State on imports or exports, shall be for the use of the treasury of the United States; and all such laws shall be subject to the revision and control of the Congress.

No State shall, without the consent of Congress, lay any duty of tonnage, keep troops, or ships of war in time of peace, enter into any agreement or compact with another State, or with a foreign power, or engage in war, unless actually invaded, or in such imminent danger as will not admit of delay.

Article II

Section 1 The executive power shall be vested in a President of the United States of America. He shall hold his office during the term of four years, and, together with the Vice-President, chosen for the same term, be elected as follows:

Each State shall appoint, in such manner as the legislature thereof may direct, a number of electors, equal to the whole number of Senators and Representatives to which the State may be entitled in the Congress; but no Senator or Representative, or person holding an office of trust or profit under the United States, shall be appointed an elector.

The electors shall meet in their respective States, and vote by ballot for two persons, of whom one at least shall not be an inhabitant of the same State with themselves. And they shall make a list of all the persons voted for, and of the number of votes for each; which list they shall sign and certify, and transmit sealed to the seat of government of the United States, directed to the President of the Senate. The President of the Senate shall, in the presence of the Senate and House of Representatives, open all the certificates, and the votes shall then be counted. The person having the greatest number of votes shall be the President, if such number be a majority of the whole number of electors appointed; and if there be more than one who have such majority, and have an equal number of votes, then the House of Representatives shall immediately choose by ballot one of them for President; and if no person have a majority, then from the five highest on the list said house shall in like manner choose the President. But in choosing the President the votes shall be taken by States, the representation from each State having one vote; a quorum for this purpose shall consist of a member or members from two-thirds of the States, and a majority of all the States shall be necessary to a choice. In every case, after the choice of the President, the person having the greatest number of votes of the electors shall be the Vice-President. But if there should remain two or more who have equal votes, the Senate shall choose from them by ballot the Vice-President.

The Congress may determine the time of choosing the electors, and the day on which they shall give their votes; which day shall be the same throughout the United States.

No person except a natural-born citizen, *or a citizen of the United States at the time of the adoption of this Constitution,* shall be eligible to the office of President; neither shall any person be eligible to that office who shall not have attained to the age of thirty-five years, and been fourteen years a resident within the United States.

In cases of the removal of the President from office or of his death, resignation, or inability to discharge the powers and duties of the said office, the same shall devolve on the Vice-President, and the Congress may by law provide for the case of removal, death, resignation, or inability, both of the President and Vice-President, declaring what officer shall then act as President, and such officer shall act accordingly, until the disability be removed, or a President shall be elected.

The President shall, at stated times, receive for his services a compensation, which shall neither be increased nor diminished during the period for which he shall have been elected, and he shall not receive within that period any other emolument from the United States, or any of them.

Before he enter on the execution of his office, he shall take the following oath or affirmation:—"I do solemnly swear (or affirm) that I will faithfully execute the office of the President of the United States, and will to the best of my ability preserve, protect and defend the Constitution of the United States."

Section 2 The President shall be commander in chief of the army and navy of the United States, and of the militia of the several States, when called into the actual service of the United States; he may require the opinion, in writing, of the principal officer in each of the executive departments, upon any subject relating to the duties of their respective offices, and he shall have power to grant reprieves and pardons for offenses against the United States, except in cases of impeachment.

He shall have power, by and with the advice and consent of the Senate, to make treaties, provided two-thirds of the Senators present concur; and he shall nominate, and by and with the advice and consent of the Senate, shall appoint ambassadors, other public ministers and consuls, judges of the Supreme Court, and all other officers of the United States, whose appointments are not herein otherwise provided for, and which shall be established by law: but Congress may by law vest the appointment of such inferior officers, as they think proper, in the President alone, in the courts of law, or in the heads of departments.

The President shall have power to fill up all vacancies that may happen during the recess of the Senate, by granting commissions which shall expire at the end of their next session.

Section 3 He shall from time to time give to the Congress information of the state of the Union, and recommend to their consideration such measures as he shall judge necessary and expedient; he may, on extraordinary occasions, convene both houses, or either of them, and in case of disagreement between them, with respect to the time of adjournment, he may adjourn them to such time as he shall think proper; he shall receive ambassadors and other public ministers; he shall take care that the laws be faithfully executed, and shall commission all the officers of the United States.

Section 4 The President, Vice-President and all civil officers of the United States shall be removed from office on impeachment for, and on conviction of, treason, bribery, or other high crimes and misdemeanors.

Article III

Section 1 The judicial power of the United States shall be vested in one Supreme Court, and in such inferior courts as the Congress may from time to time ordain and establish. The judges, both of the Supreme and inferior courts, shall hold their offices during good behavior, and shall, at stated times, receive for their services a compensation which shall not be diminished during their continuance in office.

Section 2 The judicial power shall extend to all cases, in law and equity, arising under this Constitution, the laws of the United States, and treaties made, or which shall be made, under their authority;—to all cases affecting ambassadors, other public ministers and consuls;—to all cases of admiralty and maritime jurisdiction;—to controversies to which the United States shall be a party;—to controversies between two or more States;—*between a State and citizens of another State;*—between citizens of different States;—between citizens of the same State claiming lands under grants of different States, and between a State, or the citizens thereof, and foreign states, citizens or subjects.

In all cases affecting ambassadors, other public ministers and consuls, and those in which a State shall be party, the Supreme Court shall have original jurisdiction. In all the other cases before mentioned, the Supreme Court shall have appellate jurisdiction, both as to law and fact, with such exceptions, and under such regulations, as the Congress shall make.

The trial of all crimes, except in cases of impeachment, shall be by jury; and such trial shall be held in the State where said crimes shall have been committed; but when not committed within any State, the trial shall be at such place or places as the Congress may by Law have directed.

Section 3 Treason against the United States shall consist only in levying war against them, or in adhering to their enemies, giving them aid and comfort. No person shall be convicted of treason unless on the testimony of two witnesses to the same overt act, or on confession in open court.

The Congress shall have power to declare the punishment of treason, but no attainder of treason shall work corruption of blood, or forfeiture except during the life of the person attainted.

Article IV

Section 1 Full faith and credit shall be given in each State to the public acts, records, and judicial proceedings of every other State. And the Congress may by general laws prescribe the manner in which such acts, records, and proceedings shall be proved, and the effect thereof.

Section 2 The citizens of each State shall be entitled to all privileges and immunities of citizens in the several States.

A person charged in any State with treason, felony, or other crime, who shall flee from justice, and be found in another State, shall on demand of the executive authority of the State from which he fled, be delivered up, to be removed to the State having jurisdiction of the crime.

No Person held to service or labor in one State, under the laws thereof, escaping into another, shall, in consequence of any law or regulation therein, be discharged from such service or labor, but shall be delivered up on claim of the party to whom such service or labor may be due.

Section 3 New States may be admitted by the Congress into this Union; but no new State shall be formed or erected within the jurisdiction of any other State; nor any State be formed by the junction of two or more States, or parts of States, without the consent of the legislatures of the States concerned as well as of the Congress.

The Congress shall have power to dispose of and make all needful rules and regulations respecting the territory or other property belonging to the United States; and nothing in this Constitution shall be so construed as to prejudice any claims of the United States, or of any particular State.

Section 4 The United States shall guarantee to every State in this Union a republican form of government, and shall protect each of them against invasion; and on application of the legislature, or of the executive (when the legislature cannot be convened), against domestic violence.

Article V

The Congress, whenever two-thirds of both houses shall deem it necessary, shall propose amendments to this Constitution, or, on the application of the legislatures of two-thirds of the several States, shall call a convention for proposing amendments, which, in either case, shall be valid to all intents and purposes, as part of this Constitution, when ratified by the legislatures of three-fourths of the several States, or by conventions in three-fourths thereof, as the one or the other mode of ratification may be proposed by the Congress; provided *that no amendments which may be made prior to the year one thousand eight hundred and eight shall in any manner affect the first and fourth clauses in the ninth section of the first article;* and that no State, without its consent, shall be deprived of its equal suffrage in the Senate.

Article VI

All debts contracted and engagements entered into, before the adoption of this Constitution, shall be as valid against the United States under this Constitution, as under the Confederation.

This Constitution, and the laws of the United States which shall be made in pursuance thereof; and all treaties made, or which shall be made, under the authority of the United States, shall be the supreme law of the land; and the judges in every State shall be bound thereby, anything in the Constitution or laws of any State to the contrary notwithstanding.

The Senators and Representatives before mentioned, and the members of the several State legislatures, and all executive and judicial officers, both of the United States and of the several States, shall be bound by oath or affirmation to support this Constitution; but no religious test shall ever be required as a qualification to any office or public trust under the United States.

Article VII

The ratification of the conventions of nine States shall be sufficient for the establishment of this Constitution between the States so ratifying the same.

Done in convention by the unanimous consent of the States present, the seventeenth day of September in the year of our Lord one thousand seven hundred and eighty-seven and of the Independence of the United States of America the twelfth. In witness whereof we have hereunto subscribed our names.

GEORGE WASHINGTON
PRESIDENT AND DEPUTY FROM VIRGINIA

New Hampshire
John Langdon
Nicholas Gilman

Massachusetts
Nathaniel Gorham
Rufus King

Connecticut
William Samuel
  Johnson
Roger Sherman

New York
Alexander Hamilton

New Jersey
William Livingston
David Brearley
William Paterson
Jonathan Dayton

Pennsylvania
Benjamin Franklin
Thomas Mifflin
Robert Morris
George Clymer
Thomas FitzSimons
Jared Ingersoll
James Wilson
Gouverneur Morris

Delaware
George Read
Gunning Bedford, Jr.
John Dickinson
Richard Bassett
Jacob Broom

Maryland
James McHenry
Daniel of St. Thomas
  Jenifer
Daniel Carroll

Virginia
John Blair
James Madison, Jr.

North Carolina
William Blount
Richard Dobbs Spaight
Hugh Williamson

South Carolina
John Rutledge
Charles Cotesworth
  Pinckney
Charles Pinckney
Pierce Butler

Georgia
William Few
Abraham Baldwin

AMENDMENTS TO THE CONSTITUTION WITH ANNOTATIONS
(including the six unratified amendments)

IN THEIR EFFORT TO GAIN Antifederalists' support for the Constitution, Federalists frequently pointed to the inclusion of Article 5, which provides an orderly method of amending the Constitution. In contrast, the Articles of Confederation, which were universally recognized as seriously flawed, offered no means of amendment. For their part, Antifederalists argued that the amendment process was so "intricate" that one might as easily roll "sixes an hundred times in succession" as change the Constitution.

The system for amendment laid out in the Constitution requires that two-thirds of both houses of Congress agree to a proposed amendment, which must then be ratified by three-quarters of the legislatures of the states. Alternatively, an amendment may be proposed by a convention called by the legislatures of two-thirds of the states. Since 1789, members of Congress have proposed thousands of amendments. Besides the seventeen amendments added since 1789, only the six "unratified" ones included here were approved by two-thirds of both houses and sent to the states for ratification.

Among the many amendments that never made it out of Congress have been proposals to declare dueling, divorce, and interracial marriage unconstitutional as well as proposals to establish a national university, to acknowledge the sovereignty of Jesus Christ, and to prohibit any person from possessing wealth in excess of $10 million.*

Among the issues facing Americans today that might lead to constitutional amendment are efforts to balance the federal budget, to limit the number of terms elected officials may serve, to limit access to or prohibit abortion, to establish English as the official language of the United States, and to prohibit flag burning. None of these proposed amendments has yet garnered enough support in Congress to be sent to the states for ratification.

Although the first ten amendments to the Constitution are commonly known as the Bill of Rights, only Amendments 1–8 actually provide guarantees of individual rights. Amendments 9 and 10 deal with the structure of power within the constitutional system. The Bill of Rights was promised to appease Antifederalists who refused to ratify the Constitution without guarantees of individual liberties and limitations to federal power. After studying more than two hundred amendments recommended by the ratifying conventions of the states, Federalist James Madison presented a list of seventeen to Congress, which used Madison's list as the foundation for the twelve amendments that were sent to the states for ratification. Ten of the twelve were adopted in 1791. The first on the list of twelve,

---

*Richard B. Bernstein, *Amending America* (New York: Times Books, 1993), 177–81.

known as the Reapportionment Amendment, was never adopted (see page A-15). The second proposed amendment was adopted in 1992 as Amendment 27 (see page A-24).

Amendment I

Congress shall make no law respecting an establishment of religion, or prohibiting the free exercise thereof; or abridging the freedom of speech, or of the press; or the right of the people peaceably to assemble, and to petition the government for a redress of grievances.

♦♦♦

The First Amendment is a potent symbol for many Americans. Most are well aware of their rights to free speech, freedom of the press, and freedom of religion and their rights to assemble and to petition, even if they cannot cite the exact words of this amendment.

The First Amendment guarantee of freedom of religion has two clauses: the "free exercise clause," which allows individuals to practice or not practice any religion, and the "establishment clause," which prevents the federal government from discriminating against or favoring any particular religion. This clause was designed to create what Thomas Jefferson referred to as "a wall of separation between church and state." In the 1960s, the Supreme Court ruled that the First Amendment prohibits prayer (see Engel v. Vitale, *online) and Bible reading in public schools.*

Although the rights to free speech and freedom of the press are established in the First Amendment, it was not until the twentieth century that the Supreme Court began to explore the full meaning of these guarantees. In 1919, the Court ruled in Schenck v. United States *(online) that the government could suppress free expression only where it could cite a "clear and present danger." In a decision that continues to raise controversies, the Court ruled in 1990, in* Texas v. Johnson, *that flag burning is a form of symbolic speech protected by the First Amendment.*

Amendment II

A well-regulated militia being necessary to the security of a free State, the right of the people to keep and bear arms shall not be infringed.

♦♦♦

Fear of a standing army under the control of a hostile government made the Second Amendment an important part of the Bill of Rights. Advocates of gun ownership claim that the amendment prevents the government from regulating firearms. Proponents of gun control argue that the amendment is designed only to protect the right of the states to maintain militia units.

In 1939, the Supreme Court ruled in United States v. Miller *that the Second Amendment did not protect the right of an individual to own a sawed-off shotgun, which it argued was not ordinary militia equipment. Since then, the Supreme Court has refused to hear Second Amendment cases, while lower courts have upheld firearms regulations. Several justices currently on the bench seem to favor a narrow interpretation of the Second Amendment, which would allow gun control legislation. The controversy over the impact of the Second Amendment on gun owners and gun control legislation will certainly continue.*

Amendment III

No soldier shall, in time of peace, be quartered in any house without the consent of the owner, nor in time of war, but in a manner to be prescribed by law.

♦♦♦

The Third Amendment was extremely important to the framers of the Constitution, but today it is nearly forgotten. American colonists were especially outraged that they were forced to quarter British troops in the years before and during the American Revolution. The philosophy of the Third Amendment has been viewed by some justices and scholars as the foundation of the modern constitutional right to privacy. One example of this can be found in Justice William O. Douglas's opinion in Griswold v. Connecticut *(online).*

Amendment IV

The right of the people to be secure in their persons, houses, papers, and effects, against unreasonable searches and seizures, shall not be violated, and no warrants shall issue but upon probable cause, supported by oath or affirmation, and particularly describing the place to be searched, and the persons or things to be seized.

♦♦♦

In the years before the Revolution, the houses, barns, stores, and warehouses of American colonists were ransacked by British authorities under "writs of assistance" or general warrants. The British, thus empowered, searched for seditious material or smuggled goods that could then be used as evidence against colonists who were charged with a crime only after the items were found.

The first part of the Fourth Amendment protects citizens from "unreasonable" searches and seizures. The Supreme Court has interpreted this protection as well as the words search *and* seizure *in different ways at different times. At one time, the Court did not recognize electronic eavesdropping as a form of search and seizure, though it does today. At times, an "unreasonable" search has been almost any search carried out without a warrant, but in the two decades before 1969, the Court sometimes sanctioned warrantless searches that it considered reasonable based on "the total atmosphere of the case."*

The second part of the Fourth Amendment defines the procedure for issuing a search warrant and states the requirement of "probable cause," which is generally viewed as evidence indicating that a suspect has committed an offense.

The Fourth Amendment has been controversial because the Court has sometimes excluded evidence that has been seized in violation of constitutional standards. The justification is that excluding such evidence deters violations of the amendment, but doing so may allow a guilty person to escape punishment.

Amendment V

No person shall be held to answer for a capital, or otherwise infamous crime, unless on a presentment or indictment of a grand jury, except in cases arising in the land or naval forces, or in the militia, when in actual service in time of war or public danger; nor shall any person be subject for the same offence to be twice put in jeopardy of life or limb; nor shall be compelled in any criminal case to be a witness against himself, nor be deprived of life, liberty, or property, without due process of law; nor shall private property be taken for public use without just compensation.

♦♦♦

The Fifth Amendment protects people against government authority in the prosecution of criminal offenses. It prohibits the state, first, from charging a person with a serious crime without a grand jury hearing to decide whether there is sufficient evidence to support the charge and, second, from charging a person with the same crime twice. The best-known aspect of the Fifth Amendment is that it prevents a person from being "compelled . . . to be a witness against himself." The last clause, the "takings clause," limits the power of the government to seize property.

Although invoking the Fifth Amendment is popularly viewed as a confession of guilt, a person may be innocent yet still fear prosecution. For example, during the Red-baiting era of the late 1940s and 1950s, many people who had participated in legal activities that were associated with the Communist Party claimed the Fifth Amendment privilege rather than testify before the House Un-American Activities Committee because the mood of the times cast those activities in a negative light. Since "taking the Fifth" was viewed as an admission of guilt, those people often lost their jobs or became unemployable. (See chapter 26.) Nonetheless, the right to protect oneself against self-incrimination plays an important role in guarding against the collective power of the state.

Amendment VI

In all criminal prosecutions, the accused shall enjoy the right to a speedy and public trial, by an impartial jury of the State and district wherein the crime shall have been committed, which district shall have been previously ascertained by law, and to be informed of the nature and cause of the accusation; to be confronted with the witnesses against him; to have compulsory process for obtaining witnesses in his favor, and to have the assistance of counsel for his defence.

♦♦♦

The original Constitution put few limits on the government's power to investigate, prosecute, and punish crime. This process was of great concern to the early Americans, however, and of the twenty-eight rights specified in the first eight amendments, fifteen have to do with it. Seven rights are specified in the Sixth Amendment. These include the right to a speedy trial, a public trial, a jury trial, a notice of accusation, confrontation by opposing witnesses, testimony by favorable witnesses, and the assistance of counsel.

Although this amendment originally guaranteed these rights only in cases involving the federal government, the adoption of the Fourteenth Amendment began a process of applying the protections of the Bill of Rights to the states through court cases such as Gideon v. Wainwright *(online).*

Amendment VII

In suits at common law, where the value in controversy shall exceed twenty dollars, the right of trial by jury shall be preserved, and no fact tried by a jury shall be otherwise reexamined in any court of the United States, than according to the rules of the common law.

♦♦♦

This amendment guarantees people the same right to a trial by jury as was guaranteed by English common law in 1791. Under common law, in civil trials (those involving money damages) the role of the judge was to settle questions of law and that of the jury was to settle questions of fact. The amendment does not specify the size of the jury or its role in a trial, however. The Supreme Court has generally held that those issues be determined by English common law of 1791, which stated that a jury consists of twelve people, that a trial must be conducted before a judge who instructs the jury on the law and advises it on facts, and that a verdict must be unanimous.

Amendment VIII

Excessive bail shall not be required, nor excessive fines imposed, nor cruel and unusual punishments inflicted.

♦♦♦

The language used to guarantee the three rights in this amendment was inspired by the English Bill of Rights of

1689. The Supreme Court has not had a lot to say about "excessive fines." In recent years it has agreed that despite the provision against "excessive bail," persons who are believed to be dangerous to others can be held without bail even before they have been convicted.

Although opponents of the death penalty have not succeeded in using the Eighth Amendment to achieve the end of capital punishment, the clause regarding "cruel and unusual punishments" has been used to prohibit capital punishment in certain cases (see Furman v. Georgia, *online*) and to require improved conditions in prisons.

Amendment IX

The enumeration in the Constitution, of certain rights, shall not be construed to deny or disparage others retained by the people.

♦♦♦

Some Federalists feared that inclusion of the Bill of Rights in the Constitution would allow later generations of interpreters to claim that the people had surrendered any rights not specifically enumerated there. To guard against this, Madison added language that became the Ninth Amendment. Interest in this heretofore largely ignored amendment revived in 1965 when it was used in a concurring opinion in Griswold v. Connecticut *(online). While Justice William O. Douglas called on the Third Amendment to support the right to privacy in deciding that case, Justice Arthur Goldberg, in the concurring opinion, argued that the right to privacy regarding contraception was an unenumerated right that was protected by the Ninth Amendment.*

In 1980, the Court ruled that the right of the press to attend a public trial was protected by the Ninth Amendment. While some scholars argue that modern judges cannot identify the unenumerated rights that the framers were trying to protect, others argue that the Ninth Amendment should be read as providing a constitutional "presumption of liberty" that allows people to act in any way that does not violate the rights of others.

Amendment X

The powers not delegated to the United States by the Constitution, nor prohibited by it to the States, are reserved to the States respectively, or to the people.

♦♦♦

The Antifederalists were especially eager to see a "reserved powers clause" explicitly guaranteeing the states control over their internal affairs. Not surprisingly, the Tenth Amendment has been a frequent battleground in the struggle over states' rights and federal supremacy. Prior to the Civil War, the Democratic Republican Party and Jacksonian Democrats invoked the Tenth Amendment to prohibit the federal government from making decisions about whether people in individual states could own slaves. The Tenth Amendment was virtually suspended during Reconstruction following the Civil War. In 1883, however, the Supreme Court declared the Civil Rights Act of 1875 unconstitutional on the grounds that it violated the Tenth Amendment. Business interests also called on the amendment to block efforts at federal regulation.

The Court was inconsistent over the next several decades as it attempted to resolve the tension between the restrictions of the Tenth Amendment and the powers the Constitution granted to Congress to regulate interstate commerce and levy taxes. The Court upheld the Pure Food and Drug Act (1906), the Meat Inspection Acts (1906 and 1907), and the White Slave Traffic Act (1910), all of which affected the states, but struck down an act prohibiting interstate shipment of goods produced through child labor. Between 1934 and 1935, a number of New Deal programs created by Franklin D. Roosevelt were declared unconstitutional on the grounds that they violated the Tenth Amendment. (See chapter 24.) As Roosevelt appointees changed the composition of the Court, the Tenth Amendment was declared to have no substantive meaning. Generally, the amendment is held to protect the rights of states to regulate internal matters such as local government, education, commerce, labor, and business, as well as matters involving families such as marriage, divorce, and inheritance within the state.

Unratified Amendment

Reapportionment Amendment (proposed by Congress September 25, 1789, along with the Bill of Rights)

After the first enumeration required by the first article of the Constitution, there shall be one Representative for every thirty thousand, until the number shall amount to one hundred, after which the proportion shall be so regulated by Congress, that there shall be not less than one hundred Representatives, nor less than one Representative for every forty thousand persons, until the number of Representatives shall amount to two hundred; after which the proportion shall be so regulated by Congress, that there shall not be less than two hundred Representatives, nor more than one Representative for every fifty thousand persons.

♦♦♦

If the Reapportionment Amendment had passed and remained in effect, the House of Representatives today would have more than 5,000 members rather than 435.

Amendment XI
[Adopted 1798]

The judicial power of the United States shall not be construed to extend to any suit in law or equity, commenced or prosecuted against one of the United States by citizens of another State, or by citizens or subjects of any foreign state.

◆ ◆ ◆

In 1793, the Supreme Court ruled in favor of Alexander Chisholm, executor of the estate of a deceased South Carolina merchant. Chisholm was suing the state of Georgia because the merchant had never been paid for provisions he had supplied during the Revolution. Many regarded this Court decision as an error that violated the intent of the Constitution.

Antifederalists had long feared a federal court system with the power to overrule a state court. When the Constitution was being drafted, Federalists had assured worried Antifederalists that section 2 of Article 3, which allows federal courts to hear cases "between a State and citizens of another State," did not mean that the federal courts were authorized to hear suits against *a state by citizens of another state or a foreign country. Antifederalists and many other Americans feared a powerful federal court system because they worried that it would become like the British courts of this period, which were accountable only to the monarch. Furthermore, Chisholm v. Georgia prompted a series of suits against state governments by creditors and suppliers who had made loans during the war.*

In addition, state legislators and Congress feared that the shaky economies of the new states, as well as the country as a whole, would be destroyed, especially if loyalists who had fled to other countries sought reimbursement for land and property that had been seized. The day after the Supreme Court announced its decision, a resolution proposing the Eleventh Amendment, which overturned the decision in Chisholm v. Georgia, was introduced in the U.S. Senate.

Amendment XII

[Adopted 1804]

The electors shall meet in their respective States, and vote by ballot for President and Vice-President, one of whom, at least, shall not be an inhabitant of the same State with themselves; they shall name in their ballots the person voted for as President, and in distinct ballots the person voted for as Vice-President, and they shall make distinct lists of all persons voted for as President, and of all persons voted for as Vice-President, and of the number of votes for each, which lists they shall sign and certify, and transmit sealed to the seat of government of the United States, directed to the President of the Senate;—the President of the Senate shall, in the presence of the Senate and House of Representatives, open all the certificates and the votes shall then be counted;—the person having the greatest number of votes for President

shall be the President, if such number be a majority of the whole number of electors appointed; and if no person have such majority, then from the persons having the highest numbers not exceeding three on the list of those voted for as President, the House of Representatives shall choose immediately, by ballot, the President. But in choosing the President, the votes shall be taken by States, the representation from each State having one vote; a quorum for this purpose shall consist of a member or members from two-thirds of the States, and a majority of all the States shall be necessary to a choice. And if the House of Representatives shall not choose a President whenever the right of choice shall devolve upon them, before *the fourth day of March* next following, then the Vice-President shall act as President, as in the case of the death or other constitutional disability of the President.

The person having the greatest number of votes as Vice-President shall be the Vice-President, if such number be a majority of the whole number of electors appointed; and if no person have a majority, then from the two highest numbers on the list the Senate shall choose the Vice-President; a quorum for the purpose shall consist of two-thirds of the whole number of Senators, and a majority of the whole number shall be necessary to a choice. But no person constitutionally ineligible to the office of President shall be eligible to that of Vice-President of the United States.

◆ ◆ ◆

The framers of the Constitution disliked political parties and assumed that none would ever form. Under the original system, electors chosen by the states would each vote for two candidates. The candidate who won the most votes would become president, while the person who won the second-highest number of votes would become vice president. Rivalries between Federalists and Antifederalists led to the formation of political parties, however, even before George Washington had left office. Though Washington was elected unanimously in 1789 and 1792, the elections of 1796 and 1800 were procedural disasters because of party maneuvering (see chapters 9 and 10). In 1796, Federalist John Adams was chosen as president, and his great rival, the Antifederalist Thomas Jefferson (whose party was called the Republican Party), became his vice president. In 1800, all the electors cast their two votes as one of two party blocs. Jefferson and his fellow Republican nominee, Aaron Burr, were tied with 73 votes each. The contest went to the House of Representatives, which finally elected Jefferson after 36 ballots. The Twelfth Amendment prevents these problems by requiring electors to vote separately for the president and vice president.

AMENDMENTS TO THE CONSTITUTION WITH ANNOTATIONS

Unratified Amendment

Titles of Nobility Amendment (proposed by Congress May 1, 1810)

If any citizen of the United States shall accept, claim, receive or retain any title of nobility or honor or shall, without the consent of Congress, accept and retain any present, pension, office or emolument of any kind whatever, from any emperor, king, prince or foreign power, such person shall cease to be a citizen of the United States, and shall be incapable of holding any office of trust or profit under them or either of them.

◆◆◆

This amendment would have extended Article 1, section 9, clause 8 of the Constitution, which prevents the awarding of titles by the United States and the acceptance of such awards from foreign powers without congressional consent. Historians speculate that general nervousness about the power of the emperor Napoleon, who was at that time extending France's empire throughout Europe, may have prompted the proposal. Though it fell one vote short of ratification, Congress and the American people thought the proposal had been ratified and it was included in many nineteenth-century editions of the Constitution.

The Civil War and Reconstruction Amendments (Thirteenth, Fourteenth, and Fifteenth Amendments)

In the four months between the election of Abraham Lincoln and his inauguration, more than 200 proposed constitutional amendments were presented to Congress as part of a desperate attempt to hold the rapidly dissolving Union together. Most of these were efforts to appease the southern states by protecting the right to own slaves or by disfranchising African Americans through constitutional amendment. None were able to win the votes required from Congress to send them to the states. The relatively innocuous Corwin Amendment seemed to be the only hope for preserving the Union by amending the Constitution.

The northern victors in the Civil War tried to restructure the Constitution just as the war had restructured the nation. Yet they were often divided in their goals. Some wanted to end slavery; others hoped for social and economic equality regardless of race; others hoped that extending the power of the ballot box to former slaves would help create a new political order. The debates over the Thirteenth, Fourteenth, and Fifteenth Amendments were bitter. Few of those who fought for these changes were satisfied with the amendments themselves; fewer still were satisfied with their interpretation. Although the amendments put an end to the legal status of slavery, it took nearly a hundred years after the amendments' passage before most of the descendants of former slaves could begin to experience the economic, social, and political equality the amendments had been intended to provide.

Unratified Amendment

Corwin Amendment (proposed by Congress March 2, 1861)

No amendment shall be made to the Constitution which will authorize or give to Congress the power to abolish or interfere, within any State, with the domestic institutions thereof, including that of persons held to labor or service by the laws of said State.

◆◆◆

Following the election of Abraham Lincoln, Congress scrambled to try to prevent the secession of the slaveholding states. House member Thomas Corwin of Ohio proposed the "unamendable" amendment in the hope that by protecting slavery where it existed, Congress would keep the southern states in the Union. Lincoln indicated his support for the proposed amendment in his first inaugural address. Only Ohio and Maryland ratified the Corwin Amendment before it was forgotten.

Amendment XIII

[Adopted 1865]

Section 1 Neither slavery nor involuntary servitude, except as a punishment for crime whereof the party shall have been duly convicted, shall exist within the United States, or any place subject to their jurisdiction.

Section 2 Congress shall have power to enforce this article by appropriate legislation.

◆◆◆

Although President Lincoln had abolished slavery in the Confederacy with the Emancipation Proclamation of 1863, abolitionists wanted to rid the entire country of slavery. The Thirteenth Amendment did this in a clear and straightforward manner. In February 1865, when the proposal was approved by the House, the gallery of the House was newly opened to black Americans who had a chance at last to see their government at work. Passage of the proposal was greeted by wild cheers from the gallery as well as tears on the House floor, where congressional representatives openly embraced one another.

The problem of ratification remained, however. The Union position was that the Confederate states were part of the country of thirty-six states. Therefore, twenty-seven states were needed to ratify the amendment. When Kentucky and Delaware rejected it, backers realized that without approval from at least four former Confederate states, the amendment would fail. Lincoln's successor, President Andrew Johnson, made ratification of the Thirteenth Amendment a condition for southern states to rejoin the Union. Under those terms, all the former Confederate states except Mississippi accepted the Thirteenth Amendment, and by the end of 1865 the amendment had become part of the Constitution and slavery had been prohibited in the United States.

Amendment XIV

[Adopted 1868]

Section 1   All persons born or naturalized in the United States, and subject to the jurisdiction thereof, are citizens of the United States and of the State wherein they reside. No State shall make or enforce any law which shall abridge the privileges or immunities of citizens of the United States; nor shall any State deprive any person of life, liberty, or property, without due process of law; nor deny to any person within its jurisdiction the equal protection of the laws.

Section 2   Representatives shall be appointed among the several States according to their respective numbers, counting the whole number of persons in each State, excluding Indians not taxed. But when the right to vote at any election for the choice of Electors for President and Vice-President of the United States, Representatives in Congress, the executive and judicial officers of a State, or the members of the legislature thereof, is denied to any of the male inhabitants of such State, being twenty-one years of age and citizens of the United States, or in any way abridged, except for participation in rebellion, or other crime, the basis of representation therein shall be reduced in the proportion which the number of such male citizens shall bear to the whole number of male citizens twenty-one years of age in such State.

Section 3   No person shall be a Senator or Representative in Congress, or Elector of President and Vice-President, or hold any office, civil or military, under the United States, or under any State, who, having previously taken an oath, as a member of Congress, or as an officer of the United States, or as a member of any State legislature, or as an executive or judicial officer of any State, to support the Constitution of the United States, shall have engaged in insurrection or rebellion against the same, or given aid or comfort to the enemies thereof. Congress may, by a vote of two-thirds of each house, remove such disability.

Section 4   The validity of the public debt of the United States, authorized by law, including debts incurred for payment of pensions and bounties for services in suppressing insurrection or rebellion, shall not be questioned. But neither the United States nor any State shall assume or pay any debt or obligation incurred in aid of insurrection or rebellion against the United States, or any claim for the loss or emancipation of any slave; but all such debts, obligations, and claims shall be held illegal and void.

Section 5   The Congress shall have power to enforce, by appropriate legislation, the provisions of this article.

◆ ◆ ◆

Without Lincoln's leadership in the reconstruction of the nation following the Civil War, it soon became clear that the Thirteenth Amendment needed additional constitutional support. Less than a year after Lincoln's assassination, Andrew Johnson was ready to bring the former Confederate states back into the Union with few changes in their governments or politics. Anxious Republicans drafted the Fourteenth Amendment to prevent that from happening. The most important provisions of this complex amendment made all native-born or naturalized persons American citizens and prohibited states from abridging the "privileges or immunities" of citizens; depriving them of "life, liberty, or property, without due process of law"; and denying them "equal protection of the laws." In essence, it made all ex-slaves citizens and protected the rights of all citizens against violation by their own state governments.

As occurred in the case of the Thirteenth Amendment, former Confederate states were forced to ratify the amendment as a condition of representation in the House and the Senate. The intentions of the Fourteenth Amendment, and how those intentions should be enforced, have been the most debated point of constitutional history. The terms due process *and* equal protection *have been especially troublesome. Was the amendment designed to outlaw racial segregation? Or was the goal simply to prevent the leaders of the rebellious South from gaining political power?*

The framers of the Fourteenth Amendment hoped Article 2 would produce black voters who would increase the power of the Republican Party. The federal government, however, never used its power to punish states for denying blacks their right to vote. Although the Fourteenth Amendment had an immediate impact in giving black Americans citizenship, it did nothing to protect blacks from the vengeance of whites once Reconstruction ended. In the late nineteenth and early twentieth centuries, section 1 of the Fourteenth Amendment was often used to protect business interests and strike down laws protecting workers on the grounds that the rights of "persons," that is, corporations, were protected by "due process." More recently, the Fourteenth Amendment has been used to justify school desegregation and affirmative action programs, as well as to dismantle such programs.

AMENDMENTS TO THE CONSTITUTION WITH ANNOTATIONS

Amendment XV

[Adopted 1870]

Section 1 The right of citizens of the United States to vote shall not be denied or abridged by the United States or by any State on account of race, color, or previous condition of servitude.

Section 2 The Congress shall have power to enforce this article by appropriate legislation.

◆◆◆

The Fifteenth Amendment was the last major piece of Reconstruction legislation. While earlier Reconstruction acts had already required black suffrage in the South, the Fifteenth Amendment extended black voting rights to the entire nation. Some Republicans felt morally obligated to do away with the double standard between North and South since many northern states had stubbornly refused to enfranchise blacks. Others believed that the freedman's ballot required the extra protection of a constitutional amendment to shield it from white counterattack. But partisan advantage also played an important role in the amendment's passage, since Republicans hoped that by giving the ballot to northern blacks, they could lessen their political vulnerability.

Many women's rights advocates had fought for the amendment. They had felt betrayed by the inclusion of the word male *in section 2 of the Fourteenth Amendment and were further angered when the proposed Fifteenth Amendment failed to prohibit denial of the right to vote on the grounds of sex as well as "race, color, or previous condition of servitude." In this amendment, for the first time, the federal government claimed the power to regulate the franchise, or vote. It was also the first time the Constitution placed limits on the power of the states to regulate access to the franchise. Although ratified in 1870, the amendment was not enforced until the twentieth century.*

The Progressive Amendments (Sixteenth–Nineteenth Amendments)

No amendments were added to the Constitution between the Civil War and the Progressive Era. America was changing, however, in fundamental ways. The rapid industrialization of the United States after the Civil War led to many social and economic problems. Hundreds of amendments were proposed, but none received enough support in Congress to be sent to the states. Some scholars believe that regional differences and rivalries were so strong during this period that it was almost impossible to gain a consensus on a constitutional amendment. During the Progressive Era, however, the Constitution was amended four times in seven years.

Amendment XVI

[Adopted 1913]

The Congress shall have power to lay and collect taxes on incomes, from whatever source derived, without apportionment among the several States, and without regard to any census or enumeration.

◆◆◆

Until passage of the Sixteenth Amendment, most of the money used to run the federal government came from customs duties and taxes on specific items, such as liquor. During the Civil War, the federal government taxed incomes as an emergency measure. Pressure to enact an income tax came from those who were concerned about the growing gap between rich and poor in the United States. The Populist Party began campaigning for a graduated income tax in 1892, and support continued to grow. By 1909, thirty-three proposed income tax amendments had been presented in Congress, but lobbying by corporate and other special interests had defeated them all. In June 1909, the growing pressure for an income tax, which had been endorsed by Presidents Roosevelt and Taft, finally pushed an amendment through the Senate. The required thirty-six states had ratified the amendment by February 1913.

Amendment XVII

[Adopted 1913]

Section 1 The Senate of the United States shall be composed of two Senators from each State, elected by the people thereof, for six years; and each Senator shall have one vote. The electors in each State shall have the qualifications requisite for electors of [voters for] the most numerous branch of the State legislatures.

Section 2 When vacancies happen in the representation of any State in the Senate, the executive authority of such State shall issue writs of election to fill such vacancies: Provided, that the Legislature of any State may empower the executive thereof to make temporary appointments until the people fill the vacancies by election as the Legislature may direct.

Section 3 This amendment shall not be so construed as to affect the election or term of any Senator chosen before it becomes valid as part of the Constitution.

◆◆◆

The framers of the Constitution saw the members of the House as the representatives of the people and the members of the Senate as the representatives of the states. Originally senators were to be chosen by the state legislators. According to reform advocates, however, the growth of private industry and transportation conglomerates during the Gilded Age had created a network of corruption in which wealth and power were exchanged for influence and votes in the Senate. Senator Nelson Aldrich, who represented Rhode Island in the late nineteenth and early twentieth centuries, for example, was known as "the senator from Standard Oil" because of his open support of special business interests.

Efforts to amend the Constitution to allow direct election of senators had begun in 1826, but since any proposal had to be approved by the Senate, reform seemed impossible. Progressives tried to gain influence in the Senate by instituting party caucuses and primary elections, which gave citizens the chance to express their choice of a senator who could then be officially elected by the state legislature. By 1910, fourteen of the country's thirty senators received popular votes through a state primary before the state legislature made its selection. Despairing of getting a proposal through the Senate, supporters of a direct-election amendment had begun in 1893 to seek a convention of representatives from two-thirds of the states to propose an amendment that could then be ratified. By 1905, thirty-one of forty-five states had endorsed such an amendment. Finally, in 1911, despite extraordinary opposition, a proposed amendment passed the Senate; by 1913, it had been ratified.

Amendment XVIII

[Adopted 1919; repealed 1933 by Amendment XXI]

Section 1   After one year from the ratification of this article the manufacture, sale, or transportation of intoxicating liquors within, the importation thereof into, or the exportation thereof from the United States and all territory subject to the jurisdiction thereof, for beverage purposes, is hereby prohibited.

Section 2   The Congress and the several States shall have concurrent power to enforce this article by appropriate legislation.

Section 3   This article shall be inoperative unless it shall have been ratified as an amendment to the Constitution by the legislatures of the several States, as provided by the Constitution, within seven years from the date of the submission thereof to the States by the Congress.

♦♦♦

The Prohibition Party, formed in 1869, began calling for a constitutional amendment to outlaw alcoholic beverages in 1872. A prohibition amendment was first proposed in the Senate in 1876 and was revived eighteen times before 1913. Between 1913 and 1919, another thirty-nine attempts were made to prohibit liquor in the United States through a constitutional amendment. Prohibition became a key element of the progressive agenda as reformers linked alcohol and

drunkenness to numerous social problems, including the corruption of immigrant voters. While opponents of such an amendment argued that it was undemocratic, supporters claimed that their efforts had widespread public support. The admission of twelve "dry" western states to the Union in the early twentieth century and the spirit of sacrifice during World War I laid the groundwork for passage and ratification of the Eighteenth Amendment in 1919. Opponents added a time limit to the amendment in the hope that they could thus block ratification, but this effort failed. (See also Amendment XXI.)

Amendment XIX

[Adopted 1920]

Section 1   The right of citizens of the United States to vote shall not be denied or abridged by the United States or by any State on account of sex.

Section 2   Congress shall have the power to enforce this article by appropriate legislation.

♦♦♦

Advocates of women's rights tried and failed to link woman suffrage to the Fourteenth and Fifteenth Amendments. Nonetheless, the effort for woman suffrage continued. Between 1878 and 1912, at least one and sometimes as many as four proposed amendments were introduced in Congress each year to grant women the right to vote. While over time women won very limited voting rights in some states, at both the state and federal levels opposition to an amendment for woman suffrage remained very strong. President Woodrow Wilson and other officials felt that the federal government should not interfere with the power of the states in this matter. Others worried that granting suffrage to women would encourage ethnic minorities to exercise their own right to vote. And many were concerned that giving women the vote would result in their abandoning traditional gender roles. In 1919, following a protracted and often bitter campaign of protest in which women went on hunger strikes and chained themselves to fences, an amendment was introduced with the backing of President Wilson. It narrowly passed the Senate (after efforts to limit the suffrage to white women failed) and was adopted in 1920 after Tennessee became the thirty-sixth state to ratify it.

Unratified Amendment

Child Labor Amendment (proposed by Congress June 2, 1924)

Section 1   The Congress shall have power to limit, regulate, and prohibit the labor of persons under eighteen years of age.

Section 2   The power of the several States is unimpaired by this article except that the operation of

AMENDMENTS TO THE CONSTITUTION WITH ANNOTATIONS

State laws shall be suspended to the extent necessary to give effect to legislation enacted by Congress.

◆◆◆

Throughout the late nineteenth and early twentieth centuries, alarm over the condition of child workers grew. Opponents of child labor argued that children worked in dangerous and unhealthy conditions, that they took jobs from adult workers, that they depressed wages in certain industries, and that states that allowed child labor had an economic advantage over those that did not. Defenders of child labor claimed that children provided needed income in many families, that working at a young age developed character, and that the effort to prohibit the practice constituted an invasion of family privacy.

In 1916, Congress passed a law that made it illegal to sell goods made by children through interstate commerce. The Supreme Court, however, ruled that the law violated the limits on the power of Congress to regulate interstate commerce. Congress then tried to penalize industries that used child labor by taxing such goods. This measure was also thrown out by the courts. In response, reformers set out to amend the Constitution. The proposed amendment was ratified by twenty-eight states, but by 1925, thirteen states had rejected it. Passage of the Fair Labor Standards Act in 1938, which was upheld by the Supreme Court in 1941, made the amendment irrelevant.

Amendment XX

[Adopted 1933]

Section 1 The terms of the President and Vice-President shall end at noon on the 20th day of January, and the terms of Senators and Representatives at noon on the 3rd day of January, of the years in which such terms would have ended if this article had not been ratified; and the terms of their successors shall then begin.

Section 2 The Congress shall assemble at least once in every year, and such meeting shall begin at noon on the 3rd day of January, unless they shall by law appoint a different day.

Section 3 If, at the time fixed for the beginning of the term of the President, the President-elect shall have died, the Vice-President-elect shall become President. If a President shall not have been chosen before the time fixed for the beginning of his term, or if the President-elect shall have failed to qualify, then the Vice-President-elect shall act as President until a President shall have qualified; and the Congress may by law provide for the case wherein neither a President-elect nor a Vice-President-elect shall have qualified, declaring who shall then act as President, or the manner in which one who is to act shall be selected, and such person shall act accordingly until a President or Vice-President shall have qualified.

Section 4 The Congress may by law provide for the case of the death of any of the persons from whom the House of Representatives may choose a President whenever the right of choice shall have devolved upon them, and for the case of the death of any of the persons from whom the Senate may choose a Vice-President whenever the right of choice shall have devolved upon them.

Section 5 Sections 1 and 2 shall take effect on the 15th day of October following the ratification of this article.

Section 6 This article shall be inoperative unless it shall have been ratified as an amendment to the Constitution by the Legislatures of three-fourths of the several States within seven years from the date of its submission.

◆◆◆

Until 1933, presidents took office on March 4. Since elections are held in early November and electoral votes are counted in mid-December, this meant that more than three months passed between the time a new president was elected and when he took office. Moving the inauguration to January shortened the transition period and allowed Congress to begin its term closer to the time of the president's inauguration. Although this seems like a minor change, an amendment was required because the Constitution specifies terms of office. This amendment also deals with questions of succession in the event that a president- or vice president-elect dies before assuming office. Section 3 also clarifies a method for resolving a deadlock in the electoral college.

Amendment XXI

[Adopted 1933]

Section 1 The eighteenth article of amendment to the Constitution of the United States is hereby repealed.

Section 2 The transportation or importation into any State, Territory, or Possession of the United States for delivery or use therein of intoxicating liquors, in violation of the laws thereof, is hereby prohibited.

Section 3 This article shall be inoperative unless it shall have been ratified as an amendment to the Constitution by conventions in the several States, as provided in the Constitution, within seven years from the date of the submission thereof to the States by the Congress.

◆◆◆

Widespread violation of the Volstead Act, the law enacted to enforce prohibition, made the United States a nation of lawbreakers. Prohibition caused more problems than it solved by encouraging crime, bribery, and corruption. Further, a coalition of liquor and beer manufacturers, personal liberty advocates, and constitutional scholars joined forces to challenge the amendment. By 1929, thirty proposed repeal amendments had been introduced in Congress, and the Democratic Party made repeal part of its platform in the 1932 presidential campaign. The Twenty-first Amendment was proposed in February 1933 and ratified less than a year later. The failure of the effort to enforce prohibition through a constitutional amendment has often been cited by opponents to subsequent efforts to shape public virtue and private morality.

Amendment XXII

[Adopted 1951]

Section 1 No person shall be elected to the office of the President more than twice, and no person who has held the office of President, or acted as President, for more than two years of a term to which some other person was elected President shall be elected to the office of President more than once. But this article shall not apply to any person holding the office of President when this Article was proposed by the Congress, and shall not prevent any person who may be holding the office of President, or acting as President, during the term within which this Article becomes operative from holding the office of President or acting as President during the remainder of such term.

Section 2 This article shall be inoperative unless it shall have been ratified as an amendment to the Constitution by the legislatures of three-fourths of the several States within seven years from the date of its submission to the States by the Congress.

♦♦♦

George Washington's refusal to seek a third term of office set a precedent that stood until 1912, when former President Theodore Roosevelt sought, without success, another term as an independent candidate. Democrat Franklin Roosevelt was the only president to seek and win a fourth term, though he did so amid great controversy. Roosevelt died in April 1945, a few months after the beginning of his fourth term. In 1946, Republicans won control of the House and the Senate, and early in 1947 a proposal for an amendment to limit future presidents to two four-year terms was offered to the states for ratification. Democratic critics of the Twenty-second Amendment charged that it was a partisan posthumous jab at Roosevelt.

Since the Twenty-second Amendment was adopted, however, the only presidents who might have been able to seek a third term, had it not existed, were Republicans Dwight Eisenhower and Ronald Reagan, and Democrat Bill Clinton. Since 1826, Congress has entertained 160 proposed amendments to limit the

president to one six-year term. Such amendments have been backed by fifteen presidents, including Gerald Ford and Jimmy Carter.

Amendment XXIII

[Adopted 1961]

Section 1 The District constituting the seat of Government of the United States shall appoint in such manner as the Congress may direct: A number of electors of President and Vice-President equal to the whole number of Senators and Representatives in Congress to which the District would be entitled if it were a State, but in no event more than the least populous State; they shall be in addition to those appointed by the States, but they shall be considered for the purposes of the election of President and Vice-President, to be electors appointed by a State; and they shall meet in the District and perform such duties as provided by the twelfth article of amendment.

Section 2 The Congress shall have the power to enforce this article by appropriate legislation.

♦♦♦

When Washington, D.C., was established as a federal district, no one expected that a significant number of people would make it their permanent and primary residence. A proposal to allow citizens of the district to vote in presidential elections was approved by Congress in June 1960 and was ratified on March 29, 1961.

Amendment XXIV

[Adopted 1964]

Section 1 The right of citizens of the United States to vote in any primary or other election for President or Vice-President, for electors for President or Vice-President, or for Senator or Representative in Congress, shall not be denied or abridged by the United States or any State by reason of failure to pay any poll tax or other tax.

Section 2 The Congress shall have the power to enforce this article by appropriate legislation.

♦♦♦

In the colonial and Revolutionary eras, financial independence was seen as necessary to political independence, and the poll tax was used as a requirement for voting. By the twentieth century, however, the poll tax was used mostly to bar poor people, especially southern blacks, from voting. While conservatives complained that the amendment interfered with states' rights, liberals thought that the amendment did not go far enough because it barred the poll tax only in national elections and not in state or local elections. The amendment was ratified in 1964,

AMENDMENTS TO THE CONSTITUTION WITH ANNOTATIONS

however, and two years later, the Supreme Court ruled that poll taxes in state and local elections also violated the equal protection clause of the Fourteenth Amendment.

Amendment XXV

[Adopted 1967]

Section 1   In case of the removal of the President from office or of his death or resignation, the Vice-President shall become President.

Section 2   Whenever there is a vacancy in the office of the Vice-President, the President shall nominate a Vice-President who shall take office upon confirmation by a majority vote of both Houses of Congress.

Section 3   Whenever the President transmits to the President pro tempore of the Senate and the Speaker of the House of Representatives his written declaration that he is unable to discharge the powers and duties of his office, and until he transmits to them a written declaration to the contrary, such powers and duties shall be discharged by the Vice-President as Acting President.

Section 4   Whenever the Vice-President and a majority of either the principal officers of the executive departments or of such other body as Congress may by law provide, transmit to the President pro tempore of the Senate and the Speaker of the House of Representatives their written declaration that the President is unable to discharge the powers and duties of his office, the Vice-President shall immediately assume the powers and duties of the office as Acting President.

Thereafter, when the President transmits to the President pro tempore of the Senate and the Speaker of the House of Representatives his written declaration that no inability exists, he shall resume the powers and duties of his office unless the Vice-President and a majority of either the principal officers of the executive department[s] or of such other body as Congress may by law provide, transmit within four days to the President pro tempore of the Senate and the Speaker of the House of Representatives their written declaration that the President is unable to discharge the powers and duties of his office. Thereupon Congress shall decide the issue, assembling within forty-eight hours for that purpose if not in session. If the Congress, within twenty-one days after receipt of the latter written declaration, or, if Congress is not in session, within twenty-one days after Congress is required to assemble, determines by two-thirds vote of both Houses that the President is unable to discharge the powers and duties of his office, the Vice-President shall continue to discharge the same as Acting President; otherwise, the President shall resume the powers and duties of his office.

♦ ♦ ♦

The framers of the Constitution established the office of vice president because someone was needed to preside over the Senate. The first president to die in office was William Henry Harrison, in 1841. Vice President John Tyler had himself sworn in as president, setting a precedent that was followed when seven later presidents died in office. The assassination of President James A. Garfield in 1881 posed a new problem, however. After he was shot, the president was incapacitated for two months before he died; he was unable to lead the country, while his vice president, Chester A. Arthur, was unable to assume leadership. Efforts to resolve questions of succession in the event of a presidential disability thus began with the death of Garfield.

In 1963, the assassination of President John F. Kennedy galvanized Congress to action. Vice President Lyndon Johnson was a chain smoker with a history of heart trouble. According to the 1947 Presidential Succession Act, the two men who stood in line to succeed him were the seventy-two-year-old Speaker of the House and the eighty-six-year-old president of the Senate. There were serious concerns that any of these men might become incapacitated while serving as chief executive. The first time the Twenty-fifth Amendment was used, however, was not in the case of presidential death or illness, but during the Watergate crisis. When Vice President Spiro T. Agnew was forced to resign following allegations of bribery and tax violations, President Richard M. Nixon appointed House Minority Leader Gerald R. Ford vice president. Ford became president following Nixon's resignation eight months later and named Nelson A. Rockefeller as his vice president. Thus, for more than two years, the two highest offices in the country were held by people who had not been elected to them.

Amendment XXVI

[Adopted 1971]

Section 1   The right of citizens of the United States, who are eighteen years of age or older, to vote shall not be denied or abridged by the United States or by any State on account of age.

Section 2   The Congress shall have power to enforce this article by appropriate legislation.

♦ ♦ ♦

Efforts to lower the voting age from twenty-one to eighteen began during World War II. Recognizing that those who were old enough to fight a war should have some say in the government policies that involved them in the war, Presidents Eisenhower, Johnson, and Nixon endorsed the idea. In 1970, the combined pressure of the antiwar movement and the demographic pressure of the baby boom generation led to a Voting Rights Act lowering the voting age in federal, state, and local elections.

In Oregon v. Mitchell (1970), the state of Oregon challenged the right of Congress to determine the age at which people could vote in state or local elections. The Supreme Court agreed with Oregon. Since the Voting Rights Act was ruled unconstitutional, the Constitution had to be amended to allow passage of a law that would lower the voting age. The amendment was ratified in a little more than three months, making it the most rapidly ratified amendment in U.S. history.

Unratified Amendment

Equal Rights Amendment (proposed by Congress March 22, 1972; seven-year deadline for ratification extended June 30, 1982)

Section 1 Equality of rights under the law shall not be denied or abridged by the United States or by any State on account of sex.

Section 2 The Congress shall have the power to enforce, by appropriate legislation, the provisions of this article.

Section 3 This amendment shall take effect two years after the date of ratification.

◆◆◆

In 1923, soon after women had won the right to vote, Alice Paul, a leading activist in the woman suffrage movement, proposed an amendment requiring equal treatment of men and women. Opponents of the proposal argued that such an amendment would invalidate laws that protected women and would make women subject to the military draft. After the 1964 Civil Rights Act was adopted, protective workplace legislation was removed anyway.

The renewal of the women's movement, as a by-product of the civil rights and antiwar movements, led to a revival of the Equal Rights Amendment (ERA) in Congress. Disagreements over language held up congressional passage of the proposed amendment, but on March 22, 1972, the Senate approved the ERA by a vote of 84 to 8, and it was sent to the states. Six states ratified the amendment within two days, and by the middle of 1973 the amendment seemed well on its way to adoption, with thirty of the needed thirty-eight states having ratified it. In the mid-1970s, however, a powerful "Stop ERA" campaign developed. The campaign portrayed the ERA as a threat to "family values" and traditional relationships between men and women. Although thirty-five states ultimately ratified the ERA, five of those state legislatures voted to rescind ratification, and the amendment was never adopted.

Unratified Amendment

D.C. Statehood Amendment (proposed by Congress August 22, 1978)

Section 1 For purposes of representation in the Congress, election of the President and Vice-President, and article V of this Constitution, the District constituting the seat of government of the United States shall be treated as though it were a State.

Section 2 The exercise of the rights and powers conferred under this article shall be by the people of the District constituting the seat of government, and as shall be provided by Congress.

Section 3 The twenty-third article of amendment to the Constitution of the United States is hereby repealed.

Section 4 This article shall be inoperative, unless it shall have been ratified as an amendment to the Constitution by the legislatures of three-fourths of the several states within seven years from the date of its submission.

◆◆◆

The 1961 ratification of the Twenty-third Amendment, giving residents of the District of Columbia the right to vote for a president and vice president, inspired an effort to give residents of the district full voting rights. In 1966, President Lyndon Johnson appointed a mayor and city council; in 1971, D.C. residents were allowed to name a nonvoting delegate to the House; and in 1981, residents were allowed to elect the mayor and city council. Congress retained the right to overrule laws that might affect commuters, the height of federal buildings, and selection of judges and prosecutors. The district's nonvoting delegate to Congress, Walter Fauntroy, lobbied fiercely for a congressional amendment granting statehood to the district. In 1978, a proposed amendment was approved and sent to the states. A number of states quickly ratified the amendment, but, like the ERA, the D.C. Statehood Amendment ran into trouble. Opponents argued that section 2 created a separate category of "nominal" statehood. They argued that the federal district should be eliminated and that the territory should be reabsorbed into the state of Maryland. Although these theoretical arguments were strong, some scholars believe that racist attitudes toward the predominantly black population of the city was also a factor leading to the defeat of the amendment.

Amendment XXVII

[Adopted 1992]

No law, varying the compensation for the services of the Senators and Representatives, shall take effect, until an election of Representatives shall have intervened.

♦ ♦ ♦

While the Twenty-sixth Amendment was the most rapidly ratified amendment in U.S. history, the Twenty-seventh Amendment had the longest journey to ratification. First proposed by James Madison in 1789 as part of the package that included the Bill of Rights, this amendment had been ratified by only six states by 1791. In 1873, however, it was ratified by Ohio to protest a massive retroactive salary increase by the federal government. Unlike later proposed amendments, this one came with no time limit on ratification. In the early 1980s, Gregory D. Watson, a University of Texas economics major, discovered the "lost" amendment and began a single-handed campaign to get state legislators to introduce it for ratification. In 1983, it was accepted by Maine. In 1984, it passed the Colorado legislature. Ratifications trickled in slowly until May 1992, when Michigan and New Jersey became the thirty-eighth and thirty-ninth states, respectively, to ratify. This amendment prevents members of Congress from raising their own salaries without giving voters a chance to vote them out of office before they can benefit from the raises.

THE CONSTITUTION OF THE CONFEDERATE STATES OF AMERICA

In framing the Constitution of the Confederate States, the authors adopted, with numerous small but significant changes and additions, the language of the Constitution of the United States, and followed the same order of arrangement of articles and sections. The revisions that they made to the original Constitution are shown here. The parts stricken out are enclosed in brackets, and the new matter added in framing the Confederate Constitution is printed in italics.

Adopted March 11, 1861

WE, the People of the [United States] *Confederated States, each State acting in its sovereign and independent character,* in order to form a [more perfect Union] *permanent Federal government,* establish Justice, insure domestic Tranquillity [provide for the common defense, promote the general Welfare], and secure the Blessings of Liberty to ourselves and our Posterity, *invoking the favor and guidance of Almighty God,* do ordain and establish this Constitution for the [United] *Confederate* States of America.

Article I

Section I All legislative Powers herein [granted] *delegated,* shall be vested in a Congress of the [United] *Confederate* States, which shall consist of a Senate and House of Representatives.

Section II The House of Representatives shall be composed of Members chosen every second Year by the People of the several States, and the Electors in each State shall *be citizens of the Confederate States, and* have the Qualifications requisite for Electors of the most numerous Branch of the State Legislature; *but no person of foreign birth, and not a citizen of the Confederate States, shall be allowed to vote for any officer, civil or political, State or federal.*

No Person shall be a Representative who shall not have attained to the Age of twenty-five Years, and [been seven Years a Citizen of the United] *be a citizen of the Confederate* States, and who shall not, when elected, be an Inhabitant of that State in which he shall be chosen.

Representatives and direct Taxes shall be apportioned among the several States which may be included within this [Union] *Confederacy,* according to their respective Numbers, which shall be determined by adding to the whole Number of free Persons, including those bound to Service for a Term of Years, and excluding Indians not taxed, three-fifths of all [other Persons] *slaves.* The actual Enumeration shall be made within three Years after the first Meeting of the Congress of the [United] *Confederate* States, and within every subsequent Term of ten Years, in such Manner as they shall by Law direct. The Number of Representatives shall not exceed one for every [thirty] *fifty* Thousand, but each State shall have at Least one Representative; and until such enumeration shall be made, the State of [New Hampshire shall be entitled to choose three, Massachusetts eight, Rhode Island and Providence Plantations one, Connecticut five, New York six, New Jersey four, Pennsylvania eight, Delaware one, Maryland six, Virginia ten, North Carolina five, South Carolina five, and Georgia three] *South Carolina shall be entitled to choose six, the State of Georgia ten, the State of Alabama nine, the State of Florida two, the State of Mississippi seven, the State of Louisiana six, and the State of Texas six.*

When vacancies happen in the Representation from any State, the Executive Authority thereof shall issue Writs of Election to fill such Vacancies.

The House of Representatives shall choose their Speaker and other Officers; and shall have the sole Power of Impeachment; *except that any judicial or other federal officer resident and acting solely within the limits of any State, may be impeached by a vote of two-thirds of both branches of the Legislature thereof.*

Section III   The Senate of the [United] *Confederate* States shall be composed of two Senators from each State, chosen by the Legislature thereof, for six Years, *at the regular session next immediately preceding the commencement of the term of service;* and each Senator shall have one Vote.

Immediately after they shall be assembled in Consequence of the first Election, they shall be divided as equally as may be into three Classes. The Seats of the Senators of the first Class shall be vacated at the Expiration of the second Year, of the second Class at the Expiration of the fourth Year, and of the third Class at the Expiration of the sixth Year, so that one-third may be chosen every second Year; and if Vacancies happen by Resignation, or otherwise, during the Recess of the Legislature of any State, the Executive thereof may make temporary Appointments until the next Meeting of the Legislature, which shall then fill such Vacancies.

No Person shall be a Senator who shall not have attained to the Age of thirty Years, and [been nine Years a Citizen of the United] *be a citizen of the Confederate* States, and who shall not, when elected, be an Inhabitant of that State for which he shall be chosen.

The Vice President of the [United] *Confederate* States shall be President of the Senate, but shall have no Vote, unless they be equally divided.

The Senate shall choose their other Officers, and also a President *pro tempore,* in the Absence of the Vice President, or when he shall exercise the Office of President of the United States.

The Senate shall have the sole Power to try all Impeachments. When sitting for that Purpose, they shall be on Oath or Affirmation. When the President of the [United] *Confederate* States is tried, the Chief Justice shall preside: And no Person shall be convicted without the Concurrence of two-thirds of the Members present.

Judgment in Cases of Impeachment shall not extend further than to removal from Office, and Disqualification to hold and enjoy any Office of honour, Trust or Profit under the [United] *Confederate* States; but the Party convicted shall nevertheless be liable and subject to Indictment, Trial, Judgment and Punishment, according to Law.

Section IV   The Times, Places and Manner of holding Elections for Senators and Representatives, shall be prescribed in each State by the Legislature thereof, *subject to the provisions of this Constitution;* but the Congress may at any time by Law make or alter such Regulations, except as to the *times and places* of choosing Senators.

The Congress shall assemble at least once in every Year, and such Meeting shall be on the first Monday in December, unless they shall by Law appoint a different Day.

Section V   Each House shall be the Judge of the Elections, Returns and Qualifications of its own Members, and a Majority of each shall constitute a Quorum to do Business; but a smaller Number may adjourn from day to day, and may be authorized to compel the Attendance of absent Members, in such Manner, and under such Penalties as each House may provide.

Each House may determine the Rules of its Proceedings, punish its Members for disorderly Behaviour, and, with the Concurrence of two-thirds *of the whole number* expel a Member.

Each House shall keep a Journal of its Proceedings, and from time to time publish the same, excepting such Parts as may in their Judgment require Secrecy; and the Yeas and Nays of the Members of either House on any question shall, at the Desire of one-fifth of those Present, be entered on the Journal.

Neither House, during the Session of Congress, shall, without the Consent of the other, adjourn for more than three days, nor to any other Place than that in which the two Houses shall be sitting.

Section VI   The Senators and Representatives shall receive a Compensation for their Services, to be ascertained by Law, and paid out of the Treasury of the [United] *Confederate* States. They shall in all Cases, except Treason [Felony] and Breach of the Peace, be privileged from Arrest during their Attendance at the Session of their respective Houses, and in going to and returning from the same; and for any Speech or Debate in either House, they shall not be questioned in any other Place.

No Senator or Representative shall, during the Time for which he was elected, be appointed to any civil Office under the Authority of the [United] *Confederate* States, which shall have been created, or the Emoluments whereof shall have been increased during such time; and no Person holding any Office under the [United] *Confederate* States, shall be a Member of either House during his Continuance in Office. *But Congress may, by law, grant to the principal officers in each of the executive departments a seat upon the floor of either House, with the privilege of discussing any measures appertaining to his department.*

Section VII   All Bills for raising Revenue shall originate in the House of Representatives; but the Senate may propose or concur with Amendments as on other Bills.

Every Bill which shall have passed [the House of Representatives and the Senate] *both Houses,* shall, before it become a Law, be presented to the President of the [United] *Confederate* States; If he approve he shall sign it, but if not he shall return it, with his Objections to that House in which it shall have originated, who shall enter the Objections at

THE CONSTITUTION OF THE CONFEDERATE STATES OF AMERICA

large on their Journal, and proceed to reconsider it. If after such Reconsideration two-thirds of that House shall agree to pass the Bill, it shall be sent, together with the Objections, to the other House, by which it shall likewise be reconsidered, and if approved by two-thirds of that House, it shall become a Law. But in all *such* Cases the Votes of both Houses shall be determined by Yeas and Nays, and the Names of the Persons voting for and against the Bill shall be entered on the Journal of each House respectively. If any Bill shall not be returned by the President within ten Days (Sundays excepted) after it shall have been presented to him, the Same shall be a law, in like Manner as if he had signed it, unless the Congress by their Adjournment prevent its return, in which Case it shall not be a Law. *The President may approve any appropriation and disapprove any other appropriation in the same bill. In such case he shall, in signing the bill, designate the appropriation disapproved, and shall return a copy of such appropriation, with his objections, to the House in which the bill shall have originated; and the same proceedings shall then be had as in case of other bills disapproved by the President.*

Every Order, Resolution, or Vote to which the Concurrence of [the Senate and House of Representatives] *both Houses* may be necessary (except on a question of Adjournment), shall be presented to the President of the [United] *Confederate* States; and before the Same shall take Effect, shall be approved by him, or being disapproved by him, [shall] *may* be repassed by two-thirds of [the Senate and House of Representatives] *both Houses,* according to the Rules and Limitations prescribed in the Case of a Bill.

Section VIII   The Congress shall have Power

To lay and collect Taxes, Duties, Imposts and *Excises, for revenue necessary* to pay the Debts [and], provide for the common Defense [and general Welfare of the United States; but], *and carry on the government of the Confederate States; but no bounties shall be granted from the treasury, nor shall any duties, or taxes, or importation from foreign nations be laid to promote or foster any branch of industry; and* all Duties, Imposts and Excises shall be uniform throughout the [United] *Confederate* States;

To borrow Money on the credit of the [United] *Confederate* States;

To regulate Commerce with foreign Nations, and among the several States, and with the Indian Tribes; *but neither this, nor any other clause contained in this Constitution, shall ever be construed to delegate the power to Congress to appropriate money for any internal improvement intended to facilitate commerce; except for the purpose of furnishing lights, beacons, and buoys, and other aids to navigation upon the coasts, and the improvement of harbors, and the removing of obstructions in river navigation; in all such cases such duties shall be laid on the navigation facilitated thereby, as may be necessary to pay the costs and expenses thereof;*

To establish an uniform Rule of Naturalization, and uniform Laws on the subject of Bankruptcies throughout the [United] *Confederate* States; *but no law of Congress shall discharge any debt contracted before the passage of the same;*

To coin Money, regulate the Value thereof, and of foreign Coin, and fix the Standard of Weights and Measures;

To provide for the Punishment of counterfeiting the Securities and current Coin of the [United] *Confederate* States;

To establish Post Offices and post [Roads] *routes; but the expenses of the Postoffice Department, after the first day of March, in the year of our Lord eighteen hundred and sixty-three, shall be paid out of its own revenues;*

To promote the progress of Science and useful Arts, by securing for limited Times to Authors and Inventors the exclusive Right to their respective Writings and Discoveries;

To constitute Tribunals inferior to the supreme Court;

To define and punish Piracies and Felonies committed on the high Seas, and Offences against the Law of Nations;

To declare War, grant Letters of Marque and Reprisal, and make Rules concerning Captures on Land and Water;

To raise and support Armies, but no Appropriation of Money to that Use shall be for a longer Term than two Years;

To provide and maintain a Navy;

To make Rules for the Government and Regulation of the land and naval Forces;

To provide for calling forth the Militia to execute the Laws of the [Union] *Confederate States,* suppress Insurrections and repel Invasions;

To provide for organizing, arming, and disciplining the Militia and for governing such Part of them as may be employed in the Service of the [United] *Confederate* States, reserving to the States respectively, the Appointment of the Officers, and the Authority of training the Militia according to the Discipline prescribed by Congress;

To exercise exclusive Legislation in all Cases whatsoever, over such District (not exceeding ten Miles square) as may, by Cession of particular States, and the Acceptance of Congress, become the Seat of the Government of the [United] *Confederate* States, and to exercise like Authority over all Places purchased by the Consent of the Legislature of the State in which the Same shall be, for the Erection of Forts, Magazines, Arsenals, Dock Yards, and other needful Buildings;—And

To make all Laws which shall be necessary and proper for carrying into Execution the foregoing Powers, and all other Powers vested by this Constitution in the Government of the [United] *Confederate* States or in any Department or Officer thereof.

Section IX [The Migration or Importation of such Persons as any of the States now existing shall think proper to admit, shall not be prohibited by the Congress prior to the Year one thousand eight hundred and eight, but a Tax or Duty may be imposed on such Importation, not exceeding ten dollars for each Person.] *The importation of negroes of the African race from any foreign country other than the slaveholding States or territories of the United States of America, is hereby forbidden; and Congress is required to pass such laws as shall effectually prevent the same. Congress shall also have power to prohibit the introduction of slaves from any State not a member of, or territory not belonging to, this Confederacy.*

The Privilege of the Writ of Habeas Corpus shall not be suspended, unless when in Cases of Rebellion or Invasion the public Safety may require it. No Bill of Attainder or ex post facto Law, *or law denying or impairing the right of property in negro slaves,* shall be passed.

No Capitation, or other direct, Tax shall be laid, unless in Proportion to the Census or Enumeration herein before directed to be taken.

No Tax or Duty shall be laid on Articles exported from any State, *except by a vote of two-thirds of both Houses.*

No Preference shall be given by any Regulation of Commerce or Revenue to the Ports of one State over those of another; nor shall Vessels bound to, or from, one State, be obliged to enter, clear, or pay Duties in another.

No Money shall be drawn from the Treasury, but in Consequence of Appropriations made by Law; and a regular Statement and Account of the Receipts and Expenditures of all public Money shall be published from time to time.

Congress shall appropriate no money from the Treasury except by a vote of two-thirds of both Houses, taken by yeas and nays, unless it be asked and estimated for by some one of the heads of departments and submitted to Congress by the President; or for the purpose of paying its own expenses and contingencies; or for the payment of claims against the Confederate States, the justice of which shall have been officially declared by a tribunal for the investigation of claims against the Government, which it is hereby made the duty of Congress to establish.

All bills appropriating money shall specify in Federal currency the exact amount of each appropriation and the purposes for which it is made; and Congress shall grant no extra compensation to any public contractor, officer, agent or servant, after such contract shall have been made or such service rendered.

No Title of Nobility shall be granted by the [United] *Confederate* States; and no Person holding any Office of Profit or Trust under them, shall, without the Consent of the Congress, accept of any present, Emolument, Office, or Title, of any kind whatever, from any King, Prince or foreign State.

[Here the framers of the Confederate Constitution insert the U.S. Bill of Rights.]

Congress shall make no law respecting an establishment of religion, or prohibiting the free exercise thereof; or abridging the freedom of speech, or of the press; or the right of the people peaceably to assemble, and to petition the Government for a redress of grievances.

A well-regulated Militia, being necessary to the security of a free State, the right of the people to keep and bear Arms shall not be infringed.

No Soldier shall, in time of peace, be quartered in any house, without the consent of the Owner, nor in time of war, but in a manner to be prescribed by law.

The right of the people to be secure in their persons, houses, papers, and effects, against unreasonable searches and seizures, shall not be violated, and no Warrants shall issue, but upon probable cause, supported by Oath or affirmation, and particularly describing the place to be searched, and the persons or things to be seized.

No person shall be held to answer for a capital, or otherwise infamous crime, unless on a presentment or indictment of a Grand Jury, except in cases arising in the land or naval forces, or in the Militia, when in actual service in time of War or public danger; nor shall any person be subject for the same offence to be twice put in jeopardy of life or limb; nor shall be compelled in any Criminal Case to be a witness against himself, nor be deprived of life, liberty or property without due process of law; nor shall private property be taken for public use, without just compensation.

In all criminal prosecutions, the accused shall enjoy the right to a speedy and public trial, by an impartial jury of the State and district wherein the crime shall have been committed, which district shall have been previously ascertained by law, and to be informed of the nature and cause of the accusation; to be confronted with the witnesses against him; to have Compulsory process for obtaining Witnesses in his favour, and to have the Assistance of Counsel for his defence.

In Suits at common law, where the value in controversy shall exceed twenty dollars, the right of trial by jury shall be preserved, and no fact tried by a jury shall be otherwise reexamined in any Court of the [United] *Confederate* States, than according to the rules of the common law.

Excessive bail shall not be required, nor excessive fines imposed, nor cruel and unusual punishments inflicted.

Every law or resolution having the force of law, shall relate to but one subject, and that shall be expressed in the title.

Section X No State shall enter into any Treaty, Alliance, or Confederation; grant Letters of Marque and Reprisal; coin Money; [emit Bills of Credit;] make any Thing but gold and silver Coin a Tender in Payment of Debts; pass any Bill of Attainder, *or*

THE CONSTITUTION OF THE CONFEDERATE STATES OF AMERICA

ex post facto Law, or Law impairing the Obligation of Contracts, or grant any Title of Nobility.

No State shall, without the consent of the Congress, lay any Imposts or Duties on Imports or Exports, except what may be absolutely necessary for executing its inspection Laws: and the net Produce of all Duties and Imposts, laid by any State on Imports or Exports, shall be for the Use of the Treasury of the [United] *Confederate* States; and all such Laws shall be subject to the Revision and Control of the Congress.

No State shall, without the Consent of Congress, lay any Duty of Tonnage, *except on sea-going vessels, for the improvement of its rivers and harbors navigated by the said vessels; but such duties shall not conflict with any treaties of the Confederate States with foreign nations; and any surplus of revenue thus derived shall, after making such improvement, be paid into the common treasury; nor shall any State* keep Troops, or Ships of War in time of Peace, enter into any Agreement or Compact with another State, or with a foreign Power, or engage in War, unless actually invaded, or in such imminent Danger as will not admit of Delay. *But when any river divides or flows through two or more States, they may enter into compacts with each other to improve the navigation thereof.*

Article II

Section I [The executive Power shall be vested in a President of the United States of America. He shall hold his Office during the Term of four Years, and, together with the Vice President, chosen for the same Term, be elected, as follows:] *The executive power shall be vested in a President of the Confederate States of America. He and the Vice President shall hold their offices for the term of six years; but the President shall not be re-eligible. The President and Vice President shall be elected as follows:*

Each State shall appoint in such Manner as the Legislature thereof may direct, a Number of Electors, equal to the whole Number of Senators and Representatives to which the State may be entitled in the Congress; but no Senator or Representative, or Person holding an Office of Trust or Profit under the [United] *Confederate* States, shall be appointed an Elector.

The Electors shall meet in their respective States, and vote by ballot for President and Vice President, one of whom, at least, shall not be an inhabitant of the same State with themselves; they shall name in their ballots the person voted for as President, and in distinct ballots the person voted for as Vice President, and they shall make distinct lists of all persons voted for as President, and of all persons voted for as Vice President, and of the number of votes for each, which lists they shall sign and certify, and transmit sealed to the seat of the government of the [United] *Confederate* States, directed to the President of the Senate;—The President of the Senate

shall, in the presence of the Senate and House of Representatives, open all the certificates and the votes shall then be counted;—The person having the greatest number of votes for President shall be the President, if such number be a majority of the whole number of Electors appointed; and if no person have such majority, then from the persons having the highest numbers not exceeding three on the list of those voted for as President, the House of Representatives shall choose immediately, by ballot, the President. But in choosing the President, the votes shall be taken by States, the representation from each State having one vote; a quorum for this purpose shall consist of a member or members from two-thirds of the States, and a majority of all the States shall be necessary to a choice. And if the House of Representatives shall not choose a President whenever the right of choice shall devolve upon them, before the fourth day of March next following, then the Vice President shall act as President, as in the case of the death or other constitutional disability of the President. The person having the greatest number of votes as Vice President shall be the Vice President, if such number be a majority of the whole number of Electors appointed, and if no person have a majority, then from the two highest numbers on the list the Senate shall choose the Vice President; a quorum for the purpose shall consist of two-thirds of the whole number of Senators, and a majority of the whole number shall be necessary to a choice. But no person constitutionally ineligible to the office of President shall be eligible to that of Vice President of the [United] *Confederate* States.

The Congress may determine the Time of choosing the Electors, and the Day on which they shall give their Votes; which Day shall be the same throughout the [United] *Confederate* States.

No Person except a natural-born Citizen [or a Citizen of the United States] *of the Confederate States, or a citizen thereof,* at the time of the Adoption of this Constitution, *or a citizen thereof born in the United States prior to the 20th of December, 1860,* shall be eligible to the Office of President; neither shall any Person be eligible to that Office who shall not have attained to the Age of thirty-five Years, and been fourteen Years a Resident within the [United States] *limits of the Confederate States, as they may exist at the time of his election.*

In Cases of the Removal of the President from Office, or of his Death, Resignation, or Inability to discharge the Powers and Duties of the said Office, the same shall devolve on the Vice President, and the Congress may by Law provide for the Case of Removal, Death, Resignation, or Inability, both of the President and Vice President, declaring what Officer shall then act as President, and such Officer shall act accordingly, until the Disability be removed, or a President shall be elected.

The President shall, at stated Times, receive for his Services, a Compensation, which shall neither be increased nor diminished during the Period for which he shall have been elected, and he shall not receive within that Period any other Emolument from the [United] *Confederate* States or any of them.

Before he enters on the Execution of his Office, he shall take the following Oath or Affirmation—"I do solemnly swear (or affirm) that I will faithfully execute the Office of President of the [United] *Confederate* States, and will to the best of my Ability, preserve, protect and defend the Constitution [of the United States] *thereof.*"

Section II   The President shall be Commander in Chief of the Army and Navy of the [United] *Confederate* States, and of the Militia of the several States, when called into the actual Service of the [United] *Confederate* States; he may require the Opinion, in writing, of the principal Officer in each of the executive Departments, upon any Subject relating to the Duties of their respective Offices, and he shall have Power to grant Reprieves and Pardons for Offenses against the [United] *Confederate* States, except in Cases of Impeachment.

He shall have Power, by and with the Advice and Consent of the Senate, to make Treaties, provided two-thirds of the Senators present concur; and he shall nominate, and by and with the Advice and Consent of the Senate, shall appoint Ambassadors, other public Ministers and Consuls, Judges of the supreme Court, and all other Officers of the [United] *Confederate* States, whose Appointments are not herein otherwise provided for, and which shall be established by Law: but the Congress may by Law vest the Appointment of such inferior Officers, as they think proper, in the President alone, in the Courts of Law, or in the Heads of Departments. *The principal officer in each of the executive departments, and all persons connected with the diplomatic service, may be removed from office at the pleasure of the President. All other civil officers of the executive department may be removed at any time by the President, or other appointing power, when their services are unnecessary, or for dishonesty, incapacity, inefficiency, misconduct, or neglect of duty; and when so removed, the removal shall be reported to the Senate, together with the reasons therefor.*

The President shall have Power to fill [up] all Vacancies that may happen during the Recess of the Senate, by granting Commissions which shall expire at the End of their next Session.

Section III   [He] *The President* shall from time to time give to the Congress Information of the State of the [Union] *Confederacy,* and recommend to their Consideration such Measures as he shall judge necessary and expedient; he may, on extraordinary Occasions, convene both Houses, or either of them, and in Case of Disagreement between them, with Respect to the Time of Adjournment, he may adjourn them to such Time as he shall think proper;

he shall receive Ambassadors and other public Ministers; he shall take Care that the Laws be faithfully executed, and shall Commission all the officers of the [United] *Confederate* States.

Section IV   The President, Vice President and all civil Officers of the [United] *Confederate* States, shall be removed from Office or Impeachment for, and Conviction of, Treason, Bribery, or other high Crimes and Misdemeanors.

Article III

Section I   The judicial Power of the [United] *Confederate* States shall be vested in one [supreme] *Superior* Court, and in such inferior Courts as the Congress may from time to time ordain and establish. The Judges, both of the supreme and inferior Courts, shall hold their Offices during good Behavior, and shall, at stated Times, receive for their Services a Compensation, which shall not be diminished during their Continuance in Office.

Section II   The judicial Power shall extend to all cases [in Law and Equity, arising under this Constitution], *arising under this Constitution, in law and equity,* the Laws of the [United] *Confederate* States, and Treaties made, or which shall be made, under their Authority;—to all Cases affecting Ambassadors, other public Ministers, and Consuls;—to all Cases of admiralty and maritime Jurisdiction;—to Controversies to which the [United] *Confederate* States shall be a Party;—to Controversies between two or more States;—between a State and Citizens of another State *where the State is plaintiff;*—*between* Citizens *claiming lands under grants* of different States,—[between Citizens of the same State claiming Lands under Grants of different States,] and between a State, or the Citizens thereof, and foreign States, Citizens or Subjects; *but no State shall be sued by a citizen or subject of any foreign State.*

In all Cases affecting Ambassadors, other public Ministers and Consuls, and those in which a State shall be Party, the supreme Court shall have original Jurisdiction. In all the other Cases before mentioned, the supreme Court shall have appellate Jurisdiction, both as to Law and Fact, with such Exceptions, and under such Regulations as the Congress shall make.

The Trial of all Crimes, except in Cases of Impeachment, shall be by Jury; and such Trial shall be held in the State where the said Crime[s] shall have been committed; but when not committed within any State, the Trial shall be at such Place or Places as the Congress may by Law have directed.

Section III   Treason against the [United] *Confederate* States shall consist only in levying War against them,

THE CONSTITUTION OF THE CONFEDERATE STATES OF AMERICA

or in adhering to their Enemies, giving them Aid and Comfort. No Person shall be convicted of Treason unless on the Testimony of two Witnesses to the same overt Act, or on Confession in open Court.

The Congress shall have Power to declare the Punishment of Treason, but no Attainder of Treason shall work Corruption of Blood, or Forfeiture except during the Life of the Person attainted.

Article IV

Section I Full Faith and Credit shall be given in each State to the public Acts, Records, and judicial Proceedings of every other State. And the Congress may by general Laws prescribe the Manner in which such Acts, Records and Proceedings shall be proved, and the Effect thereof.

Section II The Citizens of each State shall be entitled to all Privileges and Immunities of Citizens in the several States, *and shall have the right of transit and sojourn in any State of this Confederacy, with their slaves and other property; and the right of property in such slaves shall not be impaired.*

A Person charged in any State with Treason, Felony, or other Crime, who shall flee from Justice, and be found in another State, shall on Demand of the executive Authority of the State from which he fled, be delivered up, to be removed to the State having Jurisdiction of the Crime.

No *slave or* Person held to Service or Labor in [one State] *any State or Territory of the Confederate States* under the Laws thereof, escaping *or unlawfully carried* into another, shall, in Consequence of any Law or Regulation therein, be discharged from such Service or Labor, but shall be delivered up on Claim of the Party to whom such *slave belongs, or to whom such* Service or Labor may be due.

Section III [New States may be admitted by the Congress into this Union;] *Other States may be admitted into this Confederacy by a vote of two-thirds of the whole House of Representatives and two-thirds of the Senate, the Senate voting by States;* but no new State shall be formed or erected within the Jurisdiction of any other State; nor any State be formed by the Junction of two or more States, or Parts of States, without the Consent of the Legislatures of the States concerned as well as of the Congress.

The Congress shall have Power to dispose of and make all needful Rules and Regulations [respecting the Territory or other Property belonging to the United States; and nothing in this Constitution shall be so construed as to Prejudice any Claims of the United States, or of any particular State] *concerning the property of the Confederate States, including the lands thereof.*

The Confederate States may acquire new territory, and Congress shall have power to legislate and provide governments for the inhabitants of all territory belong- *ing to the Confederate States lying without the limits of the several States, and may permit them, at such times and in such manner as it may by law provide, to form States to be admitted into the Confederacy. In all such territory the institution of negro slavery as it now exists in the Confederate States shall be recognized and protected by Congress and by the territorial government, and the inhabitants of the several Confederate States and territories shall have the right to take to such territory any slaves lawfully held by them in any of the States or Territories of the Confederate States.*

[Section IV] The [United] *Confederate* States shall guarantee to every State [in this Union] *that now is, or hereafter may become, a member of this Confederacy,* a Republican Form of Government, and shall protect each of them against Invasion; and on Application of the Legislature, or of the Executive (when the Legislature [cannot be convened] *is not in session*) against domestic Violence.

Article V

[The Congress, whenever two-thirds of both Houses shall deem it necessary, shall propose Amendments to this Constitution, or on the Application of the Legislatures of two-thirds of the several States, shall call a Convention for proposing Amendments, which, in either Case, shall be valid to all Intents and Purposes, as Part of this Constitution, when ratified by the Legislatures of three-fourths of the several States, or by Conventions in three-fourths thereof, as the one or the other Mode of Ratification may be proposed by the Congress; Provided that no Amendment which may be made prior to the Year one thousand eight hundred and eight shall in any Manner affect the first and fourth Clauses in the Ninth Section of the first Article; and that no State, without its Consent, shall be deprived of its equal Suffrage in the Senate.]

Upon the demand of any three States, legally assembled in their several Conventions, the Congress shall summon a Convention of all the States, to take into consideration such amendments to the Constitution as the said States shall concur in suggesting at the time when the said demand is made; and should any of the proposed amendments to the Constitution be agreed on by the said Convention—voting by States—and the same be ratified by the Legislatures of two-thirds of the several States, or by Conventions in two-thirds thereof—as the one or the other mode of ratification may be proposed by the general Convention—they shall henceforward form a part of this Constitution. But no State shall, without its consent, be deprived of its equal representation in the Senate.

Article VI

The Government established by this Constitution is the successor of the Provisional Government of the

Confederate States of America, and all laws passed by the latter shall continue in force until the same shall be repealed or modified; and all the officers appointed by the same shall remain in office until their successors are appointed and qualified or the offices abolished.

All Debts contracted and Engagements entered into, before the Adoption of this Constitution, shall be as valid against the [United] *Confederate* States under this Constitution, as under the [Confederation] *Provisional Government.*

This Constitution and the Laws of the [United] *Confederate* States [which shall be] made in Pursuance thereof; and all Treaties made, or which shall be made, under the authority of the [United] *Confederate* States, shall be the supreme Law of the Land; and the Judges in every State shall be bound thereby, any Thing in the Constitution or Laws of any State to the Contrary notwithstanding.

The Senators and Representatives before mentioned, and the Members of the several State Legislatures, and all executive and judicial Officers, both of the [United] *Confederate* States and of the several States, shall be bound by Oath or Affirmation, to support this Constitution; but no religious Test shall ever be required as a Qualification to any Office or public Trust under the [United] *Confederate* States.

The enumeration in the Constitution, of certain rights, shall not be construed to deny or disparage others retained by the people *of the several States.*

The powers not delegated to the [United] *Confederate* States by the Constitution, nor prohibited by it to the States, are reserved to the States respectively, or to the people.

Article VII

The Ratification of the Conventions of [nine] *five* States shall be sufficient for the Establishment of this Constitution between the States so ratifying the same.

When five States shall have ratified this Constitution, in the manner before specified, the Congress under the Provisional Constitution shall prescribe the time for holding the election of President and Vice President; and for the meeting of the electoral college; and for counting the votes and inaugurating the President. They shall also prescribe the time for holding the first election of members of Congress under this Constitution, and the time for assembling the same. Until the assembling of such Congress, the Congress under the Provisional Constitution shall continue to exercise the legislative powers granted them, not extending beyond the time limited by the Constitution of the Provisional Government.

[Done in Convention by the Unanimous Consent of the States present, the Seventeenth Day of September in the Year of our Lord one thousand seven hundred and eighty-seven and of the Independence of the United States of America the Twelfth.] *Adopted unanimously March 11, 1861.*

Facts and Figures: Government, Economy, and Demographics

U.S. Politics and Government

PRESIDENTIAL ELECTIONS

Year	Candidates	Parties	Popular Vote	Percentage of Popular Vote	Electoral Vote	Percentage of Voter Participation
1789	**GEORGE WASHINGTON (Va.)***				69	
	John Adams				34	
	Others				35	
1792	**GEORGE WASHINGTON (Va.)**				132	
	John Adams				77	
	George Clinton				50	
	Others				5	
1796	**JOHN ADAMS (Mass.)**	Federalist			71	
	Thomas Jefferson	Democratic-Republican			68	
	Thomas Pinckney	Federalist			59	
	Aaron Burr	Dem.-Rep.			30	
	Others				48	
1800	**THOMAS JEFFERSON (Va.)**	Dem.-Rep.			73	
	Aaron Burr	Dem.-Rep.			73	
	John Adams	Federalist			65	
	C. C. Pinckney	Federalist			64	
	John Jay	Federalist			1	
1804	**THOMAS JEFFERSON (Va.)**	Dem.-Rep.			162	
	C. C. Pinckney	Federalist			14	
1808	**JAMES MADISON (Va.)**	Dem.-Rep.			122	
	C. C. Pinckney	Federalist			47	
	George Clinton	Dem.-Rep.			6	
1812	**JAMES MADISON (Va.)**	Dem.-Rep.			128	
	De Witt Clinton	Federalist			89	
1816	**JAMES MONROE (Va.)**	Dem.-Rep.			183	
	Rufus King	Federalist			34	
1820	**JAMES MONROE (Va.)**	Dem.-Rep.			231	
	John Quincy Adams	Dem.-Rep.			1	
1824	**JOHN Q. ADAMS (Mass.)**	Dem.-Rep.	108,740	30.5	84	26.9
	Andrew Jackson	Dem.-Rep.	153,544	43.1	99	
	William H. Crawford	Dem.-Rep.	46,618	13.1	41	
	Henry Clay	Dem.-Rep.	47,136	13.2	37	
1828	**ANDREW JACKSON (Tenn.)**	Democratic	647,286	56.0	178	57.6
	John Quincy Adams	National Republican	508,064	44.0	83	

*State of residence when elected president.

Year	Candidates	Parties	Popular Vote	Percentage of Popular Vote	Electoral Vote	Percentage of Voter Participation
1832	**ANDREW JACKSON (Tenn.)**	Democratic	687,502	55.0	219	55.4
	Henry Clay	National Republican	530,189	42.4	49	
	John Floyd	Independent			11	
	William Wirt	Anti-Mason	33,108	2.6	7	
1836	**MARTIN VAN BUREN (N.Y.)**	Democratic	765,483	50.9	170	57.8
	W. H. Harrison	Whig			73	
	Hugh L. White	Whig	739,795	49.1	26	
	Daniel Webster	Whig			14	
	W. P. Mangum	Independent			11	
1840	**WILLIAM H. HARRISON (Ohio)**	Whig	1,274,624	53.1	234	80.2
	Martin Van Buren	Democratic	1,127,781	46.9	60	
	J. G. Birney	Liberty	7,069		—	
1844	**JAMES K. POLK (Tenn.)**	Democratic	1,338,464	49.6	170	78.9
	Henry Clay	Whig	1,300,097	48.1	105	
	J. G. Birney	Liberty	62,300	2.3	—	
1848	**ZACHARY TAYLOR (La.)**	Whig	1,360,967	47.4	163	72.7
	Lewis Cass	Democratic	1,222,342	42.5	127	
	Martin Van Buren	Free-Soil	291,263	10.1	—	
1852	**FRANKLIN PIERCE (N.H.)**	Democratic	1,601,117	50.9	254	69.6
	Winfield Scott	Whig	1,385,453	44.1	42	
	John P. Hale	Free-Soil	155,825	5.0	—	
1856	**JAMES BUCHANAN (Pa.)**	Democratic	1,832,995	45.3	174	78.9
	John C. Frémont	Republican	1,339,932	33.1	114	
	Millard Fillmore	American	871,731	21.6	8	
1860	**ABRAHAM LINCOLN (Ill.)**	Republican	1,865,593	39.8	180	81.2
	Stephen A. Douglas	Democratic	1,382,713	29.5	12	
	John C. Breckinridge	Democratic	848,356	18.1	72	
	John Bell	Union	592,906	12.6	39	
1864	**ABRAHAM LINCOLN (Ill.)**	Republican	2,206,938	55.0	212	73.8
	George B. McClellan	Democratic	1,803,787	45.0	21	
1868	**ULYSSES S. GRANT (Ill.)**	Republican	3,012,833	52.7	214	78.1
	Horatio Seymour	Democratic	2,703,249	47.3	80	
1872	**ULYSSES S. GRANT (Ill.)**	Republican	3,597,132	55.6	286	71.3
	Horace Greeley	Democratic; Liberal Republican	2,834,125	43.9	66	
1876	**RUTHERFORD B. HAYES (Ohio)**	Republican	4,036,572	48.0	185	81.8
	Samuel J. Tilden	Democratic	4,284,020	51.0	184	
1880	**JAMES A. GARFIELD (Ohio)**	Republican	4,454,416	48.5	214	79.4
	Winfield S. Hancock	Democratic	4,444,952	48.1	155	
1884	**GROVER CLEVELAND (N.Y.)**	Democratic	4,879,507	48.5	219	77.5
	James G. Blaine	Republican	4,850,293	48.2	182	
1888	**BENJAMIN HARRISON (Ind.)**	Republican	5,439,853	47.9	233	79.3
	Grover Cleveland	Democratic	5,540,309	48.6	168	
1892	**GROVER CLEVELAND (N.Y.)**	Democratic	5,555,426	46.1	277	74.7
	Benjamin Harrison	Republican	5,182,690	43.0	145	
	James B. Weaver	People's	1,029,846	8.5	22	
1896	**WILLIAM McKINLEY (Ohio)**	Republican	7,104,779	51.1	271	79.3
	William J. Bryan	Democratic-People's	6,502,925	47.7	176	
1900	**WILLIAM McKINLEY (Ohio)**	Republican	7,207,923	51.7	292	73.2
	William J. Bryan	Dem.-Populist	6,358,133	45.5	155	

Year	Candidates	Parties	Popular Vote	Percentage of Popular Vote	Electoral Vote	Percentage of Voter Participation
1904	**THEODORE ROOSEVELT (N.Y.)**	Republican	7,623,486	57.9	336	65.2
	Alton B. Parker	Democratic	5,077,911	37.6	140	
	Eugene V. Debs	Socialist	402,283	3.0	—	
1908	**WILLIAM H. TAFT (Ohio)**	Republican	7,678,908	51.6	321	65.4
	William J. Bryan	Democratic	6,409,104	43.1	162	
	Eugene V. Debs	Socialist	420,793	2.8	—	
1912	**WOODROW WILSON (N.J.)**	Democratic	6,293,454	41.9	435	58.8
	Theodore Roosevelt	Progressive	4,119,538	27.4	88	
	William H. Taft	Republican	3,484,980	23.2	8	
	Eugene V. Debs	Socialist	900,672	6.1	—	
1916	**WOODROW WILSON (N.J.)**	Democratic	9,129,606	49.4	277	61.6
	Charles E. Hughes	Republican	8,538,221	46.2	254	
	A. L. Benson	Socialist	585,113	3.2	—	
1920	**WARREN G. HARDING (Ohio)**	Republican	16,143,407	60.5	404	49.2
	James M. Cox	Democratic	9,130,328	34.2	127	
	Eugene V. Debs	Socialist	919,799	3.4	—	
1924	**CALVIN COOLIDGE (Mass.)**	Republican	15,725,016	54.0	382	48.9
	John W. Davis	Democratic	8,386,503	28.8	136	
	Robert M. La Follette	Progressive	4,822,856	16.6	13	
1928	**HERBERT HOOVER (Calif.)**	Republican	21,391,381	58.2	444	56.9
	Alfred E. Smith	Democratic	15,016,443	40.9	87	
	Norman Thomas	Socialist	267,835	0.7	—	
1932	**FRANKLIN D. ROOSEVELT (N.Y.)**	Democratic	22,809,638	57.4	472	56.9
	Herbert Hoover	Republican	15,758,901	39.7	59	
	Norman Thomas	Socialist	881,951	2.2	—	
1936	**FRANKLIN D. ROOSEVELT (N.Y.)**	Democratic	27,751,597	60.8	523	61.0
	Alfred M. Landon	Republican	16,679,583	36.5	8	
	William Lemke	Union	882,479	1.9	—	
1940	**FRANKLIN D. ROOSEVELT (N.Y.)**	Democratic	27,244,160	54.8	449	62.5
	Wendell Willkie	Republican	22,305,198	44.8	82	
1944	**FRANKLIN D. ROOSEVELT (N.Y.)**	Democratic	25,602,504	53.5	432	55.9
	Thomas E. Dewey	Republican	22,006,285	46.0	99	
1948	**HARRY S. TRUMAN (Mo.)**	Democratic	24,105,695	49.5	303	53.0
	Thomas E. Dewey	Republican	21,969,170	45.1	189	
	J. Strom Thurmond	States'-Rights Democratic	1,169,021	2.4	38	
	Henry A. Wallace	Progressive	1,156,103	2.4	—	
1952	**DWIGHT D. EISENHOWER (N.Y.)**	Republican	33,936,252	55.1	442	63.3
	Adlai Stevenson	Democratic	27,314,992	44.4	89	
1956	**DWIGHT D. EISENHOWER (N.Y.)**	Republican	35,575,420	57.6	457	60.6
	Adlai Stevenson	Democratic	26,033,066	42.1	73	
	Other	—	—		1	
1960	**JOHN F. KENNEDY (Mass.)**	Democratic	34,227,096	49.9	303	62.8
	Richard M. Nixon	Republican	34,108,546	49.6	219	
	Other	—	—		15	
1964	**LYNDON B. JOHNSON (Texas)**	Democratic	43,126,506	61.1	486	61.7
	Barry M. Goldwater	Republican	27,176,799	38.5	52	
1968	**RICHARD M. NIXON (N.Y.)**	Republican	31,770,237	43.4	301	60.9
	Hubert H. Humphrey	Democratic	31,270,533	42.7	191	
	George Wallace	American Indep.	9,906,141	13.5	46	
1972	**RICHARD M. NIXON (N.Y.)**	Republican	47,169,911	60.7	520	55.2
	George S. McGovern	Democratic	29,170,383	37.5	17	
	Other	—	—		1	

Year	Candidates	Parties	Popular Vote	Percentage of Popular Vote	Electoral Vote	Percentage of Voter Participation
1976	**JIMMY CARTER (Ga.)**	Democratic	40,828,587	50.0	297	53.5
	Gerald R. Ford	Republican	39,147,613	47.9	241	
	Other	—	1,575,459	2.1	—	
1980	**RONALD REAGAN (Calif.)**	Republican	43,901,812	50.7	489	54.0
	Jimmy Carter	Democratic	35,483,820	41.0	49	
	John B. Anderson	Independent	5,719,722	6.6	—	
	Ed Clark	Libertarian	921,188	1.1	—	
1984	**RONALD REAGAN (Calif.)**	Republican	54,455,075	59.0	525	53.1
	Walter Mondale	Democratic	37,577,185	41.0	13	
1988	**GEORGE H. W. BUSH (Texas)**	Republican	47,946,422	54.0	426	50.2
	Michael S. Dukakis	Democratic	41,016,429	46.0	112	
1992	**WILLIAM J. CLINTON (Ark.)**	Democratic	44,908,254	42.3	370	55.9
	George H. W. Bush	Republican	39,102,282	37.4	168	
	H. Ross Perot	Independent	19,721,433	18.9	—	
1996	**WILLIAM J. CLINTON (Ark.)**	Democratic	47,401,185	49.2	379	49.0
	Robert Dole	Republican	39,197,469	40.7	159	
	H. Ross Perot	Independent	8,085,294	8.4	—	
2000	**GEORGE W. BUSH (Texas)**	Republican	50,456,062	47.8	271	51.2
	Al Gore	Democratic	50,996,862	48.4	267	
	Ralph Nader	Green Party	2,858,843	2.7	—	
	Patrick J. Buchanan	—	438,760	.4	—	

PRESIDENTS, VICE PRESIDENTS, AND SECRETARIES OF STATE

The Washington Administration (1789–1797)

Vice President	John Adams	1789–1797
Secretary of State	Thomas Jefferson	1789–1793
	Edmund Randolph	1794–1795
	Timothy Pickering	1795–1797

The John Adams Administration (1797–1801)

Vice President	Thomas Jefferson	1797–1801
Secretary of State	Timothy Pickering	1797–1800
	John Marshall	1800–1801

The Jefferson Administration (1801–1809)

Vice President	Aaron Burr	1801–1805
	George Clinton	1805–1809
Secretary of State	James Madison	1801–1809

The Madison Administration (1809–1817)

Vice President	George Clinton	1809–1813
	Elbridge Gerry	1813–1817
Secretary of State	Robert Smith	1809–1811
	James Monroe	1811–1817

The Monroe Administration (1817–1825)

Vice President	Daniel Tompkins	1817–1825
Secretary of State	John Quincy Adams	1817–1825

The John Quincy Adams Administration (1825–1829)

Vice President	John C. Calhoun	1825–1829
Secretary of State	Henry Clay	1825–1829

The Jackson Administration (1829–1837)

Vice President	John C. Calhoun	1829–1833
	Martin Van Buren	1833–1837
Secretary of State	Martin Van Buren	1829–1831
	Edward Livingston	1831–1833
	Louis McLane	1833–1834
	John Forsyth	1834–1837

The Van Buren Administration (1837–1841)

Vice President	Richard M. Johnson	1837–1841
Secretary of State	John Forsyth	1837–1841

The William Harrison Administration (1841)

Vice President	John Tyler	1841
Secretary of State	Daniel Webster	1841

The Tyler Administration (1841–1845)

Vice President	None	
Secretary of State	Daniel Webster	1841–1843
	Hugh S. Legaré	1843
	Abel P. Upshur	1843–1844
	John C. Calhoun	1844–1845

The Polk Administration (1845–1849)

Vice President	George M. Dallas	1845–1849
Secretary of State	James Buchanan	1845–1849

The Taylor Administration (1849–1850)

Vice President	Millard Fillmore	1849–1850
Secretary of State	John M. Clayton	1849–1850

The Fillmore Administration (1850–1853)

Vice President	None	
Secretary of State	Daniel Webster	1850–1852
	Edward Everett	1852–1853

The Pierce Administration (1853–1857)

Vice President	William R. King	1853–1857
Secretary of State	William L. Marcy	1853–1857

The Buchanan Administration (1857–1861)

Vice President	John C. Breckinridge	1857–1861
Secretary of State	Lewis Cass	1857–1860
	Jeremiah S. Black	1860–1861

The Lincoln Administration (1861–1865)

Vice President	Hannibal Hamlin	1861–1865
	Andrew Johnson	1865
Secretary of State	William H. Seward	1861–1865

The Andrew Johnson Administration (1865–1869)

Vice President	None	
Secretary of State	William H. Seward	1865–1869

The Grant Administration (1869–1877)

Vice President	Schuyler Colfax	1869–1873
	Henry Wilson	1873–1877
Secretary of State	Elihu B. Washburne	1869
	Hamilton Fish	1869–1877

The Hayes Administration (1877–1881)

Vice President	William A. Wheeler	1877–1881
Secretary of State	William M. Evarts	1877–1881

The Garfield Administration (1881)

Vice President	Chester A. Arthur	1881
Secretary of State	James G. Blaine	1881

The Arthur Administration (1881–1885)

Vice President	None	
Secretary of State	F. T. Frelinghuysen	1881–1885

The Cleveland Administration (1885–1889)

Vice President	Thomas A. Hendricks	1885–1889
Secretary of State	Thomas F. Bayard	1885–1889

The Benjamin Harrison Administration (1889–1893)

Vice President	Levi P. Morton	1889–1893
Secretary of State	James G. Blaine	1889–1892
	John W. Foster	1892–1893

The Cleveland Administration (1893–1897)

Vice President	Adlai E. Stevenson	1893–1897
Secretary of State	Walter Q. Gresham	1893–1895
	Richard Olney	1895–1897

The McKinley Administration (1897–1901)

Vice President	Garret A. Hobart	1897–1901
	Theodore Roosevelt	1901
Secretary of State	John Sherman	1897–1898
	William R. Day	1898
	John Hay	1898–1901

The Theodore Roosevelt Administration (1901–1909)

Vice President	Charles Fairbanks	1905–1909
Secretary of State	John Hay	1901–1905
	Elihu Root	1905–1909
	Robert Bacon	1909

The Taft Administration (1909–1913)

Vice President	James S. Sherman	1909–1913
Secretary of State	Philander C. Knox	1909–1913

The Wilson Administration (1913–1921)

Vice President	Thomas R. Marshall	1913–1921
Secretary of State	William J. Bryan	1913–1915
	Robert Lansing	1915–1920
	Bainbridge Colby	1920–1921

The Harding Administration (1921–1923)

Vice President	Calvin Coolidge	1921–1923
Secretary of State	Charles E. Hughes	1921–1923

The Coolidge Administration (1923–1929)

Vice President	Charles G. Dawes	1925–1929
Secretary of State	Charles E. Hughes	1923–1925
	Frank B. Kellogg	1925–1929

The Hoover Administration (1929–1933)

Vice President	Charles Curtis	1929–1933
Secretary of State	Henry L. Stimson	1929–1933

The Franklin D. Roosevelt Administration (1933–1945)

Vice President	John Nance Garner	1933–1941
	Henry A. Wallace	1941–1945
	Harry S. Truman	1945
Secretary of State	Cordell Hull	1933–1944
	Edward R. Stettinius Jr.	1944–1945

The Truman Administration (1945–1953)

Vice President	Alben W. Barkley	1949–1953
Secretary of State	Edward R. Stettinius Jr.	1945
	James F. Byrnes	1945–1947
	George C. Marshall	1947–1949
	Dean G. Acheson	1949–1953

The Eisenhower Administration (1953–1961)

Vice President	Richard M. Nixon	1953–1961
Secretary of State	John Foster Dulles	1953–1959
	Christian A. Herter	1959–1961

The Kennedy Administration (1961–1963)

Vice President	Lyndon B. Johnson	1961–1963
Secretary of State	Dean Rusk	1961–1963

The Lyndon Johnson Administration (1963–1969)

Vice President	Hubert H. Humphrey	1965–1969
Secretary of State	Dean Rusk	1963–1969

The Nixon Administration (1969–1974)

Vice President	Spiro T. Agnew	1969–1973
	Gerald R. Ford	1973–1974
Secretary of State	William P. Rogers	1969–1973
	Henry A. Kissinger	1973–1974

The Ford Administration (1974–1977)

Vice President	Nelson A. Rockefeller	1974–1977
Secretary of State	Henry A. Kissinger	1974–1977

The Carter Administration (1977–1981)

Vice President	Walter F. Mondale	1977–1981
Secretary of State	Cyrus R. Vance	1977–1980
	Edmund Muskie	1980–1981

The Reagan Administration (1981–1989)

Vice President	George H. W. Bush	1981–1989
Secretary of State	Alexander M. Haig	1981–1982
	George P. Shultz	1982–1989

The George H. W. Bush Administration (1989–1993)

Vice President	J. Danforth Quayle	1989–1993
Secretary of State	James A. Baker III	1989–1992
	Lawrence S. Eagleburger	1992–1993

The Clinton Administration (1993–2001)

Vice President	Albert Gore	1993–2001
Secretary of State	Warren M. Christopher	1993–1997
	Madeleine K. Albright	1997–2001

The George W. Bush Administration (2001–)

Vice President	Richard Cheney	2001–
Secretary of State	Colin Powell	2001–

ADMISSION OF STATES TO THE UNION

State	Date of Admission	State	Date of Admission
Delaware	December 7, 1787	Rhode Island	May 29, 1790
Pennsylvania	December 12, 1787	Vermont	March 4, 1791
New Jersey	December 18, 1787	Kentucky	June 1, 1792
Georgia	January 2, 1788	Tennessee	June 1, 1796
Connecticut	January 9, 1788	Ohio	March 1, 1803
Massachusetts	February 6, 1788	Louisiana	April 30, 1812
Maryland	April 28, 1788	Indiana	December 11, 1816
South Carolina	May 23, 1788	Mississippi	December 10, 1817
New Hampshire	June 21, 1788	Illinois	December 3, 1818
Virginia	June 25, 1788	Alabama	December 14, 1819
New York	July 26, 1788	Maine	March 15, 1820
North Carolina	November 21, 1789	Missouri	August 10, 1821

ADMISSION OF STATES TO THE UNION

State	Date of Admission	State	Date of Admission
Arkansas	June 15, 1836	Colorado	August 1, 1876
Michigan	January 16, 1837	North Dakota	November 2, 1889
Florida	March 3, 1845	South Dakota	November 2, 1889
Texas	December 29, 1845	Montana	November 8, 1889
Iowa	December 28, 1846	Washington	November 11, 1889
Wisconsin	May 29, 1848	Idaho	July 3, 1890
California	September 9, 1850	Wyoming	July 10, 1890
Minnesota	May 11, 1858	Utah	January 4, 1896
Oregon	February 14, 1859	Oklahoma	November 16, 1907
Kansas	January 29, 1861	New Mexico	January 6, 1912
West Virginia	June 19, 1863	Arizona	February 14, 1912
Nevada	October 31, 1864	Alaska	January 3, 1959
Nebraska	March 1, 1867	Hawaii	August 21, 1959

SUPREME COURT JUSTICES

Name	Service	Appointed by	Name	Service	Appointed by
John Jay[*]	1789–1795	Washington	Philip P. Barbour	1836–1841	Jackson
James Wilson	1789–1798	Washington	John Catron	1837–1865	Van Buren
John Blair	1789–1796	Washington	John McKinley	1837–1852	Van Buren
John Rutledge	1790–1791	Washington	Peter V. Daniel	1841–1860	Van Buren
William Cushing	1790–1810	Washington	Samuel Nelson	1845–1872	Tyler
James Iredell	1790–1799	Washington	Levi Woodbury	1845–1851	Polk
Thomas Johnson	1791–1793	Washington	Robert C. Grier	1846–1870	Polk
William Paterson	1793–1806	Washington	Benjamin R. Curtis	1851–1857	Fillmore
John Rutledge[†]	1795	Washington	John A. Campbell	1853–1861	Pierce
Samuel Chase	1796–1811	Washington	Nathan Clifford	1858–1881	Buchanan
Oliver Ellsworth	1796–1799	Washington	Noah H. Swayne	1862–1881	Lincoln
Bushrod Washington	1798–1829	J. Adams	Samuel F. Miller	1862–1890	Lincoln
			David Davis	1862–1877	Lincoln
Alfred Moore	1799–1804	J. Adams	Stephen J. Field	1863–1897	Lincoln
John Marshall	1801–1835	J. Adams	**Salmon P. Chase**	1864–1873	Lincoln
William Johnson	1804–1834	Jefferson	William Strong	1870–1880	Grant
Henry B. Livingston	1806–1823	Jefferson	Joseph P. Bradley	1870–1892	Grant
Thomas Todd	1807–1826	Jefferson	Ward Hunt	1873–1882	Grant
Gabriel Duval	1811–1836	Madison	**Morrison R. Waite**	1874–1888	Grant
Joseph Story	1811–1845	Madison	John M. Harlan	1877–1911	Hayes
Smith Thompson	1823–1843	Monroe	William B. Woods	1880–1887	Hayes
Robert Trimble	1826–1828	J. Q. Adams	Stanley Matthews	1881–1889	Garfield
John McLean	1829–1861	Jackson	Horace Gray	1882–1902	Arthur
Henry Baldwin	1830–1844	Jackson	Samuel Blatchford	1882–1893	Arthur
James M. Wayne	1835–1867	Jackson	Lucius Q. C. Lamar	1888–1893	Cleveland
Roger B. Taney	1836–1864	Jackson	**Melville W. Fuller**	1888–1910	Cleveland
			David J. Brewer	1889–1910	B. Harrison
			Henry B. Brown	1890–1906	B. Harrison
			George Shiras	1892–1903	B. Harrison
			Howell E. Jackson	1893–1895	B. Harrison

[*]Chief Justices appear in bold type.
[†]Acting Chief Justice; Senate refused to confirm appointment.

Name	Service	Appointed by	Name	Service	Appointed by
Edward D. White	1894–1910	Cleveland	Harold H. Burton	1945–1958	Truman
Rufus W. Peckham	1896–1909	Cleveland	**Frederick M. Vinson**	1946–1953	Truman
Joseph McKenna	1898–1925	McKinley	Tom C. Clark	1949–1967	Truman
Oliver W. Holmes	1902–1932	T. Roosevelt	Sherman Minton	1949–1956	Truman
William R. Day	1903–1922	T. Roosevelt	**Earl Warren**	1953–1969	Eisenhower
William H. Moody	1906–1910	T. Roosevelt	John Marshall Harlan	1955–1971	Eisenhower
Horace H. Lurton	1910–1914	Taft	William J. Brennan Jr.	1956–1990	Eisenhower
Charles E. Hughes	1910–1916	Taft	Charles E. Whittaker	1957–1962	Eisenhower
Willis Van Devanter	1910–1937	Taft	Potter Stewart	1958–1981	Eisenhower
Edward D. White	1910–1921	Taft	Byron R. White	1962–1993	Kennedy
Joseph R. Lamar	1911–1916	Taft	Arthur J. Goldberg	1962–1965	Kennedy
Mahlon Pitney	1912–1922	Taft	Abe Fortas	1965–1969	L. Johnson
James C. McReynolds	1914–1941	Wilson	Thurgood Marshall	1967–1991	L. Johnson
Louis D. Brandeis	1916–1939	Wilson	**Warren E. Burger**	1969–1986	Nixon
John H. Clarke	1916–1922	Wilson	Harry A. Blackmun	1970–1994	Nixon
William H. Taft	1921–1930	Harding	Lewis F. Powell Jr.	1972–1988	Nixon
George Sutherland	1922–1938	Harding	William H. Rehnquist	1972–1986	Nixon
Pierce Butler	1923–1939	Harding	John Paul Stevens	1975–	Ford
Edward T. Sanford	1923–1930	Harding	Sandra Day O'Connor	1981–	Reagan
Harlan F. Stone	1925–1941	Coolidge	**William H. Rehnquist**	1986–	Reagan
Charles E. Hughes	1930–1941	Hoover	Antonin Scalia	1986–	Reagan
Owen J. Roberts	1930–1945	Hoover	Anthony M. Kennedy	1988–	Reagan
Benjamin N. Cardozo	1932–1938	Hoover	David H. Souter	1990–	G. H. W. Bush
Hugo L. Black	1937–1971	F. Roosevelt			
Stanley F. Reed	1938–1957	F. Roosevelt	Clarence Thomas	1991–	G. H. W. Bush
Felix Frankfurter	1939–1962	F. Roosevelt			
William O. Douglas	1939–1975	F. Roosevelt	Ruth Bader Ginsburg	1993–	Clinton
Frank Murphy	1940–1949	F. Roosevelt			
Harlan F. Stone	1941–1946	F. Roosevelt	Stephen Breyer	1994–	Clinton
James F. Byrnes	1941–1942	F. Roosevelt			
Robert H. Jackson	1941–1954	F. Roosevelt			
Wiley B. Rutledge	1943–1949	F. Roosevelt			

SIGNIFICANT SUPREME COURT CASES

Marbury v. Madison (1803)

This case established the right of the Supreme Court to review the constitutionality of laws. The decision involved judicial appointments made during the last hours of the administration of President John Adams. Some commissions, including that of William Marbury, had not yet been delivered when President Thomas Jefferson took office. Infuriated by the last-minute nature of Adams's Federalist appointments, Jefferson refused to send the undelivered commissions out, and Marbury decided to sue. The Supreme Court, presided over by John Marshall, a Federalist who had assisted Adams in the judicial appointments, ruled that although Marbury's commission was valid and the new president should have delivered it, the Court could not compel him to do so. The Court based its reasoning on a finding that the grounds of Marbury's suit, resting in the Judiciary Act of 1789, were in conflict with the Constitution.

For the first time, the Court had overturned a national law on the grounds that it was unconstitutional. John Marshall had quietly established the concept of judicial review: The Supreme Court had given itself the authority to nullify acts of the other branches of the federal government. Although the Constitution provides for judicial review, the Court had not exercised this power before and did not use it again until 1857. It seems likely that if the Court

SIGNIFICANT SUPREME COURT CASES

had waited until 1857 to use this power, it would have been difficult to establish.

McCulloch v. Maryland (1819)

In 1816, Congress authorized the creation of a national bank. To protect its own banks from competition with a branch of the national bank in Baltimore, the state legislature of Maryland placed a tax of 2 percent on all notes issued by any bank operating in Maryland that was not chartered by the state. McCulloch, cashier of the Baltimore branch of the Bank of the United States, was convicted for refusing to pay the tax. Under the leadership of Chief Justice John Marshall, the Court ruled that the federal government had the power to establish a bank, even though that specific authority was not mentioned in the Constitution.

Marshall maintained that the authority could be reasonably implied from Article 1, section 8, which gives Congress the power to make all laws that are necessary and proper to execute the enumerated powers. Marshall also held that Maryland could not tax the national bank because in a conflict between federal and state laws, the federal law must take precedence. Thus he established the principles of implied powers and federal supremacy, both of which set a precedent for subsequent expansion of federal power at the expense of the states.

Scott v. Sandford (1857)

Dred Scott was a slave who sued for his own and his family's freedom on the grounds that, with his master, he had traveled to and lived in free territory that did not allow slavery. When his case reached the Supreme Court, the justices saw an opportunity to settle once and for all the vexing question of slavery in the territories. The Court's decision in this case proved that it enjoyed no special immunity from the sectional and partisan passions of the time. Five of the nine justices were from the South and seven were Democrats.

Chief Justice Roger B. Taney hated Republicans and detested racial equality; his decision reflects those prejudices. He wrote an opinion not only declaring that Scott was still a slave but also claiming that the Constitution denied citizenship or rights to blacks, that Congress had no right to exclude slavery from the territories, and that the Missouri Compromise was unconstitutional. While southern Democrats gloated over this seven-to-two decision, sectional tensions were further inflamed and the young Republican Party's claim that a hostile "slave power" was conspiring to destroy northern liberties was given further credence. The decision brought the nation closer to civil war and is generally regarded as the worst decision ever rendered by the Supreme Court.

Butchers' Benevolent Association of New Orleans v. Crescent City Livestock Landing and Slaughterhouse Co. (1873)

The *Slaughterhouse* cases, as the cases docketed under the *Butchers'* title were known, were the first legal test of the Fourteenth Amendment. To cut down on cases of cholera believed to be caused by contaminated water, the state of Louisiana prohibited the slaughter of livestock in New Orleans except in one slaughterhouse, effectively giving that slaughterhouse a monopoly. Other New Orleans butchers claimed that the state had deprived them of their occupation without due process of law, thus violating the Fourteenth Amendment.

In a five-to-four decision, the Court upheld the Louisiana law, declaring that the Fourteenth Amendment protected only the rights of federal citizenship, like voting in federal elections and interstate travel. The federal government thus was not obliged to protect basic civil rights from violation by state governments. This decision would have significant implications for African Americans and their struggle for civil rights in the twentieth century.

United States v. E. C. Knight Co. (1895)

Also known as the *Sugar Trust* case, this was among the first cases to reveal the weakness of the Sherman Antitrust Act in the hands of a pro-business Supreme Court. In 1895, American Sugar Refining Company purchased four other sugar producers, including the E. C. Knight Company, and thus took control of more than 98 percent of the sugar refining in the United States. In an effort to limit monopoly, the government brought suit against all five of the companies for violating the Sherman Antitrust Act, which outlawed trusts and other business combinations in restraint of trade. The Court dismissed the suit, however, arguing that the law applied only to commerce and not to manufacturing, defining the latter as a local concern and not part of the interstate commerce that the government could regulate.

Plessy v. Ferguson (1896)

African American Homer Plessy challenged a Louisiana law that required segregation on trains passing through the state. After ensuring that the railroad and the conductor knew that he was of mixed race (Plessy appeared to be white but under the racial code of Louisiana was classified as "colored" because he was one-eighth black), he refused to move to the "colored only" section of the coach. The Court ruled against Plessy by a vote of seven to one, declaring that "separate but equal" facilities were permissible according to section 1 of the Fourteenth Amendment, which calls upon the states to provide "equal protection of the laws" to anyone within their jurisdiction. Although the case was viewed as relatively insignificant at the time, it cast a long shadow over several decades.

Initially, the decision was viewed as a victory for segregationists, but in the 1930s and 1940s civil rights advocates referred to the doctrine of "separate but equal" in their efforts to end segregation. They argued that segregated institutions and accommodations were often *not* equal to those available to whites, and finally succeeded in overturning *Plessy* in *Brown v. Board of Education* in 1954 (see below).

Lochner v. New York (1905)

In this case, the Court ruled against a New York state law that prohibited employees from working in bakeries more than ten hours a day or sixty hours a week. The purpose of the law was to protect the health of workers, but the Court ruled that it was unconstitutional because it violated "freedom of contract" implicitly protected by the due process clause of the Fourteenth Amendment. Most of the justices believed strongly in a laissez-faire economic system that favored survival of the fittest. They felt that government protection of workers interfered with this system. In a dissenting opinion, Justice Oliver Wendell Holmes accused the majority of distorting the Constitution and of deciding the case on "an economic theory which a large part of the country does not entertain."

Muller v. Oregon (1908)

In 1905, Curt Muller, owner of a Portland, Oregon, laundry, demanded that one of his employees, Mrs. Elmer Gotcher, work more than the ten hours allowed as a maximum workday for women under Oregon law. Muller argued that the law violated his "freedom of contract" as established in prior Supreme Court decisions.

Progressive lawyer Louis D. Brandeis defended the Oregon law by arguing that a state could be justified in abridging freedom of contract when the health, safety, and welfare of workers was at issue. His innovative strategy drew on ninety-five pages of excerpts from factory and medical reports to substantiate his argument that there was a direct connection between long hours and the health of women and thus the health of the nation. In a unanimous decision, the Court upheld the Oregon law, but later generations of women fighting for equality would question the strategy of arguing that women's reproductive role entitled them to special treatment.

Schenck v. United States (1919)

During World War I, Charles Schenck and other members of the Socialist Party printed and mailed out flyers urging young men who were subject to the draft to oppose the war in Europe. In upholding the conviction of Schenck for publishing a pamphlet urging draft resistance, Justice Oliver Wendell Holmes established the "clear and present danger" test for freedom of speech. Such utterances as Schenck's during a time of national peril, Holmes wrote, could be considered the equivalent of shouting "Fire!" in a crowded theater. Congress had the right to protect the public against such an incitement to panic, the Court ruled in a unanimous decision. But the analogy was a false one. Schenck's pamphlet had little power to provoke a public firmly opposed to its message. Although Holmes later modified his position to state that the danger must relate to an immediate evil and a specific action, the "clear and present danger" test laid the groundwork for those who later sought to limit First Amendment freedoms.

Schechter Poultry Corp. v. United States (1935)

During the Great Depression, the National Industrial Recovery Act (NIRA), which was passed under President Franklin D. Roosevelt, established fair competition codes that were designed to help businesses. The Schechter brothers of New York City, who sold chickens, were convicted of violating the codes. The Supreme Court ruled that the NIRA unconstitutionally conferred legislative power on an administrative agency and overstepped the limits of federal power to regulate interstate commerce. The decision was a significant blow to the New Deal recovery program, demonstrating both historic American resistance to economic planning and the refusal of the business community to yield its autonomy unless it was forced to do so.

Brown v. Board of Education (1954)

In 1950, the families of eight Topeka, Kansas, children sued the Topeka Board of Education. The children were blacks who lived within walking distance of a whites-only school. The segregated school system required them to take a time-consuming, inconvenient, and dangerous route to get to a black school, and their parents argued that there was no reason their children should not be allowed to attend the nearest school. By the time the case reached the Supreme Court, it had been joined with similar cases regarding segregated schools in other states and the District of Columbia. A team of lawyers from the National Association for the Advancement of Colored People (NAACP), led by Thurgood Marshall (who would later be appointed to the Supreme Court), urged the Court to overturn the fifty-eight-year-old precedent established in *Plessy v. Ferguson*, which had enshrined "separate but equal" as the law of the land. A unanimous Court, led by Chief Justice Earl Warren, declared that "separate educational facilities are inherently unequal" and thus violate the Fourteenth Amendment. In 1955, the Court called for desegregation "with all deliberate speed" but established no deadline.

Roth v. United States (1957)

In 1957, New Yorker Samuel Roth was convicted of sending obscene materials through the mail in a case that ultimately reached the Supreme Court. With a six-to-three vote, the Court reaffirmed the historical view that obscenity is not protected by the First Amendment. Yet it broke new ground by declaring that a work could be judged obscene only if, "taken as a whole," it appealed to the "prurient interest" of "the average person."

Prior to this case, work could be judged obscene if portions were thought able to "deprave and corrupt" the most susceptible part of an audience (such as children). Thus, serious works of literature such as Theodore Dreiser's *An American Tragedy*, which was banned in Boston when first published, had received no protection. Although this decision continued to pose problems of definition, it did help to protect most works that attempt to convey ideas, even if those ideas have to do with sex, from the threat of obscenity laws.

Engel v. Vitale (1962)

In 1959, five parents with ten children in the New Hyde Park, New York, school system sued the school board. The parents argued that the so-called Regents' Prayer that public school students in New York recited at the start of every school day violated the doctrine of separation of church and state outlined in the First Amendment. In 1962, the Supreme Court voted six to one in favor of banning the Regents' Prayer.

The decision threw the religious community into an uproar. Many religious leaders expressed dismay and even shock; others welcomed the decision. Several efforts to introduce an amendment allowing school prayer have failed. Subsequent Supreme Court decisions have banned reading of the Bible in public schools. The Court has also declared mandatory flag saluting to be an infringement of religious and personal freedoms.

Gideon v. Wainwright (1963)

When Clarence Earl Gideon was tried for breaking into a poolroom, the state of Florida rejected his demand for a court-appointed lawyer as guaranteed by the Sixth Amendment. In 1963, the Court upheld his demand in a unanimous decision that established the obligation of states to provide attorneys for indigent defendants in felony cases. Prior to this decision, the right to an attorney had applied only to federal cases, not state cases. In its ruling in *Gideon v. Wainwright*, the Supreme Court applied the Sixth through the Fourteenth Amendments to the states. In 1972, the Supreme Court extended the right to legal representation to all cases, not just felony cases, in its decision in *Argersinger v. Hamlin*.

Griswold v. Connecticut (1965)

With a vote of seven to two, the Supreme Court reversed an "uncommonly silly law" (in the words of Justice Potter Stewart) that made it a crime for anyone in the state of Connecticut to use any drug, article, or instrument to prevent conception. *Griswold* became a landmark case because here, for the first time, the Court explicitly invested with full constitutional status "fundamental personal rights," such as the right to privacy, that were not expressly enumerated in the Bill of Rights. The majority opinion in the case held that the law infringed on the constitutionally protected right to privacy of married persons.

Although the Court had previously recognized fundamental rights not expressly enumerated in the Bill of Rights (such as the right to procreate in *Skinner v. Oklahoma* in 1942), *Griswold* was the first time the Court had justified, at length, the practice of investing such unenumerated rights with full constitutional status. Writing for the majority, Justice William O. Douglas explained that the First, Third, Fourth, Fifth, and Ninth Amendments imply "zones of privacy" that are the foundation for the general right to privacy affirmed in this case.

Miranda v. Arizona (1966)

In 1966, the Supreme Court, by a vote of five to four, upheld the case of Ernesto Miranda, who appealed a murder conviction on the grounds that police had gotten him to confess without giving him access to an attorney. The *Miranda* case was the culmination of the Court's efforts to find a meaningful way of determining whether police had used due process in extracting confessions from people accused of crimes. The *Miranda* decision upholds the Fifth Amendment protection against self-incrimination outside the courtroom and requires that suspects be given what came to be known as the "Miranda warning," which advises them of their right to remain silent and warns them that anything they say might be used against them in a court of law. Suspects must also be told that they have a right to counsel.

New York Times Co. v. United States (1971)

With a six-to-three vote, the Court upheld the right of the *New York Times* and the *Washington Post* to print materials from the so-called *Pentagon Papers*, a secret government study of U.S. policy in Vietnam, leaked by dissident Pentagon official Daniel Ellsberg. Since the papers revealed deception and secrecy in the conduct of the Vietnam War, the Nixon administration had quickly obtained a court injunction against their further publication, claiming that suppression was in the interests of national security. The Supreme Court's decision overturning the injunction strengthened the First Amendment protection of freedom of the press.

Furman v. Georgia (1972)

In this case, the Supreme Court ruled five to four that the death penalty for murder or rape violated the cruel and unusual punishment clause of the Eighth Amendment because the manner in which the death penalty was meted out was irregular, "arbitrary," and "cruel." In response, most states enacted new statutes that allow the death penalty to be imposed only after a postconviction hearing at which evidence must be presented to show that "aggravating" or "mitigating" circumstances were factors in the crime. If the postconviction hearing hands down a death sentence, the case is automatically reviewed by an appellate court.

In 1976, the Court ruled in *Gregg v. Georgia* that these statutes were not unconstitutional. In 1977, the Court ruled in *Coker v. Georgia* that the death penalty for rape was "disproportionate and excessive," thus allowing the death penalty only in murder cases. Between 1977 and 1991, some 150 people were executed in the United States. Public opinion polls indicate that about 70 percent of Americans favor the death penalty for murder. Capital punishment continues to generate controversy, however, as opponents argue that there is no evidence that the death penalty deters crime and that its use reflects racial and economic bias.

Roe v. Wade (1973)

In 1973, the Court found, by a vote of seven to two, that state laws restricting access to abortion violated a woman's right to privacy guaranteed by the due process clause of the Fourteenth Amendment. The decision was based on the cases of two women living in Texas and Georgia, both states with stringent antiabortion laws. Upholding the individual rights of both women and physicians, the Court ruled that the Constitution protects the right to abortion and that states cannot prohibit abortions in the early stages of pregnancy.

The decision stimulated great debate among legal scholars as well as the public. Critics argued that since abortion was never addressed in the Constitution, the Court could not claim that legislation violated fundamental values of the Constitution. They also argued that since abortion was a medical procedure with an acknowledged impact on a fetus, it was inappropriate to invoke the kind of "privacy" argument that was used in *Griswold v. Connecticut* (see page A-43), which was about contraception. Defenders suggested that the case should be argued as a case of gender discrimination, which did violate the equal protection clause of the Fourteenth Amendment. Others said that the right to privacy in sexual matters was indeed a fundamental right.

Regents of the University of California v. Bakke (1978)

When Allan Bakke, a white man, was not accepted by the University of California Medical School at Davis, he filed a lawsuit alleging that the admissions program, which set up different standards for test scores and grades for members of certain minority groups, violated the Civil Rights Act of 1964, which outlawed racial or ethnic preferences in programs supported by federal funds. Bakke further argued that the university's practice of setting aside spaces for minority applicants denied him equal protection as guaranteed by the Fourteenth Amendment. In a five-to-four decision, the Court ordered that Bakke be admitted to the medical school, yet it sanctioned affirmative action programs to attack the results of past discrimination as long as strict quotas or racial classifications were not involved.

Webster v. Reproductive Health Services (1989)

By a vote of five to four, the Court upheld several restrictions on the availability of abortions as imposed by Missouri state law. It upheld restrictions on the use of state property, including public hospitals, for abortions. It also upheld a provision requiring physicians to perform tests to determine the viability of a fetus that a doctor judged to be twenty weeks of age or older. Although the justices did not go so far as to overturn the decision in *Roe v. Wade* (see at left), the ruling galvanized interest groups on both sides of the abortion issue. Opponents of abortion pressured state legislatures to place greater restrictions on abortions; those who favored availability of abortion tried to mobilize public action by presenting the decision as a major threat to the right to choose abortion.

SIGNIFICANT SUPREME COURT CASES

Cipollone v. Liggett (1992)

In a seven-to-two decision, the Court ruled in favor of the family of Rose Cipollone, a woman who died of lung cancer after smoking for forty-two years. The Court rejected arguments that health warnings on cigarette packages protected tobacco manufacturers from personal injury suits filed by smokers who contract cancer and other serious illnesses.

Miller v. Johnson (1995)

In a five-to-four decision, the Supreme Court ruled that voting districts created to increase the voting power of racial minorities were unconstitutional. The decision threatens dozens of congressional, state, and local voting districts that were drawn to give minorities more representation as had been required by the Justice Department under the Voting Rights Act. If states are required to redraw voting districts, the number of black members of Congress could be sharply reduced.

Romer v. Evans (1996)

In a six-to-three decision, the Court struck down a Colorado amendment that forbade local governments from banning discrimination against homosexuals.

Writing for the majority, Justice Anthony Kennedy said that forbidding communities from taking action to protect the rights of homosexuals and not of other groups unlawfully deprived gays and lesbians of opportunities that were available to others. Kennedy based the decision on the guarantee of equal protection under the law as provided by the Fourteenth Amendment.

Bush v. Palm Beach County Canvassing Board (2000)

In a bitterly argued five-to-four decision, the Court reversed the Florida Supreme Court's previous order for a hand recount of contested presidential election ballots in several counties of that battleground state, effectively securing the presidency for Texas Republican governor George W. Bush. The ruling ended a protracted legal dispute between presidential candidates Bush and Vice President Al Gore while inflaming public opinion: For the first time since 1888, a president who failed to win the popular vote took office. Critics charged that the Supreme Court had applied partisanship rather than objectivity to the case, pointing out that the decision went against this Court's customary interpretation of the Constitution to favor state over federal authority.

The American Economy

THESE FIVE "SNAPSHOTS" of the U.S. economy show significant changes over the past century and a half. In 1849, the agricultural sector was by far the largest contributor to the economy. By the turn of the century, with advances in technology and an abundance of cheap labor and raw materials, the country had experienced remarkable industrial expansion and the manufacturing industries dominated. By 1950, the service sector had increased significantly, fueled by the consumerism of the 1920s and the post–World War II years, and the economy was becoming more diversified. Note that by 1990, the government's share in the economy had grown to more than 10 percent and activity in both the trade and manufacturing sectors had declined, partly as a result of competition from Western Europe and Asia. Manufacturing continued to decline, and by 2001 the service and finance, real estate, and insurance sectors had all grown steadily to eclipse it.

Main Sectors of the U.S. Economy: 1849, 1899, 1950, 1990, 2001

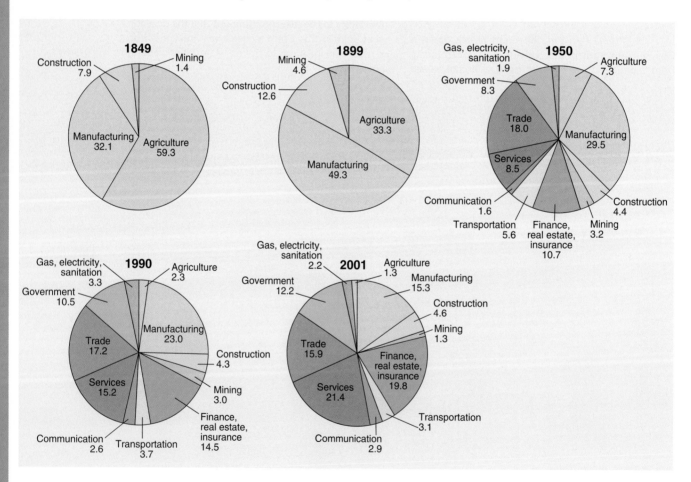

SOURCE: Data from *Historical Statistics of the United States, Colonial Times to 1970* (1975); *Statistical Abstract of the United States, 1998;* U.S. Bureau of Economic Analysis, *Industry Accounts Data, 2001.*

THE AMERICAN ECONOMY

FEDERAL SPENDING AND THE ECONOMY, 1790–2002

Year	Gross National Product (in billions)	Foreign Trade (in millions)		Federal Budget (in billions)	Federal Surplus/Deficit (in billions)	Federal Debt (in billions)
		Exports	Imports			
1790	NA	20	23	0.004	0.00015	0.076
1800	NA	71	91	0.011	0.0006	0.083
1810	NA	67	85	0.008	0.0012	0.053
1820	NA	70	74	0.018	−0.0004	0.091
1830	NA	74	71	0.015	0.100	0.049
1840	NA	132	107	0.024	−0.005	0.004
1850	NA	152	178	0.040	0.004	0.064
1860	NA	400	362	0.063	−0.01	0.065
1870	7.4	451	462	0.310	0.10	2.4
1880	11.2	853	761	0.268	0.07	2.1
1890	13.1	910	823	0.318	0.09	1.2
1900	18.7	1,499	930	0.521	0.05	1.2
1910	35.3	1,919	1,646	0.694	−0.02	1.1
1920	91.5	8,664	5,784	6.357	0.3	24.3
1930	90.4	4,013	3,500	3.320	0.7	16.3
1940	99.7	4,030	7,433	9.6	−2.7	43.0
1950	284.8	10,816	9,125	43.1	−2.2	257.4
1960	503.7	19,600	15,046	92.2	0.3	286.3
1970	977.1	42,700	40,189	195.6	−2.8	371.0
1980	2,631.7	220,600	244,871	590.9	−73.8	907.7
1990	5,832.2	393,600	495,300	1,253.2	−221.2	3,266.1
2000	9,848.0	1,070,054	1,445,438	1,788.8	236.4	5,701.9
2002	10,436.7	974,107	1,392,145	2,011.0	−157.8	6,255.4

SOURCE: *Historical Statistics of the U.S., Colonial Times to 1970* (1975), *Statistical Abstract of the U.S., 1996* (1996), *Statistical Abstract of the U.S., 1999* (1999), and *Statistical Abstract of the U.S., 2003* (2003).

A Demographic Profile of the United States and Its People

Population

FROM AN ESTIMATED 4,600 white inhabitants in 1630, the country's population grew to a total of just under 250 million in 1990. It is important to note that the U.S. census, first conducted in 1790 and the source of these figures, counted blacks, both free and slave, but did not include American Indians until 1860. The years 1790 to 1900 saw the most rapid population growth, with an average increase of 25 to 35 percent per decade. In addition to "natural" growth—birthrate exceeding death rate—immigration was also a factor in that rise, especially between 1840 and 1860, 1880 and 1890, and 1900 and 1910 (see table on page A-51). The twentieth century witnessed slower growth, partly a result of 1920s immigration restrictions and a decline in the birthrate, especially during the depression era and the 1960s and 1970s. The U.S. population is expected to reach almost 300 million by the year 2010.

POPULATION GROWTH, 1630–2000

Year	Population	Percent Increase	Year	Population	Percent Increase
1630	4,600	—	1820	9,638,453	33.1
1640	26,600	473.3	1830	12,866,020	33.5
1650	50,400	89.1	1840	17,069,453	32.7
1660	75,100	49.0	1850	23,191,876	35.9
1670	111,900	49.1	1860	31,443,321	35.6
1680	151,500	35.4	1870	39,818,449	26.6
1690	210,400	38.9	1880	50,155,783	26.0
1700	250,900	19.3	1890	62,947,714	25.5
1710	331,700	32.2	1900	75,994,575	20.7
1720	466,200	40.5	1910	91,972,266	21.0
1730	629,400	35.0	1920	105,710,620	14.9
1740	905,600	43.9	1930	122,775,046	16.1
1750	1,170,800	30.0	1940	131,669,275	7.2
1760	1,593,600	36.1	1950	150,697,361	14.5
1770	2,148,100	34.8	1960	179,323,175	19.0
1780	2,780,400	29.4	1970	203,302,031	13.4
1790	3,929,214	41.3	1980	226,542,199	11.4
1800	5,308,483	35.1	1990	248,718,302	9.8
1810	7,239,881	36.4	2000	281,422,509	13.1

Source: Historical Statistics of the U.S. (1960), Historical Statistics of the U.S., Colonial Times to 1970 (1975), Statistical Abstract of the U.S., 1996 (1996), and Statistical Abstract of the U.S., 2003 (2003).

A DEMOGRAPHIC PROFILE OF THE UNITED STATES AND ITS PEOPLE

Birthrate, 1820–2000

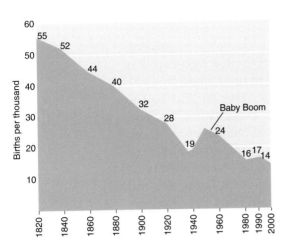

SOURCE: Data from *Historical Statistics of the U.S., Colonial Times to 1970* (1975) and *Statistical Abstract of the U.S., 2003* (2003).

Death Rate, 1900–2000

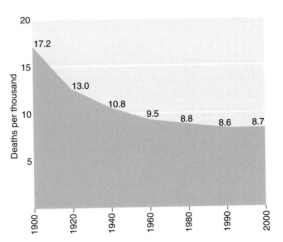

SOURCE: Data from *Historical Statistics of the U.S., Colonial Times to 1970* (1975) and *Statistical Abstract of the U.S., 2003* (2003).

Life Expectancy, 1900–2000

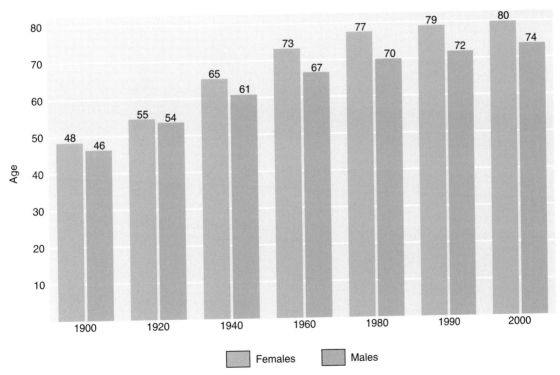

SOURCE: Data from *Historical Statistics of the U.S., Colonial Times to 1970* (1975) and *Statistical Abstract of the U.S., 2003* (2003).

MIGRATION AND IMMIGRATION

WE TEND TO ASSOCIATE INTERNAL MIGRATION with movement westward, yet equally significant has been the movement of the nation's population from the country to the city. In 1790, the first U.S. census recorded that approximately 95 percent of the population lived in rural areas. By 1990, that figure had fallen to less than 25 percent. The decline of the agricultural way of life, late-nineteenth-century industrialization, and immigration have all contributed to increased urbanization. A more recent trend has been the migration, especially since the 1970s, of people to the Sun Belt states of the South and West, lured by factors as various as economic opportunities in the defense and high-tech industries and good weather. This migration has swelled the size of cities like Houston, Dallas, Tucson, Phoenix, and San Diego, all of which in recent years ranked among the top ten most populous U.S. cities.

Rural and Urban Population, 1750–2000

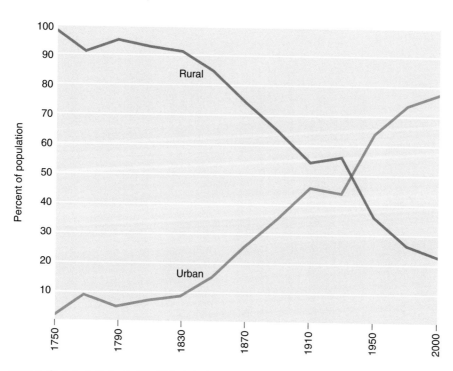

SOURCE: *Statistical Abstract of the U.S., 1991* (1991), *Statistical Abstract of the U.S., 2002* (2002).

MIGRATION AND IMMIGRATION

THE QUANTITY AND CHARACTER OF IMMIGRATION to the United States has varied greatly over time. During the first major influx, between 1840 and 1860, newcomers hailed primarily from northern and western Europe. From 1880 to 1915, when rates soared even more dramatically, the profile changed, with 80 percent of the "new immigration" coming from central, eastern, and southern Europe. Following World War I, strict quotas reduced the flow considerably. Note also the significant falloff during the years of the Great Depression and World War II. The sources of immigration during the last half century have changed significantly, with the majority of people coming from Latin America, the Caribbean, and Asia. The latest surge during the 1980s and 1990s brought more immigrants to the United States than in any decade except 1901–1910.

RATES OF IMMIGRATION, 1821–2002

Year	Number	Rate per Thousand of Total Resident Population
1821–1830	151,824	1.6
1831–1840	599,125	4.6
1841–1850	1,713,521	10.0
1851–1860	2,598,214	11.2
1861–1870	2,314,824	7.4
1871–1880	2,812,191	7.1
1881–1890	5,246,613	10.5
1891–1900	3,687,546	5.8
1901–1910	8,795,386	11.6
1911–1920	5,735,811	6.2
1921–1930	4,107,209	3.9
1931–1940	528,431	0.4
1941–1950	1,035,039	0.7
1951–1960	2,515,479	1.6
1961–1970	3,321,677	1.8
1971–1980	4,493,300	2.2
1981–1990	7,338,100	3.0
1991	1,827,167	7.2
1992	973,977	3.8
1993	904,292	3.5
1994	804,416	3.1
1995	720,461	2.7
1996	915,900	3.4
1997	798,378	2.9
1998	654,451	2.4
1999	646,568	2.3
2000	849,807	3.0
2001	1,064,318	3.7
2002	1,063,732	3.7

Source: Historical Statistics of the U.S., Colonial Times to 1970 (1975), Statistical Abstract of the U.S., 1996 (1996), Statistical Abstract of the U.S., 1999 (1999), 2002 Yearbook of Immigration Statistics (2002), and Statistical Abstract of the U.S., 2003. (2003).

Major Trends in Immigration, 1820–2000

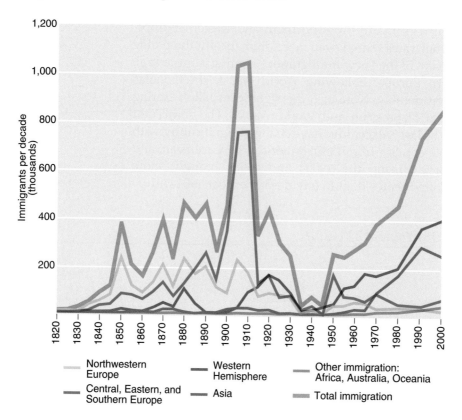

SOURCE: Data from *Historical Statistics of the U.S., Colonial Times to 1970* (1975), *Statistical Abstract of the U.S., 1999* (1999), and *Statistical Abstract of the U.S., 2003* (2003).

Research Resources in U.S. History

For help refining your research skills, finding what you need on the Web, and using it effectively, see "Other Resources at Bedford/St. Martin's" at bedfordstmartins.com/roark.

WHILE DOING RESEARCH IN HISTORY, you will use the library to track down primary and secondary sources and to answer questions that arise as you learn more about your topic. This appendix suggests helpful indexes, references, periodicals, and sources of primary documents. It also offers an overview of electronic resources available through the Internet. The materials listed here are not carried at all libraries, but they will give you an idea of the range of sources available. Remember, too, that librarians are an extremely helpful resource. They can direct you to useful materials throughout your research process.

Bibliographies and Indexes

American Historical Association Guide to Historical Literature. 3rd ed. New York: Oxford University Press, 1995. Offers 27,000 citations to important historical literature, arranged in forty-eight sections covering theory, international history, and regional history. An indispensable guide recently updated to include current trends in historical research.

American History and Life. Santa Barbara: ABC-Clio, 1964–. Covers publications of all sorts on U.S. and Canadian history and culture in a chronological/regional format, with abstracts and alphabetical indexes. Available in computerized format. The most complete ongoing bibliography for American history.

Freidel, Frank Burt. *Harvard Guide to American History.* Cambridge: Harvard University Press, Belknap Press, 1974. Provides citations to books and articles on American history published before 1970. The first volume is arranged topically, the second chronologically. Though it does not cover current scholarship, it is a classic and remains useful for tracing older publications.

Prucha, Francis Paul. *Handbook for Research in American History: A Guide to Bibliographies and Other Reference Works.* 2nd rev. ed. Lincoln: University of Nebraska Press, 1994. Introduces a variety of research tools, including electronic ones. A good source to consult when planning an in-depth research project.

General Overviews

Dictionary of American Biography. New York: Scribner's, 1928–1937, with supplements. Gives substantial biographies of prominent Americans in history.

Dictionary of American History. New York: Scribner's, 1976. An encyclopedia of terms, places, and concepts in U.S. history; other more specialized sets include the *Encyclopedia of North American Colonies* and the *Encyclopedia of the Confederacy.*

Dictionary of Concepts in History. New York: Greenwood, 1986. Contains essays defining concepts in historiography and describing how the concepts were formed; excellent bibliographies.

Encyclopedia of American Social History. New York: Scribner's, 1993. Surveys topics such as religion, class, gender, race, popular culture, regionalism, and everyday life from pre-Columbian to modern times.

Encyclopedia of the United States in the Twentieth Century. New York: Scribner's, 1996. An ambitious overview of American cultural, social, and intellectual history in broad articles arranged topically. Each article is followed by a thorough and very useful bibliography for further research.

Specialized Information

Black Women in America: An Historical Encyclopedia. Brooklyn: Carlson, 1993. A scholarly compilation of biographical and topical articles that constitute a definitive history of African American women.

Carruth, Gordon. *The Encyclopedia of American Facts and Dates.* 10th ed. New York: HarperCollins, 1997. Covers American history chronologically from 1986 to the present, offering information on treaties, battles, explorations, popular culture, philosophy, literature, and so on, mixing significant events with telling trivia. Tables allow for reviewing a year from a variety of angles. A thorough index helps pinpoint specific facts in time.

Cook, Chris. *Dictionary of Historical Terms*. 2nd ed. New York: Peter Bendrick, 1990. Covers a wide variety of terms—events, places, institutions, and topics—in history for all periods and places in a remarkably small package. A good place for quick identification of terms in the field.

Dictionary of Afro-American Slavery. New York: Greenwood, 1985. Surveys important people, events, and topics, with useful bibliographies; similar works include *Dictionary of the Vietnam War, Historical Dictionary of the New Deal*, and *Historical Dictionary of the Progressive Era*.

Knappman-Frost, Elizabeth. *The ABC-Clio Companion to Women's Progress in America*. Santa Barbara: ABC-Clio, 1994. Covers American women who were notable for their time as well as topics and organizations that have been significant in women's quest for equality. Each article is brief; there are a chronology and a bibliography at the back of the book.

United States Bureau of the Census. *Historical Statistics of the United States, Colonial Times to 1970*. Washington, D.C.: Government Printing Office, 1975. Offers vital statistics, economic figures, and social data for the United States. An index at the back helps locate tables by subject. For statistics since 1970, consult the annual *Statistical Abstract of the United States*.

Primary Resources

There are many routes to finding contemporary material for historical research. You may search your library catalog using the name of a prominent historical figure as an author; you may also find anthologies covering particular themes or periods in history. Consider also the following special materials for your research.

THE PRESS

American Periodical Series, 1741–1900. Ann Arbor: University Microfilms, 1946–1979. Microfilm collection of periodicals from the colonial period to 1900. An index identifies periodicals that focused on particular topics.

Herstory Microfilm Collection. Berkeley: Women's History Research Center, 1973. A microfilm collection of alternative feminist periodicals published between 1960 and 1980. Offers an interesting documentary history of the women's movement.

New York Times. New York: New York Times, 1851–. Many libraries have this newspaper on microfilm going back to its beginning in 1851. An index is available to locate specific dates and pages of news stories; it also provides detailed chronologies of events as they were reported in the news.

Readers' Guide to Periodical Literature. New York: Wilson, 1900–. This index to popular magazines started in 1900; an earlier index, *Poole's Index to Periodical Literature*, covers 1802–1906, though it does not provide such thorough indexing.

DIARIES, PAMPHLETS, BOOKS

The American Culture Series. Ann Arbor: University Microfilms, 1941–1974. A microfilm set, with a useful index, featuring books and pamphlets published between 1493 and 1875.

American Women's Diaries. New Canaan: Readex, 1984–. A collection of reproductions of women's diaries. There are different series for different regions of the country.

The March of America Facsimile Series. Ann Arbor: University Microfilms, 1966. A collection of more than ninety facsimiles of travel accounts to the New World published in English or English translation from the fifteenth through the nineteenth century.

Women in America from Colonial Times to the Twentieth Century. New York: Arno, 1974. A collection of reprints of dozens of books written by women describing women's lives and experiences in their own words.

GOVERNMENT DOCUMENTS

Congressional Record. Washington, D.C.: Government Printing Office, 1874–. Covers daily debates and proceedings of Congress. Earlier series were called *Debates and Proceedings in the Congress of the United States* and *The Congressional Globe*.

Foreign Relations of the United States. Washington, D.C.: Department of State, 1861–. A collection of documents from 1861, including diplomatic papers, correspondence, and memoranda, that provides a documentary record of U.S. foreign policy.

Public Papers of the Presidents. Washington, D.C.: Office of the Federal Register, 1957–. Includes major documents issued by the executive branch from the Hoover administration to the present.

Serial Set. Washington, D.C.: Government Printing Office, 1789–1969. A huge collection of congressional documents, available in many libraries on microfiche, with a useful index.

LOCAL HISTORY COLLECTIONS

State and county historical societies often house a wealth of historical documents; consider their resources when planning your research—you may find yourself working with material that no one else has analyzed before.

Internet Resources

The Internet has been a useful place for scholars to communicate and publish information in recent years. Electronic discussion lists, electronic journals,

INTERNET RESOURCES

and primary texts are among the resources available to historians. The following sources are good places to find historical information. You can also search the World Wide Web using any of a number of search engines. However, bear in mind that there is no board of editors screening Internet sites for accuracy or usefulness, and the search engines generally rely on free-text searches rather than subject headings. Be critical of all of your sources, particularly those found on the Internet. Note that when this book went to press, the sites listed below were active and maintained.

American Memory: Historical Collections for the National Digital Library Program. <http://rs6.loc.gov/amhome.html> An Internet site that features digitized primary source materials from the Library of Congress, among them African American pamphlets, Civil War photographs, documents from the Continental Congress and the Constitutional Convention of 1774–1790, materials on woman suffrage, and oral histories.

Douglass Archives of American Public Address. <http://douglassarchives.org> An electronic archive of American speeches and documents by a variety of people from Jane Addams to Jonathan Edwards to Theodore Roosevelt.

Historical Text Archive. <http://historicaltextarchive.com/> A Web interface for the oldest and largest Internet site for historical documents. Includes sections on Native American, African American, and U.S. history, in which can be found texts of the Declaration of Independence, the U.S. Constitution, the Constitution of Iroquois Nations, World War II surrender documents, photograph collections, and a great deal more. These can be used online or saved as files.

History Links from Yahoo! <http://dir.yahoo.com/arts/humanities/history/> A categorically arranged and frequently updated site list for all types of history. Some of the sources are more useful than others, but this can be a helpful gateway to some good information.

Index of Civil War Information on the Internet. <http://www.cwc.lsu.edu/cwc/civlink.htm> Compiled by the United States Civil War Center, this index lists everything from diaries to historic battlefields to reenactments.

Index of Native American Resources on the Internet. <http://www.hanksville.org/NAresources> A vast index of Native American resources organized by category. Within the history category, links are organized under subcategories: oral history, written history, geographical areas, timelines, and photographs and photographic archives. A central place to come in the search for information on Native American history.

Internet Resources for Students of Afro-American History and Culture. <http://www.libraries.rutgers.edu/rul/rr_gateway/research_guides/history/afrores.shtml> A good place to begin research on topics in African American history. The site is indexed and linked to a wide variety of sources, including primary documents, text collections, and archival sources on African American history. Individual documents such as slave narratives and petitions, the Fugitive Slave Acts, and speeches by W. E. B. Du Bois, Booker T. Washington, and Martin Luther King Jr. are categorized by century.

The Martin Luther King Jr. Papers Project. <http://www.stanford.edu/group/King> Organized by Stanford University, this site gives information about Martin Luther King Jr. and offers some of his writings.

NativeWeb. <http://www.nativeweb.org> One of the best organized and most accessible sites available on Native American issues, *NativeWeb* combines an events calendar and message board with history, statistics, a list of news sources, archives, new and updated related sites each week, and documents. The text is indexed and can be searched by subject, nation, and geographic region.

Perry-Castañeda Library Map Collection. <http://www.lib.utexas.edu/maps/index.html> The University of Texas at Austin library has put over seven hundred United States maps on the Web for viewing by students and professors alike.

Smithsonian Institution. <http://www.si.edu> Organized by subject, such as military history or Hispanic/Latino American resources, this site offers selected links to sites hosted by Smithsonian Institution museums and organizations. Content includes graphics of museum pieces and relevant textual information, book suggestions, maps, and links.

Supreme Court Collection. <http://supct.law.cornell.edu/supct/> This database can be used to search for information on various Supreme Court cases. Although the site primarily covers cases that occurred after 1990, there is information on some earlier historic cases. The justices' opinions, as originally written, are also included.

United States History Index. <http://www.ukans.edu/history/VL/USA> Maintained by a history professor and arranged by subject, such as women's history, labor history, and agricultural history, this index provides links to a variety of other sites. Although the list is extensive, it does not include a synopsis of each site, which makes finding specific information a time-consuming process.

United States Holocaust Memorial Museum. <http://www.ushmm.org> This site contains information about the Holocaust Museum in Washington, D.C., in particular and the Holocaust in general, and it lists links to related sites.

Women's History Resources. <http://www.mcps.k12 .md.us/curriculum/socialstd/Women_Bookmarks .html> An extensive listing of women's history sources available on the Internet. The site indexes resources on subjects as diverse as woman suffrage, women in the workplace, and celebrated women writers. Some of the links are to equally vast indexes, providing an overwhelming wealth of information.

WWW-VL History Index. <http://www.ukans.edu/ history/VL> A vast list of more than 1,700 links to sites of interest to historians, arranged alphabetically by general topic. Some links are to sources for general reference information, but most are on historical topics. A good place to start an exploration of Internet resources.

GLOSSARY OF HISTORICAL VOCABULARY

A Note to Students: This list of terms is provided to help you with historical and economic vocabulary. Many of these terms refer to broad, enduring concepts that you may encounter not only in further studies of history but also when following current events. The terms appear in bold at their first use in each chapter. In the glossary, the page numbers of those chapter-by-chapter appearances are provided so you can look up the terms' uses in various periods and contexts. For definitions and discussions of words not included here, consult a dictionary and the book's index, which will point you to topics covered at greater length in the book.

antebellum A term that means "before a war" and commonly refers to the period prior to the Civil War. (pp. 402, 438, 541, 573)

antinomian A person who does not obey societal or religious law. In colonial Massachusetts, Puritan authorities accused Anne Hutchinson of antinomianism because she believed that Christians could achieve salvation by faith alone; they further asserted, incorrectly, that Hutchinson also held the belief that it was not necessary to follow God's laws as set forth in the Bible. (p. 118)

archaeology A social science devoted to learning about people who lived in the past through the study of physical artifacts created by humans. Most but not all archaeological study focuses on the history of people who lived before the use of the written word. (pp. 3, 79, 271, 533)

Archaic America Various hunting and gathering cultures that descended from Paleo-Indians. The term also refers to the period of time when these cultures dominated ancient America, roughly from 8000 BC to between 2000 and 1000 BC. (p. 11)

artifacts Material remains studied and used by archaeologists and historians to support their interpretations of human history. Examples of artifacts include bones, pots, baskets, jewelry, furniture, tools, clothing, and buildings. (pp. 3, 73, 271)

artisan A term commonly used prior to 1900 to describe a skilled craftsman, such as a cabinetmaker. (pp. 57, 126, 139, 218, 270, 413, 447)

Bill of Rights The commonly used term for the first ten amendments to the U.S. Constitution. The Bill of Rights (the last of which was ratified in 1791) guarantees individual liberties and defines limitations to federal power. Many states made the promise of the prompt addition of a bill of rights a precondition for their ratification of the Constitution. (pp. 279, 287)

bloody shirt A refrain used by Republicans in the late nineteenth century to remind the voting public that the Democratic Party, dominated by the South, was largely responsible for the Civil War and that the Republican Party had led the victory to preserve the Union. Republicans urged their constituents to "Vote the way you shot." (p. 585)

Calvinism The religious doctrine of which the primary tenet is that salvation is predestined by God. Founded by John Calvin of Geneva during the Protestant Reformation, Calvinism required its adherents to live according to a strict religious and moral code. The Puritans who settled in colonial New England were devout Calvinists. (p. 112) *See also* predestination.

checks and balances A system in which the executive, legislative, and judicial branches of the government curb each other's power. Checks and balances were written into the U.S. Constitution during the Constitutional Convention of 1787. (p. 280)

civil service The administrative service of a government. This term often applies to reforms following passage of the Pendleton Act in 1883, which set qualifications for U.S. government jobs and sought to remove such jobs from political influence. (p. 585) *See also* spoils system.

colonization The process by which a country or society gains control over another, primarily through settlement. (pp. 39, 69, 107, 376, 533)

Columbian exchange The transatlantic exchange of goods, peoples, and ideas that began when Columbus arrived in the Caribbean, ending the age-old separation of the hemispheres. (p. 44)

conscription Compulsory military service. Americans were first subject to conscription during the Civil War. The Draft Act of 1940 marked the first peacetime use of conscription. (p. 536) *See also* draft.

conservatism A political and moral outlook dating back to Alexander Hamilton's belief in a strong central government resting on a solid banking foundation. Currently associated with the Republican Party, conservatism today places a high premium on military preparedness, free-market economics, low taxes, and strong sexual morality. (pp. 478, 534, 568)

covenant An agreement or pact; in American history, this refers to a religious agreement. The Pilgrims used this term in the Mayflower Compact to refer to the agreement among themselves to establish a law-abiding community in which all members would work together for the common good. Later, New England Puritans used this term to refer to the agreement they made with God and each other to live according to God's will as revealed through Scripture. (pp. 104, 139) *See also* Halfway Covenant.

democracy A system of government in which the people have the power to rule, either directly or indirectly through their elected representatives. Believing that direct democracy was dangerous, the framers of the Constitution created a government that gave direct voice to the people only in the House of Representatives and that placed a check on that voice in the Senate by offering unlimited six-year terms to senators, elected by the state legislatures to protect them from the whims of democratic majorities. The framers further curbed the perceived dangers of democracy by giving each of the three branches of government (legislative, executive, and judicial) the ability to check the power of the other two. (pp. 219, 254, 287, 340, 366, 468, 478, 519, 578) *See also* checks and balances.

draft (draftee) A system for selecting individuals for compulsory military service. A draftee is an individual selected through this process. (pp. 221, 535) *See also* conscription.

emancipation The act of freeing from slavery or bondage. The emancipation of American slaves, a goal shared by slaves and abolitionists alike, occurred with the passage of the Thirteenth Amendment in 1865. (pp. 261, 344, 376, 462, 515, 559)

English Reformation *See* Reformation.

Enlightenment An eighteenth-century philosophical movement that emphasized the use of reason to reevaluate previously accepted doctrines and traditions. (p. 159)

evangelicalism The trend in Protestant Christianity stressing salvation through conversion, repentance of sin, adherence to Scripture, and the importance of preaching over ritual. During the Second Great Awakening, in the 1830s, evangelicals worshipped at camp meetings and religious revivals led by exuberant preachers. (pp. 342, 356, 426, 459) *See also* Second Great Awakening.

feminism The belief that men and women have the inherent right to equal social, political, and economic opportunities. The suffrage movement and second-wave feminism of the 1960s and 1970s were the most visible and successful manifestations of feminism, but feminist ideas were expressed in a variety of statements and movements as early as the late eighteenth century and continue to be expressed in the twenty-first. (pp. 292, 576)

franchise The right to vote. The franchise was gradually widened in the United States to include groups such as women and African Americans, who had no vote when the Constitution was ratified. (pp. 429, 577) *See also* suffrage.

free labor Work conducted free from constraint and in accordance with the laborer's personal inclinations and will. Prior to the Civil War, free labor became an ideal championed by Republicans (who were primarily Northerners) to articulate individuals' right to work how and where they wished, and to accumulate property in their own name. The ideal of free labor lay at the heart of the North's argument that slavery should not be extended into the western territories. (pp. 377, 421, 443, 493, 541, 562)

free soil The idea advanced in the 1840s that Congress should prohibit slavery within western territories. "Free soil, free speech, free labor, and free men" became the rallying cry of the short-lived Free-Soil Party. (pp. 477, 531)

frontier A borderland area. In U.S. history this refers to the borderland between the areas primarily inhabited by Europeans or their descendants and the areas solely inhabited by Native Americans. (pp. 40, 85, 119, 137, 174, 220, 302, 334, 355, 396, 476)

government bonds Promissory notes issued by a government in order to borrow money from members of the public. Such bonds are redeemable at a set future date. Bondholders earn interest on their investment. (p. 229)

Great Awakening The widespread movement of religious revitalization in the 1730s and 1740s that emphasized vital religious faith and personal choice. It was characterized by large, open-air meetings at which emotional sermons were given by itinerant preachers. (pp. 159, 342)

guerrilla warfare Fighting carried out by an irregular military force usually organized into small, highly mobile groups. Guerrilla combat was common in the Vietnam War and during the American Revolution. Guerrilla warfare is often effective against opponents who have greater material resources. (pp. 212, 496, 518, 580)

Halfway Covenant A Puritan compromise that allowed the unconverted children of the "visible saints" to become "halfway" members of the church and to baptize their own children even though they were not full members of the church themselves because they had not experienced full conversion. Massachusetts ministers accepted this compromise in 1662, though the compromise remained controversial throughout the seventeenth century. (p. 120)

hard currency (hard money) Money coined directly from, or backed in full by, precious metals (particularly gold). (pp. 229, 262, 294, 364)

impeachment The process by which formal charges of wrongdoing are brought against a president, a governor, or a federal judge. (p. 575)

imperialism The system by which great powers gain control of overseas territories. The United States became an imperialist power by gaining control of Puerto Rico, Guam, the Philippines, and Cuba as a result of the Spanish-American War. (pp. 491, 586)

indentured servitude A system that committed poor immigrants to four to seven years of labor in exchange for passage to the colonies and food and shelter after they arrived. An indenture is a type of contract. (pp. 71, 138)

Jim Crow The system of racial segregation that developed in the post–Civil War South and extended well into the twentieth century; it replaced slavery as the chief instrument of white supremacy. Jim Crow laws segregated African Americans in public facilities such as trains and streetcars and denied them basic civil rights, including the right to vote. It was also at this time that the doctrine of "separate but equal" became institutionalized. (p. 582)

land grant A gift of land from a government, usually intended to encourage settlement or development. The British government issued several land grants to encourage development in the American colonies. In the mid-nineteenth century the U.S. government issued land grants to encourage railroad development and through passage of the Land-Grant College Act (also known as the Morrill Act) in 1863 set aside public lands to support universities. (pp. 72, 121, 175, 220, 421, 491)

liberty The condition of being free or enjoying freedom from control. This term also refers to the possession of certain social, political, or economic rights such as the right to own and control property. Eighteenth-century American colonists evoked the principle to argue for strict limitations on government's ability to tax its subjects. (pp. 104, 174, 211, 254, 290, 322, 356, 430, 443, 493, 520, 566)

manifest destiny A term coined by journalist John O'Sullivan in 1845 to express the popular nineteenth-century belief that the United States was destined to expand westward to the Pacific Ocean and had an irrefutable right and God-given responsibility to do so. This idea provided an ideological shield for westward expansion and masked the economic and political motivations of many of those who championed it. (pp. 397, 486)

mercantilism A set of policies that regulated colonial commerce and manufacturing for the enrichment of the mother country. Mercantilist policies ensured that the American colonies in the mid-seventeenth century produced agricultural goods and raw materials to be shipped to Britain, where they would increase wealth in the mother country through reexportation or manufacture into finished goods that would then be sold to the colonies and elsewhere. (p. 89)

Middle Passage The crossing of the Atlantic (as a slave destined for auction) in the hold of a slave ship in the eighteenth and nineteenth centuries. Conditions were unimaginably bad, and many slaves died during these voyages. (pp. 97, 149)

miscegenation The sexual mixing of races. In slave states, despite social stigma and legal restrictions on interracial sex, masters' almost unlimited power over their female slaves meant that liaisons inevitably occurred. Many states maintained laws against miscegenation into the 1950s. (p. 450)

monopoly Exclusive control and domination by a single business entity over an entire industry through ownership, command of supply, or other means. Gilded Age businesses monopolized their industries quite profitably, often organizing holding companies and trusts to do so. (pp. 37, 357, 592)

Monroe Doctrine President James Monroe's 1823 declaration that the Western Hemisphere was closed to any further colonization or interference by European powers. In exchange, Monroe pledged that the United States would not become involved in European struggles. Although Monroe could not back his policy with action, it was an important formulation of national goals. (p. 347)

nationalism A strong feeling of devotion and loyalty toward one nation over others. Nationalism encourages the promotion of the nation's common culture, language, and customs. (pp. 340, 407, 540)

nativism Bias against immigrants and in favor of native-born inhabitants. American nativists especially favor persons who come from white, Anglo-Saxon, Protestant lines over those from other racial, ethnic, and religious heritages. Nativists may include former immigrants who view new immigrants as incapable of assimilation. Many nativists, such as members of the Know-Nothing Party in the nineteenth century and the Ku Klux Klan through the contemporary period, voice anti-immigrant, anti-Catholic, and anti-Semitic sentiments. (p. 492)

New South A vision of the South, promoted after the Civil War by Henry Grady, editor of the *Atlanta Constitution*, that urged the South to abandon its dependence on agriculture and use its cheap labor and natural resources to compete with northern industry. Many Southerners migrated from farms to cities in the late nineteenth century, and northerners and foreigners invested a significant amount of capital in railroads, cotton and textiles, mining, lumber, iron, steel, and tobacco in the region. (p. 560)

nullification The idea that states can disregard federal laws when those laws represent an overstepping of congressional powers. The controversial idea was first proposed by opponents of the Alien and Sedition Acts of 1798 and later by South Carolina politicians in 1828 as a response to the Tariff of Abominations. (pp. 311, 325, 386, 480)

paternalism The idea that slavery was a set of reciprocal obligations between masters and slaves, with slaves providing labor and obedience and masters providing basic care and direction. The concept of paternalism denied that the slave system was brutal and exploitative. While paternalism did provide some protection against the worst brutality, it did not guarantee decent living conditions, reasonable work, or freedom from physical punishment. (pp. 448, 540)

planters Owners of large farms (or more specifically plantations) that were worked by twenty or more slaves. By 1860, planters had accrued a great deal of local, statewide, and national political power in the South despite the fact that they represented a minority of the white electorate in those states. Planters' dominance of southern politics demonstrated both the power of tradition and stability among southern voters and the planters' success at convincing white voters that the slave system benefited all whites, even those without slaves. (pp. 80, 128, 149, 183, 213, 305, 335, 376, 443, 477, 520, 562)

popular sovereignty   The idea that government is subject to the will of the people; before the Civil War, this was the idea that the residents of a territory should determine, through their legislatures, whether to allow slavery. (p. 478)

predestination   The idea that individual salvation or damnation is determined by God at, or just prior to, a person's birth. The concept of predestination invalidated the idea that salvation could be obtained through either faith or good works. (p. 112) *See also* Calvinism.

Protestant Reformation   *See* Reformation.

Protestantism   A powerful Christian reform movement that began in the sixteenth century with Martin Luther's critiques of the Roman Catholic Church. Over the centuries, Protestantism has taken many different forms, branching into numerous denominations with differing systems of worship. (pp. 62, 87, 106, 138, 199, 276, 342, 373, 425, 438, 492)

Puritanism   The ideas and religious principles held by dissenters from the Church of England, including the belief that the church needed to be purified by eliminating the elements of Catholicism from its practices. (pp. 87, 104, 138)

Reformation   The reform movement that began in 1517 with Martin Luther's critiques of the Roman Catholic Church, which led to the formation of Protestant Christian groups. The English Reformation began with Henry VIII's break with the Roman Catholic Church, which established the Protestant Church of England. Henry VIII's decision was politically motivated; he had no particular quarrel with Catholic theology and remained an orthodox Catholic in most matters of religious practice. (pp. 60, 105)

republicanism   The belief that the unworkable model of European-style monarchy should be replaced with a form of government in which supreme power resides in the hands of citizens with the right to vote and is exercised by a representative government answerable to this electorate. In Revolutionary-era America, republicanism became a social philosophy that embodied a sense of community and called individuals to act for the public good. (pp. 219, 250, 287, 321, 469, 510)

Second Great Awakening   A popular religious revival that preached that salvation was available to anybody who chose to take it. The revival peaked in the 1830s, and its focus on social perfection inspired many of the reform movements of the Jacksonian era. (p. 373) *See also* evangelicalism.

separate spheres   A concept of gender relations that developed in the Jacksonian era and continued well into the twentieth century, holding that women's proper place was in the private world of hearth and home (the private sphere) and men's was in the public world of commerce and politics (the public sphere). The doctrine of separate spheres eroded slowly over the nineteenth and twentieth centuries as women became more and more involved in public activities. (p. 369)

spoils system   An arrangement in which party leaders reward party loyalists with government jobs. This slang term for *patronage* comes from the phrase "To the victor go the spoils." Widespread government corruption during the Gilded Age spurred reformers to curb the spoils system through the passage of the Pendleton Act in 1883, which created the Civil Service Commission to award government jobs on the basis of merit. (pp. 369, 585) *See also* civil service.

state sovereignty   A state's autonomy or freedom from external control. The federal system adopted at the Constitutional Convention in 1787 struck a balance between state sovereignty and national control by creating a strong central government while leaving the states intact as political entities. The states remained in possession of many important powers on which the federal government cannot intrude. (p. 522)

states' rights   A strict interpretation of the Constitution that holds that federal power over states is limited and states hold ultimate sovereignty. First expressed in 1798 through the passage of the Virginia and Kentucky Resolutions, which were based on the assumption that states have the right to judge the constitutionality of federal laws, the states' rights philosophy became a cornerstone of the South's resistance to federal control of slavery. (pp. 272, 347, 385, 537, 566)

suffrage   The right to vote. The term *suffrage* is most often associated with the efforts of American women to secure voting rights. (pp. 256, 366, 428, 468, 561) *See also* franchise.

temperance movement   The reform movement to end drunkenness by urging people to abstain from the consumption of alcohol. Begun in the 1820s, this movement achieved its greatest political victory with the passage of a constitutional amendment in 1919 that prohibited the manufacture, sale, and transportation of alcohol. That amendment was repealed in 1933. (pp. 375, 426)

virtual representation   The notion, propounded by British Parliament in the eighteenth century, that the House of Commons represented all British subjects— wherever they lived and regardless of whether they had directly voted for their representatives. Prime Minister George Grenville used this idea to argue that the Stamp Act and other parliamentary taxes on colonists did not constitute taxation without representation. American colonists rejected this argument, insisting that political representatives derived authority only from explicit citizens' consent indicated by elections, and that members of a distant government body were incapable of adequately representing their interests. (p. 187)

War Hawks   Young Republicans elected to the U.S. Congress in the fall of 1810 who were eager for war with England in order to legitimize attacks on Indians, end impressment, and avenge foreign insults. (p. 336)

yeoman   A farmer who owned a small plot of land sufficient to support a family and tilled by family members and perhaps a few servants. (pp. 88, 153, 388, 464, 477, 536, 578)

A note about the index:

Names of individuals appear in boldface; biographical dates are included for major historical figures.

Letters in parentheses following pages refer to:
(i)   illustrations, including photographs and artifacts, as well as information in picture captions
(f)   figures, including charts and graphs
(m) maps
(b)   boxed features (such as "Historical Question")
(t)   tables

Spot Artifact Credits

p. 18 (mica hand) Ohio Historical Society; p. 23 (dolls) Photo courtesy of the Oakland Museum, California; p. 39 (caravel) National Maritime Museum, London; p. 55 (crucifix) Courtesy of the Historical Archaeology Collections of the Florida Museum of Natural History; p. 75 (pot) Valentine Museum, Cook Collection; p. 88 (pipe) Niemeyer Nederlands Tabacologisch Museum; p. 94 (stirrup) © George H. H. Huey; p. 113 (die) Courtesy of Association for the Preservation of Virginia Antiquities; p. 120 (cradle) Wadsworth Atheneum, Hartford, Wallace Nutting Collection, Gift of J. Pierpont Morgan; p. 128 (scales) Concord Musuem; p. 139 (pitcher) Pocumtuck Valley Memorial Association, Memorial Hall Museum, Deerfield, MA; p. 147 (*Poor Richard's Almanack*) Courtesy, American Antiquarian Society; p. 152 (slave's doll) The Stagville Center, Division of Archives and History, North Carolina Department of Cultural Resources; p. 155 (mirror) Concord Museum; p. 186 (stamps) Courtesy of the Trustees of the British Library; p. 190 (teapot) Peabody Essex Museum, Salem, MA; p. 203 (pistol) Concord Museum; p. 203 (musket) Concord Museum; p. 205 (Wheatley title page) Library of Congress; p. 216 (drum) Massachusetts Historical Society; p. 226 (broadside) Courtesy, American Antiquarian Society; p. 229 (currency) Smithsonian Institution, Washington, D.C., photo by Douglas Mudd; p. 233 (Howitzer) West Point Museum, United States Military Academy, West Point, N.Y.; p. 262 (penny note) Library of Congress;

p. 274 (inkwell) Independence National Historic Park; p. 290 (ballot box) Independence National Historic Park; p. 291 (barrel) Peabody Essex Museum, Salem, MA; p. 305 (kettle) Ohio Historical Society; p. 326 (compass) Smithsonian Institution, Washington, D.C.; p. 349 (telescope) Thomas Jefferson Memorial Foundation, Inc.; p. 368 (spittoon) Courtesy, The Henry Francis du Pont Winterthur Museum; p. 388 (bank note) Miriam and Ira D. Wallach Division of Art, Prints and Photographs, The New York Public Library, Astor, Lenox and Tilden Foundations; p. 389 (miniature log cabin) National Museum of American History, Smithsonian Institution, Behring Center; p. 405 (flag) Texas Memorial Museum; p. 417 (plow) Smithsonian Institution, Washington, D.C.; p. 418 (watch) Smithsonian Institution, Washington, D.C.; p. 426 (sheet music) Special Collections, Milton S. Eisenhower Library, The Johns Hopkins University; p. 449 (shoe) Valentine Museum, Cook Collection; p. 467 (fiddle) National Museum of American History, Smithsonian Institution, Washington, D.C.; p. 479 (poster) Courtesy, American Antiquarian Society; p. 496 (cane) Collection of McKissick Museum, University of South Carolina; p. 502 (shackles) Private Collection; p. 506 (revolver) Ohio Historical Society; p. 523 (jacket) Smithsonian Institution, Washington, D.C.; p. 543 (potholder) Chicago Historical Society; p. 563 (bible) Anacostia Museum, Smithsonian Institution, Washington, D.C.; p. 575 (ticket) Collection of Janice L. and David J. Frent; p. 584 (plow) Courtesy Deere & Company.

ATLAS OF THE TERRITORIAL GROWTH OF THE UNITED STATES

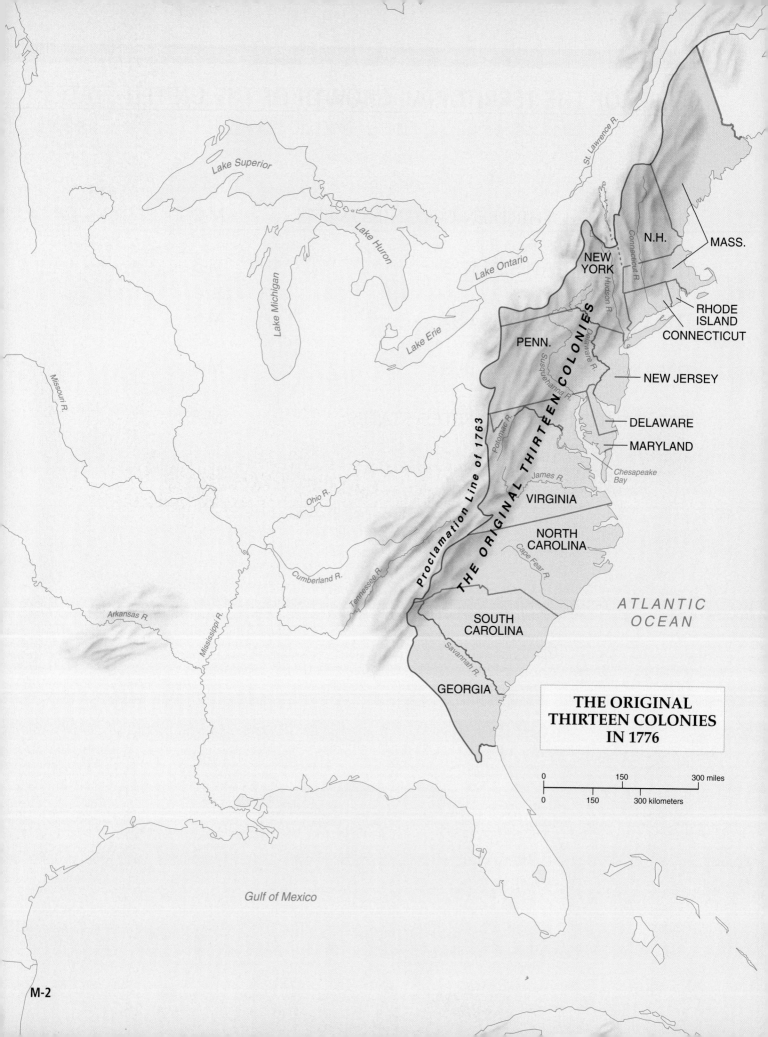

Lake Superior

Lake Michigan

Lake Huron

Lake Ontario

Lake Erie

Missouri R.

Ohio R.

Mississippi R.

Cumberland R.

Tennessee R.

Arkansas R.

St. Lawrence R.

N.H.

MASS.

NEW YORK

Connecticut R.

Hudson R.

RHODE ISLAND

CONNECTICUT

PENN.

Delaware R.

Susquehanna R.

NEW JERSEY

DELAWARE

MARYLAND

Potomac R.

Chesapeake Bay

James R.

VIRGINIA

NORTH CAROLINA

Cape Fear R.

Proclamation Line of 1763

THE ORIGINAL THIRTEEN COLONIES

SOUTH CAROLINA

ATLANTIC OCEAN

Savannah R.

GEORGIA

THE ORIGINAL THIRTEEN COLONIES IN 1776

0   150   300 miles

0   150   300 kilometers

Gulf of Mexico

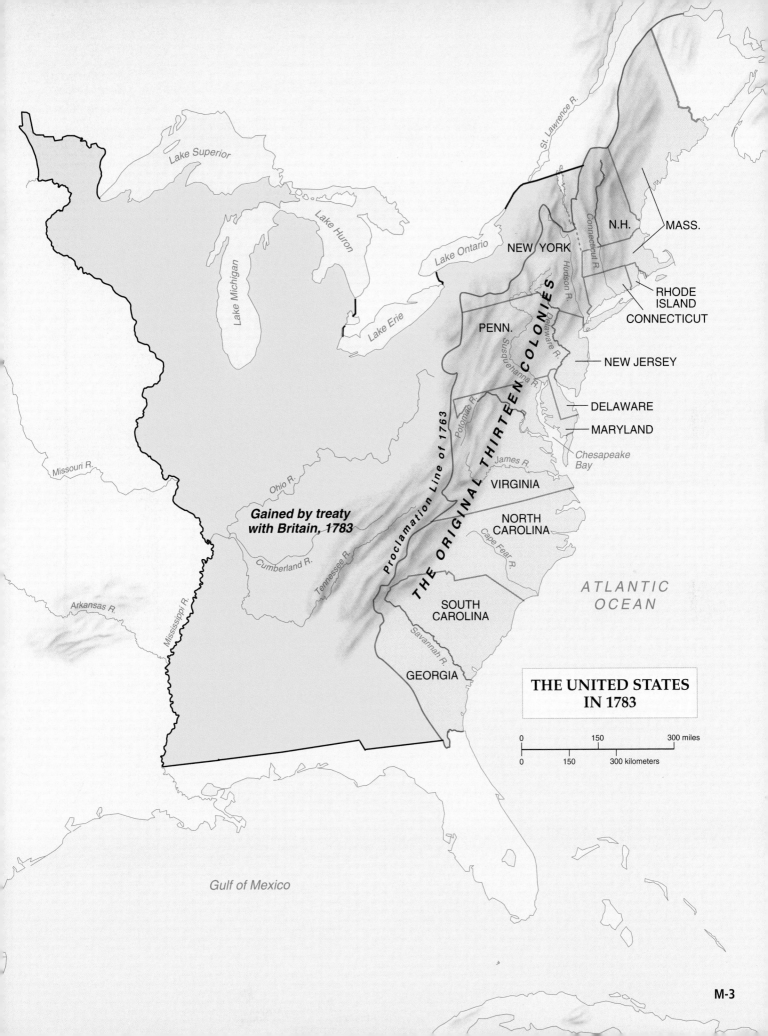

Lake Superior

Lake Huron

Lake Michigan

Lake Ontario

Lake Erie

St. Lawrence R.

Connecticut R.

N.H.

MASS.

NEW YORK

Hudson R.

RHODE ISLAND

CONNECTICUT

PENN.

Delaware R.

Susquehanna R.

NEW JERSEY

DELAWARE

MARYLAND

Chesapeake Bay

Missouri R.

Ohio R.

Gained by treaty with Britain, 1783

Potomac R.

James R.

VIRGINIA

Cumberland R.

Tennessee R.

NORTH CAROLINA

Cape Fear R.

Proclamation Line of 1763

THE ORIGINAL THIRTEEN COLONIES

ATLANTIC OCEAN

Arkansas R.

Mississippi R.

SOUTH CAROLINA

Savannah R.

GEORGIA

THE UNITED STATES IN 1783

0   150   300 miles

0   150   300 kilometers

Gulf of Mexico

M-3

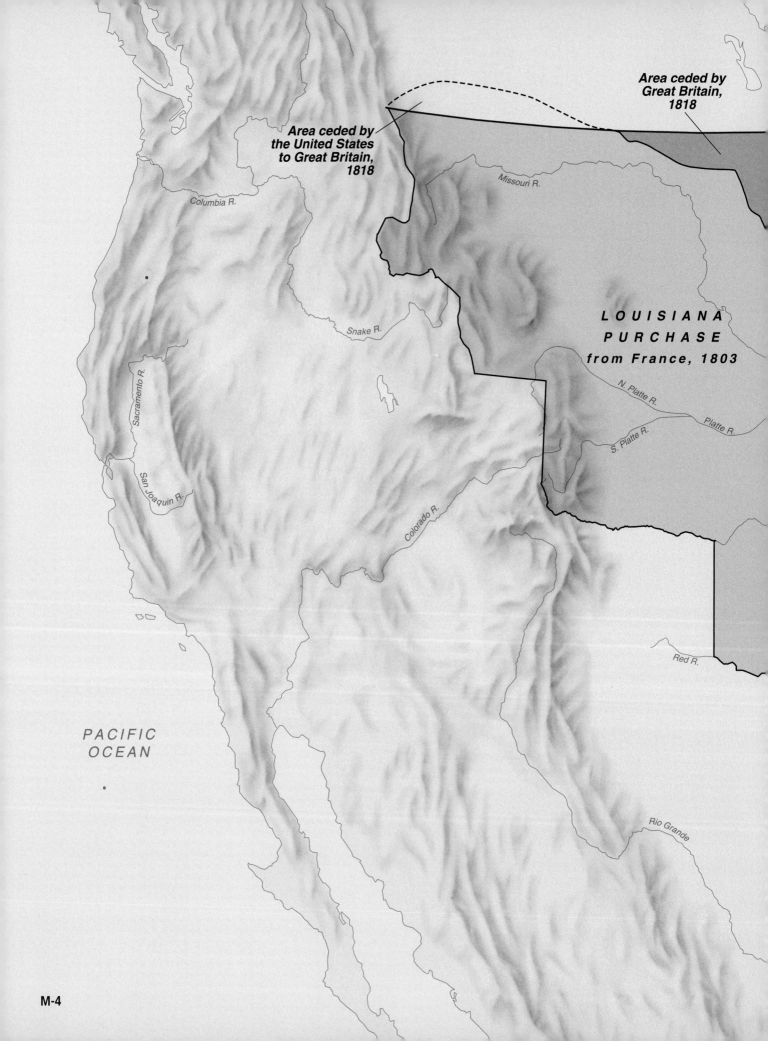

Area ceded by
the United States
to Great Britain,
1818

Area ceded by
Great Britain,
1818

LOUISIANA
PURCHASE
from France, 1803

Columbia R.

Missouri R.

Snake R.

N. Platte R.

Platte R.

S. Platte R.

Sacramento R.

San Joaquin R.

Colorado R.

Red R.

PACIFIC
OCEAN

Rio Grande

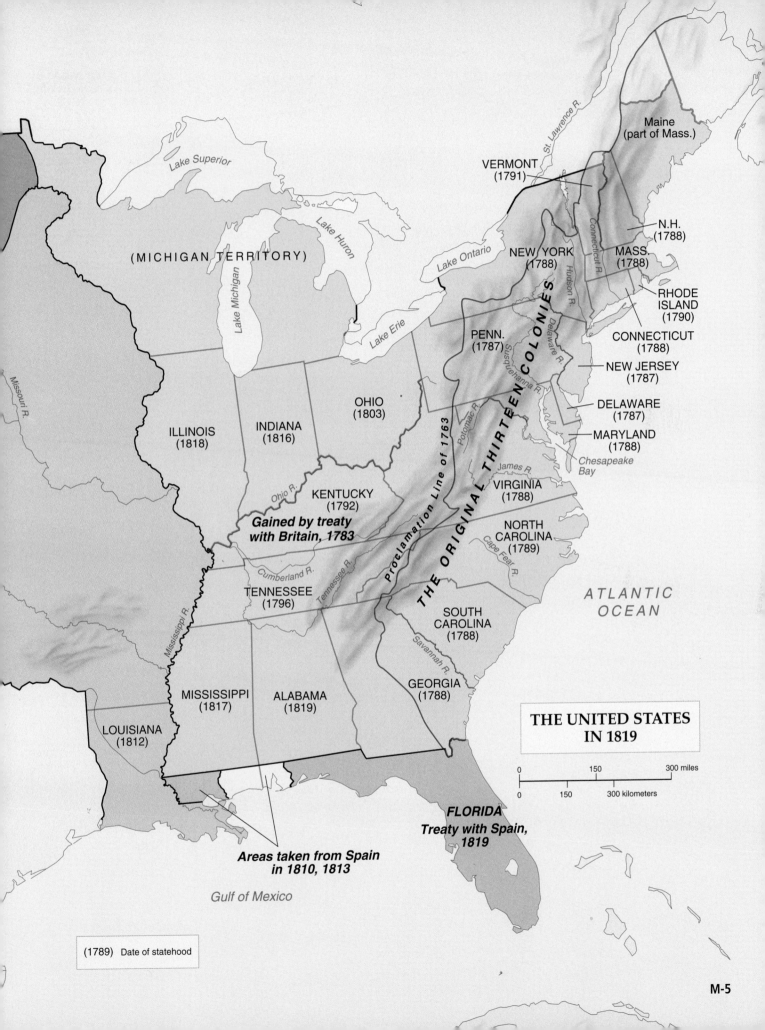

Lake Superior

Lake Huron

Lake Michigan

(MICHIGAN TERRITORY)

Lake Ontario

Lake Erie

St. Lawrence R.

Maine
(part of Mass.)

VERMONT
(1791)

Connecticut R.

N.H.
(1788)

NEW YORK
(1788)

MASS.
(1788)

Hudson R.

RHODE
ISLAND
(1790)

CONNECTICUT
(1788)

PENN.
(1787)

Susquehanna R.

Delaware R.

NEW JERSEY
(1787)

DELAWARE
(1787)

MARYLAND
(1788)

Chesapeake
Bay

Potomac R.

ILLINOIS
(1818)

INDIANA
(1816)

OHIO
(1803)

THE ORIGINAL THIRTEEN COLONIES

Missouri R.

Ohio R.

KENTUCKY
(1792)

**Gained by treaty
with Britain, 1783**

Proclamation Line of 1763

James R.

VIRGINIA
(1788)

NORTH
CAROLINA
(1789)

Cape Fear R.

ATLANTIC
OCEAN

Cumberland R.

Tennessee R.

TENNESSEE
(1796)

SOUTH
CAROLINA
(1788)

Savannah R.

Mississippi R.

MISSISSIPPI
(1817)

ALABAMA
(1819)

GEORGIA
(1788)

LOUISIANA
(1812)

**THE UNITED STATES
IN 1819**

0   150   300 miles

0   150   300 kilometers

FLORIDA
**Treaty with Spain,
1819**

**Areas taken from Spain
in 1810, 1813**

Gulf of Mexico

(1789)   Date of statehood

M-5

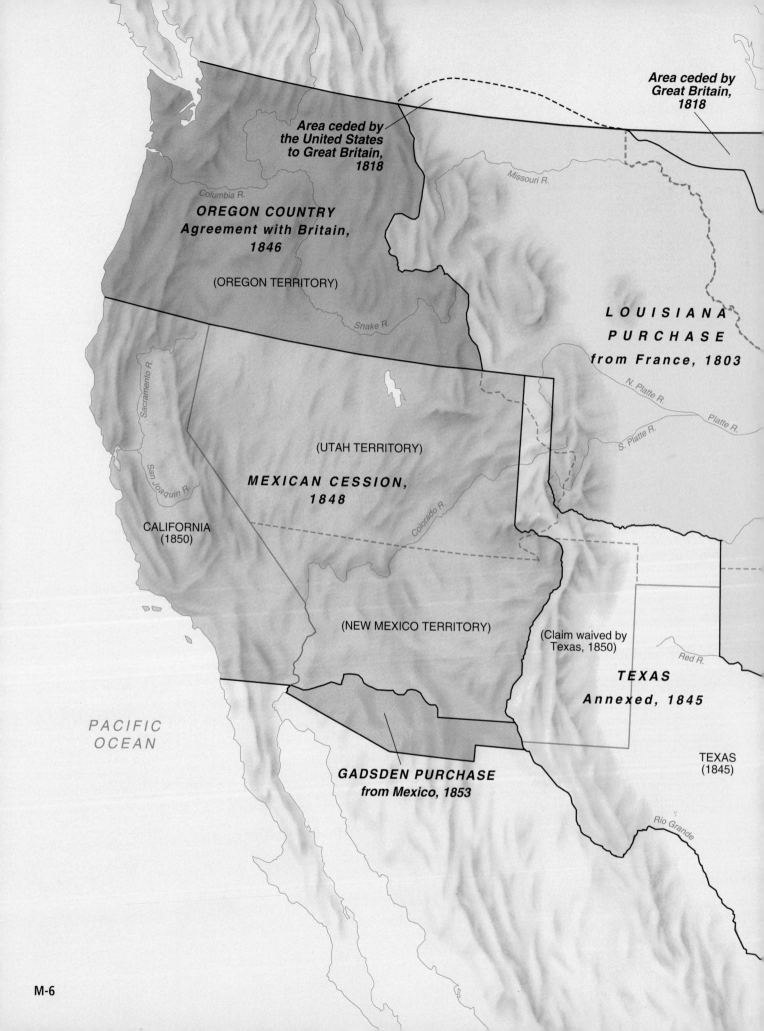

Area ceded by Great Britain, 1818

Area ceded by the United States to Great Britain, 1818

Columbia R.

Missouri R.

OREGON COUNTRY
Agreement with Britain,
1846

(OREGON TERRITORY)

Snake R.

L O U I S I A N A
P U R C H A S E
from France, 1803

N. Platte R.

Platte R.

Sacramento R.

S. Platte R.

(UTAH TERRITORY)

San Joaquin R.

MEXICAN CESSION,
1848

Colorado R.

CALIFORNIA
(1850)

(NEW MEXICO TERRITORY)

(Claim waived by Texas, 1850)

Red R.

T E X A S
Annexed, 1845

TEXAS
(1845)

GADSDEN PURCHASE
from Mexico, 1853

PACIFIC
OCEAN

Rio Grande